W9-ANK-415

FOR REFERENCE

Do Not Take From This Room

modern
architecture

since
1900

william j. r. curtis

modern
architecture

since
1900

third edition

Phaidon Press Limited
Regent's Wharf
All Saints Street
London N1 9PA

Phaidon Press Inc.
180 Varick Street
New York, NY 10014

www.phaidon.com

First published 1982
Second edition 1987
Third edition
(revised, expanded
and redesigned) 1996
Reprinted 1997, 1999,
2001 (twice), 2005, 2006

© 1982, 1987, 1996
Phaidon Press Limited

Text © 1982, 1987, 1996
William J.R. Curtis

ISBN-13: 978 0 7148 3524 2
ISBN-10: 0 7148 3524 2
(hardback)
ISBN-13: 978 0 7148 3356 9
ISBN-10: 0 7148 3356 8
(paperback)

A CIP catalogue record for
this book is available from
the British Library

Printed in Hong Kong

Illustrations to part-openers

pp. 18–19
Frank Lloyd Wright, Robie
House, South Woodlawn,
Chicago, 1908–10, perspective
drawing

pp. 160–1
Le Corbusier, project for a
house near Carthage (Maison
Baizeau), 1927–9, sketch

pp. 392–3
Louis I. Kahn, Salk Institute
for Biological Sciences,
La Jolla, California, 1959–65,
sketch

pp. 614–15
Frank Gehry, Schnabel House,
Brentwood, California, 1990,
sketch

preface
to
the
first
edition

Modern architecture was evolved less than a century ago to reconcile an idealized vision of society with the forces of the Industrial Revolution. While it made drastic breaks with the past it also allowed the basic principles of architecture to be rethought in new ways. The reverberations of this major change are only just being felt world-wide, and it may be that we are nearer the beginning of a tradition than the end of one. Even the recent reactions against modern architecture rely for the most part on their enemy for intellectual definition: as soon as forms are produced, they are seen to be extensions of the discoveries made earlier in this century. It seems a good moment to pause and to reflect on the shape of this new tradition. That is what this book sets out to do by examining the architecture of the past eighty years in detail.

I make no apologies for concentrating on buildings of high visual and intellectual quality: a tradition is formed from a sequence of such high points which hand on their discoveries to lesser followers. I have emphasized the problem of architectural language and have tried to show how a number of extraordinarily imaginative individuals expressed the deeper meanings of their times in symbolic forms. I thought it would be a good thing to strip away myths and to present the complex picture of modern architecture as simply and honestly as possible. As far as I know the views presented here do not belong to a particular 'school'. I have posed the same basic historical questions – 'what, why and how?' – that one would ask for any period.

While the book does not set out to substantiate a historical dogma or to persuade the reader that one style is better than another, it does reflect a point of view and does possess a strategy of its own. I have been concerned throughout with the ways in which ideas may be given form, and with the vital interplay between individual invention and the conventions provided by period style and tradition. At the core is a concern for authenticity within a personal vocabulary, in which form, function, structure and meaning are bound together with a certain conviction and character of inevitability. The reliance on 'movements' of the stock-in-trade survey, with its flat treatment of individual buildings and architects, has been avoided. Instead, the scale of approach has been deliberately varied from chapter to chapter, sometimes to give a close-up, sometimes to give a long or broad view. For a tradition is never an even, linear development of uniform impulse and intensity. It blends personal expressions of depth with lazy repetitions of formula and glib flashes of fashion; it draws together the cosmopolitan and the regional over certain embedded patterns of formal thinking; it links past principles and schemata with new solutions and intentions. To grasp the complex inner structure of a tradition, then, various approaches and intellectual tools will be necessary; and since a central obsession is the power of architectural abstraction to bind together levels of meaning, I have found it essential to concentrate on a few individual buildings in depth.

This book was conceived in the late 1970s and written between early 1980 and early 1981, a time during which I travelled a good deal. The last third of the manuscript was nearly lost at the bottom of the River Hawkesbury in Australia when a canoe tilted over, and Chapter 16 was in process when the author luckily escaped annihilation in Beirut. It is an odd turn of fate that Le Corbusier's Villa Savoye should be associated in my mind with the sound of gun-fire, and that Aalto's Villa Mairea will always recall the smell of Kentish blossoms. I mention these wanderings to emphasize that the book was written well outside the poky confines of the architectural fashion houses of our time. In it I have tried to convey the character of fine building, to look for lasting qualities, to keep the long historical view. I have attempted to show what modern architecture may mean in remote parts of a rapidly changing world.

History is a communal activity in the sense that one is bound to draw on past models, and the bibliographical notes at the end of this volume are reserved for specifically scholarly acknowledgements. But there are more immediate debts. I am grateful to Mark Ritchie of Phaidon for introducing me and my ideas to a firm it was a pleasure to work with; and to all the staff at the publisher's who have been involved in steering the scheme through. James Ackerman read the penultimate draft and made some good suggestions, while Karen Harder diligently transformed my scrawl into an elegant typescript.

Finally I thank Catherine, my wife, for calmly and easily putting up with the odd states of mind that are bound to accompany the writing of a big book in a short time. I dedicate this book to her with a thought from Le Corbusier: to fix a plan is to have had ideas.

William J. R. Curtis, Boston, Massachusetts, 1981

preface
to
the
third
edition

It is over a decade now since *Modern Architecture Since 1900* was first published. There was a second edition in 1987 but, apart from an addendum on recent world architecture, the book remained the same. The time has now come for some major additions and revisions. A book of this nature is by definition an evolving project, a working hypothesis, that must be tested, reordered and refined. The author welcomes the chance to take into account his own and other people's intervening researches and discoveries. With the third edition the aim has been to integrate new knowledge and experience in an existing structure and to accentuate themes that were left underdeveloped. The intention is to reveal more of the original soul while giving a better shape to the body.

In the period since this book was first written there have been several studies and monographs which have underlined the internal complexity of modern architecture and the richness and range of its theoretical intentions and formal sources. Major inventors such as Frank Lloyd Wright, Le Corbusier, Mies van der Rohe, Alvar Aalto or Louis Kahn, generated entire symbolic worlds and engaged with society on mythical as well as practical levels; they drew upon several cultures and traditions in formulating their respective versions of a modern architecture, and their contribution needs to be seen in the long term. While the polemical oversimplifications of the earlier histories have become less and less tenable, the need remains for texts charting large-scale developments. It is increasingly clear that modern architecture combines numerous strands and inflections which evade monolithic descriptions of either a stylistic or an ideological kind. The prototypes and principles defined earlier in this century continue to be transformed, inverted, cross-bred, mannered and regionalized in unexpected ways. In effect the present is heir to a diverse tradition.

When the first edition of *Modern Architecture Since 1900* was published, it was common to hear that 'modern architecture is dead'. But intellectual fashions come and go and substantial buildings remain: 'postmodernism' proved to be a temporary and localized phenomenon, while the string of 'isms' since then have continued in the usual way to distort history for their own purposes. Nevertheless, the ground has shifted and new questions have come to the surface. Certain of the 'set-pieces' of earlier modern architectural literature are no longer adequate. The concept of an 'International Style', for example, tends to obscure the richness and regional diversity of modernism between the wars. Liberal assumptions about the 'democratic' nature of modern architecture require ever greater revision the more is known about Italy in the 1930s or Spain in the 1950s. A historiography based upon the cultural biases and power structures of the North Atlantic region cannot be justified when dealing with the world-wide dissemination of modern architecture in places like Latin America, the Middle East or India. Much still needs to be done on the intermingling and collision of 'universalizing' types with national and regional traditions, a basic feature of modernism (and possibly of modernization itself) from the beginning. Greater precision has to be given to the personal and period elements of style, and to the interplay between individual inventions, vernacular types and technological norms. Modernism needs to be examined in relation to a variety of world-views and social projects, but while the political context may be crucial, a distinction must be made between the outline of a task and the symbolization which leads to architectural form.

Many of these points were raised in the first edition of *Modern Architecture Since 1900* , but the time has come to pursue them further. The simplest way of demonstrating how the third edition differs from the first is to list the main changes and additions. (A more detailed rationale is supplied in the Bibliographical Note at the end of the book on page 691.) There are seven new chapters in all, dealing with such subjects as: the industrial city and the invention of the skyscraper in the late nineteenth century (Chapter 2); national myths and classical transformations in the early twentieth (Chapter 8); the dissemination of modern architecture in several continents in the 1930s (Chapter 21); disjunctions and continuities in European architecture soon after the Second World War (Chapter 26). The final three chapters (33, 34, 35) form an entirely new Part IV on recent world architecture, organized around such general themes as the re-evaluation of the past, the response to local climates and cultures, the celebration of technology, and the re-emergence of abstraction. Rather than relying upon the usual

transient 'isms', this part of the book selects individual buildings and ideas that seem to add to an architectural culture of long-term value. Beyond the advertised fashions, the years since 1980 have yielded up an architecture of great diversity and richness, even if this has been realized against a background of growing urban disruption and mounting ecological crisis.

The creation of the third edition has been a massive undertaking for all concerned – author, publisher, editors, picture researchers and designer – and represents something like a collective act of faith. When Richard Schlagman took over Phaidon Press in 1990, he and his new architectural editor David Jenkins immediately expressed interest in the long-term future of this book. The initiative for a new edition came at the right time, as there was just about the distance necessary to allow a major revision. The project could not have been carried through without the skill and tact of the same editor who oversaw first and second editions, namely Bernard Dod. I also wish to thank the picture research department (Philippa Thomson in particular) for tracking down photographic treasures in remote parts of the world, and the designer Isambard Thomas for his patience and sensitivity in finding the right form. Last, but not least, I am grateful to my family, Catherine, Louise and Bruno, for sustaining me through a testing transition.

William J. R. Curtis, Cajarc, 1995

introduction

We have long come to realize that art is not produced in an empty space, that no artist is independent of predecessors and models, and that he no less than the scientist and the philosopher is part of a specific tradition and works in a structured area of problems.
Ernst Kris, 1952

The historian who sets out to write a history of modern architecture has necessarily to begin with a definition of his subject. Many past eras have referred to their own architectures as 'modern', so that the term on its own is scarcely discriminating. The 'modern architecture' which is the main topic of this book was an invention of the late nineteenth and early twentieth centuries and was conceived in reaction to the supposed chaos and eclecticism of the various earlier nineteenth-century revivals of historical forms. Basic to the ideal of a modern architecture was the notion that each age in the past had possessed its own authentic style, expressive of the true tenor of the epoch. According to the same outlook, a break was supposed to have occurred somewhere around the middle of the eighteenth century, when the Renaissance tradition had faltered, leaving a vacuum into which had flowed numerous 'inauthentic' adaptations and recombinations of past forms. The task, then, was to rediscover the true path of architecture, to unearth forms suited to the needs and aspirations of modern industrial societies, and to create images capable of embodying the ideals of a supposedly distinct 'modern age'.

Already around the mid-nineteenth century such theorists as César Daly, Eugène Viollet-le-Duc and Gottfried Semper were discussing the possibility of a genuine modern style, but they had little conception of its form. It was not until just before the turn of this century, with considerable stimulus from a variety of intervening structural inventions, that imaginative leaps were made in an attempt at visualizing the forms of a new architecture. This pioneer phase, which resulted in (among other things) Art Nouveau and the Chicago School, was the property of the 'advanced' industrial nations of Western Europe and the United States. Even then there was relatively little consensus concerning the appearance of a new architecture; there were, rather, broadly shared aspirations capable of visual translation in a variety of ways. 'Modern architecture', it was intimated, should be based directly on new means of construction and should be disciplined by the exigencies of function; its forms should be purged of the paraphernalia of historical reminiscence, its meanings attuned to specifically modern myths and experiences; its moralities should imply some vision of human betterment and its elements should be capable of broad application to certain unprecedented situations arising from the impact upon human life and culture of the machine. Modern architecture, in other words, should proffer a new set of symbolic forms more directly reflecting contemporary realities than had the rag-bag of 'historical styles'.

In actuality, between about 1890 and the 1920s a number of positions emerged which claimed 'modernity' as a chief attribute, until by the latter decade it seemed as if a broad consensus had at last been achieved. At any rate, this is what some practitioners and propagandists wished their contemporaries to believe. They thus invested considerable effort in distinguishing the characteristics of the 'International Style' – that expressive language of simple, floating volumes and clear-cut geometries which seemed to be shared by such diverse architects as Le Corbusier, J. J. P. Oud, Gerrit Rietveld, Walter Gropius, Ludwig Mies van der Rohe, and the rest. *This* they claimed was the one true architecture for the twentieth century. Other contemporary developments were conveniently overlooked, and everything was done to plaster over differences and preserve the façade of a unified front.

But history did not stand still, and the same creative individuals who had seemed to be pushing towards a common aim went their own separate ways; in turn, seminal ideas were transformed by followers. Thus the architecture which was supposed (wrongly, it turns out) to have expunged tradition founded a tradition of its own. In the years after the Second World War, many tributaries and transformations were developed around the world. Reactions, critiques and crises – not to mention widely differing circumstances and intentions – compounded the variety. If a historian were to look back in a century's time at the period 1900–95, he would not, therefore, be overwhelmed by some single, monolithic main line of development running from the 'pioneers of modern design' (to use Nikolaus Pevsner's phrase) up to the architecture of the last quarter of the twentieth century. But he would be struck by the emergence and domination of new traditions gradually overrunning the inheritance of attitudes and vocabularies bequeathed by the nineteenth century. Moreover, this insinuation of new ideas might be

seen in global terms, working its way bit by bit into different national and regional traditions, transforming them and being transformed by them. This book takes such a long view.

Here it has to be admitted that there are particular difficulties of a sort which confront any interpreter of the recent past. The historian who sets out to write a history of modern architecture will be describing and interpreting traditions which have not yet come to an end. There is the danger that he may impose too exclusive a pattern on recent events, so making them point inevitably to whatever aspects of the architecture of his own time he happens to admire. History then degenerates into polemic. This is to be expected in the fashion-conscious literature which always seems to follow in the wake of contemporary movements, but similar faults are found to lie in the carefully pondered scholarly works which pass as the standard books on modern architecture. For all the force and clarity of their achievement, such early chroniclers as Sigfried Giedion, Henry-Russell Hitchcock and Nikolaus Pevsner tended to share the progressivist fervour of their protagonists. Committed in advance to the idea of a unified 'spirit of the age', they felt they recognized its architectural expression in the works of the modern movement of the 1920s, and saw it as their job to write books of revelation, charting the unfolding world drama of the 'true architecture of the times'. (See Bibliographical Note, p. 690.) It is obvious from my earlier remarks that I do not wish to add some glowing extra chapters to such a saga; nor, let it be said, do I wish to add to the ever-growing heap of those 'revisionist' histories intent on demonstrating that modern architecture was some temporary fall from architectural grace. The historian of the present perhaps has a unique and almost unprecedented opportunity to see his subject (or, at any rate the early stages of it) with a certain dispassionate distance, and this should not be thrown away by indulgence in propaganda. Each year more buildings are created and more quarries of evidence on developments earlier in the century are unearthed, and this alone necessitates a revision of the broad picture. But history involves constant reinterpretation as well as the presentation of new facts, and even buildings, personalities and events that once seemed to have some immutable status must be rescrutinized and reconsidered. Between the ever-growing collection of specialist monographs of quality and the broader but somewhat biased surveys, there is little that can stand scrutiny as a balanced, readable overall view of the development of modern architecture from its beginnings until the recent past. This book is an attempt at bridging the gap.

The earliest historians of modern architecture (perhaps one should call them 'mythographers') tended to isolate their subject, to oversimplify it, to highlight its uniqueness in order to show how different the new creature was from its predecessors. Parallel developments, like Art Deco, National Romanticism, or the continuation of the classical Beaux-Arts, were relegated to a sort of limbo, as if to say that a building in the 'wrong style' could not possibly be of value. This was both heinous and misleading. It seems to me that the various strands of modern architecture are best understood and evaluated by being set alongside other architectural developments parallel with them, for only then can one begin to explain what patrons and social groups used modern forms to express. Moreover, artistic quality, as always, transcends mere stylistic usage.

Another myth that the earliest writers on modern architecture tended to maintain – again to distinguish the new forms from their 'eclectic' predecessors – was the notion that these forms had emerged somehow 'untainted' by precedent. Again this married well with the progressivist bias in their history-writing, but it was scarcely a sensible way of explaining forms. In their eagerness to demonstrate their 'fresh new start', numerous architects between 1900 and 1930 certainly played down the influence of earlier architecture upon them, but this does not mean that one should take their claims at face value. Indeed, the most profound architects of the past hundred years were steeped in tradition. What they rejected was not so much history *per se*, as the facile and superficial reuse of it. The past was not, therefore, rejected, but inherited and understood in new ways. Moreover, modern architecture itself eventually created the basis for a new tradition with its own themes, forms and motifs.

Architecture is a complex art embracing form and function, symbol and social purpose, technique and belief. It would be as inadequate in this case simply to catalogue the ins and outs of style as it would be to reduce modern architecture to a piece in a chess game of class interests and competing social ideologies. It would be as mistaken to treat technical advances in isolation as it would be to overstress the role of social changes or the importance of individual imagination. It may be that facts of biography are most appropriate (as in the case of Le Corbusier or Frank Lloyd Wright) or that analysis of structure or type is more in order (as with the American skyscraper); it may be right to work at the scale of the individual building in one case, the scale of the city in another; and while a book of this kind obviously cannot portray the entire cultural setting of twentieth-century architecture, it can avoid suggesting that buildings come about in a social vacuum by concentrating on patronage, political purpose and ideological expression in some instances.

Modern architecture has emerged against a setting of major social and technological transformations; it has registered a gradual shift from rural to urban existence in the industrializing world. It has served a multitude of interests and functions from mass housing to the glorification of capitalist institutions, from rarefied private villas to spaces of sacred meaning. It has been used both to break with the immediate past and to reinstate older continuities, both to handle the problems of the big city and to serve the aims of contemplative mysticism. In the circumstances it would be unwise to insist upon a simplistic formula governing the connection between 'ideology' and forms. Architecture is rooted in the processes and paradoxes of society, but it also transforms these into its own terminology: it works by parallel but different rules. The trick is to find the right balance between the internal logic of the discipline and the influence of cultural forces, between the social and the personal dimensions, between the unique order of the individual invention and that which is normative or typical.

Here I must confess to a certain focused interest on questions of form and meaning. Most of the buildings to be discussed in this book are outstanding works of art which therefore defy simplistic pigeon-holing. They are neither direct expressions of political beliefs, nor mere stylized containers of functions, but rich compounds of ideas and forms, which achieve symbolic resonance beyond the level of mere 'signs'. They may be thought of as dense emblems, microcosms, combining idealized visions of society with three-dimensional interpretations of the human condition. They transcend obvious representation, working on levels that touch mind and senses through the abstract control of space, light, structure, geometry, material and movement. I believe it should be a central aim of any history of architecture to explain why certain configurations and technical solutions were felt appropriate to a particular task, and to probe into underlying meanings and intentions. That simple and misleading word 'style' masks a multitude of sins, and when one investigates an artist of any depth one discovers a sort of mythical content which pervades the forms. We have to do with the ways in which fantasies, ideas, even intuitions of a moral order, are translated into architectural terms.

Next there is the tricky problem of where to begin: when does a specifically 'modern architecture' appear? Enough has been said to suggest that there is no easy answer to this question. It is interesting to note the variety of starting-points of earlier histories, naturally reflecting the writers' various notions of modern architecture. Thus, Nikolaus Pevsner, who wished to stress the social and moral basis of the new architecture, began his *Pioneers of the Modern Movement* (1936) with William Morris and the Arts and Crafts of the 1860s. Sigfried Giedion, who was obsessed with the spiritual fragmentation of his own time and saw modern architecture as a unifying agent, portrayed the nineteenth century, in his *Space, Time and Architecture* (1941), as a split era – on the one hand the 'decayed' forms of eclecticism, on the other those 'emergent tendencies' (many of them in engineering) which pointed to a new synthesis of form, structure and cultural probity. Henry-Russell Hitchcock, who was preoccupied with describing the visual features of the new architecture, suggested in *The International Style* (1932, co-author Philip Johnson), that modern architecture synthesized classical qualities of proportion with Gothic attitudes to structure. In his later writings, though, Hitchcock became less adventurous, preferring to avoid sweeping theories of origins in favour of a meticulous, encyclopedic cataloguing of the sequence of styles.

The emphasis of history-writing was bound to change as the modern tradition itself grew longer and more varied. Historians after the Second World War perceived their subject in a longer perspective and constructed more complex lineages. Bruno Zevi (e.g. *Storia dell'architettura moderna*, 1950) advocated an 'organic' cultural synthesis extending the spatial principles of Frank Lloyd Wright. Colin Rowe (in celebrated articles of the late 1940s) explored classical continuities within modernism and probed the ideas behind the forms. Reyner Banham, in *Theory and Design in the First Machine Age* (1960), re-created the theoretical background to the first three decades of the twentieth century and investigated the visual conventions and symbolic meanings of the 'machine aesthetic' of the 1920s. Peter Collins's *Changing Ideals in Modern Architecture* (1965) concentrated more upon theories than actual buildings, tracing several of the intellectual components of the modern movement to nineteenth-, even eighteenth-century texts. The writings of Leonardo Benevolo (e.g. *Storia dell'architettura moderna*, 1960) stemmed from an entirely different historiographical tradition, dealing with social factors and the reception of architecture by the public. For him the crucial fact was the Industrial Revolution, modernism emerging as a doomed effort at solving the problems of the expanding city. Later writers preoccupied with the crisis of industrialization such as Manfredo Tafuri and Francesco Dal Co (1976) or Kenneth Frampton (1980), built upon these foundations to articulate their own versions of a pre-history but with a greater awareness of the political and ideological contradictions of modern architecture (see Bibliographical Note, p. 690).

Here I must emphasize that the stress of this book is less on the theoretical roots of modern architecture than on its emergence and ensuing development. This is quite deliberate. For one thing I wish to insist upon a distinction between inherited theories and actual architectural ideas; for another it is the later (rather than the earlier) phases of modern architecture which have been neglected. It is now nearly three-quarters of a century since such seminal works as the Villa Savoye or the Barcelona Pavilion were created; but the past 45 years are still navigable only with the aid of a few treacherous maps distorted by fashionable tags and 'isms'. A comprehensive treatment of the post-Second World

War period is still impossible, but one can at least suggest a scheme which is not simply a one-way road towards some tendency or other of the very recent past. Moreover, history does not work like a conveyor belt moving between one point and another. A tradition may be ruled by dominant forms or governing principles, but it may also contain diverse strands, regional emphases, internal loops, disjunctions and continuities. In turn each artist develops a special relationship with the past. A personal language may crystallize features of its period and society, yet draw inspiration from several sources inside and outside architecture. Buildings of any depth occupy time on several levels, transmuting traditions near and far, transforming other realities in inner and outer worlds. It is misleading to treat them merely as parts or products of movements; the more interesting the individual creation, the harder it is to locate it in a particular chronological slot.

Thus the problem of origins is handled in the first part of this book, not through some hapless search for the first truly modern building (or something of the kind), but through the more fruitful approach of tracing the way inherited strands of thought come together in various individual minds in the last few years of the nineteenth century and the first few years of the twentieth, for it was then that *forms* were invented to express, simultaneously, a revulsion against superficial revivalism, and confidence in the energies and significance of modern life. It was the era of Art Nouveau, of Horta, Gaudí and Mackintosh; of Wagner, Hoffmann and Loos; of Sullivan's and Root's Chicago skyscrapers, and Wright's early houses with their new sense of space; of Behrens's and Perret's attempts at employing new methods and materials in the service of sober ideas abstracting basic classical values. It was the era too of Cubist and Futurist experimentation in the arts. Pevsner justly described it as the 'pioneer' phase of modern design, and this seems fair enough so long as one is not tempted to write off its creations as mere 'anticipations' of what came later, and so long as one does not imagine that the path from this exploratory period to the 1920s to have been straightforward. The future 'modern masters' both rejected and extended their immediate predecessors as they steered their way through a legacy of nineteenth-century dilemmas:

how to reconcile old and new, mechanical and natural, utilitarian and ideal? In turn they grappled with the contradictions of the industrial city and with conflicts between national and international definitions of culture. Most of them were exposed to regionalist formulations or versions of classicism during their formative years, and these influences were gradually absorbed into their work through a process of abstraction.

The second part of the book concentrates upon the crystallization of modern architecture between the wars. One does not have to be an advocate of the notion of 'classic moments' in art to single out the 1920s as a remarkable period of consolidation, particularly in the Netherlands, Germany, France, the United States and the Soviet Union. In retrospect this has been called the 'heroic period' of modern architecture; during it Le Corbusier, Mies van der Rohe, Walter Gropius, Erich Mendelsohn, Gerrit Rietveld, Konstantin Melnikov, Rudolph Schindler and Richard Neutra (to mention only a few) created buildings of such innovatory force that they dislodged the hold of previous traditions, laying down new definitions of architecture for the future. It is precisely because this decade has been endowed with epic significance that one must be wary of over-selective treatments of it. In reality several ideals and definitions of 'the modern' coexisted in the 1920s, sometimes overlapping, sometimes conflicting: the functionalism and 'new objectivity' of Hannes Meyer; the lofty idealism of Le Corbusier; the controlled expressionism of Erich Mendelsohn; the primitivism and nature worship of Wright. To find the right balance between period concerns, personal style and the intentions of individual works, it is necessary to probe beyond appearances to the level of spatial organization and generating ideas.

The modern movement was a revolution in social purpose as well as architectural forms. It tried to reconcile industrialism, society and nature, projecting prototypes for mass housing and ideal plans for entire cities (e.g. Wright's Broadacre City or Le Corbusier's Ville Radieuse). But there were several ideological roots to these Utopian aspirations and efforts at reform, and they were in turn implicated in a wide range of political agendas. The middle part of the book analyses the problematic relationship between ideology and modern architecture in the Soviet Union of the 1920s, as well as totalitarian reactions against modernism in the following decade. It also considers the transformation of classicism in Fascist Italy and in social democracies like Finland and Sweden, and the interweaving of nationalism, internationalism and regionalism in several parts of the Mediterranean, Asia, Latin America and Africa. The conflicts of this period constitute much more than a battle of styles: modernism challenged the status quo, articulated new social visions and suggested alternative ways of life; it played an active role in the process of modernization.

Once a tradition has been founded it is transformed as new possibilities of expression are sensed, as values change, or as new problems are encountered. Moreover, new individuals inherit the altered principles and cultural definitions implicit in the prototypes and extend these in their own directions. By the outbreak of the Second World War branches of the modern movement had been founded in places as diverse as Finland and Britain, Brazil and South Africa, Mexico and Japan. A 'second generation', including figures such as Alvar Aalto, Berthold Lubetkin, Giuseppe Terragni and Oscar Niemeyer, modified seminal ideas to fit new intentions and to deal with entirely different climates, cultures, traditions. Meanwhile the originators themselves pursued their researches, reacting to the political and economic crises of the 1930s with less dogmatic versions of machinism, and with more accommodating versions of the 'natural', the vernacular and the 'primitive'. No single tag such as the 'International Style' will do justice to the range and depth of modern architecture produced between the wars.

The third part of the book examines the global dissemination of modern architecture from the 1940s to the late 1970s. Here we come face to face with problems attached to the phenomena of transplantation (as modernism was grafted into cultures quite different from those in which it began), devaluation (as symbolic forms were gradually emptied of their original polemical content, and cheapened by commercial interests or state bureaucracies), and regeneration (as basic concepts were re-examined or rejected, and as new expressive territories were opened up). As well as the late works of the ageing 'masters' of modern

architecture, this part of the book considers the gradual modification of earlier Utopian models of urbanism; the emergence of groups seeking a less absolutist approach to planning, such as Team X; the development of new 'strains' of modernism in diverse national cultures (e.g. Spain, Australia, India, Japan); general themes such as 'regionalism' and the reading of urban context; adaptation to local climates and cultures in developing countries; building types, like the high-rise apartment block and the glass-box skyscraper; and individual designers such as Louis Kahn, Jørn Utzon, Luis Barragán, Aldo van Eyck, Carlo Scarpa, Alejandro de la Sota, José Antonio Coderch and Denys Lasdun.

In the 1960s and 1970s crises and critiques occurred both inside and outside the modern movement, suggesting a more overt reliance on the past and on lessons to be learned from the traditional city; the progressive ethos of the 'modern project' also came under attack. Theoretical writings of the period encouraged a return to historical examples, through the manipulation of signs and references, or through the abstraction and transformation of long-established urban types. By the end of the 1970s it was fashionable to suggest that the way forward lay in going back. 'Postmodernism' emerged with its arbitrary recipes and quotations, and was soon accompanied by a collection of revivalisms and mannerisms in which any period of the past was game. When the Introduction to the first edition of this book was written in 1981 it stated : 'Modern architecture is at present in another critical phase, in which many of its underlying doctrines are being questioned and rejected. It remains to be seen whether this amounts to the collapse of a tradition or another crisis preceding a new phase of consolidation.'

Despite the rhetoric about the 'end of an era', postmodernism proved to be ephemeral. In reality there was yet another reorientation in which certain core ideas of modern architecture were re-examined but in a new way. For the third edition (1996) a fourth part has been added which deals with the complex development of world architecture since around 1980. This avoids standard critical postures and largely fictional 'movements' and tries to single out buildings and tendencies of lasting value. The net is cast wide and includes the Third World as well as the First. Examples are drawn from places as diverse as Spain and India, Finland and Australia, France and Mexico, the United States, Switzerland and Japan. It seems that there are several 'cultures of modernity' in the recent past, and that these blend together long-term patterns and agendas with contemporary problems and preoccupations. Increasingly, architectural ideas are crossing frontiers, and this part of the book is concerned with the intermingling of new and old, local and universal. It postulates the idea of a modern tradition with several strands and considers diverse ways in which ideas generated earlier in this century are being cross-fertilized and transformed in response to context and cultural memory as well as to rapidly changing social and technological conditions. The backdrop here is the exploding 'information' metropolis, a system of visible and invisible networks which is demolishing old definitions of country and city, and which is requiring a new scale of thinking somewhere between architecture, urbanism, landscape art and territorial planning.

It is through the close analysis of individual works of high intensity – their guiding ideas, their spatial structure, their societal myths, their responses to culture, technology and nature – that one may begin to sense the deeper currents of a period. If the last part of the book singles out buildings like Juan Navarro Baldeweg's Congress Hall in Salamanca, Spain (1985–92), Norman Foster's Hong Kong and Shanghai Bank (1979–85), Balkrishna Doshi's studio 'Sangath' in Ahmadabad, India (1979–81), Juha Leiviskä's Myyrmäki Church, near Helsinki, Finland (1984–7), or Tadao Ando's Chikatsu-Asuka Museum, in Japan (1989–93), it is not just because they are outstanding recent achievements judged in purely architectural terms. It is also because they are among the recent buildings to draw meaning from their respective places and societies, while contributing to a global architectural culture of substance. They remind us that modernism in the late twentieth century possesses a complex identity; continuing to aspire to a certain universality, even as it reacts to different territories and traditions; stimulating radical innovation even as it reactivates its own generating principles; inspiring new visions for the future, even as it transforms the past.

Perhaps it is inevitable that, as the book draws towards the present, the author will fall into some of the pitfalls of his predecessors in championing some aspects, and chastising others of the contemporary situation. I can at least say that it has been my aim to present a balanced picture, maintain a long historical perspective, and make the basis of any judgements clear. We live in a confused architectural present which views its own past through a veil of myths and half-truths (a number of them manufactured by historians) with a mixture of romanticism, distortion and bewilderment. A freedom of choice for the future is best encouraged by a sensible, accurate and discriminating understanding of one's place in tradition. This book was written partly with the idea that a historical bridge might be built across the stream of passing intellectual fashions to a more solid philosophical ground, partly with the hope that this might encourage a return to basic principles. But such aims have been secondary: the first thing a historian ought to do is to explain what happened and why, whatever people may now think of it.

part 1 the formative strands of modern architecture

1

the idea of a modern architecture in the nineteenth century

Suppose that an architect of the twelfth or thirteenth century were to return among us, and that he were to be initiated into our modern ideas; if one put at his disposal the perfections of modern industry, he would not build an edifice of the time of Philip Augustus or St Louis, because this would be to falsify the first law of art, which is to conform to the needs and customs of the times.
Eugène Viollet-le-Duc,
1863

1 Joseph Paxton, Crystal Palace, London, 1851

There is a tidy and misleading analogy between history and human life which proposes that architectural movements are born, have youth, mature, and eventually die. The historical process which led to the creation of the modern movement in architecture had none of this biological inevitability, and had no clear beginning which can be pinpointed with precision. There were a number of predisposing causes and strands of ideas, each with its own pedigree. Although the critical synthesis began around the turn of this century, the idea of a *modern* architecture, in contrast to a revived style from some earlier period, had been in existence for more than half a century.

But this notion of a 'modern' architecture was in turn rooted in developments of the late eighteenth century, in particular the emphasis on the idea of progress. For basic to the conception was a sense of history as something which moves forward through different 'epochs', each with a spiritual core manifesting itself directly in the facts of culture. From this intellectual standpoint it was possible to speak of the way a Greek temple or a Gothic cathedral had 'expressed their times' and to assume that modern buildings should do the same. It followed that revivals should be regarded as failures to establish a true expression. Destiny therefore required the creation of an authentic style 'of the times', unlike past ones, but as incontrovertible, as inevitable-seeming, as they. The question was: how could the forms of this 'contemporary' style be discovered?

Related to the birth of progressive ideals was another eighteenth-century development that left its legacy to the nineteenth: the loss of confidence in the Renaissance tradition and the theories which had supported it. This erosion was caused, in part, by the growth of an empiricist attitude which undermined the idealistic structure of Renaissance aesthetics, and by the development of history and archaeology as disciplines. These brought with them a greater discrimination of the past and a relativist view of tradition in which various periods could be seen as holding equal value. The notion of a single point of reference, 'Antiquity', thus became increasingly untenable. The situation has been characterized as 'the loss of absolute authority' of Renaissance norms. A vacuum of sorts was created into which numerous temporary stylistic dictatorships would step, none of them with the force of conviction, or with the authority, of their predecessor. A point would eventually be reached in the nineteenth century when a revival of a Greek, a Renaissance, an Egyptian or a Gothic prototype might seem equally viable in the formulation of a style.

Another major force in the creation of the idea of modern architecture was the Industrial Revolution. This created new patrons, generated new problems, supplied new methods of construction (e.g. in iron), and suggested new forms. A split of sorts was created between engineering and architecture, with the former often appearing the more inventive and responsive to contemporary needs. At a deeper level still, industrialization transformed the very patterns of life in country and city and led to the proliferation of new building tasks – railway stations, suburban houses, skyscrapers – for which there was no obvious convention or precedent. Thus the crisis concerning the use of tradition in invention was exacerbated by the creation of novel types of building with no certain pedigree.

Moreover, industrialization disrupted the world of crafts and hastened the collapse of vernacular traditions. Machine work engendered a split between hand, mind and eye in the creation of utilitarian objects, and standardization brought with it a loss of vital touch and impulse. Mid-nineteenth-century moralists such as A.W.N. Pugin, John Ruskin and William Morris felt that mechanization was bound to cause degradation in all compartments of life, at the smallest and largest scales of design. They therefore advocated a reintensification of the crafts and a reintegration of art and utility. Their aim was to stem the alienation they felt grew automatically from the disruptive effects of capitalist development. Those who were later to formulate the ideologies of modern architecture felt that this was too nostalgic and tried instead to co-opt the potentials of mechanization by infusing them with a new sense of form. This drama was to remain basic to the twentieth century: in essence the question was how to evolve a genuine culture in the face of the more brutish aspects of mass production.

Industrialization also created new economic structures and centres of power. Where the patronage of architecture in eighteenth-century Europe had relied principally on the Church, the state, and the aristocracy, it came increasingly to rely on the wealth and purposes of the new middle classes. As always, élites found in architecture a means to authenticate their own position. The multiple reuses of the past which characterize the nineteenth-century cultural landscape cannot be dissociated from the need to create and perpetuate entirely new institutions such as museums, opera houses, libraries, parliament buildings, banks, casinos, lawcourts, prisons and centres of colonial authority; these were in addition to the new instruments of commerce such as the factory, the mill, the railway station, the market hall, the department store and the skyscraper. Historical references might be manipulated to evoke connections between the current cultural condition and past 'golden ages'. The neo-classical monuments created by Karl Friedrich Schinkel in Berlin in the 1820s were to reiterate a Greek ideal for the modern state of Prussia. The neo-Gothic Palace of Westminster in London (designed by Charles Barry and A.W.N. Pugin a decade later) was to recall, if not re-create, the moral tone, national integrity and high civilization supposedly represented by the English Perpendicular Gothic style of the fifteenth century. By the later decades of the nineteenth century the new technologies in iron and glass had developed their own iconographical capacity to express notions of progress or national ascendancy in science, as may be seen, for example, in the Eiffel Tower constructed for the 1889 Paris Exhibition (Fig. 15).

In turn, mechanization remoulded the lower orders of society, made inroads on the form of the city, and transformed the surrounding countryside into a wider field of industrial production. The infrastructures of railways and steamship lines modified relations of space and time, changed the whole concept of place, and permitted new divisions of labour. The mining of raw materials, the manufacture of objects, the management of processes, and the marketing of products could now be separated from each other by great distances. These changes in the economic order relied upon technological inventions which overran both rural and urban traditions. Local vernaculars were gradually invaded by standardized systems in iron,

2 The nineteenth-century
dilemma of style: Thomas
Cole, *The Dream of the
Architect*, 1840. Oil on
canvas, 53 × 84 in (134.7
× 213.4 cm). Toledo
Museum of Art, gift of
Florence Scott Libbey

glass and (at the end of the nineteenth century) steel. Old relations and hierarchies in the city were exploded through the impact and incision of routes of circulation and drastic increases in size and scale. Machine production absorbed the peasant into the city, but the price paid for leaving rural poverty and joining the money economy was only too often unsanitary and dangerous living and working conditions. The contrast between rich and poor, between the splendid city centres with their monuments to consumption and cultural display, and the squalid factories, slums and tenements on the fringes was dramatic and destabilizing.

Once again, architecture was affected, not only by the status quo to which it had to cater, but also by the emergence of moral and political critiques of these monstrous social conditions. A major theme of modern architecture in the early twentieth century would be the reform of the materialist city, and its replacement by a supposedly more humane and harmonious order enriched through contact with 'nature'. The roots of these positions lay in religious, revolutionary or Utopian thought, of which several strands wove their way through the nineteenth century. Among these was a type of Christian radicalism (represented by Pugin and Ruskin, for example) which rejected the fragmentation and brutality of the modern world, and posited instead images of the supposedly 'integrated' societies of the late Middle Ages. But there were also Utopian socialists like the Frenchmen Charles Fourier and Henri Saint-Simon who looked forward, rather than back, towards a resolution of conflicts in a 'rational' social order. The latter point of view stemmed from the Enlightenment, and combined a progressive idea of history with a commitment to universal liberation from obsolete authority. Echoes of this futurist fervour and this moralizing standpoint would be found in Utopian city projects of the early twentieth century. The search for alternative social and urban structures would lie close to the driving ethos of later modern architectural endeavour.

The very conception of a 'modern architecture' implied a frank engagement with the new social and technological realities brought about by industrialization. It also implied the rejection of superficial imitations of past forms, and a more 'direct' or 'honest' portrayal of the contemporary world, if not a vague anticipation of a better future. Here there lurked several basic difficulties – who was to say which 'facts' in the present were the most significant? Were they to be found in the emerging social order, in new materials, in the forces of the great metropolis? And even if there could be a consensus about such things, there was no automatic step from a particular set of conditions to a particular set of forms. The architect, as always, needed a language and a set of conventions through which to make his reading of the situation visible. Given the flux of conditions in the industrial city, and the deterioration of earlier metaphysical foundations of architectural meaning, it is not surprising that there should have been a nagging uncertainty about what the true content of architecture should be. Thus there was a tendency to locate the ideal in some compartment or other of the past, or else to dream of some hazy, ill-defined future as an alternative to a grimy, unconsoling present.

Arguably the concept of a modern architecture preceded by several decades the conditions that would make the fact of modern architecture a probability, if not a necessity. The idea itself relied upon a 'historicist' view of world development stemming from philosophers like Hegel, who conceived the facts of culture as direct expressions of an evolving historical 'spirit'. This notion was interwoven with another, according to which a modern style might be a 'direct' expression of function and structure. As early as 1828, the German theorist Heinrich Hübsch had put forward the case for forms based upon need: 'a strictly *objective skeleton* for the new style'. In the 1830s, Schinkel broached the idea of expressing construction directly without stylistic filters, but shied away from functionalism on the grounds that it lacked 'the historic and the poetic'. When dealing with the past, Schinkel was quite clear that the imitation of old forms was insufficient, that a 'new element' should enter on the high level of the guiding architectural idea, and that there should be a profound transformation. Similar dilemmas resurfaced in the writings of the French theorist César Daly and the German Gottfried Semper towards the middle of the century. Both were preoccupied with defining the relationship between construction, craft and architectural language in the past, and with the theoretical basis of a possible

language for their own time. Semper was sceptical about the idea of jettisoning precedent (he complained of 'futurists and schematists'), but was also wary of slavish imitation. He took a long-term view of the history of forms, considering the ways in which basic 'types' might be reinterpreted in fresh ways period by period; he worked towards a definition of the present by drawing parallels with the past.

Writing in the 1860s and 1870s, the French architect and theorist Eugène Viollet-le-Duc formulated a model of architectural history linking the frank expression of building construction and materials to the progressive march of history. Viollet-le-Duc was increasingly aware of the impact of new materials like iron and plate glass, and felt that the nineteenth century must try to formulate its own style by finding forms 'appropriate' to the new techniques, and to altered social and economic conditions. This was fair enough in theory, but the question still remained: where should the forms of this new style be found? To this there were a number of possible answers. At one extreme were those who believed in great individual leaps of invention; at the other were those who thought the matter would somehow look after itself if architects just got on with solving new problems logically and soundly. There was relatively little admission that even a 'new' architecture was likely, ultimately, to be assembled out of old elements, albeit highly abstracted ones.

The very notion of a modern architecture contradicted traditionalist views of design which relied upon an overt use of past models in the genesis of forms. In one version of revivalism, some historical styles were regarded as intrinsically superior to others, partly on aesthetic grounds but also because some historical periods were seen as culturally superior to others. By imitating the chosen style it was lamely hoped that one might also reproduce its supposed excellences and attendant moral virtues. But, there was the obvious danger that one might copy the externals without reproducing the core qualities, and so end up with tired academicism or pastiche. Moreover, the question naturally occurred: if a set of forms had been right for one context (be it Greek, Gothic, Egyptian, or Renaissance), could it possibly be right for another?

3

There was quite another way of handling the dilemmas and opportunities provided by a wider perspective on the past. Rather than aiming at the supposed values of a single style, this position advocated that one should evolve a language based upon the qualities of several. Here the hope was to fuse precedents and to create new combinations out of diverse lineages. This position was known as 'eclecticism' and it permitted some of the most absurd, but also inspired some of the richest, nineteenth-century buildings. At its worst it could lead to superficial and bizarre concoctions of elements without underlying integration. At its best it could lead to works of dense meaning combining, say, classical disciplines in plan, Gothic clarity in structure, Romantic effects in silhouette, and inventive uses of modern materials. Eclecticism provided no automatic rules for combination, and supplied no obvious linkage between function and form, but if a real transformation could be effected it was a powerful instrument for extracting lessons from history. The eclectic method was well characterized by one writer who spoke of 'the tireless mind of the designer' which 'having attained a great many ideas bearing on the subject, melts these very ideas in the crucible of the imagination'.

The problem of revival could not really be considered apart from the question of appropriateness in the present; here it was hard to avoid looseness because there were few guiding conventions binding functions, meanings and forms. It was all very well for the English architect A.W.N. Pugin to have argued with such deep moral fervour in the 1830s that Gothic was the most spiritually uplifting and the most structurally rational of styles; but counter-arguments of a similar kind in favour of classical forms could just as easily be made. Intellectual gambits were thus often used to post-rationalize what were really intuitive preferences. The lure of determinist arguments was strong because they seemed to bring certainty to a situation of extreme flux. If one could claim (and possibly believe) that one's forms were ordained by the predestined course of history, the national spirit, the laws of nature, the dictates of science, or some other impressive entity, then one could temporarily assuage doubts concerning arbitrariness in the choice of an architectural language.

Within the confused pluralism of the 'battle of styles', it tended to be forgotten that the lasting qualities of architecture were liable, as ever, to transcend obvious features of style, such as the use of columns in one instance, or pointed arches in another. The nineteenth century had its share of masterworks which were not categorizable by their stylistic uniform or by their allegiance to a particular historical camp ('neo-classical', 'neo-Gothic', 'neo-Romanesque' or whatever). The outstanding architectural quality of Henri Labrouste's Bibliothèque Ste-Geneviève in Paris of 1843–50 (Fig. 17) was not, after all, so much a function of its reliance upon this or that edifying classical prototype, as it was a result of an extraordinarily deep synthesis of form and content attuned to the culture, technology and institutional ideals of its place and period. Similarly, the architectural feebleness of Sir George Gilbert Scott's Foreign Office in London (1857–63) was traceable not to the use of inferior sources, but to an inability on the part of the architect to transform his sanctioned examples (medieval in his first project, Renaissance in his final one) into a cogent new expression. The major architectural talents of the nineteenth century – one thinks of figures such as Schinkel, Labrouste, or Henry Hobson Richardson – were able to probe the *principles* of past styles (not just to parrot their effects), then to translate these into authentic vocabularies of their own and achieve a prodigious imaginative unity in their results. One reason they were able to do this was that they possessed an intuitive vision of what was most appropriate to the social state of their time.

Beyond the outer conventions of historical styles it might be possible to discover a more elemental levels of continuity, and to reinterpret these 'essential' values in present-day terms. Schinkel seemed to acknowledge this when he wrote, 'If one could preserve the spiritual principle of Greek architecture, [and] bring it to terms with the conditions of our own epoch … then one could find the most genuine answer to our discussion.' At the same time he insisted that: 'Each work of art, of whatever kind, must always contain a new element, and be a living addition to the world of art …' Tradition was to inspire invention, but invention was also to keep tradition alive.

Another way of approaching the past was to construct myths of 'origins' and to suggest that one might achieve the most authentic results by returning to 'beginnings'. Known as 'primitivism', this position emerged in the mid-eighteenth century,

particularly in the writings of the Jesuit monk, Abbé Marc-Antoine Laugier. Following a Vitruvian tradition, he conceived of the beginnings of architecture in an archetypical 'primitive hut' from which, it was held, the more ornate elements of the classical system had evolved. But in his case the 'primitive' was valued more highly than the later, more 'artificial' elaborations. It tended to be implied that simpler also meant better, and that the further back one went the more authentic the form was bound to be. However, Laugier's 'primitive hut' had little basis in archaeology, and only a slight basis in texts which had speculated on the beginnings of architecture, and his version of the prototype reflected an essentially classical bias. Thus primitivism could all too easily end up as a battle of the styles simply played out on a more abstract plane. In effect, it reinforced an old ideal: the notion that architecture should 'imitate' nature.

Laugier denied that there were absolute rules in architecture and spurned mere educated taste, arguing instead that the best forms were rooted in functional or structural demands. This so-called 'Rationalist' doctrine would re-emerge under various guises in the nineteenth and twentieth centuries. It underlay the materialistic and systematic views on architecture espoused by Jean-Nicolas-Louis Durand soon after 1800, and was further nourished by the disciplined (though by no means unintuitive) methods of engineers. At its most extreme, Rationalism tended to lead to the dubious proposition that beautiful and appropriate forms would arise automatically if only problems were analysed 'on their own merits' instead of through the filter of precedent. There were a number of fallacies in this position, such as the notion that forms might arise from functional analysis alone without the intervention of some a priori image, but it was still a weapon with which to attack the whimsies of the most arbitrary revivalists.

Viollet-le-Duc's viewpoint belonged, broadly speaking, in this 'Rationalist' tradition, but unlike Laugier he tended to value medieval examples over classical ones on the grounds that they presented evidence of a more 'honest' expression of materials and construction. He was disturbed by the inability of the nineteenth century to find its own style and felt that the answer must lie in the creation of forms

'true to the programme and true to the methods of construction'. In his *Entretiens sur l'architecture* of 1863–72 (translated as *Discourses on Architecture*, 1877–81) he declared:

In architecture there are two necessary ways of being true. It must be true according to the programme and true according to the methods of construction. To be true according to the programme is to fulfil, exactly and simply, the conditions imposed by need; to be true according to the methods of construction is to employ the materials according to their qualities and properties … purely artistic questions of symmetry and apparent form are only secondary conditions in the presence of our dominant principles.

Viollet-le-Duc remained a little vague on the nature of these 'truths' and tended to assume (probably erroneously) that the conspicuous excellence of great past works was due mainly to their capacity for expressing the programmatic and structural 'truths' of their own time. Thus while he was committed to an indistinct vision of some new architecture, he none the less believed that the past could have its uses in discovering this new style; he even imagined a situation in which one of the designers of the great Gothic cathedrals had been resuscitated and confronted with a modern building problem and modern means of construction. He argued that the result would not have been an imitation Gothic building, but an authentically modern one based on analogous intellectual procedures. The past must not be raided for its external effects, then, but for its underlying principles and processes.

It is quite likely that many architects of note in earlier periods had always known that the past must be understood for its principles, but they had still had the guidance of a prevalent style phase, a shared architectural language, in which to incorporate their findings. Viollet-le-Duc outlined a probing method for the intellectual analysis of precedent but could still do little to supply the essential 'leap to form'. His imagination was not as strong as his intellect, and the buildings and projects which he left behind him were uneven combinations of old images and modern constructional means, usually reflecting his underlying taste for medieval structures (Fig. 4). There was little of that sense of 'inevitable unity' – of part linking with part in an ordered yet intuitive system – which distinguishes the true sense of style.

If Viollet-le-Duc's forms did little to solve the problem of a modern architecture, his ideas lived on and were destined to have a major influence upon

5

the 'pioneers' of modern architecture who came to maturity in the decades either side of 1900. He gave new status to vernacular forms and encouraged the study of pre-Renaissance examples which were often perceived, in the late nineteenth century, as indices of 'true' national or regional identities. He also supplied a strong counter-tendency against the worst excesses of Beaux-Arts teaching, which he accused (not always fairly) of erring in the direction of academicism. Most importantly, Viollet-le-Duc gave currency to the idea that the great style of modern times would somehow emerge on the basis of new constructional techniques – not through some merely personal formal experiment – just as the great styles of the past had done.

Viollet-le-Duc's historical parallels supplied further scaffolding to the idea of a modern architecture, but the question still remained: what should this modern architecture look like? From where should its forms be derived? Obviously tradition could not be rejected completely, otherwise there would be no forms at all; the notion of an entirely new architecture was simply illusory. Perhaps, then, it might be possible to abstract the essential lessons of earlier architecture in such a manner that a genuinely new synthesis would be achieved? Indeed, if one jumps forward to the first decades of the twentieth century and examines the pioneering works of the modern movement, one finds that they relied on tradition in this more universal sense. One is struck by the confidence of architects such as Frank Lloyd Wright, Le Corbusier and Mies van der Rohe that they had, so to speak, unearthed the central, abstract values of the medium of architecture itself; that they had created not so much a new style, as the quality of style in general – a quality central to all outstanding works of the past.

This universalizing view of the history of architecture, this notion that the important features of past buildings lay in their proportions, their arrangement, their articulation of formal themes, their basic ideas (and the like) rather than in their use of stylistic elements, may itself have had some basis in earlier tendencies towards simplification. One thinks in this instance of schematizations of the past implicit in the geometrical visions of Claude-Nicolas Ledoux and Étienne-Louis Boullée in the late eighteenth century, or of the reduction of

6

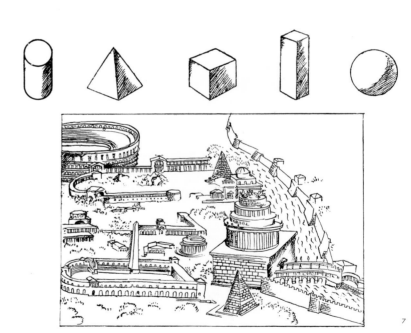

7

6 Claude-Nicolas
Ledoux, proposal for a
sluice house over the River
Loue, from *L'Architecture
considerée sous le rapport
de l'art, des mœurs et de
la législation*, 1804

7 The abstraction of
fundamental lessons from
the past: Le Corbusier,
sketch of primary
geometrical solids
alongside a view of
ancient Rome, from *Vers
une architecture*, 1923

structure to the most elemental piers and beams in the sketches of Friedrich Gilly around the same time. The idea of reading tradition for its supposed 'universal' formal values was given extra weight in the late nineteenth century by art historians such as Heinrich Wölfflin and Adolf Hildebrand, who rejected literary values in art in favour of underlying architectonic qualities, and who described past styles in terms of formal and spatial patterns. It is no accident that this way of perceiving the past should have coincided so closely with the emergence of abstract art: as we shall see, both this manner of viewing precedent, and the new language of space and form visualized by painters and sculptors, were to have an eventual influence on the creation of modern architecture.

Equally it was possible to think of the history of architecture, less as a sequence of styles, than as a series of transformations of basic types stretching back far in time and arising from a few archetypal elements and configurations. Writing at the beginning of the nineteenth century, the French theoretician Antoine-Chrysostome Quatremère de Quincy suggested that 'nothing whatsoever comes from nothing' and that 'the act of building is born out of a pre-existing germ'. For him a 'type' was 'a sort of kernel around, and in accordance with, which the variations that the object is susceptible to, are ordered'. According to this view, several inventions of different style and period might rest upon the same typological pattern, and share a common root. For example, Schinkel's Altes Museum of 1824–8, Asplund's Woodland Chapel of 1918–20 and Le Corbusier's Parliament Building in Chandigarh of 1951–63, although varying in function, material and style, might none the less all be seen as transformations of the same basic idea, portico and dome – a type exemplified most clearly in antiquity in the Pantheon in Rome of the second century AD.

The notion of type was inherited by Gottfried Semper who, writing in the mid-nineteenth century (and influenced by the evolutionists Lamarck and Darwin) could not resist linking it to the idea of natural species:

Just as nature is ever thrifty of motifs, even in her endless abundance, constantly repeating her basic forms, but modifying them in a thousand different ways according to the condition of her creatures and their mode of life … so art lies within the scope of a few Norms or Types, that derive from old tradition, each constantly reappearing in diverse forms …

Semper considered that the later symbolic forms of architecture such as column and entablature were elaborations of fundamental structural ideas such as post, beam and frame. Guided by knowledge of real peasant huts (rather than just mythical ones), he even posited the idea of four basic elements in architecture: platform, hearth, roof and enclosure. His own buildings were not so inspired or inspiring, but his ideas would be of great interest to those trying to find the best form for new 'species' like skyscrapers, or for new devices such as the steel frame or the concrete skeleton. Semper's message to the nineteenth-century architect was clear enough. Confronted by the 'mode of life' of his own time, and by the need to give appropriate form to new types, he should rely upon genetic recombinations of old ones. A version of natural adaptation was crossbred with an idea of historical progress.

While evolutionary and functionalist theories sometimes relied upon analogies with natural processes, there was a parallel line of thought which descended from Romanticism and from the writings of Ruskin, whereby nature was regarded as being the physical evidence of God's creation and laws, and thus as being a primary source of inspiration and of moral reflection. Traces of this outlook may be discerned in the thought of several major twentieth-century architects, notably Frank Lloyd Wright, Le Corbusier and Alvar Aalto who, far from being just 'materialists', had a lofty vision of 'nature' as a counterforce to banal mechanization. Natural phenomena might provide analogies and metaphors in design, or serve as the basis for abstractions and conventionalizations of form. They might also yield up general principles for guiding technology, architecture and urbanism. It was in this more general sense that Aalto could declare: 'Nature, rather than the machine, should serve as the model for architecture.'

With the 'loss of authority of the classical norms', ideas of nature were sometimes invoked as a supposed bedrock of certainties beyond the merely artificial and transient. Louis Sullivan and Frank Lloyd Wright tended to see the matter in this way, and each of them evolved 'generative grammars' based upon metamorphoses of natural forms that

8

became 'microcosms' of a kind. Something like this
procedure was already suggested in Owen Jones's
Grammar of Ornament of 1856, in which the
author argued that the ornamental systems and
vocabularies of the past were based upon the
geometrical idealizations of local plant forms. The
Egyptian column, for example, was traced to the
lotus and papyrus plants of the Nile valley. The
appeal of such ideas to the designers who pioneered
the tendrils and vegetal curves of Art Nouveau
should be obvious, but the notion of penetrating
nature for its underlying lessons had longer-range
implications and would recur within several frames
of reference. Analogy has always played a part in
the genesis of architectural forms, and in the late
nineteenth century 'natural' analogies joined with
'mechanical' ones to supply a model of perfectly
embodied function. In the twentieth century, ideas
of nature took on different guises in the work and
ideas of individual architects, sometimes with
reference to structure, sometimes with reference to
poetic perceptions of underlying order, sometimes

8 Charles Garnier,
Opéra, Paris, 1861:
Beaux-Arts classicism in
the grand manner that
was rejected in the early
twentieth century by the
avant-garde

9 'La Recherche du Style
Nouveau', from the *Revue
des Arts Décoratifs*, 1895:
the slow progress towards
a new style

9

in the context of 'organic' models of culture.

Thus, in finding forms to fit the emerging aspirations towards a modern architecture, the architects of the end of the nineteenth century and the beginning of the twentieth drew upon a rich fund of theories and ideas when formulating their task. They also drew repeatedly on both nature and tradition when grappling with the problem of style. But they looked upon these recurrent and ever-evolving sources of inspiration in quite new ways that were at variance with their immediate predecessors, for their method involved a greater degree of abstraction. In that respect their quests for new forms were not unconnected with avant-garde developments in the other arts, which dispensed with representation and relied upon basic formal structures for expression. It can even be argued that some of the most drastic innovators (one thinks, for example, of Sullivan, Root, Gaudí, Mackintosh, Perret, Wright and Behrens in these decades) were also, in some basic way, 'traditionalists'. While they certainly hoped to create vocabularies entirely in tune with modern circumstances and means, they also wished to endow their results with a certain universality: they sought to create architectural languages with the depth, rigour, and range of application of the great styles of the past.

So it was not tradition that was jettisoned, but a slavish, superficial, and irrelevant adherence to it. The rogue in all these respects was frequently (and often inaccurately) identified as the École des Beaux-Arts in Paris which was lampooned as the symbol of all that was tired and retardative. This caricature of academe aside, it is essential to see the vital developments of the 1890s against a backdrop of confusion and caprice in which the problem of style was much discussed but rarely resolved. To the young architectural minds which were to pioneer the skyscraper, Art Nouveau and the substantial new developments up to the First World War, writers like Viollet-le-Duc, Ruskin and Semper were powerful catalysts. The architects of the fin-de-siècle had little to stand on in the immediate past except facile revivalism and eclecticism, and therefore sought a new direction by going back to basics and forward to new inspirations simultaneously. In sources they were abundant; the question was how to forge these into a new synthesis appropriate to modern conditions.

2

industrialization and the city: the skyscraper as type and symbol

The architects of this land and generation are now brought face to face with something new under the sun – namely that evolution and integration of social conditions, that special grouping of them, that results in a demand for tall office buildings … Problem: How shall we impart to this sterile pile, this stark, staring exclamation of eternal strife, the graciousness of those higher forms of sensibility and culture that rest on the lower and fiercer passions? How shall we proclaim from the dizzy height of this strange, weird modern housetop, the peaceful evangel of sentiment, of beauty, the cult of a higher life?
Louis Sullivan, 1896.

10 Louis Sullivan and Dankmar Adler, Guaranty Building, Buffalo, 1894–5, detail

While the ideas which formed the theoretical scaffolding of modern architecture were first assembled in rarefied treatises, the realization of forms occurred within the calculations and mechanisms of the industrial city. It would be pointless to try to single out a particular time, place or personality as the exact starting point of a later worldwide movement, but it is striking how many tendencies professing the value of the 'new' came into being in the 1890s. Evidently a reaction against tired social, philosophical and aesthetic values was rumbling into life in urban centres as diverse as Paris, Vienna, Glasgow, Brussels, Barcelona and Chicago. The very notion and significance of 'modernity' differed from place to place, even from mind to mind, but the essential pre-conditions included the mechanization of the city, the introduction of materials like iron, glass and steel, experimental clients, and creative architects intent on expressing the new state of things in spaces and forms.

The above-mentioned cities were among the places to combine these conditions, but they each lived in different national histories which influenced the way in which architecture was perceived. The Viennese avant-garde emerged from the cracks of a declining imperial system as part of a short-lived revolt against the deadweight of previous cultural forms. The Art Nouveau which sprouted in Brussels was related to new industrial wealth, both its celebration in the world of the effete, aesthetic interior, and its critique in the politics of social reform. The formal innovations of both Glasgow and Barcelona were rooted in a consciousness of regional difference and in the evocation of 'identity' through the vernacular and natural analogies. The new tendencies in France necessarily took stock of an Enlightenment tradition, a technocratic model of national development, and the stifling effects of an 'official' Beaux-Arts view. In short, European aspirations towards a new architecture derived part of their point, much of their tension, and even some of their meaning from the destabilization or inversion of immediately preceding norms.

In North America the situation was somewhat different for the obvious reason that traditions were shorter, imported, and much less entrenched. The eventual elaboration of modern architectural ideals occurred against the backdrop of energetic *laissez-faire* economic development, technological pragmatism and chaotic urbanization. The new cities were themselves the hubs of vast new railway or steamship routes linked to westward expansion one way, and to immigration from the Old World the other. Nothing expresses the instrumentalism of American growth more directly than the land ordinance grid of the late eighteenth century mapping out future national territory for colonial expansion and occupation: a total abstraction ignoring differences of topography and obliterating all traces of indigenous memory. As a rule, the North American town was also laid out following a rectilinear system (Figs. 20, 21) and (unlike its Catholic colonial relative to the south) was based upon the principle of free-standing objects surrounded by spaces (rather than patios and plazas surrounded by buildings). Translated into the grids and blocks of the American industrial city, and the rectangular boxes and structural frames of commercial buildings, this mentality produced a neutral vernacular of a kind – a straightforward graph of land speculation and standardized modules of space: virtually an unconscious American style.

While the North American industrial city was different in plan and constitution from its European relatives (which normally possessed layers of urban fabric deposited over the centuries), the processes of technological modernization had certain broad features in common wherever they occurred. Coal and steam power, ferrous metals and engineering know-how were at the core of it all, and together with the concentration of capital, the transposition of labour from country to city, and the opening up of both national and international lines of trade and communication, they transformed the cultural landscape in a matter of decades. The large urban centres on both sides of the Atlantic expanded upwards, outwards, even underground, to cope with the pressure of people, traffic and goods. Baron Georges Haussmann characterized mid-nineteenth-century Paris as 'a great consumer's market, a vast workshop, an arena of ambitions'. His plans for the city (dating from the 1850s) cut wide boulevards through the old fabric and combined the agendas of the time: to render the capitalist instrument of the city more efficient by liberating its circulation; to celebrate the monuments and glory of empires past and present by linking focal points with vistas; to let

in light, air and greenery for the bourgeoisie, but push the poor elsewhere; to turn the boulevard into a social stage, but also a vector of military control.

Mobility was the key to the new kind of city, and circulation had a major impact on its form. The railway which permitted such concentrations of goods and people was both fact and symbol: it caused change but also represented it. It cut the finite city in pieces, demolished old boundaries between urban and rural worlds and brought the slag of the mine and the waste of the factory to the outskirts. If one result was a new 'middle landscape', another was a civic chaos in which old hierarchies between institutions were confused. Industrialization changed the size, shape and relationship of buildings in the cityscape, disturbing pre-existing conventions of representation and exacerbating uncertainties about the basis of style. The railway station itself epitomized the semantic confusion: a utilitarian shed on one side, an urban façade of uncertain form on the other. If George Gilbert Scott's Midland Hotel fronting St Pancras Station (1865–71) in London took the form of a Gothic château, Lewis Cubitt's King's Cross Station

12

importance. The city of process gradually replaced the city of finite form.

The very image of the machine could excite contrasting reactions in nineteenth-century minds. On the one hand it could be seen as the instrument of progress, offering new frontiers over land and sea, generating wealth, creating a new culture based upon science and rationality. On the other it could be seen as the great destroyer which raped nature, obliterated identity and region, and enslaved the working classes in an endless cycle of drudgery. In Pugin's *Contrasts*, published in 1836, there had been a comparison between the 'modern', 'utilitarian' way of handling the poor – the centralized mechanism of a *Panopticon* in which a single guard could survey all inmates from a single point – and the supposed medieval approach combining monastery and Christian charity. In this vision of things the machine was the epitome of inhuman authoritarianism and social alienation. The commercial structures of capitalism may have produced daring new architectural forms, but they rested upon a grimy and exploitative base. The slum, no less than the railway, the mill and the skyscraper, had a repetitive and standardized character wherever it appeared:

… row above row of windows in the mud coloured surface, upwards, upwards, lifeless eyes, murky openings that tell of barrenness, disorder, comfortlessness within … Acres of these edifices, the tinge of grime declaring the relative dates of their erection; millions of tons of brute brick and mortar, crushing the spirit as you gaze. Barracks in truth; housing for the army of industrialism, an army fighting with itself, rank against rank, man against man, that the survivors may have whereon to feed.

(1851–2) alongside took the more direct solution of a large frontispiece of wide brick arches signalling the presence of the sheds behind. This was not 'functionalism' so much as the representation of function: a bold and direct image evoking associations with viaducts and bridges.

The infrastructures of industry obeyed none of the traditional rules for the handling of urban space and made it more and more difficult to formulate a coherent image of the city as a whole. When designing for Berlin in the 1820s and 1830s, Schinkel had adapted the ideas of classical decorum to handle the transition from monumental to utilitarian and from city to country: the Altes Museum (Fig. 3) being given the full regalia of a classical order, the Bauakademie (Fig. 33) being treated to stripped pilasters almost like an industrial frame, and the Court Gardener's House at Potsdam working with a combination of picturesque, rustic and primitivist modes. But the concentration of new industrial functions upset the scale of values, so that private buildings for trade and business such as warehouses, factories and (later) skyscrapers towered above public buildings of civic or religious

13

14 Joseph Paxton,
Crystal Palace, London,
1850–1, from *Dickinsons
Comprehensive Pictures of
the Great Exhibition of
1851*, 1854

15 Gustave Eiffel,
Eiffel Tower, Paris, 1889

16 Victor Contamin and
Charles Louis Ferdinand
Dutert, Palais des
Machines, Paris, 1889

14

In the mid-nineteenth century squalid conditions were the source of both revolutionary fervour and reformist fantasy. For Karl Marx and Friedrich Engels, the question of an improved physical environment could only be answered in a post-revolutionary state; they tended to regard plans for alternative cities as hopeless attempts at imposing individual will on the unavoidable forces of history. For Utopian socialist visionaries with their ideal communities the problem was to release the working class from the alienation and exploitation of machine work and to rediscover the total personality split by the division of labour. And so the possibilities were considered of taking the town out to nature, or of putting nature in the town; of installing people in communal villages or collective palaces; of reordering the modern city so that it would function as a perfect machine or as a healthy, breathing organism (see Chapter 14). Given the nineteenth-century background of soot, disease, overcrowding and lack of open space, it is not altogether surprising that schemes of urban reform in the early twentieth century should have made so much of light, space, greenery, hygiene and transparency.

But the later images of salvation relied upon technologies that emerged in mostly pragmatic circumstances. The glazed shed fabricated with standardized iron components was a virtual leitmotif of the industrial city after mid-century on both sides of the Atlantic. Variations on this type occurred in railway stations, market halls, exhibition structures, shopping arcades, galleries, museums, even conservatories in the houses of the rich. Iron was molten and fluid and obeyed none of the traditional rules of masonry construction. It allowed wide spans and large areas of glass; it dissolved away mass and opened up space; it reduced supports from columns or piers to slender stanchions; it allowed girders to be made from standard flats and small fillets welded or riveted together; it encouraged the invention of new structural systems in bridges and towers and recast the roles of architect and engineer; it permitted tensile curves of unusual profile and prompted analogies not only with the skeletons of Gothic architecture, but also with those of nature. The Crystal Palace of 1850–1, which housed the Great Exhibition, was designed by a horticulturalist/ engineer, Joseph Paxton, who, in effect, transferred the greenhouse from one context to another. This vast glazed shed was assembled entirely from standardized pieces of iron, wood and glass, and was built to display the gadgetry and products of competing economic powers, but it soared above these mundane concerns, dissolving into trees and sky and revealing a virtually unprecedented sense of space, transparency and lightness.

We see a delicate network of lines without any clue by means of which we might judge their distance from the eye or the real size … the eye sweeps along an unending perspective which fades into the horizon. We cannot tell if this structure towers a hundred or a thousand feet above us, or whether the roof is a flat platform or is built up from a succession of ridges, for there is no play of shadows to enable our optic nerves to gauge the measurements … all materiality is blended into atmosphere …

The Crystal Palace forced many to realize that 'the standards by which architecture had hitherto been judged no longer held good'. To Rationalists it was evidence of a new architecture. Romantics compared the effects of light and space to the dissolution of the elements in J. M. W. Turner's late paintings. Semper (in an essay of 1852 entitled *Science, Industry and Art – Wissenschaft, Industrie und Kunst*) deplored the vulgarity of objects on show and warned against 'the depreciation of material that results from its treatment by machines'. Ruskin equated engineering standardization with brutal materialism and the death of craft. Meanwhile, the structure itself evaded easy categorization. It stood in Hyde Park with trees inside it, like a colossal conservatory, evoked a shopping arcade with the crowds of people pouring through, and was constructed rapidly following a method of serial production, like a railway. 'It should not be suggestive of a pyramid, a temple, or a palace,' the Building Committee in charge of the competition had stated: 'The object should determine the design. That is to say, the design should be altogether subordinate to the uses of the building, and should be of the kind that would express them, or at least, harmonize with them.'

The Crystal Palace took over a standard technology and gave it a coherent form. The rolled iron girder was the unit from which much of the industrial world was made: the railways themselves, the iron bridges of huge span, the stations and sheds, even the frames of the skyscrapers in the 1880s and 1890s, which could be thought of as vertical railways with elevators replacing the trains. Iron had revealed its formidable potential in the bridges of Telford and Brunel earlier in the century, and would do so again in the masterly designs of Gustave Eiffel, not only in the bridge over the Douro in Portugal of 1876, and the Pont du Garabit of 1880–4 in the Massif Central, but also in the Eiffel Tower, centrepiece of the Paris 1889 Exhibition, where Victor Contamin and Charles Louis Ferdinand Dutert's huge steel spans in the Palais des Machines also lent ferrous metals a monumental presence. Iron, and its relative steel

(the Bessemer process allowing economic production of this second material was patented in 1856), were increasingly able to establish their own aesthetic conventions, and in the 1889 exhibition were even involved in the expression of technological power as an instrument of national progress. In an essay written in the 1930s entitled 'Paris, Capital of the Nineteenth Century', Walter Benjamin evoked the crisis of representation brought about by rapid technological change:

The development of the forces of production reduced the wish symbols of the previous century to rubble even before the monuments representing them had crumbled. In the nineteenth century this development emancipated constructional forms from art, as in the sixteenth century the sciences freed themselves from philosophy.

If the objects of engineering could be portrayed as brute equipment lacking the ennobling endowments of the art of architecture, the opposite case could also be made that the historically bound activities of the architectural profession were being made redundant by the verve and skill of the engineers. The latter point of view was to become a standard piece of the folklore of the modern movement in the twentieth century, and was well represented eventually in the writings of Sigfried Giedion, who saw the nineteenth century as a schizophrenic age,

torn between the 'true' culture of structural integrity and the 'false' one of dying schemes of architectural representation. In fact this overstated the case, since architects as varied in their persuasions as Henri Labrouste (the Bibliothèque Ste-Geneviève of 1843–50) and Thomas Deane and Benjamin Woodward (the Oxford Museum of 1855–60) had effective and deliberate recourse to skeletal iron structures on the insides of their buildings. These were carefully conceived works in which the juxtaposition and contrast of slender metal members and articulated masonry walls was an essential and complementary aspect of the architectural idea. Labrouste's building submitted technology and craft to the governing image of a civic institution of learning with sober, arcuated stone exteriors of no particular historical style, and a single airy, well-lit interior space for 'enlightenment' (permitted by the spanning capacities of iron). Deane and Woodward's Museum worked with the bold contrast between Ruskinian Gothic ornament, geological associations and a slender metal and glass roof illuminating the natural specimens in the central court. Whatever the medieval pedigree of the design as a whole, the iron was forged to fit a Rationalist vision of Gothic, and even to echo the skeletons of creatures on display. The combination

17 Henri Labrouste, Bibliothèque Ste-Geneviève, Paris, 1843–50

18 Joseph Paxton, Crystal Palace, London 1851, under construction

19 Thomas Deane and Benjamin Woodward, Oxford Museum, Oxford, 1855–60

17

of 'natural', traditional and mechanical was integral to the institutional interpretation, and added to the material and metaphorical richness of the result.

The stone or brick casket with a metallic cage or frame let down inside it was a recurrent and basic structural type throughout the nineteenth century which even continued into the early twentieth. The fact that several notable engineers succeeded in demonstrating the intrinsic qualities of iron and steel in their designs for towers and bridges did not automatically render this type obsolete. What really changed was the nature of the relationship between load and support, cladding and frame, especially when much taller buildings like skyscrapers were needed towards the end of the century. For in these circumstances masonry could only go so high before it became an impractical encumbrance, and so iron and steel were commandeered to do more and more of the actual work. By degrees the skeleton made its presence felt in the overall form, in the façade composition and in the tectonic stresses of the building – but not directly, for it was usually sheathed in protective layers of brick, stone or terracotta which served as fireproofing, insulation or ornament. The actual structural frame was made manifest as some sort of *visual* frame in which the interplay between pier, spandrel, moulding,

19

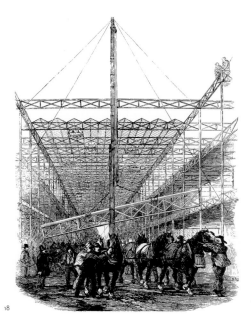

18

plate glass, lintel and arch afforded a new aesthetic.

Nothing reveals the struggle to reconcile engineering and architecture more clearly than the commercial buildings produced in the Midwest of the United States in the last two decades of the nineteenth century. The problem was to find forms for a range of mercantile functions from warehouse to tall office building. Needed were cheap, utilitarian buildings that were quick to construct, flexible in use, and fireproof. As the rectangular perimeters should be filled out to maximize floor space, and as light courts were wasteful, large apertures were desirable to admit light and air deep into the blocks. The typical arrangement combined a utilitarian cage with wide-bayed windows, elevators tucked out of the way, and a grid of structural supports in plan. This skeleton posed teasing problems of architectural expression. Should it be left alone as engineering dictated? Should it be clothed or decorated in some appeasing historical style? Or should it be interpreted as a cultural fact worthy of a new symbolic expression? At issue was the question of appropriateness. What were these new buildings supposed to look like and what did they really represent?

Although the skyscraper had become a general phenomenon in America by the end of the nineteenth century, the first major proliferation of the type was in the Chicago of the 1880s and 1890s. Chicago was the main depot, nerve centre and clearing house for the great railroad expansion to the West which occurred from mid-century onwards. It was the diagram of capitalism in its crude form and, after the fire of 1871, the flat site by Lake Michigan offered a *tabula rasa* for a boom in rapid construction. The skyscraper was, essentially, a white-collar building type, a direct expression of the division of labour between management and manufacturing. It was part of the same world as the typewriter, the telegraph, the electric light and the mechanical heating system – all of which contributed to its own commercial viability. The pressure to build upwards came from the

desirability of concentrating everybody in the downtown 'loop', an area only nine blocks long and wide, delineated by the Chicago river and the railroad yards, but it also arose from the desire to extract maximum profit from single, rectangular lots of land in the urban grid. The steel wire and the Otis elevator permitted the tall office building to happen.

The skyscraper's uncertain identity touched upon the very problem of a modern architecture, and upon an inheritance of American dilemmas concerning the relative values of 'cultural', 'vernacular', and 'industrial' forms. The country was, after all, a colonial invention: it had imported European styles from the start, gradually adjusting them to deal with local conditions. In the early nineteenth century, classicism was given the stamp of approval for the new Republic by Thomas Jefferson, and it returned later under various guises. In the ensuing decades America experienced some of the same architectural crises as Europe, with Greek, Roman, Gothic and other revivals taking on a slightly different accent. It was in the years immediately following the Civil War that a new

20 Bird's-eye view of the business district of Chicago, c.1898

21 Map of New York City, showing the grid of streets on Manhattan Island, with Frederick Law Olmsted's Central Park, designed in the 1850s

20

mood of integration and national identity influenced the arts, emphasizing the 'falsehood' of imported imitations. The writings of Horatio Greenough, praising the craft, elegance and economy of ships, gave expression to a native functionalism. The speculations of Ralph Waldo Emerson, David Thoreau and Walt Whitman opened vistas on a transcendentalism rooted in the American landscape. These antidotes to fickle revivalism and vulgar materialism were accompanied by other signs of cultural independence: in the democratic 'wildernesses' of Frederick Law Olmsted's urban parks (which invaded the grid of the capitalist city in order to make it more humane) and in the architecture of Henry Hobson Richardson, models of 'nature' were used to civilize the machine.

Richardson was a special case of his own: a 'modern' architect with the ancient sense who was broad enough to encompass the energy of the railway age while returning to first principles in tradition. He worked with bold masses of brick or stone that were cut by arches, abutted by towers and surmounted by dramatic roofs. His polychrome

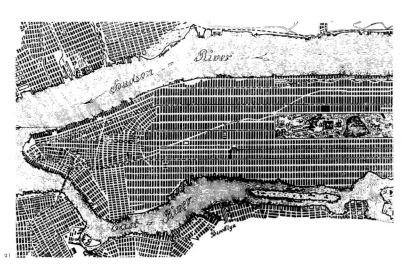

21

surfaces, romantic silhouettes, and ornamental patterns celebrated craft, while the robust order of his buildings transcended matters of personal style to evoke the social forces of an America in transition from rural to urban realities. Having studied at the École des Beaux-Arts in Paris in the 1860s, he never lost sight of the hierarchical plan or the discipline of the conceptual sketch, an inner image making itself felt in every part and detail. But his sources were medieval and vernacular as well as classical, and his 'system' could be adjusted to handle a wide range of tasks in the new cultural landscape – from churches and commercial buildings in the city to railway stations and libraries in suburbia, to rural retreats and wealthy homes in the countryside. Richardson's architecture straddled the Old World and the New, recalling both the elemental values of the French Romanesque and the rock formations of the American landscape: his colossal semicircles in stone were capable of alluding to the huge wheels of locomotives, or of rhyming with Roman aqueducts. Without theoretical pretension or undue show, he took on nineteenth-century dilemmas over the basis of style and forged an eclectic solution in the deepest sense.

Richardson was first in a line of proudly 'American' architects which included Louis Sullivan, John Wellborn Root and Frank Lloyd Wright; he also supplied the rock on which the Chicago School would stand. For a viable commercial style would result only when some coherent way had been discovered for combining the sculptural masonry tradition with skeletal thinking about the structural frame. The latter was well represented by William Le Baron Jenney's First Leiter Building of 1879, a cut-to-the-bone rectangular solution shorn of adornment which reflected the sensibility of a Civil War engineer and relied upon Viollet-le-Duc's notion of a new architecture based upon a direct expression of structure and programme. It avoided the fussiness of the cast-iron storefronts designed by James Bogardus and others in the 1850s in New York, and concentrated upon a stark rectangular aesthetic of spandrel and pier. There was a faint reminiscence of pilasters and a cipher of a cornice, but that is as far as history was allowed to go. If there were antecedents, they probably lay in the realm of mill and factory design, or possibly in new – reached a point of tense coexistence and equilibrium. Louis Sullivan described the building in these terms:

Four-square and brown, it stands, in physical fact, a monument to trade, to the organized commercial spirit, to the power and progress of the age, to the strength and resource of individuality and force of character; spiritually it stands as the index of a mind, large enough, courageous enough, to cope with these things, master them, absorb them and give them forth again, impressed with the stamp of large and forceful personality; artistically it stands as the oration of one who knows well how to chose his words, who has something to say and says it – and says it as the outpouring of a copious, direct, large and simple mind.

Richardson not only had something to say, he also had a mature language with which to say it. The Marshall Field Store worked its way towards civic monumentality on his scale of values, while holding to the stark 'objectivity' of American vernacular construction; palatial and stately, it none the less evoked 'the vitality of the rising city'. It stood midway between the age of the machine and the age of craft; between the world of industrialism and the wide western wilderness full of raw materials where Richardson had only recently erected the Ames Monument as a rugged stone cairn to mark the meeting of the railway lines between east and west. But if the building had a continental grandeur about it, it was also pervaded by a general classical sense. Its immediate nineteenth-century ancestor may have been Labrouste's Bibliothèque Ste-Geneviève, but its longer-range pedigree surely included the

22 William Le Baron Jenney, First Leiter Building, Chicago, 1879

23 William Le Baron Jenney, the steel frame of the Fair Store, Chicago, from *Industrial Chicago*, 1891

24 Henry Hobson Richardson, Marshall Field Wholesale Store, Chicago, 1885–7

25 Pont du Gard, near Nîmes, Roman aqueduct, 1st century AD

26 Henry Hobson Richardson, early sketch for the Marshall Field Wholesale Store, 1885. Pencil, crayon and wash on buff paper, heightened with white 11¼ x 20 in (28.5 x 50.1 cm). Houghton Library, Harvard University, Cambridge

22

the kind of restrained cast-iron compositions achieved in some warehouse and shop designs in Glasgow and Liverpool in the 1860s.

Richardson's major contribution to American commercial architecture was the Marshall Field Wholesale Store constructed in Chicago between 1885 and 1887. Here the utilitarian requirements of a giant purchasing warehouse were submitted to the rigours of a symmetrical and hierarchical plan and a dominant sculptural idea. The internal construction followed that of the typical elevator building with cast-iron columns carrying floors and roof, and wrought-iron beams increasing the structural spans, but the exterior was made from weight-bearing walls in sandstone resting on a rough granite base. The block as a whole was treated as a single monolith into which a dignified row of arches was cut. The combination of an exterior masonry armature and interior 'shelves' of floors was expressed deftly in the spandrels and horizontals of the fenestration system. Two entirely different technologies and ideas of construction, stone arch, trabeated metal frame – one old, the other

23

24

25

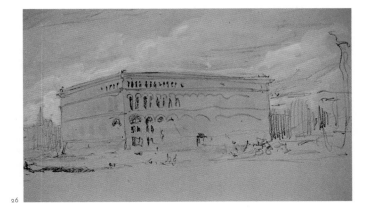

26

27 Louis Sullivan and
Dankmar Adler,
Auditorium Building,
Chicago, 1886–9

28 Auditorium Building,
longitudinal section

brown-textured stone palaces of the Florentine
quattrocento (built for an earlier mercantile class),
if not the basic type of the Roman aqueduct (the
Pont du Gard comes to mind). Richardson was
here on the knife edge between utilitarian form
and symbolic representation.

The Auditorium Building in Chicago of 1886–9
by Louis Sullivan and the engineer Dankmar Adler
was one of several buildings to extend Richardson's
seminal lessons for ennobling 'industrial
civilization'. The programme had a civic aspect,
since it was necessary to combine an opera house
and a hotel with offices in a single structure. The site
offered breathing space, views and a façade in an
easterly direction towards Lake Michigan. Whatever
his theoretical claims at making form 'follow'
function, Sullivan (who had spent a short time at the
École des Beaux-Arts, and also at the new school at
Massachusetts Institute of Technology) was aware
of the need to transform types from history when
dealing with the unprecedented problems of

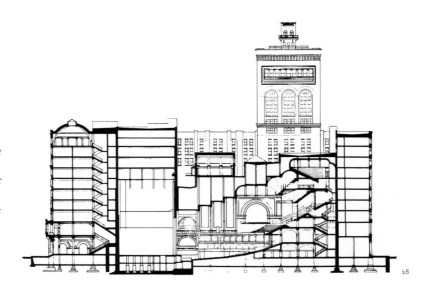

commercial construction. The overall massing of the Auditorium Building, with its tower to one side, suggested an ingenious transposition of a medieval *palazzo pubblico*. Crammed into this shape was a very different creature, relying upon wide spans in iron, and incorporating modern heating and ventilation equipment. Adler's solution to the spanning of the auditorium allowed uninterrupted visibility and an arched acoustic ceiling, while the entire structure was brought down on to wide-footed foundations dealing with the marshy subsoil conditions. As subsidence was expected to be uneven, the building was weighted unequally.

The exteriors of the Auditorium Building reveal Sullivan's struggle to reconcile a masonry syntax with the stretching of internal possibilities permitted by the structural frame. The bold sculptural massing, the varying degrees of rustication, the huge arches and the visual expression of inner tension, placed the building broadly in a Richardsonian lineage, but the vertical attenuation and flattening of the main shafts and piers anticipated some of Sullivan's later solutions for the tall building. The dense and vegetal ornament in the bar (vaguely like Art Nouveau) also hinted at his interest in geometrical systems based upon nature. The Auditorium was a transitional work in Sullivan's search for an adequate tectonic expression for the new means of construction; the division of the block into base, middle and top, and the accentuation of vertical lines of force with linear ornament would be developed and clarified in later designs. But the building revealed broader dilemmas related to industrialization itself. It grappled with the problem of imposing a civic image on raw standardized technology, and with the role of 'higher sensibility' in a commercial setting.

The Monadnock Building by John Wellborn Root and Daniel Burnham of 1884–91 also confronted these questions but, by contrast, was a completely resolved sculptural entity – a work of invincible directness and clarity. It was also the end of the line for monolithic masonry construction on this scale in Chicago office buildings of the late nineteenth century. The design was evolved gradually between 1884 and 1890, then constructed in the following year. The client Peter Brooks (a Boston real estate developer) insisted throughout on simple lines and an avoidance of unnecessary clutter. The Monadnock stood on a narrow half-block, so presenting a slender profile at each end, and a cliff-like façade on the longer sides. As the site was oblong, there was no need to include a light court, and the office windows were bowed to draw light and air into the dense mass of the shaft. The main weight of the Monadnock was born by the colossal brick walls, which were battered outwards towards the base to supply an earth-bound socle in granite. There was also some lateral steel bracing in the structure to stabilize the building in high winds, and to lock in the window bays. The uniform brick surfaces were sliced and cut to deny the sense of mass, and tapered gradually before being flared outwards at the top where the wall was coextensive with a completely abstracted 'cornice'. The tension of the design relied, in part, on the interplay between glass planes and sheer masonry. The Monadnock Building combined grim solemnity and stern utilitarianism; it had the inevitability of a geological fact.

Montgomery Schuyler, a perceptive American critic of the time, called the Monadnock 'the most effective and successful of the commercial structures to which the elevator has literally "given rise"'. He suggested that its quality relied upon 'a series of subtle refinements and nuances that bring out the latent expressiveness of what without them would be as bald as a factory'. Among these 'refinements' was the detailing of the corners, which were sharp and angular at the base, but increasingly flared, flattened and rounded towards the top. The vertical bays introduced a sober rhythm and seemed to swell from the primary mass. The windows were handled in such a way that one had the sensation of an entire glass skin inside a sheath of masonry. Thus the tectonic order of the whole building relied upon denials of visual weight, as well as their emphasis. The resulting form possessed a muscular sense of pressure and resistance, an inner energy, as if it were alive. The Monadnock took the mundane facts of construction and spiritualized them through a control of form and idea and through a distillation of principles drawn from history. Root was sophisticated and well-read in theoretical matters, knew Semper's ideas on 'origins' and types, and was surely aware of the plate in Owen Jones's *Grammar of Ornament* (1856) tracing the Egyptian column to Nile valley plant forms such as the lotus and the

29

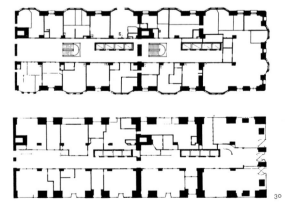

30

papyrus. He was initially hesitant about working with a brick box but revealed that 'the heavy sloping lines of an Egyptian pylon had gotten into his mind as the basis of this design, and that he would throw the whole thing up without a single ornament'.

Root was determined to see beyond the transient facts of the capitalist city to some realm of higher values and spoke of the 'Ideals of modern business life – simplicity, stability, breadth, dignity', and of the need for skyscrapers to convey 'by their mass and proportion ... in some large elemental sense an idea of the great, stable, conserving forces of modern civilization'. Root fully understood the broader implications of what he and his Chicago colleagues were doing. In response to unprecedented American conditions they were realizing an architecture that was distinctly modern, yet based upon fundamentals:

In America we are free of artistic traditions. Our freedom begets licence, it is true. We do shocking things; we produce works of architecture irremediably bad; we try crude experiments that result in disaster. Yet somewhere in this mass of ungoverned energies lies the principle of life. A new spirit of beauty is being developed and perfected, and even now its first achievements are beginning to delight us. This is not the old thing made over; it is new. It springs out of the past, but it is not tied to it; it studies the traditions, but is not enslaved by them. Compare the best of our recent architecture – some of Richardson's designs for example – with the most pretentious buildings recently erected in Europe. In the American works we find strength and fitness, and a certain spontaneity and freshness …

With the Reliance Building in Chicago of 1890–4 (by Burnham and Root, main designer of project Charles Atwood), the steel frame broke free of masonry traditions altogether and opened up an entirely new world of delicate transparency and reflective planes. The bay window, a constituent feature of both business and apartment blocks, became an object in its own right, a perforated membrane with faceted sides for ventilation, a fixed central pane for illumination, and slender vertical mullions (a type known as the 'Chicago window'). The spandrels were coated in light-coloured terracotta and made to read as continuous horizontal bands. The image of the whole was an apparently weightless cage, hovering above a shadowy base, with a slender slab closing off the top of the composition. As usual, the design was rooted in practical considerations such as the maximum provision of light, and the increase in office space

29 John Wellborn Root and Daniel Burnham, Monadnock Building, Chicago, 1884–91

30 Monadnock Building, plans of typical floor and ground floor

31 Burnham and Root, main designer Charles Atwood, Reliance Building, Chicago, 1890–4

31

or Le Corbusier's Utopian projects for glass skyscrapers. However, it needs saying that the sentiments were altogether different: the Chicago School scarcely anticipated the radical social content of the later European modern movement.

Aside from Root, Louis Sullivan was the most theoretically minded of the Chicago architects, and in an essay published in 1896, entitled 'The Tall Office Building Artistically Considered', he outlined his ideas on the skyscraper. These reflections relied upon discoveries made in his Wainwright Building in St Louis, Missouri of 1890–1 and in his Guaranty Building in Buffalo, New York of 1894–5 (both designed with Adler) and had the character of post-rationalizations. For Sullivan, the skyscraper was the inevitable product of social and technological forces, truly a new type in search of an appropriate morphology. Armed with ideas derived from Viollet-le-Duc, Semper, Greenough and others, he tended to look at the situation in 'organic' terms, meaning that the function must have an inherent and specific identity striving for direct and honest expression. He described the elements of the problem in a pragmatic way – a lower portion for shops and entrance, a mezzanine, a repeating stack of offices, a turn-around for elevators at the top, a core for vertical circulation, a frame for the structure – and decided that this functional layout led 'naturally' to a tripartite division of base, middle and top. Beyond function there was expression, and Sullivan decided that the skyscraper should have a *vertical* emphasis:

We must now heed the imperative voice of emotion. It demands of us, what is the chief characteristic of the tall office building? And at once we answer, it is lofty … It must be tall. The force and power of altitude must be in it, the glory and pride of exultation must be in it. It must be every inch a proud and soaring thing, rising in sheer exultation that from top to bottom it is a unit without a single dissenting line …

The steps in the argument from function and structure to idea and expression suggest a progression from a 'Rationalist' definition of the task to a 'symbolic' interpretation in a manner that recalls Semper's observations on the way utilitarian constructions were elevated to the level of art in past eras. Sullivan did not hesitate to accentuate or deny 'objective' structure to suit his sculptural instincts, and in the Wainwright Building, for example, every other pier in the office shaft was structurally

achieved by cantilevering the bays from the slabs. The Reliance Building was a drastic simplification of certain of the façade ideas expressed in William Holabirde and Martin Roche's Tacoma Building of 1887–8, a breakthrough design technically, since it hung the façades off the metal structure as a type of 'curtain wall'. Equally the Reliance seemed to reconfirm some of the aesthetic potentials of skeleton construction announced in earlier structures such as the Crystal Palace: ordered repetition, lightness, a network of visual stresses. It is understandable that Giedion should have looked upon it as a 'true ancestor' of the transparent buildings of the 1920s, such as Mies van der Rohe's

32   Louis Sullivan and
Dankmar Adler,
Wainwright Building,
St Louis, 1890–1

33   Karl Friedrich
Schinkel, Bauakademie,
Berlin, 1831–6

34   Louis Sullivan
and Dankmar Adler,
Guaranty Building,
Buffalo, 1894–5

32

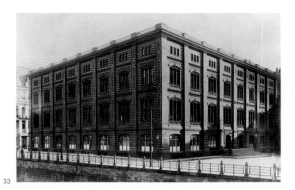

33

redundant. Moreover, despite the rejection of
'rules and other impedimenta', it was obvious that
Sullivan's theorem and image of the skyscraper
relied upon an elemental redefinition of the classical
column or pilaster, if not a more general tripartite
principle in nature (feet, body, head; roots, trunk,
branches). As for Sullivan's actual architectural
elements, they recalled early nineteenth-century
neo-classicism, especially Schinkel's distillations of
classical piers and mouldings. Schinkel's
Bauakademie in Berlin of 1831–6 takes its place in
the pedigree of the Chicago inventions of the 1890s
without too much difficulty.

Although the Wainwright Building in St Louis
preceded Sullivan's theoretical generalizations by
several years, it amounted to a polemical definition
of the tall building as a type. It was not so much
the frame, as an *idea* of the frame which was
orchestrated and accentuated through plastic means
to convey the underlying impulse of an aspiring
vertical form. While the basic scheme was tripartite,
the corner piers rose straight from street to cornice,
a secondary rhythm being set in motion by
alternating ground-level piers. The main office shaft
was expressed as a vertical grid of smaller piers
resting on a projecting ledge above the mezzanine,
the textured spandrels of the windows being
recessed behind the façade plane. Material and
ornament were used to reveal the underlying pattern
of visual stresses. The ground floor was treated to a
smooth, warm-coloured ashlar that blended almost
imperceptibly into the brick of the middle portion,
while the vegetal motifs in the spandrels and upper
registers were in richly modelled terracotta. The
slender piers of the office shaft were in turn detailed

with small brick roundels and grooves on their
corners (a typical St Louis vernacular device),
and with capitals and bases which seemed to be
'stretched'. Thus the web of masonry cladding over
the skeletal structure was reduced to a tense pattern
of piers, lintels and shafts incised with lines of
shadow to enhance the 'force and power of altitude'
and to reinforce the sense of 'a proud and soaring
thing'.

Sullivan's Guaranty Building (designed with
Adler) of 1894–5 belonged to a parallel, but slightly
different line of research, using arches. The
Walker Warehouse of 1889 was one of the clearest
statements of this theme, but it was reused in a more
'elastic' way in the Schiller Building of 1892, and
with more pomp in the Stock Exchange Building of
1893. Ultimately these solutions were haunted by
the seminal image of Richardson's Marshall Field
Store, but with the important difference that they
symbolized and expressed the skeletal nature of the
new steel construction, albeit through the medium
of masonry cladding or ceramic ornament. The
Guaranty made much of the transparency of the
lowest floor, and of the free-standing nature of the
supporting columns, which were cylindrical and

34

took on a truly anthropomorphic character. The vegetal ornament and the punctured roundels at the crest of each bay emphasized the character of growth, and dramatized the turnaround of elevators and pipes in the actual anatomy of the structure. There was a shift from the notion of mechanism to the idea of a tall building as a living organism, whose weight, pressure, tension and resistance might be experienced through empathy in a direct, almost physical way.

The architects of the Chicago School devoted their attention to the form of the individual skyscraper, but gave relatively little thought to the form of the skyscraper city with its increasingly cavernous, noisy and polluted streets, its lack of civic amenities and its curious overall impression of an endless repetition of mute rectangles. The dilemma of the industrial city as a whole was not so very different from that of the individual building – at what point should *laissez-faire* forces be bridled by aesthetic considerations? Still, the new geometrical urban landscape had an odd presence of its own. Like the grid of the American landscape and the grid of the American city, it was a reminder that America was an Enlightenment invention, a projection of rationalism as well as pragmatism: a phenomenon of daring abstraction. Just before the turn of the century, the French novelist Paul Bourget described the skyscraper city of the New World in these terms:

At one moment you have around you only 'buildings'. They scale the sky, with their eighteen, their twenty storeys. The architect who has built them, or rather who has plotted them, has renounced colonnades, mouldings, classical embellishments. He has frankly accepted the conditions imposed by the speculator; multiplying as many times as possible the value of the bit of ground at the base in multiplying the supposed offices. It is a problem capable of interesting only an engineer, one would suppose. Nothing of the kind. The simple force of need is such a principle of beauty, and these buildings so conspicuously manifest that need, that in contemplating them you experience a singular emotion. The sketch appears here of a new kind of art, an art of democracy, made by the crowd and for the crowd, an art of science in which the certainties of natural laws give to the most unbridled audacities in appearance the tranquillity of geometrical figures .

In 1893, the World's Columbian Exposition or Chicago World's Fair took place. Most of the structures were designed in a frankly Beaux-Arts, grand classical manner, a popularized version of the Second Empire mode. They revealed the full impact of Parisian taste on the American architectural

establishment and the general public. The 'White City' also introduced a new model of urbanism combining axes, boulevards, focal points, and the full panoply of classical rhetoric for civic spaces and public institutions. Louis Sullivan designed the Transportation Building at the Fair in a restrained but formal style with a portal of telescoped golden arches, inspired by 'exotic' sources such as Abbasid gateways and Moghul domes, but it was to become increasingly obvious that the ideals for which he stood would remain localized in the Midwest, or else in the fields of commercial or small-scale construction. The architects of the Chicago School found themselves confronted at the Fair by a different set of prescriptions which promised 'instant' beautification and urbanity: plaster-of-Paris classicism that was supposed to 'civilize' the machine.

The immediate future for civic buildings lay with the more 'scholarly' architects, such as McKim, Mead and White, Richard Morris Hunt, Cass Gilbert, or Daniel Burnham (who straddled several fences). Sullivan's own capacities for monumentality were confined to several tombs in the 1890s (Wainwright, Getty etc.) and to small town banks in the rural Midwest in the first two decades of the twentieth century; in these he revealed a prodigious capacity to fuse sources from diverse cultures (including Islamic in the case of the tombs) into a species of universal grammar. Meanwhile, his design for the Schlesinger Mayer (later Carson Pirie Scott)

35   Louis Sullivan, Carson Pirie Scott store, Chicago, 1899–1904

36   Chicago World's Fair, 1893, contemporary print

35

36

Store in Chicago of 1899 to 1904 revealed him at the
height of his powers. Here the frame was given a
notably horizontal emphasis with subtle variations
in the height of bays vitalizing the overall form. But
this was Sullivan's last major Chicago commission.
In ensuing years he withdrew increasingly into
the hermetic world of his elaborate ornament, a
microcosm of pantheistic and cosmic themes.
American industrial society seemed to have less
and less place for this artist's 'cult of a higher life'.

The Chicago of the late nineteenth century
demonstrated with diagrammatic crudity the
fundamental forces and typical components of
the capitalist city in the age of steam and steel. It
also laid out the generic problems and cultural
contradictions of the skyscraper as a type, and
identified several possible solutions. In reality,
the skyscraper was part of a wider system which
included the railroads at a distance, and the suburbs

closer to. For the pastoral atmosphere and romantic
domesticity of the middle-class world at the end of
the trolley lines was the essential 'counterform'
to the white-collar business city in its harsh
environment of rectangular grids. While the terms
might change, and the formal definitions vary, the
skyscraper would henceforth play a central role
in most industrial cities to come, even in Utopian
images that tried to put these cities right. Through
a happy coincidence of circumstance and talent,
Chicago was the forcing ground of a new synthesis
of technology and form. Here and there, the
raw conditions and standardized equipment of
capitalism were transformed into architectural
works of high poetic intensity. By facing industrial
realities head on, and reflecting on the essence of
their art, the Chicago architects contributed a major
foundation to a more universal ideal, that of a
modern architecture.

3

the search for new forms and the problem of ornament

… the whole basis of the views of architecture prevailing today must be displaced by the recognition that the only possible point of departure for our artistic creation is modern life.
Otto Wagner, 1895

37 Charles Rennie Mackintosh, Glasgow School of Art, 1897–1909, library wing, *c.* 1908

There is an old debate in the history of architecture concerning the relative primacy of formal and structural inventions. On the one side are those who see major revolutions in style as the direct result of new materials or methods of construction; on the other are those who argue that changes in world-view or aesthetic intention adapt techniques to their expressive aims. Where the emergence of modern architecture is concerned there is truth in both positions, although the previous chapter should be enough to warn against determinism. The iron or steel frame and the commercial programme suggested some directions more than others, but it was because there were also architects who could see these raw data as relevant to the quest for a new architecture that the Chicago School arrived at its results. Nor should it be forgotten that two of the greatest works of the period, the Marshall Field Store and the Monadnock Building, were realized by relatively conservative structural means.

The economic and cultural conditions that permitted all this to happen in the American Midwest did not find a direct equivalent in Europe, but there were some areas of overlap. The pioneer stages of modern architecture took several routes, but they all shared a revulsion against weak and arbitrary reuses of the past, and against dead cultural forms. As early as 1873, Friedrich Nietzsche had written in an essay, 'The Use and Abuse of History', of Europe's need to rid itself of its historical baggage, and to liberate a repressed inner potential. Time and again in the years around the turn of the century one encounters the theme of renewal after a period of supposed corruption and decay; time and again one hears the rallying cry that a new, modern man is emerging, whose character an avant-garde is best able to intuit. Thus, in assembling the fragments of the pre-First World War architectural world into a larger picture, it is essential to balance up the local contexts and individual intentions of architects with their piecemeal contributions to a new tradition. We have to deal here not with a simple evolutionary path, but with the tentative groundwork towards a later rough consensus.

Since the emphasis is on forms and not just ideas or techniques, it seems reasonable to concentrate next on Art Nouveau, and therefore to concur with Henry-Russell Hitchcock's assessments that 'it offered the first international programme for a basic renewal that the nineteenth century actually set out to realize' and that 'Art Nouveau was actually the first stage of modern architecture in Europe, if modern architecture be understood as implying primarily the total rejection of historicism.' But if Art Nouveau artists rejected historicism, they could not altogether reject tradition, for even the creator intent on producing new forms will rely, in some degree, on old ones. Indeed, what is often meant when the claim is made that such-and-such a movement was 'new' is that it switched its allegiances from recent and nearby traditions to ones more remote in space or time.

Even so, it is possible to distinguish between innovations which extend the premises of a pre-existing tradition, and more drastic breaks. Art Nouveau was of this second sort and embodied a strong reaction against the Beaux-Arts classicism widely practised in the 1870s and 1880s. Instead of ponderous monumentality it proposed fresh inventions exploiting the lightness and airiness permitted by glass and metal construction, and drawing inspiration from nature. As such it was a major step towards the intellectual and stylistic emancipation of modern architecture. However, the path from the curved abstractions and slender vegetal forms in metal of Art Nouveau to the stripped, white rectangular geometries of the 1920s was neither simple nor straightforward.

In architecture the most creative phase of Art Nouveau was from 1893 to about 1905 – a little more than a decade. The beginnings of the style have been variously dated. Arguably it first emerged in graphics and the decorative arts. Pevsner claimed a start in the early 1880s in England.

If the long, sensitive curve, reminiscent of the lily's stem, an insect's feeler, the filament of blossom, or occasionally a slender flame, the curve undulating, flowing and interplaying with the others, sprouting from the corners and covering asymmetrically all available surfaces, can be regarded as a leitmotif of Art Nouveau, then the first work of Art Nouveau which can be traced is Arthur H. Mackmurdo's cover of his book on Wren's city churches published in 1883.

Of course this is said with the knowledge of hindsight: Mackmurdo's design would be written off as a minor incident stemming from certain arabesques of the Pre-Raphaelites, the linear patterns of William Blake, and the fascination with natural forms of John Ruskin, if there had not

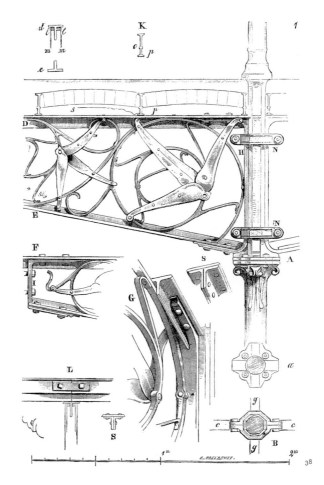

38

subsequently been a broader indulgence in the formal qualities Pevsner outlines. There is little evidence that Mackmurdo's design was the start of a sequence. Rather it was an early manifestation of a broad shift in sensibility in the 1880s, also sensed in such diverse examples as the ornamental designs of Louis Sullivan, Antoni Gaudí, and William Burges, the melancholic and erotic drawings of Aubrey Beardsley, the symbolist paintings of Paul Gauguin and Maurice Denis. A consolidation did not occur until the early 1890s, particularly in Brussels, in the work of Fernand Khnopff, Jan Toorop, and a group of painters known as 'Les Vingt', and in the architecture of Victor Horta, which seemed a three-dimensional equivalent to the painters' two-dimensional linear inventiveness.

38 Eugène Viollet-le-
Duc, proposal for a
wrought iron bracket,
from *Entretiens sur
l'architecture*, 1863–72

39 Aubrey Beardsley,
Toilet of Salome II, 1894.
Drawing, 8³/₄ × 6¹/₄ in
(22.2 × 16 cm). British
Museum, London

40 Victor Horta, Hôtel
Tassel, Brussels, 1892–3

39

40

So revolutionary does Horta's breakthrough appear in retrospect that it is irritating that so little is known about his preceding development. He was born in 1861 in Ghent, studied art and architecture at the local academy, worked in the studio of an architect by the name of Jules Debuysson in Paris, entered the École des Beaux-Arts in Brussels, and then became a draughtsman for a minor neo-classical architect, Alphonse Balat. In the mid-1880s he designed some uninteresting houses in Brussels. Next we have the Hôtel Tassel of 1892–3, a work of complete assurance, outstanding for its synthesis of architecture and the decorative arts and its declaration of new formal principles.

These were evident not in the somewhat bald façade with its bowing central volume, its restrained use of stonework and its discreet introduction of an exposed iron beam, but in the ample space of the stairwell. The principal innovations lay in the frank expression of metal structure and in the tendril-like ornamentation which transformed gradually into the vegetal shapes of banisters, wallpaper, and floor mosaics. The emphasis on the direct use of a modern material, and even the inspiration of natural forms for the metal ornament, recall Viollet-le-Duc's explorations in iron, while the expression of the effects of growth and tension call to mind the contemporary interests in 'empathy' and fascinations with organic analogies. Evidently Horta knew of wallpaper designs by C. F. A. Voysey and perhaps even of Owen Jones's *Grammar of Ornament* (1856); in either case he will have sensed a feeling for natural forms combined with a deliberate freshness and exoticism. Thus the first mature statement in the new style was a synthesis of formal inspiration from the English Arts and Crafts, of the structural emphasis of French Rationalism, and of shapes and structures abstracted from nature.

Horta extended his style in a number of other town house designs in Brussels in the 1890s. These subtly evoked an inward-looking world by creating scenarios for a well-to-do, urbane, fin-de-siècle clientele which could afford the indulgence of exotic tastes and delicate aestheticism. The props for the mood were the spacious stairwells, the long internal vistas through dining rooms and over winter gardens; the rich contrasts of coloured glass, silk stuffs, gold, bronze, and exposed metal, and vegetal forms of vaguely decadent character. Yet Horta's

buildings never lapsed into mere theatricality; there was always a tense, underlying formal order; and the sequence of spaces from halls, up stairs, over galleries was tightly orchestrated. In the Hôtel Solvay of 1895–1900, his newly found style was successfully carried through in all aspects of the design, including the linking of interior volumes and the treatment of the façade, where an appropriately linear ornament was displayed.

While Horta clearly grasped the meaning of the way of life of his luxurious clients, his social concerns and range of expression were not restricted to this class. This is clear from his design for the Maison du Peuple of 1896–9, also in Brussels, built as the headquarters of the Belgian Socialist Party. The site was a difficult one, extending around a segment of a circular urban space and part of the way along two radial streets. The façade combined convex and concave curves, and the main entrance was placed on one of the shorter convex protrusions. The visible expression of the iron skeleton was every bit as 'radical' as Sullivan's contemporary skyscraper designs in

Chicago (where the structure was usually immersed in masonry cladding, brick or terracotta sheathing). In part this treatment was no doubt inspired by earlier nineteenth-century engineering structures like train-sheds and exhibition buildings, but the choice of materials and the emphasis on lighting the interiors through infill panes of glass seem to have had moral overtones related to the institution as well:

… it was an interesting commission as I saw straight away – building a palace that wasn't to be a palace but a 'house' whose luxury feature would be the light and air that had been missing for so long from the working-class slums …

The integration of material, structure, and expressive intentions was even more successful in the interior, especially in the main auditorium at the top of the building where the roof was formed from a sort of hammer-beam system in steel. The side walls and fenestration were reduced to thin infill screens, and the effect of the whole was an organic unity in which ornamentation and the visual accentuation of actual structure worked tightly together. The ceilings were ingeniously corrugated

41 Victor Horta, Maison du Peuple, Brussels, 1896–9, auditorium

42 Furniture designed by Henry van de Velde for his own house at Uccle, near Brussels, 1895. The embroidery on the wall, *Angels Keep Watch*, was also designed by Van de Velde, 1893

to control reverberation, and a double gallery was hung from the roof trusses and used to contain heating pipes. Thus despite its fantastic character, this 'attic' space was strongly conditioned by practical demands. As the architect himself exclaimed, paraphrasing an observer,

'What a fantasist this architect is – he must have his alternating lines and curves – but he really is a "master" at them.' … but I am fuming: – 'You idiot, don't you see that everything is thought out in terms of architecture as construction, faithful to the brief to the point of sacrifice?'

Horta's experimentation with iron and steel was continued in another large-scale scheme, also for Brussels, the À l'Innovation Department Store of 1901, in which these materials were chosen for their capacity for large internal spans and wide openings. Practical considerations were again transcended in a façade composition in which delicate screens and large plates of glass provided a forward-looking image to a relatively new building type. One has to turn to Chicago to find any equivalent to this frankness of expression, and probably to the work of Louis Sullivan in particular (e.g. the near-contemporary Carson Pirie Scott Store). However, with the European example there is not the same sense of the frame as a normative, almost vernacular product, nor the underlying classical discipline. Horta's building has more the aspect of deliberate personal gesture, even of a manifesto. In Belgium, at least, Art Nouveau could be perceived as virtually a national, if not a Flemish invention, and therefore a

cultural expression of independence from the dominance of French Beaux-Arts models.

Horta continued to work in Brussels for another thirty years but rarely achieved the freshness of his earliest experiments. Another Belgian artist to continue the new-found mode well into the twentieth century was Henry van de Velde, who seems to have had a more theoretical turn of mind than Horta, and to have turned his hand to a broader range of activities. The son of a chemist in Antwerp, Van de Velde became a painter and was much influenced by the Impressionists, the social-realist imagery of Millet, and eventually the paintings of Gauguin. In the 1890s his interest in the crafts grew, under the impact of William Morris's theoretical teachings, and he devoted himself to the applied arts. If Viollet-le-Duc was important to one branch of Art Nouveau for having encouraged the notion of a new style based on the expression and accentuation of the constructional possibilities of new materials like iron, Morris was crucial as another forefather for having expressed the ideal of aesthetic and moral quality in all the objects of daily use. In due course one of the aims of Art Nouveau designers (one senses it already in Horta's houses) would be 'the total work of art' in which every detail, down to the last light fixture, would bear the same aesthetic character as the overall building.

In 1894–5, Van de Velde designed a house for himself at Uccle, near Brussels, for which the furniture was specially created. His chair designs manifested an interest in expressive, organic structure; dynamic forces were intended to heighten the functions of the various members, giving the chairs a consciously lifelike or anthropomorphic character. Van de Velde made a distinction between 'ornamentation' and 'ornament', the former being attached, the latter being a means for frankly revealing the inner structural forces or functional identity of a form. This interest in the frank expression of structure and function led him in his interior for Haby's Barber Shop in Berlin (1901) to expose water pipes, gas conduits and electrical ducts. Van de Velde admired what the machine might do in mass production, so long as a strong control over quality was maintained by the craftsman who designed the prototype; he felt that a subjective artistic element must always be present if banality was to be avoided. The French critic,

42

Edmond de Goncourt, coined the phrase 'yachting style' in assessing Van de Velde's designs when they were first made known in Paris. The artist himself claimed that his means were:

… the same as those which were used in the very early stages of popular arts and crafts. It is only because I understand and marvel at how simply, coherently and beautifully a ship, weapon, car or wheelbarrow is built that my work is able to please the few remaining rationalists … unconditionally and resolutely following the functional logic of an article and being unreservedly honest about the materials employed …

Van de Velde was a socialist and hoped that industrial mass production of his objects might make visual quality available to the broad masses; yet his statements of architectural intent remained within a fairly rarefied circle of patronage. In the Cologne Theatre of 1914, he attempted to create his version of a communal building celebrating widely held social values. But this *Gesamtkunstwerk* (total work of art) was still the property of a cultivated élite.

Art Nouveau did not always remain the aloof creation of an avant-garde. Indeed, the style was quickly popularized in graphic and industrial design, in glassware, furniture, jewellery, and even clothing. The rapid spread of ideas was encouraged by the emergence of periodicals like *The Studio*, which had a great impact on fashion, and by the pioneering commercial attitudes of men like Samuel Bing, who opened a shop for modern art called Salon de l'Art Nouveau on the rue de Provence in Paris in 1895. Bing, and the German art critic Julius Meier-Graefe, had discovered Van de Velde's house at Uccle and invited the artist to design some rooms for the shop. The fashion caught on quickly; and among those influenced were Émile Gallé the glass-maker, and Hector Guimard the architect. In New York, meanwhile, L. C. Tiffany was designing glass with delicate vegetal forms and rich stains of colour. In fact, he had come upon this manner independently, which tended to lend weight to the notion that here at last was a true expression of the underlying spirit of the age. The full triumph of the new style in the public taste was clearly evident at the Paris Exhibition of 1900 and the Turin Exhibition of 1902, in which 'Art Nouveau', 'Jugendstil', or the 'Style Liberty' (such were its various names), was dominant. By the turn of the century, then, Art Nouveau, which may have started in Belgium with a vaguely nationalist agenda, had

43

taken on an international character. It was perceived to be a way out of the interminable jumbling of eclectic styles, and a valid reflection of exotic, somewhat escapist, somewhat progressive, *fin-de-siècle* attitudes of mind. This is the way the Italian critic Silvius Paoletti responded to the Turin Exhibition:

To take the place of pitiless authoritarianism, rigid and regal magnificence, burdensome and undecorated display, we have delicate and intimate refinement, fresh freedom of thought, the subtle enthusiasm for new and continued sensations. All man's activities are more complex, rapid, intense and capture new pleasures, new horizons, new heights. And art has new aspirations, new voices and shines with a very new light.

While one ideal of Art Nouveau was the perfectly crafted and unified interior, the style also revealed its possibilities for much broader public applications. Most notable of these, perhaps, were Hector Guimard's designs for the Paris Métro begun in 1900, in which naturally-inspired forms were used to create arches and furnishings in iron which were then mass-produced from moulds. Like Horta, Guimard had passed through the academy, having been at the Paris École des Beaux-Arts from 1885 to the early 1890s. At the École des Arts Décoratifs from 1882 to 1885, he had already become acquainted with Viollet-le-Duc's Gothic Rationalism, which he had then sought to reinterpret in a highly personal way. In 1898 he wrote that he had 'only applied the theories of Viollet-le-Duc without being fascinated by the

Middle Ages'. Another key influence was the British Arts and Crafts movement, which he studied while visiting England and Scotland in the 1890s. He also visited Horta, and this provided the essential catalyst.

Guimard began experimenting with the new style in his design of 1894–8 for an exclusive block of flats known as the Castel-Béranger, in rue la Fontaine in the recently developed sixteenth arrondissement. Here the entrance details and ornamental flourishes were somewhat isolated Art Nouveau incidents in an otherwise inconsistent design. Working a decade later at a much smaller scale in his own house and studio nearby, Guimard was able to infuse the whole design with the bulbous and swelling character of a natural growth, and to model brick surfaces and iron details so that they seemed subservient to a single aesthetic impulse. The plan, with its suave links between oval forms and different diagonal axes, suggests that Guimard may have consulted the sophisticated solutions for tight urban sites of eighteenth-century Parisian *hôtels*; indeed, the playfulness and curvilinear tracery of the Rococo may be counted among the possible sources of Art Nouveau ornament.

44

In the hands of major talents, Art Nouveau was far more than a change in architectural dress, far more than a new system of decoration. In the best works of Horta, Guimard, and Van de Velde, the very anatomy and spatial character of architecture were fundamentally transformed. Their forms were usually tightly constrained by functional discipline and by a Rationalist tendency to express structure and material. Furthermore, each artist in his own way attempted to embody a social vision and to enhance the institutions for which he built.

Similar points can be made about the Catalan architect Antoni Gaudí, whose extreme originality and idiosyncrasies show him to have been only a loose affiliate of Art Nouveau ideals. Indeed, one has to beware of pushing a historical abstraction too hard: a stylistic phase in architecture is a sort of broad base of shared motifs, modes of expression, and themes, from which a great variety of personal styles may emerge.

Gaudí was born in 1852 and died in 1926. His earliest works date from the 1870s and indicate his reaction against the prevalent Second Empire mode towards the neo-Gothic. He was an avid reader of Ruskin's works and the inspiration of his early designs is clearly medieval, but there emerges early on that sense of the bizarre which was to characterize his highly personal style after the turn of the century. In the Palau Güell of 1885–9 the interiors were transformed into spaces of an almost ecclesiastical character, while the façades were elaborately ornamented with wave-like ironwork preceding Horta's experiments in Brussels by some years. Thus Gaudí's style, like Guimard's, was in part an abstraction of medieval forms. It seemed to elaborate a distinction that Ruskin had made between the evident stylistic traits of Gothic architecture, which varied considerably from region to region and period to period, and the deeper, ordering principles which remained more consistent from place to place over time. The imaginative transformation of these prototypes was motivated by Gaudí's private imagery and by his obsession with finding a truly Catalan 'regional' style. In fact this was conceived locally as a 'national' style, since Catalonia was understood by sectors of the new industrial bourgeoisie to be on the point of reclaiming its ancient culture and language in reaction against the hegemony of Madrid and the

surreal forms were not entirely without precedent, since it seems clear that Gaudí (who had worked briefly in North Africa) knew of the mud constructions of the Berbers, with their own inspiration in natural forms, their curious hermetic imagery, and their manifestation of animist beliefs. Sagrada Familia derives part of its presence and significance from the contrast of its geometry with the sharp diagonals and rectangles of the Barcelona street grid established in Ildefons Cerdà's urban plan of 1859, and from the way that its spires pick up the energies of the irregular, hillside topography of the hinterland, transmitting them towards the sea. As a young man Gaudí had worked on the paths and grottoes approaching the sacred site of Montserrat behind Barcelona, a place combining Catalan and Catholic legend, and he remained haunted by the distinctive peaks of this mythical landscape.

The richness of Gaudí's art lies in the reconciliation of the fantastic and the practical, the subjective and the scientific, the spiritual and the material. His forms were never arbitrary, but rooted in structural principles and in an elaborate private world of social and emblematic meanings. The structure of the Sagrada Familia and the designs like that for the crypt of the Chapel of the Colonia Güell (begun in 1898) were based on the optimization of structural forms which led the architect to variations on the parabola. Gaudí was thus much more of a 'Rationalist' than his work would lead one to believe on superficial inspection, and the sections of the church bear comparison not only with those of Gothic cathedrals, but also with some of Viollet-le-Duc's skeletal drawings. But the appellation 'Rationalist' does not do Gaudí justice

45 Antoni Gaudí, Palau Güell, Barcelona, 1885–9, interior

46 Antoni Gaudí, wire model of the structure of the Chapel of the Colonia Güell, Barcelona, 1898–1900

47 Antoni Gaudí, Expiatory Church of the Holy Family, Barcelona (Sagrada Familia), 1884–present

48 Sagrada Familia, drawing of the nativity façade, based on Rubió's sketch, published in 1906

Castilian language. Gaudí was one of several architects (see Chapter 8) intent upon crystallizing these cultural aspirations. In his case it was a matter of understanding local structural types and construction techniques in brick and ceramic, but also of reacting poetically, not to say mystically, to the hedonistic Mediterranean landscape and vegetation, as well as to the maritime character and traditions of Barcelona.

In 1884, Gaudí was commissioned to continue Francisco del Villar's designs for the Expiatory Church of the Holy Family (the 'Sagrada Familia') on the outskirts of Barcelona. The crypt followed Villar's design, based on thirteenth- and fourteenth-century Gothic prototypes. The lowest visible levels were completed to Gaudí's design by 1893 in a transitional Gothic manner. To then move upwards through the various stages of the termination of the crossing is to be confronted bit by bit with the architect's flowering into one of the most curious and original architects of the past two hundred years. Elements which suggest a vague affinity with Art Nouveau give way finally to a language of utter fantasy, evocative of vegetable stems and dreamlike anatomies. In fact, these

47

48

either, for he was deeply religious and believed that the material qualities of architecture must be the outer manifestation of a spiritual order. He intuited the presence of this order in the structures of nature which he felt to be a direct reflection of the Divine Mind. The 'laws' of structure, then, were not those of a merely materialist physics, but were evidence of the Creator. The parabola, in particular, with its beautiful economy, became an emblem for the sacral.

Thus Gaudí's vocabulary was infused with an elaborate symbolism for which the Gothic revival of his youth had provided a useful, conventional starting-point. His pantheism, like Ruskin's, extended to the smallest mineralogical wonders and to the grandest of natural forces. These features of nature were abstracted and expressed in a vocabulary loaded with metaphor and association. It is little wonder that the Surrealist generation of the 1920s (particularly his fellow Catalan Salvador Dalí) should have felt such an affinity with his work. For in Gaudí at his most bizarre there is a sensation of contact with deep psychic forces and irrational patterns of imaginative thought. His dense calligraphy was capable of carrying several simultaneous meanings, as one may judge from the complex curves in iron of Gaudí's baldachino over the main altar in the Cathedral of Palma, Majorca, which were guided into shape by an internal imagery combining associations with a tent, a ship, and (possibly) a crown of thorns. The 'open book' above this curved and linear armature supporting ship-like

50

lamps could also be read as a sail; the baldachino in its entirety as a vessel from the time of the Crusades, an icon of the Church triumphant.

Gaudí's completely personal late style first emerged in the design for the Park Güell, carried out between 1900 and 1914. Beast-like benches embedded with fragments of coloured tile mark off the edges of the stepped terraces offering views over the city. There are nightmarish underground grottoes suggestive of dark clearings in some subterranean forest, and steps which flow like lava. The main terrace is supported by a hypostyle hall of hollow concrete columns with drains running through their cores, while curved buttresses textured with scales suggest the gnarled forms of trees or some natural origin of the Gothic flying buttress. Both the sinuous Park Güell landscape and the encrusted towers of Sagrada Familia give the impression of an undersea world of coral accretions which has been left high and dry when the ocean has subsided.

Gaudí's principal secular works were conceived in parallel with the park, beginning with the Casa Batlló of 1904–7, a remodelling of a block of flats.

49

49 Antoni Gaudí, Park Güell, Barcelona, 1900–14, undercroft with buttresses

50 Antoni Gaudí, Casa Batlló, Barcelona, 1904–7

51 Antoni Gaudí, Casa Milá, Barcelona, 1905–10

51

Here a virtual sport of spotting analogies can be (and has been) played. Thus some critics have emphasized the maritime references of waves, corals, fishbones, and gaping jaws, while others have commented on the dragon-like roof and the possible religious significance of this as an allegory of good and evil. Whether such analogies strike close to Gaudí's intentions may never be known, but they suggest the powerful impact on the imagination of the architect's forms.

In the Casa Milá of 1905–10, the plastic conception of swirling curves was applied not just to the façade, but to the plan and interior spaces as well. The elevation is in constant motion with its deep-cut, overlapping ledges. Once again wave and cliff images come to mind (the building was known locally as 'La Pedrera' – the quarry), but it is a naturalism achieved by the most sophisticated ornamentation and stone-cutting. The contrived textures of the ledges give the impression that these forms have come about over the years through a process of gradual erosion.

Gaudí's buildings were so bizarre as to be inimitable, which naturally inhibited the immediate propagation of his style in a local tradition. One of the complaints lodged against Art Nouveau in the first decade of this century was that its propositions relied too completely on a subjective approach, and that they were not geared sufficiently to the ideal of designing types for standardized mass production. This criticism has to be taken with some salt, for, as has been shown, both Guimard and Van de Velde were able to mass-produce standardized profiles of some visual complexity. Even some of Gaudí's most complex structural sections could be realized following normal Catalan vaulting techniques using overlapping ceramic tiles. Moreover, Art Nouveau proved itself well suited to repeating print processes in such things as posters, and became a sort of popular style related to consumerism. By the turn of the century it had spread to many provincial centres which contributed their own regional accent. However, there was some resistance. In England, for example, Art Nouveau was regarded with suspicion as a wily and decadent departure from the sober aims of the Arts and Crafts. But in Scotland a style of enormous originality, related to Art Nouveau, was created by another uncategorizable individual, the Glasgow architect Charles Rennie Mackintosh.

Mackintosh is important at this juncture not
only because of the imaginative force of his own
designs, particularly the Glasgow School of Art,
of 1897–1909, but because his development
encapsulated the path beyond Art Nouveau towards
a more sober form of expression in which broad
dispositions of simple masses and sequences of
dynamic spaces were stressed. His style emerged
independently of Horta's but from loosely similar
sources and concerns, and appeared first in his
decoration of Miss Kate Cranston's various
'tearooms' in Glasgow of 1897–8. These designs
were linear, abstract and heavily laden with Gaelic
symbolism and Celtic reference; it comes as no
surprise to discover that the term 'Spook School'
was invented to characterize Mackintosh and his
circle (including his wife). In 1897 he won the
competition to design the new School of Art in
Glasgow. The building was to stand on an almost
impossibly steep slope, which seemed to suggest
that the main façade should be set at the highest part
of the site. The functions to be included were several
studios, a lecture theatre, a library, a room and
private studio for the director. Spaces to display
work and to house a permanent collection of casts
were also needed.

Mackintosh dealt with these constraints by laying
out two tiers of studios along the north side facing
Renfrew Street (the high end of the site) with
further studios, the anatomy school, the life
modelling room, the architecture school, and the
design and composition rooms facing east and west.
The director's room and studio were placed over
the entrance, while the museum was set to the rear
of the scheme at an upper level where it could be
top lit. The richness of the scheme arose from
the juxtaposition and sequence of rooms of
different sizes, and the orchestration of different
qualities of light; from the clever overlapping
down the slope in section; and from the way the
stairs, corridors, and display rooms were modelled
as if from a continuous volume of space. The School
of Art worked with the theme of a transparent
lattice of wood or metal slats – a species of
luminous cage – which had been set down into a
faceted stone armature. Windows, walls, chimneys,
steel brackets and other functional elements were
handled with an uncompromising directness: there

52

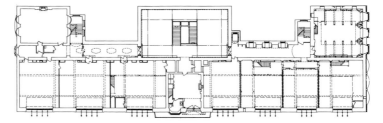

53

was a concentration on things in themselves, without distracting rhetoric. Poetry arose from strong juxtapositions, and from a tense interplay between solid and void, mass and plane. The interior movements and structural tensions were sensed in the dynamics of the exteriors. Thus the north elevation was a subtle fusion of symmetry and asymmetry, in which the grand upper windows of the main studios were set into massive, grim masonry forms. The entrance-way was emphasized by a cluster of motifs and an arch, over which the director's study was set in a recess (an arrangement suggesting a schematization of H. H. Richardson's Austin Hall, Harvard University, of 1881). To the sides, the building's flanking walls fell away to the lower portion of the site as large expanses of subtly articulated stone surface, recalling (among other things) the architect's interest in regional farmhouse prototypes and Scottish baronial halls. The ironwork on the exterior, in the railings and in the cleaning brackets on the main windows, was loosely analogous to Art Nouveau in its abstraction of natural motifs but, like the building as a whole, these details spoke less of effete curves and more of a taut, sculptural discipline. The direct handling of glass and metal introduced a frank evocation of industrial technology, not out of place in a shipbuilding city.

These qualities were brought to the fore without distracting fussiness in the library wing of the school, designed around 1908, in which chiselled abstract shapes and groups of austere vertical windows on the outside were supplemented by rectangular wooden brackets in the reading-room interiors. The verticality of the proportions recalls Art Nouveau, but the stern rectangular forms speak of a new direction. It is understandable that Pevsner should have singled out this interior as an early example of the sort of spatial effects which were later to be central to the modern movement, and, in retrospect, there are parallels with the spatial inventions of Frank Lloyd Wright in the same period (chapter 7). Looking back from a distance of more than three-quarters of a century, the British architect Denys Lasdun spoke of 'the brooding mystery of a Japanese temple':

In the library, there is an extraordinary air of frozen excitement. The lines are dynamic and everywhere the stress is on the manipulation and control of space. The structural form is revealed and emphasized; the timber itself speaks. Posts, brackets, rafters organized within recognizable modules of measurement, speak of timeless space, of a place of assembly which would be appropriate to any age.

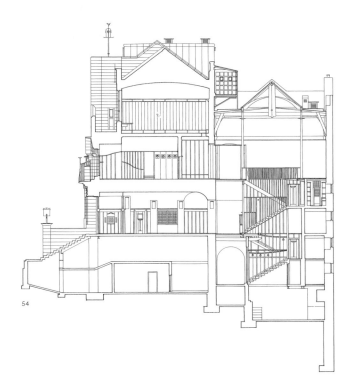

54

55

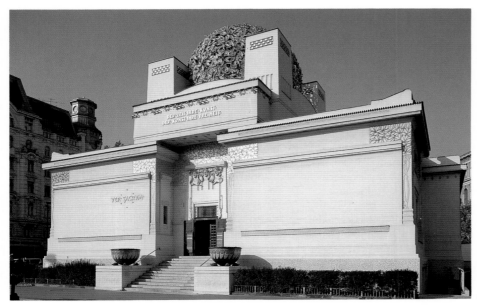

56

It is ironic that Mackintosh should have been written off by English critics of his own day as dangerously exotic, since it was precisely his geometrical control and tendency to abstraction which appealed in European artistic centres – partly as a support for their own revulsion at the excesses of Art Nouveau. Mackintosh was less appreciated in London than in Vienna, where publications of his plans and drawings made him known and influential, especially in Secessionist circles around Josef Maria Olbrich. Olbrich and the older Otto Wagner disliked both the pomposities of classical academic design, and the 'new decadence' of Art Nouveau. Indeed, Olbrich's Vienna Secession Exhibition Building of 1897–8 was a somewhat bizarre attempt at formulating an expressive language of pure geometries and massive pylon forms. Decorated on the interiors with paintings by Gustav Klimt, this building was dedicated to the aesthetic cult of the 'Sacred Spring' (*Ver Sacrum*) and was a critical manifesto against the somewhat ponderous, official, imperial cultural monuments created in a grand classical manner in the Ringstrasse a generation earlier. Wagner's Majolica House, a block of flats built between 1898 and 1899, also implied a return to fundamental architectonic values and to strict rectilinear proportions, despite

the lingering feeling of vegetal motifs in some of the detailing. In the late 1890s, in an article published in *Dekorative Kunst* (Munich), the German architect August Endell wrote of a 'non-historical' style of pure forms capable of moving the spirit in a manner similar to the rhythms of music.

They teach us that there can be no new form, that all possibilities have been exhausted in the styles of the past, and that all art lies in an individually modified use of old forms. It even extends to selling the pitiful eclecticism of the last decades as the new style.
   To those with understanding, this despondency is simply laughable. For they can clearly see that we are not only at the beginning of a new stylistic phase, but at the same time at the threshold of a completely new Art. An Art with forms which signify nothing, and remind us of nothing, which arouse our souls as deeply and as strongly as music has always been able to do …
   This is the power of form upon the mind, a direct, immediate influence without any intermediary stage … one of direct empathy.

In 1895, Otto Wagner published *Moderne Architektur*, in which he spoke of the need for architecture to orientate itself to 'modern life', alluded to the new cultural stimulus to be drawn from the day-to-day experience of the Großstadt (the metropolis), and recommended qualities of simplicity and 'almost military uniformity'. Moreover, he argued that the new style should be a 'realist' one, which seems to have implied a direct expression of the means of construction, an admiration for modern techniques and materials, and responsiveness to the changing aspirations of society. Wagner's ideas owed more than a little to Semper, but also to the sensation of a new age of industrialism and engineering erupting through the confectionery of earlier Viennese architecture. He insisted that: 'new purposes must give birth to new methods of construction, and by this reasoning to new forms.'

If we follow Wagner from his late nineteenth-century designs to the Vienna Post Office Savings Bank of 1904–6, we enter an entirely different world from that of Art Nouveau, a world in which a nuts and bolts rationality and a stable and dignified order have replaced the dynamic tendrils and curvaceous effects. This was to be a people's institution, a bank for the little man, and Wagner invoked and subverted norms of monumentality in his solution. Compared with the neo-Baroque monuments in the vicinity, the building would have seemed stern and simplified, even if its plan relied upon an essentially classical discipline. Certain of its details, such as the abstracted rustication or the slender metallic columns of the entrance canopy, involved subtle

inversions of familiar elements of construction. The façades themselves were covered in thin marble sheets with bolt-heads expressed and dramatized by shiny aluminium caps. In fact these plain surfaces of stone (and the rustication below them) were mortared to a brick wall, the caps having only a temporary function during the fixing. None the less, these bolt-heads underlined that the cladding was merely a veneer, and hinted at the presence of the glass and metal skeleton making up the main banking hall at the heart of the building. Rather like Sullivan, Wagner was concerned not just to 'express' function and structure, but to symbolize them; even to use artifice to convey 'truth'. The banking hall at the heart of the building was bathed in natural light and could be seen at the top of the main stairs the moment one entered. In effect it was a transformation of a prevalent nineteenth-century urban type – the glazed railway shed – into a translucent social metaphor evoking honesty, transparency, lightness, efficiency and availability; all values appropriate to the building's social purpose. The tapered steel supports and curious upstanding ventilating stacks suggested a slight

57

machinist rhetoric rather than just an engineering objectivity, but also implied inversions of the usual expectations of load and support. The glass was detailed to supply a milky white, weightless skin diffusing the daylight, while the floor (which had the bank-vaults directly beneath it) was made from translucent glass bricks. The 'modernity' of Wagner's solution relied upon the freshness and luminosity of his institutional interpretation and on his radical reinterpretation of pre-existing norms for public architecture.

Vienna, and a little later Berlin and Paris, were to be among the strongholds of a reaction against Art Nouveau which acquired increasing momentum in the first decade of the twentieth century. This reaction was fed in part by the Arts and Crafts ideals of simplicity and integrity; in part by an abstract conception of classicism as something less to do with the use of the Orders than with a feeling for the 'essential' classical values of symmetry and clarity of proportion; and in part by a sense that the architect must strive to give expression to the values of the modern world through frank and straightforward solutions to architectural problems in which disciplines of function and structure must play an increasing, and attached ornament a decreasing, role.

Apart from Wagner, who was already in his early sixties at the turn of the century, the two chief exponents of a new architecture in Vienna were Josef Hoffmann and Adolf Loos. Hoffmann was a founder of the Wiener Werkstätte in 1903 as a centre of activity in the field of decoration. In his design for the Purkersdorf Convalescent Home (1904–6), he reduced the walls to thin planar surfaces. His greatest opportunity came in 1905 with the commission for a luxurious mansion to be built outside Brussels for a Belgian financier who had lived in Vienna. The Palais Stoclet was to be a sort of suburban palace of the arts in which Adolphe and Suzanne Stoclet would assemble their treasures and entertain the artistic élite of Europe. It had thus to combine the moods of a museum, a luxury residence, and an exemplary setting of modern taste.

58 Josef Hoffmann, Palais Stoclet, Brussels, 1905–11

59 Palais Stoclet, dining room, with mosaics by Gustav Klimt

60 Charles Rennie Mackintosh, House for an Art Lover, 1900, design for a competition sponsored by the German periodical *Zeitschrift für Innendekoration*, and published in 1902

58

Hoffmann was able to respond to the 'aura' of the programme in a house of immense sophistication, combining devices of formality and informality, characteristics of an honorific and a more humble sort. The rooms were linked en suite in a plan employing ingenious changes of direction and axis, in which such major spaces as the hall, the dining room and the music room (with its little stage) were expressed as protruding volumes in the façades. The overall composition was balanced, but asymmetrical, the main points of emphasis being the fantastic stepped stair-tower with its attached statuary, the bow windows, and the *porte-cochère*. The forms were coated in thin stone-slab veneers detailed with linear mouldings to accentuate their planarity. In the interiors materials were stern, rectilinear and precise, and included polished marbles and rich wood finishes. The influence of Mackintosh is felt in this house (a prototype for the design was clearly the Scot's 'House for an Art Lover' of 1900), but where he would have stressed the rustic and the humble, Hoffmann emphasized

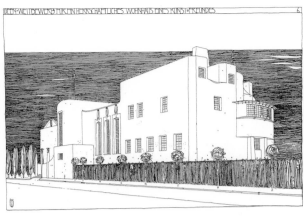

the grandiose and the cosmopolitan. The disciplined elegance of the Palais Stoclet is enhanced by the furnishings and by Klimt's splendid mural decorations. As well as echoes from Mackintosh, there are also memories of Olbrich, perhaps even of Schinkel. But the Palais Stoclet is one of those designs where there is little point in listing the sources and influences, as these have been absorbed and restated in a convincing personal style. In its imagery and mood it portrayed an exclusive way of life of a kind which was to be swept away by the devastation of the First World War – a sort of aristocratic bohemianism.

Adolf Loos's move towards a rectilinear and volumetric simplification was even more drastic than Hoffmann's. Loos was little affected by Art Nouveau, in part because he spent the mid-1890s in America (a country he praised highly for its plumbing and its bridges); in part because he seems to have sensed that that movement's reaction against the 'dead forms' of the academy was swinging too far towards the wilful, the personal and the decorative – all of which he felt to be inimical to lasting achievement in art. But Loos brought the perspective too of someone who had reflected on the form of many simple everyday objects, which he contrasted to the pretentious inventions of much self-conscious art. Some of his most penetrating essays are on such things as gentlemen's suits, sportswear, and Michael Thonet's mass-produced wooden chairs. He seems to have felt that these

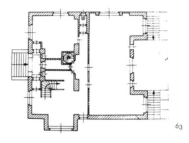

were the objects which gave evidence of, as it were, an unconscious style. Loos also admired the simplicity and directness of peasant architecture, and even of modern engineering, both of which he compared favourably to the painful stylistic excesses of the architecture and product design created for the Vienna bourgeoisie. It had been Nietzsche's suggestion that modern European man should strip away the mask, and in the Vienna of Freud Loos advocated a removal of conventional disguises to discover the 'honest' being within.

If Loos detested the mass fakery of the false façades clamped on to the apartment buildings of the new arriviste classes of Vienna, he also reviled the cultivated aestheticism of Secessionists like Olbrich, who appeared to him to express the nervous rootlessness of the grand metropolis and its lack of a foundation in common usage. Beyond Loos's acerbic witticisms, there was a serious reflection on the difficulty of evolving a genuine culture on the basis of a mass production which seemed doomed to create nothing but kitsch. In a manner that anticipated Le Corbusier's later use of 'pure', mechanized objects such as steamships

and cars to reveal a 'truer' modernism than that produced by architects, Loos singled out railway engines and bicycles for qualities that had little to do with 'personality' or aesthetic taste. He declared: 'To seek beauty only in form and not in ornament is the goal to which all humanity is striving.'

Up to 1910 much of Loos's design effort went into small-scale conversions. In his few house designs of that period he reduced the external vocabulary to rectangular stucco boxes punctured by simple openings, without even the reminiscence of a cornice or a plinth. Usually his interiors were more elaborate, some of them achieving interpenetrations of space (later elaborated as what he called a '*raumplan*'), yet they were still distinguished by an overall rectangular control. Despite his polemics, Loos had recourse to a reductivist ornament (the interior of the Kärntner Bar of 1907 (Fig. 154) even had stripped classical mouldings), but by the Viennese standards of the day this treatment would have seemed restrained, if not minimal. Perhaps the outstanding design of Loos's middle years was the Steiner House in Vienna of 1910, where the external architectural

61 Adolf Loos, Steiner
House, Vienna, 1910

62 Steiner House, section

63 Steiner House, plan at
entrance level

effect relied on the adroit placement of large
plate-glass windows in undecorated planar surfaces.
Although it was a long way (in meaning as well as
form) from this villa, with its 'neo-classical' plan and
its strict symmetry, to the interpenetrating planes
and dynamic asymmetries of the International Style
of the 1920s, the achievement of such a drastic
simplicity within a decade and a half of the
beginnings of Art Nouveau, and a full decade before
Le Corbusier's white, cubic villa designs of the
1920s, is worthy of comment.

In fact, it is by no means certain that Loos's
pre-war designs had much influence on the
emergence of the modern movement after the
First World War. His theories, especially on
ornament, were far better known, perhaps because
they put into words a number of concurrent but
not necessarily connected prejudices, which the
later generation was determined should be a
unified doctrine. As a polemicist, Loos was
brilliant; in an article entitled 'Ornament and
Crime' (1908), he inveighed against the very notion
of ornament on the grounds that it was evidence
of a decadent culture:

Children are amoral, and – by our standards – so are Papuans. If a
Papuan slaughters an enemy and eats him, that doesn't make him a
criminal. But if a modern man kills someone and eats him, he must
be either a criminal or a degenerate. The Papuans tattoo themselves,
decorate their boats, their oars, everything they can get their hands
on. But a modern man who tattoos himself is either a criminal or a
degenerate. Why, there are prisons where 80 per cent of the convicts
are tattooed, and tattooed men who are not in prison are either latent
criminals or degenerate aristocrats. When a tattooed man dies at
liberty, it simply means that he hasn't had time to commit his crime…
What is natural to children and Papuan savages is a symptom of
degeneration in modern man.
    I have therefore evolved the following maxim, and pronounce it to
the world: the evolution of culture marches with the elimination of
ornament from useful objects.

Translated into the situation in which Loos found
himself, this meant that Art Nouveau, for all its
emancipation from academic formulas, had to be
seen as yet another superficial and transitory 'style'.
A true style for the times would be discovered
when ornament was done away with, and essential
underlying qualities of form, proportion, clarity
and measure were allowed to emerge unadorned.
At least this is what Adolf Loos believed, and there
was a generation of later architects ready to follow
a similar direction in the search for the supposed
'universal style' for modern times.

4

rationalism, the engineering tradition and reinforced concrete

Living architecture is
that which faithfully
expresses its time. We
shall seek it in all
domains of
construction. We shall
choose works that,
strictly subordinated to
their use and realized by
the judicious use of
material, attain beauty
by the disposition and
harmonious proportions
of the necessary
elements of which they
are made up.
Auguste Perret, 1923

While Art Nouveau appeared to break with the bonds of the past, to be a new style, it was soon perceived to be a subjective creation insufficiently rooted in lasting principles and incompletely attuned to the means and needs of an industrial society. In this view even architects like Horta and Guimard, who had approached the heart of the matter of a new architecture, were lumped together with the most facile Art Nouveau decorators. In part the reaction was impelled by vaguely moral yearnings for the stern and unadorned, in part by Rationalist ideas which required a practical justification for formal effects. This was somewhat ironic because, as has been shown, Rationalism inspired some of the more disciplined creations of Art Nouveau.

By 1905, then, the style which had so quickly flowered was already beginning to wither; but after it, things could not be the same again. It opened up a language of abstraction and implied new ways in which nature's lessons could be incorporated into architecture. A tradition of emotive, organic form was founded, which would develop further in the free experimentation of the 'Amsterdam School' around the end of the First World War and in the so-called 'Expressionism' of the 1920s. More important in the shorter term was the reaction *against* Art Nouveau. This took a number of different forms. In Vienna, Hoffmann and Loos suggested that the way forward to a true modern style lay in increasing formal simplification; in Berlin, Peter Behrens resorted to classical principles, which he attempted to restate in a new form responsive to the modern industrial state; in Paris, Auguste Perret (yet another inheritor of Rationalism) sought a formal discipline in the constraints and creative potentials of new constructional systems, especially reinforced concrete, in the belief that this would lead to genuine architectural forms of lasting quality.

This last notion, of course, stemmed from the ideas of Viollet-le-Duc, who had influenced some of the structural inventiveness of Art Nouveau. It has already been suggested that his theories were at times over-mechanical, but they still had an immense impact on those who felt, at the turn of the century, that a language based on 'truth to the programme and truth to the methods of construction' might be the best antidote to academic revivalism on the one hand and to personal whimsy on the other. Here one must mention the role of the nineteenth-century engineering tradition, which had already demonstrated the possibility of new forms in new materials, and which Viollet-le-Duc had himself singled out in contrast to the 'dead languages' of the architects:

… naval architects and mechanical engineers do not, when building a steamship or a locomotive, seek to recall the forms of sailing ships or harnessed stage-coaches of the Louis XIV period. They obey unquestioningly the new principles which are given them and produce their own character and proper style.

One effect of Viollet-le-Duc's opinions was to found a tradition of architectural history in which the role of practicality in great works of the past was overstressed. Thus Auguste Choisy, in his *Histoire de l'architecture* of 1899, spoke of Gothic architecture as 'the triumph of logic in art', whose form was 'governed not by traditional models, but by its function and by its function alone'. This view was reinforced by simple geometrical drawings in which buildings were portrayed as structural diagrams, as if structure and only structure had been the architect's concern (Fig. 68). The implication of the Rationalist position seemed to be: if only modern architects would think as clearly as these predecessors and concentrate on function and structure, then their results would have the same authenticity.

In a sense both Viollet-le-Duc and Choisy were projecting backwards the values of

nineteenth-century engineers. The stunning new effects of visual lightness and transparency in buildings like Paxton's Crystal Palace of 1851, or Victor Baltard's market sheds at Les Halles in Paris of 1853, seemed indeed to be traceable to a judicious attention to the demands of programme and structure: but did these buildings in iron, and later utilitarian structures in steel, constitute a new *architecture*? Even those who could admire the structural feats (and the occasional formal elegance) of engineering realized that a certain poetic character of form might be missing. Thus, while the Rationalists and the engineers, each in their different ways, seemed able to emancipate themselves from revivalism, they faced another danger: the proliferation of a bland, materialistic functionalism lacking the quality of a true expressive style.

This problem had already preoccupied some writers and practitioners in the early nineteenth century. In his *Précis des leçons d'architecture données à l'école polytechnique* of 1804–9, J.-N.-L. Durand had advocated a system of design based upon the addition and combination of basic structural and functional elements, resorting time and again to grids of simplified supports laid out on symmetrical plans. In effect this was a desiccated version of classical arrangement with the expressive and metaphysical removed. In the 1820s, the theorist Heinrich Hübsch had discussed the notion of basing form directly on need, while Schinkel, who

65 Gustave Eiffel, Pont du Garabit, near St-Flour, 1880–4

66 John A. Roebling, Brooklyn Bridge, New York, 1869–83

65

66

overall order of visual stresses; the transparent lattices and spans through which the sky and the landscape could be seen.

John A. Roebling, the designer of the Brooklyn Bridge in New York of 1869–83, considered that engineering might contribute to a new, democratic culture where usefulness and higher values of form would be united. The Brooklyn Bridge was based upon a suspension principle and combined a gossamer structure of steel wires with two massive stone piers. Diagonal lines complemented the main curved cables and added to both the lateral stability and the visual drama of the design. The Brooklyn Bridge raised engineering to a high poetic plane. Montgomery Schuyler (the same critic who praised the Monadnock Building) spoke of it as 'an aerial bow … between the busy cities' and as '… a skeletonized structure in which, as in a scientific diagram, we see – even the layman sees – the interplay of forces represented by an abstraction of lines'. For him the Brooklyn Bridge was as 'perfect as an organism of nature …'

The Chicago architects discussed in Chapter 2 also sought a 'higher synthesis' of technique, material and form in their skyscraper designs. It will be recalled that Sullivan, for example, had attempted to suggest that form should 'follow' from function, but had discovered that a number of arrangements might be equally tenable and that the brute heap of matter which was the tall building could only acquire aesthetic value through an intuitive intervention on the part of the artist. Although Sullivan disclaimed the value of 'rules and other impedimenta', he had in fact discovered that function and structure could not on their own 'generate' an adequate form, without the intervention of highly abstracted historical or natural prototypes. Indeed, Viollet-le-Duc's own clumsy attempts at evolving a system 'true to iron' had been influenced by medieval precedents, and perhaps even by the forms of bones. So history had not dropped out of the picture completely. Quite the contrary, the question in a sense became: which qualities abstracted from tradition might best serve the forms suggested inherently by new construction techniques? At any rate, a query of this sort underlay many of the experiments of the early pioneers of a reinforced-concrete architecture.

welcomed the discipline of strict construction, none the less felt that the 'historic and poetic' must be present if architecture, rather than just building, was to result.

Moreover, it is not as if the great nineteenth-century engineers were ignorant of the problem of formal expression in their designs. Considered by any standards, the Pont du Garabit by Eiffel of 1880–4 would have to be judged a sculptural triumph as well as a practical solution to the problem of bridging a ravine. The structural forms were dramatized in visual terms: the dynamics of the arch leaping from one side to the other; the strong horizontal of the upper raft holding the railway line as a virtually independent element flowing in space; the hierarchies of girders embedded in a clear

Concrete had been employed by Roman and Early Christian architects but had then dropped out of use through most of the Middle Ages and Renaissance. It was not until the second half of the nineteenth century that the material was fully explored again, but usually for mundane purposes where its cheapness, its wide spans and its fireproof character all recommended it. The invention of reinforcing, whereby steel rods were inserted to increase the strength, belonged to the 1870s. Ernest Ransome in America and François Hennebique in France each evolved frame systems employing this principle. These proved to be well-suited to the creation of open-plan work spaces with large windows where fire had previously been a danger. Hennebique's system employed slender vertical posts, thin lateral beams on brackets, and floor slabs. The result was somewhat like a timber frame, which was scarcely surprising since the form-work was generally made from wood. But concrete, of all materials, was one of the most flexible, one of the least determining of form. It relied on the shape of the mould and the shaping intelligence of the designer. Some forms rather than others were certainly more logical in certain situations; but the material did not in and of itself generate a vocabulary.

This became all the more obvious when architects in the last few years of the nineteenth century attempted to discover a style based on the material. Where one designer might argue that its malleable character made it natural for Art Nouveau expression, another might emphasize the role of a frame and panel system and claim the value of Gothic antecedents – or even of steel and glass ones. A similar range of positions might be taken with regard to the external expression of the material. Where one architect might regard it as commonplace and in need of covering with tiles or brick veneers, another might claim that it had its own inherent beauty and that it should be exposed.

Among the seminal experiments in France was the church of St-Jean-de-Montmartre, begun in 1894 and completed in 1904, designed by Anatole de Baudot. In fact the church was constructed with reinforced cement, rather than concrete, but the effects of lightness and the breadth of the spans with apparently slender supports were of a kind that either material would have been well suited to achieve. On the exterior relatively little attempt was made at expressing the skeleton, but inside a system was adopted which made clear the distinction between supports and infill panels. The pointed arches and the expression of the ribs suggested medieval prototypes, and it comes as no surprise to discover that Viollet-le-Duc had been De Baudot's mentor. But St-Jean lacks a formal resolution; it is an odd hybrid of medieval and exotic sources, a loosely Art Nouveau accentuation, and entirely novel ideas

67 François Hennebique, trabeated system for reinforced concrete, 1892

68 Auguste Choisy, plate from *Histoire de l'architecture*, 1899, showing Hagia Sophia

69 Anatole de Baudot, St-Jean-de-Montmartre, Paris, 1894–1904, interior

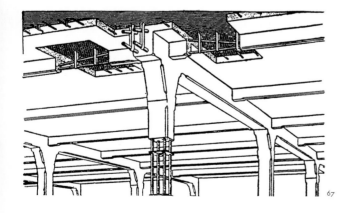

67

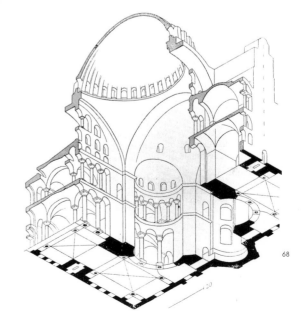

68

69

related to the construction. The structure may be logical, but the visual *expression* of the structure is indecisive. None the less, the church suggested some ways in which the lessons of earlier styles could be applied to a modern situation.

In essence, this was the problem which would preoccupy Auguste Perret as well in the same years. Perret was forty years De Baudot's junior, but was no less influenced by the ideas of Viollet-le-Duc. However, he had also undergone indoctrination in classical principles at the École des Beaux-Arts in the 1890s under the tutelage of Julien Guadet, author of *Éléments et théorie de l'architecture* (1902). The method that Guadet attempted to instil in his students was the opposite of the slavish imitation of precedents that those hostile to the

École liked to parody; his lectures were concerned with the classical principles of composition and proportion, and with the analysis of building types. He tried to convey a feeling for essential qualities of classicism, rather than a respect for superficial grammatical usages. A further element of Perret's formation needs to be stressed: both he and his brother Gustave were early trained in the basics of building construction in their father's firm. This blend of practicality, a Rationalist theoretical outlook and a firm, intuitive grasp of fundamental classical principles was to inform Perret's lifelong production.

The apartments designed by the architect at 25 bis rue Franklin, Paris in 1902 were based on the potentials of a trabeated, rectangular concrete-frame construction. The building stands in a row of vertical, rather gaunt, grey stone neighbours, with fine views down towards the Seine and the Eiffel Tower in the distance. Perret maximized these views by making the window openings as large as zoning laws allowed and by the effective device of placing the statutory light-court in the front of his building instead of at the back. The building was polite and well-behaved towards its neighbours, and respected several of their visual conventions, but also announced new departures, especially in the enlarged proportion of windows to supporting masses. The plan conformed to the standard expectations of middle-class occupancy, and placed the salons at the centre of the façade, but the concrete-frame system allowed thin wall partitions, and some saving in space. This potential was most obvious at the ground level where the Perret firm moved its studio, and where the stanchions appeared in free space as premonitions of the *pilotis* so important to the architecture of the 1920s. Perret exploited the setbacks on top of the building, and the flat roofs provided by his constructional system, to create a roof terrace.

What made the rue Franklin flats architecture, instead of just construction, was the way these practical intentions were given a clear, tectonic form. The lowest storey was emphasized as a separate unit, higher than those above it, while the next six storeys were expressed by slight overhangs and a variable placement of window depths within the U-shaped recess. The underlying rectangular frame was not exposed directly, but its presence was

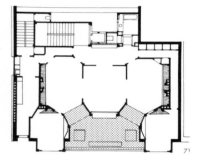

70 Auguste Perret,
apartments at 25bis
rue Franklin, Paris, 1902

71 Apartments at 25bis
rue Franklin, plan of
typical apartment

72 Auguste Perret,
garage at 51 rue de
Ponthieu, Paris, 1905

73 Auguste Perret,
Théâtre des Champs-
Élysées, Paris, 1911–13,
diagram of concrete
frame

70

71

suggested by contrasting colours and textures in the tiles of the façade, while the theme of infill, non-weight-bearing panels, was suggested by recessed, floral-designed ceramic surfaces. At the sixth storey, though, the frame broke free of the wall surfaces, giving some hint of the sort of airy and transparent effects to be pursued in modern architecture a generation later. The result of Perret's careful attention to proportion, detail and interval was a calculated work of great sobriety and repose. The whole was suffused with a serene classicism, yet without the overt use of the classical Orders. The rue Franklin apartments, along with the slightly later library wing of the Glasgow School of Art by Mackintosh, the Palais Stoclet by Hoffmann, the Larkin Building by Wright, the AEG Turbine Factory in Berlin by Behrens, and perhaps a handful of others, must certainly rank as one of the seminal works of the early modern movement. However, part of its strength lay, precisely, in the authoritative way in which it announced the potentials of a new material in a phraseology rooted in tradition.

In 1905, Perret made a further step by leaving the concrete completely exposed (though, admittedly, protected by white paint) in the garage design at 51 rue de Ponthieu. It is possible that he felt freer to do this in a building whose function lay closer to the concrete 'warehouse aesthetic' of Hennebique than did bourgeois apartments. And it may be that in his

articulation of the garage façade, Perret was working with second-hand knowledge of Chicago frame buildings. In any case, the result transcends its influences in a clear statement infused with a true personal style. The concrete frame of the interior allowed considerable flexibility in planning to facilitate the circulation and parking of cars. In less sensitive hands this interior organization might well have led to a crude assemblage of rectangular openings and stanchions in the façade. Perret brought order to the design by subtle placement of the window panes to give the right sense of depth, and by organizing the pattern of vertical and horizontal visual stresses – the apparent, not just the actual structure – in a simple rhythm of primary and secondary accents. The armature of the whole composition was defined by the stripped 'pilasters' rising from top to bottom supporting the abstracted 'cornice' at the top.

There can be little doubt that Perret had by this time decided that the 'correct' forms for concrete were rectangular ones, in part because of his aesthetic prejudices, in part because of the simplicity of making rectangular timber form-work from which the concrete was cast in simple standard sections; thus his concrete vocabulary was reminiscent in some ways of wooden-frame buildings of the past. But his father had trained him in the intricacies of stone-cutting and stereotomy, and the mouldings and details of Perret's designs,

72

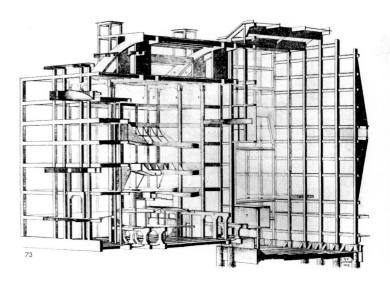

73

74   Albert Kahn, Ford
Motor Company factory,
Highland Park, Michigan,
1909

75   Eugène Freyssinet,
airship hangars, Orly,
1916–21, parabola drawn
on photograph of
unfinished building

76   Freyssinet, airship
hangars, Orly, 1916–21

74

which he could usually justify on extremely practical grounds (e.g. as drip mouldings), seem to be historical relatives of the flat wall and bracket elements observable in the French classical tradition running back to the seventeenth century. It is intriguing to speculate how the Abbé Laugier (the mid-eighteenth-century theorist mentioned in Chapter 1) might have reacted to Perret's work if he could have been brought back to life in the first decade of the twentieth century. One suspects that he would have recognized immediately the intention of restating certain essentials of classicism for new purposes and in new materials. One imagines, too, that he might have respected the sentiments underlying Perret's dictum that 'one must never allow into a building any element destined solely for ornament, but rather turn to ornament all the parts necessary for the support'.

By 1911 the Perret brothers were among the leaders of concrete construction in France. They were approached by the impresario Gabriel Anstuc, who wished to erect a new theatre and hoped that Perret might help to implement a design by Henry van de Velde. This collaboration was short-lived – as might have been expected – and the Champs-Élysées Theatre of 1911–13 was carried out to Perret's design, with façades based on Van de

Velde's elevations. Once again Perret demonstrated the depth of his classical allegiances in the use of elements recalling stripped pilasters and cornices. In the interior, the spanning power of concrete was used to minimize interruptions of the view of the stage. The building's concrete frame was almost a work of art in its own right, and was certainly to become a major inspiration to the generation which created the modern movement of the 1920s; the external treatment of the theatre they preferred to forget, as its traditionalism was not in tune with their aims.

In the United States, in parallel with Hennebique's pioneering experiments, the engineer Ernest Ransome and the architect Albert Kahn discovered many applications for the new material in factory, warehouse, and even grain silo design. Cylindrical concrete grain silos were easy and economical to construct, avoided fire problems, and could be taken to great heights, so allowing for high concentration in storage alongside railway lines. They also had an indisputable purity and beauty that was captured in later years by the painters Charles Sheeler and Edward Hopper. They were as much instruments for the industrialization of the countryside as skyscrapers were devices for the industrialization of the city.

Concrete also recommended itself for the design of wide-span factories to accommodate the new techniques of 'Taylorization', whereby all steps of fabrication were submitted to a scientific rationalization for the mass production of goods. Albert Kahn devoted much of his life to the design of car factories, worked closely with Henry Ford, and, by 1908, was already producing his characteristic framed buildings in and around Detroit. He found concrete to be almost ideal in meeting such fundamental requirements as cheapness, standardization, clear lighting, fireproofing, extensive ventilation, and unobstructed, flexible interiors through which the assembly line could be threaded. A characteristic morphology of grid plans and simple rectangular elevations of pleasing proportion resulted. But Kahn never thought of his utilitarian designs as Architecture with a capital 'A'; the same was true of the engineers who designed grain silos; it was the European avant-garde, seeing these objects in photographs, who referred to them as icons of a new, universal language of architecture.

One of the few American architects to grapple with the potentials of the new material was Frank Lloyd Wright. He was certainly attracted to it because of its cheapness and because it could create wide spans, but also because it could be moulded to his spatial ideas. With his 'Arts and Crafts' emphasis on the nature of materials, Wright thought it best to leave the surfaces of concrete bare. One of his early masterpieces, the Unity Temple in Oak Park of 1905–8, was constructed in concrete. This building is best discussed in more detail in the context of Wright's philosophy and evolving vocabulary of abstract form (pp. 127–9 below); here it is enough to say that the building, like Perret's apartments, gave enhanced status to the material, and lent further weight to the impression that the 'correct' forms for concrete were rectangular, stripped, and abstract, although Wright did not, like Perret, rely on the frame.

But rectangular forms were by no means the only ones suitable to concrete, as was well demonstrated by the engineering feats of Eugène Freyssinet in France and Robert Maillart the bridge builder in Switzerland, in the first two decades. Freyssinet's vast airship hangars at Orly (1916–21) were parabolic in section and relied upon pre-stressed members, while Maillart's bridges tended to rest on attenuated curved supports, slabs or slender beams; Maillart's experiments helped to emancipate reinforced concrete from traditional masonry thinking, but were also in conflict with that version of engineering which insists upon calculations at the expense of conceptual and visual economy. His Tavanasa Bridge (1905) over the Verder-Rhine in Switzerland employed a three-hinged arch to allow

75

76

for expansion and contraction. It was the way in which structural stresses were accentuated directly in the material employed with a complete sense of visual coherence, that raised this rigorous engineering form to the level of structural art. Sharp slab details picked out shadows and provided vectors for the eye. The roadway was expressed as a thin plane with a life independent of the structure actually holding it up. The curves beneath were also dematerialized through careful detailing of rims and extruded ridges. Overall, there was the sense of forces intersecting and counteracting one another in space. Lines and surfaces seemed to hover. Max Berg's Jahrhunderthalle at Breslau, of 1912, also made much of the vast spanning potential of arcuated construction, but revealed an expressionist, dynamic tendency far away from Perret's sobriety, or from Maillart's restraint. This great variation of possible forms for concrete only serves to emphasize that the tendency to think of the rectangular forms of the modern movement as somehow indelibly linked to concrete is an oversimplification. The generation which, for a variety of aesthetic and symbolic reasons, sought effects of thin planarity, overhanging horizontality, and geometrical simplicity, saw its forefathers as being Perret and Wright, while ignoring an equally viable curvilinear tradition.

Among the architects to provide a pedigree for the later rectangular aesthetic was the Frenchman Tony Garnier, who also linked the new material to another development to become crucial in the 1920s: town planning for an industrial society. Garnier was born five years earlier than Perret, in 1869, and also attended Guadet's lectures at the École des Beaux-Arts in the 1890s. In 1899 he won the Prix de Rome with a design for a 'State Banking House' which was an exemplary demonstration of Beaux-Arts planning in the use of primary and secondary axes, absolute symmetry and the separation of circulation from areas served. Ostensibly Garnier was to have spent his time in Rome studying the monuments of antiquity, and making reconstructions of Herculaneum; instead he turned his mind to the design of a modern ideal city known simply as the 'Cité Industrielle'. This project was not published until 1917, by which time the architect had managed to implement some of his ideas in a new quarter on the outskirts of Lyons

77

under the socialist patronage of the mayor of the city, Edouard Herriot. The Cité Industrielle was based on the notion of distinct zoning for residential, industrial, transport and recreational areas, and drew together French urbanistic precedents in its use of grandiose axes, English Garden City ideals, and social ideas from the Utopian-socialist tradition. But the houses in the drawings for the Cité Industrielle were far from the Arts and Crafts in their use of flat roofs, their simple cubic geometries, and their use of concrete and standardization. If anything, the style was a sort of stripped 'Grecian', but the minimum reference was made to classical mouldings. The dwellings had simple rectangular windows punched through their surfaces, and in places concrete frames rose clear of the roofs and supported horizontal parasol slabs, lending an air of transparency to the imagery. The central railway station was also constructed from concrete and made dramatic use of cantilevers and horizontal overhangs. Garnier's Cité gave a convincing imagery to the functions of a modern town and lent extra weight to the notion that rectangular cubic forms were the most suitable for reinforced-concrete construction and for standardization. Moreover, there was the further suggestion that sober values of clear geometrical

77 Robert Maillart,
Tavanasa Bridge,
Switzerland, c.1905

78 Tony Garnier, Cité
Industrielle, residential
quarter, from *Cité
Industrielle*, 1917

79 Tony Garnier, Cité
Industrielle, railway
station, from *Cité
Industrielle*, 1917

repetition were the 'correct' ones for an emergent machine-age society.

Among those to be convinced of these patterns of thought, and to adhere to some of the principles behind Perret's vision of a reinforced-concrete architecture, was Charles Edouard Jeanneret, later to become Le Corbusier. So important is this figure to the history to be covered by this book, that it seems best to treat his formation individually (chapter 10). Here it is enough to say that Jeanneret was born in La Chaux-de-Fonds, Switzerland, in 1887; that his early designs reveal a mixture of Art Nouveau and Regionalist influences; that he spent part of his early twenties working in Perret's atelier where he learned the basic lessons of reinforced concrete, and imbibed Viollet-le-Duc's ideas; and that two years later (1910) he worked in the office of Peter Behrens in Berlin, where he absorbed the idea that a new architecture must rest on the idealization of types and norms designed to serve the needs of modern society, while being in harmony with the

means of mass production. At least this is sufficient to supply a context to his seminal 'Dom-ino' concrete housing system of 1914–15.

This was designed as a housing kit to help in the rapid reconstruction of war-ravaged Flanders. Jeanneret optimistically expected that the war would end quickly and his ideal was to mass-produce a basic set of components, including the necessary moulds, to make a simple, six-point support concrete skeleton with cantilevered slabs. The framework of the dwelling could then be assembled in less than three weeks, and rubble walls made from ruined buildings could be used as an infill. Windows and furnishings, all mass produced, were to be modelled on local precedents, and inserted into the skeleton. The very name 'Dom-ino' implied the Latin word for house (*domus*) and the game 'dominoes' (the plan of a whole suburb did loosely resemble a row of number six dominoes). Intrinsic was the idea that simple, rectangular, mass-producible components could be arranged to make modern dwellings and communities. From the very beginning we can sense the future of Le Corbusier's preoccupation with defining the elements of a new architectural and urbanistic language.

The central generator of the Dom-ino system and of both the architecture *and* the urbanism of the later Le Corbusier was the skeleton itself (designed with the help of Max Dubois). This was a structural unit consisting of three horizontal slabs, smooth below and above, each of the upper two supported on square sectional posts of concrete, the lower level lifted from the ground on squat concrete blocks. In the perspective of this skeleton (which was published only in the 1920s) concrete stairs were shown connecting the levels. It was noticeable that the Dom-ino, by contrast with, say, the system of Hennebique, made no use of brackets or beams. The slabs and posts were entirely clean, and contributed to an entirely pure structural idea. Employing the principle of the cantilever, the slabs, moreover, extended well beyond the line of supports. In fact they were not to be monolithic concrete, but pot-tile, covered over with concrete and reinforced with interior beams of steel.

One advantage of Jeanneret's system would have been its rapid construction, but this was not put to the test. Another was intrinsic and indubitable: it did with concrete what Perret's system had not. It separated out the structural and the screening functions of the wall by removing the fill from the frame. Now the fill was attached to the end of the slabs, with the possibility of its existing as a planar surface hovering in space above a void. As the weight of the building was now borne by the skeleton, the external 'wall' (or other form of cladding) could be arranged without thought for the load on it and without the interruption of the frame. It could become effectively a sort of membrane to be punctured as functional necessities or compositional instincts required. In the drawings for Dom-ino houses glass was placed tantalizingly at the corners in some places, just where a traditional masonry structure would have been structurally most solid.

In the interior the Dom-ino system also allowed new freedoms. Partitions could be positioned as one wished, in or out of line with the grid of supports. Space was saved and a new degree of functional flexibility achieved. Aesthetically the emphasis could now shift from the subtraction of voids from masses,

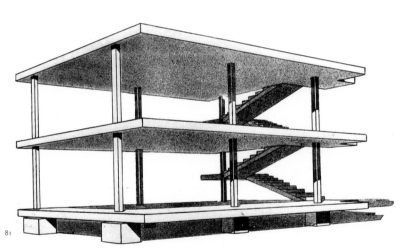

81

to the modulation of spaces with minimal supports. Parts of the slabs could be removed to create double- or even triple-height volumes. The lower level could be liberated entirely to let public circulation pass through, while the flat top could be used as a terrace. In an embryonic form, the Dom-ino skeleton spelled out certain generating principles – the free plan, the free façade, the flat-roof terrace – that were to be of cardinal importance to Le Corbusier in ensuing years.

However, this is to look at the Dom-ino skeleton with hindsight, and with the knowledge of the transparent, planar, and lightweight effects of the later works of the modern movement in the 1920s. It is therefore only fair to point out that the Dom-ino houses proposed in 1914–15 were dumpy in visual effect, for all their simplicity of volume, and that their interiors were confined and traditional for all the spatial potential of the structural skeleton. They probably reflected Jeanneret's admiration for the unadorned dwellings of the Mediterranean, with their flat roofs and cubic shapes modelled by light. Indeed, the Dom-ino houses were the first of a number of attempts by the architect at founding a modern, industrialized equivalent to the vernaculars of the past.

But if the Dom-ino ideas anticipated some aspects of the architecture of the 1920s, they also rested firmly in the Rationalist tradition. When Jeanneret worked for Perret in 1908, he had used his first pay-packet to buy Viollet-le-Duc's *Dictionnaire de l'architecture*. In one of the margins, alongside an illustration of a Gothic flying buttress, he referred in a note to Perret's insistence on the structural skeleton: 'grasp the skeleton and you grasp the art.' Equally, the purified diagram of structure represented by the Dom-ino could be seen as the very distillation of the *idea* of load and support: the essence of column, floor and roof expressed in pure, virtually ideal forms. It was like a genotype, an image of origins, out of which a symbolic architecture might be developed. In his own Dom-ino theorem the young man laid the basis for his future architectural and urbanistic systems, but with help from his mentors, past and contemporary. In much the same way, Rationalism and reinforced concrete were two elements, but only two among several, which would eventually coalesce in the 'heroic' period of modern architecture, the 1920s.

5

arts and crafts ideals in britain and the u.s.a.

82 Charles and Henry Greene, Gamble House, Pasadena, 1907–8, detail of stair

The search for values of simplicity and directness which motivated so many artistic developments in the first decade of the twentieth century had its roots in a variety of earlier intellectual positions. The last chapter traced one of these – Rationalism – and suggested how this aided the discovery of forms based on reinforced-concrete construction. There was another strand of ideas, however, which stemmed from Pugin, Ruskin, and William Morris, according to which the 'corruption of nineteenth-century styles' would be counteracted by inspired craftsmanship, and which maintained that an authentic architecture would be achieved through the direct expression of pristine moral virtues. Each of these English thinkers was disgusted in his own way with the impact of the Industrial Revolution on the social organization, the methods of building, and the very moral basis of culture. Morris, in particular, had hoped to usher in a new period of integrated wholeness in which the highest aesthetic qualities would be ripped from the museum pedestal and linked again with the tools and artefacts of everyday use. The architect must therefore become a master of craft; and, to judge by Philip Webb's and Morris's Red House of 1859, this attitude tended to be translated formally into a medievalizing vocabulary in which the direct qualities of vernacular design were emulated to create a suitable emblem of the simple, good life.

Nikolaus Pevsner has traced the evolution of Arts and Crafts ideals through the last three decades of the nineteenth century and has demonstrated the impact of Morris's thinking on Walter Gropius and the Deutscher Werkbund in Germany in the first decade of this century. It was only when Morris's ideals concerning the reintegration of art and life, craft and utility, were transformed to allow for mechanization that they became directly useful to the creation of the modern movement. But history does not work in straight lines, and the Arts and Crafts inheritance permeated a number of developments around the turn of the century which did not, it so happens, bear fruit in specifically 'modern' architecture.

It is natural to begin the story in Britain with the legacy of domestic architectural ideals handed down from Webb, Richard Norman Shaw, Edward Godwin, and Arthur Heygate Mackmurdo to a later generation including Voysey, Edwin Lutyens,

83

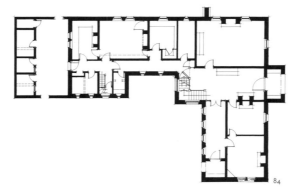

84

Mackay Hugh Baillie Scott, Edward Prior, Mackintosh, Charles Robert Ashbee, and William Richard Lethaby. Charles Francis Annesley Voysey was born in 1857 and produced his own unique style just before the turn of the century in designs like that for a house in Bedford Park of 1890–1 or for a studio in St Dunstan's Road, West Kensington, of the same year. In these, the aesthetic effect arose from the disposition of simple pebble-dashed and whitewashed volumes punctured by rows of windows and enhanced by the geometrical play of chimneys and low-angled roofs. It is not hard to understand how formalist historians seeking a pedigree for the stripped white forms of later modern architecture should have turned to Voysey; however, the architect expressed embarrassment at having this role of 'pioneer of modern design' thrust upon him. His immersion in the simple joys of English vernacular design, his lack of fuss, his almost childlike obsession with the composition of rain barrels and gutters in façades, have very little in common with the ideas of a later generation for whom simplicity had a very different universal and mechanistic significance.

Voysey's vision seems to have come to full maturity in his large houses in rural settings, such as Perrycroft, designed for a site in the Malvern hills in 1893, or Greyfriars of 1896, built on a ridge in

Surrey known as the Hog's Back. The first of these made much use of sloping buttresses and deeply overhanging eaves, not only as structural, climatic and compositional devices, but also as ways of linking the building to the ground and suggesting continuity with local vernacular design. This was a central idea of Arts and Crafts architectural doctrine: indigenous materials and usages were to be translated to good use by the modern practitioner.

Although Voysey was not a craftsman himself, he turned his mind to the design of wallpapers, furniture, fixtures and fittings, for he felt that the same impulses should permeate all the interiors of a house as conditioned the overall form. Here again he pursued a rhetorical simplicity, which made a pointed contrast with the clutter and complexity of earlier Victorian design. In The Orchard, Chorleywood (1899–1900), walls and stair-rails were stripped down, and door latches and hinges were modelled on rural examples; the interiors were bathed in light. Pevsner tended to associate this straightforwardness and youthfulness with a wider reaction in values. 'It is well known that everywhere in English cultural life a longing for fresh air and gaiety expressed itself at the end of Queen Victoria's reign.' Another novel feature of Voysey's designs was the way they liberated interior volumes so that they tended to flow into one another. In Broadleys (1898), a house overlooking Lake Windermere, the hall was carved out as a double space. In plan the main elements were subtly disposed with an order combining some degree of symmetry and formality

85

with informal and asymmetrical qualities. In these ways Voysey succeeded in giving form to the patterns of social life of the English well-to-do at the turn of the century. It was a sort of procured rusticity, an emulation of the 'common speech' of the vernacular which was, of course, very self-conscious.

M. H. Baillie Scott was nine years Voysey's junior and, unlike him, did much work on the continent. In his Blackwell House of 1900, also on Lake Windermere, he attempted to open up the interior space. Of course, this was not simply an aesthetic matter, but an attempt at expressing a way of life. Baillie Scott has left evocative descriptions conjuring up the life of the middle-class home with the fire crackling in a central hall, the living rooms opening out into one another, the inglenooks, the music gallery, the broad, winding stairs. Such arrangements were heavily loaded with deliberate manorial associations, referring to a romanticized national past. Both Voysey and Baillie Scott managed to conjure up a powerful image of the Englishman's home which would eventually be disseminated through the building catalogues to provide many of the standard clichés of inter-war domestic suburban building.

Another feature of creative domestic design in the Edwardian period was the fusion of the house with its garden setting through the use of pergolas, pathways, sunken gardens and the like. To be sure, the 'rusticity' of the Arts and Crafts dwelling was not allowed to be too rude or too removed from the gentility and urbanity of the middle-class users. In

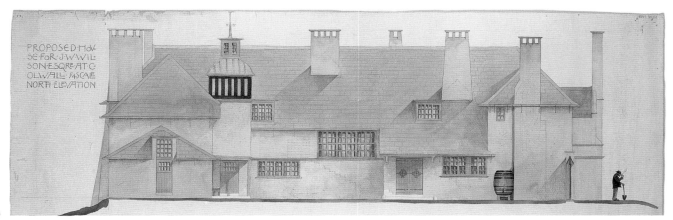

86

Hill House at Helensburgh of 1903, built for Walter Blackie the publisher, Charles Rennie Mackintosh designed not only the house and all its fixtures and fittings, but the outbuildings, the garden gates, the walls, the terraces, and the pergolas as well – all as part of a unified aesthetic conception. The result was a total work of art, an aesthetic enhancement of all the rituals of family life, from the 'public face' presented to arriving guests in the hall, to the relative formality of dining room and living room, to the more informal and private worlds of inglenooks, bedrooms, library and garden seats. The echoes were local and traditional, the reverberations international, even universal, for Hill House was one of several Mackintosh designs to inspire new tendencies abroad. It was the sharp interplay of wall planes and openings, silhouettes and surfaces, as well as the direct celebration of functional elements like chimneys, which recommended this building to the Viennese avant-garde. In effect 'Mackintosh

developed the somewhat thin and frosty air of the Scottish vernacular and transformed it into a living style of the early twentieth century …'

Some of the richest creations of this type in England were designed by Edwin Lutyens, who frequently worked closely with his cousin, the garden designer Gertrude Jekyll, for whom he built one of his earliest houses, at Munstead Wood near Godalming, Surrey (1896). This was soon followed by a number of other outstanding houses in the area, including the Orchards at Godalming, and Tigbourne Court, also in Surrey and also of 1898. Lutyens received direct inspiration from Shaw and Webb but exceeded both in the breadth of his sources, the range of his imagination, and his capacity for wittily turning a vernacular usage to his own advantage. He believed strongly in the use of local crafts and materials, both because this was practical and because it was liable to lead to a harmony between the house and its architectural or

87   Charles Rennie Mackintosh, Hill House, Helensburgh, 1902–3

88   Edwin Lutyens, The Pleasaunce, Overstrand, Norfolk, 1899–1901, view of garden steps

89   Edwin Lutyens, Tigbourne Court, Surrey, 1898

87

88

89

natural setting. Thus in his early designs one finds him employing Surrey tile fascias and wooden frames based on yeomen's houses, and varying the depth of his eaves according to local character and precedent. In Overstrand Hall, Norfolk (1901), typical indigenous combinations of flint and red-brick courses were employed, but adeptly transformed into a vocabulary suave in its accents and enhanced by clever collisions of classical and medieval fragments.

It would be entirely inadequate, however, to reject Lutyens as a mere eclectic who raided the rag-bag of history in order to satisfy the taste for exotic weekend scenarios of his extremely wealthy patrons. Underlying the play was a controlling sense of proportion and organizational principle; beneath the sparkle was a sober and probing mind, which was eventually to seek the certainties of classical design. Moreover, the unity of Lutyens's designs was achieved by a judicious combination of axes and repeating geometrical motifs. Thus one finds 'themes' played out in plan, elevation, and volume, as when an arch turns into a semicircular step, to be rediscovered as a wall niche, a dome, or a luxurious hemispherical Edwardian bath lined with mosaic. Geometrical play could extend to the elements of garden design as well. At The Pleasaunce (also in

Norfolk, 1899–1901) the convex spherical form of the baking oven was restated in the concave hemisphere of the brick garden-seat canopy; the sunken gardens were in turn linked to the house by amphitheatre-like steps, circular ground patterns and curved levels.

Lutyens was also fascinated by the special character of each client and site, and always attempted to produce a unique response to these. At Lindisfarne he was requested to remodel a Scottish castle on the promontory overlooking the North Sea. He transformed it into a bijou fortress, whose parapets harmonized with the surrounding rocks and whose imagery was entirely at one with the spirit of the place. At Heathcote, Ilkley (1906), the client required a more magnificent and prestigious imagery than was usual for Lutyens, and the site, being almost suburban and hemmed in by buildings on both sides, suggested the qualities of a formal villa. Thus the architect varied his manner to include something of the character of the English Baroque, with quotations from Vanbrugh and Hawksmoor. The body of the house was ingeniously linked to the setting by parterres, an apsidal 'great lawn' and subtle cross axes. The materials, meanwhile, were local ones: Guiseley stone with grey dressings from the Morley quarries. The result was a massive heap of a certain dour quality, perfectly suited to its region and placement. In The Salutation (1912) at Sandwich, Kent, the gate lodge was made to harmonize with the character of a Kentish riverside town through the use of local tiles and white woodwork, which were handled with a sort of procured irregularity blending superbly with the ageing character of the surroundings. Nowhere in Lutyens's work is there the disturbance of new social forces or of the industry whose very owners were frequently his clients. His designs evoked a safe and stable world of national continuity. They implied the conceit that the crafts had remained perpetually the same from region to region over the ages.

Voysey, Lutyens, Baillie Scott, Prior and the other English architects who might be loosely grouped as 'Arts and Crafts' in the first decade of the twentieth century were bold innovators in domestic design, but in most respects were traditionalists. The 'freedom' of their planning and the directness and 'honesty' of their use of materials were perhaps emblematic of a reaction against the clutter and pomposity of earlier English domestic architecture, but these architects were certainly far from attempting the creation of a brave new world. In a sense, their designs were microcosms of deeply felt values concerning the meaning of the home: worlds in miniature in which details like door latches or dovecots, as well as the overall mood, were infused with a sense of reverence for the ideal of a happy family life in a natural setting.

It was customary before the First World War to refer to the new style as 'the English Free Architecture', but by 1910 a strong reaction had set in, in favour of a direct neo-classical revival and a dependence on foreign and 'cosmopolitan' models rather than native, vernacular ones. At about the same time that the French Beaux-Arts was beginning to exert its influence in England, Arts and Crafts values were being, as it were, exported to Germany. A key personality here was Hermann Muthesius, who was posted to the German embassy in London precisely to study English domestic design. His book Das englische Haus of 1904 was a masterly survey of the national tradition of houses. Undoubtedly he was catering to a taste in Germany, stretching well back into the nineteenth century, for the English cottage and garden. But there were weightier ideals at work as well. Muthesius was

working for a German élite who felt strongly the inferiority of their culture, and its disruption by industrialization. They sensed in the English movement an unruffled, sober character, as well as an intelligent application of formal quality to everyday design. Muthesius mythologized the Englishman and his home in this way:

… let me repeat once more that the Modern English artistic movement has no trace of those fanciful, superfluous, and often affected ideas with which a part of the new continental movement is still engaged. Far from this, it tends more towards the primitive and the rustic; and here it fits perfectly well with the type of traditional rural house. Moreover, this outcome is perfectly to the taste of the Englishman for whom there is nothing better than plain simplicity … A minimum of 'forms', and a maximum of peaceful, comfortable and yet lively atmosphere, that is what he aims for … Such accord seems to him to be a link with beloved Mother Nature, to whom, despite all higher cultures, the English nation has remained more faithful than any other people. And today's house is proof of this … The way in which it fits so admirably into surrounding Nature in the happiness of its colouring and the solidity of its form: in all these ways it stands there today as cultural proof of the healthy tendencies of a nation which amid all its wealth and advances in civilization has retained, to a remarkable degree, its appreciation of what is natural. Urban civilization, with its destructive influences, with its senseless haste and press, with its hothouse stimulation of those impulses towards vanity which are latent in man, with its elevation of the refined, the nervous, the abnormal to unnatural proportions, all this has had practically no harmful effect on the English nation.

German admiration for the English Arts and Crafts went further than this. It included an attempt at emulating the values of honesty of materials, simplicity etc. in the design of everyday objects and in the teaching programmes of schools of design, and it eventually extended to a wholesale national obsession with the ideal of good formal quality in *industrial* design. Looking back in 1915, William Lethaby, who had been deeply involved with the English movement, could express his sadness at the 'timid reaction and the re-emergence of the catalogued styles' in England and his admiration for 'advances in German industrial design founded on the English arts and crafts'. The manner in which a movement which had been conceived, in part, as a reaction against the crudities of mechanization became the basis of a national industrial design philosophy, must be explained in a later chapter; suffice it to say that Arts and Crafts values, once exported and transformed, were another major element in the jigsaw puzzle of the modern movement.

This was true not only in Europe, but also in

Hobson Richardson – Beaux-Arts trained, with a deep appreciation of medieval sources and a rare instinct for what was most relevant to the emergent social order of the United States – that one finds a forceful synthesis of the indigenous and the imported. The Ames Gate Lodge of 1880–2 at North Easton, Massachusetts, is linked to its site and its region by a strong sense of place and by an exaggerated use of indigenous stonework; yet the rusticity of the imagery is ennobled, formalized and enhanced by the architect's knowledge of far-distant traditions including such exoticisms as Early Christian arches from Syria and French medieval farm buildings. This was the 'rural' end of the scale for Richardson, and the Ames Gate Lodge even courted the idea of architectural origins in geological formulations or primitive shelters made from huge boulders.

Thus the search for a model domestic architecture in America was never very far from the larger question of defining an American architecture in general. There followed a series of formulations and emotions unfolding around such ideas as: the search for a pastoral or middle-landscape ideal; the notion of an honest expression unfettered by European decadence; a conception of native functionalism; an aspiration towards a fitness and commodity mirroring nature's, which would lead by a short route to beauty and deeper meanings. Tinged with nostalgia for an earlier search for paradise in the 'New World', this sophisticated quest for a simplicity in touch with natural values crystallized in that most cultivated and artificial of 'natural' settings, the suburbia which began to proliferate around the mechanized American cities from the 1880s onwards.

As we shall see in Chapter 7, Wright grasped the full meaning of this situation and managed to take the suburban family house and weave a mythology around it. His earliest designs were drawn from the Shingle Style, from Japanese sources, from the Midwestern vernacular, and from the Queen Anne and Colonial revivals which briefly touched the Midwest of his youth in the 1880s and early 1890s. Arts and Crafts ideals imported from Britain, concerning the direct response to the nature of materials and the total design of furnishings and building, including the setting, early permeated his outlook. However, unlike Morris and his British

America, where the catalyst of transformation was Frank Lloyd Wright. He was undoubtedly the most original architect to be influenced by Arts and Crafts ideals and, to that extent, can scarcely be considered typical. None the less, his formulation occurred in a milieu of ideas derived from the earlier nineteenth century. There was no direct equivalent to William Morris in the American tradition, but his ideas were certainly well known. In the figure of Andrew Jackson Downing one has a mid-century thinker and designer who put great store by the image of the individual wooden-battened house – the rustic retreat – as somehow quintessentially American and democratic. Vincent Scully has traced the ensuing development in the last three decades of the nineteenth century of the so-called 'Stick' and 'Shingle' styles, in which the direct expression of wooden construction, informal open-planning, verandas, and a romantic display of hipped roofs, chimneys, and gazebo elements all played a part. Arguably Norman Shaw's influence on these developments was considerable; certainly local traditions of wooden construction had a role; but there was also something less definable – an ethos of freedom, and a concern for the relationship of the individual dwelling to its natural setting. As always, American architectural development was both helped and hindered by the lack of a long, coherent national tradition: helped because this situation encouraged a degree of experimentation; hindered because there was relatively little guidance from earlier norms. It is in the figure of Henry

developments in bungalow and furniture design and illustrated ideal projects for individual homes. Among these suggestions were ones for single- and double-storey homes with deep overhanging eaves, verandas, climbing plants, and rusticated chimneys. The interiors were simple evocations of 'home', to which bare beams and wooden uprights, inglenooks and built-in benches, 'humble' materials and fireplaces in the hallway all contributed. The sources for this imagery were diverse, and seemed to include Swiss chalets, Japanese wooden houses, and a variety of American regional cabin and shack prototypes.

In California there was not only the sense of a new society, unbounded by conventions and as yet untainted by industry; there were also plentiful lots of land. Moreover, the climate encouraged an architecture opening to the outside. The masters of the genre of the luxurious, but still 'simple', California bungalow were the brothers Charles and Henry Greene (born in 1868 and 1870) who were educated in Calvin Woodward's Manual Training School in St Louis in the late 1870s, where they were encouraged to handle natural materials (especially wood) and to give their conceptions visual form. In the late 1880s the brothers went East and studied at the Massachusetts Institute of Technology, where they learned some of the axial devices and intellectual strategies of Beaux-Arts design. After graduating they spent some time working in the Boston area, where they no doubt examined the works of H. H. Richardson and a variety of local Stick and Shingle Style examples. Finally they moved to the West. It was to take them a decade to work out a style based on their earlier influences, on the hybrid indigenous styles of California (especially those using simple wooden construction and deep overhanging balconies), and even on Japanese prototypes in which elegant proportions, finely handled joints and a superb combination of the formal and the informal were achieved.

The masterpiece of their new regional style was the Gamble House in Pasadena of 1907–8, built for one of the millionaire partners of the soap firm Procter and Gamble. The house represented the full aggrandizement and ennoblement of the California bungalow image, yet the building was still striking for its intimacy and human scale. An effect of

91 Frank Lloyd Wright's own house, Oak Park, near Chicago, Illinois, 1893

92 Gustav Stickley, bungalow design from *The Craftsman*, c.1905, interior

93 Charles and Henry Greene, Gamble House, Pasadena, California, 1907–8

94 Gamble House, Pasadena, ground-floor plan with planting

contemporaries, he grasped the positive importance of mechanization as well. In his essay 'The Art and Craft of the Machine', of 1901, he acknowledged that 'the machine is here to stay' and that this would influence not only the artist's techniques in building (e.g. straight lines of simple cut wood) but the entire fabric of the society for which he would build. A traditionalist in many senses, Wright remained; but his powerful feeling for abstract form and his vision of a new social order made him a link between the nineteenth-century craft ideal and the propelling ideas of the later modern movement in Europe.

In addition to Wright's own architecture and the 'Prairie School' which developed some of his ideas (see p. 138), there were other developments in the United States which extended the Arts and Crafts movement, especially on the West Coast. The West was still regarded as a last frontier and thus collected the detritus of over a century of pioneer mythology. From 1901 to 1916, Gustav Stickley spread the message of the 'Craftsman's Movement' in a magazine called *The Craftsman*. This recorded

93

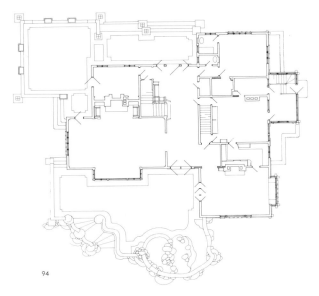

94

nobility was conferred on the whole by its placement on a sort of terrace plinth, lifted slightly above the level of the surrounding lawns and banks of ferns. The relative solidity of the main gabled portions was heightened by the delicate transparency of the sprawling Stick Style balconies containing sleeping porches, with their overlapping struts and deep reveals of shadow. The main materials on the exterior were the redwood of the beams and frame, and the redwood 'shakes' (giant shingles) which blended well with the surrounding natural colours. In the interior these material qualities and textures were supplemented by glistening stained-glass panels, hand-polished maple, and the glow of Tiffany lamps. The elegance of the overall proportions was continued into the smallest parts and details – the articulation of earthquake-proof sliding joints with pegs and thongs, and the visual subtlety of tapering beam ends in the balconies. One is not surprised to discover that the house was modified (as were most of the Greene brothers' designs) in the course of construction, with the architects themselves frequently fashioning the wooden details on site to ensure a precise effect.

The Gamble House plan gives further clues to the architects' intentions. One arrives by way of an open terrace; the front door gives straight on to a wide open hall passing right through the house to another terrace at the rear. The stairs, dining room, and living room (the latter two looking out over the pool and fernery) are all linked by this major space. The living room, as in so many of Wright's contemporary designs, is symmetrical and on an axis with the main fireplace, which is conceived as a major incident. The plan, and the spaces generated from it, admittedly lack the tension and control of Wright's Prairie Houses, but the combination of formal and informal qualities so appropriate to the social role and meaning of such a dwelling is a widely shared feature of much Arts and Crafts design of the period. So is the attempt at unifying the building with its setting, achieved in this case by the prevalent horizontality, the ambiguous situation of porches half inside, half outside, the sympathy for the nature of the materials, the provision made for planting, and the irregularly edged plan blending with the garden. It is the theme of the 'natural house' taken to an extreme which the California climate and flora encouraged.

While 'craftsmen's' ideals were usually carried through in domestic contexts, this was not their only outlet, and both Mackintosh's School of Art and Wright's Unity Temple were notable examples of similar ideas being worked through in institutional settings. In Northern California, Bernard Maybeck produced an exemplary craftsman's building in his First Church of Christ, Scientist, in Berkeley of 1910. Actually, the building defies simple categorization; it is unique and eccentric. Maybeck had been trained as a furniture-maker and had then revelled in his Beaux-Arts education in Paris. The church is steeped in tradition and relies strongly on the ceremonial axial compositional ideas basic to the Beaux-Arts outlook. But the architectural elements assembled above this hieratic plan have little to do with the grand classical manner (although the same architect's designs at the Pacific Exhibition of 1915 reveal a personal and effective reinterpretation of classical prototypes). Rather we are confronted by a jumble of styles and allusions – Gothic, suburban

95

California, Stick Style, Japanese, and an almost fantastic range of materials and effects, including carved wood, industrial sash glazing, asbestos panels and trellises carrying festoons of wisteria. This profusion of associations was held together by a consistent development of geometrical themes. The design rested upon an armature of types – pergola and aedicule, roof and pediment, house and temple – making analogies between vernacular and honorific forms. Despite the complexity of its sources, the First Church of Christ, Scientist, Berkeley, maintained a convincing unity.

If Maybeck represents a rugged and obsessive extreme of the Craftsman's Movement in the western United States, then Irving Gill must be taken as the complement because of the sobriety and broad simplicity of his approach. Born in 1870, he was largely self-taught and much influenced by the fact that his father was a building contractor with a knack for finding short cuts in construction. Gill himself was an early advocate of reinforced concrete in domestic design, especially using 'tilt-slab' techniques, and like Perret thought that the material required a simple rectangular vocabulary. He was confirmed in this view by his personal reactions to the regional traditions of the south-western United States, especially the mud adobe constructions of the area and the white-walled Mission Style dwellings with their planar, white surfaces gashed by shadows, their low roofs, their extending pergolas, and their sequences of patios. But Gill's was no mere grass-roots

95 Bernard Maybeck,
First Church of Christ,
Scientist, Berkeley,
California, 1910

96 Irving Gill, Dodge
House, Los Angeles,
California, 1915–16

romanticism; his work was motivated by a social vision of considerable breadth. He understood the suburban condition, and how best to respond to the topography, vegetation, climate and society of rapidly expanding cities like San Diego. He thought of California as the last frontier, and therefore as a suitable place for the expression of a new way of life based on the best of old American democratic ideals. The significance of stripped simplicity in his work was therefore partly moral, but very far in its meanings from the machine idolization of the avant-garde in Europe who were to create the modern movement of the 1920s. On the contrary, Gill (who had absorbed something of Sullivan's pantheism and feeling for symbolic geometries) sought to make the broad masses of his own designs an equivalent to the structures of nature:

We should build our house simple, plain and substantial as a boulder, then leave the ornamentation of it to Nature, who will tone it with lichens, chisel it with storms, make it gracious and friendly with vines and flower shadows as she does the stone in the meadow. I believe also that houses should be built more substantially and should be made absolutely sanitary. If the cost of unimportant ornamentation were put into construction, then we would have a more lasting and a more dignified house.

Gill's interpretation of 'Nature' went deeper than an interest in sensitive siting and the effects of weathering on surfaces. Like Wright and Sullivan, he believed that the best geometries were those abstracted from nature's structures and processes; and that the forms of art should emulate the fitness to purpose of natural forms. In Gill's mind, the basic shapes of architectural grammar were analogous to natural features and capable of impressing the emotions of a spectator in precise ways.

Every artist must sooner or later reckon directly, personally with these four principles – the mightiest of lines. The straight line borrowed from the horizon is a symbol of greatness, grandeur and nobility; the arch patterned from the dome of the sky represents exultation, reverence, aspiration; the circle is the sign of completeness, motion and progression, as may be seen when a stone touches water; the square is the symbol of power, justice, honesty, and firmness. These are the bases, the units of architectural language, and without them there can be no direct or inspired architectural speech.

In the broad picture of the transition from the 'styles' of the nineteenth century to the creation of modern architecture, the continuation of the Arts and Crafts movement into the twentieth century played a partial role, and inspired individual work of outstanding quality. Rather than a unified style, there were broadly shared concerns. It so happened that Gill anticipated some superficial aspects of the white, geometrical architecture of the 1920s, but his work was virtually unknown in Europe and his outlook quite different. Indeed much of the effort of the generation which was to create the modern movement in Europe was directed *against* handicraft aspirations. None the less, Arts and Crafts ideals had an important purgative function by stressing the values of simplicity, honesty, and necessity. Ideals such as these were to be fundamental to the Deutscher Werkbund in Germany, an organization which sought a more direct confrontation with mechanization.

96

6

responses to mechanization: the deutscher werkbund and futurism

97 Bruno Taut, Glass Pavilion, Cologne, 1914

From the beginning, the Arts and Crafts movement had been permeated with preservationist sentiments and a nostalgia for a supposedly integrated society preceding the chaotic effects of industrialization. By contrast, in the decade before the First World War, especially in Germany and Italy, philosophical, poetic, and eventually formal attitudes emerged in which an adulatory view of mechanization was to be found. It has already been suggested that the very notion of 'modern' architecture presupposed a progressivist sense of history; it is only by examining the theories of the Deutscher Werkbund in Germany and of the Futurists in Italy (which contrasted considerably) and the parallel architectural ideas of men like Peter Behrens, Walter Gropius, and Antonio Sant'Elia that one may grasp how mechanization came to be regarded as a sort of essential motor to the forward march of history, requiring an appropriate expression in architecture and design.

This is not to suggest for one minute that a consensus was reached on just how this should be done. In Germany, which industrialized later than Britain and France, and experienced some of the opportunities and traumas of the process deeply, there was much debate concerning the ideal relationship between the artist and industry. Broadly speaking there were four main strands of opinion. One of these was a direct continuation of Arts and Crafts values in the Kunstgewerbeschulen (Schools of Applied Art), where the belief was maintained that quality goods would be achieved only through a concentration on handicrafts. Closely related to this view was a highly individualistic idea of the role of artistic invention which held that authentic forms in architecture could arise only from the imprint of the expressive temperament; this position tended to extend the most subjective aspects of Art Nouveau and led to the 'Expressionist' outlook. A third position was materialist and down-to-earth by contrast, and tended to hold that the best forms would be those emerging from the logical and direct use of new materials to solve building problems; it was, in other words, a functionalist outlook. The fourth position (the one which will principally concern us) tended to regard the functionalist as an uncultivated brute, the Expressionist as an irrelevant remnant of the cult of genius, and the craftsman as an extinct entity unless directed to the problems of designing objects for mass production. Thus it became the business of the artist/architect to design the 'type forms' – be they objects of industrial design, building elements, or pieces of urban structure – of a new, mechanized and, let it be said, German civilization. It was an ideology in which the artist had to function as a sort of mediator between formal invention and standardization, between personal style and the appropriate form for the *Zeitgeist* (or 'spirit of the times'), between a sense of the contemporary world and reliance on age-old artistic principles.

One of the most vocal proponents of such an outlook was Hermann Muthesius (author of *Das englische Haus*), who founded the Deutscher Werkbund in 1907. This organization was set up precisely to forge closer links between German industry and artists, and thereby upgrade the quality of national product design in emulation of what Muthesius had seen in England. From the start this was seen as being far more than a commercial matter; rather it was one involving deep probings into the nature of 'the German spirit', the role of form in history and the psychic life of the nation. Muthesius wrote:

Far higher than the material is the spiritual; far higher than function, material and technique, stands Form. These three aspects might be impeccably handled but – if Form were not – we would still be living in a merely brutish world. So there remains before us an aim, a much greater and more important task – to awaken once more an understanding of Form, and the renewal of architectonic sensibilities.

Muthesius put his faith in the cultivated industrial élite who, he hoped, could be educated to lead the German nation on its innate mission: the elevation of a general taste to a position of supremacy in world markets and affairs, and the efflorescence of an influential and genuine *Kultur*. The moral tenor of life was to be raised through the impact of well-designed objects in the marketplace, in the home, and in the workplace – indeed, in the environment as a whole. Evidently he envisaged a sort of unified style to replace the confectionery of nineteenth-century eclecticism, which should be expressed with equal clarity in a lamp-post, a teacup, a monument, or even a factory building. Central to his outlook was a belief in the return to fundamental formal qualities which would express architectonically the dignity and the calm endeavour of a new, confident national German spirit. There

are echoes in this outlook of the writings of Semper, who had forecast the necessity of a style appropriate to machine methods after his visit to the Crystal Palace and the Great Exhibition of 1851. And it comes as no surprise to find that Muthesius had a considerable sympathy for the grandeur of the classical tradition (especially as manifested in the work of Schinkel), for this seemed to sum up so well the combination of martial values and impersonal power, scholarship and formal abstraction, that Muthesius perhaps envisaged as essential to the necessary style for his own times: '... the re-establishment of an architectonic culture is a basic condition of all the arts ... It is a question of bringing back into our way of life that order and discipline of which good Form is the outward manifestation.'

From the English Arts and Crafts tradition Muthesius inherited a concern for the moral power of design to influence people's lives, a sense of integrity in the expression of the nature of materials, a feeling for the dignified embodiment of function, and an obsession with the 'dishonesty' of false revivalism. However, these notions were cross-bred, as it were, with the ideal of designing for the machine and with philosophical concepts derived from the German Idealist tradition (notably the writings of Hegel). Central to these was the notion that it was the destiny of Germany to realize some higher idea in the historical scheme of things, and a related notion that a sort of 'will-to-form' with a strong national taint would realize the forms of a genuine style. Such a style would not then be seen

98

99

as a merely personal, conventional or wilful matter, but as an inevitable force of destiny: a universal necessity.

It is evident that the ephemeral is incompatible with the true essence of architecture. The peculiar qualities of architecture, constancy, tranquillity and permanence and its thousand-year-old traditions of expression, have almost come to represent what is eternal in human history … Of all the arts architecture is the one which tends most readily towards the typical and only thus can it really fulfil its aims. It is only by steadily striving for a single target that we shall be able to recover the quality and the unerring surety of touch that we admire in the achievements of the past, where singleness of purpose was inherent in the age.

It would be too simple, and too convenient, to see the architecture of Peter Behrens as a direct illustration of Muthesius's aspirations; but after about 1907 there was a considerable consonance in their positions, especially in the designs that Behrens executed for the giant electrical concern, AEG; these included objects for mass production, like lamps, posters, and furniture, as well as buildings. His artistic career to that date had been symptomatic of more general developments, starting with an immersion in Arts and Crafts ideals during his time at the Darmstadt Artists' Colony, founded

by the Grand Duke Ernst Ludwig von Hessen in 1899. Behrens, while one of the seven founding inmates of the colony (J. M. Olbrich was another), wrote of the 'physical pleasure existing in the useful and the suitable' and stressed the need for a new integration of the two. His own house of 1901 shows him to have passed through a dreamy Art Nouveau phase, with a rich fusion of curvilinear forms and melancholic emotions of the sort which appealed to an inward-looking frame of mind. Behrens's search for a genuine German art then seems to have taken him through a 'recall to order' which manifested itself in the stereometric and planar geometries of his Romanesque-inspired buildings at the Oldenburg Exhibition of 1905. By the time he worked for the AEG, his outlook had matured considerably and his vocabulary began to exhibit overtly neo-classical characteristics. Like Muthesius, Behrens sensed in Schinkel a combination of nationalist and idealistic associations suitable to his own task of formulating an imagery for the industrial élite. He was fortunate in the attention and interest of Emil Rathenau as his chief AEG patron, for here was a man who combined cultural

and technical interests in a single outlook.

Both Rathenau and Behrens felt that industrial tasks must be seen as the essential cultural ones of the time. The factory thus took on a far greater significance than it had usually possessed. Behrens realized that his client required impressive and cultivated-looking buildings in the grand manner. Many of the factories and warehouses he designed for the AEG between 1908 and 1914 were ingenious fusions of abstracted classical vocabulary and straightforward structural skeletons. The Berlin Turbine Factory of 1908–9, for example, had the character of a temple dedicated to some industrial cult. The colossal turbines had to be lifted and moved from one end of the hall to the other while work was done on them, a process requiring an uninterrupted central aisle and an overhead moving gantry. Behrens's solution was to make the whole building a series of elegant, parallel two-sided cranes meeting at the peak of the roof. There was a grand, even ennobling character to the whole, and effects of visual lightness and massiveness were cleverly orchestrated to emphasize the overall lines. Had Behrens been a mere functionalist he might simply have optimized the functions and clothed the resulting structure in cheap materials without

concern for proportion, let alone the impact of forms on the spirit; had he been an 'Expressionist' (like his contemporary Hans Poelzig in Breslau) he might have sought to dramatize the process of movement with a highly sculptural formal arrangement. But Behrens steered a way between these approaches in a search for a sober and, indeed, 'typical' form in the 'classical/German spirit'. The supports and profile were adjusted to give a dignified rhythm and impression of repose; the gantry shape was blended ingeniously with the image of a classical pediment; and the repeated exposed steel supports along the side elevations were given the character of a *travée* of classical supports. But the usual expectations of load and support were reversed, since these steel stanchions were tapered, being thinner at the bottom than at the top. Where they met the base on which the building sat there were bolted knuckle joints. Meanwhile the vast areas of glass in the main façade were laid flush with the pediment plane, so as to give the sense of a thin screen hovering in front of the massive corner quoins in concrete, which provided a suitable sense of structural stability to the eye.

Behrens's intuition for primary geometrical volumes in the classical tradition (perhaps enhanced by his reading of formalist art historians such as Heinrich Wölfflin) allowed him to bring a sense of proportion to numerous other categories of industrial structure. His design for a gasworks at Frankfurt of 1911–12, for example, was composed of simple cylinders in dramatic juxtaposition. Indeed engineering aesthetics were a topic of

100 Peter Behrens, Gasworks, Frankfurt, 1911–12

101 American grain silos, from the *Deutscher Werkbund Jahrbuch*, 1913

102 Hans Poelzig, Chemical Factory, Luban, Germany (now Poland), 1911

recurrent interest to the Deutscher Werkbund, and it was not unusual for debates to be held comparing the relative aesthetic value of one signal gantry over another. The Deutscher Werkbund *Jahrbücher* of 1913–14 illustrated battleships and grain silos as examples of designs combining functional logic with impressive qualities of abstract form.

In the 1913 *Jahrbuch* there was an article entitled 'The Development of Modern Industrial Architecture' by a young architect called Walter Gropius, who praised the AEG factories as 'monuments of sovereign strength, commanding their surroundings with truly classical grandeur', and spoke too of 'the compelling monumentality of the Canadian and American grain silos … and the totally modern workshops of the North American firms which bear comparison with the buildings of Ancient Egypt …' He further praised the 'natural feeling for large compact forms, fresh and intact', and suggested that modern European architects might 'take this as a valuable hint and refuse to pay any more heed to fits of historical nostalgia or other intellectual considerations … which stand in the way of true artistic naïveté'. Gropius went further still and claimed that the spirit of modern times required its own expression in a new style characterized by 'exactly stamped form … clear contrasts, the ordering of members … unity of form and colour', a style that would be 'appropriate to the energy and economics of public life'. Among those 'to take this valuable hint' was the young Charles Édouard Jeanneret (later Le Corbusier), who worked in Behrens's office in 1910 and remained in touch with German developments after that date.

It is instructive to contrast Behrens's gasworks design with Hans Poelzig's for a water-tower in Breslau of 1908, or with the same architect's design for a chemical works at Luban of 1911, as this gives some sense of what is meant by the 'Expressionist' wing of the Werkbund. 'Expressionism' is a blurred term at best, and has little validity as a stylistic label. In this context of industrial design it refers to an attitude in which sobriety and stability were eschewed in favour of restless, dynamic and highly emotive forms. In fact the functional rationale behind Poelzig's designs was every bit as tight as that governing Behrens's, but the emphasis of formal expression was different. The roots of Expressionist vocabulary lie in this case in Art

102

Nouveau, and it was Art Nouveau with its emphasis on individualism which most disturbed Muthesius. Indeed, at the Werkbund Congress of 1914 there was a celebrated debate between Henry van de Velde and Muthesius which tended to be framed in terms of the individualist outlook versus the philosophy of 'the typical'. Ultimately, such a discussion was one over appropriateness: what should the 'true' modern style be like?

Behrens's office, with its stress on all aspects of industrial design, was the training ground of a number of artists who were to inherit the tensions and successes of the pre-1914 period and to contribute to the extremely creative phase of the 1920s. Chief among these were the future Le Corbusier, Ludwig Mies van der Rohe, and Walter Gropius himself; indeed, these three may have 'overlapped' briefly in 1910. Gropius was born in 1883 and trained at the Charlottenburg Hochschule, Berlin, and in Munich; his earliest designs for housing show a marked concentration on simple volumes and shapes. In 1911, after a thorough training in Behrens's office, he received his own commission to redesign the Fagus shoe-last factory at Alfeld. This belonged to Karl Benscheidt, who had already overseen a design by one Eduard

Werner, an industrial architect from Hanover. The plan and elevations had been fixed and had even passed the local building authorities when Gropius was brought in to provide improvements to the external treatment. He modified the interior suggestions of his predecessor only slightly. It is the visual treatment of the workshop block which is significant in the creation of an industrial style, indeed in the formation of a 'factory aesthetic' that would eventually influence the universal 'machine style' of a decade later. The devices of the external wrapping of the building are intelligent adaptations of Behrens, but the effect is absolutely different, as here everything conspires to give a sense of weightlessness and transparency rather than of mass. The wall piers have been recessed so that the glazing appears to float as a transparent skin. Window bars, brick mouldings and joints reinforce the main proportions, and the image successfully incorporates a symbolic reaction to mechanization as an idea. To be sure, Gropius seems to have grasped the essential mood of the programme of his client, which included the provision of the latest that modern American industrial planning could offer: good ventilation, a logical, open plan for machine serial-production, and well-lit spaces for draughtsmen and managers to go about their business of helping improve the condition of those with foot problems.

However, it is interesting to contrast the Faguswerk with Albert Kahn's contemporaneous Ford factory designs in Detroit (mentioned in Chapter 4 in connection with reinforced-concrete construction). These factories were built around naked commercial and functional considerations. Admittedly, due attention was given to the relationship of solids and voids, but it does not seem to have occurred to either Kahn or Ford that their buildings might be the 'index to the spirit of the new times'! In Germany the attitude to factory design was quite different, and clothed in philosophical speculation. As Gropius was to put the matter after the war: his architecture was an attempt not only at accommodating the functions of the modern world, but at symbolizing that world as well.

In 1914 Gropius and Adolf Meyer were given the important task of designing the Werkbund Pavilion for the Cologne Exhibition. This was to house objects of German industrial design in a framework which would itself be an exemplary demonstration of Werkbund ideals. The largest building was the Machine Hall, placed on the main axis and expressed as a simple, neo-classical railway shed. This was approached through a courtyard enclosed by a symmetrical entrance pavilion flanked by open glazed staircases. The symmetry of the scheme was broken by the Deutzer Gasmotoren Pavilion, attached to the rear end of the machine hall on the cross axis. The discipline and axes of the plan recalled Beaux-Arts procedures, and the arrangement had a marked processional character.

The forms rising into space above this plan, however, had no obvious historical precedent. The stripped brick volumes of the entrance block with overhanging roofs and sharp horizontal parapets were perhaps an echo of Wright in a formal mood. But the glazed wrapping to the rear and the transparent, streamlined stair-towers (with the spiral stairs visible inside them) were stunning inventions which created not only a sense of weightlessness and space, but also an aura of crisp and disciplined machinery, of elegant and dignified industrial

103 Walter Gropius and Adolf Meyer, Fagus Shoe-last Factory (Faguswerk), Alfeld, 1911–12

104 Walter Gropius and Adolf Meyer, Werkbund Pavilion, Cologne, 1914, front view showing glass stairs, Machine Hall and the Deutzer Gasmotoren Pavilion

105 Werkbund Pavilion, plan

106 Werkbund Pavilion, rear view showing Machine Hall and Deutzer Gasmotoren Pavilion

103

104

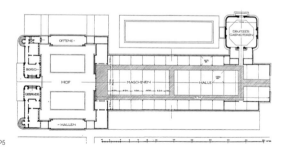

105

106

control. Here was another quasi-sacral building dedicated to the values of Germany's industrial élite, and it was typical of the mood and taste of the whole, that a reclining classical statue should have been placed at the end of a pool leading up to the Deutz Pavilion while, on the opposite side of the same structure, there stood a 'sacral object': a gas turbine engine.

This transparent pavilion may well have been inspired by an even more fantastic evocation of industrialization, Bruno Taut's Steel Industry Pavilion at the Leipzig Fair of 1913. This had been built in the form of a ziggurat surmounted by a sphere, the whole being constructed out of an elegant frame in the material the pavilion had been built to celebrate and advertise. Taut's work had more affinities with the 'Expressionist' wing of the Werkbund than with Gropius, and was pervaded by a mystical, if not Utopian, spirit somewhat at odds with the restraint and sobriety, the belief in standardization and normative solutions, of men like Behrens and Muthesius. Taut's design for the Glass Pavilion (1914) at Cologne made the contrast even more clear. This was in the form of a sort of industrial mausoleum – a dome of different-coloured glass standing on a high plinth and reached by a grand flight of stairs. The interior was dappled with different-coloured patches of light which reflected off glass-brick stair-risers set into slender steel supports, and which were accentuated by moving lenses. There was all the craft there, and something of the atmosphere, of an elaborately chased, carefully made piece of Art Nouveau tableware. But the *fin-de-siècle* qualities were transcended by a Utopian, forward-looking aspiration: indeed the poet and fantastic novelist Paul Scheerbart, who saw glass as the material of the future, surely influenced Taut's imagery.

We live for the most part in closed rooms. These form the environment from which our culture grows. Our culture is to a certain extent the product of our architecture. If we want our culture to rise to a higher level, we are obliged, for better or for worse, to change our architecture. And this only becomes possible if we take away the closed character from the rooms in which we live. We can only do that by introducing glass architecture, which lets in the light of the sun, the moon, and the stars, not merely through a few windows, but through every possible wall, which will be made entirely of glass – of coloured glass. The new environment which we thus create must bring us a new culture.

It scarcely needs emphasizing that Gropius and

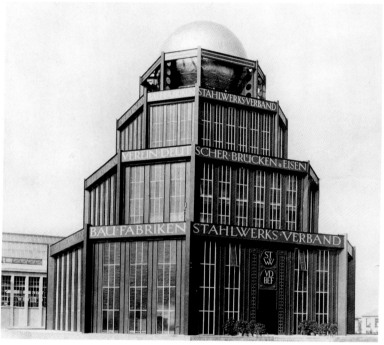

107

Taut, each in his own way, were attempting to celebrate industrialization, to reveal its capacity for poetry, and to suggest its genuine, progressive cultural potential. It was to be the Gropius outlook and vocabulary, however, with the inherent suggestion that rectangularity and transparency were appropriate visual features of a new industrial architectonic order, which would be more influential. However, before these fragmentary suggestions of Gropius's pre-war buildings could congeal as the mature style of the 1920s, other catalysts would be necessary, particularly the spatial and formal devices of abstract art, and the poetic attitudes of Futurism, which would themselves be fused in the philosophy and form of De Stijl at the end of the 1910s.

Futurism was a poetic movement before it became a movement in painting and sculpture, and an architectural movement in the limited sense that there was a Futurist Manifesto of Architecture of 1914, and an architect, Antonio Sant'Elia, whose drawings attempted to translate Futurist ideals into a new urban imagery – 'La Città Nuova' ('The New City'). The Foundation Manifesto of Futurism was published in *Le Figaro* of 20 February 1909, and was the creation of the poet Filippo Tommaso Marinetti. The manifesto was a lively attack on traditionalism in culture, and championed an expression nourished by contemporary forces and the poetic sensations released by a new industrial environment. Anarchist in inspiration, the Futurist outlook had no particular political affiliation, but was in favour of

108

109

revolutionary change, speed, dynamism of all sorts, and an aggressive adulation of the machine. Typically, the Foundation Manifesto suggested the destruction of museums and academies; the vitality of contemporary life was opposed to the tiredness of inherited art forms:

We declare that the splendour of the world has been enriched by a new beauty – the beauty of speed. A racing car with its bonnet draped with exhaust pipes, like fire-breathing serpents – a roaring racing car, rattling along like a machine gun, is more beautiful than the winged Victory of Samothrace.

Of course Marinetti's writing did belong to an aesthetic tradition, one stretching back through French Symbolism to Baudelaire, the 'poet of modern life'. In a sense, then, the aim was to make the frontiers of art broader and more inclusive, rather than to do away with them altogether. The typical subject-matter of Futurism was the modern metropolis, seen as a sort of collective expression of the forces of society.

We will sing of the stirring of great crowds – workers, pleasure-seekers, rioters – and the confused sea of colour and sound as revolution sweeps through a modern metropolis. We will sing the midnight fervour of arsenals and shipyards blazing with electric moons; insatiable stations swallowing the smoking serpents of their trains; factories hung from the clouds by the twisted threads of their smoke; bridges flashing like knives in the sun, giant gymnasts that leap over rivers; adventurous steamers that scent the horizon; deep-chested locomotives that paw the ground with their wheels, like stallions harnessed with steel tubing; the easy flight of aeroplanes, their propellers beating the wind like banners, with a sound like the applause of a mighty crowd.

The Futurist Manifestos of Painting (1910) and Sculpture (1912) attempted to extend Futurist sensibility still further. Dynamism was the shared central conception, and the early painters in the movement, among them Umberto Boccioni and Gino Severini, attempted to translate the Futurist ethos not only by choosing such subjects as trains leaving stations, building sites on the edge of industrial cities, and strikes, but also by treating these themes in a vital play of complementary colours, divisionist lighting effects and unstable diagonal compositions. In 1911 the devices of Analytical Cubism began to be absorbed by the Futurist painters, with the result that fragmentation, interpenetrations of space and form, abstraction and elements of reality were incorporated. The Cubist device of showing different viewpoints of an object was co-opted to express duration and the different states of objects unfolding in their environment. This was a key element of Futurist doctrine, related no doubt to the artists' adulation of Henri Bergson's philosophical ideas on time and flux. Bergson emphasized the primacy of change in all reality and the role of intuition in perceiving it. Futurist painters far transcended any banal 'realism of contemporary appearances' by attempting to create *symbolic equivalents* to their excited state of mind when faced by entirely new stimuli like speed, artificial light, steel and fast car rides.

Futurist sculpture likewise opened up new expressive territory in an attempt at expressing 'the universal dynamism' – the flux of modern life. The Sculpture Manifesto announced that the basis of this new form would be 'architectonic': '... not only as a construction of masses, but also because the sculptural block will contain within itself architectonic elements from the sculptural environment in which the object exists.' Boccioni's drawing *Bottle + Table + Block of Houses* of 1912 seems to demonstrate this 'field' conception of space, and suggests how important transparency and the intersection of planes were as principles of Futurist composition. When he came to translate

these ideas into sculpture, the artist had to adopt different techniques, obviously, and his *Bottle Unfolding in Space* (1912) attempted to evoke the shifting energies of an object, its palpitation and movement in its surroundings. *Unique Forms of Continuity in Space* (1913) – a dynamic human figure striding forward with flailing planes of bronze rushing from its edges – used the evanescent lighting effects of polished surfaces to evoke dynamism. However, the Sculpture Manifesto was in theory opposed to traditional hierarchies of material value (bronze, marble, etc.) and suggested (again, no doubt, following the juxtaposition of humble and heroic values in Cubism) the incorporation of new synthetics:

Destroy the purely literary and traditional nobility of bronze and marble. Deny that only one material should be used exclusively for the whole of a sculptural construction. Affirm that even twenty different materials can join in one work to increase the scope of its plastic emotion. We enumerate some: glass, wood, iron, cement, hair, leather, cloth, electric light, etc.

Although there was not, properly speaking, a 'Futurist Architecture', there was a Futurist Manifesto on the subject. This was perhaps composed by the young architect Antonio Sant'Elia,

110

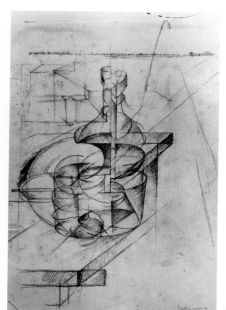

111

with the help of Marinetti. In its first version –
known as the 'Messaggio' – it functioned as the
introduction to a show of Sant'Elia's drawings
of the Città Nuova in 1914. Not surprisingly, this
theoretical architecture was conceived as a direct
expression of contemporary forces, and a dynamic
celebration of the uprooted, anti-natural tendencies
of the modern city.

Such an architecture cannot be subject to any law of historical
continuity. It must be new as our state of mind is new … In modern
life the process of consequential stylistic development comes to a
halt. Architecture, exhausted by tradition, begins again, forcibly from
the beginning.

Thus the new architecture was to express 'new
spiritual attitudes'; but it was also to find new forms
appropriate to new materials and means of
construction:

Calculations of the resistance of materials, the use of reinforced
concrete and iron, exclude 'Architecture' as understood in the
Classical and traditional sense. Modern structural materials and
our scientific concepts absolutely do not lend themselves to the
disciplines of historical styles, and are the chief cause of the grotesque
aspect of modish constructions where we see the lightness and proud
slenderness of girders, the slightness of reinforced concrete, bent to
the heavy curve of the arch, aping the solidity of marble.

So far this was a negative definition which did
not imply a precise form beyond saying that new
buildings should be lighter and more open in
expression, and no longer fettered by inappropriate
inherited ideas. Later in the Messaggio, a clearer
idea was given of the *style* of this new expression of
the times:

We must invent and rebuild ex novo our modern city like an
immense and tumultuous shipyard, active, mobile, and everywhere
dynamic, and the modern building like a gigantic machine. Lifts must
no longer hide away like solitary worms in the stairwells, but the
stairs – now useless – must be abolished; and the lifts must swarm up
the façades like serpents of glass and iron. The house of cement, iron,
and glass, without curved or painted ornament, rich only in the
inherent beauty of its lines and modelling, extraordinarily brutish in
its mechanical simplicity … must rise from the brink of a tumultuous
abyss; the street itself will no longer lie like a doormat at the level of
the thresholds, but plunge storeys deep into the earth, gathering up
the traffic of the metropolis, connected for necessary transfers to
metal catwalks and high-speed conveyor belts.
    For these reasons I insist that we abolish the monumental
and the decorative; that we must resolve the problem of modern
architecture without cribbing photographs of China, Persia or Japan,
not stultifying ourselves with Vitruvian rules, but with strokes of
genius, equipped only with a scientific and technological culture;
that everything must be revolutionized; that we must exploit our
roofs and put our basements to work; depreciate the importance of
façades; transfer questions of taste out of the field of petty mouldings,

112

fiddling capitals and insignificant porticoes, into the vaster field
of the grouping of masses on the grandest scale … That the new
architecture is the architecture of cold calculation … boldness and
simplicity; the architecture of reinforced concrete, iron, glass, textile
fibres and all those replacements for wood, stone and brick that make
for the attainment of maximum elasticity and lightness.

The Messaggio then draws to a close with a plea for
'raw, naked and violently coloured materials'; with
an affirmation that 'real architecture' transcends
functionalism by being 'synthesis and expression';
with the suggestion that inspiration be found in 'the
new mechanical world we have created, of which
architecture must be the fairest expression, the
fullest synthesis, the most effective artistic
integration.'
    It is probable that the Messaggio was inspired
by Sant'Elia's sketches rather than the other
way round, but these were themselves intuitive
responses to earlier Futurist attitudes. Although
the theme of the exhibition was La Città Nuova,
there was no overall plan, rather a collection of new

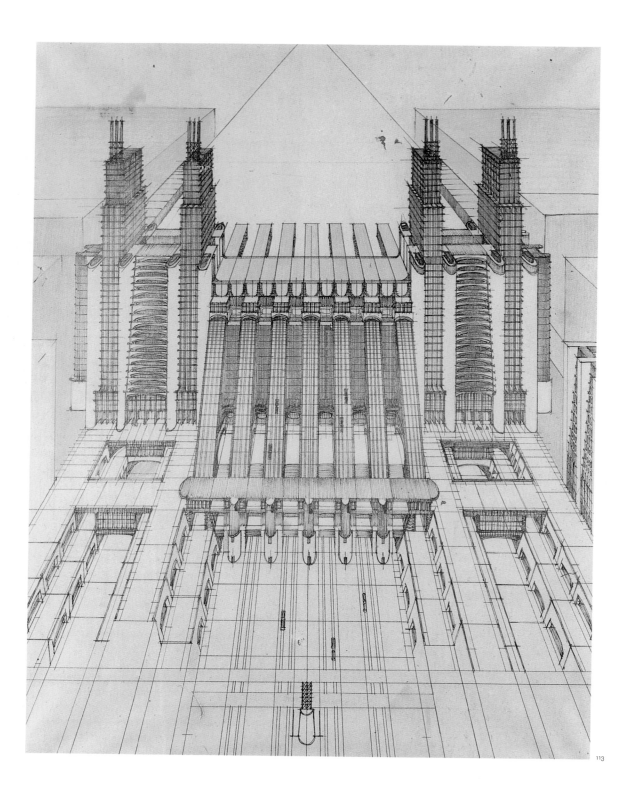

113

113 Antonio Sant'Elia,
La Città Nuova, central
railway station and
airport, 1913–14. Ink
and pencil on paper,
19³/₄ × 15¹/₄ in (50 × 39
cm). Musei Civici, Como

114 Antonio Sant'Elia,
*La Città Nuova, Casa
a Gradinate*, 1914. Ink
and pencil on paper,
11¹/₄ × 7 in (28.8 × 17.9
cm). Musei Civici, Como

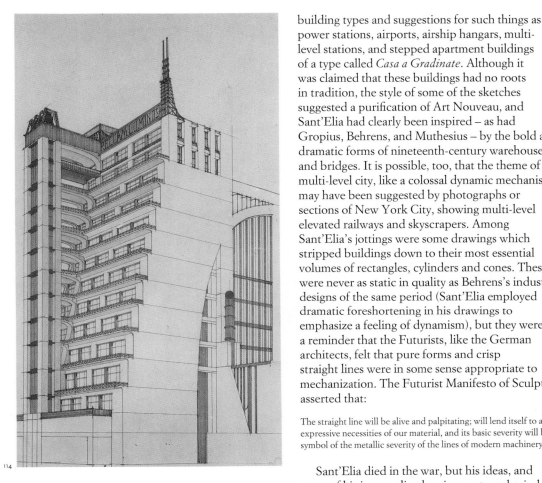

114

building types and suggestions for such things as power stations, airports, airship hangars, multi-level stations, and stepped apartment buildings of a type called *Casa a Gradinate*. Although it was claimed that these buildings had no roots in tradition, the style of some of the sketches suggested a purification of Art Nouveau, and Sant'Elia had clearly been inspired – as had Gropius, Behrens, and Muthesius – by the bold and dramatic forms of nineteenth-century warehouses and bridges. It is possible, too, that the theme of the multi-level city, like a colossal dynamic mechanism, may have been suggested by photographs or sections of New York City, showing multi-level elevated railways and skyscrapers. Among Sant'Elia's jottings were some drawings which stripped buildings down to their most essential volumes of rectangles, cylinders and cones. These were never as static in quality as Behrens's industrial designs of the same period (Sant'Elia employed dramatic foreshortening in his drawings to emphasize a feeling of dynamism), but they were a reminder that the Futurists, like the German architects, felt that pure forms and crisp straight lines were in some sense appropriate to mechanization. The Futurist Manifesto of Sculpture asserted that:

The straight line will be alive and palpitating; will lend itself to all the expressive necessities of our material, and its basic severity will be a symbol of the metallic severity of the lines of modern machinery.

Sant'Elia died in the war, but his ideas, and some of his images, lived on in avant-garde circles in Holland, Russia, Germany, and France. The importance of Futurism in the context of the history of modern architecture is clear: it pulled together a collection of progressivist attitudes, anti-traditional positions and tendencies towards abstract form, with the celebration of modern materials, and an indulgence in mechanical analogies. The contrast between the dynamic and anarchical values of Futurism and the more stolid, organized thought of the Deutscher Werkbund is obvious; but both movements rested on the central assumption that the spirit of the times was inevitably tied to the evolution of mechanization, and that an authentic modern architecture must take this into account in its functions, its methods of construction, its aesthetics, and its symbolic forms.

7
the architectural system of frank lloyd wright

Radical though it may be, the work here illustrated is dedicated to a cause conservative in the best sense of the word. At no point does it involve denial of the elemental law and order inherent in all great architecture, rather it is a declaration of love for the spirit of that law and order, and a reverential recognition of the elements that made its ancient letter in its time vital and beautiful.
Frank Lloyd Wright, 1908

115   Frank Lloyd Wright, Robie House, South Woodlawn, Chicago, Illinois, 1908–10

Occasionally a single artist emerges who so profoundly reorganizes the basic assumptions of a period that he deserves to be considered in isolation. The creations of such individuals are marked by an extraordinary consistency and integrity traceable to both a mastery of means and a capacity to give an idealistic world-view a deep expression. The solutions embodied in their work seem to solve problems that are relevant far beyond their particular circumstances. They crystallize the preoccupations of a period, and influence others distant in space and time. Whether they intend it or not, artists with such charisma become the founders of new traditions. In the formation of modern architecture two figures of this imaginative and intellectual calibre stand out: Le Corbusier and Frank Lloyd Wright.

Frank Lloyd Wright's architecture has occupied a curious position in the histories of modern design. He has been portrayed as one of the first architects to break with eclecticism and to found a new style based on a spatial conception of interpenetrating planes and abstract masses, which (the story runs) then evolved, especially through its influence on Dutch developments, into the International Style. In this view, Wright's scattered remarks on the relevance of machine production to architecture are to be taken as evidence of his 'forward-looking' stance. But there is another version of Wright which emphasizes his roots in American social ideals and plays up his regional sensitivities and Arts and Crafts allegiances. In this scenario he emerges as a traditionalist intent on preserving the values of an individualist yet democratic frontier America against the onslaughts of mechanization. Both views contain some truth – and the very fact that so much can be seen in the work and thought of a single artist should alert us to possible polarities in a single outlook.

Wright's long-range importance far outstrips these limited scenarios which earlier historiography has imposed upon him. His starting point may have been the material and cultural conditions of the Midwest around the turn of the century, and the inheritance of the Chicago School, but his activity and his vision eventually extended far beyond this towards a wider reading of the American landscape and city, to include a universalizing interpretation of several traditions East and West. Within the body of

Wright's intuitions and world-view, there was a Utopian dream concerning the portrayal of human relationships and institutions, and the harmonization of modern space with nature. Wright managed to evolve an architectural language of symbolic geometries that gave shape to a mythical view of society, that absorbed images and ideas from diverse sources, and that had its own internal 'rules' as a formal system.

Wright was born in 1867. His father was a preacher and his mother held the fervent belief that her son would be a great architect. His parents eventually separated, and it is arguable that Wright's later obsession with the expression of idealized family relationships may have owed something, in a compensatory way, to the effect on a sensitive nature of an unhappy and uprooted home life. A strong early influence was the experience of working on his uncle's farm in Wisconsin; Wright later recalled how he would fix his attention on a tree, a hill or a flower and wander off into reveries of abstract forms and shapes. Another crucial formative influence was some 'Froebel' blocks which his mother acquired for him at the Philadelphia Exhibition of 1879. Wright derived great delight from arranging these simple geometrical shapes into formal patterns that matched his intuitive compositional sense. It was part of the Froebel method that a configuration should be linked to a cosmic theme. The architect's later formal strategies in design, and his belief in the universality of fundamental geometrical forms may be traced in part to these early experiences.

Wright's architectural training was far from orthodox. He began by studying engineering in 1885 at the University of Wisconsin, but did not stay the course. Instead he moved to Chicago where he worked in the office of Joseph Lyman Silsbee, a designer of suburban houses. Here he learned much about the basic business of domestic design and immersed himself in the prevalent modes of suburban architecture. In 1888 Wright moved on to work for Louis Sullivan, who at the time was occupied with evolving the principles and forms of an organic architecture, especially for the design of skyscrapers. As was suggested in an earlier chapter (pp. 47–50), Sullivan was an idealist who believed that the architect in the Midwest had a unique opportunity to generate the images of a culture, uncluttered by imported and foreign models, yet founded upon the ancient principles of architecture. His frequent use of organic analogies in his writings, his building forms and ornamental designs was the outward expression of a belief that architecture and society had their roots in a natural order. By a feat of visionary abstraction the artist was to dig below the surface of his society and see the 'inner meaning' of human institutions, then give them an appropriate shape. He was obsessed with the idea that the architect was specially endowed with the gift of prophesying the 'true' form of democracy.

Much of this Wright absorbed and eventually elaborated in his own way, but in the realm of the individual family dwelling. He was quickly given much responsibility in the office but broke away after a period of about five years to set up his own practice in his studio alongside his home in Oak Park, a suburb of Chicago. His own house, designed when he was 22, gives some idea of his formative period (Fig. 91). Shingle Style influences stemming from Silsbee were controlled by a strong formal discipline; elements like the porch and the overhanging roof were intrinsic to the Chicago suburban vernacular, being sensible ways of dealing with the extremes of climate and linking house to garden; the focal position of the hearth was another traditional feature of the American home, which Wright was gradually to infuse with his own meanings. But the spaces of the lower floor flowed into one another more than was usual in a design of this kind, and the whole form was ingeniously controlled by axes in such a way that there was the feeling of rotation about the central core. With hindsight, one may begin to grasp here certain underlying tendencies which were to become clearer later on.

Wright's breakthrough building was the Winslow House of 1893–4, built in River Forest, a suburb of Chicago near Oak Park. Mr Winslow was a businessman who had recently moved to Chicago and who wanted a house devoid of frills, but with a solid elegance. The formality of the building is evident in the first view. The main façade is entirely symmetrical about the front door, which is set into a stone panel brought forward slightly from the wall plane. The second level is set back and textured in dark terracotta, and by contrast with the light-coloured bricks of the lower storey this zone appears to recede. The composition is capped by a

116 Frank Lloyd Wright,
Winslow House, River
Forest, near Chicago,
Illinois, 1893–4

117 Winslow House,
ground-floor plan

118 Winslow House,
rear view

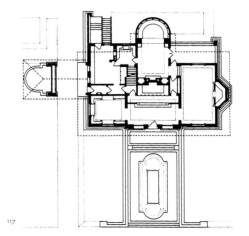

third element, also strongly horizontal in emphasis, an overhanging roof with deep eaves. The detail is crisp, the lines are sharp, the joints are clearly expressed; the form is sober and dignified, but not lacking in vitality.

At the front the chimney is visible above the centre of the house, and when one passes to the interior one comes face to face with a fireplace set back behind a sort of rood screen; an image suggesting that the hearth be seen in quasi-sacral terms as the emblem of the morally upright home. Formally the hearth stands at the core of the dwelling and forces the visitor into a rotational sequence through the reception spaces, culminating in the dining room on the main axis to the rear, expressed externally as an apsidal volume. The rear elevation lacks the coherence of the front as it presents an asymmetrical, rather sprawling arrangement of forms. It was typical of Wright's planning approach that he should have placed the master bedroom over the most formal room below – the dining-room – and on the same axis. To the rear of the site, beyond the *porte-cochère*, is a little stable restating the vocabulary of the main house in miniature. It was here that Mr Winslow and Wright together produced a limited edition of exquisitely printed and illustrated volumes of William Channing Gannett's *House Beautiful* (1896–7). The themes of this book have some bearing on Wright's own attitudes to the home, which he seems to have regarded as an almost sacred institution, requiring a noble and formal architectural treatment. The sense of the dwelling as a moral and religious influence was embedded in the culture in which Wright worked, but probably had a special personal relevance to him. Norris Kelly Smith has even gone so far as to claim that the combination of formality and informality in Wright's house designs should be read as an institutional metaphor expressing the artist's vision of the nature of freedom and dependence intrinsic to family life.

But themes on their own do not make an architecture without forms. What made the Winslow House so remarkable was the way it combined influences, yet transcended them, so implying the ingredients of Wright's own style. Silsbee was left far behind; the classical tradition was raided for its axial control, the Shingle Style for its rotating plans; Sullivan's nature abstraction was reinterpreted, as was the master's intuition that buildings should have a base, a middle, and a head (also an idea with classical overtones – the column with base, shaft, and capital). The formal entrance of the Winslow House was close in spirit, and even in some of its stone details, to Sullivan's Wainwright Tomb in St Louis of the same period. However, Wright's forms probed beyond the inherited schemata to an instinctive sense of the order in nature, as one commentator well understood:

… it is the broadest, most satisfying thing that he has done … Upon the chosen site, nature has been at work for years, building the wonderful elm – and the character of the house was somewhat determined by the character of this tree. The sympathy that has been cultivated between them is felt by the cultivated and the uncultivated … the impression conveyed by the exterior is the impression conveyed by the elm … a certain simple power of an organic nature that seems to have as much right to its place and is as much part of the site as the tree. The analogy begins there and continues, for the details of the house are as much in their place and as constant in themselves and in relation to each other as the whole house is to its surroundings … The architect shows his sympathy with nature.

This critic might have gone further in his suggestions of analogies with nature. The metaphor of the tree was to become a central one in Wright's thought (just as it had been in Ruskin's), with implications of order and rootedness yet a capacity

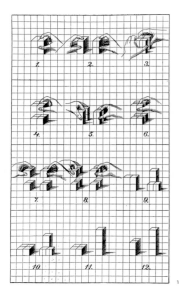

119

for growth and change. The tripartite scheme of roots, trunk, and branches was in turn to infiltrate his formal arrangements. At the Winslow House the triple division of base, middle and overhanging roof was spelled out with great clarity.

Without clients there would be no architecture, and it is intriguing to speculate just what it was about Wright's buildings which brought him over a hundred commissions in the ensuing fifteen years. At the time Chicago was developing rapidly and so were its suburbs. These formed prosperous middle-class communities of new money, but, on the whole, conservative values. Many of Wright's clients were self-made men whom the architect himself described as having 'unspoiled instincts and untainted ideals'. Leonard K. Eaton more recently attempted to characterize them as 'outwardly conventional [but tending] to possess a streak of artistic or technological interest which predisposed them to accept new and radical solutions to the architectural problem of the dwelling house'. Moreover, Wright's clients wanted value for money and his was an architecture devoid of the elaborate trappings typical of much domestic design in the area. His plans were logical and well worked out to match each client's requirements, and were fitted to their sites so as to make the most of the small rectangular lots typically available. He responded to the new phenomenon of the automobile by transforming the previous type of the carriage house into a garage. Considerable attention was devoted to the design of hot and cold water systems, and a crude form of air conditioning was sometimes incorporated. Wright was an architect who liked to oversee building work closely and to supervise the very details of his designs.

However, one suspects that the appeal went deeper than just these practical considerations. With their ample horizontal lines, their elegantly proportioned details, their built-in furniture and overhanging eaves, their ever-changing moods and qualities of space, Wright's designs possessed sobriety, fantasy, and a noble quality of scale. In contrast to the harshness of downtown Chicago, where many of the owners worked, the house supplied a soothing domestic world, a space of calm and retreat. At the heart, a broad fireplace finished with thin Roman bricks could be set with logs on the very floor of the prairie, while in summer the stained-glass windows with their abstracted vegetal forms let the changing light dapple the interiors. Kitchens were designed to make the lot of servants or of housewives (depending upon the wealth of the clients) easier. Living rooms were wide and relaxed for informal afternoon gatherings. Sometimes separate playrooms were planned, in which case there was independent access to the adult regions of the house. For the more extravagant and cultured, music wings or conservatories were included. Wright's houses responded to the rituals and aspirations of a new suburban bourgeoisie (dinner parties and the like) but also evoked a traditional image of the American home; in a sense, they helped an emergent class to find its own identity.

The path from the Winslow House to the fully developed type of the 'Prairie House', nearly a decade later, was not straightforward. It was a process of endless experiment in which each new task allowed the extension and refinement of principles. Wright's domestic ideas were obviously stamped with Arts and Crafts values of the sort which encouraged restrained simplicity, the honest and direct use of materials, the integration of the building with nature, the unification of fixtures and fittings, and the expression of an elevated moral ideal. But he set out to reinterpret these premises radically. He was more concerned with mechanization than most of his predecessors and contemporaries within the Arts and Crafts tradition. In 1901, in a paper entitled 'The Art and Craft of the Machine', Wright explained that simple geometrical forms could most easily be turned out by machine saws, and suggested that the architect must remain open to the tremors of a new mechanized age. By this he intended to imply not that the machine should be celebrated directly in mechanical analogies or images, but that industrialization be understood as a means to the larger end of providing a decent and uplifting environment for new patterns of life.

It was Japanese architecture which helped Wright achieve his synthesis. He did not visit the country until 1905, but long before that he had studied oriental examples in books and in representations in Japanese prints. Wright probably saw the reconstruction of the Ho-o-den Temple at the Chicago World's Columbian Exposition of 1893, which can only have confirmed an interest in overhanging roofs and a grammar based upon timber frames, transomes and screens. Grant

120

121

Manson has suggested that the *tokonoma*, 'the permanent element of a Japanese interior and the focus of domestic contemplation and ceremony', may have influenced Wright's concentration upon the hearth as the fixed element in otherwise fluid spaces. Evidently the architect admired the refined proportions, the exquisite carpentry, the use of humble materials, and the subtle placement in nature which he found in certain Japanese examples. This was an architecture which modulated space and charged it with a spiritual character: the opposite, in his mind, of the Renaissance tendency to put up walls around box-like rooms and to decorate them with ornament. Wright was seeking an integral, three-dimensional expression in which the exterior would convey interior volumes, and in which human scale would permeate all the parts. Moreover, Japanese prints – aside from their representation of architecture – suggested a language of shape and colour directly attuned to the feelings (rather as the Froebel blocks had done in earlier life). In other words, the prints provided further lessons in *abstraction*: they gave Wright deeper insight into the intuitive apprehension of 'higher' spiritual values.

More than that, the prints encouraged Wright to try to formulate a sort of ideal type for the dwelling above the particulars of any one case; Sullivan had attempted something similar for the skyscraper, a formulation 'so broad as to admit no exception'. For Wright the key phase of crystallization seems to have been around 1901 when he published his idea for 'A Home in a Prairie Town' in the *Ladies' Home Journal*. In retrospect, one may see this as a sort of 'theorem' summing up his discoveries to date,

and laying the basis of a great period of creativity running from 1901 to 1910, and including such masterpieces as the Martin House, the Coonley House, the Robie House, the Larkin Building, and the Unity Temple. The 'Home in a Prairie Town' was formed from long low horizontals stretching parallel to the flat land of the site. The sprawling roofs extended to the surroundings and drew the porches, the *porte-cochère* and the main volumes into a vital, asymmetrical unity. Windows were reduced to simple screens – there were few solid walls – and the spaces inside were linked together. Much of the furniture was built-in and the character of the interiors was commodious yet elegant. At the heart was the hearth, and all the diverse spaces of the house were placed relative to this centripetal element. There was still axial control and hierarchy, but the rotational and asymmetrical were combined with these in an architecture of sliding and overlapping planes enlivened by an intense rhythm.

The Ward Willits House of 1902, built in the north Chicago suburb of Highland Park, was one of the first in the mature phase of Wright's work. It stands back from the road, and the first impression is of low roofs extending behind the nearby trees and of hooded windows with dark chinks of glass set under eaves. The building is divided into four main wings, so that the size is never overwhelming. One enters from a *porte-cochère* to the right of the building up some steps. Wright's houses usually had a 'path' running through them; in this case there is the instant choice of either turning back up the square spiral stairs to the bedroom level, or taking the more prominent route out of the vestibule by following the diagonal view into the living room.

122 Frank Lloyd Wright, Martin House, Buffalo, New York, 1904, aerial view, from the *Wasmuth Volumes*, 1910–11

123 Frank Lloyd Wright, project for 'A Home in a Prairie Town', *Ladies' Home Journal*, February, 1901

124 'A Home in a Prairie Town', ground- and first-floor plans

TAFEL XXXII VILLA D. D. MARTIN, BUFFALO, N.Y.   GEDRUCKT UND VERLEGT VON ERNST WASMUTH A.-G., BERLIN

122

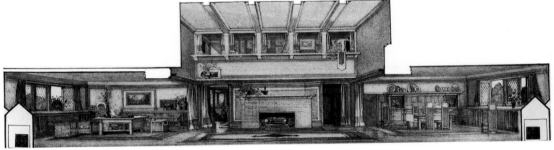

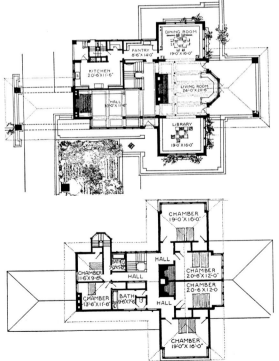

123

124

This is on the main axis and is one and a half storeys high. It has the chimney on its axis and vertical screen windows. The walls are plastered and smooth and there are slats of wood which bring down the scale and relate structure, furnishings and details to the main proportions. From this space one can see in turn along another diagonal into the dining-room, situated on a cross axis, with views on three sides into the garden; in the rear wing of the house is the kitchen.

Details such as grilles, brick textures in the fireplace, window mullions, even the leaded lines of the glass, bear the imprint of the same formal intelligence which conceived the whole, as if the smallest parts all had the generating idea implicit within them. Thus the abstract shapes of the plan, and the ornamentation of the windows are sensed as variants on the same geometrical patterns. Indeed, the plan is almost a work of art in its own right and serves to illustrate Wright's compositional principles. There are primary and secondary axes which are reinforced by the centre lines of the roofs and the placement of the chimney, but many of the rooms are shifted on to subsidiary axes parallel to the main ones. The result is a sort of 'pinwheel'

125

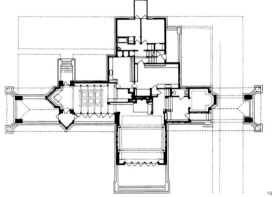

126

rotation, experienced in three dimensions as a
spatial tension which varies as one moves through
the interior spaces. The section is stratified, and
elements slide past each other. Parts and whole
are held in a vital equilibrium. To Wright this
dynamism was perhaps equivalent to the life force
he sensed in nature; it gave his dwellings something
of the quality of a spatial music in which rhythm,
movement, repetition, and variation of similar
elements achieved moods and emotions of different
pitch and intensity.

The Ward Willits House was an early experiment
with Wright's recently conceived theories. In it he
tried out the various pieces of his 'Prairie House'
type. Over twenty years later he looked back on this
period and attempted to put in writing the guiding
principles of his domestic designs.

First.
To reduce the number of necessary parts of the house and the
separate rooms to a minimum, and make all come together as
enclosed space so divided that light, air and vista permeated the
whole with a sense of unity.
Second.
To associate the building as a whole with its site by extension and
emphasis of all the planes parallel to the ground, but keeping the
floors off the best part of the site, thus leaving that better part for use
in connection with the life of the house. Extended level planes were
found useful in this connection.
Third.
To eliminate the room as a box and the house as another by making
all walls enclosing screens – the ceilings and floors and enclosing
screens to flow into each other as one large enclosure of space, with
inner subdivisions only. Make all house proportions more liberally

human, with less wasted space in structure, and structure more
appropriate to material, so the whole more liveable. Liberal is the
best word. Extended straight lines or streamlines were useful in this.
Fourth.
To get the unwholesome basement up out of the ground, entirely
above it, as a low pedestal for the living-position of the home, making
the foundation itself visible as a low masonry platform on which the
building should stand.
Fifth.
To harmonize all necessary openings to 'outside' or to 'inside' with
good human proportions and make them occur naturally – singly or
as a series in the scheme of the whole building. Usually they appeared
as 'light-screens' instead of walls, because all the 'Architecture' of the
house was chiefly the way these openings came in such walls as were
grouped about the rooms as enclosing screens. The room as such was
now the essential architectural expression, and there were to be no
holes cut in walls as holes are cut in a box, because this was not in
keeping with the ideal of 'plastic'. Cutting holes was violent.
Sixth.
To eliminate combinations of different materials in favour of mono
materials so far as possible; to use no ornament that did not come out

of the nature of the materials, to make the whole building clearer and
more expressive as a place to live in, and give the conception of the
building appropriate revealing emphasis. Geometrical or straight
lines were natural to the machinery at work in the building trades
then, so the interiors took on this character naturally.
Seventh.
To incorporate all heating, lighting, plumbing so that these systems
became constituent parts of the building itself. These service features
became architectural and in this attempt the ideal of an organic
architecture was at work.
Eighth.
To incorporate as organic architecture – as far as possible –
furnishings, making them all one with the building and designing
them in simple terms for machine work. Again all straight lines and
rectangular forms.
Ninth.
Eliminate the decorator. He was all curves and all efflorescence, if
not all 'period'.

This is not to suggest that Wright's 'system' was
rigid and prescribed. On the contrary, it allowed

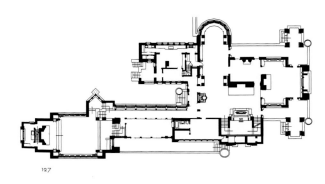

127

128

him a firm base from which to experiment. Its
flexibility was well demonstrated in his responses to
different sizes of dwelling. Many of his early houses
were modest, but as his reputation grew, so did the
size of his commissions, to the point where he was
soon building for the extremely wealthy.

The Dana House in Springfield, Illinois (1902–4),
covered an entire suburban lot and included not
only the main house, a music wing, and a covered
conservatory walkway, but also remnants of the
previous family residence which it replaced. This
was incorporated as a sort of family shrine. The
main entrance was given a formal treatment by
means of a pedimented roof and a low archway
(lending the whole the air of a tomb), preceding
a formal sequence through expanding and
converging spaces culminating in the barrel-vaulted
dining room on the main axis. The music room was
a more perforated version of the vaulted theme, and
was placed on a cross axis at the end of a half-glazed
pergola. The family had gained its wealth from the
prairies and had retired to Springfield (the Illinois
state capital) for a more urbane existence, and the
ensemble was given an almost institutional stance,
for it could be expected to function virtually as a
cultural centre in this small but rapidly expanding
Midwestern town. Flat, buff-coloured Roman bricks
were used on the exterior with copper trim (now
verdigris) for the rims of the roofs. The interiors
orchestrated a visual equivalent to Whitman's
hymns to the prairies, with gold, brown and russet
finishes, and with light fixtures and leaded glazing
based upon a triangular stylization of the sumac
plant. For this type of project, Wright separated out
the individual pieces, then submitted them to a
consistent formal discipline based upon dominant
metaphorical themes.

For the Martin House in Buffalo, New York
(1904), Wright had to accommodate all the
functions of a luxurious estate: stables, a
guest-house, a large main dwelling, pergolas,
gardens, a conservatory, etc. He monumentalized
his usual vocabulary of piers, roofs, and garden
urns to lend an appropriate air of importance,
and worked downwards in scale in several linked
hierarchies. This is where Wright's method of
organizing a plan with the help of a geometrical grid
helped him to maintain uniform dimensions and
to orchestrate axes and directions. The plan of the

Martin House is a most sophisticated abstract pattern, not unlike a Mondrian painting, in which interior and exterior spaces, figure and ground have equal value (see Fig. 166). In other words, the lawns, pergolas, and spaces between were organized by the same formal principles as those in the main buildings.

The Coonley House of 1908 in Riverside was another case where an entire wealthy precinct was unified but with full respect for different functional demands. These larger Prairie Houses combined an aura of magnificence and dignity suitable to their patrons, with subtle and refined control of detail and scale. In them Wright demonstrated that he could 'stretch' his vocabulary without loss of coherence. They have been referred to as 'palaces', but it would be more precise to place them in the long tradition of the *villa*, and particularly the '*villa suburbana*', a type combining the virtues of urban and country life within a modulated pattern of living spaces responding to both. Wright's handling of formality and informality, block and garden, pergola and roof, picturesque and classical, urbane and primitive, suggests more than a slight acquaintance with such seminal examples of the type as Schinkel's Court Gardener's House at Charlottenhof of 1836. Wright's archetypal image of the suburban home, whether large or small, with its sense of enclave, its sprawling roofs, its fluid transitions, and its romantic aura, was, in effect, a 'counterform' to the rigidity of the urban grid, and to the duress and harshness of the industrial city. It was as much the distillation of a social type as was Sullivan's theorem of the tall office building.

Wright had to cope with variations of site as well as of size. Many of his early houses were situated on flat, rectangular lots of small to medium area. But in 1904 he encountered an entirely new character of terrain when he was asked to design the small Glasner House in Glencoe on the North Shore of Chicago. The site was perched on the edge of a ravine which was heavily wooded. The habitual arrangement of a plinth-based, basementless house simply would not fit. Wright therefore planned the house so that the horizontal datum was supplied by the roofline; the forms of the building cascaded downwards from this line to meet the ravine at various levels. One entered on the upper level from the rear past the kitchen, to find the combined living/dining room and the master bedroom; the other rooms were placed downstairs. The volumes were anchored in place by three vertical elements, polygonal in plan: a library at one end, a teahouse (not built) over a bridge at the other, and a sewing room alongside the master bedroom.

As the living room was at tree-top height and surrounded by bushes, flies and insects could be expected in the summer months. If all the windows had been made openable, they would have needed insect screens, which would have blocked the view. Wright solved the problem by cross-breeding his usual 'Prairie House' fenestration with the well-tried 'Chicago window' (a central, fixed pane exclusively for light, and two small, side, vertical panes with screens exclusively for ventilation), which he stole from its usual commercial context; in this way it was possible to keep large areas free of insect meshes. The view through the long *travée* of windows with abstracted stained-glass tree motifs in them was quite magical. The interior was rendered sensitive to every change of light and colour in the ravine. The resulting character was rustic rather than suburban, and was reinforced by the horizontal batten-boarding of the lower portion, as well as the gazebo

129 Frank Lloyd Wright, Glasner House, Glencoe, near Chicago, Illinois, 1905

130 Glasner House, ground-floor plan; the bridge and teahouse on the right were not built

131 Frank Lloyd Wright, Coonley House, Riverside, Illinois, 1908

132 Coonley House, living room, from the *Wasmuth Volumes*, 1910–11

129

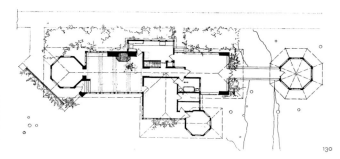

130

131

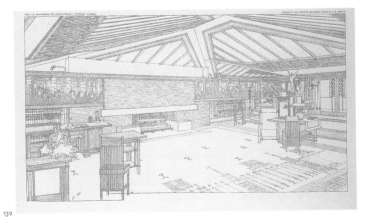

132

imagery of the polygonal volumes. The rich effect of a cantilevered roofline hovering above uneven terrain was one which Wright would employ again.

The artist's style may be thought of as a set of typical elements organized into wholes which themselves take on characteristic, generic patterns. A style based on principle will embody a sort of 'system' of building forms which combine and recombine according to grammatical and intuitive rules. Such a 'formula' is the opposite of a dry, repetitive 'cliché'; it is an abstraction which allows many creative possibilities around a few central themes. For such an artist – and Wright was such an artist – each new building task is a further opportunity to explore the ideal type while also unearthing new meanings. On occasion, an opportunity may arise which prompts the clarification of the artist's guiding vision.

The Robie House of 1908–10 was among the

clearest of Wright's expressions of the Prairie House ideal; rather as the Villa Malcontenta was one of the most complete realizations of Palladio's dream of the villa. The client, Mr Robie, was a bicycle manufacturer and only 27 years old when he employed Wright to design a home for him on an extremely tight corner site in south Chicago. He required a servants' wing and a billiard room, as well as the usual dining and living rooms, bedrooms, kitchen and bathrooms, and indicated that he wanted to 'see his neighbours on the sidewalk without being seen' and that he would also like, if possible, views of a park situated diagonally opposite, but a block away. Wright interpreted these givens by translating them into form via his evolving vocabulary. In plan he arranged the building as two bands, sliding alongside one another, with some degree of overlap between. The smaller of these was to the rear of the site and contained the garage, boiler room, laundry and entrance on the ground floor, servants' rooms,

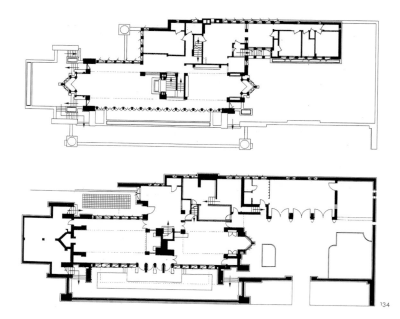

133 Frank Lloyd Wright,
Robie House, South
Woodlawn, Chicago,
Illinois, 1908–10

134 Robie House,
first-floor and semi-
basement plans

135 Robie House, first-
floor living/dining room

136 Robie House, detail
of leaded-glass window

the kitchen and a guest room on the first level. The other 'strip' was more prominent and arranged with chimney and stairs as a unit passing up through the centre. The billiard room and children's room were in the semi-basement, while the living and dining rooms were on the first level, which became a sort of *piano nobile*. Indeed, it was not so much two rooms as one – a single space partially divided by the chimneypiece, detailed so as to give the effect that the ceiling hovered above it as a single, continuous element running from one end to the other. At the ends were window seats in prow-like protrusions, reinforcing the sense of the longitudinal axis, and echoing the triangular forms of the pitched roofs above. From here, Mr Robie could look down but not be seen, for the parapets and overhangs ensured visual protection.

The main interior space of the Robie House illustrates how ingeniously Wright could attune his customary solutions to a new individual case on formal, functional, structural and symbolic levels simultaneously. Along each side was a rim set even lower than the rest of the ceiling. This reinforced the character of enclosure and accentuated the horizontality of the room. But it also served a number of functions because small 'Japanese' globe

lights were attached to the rim, and electrical wires were concealed within it, as were ducts and vents for moving air. The roof as a whole was an ingenious environmental device capable of being a heating cushion in winter or an extract flue in summer. The overhangs extended dramatically into the setting, the longest span supported with the help of a steel beam ordered from a shipyard. But these wide cantilevers were not just for visual effect. The extending planes enhanced the feeling of shelter, protected the windows from rain, snow, and glare, released the edges of the building from any great structural load (permitting the extensive screen-windows), and mediated between inside and outside. The result of all these devices together was the antithesis of the closed box, it was as if the Winslow House of fifteen years before had been exploded outwards.

An architectural system requires a consistent attitude in detailing, as well as in the disposition of the main forms, and just as the overall 'formula' must adjust as each new unity is found, so typical details must be attuned to the unique work. In the Robie House, Wright used elongated 'Roman' bricks laid with deep reveals of shadow in the joints so as to rhyme with the predominant horizontals.

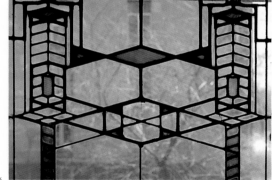

136

135

Another characteristic detail was the urn with a coping-stone top; in the Robie House these were made integral to the composition and adjusted to echo rooflines and parapets. Yet another customary Wrightian element was the leaded, stained-glass window with motifs abstracted from natural forms; in the Robie House the patterns were harmonized with the dominant horizontality, and with the triangular themes of the plan. Thus all the parts were drawn into a symphony: an orchestration of ideas and forms, moods and materials, which transcended merely period concerns. Alongside it, the designs of the so-called 'Prairie School' – the followers of Wright – were mere shadows.

The Robie House captured a moment in the history of American culture in the years leading up to the First World War, and was seminal in the development of a modern concept of space, but it also engaged with a wide field of meanings and resonances in the history of architecture. The combination of axial control and romantic, expanding silhouette perhaps linked the building to works of an earlier generation, such as H. H. Richardson's Ames Gate Lodge of 1880–2 (Fig. 90). Lessons of Japanese religious and domestic design were absorbed, as were features of the Midwestern vernacular. In the expansive horizontal lines floating above striations of shadow and a base of stone lintels and brick, there were perhaps long-distant recollections of the geological strata which had so intrigued Wright in childhood, though analogies can also be made with steam yachts and other objects of the modern age. The Robie House engaged with the very idea of a dwelling, its practical needs, its rituals, its psychological nuances. It was a work which, while modern, pitched towards the idea of origins. It even called to mind Semper's archetypal elements (which Wright certainly knew): the plinth, the hearth, the roof and the enclosure. The Robie House was rich in hidden implications. The propositions which it contained, and the formal devices which articulated them, were capable of almost endless elaboration in Wright's later work.

While most of Wright's works up to 1910 were houses, he also received other types of commission. His 'system' had then to stretch to accommodate new functional and expressive demands. In 1902, for example, the Larkin mail order company in Buffalo, New York, asked him to design an office

137

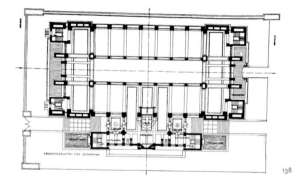

138

building around their requirements. The site was almost completely surrounded by railroads with factories in the background and a gasworks nearby. An inward-looking, hermetically sealed solution seemed advisable. From the Prairie House vocabulary Wright adopted the theme of trays slung from vertical piers, which he arranged around a high, top-lit atrium space. The stairs and ventilating equipment were set in tall towers to the corners from which the inner system was slung. These gave a massive and monumental character to the exterior and provided vertical emphases sufficient to unify the smaller parts and to make the overall form coherent. With its severe, dominating silhouette, its strong axial character and its airy, nave-like interior space (Fig. 170), it was perhaps understandable that the Larkin Building should have been dubbed 'a cathedral of work' (it was inscribed with moralistic mottoes suggesting the religious value of labour), but the building also suggested Wright's designs for sideboards or other domestic furniture. Large or small, every design was handled according to consistent formal principles.

Equally, the Larkin Building revealed Wright's stance in relation to contemporaries and predecessors. In effect it was a more vertical version of a pre-existing urban type: the office building with a top-lit, glazed atrium in the middle. Grammatically it was a descendant of Sullivan's Wainwright Building (Fig. 32), but turned, so to speak, outside in. The massing suggested an abstracted version of an Egyptian pylon gateway, while the overall lines perhaps revealed the influence of Olbrich's Viennese Secession Building of 1897–8 (Fig. 56). The starkness and boldness were in character with industrial types such as grain silos, and yet the whole thing had a daring monumentality. The Larkin Building received lavish praise from European designers in search of a modern architecture, but was censured by several notable American critics (e.g. Russell Sturgis) for being too naked. Wright defended his approach in these terms:

There is a certain aesthetic joy in letting the thing alone which has for centuries been tortured, distorted, and dickered with in the name of Art, letting its native dignity show forth once more. I confess to a love for the clean arris; the cube I find comforting; the sphere, inspiring. In the opposition of the circle and the square I find motives for architectural themes … combining these with the octagon I find sufficient materials for symphonic development. I can marry these forms in various ways without adulterating them, but I love them pure, strong and undefiled … There is quite room enough within these limitations for one artist to work, I am sure, and to accord well with the instinct for first principles.

In 1905 Wright was commissioned to design a building with a truly sacral function. The Unitarians in Oak Park needed a new meeting place. Evidently they thought of it in traditional terms involving a spire. But Wright insisted on redefining the programme and on reinterpreting the fundamental idea of a place of assembly. He decided to 'abolish in the art and craft of architecture, literature in any symbolic form whatsoever', and to provide a dignified space 'in which to study man himself for his God's sake'. He started with a *room* not unlike

the most formal spaces for public reception or dining in his houses – symmetrical, hieratic, focused by means of balconies on the pulpit: '… a noble room for worship in mind, and let that great room shape the whole edifice. Let the room inside be the architecture outside.' During the course of the design, Wright may have been partly inspired by Kakuzo Okakura's *Book of Tea* (1906) in which the author described the rituals of the traditional Japanese tea ceremony, and referred to the space of the teahouse as 'the abode of vacancy'. For the main room of the Unity Temple Wright chose a square as a generator, perhaps because this was a centralized, focal and stable shape with an inherent suggestion of wholeness and unity. This he endowed with a numinous character through the subtle control of proportion and the filtering of light. The presence of this main volume was sensed directly on the exterior through the straightforward expression of the building's geometry and hierarchy of supports.

As well as a 'temple', the Unitarians needed a children's Sunday School and a meeting hall for get-togethers. These Wright placed in a lateral oblong, which he set with its short axis aligned to the square. The entrance hall to both spaces was placed as a 'neck' between them and was reached from the street up some steps on to a terrace. Over thirty-four studies were made before Wright was satisfied with the relationship between these main volumes. The power of the result lies in tense and elemental relationships and in the way the main themes are restated in all the smaller parts. Wright chose concrete as his building material because it was cheap and easy to use: an extremely bold step for someone to take in 1905, especially for a religious building, the more so because he decided to leave the material bare on the exterior.

The main elements recalled the Prairie House formula and handled transitions in size between the overall volumes and smaller parts. They included corner piers (with stairs and ducts), walls, screen-windows, and thinner versions of the main piers to support the structure of the roof. This was flat and lifted free of the box beneath it, giving the impression of a sort of classical overhang at the top of the composition outside, and of a parasol pierced by rectangles of light inside. The building had a clearly defined base as well, so that the tripartite

139

'grammar' of the elevation was once again employed. The significance of this abstraction of tradition was not lost on Wright's contemporaries; one of his draughtsmen commented in 1904 on 'his tendency in the last two years … to simplify and reduce to the "lowest elements" (as he says) his designs. His grammar, which he may be said to have invented, is such as he used in the Winslow House, consisting of a base, a straight piece of wall up to the second-storey window sills, and frieze from this point to the roof, and a cornice with a wide overhang …' The Unity Temple was a complete distillation of just such elements as these, and in 1906 the same writer could be found comparing the building with a classical temple (an analogy which is strongest in section). It seems that Wright was entirely conscious of classical resonances in his design, which would not be so unusual for an architect who had worked with Sullivan, and had probably studied Schinkel's work in publications. In Wright's mind, no doubt, the Unity Temple was an exercise in 'first principles'.

Part of the richness of the Unity Temple arose from the contrast between the solid exteriors and the luminous interiors in which masses dissolved away. Although the layout of the main rooms was symmetrical, the volumes were in fact perceived on diagonals from the circuitous route passing through

them: another theme from the houses. The path to the interior passed through the entrance hall, then down some steps into a half-level access cloister under the side balconies. These were hung from four burly piers into which service ducts were run. The vitality of the interior space was created, in part, by the secondary rhythm of the half levels, and the light filtering in through leaded screen-windows at clerestory level; these were detailed to give the impression that the roof slab was floating. Once the visitor was seated, the geometry focused attention on the pulpit, and on the main axis of the scheme.

Thus the solution to the Unity Temple was found by the application of the principles Wright had already been pursuing, and their reconsideration in the light of a sacred institution. He did not rely on a spurious symbolism, but on the direct impact of spaces and volumes in light, suffused with a spiritual character. Whether Wright really regarded a 'church' as more sacred than a 'home' is, perhaps, open to question, but his response was to lend his domestic system an unusually hieratic, formal, and symmetrical grandeur. As in the Winslow House, classical values were abstracted and transformed to the point where the architect's forms seemed to possess an almost natural character. This magnificent synthesis was a further reminder that Wright, for all his power of innovation, was also

139 Frank Lloyd Wright,
Unity Temple, Oak Park,
Illinois, 1905–8,
perspective drawing.
Sepia ink and
watercolour. Frank
Lloyd Wright Archives,
Taliesin West, Arizona

140 Unity Temple,
ground-floor plan
showing entrance zone
between main space (left)
and Sunday School (right)

141 Unity Temple,
interior

drawn to what he called 'the elemental law and order inherent in all great architecture'.

In 1909 Wright left his wife to live with Mamah Borthwick Cheney, the wife of one of his clients. The following year he went with her to Europe for some months, during which he assembled drawings of his past years of activity. These he published in the so-called *Wasmuth Volumes* of 1910–11. On his return to the United States, he withdrew from the framework of suburban life and family responsibilities to the Wisconsin countryside, where he built 'Taliesin', a 'house on the hill', in which the Prairie House system was further extended to meet the irregular levels of the land. Indeed, echoes of the rural vernacular and even of rock strata emerged ever more clearly; one might be justified in calling this Wright's 'rustic' manner. Taliesin became his retreat, and his celebration of the ideal life lived in a 'natural' setting.

Divorced from the milieu in which he had first formed his architecture, Wright was ever more disposed to explore new directions. The Midway Gardens of 1913, a place for entertainment on the South Side of Chicago (combining stages, open air restaurants and bars), expanded the theme of interpenetrating horizontals to make a species of social theatre of courts, terraces, pergolas and levels. The ornaments and interlacing pergolas of this scheme took on a fantastic character like abstract sculptures referring to hidden figures. Wright's

mural decorations for the Coonley Playhouse (1911–12) worked with overlapping discs of colour, and explored themes similar to those emerging in avant-garde painting in Europe. But Wright's new way of life was cut short by a tragedy in 1914 when his adopted family was massacred by a mad servant at Taliesin and the house was burned to the ground. The ensuing psychological disorientation had a considerable impact on Wright's later direction as an architect (Chapter 13).

By the outbreak of the First World War, Wright had established an architectural language based on principle and created a number of individual works that could be fairly called masterpieces. He had inherited the confusions of the 'historical styles' and drawn lessons from diverse cultures as well as uniquely American influences, to formulate a grammar of design which far transcended his local situation in its universal implications. His influence in America was already considerable, especially among those Midwestern followers of the 'Prairie School' (below, p. 138), but the *Wasmuth Volumes*, and the occasional foreign visitor, ensured that his work also became known in Europe. This happened mainly through photographs and drawings. Thus a sort of 'mythological' version of Wright was created in various architects' minds, particularly in Holland, and was used to encourage a range of emergent theories and ideals in the general quest for a modern architecture.

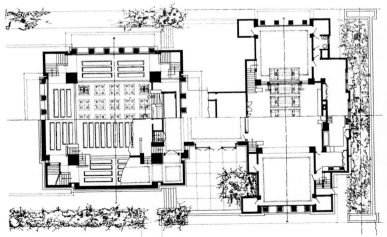

140

141

8

national
myths
and
classical
transformations

The nobility of each
building depends on
its special fitness for its
own purposes; and
these purposes vary
with every climate,
every soil, and every
national custom ...
John Ruskin, 1853

One of the risks of treating individual architects as players putting in brief appearances in the saga of 'movements' is that one may oversimplify their work and so underrate their uniqueness in order to make them fit a historical role. While Frank Lloyd Wright supplied some of the essential bridges between the architectural culture of the nineteenth century and that of the twentieth, he also invented a language, revealed a new conception of space, and opened vistas on traditions near and far. Each of the major 'modern masters' established his own world within a broadly shared endeavour. One way of establishing the identity of figures such as Le Corbusier, Mies van der Rohe, Alvar Aalto, Giuseppe Terragni, Erik Gunnar Asplund and Louis Kahn, is to investigate their formative years, when each of them passed through traditionalist phases corresponding to the state of architecture in their respective places and times. This reveals the foundations on which they built, and suggests how they absorbed impressions and principles for later use. It also focuses attention on two major, though often contradictory, streams within the architecture of the early twentieth century – the one regionalist in tendency, the other classicizing.

The former was concerned with the character, climate, and culture of particular places, with national myths and territorial continuities. It responded to currents of nationalism in the political culture around the turn of the century, and represented a reaction against both the uprootedness and homogeneity of industrialism and the imposition of cosmopolitan formulas derived from the classical Beaux-Arts. The writings of Ruskin and Viollet-le-Duc were sometimes cited to sustain an ideal of indigenous authenticity rooted (supposedly) in local vernaculars or in pre-Renaissance examples, which were believed to have grown from the cultural subsoil. But while medieval and rural worlds were both idealized, it was never the intention to imitate the forms directly. Rather, native sources were to be transformed to respond to a new cultural atmosphere in which urbanized societies looked back at national history and the rural base through a haze of politicized romanticism. Mechanization was notably absent from the agenda, and Arts and Crafts ideals were often exaggerated to procure effects of rusticity. Inspiration was even sought in the landscape itself,

142 Peder Vilhelm
Jensen-Klint, Grundtvig
Church, Copenhagen,
1913–40, detail of façade

for example in typical plant or rock formations. In these cases, 'nature' was implicated in myths about the roots of culture in particular geographies. It is scarcely an accident that this obsesssion with the land and its meaning should have emerged at precisely the same time that industrialization was rapidly destroying rural traditions.

The term 'National Romanticism' has sometimes been used to refer to a disparate set of buildings created around 1890–1910 in which allusions to national traditions played a major part. But the term is never very precise and can scarcely be used to designate a style, since by definition this was a tendency which addressed local and regional differences. Moreover, sensitivity to locale was implicit in the work of several architects whom it would be pointless to group together under an 'ism': Wright, Gill, Lutyens, Gaudí among others. But if there was no unified style, there were nevertheless some shared concerns, possibly even some recurrent visual emphases. Forms which drew their life initially from medieval towers, log cabins or the iconography of national sagas were gradually attenuated and schematized to become highly charged abstract shapes. One finds a preoccupation with handicraft, textured surfaces, evocative silhouettes, emblematic details, and masses stimulating mood. A cultivated 'naturalism' accentuated by coarse brickwork, rough masonry or tendrils of ironwork might be used to root the building to its site and to its place. Ornament might illustrate well-known national themes, or refer in a more abstract way to local vegetation and geology. The reading of regional traditions was necessarily selective and subjective, but the aim was to reveal typical patterns of adaptation in the vernacular and the monumental alike. Despite the rhetorical insistance on local roots, contemporary filters through which the past was seen were drawn from a range of late nineteenth-century international examples: works by H. H. Richardson and Louis Sullivan; the English Arts and Crafts; the American Shingle Style; even Art Nouveau.

National Romantic ideals emerged in several parts of Europe just before the turn of the century and remained active in some cases until the 1920s. They also exerted an influence in the United States, particularly in the Midwest (the 'Prairie School') and in the southwest. They resurfaced later in the

143

twentieth century under different guises, usually when it was a question of affirming a distinct cultural identity. In the European context of the late nineteenth and early twentieth centuries, the insistence on local continuities touched upon deep-rooted conflicts between the languages of different regions and the centralized 'universalism' of classical order; as if an old argument about the relative value of vernacular languages and of Latin had found a new outlet after the lapse of centuries. The idea of a local dialect found an approximate visual equivalent in the common usage of peasant forms and in regional traditions of building. Response to particular climates was also important; it was one thing to construct for the snow, ice and forest of Finland, another to build in the strong sunlight and lush vegetation of Mediterranean Spain.

Identity did not always coincide with nationality, and cultural territory did not always fit neatly within the boundaries of the nation state. In Spain, for example, the idea of a distinctly Catalan expression in architecture was already formulated in theory in the 1870s, and corresponded to a renewed assertion of independence of the Catalan language and of Catalonia as a political and cultural entity. Gaudí responded in his own way to these conditions in an architecture which combined a metaphorical transformation of medieval types, an inventive exploitation of indigenous construction techniques, and a poetic interpretation of the myths and memories of the local landscape (see above, pp. 59–63). Gaudí understood that Barcelona and its surroundings belonged to a wider Mediterranean world, not just the landmass of Spain, and his images were not without Arab and African echoes. While his own architecture was utterly unique, the cultural predicaments that it reflected were shared with other Catalan architects, for example, Francesco Berenguer and Lluís Domènech i Montaner. The former's Celler dal Garraf of 1888–90 explored parabolic structure, rough masonry, folk motifs (especially in its bizarre, conical chimneys) and surreal, vegetal forms. The latter's Café-Restaurant in the Ciutadella Park (1888) combined an imaginative reinterpretation of local medieval precedents with an accentuated brick articulation, steel trusses and an ornament of crenellations and mouldings. In both cases an armature of structural Rationalism was cloaked in romantic allusions; classicism was nowhere to be seen.

Brick and ceramic tile were the prevalent construction materials in the Barcelona region, and over the centuries a normative set of structural types – thick buttresses, screen walls, arches, cross vaults – had gradually emerged. The Dipòsit de Les Aigües in Barcelona of 1874–80 by Josep Fontserè, a monumental reservoir, relied upon this well-tried

system. The vast water tank was placed on the roof, supported by a hypostyle hall of sober brick piers and arches. The Dipòsit de Les Aigües evoked a timeless engineering tradition quite beyond matters of style, in which modular units and bays were repeated over and over again on a grid plan. The medieval shipyards in Barcelona were one variation on this pattern, but Fontserè's structure also seemed to hark back to Arab columnar halls such as the eighth-century Mosque at Cordoba (the 'Mezquita'), itself a fusion of Islamic, multicellular conceptions of space, and of the Roman aqueduct as a type. To penetrate the substructures of Spanish architectural tradition might mean unearthing several layers of memory, while also discovering long-range continuities and consistent accents in the way that forms were constructed and composed.

In addition to the traditional masonry kit of parts, there was the distinctive Catalan vault which was made from laminated layers of tile. Combined with reinforced concrete, the Catalan vault was well suited to factories and warehouses in which fireproofing was necessary, and a species of industrial vernacular emerged in the Barcelona area based upon the top-lit vaulted hall with parallel bays and low curved ceilings on piers. The laminated tile could also be used in a sinuous geometry so that the wafer-thin surface could carry over considerable distances without the need for ribs or beams. Gaudí explored this technology in the roof of the school next to the Sagrada Familia (a 'saddle vault' combining convex and concave curvatures), but there were others who made of the serpentine or jagged roof shell a virtual Barcelona signature. The Aymerich i Amat Factory at Terrassa, designed by Lluís Muncunill in 1907, combined a wave-like roof with a skeletal armature; other warehouses of the time cut skylights into the apertures left between the parallel rows of protruding roofs. Here was a case of a distinctive local technology which combined artisanry and industrialism, and which opened the way to extraordinary spatial effects.

One architect to grasp the expressive possibilities of complex surfaces and structures was Josep Maria Jujol, who clearly learned much from Gaudí (with whom he worked) but who established an eclectic and emotive style of his own. Jujol rejoiced in the calligraphy of ironwork, the layering of stucco, brick and masonry, and the interpenetration of different

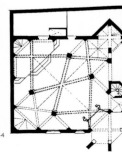

144

145

curved geometries in section and plan. He was attracted to Catalan medieval examples which he perceived in his own way, but in fact drew upon a much wider tradition, and was able to splice together several spatial ideas in a single design. Jujol extended the discoveries of his Catalan predecessors, evoked the surrealist aspects of Catalan peasant folklore, and even stirred the underground memory of Arab space, in a language which also owed something to the international currency of Art Nouveau. The Church at Vistabella, near Tarragona, of 1918–23 used splayed diagonal geometry, criss-cross ribbed vaults, and dissolving effects of light, and transformed Gothic and Moorish precedents. Jujol's buildings brought together industrialism and handicraft, materials like concrete and iron with customary ceramic and brick. His elaborate hieroglyphs and 'organic' shapes were infused with a private sensibility for plants and organisms, and amounted almost to a mystical handwriting; but they also registered a poetic and sensuous reaction to the *genius loci* and landscape of this maritime, Mediterranean region.

It was in the entirely contrasting geographical conditions of the northern European countries that some of the most remarkable 'National Romantic' buildings were produced. The Copenhagen Town Hall by Martin Nyrop, of 1892–1902, introduced some of the ingredients and visual conventions for the handling of a public building. This was eclecticism of a high order, blending together medieval and modern inspirations over a body

possessed of a calm sense of classical repose. The bold massing (which may have owed something to the example of H. H. Richardson) was articulated by a well-controlled roofscape of undulations and spires evoking, yet also simplifying, Danish prototypes. In plan, the building was organized as two courts, one of them glassed in. The most important public functions were situated along the main axis, and the main chamber (rather as in the medieval Town Hall of Siena) was placed looking over the public square. The principal material of the exterior was brick, the overall palette working its way through a range of reds and browns. As in Hendrik Petrus Berlage's slightly later Stock Exchange in Amsterdam, a work which pursued the route towards pure geometry much further, an urban building was treated as a bold medievalizing mass, unmistakably departing from any vestige of classical representation in its character and associations.

The Stockholm Town Hall of 1909–23 by Ragnar Östberg also engaged with the problem of civic rhetoric by employing a vocabulary of a generalized traditional character. It was a simplified eclecticism which evoked several pertinent urban and institutional models in the history of architecture. The building was organized as a wide block perforated by courtyards and placed upon a platform between city and sea, with a brooding and tapered brown-brick tower rising to one corner. The tower was surmounted by a delicate spire, an ingenious reworking of a traditional form used in

146 Martin Nyrop, Copenhagen Town Hall, 1892–1902

147 Ragnar Östberg, Stockholm Town Hall, 1909–23

148 Lars Sonck, St John's (later the cathedral), Tampere, Finland, 1899–1907, drawing of final design, 1901. Museum of Finnish Architecture, Helsinki

146

147

148

incident and dense in local imagery, it none the less maintained a clear sense of overall order. Windows, walls and profiles were attenuated and stretched to enhance the sculptural life of the primary forms.

This interest in the visual expression of structural forces and in the movement of the body through spaces was to be found in several key buildings of the National Romantic tendency. Sigfrid Ericson's Masthugg Church at Göteborg, Sweden of 1910–14 seemed to grow directly from its rocky site, its battered and rusticated walls rising from a dense stone base to ever more simplified and chiselled forms higher up. Lars Sonck's Tampere Cathedral (originally St John's Church) in Finland of 1899–1907 gave shape to the visual tensions of load and support in its overall pyramidal massing, and in its compression and expression of space and structure. The secondary articulation of steeply-angled roofs, windows and masonry joints communicated a vital inner image, while the interior columns were muscular in effect. The building achieved a primal presence through a rigorous control of plan, geometry and materials, which was more than just a matter of Richardsonian influence. The varied rustication evoked a textured, cliff-like surface responsive to weather and to the low angle of northern sunlight. The aim was to move beyond any obvious Romanesque or Gothic references to something more primitive. Sonck's inspirations came from several places, among them the medieval stone churches of Åland – buildings of a rugged and timeless quality. St John's, Tampere, was a celebration of granite construction by local craftsmen, and took on the quality of a collective statement for its city.

It was also an affirmation of cultural identity and independence for Finland. Finnish architects such as Sonck and the younger Eliel Saarinen asserted autonomy from the Russian classicizing influence by returning to old indigenous themes arising from a poetic 'reaction' to the glacial landscape, to traditional timber and stone construction, and to the Nordic climate. They took Finnish epics such as the *Kalevala* as their inspiration. They were also touched by popular sentiments which expressed a violent reaction against Tsar Nicholas II's attempts to violate the Finnish constitution. To follow the design process of St John's, Tampere, from its original competition-winning stage (called

various stages of Swedish architecture, and visible in several earlier metamorphoses in the surrounding, and irregular, Stockholm skyline. The Town Hall combined the type of a medieval Italian *palazzo pubblico* with some vague evocations of Venice, and yet contained numerous allusions to Swedish vernacular traditions in its massing, its details and its craftsmanship. The democratic gestures of a wide arcade and an open court linking the urban side to the water were reinforced by an avoidance of dominant axiality in the plan. The court was treated as a space of dispersal in which the visitor was subtly turned towards a lateral flight of steps flanked by diagonal towers, before moving into the interior. While Östberg's design was rich in decorative

'Aeternitas') to its final stage, is to see how Sonck moved gradually from a simplified form of Gothic Revival, through a stage influenced by the organicism of Art Nouveau, to an idea with a distinct character of its own: what one might be tempted to call a Finnish style. But this would be to put limits on a work of architecture that had a certain universal quality, both earthbound and aspiring.

There can be no doubt that the example of H. H. Richardson played its part in Sonck's crystallization of a personal yet national expression, and he was far from being the only architect to grasp the relevance of this American architect to Nordic European conditions. Richardson's institutional buildings combined a Beaux-Arts planning discipline with an elemental masonry vocabulary of formal geometries and medieval associations. He showed himself adaptable to the new tasks of an emergent nation in the whole range from city to country. The rusticated forms of his buildings suggested several ways for dealing with precisely the kind of rocky, suburban

sites that the expanding Baltic cities offered in abundance. His massive integrity was felt to possess an almost geological inevitability which appealed to Scandinavian and Finnish sensibilities.

Among those to be touched by Richardson's example was Eliel Saarinen, who was born in 1873, moved to the United States in the 1920s, and died in 1950. Saarinen's earliest works such as the National Museum in Helsinki of 1902 (designed with Armas Lindgren) were sophisticated reworkings of Richardsonian themes, in which there was evident enjoyment of the transition through stone of several degrees of roughness to textured brick and hewn timber. The full impact of this rugged vocabulary is felt in the complex of residences and studios that Saarinen designed with Lindgren and Herman Gesellius in 1902 for their combined use at Hvitträsk, some distance to the west of Helsinki on a hillside site overlooking forest and lake. Hvitträsk combined international sources derived from Glasgow, Boston and Vienna with an evocative image of the Finnish rural homestead, replete with pergolas, stone platforms, log walls and monumental fireplaces. In both massing and materials, the building responded to its natural setting.

151

Saarinen won the competition in 1904 for the Helsinki Railway Station with a flagrantly romantic scheme that had textured stone façades capped by statues of bears. This was fiercely attacked as an excessive exercise in pictorialism by Gustaf Strengell and Sigurd Frosterus, two architects aware of the major changes taking place abroad. Using terms derived from Otto Wagner, they advocated 'a brawn-and-brain style' reflecting the needs and aspirations of the modern age. Evidently Saarinen reacted to these criticisms, for he gradually stripped his formal system of cloying rusticity, disposing purified elements over an almost classical plan and using a language of abstract striation in the façades which no longer referred to any particular style. It was this 'mineralogical' vocabulary that was simplified still further when the architect became active in the United States a decade and a half later (e.g. his entry to the *Chicago Tribune* competition of 1922 which won second prize).

The Grundtvig Church outside Copenhagen, designed by Peder Vilhelm Jensen-Klint just before the First World War (but not brought to completion until 1940), reveals another aspect of National Romanticism: the abstraction of a regional way of building in bold, tectonic forms. Jensen-Klint's design relied upon a radical simplification of Danish church and vernacular prototypes using brick-wall and timber construction, but its jagged silhouette and stepping vertical forms also suggested a geological formation. Indigenous cues were translated into an angular, almost crystalline system of walls, piers and splayed shafts. The interior read as a highly simplified version of Danish Gothic, but carried out in naked brick and bathed in an even light. The basic source was a type of Zeeland country church in which stepped gable ends in brick were used not only for nave and entrance, but also for towers. Similar devices were to be found in the farmhouse and barn vernacular, so that in probing this area of the collective memory Jensen-Klint felt he was reaching towards an archetypal response to the flat Danish landscape and its long rural traditions. However, his building avoided any descent into mere provincialism, and transcended its 'regionalist' agenda with an evocative geometrical order of its own. The Grundtvig Church took its place in a small family of 'traditionalist' buildings conceived in the early decades of this century which relied upon fundamentals of form, light, proportion and material (the War Memorial at Thiepval of 1924 by Lutyens would be another), and which worked towards the utmost simplicity without making any claims on 'modernity'.

While the very idea of national identity tended to imply unity and consistency, the fact was that most countries were divided into different regions, some of them with cultural affinities remote from those of the capital. This broad generalization applies well enough to the United States in the years leading up to the First World War, the period in which Wright invented the 'Prairie House' for Midwestern conditions, and in which Gill evolved a modern architecture attuned to the climate, landscape and Hispanic memories of southern California. The architects loosely grouped under the heading 'Prairie School' (most of them followers of Sullivan and Wright) considered themselves to be in touch with the values of the American heartland and therefore to be closer to the country's 'true' spirit and identity than the American Beaux-Arts architects whom they criticized for continuing the usual pattern of European importation. Working for the most part in Midwestern states such as Iowa, Illinois and Minnesota, the Prairie School architects (including George Maher, Marion Mahony, William Drummond, George Elmslie, William Purcell, Barry Byrne and Walter Burley Griffin) attempted to produce an authentic reaction to the flat landscape, the extremes of the climate and the cultural ethos of the small country town – a world which they considered to be 'purer' than that of the big city. While the personal styles differed, there was a distinctly Wrightian feeling to most of the production. The Prairie School (which dwindled soon after the United States entered the First World War in 1917) concentrated on the individual home, but also turned its attention to the institutions of small-town America: the schoolhouse, the public library, the bank. Writing in 1918, Irving K. Pond caught the atmosphere behind this short-lived movement already on the wane:

In imitation of a certain broad and horizontal disposition of lines individually employed, a school of design has sprung up for which its authors claim the title 'American'. The horizontal lines of the new expression appeal to the disciples of the school as echoing the spirit of the prairies of the great Middle West, which to them embodies the essence of democracy.

If there was a single work to distil the American dream of a democratic capitalism rooted in the land, it was surely the National Farmers' Bank in Owatonna, Minnesota, of 1906–8 by Louis Sullivan, a building that was seminal for the Prairie School architects. A low cubic mass in rough brown brick, the main volume of the bank was penetrated by bold arches bringing light to the banking-hall within. Although modest in size, Sullivan's building was monumental in effect, and portrayed the enclosed institution as a sentinel of security and decency in its local farming community. As with Sullivan's tombs, there were echoes of Richardson, though compressed into something more abstract. The tripartite system which Sullivan had used in his skyscrapers was reiterated: a sandstone base with deep openings (suggesting storage boxes or tellers' windows); the grand sweep of the arches up above (enhanced by copper mouldings); the flare of the wall surface at the top into a species of cornice. While there were hints of Roman, Byzantine, even Islamic inspirations, these were blended into something else: an eclectic synthesis of a profound sort, infused with Sullivan's transcendentalist sentiments, and his intention of 'deifying American daily life'. Beyond any particular stylistic designation, the Owatonna Bank was pervaded by a generalized classical sense expressed through the 'primordial' elements of pier, lintel and arch. Perhaps this was Sullivan's 'authentic American' answer to the cosmopolitan superficialities (as he

152

152 Louis Sullivan, National Farmers' Bank, Owatonna, Minnesota, 1906–8, interior

153 National Farmers' Bank

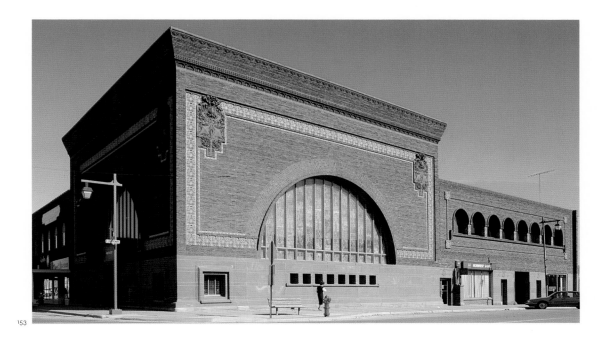

153

perceived them) of the Beaux-Arts monuments being erected in larger American cities at the time.

Whatever the local cultural agenda of the Owatonna Bank (and of its several cousins designed by Sullivan in small Midwestern towns in the 1910s), the building was like an inclusive emblem of Sullivan's preoccupations in his later years, especially his hope of forming a universal architectural language based upon the abstraction of natural forces and principles. Mechanical processes of electroplating, rolling steel, or even casting bricks, were to be pressed into the service of a 'prose poem' of many tones in which the given character of materials would be transformed by the myth of the American Prairie and of the endless abundance of nature. The inheritance of Arts and Crafts values is sensed in Sullivan's own description of the flecked brickwork of the Owatonna Bank, which combined rough and smooth, light and dark, in a sort of shimmering tapestry, a surface that was virtually alive:

Manufacturers, by grinding the clay and shale coarse, and by the use of cutting wires, produced on its face a new and most interesting texture … with a nap-like effect, suggesting somewhat an Anatolian 'rug', a texture giving innumerable highlights and shadows, and a moss-like softness of appearance.

In the interior, the usually secretive activities of banking were rendered open and transparent in a single unified space bathed in light. The sober browns of the outside walls were left behind for russet golds and yellowy greens – colours inspired by the prairie in its different seasons. The ornament was far more elaborate too, especially in the suspended light fixtures with their festoons of metallic vegetation, and their small white globular bulbs resembling oozing drops of sap. These lamps were vaguely phallic in form, and suggested both the peeling away of foliage from stalks, and seed-drills coming down to sharp points. It was as if money should be thought of as a 'seed' embedded in the land, then brought to fruition by the skill of agriculture. Capitalism was to sow, then reap, the abundance of nature. Equally there were polarities between 'male' and 'female' principles: the earth being furrowed and ploughed by the machine. A casket of riches, the Owatonna Bank also suggested an abstracted sky floating above an earthbound base. While these cosmic overtones were perhaps more at home in a rural institution than in the shafts of Sullivan's skyscrapers in the big cities, they still sat awkwardly in what was, in reality, a mundane building type. Sullivan's last stand, his dream of generating a new American culture, blending populism and transcendentalism, rooted in the heartlands, was doomed to failure, swept aside by a national destiny that no longer had a place for idealistic sentiments of this kind.

In the period between roughly 1910 and 1920 there was a widespread swing in several European centres against National Romanticism, Art Nouveau and their Expressionist legacy, in favour of classical values. This took many guises and gave shape to diverse social ideologies and aesthetic points of view. Broadly speaking it was a *rappel à l'ordre* which rejected subjectivism, caprice, and national parochialism in favour of supposedly more 'universal' ideals rooted in several phases of the classical past. From the vantage point of the early years of the twentieth century, the classical tradition was seen as anything but monolithic. The most inventive interpretations involved the transformation and fusion of past types and schemes of order to serve fresh creative impulses. Alongside the somewhat routine and tired productions of academic revivalism there were several developments – both 'modern' and 'traditional' – which relied upon a more 'abstract' interpretation. Beaux-Arts classicism continued to be the dominant mode in the field of public, institutional and monumental architecture in much of Europe and the United States well into the first half of the twentieth century. Even a major international competition such as that for the League of Nations of 1927 was won, eventually, by a design with this pedigree. Beyond the evident use of classical elements (columns, domes, pediments etc.) and ornamented façades, this tended to mean symmetrical plans with major and minor axes marking out the rooms of greatest importance, generous areas for circulation, thick walls articulated by niches or pilasters, and a combination of revered and well-studied classical examples from several periods.

In reality, classicism in the early twentieth century took on different meanings in different national traditions. In the United States it had a worthy pedigree stretching back to the foundation of the Republic, although the efflorescence of the grand manner and the vision of the 'White City' towards the end of the nineteenth century did seem to coincide with the great white fleet, and with the expansion of American power. In Russia, Italianate

classicism had the imprimatur of the Tsars and the aristocracy, and so was associated with centralized royal authority. (After the Revolution in 1917 a short-lived *avant-garde* experiment in modernism was soon replaced by another version of classicism within the state apparatus of Stalin.) In Britain the period of free experiment initiated by the Arts and Crafts movement and by Mackintosh was interrupted by a phase of classical cosmopolitanism which served the purposes of several London banks and shops and fitted the mood of late British Imperialism. But Reginald Blomfield's 'not too French', French manner and Herbert Baker's overblown South Africa House (1922) in Trafalgar Square were evidence of the degradation of a tradition rather than its reinvigoration. The great exception was Edwin Lutyens, whose unerring sense of mass, proportion, material, silhouette and siting assured him an easy transition from the Arts and Crafts values of his early houses to the more grandiose gestures and classical innuendoes that larger state and commercial commissions seemed to require. Lutyens looked deeper into the past than his more 'scholarly' colleagues, and his instincts took him back to the bold sculptural inventions of the English Baroque of the early eighteenth century, the work of Hawksmoor and Vanbrugh in particular. This fitted no simple classical category, and fused together the European influences with a national medieval tradition. Lutyens's capacity to grasp the inner connections between different formal lineages served him particularly well in the design of the Viceroy's House in New Delhi, India, between 1912 and 1931 (Chapter 17).

Attacks against the decadence and irrelevance of the École des Beaux-Arts were part of the standard rhetoric of early modernism, but the matter was not so simple. Some of the key figures of the early modern movement like Tony Garnier were thoroughly grounded in the planning disciplines of the École. Moreover, the rejection of the highly ornamental Second Empire mode (e.g. the Paris Opéra) was often accompanied by a desire to return to some more naked 'essentials' of classical order. As has been shown already, 'schematizations' of classicism even played a significant role in the pioneer phase of modern architecture. Sullivan's reformulation of a tripartite, column-like theme for the skyscraper; Wright's radical simplification of

154 Adolf Loos, Kärntner
Bar, Vienna, 1907,
interior

155 Adolf Loos,
Goldman and Salatsch
Store, Michaelerplatz,
Vienna, 1910–11

base, middle and top in domestic and institutional designs; Perret's Rationalist fusion of reinforced-concrete framing and traditional proportion and trabeation; Behrens's reconsideration of the modern factory in the light of the temple type – all these might be considered as vital reinterpretations of basically classical ideas. Even so unexpected an example as Gropius's Werkbund Pavilion of 1914, with its 'forward-looking' machinist iconography and its play with transparency, is found on close inspection to rest upon a plan with a marked Beaux-Arts character: with primary and secondary axes, a processional hierarchy, and a latterday version of a symmetrical façade. Beyond allusions and ordering devices, the engagement with 'classical values' tended to imply a search for 'ideal' forms and 'immutable' qualities. The painter and writer Amédée Ozenfant suggested: 'Deep in every revolution, discreetly hidden, resides a classicism which is a form of constant.'

The reconsideration of classicism in the years around 1910 to 1920 took several directions. Among those to be affected by the change in mood was the Viennese architect Josef Hoffmann, who had conceived works like the Palais Stoclet in the 'new spirit' around 1905, but who five years later was designing buildings such as the Austrian Pavilion in Rome of 1910–11 with highly simplified classical

elements of load and support, striations evoking fluting, and mouldings. His houses of the period around 1912 to 1915 (the Villa Primavesi, the Villa Ast) also registered a marked shift of emphasis, evoking a monumental, almost stately presence by using primary volumes and abbreviated versions of classical pilasters and brackets that were highly inventive in their transpositions and inversions. Adolf Loos, despite his theoretical attacks on ornament, was content in his Viennese works of 1907–12 to make frequent classical allusions; the marble ceiling details of the Kärntner Bar suggested classical coffering, and the façade of the Goldman and Salatsch Store of 1910–11 in Vienna included Doric columns. In Austria, in particular, the return to classical values was intended to evoke the sobriety and supposed cultural integrity of the Biedermeier period of the early nineteenth century. In effect it constituted a reaction against both the innovatory upheavals of the turn of the century *and* the grandiose and rhetorical modes of classicism employed for the main monuments on the Ringstrasse in the 1870s and 1880s.

In Germany there was a parallel tendency to invoke the epoch of neo-classicism as a lost golden age in which 'higher' values were supposed to have been made manifest through a distillation of classical essentials. This was the way that Behrens

154

155

tended to look upon his early nineteenth-century predecessor Schinkel, presumably in the hope that the ideology and patronage of the Deutscher Werkbund might orchestrate a similar 'classic moment' for the modern industrial state of Germany. The houses designed by Behrens around the same time as his AEG factories (e.g. the Cuno Residence at Hagen-Eppenhausen, 1910–11) were markedly neo-classical in spirit, though devices such as the striated cornice revealed the extent to which the architect was willing to depart from any obvious precedent. In later buildings, such as that for the German Embassy in St Petersburg of 1912, Behrens adapted an obvious and relatively mute usage of classical columns and piers. Where Behrens looked to the classical tradition for its lessons in monumentality, Heinrich Tessenow sought out the common bonds between temple and house, classical types and simplified vernacular forms. This was most evident in his works at Hellerau of 1910–12, where the allusions to the classical language were subliminal, and the attitude verged on primitivism.

The earliest works of Ludwig Mies van der Rohe (born 1886 in Aachen) were also frankly classical in spirit (e.g. the Riehl House of 1907 or the Perls House of 1911, both in Berlin). Mies worked in Behrens's office over the period 1908–11 and was exposed to the idea of a 'normative' synthesis for modern industrial design and to the entire question of an industrial culture uniting the pragmatic and the ideal. The stripped-down forms, simplified piers and lintels, and reductivist geometry of his unbuilt project for the Kröller-Müller House of 1912 (to stand on open land outside The Hague, in the

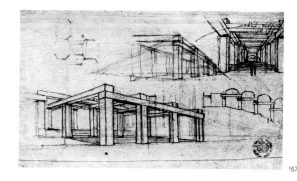

Netherlands) suggested the extent to which he had already absorbed lessons from Schinkel, if not from Friedrich Gilly. His proposal of 1912 for a Bismarck Monument to stand on a platform above the Rhine at Bingen was even more clearly indebted to the simplified neo-classicism of the late eighteenth or early nineteenth century. Schinkel supplied Mies van der Rohe with ways for dealing with a wide range of building types (suburban villa, pavilion, industrial structure, museum, monument), and with a radical redefinition of basic architectural elements such as the pedestal, the wall, the opening, the column, the pier, the pilaster, the soffit, the pergola and the entablature. Influenced by writings in a

German Idealist tradition, and by art historians such as Heinrich Wölfflin (whose *Classic Art* appeared in 1899), Mies tended to see classicism in lofty terms as a sublime, geometrical manifestation of the spiritual world. These early experiences would prove critical in later life, especially when he investigated parallels between the modern steel frame and the tectonics of column and load in classical architecture. It was Mies's later suggestion that 'it must be possible to fuse into a harmonious whole the old and new energies of our civilization'.

The early historians of modern architecture concentrated on the mature works of the 'modern masters' and did next to nothing to reveal their formative efforts and their debts to the past. This accorded with the need to project modernism as a direct expression of the spirit of the modern age, but it also had the effect of obscuring an essential tension between inherited ideas and radical inventions. It is as well to be reminded that Le Corbusier's (Charles Edouard Jeanneret's) first work, the Villa Fallet of 1907, in his native La Chaux-de-Fonds, Switzerland, was in a 'Jura Regionalist' mode that fulfilled many of the agendas of National Romanticism. This building evoked the local vernacular farmhouses with steep roofs, abstracted the forms of conifer trees and rock strata in its overall shape and detail, and embodied Ruskin's ideas on the use of natural motifs. Le Corbusier's formative years are dealt with in Chapter 10, but here it is valuable to mention his debt to Perret and Behrens; his early travels to Greece and Rome; his passion for ideal form; and

his capacity to transform lessons from history into vocabularies directed at contemporary cultural realities. Much of this was visible at an early stage in Le Corbusier's development, and even a youthful project such as the Maison Favre-Jacot at Le Locle, of 1912, already reveals the architect's capacity to blend diverse classical influences (from Behrens, from Palladio, from Parisian *hôtels particuliers*, from the Roman houses in Pompeii) in a coherent statement. Interestingly, this same design was intended to fulfil a 'Regionalist' programme, since the architect had absorbed the writings of a certain Alexandre Cingria-Vaneyre who advocated a purified classicism as the appropriate style for the Suisse-Romande. In the Maison Favre-Jacot the architect even invented an Alpine version of classical ornament.

Beyond particular phases of history, Le Corbusier wished to uncover underlying constants and continuities. The same architect who announced a machine-age Utopia and who learned so much from Cubism, regarded the Parthenon as the supreme architectural creation and enthused over the naked structure of Roman ruins. While his seminal works of the 1920s apparently abandoned the apparatus of historical forms, he never lost touch with tradition. Perhaps he was referring to the foundations laid down in his early years when he stated in 1929 (at the peak of his modernist experimentation): 'Today I am accused of being a revolutionary. Yet I confess to having only one master – the past; and only one discipline – the study of the past.'

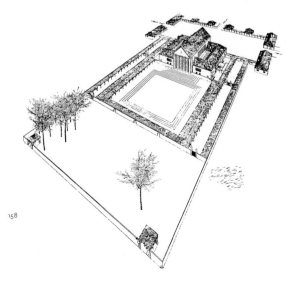

158

159

Paradoxically, the very capacity to look at history with this sort of long-range perspective and breadth of vision relied upon the range of eclectic options supplied by the nineteenth century. It also presumed the ability to think of architecture in terms of its primary, abstract values without the intermediary of a particular language or convention. Henry van de Velde, who had been such a key figure in the development of Art Nouveau, later moved towards an 'a-stylar' style which made no particular allusions, and which relied upon a radical simplification of basic elements such as the wall. His design for the Kröller-Müller Museum at Otterlo in the Netherlands (designed from 1919 to the 1930s) was laid out as a formal, symmetrical plan, and was classical in spirit, but abandoned the apparatus of the classical language. Its calm interiors and courts, and its lucid clarity of form, put it at odds with his earlier dynamic and restless buildings. It was one of several buildings conceived in Holland (J. J. P. Oud and Rob van t'Hoff proposed slightly earlier ones) which showed how the stripping down of volumes and planes might open the way to a new kind of reductivism.

The search for elemental values in classicism and in the vernacular contributed to a formal simplification in Scandinavian architecture that supplied a foundation for eventual modernism. In Denmark and Sweden, the shift towards neo-classicism after 1910 was drastic and decisive. Here it was a direct reaction against the medievalism and forced populism of National Romanticism. In Denmark, the change of direction even had the character of a purge involving a return to the qualities of noble simplicity and primary geometry evident in the work of Christian Frederik Hansen, the Danish neo-classicist of the late eighteenth and early nineteenth centuries. The new direction was signalled most clearly by Carl Petersen's Fåborg Museum of 1912–15, a highly concentrated exercise in the fusion of Doric sensibility and stripped vernacular form. Around 1920, the Danish Co-operative Housing Societies constructed several five-storey urban blocks with surrounding gardens in which the architectural effect was created by an almost neutral repetition of windows and smooth stucco wall surfaces, yet with a basically classical rhythm and articulation. The matter-of-fact neutrality of these buildings was not at odds with the aesthetic and social aims of the next generation.

The Copenhagen Police Headquarters of 1919–24 (designed by Hack Kampmann and brought to completion by Aage Rafn, with Hans Kampmann and Holger Jacobsen as collaborators) worked with similar neutral exteriors of impressive starkness, reserving the interior round court and the rectangular atrium for a more ornate treatment, using a twin Doric order in the first case and a Corinthian order in the second. Evidently, the design was inspired by round-court models such as the Palace of Charles V in Granada, although this solution also responded to the need for combining large numbers of offices with an institutional image. The design also paid homage to the Pantheon by repeating the radius in the geometry of the court. Among the most notable features of the Police Headquarters were its impeccable control of circulation, and the ingenious way in which light was brought in at the main junctions of the triangle and dropped the full height of the building through the stair-wells. Edvard Thomsen and G. B. Hagen's Øregård School in Hellerup of 1922–4 worked with more restrained means. It was built around a glazed atrium, with an internal structure reduced to the strictest expression of load and support, and yet the

160   Hack Kampmann and Aage Rafn, Police Headquarters, Copenhagen, 1919–24

161   Police Headquarters, plan

160

161

whole was pervaded by a basically classical sense. As a rule, the Danish neo-classicism of the early twentieth century avoided excessive pomp and decoration, and was intended to transmit a sense of social democracy. It was:

… not so much an eclectic selection of earlier architectural devices as it was a search to analyse and reformulate the essential tendencies which have always characterized architecture everywhere … The relation between space and mass, the penetration of surface, form's delineation in light, and the mutual proportional relationship between elements.

It was precisely generic qualities of this kind which allowed the stripped neo-classicism of the 1910s to form a potential link to the reductivist and normative aspects of later modern architecture. The career of the Swedish architect Erik Gunnar Asplund, who was born in Stockholm in 1885, is revealing in this respect, since he eventually managed a transition from classicist beginnings to an allusive and concentrated modern style rich in echoes from tradition. Sweden was industrialized later than most of the rest of Europe, and even in the late nineteenth century the economy was largely rural, based upon forestry, agriculture and mining. Between the 1880s and about 1910, the urban architecture of the country went through rapid changes representing a variety of imported eclectic and Art Nouveau positions, against which the Stockholm Town Hall by Östberg stood out like a sentinel of consistency. But a younger generation was seeking new directions and a simpler expression. Soon after 1910, Asplund's contemporary Sigurd Lewerentz adopted a direct and restrained manner using board-and-batten timber and rectangular windows. In the same years Carl Bergsten, who was born in 1879, evolved an architecture of sober rationality, absorbing ideas from Berlage and Wright (e.g. the Liljevalch Gallery in Stockholm of 1916). Asplund's own studies had drawn him towards classical models, and in 1913–14 he travelled in Italy and Greece drawing inspiration from the ancient sites and from the Mediterranean vernacular.

In 1915, Asplund and Lewerentz together won the competition for the Woodland Cemetery at Enskede on the outskirts of Stockholm, a project that would continue to absorb them for the better part of the next 25 years. The earliest proposals for the cemetery were in an informal style with curved roads, knolls and groves carved out of the pine forest. Some of the inspiration came from German Romantic landscape paintings such as the desolate vistas of Caspar David Friedrich. But in the early 1920s Lewerentz altered his landscape style to incorporate a propylaeum, a grand axis, a necropolis, and a series of outdoor spaces defined by formal planting. The intentions behind the landscape were now increasingly related to his and Asplund's study of classical antiquity, and it is possible to sense the influence of diverse ancient complexes such as Hadrian's Villa, or, possibly, the ruins of the Roman Forum. But the whole was also guided by underlying mythical themes to do with the transition from life to death, the procession of burial and redemption and the transubstantiation of natural elements such as water and light. There were echoes too of Nordic burial mounds, and of Christ's route to Calvary. Among the sketches was one for a large, stark stone cross to be seen against the sky (Fig. 162). This was landscape in a tragic mode.

The most compelling individual building to emerge from these early stages in the creation of the cemetery was the Woodland Chapel, designed by Asplund alone between 1918 and 1920. This was placed on a cross axis of the cemetery at the end of an alleyway through the conifer trees and was preceded by a small, sharply defined rectangular portal carrying a totally simplified pediment. The chapel itself was an ingenious blend of classical temple and Nordic hut. The enclosure blended the idea of a Scandinavian country church with a classical *temenos*. To one side was a small burial mound, to the other a low gateway with a disc-shaped floor. In effect, the chapel itself was a miniature and rustic version of the Pantheon, over which had been placed a steeply angled roof covered in wooden shingles. The roof was detailed to come down to a sharp edge which cut off from view the Doric capitals of the slender wooden columns in the portico. Thus, seen from the front it appeared to hover on white wooden cylinders which echoed the trunks of the surrounding trees. The depressed diagonal lines of the roof with their textured wooden surfaces also rhymed with the downward slope of the surrounding conifer branches. The triangular shape inevitably recalled the image of a schematic classical pediment, and so touched off a string of primitivist associations concerning the possible origins of classical elements in the forms of huts or even the forms of nature. At the same time it evoked the idea of a pyramid floating slightly above the ground.

In contrast to the rustic and textured exterior, the interior of the chapel was smooth, luminous and clear. The dome was flat in profile but top-lit through a lantern, while the floor below was cut to echo the circular form above. This not only reiterated a cylindrical theme found elsewhere in the cemetery, where circular wells were sunk into the ground, but it also created a formal version of a forest clearing under a symbolic sky. The plan responded to the rituals of interment: arrival, condolence, gathering, transition, concentration, last rite, return, procession, burial. The section was a microcosm of themes found elsewhere in the cemetery connecting the underworld to the heavenly realm. Asplund was able to breathe new life into familiar classical types with a content related to the function the building was to serve.

The combination of primary geometries, classical archetypes, vernacular inspirations and natural analogies aligned Asplund with the eighteenth century: with Laugier's ideas about the beginnings of architecture, or perhaps with 'revolutionary classicists' such as Ledoux whose unbuilt, Utopian projects included furnaces, woodmen's huts and houses for rural guards based upon cone, cube, pyramid and sphere. The Woodland Chapel, and

the projects which followed it – the Lister Courthouse of 1917–21 and the Stockholm Public Library of 1920–8 (Figs. 365–6) – gave a fresh impetus to this Enlightenment inheritance, but also opened the way to an architecture simple in form but complex in meaning. Asplund revealed ways for fusing the vernacular and classicism, and for bridging the gap between Nordic and Mediterranean worlds.

Among those to grasp the implications was the young Finnish architect Alvar Aalto, who was born in 1898, and who passed through a simplified classicism of his own before absorbing the lessons of the international modern movement (with its own aspirations towards 'universality') in the late 1920s. Theoretically modernism rejected National Romanticism and neo-classicism, but it is probably truer to say that it pushed underground certain of the impulses which had created these tendencies. When both Asplund and Aalto attempted to sensitize modern architecture to their respective cultural and geographical conditions in the 1930s, some of these subterranean streams resurfaced, but in a new form. In a similar way, the mature works of the other 'modern masters' continued to draw sustenance from their early perceptions of nature and tradition. It may be that this reveals a broader principle of radical innovation: 'Every truly powerful period in architecture brings the core back to the surface.'

162

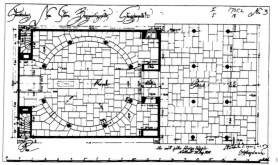

163

national myths and classical transformations

9
cubism, de stijl and new conceptions of space

The new architecture is anti-cubic; that is, it does not seek to fix the various space cells together within a closed cube, but throws the functional space cells ... away from the centre ... towards the outside, whereby height, width, depth + time tend towards a wholly new plastic expression in open space. In this way architecture acquires a more or less floating aspect that, as it were, works against the gravitational forces of nature.
Theo van Doesburg, 1924

165 Gerrit Thomas Rietveld, Schröder House, Utrecht, 1923–4

If an architectural historian highly attuned to the significant traits of his own time had positioned himself in 1914 and looked back over the previous two decades in Western Europe and the United States, his main impression would have been of a rich and varied pluralism. In France, the United States, and England Beaux-Arts classicism would have been seen extending its influence, alongside pockets of continued medieval revival; strands of National Romanticism linked to Arts and Crafts and Regionalist ideals would also have been prominent. Against this varied backdrop, the innovations defined in earlier chapters – from Art Nouveau to Futurism, from Gaudí to Wright – would have stood out with relative degrees of firmness. But even these 'modern' tendencies would have revealed a great diversity of approach.

Had the same historian positioned himself twenty years later and surveyed the scene of the preceding few decades, he might have been struck by the way pre-war strands of modern architecture tended to converge in the early to mid-1920s, culminating, in some cases, in the broadly shared qualities of the International modern movement. Admittedly the historical landscape would still have contained major tributaries of revivalism, but these would have flowed with less force. Moreover, Art Deco and the various forms of Expressionism would have appeared as parallel movements of modern architecture occasionally diverging from, occasionally overlapping with, the visual conventions of the 'International Style'. Individual works of high intensity do not lend themselves to superficial stylistic description, and each architect had his own trajectory in these overall developments; nevertheless, for a brief period in the second half of the 1920s, there was something like a shortlived consensus.

Some of the elements which contributed to the synthesis of the post-war era have been singled out already: the very idea of a modern architecture; Rationalist approaches to history and construction; visual and philosophical concerns with mechanization; attempts at distilling certain essentials from tradition; moral yearnings for honesty, integrity and simplicity; interpretations of new institutions and building types in major industrial cities; aspirations towards internationalism and 'universality'. However, without the influence of Cubism and abstract art, the architecture of the 1920s would probably have been very different. This was not so much a matter of architects lifting motifs from paintings and aping their forms, as it was a matter of infusing the entire three-dimensional anatomy of architecture with a geometrical and spatial character *analogous* to that first discovered in the illusionistic world behind the picture plane.

In fact the various paths from the discoveries of painters and sculptors to the vocabularies of architectural design were rarely straightforward. Aside from particular routes of influence from, say, Cubism to Russian geometrical abstraction to Constructivist design, or from Cubism to Purism to the architecture of Le Corbusier, it is possible to divine broad underlying areas of shared concern between the artists and architects of the avant-garde in the first part of this century. One finds the recurrent theme of purification of the means of expression through the device of abstraction. The emphasis on the underlying 'architectonic' order of the visual work of art is, in turn, often linked to a belief in 'higher', more spiritual meanings, transcending the mere reproduction of appearances. The rejection of traditional means of representation like perspective is in turn often linked to rediscoveries of 'primitive' and 'exotic' sources – African sculpture, Japanese prints, oriental carpets. Considerable emotional investment is made in the idea of the creative individual preserving his authenticity in the face of the supposedly decaying forms of official, academic and bourgeois culture.

Another feature of this intellectual scenario was the very idea of an avant-garde whose business was seen as the rejection of dead forms in a constant quest for innovation. Curiously, however, the impetus towards permanent iconoclasm, accompanied by a contempt for the recent past, was often also linked to a generalized respect for far distant history. It was as though being 'modern' required that one should return to the fundamentals of one's art, and rethink it from the ground up. Moreover, the modern artist – as Wassily Kandinsky put the matter overtly in *Concerning the Spiritual in Art* (1912) – should function as a sort of high priest and prophet of a new culture. Once again one glimpses the progressivist notion of history, the pervasive belief in a *Zeitgeist* – the myth of the

modern artist as someone who is supposed to make the inner meaning of his own times visible. Past styles were therefore, at least in theory, barriers against the deep mission of revealing abstract form in its universal character. It was as if the true modern style was to be the style to end all styles, as if it was supposed to be privy to some esperanto of expression, transcending countries and conventions, and rooted in central structures of the mind. The stripped white geometries of the modern movement and the recurrent obsession with 'essentials' in surrounding polemics can scarcely be understood apart from such trans-historical and pan-cultural aspirations.

It is ironical that rebellious avant-garde positions should have been influenced by scholars and historians of art. In the late nineteenth century, such writers as Heinrich Wölfflin and Konrad Fiedler had discussed style as if it could be defined in terms of dominant modes of spatial or formal patterning, and had gone so far as to suggest that such underlying visual structures were the key way in which past *Zeitgeist*s had been expressed. The lesson for someone in the present who held a similar view of the relationship between culture and form was therefore obvious: he should seek the true sense of a modern style in some new spatial conception which (supposedly) gave direct expression to 'the spirit of modern times'.

Another strand contributing to the ideal of abstraction stemmed from late nineteenth-century Symbolist ideas and from the notion of 'empathy'. We have seen how August Endell (p. 66) in Munich could write of a 'new art' capable of expression without anecdote; at the turn of the century there were numerous other suggestions of a painting equivalent to music, and of a pure language of lines, shapes, volumes, colours and tones. This no doubt betokened a strong reaction against the moral and literary emphases of mid-nineteenth-century art. In his *Notes of a Painter* of 1908, Henri Matisse suggested that: 'A work of art must carry in itself its complete significance and impose it upon the beholder even before he can identify the subject-matter,' and that nature should not be copied but interpreted and submitted 'to the spirit of the picture' resulting in 'a harmony not unlike that of a musical composition'. Even a champion of classicism like Geoffrey Scott, in *The Architecture of*

166 Frank Lloyd Wright, Martin House, Buffalo, New York, 1904, site plan

167 Pablo Picasso, *L'Aficionado*, 1912. Oil on canvas, 53$^1/_4$ × 32$^1/_4$ in (135 × 82 cm). Öffentliche Kunstsammlung, Basle

168 Piet Mondrian, *Composition in Blue*, 1917. Oil on canvas, 19$^1/_4$ × 17$^1/_4$ in (50 × 44 cm). Kröller-Müller Museum, Otterlo

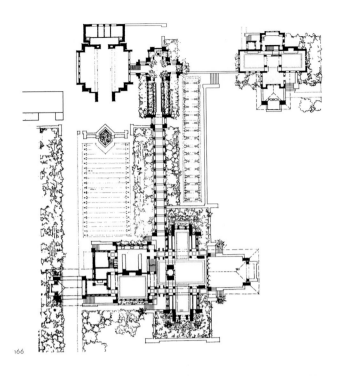

166

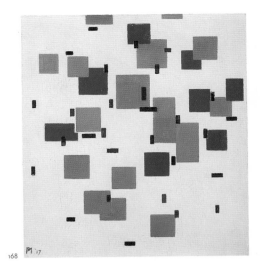

168

167

Humanism of 1914, could write: 'Architecture directly and immediately perceived, is a combination of masses, of spaces and of lines.'

The influence of Cubism on architectural form was not direct, but through derivative artistic movements. In the crucial, formative stage between about 1907 and 1912, Pablo Picasso and Georges Braque, following certain hints in the late works of Cézanne and in Negro sculpture, developed a visual language blending abstraction with fragments of observed reality, allowing space and form to come to new terms, forcing heroic and humble subject-matter into new combinations. The effects of this visual revolution would be felt in sculpture, film, the graphic arts and, eventually, architecture. One crucial transition between Cubism and a more ordered vocabulary took place in France between 1912 and 1920, culminating (as will be shown in the next chapter) in the doctrines and forms of Purism, and, eventually, in the architecture of Le Corbusier. This general development, in which Cubist-derived forms were gradually simplified and infused with a machine-age content, would be repeated in Germany and Russia in the late 1910s and early

169

170

1920s (one thinks of the abstractions of Kasimir
Malevich, Lázló Moholy-Nagy and El Lissitzky and
their eventual role as sources of architectural form),
but only after the ground had been prepared by the
De Stijl movement in Holland. This was founded in
1917 and brought together painters, sculptors, a
furniture-maker and architects in a loose affiliation
of beliefs, and a broadly shared style of abstract and
rectangular emphasis; chief among the painters were
Theo van Doesburg and Piet Mondrian.

As early as 1907 Mondrian had already been
tending towards abstraction in his paintings of
trees and natural scenes. By 1914, with the help of
Cubism, he had managed to simplify the language of
painting to the point where he used combinations of
vertical and horizontal lines; but these still referred,
schematically, to observed phenomena such as the
sea, flat landscapes or trees. Increasingly, though,
the elements of his paintings achieved their own
autonomy, as Mondrian began to sense that a
pure language of form, colour and rhythm – a
visual music in touch with the emotions – might be
possible. His theosophical beliefs and his reading of
Schoenmaeker's writings on 'spiritual mathematics'

were certainly a stimulus here; the painter was in
search of 'thought forms' to match his intuitions
of a higher order transcending mere appearances.
Indeed, the De Stijl movement as a whole – to which
Mondrian would be loosely affiliated – would claim
for abstract art a lofty role as a sort of tool of
revelation.

It was Theo van Doesburg and Gerrit Rietveld
who grasped most clearly the three-dimensional
implications of such a geometrical abstraction.
The general aim was not to decorate the modern
building with painted murals, but to treat it as a
sort of abstract sculpture, a 'total-work-of-art', an
organism of colour, form, and intersecting planes.
By 1918–20 Mondrian's and Van Doesburg's
paintings had become distillations of black, white,
and primary colours with the simplest rectangular
geometries, which made it all the easier to think
of translating such qualities into the shapes of a
functioning architecture, where walls, floor planes,
roofs, or windows might have an analogous formal
character to the elements in the paintings. By 1923,
Van Doesburg was able to produce a remarkable set
of models and diagrams for a house in which earlier

169 Hendrik Petrus
Berlage, Stock Exchange,
Amsterdam, 1897–1904,
main hall

170 Frank Lloyd Wright,
Larkin Building, Buffalo,
1902–6, interior
(demolished)

171 Michel de Klerk,
Zaanstraat Post Office,
Eigen Haard, Amsterdam,
1917

De Stijl experiments were synthesized (Fig. 176).
The resulting order represented a complete break
with the axial schemata of Beaux-Arts classicism.
Instead of simple symmetry, there was dynamic,
asymmetrical balance; instead of voids set into
solids, there were tense interactions of form and
space; instead of closed forms, there were dynamic
extensions of coloured planes into the surroundings.

The achievement of this novel 'spatial
conception' was more than a three-dimensional
projection of Mondrian's painting ideas, however;
it reflected too the absorption of Frank Lloyd
Wright's architectural ideas by the European
avant-garde. These were known in Holland by
1910–11 through the superb plates of the *Wasmuth
Volumes*, published in these years, and through
the praise lavished on Wright by Hendrik
Petrus Berlage, a sort of father-figure of modern
architecture in Holland, whose bold and simple
forms (e.g. the Amsterdam Stock Exchange of
1897–1904) bear some comparison with those of
Mackintosh or H. H. Richardson. Berlage was
deeply concerned with the problem of a genuine
modern style, which he spoke of in terms of clear
proportions, planar walls, the direct expression of
materials and the primacy of space. In 1908, the
same year that Loos's essay 'Ornament and Crime'
was published, Berlage stated that: 'In architecture,
decoration and ornament are quite inessential while
space-creation and the relationships of masses are its
true essentials.' It is not too surprising to discover
how deeply he admired the architecture of Wright,

which he had actually seen at first hand; this was
his reaction to the Larkin Building of 1902–6: 'I
came away with the conviction that I had seen a
truly modern building, and was filled with respect
for a master who could create such a work, whose
equal is yet to be found in Europe.'

In other words, Berlage found in Wright qualities
which corroborated his own ideals. Certain Dutch
'Expressionists' – notably Michel de Klerk and
Piet Kramer – also found much to admire in the
American's work that supported aims which
diverged considerably from those of Berlage. Even
so idiosyncratic a building as De Klerk's Zaanstraat
Post Office in Amsterdam of 1917, with its bizarre
brick patterns, its humped roof profiles and its
textured tower, recalls the example of Wright in
its horizontal dynamism, its layering of space and
its use of materials. In this case, it was, perhaps,
the 'handicraft Wright', rather than the 'abstract
Wright', who was being appreciated. When one
examines the textured brick surfaces, undulating
walls and curious bulbous towers produced by the
architects of the Amsterdam School, one senses how
features of local style were metamorphosed to carry
a high emotional charge. The visual conventions of
an earlier National Romantic phase – buttressed
towers, jagged silhouettes, faceted masonry, etc. –
were taken over and schematized still further,
leaving less and less sign of historical influence.
The example of Wright was helpful in precisely
this process of simplification.

The generation of Gerrit Rietveld, Theo van
Doesburg and J. J. P. Oud, who were to contribute
to De Stijl and who rejected Expressionism as an
outmoded manner from the era of individualism
and handicraft, also claimed Wright as one of their
guiding lights. They ignored his suburban and
naturalistic imagery as well as his sometimes lavish
use of materials, and concentrated on the spatial
character and the vocabulary of hovering and
intersecting planes, which they perceived almost
entirely divorced from the original physical and
social context. The fact that they knew the work
chiefly through drawings and photographs was
probably important here, and it may be, as Reyner
Banham has suggested, that they were influenced by
the introduction to the second *Wasmuth Volume* of
1911 written by C. R. Ashbee, who emphasized the
architect's 'struggle for mastery over the machine'.

171

The 'De Stijl version of Wright' was an oddly distorted but fruitful one, for it implied that his forms symbolized the advance of machine civilization. Thus, writing in the first volume of the journal *De Stijl* in 1918, the Dutch architect J. J. P. Oud praised the way in which the Robie House worked with 'the primary means: the effect of the masses themselves'. Conveniently overlooking Wright's use of ornament, Oud also spoke of the way that Wright 'detaches the masses from the whole', creating 'a new plastic architecture' in which 'masses slide back and forth and left and right'. Oud considered this 'more modern' than the Amsterdam School and a truer expression of 'the spirit of the age'.

Holland had the benefit of peace between 1914 and 1918, and this allowed a gradual maturation of pre-war ideas such as was scarcely possible elsewhere in Europe. The fusion of Wrightian and Mondrianesque abstraction occurred in an atmosphere of continuous experimentation. Typical of this exploratory stage is the Villa at Huis ter Heide of 1916 by Rob van 't Hoff. This was flat-roofed, formed from simple rectangles, and made from reinforced concrete; in some respects it was similar to Le Corbusier's slightly earlier Dom-ino house projects. The influence of Wright was clear in the overhangs, the extending horizontals and the sliding volumes. In fact, Van t'Hoff was one of the few European modern architects to have seen the American's work at first

hand. It is tempting to suggest that the Dutch felt a special affinity for Wright, because they saw how well his work sat on a flat, 'artificial', gridded landscape, a condition they understood only too well. There was little applied ornament in Van 't Hoff's villa; the main effects arose from the subtle division of masses and voids, the play of light and shade. Ideas which had permeated European and American avant-garde discussions just before the war were here able to find expression in an actual building.

J. J. P. Oud's project for seaside housing of 1917 was also stripped to the most essential geometrical forms, with flat roofs and a rhythm arising from repetition of similar parts. His scheme for a small factory of 1919 attempted an interrelationship of planes about the corner in an overlapping, asymmetrical fashion, but the effect was earth-bound and contrived in comparison to Wright's accomplished works of over a decade before. It would be some years before the full implications of an open-form, dynamic spatial conception would be sensed, then drawn together in three dimensions, in Van Doesburg's above-mentioned models, in the architectonic constructions of Malevich and Lissitzky, in the Schröder House by Rietveld of 1923–4, in Friedrich Kiesler's extraordinary hovering three-dimensional structure *Cité dans l'espace* (*City in Space*) of 1926, and eventually in Gropius's Bauhaus buildings at Dessau of the same year. Even Oud's remarkable housing at the Hook

172   Rob van 't Hoff, Villa at Huis ter Heide, The Netherlands, 1916

173   Villa at Huis ter Heide, plan

174   J. J. P. Oud, project for a factory, 1919. Pencil and watercolour on paper, 6 x 17³/₄ in (15 × 45 cm). Netherlands Architecture Institute, Rotterdam

175   J. J. P. Oud, 'Strandboulevard', seaside housing project, Scheveningen, 1917

172

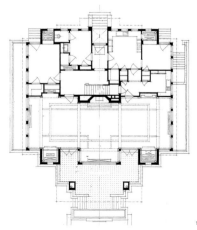

173

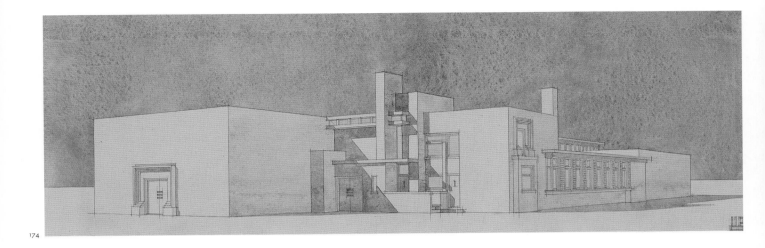

174

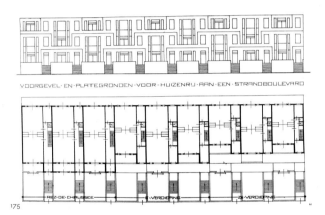

VOORGEVEL·EN·PLATEGRONDEN·VOOR·HUIZENRIJ·AAN·EEN·STRANDBOULEVARD

175

of Holland of 1924–7 relied on traditional planning devices of regular symmetry.

The period between the end of the war and the creation of these seminal works was characterized in Holland by an active exchange of ideas between the main artists of the De Stijl group, who were capable – through their various roots and experiences – of drawing on most strands of pre-war, avant-garde theory. De Stijl means simply 'The Style', or to be more precise '*The* Style', for it was the common aim of all the participants to create a language of forms appropriate to contemporary realities, and free of the supposed bogus historical residues of nineteenth-century eclecticism. By 1917, it so happened, the influences of Wright and Mondrian had tended to foster a vocabulary in which simple

geometrical forms, rectilinear grids, and intersecting planes were indeed part of a shared style; moreover, it was a style which seemed to have an almost universal application from painting to typography, to sculpture, to furniture design, to architecture. Typically, the early polemics of De Stijl claimed for this coincidental and happy unity of aim an almost divine sanction, as if the *Zeitgeist* of the modern era had singled out a group of men in Holland for some epic intervention. Thus the emergent shared vocabulary was claimed as the most true one for the times and clothed in a moral rectitude and Utopian sentiment which contrasted it with the 'archaistic confusion' of 'modern baroque' (i.e. the sort of husky brick 'Expressionism' of Kramer and De Klerk). By 1920 De Stijl had succeeded in drawing together devices of abstract art and fusing them with a multi-layered content including Futurist ideals, the spiritualism of Mondrian, the drive towards simple and typical forms espoused by Gropius in the pre-war years, and a Utopian slant that took these forms to be appropriate to the social emancipation of the post-war era. There is here a loose parallel to the Parisian development of Purism in the same period, where a *rappel à l'ordre* also succeeded in drawing together the Cubist tradition with a language of symbolic forms felt to be appropriate to the 'machine age'; the difference, obviously, lay in the 'non-objective' character of De Stijl, and in the tendency of the Dutch movement to avoid using curves.

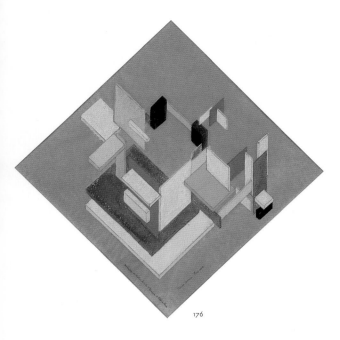

176

as the correct mode for revealing the nature of the emergent epoch.

Spatial ideas that were later to be drawn into architecture were often first revealed at the smaller scale of painting or sculpture, or in mere drawings of buildings where technical problems of realization could be avoided. A pivotal work of early De Stijl was Rietveld's Red/Blue Chair design of 1917–18, because here an attempt was made to find a functioning equivalent in three dimensions to a rectilinear abstract painting. There can be no doubt that Rietveld received some stimulus from Wright's earlier furniture designs (with their own pedigree in Arts and Crafts ideals, machine-cut wood, and Japanese simplicity), but here the meaning was a little different. Despite the fact that the chair was clearly a one-off, handmade object, it was intended to have the symbolic significance of a prototype of machine art and the character of a standardized object, manifesting 'the need for number and measure, for cleanliness and order, for standardization and repetition, for perfection and

176   Theo van Doesburg, *Spatial Diagram for a House*, 1924. Gouache, 22¼ × 22 in (56.3 × 56 cm). Stedelijk Museum, Amsterdam

177   Gerrit Thomas Rietveld, Red/Blue Chair, 1917–18

178   Gerrit Thomas Rietveld, Schröder House, Utrecht, 1923–4, plans of upper floor, 'closed' (above) and 'open'

179   Schröder House

From the beginning, De Stijl proclamations emphasized the emergence of a new order in which 'materialism' was to be left behind and replaced by spiritualized, mechanized abstraction.

The machine is par excellence a phenomenon of spiritual discipline. Materialism as a way of life and art took handicraft as its direct psychological expression. The new spiritual artistic sensibility of the twentieth century has not only felt the beauty of the machine, but has also taken cognizance of its unlimited possibilities for the arts … Under the supremacy of materialism, handicraft reduced men to the level of machines; the proper tendency for the machine (in the sense of cultural development) is as the unique medium of the very opposite, social liberation.

The appropriate symbolic visual expression of this outlook was felt to lie in what Oud later characterized as 'an unhistorical classicism' – in other words a style which took simplification even further than it had gone in the pre-war generation. Here, indeed, was the value of Mondrian's paintings and Wright's architecture to De Stijl, for each seemed to imply a formal language of tensely related, simple forms and shapes resolved into compelling unities. Controlled asymmetry and the enlivened contrast of hovering planes seem to have taken on an almost sacral meaning for De Stijl artists

177

178

179

high finish …' The struts and rails of the chair were detailed to suggest that one element was floating independently of another, with the implication that all the parts were hovering in a tangible, continuous space. Probably this was conceived as a sort of three-dimensional equivalent to the space of Mondrian's paintings with their lines 'extending to infinity'. But the significance of this spatial conception in the minds of De Stijl artists was nothing less than epochal. It was seen as the true one for the twentieth century – an 'optically immaterial, almost hovering appearance'. Such an ideal was to blend particularly well with the possibilities of cantilevered concrete construction, and the shimmering, transparent effects of industrial glazing in architecture.

Van Doesburg's remarkable spatial diagrams and models of 1923 have been mentioned already, but these were never realized directly as architecture. Probably the first actual building to embody the full range of De Stijl formal, spatial, and iconographic intentions was therefore the Schröder House of 1923–4, designed by Rietveld as a family dwelling for a site at the end of a suburban row in Utrecht. With its rectangular, smooth shapes and the bright primary colours of its elements, the Schröder House stands out dramatically from its sober brick neighbours. The building is formed from intersecting planar walls detailed in such a way that some of them appear to hover in space, while others extend horizontally, and still others join to define thin volumes. There is no single axis or simple symmetry: rather one part is held in tenuous, dynamic and asymmetrical relationship to the other, as had been suggested in Mondrian's paintings seven years earlier. The planes are in turn articulated by the thin lines of window mullions, balcony railings and attached struts, which are coloured black, blue, red, and yellow, and stand out cleanly against the grey and white wall surfaces. Again De Stijl painting comes to mind, but the manner in which one element is expressed independently, and made to stand discretely in space, also recalls the 'Elementarism' of Rietveld's chair. Some of the thin metal supports are in fact attached girders – quotations from the world of industrial standardization – detailed to give the sense that all parts of the building are weightless. Voids and volumes of space are integrated in the composition as active constituents.

The interiors of the Schröder House continue the same aesthetic themes. Details like the light fixtures or the glass staircasing are integrated with the building's overall style and proportions. The downstairs contains two bedrooms and a studio, with the kitchen/living area to the south-east corner, where it originally afforded views over the neighbouring flat landscape (a motorway now blocks the view). Upstairs there are working / sleeping areas giving on to balconies, and a living room, but partitions may be removed altogether to give an entirely free plan. The client, Mme Schröder, was herself a painter and something of a pioneer, and wanted an unconventional environment for her three children which would also give her a place to work at her own art. It seems probable that she

inspired some of the more 'revolutionary' aspects of the building, like the openness of the upstairs 'free plan' and some of the ingenious built-in furniture.

Rietveld worked closely with his client in the course of design by using demountable cardboard and wooden models. The earliest scheme was more cubic and closed in character than the final one, and it was only gradually that the three-dimensional vitality was achieved. One advantage of this method of work was that it allowed a consistency of approach from small to large. The scale of the building is in fact quite petite and intricate, considerable attention being given to small touches like ledges, stairs, shelves, window ledges and mullions. Details inside and out are themselves like

180 Gerrit Thomas Rietveld, Schröder House, Utrecht, 1923–4, detail of upper level with screens removed

181 Schröder House, light fixture designed by Rietveld

180

181

small 'models' of the whole and have been fashioned to reveal the life of the underlying form. One is reminded constantly of Rietveld's artistry as a cabinet-maker; it is as if the whole was some oversized intricate piece of De Stijl furniture. The Schröder House is thus a 'total work of art' in which fixtures and overall form are consistent expressions of the same idea, and in which painting, sculpture, architecture, and the practical arts are all fused.

While the Schröder House, like Rietveld's earlier furniture designs, was built through the most careful handicraft, carpentry, and intuitive trial and error, its symbolic message concerned a way of life created by the supposed spiritual liberation of mechanization. If these crisp, well-proportioned planes and volumes had been merely pleasing shapes, they would probably have had no lasting power; as it is, they are the outward manifestation of a polemical content, of a transcending social ideal. They embody a vision of 'the way life ought to be', and this adds extra force to the formal arrangement. Architecture is, after all, an art, an expressive language for the articulation of ideas and feelings as well as for the service of utilitarian functions. Part of the richness of the Schröder House lies precisely in the way function and structure, and such 'straightforward facts' as the girders or the simple slabs, have been rarefied, given a deeper significance. As Oud had written some

years earlier, anticipating such an architecture: 'Without falling into barren rationalism, it would remain above all objective, but within this objectivity would experience higher things …' He had gone on to say that:

… an architecture rationally based on the circumstances of life today would be in every sense opposed to the sort of architecture that has existed until now … its ordained task will be, in perfect devotion to an almost impersonal method of technical creation, to shape organisms of clear form and pure proportions. In place of the natural attractions of uncultivated materials … the weathering of walls etc… it would unfold the stimulating qualities of sophisticated materials, the limpidity of glass, the shine and roundness of finishes, lustrous and shining colours, the glitter of steel and so forth.

Thus the development of the art of building goes towards an architecture more bound to matter than ever before in essence, but in appearance rising clear of material considerations; free from all Impressionist creation of atmosphere, in the fullness of light, brought to purity of proportion and colour, organic clarity of form; an architecture that, in its freedom from inessentialism, could surpass even Classical purity.

There is much in this passage which could be applied without much distortion to the seminal works of Walter Gropius, Le Corbusier and Mies van der Rohe in the early 1920s. Each of these architects was seeking in his own way to give form to his poetic reactions to the technological and social realities of his time; each had grown up in the dusk of Art Nouveau and had been exposed to the ideas of Rationalism and the Deutscher Werkbund; each too had imbibed spiritual conceptions of the typical and of abstraction. Moreover, each had learned crucial lessons from the stripped classicism of the first decade of the century, and from the syntax of Cubism, before achieving his own version of an architecture that 'in its freedom from inessentialism could surpass even classical purity'. In turn, each architect had experienced the traumas of the First World War, and optimistically hoped to encourage a new world to rise out of the ashes. It is scarcely surprising therefore – given the community of formative ideas – that there should have emerged a certain consonance of expression in the latter half of the 1920s. However, it is insufficient simply to lump the whole matter together as 'the New Objectivity' or 'the International Style'. As was suggested in the Introduction, shared themes are best understood in the light of particular intentions, singular conditions and the unique order of individual works.

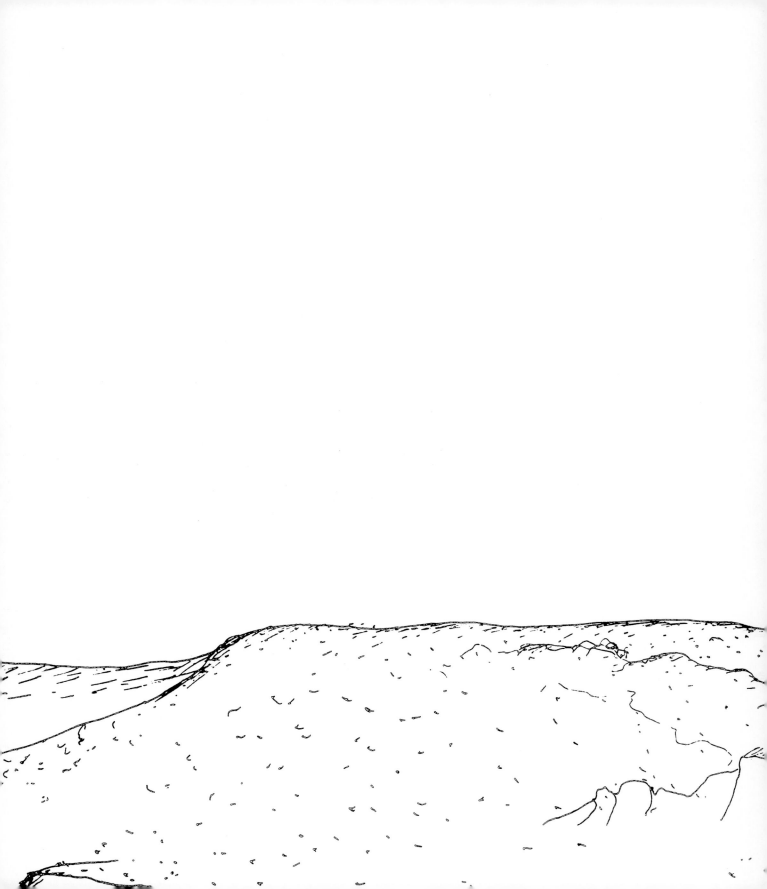

part 2

the crystallization of modern architecture between the wars

10

le corbusier's quest for ideal form

Architecture is the masterly, correct and magnificent play of volumes brought together in light.
Le Corbusier, 1923

182 Le Corbusier, Maison La Roche/ Jeanneret, Paris, 1923–5

The 1920s in Europe, Russia and, to some degree, the United States was one of those rare periods in the history of architecture when new forms were created which seemed to overthrow previous styles and set a new, common basis for individual invention. Sometimes called the 'International Style', this shared language of expression was more than a mere style; it was also more than a revolution in building technique, though its characteristic effects of interlocking spaces, hovering volumes and interpenetrating planes admittedly relied on the machine-age materials of concrete, steel, and glass. Like most major shifts in the history of forms, the new architecture gave body to new ideas and visions of the world. It expressed polemical attitudes and Utopian sentiments; and whatever qualities individual buildings may have shared, they were still the products of artists with personal styles and private preoccupations. It is only by probing into the ideals and fantasies behind the forms that one may begin to understand their meaning. This applies particularly to Le Corbusier, whose vast imaginative world included a vision of the ideal city, a philosophy of nature, and a strong feeling for tradition. He was one of those rare individuals who succeed in investing their creations with a universal tone.

Le Corbusier (Charles Edouard Jeanneret) was born in the Swiss watchmaking town of La Chaux-de-Fonds in 1887 and was therefore twenty years younger than Frank Lloyd Wright, a generation younger than Hoffmann and Perret, and almost the same age as Walter Gropius and Mies van der Rohe. He trained as an engraver, and a watchcase he made at the age of 15 won a prize at the Turin Exhibition of 1902. It shows clearly the impact of Art Nouveau, as do the decorations of a number of chalet-like structures he designed in his late teens and early twenties around his native town: for example the Villa Fallet of 1907, or the Villas Jacquemet and Stotzer of 1908. His teacher at the local art school, Charles L'Eplattenier, encouraged Jeanneret's habit of the close study and observation of nature, prompting his student to look beyond appearances to the underlying structures of plants and fossils, and stressing the beauty of simple geometrical forms. L'Eplattenier was an avid follower of Ruskin, but his teaching method may also have reflected knowledge of Owen Jones's

Grammar of Ornament of 1856 or Eugène Grasset's *Méthode de composition ornamentale* of 1905, both of which suggested ways of 'conventionalizing' natural forms and generating 'shape' grammars based upon a few rules of transformation. Thus, while the future Le Corbusier had 'Regionalist' beginnings, he was introduced to a whole way of thinking that had far more universal implications, and that would continue to enrich his creative procedures in all media until the end of his life.

Jeanneret's design for an art school of 1910 is a useful gauge of his early thinking, with its emphasis on simple cubes and a pyramid, and its unadorned surfaces. It perhaps shows debts to Egyptian architecture or even to the simplified geometrical 'classicism' of the eighteenth-century architect C.-N. Ledoux. It also reveals Jeanneret's inherent disposition for primary forms and his way of looking at the past for its general lessons. In his formative years he read several works whose ideas belonged, broadly speaking, in an 'Idealist' tradition, and which stressed the revelatory and spiritual functions of art. For him, geometry would be a symbolic medium for expressing 'higher truths'. But one should beware of reading too clear a development into Jeanneret's early years; he absorbed many different influences and tried many different forms of expression before he found his true way.

The young Jeanneret was deeply introspective. He oscillated between periods of great uncertainty and periods of exaggerated confidence when he sensed he must have some Olympian destiny. He read Nietzsche and absorbed a messianic view of the artist as someone in touch with a higher order who produces redemptive forms for the world below. Jeanneret was suspicious of the conventional system of Beaux-Arts education and avoided it (though some of its lessons later crept into his work). He preferred to learn by doing and his erratic self-education included much reading, extensive travel, and experience in a variety of architectural ateliers. He seems to have had an uncanny talent for turning up in what history has since proved to be the 'right' places. By the time he was 24, he had managed to work in the offices of two of Pevsner's 'Pioneers' of modern architecture: Auguste Perret in Paris and Peter Behrens in Berlin.

Perret taught Jeanneret the business of reinforced-concrete construction and introduced

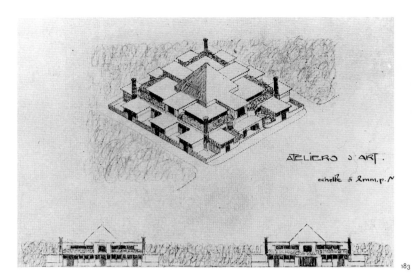

183

him to the tradition of French Rationalist theory stemming from Auguste Choisy, Eugène Viollet-le-Duc and the Abbé Laugier (above, pp. 24–7, 74, 83). Jeanneret was only 20 when he worked for a few months in Perret's office, but it was enough to convince him that this material should, in a sense, become his own. By 1914, with the aid of Max Dubois, he had invented the 'Dom-ino' skeleton, which went far beyond Perret in its exploitation of the cantilever principle and which would become a central instrument of Le Corbusier's urbanism as well as his architecture. Jeanneret's curious blend of Rationalism and Idealism was next enriched by working in Germany in 1910 for Peter Behrens, who was then designing his factories for the AEG. Behrens had connections with Hermann Muthesius and the Deutscher Werkbund, and tended to see mechanization as a central, positive force in the creation of a new culture, so long as the artist could inject the higher values of form into the industrial process (above, pp.101–2). In Germany, Jeanneret encountered the forces of big business and the idea that an architect should oversee the smallest and largest articles of design. It may have been there that he came to believe in the necessity for 'types' – standard elements of design amenable to mass

183 Charles Edouard
Jeanneret (Le Corbusier),
project for an art school,
1910

184 Le Corbusier, sketch
of the Acropolis, Athens,
done during the 'voyage
d'Orient', 1911

production on the one hand, and to the uses of
society on the other. He saw and admired the
Faguswerk and the Werkbund Pavilion by Gropius,
with their exciting use of glass envelopes (Figs.
103–6), and began to grasp the necessity for an
alliance between art and the machine.

But in considering the early influences on the
artist one cannot be restricted to developments
which were contemporary with his formation.
From his early days Jeanneret had been in the habit
of sketching buildings of all periods in order to
understand their organization and underlying
principles. In 1911, he set out on a long journey
through Italy, Greece, and Asia Minor. This was
very much in the tradition of the Northern
Romantic who goes to the Mediterranean in search
of Western cultural roots, and he later called it his
'voyage d'Orient'. It was a quest for the perennial
values of architecture, and his sketchbooks are filled
with drawings of mosques in Istanbul, Greek and
Turkish vernacular buildings and the Roman
houses at Pompeii. But the greatest impression was
made by the Acropolis at Athens. He visited the
Parthenon daily for nearly a month, sometimes for

hours at a time, sketching it from many angles. He
was impressed by the strength of the underlying
idea, by the sculptural energy, by the precision of
the forms (even then he compared the Parthenon to
a 'machine'), and by the relationship to the site and
far distant views of mountain and sea. There was
something, too, about the processional route over
rising strata of rock which Jeanneret never forgot.
The Parthenon gave him a glimpse of an elusive
absolute which continued to haunt him.

Jeanneret's attitude to tradition was far from
that of the superficial copyist. He drew incisive
thumbnail sketches to help him pick out salient
features and to lock images in his memory. He
attempted to cut through to the *anatomy* of past
architecture, to reveal principles of organization,
and to relate plan shapes to the dynamic and
sensuous experience of volumes in sequence and in
relation to setting. One minute it might be a Turkish
wooden interior which captured his attention, the
next it might be the symphonic character of the
volumes of Sinan's Mosque of Suleyman in Istanbul
(which, revealingly, he drew as an axonometric
projection, perhaps following the schematic

184

guidance of Choisy's drawings). All these impressions then blended together to become part of a rich stock of forms – the stuff of the later Le Corbusier's imagination.

In Italy he was repelled by the encrustations of the decadent phase of the Baroque and by various nineteenth-century horrors; he was repelled too by the *intellectual* 'encrustations' formed by academic opinion which he felt distorted classical antiquity by serving it up as a series of 'tasteful' and 'correct' recipes. Jeanneret took his intellectual revenge on this position by pursuing the underlying formal vitality and structural order of the classical buildings he experienced and analysed in their naked, ruined state. If it is true, as one notable historian of Renaissance architecture has claimed, that 'every great artist finds his own Antiquity', then Jeanneret's 'version' lay in the giant brick volumes of the baths, in the cylinder of the Pantheon, in the spatial dramas of Hadrian's Villa at Tivoli, and in the systematic and ordered standardization of the classical devices of construction and support. In 1911, he wrote revealingly of the Italian phase of his great journey:

Italy is a graveyard where the dogma of my religion now lies rotting. All the bric-à-brac that was my delight now fills me with horror. I gabble elementary geometry; I am possessed with the colour white, the cube, the sphere, the cylinder and the pyramid. Prisms rise and balance each other, setting up rhythms ... in the midday sun the cubes open out into a surface, at nightfall a rainbow seems to rise from the forms, in the morning they are real, casting light and shadow and sharply outlined as a drawing ... We should no longer be artists, but rather penetrate the age, fuse with it until we are indistinguishable ... We too are distinguished, great and worthy of past ages. We shall even do better still, that is my belief ...

Jeanneret spent the next few years in Switzerland, working towards the foundation of a Jura Regionalist movement that would draw together a supposed 'Mediterranean' synthesis of Germanic and French ideas, but this did not come to much. Even so, it was to this phase that the Maison Favre-Jacot belonged (Fig. 159). In the same period, around 1912, Jeanneret also designed a house for his parents in La Chaux-de-Fonds, which combined several up-to-the-minute classicizing influences from Vienna and Germany with his own reading of contemporary Swiss conditions. For the next three years, Jeanneret was increasingly preoccupied with reinforced concrete and the problem of using this material in the context of increasing industrialization; he also wished to combine the potentials of concrete with the lessons he had learned from tradition. These aims are relevant to an understanding of the Villa Schwob, a private house which he was asked to design for a site on the edge of La Chaux-de-Fonds in 1916. It was made from a reinforced-concrete armature, had a double-height central space with overhanging galleries, a flat roof and double glazing in its windows. Perret's, Behrens's, and perhaps Hoffmann's influences can be seen in the elevations and the use of concrete; Wright's in the spacious interiors (Jeanneret certainly knew the *Wasmuth Volumes*); and it is possible to discern, in the cornice, symmetry and proportions, a pervading classical sense. Among the architect's sketches, some indicate that he was thinking of this as an up-to-date version of a Palladian type of villa with symmetrical wings and a central block. There are features about the interior sequence and the plan which echo Jeanneret's description of Roman houses at Pompeii. The splayed cornice may have been partly inspired by Turkish wooden houses (the building was known locally as the 'Villa Turque'). But this building was more than the sum of its sources; its powerful combinations of curved and rectangular forms pointed to a strong organizing talent, a talent still trying to find its true mode of expression. Jeanneret's mind was well stocked with classical types, and in later life these would re-emerge in unexpected ways within the body of his 'modern' work.

By 1917 Jeanneret had settled in Paris. There had been legal wrangles over the Villa Schwob, and in any case he may have found provincial life too stifling. Soon he met Amédée Ozenfant, who introduced him to the post-Cubist avant-garde, including such artists as Fernand Léger and the poet Guillaume Apollinaire. Ozenfant, the eventual author of *Foundations of Modern Art* (1931), had many interests: painting, photography, psychology, anthropology, and pamphleteering. Like Jeanneret he was intrigued by the beauty of machines. He tended to see them as the Futurists had done a little earlier, as purveyors of romantic sensations. However, in this intellectual milieu, which was much preoccupied with the Golden Section and the supposed constant laws of perception, Futurist attitudes were given a geometrically disciplined

185 Charles Edouard Jeanneret (Le Corbusier), Villa Schwob, La Chaux-de-Fonds, Switzerland, 1916

186 Villa Schwob, ground-floor plan

185

186

visual form. The synthesis of industrial subject-matter and a hieratic manner can be found, for example, in some of Fernand Léger's paintings of the period, such as *The City* of 1919.

Ozenfant encouraged Jeanneret to paint and introduced him to the ideas of modern art which had been evolving in Paris since the days of Cézanne; evidently Jeanneret had known little about these developments during his 1908 stay in the city, when he had worked with Perret and had spent lonely hours wandering around the museums or looking at the recent steel and glass structures. Jeanneret felt at home with the new medium immediately, and by 1918 he and Ozenfant had collected enough work together to exhibit. They called themselves 'Purists' and their catalogue was a sort of manifesto entitled *Après le Cubisme* (*After Cubism*). While their paintings took from Cubism such devices as the combination of abstract forms with representational fragments, and the handling of space in tight, ambiguous layers, their new direction implied a rejection of the bizarre and fragmented world of Picasso and Braque in favour of

mathematical order and precision. This *rappel à l'ordre* perhaps expressed a feeling of consolidation after the chaos of the war. The Purists, moreover, established their pedigree in the classical tradition: they revered Poussin, Seurat and Piero della Francesca, and praised the dignity and calm intellectual control of their works.

Ozenfant and Jeanneret were aware of the abstraction of De Stijl but rejected a non-objective art. Their subject-matter followed Cubism in being drawn from the banal objects of the café table, the studio and the machine shop: guitars, bottles, and pipes were presented in their most typical forms. Their interest in the 'morality' of the simple object puts one in mind of Adolf Loos's praise of both unselfconscious craftsmanship and the 'objectivity' of engineering. A strain of Platonism in the Purist outlook led the artists to pursue essential underlying ideas and to be preoccupied with the classification of ideal types in design. They explored the tension between 'ordinariness' and spirituality. Jeanneret's *Still Life* of 1920 is representative of his work in this period. The outlines of bottle and guitar have been reduced to geometrical shapes laid out parallel to the picture surface; outlines and colours are crisp and distinct; visual tension is introduced by overlaps and spatial ambiguities; the Cubist principle of fusing different views of an object has been regularized – the bottle top, for example, is a pure circle. An attempt is made to reveal the heroic qualities of simple, everyday, mass-produced things.

Jeanneret's activity as a painter was to be most important to him when he became Le Corbusier the architect, because it provided him with a filter of experiences and a laboratory of forms. Dissatisfied with the eclecticism of the nineteenth century, with Art Nouveau and with the various 'styles', he required a vocabulary which conformed to his private ideas and his taste for geometry, but which also seemed to have relevance to the mechanized world in which he lived. As much as possible, too, he required forms with a universal character which addressed, over time, the basic aesthetic values he had sensed in tradition. Now Purist paintings provided all these things, and henceforth he was to believe that pure, precise geometrical forms were the appropriate ones for the machine age.

Jeanneret's first years in Paris brought him no commissions and much anxiety, but by 1920 he was at last beginning to sense his true direction as an architect. It was then that he took the name 'Le Corbusier' (a conflation of 'Le Corbesier', an ancestral name, and of 'Corbeau' or 'Crow', a nickname) and founded the magazine *L'Esprit nouveau* (*The New Spirit*) with Ozenfant. This opened on a positive note which, again, suggested a consolidation after the upheaval of the war years:

There is a new spirit; it is a spirit of construction and synthesis guided by a clear conception.

Some of the articles which Le Corbusier had published in the magazine were later gathered together as a book which appeared in 1923 with the title *Vers une architecture* (literally *Towards an Architecture* though mistranslated as *Towards a New Architecture* in the English edition of 1927). This has been one of the most influential architectural books of the century, combining deep wisdom, poetic observation, rich illustration of ideas, and a confident call for an architectural language in tune with the machine era that Le Corbusier sensed rising around him. But as well as putting the case for a new architecture, and providing some hints (for himself as well as others) concerning its eventual appearance, Le Corbusier also stressed the role of tradition in providing great examples whose lessons might be transformed to contemporary purposes. *Vers une architecture* was certainly far from being a defence of 'functionalism' (as some commentators have complained); indeed, it was permeated with a lofty view of the role of art and emphasized the poetic value of sculptural form.

The Architect, by his arrangement of forms, realizes an order which is a pure creation of his spirit; by forms and shapes he affects our senses to an acute degree and provokes plastic emotions; by the relationships which he creates, he wakes profound echoes in us …

187 Charles Edouard Jeanneret (Le Corbusier), *Still Life*, 1920. Oil on canvas, 32 x 39¹/₄ in (80.9 x 99.7 cm). The Museum of Modern Art, New York, Van Gogh Purchase Fund

188 Ocean liner, from Le Corbusier, *Vers une architecture*, 1923

189 Greek temples and cars, from Le Corbusier, *Vers une architecture*, 1923

187

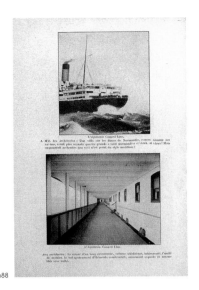

Extending some of the ideas of Purist painting to architecture, and revealing the underlying Platonism of his outlook, Le Corbusier argued that there were basic and absolutely beautiful forms transcending the mere conventions of period and style. Like his contemporaries in Holland, the artists of De Stijl, he believed in a sort of universal visual language of the spirit.

Architecture is the masterly, correct and magnificent play of volumes brought together in light. Our eyes are made to see forms in light; light and shade reveal these forms; cubes, cones, spheres and cylinders or pyramids are the great primary forms which light reveals to advantage. The image of these is distinct and tangible within us and without ambiguity. It is for this reason that these are beautiful forms, the most beautiful forms. Everybody is agreed to that, the child, the savage and the metaphysician. It is of the very nature of the plastic arts.

While Le Corbusier found evidence of the underlying primary forms in the Pyramids, the Parthenon, the Roman baths, the Pantheon, the Pont du Gard, Michelangelo, Mansart, etc., he felt the architecture of the recent past to be impoverished and lacking in lasting value. It was in certain *engineering* objects that he sensed the presence of the harmony he desired – grain silos, factories, ships, aeroplanes and cars – and these were illustrated extensively in the book. Silos and factories, for example, were praised for their clear and distinct articulation of volumes and surfaces; ships and aeroplanes for their rigorous expression of function. It was obvious that all the objects he chose to illustrate conformed with his Purist prejudices, but he also believed them to be symptoms of the emerging spirit of the age; in this, of course, he was certainly reflecting a knowledge of Deutscher Werkbund speculations on engineering aesthetics, and a fairly long nineteenth-century tradition for treating mechanisms as the 'true' design expression of the times. The solution to the problem of defining the architecture of 'the new era' seemed, then, to lie in the *transformation* of such images as ships, automobiles and aeroplanes into the symbolic forms of art. Purism pointed the way here, and it was clear too that the resultant vocabulary should also exhibit the classical values the architect had intuited in the past.

The equation of machine art and classicism came to a head towards the centre of the book where pictures of one of the temples at Paestum (dated by Le Corbusier as 600–500 BC) and the later Parthenon were placed on opposite pages, with a Humber automobile of 1907 confronting a Delage car of 1921 in a similar fashion underneath. This brilliant use of the photograph was supposed to reinforce the idea of 'standards' – such basic elements as columns, triglyphs, etc. in the temples, and wheels, lamps, chassis, etc. in the cars – 'type forms' which, once defined and related as a system, might then evolve towards perfection.

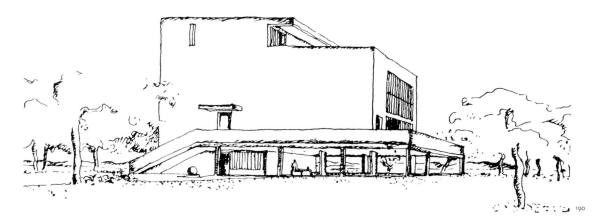

190

Let us display, then, the Parthenon and the motor car so that it may
be clear that it is a question of two products of selection in different
fields, one which has reached its climax and the other which is
evolving. That enriches the automobile. And what then? Well it
remains to use the car as a challenge to our houses and our greatest
buildings. It is here that we come to a stop.

What, then, would be the modern equivalents to
the standard elements of the classical system of the
past? Le Corbusier was to find this out, precisely, by
using the car as a challenge to the house, and the
resulting prototype, the Maison Citrohan of 1922,
was to be a sort of Paestum or Humber to the later
villas, which were much more refined versions of
the same system. 'Citrohan' was a deliberate pun
on 'Citroën', and it is clear that Le Corbusier, like
Gropius and Oud in the same period, was intent on
using mass-production processes, like those which
Ford had used for cars, to solve the housing crisis
of the post-war years. His prototype was a white
box on stilts with a flat roof, planar, rectangular
windows of an industrial kind, and a double-height
living room behind a huge studio window. The back
part of the house contained the kitchen, bathroom
and bedrooms in smaller compartments, and
at the lowest level was a heating plant; cars meanwhile could tuck into the space created by the
reinforced-concrete columns or *pilotis*. Halfway
up and on top were terraces. The building as a
whole was made of concrete – hence the large
uninterrupted spans of the interior – and much of
it would, in fact, have to have been constructed on
site. But the *idea* of mass-production dwelling was as
important as the fact, and the Citrohan envisaged a
way of life freed from the unnecessary clutter of the

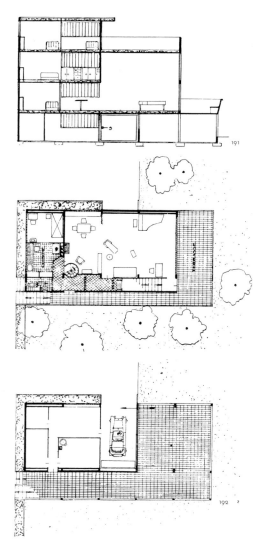

191

192

customary bourgeois dwelling of the time. In *Vers une architecture* Le Corbusier had spoken of the new dwelling as a 'machine for living in', and by this he meant a house whose functions had been examined from the ground floor up and stripped to the essentials. Healthy in mind and body, the ideal inhabitant would no doubt have been suffused with 'L'Esprit Nouveau' as he looked out past pure white walls to the 'essential joys' of light, space, and greenery. Of course, for all its claims at universal relevance, the way of life symbolized by the Citrohan was a projection of the rather odd values of a monastic and reclusive artist of the Parisian avant-garde.

The Citrohan was a conflation of earlier Le Corbusier concerns: the mass-producible Dom-ino houses; the Mediterranean cubic dwellings with whitewashed surfaces he had seen on his travels; the ocean liners he so admired for their 'tenacity and discipline'. There were lingering debts as well to the unornamented forms of Adolf Loos and the flat-roofed concrete houses illustrated in Garnier's 'Cité Industrielle' (Fig. 78). Le Corbusier had also been impressed by the studio houses built in Paris in the early part of the century, with their large areas of glazing; and the double-height room with a balcony at the back was inspired by a similar arrangement in a Paris café. This 'normative', vernacular background helps to explain the choice of white, planar surfaces in Le Corbusier's Parisian houses.

The architect wrote revealingly of old houses 'with façades of smooth plaster, pierced regularly by uniform windows … ageless houses in which Paris is so rich and which offer us an accomplished model of the "standard" dwelling; or at least the pre-machinist standard running back to Henry IV.'

It was only in 1924 that Le Corbusier managed to find someone willing to carry out his ideas for mass-production houses on a large scale, for it was then that he persuaded an eccentric Bordeaux industrialist, Henri Frugès, to build housing for his workers at Pessac along the guidelines of the Citrohan. Despite cost overruns and some erratic experimentation with concrete 'spray-gun' techniques, part of this Garden City suburb was constructed. The smooth walls of the cubic houses were painted in a rich palette of bold greens, blues and browns, as well as white.

In the France of the 1920s (unlike the German Weimar Republic), there was relatively little opportunity for public housing, so the architect had to be content with transforming his prototype as circumstances allowed. Since his clients tended to come from that sector of Parisian society which Wyndham Lewis aptly called 'upper-middle-class bohemia', Le Corbusier had to forgo his ambition of effecting a major transformation of the modern environment and be content with designing elegant demonstrations of his general principles on small suburban lots around Paris. Thus between 1920 and

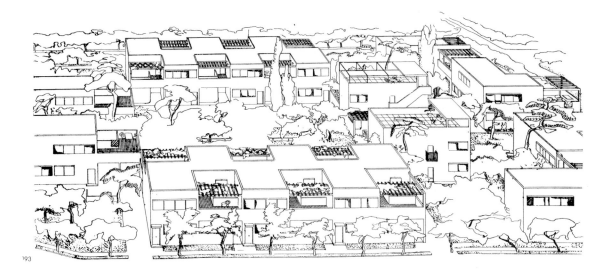

193

194

195

1924 we find him building houses or studios for his friend Ozenfant, for the sculptor Lipchitz, and for the Swiss banker and collector of paintings, Raoul La Roche. In these early experiments, Le Corbusier developed a technique for moving things out of their usual contexts, and setting up new vibrations of meaning for them. Thus, for example, factory windows or saw-toothed industrial skylights were suddenly thrust into the domestic setting. Whitewashed cubic dwellings with flat roofs and terraces evoking distant Mediterranean echoes were found in Paris. Salons, kitchens, bedrooms occurred in new and unexpected relationships, often on floors that were not usually reserved for them. Arguably this technique of 'disturbance' was used to force a rejection of old habits and stale customs.

The Maison La Roche/Jeanneret was designed in 1923 just as Le Corbusier's architectural ideas were beginning to crystallize. It stands at the end of a cul-de-sac in the sixteenth *arrondissement* and its L-shaped plan fits into two sides of the oblong site. In fact two houses are combined – one for La Roche, the other for Le Corbusier's brother Albert and sister-in-law Lotti Raaf – and one of the major problems of the commission was to unify the demands of Le Corbusier's relatives, who were newly married and wanted a compact house, with those of a bachelor collector who wanted to use his dwelling to display his superb Purist and Cubist works of art. The main volumes of the house are, first, the long oblong which contains Jeanneret's dwelling and the private areas of La Roche, and, second, a curved element lifted free of the ground on slender *pilotis* which contains a studio, in fact an exhibition space for La Roche's paintings. Between the two is La Roche's entrance hall, also used as an exhibition space. This is three storeys high and is penetrated by overhanging balconies and a sort of bridge that runs just inside the glass and provides a variety of elevated viewpoints, calling to mind a liner's deck illustrated in *Vers une architecture* with the caption:

Architects note: The value of a long gallery or promenade – satisfying and interesting volume; unity in materials; a fine grouping of the constructional elements, sanely exhibited and rationally assembled.

Windows are set flush with the façade plane so that the effect is of a thin skin wrapped tautly around the sequence of interior spaces. These have sparse surfaces and uncluttered walls painted white, green or brown. The overlapping of planes and transparent areas of glazing recalls the analogous qualities of interpenetration in Purist pictures. But there is also a connection with the subject-matter of Purism, for the fixtures of the house – radiators, naked light bulbs, simple Thonet chairs, door latches, metal windows – are obviously of industrial extraction. Like the bottles and machine parts in the pictures, they are *objets-types* – objects that 'tend towards a type which is determined by the evolution of forms between the ideal of maximum utility, and the necessities of economic manufacture'. Some rhetoric was involved here, as the main window-frames had to be specially made to look like mass-produced factory ones.

196

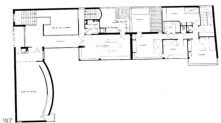

197

198

The spaces of Maison La Roche have been ingeniously linked in sequence to allow the gradual exploration of the interior. Le Corbusier christened such a route the *promenade architecturale* and criticized the star shapes and axes of the plans of the École des Beaux-Arts because they were mere patterns on paper; a good plan would 'contain an enormous quantity of ideas and the impulse of an intention', and would project volumes into space in an ordered hierarchy of a more subtle kind, taking into account the site, the play of light, and the gradual revelation of a building's form and idea over time. As one passes through the triple volume of Maison La Roche one begins to grasp Le Corbusier's intentions. The elements slide by into new relationships, and interior and exterior are temporarily fused; one glimpses the outer white wall of the curved studio dappled with shadows, juxtaposed to interior walls of analogous character. The promenade then continues round into this curved volume and up to the highest level of the house by means of a curved ramp fitted into the profile of the wall. One doubles back, sees the intersecting balconies down below, and emerges on the roof terrace, which recalls immediately the deck of a ship; a small garden set about with evergreens is created at the level of the surrounding rooftops.

Much play is also made with the idea of a building as an object poised in space, especially in the studio wing. The curved surfaces in light contrast strongly with the recess of shadow beneath, and a single, cylindrical *piloti* stands at the centre, set back under the slab; this is on the axis of the long access road and is seen against the background of an ivy-covered wall terminating the site. In effect, the studio wing was a demonstration of urbanistic doctrine, for it was already part of Le Corbusier's thinking that the entire modern city should be lifted up a level, leaving the ground clear for the circulation of cars. The horizontal strip windows and planar walls of Maison La Roche/Jeanneret help to engender a feeling of weightlessness (precisely the sort of illusion praised by De Stijl artists) and the curved volume of the studio wing in particular appears to hover in the air. If there are rough analogies with the interlocking planes of the Schröder House (for example), they are to be found in the triple volume of the entrance hall where white and coloured surfaces of no apparent thickness slide past one another in a play of ambiguities and transparencies. But Le Corbusier's building also contains its hidden echoes of the past. Soon after the completion, the architect wrote: 'Here, brought to life under our modern eyes, are architectural events from history.'

It was typical of Le Corbusier's intellectual approach that at the same time as he conceived the Citrohan, he should have outlined plans for an entire modern city, 'The Contemporary City for Three Million Inhabitants'. This was exhibited at the Salon d'Automne in 1922. The political and philosophical ideas behind Le Corbusier's urbanism are examined in more detail in Chapter 14. Here it is enough to point out that architecture and urbanism were overlapping concerns for him, propelled by a single vision of technology as a progressive force which, if guided by the right ideals, might reinstate a natural and harmonic order. This Utopian vision, with its roots in such nineteenth-century thinkers as Charles Fourier, Henri Saint-Simon and Ebenezer Howard, was given a body in the 'Contemporary City', a city of skyscrapers in a park, where techniques of modern construction, automobiles and aeroplanes were brought together in an ordered diagram, with nature and the machine reconciled

and harmonized. A later vision of the same kind, the 'Ville Voisin', in which Le Corbusier's pro-capitalist stance was dramatically revealed in a scheme for inserting huge glass skyscrapers into the centre of Paris, was exhibited at the Exposition des Arts Décoratifs in 1925 in the Pavillon de l'Esprit Nouveau. The pavilion was in the form of an apartment (in effect, a rephrased Citrohan) from the ideal city and was furnished with modern machine-age objects and Purist works of art. It was as if the Utopian wished to carry his vision of the millennium – his poem to modern life – simultaneously into the smallest details of the private interior and the largest settings of public life. As we shall see, the dictatorial implications of Le Corbusier's paradise on earth only emerged later on.

The period between about 1918 and 1923 was extraordinarily turbulent and creative for Le Corbusier, for it was then that he laid down the basic themes of his life's work. By the mid-1920s, he was in far greater control of his means of expression, one reason being that he had a better idea of how to transform his intentions into actual construction. In this regard he worked closely with his cousin Pierre Jeanneret, and together they established regular contacts with carpenters, metalsmiths, contractors and suppliers who also 'learned the language'. While Rationalism may have been one of Le Corbusier's starting points, it is obvious that it was a springboard towards a lyrical expression. Structure was always adjusted as necessary to fit formal

199   Le Corbusier, Maison Cook, Boulogne-sur-Seine, 1926–7, axonometric drawing showing double-height living room on second floor, and library with adjacent roof terrace on third. Print heightened with gouache, 35³/₄ × 33³/₄ in (91 × 86 cm). Fondation Le Corbusier, Paris

200   Le Corbusier, diagram demonstrating the 'Five Points of a New Architecture'

201   Maison Cook, façade

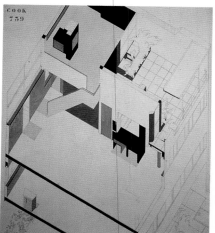

199

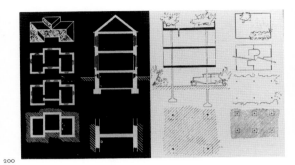

200

201

intentions, and the pristine 'machine-age' surfaces of the buildings were achieved by the relatively crude techniques of pot-tile walls placed into concrete frames, that were then plastered over by hand.

The refinement of Le Corbusier's formal language was also traceable, in part, to his daily experience of painting. The precise control of volume, surface and profile may be sensed in the Maison Cook of 1926–7 in the western Paris suburb of Boulogne-sur-Seine. The site was once again cramped, being part of a row of houses, but it did offer views towards the Bois de Boulogne nearby. Only the main façade would be seen and much effort would obviously have to go into this single view. The client was an American painter called Cook, who was willing to let Le Corbusier experiment. The façade as it stands today is almost square; so is the plan. Thus the form is almost a cube, one of those ideal forms singled out in the aesthetic speculations of the magazine *L'Esprit nouveau*. The symmetry of this overall shape is reinforced by the strip windows which run from one side to the other, and by a single cylindrical *piloti* on the central axis. Within this stable outline are a variety of asymmetrical rhythms. The curved entry cabin at ground level contrasts with the rectangular surfaces above, and the balcony at the top left pulls

away from the façade. The main relationships and tensions of the design are enlivened by areas of shadow and light, taut rectangles of glazing alongside stucco, and the thin lines of the railings, edges and joints. Pushes and pulls, laterally and in depth, are seen to resolve around the pivotal element of the central *piloti*.

But this is to discuss Maison Cook in mainly formal terms. As one passes under the raised body of the building and on into the interior, or examines a section or plan, one sees how the functions of the house have been ingeniously slotted, like the pieces of some three-dimensional jigsaw puzzle, into the overall cubic shape. The traditional arrangement is turned upside-down, as the bedrooms and maid's room are on the first floor, and the living room, kitchen and dining room are on the second. The living room is double-height and at its back is a stairway up to the little library on top, adjacent to the roof terrace, with long views towards the Bois de Boulogne. As one passes up the stairs, which stand at the rear of the building alongside the central axis, one is fed into a variety of rooms at each level. The architect has employed the concrete skeleton to sculpt a sequence of compressed and expanding spaces of variable character, proportion, lighting and view. The curved partitions dramatize the 'free plan', catch the light, and stand like objects in the lucid space; inevitably they call to mind the bottles and guitars of Purist pictures. Unity and control are maintained by the rule of geometry and proportion, and by the consistent dimensioning of such elements as the strip windows.

But there is the clarity too of an artist who has gained full control of his vocabulary. 'Sources' (such as the Farman Goliath aeroplane cockpit echoed in the little cabin underneath) have been totally integrated and the style is now assured. Le Corbusier seems to have recognized this since he later wrote:

Here are applied with great clarity the certainties from discoveries to date: the pilotis, the roof garden, the free plan, the free façade, the ribbon window sliding sideways. Regulating lines are automatically generated by simple architectural elements at a human scale, which also controls the floor heights, the window dimensions, doors, and railings. The classic plan is turned upside down: the underneath of the house is free. The main reception room is right on top of the house. You step directly on to the roof garden from which you have a commanding view of the Bois de Boulogne. One is in Paris no longer; it is as if one were in the countryside.

The 'certainties to date' of *pilotis*, roof garden, free plan, free façade, and ribbon windows were christened the 'Five Points of a New Architecture' by the architect in 1926. They were an extension of the Dom-ino principles and were to remain one of Le Corbusier's major devices for the rest of his life. It was typical of him that he should have endeavoured to create a generic solution, one which transcended particular cases. Perhaps the choice of *five* points is significant – as if he were trying to canonize a modern equivalent to the five classical Orders. Certainly his system was a solution to the problem he had set himself many years before: the creation of a vocabulary based on reinforced-concrete construction and applicable to all the tasks of modern industrial civilization.

It is worth examining the 'Five Points' in the abstract. The *piloti* was the central element from which the others evolved; it lifted buildings off the ground allowing the natural ground surface or traffic to pass underneath, and was the basic device in both city planning and architecture. This typified Le Corbusier's tendency to invert normal expectations, since the ground floor of a masonry building was exactly where one would expect to find the most impenetrable mass. The roof terrace also had several functions, being one of the means by

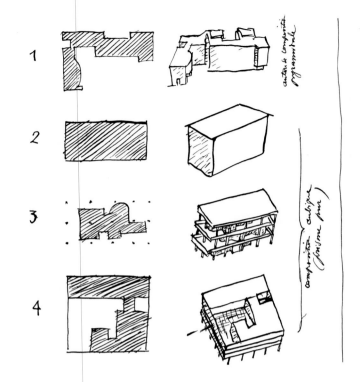

202

which the architect intended to reintroduce nature into the city; in turn, planting could supply insulation for the flat concrete roof. With *pilotis* supporting the weight of a building, its interior and exterior walls could pass anywhere according to functional demand or aesthetic intention, and the free plan allowed rooms of different sizes to be slotted into the skeleton, and spaces to be orchestrated in sequence. The free façade, meanwhile, could be a total void running from slab to slab, a thin membrane, or a window of any size. Theoretically any sort of opening could be left, depending on the demands of view, climate, privacy and composition. In fact, through most of the 1920s, Le Corbusier preferred a horizontal strip window running the full length of his buildings. Ostensibly this was because the *fenêtre en longueur* or 'strip window' let in most light; but it had as much to do with the feeling of repose of horizontal bands in a façade, and the effects of transparency and planarity that the strip window allowed. Most of these ideas had existed discretely in earlier architecture: Le Corbusier's innovation was to put them all together in a single system with a broad range of application

203

– a system which worked on formal, symbolic, and structural levels.

If one returns to Maison Cook it is evident that Le Corbusier has not only employed the 'Five Points', but has also emphasized them rhetorically as a sort of demonstration. The *piloti* is the centre of attention and is set back from the façade plane, dramatizing the separation of structure from external cladding. The passage under the house is also shown by the pedestrian path on one side and the car tracks on the other, as if to imply a new form for the city as well as for the building; moreover, a little planter is set underneath the overhang suggesting that nature too might pass underneath. The roof garden is rendered visible on top by means of penetrations, and the free façade is accentuated by the windows running from one end to the other. It is even possible to sense the character of the free plan inside, through the curved shapes which imply concave and convex objects within the 'box'.

Having assured himself of the 'Five Points' in the design of Maison Cook, Le Corbusier was on firm ground to explore further possibilities of his system. The particular incidents and complex curves of his free plan were not unlike updated versions of the

Rococo niches and interlocking chambers of a Parisian eighteenth-century *hôtel particulier*, and in several of his domestic designs of the 1920s Le Corbusier packed in sinuous internal routes of stairs, ramps and piano-shaped partitions which were 'set off' against the abstraction of the enclosing box. The Maison Planeix in Paris of 1925–6 was one variation on the idea of a miniature urban palace ('une maison, un palais'), while the unbuilt project of 1925 for a luxury house for Madame Meyer to stand in Neuilly was another. The latter involved an elaborate ascending route, shifting back and forth, on and off axis, and culminating in a fantasy roof terrace not unlike an outdoor room, with carefully controlled views of the park and Folie-St-James opposite. The Maison Guiette at Anvers (1926) devoted an entire narrow slot alongside the 'box' to a stair which cut through the whole section of the building, giving access to the double-height atelier, and the roof terrace on top. In a scheme for a house near Carthage in Tunisia in 1927–9 (Maison Baizeau), Le Corbusier let the skeleton predominate so that the overhanging slabs created deeply shaded terraces open to the sea breeze and the view, the interior functions being enclosed in curved partitions which could be seen from the outside. In an earlier version of the same house, the top slab was extended as a hovering parasol, a device which would be developed much further in the 1950s in Le Corbusier's buildings in India. In 1927, in a design for the League of Nations competition, he showed how the system could be orchestrated at a monumental scale to handle a variety of different programme elements and express them separately. In short, he accentuated first one aspect, then another, of a vocabulary that was by now mature.

Le Corbusier's next major opportunity to build came in 1926 when he was asked by Michael and Sarah Stein (relatives of Gertrude Stein) and

Gabrielle de Monzie to design a large villa at Garches a few miles to the west of Paris. The site was a long and narrow stretch of land approached from one end, with room for a garden front and back. Here, at last, was the chance to make a building as a full, free-standing volume, and to orchestrate an architectural experience as a sequence starting outside. The Villa Stein/de Monzie is a virtual study in the transition from a formal entrance on one side, to an informal garden on the other, and thus touches upon old themes of villa design to do with the transition from urban to rural existence.

The first view of the Villa Stein/de Monzie at

204

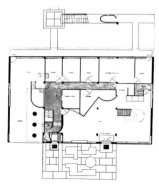
205

206

Garches (also called Les Terrasses) is from the
porter's lodge at the gateway. The drive approaches
the building off axis along a straight line, and
celebrates the arrival by car in an almost ceremonial
way. The overall impression is of a formal,
rectangular block rendered weightless by the
hovering horizontal bands of white wall and the
slender strips of glazing. Compared to Maison
Cook, the Villa Stein/de Monzie is rather grand.
As one approaches bit by bit, one is able to grasp
the subtleties of the façade articulation. Two
strip windows run from one side to the other,
surmounted by an almost top-heavy area of wall
punctured at its centre by an opening with a balcony
which hints at the presence of a roof terrace, but
which also has the character of a benediction loggia
– one would not be a bit surprised to see a royal
group appear. The lowest level has a variety of
openings cut into it: a garage far to the left; a small
entrance to the servants' quarters under a tiny
balcony (but shifted slightly off the balcony's axis);
a large area of industrial glazing suggesting the
presence of a hall; the main entrance surmounted by
a canopy; and, finally, at the right-hand extremity,
some more glazing with thin horizontal bars. As at
Maison Cook, there are advances and recessions
of varying depth, and axes and sub-axes are
discernible. Rectangles of different sizes set up
rhythms across the façade and are held in tense
equilibrium within the simple geometrical outline.
There is no *piloti* in sight, but the way the windows
extend to the edges is enough to suggest that the
façade is a non-weight-bearing skin. At the same
time, the subtle displacements and similarities of
rectangles, and the glimpses of transparency at the
corners, introduce visual ambiguities about the
actual position of things, and about the thickness of
the façade plane. In effect, the Villa Stein-de Monzie
is organized as a series of 'layers', some actual, some
suggested, some more perceptible than others.

The main entrance is signalled by the canopy
which vaguely recalls the wings and struts of an
aeroplane, but which also wittily restates the image
of a drawbridge. If one enters by the main door, one
passes into a foyer clearly marked out by four *pilotis*
with a stair rising immediately to the right. This
brings one to a sort of *piano nobile* which is set aside
for the most public and ceremonial functions. The
grand salon is situated here, and after the constricted

207

hallway beneath and the narrow gangway at the top of the stairs, the space expands dramatically. So does the view: from the moment one enters, one sees the garden and terrace on the other side. The Steins were avid collectors of modern art, and works such as a sculpture of a reclining nude by Matisse were originally placed at strategic points along the interior processional route, like household gods. The Villa Stein/de Monzie combines the lateral expansiveness of the modern free plan with an honorific measure, a regular grid of *pilotis* giving the interiors 'a constant scale, a rhythm, a cadence of repose', to use the architect's own words. Set against the grid is the countertheme of curved partitions. These channel the diagonal movement, define focal points, enclose stairs or bathrooms and set up spacial tensions of their own. They embrace the human figure and its activities, in contrast to the more regular and 'Cartesian' space suggested by the columns. Early studies for the villa reveal that Le Corbusier at one point considered an explosive and asymmetrical composition of indoor and outdoor compartments interconnected on several levels;

in parallel, he developed a scheme of almost neo-classical regularity and symmetry. In the final work these contrasting ideas coexist in high tension.

The lower level of the Villa Stein/de Monzie is given over to the servants' quarters, which are entered through the smaller door seen in the first view (Fig. 203). The kitchen, dining-room and library, though, are clustered around the salon on the *piano nobile*. The second floor, meanwhile, contains bedrooms, boudoirs and bathrooms, and its plan is arranged quite differently from the floor below it. Two of the rooms give on to an open-air deck suspended above the main platform of the rear terrace (the part of *Vers une architecture* entitled 'The Manual of the Dwelling' had made much of the idea of fresh air and view for individual rooms), while the master bedroom is entered along the main axis of the house. The small hallway in front of it is formed by two equalized curves making a kind of vestibule. The way that partitions have been arranged within the overall format recalls Le Corbusier's paintings, where curves and rectangles slide, overlap, and harmonize into a perceived unity within a rectangular frame. At the top of the house are more bedrooms and two roof terraces – one at the front, one at the back. The balcony in the main façade allows long views over the driveway towards the golf course, and restates the axis of the entire composition. Thus the *promenade architecturale* is brought to a point of stasis by a prominent device that was spelt out in the very first view of the building. A protruding, curved volume (containing storage) recalls the funnel of a liner; other nautical allusions are found in the railings, the spiral stairs, and the overall crispness of the forms. The caption under one of the ship illustrations in the chapter 'Eyes Which Do Not See' in *Vers une architecture* reads: 'An architecture pure, neat, clear, clean and healthy.' It might well be used to describe the Villa Stein/de Monzie.

The garden façade of Les Terrasses is more broken up than the front one, more horizontal in emphasis, and its windows are larger in relation to the walls. The terrace breaks into the closed box and sets the theme of stratified horizontal planes sliding, receding or stepping back towards the heart of the building. There is no doubt at all about the presence of a frame within – for the overhangs, spatial penetrations and illusions of transparency rely on the cantilevered slabs. The movement of these hovering elements is contained between the flanking side walls which are now perceived as thin planes (they were seen as volumes in the front view). Here the analogy with the idea of space intended by De Stijl designers is evident. But the agendas of the Villa Stein/de Monzie are more complex than this, since they splice several formal ideas together. There is a symmetrically divided block; the column grid is laid out in parallel slots in a 2 : 1 : 2 : 1 : 2 rhythm; the curves work in counterpoint; and the route involves serpentine and spiralling movement. In the same period that the house was designed, Le Corbusier's paintings were becoming more complex and ambiguous, the rigid forms of early Purism being replaced by a more fluid and fluent visual language. The Villa Stein/de Monzie suggests that by 1926 he was able to translate these qualities into architecture as well.

The new complexity of Le Corbusier's visual language also provided him with a more subtle means for combining several levels of significance in a single configuration. The Villa Stein/de Monzie

fused together images and types of varying pedigree. While it fulfilled his vision of a 'machine for living', its *piano nobile*, its processional entrance and sequences, its harmonic proportions and its noble mood revealed a pervasive classical sense. The idea of a processional route by car, a pinched entrance, and a series of lateral movements leading to a garden had already been present in the Maison Favre-Jacot of 1912 (Fig. 159). At Garches there were echoes too of a project of 1923 by Adolf Loos for a villa on the Venetian Lido. Colin Rowe has pointed out that the proportional system regulating the façade bays and the grid was the same as the one used by Palladio at the Villa Malcontenta. There is no evidence that this particular example was in Le Corbusier's mind, but he certainly intended to create a modern villa with something of the harmony, order and repose of a classical work. It is just as pertinent to compare the Villa Stein/de Monzie to examples of French classical 'pavillons', such as the early eighteenth-century Petit Trianon at Versailles by Gabriel (which Le Corbusier had illustrated in *Vers une architecture* to demonstrate proportions). One wonders if the Steins (who spent some of their summers in a villa near Florence), appreciated that their new acquisition was in a classical spirit as well as in 'L'Esprit Nouveau'.

By 1927, at the age of 40, Le Corbusier had thus succeeded in producing several works of a high order in a new style, but a style based on principles drawn from the past, as well as on an idealized vision of modern life. Like Wright, he had established an entire architectural system, blending logical, structural and intuitive rules: a set of 'type-forms', capable of numerous variations and combinations, and addressing all scales from that of the individual window to that of the entire city. Initially driven by a Utopian dream for the machine age, this system of ideas and forms would continue to nourish Le Corbusier's architectural inventions later in life, even if some levels underwent change. Meanwhile his discoveries transcended his personal situation, for they provided charismatic solutions as well to the larger problem of an authentic modern architectural language. This is why Le Corbusier's breakthrough must be considered in a broader context of emerging modernism in Europe, the Soviet Union and the United States.

11

walter gropius, german expressionism and the bauhaus

The new times demand their own expression. Exactly stamped form devoid of all accident, clear contrasts, the ordering of members, the arrangement of like parts in series, unity of form and colour …
Walter Gropius, 1913

208 Walter Gropius, Bauhaus, Dessau, 1926, balconies

While some of the crucial foundations for modern architecture had been laid in Germany before the war, the preparatory work had to wait until the mid-1920s to come to fruition. With the defeat of the German armies in 1918, and the collapse of the old imperial order, Muthesius's dream of a unified, national *Kultur* guided by an élite of artist technocrats was shattered. Instead of competing in the marketplace, the frightful technical ingenuities of the great industrial nations had ended up competing on the field of battle. The war may have been 'won' by the Allied side, but the bulwarks of an already sagging liberal Christian civilization had been further eroded in the process. In Germany the reaction to economic chaos was revolution, and this brought with it a polarization of the political extremes of left and right. In the arts, groups of visionaries modelled their manifestos on those of the radical workers' groups and hoped that political revolution might be accompanied by a cultural one. Gropius caught the ambivalent mood of the period – oscillating between despair at internal collapse and hope in some radiant, new social edifice – when he wrote in 1919:

Today's artist lives in an era of dissolution without guidance. He stands alone. The old forms are in ruins, the benumbed world is shaken up, the old human spirit is invalidated and in flux towards a new form. We float in space and cannot perceive the new order.

This was the perfect ground for the growth of Utopianism tinged with an underlying *Angst*. Severe economic inflation contributed to the mood by minimizing the likelihood of actual construction. Thus architects in Germany reverted to the creation of paper projects in which they foresaw the image of a new society. Bruno Taut, in the bizarre watercolours of his *Alpine Architektur* (1919), portrayed collective buildings of glass facets, rising like crystals from glaciers and mountain peaks. These were meant to embody an 'apolitical socialism', an ideal realm for the brotherhood of man, in which national boundaries and individual greed would dissolve away, and in which a 'natural' society undisturbed by inherited class divisions would emerge. In *Die Stadtkrone* (*City Crown*) of 1919, the architect even tried to embody the new collective religion in a town plan with a symbolic centre in the form of a cosmic world-mountain or a stepped pyramid. This 'centre' was clearly supposed to make up for the loss of centre of modern, alienated man, and to root him to 'deeper' meanings in an integrated society. Following such pre-war visionaries as Paul Scheerbart (author of *Glasarchitektur*, 1914) and the painter Wassily Kandinsky, Taut thought it was the business of the *artist* to reveal the form of this new polity which was to rise from the ruins of European civilization.

This tendency to believe that architectural forms might themselves have redemptive potential recalls the moralism of Pugin, who had imagined that good Christian forms (i.e. Gothic ones) would accelerate a moral regeneration. The appeal of a similar idea in circumstances where the creative individual felt cut off from his surroundings, and without bearings, is understandable. Even so, it comes as a shock to find Walter Gropius indulging in fantasies of a similar tone in the period around the founding of the Bauhaus, that is, in 1919. After all, he had been one of the champions of Muthesius's ideal of standardization; his position had seemed to stress the notion of a broad co-operation between the architect, the industrial process and the values of a technocratic clientele.

The Bauhaus was formed by the fusion of two existing institutions in Weimar: the old Academy of Fine Arts and a Kunstgewerbeschule (School of Applied Arts) founded under Van de Velde in 1906. This odd marriage had more support from the state government than from the local Weimar establishment, and was the first step towards Gropius's eventual aim of a regeneration of German visual culture through a fusion of art and craft. The first Bauhaus proclamation was permeated with the ideal of a new social and spiritual integration in which artists and craftsmen would unite to create a sort of collective symbolic building of the future:

The complete building is the ultimate aim of the visual arts … Architects, painters and sculptors must recognize once more the nature of buildings as composite entities. Only then will their works be permeated with that architectonic feeling which has become lost in the art of the salons.

A groundwork of craft discipline is essential to every artist.

Let us create a new guild of craftsmen, without the class snobbery that tries to erect a haughty barrier between artist and craftsman. Let us conceive, consider and create together the new building of the future that will bring all into one simple integrated creation: architecture, painting and sculpture rising to heaven out of the hands of a million craftsmen, the crystal symbol of the new faith of the future.

Permeating Gropius's thinking at this stage was adulation for the way in which Gothic cathedrals had supposedly represented the deepest collective aspirations of the medieval *Volk*. This myth was joined to another one in Gropius's mind: that the cathedrals had been produced by bands of inspired craftsmen without the interference of 'self-conscious designers'. Turning such beliefs around, he assumed that if a band of craftsmen could somehow be initiated into the needs and means of the modern era, then they might combine to produce the authentic collective imagery of the times. Correspondingly, the proclamation had on its cover a woodcut by Lyonel Feininger representing the 'Cathedral of Socialism' – a jagged, Expressionist image, soaked in visionary sentiments, clearly intended to be evocative rather than buildable, and in its crystal-like shapes resembling Taut's fantasies. Indeed, both Gropius and Taut were fully aware of Scheerbart's pre-war praise of glass, and of more recent pronouncements in the same vein by the German architect Adolf Behne,

209 Bruno Taut, plate from *Alpine Architektur*, 1919

210 Lyonel Feininger, 'Cathedral of Socialism', from the cover of the first Bauhaus proclamation, 1919

211 Walter Gropius, Sommerfeld House, Berlin, 1920–1

212 Students' work produced under Johannes Itten in the sculpture workshop at the Bauhaus, Weimar, 1923

209

210

who stated in 1918: 'It is not the crazy caprice of a poet that glass architecture will bring a new culture. It is a fact.'

Gropius's expressed belief in the necessity for reuniting aesthetic sensibility and utilitarian design was in line with his experiences within the Werkbund; but there was no mention in his proclamation of the design of types for mass production. It seemed as if he had returned to the roots of the Arts and Crafts movement, to William Morris, and to the belief in handicraft as the sole viable guarantee of design quality. The earliest curriculum at the Bauhaus mirrored this position: the student was regarded as a sort of apprentice to an updated version of the medieval guild and was expected to learn weaving and other crafts which might eventually be useful in the decoration or articulation of living spaces and buildings. Parallel with these courses was the *Formlehre* (study of form) – instruction in the basis of formal arrangement, including composition and the study of colour, texture, and expression; eventually this course would, in fact, be taught best by painters of easel pictures, men like Paul Klee, Wassily Kandinsky and Oskar Schlemmer. However, preceding these middle levels of the Bauhaus education, every student would have to pass through the *Vorkurs* (foundation course) in which, under the direction of Johannes Itten (and, later, Josef Albers and Lázló Moholy-Nagy), he would be encouraged to 'unlearn' the habits and clichés of European 'academic' traditions, and to make a new beginning through experimentation with natural materials and abstract forms. Thus it was hoped that each student would tap his deepest instinctive expression in the definition of forms which would not have been

'imposed' by conventions. The ideology here was primitivism of a pure type: the interior world of the psyche was to reveal itself in all its naturalness, and working together with the nature of materials was supposed to generate authentic forms mirroring the deepest collective beliefs.

Johannes Itten, the first teacher of the *Vorkurs*, was a Swiss painter who had imbibed the pre-war educational ideas of Adolf Hölzel and Franz Čižek in Vienna, and believed in the central role of form/feeling training in education. Moreover, extending Symbolist ideas of the pre-war generation (especially some of Kandinsky's theories set forth in *Concerning the Spiritual in Art*, 1912), he held that there was an inner connection between certain visual configurations and certain states of mind. It is clear that Itten believed he was conducting his students into a form of religious initiation. He actually encouraged meditation, deep breathing exercises and physical training as aids to mental relaxation and self-discovery in his classes. Many students joined the Mazdaznan cult, which involved fasting, a vegetarian diet, and various spiritual disciplines. One pauses for a moment, to guess how Muthesius, the Werkbund theorist, or Rathenau, the pre-war client, might have reacted to this idea of an education for the designers of the future!

The work produced under Itten in the earliest sessions of the *Vorkurs* had a notably primitive flavour, which perhaps mirrored a prevalent state of gloom at the decline of the West, and a tendency to clutch on to tribal and magical artefacts for guidance. While Itten insisted that these productions should not be regarded as 'finished works of art', they were influenced by productions of the Zurich Dada avant-garde, including Kurt

Schwitters's rubbish constructions and the fantastic disassembled machine-collages of Max Ernst. The mood here was one of cultivated despair underlined by a sense of absurdity at the impact of a fully mechanized war. Moreover, like the Dadaists, Itten's students were evidently interested in African masks and fetishes. Altogether 'primitivism' seems to have been a major strand in 'Expressionist' attitudes of both the pre- and post-war periods.

While the Bauhaus potters could at least sell their wares, the majority of Bauhaus students had little chance to contribute their designs to the 'new cathedral of the future' in a Germany rent by inflation and poverty. However, in 1920, Gropius received a commission to design a house for Adolf Sommerfeld, a timber merchant who had managed to acquire the entire teak lining of a ship at a time when building materials were extremely scarce. Gropius drew up his design in 1920 and used the services of some of his students in the ornamentation of the interiors and the designs of some of the fixtures. Among these was Marcel Breuer, whose wooden furniture anticipated some of the ideas that he would later carry out in steel. The Sommerfeld House is a sophisticated essay in procured naïvety; it combines aspects of Gropius's pre-war formal and compositional approaches with a medievalizing mood, a vernacular image, and elements which may well have been influenced by Wright's ornamentation of Midway Gardens (1913). The suggestion has been made that the house followed some of the ideas of Josef Strzygowski on the probable origins of Indo-Germanic timber construction. In retrospect, the building seems very far from the machine-age architecture Gropius was to create only a few years later, but the peculiarities of the commission must be taken into account to balance too exaggerated a claim for Gropius's so-called 'Expressionism' in the immediate post-war years.

'Expressionism' is, in any case, an imprecise term: it is commonly used to group together a number of diverse artists working in Holland and Germany between roughly 1910 and 1925, and to describe a so-called 'anti-rational' tendency in art which – so the argument goes – manifests itself in works of complex, jagged, or free-flowing form. The premise here tends to be an over-simple one whereby 'rational' tendencies are taken to manifest

themselves in 'opposite' stylistic qualities like simplicity, rectangularity, and stasis. The difficulty comes in assuming that the frenzied, the emotive, and the bizarre must manifest themselves in a particular style, and in ignoring the fact that most works of art of any depth are characterized by tensions between emotional expressiveness and formal control. 'Expressionism' then is a term which is all the more slippery for the way it is sometimes employed to describe attitudes of mind, sometimes forms. It is used here in a spirit of caution and as a reluctant continuation of a well-worn convention according to which architecture by men like Michel de Klerk, Pieter Kramer and Theo van Wijdeveld in Holland, and Hans Poelzig, Bruno Taut, Otto Bartning, Hugo Häring, Mendelsohn and Gropius in Germany (in a particular phase of their lives) are customarily called 'Expressionists'. Even within the fold of Expressionism there were contrasting positions. For example, Van Wijdeveld, who published the magazine *Wendingen* (*Turnings*), championed a free-flowing, organic approach which made his compatriots Kramer and De Klerk seem relatively restrained by comparison.

The simplistic nature of such characterizations is revealed all the more obviously when one confronts the major talent. This is true, for example, of Erich Mendelsohn, who was born in Allenstein, East Prussia, in 1887, and whose work passed through several stages during which the basic elements of his mature vocabulary emerged gradually. He was 27 years old when the war broke out, and so was already set in several of his attitudes, but he had had little chance to practise. Mendelsohn was drawn to the work of Henry van de Velde, especially to the notion that buildings or pieces of furniture should be like vital organisms expressing their internal forces through their structure. While in Munich in 1911, he made the acquaintance of the Blaue Reiter (Blue Rider) movement (especially of the painters

213 Erich Mendelsohn, sketch for a factory, c.1915

214 Erich Mendelsohn, Einstein Tower, Potsdam, 1920–4

213

214

crematorium. The forms are sensed in a state of extreme tension ('dynamism' was the word the artist preferred) and the structural stresses are dramatized and accentuated so that parts and whole merge together. Mendelsohn criticized Behrens's architecture for its additive 'cardboard' quality and sought instead the integration of all details into the rhythms of a controlling image; at the same time he rejected the more extreme creations of the Dutch *Wendingen* Expressionists, who delighted in sprawling and eccentric plans, on the grounds that they lacked control. For Mendelsohn the tension of a work was increased and enriched by a fusion of the organic with a strong geometrical armature employing axes, and by an accentuation of an actual structural system. He wished, for example, to exploit the tensile capacities of steel, and the compressive ones of concrete, and to express these opposing forces simultaneously.

In 1920 Mendelsohn had a chance to translate his biomorphic fantasies and intuitions about a new world order into an actual building when he was asked to design an observatory at Potsdam. The Einstein Tower was to combine a telescope with an astrophysical laboratory for the exploration of spectroanalytic phenomena. Mendelsohn organized these requirements over an axial plan, with overlapping curved forms in high tension rising to a crescendo in a tower-telescope. The 'coelostat' in the crowning cupola was to reflect beams of cosmic light vertically into a subterranean laboratory where a mirror, tilted at 45 degrees, would direct them towards instruments generating and measuring spectra. The surfaces of the building were modelled as a free-form sculpture, windows and other openings being made so as to accentuate the overall dynamism. In fact the material was not at all the single 'plastic' sculptural one it appeared, but brick cosmetically coated in plaster and cement. Evidently the *idea* of the tower was related to Einsteinian themes of matter and energy.

Since the recognition that the two conceptions hitherto kept separate by science – Matter and Energy – are only different conditions of the same basic stuff, that nothing in the Universe is without Relativity to the Cosmos, without connection with the whole – since then, the engineer has abandoned the mechanical theory of dead matter, and has reaffirmed his allegiance to Nature. From primal states he deduces the laws determining interactions … The machine, till now the pliable tool of lifeless exploitation, has become the constructive element of a new, living organism.

Franz Marc and Wassily Kandinsky), and this may have encouraged a sense that visual ideas should spring from a deep central intuition, resonant with a vaguely cosmic element. Mendelsohn was Jewish, and recent attempts at linking his forms to the geometrical symbolism of ancient Jewish mystical texts should not be dismissed out of hand. Certainly he felt that it was one of the functions of art to make a spiritual order visible and to reveal the inner processes and rhythms of nature. He absorbed the theory of empathy, according to which the essential character of forms was perceived through a translation, mimetically, of the tactile sense into the forms of architecture.

Some of these concerns are already clear in a series of remarkable sketches Mendelsohn drew while serving in the trenches during the First World War. These are of building types such as film studios, a car-body factory, an observatory and a

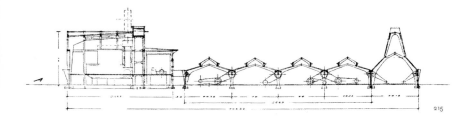

215

Mendelsohn hinted further at the intentions behind the Einstein Tower when he spoke of 'the union of the sensually appreciable mass and the transcendent mass of light'. In effect this was some modern version of a cosmic world-mountain with a divine ray penetrating to the shadows of the underworld and 'revealing' the laws of science to the initiated. Mendelsohn conceived of science and industry as sources of new social and formal energy. He wished to breathe the quality of life into his designs and to unite intellect and feeling, function and space.

In the early 1920s, in response to his own maxim 'Function plus dynamics is the challenge', Mendelsohn developed a more restrained vocabulary which avoided the extremes of dry functionalism and wilful formalism. In the design for a Hat Factory and Dye Works at Luckenwalde of 1921–3 the inert matter of an industrial programme and a standardized construction system were endowed with animistic vitality. The production process was arranged as parallel top-glazed sheds on a symmetrical plan with the Dye Works accentuating the standard section in a way which evoked, subliminally, a piece of headgear. Canted diagonal concrete beams were expressed in the sloping profiles; the tensions of belts, pulleys and rotary axles were conveyed by the overall slanting lines; and the external cladding in masonry with diagonal glazing was detailed so that all parts contributed to a dynamic and inevitable whole. The emphasis on actual and visual tension distinguished Mendelsohn's building from contemporary works by, for example, Le Corbusier or Rietveld. Moreover, like its ramshackle rural cousin, the Farm Complex at Garkau, near Lubeck (designed by Hugo Häring in 1924), Luckenwalde suggested that the supposed dichotomy between 'expression' and 'standardization' might be illusory.

Later in the 1920s, Mendelsohn's style became more stereometrical, as one may judge from the numerous department stores, cinemas and villas (many of them in and around Berlin) which he designed in this period. He resorted to some of the mechanistic analogies and characteristic forms of the new architecture (metal strip windows, hovering bands, curved cantilevered stairs, etc.), but a personal inflection and quality of inner energy made Mendelsohn's works unmistakable. He reverted time and again to parallel layers in plan and in section and to long horizontals in elevation. According to Mendelsohn: 'Contemporary man, in the excitement of his fast life, can only find balance in the stress-free horizontal.' His interest in the poetics of space aligned him more with Wright (whom he visited in 1923) than with the puritanical, 'functionalist' wing of modern German architecture. Among Mendelsohn's less-known works of the period was the Boiler House of the Rudolf Mosse Building of 1927, in which he articulated the steel frame and infills of glass and brick in a way that anticipated Mies van der Rohe's analogous treatment of IIT Chicago by more than a decade. Even in this utilitarian setting, Mendelsohn managed to bring the overall form alive.

Ludwig Mies van der Rohe (born 1886) was another German architect to pass through an 'Expressionist' phase in the years immediately following the First World War, before settling on a rectilinear style reliant upon the poetic accentuation of structure and technology. As we have seen (pp. 103, 142), Mies worked in the office of Peter Behrens from 1908 to 1911, but this apprenticeship came after experience in his father's stonemason's yard, and after time in the furniture business of Bruno Paul. He early identified the characteristics he wished to emulate in the stern and timeless structure of the ninth-century Palatine Chapel in Aachen, in the neo-classical severity and geometrical precision of Schinkel, and in the planarity and directness in the use of materials of Berlage. By the outbreak of the war, Mies had set up his own practice and designed a number of buildings,

including the Kröller-Müller House project of 1912
(Fig. 156), in a simplified classical style which laid
considerable stress on order, repose, symmetry, and
a rectilinear discipline. While still in his twenties, he
set in place many of the basic terms of his life's
work: the search for spiritual values, reduction to
simple forms, distillations from history, the order of
industrial technique.

   After the war, Mies van der Rohe directed the
architectural section of one of the radical groups
(in his case the 'Novembergruppe') and seemed
to share the visionary attitudes of Taut, Behne
and Gropius. His first entry to the Friedrichstrasse
Skyscraper competition of 1921 might almost be
read in Rationalist terms as an attempt at stripping a
tall, framed building down to its essential structure,
which was then wrapped with a glass curtain-wall
as a 'minimalist' solution – a sort of ultimate
destination of the tall, steel-framed building.
However, this would be to miss half the point. The
sharp forms, romantic silhouettes, and rich play of

218

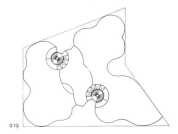

219

216

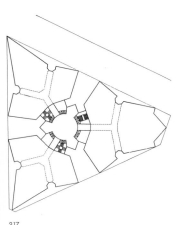

217

reflecting and transparent surfaces seem to suggest a crystal cathedral as well as an office building. The glass tower reveals Utopian sentiments not unlike those of Taut's glass visions, or Le Corbusier's drawings of transparent towers floating above the parks of the Ville Contemporaine of 1922. The suggestion is almost made that the tall building is an index of progressivist fervour, an image to be central to some vaguely defined new state. It is a sad irony of ensuing history that the pure glass prism should have started off as the symbol of a new faith and ended up as the banal formula for the housing of big business and bureaucracy.

In a further development of this scheme dating from 1922 (Fig. 218), Mies modified the plan to curved forms radiating from a circulation core and described his experiments with glass and transparency: 'At first glance the curved perimeter of the plan seems arbitrary. But these curves were determined by three factors: sufficient illumination of the interior; the massing of the building from the street; and lastly, the play of reflections.' Indeed, the fascination with *glass* recalls once again Scheerbart's poetic dreams, if not the adulation of lustrous, artificial, and floating materials in the proclamations of De Stijl. Mies seems to have been concerned with a redemption of sorts, through technological means. The forms of his architecture achieved the character of transcendental symbols. Le Corbusier explained the nature of this 'idealization' succinctly: 'Architectural abstraction has this about it which is magnificently peculiar to itself, that while it is rooted in hard fact it spiritualizes it …'

Mies van der Rohe's project for a Concrete Office Building in 1922–3 indicated a change of mood and form. Emphasis now shifted to the horizontal layering of space and to the expression of hovering planes, the building as a whole being formed from cantilevered trays on piers with brackets. The plan had a grid of structural posts with partitions inserted between them, but the arrangement still contained vestiges of classical organization in its symmetry, stress of the central axis, and articulation of a sort of 'floating' cornice plane at the top (perhaps influenced by Sullivan's similar treatment in the Carson Pirie Scott Store of 1899–1904). Visual tensions were also introduced in the way each floor was made to step out a little further than the one below; these optical 'corrections' might be related to the architect's 'Expressionist' tendencies; equally they may be seen as an intelligent reinterpretation of classical entasis. In 1923 Mies became a founding member of the G group in Berlin, which declared its opposition to 'formalism' and its theoretical support for forms closely related to practicality and construction under the banner of a 'New Objectivity' ('Neue Sachlichkeit'). He wrote of the Concrete Office Building in these terms:

… a house of work … of organization, of clarity, of economy. Bright, wide workrooms, easy to oversee, undivided except as the undertaking is divided. The maximum effect with the minimum expenditure of means. The materials are concrete, iron, glass.

Evidently the dreamer was coming back to earth. It should be mentioned that by 1923 the German economy was showing marked signs of improvement and that this made the adjustment

220

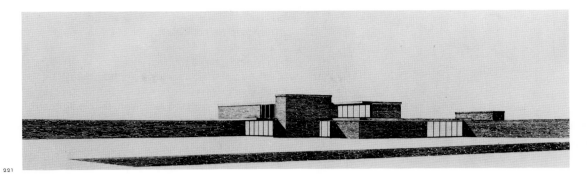

221

222

of the avant-garde to reality both desirable and tenable. Moreover, the Social Democratic leadership of the newly founded Weimar Republic was, for the most part, well disposed to modernism. There would soon be opportunities to build.

An artist's vocabulary takes time to absorb influences and mature. There may be a pivotal work in which a guiding concept is first revealed that then takes years to congeal with other discoveries. Mies van der Rohe's Brick Villa design of 1923 seems to have had this role in his evolution, for it was in this unbuilt project for a house to stand on open land near Berlin that he crystallized a key spatial idea. The plan was formed from a nexus of lines of varying length and thickness which seemed to expand gradually towards an implied infinity, or else to draw the distant views into the heart of the interior. These lines indicated wall planes which stopped in places to admit openings with full floor-to-ceiling glazing. Some of the masses rose to two storeys, and all roofs were flat with slender slabs. The spaces between the wall planes were activated by a principle of overlapping. There was no dominant axis, and the field of energies would have varied as one moved about. It was as if Mies had drawn together the rectangular restraint of the pre-war Kröller-Müller project with some of the formal concepts of modern art. The Brick Villa combined a generalized 'unhistorical' classicism in its proportions and profile with the pinwheel

223

qualities of Wright's pre-war house plans, and with a pattern of rhythmic lines and intervals inspired by the paintings of Mondrian, Van Doesburg or, perhaps, Lissitzky. Again one finds the fruitful translation of painting abstraction into architecture, although in this case the building volumes remained earth-bound; it was to take Mies some years to find a way of expressing such spatial ideas in a way that animated the whole fabric in three dimensions and that allowed some elements to float. Throughout his later career, he would oscillate continually between symmetrical axial plans and ones based on dynamic rotation and the centrifugal splay of planes.

Given the emphasis upon dematerialization and smooth planarity in the later formulation of an 'International Style', it is interesting that several of Mies van der Rohe's actual constructions of the mid-1920s should have relied upon the effects of rough, even rugged, brickwork. The Monument to the Communist Spartacist martyrs, Karl Liebknecht and Rosa Luxemburg, in Berlin of 1926 (now destroyed) was constructed from interlocking and projecting rectangular brick volumes of varying size and depth. Far from evoking the sort of machine abstraction favoured by, say, Oud or Rietveld, this work rejoiced in tactile materiality, an interplay between density, weight and shadow, and a strong handicraft feeling recalling Mies's admiration for Berlage. The

bricks themselves were purple in colour, many of them burnt rejects with snapped ends or rough shards. The Wolf House at Guben of 1925–7 took on the character of a virtual geological abstraction when seen in the context of its setting, with a cascade of rough stone terraces in the foreground and the building itself emerging in the background as so many brick platforms and cubic shapes. The Hermann Lange and Esters Houses in Krefeld (both of 1927) were both built from brick with relatively large areas of glass, and provided evidence of Mies's struggle to liberate the wall plane from the box. As late as 1924 he was still designing houses in a fully neo-classical style; his development of a consistent personal language was anything but straightforward.

The period from 1922 to 1923 seems to have been a crucial one in Germany (as in France) for the growth of modern architecture and the emergence of the International Style. For it was then too that a new orientation began to emerge at the Bauhaus and in Gropius's thinking and designing. In 1922 Van Doesburg visited Weimar and had a great impact on the school. From then on De Stijl-influenced forms became the basis of a general language of design, and a greater emphasis was again placed on reintegrating form and industry. Itten realized his time had come, and resigned. The *Vorkurs* was handed over to Lázló Moholy-Nagy, whose sophisticated 'Elementarist' vocabulary of rectilinear machine abstraction was in line with Van Doesburg and with artistic educational experiments in post-Revolutionary Russia (e.g. the Vkhutemas School). Gropius's own office design of 1923 was blatantly a three-dimensional translation of some of these ideas, as was his *Chicago Tribune* skyscraper design of 1922 (to be analysed in more detail in a later chapter). Gropius's 'style for the times', with which he sought to fulfil his dream of a new communal art, seemed increasingly to be reverting to the basic forms of circles, spheres, rectangles, cubes, triangles and pyramids. While the Bauhaus teachers may have denied strongly the existence of a 'Bauhaus style', the body of forms and ideas derived from geometrical abstract art endemic within the *Vorkurs* from 1923 onwards ensured that artists and craftsmen who later designed ceramics, fabrics, furniture, even buildings, did so on the basis of a sort of shared visual grammar.

In the year 1923 Gropius also published *Idee*

223 Ludwig Mies van der Rohe, Monument to Karl Liebknecht and Rosa Luxemburg, Berlin, 1926

224 K. J. Jucker and W. Wagenfeld, table lamp designed at the Bauhaus, 1923–4

225 Walter Gropius, director's office at the Bauhaus, Weimar, 1923

und Aufbau (*Idea and Construction*), a proclamation of Bauhaus philosophy, as the leading article accompanying the Bauhaus exhibition of that year. This was more sober and optimistic than the Foundation Manifesto had been. Once again we find Hegelian ideas concerning 'the spirit of the age' and the creation of forms appropriate to that spirit:

The dominant spirit of our epoch is already recognizable although its form is not yet clearly defined. The old dualistic world concept which envisaged the ego in opposition to the universe is rapidly losing ground. In its place is rising the idea of a universality in which all opposing forces exist in a state of absolute balance.

Gropius went on to outline the new orientation of the school: 'The Bauhaus believes the machine to be our modern medium of design and seeks to come to terms with it.'

This was clearly a shift in emphasis from the 1919 attitudes, and it appears that for Gropius 'coming to terms' with the machine included a two-level response: students should both learn about the design of types for mass production, and seek to design forms which crystallized the values of a mechanized epoch. Gropius's answer to how this might be done involved a curriculum divided between *Formlehre* and *Werklehre* (practical study). The apprentice would pass through a Vorkurs lasting six months, and instruction in a particular craft lasting three years, before being exposed to the master's programme, in which he would receive instruction in architecture and the technology of mass production. For it was central to Gropius's thesis – as it had been before the war – that the brutality of mere utilitarian design and the kitsch of consumerism might both be avoided if the most sensitive spirits could upgrade the basic formal character of the products of their period by the injection of feeling and sensitivity into utilitarian objects. As before, the highest aim was held to be the unity and synthesis of all the arts in the total work of art: a building. This would not merely have

224

225

226

other works of art attached to it, but would
synthesize the basic values of painting, sculpture,
and architecture into an emotive structure
which would symbolize the culture of the times.

By now Gropius was increasingly clear what form
this architectural synthesis might take:

Architecture in the last few generations has become weakly
sentimental, aesthetic and decorative … this kind of architecture we
disown. We aim to create a clear, organic architecture whose inner
logic will be radiant and naked, unencumbered by lying facings and
trickery; we want an architecture adapted to our world of machines,
radios and fast cars, … with the increasing strength of the new
materials – steel, concrete, glass – and with the new audacity of
engineering, the ponderousness of the old methods of building is
giving way to a new lightness and airiness.

In some ways, of course, this was a hotchpotch of
ideas derived from Futurism, the Deutscher
Werkbund, and De Stijl. What is interesting in this
context is the way the traumas of the war and the
ensuing few years had caused Gropius to infuse a
more mystical approach than in his pre-war years
and to reject the framework of Beaux-Arts axiality
in his planning. Instead, he adopted a spatial
conception which clearly derived from Van
Doesburg, Rietveld, Lissitzky, and Moholy-Nagy:

… the symmetrical relationships of the parts of the building and
their orientation towards a central axis is being replaced by a new

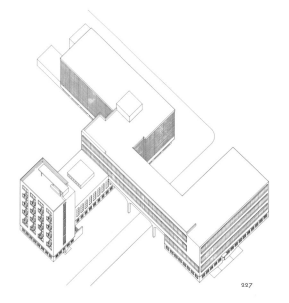

227

226 Walter Gropius,
Bauhaus, Dessau, 1926

227 Bauhaus, Dessau,
1926, axonometric
projection

228 Bauhaus, Dessau,
architectural studio,
c. 1929

229 Marcel Breuer,
'Wassily' tubular steel
armchair, designed at the
Bauhaus, 1926

conception of equilibrium which transmutes this dead symmetry of
similar parts into an asymmetrical but rhythmical balance.

Until 1925, Gropius had little chance to carry out
his new architectural ideas, apart from Bauhaus-
sponsored house-prototype experiments. But in that
year right-wing criticism of the Bauhaus reached
such a pitch that he decided to move the school.
The accusations included 'cultural degeneracy',
'Bolshevism', and a general foreignness, which some
of the good citizens of Weimar may have felt to be
irreconcilable with their genteel sense of a national
cultural tradition ornamented by Goethe and
classicism. However, some of the charges were an
eerie premonition of savage criticisms which would
return with new force in the 1930s, when they were
backed by the rising Nazi tide:

… what the Bauhaus offered in these first public displays stands so
far beyond the pale of any kind of art that it can only be considered in
pathological terms … The clearly recognizable philosophical attitude
which is entirely devoted to negating everything that exists causes the
Bauhaus people to lose all social connection, in the widest sense, with
the rest of the world … The work of the Bauhaus carries signs of the
deepest spiritual isolation and disintegration. The public therefore
rightly objects to the notion that in this manner young artists and
craftsmen in Thuringia who still have honest and sober aspirations
are simply going to be banned from a thorough education if the
Staatliche Bauhaus continues to exist in its present form. A small
band of interested persons, who for the most part are foreigners,
should not be allowed to suffocate the healthy mass of youthful
German art students like a layer of oil on clear water. Moreover,
this undertaking was only ostensibly based on artistic endeavours.

It was, in reality, intended to be politically partisan from the
beginning, for it proclaimed itself the rallying point of the
sky-storming Socialists who believed in the future and who wanted
to build a Cathedral of Socialism. Well, the reality around us shows
what this cathedral looks like.
    The Bauhaus in Weimar, too, contributes a fitting note with
its 'works of art' that are put together with the ingredients of a
junk pile …

The mayor of Dessau, by contrast, showed
considerable sympathy for the ideals of the school.
Within a year a site had been chosen on flat land
outside the town, on which to set the new building
that Gropius was to design for his institution. This
was an opportunity for him to create an exemplary
modern work in which all the arts would be
synthesized, and the philosophy of the school
expressed.
    The site was unconstricted and open; the
programme was large; so the solution would have
to break down the main volumes in such a way
that they could be experienced from any angle,
but without loss of overall coherence. Gropius
expressed the separate elements as rectangular
volumes of varying size, which were then linked
by intermediary oblongs containing corridors or
smaller rooms. Thus the art studios and the craft
workshops were linked by a bridge which crossed
over a road traversing the site. The next level of
articulation involved the accentuation of volumes
and planes, verticals and horizontals, through

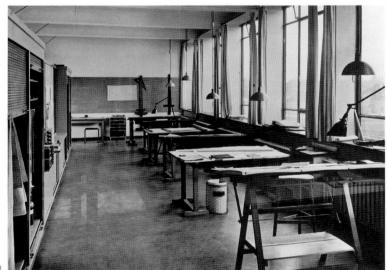

228

229

the composition of window surfaces: a set-piece Bauhaus exercise in the heightened expression of three-dimensional tensions in space, but one which still had to take practicalities into account. Gropius varied his fenestration to accentuate the largeness or smallness of the spaces within, and to admit various qualities of light according to function.

Gropius was given a large amount of plate glass at the time he commenced design, but the 'duty' of including this clearly did not violate his general aesthetic aims. The glazing far transcended its merely formal or functional characteristics, becoming an emblem of the machine age. At times the glass was laid flush with the façade, reinforcing the overall volumetric character of a space enclosed by a skin; at times it was recessed, accentuating the hovering white horizontal floor planes; and all of these choices of detail were to articulate the larger movements and themes of the design. What is so striking about the Bauhaus buildings in retrospect is the precision of the formal thinking, and the fusion of Gropius's earlier ideas and vocabulary. The experiences of pre-war Faguswerk and Deutscher Werkbund years; the spiritual idealism and Utopianism of the post-war period; the search for a language blending abstraction and mechanization – all are here, but synthesized into a statement which was paralleled in its assurance by perhaps only the Schröder House or Maison Cook at this stage in the unfolding history of the modern movement.

Indeed, the Bauhaus solution was more than a personal statement of assurance; it marked a major step in the maturing system of forms that many other architects were beginning to adopt. And just as in, say, the early phases of Gothic or Renaissance architecture there was a gradual coalescence of sources into a new, coherent system of expression, so, at the Bauhaus, the International Style came of age. There were lessons here for all who were trying to forge their own vocabulary within the shared values of the period, and soon after its completion, the building was published worldwide. Among the photographs were aerial ones which gave it the appearance of a giant Elementarist sculpture.

Gropius designed residences for the masters and for himself close to the school, so that by the end of 1926 there had grown up around Dessau a new colony which seems, initially, to have been better tolerated than it had been in Weimar. This was the Golden Age of the Bauhaus, with Wassily Kandinsky and Paul Klee teaching in the *Formlehre*, Lázló Moholy-Nagy and Marcel Breuer instructing in design, Josef Albers developing his studies in pure colour, Oskar Schlemmer producing his ballets, and the first apprentices beginning to make their mark in the outside world. The German public took a great interest in the school, which was constantly under fire for its supposed 'decadent' and 'subversive' tendencies. This public interest stemmed, in part, from the flood of articles and

230

231

232

books published by the Bauhaus staff, particularly the series of *Bauhausbücher*, which presented the ideas, in their respective fields, of Klee, Kandinsky, Moholy-Nagy and Gropius, among others.

It is instructive to examine some of the artistic and intellectual products of the later phase of the Bauhaus as a means of gauging its change of direction since the early Weimar years. In the factory workshops, for example, Marcel Breuer and Mart Stam evolved tubular-steel chair designs as models for standardized mass production; these had cantilevered overhangs and an airy and lightweight appearance in tune with Gropius's general ideal of finding forms which 'symbolized the modern world'. The contrast with Breuer's 1921 designs for chairs made of wood, with their exaggerated handicraft character and their far dumpier form, was

considerable. Similar contrasts can be seen over the six years between 1920 and 1926 for light fixtures, ashtrays, tapestries, and other objects; indeed, it is also instructive to compare the primitivist *Bauhütte* (workmen's hut) of the Sommerfeld House with 'the machine for teaching' of the Bauhaus buildings, for this reveals a similar shift in emphasis and meaning.

Now that the Bauhaus was at last settled in its new home, Gropius turned his attention increasingly to the problems of standardization in architecture. This concern was manifest in the housing studies he instituted in the school, which culminated in the rationalization of collective apartment blocks, open to space, light, air, and view. In 1928 he was employed by Siemens to build company workers' housing outside Berlin. After 1925, with the stabilization of the currency, cities like Frankfurt and Stuttgart had already employed such modern architects as Bruno Taut (who had sobered since his Expressionist days) and Ernst May to design large-scale, low-cost housing, and a variety of standard models had been evolved. In principle, the layouts frequently drew on English Garden City ideals (Chapter 14), but in form the houses were simple and cubic. This led critics to perceive in them an anti-German sentiment, and Gropius too was criticized for the supposed 'unnatural', 'anti-human' and 'mechanistic' character of his architecture. Thus as the new architecture extended beyond the scope of paper projects and private and specialized commissions, it was increasingly likely to be misunderstood, particularly when the 'factory aesthetic' invaded the sanctuary of the home. Especially in the hands of the hardest-headed Neue Sachlichkeit designers in Berlin, who eschewed 'formalism' and the pursuit of 'higher spiritual meanings', there was the constant danger that the intended aesthetic effects of sobriety and controlled repetition might be misread as blandness and lifelessness. The collision between architects' norms and the public's was often drastic.

Moreover, debates over the form of housing revealed a variety of positions within German modern architecture itself, from the die-hard attitudes of some of the adherents of the G group in Berlin, who continued to proclaim functionalist and Rationalist ideals, to the more 'spiritual' aspirations of men like Gropius and Mendelsohn, for whom formal poetics were essential to architecture. Even

233 Overall view of the
Weissenhofsiedlung,
Stuttgart, 1927

234 Hannes Meyer and
Hans Wittwer, project for
the Petersschule, Basle,
1926

233

Mies van der Rohe (who was in reality closer to
the latter camp than the former) could be found
parroting the attitudes of strict objectivity:

We reject all aesthetic speculation, all doctrine, all formalism. We
refuse to recognize problems of form; we recognize only problems of
building. Form is not the aim of our work; only the result. Form by
itself does not exist. Form as an aim is formalism, and that we reject.

In 1925, Mies had been asked by the Deutscher
Werkbund to oversee the design of the first major
exhibition of the organization since 1914. This was
to be devoted to housing prototypes, which were to
be co-ordinated in a single *Siedlung* (housing estate)
design on a brow overlooking Stuttgart (see also
Chapter 15). The majority of the contributors were
German, indeed were from Berlin (e.g. Mies
himself, Gropius, Ludwig Hilberseimer, Taut,
Scharoun), but J. J. P. Oud and Mart Stam were
invited from Holland, Victor Bourgeois from
Belgium, and Le Corbusier from France. Mies's
overall site plan was like an abstract sculpture of
different-sized blocks laid out to echo the form of
the terrain, with his own design for a block of 24

apartments at the crown. This was a simple
geometrical volume with fixed bathroom cores and
ingenious interior planning which began to explore
his later theme of a 'universal' interior space for
multiple uses. The windows were almost continuous
horizontal bands running between slender
stanchions that were flush with the façade plane. Le
Corbusier ended up designing two schemes – a
much accentuated 'Citrohan' dwelling, and a larger
version on dramatically advertised *pilotis*, both of
them polemical demonstrations of the 'Five Points
of a New Architecture'. Meanwhile, Hans
Scharoun's design at the other end of the site, with
its curved balcony forms and completely different
spatial character, was a reminder of the variety of
individual inflections within the modern movement.
Even so, the overwhelming impression when the
Weissenhofsiedlung was opened to the public in
1927 was of a general conformity of expression, in
which white, cubic volumes, stripped planar shapes,
open plans, and machine-age details were the
hallmarks. The extreme right in Germany was quick

to denounce the whole thing as further evidence of an international communist plot, and there were even caricatures of the Weissenhofsiedlung in which camels and Arabs were shown wandering around a supposedly degenerate 'kasbah' (Fig. 431). The extreme left rejected the exhibition as an irrelevant display of formalism, being particularly harsh about Mies van der Rohe's somewhat 'geological', sculptural massing in the overall layout. But to proponents and supporters of International Modern architecture, the exhibition transcended its fascinating lessons in housing by exhibiting directly the character of what was later (by Alfred Barr in 1932) to be called 'the International Style'. The same tag was adopted by Henry-Russell Hitchcock and Philip Johnson in their book *The International Style: Architecture Since 1922* (1932) (Chapter 15). In retrospect, 1927 appears to have been a crucial year of self-realization on an international front for the new architecture.

In 1928, Gropius left the Bauhaus and handed over the reins to the Swiss Hannes Meyer. Meyer's philosophy differed considerably from his predecessor's: he despised the formalist camp for its bogus 'humanism' and defined architecture laconically as the result of the equation 'function × economics'. It might be thought that this was a proclamation of the purest capitalist instrumentalism; in fact, it betokened a socialist puritanism which (despite Meyer's protests to the contrary) was expressed in an architectural style made eloquent by its lack of pretensions and its direct expression of functional volumes and the supposed 'ordinariness' of machine-produced components. To gain some idea of what Meyer's 'Marxist-materialist' position meant when translated into forms, one need only turn to his and Hans Wittwer's project for the Petersschule in Basle of 1926, in which the main rectangular volume containing the classrooms was envisaged as a neutral frame-building raised above the ground on stanchions and canted piers, and where secondary elements such as skylights and external stairs emerged directly but without any observable hierarchy or dominant compositional idea. In similar fashion the suspended terraces supporting the open-air playground (and releasing the ground level for circulation and the gymnasium) were expressed as decks in tension, pulled back towards the main volume by means of wires. Whether or not the Petersschule would have functioned well as a school can never be known, for it was not constructed, but it seems obvious that, despite the architects' claims to neutrality and analysis, this was a design imbued with a rhetoric of a kind. More than that, despite the architects' rejection of the notion of 'style', it demonstrated the character of Meyer's personal style only too clearly: a somewhat puritan and laconic rendering of Constructivist devices and preoccupations.

Meyer was far less squeamish about the radicalization of the Bauhaus than Gropius had been; he encouraged the design of cheap plywood furniture, and even pointedly changed the name of the 'architecture' department to 'building'. This lent extra support to the notion that the Bauhaus was indeed some sort of Trojan Horse of Bolshevism, and criticisms against the school became vitriolic in the late 1920s and early 1930s, especially when the Nazi party understood how much political capital was to be made from supporting aesthetic dogmas of a regionalist and nationalist bent. Finally, Mies van der Rohe oversaw the school in its last years up to its closure in 1933. Although the Bauhaus had a short life, the ideas and personalities which had activated it were not extinguished. When Gropius, Mies van der Rohe, Mohol-Nagy, Breuer and Albers emigrated to the United States in the late 1930s, they took their pedagogical methods and concepts with them. But this was merely one episode in the collapse and fragmentation of the Weimar Republic, and in the dissemination of modernism to foreign shores.

234

12

architecture and revolution in russia

We are convinced that the new forms of Soviet architecture will be found not by way of the imitation of the architectural forms of the past but on a basis of critical thinking … by way of a profound understanding of living processes and their translation into architectural form.
Alexander and Victor Vesnin, 1926

235 Ivan Leonidov, project for Lenin Institute of Librarianship, 1927, detail of model

While the forms of modern architecture created during the 1920s cannot be understood apart from the social ideals which gave rise to them, simplistic equations between ideology and formal usage should be regarded with suspicion. The German examples cited in the last chapter serve to show, among other things, a spectrum of political attitudes within the modern movement, from the spiritualized 'apolitical socialism' of Gropius to the far more hard-headed, left-wing stance of Hannes Meyer. Likewise, whatever Utopian yearnings they may have shared, the versions of an ideal life entertained by such artists as Le Corbusier, Gerrit Rietveld and Erich Mendelsohn varied considerably. One should be cautious then of imputing to the whole of modern architecture some monolithic ideology; a rich variety of values was operative, and in any case there is no direct step from a set of ideas to a set of forms.

These cautionary remarks seem pertinent to the Soviet architecture of the 1920s, since this emerged in a post-Revolutionary atmosphere which encouraged dogmatic assertions about the supposed 'truth' of modern architecture to the new social order. In fact the matter was by no means straightforward. Creative individuals were faced with the awesome task of formulating an architecture which was supposed to 'express' not so much the values of an existing order, but one it was felt *ought* to emerge from the progressive attitudes of the Revolution. Here, there were many problems. To begin with, it was clear that earlier national traditions could play little part, since these were 'tainted' with the values of the old regime or with a narrow nationalism inappropriate to the clarion call of a world revolution. Then it was uncertain what functions should be catered for to help in the general process of emancipation, and what images should be employed in the definition of a supposedly 'proletarian' culture. Perhaps even more basic: it was not entirely agreed whether architecture should follow or lead in the definition of a new order. Reviewing the various positions of the 1920s, one finds a multiplicity of reactions to these problems, all the way from those who considered architecture a minor element in social reform to those who felt, on the contrary, that artistic endeavours should be in the vanguard of change.

The turbulent artistic debates of the 1920s can scarcely be understood without some sense of the nineteenth-century background in Russia. Here the general rule was an eclecticism emulating European trends in support of the somewhat effete tastes of the aristocracy. Despite the strong hold which Slavic revivalism had on later nineteenth-century Russian architecture, the use of monumental, Western European classical prototypes continued well beyond the turn of the century; indeed, we shall see that this tradition was later co-opted to state purposes under the dictatorship of Stalin. The short burst of activity of the avant-garde in the 1920s was thus an interlude of a sort. However, it was preceded by the 'Populist' movement of the late nineteenth century, with its close attention to the realities of the masses; by the activities of the 'Ropetskaya' group (who took folklore as their guide); and by the tendencies culminating in the 'Proletcult' movement of 1918, which achieved an uneasy alliance between workers' unions and the aspirations of the avant-garde.

Thus an avant-garde culture of sorts had existed within the old order, drawing heavily on influences from Western Europe, particularly in painting and sculpture. However, these are art forms which may be created in private; in architecture there was little vital deviation from the reactionary modes of the nineteenth-century revivalists. It was not difficult for the later generation to see this tired aestheticism as a direct portrait of what they thought of as a defunct social system. Whatever the requirements of patronage, no major talent seems to have emerged, in any case, during the few decades preceding the Revolution. But the overthrow of the old order did not guarantee a vital wave in the arts, though it may have encouraged it. The period after 1917 was one of frenzied visual experimentation in which ideas tended to exist more on paper than anywhere else. This was natural, given the confused economic circumstances of the years up until about 1924, during which construction was all but impossible. It was an atmosphere that, as in Germany, encouraged a heady and impractical Utopianism.

The need to destroy all links with the reactionary past brought problems for the architect seeking a visual language of expression appropriate to new ideals. He could not create *ex nihilo* even if he did have 'a profound understanding of living processes'

(to paraphrase the Vesnin brothers). A vocabulary which fitted the situation had to be created, but where could the creator now turn for his forms? Could contemporary realities 'generate' a vocabulary on their own, or should the individual admit that he had to lay a personal interpretation on events? Should the individual building be treated as a neutral solution to a carefully analysed programme with the stress on practicality? Or should the artist seek metaphors and images which distilled his excitement at the post-Revolutionary possibilities? Perhaps he should attempt to create provocative emblems which gave a hint of the future state; or perhaps he should concentrate on the design of prototypes for later mass production in the service of the greater number. Such questions and dilemmas as these underlay the debates and formal explorations of the late 1910s and the early 1920s. Such 'bibles' as the writings of Marx and Engels supplied little guidance, since these could be pulled in to support a wide divergence of approaches: neither writer had had more than a confused idea of the way 'art' had functioned in the cultures of the past.

The first crucial discussions which would have a direct impact on architecture and town planning were held in February 1918 when the Pan-Russian executive committee abolished private property and proclaimed the socialization of the soil. Artists found an immediate outlet in the design of propaganda trains and posters, and the painting of walls with strident visual statements. Art schools newly set up in Moscow and the provinces overthrew the system of Beaux-Arts education, and introduced ideas of basic design (derived from abstract art), and theories based on a belief in a universal aesthetic language (already present in the non-objective paintings and high-minded theories of Malevich's 'Suprematism'). 'Constructive' artists like Naum Gabo and Antoine Pevsner attempted to create a scientific-technological sculpture from steel, glass and plastic, in which Cubist and Futurist conceptions of sculpture were extended to basic rhythms of space and form designed to emulate the structures of physics. Furious debates ensued concerning the legacy of bourgeois 'spiritual' aesthetics: should the artist reintegrate with social functions by concentrating on the design of utilitarian objects? The idealistic and the pragmatic were bridged by El Lissitzky, whose abstract

236 El Lissitzky, *Proun IE (City)*, 1921. Lithograph, 9 x 11 in (23.3 x 28.3 cm). Stedelijk Van Abbemuseum, Eindhoven

236

'Prouns' were conceived as ideograms with a Utopian content, and also as a basic form-language applicable to sculpture, furniture, typography or buildings. Nikolai Ladovsky's psycho-technical laboratory at the Vkhutemas School encouraged free experimentation with basic geometrical shapes to discover the rules of a new language of composition which might, when economic reconstruction allowed it, eventually pervade architectural thinking and even the form of the city.

A partial solution to the problem of originating a contemporary architectural vocabulary without reference to the institutions or images of Tsarist Russia lay in the groundwork already done in Western Europe towards the definition of a modern architecture. Futurist ideas were co-opted, shaved of their proto-Fascist character, and mated with Marxist ideals in the quest for suitable metaphors to express the supposed inner dynamism of the revolutionary process. Machine-worship became a tenet of faith, as if mechanization could be thought of as identical with the social and historical path of progress. This was not, perhaps, a curious choice of emphasis, given the 'backwardness' of the Soviet Union in industrial terms, but for this same reason it meant that an imagery was elaborated which was

quite foreign to the large majority who were peasants. Besides, the activities of the avant-garde were largely restricted to the cities, and had little to give to evolving vernacular traditions.

Thus the avant-garde – a curious minority class of its own – took on the task of formulating a visual language supposed to be alive with the aspirations of Soviet society as a whole. Intrinsic to this position was the belief that the artist must have some special intuition of the deeper processes of society, which would transcend mere populist expression. In the Soviet Union an iconography was evolved which blended the floating planes of abstract art with direct quotations from the factory floor and the production line. A rhetorical and highly demonstrative machine fetishism was often the result, in which the factory aesthetic, ships' hooters, and elaborate splays of wires might be assembled into dramatic architectural collages posing as theatrical sets (e.g. stage designs commissioned for Vsevolod Meyerhold's productions of around 1920) or as entire buildings. For the time being, the question of the possible irrelevance of all this fantasy world to a country whose technology lagged far behind that of Western Europe, and whose intelligentsia, however well

237

237 Vladimir Tatlin,
project for a Monument
to the Third International,
1919–20

238 El Lissitzky, design
for a Lenin Tribune, 1924

intentioned, was divorced from the values of the majority, was conveniently left aside.

Some sense of the new orientation in Russia is to be gleaned from Vladimir Tatlin's paper project for a Monument to the Third International of 1919–20. Inside two interlacing spirals of open structural lattice-work were suspended three volumes – a cube, a pyramid, and a cylinder – containing the various congress halls of the state. Each of these chambers was designed to revolve at a different speed – once a year, once a month, and once a day – in accordance with the supposed cosmic importance of the enclosed institutions. Tatlin intended that the monument should be 400 metres tall (even taller than the Eiffel Tower) and painted red, the colour symbolizing the Revolution. The inspiration for this romantic display of engineering seems to have come from such diverse sources as oil derricks, fairground constructions, and Futurist images such as Boccioni's spiralling *Bottle Unfolding in Space*. However, the transparent lattices and abstract sculptural forms were more than a display of private virtuosity; the spirals were intended as suitable expressions of the new order. Nikolai Punin wrote of the inherently vital and dynamic characteristics of the spiral: 'The spiral is a line of liberation for humanity: with one extremity resting on the ground,

238

it flees the earth with the other; and thereby becomes a symbol of disinterestedness, and of the converse of earthly pettiness.' In this case, though, the tilt of the main volumes was contained within a double helix drawing gradually to a resolution at the top. It may be that this was intended to have the extra significance of an image of the dialectical-historical process, between thesis and antithesis, with the eventual harmony of a synthesis. If so, Tatlin's tower must be read as an emblem of Marxist ideology, in which the actual movements of the parts, and the sculptural dynamism of the armature, symbolized the very idea of a revolutionary society aspiring to the 'highest state' of an egalitarian, proletarian Utopia.

Much like Boullée's grandiose visions of the late eighteenth century (see p. 28), Tatlin's tower was scarcely buildable at the time it was conceived; the model itself was assembled from old cigar-box wood and tin cans. But the power of the idea was still considerable. Had it been built, it would have dwarfed all nearby buildings, effectively challenging and overbearing the monumental churches and palaces of the *ancien régime*. Thus, in iconographic terms, it might be right to speak of Tatlin's design as another attempt at realizing a 'Cathedral of Socialism' (see p. 184), dedicated in this case to nothing less than a new religion. Parallels can be found in other media. There is a notable similarity of theme, for example, in Sergei Eisenstein's slightly later film *Battleship Potemkin*, in which the notion of salvation through revolution was also played out with the help of mechanistic images (e.g. the battleship), and through a scheme of alternating contrasts using montage. What is so striking about each of these works of art is the way in which revolutionary values were sublimated within the formal structure in a manner far transcending banal realist portrayal.

Although a large proportion of the small amount of building carried out in the early 1920s in Russia was conservative in nature, there were gradual incursions of the avant-garde, especially in the world of architectural competitions. The competition for the Palace of Labour of 1922–3 drew forth a rich variety of solutions. The programme envisaged a colossal 8,000-seat auditorium, another one for 2,500, a meteorological observatory, an astrophysical laboratory, a social-science museum, a museum of

239

240

labour, a library, a restaurant for 6,000 diners, and a myriad of offices. The institution was a novel one and little help could be found in consulting traditional types. The solution produced by Alexander and Victor Vesnin made much of the articulation of the different functions in simple contrasting forms linked by dramatic circulation bridges. The theatres and main social spaces were contained in an oval zone, the administrative areas in a rectangular tower. Reinforced-concrete construction was not simply employed but sculpturally heightened through the lattice-work expression of the vertical and horizontal members of the frame. A bold attempt was made to express the dynamic interpenetration of volumes, as well as a degree of axial formality appropriate to the institutional character of the scheme. The main forms were then liberally dressed with the paraphernalia of radio masts, taut wires, and ships' hooters; once again a communal building was expressed, essentially, as a social engine. But, like so many other projects of the period, this one was not built.

The Vesnin brothers also designed a scheme for the Moscow headquarters of the newspaper *Leningrad Pravda* in 1924. This exhibited a new degree of formal control – a more successful fusion of the devices of abstract art with the articulation of function and mechanistic moving parts. The building was envisaged as a sort of 'skyscraper kiosk' and succeeded in embodying the architects' excitement at the notion of a modern communications centre. The attached searchlight, the revolving billboards and the visible movement of lifts within their glass cages all recalled the Futurist notion of a building as a sort of machine, if not precisely Sant'Elian images of a new architecture made of light materials, with lifts snaking up and down. But the rhetorical imagery was here submitted to a rigorous geometrical and functional control, with the floor slabs expressed as thin planes and the roof slab as a thicker 'cornice'. It is ironical that such a celebration of modern technology should have been conceived in a country where, well into the 1920s, even reinforced-concrete buildings had to be created by the crudest mass-labour and handicraft methods. The irony is doubled when one considers that in the United States, where the appropriate technology was in existence, little attempt was made to celebrate it. Thus the architect

239   Alexander and Victor Vesnin, competition project for Palace of Labour, 1923

240   Competition project for Palace of Labour, first- and ground-floor plans

241   Alexander and Victor Vesnin, competition project for the *Leningrad Pravda* Building, Moscow, 1924

of the Soviet avant-garde found himself trapped in a Utopian hall of mirrors, dreaming up unbuildable schemes for a society of uncertain form. One senses something of the same difficulty with Lissitzky's extraordinary schemes for 'cloud-hanger' skyscrapers with dramatic horizontal overhangs cantilevered from giant vertical shafts. These bridge-like elements were to hover above key Moscow intersections.

The Exposition des Arts Décoratifs in Paris in 1925 gave the Soviet Union the opportunity to design a pavilion as a showcase of industrial goods; clearly the building would also have to be a banner of Soviet ideology. The architect chosen for the task was Konstantin Melnikov, a member of the Association of New Architects (ASNOVA), a former teacher at the Vkhutemas School, and an artist dedicated to the notion that a dynamic sculptural expression, stirring the masses, was the right style for the new order. His pavilion was a masterly propaganda instrument. The plan was traversed by a diagonally ascending way, allowing views on to the exhibits on either side and effecting the penetration of inner and outer spaces. The volumes were rhomboidal in form, rather than simply rectangular, and the illusions of perspective that this produced added to the visual tension of the design. The pavilion was demountable and made of wood, but its *imagery* was a flagrant celebration of the factory aesthetic. For those untutored in the associational meanings of modern architectural forms (presumably the majority of the visitors) the identity and meaning of the building were reinforced by a sort of pergola that straddled the walkway, made of interlacing girders and hammers and sickles. The contrast between this deliberately humble, cut-to-the-bone treatment and the chintzy, consumerist kitsch of most of the other national pavilions can only have added to the force of the messages. Only Le Corbusier's Pavillon de l'Esprit Nouveau, tucked to one side of the exhibition site, was equal to this display of probity. None the less, both artists' designs were curious microcosms of larger world-views striving for an actual social outlet; they stood like Utopian fragments alongside the sophisticated but shallow expressions of middle-class commercialized taste, exotically drenched in the new possibilities of expression revealed by Art Deco.

241

Thus the period up to 1925 was one of tentative paper experimentation, or of small-scale building hypotheses, for the Soviet avant-garde. The second half of the 1920s – as in Germany – was a period of realization as the modern architects began to imagine new social functions as well as new forms. Melnikov himself was among the first architects to design clubs or public buildings containing theatres, communal libraries, and lounges for the dissemination of ideas, the celebration of public life, and a controlled form of 'leisure'. Again Melnikov could not conceive of such functions in neutral formal terms: he sought to translate the programmes into dynamic sculptural volumes. In his design for the Rusakov Workers' Club in Moscow of 1927–8, the auditorium converged on the stage, and its rear extension was arranged to overhang the back of the building in three sections. The sharp intersections and contrasts of shape were articulated in details. Melnikov, like other members of the ASNOVA

School, tended to believe there was an underlying language of forms which could be relied upon to elicit specific emotions in the spectator. He saw it as the task of architecture to co-opt this universal language of form in the service of the vital themes of revolution.

This position was heavily attacked on the grounds that it was rooted in bogus, bourgeois, 'idealistic' aesthetics. A typical critique emerged in the theories of the Union of Contemporary Architects (OSA) – including Fedor Yalovkin, Moisei Ginzburg, Mikhail Barshch, Viacheslav Vladimirov and the Vesnin brothers – which pilloried ASNOVA for its self-indulgence and lack of attention to practicality. In a well-documented debate which took place in 1929, Yalovkin put forward the OSA 'Constructivist' position and criticized the ASNOVA descendants of the 'formalist camp':

The principal difference between the present associations consists in their very aim, i.e. for the constructivists (the OSA), the social role of architecture is essentially as one of the instruments for the building of socialism by means of the collectivization of life, by means of the rationalization of labour, by means of the utilization of scientific data and so on, whereas for [the formalists] the social role 'acquires a special significance' and the essence of this 'special significance' is that you make architecture an art, not contemplative but 'active', which 'must become a means' for the liberation of the masses, a powerful lever in the building of socialism and a new collectivist way of life, organizing the psyche and actively educating the will and feeling of the masses towards the struggle for communism … Their pathetic ejaculations about art are reminiscent of antediluvian searchings for a god; for we believe that what is needed is not the invention of an art … but work on the organization of architecture, proceeding from the data of economics, science, and technology. It is to this great work that we call all the architects of the Soviet Union.

243

At the opposite end of the spectrum from formalist tendencies were functionalist ones, according to which the new forms would be dictated by sociology and technique alone. In this case the criticism could be produced that the functionalist was imitating the debasement of life implicit in Western industrialization. The OSA group managed in their ideology and their architecture to steer carefully between these extremes, despite their tendency to veer towards a severe puritanism of expression. Such architects of the group as Moisei Ginzburg turned their attention to housing and to the creation of collectivist dwellings. Inherent in Ginzburg's plans and in the various theoretical researches of the OSA was the belief that the clear logic of planning and the sanity of orderly forms could have some limited moral effect on the gradually evolving forms of society. A typical product of the group was the Narkomfin Apartment Building built in Moscow in 1928–30. The concept marked a transition between the traditional apartment house containing entirely private flats and a new type of communal housing in which some areas were shared, and in which a judicious balance was sought between the individual, the family and the larger social group. The impact of Le Corbusier's formal vocabulary was indisputable: the housing was contained in a long low box lifted from the ground on *pilotis*, and the strip window was here used as a primary device for articulating the whole.

The OSA devoted much time to housing studies, considering such questions as the functional family cell, the minimum standards commensurate with mass production, and the meaning of different access spaces. The Narkomfin Building was a laboratory of their social researches. It incorporated a variety of 'F-type', the minimum, one-family units, with large 'K-type' units with three rooms on two levels. The section of the building as a whole was an ingenious invention using a three-over-two arrangement. Thus living rooms on one side of the building could be ample in height and well lit, while bedrooms and bathrooms could be smaller, more economic in their use of space, and contained on the other side of the building. But this functional arrangement had further properties: the 3 : 2 system allowed access decks to be threaded along the entire length of the building at every third level, and apartments to be jigsawed together so that views and

245

light on both sides could be enjoyed. These 'street decks' were more than mere functional access corridors, however; they could be seen as symbolic elements expressing communal aspirations. In the Narkomfin Building they were actually heated to encourage interaction all through the year. The other communal parts of the building, such as the canteen, kitchen, gymnasium, library and day nursery, were contained in an earthbound rectangular element linked to the main oblong by a bridge. Le Corbusier's idea of the roof terrace was here employed as a further communal space for use in the summer months.

It would be preposterous to claim that Ginzburg and his associates were not concerned with aesthetic matters in such a crisp and well-proportioned formal statement. But the contrast with the sculptural acrobatics of the ASNOVA architects is still obvious; the OSA sought to generate the overall volumes of a building from a stringent rationale taking into account living-patterns, circulation, cost, building procedure, etc. This 'diagram' was then translated into a restrained aesthetic vocabulary which suggested social values of co-operation and stability.

The arrangement with a slab for private living and distinct volumes for communal elements was much used for student hostels in Russia in the late 1920s (Fig. 248) and may have had a direct influence on Le Corbusier's Pavillon Suisse in the Cité Universitaire, Paris, of 1930–1. Indeed, by 1927 Soviet architecture was well known in European publications, and there was a regular traffic of

244

ideas to and fro. The role of Russian abstract art at the Bauhaus has already been mentioned, and was no doubt aided by the impact of an exhibition of Soviet art (including Lissitzky's Proun room), in Berlin in 1922; but influences clearly worked the other way too, and it is scarcely an exaggeration to claim that without Le Corbusier, Soviet architects of the late 1920s would have had far less idea than they did how to translate their visions into forms and then into three-dimensional realities.

In 1927, Le Corbusier was invited to design a major project in Moscow: the Central Union of Consumer Co-operatives known as the 'Centrosoyus'. The programme called for the combination of office spaces with lecture halls, conference rooms and large public forums. The challenge that this problem posed to Le Corbusier's vocabulary was in some ways analogous to the one posed by the League of Nations competition of the same period. The architect had to 'stretch' an architectural system which had been applied initially to the design of villas, and in the process was forced to discover means for articulating hierarchies of varied functions, and for breaking down the overall

form into discrete parts which still had, somehow, to be integrated harmoniously. In both schemes it was also necessary to respond to different site conditions on each side. The design process of the Centrosoyus shows the architect grappling with these problems and evolving a scheme in which circulation was a strong organizing principle, and primary and secondary axes were used to define major routes and emphases. The result relied strongly on the increased spatial complexity manifest in his paintings in the previous two or three years. The Purist language was being forced to become more ambiguous and multivalent. But the Centrosoyus seems to indicate too that Le Corbusier wished to outdo the Constructivists on their own ground, by taking over from them devices like the sculptural expression of circulation zones, and the dynamic equilibrium of asymmetrical volumes across space; indeed, he attempted to handle these elements with greater control and conviction than in the originals. The Centrosoyus also marked one of the architect's first attempts at employing a fully double-glazed façade with the help of a crude mechanical heating and ventilating system, that

246 Moisei Ginzburg and Ignati Milinis, Narkomfin Apartment Building, Moscow, 1928–30

247 OSA group, study of an 'F type' apartment, 1930, section and plans

248 Ivan Nikolayev, collective housing complex for Textile Institute apprentices, Moscow, 1930

249 Le Corbusier, Centrosoyus Building, Moscow, second project model, 1928

246

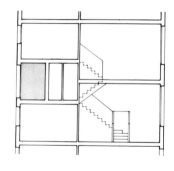

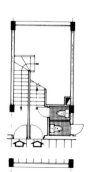
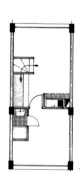

247

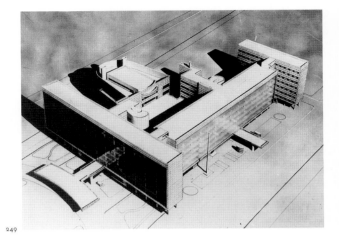

would not have been able to handle the climatic extremes of Moscow's summers and winters. The bulbous forms of the auditoriums and circulation ramps were quickly absorbed into the general vocabulary of modern architecture and devalued to the level of official cliché in numerous ensuing state projects.

The dream of a sort of secular equivalent of a cathedral – a collectivist emblem signifying an integrated culture – seems to have lain close to the surface of Soviet architectural imagination throughout the 1920s. But there were few individual artists equal to the imaginative challenge. One architect whose work far transcends the division between formal expression and functional necessity expressed in the OSA/ASNOVA debates was Ivan Leonidov. Like Le Corbusier, whom he much admired, he seems to have been able to forge a synthesis of poetry and fact, of form and function, which at the same time dug to deeper levels of aspiration than the pantomime technocrats. This is clear in his proposal for a Lenin Institute of Librarianship of 1927. The auditorium, conceived as a 'Planetarium: a scientific optical theatre' was expressed as a glass sphere, a form which conveys simultaneously a universalizing intention and a metaphor of enlightenment. But this world image is not earthbound; it has almost the character of a balloon which wishes to pull free of its cables and rise into the air. The twin themes of visual lightness and spatial hovering seem intimately connected with a content of a metaphysical sort, as if the architect

was attempting to extract an almost sacral meaning from the pantheon of Soviet heroes and Marxist ideas. The other main element is the stack tower, expressed as a slender skyscraper to which delicate power lines and radial antennae are attached in tension. The space between and around these two forms is activated by the horizontal planes of offices which intersect the round podium on which the main sculptural objects are placed. Elements slide past one another in the manner of a Lissitzky abstraction, or even a 'pinwheel' Wrightian plan, and extend towards the corners of the world. Leonidov's scheme incorporates a full range of Suprematist compositional devices and indicates the maturity of a style phase, but a mere listing of elements scarcely does credit to the power of the idea. Once again, one is left guessing as to how the architect might have translated this fantasy into material form.

So architects in the Soviet Union applied their minds to the full range of social functions in the 1920s, including housing, social clubs, theatres, offices, libraries, dams, factories, and state institutions. But they also gave thought to the ideal relationships between them all, to town planning, and even to the spatial reorganization of the countryside. Artistic imagination here attempted to work hand in hand with economic reorganization at the largest scale in the generation of a new visual and spatial culture. Of the various urban planning paradigms adopted from the West and transformed, the linear city (pioneered by the Spaniard Arturo Soria y Mata in the late nineteenth century on the

250

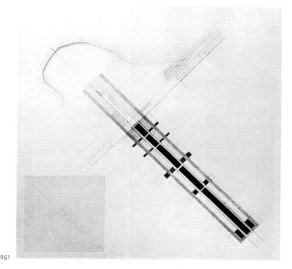

251

By the end of the 1920s, though, the various avant-garde groups had come under the increasingly close scrutiny of central state control. Some leaders of the Bolshevik Party considered that traditional images of national consolidation, including classical and eclectic monumentality in architecture, might serve the purposes of the state better than the imagery of modern architecture. Meanwhile, the divergence between avant-garde values and popular ones was becoming increasingly clear. It is ironical that the products of the Soviet modern movement should have been accused of bourgeois formalism at almost exactly the same time as the products of the German modern movement were pilloried as 'Bolshevist' and un-German. Totalitarian manipulation of visual culture took different forms, but the triple pressures of state control, emphasis on regional values, and the need for centralized traditional images of state power have eerie similarities in both Stalin's Russia and Hitler's Germany.

The drama in which the modern movement played out its final act was the Palace of the Soviets competition of 1931. The programme called for a colossal building incorporating two auditoria, press galleries, meeting rooms, libraries, and a monumental image equal to the progressivist technical and social aspirations of the Soviet state. Entries poured in from all over the world and included major ideas from Gropius, Mendelsohn, Perret, and Le Corbusier. Some of the architects chose to pack the functions into a single dynamic

250 Trifon Varentsov, urban project for regional centre, 1927

251 Vitaly Lavrov, linear city proposal, mid-1920s

252 Ivan Leonidov, project for a Lenin Institute of Librarianship on the Lenin Hills, 1927, plan

253 Project for a Lenin Institute of Librarianship, model

basis of an extendable spine of transport) was perhaps most pertinent, because it fused together the means of production (agricultural and industrial) with networks of power and circulation, allowed the interpenetration of nature and the city, and encouraged the integration of rural and industrial proletariats in spatially ordered surroundings (Chapter 14). Social 'condensers' (clubs, auditoriums, etc.) and family dwellings could be evenly distributed in bands parallel to the main routes, and the linear, non-hierarchical character of such a city form was felt to be particularly appropriate to the egalitarian aspirations of the inhabitants. Thus the linear form was adopted in the design of the new city of Magnitogorsk in the late 1920s.

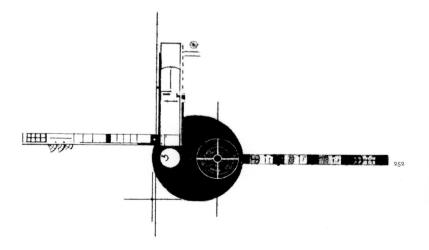

252

253

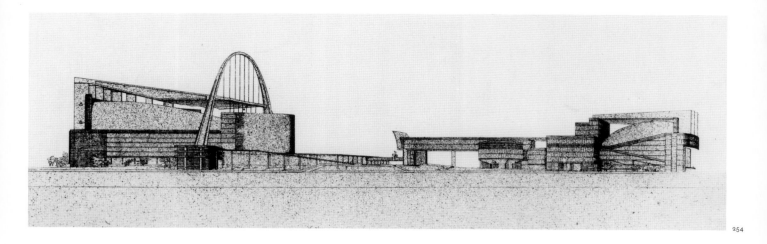

254

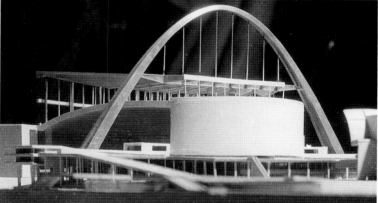

255

sculptural form, while others separated out the
volumes of the two main auditoriums and arranged
large machine-age sculptures against the existing
Moscow skyline. In principle, this was the approach
of Le Corbusier, whose entry must be ranked as
one of his masterpieces. The two auditoriums were
arranged on the same axis and were direct sculptural
expressions of the acoustically optimized forms of
the interior profiles. It was an idea the architect
had employed in his League of Nations proposal.
Instead of resorting to domes or other defunct
iconography, Le Corbusier invented a new
symbolism with, clearly, some prompting from
Tatlin and earlier fantasies of Constructivism. The
roof of the main hall was suspended on wires from
a parabolic arch which would have dominated
the skyline of Moscow (and which may have been
inspired by Freyssinet's aircraft hangars of
1916–21). The lower auditorium had a scarcely less
dramatic structural treatment: cantilevered flanges
were splayed in plan to create a focal concentration
on the space between the two main volumes. Here
there was an open-air platform – a sort of modern
agora – linked to the surrounding public space of
the city by ramps and walkways. Within were
hypostyle halls of *pilotis* where, presumably, the
business of debate and discussion would have
continued between the main sessions. With its
spaces in dynamic tension, its transparent structures,
and its great areas of assembly, the project posed
the image of a mechanism of collective life: a

participatory democratic monument. Once again
Le Corbusier demonstrated his ability to probe the
underlying meaning of a social programme and to
translate this into aesthetic forms.

But his palace was not to be. The model went
back to Paris, as Gropius's did to Berlin. Official
taste intervened and gave the prize to a Soviet
entry by Boris Iofan (having also honoured the
classicist I. V. Zholtovsky). The project eventually
approved resembled a stepped mausoleum and was
surmounted by a colossal statue of Lenin, even larger
than Manhattan's Statue of Liberty. The supporting
steel frame of the building was encased in a massive,
ill-proportioned cladding of stone, and the imagery
bordered on kitsch, for all its 'acceptable' Socialist

Realism. Evidently the dreamers of modern visions had outstripped the aspirations of their potential clientele and, in the process, had pointed to severe problems of communication between the perceptions of an avant-garde steeped in the devices of abstraction, and the values of a mass culture as envisioned by a centralized state. Indeed, in 1932, the remaining architects of the avant-garde were marshalled under state control and either left architecture, or else immersed themselves in the official but apparently uninspiring doctrines of Socialist Realism. Melnikov's project for a Ministry of Heavy Industry of 1934, with its grotesque statuary and heavy-handed machine ornaments, was an extreme and even caricatured response to the new kind of statement being demanded.

But as well as being representative of the problems of state interference, Iofan's victory in the Palace of the Soviets competition may perhaps also be seen as an epitaph to the avant-garde's premature attempt at visualizing the architectural forms of a new society without sufficient support from the wider community. Despite their constant protestations to the contrary, the Soviet modern architects – in their rise and fall – had acknowledged schisms, typical of Western industrialized culture, between history and modernity, the artist and 'the people'. All too often they had resorted to a secularized version of Kandinsky's conception of the artist as a prophet of new forms. 'The *Volk* is not with us', Klee had written in his diaries; the same was to prove true in a variety of areas of modern culture between the wars.

256

13

skyscraper and suburb: the u.s.a. between the wars

All previous experience in architecture is the inherited property of America, and should be taken every advantage of. Each beautiful thought, form, and mode that is not unsuited to the climate and the people, ought to be studied, sifted, and tested, its principles elucidated, and itself improved on; but the past should always be looked on as a servant, not as a master.
Calvert Vaux, 1857

257 Frank Lloyd Wright, Freeman House, Los Angeles, 1923–4, interior

The decade between the end of the First World War and the Wall Street crash of 1929 was a boom period for building investment in the United States. This was mirrored directly in the profile of the large cities, in the mushrooming of skyscrapers, the rapid growth of highways, and the creation of suburban sprawl. The resultant pressures on urban services were overwhelming, but perceptions of this crisis of mechanization were far from most architects' minds. Intellectual forces were co-opted in an effort of *laissez-faire* expansion whose motives and values went largely unexplored. The anxiety-laden probings and apocalyptic Utopianism of the European avant-garde had few equivalents in the United States. Reformist yearnings were reserved, on the whole, for anti-urban dreams, or for the microcosm of the individual dwelling, usually in a context isolated from the city, where time-honoured American themes concerning the individual's contemplation of the sublimities of nature could be played out once again.

The search for alternative social and urbanistic structures, which played such a central role in European modern architecture, was foreign indeed to a country in a conservative mood that could draw upon the cosy mythology that any necessary revolutionary steps in the polity had occurred over a century before. Moreover, in the visual arts there was scarcely an equivalent to the avant-gardes of the main metropolitan centres of France and Germany. The Armory Show in New York of 1913 had presented a selection of recent European painting and sculpture, and made Cubism and abstraction widely known in America, but these tendencies had been regarded by the majority as suspect, foreign imports. Even the activities of Alfred Stieglitz's magazine and art gallery '291', which cut through academic and sentimental clichés to the imaginative potentials of the New World, had little impact on architecture. Despite the Futurist overtones and urban romanticism in some of Stieglitz's and Edward Steichen's photographs, and in the work of such painters as Charles Sheeler, Joseph Stella, and Marsden Hartley, architects remained unmoved by the technological wonders of their country. Engineering continued to be seen as merely the material means for supporting historically sanctioned combinations of styles which were, so to speak, stuck on. Hartley put the matter succinctly:

I often wonder why it is that America ... has not the European courage as well as capacity for fresh developments in cultural matters ... There is ... an obvious lethargy in the appreciation of creative taste and a still lingering yet old-fashioned faith in the continual necessity for importation. America has a great body of assimilators and out of this gift for uncreative assimilation has come the type of art we are supposed to accept as our own.

Cultural critics such as Lewis Mumford (e.g. *The Brown Decades*, 1931) would write of a dreadful regression from the probity and integrity they had sensed in the architecture of Richardson, Root, Jenney, Sullivan and Wright several decades earlier. It was customary in this connection to stress the symbolic importance of the World's Columbian Exposition of 1893 as the event signalling the 'fall from grace', for it was the giant Beaux-Arts classical 'White City' which had set in motion a fashion for pompous revival that Sullivan later bemoaned (in bitter old age) as having set back the course of American architecture by fifty years. Actually, this was gross over-simplification: not only was some of Sullivan's and Wright's best work produced after that date, but the American renaissance was not always superficial. It is more to the point to recall that a variety of viable parallel tendencies were operating up until about 1914 (including the extension of the Prairie School after Wright), and to explain what needs of expression the classical Beaux-Arts fulfilled.

Here one necessarily over-simplifies: the American Beaux-Arts supplied a set of recipes for civic institutions such as museums, metropolitan libraries, opera houses, clubs, universities and monuments. It implied links with classical civilization and made available traditional imperial symbols to the institutions of the state in an era when the United States was first sensing its role as a world power. In the private sector of plutocratic patronage (Frick, Morgan, Rockefeller) instant classicism was a useful prop, an embellishment for 'the age of elegance'. In the 'City Beautiful' movement, images drawn from Imperial Rome or Haussmann's Paris were brought in to ennoble and tame the gridded, utilitarian, money-making machine of the American metropolis. The movement was well represented by Daniel Burnham's vast plans for Chicago of 1909, in which not a skyscraper was to be seen (despite the fact that this architect had done well from designing them). A

domed civic centre towered above the heart of the city. The radial boulevards and parks were supposed to supply open space and to free the traffic, but they were also conceived in theatrical terms. Burnham's plan was suffused with nostalgia for a pre-industrial culture.

Something of this cult of instant beautification lingered on into the 1920s, but with less moral concern for urban improvement. Educated taste still stood between American imaginations and the raw possibilities of indigenous technology. It was a curious situation: on the one side American architects and clients clamouring for the instant sanction of European culture; on the other a European avant-garde looking romantically to America as the promised land of all things modern. The matter was summed up by a caption in Le Corbusier's *Vers une architecture*, which appeared under an illustration of a San Francisco skyscraper encrusted with feebly executed Renaissance ornament: 'Let us listen to the counsels of American engineers. But let us beware of American architects.'

Economic expansion in the boom years relied heavily on mass production, advertising, the deliberate fostering of consumerist imagery, and such communications devices as the radio, telephone and automobile. New corporations of unprecedented size brought increasing

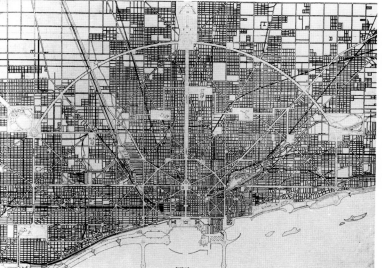

258

specialization to labour and required giant head offices in the city centres. They needed tall buildings which could also project persuasive images of themselves and their products. Many of the basic structural and fireproofing problems of the skyscraper had been solved by the previous two generations. Emphasis now switched to stylistic clothing, to the symbolic function of the building in the cityscape as institutional and corporate image.

The forces which led to the emergence of skyscrapers in the late nineteenth century were discussed in Chapter 2. The typical structural anatomy combined a skeleton or frame, a grid plan, partitioned spaces, and open façades, and this could lead to various possible vocabularies. Here was the core of an American dilemma which also stood near the heart of the problem of a modern architecture: should the creature be left virtually as an object of engineering? Should the native invention be clothed in imported cultural dress to lend a veneer of civilization? Or should some attempt be made to discover and express the 'nature' of the new type symbolically? Evidently, the seminal works of the Chicago School fitted the third category, and in the process abstracted and transposed ordering devices from both natural and past examples. But by 1900, intellectual and artistic tendencies had changed and the discipline of 'Rationalism' seemed less pertinent. Anyway, few architects working in the 1890s had had the penetration or depth of synthesis of a Sullivan or a Root. In the first two decades of the twentieth century, the general rule was eclectic experimentation which departed from the ideal of a genuine modern style. Architectural history was often treated like a used-clothes store and raided for its garments with little thought for their original purpose and still less for the new body they were to clothe. Between 1900 and 1920, Manhattan was transformed into an ersatz historical dreamscape where Mayan temples stood only feet away from Gothic spires and classical mausoleums. Among these were buildings of notable quality, such as Burnham's Flatiron Building of 1909, which was wedge-shaped in plan, and classicizing in external articulation. It continued the scale of the flanking streets, but also rose free as an object in its own right. The Woolworth Building of 1917 by Cass Gilbert transferred vertical piers, shafts and brackets from the English Perpendicular phase

259

of Gothic and used these to articulate a gradually receding vertical shaft. Here too – within another stylistic matrix – was an attempt at breaking down the bulk of the tall building and giving it civic dignity and human scale. The New York zoning law of 1916, requiring set-backs to admit light and air to the buildings and streets below, further encouraged a stepped pyramid form which often surmounted a shaft-like tower standing on a broader pedestal: ziggurats and Meso-American extravaganza wedded well with shapes of this kind.

Such, then, was the history of the skyscraper in outline, down to the *Chicago Tribune* competition of 1922. The newspaper wanted 'one of the most beautiful buildings in the world'; the site stood just north of the Chicago Loop beyond the river, where Michigan Avenue was cranked, allowing more breathing space than was usual in the gridded city, and opening up an uncustomary long, diagonal

260

261

262

263

view; the programme required mainly office space. But these requirements did little to determine a form beyond suggesting some variation on a tower, probably with elevators towards the centre and a slender shaft rising high enough to provide a striking image in contrast to the surroundings. The notes sent to competition applicants made much of the visual quality of the design: here was a chance to concentrate on matters of form and to provide a prototype for the 'beautification' of American cities.

Competitions are a useful gauge of the true outlook of a period because they give evidence of a wide variety of different responses to the same constraints. In all there were nearly 300 entries to the *Chicago Tribune* competition; they make it quite clear that in 1922 there was no American – or worldwide – consensus on style. A survey of the entries reads like a lexicon of eclecticism and half-understood prototypes with little evidence of subtle transformation from precedent. Typical was a design modelled on Giotto's campanile in Florence; in order to preserve the recognizable proportions of the prototype yet still fulfil the volumetric demands of the programme, the architect found it necessary to tack a bulky appendage on to the rear. There were also many quasi-classical solutions employing a jumble of columns, pediments, temple

motifs, and domes. These ran up against the basic incompatibility of a skyscraper's dimensions with the classical orders; columns were either attached like matchsticks with no genuine tectonic value in relation to the underlying mass, or else blown up to a colossal size to clothe some major portion of the tower, in which case their girth tended to interfere with the windows and with the clarity of the overall form. Whatever their incongruities of form, these solutions never gave adequate visual expression to the facts of steel-frame construction within. Perhaps with tongue in cheek, Adolf Loos proposed to solve the problem of incompatible dimensions by making the *entire shaft* of the skyscraper into a Doric column. This took Sullivan's suggestion of a tripartite form for the building type all too literally. Other architects descended into pantomime by pursuing the imagery of a trumped-up, populist Americanism. One entry had its top fashioned as an American Indian with his tomahawk raised above his head.

The European entries were restrained, humourless and sincere by comparison, and provided an intriguing cross-section through emergent modern architectural tendencies. Bruno Taut's design, tapering gradually towards the top, was an Expressionist hybrid combining the images of his pre-war steel and glass pavilions. It issued

260 Entry to the *Chicago Tribune* competition, 1922, modelled on Giotto's Campanile in Florence

261 Entry to the *Chicago Tribune* competition, 1922, modelled on Renaissance prototypes

262 Adolf Loos, entry to the *Chicago Tribune* competition, 1922

263 Walter Gropius, with Adolf Meyer, entry to the *Chicago Tribune* competition, 1922

264 Raymond Hood and John Mead Howells, *Chicago Tribune* Building, Chicago, 1922–5

264

from an utterly different ideological world from the American designs, and was frank and enthusiastic in its attitude to steel technology. Its true cousins were Mies van der Rohe's glass-tower 'cathedrals', rather than the eclectic piles which were its local competitors. Ludwig Hilberseimer's design was composed of stark, rectangular volumes, articulated solely by the checkerboard pattern of the frame; it embodied a strict, Rationalist outlook, a stern 'objectivity'. A Dutch entry (by Bernard Bijvoet and Johannes Duiker) was compositionally extravagant by contrast, with its extending horizontal flanges and overlapping planes. Walter Gropius's scheme also employed a vocabulary based on the rectangular frame. The entrance was indicated by a sort of portico, but the main divisions in the design were articulated by slight changes in rhythm and bay spacing, by recesses and balcony planes of varying depth. The overall impression was of a tense interrelationship of asymmetrical parts, well suited to the three-quarter view by which the building would be most easily seen. Inside, the plan was open, uncluttered, and well lit from all sides, while the elevation to the rear aligned with the frame of the pre-existing printing office. If the design showed sensitivity to the earlier Chicago School (it used the indigenous tripartite Chicago window), it also incorporated devices which were just then emerging

at the Bauhaus through the impact of Van Doesburg, Moholy-Nagy and Constructivism. Gropius's scheme was conceived as a mechanistic abstraction, celebrating the idea of a modern communications building; its effects of lightness and transparency were as hallmarks of the new architecture; in it, technological facts were infused with idealistic sentiments.

Evidently the jury did not think so; to their eyes, it probably looked more like engineering than architecture. They awarded first prize to a neo-Gothic design by Raymond Hood and John Mead Howells, who succeeded as adeptly as Gropius in solving many of the basic problems of the site and the building type. The primary emphasis was vertical, the shafts were set back at the top to become a spiky crown in which the machine rooms and a small museum were placed. Secondary piers emphasized the tall middle portion or shaft, while the lowest part, where the entrance was situated, acted as a base and responded in height to the pre-existing printing office to the rear. In fact this was a variant upon a tripartite scheme which, in its accentuation of the vertical, responded to Sullivan's theorem for the tall office building. While the frame that held up Hood's design was disguised under stonework, the sense of a vertical thrust was successfully articulated by the Gothic piers in the

265

266

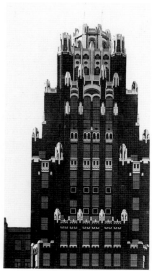

267

façades; these did not confront the architect with the same modular difficulties as classical Orders, for piers could be stretched almost indefinitely. But Hood's choice of Gothic may have had moral associations as well. One of the presentation renderings showed the *Tribune* building in perspective, riding high above the smoke and smuts of the Chicago environment – a white cathedral of enlightenment towering above base concerns. Such evocations appealed to the newspaper proprietors' sense of their own moral purpose. Hood and Howell's design brilliantly caught the right nostalgic and slightly romantic mood. The historian Sigfried Giedion later had his revenge on behalf of Gropius by publishing his colleague's scheme alongside Burnham and Root's Reliance Building of 1890–4 (as if to say that the former was the next logical step from the latter in the evolution of the 'true' modern prism) and by leaving Hood's design out of account altogether. From the point of view of the European avant-garde, of course, the jury's decision was merely evidence of reactionary tendencies.

The scheme which came in second was more influential than any of the others in the inter-war years. This was designed by the Finnish architect Eliel Saarinen and was in no easily categorizable style with its telescoping forms, slight set-backs and vertical linear articulations. Interestingly, Sullivan praised this design, perhaps because he sensed in it an abstraction of nature akin to his own earlier theories, although here the analogies were more with rocks than with plants. The following year Saarinen elaborated a proposal for the urban redevelopment of the area close to the Chicago Loop and the lake-shore, thus indicating his urbanistic understanding of the tall building and a certain naïvety with regard to the speculator's mentality, which was scarcely likely to allow open space for leisure when the same land could be exploited for profit. The forces which brought tall buildings into being ignored the character of civic space and tended to destroy not only the street as a social realm, but the complex grain of pre-existing historical and social relationships as well. To this process of disruption, most architectural suggestions were merely an affirmative veneer.

Two years after his success with the *Chicago Tribune* Building, Raymond Hood designed the American Radiator Building in New York. This followed the pattern of his earlier building, but the vocabulary was now less obviously revived, being more abstract and relying upon (among other things) the appearance of the company's radiator products. With its black-brick facing, gold finials, and elegant proportions, the building crystallized an American machine-age fantasy more whimsical and ornate than the glass and steel evocations of mechanization produced in Europe. There was little sense of a quest for type-forms in Hood's one-off designs; quite the contrary, the architect took a certain delight in posing as a dilettante, for whom consistency of style and a search for the authentic were tedious and grim burdens for those unlucky enough not to have the exuberant capitalist city as their playground. Even the images of the modern movement could be reduced to mere motifs, as is clear from Hood's design for the McGraw-Hill Building of 1928–30 with its 'appliqué' of strip windows and its plain volumetric forms. The silhouette as a whole resulted from a judicious visual composition within the rules of the set-back laws. The top was a streamlined invention, with the dynamism and populist character of Raymond Loewy's contemporary 'Moderne' industrial designs, or of Fritz Lang's Expressionist city in the film *Metropolis*. In the slightly later *Daily News* Building, Hood adopted yet another dress – one perhaps derived from Saarinen's *Tribune* design – by stressing verticality to an extreme. The lobby (along with the crown of the skyscraper, the area most likely to attract public attention) was turned into a middle-brow scenario on the theme of the *Daily News* as a network of information spreading across the world. A giant, gloomily lit globe was sunk in a central pit, while the gadgetry of thermometers, wind-speed indicators, and clocks provided the precise hour in the main cities of the world and gave the whole thing a vaguely science-fiction air. However one characterizes this phase of American design – 'Moderne', 'Art Deco', or 'Jazz Modern' – it flew in the face of European modern movement puritanism in its obsession with ornament, axial composition, gaudy polychromy, and a sort of consumerist theatricality.

The swan song of the 'roaring twenties' in New York was the Chrysler Building, designed by William van Alen between 1928 and 1930. In its celebration of financial success, this captured

perfectly the heady atmosphere of pre-crash
capitalism. It rose to 850 feet (259 metres) and so
was the tallest building in the world for a short time
(being outstripped by the Empire State Building in
the early 1930s). Light silver-grey in colour, it stood
on a base twenty storeys high. Above this was a
middle-section shaft rising another 560 feet (170
metres). Then this too began to step inwards,
tapering finally to a stainless-steel sunburst top with
scalloped windows and surmounted by a spire. The
lobby was conceived as a dream-world of revealed
lighting effects, expensive russet-coloured marbles
and lustrous metals, and had something of the
feeling of a Hollywood stage-set. Each of the lifts
was lined in a different wooden intarsia design with
ornamental motifs recalling the heraldry of the main
body of the building. The skin of the tower was
patterned with dark grey bricks against the silvery
surfaces, and the corners gave the impression of
quoins of increased mass. In the centre of each
façade, the windows were detailed to give a sense of
vertical forces rising the whole height of the shaft,
and terminating as a curved centrepiece; these
mimicked the actual movements of the elevators
running up and down at the core. The plan of
the Chrysler Building was based on primary and
secondary axes (Van Alen had been Beaux-Arts
trained), and the elaborate design of the skin
reflected his interest in a sort of new 'wall'
architecture as an appropriate treatment for the
steel frame. It seems that his ideas may have been
modelled in part on weaving, fabric, or basketwork
designs.

However one categorizes the Chrysler
Building stylistically ('Art Deco' or perhaps even
'Expressionist'), its forms were among the most
elegant in the field of skyscraper design to that date.
But these appearances were also manifestations of a
fantasy about the client, which in turn touched on
broader social meanings. At the corners on the 40th
floor, just below the base of the main shaft, were
four giant metal Chrysler radiator caps with wings.
Next to them a frieze of abstracted car wheels
with huge silver studs for hub-caps encircled the
building. The chevron logo of Chrysler occurred
in the brickwork at various levels; on top, within
the sunburst portion and beneath the spire, there
originally stood a glass case containing Walter
Chrysler's first set of tools (reportedly closed on

268

268 William van Alen, Chrysler Building, New York, 1928–30

269 Scene from the entertainment, 'Skyline of New York', presented at the 1931 Beaux Arts Ball, Astor Hotel, New York: architects dressed as their own buildings, with William van Alen (Chrysler Building) in the centre

270 Hugh Ferris, idealized skyscraper, from *The Metropolis of Tomorrow*, 1929

the day the Empire State surpassed the Chrysler Building in height). Around the base of the sunburst, projecting like gargoyles towards the horizon, were colossal American eagles. The compound message was clear: it was a celebration of self-advancement within the American economic system. Here was a 'Cathedral of Capitalism', a free-enterprise equivalent, perhaps, to the various quasi-socialist paper-project skyscrapers conceived in Europe earlier in the decade.

While the American skyscraper designs of the 1920s succeeded in the limited task of dressing up big business in attractive costume, they rarely produced work of depth. Those 'higher forms of sensibility and culture' which Sullivan had attempted to express (perhaps quixotically) in his skyscraper designs of the 1890s were notably lacking. Shortly before his death, as he had watched the eclectic heaps rise around him, Sullivan had despaired of the possibility of an authentic American architecture in the capitalist city.

These buildings, as they increase in number, make the city poorer morally and spiritually: they drag it down and down into the mire. This is not American civilization; it is the rottenness of Gomorrah. This is not Democracy – it is savagery…. So truly does this architecture reflect the causes that have brought it into being.

Sullivan's cry reflected a basic dilemma of the artist-architect designing in the commercial world: how – if at all – could the brute 'causes' of finance be translated into the lasting stuff of a profound aesthetic symbolism? A question of this kind lay near the heart of European fascination with the tall building too. Le Corbusier was appalled by the facile treatment of Manhattan's skyscrapers, and by their urban irresponsibility, but he was none the less magnetized by the romanticism of the resulting skyline and by the manifestation of financial force,

managerial organization, and technological know-how which brought such buildings into being; he described Manhattan as 'the workhouse of the new era'. By contrast with the American skyscrapers of the 1920s, his idealized images of the tall building in the Ville Contemporaine 1922 (and in the later Ville Voisin of 1925) were entirely glazed, regular in form, and conceived not only as emblems of technological power (they were to contain the Saint-Simonian élite of his city), but also as urbanistic tools for releasing the floor of the city for nature and circulation:

The skyscraper is a tool. A magnificent tool for the concentration of population and for the decongestion of the soil; a tool of classification, and for interior efficiency; a prodigious force for the improvement of working conditions and a creator of economies; for these reasons it is also a dispenser of richness.

Thus artists of the European avant-garde employed images of Manhattan as triggers in the search for Utopian alternatives to the European industrial city.

America was not without its dreamers, the most notable being Hugh Ferris, who published a book called *The Metropolis of Tomorrow* in 1929. This was liberally illustrated with his evocative conté crayon sketches of tall buildings. Some of the

270

271

272

drawings were theoretical studies of possible set-back variations within the constraints of the 1916 zoning laws; others were renderings of other architects' proposals for skyscrapers; but towards the end of the book was a sequence of extraordinary views in which Manhattan emerged in a biblical, almost Babylonian guise. Some of the buildings were even made to look like crystals or magical geological fragments. This other-worldly urban landscape was divided into three main sectors – the scientific, the cultural and the commercial – each with its own symbolic skyscraper. Each of these functions was in turn related to basic divisions in the mind with mystical triangular diagrams. Ferris tried to imply that his image of the metropolis was infused with a divine aura. Again we find the artist hoping for transcendent values beyond the crude materialism of the industrial city. A comparison between *The Metropolis of Tomorrow* and the mechanistic fetishism of the Soviet avant-garde in the 1920s serves to underline Erich Mendelsohn's suggestion of 1928 on the problem of a 'synthesis in world architecture': 'The Russian, technologically speaking still primitive, seeks salvation in the exaggeration of a form of intelligence alien to him, whereas the technologically highly developed American seeks his in the intensification of a spirituality that is alien to him.'

After the financial crash of 1929, fewer tall buildings were constructed in the USA, but two major skyscraper projects did emerge in mid-Manhattan. The Empire State Building by Shreve, Lamb and Harmon became the tallest building in the world in 1931 and enclosed an entire vertical city of functions, but the visual solution lacked the subtlety and elegance of the Chrysler Building. The other major scheme of the period was the Rockefeller Center – a group of buildings incorporating rental office space, the RCA Building, a popular music hall and movie palace (Radio City), and a sunken square (which later became an ice rink) with a perimeter of shops. An extensive team of architectural firms was involved in the design – Reinhard & Hofmeister; Corbett, Harrison, MacMurray; Hood, Godley & Fouilhoux – Raymond Hood being the overseeing designer. Here at last was an attempt at sensitizing the spaces around the base of the skyscraper; Hood's design even included roof terraces on the lowest buildings.

Perhaps the most exploratory skyscraper designs of the 1920s in the United States were never built. These were by Frank Lloyd Wright, who had a notorious distaste for the modern city, but who still admitted the role of tall buildings in his ideal scheme of things. His National Life Insurance project of 1924–5 extended some of the propositions and elements of his pre-war architecture, including the idea of overhanging trays held up by piers, and the conception of a stratified interior space. The slabs were made sufficiently narrow for all offices to have daylight and direct contact with the outside. The façades were clad in copper grilles, which provided a vibrant skin when seen from outside, and intimate, screen-like windows when seen from within. If, for Sullivan, the idealized image of a tower was a vertically emphasized shape, for Wright it was an assembly of interlocking horizontal levels. In the St Mark's-in-the-Bouwerie Tower project of 1927–31 for Manhattan, the box-frame vision of the tall building was rejected in favour of a central core with radiating platforms, split levels, mixed working and living functions, and triangular geometries. The skyscraper became a textured object, registering human use and the reaction to light and climate in the angles and membranes of its façades. An old Wrightian metaphor was given a new emphasis: the tree with its central trunk and extending branches.

The 1920s was a troubled decade for Wright in which he lived an uprooted existence plagued by personal, legal and financial difficulties. After the disastrous burning of Taliesin in 1914, he spent much of his time in Japan overseeing the design and construction of the Imperial Hotel in Tokyo (1912–23), a complex, Orientalist building over a formal, classical plan, with ingenious taproot foundations which successfully withstood the earthquake of 1922. Taliesin was gradually rebuilt and extended, even surviving another fire in the 1920s. It was like a living laboratory in which Wright could try out architectural and landscaping ideas. Taliesin hugged its hillside site, its extending horizontals echoing the rock strata, the whole taking on the character of a Japanese complex not unlike the Katsura Palace. At the same time it was a poem on the 'conventionalization' of natural inspirations in architecture, in which artificial and natural ledges were woven together at large and small scales. From this remote eyrie, Wright surveyed the world with a vision that was more sweeping, less localized than that which had guided him during the relatively

273

SECOND FLOOR
MEZZANINE
GROUND FLOOR

274

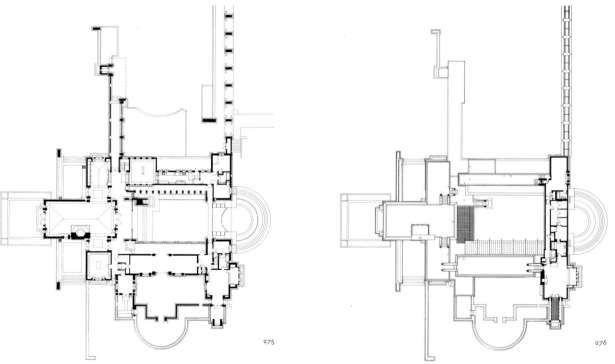

275

276

stable family years in suburban Chicago. He became increasingly interested in the vast landscape of the American continent, its sense of place, topography, memory. His historical range was extended to include the traces of indigenous American civilizations, especially those of the south-western states, but also the pre-Columbian ruins of Meso-America.

Although Wright made proposals for large-scale projects in the 1920s, it was in the field of the individual dwelling that he received the majority of his commissions. Several of these were for southern California on the outskirts of Los Angeles, where the city was expanding rapidly into the surrounding desert, past olive groves and orange orchards created by irrigation. Chief among them was the Barnsdall House (1916–21) on Olive Hill, known as the 'Hollyhock House', and designed for a client almost as eccentric and itinerant as the architect himself: Aline Barnsdall, heiress to an oil fortune. In fact, the project called for an entire enclave with an experimental theatre (on which Aline Barnsdall and Wright had been meditating for several years, but which was never built), artists' studios and houses,

secondary residences, and the main house itself on the crest of the hill. From the highest point of the site it was possible to enjoy long views of mountains and sea, and Wright organized the Hollyhock House as a series of horizontal bars with upper terraces on their flat roofs. The oblong volumes of the house were grouped to form a patio, but on its outer perimeter the building radiated in all directions, towards landscape, city and sea. A small artificial stream was made to rise on one side, then to pass through the interior where it circled the central fireplace, before crossing the patio and passing into an open-air 'water theatre' under a proscenium-like portal formed by one end of the house. From that point on, the stream was to continue the west/east axis down to the Barnsdall Theatre on the eastern perimeter of the lot. This compact little monument would have completed the themes by blending together rectangular stepped forms and arc-shaped steps. In effect, this was architecture conceived as landscape sculpture on a broad topographical scale. The Hollyhock House itself was a species of cosmic theatre for unknown rituals, open to the sky and the realm of the planets.

On first inspection the massive, fortress-like forms with their sloping walls, inward-looking courts, ponds and flat roofs would seem to suggest a strong break with the Prairie Houses. However, if one consults the plan one finds the usual organizational principles combining axes and cross-axes, effects of formality and informality, and a unity of conception between interiors and exteriors (Chapter 7). Even so, the changes are significant. Wright's emphasis on the enclosing wall, instead of the screen-window with horizontal overhang of the Prairie House period, must be seen in the context of a new mood, if not a new ideological direction. It expressed a remoteness from the outside world which may well have been in tune with the outlook of his rather aloof new patrons and with the architect's own feelings of isolation. Wright was now estranged from the tight-knit suburban community of Oak Park which had sustained him in the early years, and it was in the 1920s that the image of the architect as an erratic, aristocratic genius at odds with 'mobocracy' gained currency.

Surely one reason for the protected exteriors and the patios was the hot dry climate. Wright's Prairie

House ideas had been worked out for an entirely different setting, and the natural conditions of southern California required a new response. He seems to have followed some cues supplied by traditional adobe structures with thick, sloping walls and flat roofs. Possibly in transforming tradition, Wright was aware of the pioneering work of Irving Gill, who had already evolved an ingenious concrete architecture for local conditions (see pp. 96–7). But then the Barnsdall House was only cement-rendered to resemble concrete, its actual structure being of brick and wood, and its stylized ornamentation (based on hollyhock motifs) cast in moulds. However, one guesses that more was at stake in Wright's vision. Hollyhock House seemed to fuse together several themes to do with landscape and theatre, and to draw lessons from sources as diverse as Raphael's early sixteenth-century Villa Madama in Rome (a theatre/villa of a kind), and the Nun's Quadrangle at Uxmal (a Mayan complex of the ninth century). It caught the Hollywood atmosphere of the 1920s, in its odd blend of the popular and the exotic, but also crystallized Wright's emerging pan-American dream: In *A Testament* (1957), he wrote:

'I remember how, as a boy, primitive American architecture – Toltec, Aztec, Mayan, Inca – stirred my wonder, excited my wishful admiration … Those great American abstractions were all earth-architectures; gigantic masses of masonry raised up on one great stone-paved terrain …'

The Millard House in Pasadena of 1923 was treated as if it were a contrived ruin, the textured ornamental effects of its concrete-block construction being incomplete without clambering foliage and weathering. The Ennis House (1923–4), which stood on a prominent site with long views, was surrounded by almost ceremonial terraces; its domestic purpose overriden by a grandiose, almost monumental scale. The Freeman House of 1923–4 emerged from the ground like an ancient tomb, the route through the building passing along dimly lit passages and stairs prior to the expansive view through the living room glazing. In all these Californian buildings one senses Wright's preoccupation with primal qualities of space, with archetypes of dwelling, and with the notion of

278 Frank Lloyd Wright, Ennis House, Los Angeles, 1923–4

279 Frank Lloyd Wright, Millard House, Pasadena, 1923

280 Frank Lloyd Wright, Freeman House, Los Angeles, 1923–4, ground-floor plan

281 Freeman House

278

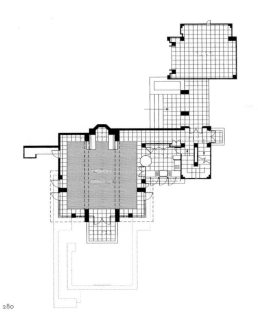

280

281

279

origins. The images and associations are far indeed from the mechanistic obsessions and 'weightless' transparencies of the European avant-garde in the same period.

Nevertheless, the 'concrete-block houses' (as they were sometimes called) did reveal Wright's engagement with technological experimentation and standardization. The idea was to create buildings on the basis of a few geometrical modules and pre-cast concrete units. The blocks were to be cemented and sealed on site, once steel reinforcing had been run through prepared grooves. Glass could be inserted in the blocks themselves, or else treated independently as panes. If the exterior of Wright's houses of this period appeared massive, the interiors dissolved through diapered geometrical patterns, giving an evocative and mysterious light. The architect was intrigued by the idea of interweaving plate glass and concrete, by the notion of the perforated wall, a theme which is celebrated in the Freeman House by a gradual transition from mural enclosure to transparent, glazed corners. Possibly Wright was here making analogies with plaiting

or the weft and warp of fabrics (recalling both Semper's theories about the origins of cladding and the kind of geometrical ornament incised in the stone friezes of ancient Mexican examples such as Mitla or Uxmal). Whatever the historical parallels, the abstract motifs of the blocks often repeated those of the building as a whole: 'microcosms' of larger themes.

During the 1910s and 1920s two Austrian-born architects who passed through Wright's atelier imbibed his principles while still preserving their own artistic identities (a rare combination). The first was Rudolf Schindler, who came from Vienna in 1914, after grappling with the influence of Otto Wagner, the Secession and Adolf Loos. Schindler had a strong intuitive grasp of the tendencies towards abstract form already manifest in pre-war Viennese architecture, and after a period supervising some of Wright's California projects, set out on his own. The Schindler/Chase House of 1921–2 shows how he reacted to the California setting, which it was then still just possible to celebrate as a virgin land. He responded to the landscape, the earth colours, the trees and the vast spaces, and attempted to translate his grasp of these characteristics into an inward-looking shelter of low-ceilinged spaces giving on to densely

planted inner courts reached through sliding screens. The house was designed for himself and his wife, and another newly married couple, the Chases; there were separate private spaces for each person. The plan expressed the idea of a community as a free association of individuals, either guarding their autonomy or else blending into the larger framework. The life of the house was seen as flowing back and forth between the patios (which had external fireplaces and could be covered by awnings), and the areas more solidly enclosed by roof and walls. Schindler added wood and canvas 'sleeping-baskets' on the roofs, for the warmer months. The rectangular gardens and hedges were accorded as much importance as the interiors. Schindler thought of the dwelling as 'a simple weave of a few structural materials which retain their natural color and texture throughout'.

The Schindler/Chase House distilled many lessons from Wright, but took the process of simplification still further. It was like a miniature essay on the theme of the origins of the dwelling. The walls were tapered slightly and this gave an inward-sloping profile to the exteriors, an effect recalling the architect's interest in the adobe vernacular forms of Indian *pueblos*. He used a

282 Rudolph Schindler,
Schindler/Chase House,
Hollywood, California,
1921–2

283 Schindler/Chase
House, plan

284 Schindler/Chase
House, interior

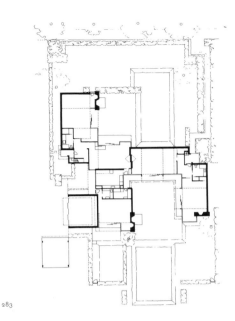

283

concrete tilt-slab technology similar to the one developed by Irving Gill, casting the wall slabs on the ground then hauling them into place. Small window chinks were left between the concrete elements, so that on the inside there was little sense of mass, only a feeling of warm, coloured planes producing a tranquil rhythm and a luminous calm. The eye was kept down by a continuous horizontal transome above which there was a clerestory. Low beams braced the wooden fenestration to the walls and enhanced the feeling of continuity between inside and outside. The interiors were probably indebted to Japanese architecture, especially the contrived incompleteness of the teahouse. The movable wooden screens (which were initially of canvas and only later of glass) were inspired by a temporary camp in which Schindler and his wife stayed while the house was being designed. The sense of a primeval shelter – a curious blend of cave and tent – seems to have been deliberate, for

284

Schindler (like Wright) was much concerned with the basic need for protection and with the psychological nuances of space. In 1912, shortly before leaving Vienna for the United States, Schindler had written:

A hollow adobe pile was the first permanent house … The old problems have been solved and the old styles are dead. Our efficient way of using materials eliminated the plastic structural mass. The contemporary architect conceives the 'Room' and forms it with ceilings and wall slabs. The architectural design concerns itself with 'Space' as its raw material … the shape of the inner room defines the exterior of the building … The architect has finally discovered the medium of his art: SPACE. A new architectural problem has been born.

Analogous themes can be sensed in the Pueblo Ribera Courts designed by Schindler in 1923–5 for a beautiful oceanside site at La Jolla. Here the individual units each had a patio, an upper level terrace with an open air fireplace, and a wooden pergola. The concrete walls were poured in place between movable shuttering which left deep horizontal grooves inside and out, and there were pebbles from the sea-shore in the aggregate. The internal angles were defined by voids left by vertical shuttering posts, and these 'absent corners' gave a curious weightless feeling to the interiors (Otto Wagner's clever denials of visual weight come to mind). The grain of horizontal imprints was made continuous with woodwork, fixtures and sliding screen doors, so that each unit read as a network of glass, timber and concrete. The wooden trellises up above seemed to grow naturally from the construction system beneath, so that the pergolas even hinted at the geometry on which the whole was based. Out of a limited number of pieces, Schindler was able to generate a labyrinth. The units themselves allowed a relaxed transition between inside and outside. They were in turn locked together in a lattice of external spaces, courts and interstitial paths, allowing gradual transitions from public to private.

Schindler's El Pueblo Ribera complex celebrated a healthy way of life in contact with sea, fresh air, surf and vegetation, but beyond this evocation of the contemporary Californian condition, it also touched memories of ancient south-western settlements with mud walls, flat log roofs, and stepping forms, evolved in response to climate, myth and landscape. As the name 'Pueblo Ribera' suggests, Schindler was deeply impressed by the very idea of the native

285

286

American *pueblo*. His own project, with its tawny concrete walls, low terraces, projecting timberwork and modular geometry, was like an abstraction of this prototype. But beyond any specifically 'regional' interpretation, Schindler was really seeking out an archetypal conception of shelter. In 1928 he wrote in his notebook: 'Technik = type based on human laws. Art = variation seen through a human mind.' The interwoven courts and floating pergolas of Pueblo Ribera gave shape to a dream, a vision of human liberation, conceived first in the intellectual ferment of Vienna, but realized on the Pacific rim of the New World.

The weekend house designed for Dr Phillip Lovell at Newport Beach in 1923–6 also fused together a social vision with a strong structural concept. Wishing to exploit the views to the sea, and needing to deal with earthquakes, Schindler conceived the house as a reinforced concrete armature of five perforated lateral piers, from which walls and secondary elements were, in effect, suspended so that they could move without crumbling. To execute his idea, he chose concrete for its cheapness, its durability, and (through the use of cantilevers) its space-creating capacity. The upper portions of the Lovell Beach House were formed from interlocking trays which gave a bold, horizontal overhang to the main elevation and provided a lofty, double-height living space with a correspondingly large window to the sea side. The sleeping lofts were placed on the upper tray at the outer extremity; the same tray then extended inwards to create a gallery looking down into the living room. The undercrofts could be used to store such items as surfboards or boats, and echoed local seaside-pier architecture. The solution was unpretentious and simple. The building form was a direct expression of the section. There were obviously lingering debts to Wright, but the house was still stamped with a uniquely Schindlerian character. Moreover, the spatial ideas behind the scheme and the reduction to hovering horizontal volumes bore some obvious similarities to European progressive work. Schindler's outlook lay closer to Wright's organic philosophy than to the mechanistic abstractions of the European avant-garde, and he seems to have come to his conclusions by his own route without knowledge of contemporary developments abroad. When he did eventually see pictures of the architecture of the 1920s created 6,000 miles away, he spoke of its apparent starkness, emptiness of spirit and lack of warmth. For him, it was the work of men who had had to go through the horror and alienation of trench warfare. Schindler combined a sophisticated ideal of the 'simple' life with reverence for the order of 'nature', which he

287

288 Richard Neutra,
Lovell House, Los Angeles,
1927–9

289 Lovell House, plans
at upper entrance
(second) level showing
access terrace and
bedrooms, and at living
room (first) level

290 Lovell House,
interior showing double-
height living room

288

conceived in virtually spiritual terms. Dr Lovell, an
intellectual progressive who ran a 'Physical Culture
Center' and wrote about natural health remedies,
was exactly the sort of client to allow Schindler's
own convictions to take form.

The other Viennese architect to come to
California via Wright's office was Richard Neutra,
who worked with Schindler until he secured some of
his own commissions. They made a joint entry to the
League of Nations competition in 1927, and then
Neutra embarked on the design of another house
for Lovell, this time to stand on the side of a spur
looking over a lush valley in Los Angeles. The
building was organized as a series of horizontal
levels and interlocking indoor and outdoor spaces.
It grew away from the hillside, so that one entered at
an upper level and passed along a landing into the
airy upper part of a triple-volume stairwell before
coming to the more private areas, perched above
the landscape with fine views over the valley. The
different functions were expressed in varying
window sizes unified by floating white horizontals in
concrete that were set off against the steel supports,
window frames and dark areas of shadow, and
detailed to give the maximum effects of lightness
and planarity. In places these bands ceased to

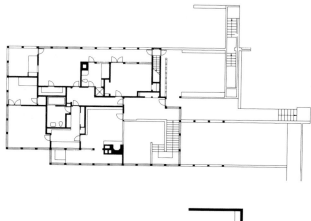

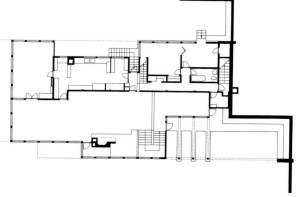

289

have any enclosing function, becoming instead the loose boundaries of exterior terraces, the overhangs of sunshades, or the partial shelter of a swimming pool. The details had a more precise and mechanistic character than Schindler's, traceable, in part, to the steel skeleton. Neutra was also aware of recent work in Europe, so was able to draw lessons from a broader range of experiments. He had himself contributed to transatlantic mythologies in a book entitled *Wie Baut Amerika?*, 1926 (*How Does America Build?*, 1927). Thus the Lovell House was an intriguing hybrid of International modern architecture, the organicism of Wright, and Neutra's own vision of the 'natural' way of life. In the ensuing designs of both Schindler (e.g. the Sachs Apartments, 1929; the Wolfe House, 1928; the Oliver House, 1933) and Neutra (the Kaufmann Desert House, 1946–7), one may tentatively speak of a 'regional' strand of modern architecture.

A review of modern architectural experimentation in the United States during the 1920s would be incomplete without the Philadelphia Savings Fund Society (PSFS) skyscraper designed by George Howe and William Lescaze between 1926 and 1932. Here inherited typological thinking about the American skyscraper and the emergent vocabulary of the International Style came together in a way which modified each. Howe had been trained in the Beaux-Arts system while Lescaze had first-hand experience of designing with the new forms in Europe. To trace the sketches of the PSFS project from the earliest in 1926 (when Lescaze had not yet come into the picture) to the latest in 1930, is to gauge not only the vicissitudes of an individual design process in which formal and functional conflicts were gradually resolved, but also the transition from one architectural style phase to another. An axial,

290

291

encrusted, eclectic skyscraper of the kind all too familiar from the *Chicago Tribune* competition gave way bit by bit to an asymmetrical, machine-age design, in which structure, volume, and differentiations of function were articulated in a disciplined yet subtle way. Even within the emerging confines of the International Style, there were many possible variations of treatment. For example, the architects spent much time studying alternative ways of reconciling the structural verticals (which they wished to 'express honestly') with a horizontal planar expression (which they felt to be associatively right for a building of modern and efficient image). The relationship of the large vertical volumes of the main slab to the attached elevator zone to the rear, and to the 'pedestal' of the banking area, also took a long time to resolve.

The finished PSFS Building (1932) was one of the first skyscrapers actually to be built in the new style. It can be distinguished immediately from those designs in the late 1920s which simply picked up period clichés like strip windows or streamlined horizontals, and applied them as a form of styling (e.g. Raymond Hood's McGraw-Hill Building of 1928–30). PSFS was modern to its very bones: in its dynamic spatial concept, its image of urban life, and its formal and structural articulation. The design of the lower portion of the building combined subway access, shops, and a raised-level banking floor

reached by escalator. These, the honorific zones of the structure, were amplified in scale and treated in dignified materials such as marble veneers and chrome. The upper floors were well-lit, open, plush offices which were also air-conditioned (the mechanical services floor made a clear caesura in the façade composition). The overall image conveyed efficiency and crispness. This was not a question of 'stylism', of packaging into preconceived forms, nor was it mere 'functionalism'. The PSFS form was backed by a rigorous architectural philosophy which, at its most high-flown, embraced abstruse notions of 'space/time' appropriate to modern life, but on a more down-to-earth level manifested a deep concern for the touchstones of functional design. Howe wrote revealingly of the PSFS:

Sound architecture must be able to bear the closest analytical examination externally, internally, structurally, and mechanically, and the solution of each problem which presents itself in the development of a design must be not only possible, but possible in a concise and orderly form as a consequence of the organic foundation of the original conception ...

Modern architecture originated not in a search for a purely practical solution of modern problems but in a dissatisfaction with the superficial, inorganic beauty of superimposed traditional architectural elements and ornament. As would naturally be the case, the search for an organic beauty led back to the very conception of design and it was found that the beauty sought could be found ... only in an expression of the human, structural and mechanical functions of architecture. Our purpose as artists, as opposed to mere builders, in moulding these functions ... has been to achieve beauty... .

The experimental works of modern architecture created in the United States in the 1920s were backed by a variety of ideologies and were genuine attempts at coming to terms with the problem of a serious architectural culture. Curiously, though, the Museum of Modern Art show on modern architecture of 1932 organized by Alfred Barr, Henry-Russell Hitchcock, and Philip Johnson, which gave popular currency to the term 'International Style', did not include the work of Schindler, was forced by its own restrictive criteria to exclude Wright, and was silent on the social content of the new architecture altogether. Hitchcock and Johnson's catalogue, *The International Style: Architecture since 1922*, attempted instead to illustrate and define the shared visual motifs and modes of expression irrespective of differences in function, meaning, and belief. Perhaps influenced by historians of Renaissance art like Heinrich Wölfflin, who had tried to define the most characteristic general forms of an earlier epoch, the authors outlined the main visual principles of what they took to be a new style:

There is first of all a new conception of architecture as volume, rather than as mass. Secondly, regularity rather than axial symmetry serves as the chief means of ordering design. These two principles with a third proscribing arbitrary applied decoration mark the productions of the International Style.

It is ironical that this formalist emphasis should have been made in the Depression years and just before the launching of Roosevelt's New Deal, an atmosphere in which stylistic niceties scarcely seemed relevant, but a situation to which the ideological probings of the modern movement might well have been appropriate. In a sense, Hitchcock and Johnson did modern architecture a severe disservice by presenting it in the way they did. Wright denounced the abstract box-architecture for its lack of an integrated view of man, and its superficial formalism; Regionalists bemoaned the importation of yet another cosmopolitan gloss; the engineer/inventor Richard Buckminster Fuller inveighed against the lack of a real functionality, the superficial flirtation with technology; and in the field of civic design various branches of Revivalism went virtually untouched. Apart from some interesting experiments by A. Lawrence Kocher and Albert Frey (e.g. their lightweight 'Aluminaire House' on Long Island of

1931–2), and by Frederick Keck in the mid-1930s, and the continuing (but little-known) works of Schindler and Neutra on the West Coast, that is about where the matter of 'the International Modern movement' in the United States was left until the end of the 1930s. Meanwhile, of course, Wright proceeded to produce some of his most profound and uncategorizable creations in the same years.

Taking the period 1920–40 in the United States as a whole, it is clear that there were many parallel trends in architecture, and that the innovators, as usual, were atypical. The most probing modern work was carried out far away from the cultural opinion-makers of the East Coast, under somewhat eccentric patronage. Some of the key civic and monumental programmes were still handled with classical forms (e.g. John Russell Pope's Jefferson Memorial in Washington DC of 1937), while both domestic and collegiate buildings continued to emerge within traditionalist conventions. The Beaux-Arts system of education remained virtually unchallenged in America until the late 1930s; it was the arrival of Mies van der Rohe, Walter Gropius and Marcel Breuer towards the end of the decade which set the scene for the growth of a modern architectural educational establishment after the Second World War. Paradoxically – as we shall see – the eventual 'victory' of the modern movement in the United States ran the risk of producing just another style, even a commercial fashion. The Utopian glass towers envisaged on paper by the fantasists of the 1920s were destined to become signs of the corporate status quo; the idealism of the early modern movement would be absorbed by the contradictions and cycles of mass industrialism.

14

the ideal community: alternatives to the industrial city

Men who try to create
a new architecture,
a free architecture for
a free people, anticipate
the creation of a new
social order ...
Karel Teige, 1928

292 Michel de Klerk, Eigen Haard Housing Estate, Amsterdam, 1917–20, detail

The search for new ways of life basic to so much modern architecture of the 1920s was also manifest in idealistic blueprints for the replanning of the industrial city. But whereas individual commissions for villas, schools, factories, and university dormitories allowed socially committed artists to realize fragments of larger dreams in microcosm, the power to build urban totalities was rarely granted. Avant-garde visions of the city therefore usually remained on paper. Even so, they were able gradually to infiltrate the imaginations of later generations and hence to alter the very concept and image of the modern town.

The numerous ideal city plans of the 1920s suggest an ambition to build the world anew, to start afresh, to rid culture once and for all of the detritus of 'dead forms'. However, just as the new architecture often had roots in history, so the new cities were usually concoctions of existing urban elements reassembled in new ways. The fact is that Utopias are historically bound; they have ideological roots and formal precedents; and if one scratches beneath the rhetoric of the 'brave new world', one often finds a vein of nostalgia running through the futurism.

The core problems that were addressed by such urbanists as Tony Garnier, Hendrik Petrus Berlage, Le Corbusier, Walter Gropius, Ernst May and Nikolai Milyutin had a history inextricably linked to the evolution of the industrial city in the nineteenth century. Mechanization, new means of production and transportation, had then transformed the pre-existing morphology of the city into an unrecognizable and incoherent morass of institutions and infrastructures of circulation catering to capitalist development. Moreover, cities in the industrialized regions of Britain and France had grown with uncontrolled speed as the peasantry had flocked to the urban areas for employment and had been housed in the most squalid conditions. In the same period populations increased dramatically. The result was a slum landscape of factories, tenements, and grimy streets without decent communal or private amenities. They were described by Engels in 1845 after a visit to Manchester: 'a filth and a disgusting grime the equal of which is not to be found'.

But the disruptions of industrialization extended well beyond the working-class slums into other areas of the city. As discussed in Chapter 2, combined forces of land speculation and railway transport cut into the old fabric and destroyed the existing hierarchy. New building types like the skyscraper and the railway station disrupted the scale and changed the image of the city. As the case of Chicago showed only too clearly, the new middle classes required homes remote from the dirt created by the sources of their own wealth. Thus the fringes of the city extended outwards, enveloping the countryside with suburban lots and new patterns of roads. A recurrent theme of reformers throughout the nineteenth century and in the early twentieth was that a supposed harmony between the social order and 'nature' had been lost and should be reclaimed.

There were many ways in which criticism of the industrial city was framed. Marx and Engels argued that the true roots of the evil lay in the rottenness of the social order engendered by capitalism; they therefore advocated revolution as the prerequisite for a decent political *and* architectural environment. Earlier in the century, Utopian socialists such as Henri Saint-Simon and Charles Fourier had argued in favour of alternative social structures based on new forms of rule and co-operation. Saint-Simon had advocated the overthrow of the ruling classes and their replacement by technocrats who would propel society along the inevitable path of human progress. Fourier had entertained a theory of passional attractions in human nature whereby opposites would be resolved in a sort of perfect balance of forces between individual desires and social expectations. This dream of a natural co-operation untrammelled by the irrelevancies of previous social contracts was carried through in the fantasy of an ideal collective palace: a '*phalanstère*'. This was supposed to stand in a rural setting and to contain all the functions necessary to support a community of about 1,800 people, who would avoid the dangers of the 'division of labour' by spending their days developing their talents and nurturing the growth of whole, uncramped personalities. The *phalanstère* had an uncanny resemblance to a Baroque palace, as if Fourier were making available to the populace as a whole the enrichments and potentials of the pre-revolutionary aristocracy. The various quarters (including private rooms, ballrooms, a hostelry, a library and an observatory)

293

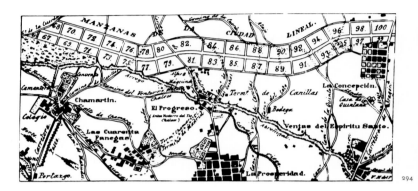

294

were to be linked by a long interior street to encourage chance contacts and to embody the idea of an egalitarian society.

There were other urban proposals for countering the pressures of industrialism which were less drastic than either the revolutionary or the Utopian models and relied more on the forces of the status quo. One thinks in this connection of the several attempts at designing decent workers' towns – from Bournville to Pullman City – in which the philanthropic side of capitalist ownership emerged. Haussmann's plans for Paris (Fig. 11) also reflected mixed motives. The new boulevards and parks offered hygienic amenities to (at least some of) the public, while also opening up routes for commerce, military control, and the spectacular display of the city's monuments past and present. Frederick Law Olmsted's Central Park in New York (designed soon after mid-century; see Fig. 21) brought a rugged version of nature to the heart of the industrial metropolis and enhanced the land values immediately adjacent, even as it embodied a 'humanist' intention. The park in Olmsted's eyes was an ideal public realm celebrating the inevitable drift of history towards an increasingly democratic state.

In Europe a number of other paradigms were created in the second half of the nineteenth century, which were destined to influence twentieth-century ideas. One of these emerged in the writings of Camillo Sitte (e.g. *Der Städtebau nach seinem künstlerischen Grundsätzen*, 1899; translated as *City Planning according to Artistic Principles*, 1965). Sitte was Viennese and opposed to the kind of grand axes and vistas which had been so evident in the carving out of the Ringstrasse around Vienna. He instead advocated a closer relationship between the irregularities of earlier city forms and the layout of spaces and squares; Sitte thus unknowingly became the father-figure for many later movements and urban theorists intent on maintaining the close-knit scale of the pre-industrial city against the onslaughts of grand *tabula rasa* plans of every stripe. If biological and mechanistic analogies were sometimes made by architects, they were also made by urbanists who might conceive of the industrial city as a large machine or else as an organism capable of ordered change. The Spanish urbanist Arturo Soria y Mata invented a prototype known as the 'linear city', to ameliorate the crush of population on large urban centres, to integrate the inevitable facts of roads and railways and to allow for a continuous pattern of extension and growth. Soria y Mata realized that the old hierarchical city was being destroyed by the demands of transport and exchange, and by a wasteful sprawl. The linear city was supposed to link living and working areas to an extendable spine of circulation, and to make for a more ordered relationship between country and city. It was to be laid out in parallel bands along roads and railways, which might link up pre-existing cities as far apart as Barcelona and Moscow; a variation of this principle was proposed by Soviet planners in the 1920s (Chapter 12).

Another model for dealing with overpopulation was decentralization. This was a central theme in several texts produced just before the turn of the century, for example, the writings of the Englishman Ebenezer Howard, particularly his book entitled *Tomorrow: A Peaceful Path to Real Reform* (1898). Howard was disturbed by the disruption and waste he saw in London and other industrial cities, and argued in favour of new communities of manageable size, in which rural and urban worlds would be brought together in a happy synthesis. Essentially his vision of local communities was a variant on the English village, but with additional amenities like railways and small-scale industry. The unit in the Garden City was the family in its individual home; these houses were to be laid out along well-planted streets, converging gradually upon the broad communal green and civic buildings towards the centre. Howard was much influenced by that moral strain of social criticism which descended from William Morris and John Ruskin. He would have agreed with the latter when he wrote in favour of: 'clean streets with free countryside all around; a belt of fine gardens and orchards, so that from every point in the city one can reach the pure air, the grass and the distant horizon'. However, Howard's thinking also stemmed from a more drastically Utopian tradition of 'alternative communities' like the one envisaged earlier in the century by Robert Owen (e.g. his 'New Lanark' of 1815). Permeating the dream was a nostalgia for a pre-industrial world, and when a version of the Garden City idea was eventually carried out in reality at Letchworth it was appropriately complemented by Raymond Unwin's Arts and Crafts architecture with hipped roofs and the imagery of English yeomen's houses.

Garden City principles were taken over and transformed by Tony Garnier in his proposals for a Cité Industrielle, conceived between about 1901 and 1917, when his ideas were published. This scheme was mentioned earlier in connection with reinforced concrete, the material most widely

295

296

employed in the plan's design (Chapter 4). It was Garnier's intention to lay out all the problems and solutions of the 'most general case' of the industrial city. He proposed a medium-sized case of about 35,000 inhabitants for which he attempted to co-ordinate all the social, productive, and transport functions. Zoning was employed to separate industry from the home, and railways were used to link the two with trade centres. The ideal site conveniently foresaw terraces in the landscape which helped to articulate the different zones, but the hierarchy of parts was also ordered and heightened by the use of axes (recalling his Beaux-Arts training and his interest in ancient classical towns). There was a large civic area towards the centre, but Garnier made no provision for religious buildings. This no doubt mirrored his socialist conviction that the new society would render such 'palliatives' unnecessary. As in Howard's Utopia, small family villas were laid out along side streets lined with trees, protected from overcrowding, the noise and smell of traffic, and industry. There were some apartment buildings on

a larger scale, also flat-roofed and rectangular. Walkways were provided alongside each building, so allowing pedestrians to filter across the city at any point and permitting a dense planting of trees. Garnier claimed that 'the land of the city, taken overall, is like a big park, without any fences to delimit the various sections'. Hygienic factors also played a major part in his plan.

Thus the Garden City was here rethought in ways which faced up to the techniques, potentials, and values of an industrial society. Garnier's imagery was pervaded by a sober yet romantic aura of the progressive potential of industrial technique to further a programme of social emancipation. Class struggles and oppositions of interest seemed to have no place in this Arcadian dream of Grecian villas, co-operative institutions and tree-lined avenues. The Arts and Crafts imagery of Unwin's sound English working-men living a healthy and moral life in a rural setting gave way to a flat-topped architecture evocative of the larger organizations of the industrial state. But for all its progressive mood, there was still a touch of nostalgia, as the historian Manfredo

297

Tafuri has suggested by referring to Garnier's Cité Industrielle as 'a New Hellas': 'For him the future was anchored in a past fondly pictured as a Golden Age, as an ideal equilibrium to be won again.' Owing to his connections with the socialist mayor of Lyons, Édouard Herriot, Garnier was able to translate part of this ideal city into reality (e.g. the Abattoir in Lyons of 1908–13, or the Quartier des États-Unis, 1920–35); but something of the dream-like character of the drawn version was lost.

Another major work of urbanism which linked nineteenth-century notions with the progressive planners of the 1920s was that undertaken by Hendrik Petrus Berlage for the extension of south Amsterdam between 1902 and about 1920. Outside the perimeter fortification walls, the growth of Amsterdam throughout the nineteenth century had continued in a pell-mell fashion. The influx of industry required a vast provision of decent housing conceived on the scale of neighbourhoods. Berlage brought order to the chaos with the help of grand avenues defining major pieces of massive and substantial character; these were in turn penetrated by secondary systems of roads and quiet squares containing shops, schools, and public institutions. The main unit of collective dwelling was the perimeter block, set around large internal courts containing gardens. Many of these were laid out on symmetrical plans with massive central elements marking entryways. The buildings were finely detailed in dark brick, and arches, windows, corners, etc. conspired to give the whole area a unity of theme and sobriety of effect, offset by the looser order of trees and pathways.

A similar basic pattern was adopted by the 'Expressionist' architects Piet Kramer and Michel de Klerk in their various collective-block designs in Amsterdam. De Klerk's Eigen Haard (literally 'Own Hearth') housing of 1917–20 was also beyond the edge of the coherent historical centre, and the architect attempted to solidify the urban fabric by virtually monumentalizing the housing and by treating the perimeter as a single sculptural unit. However, this was brilliantly articulated by changes in rhythm, texture, scale, and colour to hint at changes of interior function and disposition, and to respond to the varying pressures of a triangular site. To one end, on the centre of the baseline of the triangle, a gateway was cut through the outer edge and a steeple used to mark its presence. Once again, the mood was a sober and solid one, as if the architecture was seeking deliberately to counter the uprootedness and flux of modern urban existence with something reassuring and evocative of an earlier guild co-operation. Speaking of his plans for

298

299

He referred to the triad 'Organism, Function, Environment' which translated into such basic ideas as 'Folk, Work, Place'. While vague, these notions constituted an antithesis to a merely utilitarian notion of city-planning.

Le Corbusier tried to reduce the industrial city to its typical elements and its main relationships, seeking a grand synthesis of mechanization, geometrical order and 'nature'. In France, during the years immediately after the First World War, there was a serious housing crisis, and a need to encourage international investment. Le Corbusier's various urban studies of the period can really be seen in this immediate setting, as well as in a longer perspective, including a French commitment to centralized technocracy, and a tradition of grand classical urbanism. Polarity between the vague promise of some ideal future and the reminiscence of a more integrated past seems to have been intrinsic to the urbanistic thought processes of Le Corbusier. The 'Ville Contemporaine pour trois million habitants' ('Contemporary City for Three Million Inhabitants') of 1922 was mentioned earlier (p. 174) in the context of the architect's pervasive conception of the 'machine age' and his search for a harmony in modern culture, but it may also be seen both as a generalized hypothesis for the modern city (based upon the particular experience of Paris), and as a broader analysis of emerging forces and types in the industrial metropolis. Like Garnier, Le Corbusier was content with nothing less than a total

Amsterdam, Berlage had claimed he was instituting 'a sort of town-planning revival'; De Klerk also seems to have sought a balance between an innovative solution to new demands, and a feeling of continuity. In 1934, the American urbanist Catherine Bauer wrote an appreciation of Dutch town-planning, which she felt put the paltry efforts of her own country, of France and of Britain, to shame:

But it was in Holland that the Romantic movement left its most enduring mark. Berlage and his followers, influenced on the one hand by the medievalism of Morris and on the other by the freer and more original genius of the American, Frank Lloyd Wright, achieved the first real vernacular of modern architecture. That is, a 'style' whose monuments were not to be found merely in isolated villas or public buildings, but in whole blocks and streets of 'housing' and shops and offices, in plotting and planning, and within the dwelling of l'homme moyen sensuel as well as in those of the more advanced or Bohemian literati. This was particularly true in Amsterdam, where entire districts, including many low-cost workers' apartments put up with official assistance, and also palatial hotels and schools and bath-houses and bridges, bear witness to a fresh approach to the modern world, for the most part quite unified … The same sort of rejuvenation (for there was no complete or revolutionary break with the past until much later) was going on in the Scandinavian countries, where the early co-operative housing has a sort of decent dignity difficult to discover in the model tenements of London or Paris or New York.

It was rare for housing to be understood as an element in a larger whole, and the very complexity of the industrial city made it difficult to imagine a totality. The Scottish philosopher/biologist/planner Patrick Geddes, whose theoretical work was mostly carried out between 1892 when he founded the 'Outlook Tower' in Edinburgh and 1932 when he died, attempted to understand the city in the broadest terms, considering its relationship to the surrounding countryside and region, and reflecting upon its social and economic frameworks. Geddes was less important for any particular images or plans he may have conceived than for an overall attitude. For him human habitation had to be understood on several levels, including the processes of biology.

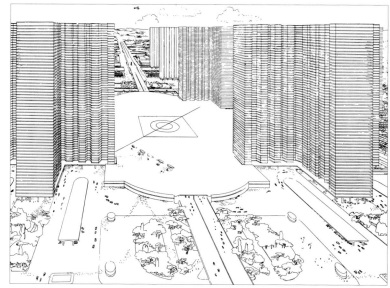

300

theorem for all the processes of industrial society. It has to be said that he over-simplified these drastically in his plans.

The Ville Contemporaine is known from a series of drawings which Le Corbusier exhibited at the Salon d'Automne in Paris in 1922. The plan was based on a regular geometry and was cut across by a main axis of road circulation coming to a transportation centre laid out on a number of levels, the topmost of which was an airport. Around this centre, and conforming to the grid of the city, were twenty-four glass skyscrapers 600 feet (183 metres) high. These were supposed to contain 'the brains' of the society – the technocrats, the managers and the bankers. Most of the rest of the city was taken up with high-density apartment buildings laid out regularly in a park-like setting. The workers' suburbs and the main industrial zone were placed some distance away, so reinforcing the distinction between a managerial élite and the lower orders. The whole was pervaded by a spirit of almost obsessive rationality and discipline: the forces of mechanization were brought to a complete resolution in a mandala-like plan embodying an 'ideal order'.

The rationale behind the Ville Contemporaine was relatively straightforward. High-density living was to be combined with the maximum of open space and fresh air through the use of new techniques like steel and concrete construction and with the help of the motor car. Mechanized traffic

was to be separated from the pedestrian by the use of *pilotis*; indeed the entire green floor of the city was to be kept free as the buildings too were lifted up. The traditional street was abolished; Le Corbusier associated it with the choking fumes and diseased areas of nineteenth-century slums. Instead of the grimy industrial city, a brave new world of light, greenery, air, cleanliness, and efficiency was to arise. Country and city were to be reintegrated so that the city became a vast park. Le Corbusier saw technology as a double-headed creature capable of good or ill; his city plan was an attempt at co-opting and harmonizing the forces and possibilities of industry in the service of human betterment and emancipation.

There were a number of ideological components; it seems clear that Le Corbusier had absorbed the ideas of Saint-Simon, especially the conception of a benevolent élite of technocrats who would act as the agents of a progress for all. This vision of the state was embodied in the skyscrapers at the city's core, and in the romanticization of technology implicit in both the grand treatment of the roads and the machine-age tenor of the other buildings. Of course, the architect could not locate a strict equivalent to a Saint-Simonian élite in his own time, and his later Ville Voisin of 1925 (in which he suggested the construction of a business district of skyscrapers in the centre of Paris) was a heavy-handed attempt at exciting the interest of big business in his schemes. It was later in the 1920s that Le Corbusier began to

301

302

realize some of the severe problems of a capitalist economy, and began to shift his political ground. But he maintained a romantic conception of technocracy as a progressive force in its own right. Once again we find an element of determinism in this artist's outlook.

The actual images of Le Corbusier's Ville Contemporaine also had a complex lineage. It was as if he had assembled fragments of the cities and urban theories which he liked and which he found pertinent over a single regular plan. The technological aura of the American grid and skyscraper city (known from photographs) was spliced together with the roads and glass buildings of Sant'Elia's Città Nuova. The boulevards, grand avenues and parks of Paris were mated with a geometrical order reminiscent of ideal city plans from the Renaissance. Howard's Garden City and Garnier's Cité Industrielle were rephrased on a far larger scale. The sensibility of Purism was blended with memories of grand classical cities of the past. The whole was infused with that love of the typical and the abstract that we have sensed in Le Corbusier's architecture. It was as if he was not content with merely defining the 'standards' of a new architecture, but also had to take on the question of the typical elements of the town – indeed the society – of the future. Was this simply a theoretical exercise or did he seriously hope to build the whole thing? Neither point is certain, but clearly Le Corbusier was not squeamish about projecting his own vision of Utopia in the belief that it was good for all. One guesses that if it had been built, the Ville Contemporaine would have possessed a crushing uniformity.

The residential buildings for Le Corbusier's élite were of two types: set-backs (to re-emerge in the 1930s as the *à redent* apartment houses of the Ville Radieuse or Radiant City) and perimeter blocks laid out around courtyards and called *immeubles villas*. The latter were made up from double-height units, each with a large garden terrace, and stacked up to a height equivalent to twelve single storeys. The interior of each double-height maisonette was similar to that envisaged in the Maison Citrohan. Evidently it was Le Corbusier's intention to turn the powers of mass production to the solution of the housing question on the widest scale. Communal facilities such as restaurants, tennis courts, roof terraces and lawns were included. The atmosphere was quite luxurious – like a middle-class hotel rather than the communist collective condensers envisaged in the Soviet Union later in the decade.

Like the city as a whole, the *immeubles villas* drew upon diverse sources that had captured Le Corbusier's imagination during his travels. Most notable was the Carthusian monastery at Ema in Tuscany which he had visited as a young man in 1907. This too was formed around a courtyard and had individual cells of double height with views over private gardens. It was an organization which was to recur in many of Le Corbusier's architectural essays on collective living in later life. The monastery was a type which fascinated him because it seemed to embody an ideal balance between public and private existence, and between the built and the natural worlds.

303

Although Le Corbusier was never to build a total version of any of his ideal cities, their spirit still informed much of his later production. This was also true of many other architects in the 1920s, who employed individual opportunities as experiments towards the larger whole. In a sense, the examples of housing at the Weissenhofsiedlung in Stuttgart in 1927 fulfilled this role for the participants. But in the Weimar Republic there were agencies which allowed the construction of modern housing on a broad front. Indeed the constitution of the new German republic of 1919 stressed state control over the use of land, one intention being the provision of homes for all. In fact, housing reforms could only become effective after about 1923 with the temporary stabilization of the economy. The results were seen most dramatically in such cities as Breslau, Hamburg, Celle, Berlin, and Frankfurt.

Frankfurt was a special case because there the aims of the trade unions and the social democratic co-operatives were most effective in influencing policy. The mayor of the city, Ludwig Landmann, had a special interest in housing, which he had expressed in a book entitled *Das Siedlungsamt der Großstadt* (*The Provision of Housing in the City*) in 1919. In 1925 he invited the architect Ernst May to Frankfurt, invested him with the powers of city architect and supported him with official machinery to appropriate land for modernization. May had already realized a series of small agricultural communities in Silesia in the early 1920s which had reflected the obvious influence of Howard's ideas;

but his new task was on a colossal scale by comparison. The numerous *Siedlungen* which he and his associates designed for Frankfurt in the next five years were only loosely based on Garden City principles, though much attention was devoted to the natural setting, the creation of hygienic living spaces, and proximity to the place of work. Equally important was the commitment to industrial mass production of rationally based housing prototypes. May and his associates undertook the most detailed researches into the logistics of use and production on all scales, from the outside spaces to the individual dwellings and the tiniest fixtures. From this emerged, for example, the compact and exceptionally functional 'Frankfurt kitchen', designed by Grete Schütte-Lihotzky. This spirit of analysis seems to have thrilled committed modern architects elsewhere in Europe, who felt that it was evidence of the divergence of technology away from the rapacious purposes of *laissez-faire* economics towards a socially responsible aim. On the other hand, opponents were quick to parody the 'inhuman' and 'scientific' invasion of the home.

In layout and appearance the *Siedlungen* were also far removed from the free-standing family houses of the Garden City with their pitched roofs and rustic overtones. A characteristic layout was a long, low block between three and five storeys high, with access ways and stairs between the paired flats that were placed on each floor. This led to an almost monotonous repetition of standardized modules and constructional elements, which the architects attempted to humanize by judicious attention to proportion, scale, light, shade and detail. The tight budgets allowed no frills, but the resulting asceticism was turned to good use as an expression of co-operative discipline and moral rigour. The planar, white or coloured surfaces were enlivened in any case by the play of shadows from trees and the juxtaposition of lawns and planting.

Thus Garden City ideas and the abstract forms of the new architecture came together in a compelling imagery which was intended to display the values of enlightened socialism. It seemed briefly as if the Utopian aspirations of the avant-garde and the social realities of the time were in step; the Römerstadt, the Bruchfeldstrasse, and the Praunheim housing schemes were widely published and eagerly upheld by left-wing champions as

305

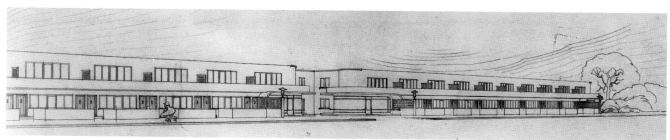

306

the crystallization of modern architecture between the wars

examples of what could be achieved when modern architecture was allowed its 'true' destination; not the aggrandizement of chic middle-class Bohemia, but the emancipation of the working class from bondage, the amelioration of environmental conditions on a wide front, the harmonization of mechanization and nature. However, the bubble soon burst at the end of the decade, when increases in the cost of materials led to a rapid decrease in quality, when it became clear (as was the case in Russia) that the imagery was by no means necessarily welcomed or understood by the populace, and when the forces of reaction turned violently on the new architecture for its supposed communist inspiration.

Although patronage in Berlin worked otherwise than in Frankfurt, it too had its share of remarkable housing schemes. Among the most notable, perhaps, were those by Gropius for the Siemensstadt, and those by Bruno Taut and Martin Wagner at the Britz-Siedlung. Taut had by this time long abandoned the Expressionist and quasi-sacral yearnings of the late 1910s. Instead he had adopted the manner of the 'New Objectivity' (Neue Sachlichkeit) which he probably thought most appropriate to the stringent social programme implicit in the new housing schemes. However, he was far from being a mere 'functionalist' in intention, and sought to imbue the standardized and repetitive forms of his designs with an aura of dignity and with a communal spirit. The Britz

plan was centred on a horseshoe-like open space embraced by a strip of housing. From this focus, parallel oblongs were disposed with layers of green space between. The image of the free-standing 'bourgeois' villa was deliberately rejected, as were the unsanitary working-class tenements of the nineteenth century. The strict form language was supposed to have a purgative effect. However, there was the perpetual danger that reductivism and repetition might degenerate into mere banality when the requisite visual control or the probity of the socialist vision were absent. This tended to happen in the many weak derivatives of the classic *Siedlungen*. The danger of applying primarily utilitarian criteria on a large scale was demonstrated by Ludwig Hilberseimer's 'Highrise City' proposals of 1924, in which eerie, uniform blocks with minimal articulation were shown receding in perspective with canyon-like roadways running between them.

The housing schemes of May, Wagner, Taut and the rest were probably influenced by the remarkable and slightly earlier housing projects of J. J. P. Oud in Holland. As early as 1918, at the age of 28, Oud had been appointed the chief architect of Rotterdam. His earliest designs in this role were clearly modelled on Berlage's prototypes. Only gradually did he manage to break away from hackneyed plan arrangements and to synthesize De Stijl discoveries with an architectural language that had still to

307

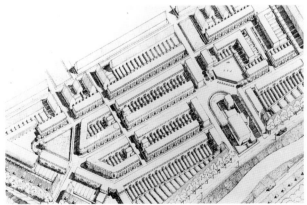

308

handle the requirements of workers' dwellings. The moment of crystallization seems to have occurred in his designs for housing at the Hook of Holland in 1924. Here sanitary intentions were transcended by a remarkably expressive formal design. The two identical blocks contained two rows of superimposed dwellings, and the extremities were rounded. The walls were plastered and whitewashed, while the low base was made of yellow brick, the doorsteps of red brick, and the doorposts of grey concrete. There were small individual gardens at the front, and communal ones at the rear. Oud was able to take on and solve many of the classic problems of the urban terrace: the expression of individual units in a perceptible whole; the separate articulation of middle and ends; the layering and differentiation of front and back façades. Doors, lamps, pillars and other details were painted in blue, red, black, and yellow, inevitably recalling the character of Mondrian's paintings or some touches in the Schröder House by Rietveld. The asymmetrical dynamism of De Stijl was not so easily translatable to the larger scale, but in the Kiefhoek housing in Rotterdam of 1925, Oud managed to slide the surrounding spaces one into another. Again the houses were kept down to two storeys. The thin, whitewashed boxes with their tight and exquisite details were a dramatic departure from the texture and weight of earlier Dutch housing experiments in the 'Expressionist' mode and stood out against their red-brick surroundings, but the possible problems of a clash with the immediate context were not an issue at the time. Oud's stark, abstract prototypes were, after all, emblematic of a new order. In Holland Oud usually had the advantage of regularized street patterns and flat terrain which wedded well with his style and approach, but there was no guarantee that the supposed universal qualities of his designs would be transferable to other conditions.

The dilemmas of social interpretation faced by European avant-garde architects were not so far removed from those faced by their counterparts in Soviet Russia at the same time. The avant-garde was in constant danger of projecting its own values on reality and indulging in over-simple environmental determinism of the kind which claimed that modern architecture must be good for all, morally and socially. As was shown in Chapter 12, groups like the OSA researched into living patterns and constructional techniques in order to seek out prototypes for workers' housing and to discover forms 'expressive' of the new state of things. This was only part of a larger vision of renewal, which was more ambitiously registered in town plans. In his book *Russia: an Architecture for World Revolution* of 1930, El Lissitzky presented a synopsis of avant-garde tendencies over the previous decade, building type by building type, and tended to imply that the clubs, housing schemes, factories, etc. were all basic elements of some new urban order. In a section entitled 'The New City', he wrote: 'Social evolution leads to the elimination of the old dichotomy between city and country. The city endeavours to draw nature right into its centre and by means of industrialization to introduce a higher level of culture into the country.' This was in the spirit of Marx's and Engels's original pleas for the abolition of the distinction between urban proletariat and rural peasantry, and also seemed to echo Lenin's call for 'the fusion of industry and agriculture', but even once the article of faith had been accepted, there were a number of possible ways to translate the idea into an urban plan.

There thus ensued a series of city-planning debates on the desirable balance between country and city, and especially on the question of decentralization. In the late 1920s Zelenko and Leonid Sabsovich conceived the theory of communal houses to be placed in new residential and industrial centres at regular intervals of 25 miles or so between existing cities; these were supposed to become nuclei of ideologically transformed peasantries, and were vaguely reminiscent of Fourier's *phalanstères*. This theorem was attacked by the 'disurbanists' (particularly Ginzburg and Mikhail Barshch) who caricatured the communal houses as rural barracks and argued that industry and agriculture should be dispersed throughout entire territories, so dissolving the old boundaries of city and country altogether. Ginzburg's and Barshch's project for a 'Green Moscow', proposed in 1929–30, suggested that the heart of the historic city should be preserved, for leisure and cultural activities, while linear cities should be created on a radial pattern expanding from the centre. These cities were to be made up of movable wooden houses on stilts, and would be linked by railways which would be free of charge. An even more extreme and anarchical faction in the 'disurbanist' school argued for complete fragmentation and for the avoidance of coherent formal structure altogether.

The case for the linear city was pursued most single-mindedly by Nikolai Milyutin in a book entitled *The Problem of Building Socialist Cities* (1932), in which he argued that industry should be built in a linear manner with a parallel residential strip separated from it by a green belt a few hundred yards wide. The railways were to be located away from the green belt on the far side of the industry, while a main road would give access to the residential zones. The linear form (derived from Soria y Mata) was recommended for its supposed flexibility and because it avoided centric images of power. It could even be seen as an egalitarian instrument, fusing together the urban proletariat and the peasantry, and demolishing some of the old distinctions between country and city. Given the range of their urban thinking, it is not surprising that the Soviet theorists should have maintained a strong critical interest in developments and ideas in

the capitalist world. It was at the beginning of the 1930s, with the general economy stunned by the world depression, that Le Corbusier promoted his idea of a Ville Radieuse and that Frank Lloyd Wright assembled his concept of Broadacre City as palliatives: the former a centralized theorem, the latter a decentralized one (chapter 18).

A review of collective housing proposals in the 1920s would be incomplete without some discussion of Vienna. A census taken in 1917 revealed that nearly three-quarters of Viennese lodgings were unhygienic and overcrowded. Under the Social Democrat Otto Bauer, rents were controlled, private properties were bought for municipal housing, and a programme for building 5,000 apartments a year was set in progress. Architects like Josef Frank and Adolf Loos responded to the crisis by suggesting low-population-density, single-home suburbs. However, the commune followed the lead of Peter Behrens in favour of colossal super-blocks with their own collective facilities. The model selected became known as the 'Hof' – a closed or semi-closed block of extremely high density, to be built according

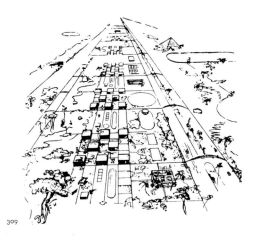

309

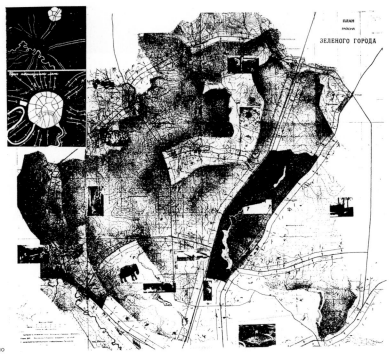

310

to traditional methods. The resulting enormous structures became known as 'workers' fortresses'; indeed, the Karl-Marx-Hof was the scene of a pitched battle in 1934 between the forces of the left and the extreme right.

This latter building was designed by Karl Ehn in 1927 and stretched for more than half a mile. It contained 1,382 apartments plus offices, laundries, green spaces, a library, an out-patients' clinic and green areas. The vast problems of scale posed by a building of this size were somewhat clumsily resolved by adopting a linear-block arrangement which was then articulated by broad entrance arches with massive surmounting towers. The whole had something of the character of a viaduct or rampart wall; in fact, each of these historical prototypes would recommend itself to later planners who attempted to design *Unités* on this scale. The

style of the Karl Marx Hof was a monumental and somewhat ungainly descendant of the Wagner School. One historian claimed to see in the building an example of 'the populist epical idiom'.

In 1928 the first meeting of the Congrès Internationaux de l'Architecture Moderne (CIAM) took place at the castle of Mme de Mandrot at La Sarraz near Lausanne, and discussions among some of Europe's leading modern architects turned to the interrelationships of architecture and town planning. The final statement of the meeting (at which Gropius and Le Corbusier were among the protagonists) argued that architecture should be put 'back in its true sphere, which is economic, sociological, and altogether at the service of humanity'. It also stated that: 'Town planning is the design of the different settings for the development of material, emotional, and spiritual life in all its

manifestations, individual and collective, and it
includes both town and country.'

The ensuing CIAM meeting took place at
Frankfurt in 1929 and discussion centred on the
problem of the '*Existenzminimum*' (the 'minimum
habitation'). In 1930, in Brussels, housing emerged
once again, when debates on the relative value of
middle- or high-rise planning occurred. Gropius
presented his studies of lighting angles and plot
ratios, while others raised once again the difficult
problem of political implementation. The fourth
congress took place in 1933 on board the SS *Patris*
between Marseilles and Athens, and on this occasion
the general announcement (later called the Charter
of Athens) returned to the problem of the modern
city and to general town-planning principles:

> Today, most cities are in a state of total chaos. These cities do
> not come anywhere near achieving their aim, which is to satisfy the
> biological and psychological needs of their inhabitants.
> From the beginnings of the machine age this situation bespeaks
> the proliferation of private interests …
> On a spiritual and material level, the city should ensure
> individual freedom and the benefits of collective action.
> Reorganization within the urban pattern must be regulated on
> the human scale only.
> The key points in town planning lie in the four functions: living,
> working, recreation (in free time), circulation …
> The basic nucleus of town planning is the living-cell (a dwelling)
> and its introduction into a group constitutes a unit of habitation of
> suitable size.
> Starting from this unit, the relations between living place, place
> of work, and place of recreation can be worked out.
> To solve this serious problem it is vital to utilize the resources of
> modern technological progress.

Once again the avant-garde had to resort to a
theoretical blueprint in the description of the ideal
urban totality. This was bound to be the case in the
absence of state authorities sympathetic to the cause.
Elsewhere in the same document it was admitted
that 'private interest' should be subordinated to
'public interest', but it was by no means clear how
this should happen. In the event, the modern
urbanist/architect was forced into the position
of making piecemeal demonstrations where
unique aesthetic qualities might well obscure the
prototypical nature of the experiment. Without a
consensus and a society in favour of the values it
represented, the ideal city was bound to remain on
paper. Here it could maintain its diagrammatic
purity, but at the risk of remaining dangerously
simplistic.

15

the international style, the individual talent and the myth of functionalism

Styles, like languages, differ in the sequence of articulation and in the number of questions they allow the artist to ask …
Ernst Gombrich, 1960

By the beginning of the 1930s, it was possible for the discerning and selective eye to survey the productions of the previous decade and to single out a new style. From Moscow to Milan, from Los Angeles to Japan, buildings of different function, size, material, meaning and expressive power could be found which none the less had obvious features in common. One could speak of the shared characteristics in terms of recurrent motifs like strip windows, flat roofs, grids of supports, cantilevered horizontal planes, metal railings and curved partitions; or, one could define the general qualities of the style by more abstract features such as the recurrent tendency to use simple rectangular volumes articulated by crisply cut openings, or to emphasize hovering planes and interpenetrating spaces. In their book *The International Style* (1932; see p. 239), Hitchcock and Johnson went still further by attempting to outline the main visual principles of the new style (the stress on volume rather than mass, regularity, the avoidance of architectural decoration, etc.). Moreover, they claimed for this new 'International Style' a major historical significance.

Now that it is possible to emulate the great styles of the past in their essence without imitating their surface, the problem of establishing one dominant style, which the nineteenth century set itself in terms of alternative revivals, is coming to a solution … There is now a single body of discipline fixed enough to integrate contemporary style as a reality and yet elastic enough to permit individual interpretation and to encourage general growth.

The authors supported their case with a selection of black-and-white photographs of buildings in places as far apart as California and Czechoslovakia. This method of presentation played down differences in size, colour and material. But the intellectual filters were just as crucial as the photographic ones in establishing a historical picture. Hitchcock and Johnson were evidently determined to honour a genuine modern style and therefore were bound to ignore such oddities as Wright or Expressionism which did not fit. Their criteria were also vague. The concept of 'regularity', for example, could never do justice to the spatial complexity of Richard Neutra's Lovell House or of Mies van der Rohe's Barcelona Pavilion. The authors' approach was strong on the general, the shared, and the typical, but weak on the personal, the practical and the particular.

312 Pierre Chareau and Bernard Bijvoet, Maison de Verre, Paris, 1928–31, detail of façade

This is not to deny the presence of a certain community of expression in the 1920s. It is rather to suggest that the major innovations of the period rested upon a deeper reorganization of the spatial and conceptual structures of architecture than can be conveyed by dealing with obvious similarities of appearance. Major revolutions in the history of architecture have usually blended together new forms and technical devices over spatial conceptions which embody an altered world-view. The hovering volumes, transparent layers and lateral interpenetrations which recurred in various guises in the modern architecture of the 1920s certainly relied upon the ambiguities of Cubism and the structural potentials of concrete and steel, but they also gave shape to Utopian sentiments exploring new relations between people, their artifacts and nature.

To come to terms with the internal life of a period style it is necessary to move back and forth between common elements, individual vocabularies and unique works of art. Some idea of what is meant by divergences of personal style may be gained by considering two seminal buildings of the 1920s analysed earlier in this book: Le Corbusier's Maison Cook of 1926 and Rietveld's Schröder House of 1923–4. These have more in common with one another than either of them has with, say, an Art Nouveau or an Expressionist dwelling, so it is reasonable to group them together; but one is still struck by the difference in spatial emphasis between Le Corbusier's planar box with its jigsaw intrusions of *pilotis* and partitions, and Rietveld's exploding planes which overlap and extend into the surroundings (a contrast which embodies some of the crucial differences between Purism and De Stijl). Each design also reflects something of its environment, the former having a certain Parisian touch about it (in its scale, hardware and linear elegance), the latter distilling the gridded, artificial Dutch landscape in its overlapping rectangular geometries. Many finer visual distinctions could no doubt be drawn between Rietveld's and Le Corbusier's other works, in order to characterize their personal styles. By degrees, one might even dig into each artist's world of meaning; on some levels it would be possible to discern shared themes to do with the spiritualization of the machine or liberation from past constraints, but if one pursued the matter further one would find contrasting private metaphors, sources of form, and ideological positions. The preceding few chapters have shown what a variety of social ideals was expressed through analogous forms during the 1920s.

Perhaps 1927 was the first year of maturity of the new style, in which forms could be assumed, and problems worked out on the basis of discoveries which were increasingly assured. It was the year of the Villa Stein/de Monzie at Garches, of the Bauhaus buildings at Dessau, of Neutra's Lovell House in California and of Golosov's Zuyev Workers' Club in Moscow; it was also the year

313 Hans Scharoun, exhibition dwelling, Weissenhofsiedlung, Stuttgart, 1927

314 Le Corbusier, exhibition dwelling, Weissenhofsiedlung, Stuttgart, 1927

315 Ludwig Mies van der Rohe, apartment house, Weissenhofsiedlung, Stuttgart, 1927

313

314

315

of two key symbolic events of international importance, the Competition for the League of Nations in Geneva, and the assembly of avant-garde tendencies at the Weissenhofsiedlung, Stuttgart. The former of these two events acted as a sharp reminder that the new forms had a long way to go before they received official acceptance; the latter, ostensibly an exhibition of housing ideas sponsored by the Deutscher Werkbund, was an affirmation that a shared language had at last been achieved. Even so the individual items in this contemporary museum of international architecture exhibited considerable divergences of approach. Hans Scharoun's house was composed of overlapping curves and was quite 'Expressionist' in character compared with the stereometric discipline of the other designs. Le Corbusier's larger building, with its *pilotis*, its taut, hovering box, its expanses of glazing, its nautical imagery and its almost obsessive demonstration of the Five Points, differed from Mies van der Rohe's far more contained, closed, earthbound and planimetric block of flats, with its structural columns running along the centre line. Le Corbusier's smaller house was a sophisticated rendering of the theme of the Maison Citrohan, employing different-coloured planes, slender *pilotis*

and carefully controlled openings. Next to it, Ludwig Hilberseimer's house was revealed to be a spiritless little box.

In part such distinctions had to do with differences of intention; in part they had to do with differences of function and size. From 1925 onwards the style which had so often been pioneered in small villas had increasingly to prove its worth in handling much larger and more complex programmes. The Bauhaus buildings at Dessau were one case where the architecture employed variations in the system to orchestrate a variety of functions and volumes. Another case, on an even larger scale, was the Van Nelle Factory of 1926–9 outside Rotterdam by Johannes A. Brinkman, Leendert Cornelis van der Vlugt and Mart Stam. The main production functions – tobacco, coffee and tea factories – were placed in three connected oblongs, each taller than the next, so that the building as a whole had a stepping form. The spaces inside were on an open plan, being supported on a grid of mushroom columns. The floor slabs were cantilevered so that the façades could be glazed without interruption to admit the maximum of light and air. The separation between the primary volumes could be sensed, but the form as a whole was unified by hovering

horizontal metallic bands floating a full 300 yards
(276 metres) without apparent support. This glazed
crescendo of weightless lines and planes was linked
laterally by dramatic conveyors and criss-cross
transparent bridges to the storage and transport
buildings along the parallel canal. Transparent
stair-towers supplied points of vertical stress and
could be read as discrete elements. The highest
volume was joined longitudinally by another glazed
bridge to the main office wing, curved to fit the
profile of the arrival street, and to provide a suitable
accentuation of its honorific meaning. The
composition was topped by a small glazed room
almost circular in shape, like some much-expanded
precision piece from a glass machine; in this,
guests could be received to survey the complex of
buildings below. In the main, curved entrance wing
a canteen was placed so that workers could come
together while the humming mechanical processes
of their joint endeavour continued alongside them.

The horizontal accent was relieved by verticals
containing lifts and pipes, but detailed to give
the sense of the thinnest possible transparent or
reflective surfaces, rather than any traditional sense
of mass.

Despite the fact that these forms had the clearest
basis in functional decisions concerning the process
of manufacture, and despite the fact that they could
be related to the naked facts of concrete and steel
construction, the pragmatic was transcended,
idealized, given a poetic, expressive presence.
We have to do here with matters far deeper than
style, matters of which style is only an outward
manifestation. These hovering glazed strips and
tense details resulted from a search for deeper
symbolic meanings in the mechanical process and in
the sphere of work. One recalls Lissitzky's panegyric
to the Vesnin brothers' project for the *Leningrad
Pravda* Building of 1924: 'the building is
characteristic of an age that thirsts after glass, steel

and concrete'. Le Corbusier, reacting to the evocative transparency of the Van Nelle Factory, sensed a social vision of emancipation:

The sheer façades of the building, bright glass and grey metal, rise up … against the sky … Everything is open to the outside. And this is of enormous significance to all those who are working, on all eight floors inside … The Van Nelle tobacco factory in Rotterdam, a creation of the modern age, has removed all the former connotations of despair from the word 'proletarian'. And this deflection of the egoistic property instinct towards a feeling for collective action leads to a most happy result: the phenomenon of personal participation in every stage of the human enterprise.

The programme of the Van Nelle Factory implied a linear arrangement of rectangular blocks; the Zonnestraal Sanatorium at Hilversum (1926–8) by Johannes Duiker and Bernard Bijvoet required a more dispersed plan as its main functions were a medical complex, an administrative block and individual linear wards requiring direct access to the outside. The principal purpose of the sanatorium was to treat eye diseases contracted by members of the diamond workers' union, and the clinical forms of modern architecture seemed well suited to the ethos and the social programme. The main volumes were disposed on a butterfly plan with the administration and communal facilities at the head and the sprawling wards in the wings. The individual functions were differentiated

by variations in form and fenestration.

Both the Van Nelle Factory and the Zonnestraal Sanatorium were influenced in part by Elementarist and Constructivist attitudes emanating ultimately from the Soviet Union, yet in order to grasp how different these buildings were from Russian work of the same period, one has only to compare them to Golosov's Zuyev Workers' Club in Moscow of 1927–8. Here the machine rhetoric of the great glass cylinder containing the stairs was more overt and less controlled than in the Van Nelle Factory. Compared to the thin, planar surfaces, the intersecting horizontal bands were chunky, even massive in appearance. The architect attempted to exploit violent contrasts of space and form, and to clash together, almost brutally, the different materials of his building, so as to dramatize functional differences and to create emotive mechanistic and revolutionary symbols.

Compared to any of the aforementioned three examples, Mendelsohn's Schocken Department Store at Chemnitz of 1928–9 presents a suave, unified and smooth appearance. The site was triangular, and the interiors were opened up by a grid of slender supports; stairs and lifts were shifted to the apexes of the triangle. The façade was a single broad curve, with an almost uninterrupted shop window at the base and continuous strip windows at the upper levels. No attempt was made to articulate the stairways or the circulation, or to dramatize changes of volume or material; rather there was a dynamic *Gestalt*, a simple yet living form subsuming all parts and details. One is reminded, of course, of Mendelsohn's earlier development, of the fusion of all the parts in his so-called 'Expressionist' phase, of his method of conceiving buildings as totalities in small, dynamic sketches. Mendelsohn's streamlined bands suggest debts to some of the pre-war works of Hans Poelzig, if not to Sullivan's Carson Pirie Scott Store in Chicago. The Van Nelle Factory belonged to a different world and stemmed from a different branch of the modern movement – the world of Elementarist, rectangular, abstract art; only the *superficialities* of style were the same.

The hovering volumes and weightless illusions of the International Style were related to the layering of space suggested by concrete cantilever construction; a building like the Van Nelle Factory did at least require a predominantly horizontal treatment. But

317

the elements of the new style had sometimes to cope with buildings of which the function implied a primarily vertical form. Such was the case with the skyscraper, where the problem of maintaining unity was severe. As with any reductivist vocabulary, the onus fell upon a clear expression of volume, plane, line and silhouette. The entire visual weight of a composition could be altered by advancing or recessing the glazing a fraction. In the *Chicago Tribune* competition, Gropius's entry employed subtle modulations of rectangular frame, vertical panel and cantilevered horizontal plane to unify the form; Mies van der Rohe's slightly earlier glass towers tended to adopt the solution of total glazing (hardly realizable at the time), the faceted panes being handled as vertical flanges attached to the extremities of the floor slabs. Le Corbusier's glass towers in the Ville Contemporaine expressed the floor slabs as thin lines (again, the glazing solution was scarcely practical but achieved a vertical articulation by bending the glazing back and forth as bays); Howe and Lescaze's design for the PSFS skyscraper in Philadelphia (1929–32) skilfully blended vertical and horizontal articulations which were rooted in functional and structural differences.

Factories, skyscrapers, blocks of flats, department stores and workers' clubs were, at least, specifically 'modern' functions; on occasion, though, the new architecture had to handle more traditional tasks like civic monuments and parliament buildings, where questions of size, hierarchy and

symbolism were crucial. The League of Nations competition of 1927 offers an intriguing insight into the way a variety of modern architects and 'traditionalists' approached the same 'monumental' programme and site. The building was to contain a species of world parliament, to express international idealism, and to contain a giant assembly hall, lobbies, a secretariat and a multiplicity of supporting bureaucratic functions; it was to stand near Geneva on the lakeside. The symbolic and rhetorical aspects of the problem were pivotal, and among the many entries were a number of half-baked attempts at a global and holistic imagery in the form of circular buildings, mandalas, and the like. Eventually, a rather clumsy Beaux-Arts scheme was chosen (designed by P.-H. Nénot), but only after a scandalous interlude in which Le Corbusier, who had appeared to be the winner, was disqualified on the grounds that he had not submitted original ink drawings, but prints.

In Le Corbusier's design the most important element, the assembly hall, was placed on a dominant axis, and the supporting functions of the secretariat were disposed as uniform lateral blocks overlooking strips of landscape and the nearby lake. The volume of the assembly was derived primarily from acoustic considerations and was curved in profile; it would have been reached gradually through a grand entrance facing the landward side, via a sequence of spaces of strongly ceremonial character linked on axis. Le Corbusier gave the lake

318 Ilya Golosov, Zuyev
Workers' Club, Moscow,
1927–8

319 Erich·Mendelsohn,
Schocken Department
Store, Chemnitz, 1928–9

320 Hannes Meyer,
competition project for the
League of Nations, Geneva,
1927,
axonometric drawing

321 Le Corbusier,
competition project for the
League of Nations, Geneva,
1927,
axonometric drawing

façade of the assembly hall a monumental treatment by using grandiose *pilotis* supporting a curved portico with a sculptural group; this element radiated to the setting, as if transmitting the deliberations of the League of Nations to the wider world. The library was another ceremonial element, and this was placed on the cross axis of the scheme. The secretariat was treated in a more neutral way, with long windows, polished granite panels, balconies and *pilotis* allowing the passage of circulation beneath. The spatial richness of Le Corbusier's building arose from the interplay between these 'sliding' horizontal slabs, and the predominant hierarchy with its latent classical order. His project suggested a communal machine for enlightened, well-meaning functionaries whose life would be daily nourished through contact with nature; a modern palace for the world élite.

It is intriguing to compare Le Corbusier's design with Hannes Meyer's entry in the same competition. Kenneth Frampton has characterized the contrast as one between 'the humanist and the utilitarian' ideals. Meyer was suspicious of the poetic Utopianism of men like Le Corbusier, and of the élitist values implicit in the programme. In his scheme, the secretariat was the dominant element

and was contained in an open-framed tower, a celebration of engineering recalling the architect's admiration for Russian Constructivism. The deliberate accentuation of the factory aesthetic and 'found' industrial objects was no doubt intended as a sort of proletarian imagery, again following the 'code' of the Russian avant-garde. There was no hankering after what the architect might have regarded as a specious traditionalism bolstering an honorific interpretation of the institution. Meyer even played down the possible hierarchical characteristics of his scheme by designing the whole on a standardized and repetitive module. Despite the denials of symbolism, these forms were loaded with the sort of social content that the 'New Objectivity' (p. 190) architects in Germany had striven to express by an 'honest' assessment of function and technique; Meyer's scheme was intended to convey the image of an entirely open, egalitarian forum: a mechanism for reaching consensus by the people and for the people. The architect wrote revealingly of it:

If the intentions of the League of Nations are sincere, then it cannot possibly cram such a novel social organization into the straitjacket of traditional architecture. No pillared reception rooms for weary monarchs but hygienic workrooms for the busy representatives of their people. No back corridors for backstairs diplomacy but open glazed rooms for public negotiation of honest men.

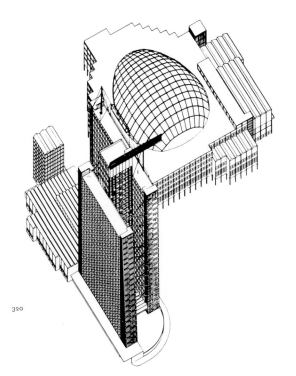

320

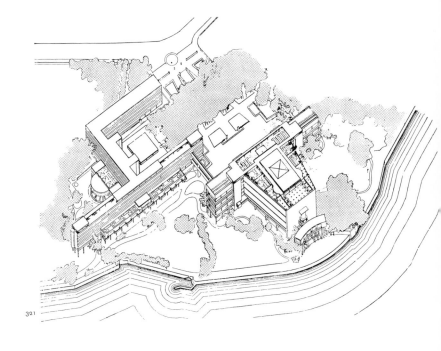

321

The contrast between Le Corbusier's and Meyer's designs, and the ideologies they articulated, calls to mind some of the debates between so-called 'formalists' and 'functionalists' in Russia (Chapter 12) and Germany (Chapter 11) at about the same time. Le Corbusier was later castigated by socialist architects committed to a functionalist line for his dangerous 'Utopianism' and for his concern with the past, and replied that he saw man's deepest aspirations as transcending the mere categories of left and right. His design for the League of Nations was a celebration of his belief in a rational, enlightened humanity, aspiring to abstract principles of justice and law. In his eyes an over-emphasis on the utilitarian aspects of the problem would have been as inappropriate as an over-emphasis on authority through monumental rhetoric. He sought to embody some of the higher ideals of the enclosed institution while also linking the rituals of a world parliament to an orchestrated experience of nature – the high peaks to the south on the other side of Lac Léman, and the barrier to the north, the Jura massif. The comparison of the two schemes is so valuable because it demonstrates different personal and ideological emphases in buildings which it might still be possible to group together under the same broad label of style.

Those architects who, like Hannes Meyer, advocated a 'New Objectivity', were emphatic about separating themselves from both 'traditionalists' using vestiges of historical forms, and modernists who relied upon what was, from their point of view, an irrelevant personal lyricism. In 1926, the magazine *ABC* bore a telling illustration which placed alongside each other Ragnar Östberg's 'National Romantic' Stockholm Town Hall of 1909–23 (Fig. 147), Paul Bonatz's traditionalist Stuttgart Railway Station of 1911–27 (Fig. 349) and a De Stijl house project of 1923 (by Theo van Doesburg and Cornelis van Eesteren) made from coloured planes exploding into the surrounding space. According to the criteria of the International Style, and by most definitions of modern architecture, the last would have been considered 'acceptable', the first two taboo; but from the point of view of the New Objectivity, *all* were anathema, and, in the illustration, all were crossed out.

Thus, by packing together things that happened to look like each other and by claiming that

they were all part of a unified phenomenon, the proponents of an 'International Style' ran the risk of ignoring considerable differences of visual inflection, and great differences of intention and of belief. The Czech modern movement, founded in the early 1920s by the Devetsil group (including such architects as Karel Teige, Jaromir Krejcar and Josef Chochol), could supply a cautionary tale here, since it was pluralist from the beginning and contained numerous battling groups along the spectrum from 'functionalism' to 'formalism'. Radical ideas were published in such magazines as *Stavba* and *Stavitel*, which served as forums for debates concerning the social role of modern architecture and as sources of information on developments east and west of Czechoslovakia. One is not surprised to find a blend of ideas from both Western European and Soviet sources. The variety of theoretical positions was matched by a certain pluralism of vocabulary. Otto Eisler's 'Double House' at Brno of 1926 employed some of the 'constituent elements' of the new architecture on the outside, but with a somewhat compartmentalized plan. Czech modern architectural expression ranged from the polychrome Constructivist drama of Bohuslav Fuch's Pavilion of the City of Brno of 1928, to the restraint of Ludvik Kysela's Bata Shop in Prague of 1928–9. At the puritan extreme of opinion was the critic Karel Teige who, in 1929, massed an attack against Le Corbusier's project, also of 1929, for a 'Mundaneum' (a sort of Acropolis of world culture dominated by a ziggurat-like museum, the whole for a site above Geneva) on the grounds that it regressed towards an Idealist Platonism and a retrograde monumentality. It was towards the end of the 1920s that Mies van der Rohe (whose luxurious Tugendhat House of 1928–30 was in Brno, Fig. 369) was also being hounded for his

322

323

'spirituality' and supposed lack of concern for the problems of the greatest number.

Modern architecture in the 1920s also articulated a variety of visions of the private sphere, revealing a spectrum of design ideas for the interior, all the way from the clinical sparseness and naked light bulbs of the New Objectivity architects, to the shot silk, polished steel and lustrous chrome of Mies van der Rohe. In his houses Le Corbusier exploited contrasts between planar walls (some white, others in uniform greens, browns, blues), industrial *objets-trouvés* (metal radiators, doorknobs, taps), bentwood Thonet chairs, and handicraft objects such as boldly coloured, geometric Berber rugs from North Africa. Working in collaboration with Charlotte Perriand, he developed an entire range of tubular steel furniture relying upon bicycle technology and fitted to the human body in sitting or reclining positions. The *chaise longue*, with its slender steel structure and leather covering, may have been partly inspired by camp furniture, but its

sinuous shape was also in harmony with the curved geometry of the 'free plan'. The architect and designer Eileen Gray also developed a refined aesthetic for the interior relying upon subtle juxtapositions of exotic, folk and machine-age finishes, and upon a sensitivity to the intimate rituals of daily existence. She brought together sliding screens (of Oriental inspiration), modular woodwork, light-weight chairs with leather upholstery (e.g. the 'Transat' chair), lacquered surfaces and woven fabrics. The house which Gray designed for herself and Jean Badovici at Cap Martin, 1926–9, revealed 'a relaxed and elastic control of the visual ambiance', a sense of human nuance and spatial incident at odds with stylistic manipulation and with the vacuity of merely functionalist design.

The International Style had some adherents who only partly understood the underlying principles, and who adopted the forms as a new external dress. In such cases, modern forms became a sort of packaging, a cosmetic application, rather than the expression of deeper meanings or the disciplined result of attention to the functional discipline suggested by a task. This was one of the dangers of speaking of the new architecture as a 'style' at all; it suggested that a set of visual formulae could be picked up and then applied. The work of the Dutch architect Willem Dudok supplies an example of this competent 'stylism'; or in France, that of Robert Mallet-Stevens. Each was capable of making of modern reductivism a sort of pleasing simplicity, which none the less lacked the transcending visionary content of the authentic modern movement.

Of course, to the die-hard functionalist, distinctions like these were not relevant; so far as he was concerned, all style was false imposition. In 1929 the engineer-philosopher Richard Buckminster Fuller designed an aluminium house around a central mast of mechanical services. He claimed that this 'Dymaxion House' was far more tightly related to functional and technological optimization than the cosmetic productions of the modern movement, which he rejected out of hand:

The 'International Style' … demonstrated fashion-inoculation without necessary knowledge of the scientific fundamentals of structural mechanics and chemistry.

The International Style 'simplification' then was but superficial. It peeled off yesterday's exterior embellishment and put on instead formalized novelties of quasi-simplicity, permitted by the same hidden structural elements of modern alloys that had permitted the discarded Beaux-Arts garmentation … The new International Stylist hung 'stark motif walls' of vast super-meticulous brick assemblage, which had no tensile cohesiveness within its own bonds, but was, in fact, locked within hidden steel frames supported by steel without visible means of support. In many such illusory ways did the 'International Style' gain dramatic sensory impingement on society as does a trick man gain the attention of children …

Running through this assessment was a belief in the 'honest' use and assemblage of technique and function, without the 'imposition' of symbolic or aesthetic filters; and as a critique of the plumbing and structural veracity of modern architecture, Fuller's criticisms may have had a point. But as architectural criticism, his remarks were, frankly, beside the point. They remind one that, for all the rhetoric used in the 1920s concerning the 'honest expression' of function, structure, and technology, the game had to go on at one remove, as it were, in

324 Willem Dudok, Town Hall, Hilversum, 1924–31

325 Richard Buckminster Fuller, Dymaxion House, 1929, model

324

the field of symbolic forms, if the pragmatic was to be translated into art. One can go further, and say that it was in the tension between such apprehended facts as, say, an industrial window, or a standardized reinforced-concrete column, and the symbolic associations they evoked, that part of the expressive power of the new architecture lay. Whether or not the washbasin in Le Corbusier's Villa Savoye entrance was good plumbing, it was a standard fixture whose meaning was transformed by juxtaposition with surrounding *objets-types* – the *pilotis*, the industrial windows, etc. – whose external form mirrored a higher ideal; modern architects sought a kind of poetry of everyday facts transcended by ideas. In the end, to claim that structure was handled 'dishonestly', or that the latest fixtures were not included or designed by the architects, would be a little like complaining of a Renaissance architect that his avowed revival of a particular ancient prototype was 'inexact'. The architects of the machine age transformed the stuff of industrial production into new forms and meanings, but in such a way that the original 'reality' of, say, a glass brick or a nautical detail would be among the layers of reference of the final form. The historian William Jordy described this 'symbolic objectivity' rather well:

The goal of symbolic objectivity was to align architecture with the pervasive factuality of modern existence, with that 'ineloquence' (to call up Bernard Berenson's tag) which characterizes the modern imagination. The aims of simplification and purification at the core of the movement, providing it with a morality of Calvinist austerity, actually stemmed from a diffuse convention on the part of many progressive designers and theorists during the nineteenth century to the effect that architecture should be 'honest', 'truthful', and 'real', especially with respect to the revelation of functional programme and of materials and structure. During the 1920s this moralistic heritage acquired an antiseptic cleanliness, and irreducible bareness, which symbolically, if not quite literally, accords with the morality of objectivity …

But the objection against taking 'functionalist' slogans at face value is even more fundamental. For even those few architects of the 1920s who saw themselves as pursuing a purely functional architecture were still stuck with the fact that functions do not, on their own, generate forms. Even the most tightly defined set of requirements may be answered in a variety of ways, and *a priori* images concerning the eventual appearance of the building will enter the design process at some point.

325

Thus functions could only be translated into the forms and spaces of architecture through the screen of a style, and in this case it was a style of symbolic forms which referred, among other things, to the notion of functionality.

Some architects rejected simplistic attempts at equating modern architecture with any particular style, not only because this was too exclusive, but also because they wished to emphasize that durable architectural values lay beyond the range of style. Rudolf Schindler criticized the 1932 exhibition at the Museum of Modern Art which gave rise to Hitchcock and Johnson's book *The International Style* on precisely these grounds. He wrote to Philip Johnson about the forthcoming show:

It seems to me that instead of showing late attempts at creative architecture, it tends towards concentrating on the so-called 'International Style'.

If this is the case my work has no place in it. I am not a stylist, not a functionalist, nor any other sloganist. Each of my buildings deals with a different architectural problem, the existence of which has been entirely forgotten in this period of rational mechanization.

If such varied and unique works of the 1920s as, say, Johannes Duiker's Open Air School in Amsterdam of 1929–30, or Alvar Aalto's *Turun Sanomat* Building of 1927, or Rudolph Schindler's Lovell Beach House of 1923–6 continued to hold attention for years after they were built, it was less because they wore some acceptable period uniform, than because of their inherent vitality as architectural creations, binding together ideas, forms and materials in the service of unique intentions. The Maison de Verre in Paris of 1928–31, designed for Dr Dalsace by Pierre Chareau and Bernard Bijvoet, was another work of the time to evade facile categorization. It was constructed to combine the functions of a medical clinic and a private house, in a quiet enclave off a Paris street. The pervasive materials were glass brick and thin steel structural elements, elegantly composed into a linear aesthetic recalling the slender wooden frames and screens of traditional Japanese construction. The interior plan was complex, reflecting the need to separate home and profession, and to get light into a tight urban site yet preserve privacy. The glass brick was made to function as a veil, filtering the silver-grey Parisian light into the interiors, but also keeping the world at bay. Plate glass was used sparingly, either in small

strips laid flush with the glass brick or else as a separate layer. The most impressive space was the double-height living room/library with its slung galleries, its adjustable louvres, its exposed bolts and its thin slabs of slate attached to the piers. Wires were threaded through metal tubes running from floor to ceiling with switches set directly into them, and heat was passed through ducts in the floor slabs then distributed through grilles. It is possible that the imagery was inspired by such things as the stacks at the mid-nineteenth-century Bibliothèque Nationale by Henri Labrouste, or the companion ladders and engine rooms of ships. Whatever the precise sources, they were transformed into an elegant and translucent *machine à habiter* with a tranquil sense of space. The Maison de Verre was like an elaborate piece of hardware or modern furniture with moving parts (a folding stair, adjustable slats, sliding doors), but it also worked with ambiguous definitions of material and with illusions of recession, depth and transparency. The Maison de Verre helped to refocus interest on metallic frames and on the culture of revealed construction, and was a major step in a line of experiments in glass and steel in the 1930s in France; but it was also poetic work full of hidden implications. Beyond the obvious mechanistic themes there was an intense involvement with the daily rituals of the dwelling, with the tactile aspects of experience, and with the metaphorical power of glass, stone, steel and light.

Materials and their associations must be considered part of the matrix of a style. The white-plaster walls and planar surfaces so often employed in the 1920s were perhaps intended to convey a non-material quality, to suggest the opposite of handicraft: the abstraction of the machine. The sheen of glass and the thinness of aluminium were likewise evocative of aeroplanes or mass-produced objects. Volumes were made to float, boundaries to dissolve – all effects evocative of new freedoms. A style may be considered a complex of formal relationships in which certain moods and meanings are most at home; it provides a set of conventions, which, in the compelling and profound work of art, come together in such a way that the conventionality is forgotten. The pedant may insist that abstract art and mechanism, that ocean liners and classical values have no necessary connection, but when he

326

327

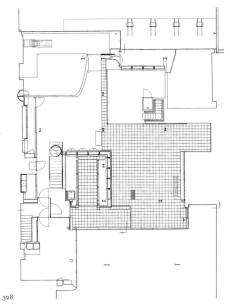

328

329

330

has experienced the Villa Stein/de Monzie at Garches, these doubts are dispelled by a poetic sense of inevitability.

It is a paradox of great works of art that they should announce with unparalleled force the imperatives of a new outlook while simultaneously invoking, at a deep level, the values which informed classic moments in the past. This is another reason why it is never adequate to characterize a work merely in terms of the style phase linking it to other works contemporary with it. Henri Focillon has suggested that 'the time that gives support to a work

of art does not give definition either to its principle or to its specific form'. This shrewd observation seems specially pertinent to two masterworks of the modern movement: the Villa Savoye at Poissy by Le Corbusier, 1928–31 (which has the next chapter to itself), and the German Pavilion in Barcelona (the Barcelona Pavilion) of 1928–9 by Mies van der Rohe.

The Pavilion was built as a temporary structure for the International Exhibition of that year, and had the honorific, not to say ambassadorial, function of representing the cultural values of a new Germany eager to distance itself from its

330 Ludwig Mies van
der Rohe, Barcelona
Pavilion, 1928–9

331 Barcelona Pavilion

332 Barcelona Pavilion,
plan

imperialist past. The Weimar Republic wished to project an image of openness, liberality, modernity, and internationalism. The Commissar General of the Reich, Georg von Schnitzler, stated that the building should 'show what we can do, what we are, how we feel and see today. We do not want anything but clarity, simplicity and honesty.' Mies van der Rohe wrote revealingly of the task:

The era of monumental expositions that make money is past. Today we judge an exposition by what it accomplishes in the cultural field.

Economic, technical and cultural conditions have changed radically. It is very important for our culture and our society, as well as for technology and industry, to find good solutions. German industry, and indeed, European industry as a whole must understand and solve these specific tasks. The path must lead from quantity towards quality, from the extensive to the intensive.

Along this path industry and technology will join with the forces of thought and culture.

There were reminiscences here of the ideological programme of the pre-war Deutscher Werkbund,

and one is not surprised to discover that Mies van de Rohe's design made a deliberate synthesis of form and technique, of modern and classical values. As a demonstration of the power of modern structural invention to create unprecedented spatial effects, the building was a *tour de force*. The thin roof-slab was poised delicately on eight cruciform steel columns clad in chrome: a conception recalling the Dom-ino skeleton, but only a single storey in height. While some of the walls were load-bearing, the *idea* expressed was of the independence of wall-planes from traditional supporting roles. In this context the structural frame was far from being a low-cost instrument of standardization; it was accompanied by expensive materials – marble and onyx walls, tinted, semi-reflecting glass, sharp-edged stainless steel and travertine. This simple trabeated and symmetrical structure was placed to one end of a raised podium in tense juxtapostion to two rectangular pools. A counterpoint was set in motion by shifting the axis of the main pool off that of the pavilion, and this visual movement was reinforced by the way that the walls were set down, some under the roof, others extending into the surroundings, all of them free of the grid of supports. The soffit was white, the junction with the top of the columns smooth, so that the roof appeared to float parallel to water and floor. The plan of the Barcelona Pavilion read like an abstract picture with lines of varying weight generating an intense rhythm of spaces and of planes.

Until recently, the only way in which the Barcelona Pavilion was known to the majority was through black-and-white photographs taken soon after completion (the building was dismantled shortly after the Exhibition). These showed it in an even light with sharp profiles and precise edges cut by shadow. As the eye of the camera moved about, the rippling chrome, glass, water, stone, steel and onyx merged identities, the solid becoming lustrous, the translucent becoming dense. The interiors were furnished with heavy leather chairs supported by criss-cross stainless-steel flanges coated in chrome ('Barcelona chairs'). Regal and luxurious, these were grouped formally, not unlike objects of antiquity, or tensile versions of thrones. The Barcelona Pavilion had the specific, honorific function of a chamber for the reception of the Spanish king and queen by the German

331

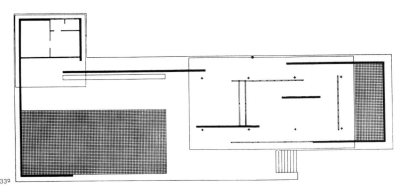

332

ambassador; it was a '*Repräsentationsraum*'.
For the rest, the interior was left uncluttered,
a demonstration perhaps of a new way of life
supposed to have a special appeal to the cultivated
industrial élite. Recalling the Deutscher Werkbund
Pavilion of 1914, there was a classical contemporary
female statue (designed by Georg Kolbe) by one of
the pools. This made an odd touch alongside the
rectangular rigours of Mies's modern forms, but it
was a further reminder that the building as a whole
was guided by a classical sense.

The Barcelona Pavilion was reconstructed in the
1980s following the original plans, but not using
the original elements which had been lost. The
simulacrum hints at the original experience of the
building and underlines the extent to which Mies
van de Rohe's architectural ideas were reliant upon
the ambiguous qualities of materials. As one moves
up on to the platform, the precisely cut stone
surfaces establish a stately rhythm, while the play of
light on water, marble, layers of semi-transparent
glass and stainless steel introduces a mercurial
quality. The transition into the building involves
working through several layers (actual or
perceptual) and in the process one understands how

the partitions blend together internal and external
'rooms'. The cruciform chrome columns (with their
latter-day version of fluting) supply vertical accents
of light, but lack tectonic density; the polished
marble and onyx surfaces are also sheer and
reflective. The glass planes (green, grey or black)
may be seen several at a time, in which case they
melt with the light, though seen obliquely they
emerge as vitreous stone. The water itself blends
with these evanescent shifts from opaque to liquid,
being either a mirror surface or else a semi-
translucent plane. The dappled patterns of reflected
light merge with the veins of onyx and marble, while
ripples activate the chrome. The coarse-grained
travertine of the base, the benches and some of the
external partitions introduces a shadow-absorbing
surface noble, even antique, in effect.

In terms of Mies van der Rohe's evolving
vocabulary, the Barcelona Pavilion was a synthesis
of the hovering horizontal slabs and grid structures
he had envisaged in his Concrete Office Building
project of 1922, and of the sort of pivotal plan he had
experimented with in the Brick Villa of 1923. In the
intervening six years he had had the opportunity to
test variations of his ideas – in the Rosa Luxemburg

Monument of 1926, in the Weissenhofsiedlung designs of 1925–7, in several houses, and in exhibition pavilions for glass and for silk products, which he designed in 1927. The Barcelona Pavilion accumulated all these discoveries in a single statement, which did not, however, suffer from the overburdening of ideas. In the mind of its creator, the pavilion may have been the purest embodiment of the *Zeitgeist*: for Mies van de Rohe the most significant spiritual artefacts were those which translated 'the will of the epoch into space'.

But the Barcelona Pavilion, like the Schröder House, the Bauhaus buildings or Le Corbusier's villas, was also a solution to broader, shared problems of expression of the period. Historians have drawn attention to the similarity of the plan to Mondrian's paintings; to the 'factuality' of the materials employed (relating Mies tangentially to the 'New Objectivity'); to the simplicity of the wall surfaces recalling Berlage's pleas for well-proportioned surfaces unadorned from top to bottom; to the novelty and richness of the space conception with its floating planes, painterly illusions and ambiguities. It is not surprising that Hitchcock and Johnson should have singled out the building as an exemplar of the International Style.

Yet the roots of Mies van der Rohe's masterwork lie deeper than this in history. Attention has already been drawn to his admiration for Schinkel, manifest particularly in his neo-classical designs of the pre-First World War years. It was the reduction of form to the most expressive simple geometries, and the radical redefinition of basic classical types, which most inspired him in the work of his Prussian predecessor. Surely one recognizes a similar concentration on classical essentials in the Barcelona Pavilion, especially in its impeccable proportions, its sense of repose, and its restatement in an abstract form of the elemental column and entablature. It distilled the image of a temple on a podium, but supplied it with the sensation of weightless liberation, enlivening it with a new kind of space (transformed from Wright and Cubism), and subverting its solidity in rippling surfaces and liquefied matter. It showed that the 'simplifications' of modern architecture could blend an imagery of contemporary relevance with a reminiscence of architecture's most enduring values.

16

the image and idea of le corbusier's villa savoye at poissy

To make a plan is to determine and fix ideas. It is to have had ideas. It is so to order these ideas that they become intelligible, capable of execution and communicable.
… A plan is to some extent a summary like an analytical contents table. In a form so condensed that it seems as clear as crystal and like a geometrical figure, it contains an enormous quantity of ideas and the impulse of an intention.
Le Corbusier, 1923

334 Le Corbusier, Villa Savoye, Poissy, 1928–31, view up last leg of ramp

The last chapter examined the validity of the notion of the 'International Style' and found it strong in some respects, weak in others. It seems that the early apologists of modern architecture were over-preoccupied with defining a generalized historical identity for the style and were not sufficiently attentive to individual and personal intentions. There *was* a broadly shared language of expression in the 1920s in certain countries of Western Europe and parts of the Soviet Union and the United States, but this possessed deeper complexities than defined by the lexicon and supplied a transitional phase for most of the architects involved. Moreover, it was only one of a number of visual options, and the most interesting works conceived within it were so individual as to remain virtually uncategorizable.

Beyond even the personal language of the artist there is another level which has to be grasped if the inner meaning of a new tradition is to be understood. This lies in the special intellectual chemistry of the individual work of a high order. Here one is interested in the unique site, context and intentions, as well as the artist's usual themes and vocabulary; in the expression of a particular social vision in resonant forms, as well as the pervasive mood of the times. In this case the Villa Savoye at Poissy of 1928–31 by Le Corbusier has been singled out for monographic scrutiny. For, like the Barcelona Pavilion, this building 'contains an enormous quantity of ideas', embodies a myth of modern life, and contains echoes of the past. To probe into its underlying meanings is to penetrate still further Le Corbusier's patterns of imaginative thinking in early maturity.

Architecture works with four dimensions, not just three. By nature it is involved with time and change. The form of a building is understood gradually as one moves through it, comparing scenographic incidents, and fitting them into a growing sense of the whole. The same building varies with weather and light, as silhouette, shape, or depth are accentuated. Movement and change lie near the heart of the Villa Savoye's conception. A description of the building is best conducted as a promenade.

The Villa Savoye (also known by the evocative name Les Heures Claires) stands some twenty miles (30 kilometres) north-west of Paris on the outskirts

335

335 Le Corbusier, Villa Savoye, Poissy, 1928–31, view from south-west

336 Villa Savoye, axonometric sketch showing relationship of roof terrace to sun and the processional character of the automobile approach

337 Villa Savoye, entrance

of the small town of Poissy; the site is bordered by trees on three sides, yet has a long view towards the softly rolling fields and valleys of the Île de France beyond the fourth. Perhaps one arrives by car, in which case one leaves the road and passes by a small, white, cubic gate-lodge guarding the entrance to the drive. The gravel way turns slowly into the trees, its destination mysterious. Then one catches the first view of the villa standing fifty yards away towards the centre of an open meadow.

The first impression is of a horizontal white box, poised on *pilotis*, set off against the rural surroundings, the far panorama and the sky. The driveway passes through the undercroft, whose walls are deep green, circles the building beneath the overhang, and re-emerges to return to the road on the other side. The main first-level box is surmounted by curved volumes (once painted in vivid colours) just visible to the rear. Bit by bit one gathers that the villa is not as detached as it first appears. It is sculpted and hollowed to allow the surroundings to enter it, and its formal energies radiate to the borders of the site and to the distant horizon.

The main 'façade' is somewhat blank and forbidding and gives the impression (later to be disproved) of a completely symmetrical building,

rooted to the ground in its middle part. The strong horizontal emphasis is supplied by the overall shape, the single strip window running from one end to the other of the (main) upper level, and the repeated horizontals of the factory glazing at the lower level (hiding the mundane functions of servants' and chauffeur's quarters). The predominant verticals at this stage are the ranks of cylindrical *pilotis* receding on each side behind the suggested façade plane; they supply an airy sense of lightness and are placed so that the box above appears to hover.

The approach to the building has a curious quality of ceremony, as if one were being drawn without choice into some Corbusian machine-age ritual. The car passes beneath the overhang as a forceful reminder of a guiding point of the artist's doctrine. The entrance is found at the apex of a curve formed by the glazed lower level. A chauffeur is assumed, and as one is put down on the main axis, the car continues to follow the curve, then to slide in diagonally beneath the rectangular superstructure.

One passes through the main doors into the vestibule, a space defined by curved glass surfaces to either side. The main choices are clear. A ramp rises straight ahead along the main axis of the building to the upper levels. To the left is a spiral stair linking the servants' zone to the world above. Ahead and

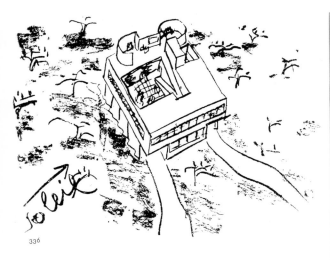

336

337

338

slightly to the left a washbasin stands mysteriously on its own in the hall leading to the chauffeur's quarters. The surfaces all around are brittle and smooth, the atmosphere clinical. The space is set about with the pure forms of cylindrical *pilotis*. Those near the door are grouped to form a sort of portico and – a subtle touch – one of them is made square in plan to correspond to the corner of an interior wall flanking the other side of the base of the ramp. Another refined detail catches the eye: the small white tiles in the floor are laid out on the diagonal, and effect a subtle link between the various curves and rectangles of the building.

The ramp is the very spine of the idea: in plan it stands on the axis and passes between the grid of *pilotis* (not so regularly spaced as one might at first

imagine); in section it suggests a dynamic passage through the horizontal floor slabs, bringing with it a gradual expansion of space the higher one goes. The plan of the Villa Savoye is nearly square, one of the ideal shapes which the architect so admired, and part of the richness of the building comes from the dynamics of curved forms within a stable perimeter. The ramp guides the '*promenade architecturale*' and links the various events; in turn it supplies an ennobling, character to the ascent.

After turning back on its original direction, the ramp emerges on the first floor, the main living-level of the house (as at Garches, a *piano nobile*), where the most formal and public spaces are situated. They stand around the roof terrace, a sort of outdoor room concealed from the exterior by a uniform strip

339

window without glass. This catches the sun at all times of the day (it faces in a southerly direction) and helps to fill the house with light. The biggest room is the salon, with a large expanse of glazing giving straight on to the terrace and a strip window facing the best view – that of the distant hills, to the north-west. To the other two sides of the roof terrace are the more 'private' areas: the kitchen (in the corner) with its own tiny terrace; the guest bedroom; Madame Savoye's bedroom, boudoir and bathroom; and her sons' bedroom and bathroom. The Villa Savoye was not an all-the-year home, but a country retreat or summer weekend residence – a villa in an old tradition, where the well-to-do might retire and enjoy the greenery and fresh air of the countryside. Among other curiosities on the main

level are the fireplace in the salon expressed as a free-standing stack, and a blue-tiled reclining seat next to the main bathroom, suggesting something of both Madame Savoye's and Le Corbusier's obsessive interest in cleanliness and athleticism.

The interrelated themes of health, fresh air, sunlight and intellectual clarity are reinforced as one continues up the ramp to the topmost level, again making a return at a middle-level landing. The floor of the ramp is finished in paving laid on the diagonal to reinforce the sense of movement, in contrast to the orthogonal details of analogous flagstones on the main terrace. It is in these upper regions that the artist's nautical fantasies are felt most vividly, especially in the delicate tubular 'ship's' railings and the curious stack containing the top of the spiral

stair. This is a relative of other cylinders in
the composition; the spiral stair can be seen
'peeling' away below it, behind liquidly dark and
semi-transparent areas of glazing. As at Garches,
and in Le Corbusier's paintings, the richness of
the effect comes from the harmony and similarity
of basic geometrical forms, from the control of
proportion and ratio, and from effects of illusion
whereby objects are glimpsed through layers of glass
or through windows cut clean through the plainest
of white surfaces. Ambiguity constantly reinforces
visual tension. Sigfried Giedion referred to the villa
as a '*construction spirituelle*', and claimed to see in
the dynamic experience of the building an example
of 'space-time' – supposedly an architectural
equivalent to notions of relativity. Be this as it may,
the Villa Savoye clearly exploits the ideas of variable
view-points and simultaneous perceptions of
multiple layers and levels.

The final slope of the ramp ascends towards the
solarium – seen first from the outside as a hovering
curved volume, but from this position as a thin,
strip-like plane with a small window cut clean into
it. It is this which now holds the attention – a
rectangle of blue sky and passing clouds, seen in an
entirely monochrome surround. As one draws level
with it, one has the breathtaking view of the distant
valleys which captured the attention in the very first
approach. Then the building was seen surrounded
by the setting; now the setting is framed by the
building. The adequate provision of greenery
was a central part of Le Corbusier's machine-age
mythology. At the Villa Savoye nature is celebrated
as dramatically as the idea of the house as a *machine
à habiter*, or the theme of procession by car; views
of trees and grass are carefully orchestrated and
framed. These vignettes of the exterior have an
almost super-real intensity, as if the artist has
clipped bits of the outside world and spliced them
together in a collage.

At the Villa Savoye several formal ideas are fused
together. There is a symmetrical armature which
is reinforced by the square plan, the central ramp
and the curvature of the drive. Within this there
is an asymmetrical counter-theme, expressed by
the dynamic action of the curves on top, by the
asymmetry of the main roof terrace, and by the
lateral expansion of the free plan. In fact the design
also contains an implied rotational movement, while

340

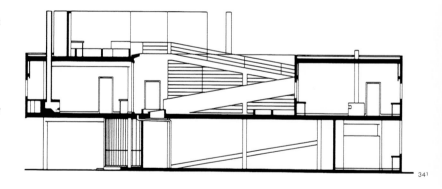

341

340 Le Corbusier, Villa
Savoye, Poissy, 1928–31,
view across terrace to
ramp

341 Villa Savoye, section
showing salon, terrace
and boudoir at first level

342 Le Corbusier,
*Still Life with Numerous
Objects*, 1923. Oil on
canvas, 48 × 57¹/₂ in
(114 × 146 cm). Fondation
Le Corbusier, Paris

the actual transition from floor to floor allows one
to link together inner vistas and events with outer
ones. The Villa Savoye might be understood
as an analogue to the flux and relativity of
modern experience; equally it might be seen as
an architectural equivalent to the transparencies,
simultaneities and illusions of Cubist painting.
Interestingly, Le Corbusier evoked the dynamism
of his conception in terms of an 'Espace Arabe':

Arab architecture provides us with a precious lesson. It is
appreciated on the move, on foot; it is in walking, in moving about,
that one sees the ordering devices of architecture develop. It is a
principle contrary to Baroque architecture which is conceived on
paper, around a fixed, theoretical point…
 In this house there is a true architectural promenade, offering
ever-changing views, some of them unexpected, some of them
astonishing. It is interesting to obtain so much diversity when
one has, for instance, admitted a constructive system based on an
absolutely rigorous schema of beams and columns.

The Villa Savoye drew together a number of the
architect's earlier themes and formal experiments.
In *Vers une architecture* Le Corbusier had referred
to the idea of setting down 'standards' and then,
through a gradual process of experiment and
refinement, 'perfecting' them by paring them down

to their most essential characteristics. He claimed
that this had occurred for the Greek temple in the
development between Paestum and the Parthenon
(Chapter 10, fig. 189). In a sense one may see the
Villa Savoye as a culmination of a similar path of
refinement but telescoped into the single decade
of the 1920s. The propositions of the Maison
Citrohan, the principles of the Five Points of a New
Architecture, the proposals of *Vers une architecture*,
the suggestions of the various intermediary schemes
(e.g. Maison Cook, the unrealized Maison Meyer,
Villa Stein/de Monzie) were here ennobled,
dignified and simplified to an extreme degree. One
is bound to say that the Villa Savoye, like the Robie
House, and like certain of Palladio's mature villas,
represents a high point of expression within a
vocabulary of type forms.

When Le Corbusier was first approached with
the commission in 1928, he had at last achieved his
synthesis; he was a mature architect of the highest
order. It is intriguing to speculate on his possible
initial responses to the Savoye's suggestions for a
country house and to a site which was not, for once,
hemmed in by other buildings. He described his

342

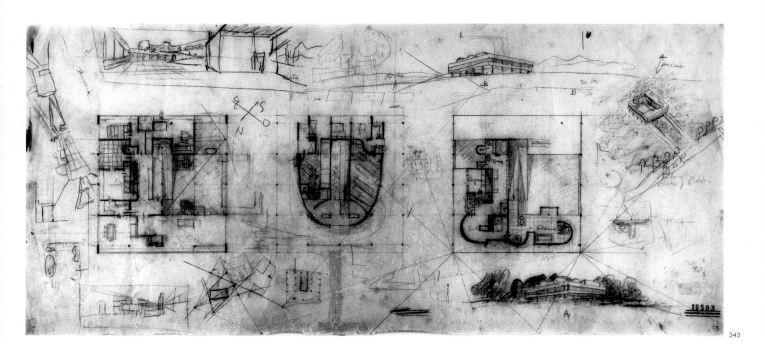

343

clients as 'completely without preconceived ideas, modern or ancient': 'Their idea was simple: they had a magnificent park formed from meadows surrounded by forest; they wanted to live in the countryside; they were linked to Paris 30 kilometres away by car.' Le Corbusier was no doubt intrigued by the possibility of weaving his own fantasy of modern life around a sort of ritualistic celebration of his client's high bourgeois habits – the arrival by car, the 'ablutions' in the chauffeur's hall, the companion stair for the servants, the ramp for the initiated or the well-to-do. One guesses, too, that he must have realized immediately that this site allowed the possibility of a sculpture in the round – rather than a building with a single façade like Maison Cook, or a front and back like 'Les Terrasses' at Garches.

Unfortunately, the evidence of Le Corbusier's sketches for the Villa Savoye is incomplete, patchy, and not firmly dated. It seems that there were five different schemes between September 1928 and April 1929. As was often the case in his design processes, some ideas which emerged early were discarded, only to be picked up again later

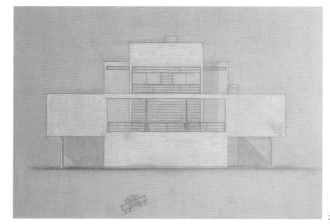

344

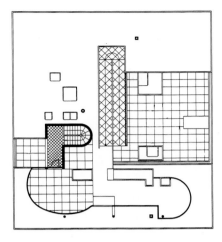

343 Le Corbusier, development sketches for the Villa Savoye, September 1928. Pencil and colour on paper, 20 x 43⁷/₈ (51 x 110 cm). Fondation Le Corbusier, Paris

344 Le Corbusier, study of symmetrical scheme for Villa Savoye, late November 1928. Pencil and colour on paper, 17³/₄ x 25¹/₂ in (45 x 65 cm). Fondation Le Corbusier, Paris

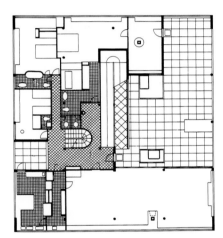

345 Villa Savoye, plans of second-, first- and ground-floor levels

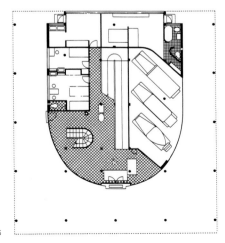

345

and reincorporated into the final project; for the earliest sketches are in fact quite close to the finished building. Among the intermediary explorations was one of an almost neo-classical formality with a symmetrical box protruding behind the screens of the façade; and another in which the top level was made curved and habitable. To follow these drawings is to see an architectural system in action. It is also to gauge the conflicts between function and form, client and architect. There were many programmatic problems along the way, among them the difficulty of garaging the cars and giving them enough room to turn at the lowest level, especially when, for a short phase, the entire scheme was reduced in size. A synthesis had to be sought which accommodated the 'external' constraints of practicality and the 'internal' requirements of the architect's own ideal intentions.

Although the Villa Savoye must be understood as a relative of Le Corbusier's earlier designs, it was not as if he simply took pieces from old designs and stuck them together. Rather, a vital new image was created, which articulated new possibilities of form and meaning in an unprecedented synthesis. This is why it is only of limited value to point out that the idea of the automobile passing under the building was first made clear – with all its urbanistic and architectural implications – at Maison Cook, or that the ramp first occurred as a principal feature in the studio wing of Maison La Roche, for in the Villa Savoye these devices were employed in a vital new combination. A similar observation can be made about the accent given the 'five points of a new architecture': the strip window had never been used so potently to unify all four sides of a design, and the *piloti* – employed as a major device in the *interior* of Garches, was here used as a dominant feature of both interior and exterior design. In 1929, in the first volume of his *Oeuvre complète* (*Complete Works*), Le Corbusier published a series of sketches of his principal villa designs of the decade, including La Roche, Stein/de Monzie at Garches, the Villa Baizeau for Carthage and, finally, the Villa Savoye (Fig. 202). In each case he attached notes describing salient features such as the pure, formal character at Garches, or the internal and external interpenetrations of the Carthage dwelling. The Villa Savoye managed to combine qualities of all the other three.

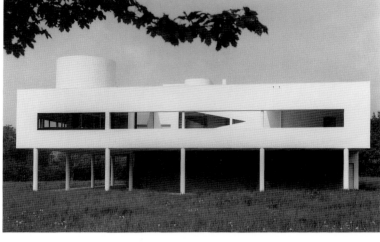

But every time Le Corbusier reused a form it had many levels of practical and mythical significance in its new context. An example of this at the Villa Savoye is the curved solarium on top of the building. Within Le Corbusier's overall syntax this screen was clearly a relative of numerous other curved 'free-plan' partitions which served to sculpt different functions independently of perimeter walls or grids of columns; here it even had a double identity as a 'partition' and a curved 'exterior wall'. In this particular design the curve began its life as the shelter for a small terrace and as the sinuous wall to the boudoir of Madame Savoye (placed suggestively at the culmination of the ramp procession in the earliest scheme). Formally it defined a counterpoint with the rectangles beneath it; perceptually it had a shifting identity, at times appearing as a cylindrical funnel floating above the glazed zones below, at times as an uncurled plane. The plan shape of the solarium had strong affinities with the guitar outlines in Le Corbusier's earlier Purist pictures, but it was not as if he traced out the discoveries of his paintings on to his building plans; rather, the same formal intelligence working in different media achieved analogous results. The long, distant view of the Villa Savoye has, understandably, been compared with a Purist still life on a table-top and the associations with ships' funnels or machine parts are not hard to make. Yet all such 'references' are held in check by a

prodigious force of intellectual abstraction, as if the curve were *all* of these things at once – or none of them, only itself.

Like any work of a high order, the Villa Savoye evades facile categorization. It is simple and complex, cerebral and sensuous. Laden with ideas, it still expresses these directly through shapes, volumes, and spaces 'in a certain relationship'. A 'classic' moment of modern architecture, it also has affinities with the architecture of the past. It was a central concern of Le Corbusier's philosophy that a vision of contemporary life be given expression in architectural forms of perennial value, and in the Villa Savoye one recognizes echoes of old classical themes: repose, proportion, clarity, simple trabeation. If the Villa Stein/de Monzie at Garches reiterates the classical French *pavillon* as a type, then the Villa Savoye surely represents Le Corbusier's reinterpretation of the basic idea of a classical temple but in machine-age terms. One may even suggest a reminiscence of the Parthenon, which had so obsessed Le Corbusier during the '*voyage d'Orient*': the mechanized procession culminating in an entrance point at the far end of the building has affinities with the ceremonial route he had noted on the Acropolis nearly twenty years before. In its tense mathematical relationships and tight contours, its clear geometry and slight optical distortions, the Villa Savoye also invoked qualities Le Corbusier had admired in this classical prototype. A caption from

346 Iktinos and Callicrates (and, according to Le Corbusier, Phidias), the Parthenon, Acropolis, Athens, 447–32 BC

347 Le Corbusier, Villa Savoye, Poissy, 1928–31

the chapter in *Vers une architecture* called 'Architecture: Pure Creation of the Mind' might apply to the ancient or the modern building equally well.

From what is emotion born? From a certain relationship between definite elements: cylinders, an even floor, even walls. From a certain harmony with the things that make up the site. From a plastic system that spreads its effects over every part of the composition. From a unity of idea that reaches from the unity of materials used to the unity of the general contour.

It is tempting to regard the *piloti*, that central element of Le Corbusier's architectural language, so resonant with meanings related to Purism, standardization, the definition of concrete, and the creation of a new urbanism, as being a reinterpretation of the idea of a column as well. The cylinder was one of those 'absolutely beautiful' Platonic forms singled out for special attention in *Vers une architecture*; it was a primary form capable of touching the mind at the deepest levels. At the same time the *piloti* was conceived as the correct expression for concrete, and an *objet-type* in the class of supports; it embodied the essential idea of a free-standing support, stripped of all accidental or ornamental effects. It supplied yet another instance of the unity of Idealism and Rationalism in Le Corbusier's thought.

Thus the Villa Savoye drew together a number of strands of its creator's philosophy and gave poetic expression to his world-view. Its language was based on a modern structural technique, as Viollet-le-Duc had required, and its imagery referred to objects of modern engineering which were regarded as symbols of the modern age. Its idealization of a way of life addressed the needs of industrial society, positing a Utopian order, while its forms were intensified through proportional expertise and the discoveries of Purist painting. Its individual elements – the *piloti*, the strip window, etc. – like the columns and triglyphs of a Greek temple, were elevated to the level of 'timeless' solutions; the abstraction of its forms implied a lofty and spiritual aim for architecture. Above all, the architectural language of the Villa Savoye was the result of a radical quest, a returning to roots, a rethinking of the fundamentals of the art. That is why it may be compared to that paradigm of simple trabeation, the 'primitive hut', an architecture supposedly reflecting natural law.

17

the
continuity
of
older
traditions

After all, architecture is
an art and from time
immemorial it has been
regarded as one of the
greatest. Beautiful
buildings, the Parthenon
for instance, the
Pantheon, Chartres or St
Paul's have moved men
more profoundly than
any but the very greatest
masterpieces of painting
and sculpture, but who
is going to be moved,
except to resentment, by
buildings such as Herr
Mendelsohn produces
in Germany or M. Le
Corbusier in France, or
by buildings of steel
and brick that purport
to be made of concrete,
buildings cased in steel
and glass, buildings that
appear to follow no
principle but that of
contradicting everything
that has ever been done
before? I suggest that
our modernists are
wrong in principle.
Reginald Blomfield, 1932

348 Jože Plečnik,
remodelling of Prague
Castle, 1921–35, base of
flagpole

The early historians and propagandists of modern architecture tended to portray it as the single true style of the times and to relegate deviants to a historical dustbin. While this historiographical exercise undoubtedly had a useful purgative function, it conveyed an extremely lopsided historical picture and encouraged a partisan view of architectural quality. In its early days the modern movement, like any other young movement, was in a minority. The majority of buildings constructed in, say, the year 1930 were continuations of earlier traditions and vernaculars. It is useful to be reminded of this pluralist background in considering the very significance of avant-garde production. Furthermore, the determinist slant of the aforementioned writers tended to leave the impression that a building which failed to ally itself to new tendencies must be inferior. But the fact that a building might be a transformation of Gothic forms (e.g. the Hood design for the *Chicago Tribune*) did not guarantee its inferiority any more than the use of the new style guaranteed quality. It has to be said, at this juncture, that writers who were opposed to modern architecture sometimes adapted counterpart tactics by automatically opposing anything new.

While modern architects as diverse as Wright, Le Corbusier and Mies van der Rohe expressed a vision of contemporary life with new spatial ideas, and threw off the garments of the nineteenth-century 'styles' in order to crystallize their version of the fundamentals of 'style' in general, they were none the less deeply indebted to tradition. Wright deserves to be taken seriously when claiming that his work was dedicated 'to a cause conservative in the best sense of the word' and insisting 'at no point does it involve denial of the elemental law and order inherent in all great architecture'. Le Corbusier's declaration that the past was his only real master (made at the height of his modernist experimentation in 1929) is not so surprising when one considers the themes of *Vers une architecture* and the metamorphoses of ideas drawn from history in his actual creations. Mies van der Rohe, no less than these two, treated the past as a source of principles and inspirations to be distilled in a modern language. And this is to speak of only three major architects out of the many who made a radical re-evaluation of tradition. The distinction between

349

'modernists' and 'traditionalists' can therefore
be overstressed. I do not believe that it is being
oversophisticated to suggest that the outstanding
works of modern architecture transcended period
concerns to become long-term relatives of other
outstanding buildings of the past which, likewise, in
their own time, cut far deeper than changing trends
or mere conventions of period style.

Be this as it may, the obvious still has to be stated:
the Villa Savoye and the Bauhaus buildings did not
employ classical orders, arches, or rib vaults; they
were part of the same general grouping in ways
that the Chrysler Building by Van Alen or Edwin
Lutyens's designs for New Delhi were not. At the
time the modern movement first emerged, its
differences from other architecture were far more
easily identified than its similarities. It was clear that
this was something new, and that both its outer
appearance and its anatomy were in profound ways
different from those of predecessors; it was not,
then, just a change of stylistic clothes. Moreover,
the 'moderns' eventually won, in the sense that their
schemata were the ones generally adopted around
the world. It was no divine law of progress that
brought this about; rather (as we have begun to
see) the reasons for adopting the new forms over
pre-existing traditions varied considerably from
place to place. Whatever the lasting qualities of
some buildings within these pre-existing traditions,

their formulations seemed less and less relevant
to changing cultural conditions and to the aims of
the next few generations. Such perhaps is the
picture after any major revolution in sensibility,
which the modern movement certainly was.

The entire subject of 'traditionalism' has
undoubtedly been influenced by the fact that
traditionalist positions were often used by the
totalitarian regimes in the 1930s to oust modern
architecture (Chapter 20). It tends to be overlooked
that several works of notable quality were realized
between the wars which, while they may have
seemed to stem from an earlier period, nevertheless
contained intrinsic value. Among these one would
surely count the Stuttgart Railway Station (1911–14,
1919–27) by Paul Bonatz and Friedrich Scholer (the
building that was explicitly rejected by the New
Objectivity architects in their magazine *ABC* in
1926, Fig. 322). Here the railway station was treated
as a civic building type, with a masonry façade and
booking hall, and steel and glass railway sheds to the
rear. The exteriors were handled in a bold, vaguely
Romanesque style, using large surfaces of rock-faced
ashlar, round arches and simplified piers. In the
booking-hall interior, Bonatz had recourse to bands
of coloured masonry, while in the sheds, the glazing
was detailed to create impressive parallel bays of
suspended planes. Bonatz was one of the most
vociferous critics of the Weissenhofsiedlung in

349 Paul Bonatz and
Friedrich Scholer, Central
Station, Stuttgart, 1911–14,
1919–27

350 Rudolf Steiner,
Goetheanum, Dornach,
second version, 1925–8

Stuttgart, taking the view that the white-painted, plaster-rendered forms were impractical as well as symbolically inappropriate, a stance which cost him dearly in the later historical literature of modernist persuasion.

Another effect of treating the history of modern architecture as a sort of conveyor belt (as the early historians tended to) was that 'survivals' from earlier 'pioneer' phases also tended to be relegated. Art Nouveau, for example, was a temporary phase for such individuals as Behrens and Le Corbusier, but its effects lingered on well into the 1920s in places as varied as Majorca and Buenos Aires. A major artist like Gaudí was still extending his personal manner up to the time of his death in 1926. Frank Lloyd Wright was 'acceptable' in the sanctioned scheme of things so long as he was 'anticipating' modern ideas of space and form (i.e. up to 1910); but when he

became awkwardly Romantic and exotic in his California works of the 1920s he no longer fitted the preordained picture and had to be regarded as an 'anachronism'. In the need to define an exclusive modernism, too much was done to pin a style to a moment, and a moment to a style. In reality, a variety of options remained open, and were often continued with conviction. After all, Auguste Perret pursued his pre-war manner with little impact from, yet in parallel with, the seminal works of the 'white architecture of the twenties'. In fact, the Church of Notre Dame, Le Raincy, of 1924 was the logical culmination of all that Perret had been pursuing for reinforced concrete for the previous three decades (see below).

Historical and critical writing about architecture naturally reflects an author's idea of what is 'significant'. 'Expressionism' was scarcely mentioned in the early literature on modern architecture, perhaps because the extreme bizarreness and emotionalism underlying some works labelled by this term were at odds with the personal taste of the historians, perhaps because the tendency to seek out a unifying *Zeitgeist* at the core of modern culture left them looking for a single 'true' modern style. A work like the Einstein Tower by Mendelsohn sat awkwardly in this scheme of things, while a curious creation like the Goetheanum at Dornach outside Basle, Switzerland, of 1925–8 (designed by Rudolf Steiner, the founder of Anthroposophy) simply had to be left out of the account altogether. This despite the fact that both were inspired by revolutionary conceptions and were capable of standing alongside much that was within the safer, supposedly more 'rational' pale of the 'International Style'. Here again, historians possibly showed how they could be influenced by the prejudices of artists, for several of the architects who were 'safe' had passed through Expressionism and rejected it as a juvenile phase before their mature flowering.

The Goetheanum was the headquarters of Steiner's World Anthroposophical movement and included an auditorium for mystical plays and congresses. It replaced a pre-war building (also designed by Steiner) which had been made almost entirely from wood and which had been destroyed by fire. Combining two domes over a radial/polygonal plan, this earlier structure had

350

been conceived as a cosmogram of sorts, marking the energy centre of Anthroposophy as a system of beliefs and ideas. There were unmistakable allusions to Oriental stupas and world-mountain themes, and some of these images may have been maintained hermetically in Steiner's later design which was made entirely from concrete, with 'mineralogical' facets ascending to a curved roof. In fact the mineral and the vegetal seemed to blend into one another in Steiner's bizarre forms. The flow of surfaces and the dynamism of elements in the Goetheanum need to be understood in the light of Steiner's intuition that all phenomena were in a transition from one state to another, that all tangible and visible things were the outward expression of inner and invisible processes. To the rear of the site was a curious abstraction of a tree, a virtual totem, an allusion, perhaps, to Goethe's theories on the origins of plant species. While the articulation of silhouettes and openings in the Goetheanum was not felicitous, and the overall expression was sometimes forced and theatrical, the interior spaces managed to evoke an other-worldly realm through the play of light on rough concrete surfaces, and to suggest some visual equivalent to the idea of transformation from the material to the spiritual. Steiner may have been influenced by Kandinsky's ideas on the spirituality of forms guided by 'inner necessity' (a notion with its own Theosophical resonances), by the crystalline, Alpine imagery of Bruno Taut, even by certain of the formal precepts of Art Nouveau.

While Art Nouveau itself was a relatively short-lived phenomenon, its influence lingered on in developments stressing the 'organic' and the abstraction of natural forms. The Einstein Tower would have been inconceivable without this legacy as would some of the outstanding buildings of Dutch Expressionists like De Klerk. However, there were other trends which stemmed, in part, from Art Nouveau. Among these was the manner of design called 'Art Deco' after its appearance at the Exposition des Arts Décoratifs in 1925. This loose affiliation of exotic and highly decorative tendencies was quite at odds with the fundamentalism and rigorous moral tenor of the new architecture, but it reached its full (and brief) efflorescence at about the same time. In the decorative arts one thinks of the glasswork of Lalique, or of spangled interiors in which neo-Egyptian motifs, chevron geometries,

and luxuriant indulgence in lustrous materials played a part. The garden designed by Gabriel Guevrekian in 1927 for the Villa Noailles on the French Riviera at Hyères relied upon an analogous aesthetic, treating tulip beds and planters as a checkerboard pattern inside a triangular perimeter, and handling the ensemble as if it were a piece of costume jewellery projected on to the ground. 'Art Deco' scarcely presents a coherent stylistic entity, and there was relatively little of lasting architectural value in it; none the less, works of considerable richness like the Richfield Building in Los Angeles (by Morgan, Walls and Clements) of 1928 or the Hoover Factory in London of 1935 (by Wallis Gilbert and Partners), not to mention the Chrysler Building in New York of 1928–30 by William van Alen were all related to Art Deco trends. In each of these, an armature of Beaux-Arts axial planning was cloaked in modern materials and elaborately decorated and coloured wall surfaces. The attitude behind such forms was far indeed from the ideals of dematerialization, 'honesty', and puritanism which were inherent in the smooth white planes and stark surfaces of the International Style. Ornament was embraced and elaborated in polychrome stripes and violent contrasts of texture; and the style was frequently and blatantly employed in the service of commercial advertising – to attract, to delight, and to persuade. It enjoyed a vogue in the design of things as diverse as cinemas and toasters. There was a notable lack of that cultural high-mindedness with

351

352

regard to industrialism which had propelled the more profound thinkers of the modern movement. Art Deco served as a middle-brow bridge between modernism and consumerism. This was also true of the streamlined 'Moderne' style prevalent in industrial design in the United States in the late 1920s and early 1930s. The market laws of obsolescence and fashion were here met with less anguish than in the moral positions of the modern mainstream.

This leads to a further point about the modern movement which, possibly, applies to other novel systems of forms: it ran the risk of staying beyond the grasp of public understanding and sympathy. Although it had been a central underlying doctrine that the architect was somehow specially endowed with the ability to intuit communal aspirations, the majority taste remained allied to traditional images and customary associations. This problem of communication was exacerbated by the very stance of the avant-garde with its haughty disdain for the clichéd and the conventional. It is not so strange that the juries of the *Chicago Tribune*, the League of Nations, and even the Palace of the Soviets competitions should have voted the way they did. There was uncertainty about the capacity of the new forms to convey generally held beliefs.

The point is even clearer for the family home. The new architecture was the cultural property either of isolated pockets of upper-middle-class bohemia, or else of large-scale planning bureaucracies with a progressive outlook. The taste of 'everyman' in the 1920s was frankly more at home with images derived from the Arts and Crafts movement, which had itself been based on time-worn notions of the dwelling. Some of the

criticisms concerning the 'factory' appearance and the lack of psychological warmth which became part of the Nazi rejection of modern architecture (Chapter 20) were not so very far away from complaints that might have been delivered by many decent home-owners elsewhere in the West at the same time. Far from being perceived as elements of a new universal language of design, the creations stemming from the Bauhaus or from Purism were as likely to be seen as emblems of a highbrow clique. It was to take over two decades for the imagery of 'the modern' to become popularized and, so to speak, vernacularized; and once this had happened much of the original meaning and polemical impulse had been lost. Perhaps a confusion of this sort was inevitable, given avant-garde premises; obsessed with the idea that a major decay was in process, the avant-garde thought it was its business to rescue the values of higher forms and to instate radical new prototypes. Divorce from obvious conventions was intrinsic to this process.

Were this a book on the architecture of the entire twentieth century, instead of a study of the traditions of modern architecture in their cultural setting, it would be necessary to devote a number of chapters to such phenomena as the continuation of the Gothic revival well into the 1930s in the United States, and the broad resurgence of the neo-classicism which occured in the Western World during the 1930s (and not just under the mantle of authoritarian regimes). Presumably, too, a representative coverage would concern itself with a variety of eclectic 'neo-colonial' styles which proliferated before the arrival of modernism in, for example, Latin America. However, the aims of this book are different, so it is necessary to single out a

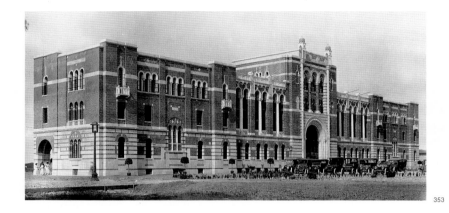

353

few key examples of 'traditions other than the modern', in an attempt at explaining why 'historical' forms were employed and to what effect.

In the majority of Western European countries, the United States and the Soviet Union, the 'official taste' against which the avant-garde launched its battles usually derived from nineteenth-century eclecticism. As shown for the American skyscraper, the hotchpotch of styles was actually capable of supporting a broad range of allusions and meanings. In 1929, the year the Villa Savoye was designed in Paris, major collegiate construction in the United States was still fully committed to neo-Georgian and neo-Gothic modes. To the avant-garde, this seemed like further evidence of retrogressive sentimentalism; however, in a situation where modern forms were not even known, this was scarcely fair criticism. Even if modern architecture had been known, it is doubtful that it would have been employed in a context where associations with past learning and with tradition were sought. The case of Rice University outside Houston, Texas (1912), designed by Ralph Adams Cram in an eclectic 'Byzantine-Gothic' manner, is revealing in this respect, for it suggests an attitude to design which was quite prevalent for institutional commissions up until the Second World War. Cram's own reflection on the dilemma of style betrays the loss of a solid foundation in the choice of forms, but it also shows how an architect might seek an appropriate symbolic solution for a particular task and site, by sifting through several periods in the history of architecture:

Here was a new situation altogether. It had been sufficiently easy to determine the stylistic basis of West Point and devise its plans, because the limiting factors were so very precise. It was equally easy in the case of Princeton, for the same reason, and in that of Sweetbriar College in Virginia, then under way, whose history, tradition, and architectural style predetermined the course to follow. But what to do here, when there was no possible point d'appui? A level and stupid site, no historical or stylistic precedent (not even that of Old Mexico of which Texas had been a frontier post so many generations ago); no ideas proposed by President or Trustees. Wild horses would not have driven us to use the 'Mission style', then so undeservedly popular; Spanish-Indian-Baroque had nothing whatever to do either with the ethnological or historical associations of Texas; the Puritan Colonial and the Cavalier Georgian of the Atlantic Seaboard was equally out of key with the temper and the climate of the place. The Modernist-functional style had not then come in, and was no more than a cloud no larger than a man's hand on the aesthetic horizon; besides, we would not have had it anyway where any cultural connotation was concerned… We wanted something that was beautiful, if we could make it so, Southern in its spirit, and with some quality of continuity with the historical and cultural past. Manifestly the only thing to do was invent something approaching a new style (though not too new) and develop a psychological excuse for it…

I had travelled much in the Mediterranean lands and was familiar with their architectural 'documents', so I reassembled all the elements I could from southern France and Italy, Dalmatia, the Peleponnesus, Byzantium, Anatolia, Syria, Sicily, Spain, and set myself the task of creating a measurably new style that, while built on a classical basis, should have the Gothic romanticism, pictorial quality, and structural integrity.

In effect, Cram was arguing in favour of 'character': the appearance of a building would be concocted from a 'relevant' amalgam of historical styles, sources, images and details. According to this point of view, centres of learning, state monuments, churches, memorials, tombs or city halls demanded some continuity of symbolism rather than a radical break. But the matter was not so straightforward, for there were rarely clear-cut conventions governing the appearance of any one type of building. The Lincoln Memorial in Washington, DC, designed in 1911 by Henry Bacon, and completed in 1922, affords an interesting case of this struggle for appropriate representation. The forms of Bacon's solution would have been inconceivable without the pre-existing tradition of Beaux-Arts classicism within the United States, stemming from Richard Morris Hunt and Charles Follen McKim. However, the pre-existing neo-classical context of Washington – not to mention various moral and political associations attached to classical forms within the American tradition – must also be taken into account. The idea of a memorial to Lincoln had first been formulated soon after his death, but it was only in the twentieth century that debates were set in motion to find a site and an architect. The former was chosen from a set of six alternatives, the latter on the recommendation of Daniel Burnham, who had already been involved with the replanning of the Washington Mall according to classical planning principles. The project was inseparable in this era

from a sense of Washington as a sort of new Rome at the centre of an emergent empire. The monument had to stand on the main axis with the Capitol and the Washington Obelisk and to be an eventual visual link between this grand avenue of presidential associations and the Arlington Cemetery on the other side of the Potomac. The scheme adopted avoided a dome, so as not to distract from the dome of the Capitol, and was a low, horizontal, elegant neo-Greek box on an elevated mound. It was a cross between a temple and a tomb, and was made from the purest of white Colorado marbles. The low attic was supported on a peristyle of sharp-cut Doric columns, while the frieze and entablature were engraved with symbols of the states and their unity. In the interior, Daniel Chester French's sculpture of the seated Abraham Lincoln faced down the main axis over a long reflecting pool (modelled on the Taj Mahal) towards the Washington Monument and the Capitol beyond. In symbolic terms the aim was to mirror the purity of Lincoln's character, to anchor his historical position in relation to his great presidential predecessors and to celebrate the guiding ideals of the Union. The synthesis of these

354

particular classical prototypes fitted no simple orthodox procedure; but the fusion had architectural value none the less. It is intriguing to speculate how this building could have handled this range of evocations and emotions without references to classical antiquity and to American reuses of classicism of the previous century and a half. As will be shown in the third section of this book, the modern movement had eventually to solve analogous rhetorical problems, sometimes by turning back to ancient precedents but without such obvious reuse of historical vocabulary.

The New York skyscrapers of the 1920s are evidence that the schemata of Beaux-Arts planning carried on well into the inter-war years in the United States, even when the full regalia of classicism was absent. Just as the Chrysler Building represented an attempt at creating a popular imagery for modern commercial architecture, so the State Capitol in Lincoln, Nebraska, of 1921–32, designed by Bertram Goodhue, embodied an effort at forging a populist and democratic language of state monumentality in the American provincial context. The central tower with its gold dome and abstract vertical shafts could be seen for miles around across the flat landscape, and in style was a hybrid between the sort of crystalline verticality suggested by Sullivan and (later) Saarinen, and some generalized apparatus for state representation. The complex

as a whole was laid out on a symmetrical and hierarchical Beaux-Arts plan, while the iconography of detail was intended to evoke local themes to do with agriculture in the prairies. Goodhue's building represented an attempt at simplifying eclecticism and 'modernizing' it in a way (Hitchcock called it 'an eclectic sort of semi-modernism'). A similar style would be absorbed into numerous small-scale Federal buildings of the 1930s, such as post offices and court-houses.

Modernist mythology implied that it was in the natural order of things that revivalism and eclecticism should be replaced by the 'truer' forms of modern architecture. But the Slovenian architect Jože Plečnik developed in the opposite direction, aligning himself initially with avant-garde Viennese tendencies at the turn of the century, then gradually evolving a complex metaphorical language enriched by classicism and regional styles in the 1920s and 1930s. Plečnik studied with Otto Wagner in the 1890s and his Zacherl House in Vienna of 1903–5 had a bold directness about it which put it at odds with the revivalist encrustations of an earlier generation, while also distancing it from the aestheticism of the Secession; like Wagner's work of the time, it attempted to evoke the constructive and social realities of the modern metropolis. By degrees, Plečnik's emphasis shifted towards an allusive transformation of historical fragments which revealed his struggle to define the syncretic, even secretive, character of central European identities re-emerging after the dissolution of the Austro-Hungarian Empire.

In the early 1920s Plečnik was invited by Tomás Masaryk, the President of the newly founded Czech Democratic Republic, to convert Prague Castle, a site of the Hapsburg *ancien regime*, into a democratic symbol crystallizing the new political order. The architect envisaged a species of pan-national acropolis inserted into the ramparts as a series of gardens, walks, monuments and historical alignments linking together the recent struggles for national liberation with events and legends in both Czech and Slovakian pasts. Platforms, courtyards, steps and gates were handled as an ascending sequence in which new emblems were juxtaposed with excavated foundations and views over the city below. In Plečnik's original design, the 'Garden of Paradise' was like a plateau open to the sky. At one

355 Bertram Goodhue, State Capitol, Lincoln, Nebraska, 1921–32

356 Jože Plečnik, remodelling of Prague Castle, 1921–35, the 'Plečnik Hall', 1926–8

355

and correspondences of its own. It blended together politics and allegory, classicism and regional folklore, high traditions and low, in a sort of promenade through time.

Plečnik avoided a descent into trivial narrative by maintaining an overall discipline and by transforming historical references into a new poetic structure. He measured out powerful architectural experiences across space, telescoping present and past with controlled perspectives. A limited number of geometrical forms took on different identities and carried forward the dominant themes of the ensemble. Basic classical elements such as columns, mouldings, pedestals, capitals, aedicules and amphitheatres were given surprising roles, sizes and combinations, sometimes fusing with shapes of local significance. Sources went through a metamorphosis, achieving new multivalent identities in objects which resonated among themselves. The whole was pervaded by an intensity which removed it from the province of superficial revivalism. Plečnik here revealed a method for unearthing the historical memories in a place; his walkways along the river-banks of his own city, Ljubljana (carried out in the 1930s), had a similar haunting quality, even evoking an idealized Slovenian past. These works, conceived at the same time that the modern movement was developing in central Europe, combined topographical and cultural symbolism with hermetic abstraction: they fused together idea, material and myth.

National Romanticism posited the idea that architecture should embody regional or national cultural identity (see Chapter 8). Curiously enough, analagous methods for blending imported with indigenous were sometimes used in countries which had been colonized and whose 'official culture' was thus largely imposed by foreigners. When one surveys the architecture built by Europeans in their African and Asian colonies in the early decades of the century, one finds cases of buildings uniting cosmopolitan, Western ideas with native, local ones. Sometimes the result was a bogus 'Orientalism', virtually a caricature of another people's monumental or vernacular heritage; sometimes it was an effective eclecticism adjusted to climate and place. Beyond matters of aesthetic expression, there were inevitably complex questions concerning the relative status of the colonizing culture and the

end a bank of steps rose towards a monument to national martyrs, an obelisk attended by an eternal flame signifying freedom. On an upper-level walkway a pyramid of ambiguous size was seen against the backdrop of Prague. There were other curious incidents. A giant cylindrical stone basin, not unlike a sliced-off piece of Doric column, rhymed with the circular geometry of flights of steps in the form of miniature amphitheatres or their reversals. Twin flagpoles fashioned from the trunks of Moravian conifers stood before the 'Plečnik Hall', the high sides of which were open screens of superimposed classical columns penetrated by light. Elsewhere a polished granite beam of oval section hovered horizontally above the ground, while an aedicule of folded metal covering a partly interred stair recalled an Ionic profile. Plečnik's idiosyncratic creation seemed to work with rules colonized one. Even when the local past was alluded to, it was not necessarily with the most noble motives in mind. British India soon after the turn of the century offers an intriguing case of these ambiguities and ambivalences. In the period leading up to the foundation of New Delhi as the new capital of the Raj in 1911, there were heated debates over the question of an appropriate architectural expression. There were those who advocated the reuse of Western forms (modified somewhat to deal with climate), an approach which had been used throughout the nineteenth century. But there were also those who advocated the support of local Indian styles and craftsmen, and who saw here an opportunity for the reinvigoration of local traditions which were, in fact, either broken or else in decline.

The main state buildings crowning the urban plan of New Delhi were designed by Edwin Lutyens and Herbert Baker. In varying degrees they were hybrids of classical Western and Indian forms drawn from several periods. Lutyens needed some persuading about the virtues of Indian architecture, but his Viceroy's House (the most important state monument in the new city) designed in 1912, and completed in 1931, was an eclectic solution of great wit and skill which amounted to an 'inclusive' emblem – a monumental piece of diplomacy engaging symbolically with the several ancient Delhis, and with certain strata of the Indian architectural past. The political task in this case

was nothing less than the authentication of the authority of the British Raj. Lutyens drew upon a range of imperial associations and symbols within both oriental and classical traditions to achieve what he considered the right tone. The Viceroy's House was placed at the end of a three-mile axis on Raisina Hill, and evoked such Baroque prototypes as Versailles, Blenheim, and Greenwich Hospital in its central focus and symmetrical wings. The vocabulary was a fusion of sources and references: classical devices for organizing plan and façade being cross-bred with the protective stone ledges ('chajjas') of Indian tradition to create a wide band of shade. The red and honey-coloured sandstone were in an obvious Delhi tradition, while the upturned basins and deep-cut ledges suggested witty inversions of typical Mogul or Rajput devices. The dome itself – marking the *axis mundi* of British power in India – was an ingenious blend of two archetypes of authority: the Roman Pantheon and a Buddhist stupa like that at Sanchi (*c.* 100 BC). Lutyens was able to discover analogies and parallels between the forms of different cultures and periods, then transform these 'grammars' into a statement of his own which crystallized the political situation facing him. According to standard, modernist critical views, this procedure should have ended up with a 'dead formula' or with a mere assemblage of quotations, but Lutyens was able to breathe new life into old forms.

357 Edwin Lutyens, Viceroy's House, New Delhi, 1912–31

358 Viceroy's House, plan

359 Viceroy's House, view of dome from the roofless staircase

357

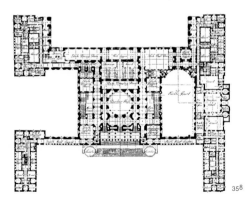

358

359

Another area in which traditionalist solutions were liable to be preferred over modern ones was the design of churches, since this was a context requiring some adherence to conventional imagery. Some of the most powerful results were achieved by paring down traditional models. St Martin's Garrison Church in New Delhi, designed in 1928 by one of Lutyens's former associates, Arthur Gordon Shoosmith, relied upon the past in this generalized sense. The stark brick walls, battered tower and regimented waterspouts evoked a martial image, something between a fort and an abstraction of a country church: an outpost of Protestantism in a foreign land. Openings were kept small to keep out the strong sunlight and the brickwork was handled without ornamental flourishes of any kind. The whitewashed interior was also stripped down to its essential structure of piers, walls, and flat domes, the whole submitted to the same clear rigour as the outside. The Garrison Church imposed its stern presence on the observer through sharp-cut mass, strong silhouette, and the action of light and shade on materials used in a sparing and logical way. The result was a work of a certain timeless quality (loosely reminiscent of some of Lutyens's war memorials); utilitarian, but grave. There was much here that would be admired by a later generation of

Indian architects brought up on the poetic severity of Louis Kahn's brick and concrete buildings in Ahmadabad over thirty years later. The Garrison Church is one of those buildings to make debates about 'modernity' and tradition seem superfluous.

While the overt revivals of Gothic architecture made in the first three or four decades of the twentieth century were usually weak relatives of their nineteenth-century predecessors (which were in any case rejected by modernist dogma), the inheritance of medieval forms and structural principles continued to be transformed in several ways. Jensen-Klint's remarkable Grundtvig Church outside Copenhagen (designed in 1913 but not completed until 1940) supplies an example of a vigorous reinterpretation achieving a new order and integration (see Fig.151). In Germany and Austria in the 1920s there were several fusions of traditional and modern forms which aspired towards an evocative setting for liturgy, worship or burial: one thinks of works such as Clemens Holzmeister's Crematorium in Vienna of 1922–3, of the Danish Church in Berlin by Otto Bartning of 1922 or of Dominikus Böhm's Church in Neu-Ulm of 1927. As a rule, these projects drew upon the Expressionist interest in elongated motifs and formal accentuations intended to evoke mood. In technological matters they were conservative, especially judged in the light of reinforced-concrete expressions such as the Church of St-Jean-de-

362

360 Arthur Gordon
Shoosmith, St Martin's
Garrison Church, New
Delhi, 1928–30

361 Dominikus Böhm,
St John the Baptist
Catholic Parish Church,
Neu-Ulm, Germany, 1927

362 Walter Burley
Griffin, Newman College,
Melbourne, 1915–18

363 Walter Burley
Griffin, competition
design for new Federal
Capital, Australia, 1912,
drawn by Marion
Mahony. Coloured
lithograph on cotton, 30 ×
6 in (76 × 15 cm).
Australian Archives,
Canberra

Montmartre by Anatole de Baudot of 1897–1905
(Fig. 69).

Walter Burley Griffin's Newman College in
Melbourne, Australia, of 1915–18 was more
adventurous in spirit than these German and
Austrian examples, but no less indebted to medieval
prototypes. Griffin had worked in Frank Lloyd
Wright's studio and was a major contributor
to the 'Prairie School', but in 1912 had won the
competition for the new capital of Australia,
Canberra, with a project which envisaged a
pyramidal, transparent, almost crystalline
Parliament at the apex of a triangular urban plan.
Although the Parliament was not built, several of
Griffin's principles were adopted for the layout of
the new city, an 'organic' conception blending a
non-authoritarian monumentality with a dispersed
Garden City ideal. The College in Melbourne
picked up some of the same institutional themes
and structural conceptions, since it was a hybrid of
modern skeletal thinking, abstracted Gothic motifs,
and vaguely geological metaphors. Rib and vault,
buttress and pinnacle, tracery and angled shaft
were reinterpreted in terms which clearly owed
something to Wright's abstraction of natural forms,
even as they invoked a sort of expressive structural
Rationalism. The refectory was covered by a
concrete ribbed dome surmounted by a lantern and
a tapering cross; masonry was employed elsewhere
in the design but with a slight exaggeration of blocks

363

·SECTION B-A · SOVTHERLY SIDE OF WATER AXIS·
·GOVERNMENT GROVP·

364

and joints. The spiky silhouettes and brooding shapes of Griffin's building carried an aura and meaning of their own, at the same time echoing traditional ideas such as the cloister, or the sort of entryway split by a column found at Vézélay (the twelfth-century pilgrimage church in Burgundy).

Auguste Perret's Notre Dame, Le Raincy, 1922–3, suggested how modern materials like reinforced concrete might be used to reinterpret traditional church typologies, but without abandoning a recognizable connection to traditional imagery. In this instance nave, aisles, columns, vaults were all present, but recast according to the logic and dimensions of an uncustomary structural system. In the same spirit, the exterior dispensed with walls altogether, being constructed instead with perforated concrete screens through which the light was filtered. The result was a work which fitted no particular stylistic category, that was neither 'Gothic' nor 'classical', but which none the less relied upon tradition at the level of generating principles. In that respect it could be contrasted with the Church of St Anthony in Basle of 1926 by Karl Moser, which also worked with a modern, reinforced-concrete structure, but which clung to

elements from another construction system (such as deep classical coffering in its vaults) that seemed gratuitous, even out of place.

As suggested in Chapter 8, several strands of classicism were operative in the first two decades of the twentieth century, including ones which contributed to the formation of modern architecture. In the 1920s and 1930s, classicism did not disappear, but took on many new guises from the most literal to the most abstract, within and without the modern movement. In this connection it is instructive to trace the work of the Swedish architect Erik Gunnar Asplund whose Woodland Cemetery Chapel of 1918–20 (Fig. 164) provides yet another example of the inventive reinterpretation of classical types. Asplund's Stockholm Public Library of 1920–8 was modelled on a cluster of themes derived from neo-classicism and the nineteenth-century tradition of library design. The reading room was set upon a round plan and expressed as a centralized cylinder poking up through a rectangular box; a formula with numerous antecedents including, ultimately, the stripped geometrical vocabulary of the French eighteenth-century architect Claude-Nicolas Ledoux (e.g. the Barrière de la Villette of 1784–9). Had Asplund been a lesser architect, he might have produced a mere pastiche. As it was, he was able to reinvigorate earlier forms with his own expressive intentions and metaphors. His vocabulary may even have been partly inspired by physiological imagery: in the case of the library, the original section emerged from a sort of reconstituted cranium – an idea that the architect presumably felt appropriate

364 Auguste Perret, Notre Dame, Le Raincy, 1922–3

365 Erik Gunnar Asplund, Stockholm Public Library, 1920–8, plan

366 Stockholm Public Library

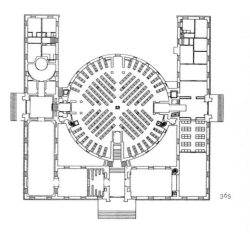

365

366

to a chamber for reading, thinking and recollection. Equally, the use of these sober and urbane forms may be seen in the context of an overall reaction against the medievalism of National Romanticism, a return to more 'universal' Enlightenment values, and an attempt at crystallizing a Social Democratic ethos. Nothing could be further from the imperialist rhetoric of Lutyens's New Delhi, though both architects drew from the same pool of classical sources. Asplund would go on to absorb the usages of the International Style at the Stockholm Exhibition of 1930, only to fuse them together with the underlying armatures of classicism in his remarkable works of the ensuing decade.

France and Britain were generally less fortunate than this with their 'traditionalist' and classical architects in the period from around 1910 to 1940. The French Academician P.-H. Nénot, for example (mentioned in Chapter 15 in connection with the League of Nations), was fully endowed with all the scholarly trappings of Beaux-Arts respectability, but lacked a gift for original synthesis, as was clear enough from the version of the League of Nations which was constructed in the 1930s. The same might be said of the British architect Reginald Blomfield, who was one of a number of exponents of a stylish Beaux-Arts classicism imported from France around 1910. His extensive façades on Regent Street of 1922, for instance, were uninspired reworkings of motifs derived from Palladio and Sansovino. One can understand, on inspection, why a younger generation felt the need for change; it is even arguable that Perret, Behrens and Wright (in one generation), and Le Corbusier, Mies van der Rohe and Aalto (in another) had a deeper insight into the essentials of classicism than their learned counterparts who made a more overt reference to the past.

Even so, Blomfield became one of the leading spokesmen of the 'traditionalist' position. In a debate which took place in 1932 between himself and the modernist Amyas Connell, Blomfield claimed that the new architecture was bound to end up in barbarism because of its stress on function and its lack of concern with the great lessons of the past.

I part company with the modernists, not for their dismissal of Gothic tracery and Classical orders or meaningless ornament, or for their use of steel and reinforced concrete or any other material suitable for building, but because they insist on our regarding architecture, no longer as an art, but only as a branch of engineering.

367

Against this, Blomfield set the position of the 'traditionalist' (which he was better able to convey in words than in his own architecture):

… civilization is far too old and complicated for a clean sweep. It runs back for thousands of years, and in all those years man has been building up certain instinctive preferences or prejudices, if you like, which lie at the back of consciousness. They may be stamped out for a time, but they will inevitably play their part again …

One suspects that if Blomfield had spent less time taking the slogans of 'functionalism' literally, and more time examining actual works of modern architecture, he might have understood that his position was not so drastically opposed to 'modern' architects as he imagined. After all, it had been one of the main messages of *Vers une architecture* that one should return to the primal signposts of the classical past in order to resolve the problem of a modern architecture. The difference between Le Corbusier and Blomfield lay, of course, not only in the divergence of their respective talents and their particular ways of interpreting the history of architecture, but also in their attitudes to the contemporary world. Le Corbusier might have argued that the *only* way to use the lessons of the past fruitfully was to rethink them in terms of the present; Blomfield, on the other hand, put forth the academic position, which required closer adherence to the classical language, but which was liable to lead to sterility, since there was insufficient transformation of precedent. Classicism was not

just a matter of style, and, as always, the most
authentic inventions were those which injected a
new meaning and formal vitality into the inheritance
of classical principles, types and underlying ideas.

The Connell/Blomfield debate was by no means
an isolated instance of a sort of caricaturing of both
'modernist' and 'traditionalist' outlooks which
recurred in the 1920s and 1930s. Unfortunately
this polemical atmosphere did little to clarify the
true relationship between modern architecture
and the past, or between traditional architecture
and modernity. The matter was scarcely helped
by the early writers about the modern movement,
Hitchcock, Pevsner and Giedion (whose seminal
works appeared in 1932, 1936 and 1941
respectively), as these lent extra weight to the
notion that the new architecture was indeed
altogether new. This attitude was entirely
understandable given the historical context, and,
in a sense, it became the official line bequeathed
to the generation who came to the fore after the
Second World War. Their upbringing occurred
under the mantle of a new tradition whose slogans
of modernity they understood, but whose subtleties
with respect to tradition they often failed to grasp.
The way to the more distant past was, then,
temporarily barred.

Far beyond mere matters of architectural style,
the struggle between traditionalism and modernism
was symptomatic of tensions between the advance
of the new and the maintenance of the old in several
areas of social and political life. It exacerbated
existing fault lines between the rural and the
industrial in some countries, between national
mythologies and international influences in others.
Modern architecture broke existing conventions
and attempted to institute new ones, but it was a
rupture which several brands of conservatism found
hard to take. In the 1930s, modernism sometimes
found itself on a collision course with the forces of
political reaction, but in any case underwent
transformations and revisions of its own, requiring
a greater sensitivity to the continuities of local
cultures and to the demands of tradition. It is one
of the ironies of the period that, precisely at the
moment that cataloguers and curators were trying
to fix the terms of the 'International Style', the
proponents of modern architecture should have
been moving on to other things.

18

nature
and the
machine:
mies van der rohe,
wright
and
le corbusier
in the
1930s

Only nature is inspiring
and true; only Nature
can be the support for
human works. But do
not render Nature,
as the landscapists do,
showing only the
outward aspect.
Penetrate the cause of
it, its form and vital
development …
Charles L'Eplattenier,
1906

368 Frank Lloyd Wright,
Johnson Wax
Administration Center,
Racine, Wisconsin,
1936–9, interior

By the early 1930s modern architecture had become a major force and public presence in the culture of the West, and its lessons were being adapted by countless new followers. The creative pressure could not be kept up indefinitely, and in the remaining years of the decade the onus shifted from the continuing revolution of forms to the extension of recently discovered prototypes. This tentative construction of a 'tradition of the new' was soon hampered by external circumstances such as economic depression and the repressive attitudes of totalitarian regimes; but there were also internal difficulties related to the problem of symbolic devaluation.

The example of buildings like the Villa Savoye was extremely hard to follow. The ideas brought together in such a synthesis had been filtered through the poetic intelligence of a single artist and represented an irreducible pattern of myth. Repetition of the same forms without sufficient transformation into a new content could only result in pastiche. One is bound to say that a vital extension of the principles of modern design of the sort achieved by (say) Aalto, Lubetkin and Terragni in the 1930s was more the exception than the rule. It is striking how quickly there emerged a sort of modern academicism, in which clichéd usages of *pilotis* or whitewashed walls became the signs that one was 'up-to-date'. This very process of 'normalization' raised the broad question of a modern vernacular. By the mid-1930s there were those ready to speculate on the 'condition of anonymity', and to consider the possibility that modern architecture might achieve the same sort of common usage and wide application that classicism had in the eighteenth century, for example in the Georgian period in Britain.

In the 1930s, the filtering down, extension and elaboration of central principles of modern architecture was complicated and enriched by the growth of new branches far from the points of origin, sometimes in places with quite different climates, traditions, social projects and ways of building. The repression of the new architecture by dictatorial regimes in Nazi Germany and Soviet Russia forced some of the most innovative designers to leave, and they took their ideas with them to foreign shores. To understand these patterns of dissemination and absorption it is really necessary to consider some cases in detail (e.g. Chapters 19–21); for the moment a rough distinction can be drawn between places which received a ready-made version of modernism from outside, and ones which, while they relied upon foreign stimulus, evolved modern movements of their own in parallel with those of the major originating centres. The reception of modern forms was rarely smooth, and was usually accompanied by debates concerning the appropriateness (or lack of it) to national cultural traditions.

Czechoslovakia was actively involved in defining a modern architecture in the 1920s. So, to a lesser degree, was Japan, a country in which modernization itself raised tricky dilemmas about the acceptable degree of Western influence. In Mexico, new architectural ideas were promoted by José Villagran in the middle of the same decade, and these were carried forward by Juan O'Gorman and others, later to be integrated with a broader social and technological transformation by the Mexican state. In Spain there were also hints of a modern movement in the late 1920s, which were consolidated by Josep Lluís Sert (a collaborator of Le Corbusier destined to become president of CIAM) until the Civil War intervened. In South Africa, Rex Martienssen and the Transvaal group made an effective translation of Purism in the early 1930s within a relatively limited social milieu, while in Brazil, the activities of Lucio Costa and Oscar Niemeyer ensured the vitality of a particular strand of modernism sensitized to a tropical way of life. In Palestine during the same years, European immigrants constructed their version of the 'International Style', and Erich Mendelsohn evolved a modern architecture responsive to local historical and geographic conditions. Finally, of course, one must mention Britain, Italy, Finland, Denmark and Sweden, all countries with isolated germs of modern ideas in the 1920s destined to come to fruition with varying degrees of social engagement, and under different ideological flags, in the 1930s.

To chart the early stages in the expansion of a new set of forms, it is necessary to find the right balance between 'internal' impulses and necessities, and 'external' pressures and stimuli. Modern architecture had a core of its own inventions which imposed limitations as well as opening new directions. In the 1930s, both the originators and the followers discovered further possibilities for primary ideas and devices such as the free plan, the hovering horizontal, the abstract, planar wall, the *piloti* and, of course, the post-Cubist conceptions of space. No less than in the early stages of Gothic or the Renaissance (or any other period of major discoveries) there were 'type-forms' to which several successive minds might devote their attention, making new discoveries and connections. In the 1930s, concrete skeleton and steel frame, *piloti* and free-plan partition, grid and extending curve, became common property. The white plaster surface with metallic strip windows (a hallmark of the 1920s) was gradually abandoned as impractical or inappropriate to new intentions. A wide range of new solutions emerged for the idea of the free façade, all the way from full glazing to sun-shading screens.

There was no single identifying feature of the architecture of the 1930s, but it was noticeable that curves became more complex and 'organic', that façades became more textured, that finishes and materials rejoiced more in 'natural' effects such as weathering. Here one should not underrate the impact of a gradual shift in values from the progressivist and machinist ideologies of the 1920s, towards various schemes of 'bio-technical' thinking in the ensuing decade. Confronted by the collapse of capitalism, by the Depression, by the emergence of totalitarianism, and by the demands for greater regional differentiation, the mechanistic Utopia of early modernism was forced to shift some of its terms. The underlying preoccupation with 'nature' as a palliative and supposed source of integrity became more overt in ideas, images and forms. This could be sensed differently with each architect, but there was a general trend none the less, and the strictures of the International Style seemed less and less pertinent, while abstract planarity tended to be replaced by something more tactile and more massive.

If the modern movement was passing into new geographical and philosophical territories, the originators still had the problem of what to do next. The work of Wright, Le Corbusier and Mies van der Rohe in this period reveals varying degrees and levels of innovation and retrospection. Wright, of course, had never abandoned 'nature' as a bedrock of certainties, but in the 1930s made several radical

369

inventions which touched upon the notion of origins. Le Corbusier changed direction, grappling with the dialectic between a pristine machine-age technology in steel and glass, and a species of rural primitivism nourished by the vernacular and by Surrealism. Aalto and Asplund both achieved a synthesis of international, classical and regional strands in buildings which were dense in mythological content (Chapter 19). Even Mies van der Rohe (who stayed in Germany until 1937) could be found making appeals to a lofty idea of 'nature': these had to do less with a wide-ranging programme for social transformation, than with the intensification of individual experience. The sense of the natural world was to be enhanced by the 'spiritual' order of architecture, and by subtle resonances between glass, stone, water and steel.

The Barcelona Pavilion was the pivotal work in Mies van der Rohe's development, summing up his discoveries to date, but also opening the way to the future. Combining the attributes of a house and a monument, it set down a range of visual conventions that he would continue to develop in later years. Broadly speaking, he adopted symmetry, frontality and axiality for civic buildings and monuments, and asymmetry, fluidity and interlocking volumes for residences, although both of these 'modes' were combined in the Barcelona building. Mies's entry to

the competition of 1930 for a War Memorial to be inserted in Schinkel's Neue Wache in Berlin of 1817 was grave and symmetrical: a restrained cubic volume of space detailed with 'lapidary clarity' and bathed in a low light. The pattern of a hieratic, stable geometry would recur at various scales, usually with an underlying classical echo, for buildings requiring a rhetorical stance (e.g. the unbuilt project for the Reichsbank in Berlin of 1933, the Seagram Building in New York of 1954–8, or the New National Gallery in Berlin of 1962–7). For individual houses or suburban pavilions, on the other hand, the informal mode was preferred (e.g. the Tugendhat House in Brno, Czechoslovakia of 1928–30, the Farnsworth House in Illinois of 1946–51). These conventions owed more than a little to Schinkel's distinctions between civic representation and rural retreat.

The Tugendhat House combined a liberating modern space with subtly placed axes and focal points; it worked with steel, stone and glass to evoke a translucent world. It stepped down a south-facing slope and opened up views over the landscape towards the city of Brno and the Schlossberg. The north side, off the road, was closed and secretive, the south one wide-open and transparent. The *pièce de resistance* was the living room/dining-room/study at the lower level – a single space

370

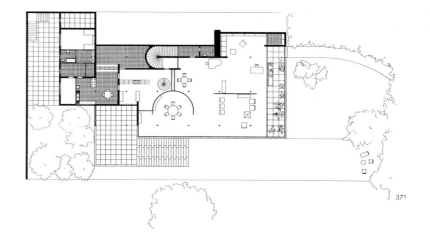

371

measuring 80 × 50 feet (25 × 15 metres) extending off the slope, with a grid of structure and curved or rectilinear partitions laid down in to it. Here the luxury of the Barcelona Pavilion was reproduced in a domestic setting, with clear, semi-reflective or tinted panes of glass, chrome-faced cruciform columns, white and gold polished onyx planes, and a curved ebony partition defining the dining-alcove. Whole areas of the south-facing glazing could be retracted into the floor at the touch of a switch, and winter sunlight could penetrate, while summer rays were excluded by an awning. The Tugendhat House combined a luxurious idea of machinism with an air of classical nobility: it was a health-giving instrument with something of the character of a villa.

Fritz and Grete Tugendhat typified the sort of progressive and wealthy clientele that made the Czech modern movement possible. They came to Mies because they admired his earlier buildings and wanted 'lightness, airiness and clarity' in their own house. The main living space was a shimmering belvedere: set about with polished machine-age materials, shot-silk curtains, and glass of varied opacity and colour. To the east end of the salon was a darkened area of glazing through which one could see a winter garden dappled in reflections from a hidden body of water. At night this same view was transformed into something hypnotic by electric light. Fritz Tugenhadt described the plants visible through the dark glass as 'gleaming solitaires' and revealed the uplifting effect that the building had upon him: 'When I allow these spaces and all that is in them to affect me as a whole, then I have the clear impression: this is beauty, this is truth.'

There was about the Tugendhat House something of the most luxurious Daimler-Benz car, and in its way the building was a celebration of industrialism. But Mies was able to take the 'facts' of the modern age and heighten their presence through a limpid control of proportion and transparency, and through a sublimation of materials. The building resumed several of his earlier ideas for houses and pavilions with terraces, and was not without classical echoes (Schinkel's pergolas and garden pavilions at Potsdam come to mind). A modern idea of continuous space was supplied

with a sense of hierarchy and incident; the usual Miesian planar walls were complemented by features of a 'free plan' such as semi-circular stairs and a curved partition, the latter demarcating the dining area and projecting it towards the landscape. These devices, and the composition of the entire south façade, suggested knowledge of Le Corbusier's Villa Stein/de Monzie. The Tugendhat House contained subtle allusions to history, but it also intensified the transition from artificial to natural worlds. The veins of marble and views through shaded glass contributed to a bizarre sense of the real. Frampton has described the effect of the winter garden seen from the interior:

The shallow glasshouse containing tropical vegetation appears to posit itself as a third term; one which is capable of mediating between the crystallized structure of the free-standing onyx plane on the interior and the natural vegetation of the garden landscape beyond. The decorative here appears as nature herself, rather than artistic invention.

If one seeks an analogy with this ambiguous 'framing' of natural phenomena, it is perhaps to be found in the mineralogical abstractions of Paul Klee, or in the Surrealistic *frottages* of Max Ernst. In the 1930s, Mies would return on several occasions to photomontages of landscapes seen through transparent structures, 'vignettes' which generated a super-real intensity. He would try out variations upon the Tugendhat scheme in several exhibition structures and unbuilt house designs in the 1930s: a model house for the Berlin Building Exhibition of 1931, and a series of proposals for 'courtyard houses', in which inside and outside were linked together as outdoor rooms or interior patios. Among these was a project of 1934 in which Mies made daring use of curves and diagonals to register the arrival by car, the position of the garage and the movement across the site. Increasingly he found ways of deflecting the eye to the far horizon, or of setting up tensions with the semi-enclosing walls. In the spidery perspectives for the Hubbe House in Magdeburg of 1935 (not built), foreground and background were compressed together by 'capturing' the distant view of the river between the edges of internal and external partitions in such a way that the middle distance was denied. In a project for a mountain house in the Tyrol of the mid-1930s, minimalist forms and transparent planes were juxtaposed to the rugged drama of

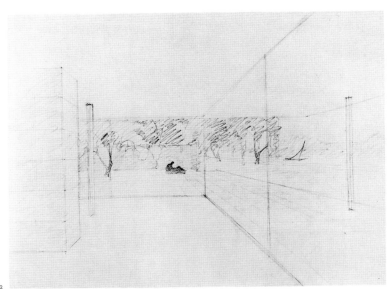

372

373

surrounding Alpine peaks. A similar principle was pursued in the project for Mies's first American house (not built) designed in 1938 for Stanley Resor to stand in a landscape of incomparable grandeur and wildness in Wyoming: here the spindly steel frame was also a frame of the view, the mountains becoming the 'wall' of the interior. With each step, new aspects of a restricted but highly concentrated language were discovered. Beyond the obvious and recurrent aspects of a Miesian style, there was an overriding intention: 'to bring Nature, man and architecture together into a higher Unity'.

This ideal was pursued in a deteriorating and increasingly barbaric social atmosphere in Germany, as the sustaining environment of the Weimar Republic gave way gradually to something sinister, even menacing. Mies found himself rejected by traditionalists for being too functionalist, and by social radicals for indulging in irrelevant luxury and 'spirituality'. When the Nazis first came to power in 1933, it seemed possible to some German modern architects that the more 'forward-looking' and 'technocratic' conservatives might wish to employ a version of modernism for state commissions: Mies was one of several (Gropius was another) to make an entry that year to the Reichsbank competition in Berlin (Fig. 432). With the forced closing of the Bauhaus (of which Mies was director) in that same year of 1933, it was becoming increasingly obvious that the new regime had little time for modernism of any kind. Official buildings would need to make a more overt reference to the past (a situation to which Mies also tried to react in his project for the German Pavilion in Brussels of 1935). In effect he was in an increasingly untenable and compromised political position. In 1937 he transferred to the

United States at the invitation of the Armour Institute (the future Illinois Institute of Technology) in Chicago. Soon after arriving, Mies van der Rohe was 'received' by Frank Lloyd Wright at Taliesin in Wisconsin. Moved by the expansive view from Wright's hillside retreat across the vast American landscape, he declared: 'Oh what a realm of freedom!'

The 1920s had been a difficult time for Wright, who was by then already in his late fifties. Dogged by personal and financial problems and a general indifference to his architectural ideals, he had adopted the quirks of the misunderstood eccentric. In the 1930s much of this changed, as his architecture went through a resurgence; as his life achieved a new stability with Olgivanna (his third wife); and as he solved his financial problems with the help of the Taliesin Foundation – a sort of rural retreat and architectural school in which young men helped about the farm and estate while learning the basics of Wright's 'organic' philosophy. It is arguable too that the intellectual atmosphere of the New Deal provided a richer soil for Wright's reformist tendencies than had the boom period of the 1920s. In the 1930s he devoted time to the design of cheap, single-family dwellings (e.g. the Usonian houses) and to a decentralized Utopia ('Broadacre City') – both intended to supply American society with a coherent social form in a period of crisis.

It was in several individual masterpieces of marginal social relevance that Wright revealed to the world at large that he was far from spent as a formal inventor of the highest order. The first of these was 'Fallingwater' (1934–7), a country retreat for the Pittsburgh millionaire Edgar J. Kaufmann, placed above a waterfall in a deep ravine in Pennsylvania known as 'the Bear Run'. The building was formed from cantilevered concrete trays rooted to a core embedded in the rocks. Its horizontal layers soared free of apparent support over the cascades and pools of the stream. Walls were avoided almost entirely, the sense of shelter being provided by the overhangs and by screen-like windows detailed to enhance the vertical and horizontal rhythms. The chimney core was made from local stone laid rough, in contrast to the smooth finish of the concrete balconies. A major part of the interior space was given over to a large living room, suitable to the

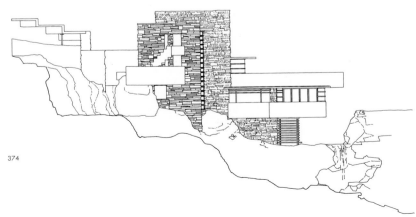

374

function of a weekend house. The effects of dappled light, surrounding foliage, and tumbling water, and the feeling of horizontal expansion in all directions, gave an exact image of Wright's well-known maxims concerning the integration of architecture and nature. There was the sense of a vital, ever-changing order as elements and context slid into new relationships. The spaces around the waterfall and the screens of the trees were drawn into the building: nature and art were made to reinforce one another. This is how Kaufmann's son (who introduced his father to Wright's work) recalled Fallingwater years later:

When Wright came to the site he appreciated the powerful sound of the falls, the vitality of the young forest, the dramatic rock ledges and boulders; these were elements to be interwoven with the serenely soaring spaces of his structure. But Wright's insight penetrated more deeply. He understood that people were creatures of nature, hence an architecture which conformed to nature would conform to what was basic in people. For example, although all of Fallingwater is opened by broad bands of windows, people inside are sheltered as in a deep cave, secure in the sense of the hill behind them. Their attention is directed toward the outside by low ceilings; no lordly hall sets the tone but, instead, the luminous textures of the woodland rhythmically enframed. The materials of the structure blend with the colorings of the rocks and trees … The paths within the house, stairs and passages, meander without formality or urgency … Sociability and privacy are both available, as are the comforts of home and the adventures of the seasons. So people are cosseted into relaxing, into exploring the enjoyment of life refreshed in nature.

A superficial reading of Wright's achievement at Fallingwater might point to the hovering horizontals in cream colours, and to the bands of glazing with metal frames, and claim that he was here

being influenced by the simplifications of the 'International Style'. This would be to fall into the sort of facile stylistic categorization warned against earlier in this book. For not only were the forms of the house rooted in Wright's earlier principles and discoveries (e.g. the landscape terraces of Taliesin, the extending levels and 'base elements' of the Prairie Houses, the pervasive stratification), they were also infused with meanings and associations at odds with the philosophical and formal precepts of much of the European avant-garde. Fallingwater celebrated the specifically American obsession with the free life lived in nature (an idea rich in pioneer mythology and ennobled by the transcendentalist writings of Thoreau and Emerson). Wright distanced himself from the International Modern movement in a display of scorn:

Human houses should not be like boxes blazing in the sun, nor should we outrage the Machine by trying to make dwelling places too complementary to machinery. Any building for humane purposes should be an elemental, sympathetic feature of the ground, complementary to its natural environment … But most 'modernistic' houses manage to look as though cut from cardboard with scissors … glued together in box-like forms – in a childish attempt to make buildings resemble steamships, flying machines or locomotives … So far I see in most of the cardboard houses of the 'modernistic' movement small evidence that their designers have mastered either the machinery or the mechanical processes which build the house … Of late they are the superficial, New 'Surface-and-Mass' Aesthetic falsely claiming French Painting as a Parent.

Opposed to this 'modernistic' style, Wright placed his own organic ideal, with its emphasis on the inner vitality of expression, on the fusion of

375 Frank Lloyd Wright, Fallingwater, Bear Run, Pennsylvania, 1934–7, living room

376 Fallingwater, living room, looking towards fireplace

377 Fallingwater, second-, first- and ground-floor plans

375

376

377

structure, function and idea, and on the inspiration of natural forms. With Fallingwater he may even have adopted the subtle position of a *corrective* to the 'box architecture' of the International Style, by demonstrating how floating horizontals might create a vital, life-enhancing space. In a talk to the Taliesin Fellowship Wright claimed:

… now you are released by way of glass and the cantilever and the sense of space which becomes operative. Now you are related to the landscape … You are as much part of it as the trees, the flowers, the ground … You are now free to become a natural feature of your environment and that, I believe, was intended by your maker.

To this vague pantheism, the various organic analogies in Wright's forms were the formal equivalent. At Fallingwater two natural elements seem to be interwoven in a fabric of imaginative abstraction: the rock strata bordering the site, and the trees with their hierarchy of supports, circulation and texture. A few years before designing the house, Wright had eulogized 'the rock ledges of a stone-quarry':

There is suggestion in the strata and character in the formations … For in the stony bone-work of the Earth, the principles that shaped stone as it lies, or as it rises and remains to be sculptured by winds and tide – there sleep forms and styles enough for all the ages for all of Man.

The tree, on the other hand, was a pervasive image in Wright's thinking from his earliest years – both an analogue for the structure and hierarchy of buildings, and (as in some of Ruskin's writings) an emblem of human freedoms rooted in moral principles. Fallingwater, no less than Richardson's Ames Gate Lodge half a century before, was an imaginative exploration of the primitivist idea of 'natural origins'. The cantilevered concrete shelves were lucid human creations of the modern age, but they seemed to emerge gradually from traditional rusticated walls, and from the rock ledges themselves. 'Nature', according to Emerson, 'offers all her creatures as a picture language, as symbols…' With this Wright might have concurred, but it was still necessary to translate the inner 'life-principle' into the forms of art. To do this he relied upon a geometrical transformation, a 'conventionalization' of the order in nature in the terms of his evolving architectural language. Fallingwater was clear evidence of his renewed vitality as a creator, but it was also an extension of his earlier discoveries. Like the Villa Savoye, the building contained 'an enormous quantity of ideas' compressed into a simple guiding image; it, too, relied on years of experimentation with an architectural system based upon principles, and upon a philosophy of life.

Wright's other *tour de force* of the mid-1930s was the Johnson Wax Administration Center in Racine, Wisconsin. Here the situation was entirely different: the building was to contain offices and to stand on a flat lot in a somewhat ugly urban setting. Unlike the managers of the giant, impersonal corporations then beginning to dominate American life, the Johnsons thought of their organization as a kind of extended family under a beneficent patriarchy. Wright grasped this at once and attempted to form an inward-looking community which would foster togetherness while mirroring the hierarchy of the firm. The administration building was designed as a large, windowless rectangle covered in brick and lit from above through a glazed ceiling and a clerestory; trays were suspended inwards from its edges and looked down on to a two-storey hall. This well-scaled, luminous space was articulated by a grid of slender mushroom columns in concrete and was given over mainly to clerks and secretaries, while management was placed on upper levels off the trays. The president and senior executives were inserted in a superstructure, visible on the exterior as two symmetrical, rounded, ziggurat forms. From here it was possible to see back into the hypostyle of tapered columns. A bridge passed on towards the research areas of the organization, to which Wright later added a glazed laboratory tower. Johnson

Wax was no ordinary office headquarters; it was a collective machine in which the social relationships were idealized in a clear diagram of institutional regulation and co-operation. If there was a model for the building in Wright's overall urban vision, it was the small regional manufacturing centres proposed in the drawings of Broadacre City.

The exteriors of the Johnson Wax Building had curved corners not unlike certain streamlined 'Moderne' trains and household objects by the industrial designer Raymond Loewy in the early 1930s. Cars swept in under the *porte-cochère* and then turned into the covered parking where the dynamism of the mushroom columns with disc-like tops was accentuated. Perhaps these touches revealed a deliberate attempt on Wright's part at designing in a 'populist' mode. The streamlined quality was continued in the interior in the horizontal attenuation of trays and parapets, and in details such as the integrated lighting made from the same materials as laboratory test tubes and resembling bundles of glass bamboo. But the mood of the interior went deeper than glossy surface effects: without being authoritarian it suggested stability and formality; in contrast to the somewhat forbidding exterior, it glowed with warmth and light. The structural grid belied the bleak repetitiveness of so many commercial offices; each column was elegant and delicate; together the rows of tapering shapes, their circular tops floating like lily-pads on a translucent surface, created a sort of underwater world. Wright despised the values represented by most business buildings –

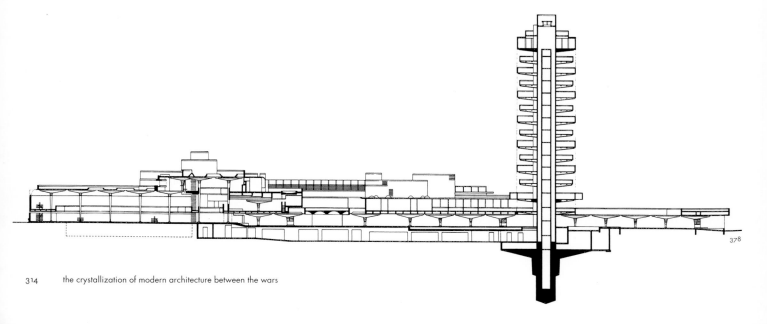

378

379

378 Frank Lloyd Wright, Johnson Wax Administration Center, Racine, Wisconsin, main building 1936–9, Laboratory Tower 1943–5, section drawing

379 Johnson Wax Administration Center

profiteering, brashness, the uniformity of the hive, and instead tried to mould spaces of a certain richness in which life, work, and art might enhance one another. The proof of the building's success lay in the way employees chose to linger in it after work, as if it were an oasis against the chaos and economic depression in the world outside. The polished glass and metal surfaces, deliberately chosen with Johnson's wax products in mind, were lavishly cared for and kept continually shiny and spick.

Like Fallingwater, the Johnson Wax building was superficially different from Wright's earlier architecture; on a deeper level, though, its organization was also rooted in his earlier experiments. The pedigree included the Larkin Building of 1902–6 (also an inward-looking, symmetrical 'Cathedral of Work'); the Unity Temple of 1905–8 (where two major volumes on axis with one another were also entered through a link between); the Tokyo Imperial Hotel of 1912–23 (in which the earthquake-proof foundations anticipated the principle of mushroom supports); and a project for the *Capital Journal* Building in Salem, Oregon, of 1931–2 (where a similar grid of structure had been intended). Wright's image of the columnated hall probably owed something to ancient Egyptian

hypostyles, just as his naturally inspired columns may have been indebted to the papyrus-like or lotiform supports in the same prototypes; he undoubtedly knew the plates in Owen Jones's *Grammar of Ornament* that investigated parallels between architectural structure and the forms of plants. The architect had to prove to his nervous clients that his slender columns could support the anticipated loads by building a mock-up and piling heavy weights on to it. This experiment only served to confirm that Wright had the practical engineering knowledge to match his intuitive structural sense.

In the early 1940s the Johnson Wax organization chose to expand and build a laboratory tower, which Wright was also commissioned to design. He adapted and fused the idea of the mushroom column with the needs of the programme, placing the services in the core and the laboratories on cantilevered trays with intervening balconies of lesser width. The result was an elegant, round-cornered building wrapped in solar-deflecting glass in which the main floor slabs registered on the exterior as horizontal bands. Although the Johnson Wax had practical problems because it swayed slightly in the wind, it still constituted a manifesto on the nature of the tall building: a concept at odds with the grid/frame/box formula. Here again was the analogy of the tree, with central trunk, deep root and extending branches.

Frank Lloyd Wright's theoretical proposal known as 'Broadacre City' (1934–5) was the fruit of many years' reflection on the problem of reconciling an ideal state with individual liberty in a mechanized society. On first inspection it might seem odd that his scheme should be called a 'city' at all, since it was the epitome of the decentralized community in which the individual family home and small holding were the basic units, and in which the only tall buildings were miles apart, separated by vast tracts of countryside. Wright argued that the telephone and the automobile were making the centralized city obsolete, and that mechanization, paradoxically, was allowing the return of Americans to their true destiny: a society of free individuals living in a rural democracy. As in most of Wright's ideas, there was about this a curious blend of the progressive and the conservative. Broadacre City was supposed to release people from the tyranny of centralized urban capitalism – of 'rent' (a word Wright used to describe all forms of alienation and exploitation) – to deliver them from the evil ways of the city and to return them to a purer and more natural state, where they would be self-reliant rural proprietors on the Jeffersonian model but living with the benefits of science. In this way individual dignity would, he hoped, be restored. Like Le Corbusier, Wright thought of himself as a prophet, able (in his case) to intuit 'the plastic form of a genuine democracy': 'The creative artist', he wrote, 'is by nature and by office the qualified leader in any society, natural, native interpreter of the visible form of any social order in or under which we choose to live.'

Broadacre City was laid out to conform with the American grid, and divided up into sites of an acre or more on which individual 'Usonian' houses were sited. Great emphasis was placed on the single family as the central bond of the community, but there were also co-operative markets, theatres and 'community centers' dotted about among the fields. The tall towers standing here and there were complex in texture and shape. They broke with the countryside grid and were like beacons in the landscape. To one side of the model which Wright and his Taliesin associates put together,

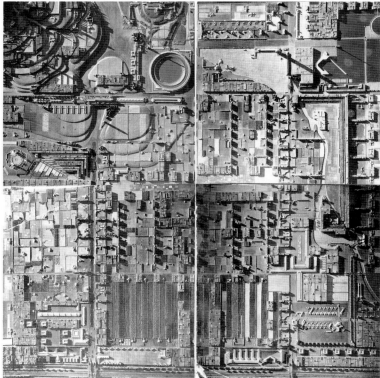

380

there was even a cathedral of no fixed denomination. Wright, like Le Corbusier, tended to think that the realization of his particular Utopia would make traditional religion obsolete. There were also schools and what he called 'Design Centers' where the young would be introduced to 'spiritual values' in nature through a training in the perception of form, and so become well-rounded citizens in the future. 'Eye and hand, body and what we call mind thus becoming more and more sensitive to nature …' Wright insisted that Broadacre City was neither 'backward-looking' nor escapist, but an intelligent response to 'excess urbanization', combining the best of a scientific culture with 'new free forms … for the accommodation of life': 'Broadacre City is the country itself come alive as a truly *great city*.'

The 'Usonian' home embodied a similar ethos and was also an attempt at dealing with the social and economic realities of the Depression. Entirely

380 Frank Lloyd Wright,
Broadacre City project,
1934–5, model

381 Frank Lloyd Wright,
Jacobs First Residence,
Madison, Wisconsin,
1936–7, plan:
a 'Usonian' house

382 Jacobs First
Residence, interior

practical, it was constructed from a kit of parts
including a concrete-slab foundation floated on a
drained bed of cinders and sand, with radiating
hot-water pipes inserted beneath. Walls were
prefabricated from three layers of board and two
of tar-paper. The roof was a simple insulated slab
containing a ventilation system, and was made to
overhang the edges of the dwelling so as to throw
water clear, to give a sense of shelter, to protect the
interior from glare, and to provide a horizontal
related to the earth plane. But there was more
to the Usonian idea than a clever labour- and
money-saving assembly. The dining room was
abolished in favour of an alcove with a table in it,
a space blending kitchen and living areas together:
a response to the servantless clients who could be
expected to buy Usonian houses, and a sign of the
rejection of pre-First World War formalities in
American life generally. Wright first tried out the
Usonian idea in the Jacobs First Residence of
1936–7, at Westmoreland, near Madison,
Wisconsin. It caught on quickly, and in the
following decades Wright would build dozens of
them. His formula was soon adopted by building
contractors and cheap home catalogues. Its
free-plan interiors and exterior decks caught the

mood of an emergent middle-class suburban
existence. The imitations lacked the judicious
proportion and detail of the originals, but the very
fact that Wright's ideas were copied so frequently
suggested that he had succeeded in crystallizing the
terms of an emergent suburban vernacular.

In 1937–8 Wright constructed 'Taliesin West'
in the Arizona desert at Maricopa Mesa, Paradise
Valley. In effect this was a small Utopian settlement
where the Taliesin community and Wright's family
would spend several months each winter. The layout
combined drafting rooms, theatre, apprentices'
court, residences and a small, centralized meeting
room in the form of an Native American 'hogan'.
The buildings were woven together over a pattern of
indoor and outdoor spaces laid into a base of rough-
hewn boulders set in mortar. The superstructure
was largely of wood, the main drafting room
having a roof of parallel tilted beams with canvas
slung between them. There were sunken areas,
breezeways, pergolas and a pool, the last being
placed on a diagonal platform guiding the eye
outwards towards the rim of surrounding peaks.
The low, earth-hugging forms of Taliesin West
combined two desert archetypes in a single idea:
the half-buried 'pit-house' and the nomadic tent.

381

382

Wright was fascinated by the archaeological remains and indigenous cultures of the southwest, and by the idea of a building as a mimetic version of landscape. The rough-hewn base was a formalized version of the water-swept gullies and canyons, while the 'peaks' of the building's timber profiles rhymed with the rim of distant mountains, and with the vertical fingers of the cacti rising from the desert floor. Arguably the geometry of the plan was influenced by Navaho sand-paintings, or even the motifs to be found in basketwork, pots and textiles. Wright was attracted to the mythopoetic vision of natural phenomena which he felt lay behind the abstract shapes of these designs, and was intrigued by the notion that the earliest buildings of the area may have derived, mimetically, from pots or baskets. The vase was a long-standing Wrightian obsession, supposedly demonstrating that the primary reality of architecture was 'the space within'. At Taliesin West (as at Taliesin North) vases were placed at key points as if to underline this lore. In this modern version of an encampment, Wright was both chief and shaman of his own tribe.

No less than its Wisconsin counterpart, or the Hollyhock House, or Fallingwater, Taliesin West was a celebration of the American landscape its ancient memories and its cosmic echoes. But it was also a summation of over a decade of architectural experiments, some adjusted to desert conditions. Its immediate predecessor was the wood and canvas Ocotillo Camp which Wright and his assistants constructed by hand in 1927 outside Chandler, Arizona, as a temporary work base to handle the ill-fated project for San Marcos in the Desert, a hotel embedded in the landscape as a latterday version of a *pueblo* with terraces, stepped levels and shaded courts. The project for a 'House on the Mesa' which was shown at the Museum of Modern Art in 1932 (surely one of his answers to the 'International Style'), showed how the concrete cantilever could be used to form a low-lying residence of deeply shaded overhangs and wide horizontals echoing the ground plane. The small Malcolm Willey House constructed in Minneapolis in 1934 reinvigorated the Prairie House vocabulary in a new context, and introduced the theme of a

383 Frank Lloyd Wright,
Taliesin West, Scottsdale,
Arizona, 1938

384 Taliesin West, plan

385 Taliesin West,
interior

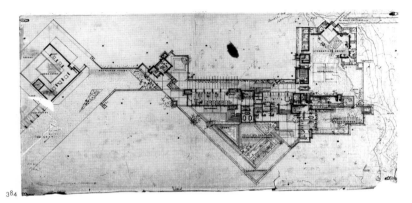

384

385

diagonal terrace and route of approach as a means
of deflecting the eye to the horizon. Taliesin West
pulled all of these discoveries together, but, in like
manner, was the parent of numerous buildings to
come in the late 1930s and 1940s: the Pauson
House of 1940 (also in Arizona) with its wooden
horizontals springing from a rock base, the Florida
State College of 1939 (in which landscaping and
architecture were fused), and a host of individual
house designs in which Wright used ever more
complex grammars of circles, diagonals and
hexagons to wed buildings to the landscape.

In 1930 Wright was 63 and in difficulties; at the
same time, Le Corbusier was 43 and on the crest of
a wave of success. The 1920s had witnessed his
rapid emergence from obscurity to a position in
the vanguard of the European modern movement.
By the time he received the commission for the
Villa Savoye he had become an international figure,
invited to design buildings as far afield as Moscow
and North Africa. He evidently thought of himself as
some kind of messiah destined to supply the forms of
a new machine-age civilization. Although the 1930s
was far sparer in actual commissions than the 1920s
had been, this did nothing to diminish the architect's
sense of a world mission. On the contrary, the scope
of his thinking continued to broaden, particularly
with regard to the design of cities. In this period he
delivered plans for places as varied as Algiers, Rio
de Janeiro and New York, and formulated the
universal principles of the *city-type* for modern
regeneration: the 'Ville Radieuse' ('Radiant City').

The Villa Savoye had summed up the researches
of the 1920s and was later canonized as a classic
work of the 'heroic period' of modern architecture.
But it also left Le Corbusier with the problem of
avoiding self-imitation. In the 1930s he extended
some features of his architectural system, left
others behind, and introduced new inventions.
This process of retrospection and selection was
not entirely rational and was effected by the tasks
and opportunities that the 1930s offered. Generic
themes such as the box on stilts required new
solutions at the larger scale of collective housing or
institutional commissions. Complex programmes
such as that for the Palace of the Soviets project of
1931 (Chapter 12) could not be handled by simply
stretching the typology of the Villas, so Le
Corbusier developed an approach in which

individual functional pieces were identified, then joined together by axes, circulation areas or flanges of open-air space. An analogous procedure lay behind the design of the Cité de Refuge of 1929–33 (a Salvation Army hostel in Paris), where the entrance sequence was expressed as a series of free-standing objects – a shelter, a bridge, a tiled cylinder – against the backdrop of a sheer, double-glazed curtain wall. This treatment of the façade may have been considered appropriate to the image of a collective *machine à habiter*, but the mechanical heating and ventilating systems did not function well, and in the course of time Le Corbusier began to rethink the nature of the free façade so as to let in light, but cut down on the glare of the sun.

Climate became a major preoccupation of Le Corbusier's in the 1930s, perhaps because he had to consider the problems of constructing in North Africa, Brazil, the tropics and the Mediterranean. The architect travelled a great deal in this period and from his sketches and notes one realizes that he was increasingly interested in folk forms, and in the harmony between people, buildings and landscapes which he sensed in the vernacular. In 1935 he wrote that he was 'attracted to the natural order of things'

388

and that he sought out 'primitive men, not for their barbarity, but for their wisdom'. It is not that Le Corbusier was totally abandoning 'the machine', but the mechanical now entered a more clearly defined polarity with the 'natural' and the 'organic'. A vein of primitivism (in tune with changing sensibilities) came closer to the surface. There were shifts in imagery, form and material which betokened a new engagement with the structures of nature. These first showed up in his sketches and paintings of the late 1920s. The human figure began to replace still lifes and machine parts. *Objets trouvés* such as shells, bones and pebbles were the starting point for metamorphoses and secret correspondences. Biomorphic abstractions, influenced no doubt by the contemporary paintings and sculptures of Picasso and Miró, became more frequent. Curves and contours became more sinuous and irregular. The rather strict, stereometric world of Purism was eased open to reveal a more complex and primordial subject matter related to the contents of the unconscious. It was around 1930 that Le Corbusier was attracted to Surrealism and to techniques of photomontage, in which objects were shifted from their normal context so generating a sense of the magical and the bizarre. Both his architecture and his paintings rejoiced more in the contrast of different textures, materials, identities and associations. One senses a transition in the architect's emotional life towards a more 'female' aspect of his nature, and in his ideological affiliations towards a vaguely defined ideal of 'natural' laws in the political and social body.

At the very moment that chroniclers and curators were canonizing Le Corbusier's 'white villas' of the 1920s as examples of the 'International Style', he was pursuing quite new directions in his

386

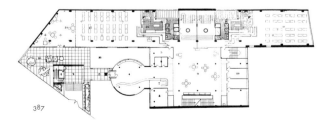

387

architecture. In parallel with the larger projects in plate glass, glass brick and steel, there were more modest schemes for buildings in the countryside which revealed a rustic strain in Le Corbusier's thinking. The Maison de Mandrot at Le Pradet in Provence of 1929–32 combined the 'universal' technology of the steel frame with the 'local' craftsmanship of masonry construction. The unbuilt proposal for the Maison Errazuris in Chile (also of 1930) recast Le Corbusier's customary vocabulary in terms of logs, rugged masonry and turf roofs. The house at Mathes (1934–5), next to the Atlantic, made use of planar stone walls, deep embrasures and a secondary structure in timber, the roof being in the form of an inward-sloping 'V' with a gutter along the centre line to sluice off the rain. This return to the solid wall and natural materials had to do with the need to use local builders, but it also recalled the Ruskinian values of Le Corbusier's formation, as well as his early interest in the basis of vernacular form. In turn, it revealed a new engagement with the problem of sensitizing modernism to the requirements of different regions and climates: it was further evidence of the eternal dialectic between nature and machine in Le Corbusier's thinking.

The Petite Maison de Weekend of 1935 at La Celle-St-Cloud returned to the vaulted, low-cost housing prototype of 1919, the Maison Monol, and restated it as a one-off design: a rustic retreat in a western suburb of Paris for a well-to-do client. Where the villas of the 1920s were poised above the ground on *pilotis*, the Petite Maison was an earth-hugging shelter – half cave, half machine-age primitive hut – with turf roof, concrete piers, rough brick walls, glass-block screens and wooden panelling. Le Corbusier made a distinction between the cubic volumes of the Citrohan prototype and the Monol with its swelling vaults: 'in the one … strong objectivity of forms, male architecture; in the other, limitless subjectivity … female architecture'. The garden of the Petite Maison de Weekend combined a neolithic ring of stones with a small aedicule. There were also hidden erotic agendas: on arrival the car fitted snugly into a rounded, womb-like enclosure of earth and rock. Inside there were deliberate 'puns' between handicraft and industrial objects: a wicker basket and a wire one, an earthenware vase and a mass-produced glass one. Analogous interactions between 'organic' and 'mechanical' could be found in Le Corbusier's contemporary paintings while the playful Beistegui roof terrace of 1930–1 derived part of its fascination from tongue-in-cheek reversals of the 'natural' and the 'artificial'. Vincent Scully caught the mood of the Petite Maison de Weekend when he referred to it as 'this elegant cavern, this ironic grotto half underground':

One says ironic because there remains a kind of intelligent distance, especially in the furniture, a marvellously active collaboration between the popular, the primitive, the high-tech, and the en série. During these same years the work of Frank Lloyd Wright was also exhibiting an exotic and consciously primitive character – very straight and serious. With Le Corbusier there is more comment and a marvellous pictorialism. A sense of ironic play still persists…

The Petite Maison probably needs to be seen in the broader context of the 1930s where 'Regionalism' often degenerated into a caricature of local architecture, but where the pressure was none the less felt to blend the universality of modernism with rural values. Indeed, the Monol type became a sort of 'generalized sign' of vernacular form in Le Corbusier's vocabulary: variations on vaults, or aggregations of vaults, would reappear in later schemes, such as the unbuilt 'Roq and Rob' holiday housing on the Riviera of 1949, the Sarabhai House

389

390

in Ahmadabad of 1951–5 or the Maisons Jaoul
outside Paris of 1951–4.

   This was but one example of the way that Le
Corbusier would invent a type-form or a motif and
then develop it through different purposes and
meanings. For example, in 1929 he proposed a
'World Museum' as the centrepiece of his unbuilt
Mundaneum to stand above Geneva. In 1931 he
flattened this out as a square spiral for a 'Museum
of Modern Art' that would begin with a small
nucleus and then grow gradually as an expanding
square of top-lit, parallel halls based on a module.
In 1939 he returned to the idea again, this time as
the more refined 'Museum of Unlimited Growth'.
Le Corbusier had long since developed the habit
of abstracting lessons from natural systems of order,
and the spiral was a basic geometrical principle
which could be found in both shells and plants.
Similar transpositions and transformations
of ideas can be found at many levels of Le
Corbusier's oeuvre, from individual elements to
overall schemes.

   One of the pivotal buildings in Le Corbusier's
transition from the 1920s to his later works was the
Pavillon Suisse in the Cité Universitaire, of 1930–1.
This was a student hostel in which the individual

rooms were placed in a steel and glass box poised
above the ground on bold concrete *pilotis* of
complex, curved shape. The communal parts of the
programme – lounge, lobby, etc. – were inserted in
free-form curves at ground level. The rear wall was
treated to a rubble surface. Between box and base
was an intermediary element, a curved tower lit
through glass bricks and containing the stairs. The
space underneath the *pilotis* was given over to
relaxation, but also functioned as a transitional
portico leading to the entrance. The fully glazed
wall of the superstructure faced south over a field
destined to become an athletics ground. The plan
of the Pavillon Suisse had all the clarity of a Cubist
picture, and the taut shapes, implying transparencies
and overlapping forms, had much to do with Le
Corbusier's discoveries as a painter. Each part was
related to the whole and every detail made a specific
response to the total image.

   In type, the Pavillon Suisse was a relative of
Soviet projects of the 1920s for 'ideal collectives',
but it was also the cousin of Le Corbusier's own Cité
de Refuge and implied a similar message of urban
reform: liberation from the soot and imprisonment
of the nineteenth-century slums; provision of the
essential joys of light, space and greenery for all.

It gave the usual Corbusian formula of the box on stilts a new robustness and materiality which contrasted with the smooth whitewashed surfaces and slender cylinders of the 1920s. While the Pavillon Suisse was based upon the principles of the Five Points of a New Architecture, it adjusted these to deal with the greater size, and to express the structural concept of a steel cage on bold concrete legs. The *pilotis* for this building were remarkable sculptural inventions (variations on a figure 8 in plan), which were referred to as 'dog bones' in the course of the design. They reconciled the need for actual and visual stability, and harmonized with the anthropomorphic shapes used elsewhere in the building. When he published Pavillon Suisse in volume 2 of the *Oeuvre complète* in 1934, Le Corbusier made much in the photographs of the way that people might linger or pass under the *pilotis*. In fact he seems to have thought of the building as a demonstration of the way that modern techniques might be employed to liberate the ground for circulation in the modern industrial city. He wrote revealingly in the introduction:

So what have we done in these years 1929–34? First of all a few buildings, then many large-scale urbanistic studies. These buildings have served the role of laboratories. We wanted each element of construction during that period to be the experimental proof which would enable us to take the necessary urbanistic initiatives.

In effect, the Pavillon Suisse was a slice of housing from the 'Ville Radieuse' (or 'Radiant City') transformed into a unique work of art.

Le Corbusier embodied his vision of an ideal society in his city plans. Underpinning his urban initiatives was a naïve faith in the power of a well-ordered environment to reunite man, nature, and the machine in an unalienated harmony. Mechanization was seen as essentially two-sided: it caused disruption and decay, undermining society and bringing it to the edge of revolution; but it also supplied the means for realizing a new order whose constitution the Utopian artist would be able to form. After his failure to 'sell' the concepts of the Ville Voisin of 1925, Le Corbusier began to lose his earlier confidence in the powers of big business and centralized technocracy to bring his ideal to the plane of reality. His experiences in Moscow in the 1920s did little to encourage a swing towards the left either, although he appears to have admired the housing experiments of the OSA group and the linear city theories of Milyutin (Chapter 12). Equally, Le Corbusier's confidence in the power of democracy to counter chaos continued to dwindle, and it was in the same period that he was attracted to 'Syndicalism'. This grew out of the trade union movement of the late nineteenth century and proposed a 'pyramid of natural hierarchies' from a base on the shop floor, through a middle level of elected managers to an apex in a regional council. In effect, an echelon of elected administrators was to replace the old state. Le Corbusier hoped (naïvely) that this would be a more effective and more representative method of government than that

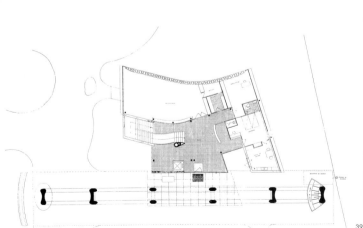

391

392

and communal functions like gymnasiums and child-care centres. These *à redent* apartment houses were a conflation of several earlier collectivist images. There were echoes of Eugène Hénard's '*Boulevards à redans*' of 1903 and of Charles Fourier's early nineteenth-century Utopian communal ideal, the '*phalanstère*' (which in turn transformed the prototype of the Baroque palace, e.g. Versailles). The continuous roof terraces for leisure activities showed how the '*toit jardin*' (roof-garden) principle could be transformed to public use, and may in turn have been influenced by the decks of ocean-liners: in the book *La Ville radieuse* (1935) Le Corbusier wrote tellingly of

393   Le Corbusier studying a model of '*à redent*' housing for the 'Ville Radieuse', early 1930s

394   Le Corbusier, Ville Radieuse, overall plan, *c.* 1930

395   Le Corbusier, sketch of nude, Algiers, *c.* 1931. Fondation Le Corbusier, Paris

provided within democracies with their perennial oscillation between right and left. Naturally, the system he envisaged gave a special place to planners and architects, who were situated near the top of the pyramid; it was their business to give form to the new society.

Such ideas as these were ripe when Le Corbusier put together a new version of his ideal city, the Ville Radieuse, in the early 1930s. The Ville Radieuse as a whole was highly centralized and densely populated, yet most of its surface was given over to zones of leisure – parks, playing-fields, etc. Following his earlier principles, Le Corbusier also created broad roads to facilitate the rapid passage of traffic to and from the countryside and from place to place within the city; pedestrians were able to circulate on separate levels; and the traditional 'corridor street' was completely destroyed. As in Renaissance Utopian plans, the 'ideal order' was expressed through symmetry and symbolic geometry. There was even an anthropomorphic image underlying it: a 'spine', 'arms', a 'heart' and a 'head'. As in the Ville Contemporaine of 1922 the main building types were skyscrapers and apartment houses, but the former were now grouped at the head of the city while the latter were laid out in long strips *à redent*, thus creating semi-courts and harbours along their length. The housing strips were in turn lifted above the continuous ground plane on *pilotis*. There was no longer a division between the élite and the working class, as there had been in the Ville Contemporaine; everyone lived in the *Unités*, which combined individual rationalized apartments

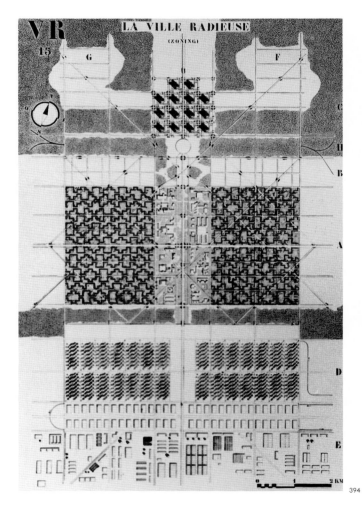

394

the good life lived in the open air and sunlight, surveying 'a sea of verdure'.

In 1933, the members of the CIAM (Congrès Internationaux de l'Architecture Moderne) met on board the SS *Patris* on a voyage between Marseilles and Athens to discuss the state of the modern city. Against the superb landscape background of the Peloponnese, the modern architects of Europe drew up the blueprints for what they hoped would be an enlightened new civilization coming to terms with mechanization (see above, pp. 254–5). Le Corbusier was adopted, in effect, as the unofficial pope. The 'Charter of Athens' was really a restatement of the Ville Radieuse philosophy but without the original poetry. The already problematic principles of Le Corbusier's urbanism were separated from a particular personal vision and rendered as a sort of catechism. Looking back from a distance of three decades the historian Reyner Banham summed up the situation succinctly:

The Mediterranean cruise was clearly a welcome relief from the worsening situation of Europe and in this brief respite from reality the delegates produced the most Olympian, rhetorical and ultimately destructive document to come out of CIAM ... the 111 propositions that comprise the Charter consist in part of statements about the conditions of towns, and in part of proposals for the rectification of those conditions, grouped under five main headings, Dwellings, Recreation, Work, Transportation, and Historic Buildings ... this persuasive generality which gives the Athens Charter its air of universal applicability conceals a very narrow conception of both architecture and town planning and committed CIAM unequivocally to (a) rigid functional zoning of city plans, with green belts between the areas reserved to different functions, and (b) a single type of urban housing, expressed in the words of the Charter as 'high, widely-spaced apartment blocks wherever the necessity of housing high density of population exists'. At a distance of thirty years we recognize this as merely the expression of an aesthetic preference, but at the time it had the power of a Mosaic commandment and effectively paralysed research into other forms of housing.

While Le Corbusier's followers seemed bent on calcifying his urban doctrines, he was, in fact, reacting with considerable flexibility in his proposals for particular places. Among the most spectacular of his many unrealized schemes were those for Rio de Janeiro (1929) and Algiers (1930–42), where he imagined long viaducts in reinforced concrete with roads running along the top to free circulation. These were veritable 'constructed sites' into which a whole range of urban functions could be inserted. In the proposal for Algiers (known as the 'Plan Obus') the viaduct was bent into a sinuous, calligraphic form following the coastline. The collective

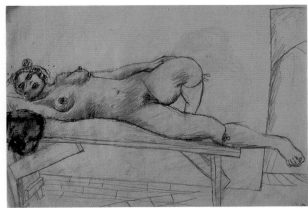

395

habitations were conceived as vast curving slabs, virtually landscape sculptures on the scale of the mountains and sea. The viaduct itself was based on a concrete skeleton and had a pedestrian street threaded through it at the middle level. Individual apartment units were plugged into the structure (one was shown in a 'Moorish' style). Le Corbusier was certainly interested in the image of ancient viaducts and aqueducts straddling cities, and intrigued by the automobile test-track on the roof of the Fiat factory in Turin (designed by Giacomo Matté Trucco, Figs. 445, 446). 'Sources' like these were combined with the idea of a linear city intended to alleviate the urban problems of Algiers and to provide rapid transportation from the interior. The eruptive contours of the scheme recalled Le Corbusier's sketches of mud buildings in the M'zab and of Algerian women in the Casbah. *Les Femmes d'Algers* had been a key subject for the nineteenth-century painter Delacroix, and in Le Corbusier's hands this theme was transformed into an interlacing calligraphy of abstract lines suggesting, simultaneously, the outlines of women and those of mountains and coastlines.

Although the Plan Obus for Algiers did not follow the precise form of the Ville Radieuse, it did show how its general principles could be adjusted to a specific topography and cultural circumstance. Probably intended to embody some notion of a 'progressive' colonial order, it corresponded to Le Corbusier's youthful dream of regenerating Mediterranean culture. It also suggested a broader programme for the integration of mechanization,

396   Le Corbusier, 'Plan Obus' for Algiers, project A, 1930

397   Le Corbusier, project for Quartier de la Marine, Algiers, drawing of skyscraper with *brise-soleil* façades, 1939. Fondation Le Corbusier, Paris

396

regional and 'natural' imperatives. These ideas converged in the large glass skyscraper containing the administration. This dominated the image of the city and was directed out towards the sea. In later versions (Algiers preoccupied Le Corbusier until the early 1940s) the skyscraper was treated to sun-protecting screens known as *brises-soleil*. The fact was that his fully glazed façades (e.g. the Cité de Refuge and the Pavillon Suisse) had proved to be environmental disasters, producing unbearable conditions in the summer months. The *brise-soleil* was a means for preserving the idea of a free façade while letting in light, reducing solar heating, and cutting down glare. It was a principle which owed something to traditional precedents (for example, Arab *claustras* and *mashrabiya* screens), but which was consistent with Le Corbusier's structural philosophy. The later versions of the Algiers skyscraper showed how the screens could be integrated with the actual fabric as a deep texture of shaded loggias; Le Corbusier sketched comparisons between his new idea and the extending branches and shading leaves of a tree.

The Olympian vision of Le Corbusier's urban plans of the 1930s owed something to the fact that the aeroplane allowed him to grasp the overall shape of a terrain from the air; but it was also reliant upon his capacity to fuse together painting, sculpture, architecture, urban form and landscape. Although he had no success with his urban proposals, this was none the less a period of epic thinking in which he delivered his message of salvation from on high and behaved as one of Nietzsche's 'historical world individuals'. In 1935 he visited the United States and criticized Manhattan, claiming that the skyscrapers were too small and too close together; of course, his essential purpose was to preach the Ville Radieuse in the hope that the American authorities might turn the most powerful technology in the world over to his plans. Again he was disappointed, pouring his dreams and regrets into his book *When the Cathedrals were White* (1937), in which he condemned the wastefulness of American suburbs and the irrationality of prevalent skyscraper forms. These he intended to replace with a new variant, 'the Cartesian skyscraper', a vast vertical building for living and for working, which would ensure that the city with a park in it (Manhattan) became a park with a city in it (the Ville Radieuse). Le Corbusier even went so far as to hope that Mussolini might build his ideal dream, and as late as 1941 was evidently attempting to persuade the Vichy government to listen to his ideas for Algiers (without success). Certainly this was a case of opportunism; equally it must be pointed out that Le Corbusier believed the inherent 'good' of his city plans would do more than justify any double-dealing that might be necessary to bring them into being.

The 1930s was a decade in which Mies van der Rohe, Le Corbusier and Frank Lloyd Wright succeeded in transforming earlier themes and enriching them in works that were microcosms of their view of things. Each in his own way reacted to the world crisis of the period by insisting upon the role of architecture in relinking individuals and societies to some sort of 'natural order', though what each meant by this varied considerably. In Mies van der Rohe's mind, it had to do with an expansion of inner awareness and with a space of individual freedom; he remained vague about the public shape of the city. Le Corbusier and Wright addressed the whole range of building types and the relations between them. For them 'nature' took on a regulative, even a cosmic, significance for the entire order of society. For the former, the roots of his view lay in the Utopian thought of the Enlightenment; for the latter it lay in a fusion of native agrarianism and an American transcendentalist tradition.

Both Frank Lloyd Wright and Le Corbusier regarded themselves as latter-day versions of the philosopher-king, who enshrines the constitution of a perfect society in the form of an ideal city. Despite obvious differences between their respective urban models, they addressed similar questions: how to overcome the schisms resulting from the division of labour, how to employ the machine yet maintain a sense of wholeness socially and visually, how to reintegrate man and 'nature'. Each had as little success as the other in persuading any influential authority to adopt his larger ideas, and each had to be content with realizing his Utopia in fragmentary experiments. In any case, as the decade wore on, it became increasingly clear that the disjunctions within modern European and American society were far too deep to be healed by soothing architectural palliatives. The era of justice and harmony seemed less and less likely to dawn. The dusty model of Broadacre City and the fading drawings of the Ville Radieuse remained the property of their creators: two individualist artist-thinkers who optimistically, but mistakenly, imagined that architectural form could fashion a new, integrated civilization.

397

19

the spread of modern architecture to britain and scandinavia

398 Berthold Lubetkin and Tecton, Penguin Pool, London Zoo, 1934

It is perhaps in the nature of major creative revolutions that the period of peak creation be followed by a phase in which the implications of recent innovations are gradually absorbed and explored. This had already begun to happen to the modern movement in the 1930s, when a 'second generation' – including Aalto, Lubetkin, Maekawa, Niemeyer, Sert and Terragni – began to make their impact. These architects were all born close to the turn of the century and so were old enough to have been brought up in the twilight of *fin-de-siècle* tendencies, yet young enough to have experienced the promise of the new architecture with full force. Like any immediate inheritors of a new faith they had the problem of absorbing and transforming novel ideas without resorting to slavish imitation or rigid dogmatism. Problems of transmission were complicated in the 1930s by the political climate and the emigration of forms to new lands. Moreover, the 'masters' were not standing idle and a young architect might be on the point of mastering certain lessons of the Villa Savoye only to be confronted by the Petite Maison de Weekend or the invention of the *brise-soleil.* With this tendency towards a slight time-lag, it is scarcely surprising that many of the key breakthroughs in the works of Wright, Mies van der Rohe and Le Corbusier of the 1930s should have waited for the post-war years to exert their broader influence.

While modern architecture was reaching its peak in the late 1920s in France, Germany, Holland and Russia, it was exerting only the slightest influence in Scandinavia and Britain. But by the mid-1930s the situation had almost reversed, and these were among the most active centres of modern experimentation left in Europe. In part this phenomenon was traceable to the influx of immigrants from countries such as Germany where modern architecture had been repressed; equally it was due to happy coincidences of talent, and to national cultural situations which virtually demanded a rejection of tired forms and an inoculation of new creative energy. However, the predisposing causes in Britain and the Nordic nations contrasted sharply. In Denmark and Sweden, modern architecture was implicated in a Social Democratic vision of emancipation, and was gradually grafted on to an existing architectural culture. In Finland, which was industrializing rapidly and asserting its independence from Russian domination, modernism was also involved in broad societal changes including the quest for a new national identity. In Britain, by contrast, modern architecture was initially remote from the concerns of the state. It set down roots with some difficulty, encountered strong resistance from traditionalists and remained somewhat marginal in the larger scheme of society. Even by the end of the 1930s, when a fair body of work had been achieved, it could still be portrayed as a cosmopolitan import from the continent.

In the 1930s in most of Europe, new strands of the modern movement were virtually obliged to come to terms with vestiges of classicism and with lingering effects of the Arts and Crafts or of National Romanticism. Usually there was a collision, though in some rare cases there was an exchange. Moreover, the extension of modernism imposed choices between existing options, and debates of the 1920s, such as that between 'formalism' and 'functionalism', took on new guises in the ensuing decades. In the 1930s architects could profit from a slight temporal or even geographical distance from the seminal works of the 'heroic period'. The Finnish architect Alvar Aalto, for example, established his vocabulary through a judicious combination of what was still valuable in his local situation and new ideas in the modern architectures of France, Germany, Holland and the Soviet Union. The Russian-born architect Berthold Lubetkin, whose main contribution was made in the 1930s as an immigrant to Britain, brought with him an international architectural culture blending French classical Rationalism and a deep understanding of the Soviet avant-garde. When charting developments in the 1930s, it is crucial to strike the right balance between original ideas and inherited elements, between stimuli of the moment and longer-term echoes in the history of architecture.

The reception of new forms was naturally affected by attitudes prevailing in the country of arrival. The modern movement in its initial phase in Britain had to deal with a certain insularity, but it could also hark back to the period of the 'pioneers' and to revered icons such as the Crystal Palace. Britain had contributed to the moral and reformist impetus behind the very idea of a modern architecture and had helped to foster Arts and Crafts values at the turn of the century. W. R.

Lethaby and his faction might almost have brought a vital architecture to full flower had their views not gone out of fashion to be replaced by a scholarly Beaux-Arts revival supported, on the whole, by architectural mediocrities. Even Mackintosh had been better understood in Vienna than in London. In Britain a cluster of predisposing factors, which seem in retrospect to have been crucial in channelling the direction of the new architecture on the continent, was missing. Apart from the short-lived impact of Wyndham Lewis's vorticism, there was no Cubist revolution in the arts. The activities of the Design and Industries Association were scarcely the equivalent of the Deutscher Werkbund's idealistic obsession with injecting 'good form' into industrial products. There was a lack of progressive clientele and talent, and a general post-war complacency. Victory had made fantasies of a 'brave new world' or a mechanized social Utopia seem neither relevant nor necessary. The intellectual radicals of the time had an almost pathological distaste for mechanization; British reformers were either pragmatic, or medievalizing, or concerned with more fundamental ills than bad architecture – if they were not of the precious 'art for art's sake' variety. Nothing could have been further from the English situation and temper than the abstract social ideology of De Stijl or the Bauhaus, the machine fetishism of Futurism, or the total solutions of Le Corbusier's Ville Contemporaine.

The period between 1910 and 1930 in Britain has been characterized variously as the 'Regency revival', 'the playboy era', or the phase of 'ancestor worship' in design. Standing clear of the prevalent mediocrity was of course Lutyens, but he, for all his unique and uncategorizable quality, stood at the end of an expiring tradition rather than at the beginning of a new one; his remarkable works in New Delhi were easily associated with the 'Indian Summer' of British Imperialism. There were a few 'modern' experiments in the late twenties, like Behrens's design for a house for J. Bassett-Lowke of 1926 in Northampton and Thomas Tait's designs for the Crittall window manufacturers' workers' housing at Silver End, Essex, of 1927; but it was typical of the situation as a whole that it should have been the 'watered-down' versions of modern architecture – e.g. those of Willem Dudok and Robert Mallet-Stevens – which received attention in Britain. It was

399

not until 1929 with the Crawfords Advertising Building in London by Frederick Etchells (translator into English of *Vers une architecture*) and the white, cubic, concrete forms of Amyas Connell's house for Bernard Ashmole, at Amersham (1928), that a more rigorous modernism was made manifest. Joseph Emberton's Royal Corinthian Yacht Club of 1931, meanwhile, was clear evidence that the new architecture was at least being understood for its structural principles. This building was even included in Hitchcock and Johnson's *The International Style* of the following year.

The outstanding architect of the 1930s in Britain was undoubtedly Lubetkin. Born in 1901 in the Caucasus in Russia, he had experienced the architectural debates following the Soviet Revolution at first hand, had studied in Paris at the Atelier Perret, where he had been initiated into the secrets of reinforced-concrete construction, and had absorbed the principles of Le Corbusier's Five Points of a New Architecture. The flats designed by Lubetkin and Jean Ginsberg at Avenue de Versailles, Paris, in 1928–31 were a suave reinterpretation of Maison Cook, mated to certain ideas derived from the Soviet context. Lubetkin maintained contacts with Russia in this period,

designed the Soviet Pavilion for Strasbourg in 1929, and kept a firm grasp on the ideological issues then being hammered out in his homeland.

In 1930 Lubetkin went to England and gathered about him six young Englishmen; the group was christened 'Tecton'. Among their earliest commissions were two for London Zoo: the Gorilla House and the Penguin Pool. The latter, designed with the aid of Ove Arup the engineer, was a shallow oval pool in reinforced concrete with two curved ramps interlacing at its centre on which the birds could parade or from which they could dive into the water. The ramps were packed with steel reinforcing and were a structural innovation for the time, but it was the imagery and the taut abstraction which were so new in the British context. The Penguin Pool recalls some of Meyerhold's Constructivist stage-sets or Gabo's scientific sculptures from the 1920s, and was further evidence of Lubetkin's indebtedness to the formal inventions of the previous decade in Russia.

Lubetkin and Tecton's next major work was High Point I flats, Highgate (1933–5), designed for a site surrounded by greenery, with long views south over the whole of London. The flats were packed into a cross-of-Lorraine plan so as to maximize views, cross-ventilation, and contact with the outside. The main eight-storey body of the building was lifted up on *pilotis* and surmounted by a shared roof terrace. The lower storey was also communal, containing lobby, winter garden, main hall, access to the lifts, a tearoom, and a fantastic curved ramp descending to the garden at the rear – a vaguely Baroque flourish. This lower zone of the building was expressed as curved, free-plan elements swinging out and back from the prevalent rectangular order of the grid of columns and the axial discipline of the main forms. The vocabulary was, once again, an intelligent adaptation of Le Corbusier's white forms of the 1920s and of the system of the Five Points of a New Architecture. In this case, though, the walls were load-bearing, and the rooms cellular and compact. More than that, High Point I was among the earliest demonstrations of the synthesis of architecture and urbanistic doctrine, derived from both Le Corbusier and Soviet collective housing of the 1920s. Le Corbusier himself visited the building and (uncharacteristically) praised it as one of the

400

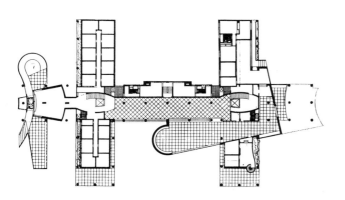
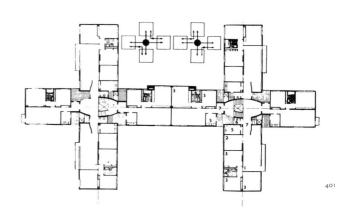

401

first 'vertical Garden Cities of the future'. A tower standing in a green park, its white wings spread out, its details tight and clear, High Point I became a rallying point of the emergent British modern movement, and a demonstration of what could be done when rigorous functional analysis, formal lyricism, and a social vision were synthesized. Of course the collectivist polemic of the building was a little uneasy in its upper-middle-class context, but the rhetoric was none the less clear; these were principles which might later be applied to collective housing on a broader scale once the necessary social transformations had occurred.

It is when one probes the underlying order of High Point I further that one appreciates the complexity of its sources. The conception owes much to those 'social condensers' designed in Russia only five years before; the radio mast at High Point was even detailed as a sort of Constructivist, high-tension sculpture. Perhaps the aeroplane imagery of the plan incorporates something of the notion of a social engine of the future. But along with these references from the machine-age imagery of the 1920s, there was a classical quality as well. The distinction between 'areas served' and 'circulation', by means of different geometries, recalls the principles of Beaux-Arts planning. Indeed the plan as a whole is a masterly exercise in the articulation of movement through a sequence of ceremonial spaces and in the control of primary and secondary axes, that will stand comparison with the plan of Charles Garnier's Paris Opéra (1861–74). Once again, we have to do with a fusion of lessons learned from various earlier periods in history.

By 1935, when High Point I was completed, a number of other modern buildings had also been erected in Britain. Lawn Road flats, Hampstead (1932–4), by Wells Coates – a Canadian born in Tokyo – was another collective statement. The individual flats were packed like the cabins on a ship into a simple oblong form served by cantilevered balconies. The memories of Le Corbusier and perhaps Mendelsohn are evident (especially in the sketches with their *tracées regulateurs* or 'regulating lines' and their dynamic perspectives), yet the building has a rigour of its own. In the British context, Lawn Road was an emblem of a new way of life. Significantly, many of its first occupants were cosmopolitan British intellectuals of leftist opinion or such immigrants from the continent as Mondrian, Gropius and Breuer. Gropius set up a partnership with Maxwell Fry, Breuer with F. R. S. Yorke, but it would be wrong to see their influence as anything other than an encouragement for a movement which had its own momentum.

Erich Mendelsohn also arrived in Britain in 1933 to escape Nazi persecution, and, in partnership with Serge Chermayeff, immediately won the competition for the De La Warr Seaside Pavilion at Bexhill in Sussex. This was to be a place for public entertainment of the usual south-coast resort type, with a theatre/cinema, bars, a cafeteria, some offices, a bandstand, and a swimming pool (later abandoned). The site was on the edge of the English Channel with southern exposure and long views. The scheme was close, programmatically, to some of the buildings Mendelsohn had designed in Berlin in the 1920s, such as cinemas, bars and canteens; he therefore felt free to experiment formally, and his early sketches show a sort of looming dynamic structure, fully fenestrated to give views over the sea. Even the rectilinear final building has the quality of dynamism of his earlier First World War sketches, a quality which upset 'functionalist' prigs who detected what they called 'formalism'.

Although the overall conception came about in organic, freely expressive sketches, the layout of the plan shows careful logic. The theatre/cinema was treated as a major entity and allowed to take up the whole west end of the building; its axial symmetry, and the fact that it scarcely needed daylight, made its exterior treatment as a closed, rectangular box appropriate. The bar, restaurant and cafeteria

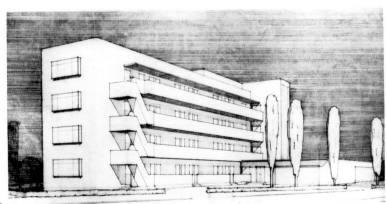

402

403

404

functions were grouped at the other end of the building on a long strip and given wide horizontal windows through the use of concrete cantilevered trays and a 'free façade'. These two main zones were joined by a hallway, which also served to link the town to the sea. This element was demonstrated on the exterior by means of curved glass projections at each end. The one on the sea side was a *tour de force* in concrete, with stairs spiralling up inside a glazed semi-cylinder linking the whole height of the building, and the main light fixture treated as an abstract sculpture suspended at the centre.

Public commissions on this scale were rare for modern architects in Britain during the 1930s, and many of them had to be content with designing small houses which took on the significance of experiments for some hoped-for future collective programme. The partnership of Amyas Connell, Basil Ward and Colin Lucas (two New Zealanders and an Englishman) developed a style of their own on the basis of Dutch, French, and Russian precedents, in which solids and voids were juxtaposed in strong contrasts, and reinforced-concrete construction was adapted to the unique demands of clients and sites. Thus New Farm at Grayswood (1932) was splayed in plan, in an attempt to maximize views and to link it to the landscape, while the house in Frognal of 1937 was more sedate, and combined the formality of an urban façade with informality to the rear, where a terrace and full-length glazing allowed a link with the garden. The model for this building was probably Le Corbusier's Villa Stein/de Monzie at Garches, and it is interesting to compare the force of a major prototype with a much softened, but creditable adaptation. The house at Frognal included brick because the local authority had insisted on some reference to typical local materials.

Indeed, 'Modern' buildings were often regarded with suspicion in Britain. In their design for a small house in the Sussex countryside of 1935, Connell, Ward and Lucas were presented by the local council with the option of using either a pitched roof with their intended white walls, or a flat roof, but with wooden cladding. They chose the second option. To compare Lubetkin's design for a bungalow at Whipsnade (1934), with its curved aerofoil forms and its tight discipline, to the house at Frognal and, say, Marcel Breuer and F. R. S. Yorke's house at Angmering of 1936 with its sculpted concrete stair, is to be impressed by the considerable variety of expression being worked out within the inherited forms of the International Style. At the same time it is to be made aware how far the imported foreign ideas were from prevalent English notions of 'the home'.

Two of the most remarkable buildings of the Modern movement in Britain served commercial purposes: the Boots Factory at Beeston by Owen Williams of 1930–2 and Peter Jones's Store in Sloane Square, London, by William Crabtree in association with Slater and Moberley and C.H. Reilly of 1936. Both were clad in glass curtain walls, and both used a concrete-skeleton construction to open up wide spaces in the interior, and to create unobstructed voids where outside and inside met at ground level. These were used as loading-bays for packing and unpacking drugs in the Boots case, and as uninterrupted shop windows for the display of merchandise in Peter Jones. There the similarities

405

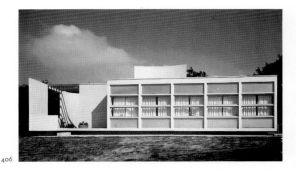
406

407

408

ended, for the Boots building had an assertive, even brutal character, quite in contrast to the elegantly proportioned mullions and urbanity of Peter Jones. Owen Williams was an engineer with a remarkable tectonic sensibility; his building had mushroom columns holding it up, which were perfectly suited to their purpose, as they created wider spans and allowed movement of goods around them. The central space of the Boots Factory was a sort of nave interrupted by cross-galleries and top-lit by a thin glass-brick and concrete membrane roof. The effect was tough but ennobling, a quality which understandably endeared it to the so-called 'New Brutalists' of the 1950s.

By the end of the 1930s, some of the avant-garde were beginning to labour and stretch inside the strait-jacket of the International Style; they were perhaps sensing its limitations visually and perhaps intuiting its foreignness, ideologically, to the British scene. The most outstanding case of the pursuit of more overtly formal values was Lubetkin's High Point II of 1936–8, designed to go alongside High Point I. Admittedly there were unusual constraints on the design (including a hostile local planning authority), but these do not account for the almost neo-Palladian façade composition; a plastic expressiveness in the overall form which reminds one of Lubetkin's admiration for the Baroque; the rich textural effect of a variety of materials; and the use of classical caryatids to support the canopy. Here there was obvious, indeed rather decorative, wilful aesthetic experimentation – what the critic J. M. Richards might have called 'celebrity architecture' in contrast to a hoped-for 'anonymous' modern vernacular. Lubetkin was expressing yearnings for the Grand Architectural tradition, and reacting, perhaps, to the greater complexity of texture and material in Le Corbusier's works of the early 1930s; the penthouse apartment at High Point II had curved, vaulted ceilings and cow-hide furnishings, and was like a suave reinterpretation of Le Corbusier's Petite Maison de Weekend of 1935. *The Architectural Review* assessed High Point II as 'an important move forward from functionalism'; but the Puritan left-wing element who espoused the utilitarian and moral qualities of modern architecture, and played down its aesthetic aspects, were outraged. This is how Anthony Cox, a young socialist architect, criticized High Point II:

408 Owen Williams, Boots Factory, Beeston, Nottinghamshire, 1930–2

409 William Crabtree with Slater and Moberly and C. H. Reilly, Peter Jones Store, Sloane Square, London, 1936

410 Berthold Lubetkin and Tecton, High Point I flats, Highgate, London, 1933–5, with High Point II flats, 1936–8, behind to the right

411 High Point II flats, entrance canopy with High Point I behind

409

Standing in the garden and looking up at the two blocks, 1935 and 1938, it is clear that something has changed, and that the change is not merely due to the higher level of building technique, or to the use of a smooth, clean tile facing to the concrete… It is as if during the three years that separate the buildings, rigid conclusions have been reached as to what is formally necessary in architecture. This tendency towards certain formal conclusions, that are very near clichés, is noticeable in the work of many modern English architects, but in Tecton's later work it is more than a tendency. It is considerably marked and mature … The intellectual approach which has produced what we know as modern architecture is fundamentally a functionalist approach … My contention is that the recent work of Tecton shows a deviation from this approach. It is more than a deviation of appearance; it implies a deviation of aim. It is more than an adjustment within legitimate limits; it is prepared to set certain formal values above use-values, and marks the re-emergence of the idea as the motive force … The change in aim must be due to personal reasons, to a turning inwards towards private formal meanings which have no general recognizable social basis … Is it really an 'important move forward from functionalism' from which development is possible; or is it a symptom of decline, an end in itself?

It is ironical that the criteria by which Lubetkin was here being judged were ones that he may himself have introduced into the British architectural world in his writings on the Soviet situation of the 1920s. However, there is some truth in Cox's assessment. High Point II has a flaccid elegance in contrast to the taut, sharp-edged polemic of the earlier building. Perhaps Lubetkin was beginning to sense the divergence between his own socialist aims and the values of the only clientele who would, or indeed could, put up his buildings. Or perhaps a tendency to formalism is inevitable at a certain stage in working out the implications of a style. However one sees it, the 'formalism' of High Point II was symptomatic of a much broader problem: given that mere imitations of the prototypes of the 1920s would be inadequate, what direction should the modern movement now take? Given that a sort of

410

411

412 Erik Gunnar
Asplund, Stockholm
Exhibition Building, 1930

413 Arne Jacobsen,
Bellavista housing,
Klampenborg, near
Copenhagen, 1934, plan

414 Bellavista housing

412

modern academicism was to be avoided, where
would sources of a new vitality lie?

Scandinavian architecture of the 1930s reveals
several ways of dealing with dilemmas of this kind.
Relations with the state and with the society at
large influenced the range and impact of imported
forms. Modernism was quickly implicated in Social
Democratic policies of institutional and urban
reform. The Stockholm Exhibition buildings of
1930 designed by Erik Gunnar Asplund revealed
a fresh interpretation of the new architecture,
achieved a wide endorsement from the general
public and supplied an image of modernity not
only for Sweden itself, but also for neighbouring
countries. The Exhibition projected a shining vision
of glass, lightness, openness, and efficiency at
just the moment that an increasingly urbanized
Scandinavia was ready to receive it. Modern
architecture was able to articulate communal
aspirations and express individual artistic visions,

but it also settled on ground that had been prepared
by state planning and by simplified versions of both
classicism and the vernacular. Imported *Siedlung*
housing types, with their modular repetition and
their strip-like configurations separated by bands of
greenery, were not so very foreign to the geometry
and social intentions which lay behind the sparse
uniformity of the more traditional public housing
blocks put up in such cities as Stockholm, Helsinki
or Copenhagen in the 1920s. The asceticism of the
modern architecture even conformed to a certain
Protestant reticence and restraint – an 'aesthetic
of poverty'.

Not that reactions to the new architecture were
exactly the same in all Scandinavian countries. In
Denmark the well rehearsed debates between
functionalism and formalism were reproduced
in a new guise. While Kay Fisker advocated a
neutral utilitarianism, Mogens Lassen embraced
the poetics of form and modelled several of his

houses of the mid-1930s on Le Corbusier's villas. The breakthrough building for Danish modern architecture was probably the Bellavista housing at Klampenborg of 1934 by Arne Jacobsen, which took the *Siedlung* theme and staggered it to make the most of the sunlight and views to the sea, and to introduce a greater degree of plasticity. While the units appeared to be made from white, rendered concrete, they were in fact constructed from traditional brick, and it was to the planar brick wall (a constituent element of the Danish vernacular) that Jacobsen would eventually return. By the end of the 1930s modern architecture had been adapted for several major public commissions, such as the Aarhus Town Hall (1937–42) by Jacobsen and Erik Møller, or the Broadcasting House in Copenhagen (1934–41) by Vilhelm Lauritzen. The latter was assembled out of several functional elements on a corner site, its fragmented plan responding to varied interior demands of acoustics and to angles in the context. As modern architecture was absorbed into Denmark it became increasingly domesticated, combining local craftsmanship in glass-ware, leather, timber and brick with a customary modesty of scale.

While Asplund's use of 'functionalist' forms in the Stockholm Exhibition seemed to imply a clean

break with his earlier work, it was only a matter of time before he was combining modern structural and spatial concepts with classical disciplines, hierarchies and types. His later development in the 1930s revealed his capacity to fuse together modernity and tradition over a basically mythical idea of architecture. The Crematorium in the Woodland Cemetery at Enskede outside Stockholm of 1935–40 continued some of the themes of his earlier Woodland Chapel but in a more abstract form. From the moment one entered the cemetery one was drawn up an incline towards a stark, grey granite cross standing out against the sky. Behind it on the crest of the ridge protruded the low rectangle of the crematorium portico, classical in spirit but modern in its simplified geometry. The overall landscape combined the ideas of Asplund and Sigurd Lewerentz and drew together aspects of Nordic Romanticism with a contemporary reading of Antiquity to establish an appropriate sense of *gravitas*. But the Crematorium was by Asplund alone and had the air of a partly ruined necropolis. It rose up the slope, with outdoor rooms displaying memorial plaques on low walls, and ante-chambers with courtyards leading to the chapels beyond. Its archaicism was contained within forms of cool abstraction, their hard edges facing the landscape

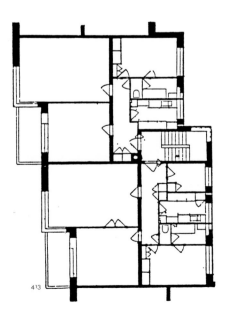

413

414

415

416

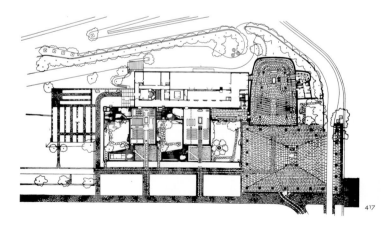

417

the crystallization of modern architecture between the wars

opposite. The portico, a Protestant palisade, stood off against a pagan mound crowned by a clump of trees: the 'Grove of Remembrance'. The approach was organized as a solemn ascent, a latterday Sacred Way or even Hill of Calvary. The dominant tone was tragic and severe, but there were also glimmers of redemption and renewal. Asplund's forms were highly charged, landscape and buildings together suggesting a hidden meaning uniting earth and water, fire and sky. Beyond historical allusions and the mood of forest and ground, there was a deeper suggestion of release from the material to the spiritual.

While the side chapels were on cross axes, the main portico of the Woodland Crematorium was more ambiguous in direction and sense: it could be read as a simplified temple, as a formal façade, as a lateral screen, as a rustic shelter, as an *impluvium* for catching the rain, even as a dignified space of assembly. No less than the tiny portico of the chapel created twenty years earlier in its woodland clearing it entered the larger life of the landscape framing views of the stern conifer trees, gathering mourners together, guiding them into the curved main chapel, and releasing them after the final separation towards soothing hillocks and ponds, and the wide open sky. The distillation of a classical idea, this structure was also a device for intensifying the experience of nature. Constructed from a concrete frame it was clad in precise stone, and its slender piers rhymed with the straight trunks of the trees beyond while affirming a human precinct. The underside of the roof was ribbed in timber and inclined towards a hole at the centre where rain water sluiced on to the sloped floor beneath. Rising through the gap towards a cut-out rectangle of sky was a sculptural group, prefiguring the release of the soul towards heaven. If Terragni in his Danteum probed archetypes of architectural order to explore societal and religious myths (Figs. 453–4), Asplund here did likewise, but in the service of a completely different political ethos: he returned to the roots of classicism in order to frame and idealize a Nordic rite involving mourning catharsis, and the transition from life to death.

The ripple effect of the Stockholm Exhibition was also felt in Finland where both Aalto and Erik Bryggman had already embraced the lessons of Modernism in the late 1920s. The importance of classical and National Romantic foundations to Aalto was suggested earlier (Chapter 8); in the 1930s he appeared to absorb these formative influences into the maturing body of his work. Bryggman's architecture was nourished by vernacular and classical traditions, by Nordic and Mediterranean sources. Even with his 'conversion' to modernism he never lost sight of this rich cultural background. Bryggman also thought of buildings as part of a larger landscape. Both the underlying topographical sensitivity and the informing substructures of the past resurfaced in a situation requiring a grave and dignified response, the Resurrection Funerary Chapel at Turku of 1938–41. Here principles of the new architecture related to dynamic asymmetry, transparency, and the flow of space were combined with a remembrance of traditional church conventions such as symmetry, massiveness, processional structure and a basilical plan with nave, aisle, and arcades. As in Asplund's Crematorium, the basic intention was to evoke the transition from life to death and from death to paradise. The lower part of the south aisle was opened out through full glazing to include the neighbouring landscape and to console mourners with a hypnotic prospect of the Garden of Paradise beyond. This heavenly realm

418

could be reached by means of a stone portal adjacent to the altar passing laterally through the membrane of glazing so that the coffin could be carried across a symbolic threshold. The complex curves and convergences of the nave were enhanced by the diagonal placement of the seats permitting a better view to the outside, and by the light falling on the altar from an unseen source. Bryggman's Chapel existed in the tension between modern and classical traditions.

The work of Alvar Aalto during the 1930s provides another example of a modernism attuned to the natural and social conditions of the North. Aalto was born in 1898 in Kuortane, Finland, studied in Helsinki, and grew up in an atmosphere fraught with questions of national identity for the Finns seeking autonomy from the Russian sphere of influence. Broadly speaking there were two main strands in the 'high' architectural culture of the late nineteenth century which influenced him: a simplified Nordic classicism stemming from certain late-eighteenth-century sources and coming to a refined twentieth-century resolution in the works of Asplund; and a National Romantic tendency, which drew on the Gothic revival and on H. H. Richardson, found inspiration in national myths and local vernaculars, and was well represented in

Finland by the work of Lars Sonck and Eliel Saarinen around the turn of the century (Chapter 8). Aalto would eventually succeed, with the help of modern architectural abstraction, in forging a synthesis between these inherited tendencies. And in that respect the true vernacular (rather than romantic interpretations of it) was a crucial trigger, since it gave evidence of type-forms adapted to the stringencies of the Finnish climate, to the character of the landscape, and to the outlook of the people. At the same time, of course, it revealed a direct and elegant use of local materials, particularly timber.

The modern movement began to seep into Finland only gradually in the 1920s. Aalto encountered the new ideas principally through Dutch, German and French examples. His *Turun Sanomat* Newspaper Building in Turku (for which design began in 1927) was conceived in the terminology of the new architecture, was based on the Five Points of a New Architecture, and in its plastic accentuation of structure, its variation of space, and the disciplined articulation of its façade even suggested the imprint of a vital new talent on received canons. Aalto's gradual growth from his neo-classical beginnings to the clarity of his 'functional' style, can be seen clearly in the evolution of three main projects for the Viipuri Library

419

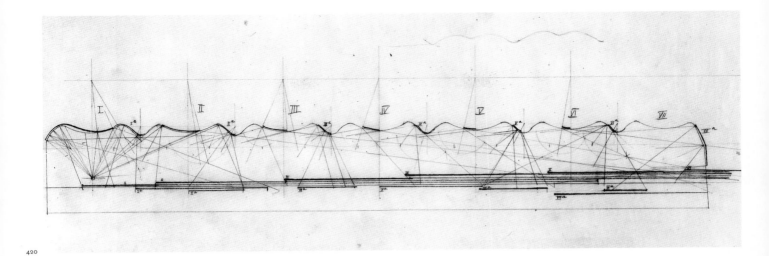

420

between 1927 and 1935. But, while Aalto rejected overt usage of the classical orders, he still retained abstract schemata from the classical tradition (e.g. the frequent use of a *piano nobile*, a processional character in circulation, a refined sense of proportion in the placement of voids and solids and, in later life, a recurrent interest in the splayed forms of ruined Antique theatres). The ground floor structural grid of the *Turun Sanomat* Building suggested a thorough knowledge of the disposition of columns in Greek temple plans, while the earliest projects for the Viipuri Library seemed to echo the arrangement of a classical *cella*, or inner rectangular precinct; the façades in these same early stages were in a stern neo-classical mode which was gradually shorn of all adornment. The final building at Viipuri retained the shifting symmetries and processional sense, while its internal volumes flowed into one another under a ceiling formed of gradually stepping planes perforated by skylights. Such rich modulations of space and light were enhanced in the meeting room by the curved and textured wooden roof, which gave some hint of the naturalism of Aalto's later development. Overall, the Library suggested already the rejection of certain mechanistic qualities of earlier modern architecture; its functional discipline had nothing to do with arid calculation but was bound up with a poetic reaction to human needs, lighting angles and the flow of sound.

In the design of the Paimio Sanatorium (1929–33), Aalto gave body to his 'humanist' aspirations in a work which must be counted one of the masterpieces of the modern movement. The building stands some fifty miles west of Helsinki on a slightly elevated site overlooking forests and lakes. At the time it was built, the best cure for tuberculosis (the Sanatorium was to specialize in the cure of this disease) was felt to be exposure to sun, fresh air, and greenery. This was one of those cases where the aims of the client and the 'sanitary' philosophical and visual aspects of the new style were in accord from the beginning. The patients' rooms were placed in a long, six-storey slab facing south; they were served by corridors running along the north side, and there was an open roof terrace, part covered by a canopy, on the top floor, where beds could be wheeled outside on particularly warm days. Precise attention was given to angles of vision on to the landscape, and to the control and admission of winter and summer light to individual patients' rooms. The structure of the stack of rest-terraces to the eastern end of the building was a tapered concrete 'trunk' from which the floors were cantilevered, thus allowing an openness of façades and a freedom of circulation. The mono-material character of this wing was accentuated by curved details and a sculptural sense of volume, which contrasted with the more cardboard qualities of certain other buildings in the International Style.

421 Alvar Aalto, Paimio
Sanatorium, Finland,
1929–33

422 Paimio Sanatorium,
ground-floor plan

423 Paimio Sanatorium,
section through rest
terraces

424 Paimio Sanatorium,
section through patients'
wards

Behind the slab were grouped the 'serving' elements of the hallway, the doctors' wing and lounge, and the nurses' wing. Each function was expressed in a slightly different form, and angled to the topography of the site. Aalto's splayed plan and slender slabs permitted light to penetrate the building at all points, and showed how a building of complex programme might be fragmented to react to variable topographical conditions. The slab and the lounge block funnelled one towards the entrance. Variations in fenestration and detail ensured that the main divisions in the form were articulated throughout. Rising like a well-proportioned ship above the Finnish landscape, the sanatorium announced its healing function through clean forms, tidy proportions, and well-lit volumes. At the same time, the horizontals of its balconies, steel-tube railings and garden terracing supplied links to the surrounding land.

It has been convincingly argued that the Paimio Sanatorium was modelled, in part, on Duiker and Bijvoet's Zonnestraal Sanatorium of 1927, outside Hilversum (Fig. 317), a building in which the various functions were also splayed in different directions on a wooded site. Moreover, there were particular details, like the extractor stack of the Zonnestraal, which were reworked by Aalto.

Probably he also drew upon the formula for collective dwellings evolved a couple of years earlier in the Soviet Union, in which individual rooms were placed in a slab, and collective functions were grouped in ancillary volumes of different geometry or form. It has already been suggested that this arrangement influenced Le Corbusier's Pavillon Suisse, too. In both the student hostel and the tuberculosis sanatorium, the discoveries of earlier modern architecture were extended into new, and more complex, formal territories.

In 1933, Aalto attended the CIAM meeting on the SS *Patris*. Here, against the setting of the Greek islands, the Parthenon and the sea, he met Le Corbusier, Mies van der Rohe, Walter Gropius – indeed the protagonists of modern architecture; and they in turn were impressed by a newly emergent talent. At home it had been possible for Aalto to convert patrons gradually to an appreciation of the new architecture, though this had not always been easy. By degrees, the practical and symbolic aspects of modernism were absorbed by leading Finnish industrialists and social institutions. Finland was a young nation which relied largely upon the timber industries for its economic life, and which was passing through a rapid urbanization; but the natural landscape with its vast forests and numerous

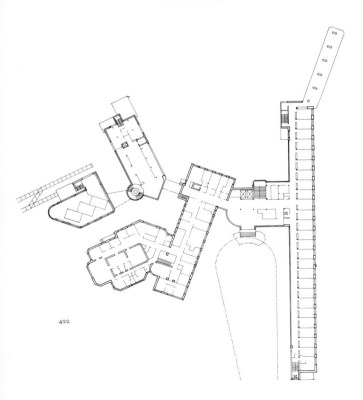

422

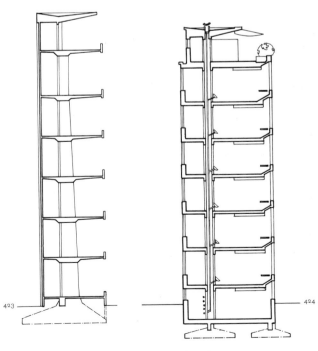

423   424

lakes was ever present in reality and imagination. Aalto was quick to grasp the salient features of this situation, and to adjust modern architecture to the topographies and social needs of small urban communities in far-flung corners of the countryside.

Between 1934 and the outbreak of the war, Aalto was kept busy with the major commission for the Sunila Pulp Mills (including workers' housing) and with entries to a variety of competitions, such as the one for the Finnish Legation Building in Moscow. In 1934 he designed a house for himself and his wife outside Helsinki which employed brick and wood and incorporated a range of textures and subtle curves; plants and natural materials were included in a work that suggested a departure from the white concrete forms of five years earlier. For the Paris International Exhibition of 1937 he designed the Finnish Pavilion using standardized sections of timber, while for the New York World Fair of 1939 he evolved a Finnish exhibit with a serpentine wooden wall, evoking the curves and contours of the Finnish waterways and landforms. On display were objects like skis and propellors which showed how Finnish technology could fabricate forms of great functional elegance out of laminated timber, and these objects were echoed in the rippling wooden slats of Aalto's structure. It was in this period, too, that Aalto created sinuous glassware and plywood furniture, the latter moulded to the form of the human figure. This anthropomorphism lay close to the heart of Aalto's idea of architecture and even to his understanding of classical forms. The transition towards greater sensitivity to the human figure moving through space, towards direct uses of materials and towards ever more complex metaphors has been called the shift to 'Romantic Modernism'; but whatever one calls it, it was a style which was increasingly able to handle psychological nuances, and in which a more accommodating relationship to both the Finnish vernacular tradition and the regional demands of climate and landscape was worked out. Aalto was later to write: 'Architecture cannot disengage itself from natural and human factors; on the contrary, it must never do so … Its function rather is to bring nature ever closer to us.'

Perhaps the most representative work of this phase in Aalto's development was the Villa Mairea of 1938–41, built for Maire and Harry Gullichsen as a villa, guest-house and rural retreat at Noormarkku.

The Gullichsens were immensely wealthy and told their architect that he should regard it as an 'experimental house'. Aalto seems to have treated the Villa Mairea as an opportunity to pull together many of the themes which had been preoccupying him in recent years, but which he had not always been able to introduce into actual buildings; in much the same way, Le Corbusier had taken the opportunity offered him by a well-to-do client to condense his driving obsessions in the Villa Savoye.

The plan of the Villa Mairea is a modified L-shape of the kind Aalto had used frequently before, and would use often again. It was a layout which automatically created a semi-private enclosure to one side, and a more exclusive, formal edge to confront the public world on the other; it recalled, loosely, Finnish farm buildings with 'semi-courtyards' defining an inward-looking community and protecting inhabitants and livestock from winter winds. In the Villa Mairea the lawn and the swimming pool were situated in the angle of the 'L', with a variety of rooms looking over them. Horizontals and overhangs in the main composition echoed the ground plane, and the curved pool wedded with the nearby forest topography. In contrast to these 'softening' devices, the main façade had a more rigid, formal mood, and even possessed a canopy restated in a garden pergola vocabulary of bindings, poles and slats.

The interiors of the Villa Mairea were richly articulated in wood, stone and brick. The spaces varied in size from the grand to the cabin-like. The master-bedroom stood at the pinnacle of the house with fine views of the forest, and the studio for Maire Gullichsen's paintings was also given prominence. The ground floor was open and in constant contact with the garden. Sitting room, dining room, library flowed easily into one another, separated only by slight changes in level or delicate, fence-like screens. The details of the Villa Mairea made much of weaving, binding, tying and matting in both natural and artificial materials. The poles holding up the entrance canopy were laced together with thongs, while those either side of the main stair were fixed together with small chocks of timber. Aalto seems to have indulged in a virtual 'forest mythology' on the nature of structure and cladding, exploring different states of wood all the way from rough branches and fibres made from split twigs, to

425 Alvar Aalto, Villa Mairea, Noormarkku, Finland, 1938–41

426 Villa Mairea, ground- and first-floor plans

425

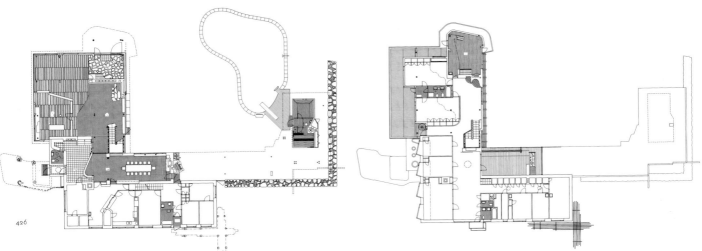

426

smooth cylinders and planks. To one end, the Villa Mairea descended to a sort of 'rustic' wing, which wrapped around two sides of the swimming pool and contained the sauna. This wing alone was emblematic of Aalto's increasingly 'naturalistic' concerns: it evoked a wooden palisade with an overhanging flat roof surmounted by a ragged band of turf. The spirit of this primitivist, Nordic hut, brooding next to a dark pool of water and surrounded by boulders, could not be further from the pristine solarium of the Villa Savoye, with its Mediterranean evocations and its crisp, machine-age imagery. But in details like these, each architect managed to condense an entire world outlook, and to reveal his ability to transform the rituals of upper-middle-class existence into the stuff of a lasting architectural dream.

The Villa Mairea was organized as a series of layers with metaphorical structural themes that unfolded as one moved from entrance, through interiors, to garden. For example, there were 'puns' between steel tubular columns, concrete stanchions, wooden posts, fences, and the trunks of trees; one moved gradually through modern structural elements towards the casual rusticity of the sticks and pickets closing off the site to the rear. These details reinforced an underlying polarity between the 'artificial' and the 'natural'. The free-form curves of the Villa Mairea also took on several identities while guiding the human figure almost physically across the building. One started at the biomorphic form of the entrance canopy and ended up in the serpentine pool, but on the way there were several other versions of curves handling multiplicities of direction: the low wall inside the entrance, the organic shape of the bottom stair, the double curvature of the Gullichsens' private wing. The meandering route perhaps represented Aalto's witty interpretation of an evening's entertainment in which the formalities of the city guest might be stripped away to lead to the naked conviviality of the sauna and to the 'natural' man within. In effect the Villa Mairea took its place in a long villa typology, addressing age-old themes to do with the contrast between the urban and the rural, the cultivated and the primitive.

It was suggested earlier (Chapter 18) in reference to Wright, Le Corbusier and Mies van der Rohe that the 1930s was a decade in which the imperatives of

427

427 Alvar Aalto, Villa
Mairea, Noormarkku,
Finland, 1938–41, interior

428 Villa Mairea, sauna
steps and door

429 Villa Mairea, turf
roof of sauna wing

'machinism' were radically reconsidered in the light of several visions and interpretations of the natural order. Aalto's transition in the 1930s seems to have followed a loosely parallel course towards a 'bio-technical' version of modernity, and an architecture of deeper physical and psychological resonances. The Villa Mairea rejected a merely 'abstract' vision of space and replaced it with an enclave encouraging a sense of belonging. The incidents and rituals of daily life were celebrated in a sequence of 'places' and stopping points. The plan of the whole evoked an organism, even a curved fish with head, body and tail; it also had the character of a Cubist collage in which different qualities, shapes, materials and identities were spliced together. The sinuous shapes were rooted in Aalto's earlier experiments in furniture and glassware design, in Le Corbusier's free-plan curves and in the 'biomorphic', abstract painting and sculpture of the 1930s. The ensemble of the Villa Mairea – with its field of structural supports, its clearings and alley ways, was like a transposition of a woodland clearing into the forms of architecture. It was the theme of the 'natural house', but arranged as a kind of show: the forest itself at a safe distance, acting as both backdrop and final reference. Once again a modern work addressed the idea of origins.

The Villa Mairea was the condensation of so many ideas that it is tempting to see it as the pivotal building for Aalto in which, so to say, he sloughed off the last inherited skin, and revealed his true nature. The formal disciplines of classicism, the philosophy and forms of the International Modern movement, and the perennial lessons of a regional vernacular all contributed to the synthesis, but its sources were utterly transformed. After the Villa Mairea, his style was assured at a deep level, variation occurring on the basis of a few fundamental themes and forms, capable of apparently endless combinations and renewed meanings. The result was deeply related to ideas about the human condition, in which weathered materials, lyrical spaces, and magical effects of light produced a lasting primal poetry far beyond merely 'modern' concerns.

Aalto's Villa Mairea also marked a stage in the development of the modern movement, for it rested upon the collective discoveries of the 'heroic period' while transcending them with a new set of impulses. It was, indeed, 'an important move forward from functionalism' and not simply a relapse into decorative formalism. It was to examples like this that post-war architects could turn, in their own attempt at breaking with the increasingly restrictive bondage of received formulae, and in their own quest for an authentic synthesis of the local and the international, the ancient and the modern.

428

429

2 0

totalitarian critiques of the modern movement

430 Giovanni Guerrini, Ernesto la Padula and Mario Romano, Palazzo della Civiltà Italiana, EUR, Rome, 1937–42, detail of façade

Throughout history, monumental architecture has been employed to embody the values of dominant ideologies and groups, and as an instrument of state propaganda. The totalitarian regimes that came to power between the wars (notably in Italy, Russia and Germany) each devoted considerable attention to the ways in which buildings and urban plans might be used to legitimize their position at home and abroad, and to convey their beliefs through symbolism and association. A persistent theme in all three countries was the reinforcement of nationalist sentiments by appeal to earlier national architectural traditions. Allied to this was a nostalgia for supposedly indigenous virtues which were to be reclaimed from the onslaughts of modern fragmentation. It was necessary for totalitarian regimes to foster the impression that their right to rule was embedded in the deepest aspirations of the people. State patronage had therefore to steer a careful way between evocations of past imperial power and suggestions of populist support. The pretence had to be maintained that official taste was a conduit, so to speak, for broader communal impulses.

In these circumstances modern architecture seemed at best marginal, at worst a dangerous threat in need of extermination. It could, after all, be portrayed as an internationalist novelty created by a fringe avant-garde working independently of dominant values; it could be claimed too that it lacked rhetorical devices capable of conveying simple messages to the majority. Modern architecture was also open to the charge that it was 'foreign', that it had not grown from national cultural roots and craft traditions; in Germany it was frequently portrayed as an 'Oriental' import from alien lands or (still worse!) as the thin edge of a Bolshevist plot originating in the East. In Russia, simultaneously, one might well find it being treated as a commodity from the West, as a last fragment of decaying European civilization. In these sweeping condemnations one has, of course, to bear in mind the distinction between intended and received meanings. The true symbolic and ideological texture of modern architecture was far more refined than blunt and imperceptive criticisms of this kind allowed. Moreover, it was not always rejected out of hand; the Nazis (for example) were quite happy to claim the structural economy and technological

431 1940 Stuttgart - Weissenhofsiedlung, Araberdorf

imagery of modern architecture when it suited them (e.g. in certain utilitarian buildings for the Luftwaffe), while in Italy, the 'progressive' character of modern design – if expressed with suitably Latin emphasis – could be acceptable to the regime. Again one has to guard against over-simple polarities: there was no clear-cut totalitarian critical position, nor a single accepted style.

In Germany political debates over the new architecture had continued throughout the 1920s. Socialist support of large housing schemes had tended to give the flat-roofed *Siedlungen*, and the architects who had designed them, the automatic stigma of Communism. It makes little difference that only some modern architects were adherents of Marxism, or that a great variety of expression for socialist ideals was possible; right-wing critics were suspicious of the new architecture and determined to tar it all with the same brush. The tone of one brand of criticism already prevalent in the late 1920s is well caught by the following:

According to the leaders of the Bauhaus – rooms must look like studios, like operating theatres; all warmth is banned from them. Therefore no wood; rugs and upholstery are sins against the Holy Ghost of 'Sachlichkeit'. Glass instead, all kinds of metal or artificial stone – these are the stylish materials! The new man is no longer a man, he is a 'geometrical animal'. He needs no dwelling, no home, only a 'dwelling machine'. This man is not an individual, not a personality, but a collective entity, a piece of mass man. And therefore they build 'housing developments', apartment blocks of desolate uniformity, in which everything is standardized. These are tenements, built not as a necessity, as in the rapidly growing cities during the second half of the nineteenth century, but as a matter of principle. They want to kill personality in men, they want collectivism, for the highest goal of these architects is Marxism, Communism.

In this version we find modern architecture portrayed as something rootless, materialistic,

uncomfortable, inhuman, Communist, and anti-German. Another style of criticism concentrated on the supposed impracticality of modern buildings, their leaking flat roofs, the peeling of their white plaster surfaces, the rusting of their windows, the ignorance manifest in them of time-worn methods for handling extremes of climate. Then again there were the racist arguments. These emphasized the way the new architecture was lifted free of the soil, and its lack of nourishment from local and regional vernacular sources. The most extreme slurs were reserved for the distortions of modern painting, which were compared to 'deformed' and 'inferior' races; with architecture this distasteful haranguing had a less easy target, none the less the flat roof was singled out as flagrant evidence of 'un-Germanness'. In one hysterical outburst this constituent feature of the new architecture was branded as 'Oriental, Jewish and Bolshevik' simultaneously. The soapbox oratory could often become extremely confused; while one criticism might try to link modern architecture to an international Socialist conspiracy, another might latch on to the industrial imagery and interpret it as an expression of ' … the unclean collaboration of certain branches of great industry, dominated by Jews, with the Marxist parties'. Finally, modern architecture could be rejected on the grounds that it was simply ugly and therefore not ennobling of German culture.

The trigger springs were thus already set when the Nazis came to power in 1933. It has to be emphasized that there was no single monolithic Nazi doctrine concerning either the criticism or the creation of architecture, that even official positions often diverged, and that these odd mixtures of opinions had been lying around for some time. One does note, however, a preponderance of the racist style of argument combined with a fairly sound general assessment that modern architectural imagery would not be suitable for grand civic monumentality or for Regionalist, *volkisch* expression. Moreover, there was another feature of the modern movement which made it unsuitable. The Reich needed to assert the hierarchy of building types as visual evidence of the hierarchy of power; an architectural system that tended to blur distinctions between building types was not ideally suited to this sort of symbolic differentiation.

431 Anonymous photograph of the 1927 Stuttgart Weissenhofsiedlung tricked-up as an 'Arab village', c.1928

432 Ludwig Mies van der Rohe, competition project for the Reichsbank, Berlin, 1933

It is interesting, therefore, to see how modern architects fared in Germany in the 1930s. The fact is that most of them were outlawed, unpopular, or simply decided to leave. Erich Mendelsohn was among the first to go, realizing immediately the anti-Semitic character of the new regime. He went first to England, then to Palestine, then, eventually, to the United States. The Bauhaus was closed in 1933, and its staff scattered in all directions, many of them to seek refuge in England and the United States. While Hitler was opposed in principle to the emptiness of 'functionalism', he was still capable of declaring in a speech made in 1933, 'from material and function new forms are found and developed that breathe more of the Greek spirit in the aesthetic of machines, for example, than in many a poorly conceived building'. Presumably it was remarks of this kind which made some members of the modern architectural world in Germany think that things were not as bad as they seemed. Among these was Mies van der Rohe, whose project for the Reichsbank competition of 1933 was mentioned earlier – a scheme distinguished by its severe monumentality, its grim elegance, its symmetry and its evocation of modern technology. Mies's façades relied upon a straightforward expression of strip windows and the building skin, with the result that the exterior was curiously lacking in the rhetoric implied by the plan. Although his design was placed among the finalists, it was rejected, perhaps because it looked too much like a department store or an industrial building. Gropius also made an entry: his project made use of clumsy vertical struts which read as feeble surrogates for classical pilasters. It was probably this competition that encouraged the regime to think in terms of a more overt use of the past. In 1935, Mies van der Rohe submitted a project for representing the Reich at the Brussels Exhibition of that year; this reverted to some of the ideas contained in his Neue Wache War Memorial proposal of 1930, abstracting elements of classical formality in plan, in structure and even in exterior representation, and yet evoking a modern sense of space. But the project (which possibly represented a deliberate manoeuvre by the Reich to avoid seeming too imperialistic and too traditional) was cancelled. Mies van der Rohe seems to have hoped that his 'idealist' view of architecture could somehow remain untainted by surrounding political realities. By the mid-1930s it was obvious, even to him, that this position was unrealistic, and in 1937 he too emigrated, in this case straight to the United States.

It is central to the story that Hitler was himself a frustrated architect and perhaps saw statecraft itself

432

as a kind of monumental design. As an adolescent he had dreamed of redesigning Linz, his home town in Austria. Towards the end of his life it became his ambition to leave behind a new imperial Berlin, testifying to the world domination of the Reich. Just as he sensed that the great buildings of the past bore witness to a coherence of belief, so he hoped that the new bonds of German unity might, almost automatically, find expression in great communal projects and a healthy vernacular rooted in native blood and soil. On this point it might be said that his thinking partially paralleled Gropius's, Wright's, and Le Corbusier's, since he too expected the individual artist to grasp the whole inner feeling of an epoch and then to give it form. He played down the actual pluralism of modern life, in a monumental belief that he had risen to power by some inherent force of the whole *Volk*. His National Socialist beliefs led him to distrust previous German élites – including, let it be said, that élite of perception, the avant-garde. His patronage was ideally suited to the production of a bathetic, banal instant culture of little lasting depth; and that is what most architecture produced under the Nazi regime usually became.

There was the further problem of representation – a problem that the other totalitarian regimes shared: what should their architecture *look* like? what appearance should a specifically *Nazi* building have? Half-baked art history was dragged in to suggest that Gothic architecture one minute, classical architecture the next, lay closest to the reconsolidated national genius of the German people. Even modern architecture could be made acceptable on occasion, so long as it was restricted to 'lower' buildings in the hierarchy: factories, office buildings, etc. It is never very precise, then, to speak of one essential 'Nazi architecture' in the 1930s.

As soon as he came to power, Hitler chose Paul Ludwig Troost as his main architectural adviser. Troost had been a member of the Nazi party since 1924 and his love for simplified but traditional classicism made him the ideal man to express the Führer's aspirations towards a monumental 'community' architecture, extolling the discipline, order and strength of the new state. Both patron and architect shared a love of Schinkel and an intuition for a supposed link between Greek and Teutonic culture. It was no anomaly, then, that the House of German Art in the Prinzregentenstrasse, Munich

433

434

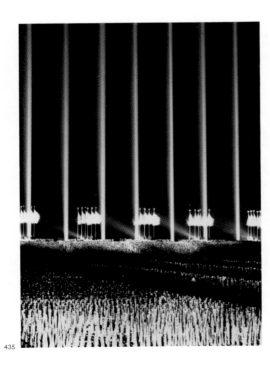

435

(1934–6) should have had a stripped Doric order, a low horizontal attic, and sharp but clean lines.

In 1934 Troost died and his place was taken by a young man named Albert Speer. Speer became the stage designer, as it were, for Nazi pageantry, by providing an instant monumentality for quick effect and mainly rhetorical emphasis. He drew on whatever sources seemed most suitable for evoking an overwhelming scale – Egyptian, Babylonian, classical, neo-classical – and pared down inherited forms into a vocabulary of stripped surfaces, stone veneers, and regimental repetition. His design for the 'Zeppelinfeld' arena at Nuremberg of 1934 is a good example of this species of monumentality. It was one of the settings for the colossal Nazi rallies, and so was a collective *Volk* building in the full sense. In the same year Speer had the stunning idea (perhaps suggested by certain festivalia used in the French Revolution) of pointing a thousand searchlights into the air during a night event. Slender shafts of light rose miles into the sky and the idea was christened 'the Cathedral of Light'. A similar bombast and militarism inspired the vast Olympic Stadium and attached buildings outside Berlin in 1936. These had the extra propaganda function of impressing the world with refound German might. Nazi monuments were a little like Hitler's oratory: forceful, repetitive, but ultimately banal. They tended to deaden opposition with statements of overwhelming conformity and force.

Speer pandered to Hitler's fantasies and became, in a sense, the Führer's own architectural interpreter. In 1938, the inner circle of the Reich decided that the Chancellery building in Berlin must be rebuilt on a scale commensurate with the increasingly imperial stature of the leader. Speer produced a suitable scenario at top speed. Hitler's personal salon and office were placed off an overbearing marble corridor almost as long as the Galerie des Glaces at Versailles. It was reached through a sequence of formal spaces – a courtyard of honour, a vestibule, a mosaic room, a round hall – while at the other end of the building was the Cabinet conference room. Admittedly, the plan was quite an elegant and ornamental composition pulling together various antique models; but when built, the stripped classical forms had a dull and drab quality. Stone was imported from all parts of Germany for this project and the buildings were erected in less than eighteen months. Nazi insignia and emblems were embossed on walls and furniture, to give added impact to the heavy-handed and obvious messages of the architecture with its overwhelming scale, its polished, rich materials, its pompous axial regimentation and its disciplined repetition. The psychological game was clear: the visiting statesman or ambassador was to see that the new Reich had become a patron of the monumental arts, and was to be placed at an instant disadvantage by a 200-yard walk over polished floors, past swastika flags and impeccably designed uniforms, before he wheeled on to the cross-axis, presumably to see the Führer waiting behind his desk in a room of grandiose proportions. It was in the bunker next to this building that Hitler came to his end in 1945 while Russian shells demolished all this Nazi handiwork.

Speer's and Hitler's megalomania did not stop there. In 1937 they launched plans for the reordering of Berlin, employing long avenues, axes, and a stage scenery drawn from Paris, ancient Rome and Washington. The focal point was to be a centralized domical monument larger than any dome yet built and known simply as the 'Great Hall'. This was to be a pantheon of sorts, containing images and inscriptions dedicated to the heroes and heroic aims of Nazism. It was to stand facing a boulevard, at the other end of which would be a triumphal arch in honour of Hitler. Had it been

436

437

built, the hall could have contained St Peter's in Rome in its vaulted interior space. This sublime scale recalls those fantasy schemes for pure geometrical cenotaphs and cathedrals painted by Étienne-Louis Boullée towards the end of the eighteenth century. Indeed, neo-classical images of funeral pyres influenced the war memorials envisaged by Wilhelm Kreis to stand as grim beacons of Nazi superiority on the conquered lands of 'inferior races'. But such Nazi emblems had about them a quality of empty gesture for all their vastness; they were a classic case of what Giedion called 'the devaluation of symbols'.

In parallel with civic monuments, domestic and rural projects were also sponsored by the Nazis in the 1930s. The recurrent themes of athletic prowess and rustic purity were nurtured in deliberately 'Regionalist' buildings. The long-standing suspicion of urban centres as infamous breeding grounds of 'uprootedness', 'cosmopolitanism', and other anti-nationalist sins could here find an outlet. It was noted earlier that the flat roof particularly excited the hostility of certain right-wing critics as evidence of alien influence; as a corollary, the type, shape, and materials of hip roofs were regarded as primary signals of a building's allegiance to the vernacular traditions of a particular region. Karl Vesser's design for a Nazi Youth Hostel at Urfeld (1935) employed the overhanging eaves and balconies of the local Bavarian village houses and stood on a stone base of a vaguely martial character; Goering's Hunting Lodge was a theatrical evocation of Teutonic memories quite at odds with the 'brave new world' and machine imagery of the new architecture. Nazi Regionalism was not a genuine vernacular but a sophisticated and procured Arts and Crafts rusticity catering to the overflow towns and suburbs. The imagery was supposed to suggest the conservation of the homeland and the local community, as opposed to the 'disturbances' of the modern metropolis and festering discontents brought on by rapid industrialization and (of course) by 'dangerous' foreign ideas. This *Heimatstil* (home style) was to foster open, healthy social relationships and conformity to the prevalent state doctrines. Even telephone buildings, electricity generating stations and other utilitarian structures could be fitted up with an appropriate thatched overhang to preserve the sense of regional continuity.

Although Nazi power was based in a large degree on rapid mechanization, on the creation of efficient factories, autobahns, and munitions industries, on the construction of a modern military and state apparatus, the 'factory aesthetic' had no place in the domestic sphere. Its intrusion into housing was seen not only as a break with decorum, but also as a sinister dislocation of family integrity by hostile and materialistic forces. It is instructive in this connection that Hitler made much of the fact that only handicrafts were employed in the construction of one of his residences. This is all the more ironical given the stress that the majority of the modern movement architects had placed on the supposed 'spirituality' of their simple abstract forms. They too had sought to transcend materialism.

However, modern doctrines did have their uses in the design of of more humble and utilitarian buildings, where qualities of discipline, clarity of structure, and clear lighting could also have moral overtones. Here the nationalist streak in previous Deutscher Werkbund theorizing permitted some cross-breeding of ideas. Herbert Rimpl's design for a Heinkel factory of 1936 is a good example of this clear-cut rationalism. In fact Rimpl had been a

438

439

440 Albert Speer, German Pavilion (left), and Boris Iofan's USSR Pavilion (right), Paris International Exhibition, 1937, contemporary coloured photograph

441 Alexei Shchusev, Marx-Engels-Lenin-Stalin Financial Institute, Tbilisi, 1934–8

442 Sergei Gerasimov, *Collective Farm Festival*, 1937. Tretyakov Gallery, Moscow

440

student of Mies van der Rohe, and the design anticipated something of the character of Mies's later buildings for the campus at Illinois Institute of Technology in Chicago. German engineers took an interest in aesthetic and even ideological matters. A supreme emblem of National Socialist industrial design was, of course, the famous 'Volkswagen' automobile; during the war the concrete fortresses and bunkers of the 'Atlantic Wall' had certain aesthetic qualities despite their grim function.

At the Paris International Exhibition of 1937 the German Pavilion stood facing the Russian one. To the unpractised eye it might have been difficult to tell the difference, since both states employed a combination of gross realism and stark monumentality as their official ambassadorial style. Speer's design stressed the vertical and was modelled on a stripped neo-classical tribune of some kind. It was surmounted by a stern eagle. Iofan's Soviet design opposite was assembled from stepped masses of vaguely streamlined character (not unlike some of New York's skyscrapers of the late 1920s) and was topped by the enormous lunging figures of a man and a woman intended to reflect the energy and populism of the Soviet state. Both

nations' design policies had clearly altered since Mies van der Rohe's Barcelona Pavilion of 1929, or since the Paris Exposition des Arts Décoratifs of 1925, when Melnikov had been allowed by his sponsors to create his daring evocation of the factory aesthetic, proclaiming the values of a forward-looking, supposedly egalitarian society. At the 1937 Paris International Exhibition it was buildings like the Pavilion of the beleaguered Spanish Second Republic (designed by Sert and Lacasa, Fig. 464) which projected a sense of liberality and modernity, in strong contrast to the heavy statements of the nearby pavilions of the authoritarian regimes.

As has been shown in Chapter 12, the intervening event of the Palace of the Soviets competition of 1931 had already offered clear signals of changing official taste in the Soviet Union, and implied too, in its outcome, that the messages of modern architecture were suspected of being too arcane for the general public. In the early 1930s Socialist Realism in the arts became the official line. In painting, this tended to mean that abstraction should be avoided on the grounds that it might become a self-indulgent filter between the artist, 'reality', and the public; the worst term of censure was 'formalism'. The 'reality' upon which artists were supposed to concentrate was largely preselected, and involved proletarian subjects of daily life or heroic deeds in the service of the state (Fig. 442). The 'appropriate' style in painting was a descendant of nineteenth-century realists such as Gustave Courbet.

How could such arguments be transposed to architecture? One way was through the decoration of buildings with suitable sculptures, paintings, and reliefs. Another was through the use of an easily legible monumentality employing devices of allusion, axiality, and grandiose scale. A shift in emphasis towards the aggrandizement of the central state and its official folk heroes seems to have accounted for Iofan's victory in the Palace of the Soviets competition, with its statue of Lenin on top and its rhetorical display of classical elements (Fig. 256). The aerodynamic forms of the 1937 Soviet Pavilion in Paris, even the decorations of the Moscow Underground system, represented other attempts at defining an official public architecture; so, eventually, did the plans for the university on the Lenin hills, approached from the centre of the city by way of an axial road starting in Red Square and running for twenty miles. In the mid-1930s the Marx-Engels-Lenin-Stalin Financial Institute in Tbilisi was designed by Alexei Shchusev with giant Corinthian columns in its façade. It was as if the grand manner of the Tsar had returned,

albeit in a more populist mode. Parallels between Marxist and Greek democratic ideals of statehood were subsumed by the slogan 'columns for the people', but imperialist overtones were obvious. Indeed, there was some convergence between Nazi and Soviet positions; in each case the avant-garde was regarded with suspicion, while continuity was sought with pre-revolutionary frames of reference; the result tended to be a banal traditionalism.

There were also some points of similarity in the attitudes towards housing and city planning. As in Germany, the pitched roof was recommended for climatic reasons and because it was supposed to be closer to 'popular' aspirations. Those avant-garde planners who had left Germany for Russia in the late 1920s to build the architecture of the World Revolution for the new society (e.g. Ernst May) were stranded, by the mid-1930s, between two tides of reaction. But the writing had been on the wall for some time, as this official Soviet pronouncement of 1930 makes clear:

It is impossible suddenly to overcome obstacles that are centuries old, the fruit of the cultural and economic backwardness of society. Yet this is the system implicit in these unrealizable and Utopian plans for the construction, at state expense, of new cities based on the total collectivization of living, including collective provisioning, collective care of children, the prohibition of private kitchens. The hasty realization of such schemes, Utopian and doctrinaire, which take no account of the material resources of our country and of the limits within which the people, with their set habits and preferences, can be prepared for them, could easily result in considerable losses and could also discredit the basic principles of the Socialist reconstruction of society.

441

442

The situation in Italy in the same decade was every bit as complex, though with the important difference that various modern architectural tendencies were quite able to flourish, and were even (on occasion) introduced into the field of state representation. Mussolini felt no constitutional restraint on his imperial ambitions and had the convenience of ancient Rome as his stage-set and plaything. Like Hitler, he took a direct interest in planning affairs. By 1925 a new plan for the renovation of Rome had been set in motion. Straight streets were to be cut through the patchwork urban fabric to link up key monuments of the distant past with ones which Mussolini himself intended to build with Marcello Piacentini as his architectural aide. The blend of theatricality, functionalism, and propaganda of this scheme recalled Haussmann's plans for Paris or the Baroque planning projects of the popes. Major historical monuments like the Colosseum were to be shorn of their encumbrances (dislodged people being forcibly rehoused), so facilitating the flow of traffic and the perception of Rome's great past. The urban scene of the 'New Rome' – centre of the 'Mediterranean Dream' – would glisten with automobiles alongside the ruins, and combine the efficiency and speed of a modern metropolis (Marinetti the Futurist was a friend of the Duce) with ancient imperial memories.

Mussolini himself soon realized the power of traditional cultural images in his projection of a new nationalist spirit. He affected a pedigree in Roman history, identifying with the Emperor Augustus , staging elaborate political events in the Campidoglio and the Palazzo Venezia, and vowing to leave the 'Third Rome' a 'city of marble'. In line with this search for parallels in antiquity, a design was drawn up and built in 1934–8 by Vittorio Ballio Morpurgo for the Piazzale Augusteo next to the Tiber. The Ara Pacis was enclosed in a glazed building opposite the Mausoleum of Augustus and juxtaposed with the new stripped classical buildings of indescribable dullness, bearing an iconography concerning the fruits of a peaceful existence brought by Fascism. The imagery suggested the basis in Roman tradition of a synthesis of peasant and soldierly virtues. It was a trumped-up mythology which suffered all the more from the lack of aesthetic conviction with which it was expressed.

443

The eventual absorption of international models of modernity needs to be understood against the background of a struggle to crystallize an industrial culture (especially in the major urban centres of the north of Italy) and against the background of a persistent, sometimes unconscious, classical continuity. Naturally this inheritance was open to different readings and interpretations all the way from an ornamental eclecticism in the late nineteenth century, to a concern with geometrical 'essentials' in the twentieth. This abstract view of classical values was sometimes mixed with a vaguely metaphysical 'Mediterraneanism'. Writing of the Novecento painters in 1924, the critic Margherita Sarfatti referred to 'a style of clarity and synthesis which is at once classical and highly modern', then went on to make a more general claim that would also be pertinent to architecture: 'To create in every great epoch a new ideal of beauty, beyond inconstant reality and eternally true, is the task of the Mediterranean: once it lay with the Egyptians and Greeks, now with the Italians.'

Modern architecture took hold later in Italy than in Germany, Holland, and France, and encountered less hostility from state taste than it did in Nazi

443 Vittorio Ballio
Morpurgo, Piazzale
Augusteo, Rome, 1934–8

444 Giovanni Guerrini,
Ernesto La Padula and
Mario Romano, Palazzo
della Civiltà Italiana, EUR,
Rome, 1937–42

Germany. In part this was due to the fact that Fascism was already well established when the Italian modern movement got under way, and so there was no automatic identification with a previous, and suspect, socialist ideology, as was the case in Germany. Then it is one of the intriguing features of the modern movement in Italy that it minimized 'functionalist' and 'machine-age' rhetoric, playing up instead an abstract aestheticism deliberately evocative of classical precedents. This was constantly in danger of degenerating into a suave formalism or, still worse, a stripped monumentality in which vast areas of travertine, with the consistency of linoleum, conjured up an instant skin-deep traditionalism. When one traces the polemics and debates of Italian architecture in the 1920s and 1930s, one is struck by the pervasive concern with the problem of symbolic representation, and with the notion of architecture as a species of 'language'. In effect there was a wide span of possibilities, all the way from a rhetorical

monumentality using simplifications of traditional tectonic elements such as the wall, the arch, the column and the pilaster (e.g. some of Piacentini's buildings for the University of Rome in the 1930s, or the crystalline cube with incised arches of the Palazzo della Civiltà Italiana by Giovanni Guerrini, Ernesto La Padula and Mario Romano at EUR just outside Rome), to a modernism of horizontality, transparency, and spatial dynamism (e.g. several of the works of Figini, Pollini and Libera and in the 1930s). At its best the consciousness of history opened up new possibilities for the modern tradition, in which the concrete frame (the *piloti*, the stripped support, the plain opening) and elemental characteristics of the classical system were mutually reinforcing at a deeper, more abstract level. It may not have been mere diplomacy, then, when the 'Gruppo 7' (an architectural group with modern leanings who launched themselves in 1926) claimed that they did not advocate a break with tradition:

444

445

In Italy there is such a pronounced Classical substratum, and the spirit of tradition – not the forms it takes, which is something quite different – is so deep that, obviously and almost mechanically, the new architecture could not fail to retain a typical national character. And this is already a great force, since tradition, as we said, does not disappear but changes appearance.

The members of the 'Gruppo 7' were Luigi Figini, Guido Frette, Sebastiano Larco, Gino Pollini, Carlo Enrico Rava, Giuseppe Terragni, and Ubaldo Castagnoli (the last being later replaced by Adalberto Libera); they declared their intention of founding an 'Architettura Razionale':

The new architecture … must be the result of a close adherence to logic and rationality … We do not claim to create a style, but from the constant application of reality, the perfect correspondence of the building to its aims, … style must inevitably result.

At an exhibition in 1928 the group none the less revealed the range of its interest in recent International Modernism. Figini and Pollini's scheme for a 'Casa di Dopolavoro' (a workers' club) had notable Constructivist affinities, while

446

Terragni's Officino per la Produzione del Gaz (Gas Company Headquarters) was an eclectic mixture of Russian, German, and French influences, with some reminiscences of Sant'Elia and a frank interest in the expression of industrial forms. Even though Sant'Elia's 'Città Nuova' sketches of 1912–14, some inventive proposals by Mario Chiattone, and such remarkable industrial buildings as Giacomo Matté-Trucco's Fiat Factory of 1923 with its test-track on the roof, preceded the 1928 exhibition, it was not until after this date that it was possible to speak of anything like a consolidated modern movement in Italy. Not surprisingly it was in the northern cities – Milan and Turin in particular – that modern architecture took root, for here a technocratic patronage sensed some reflection of its own aspirations in the new forms. Figini and Pollini's Casa di Elettricità of 1930 at Monza is an excellent example of the tasteful, almost over-elegant modernism of this period; meanwhile Figini's own house of 1934 was a taut adaptation of Le Corbusier's vocabulary. In Rome there was a greater pressure towards classical reference, but Luigi Moretti's Fencing Academy of 1934–6 with its planar stone-clad walls and horizontal slats and planes showed that it was possible to create an honorific architecture without obvious references to tradition, simply through materials and abstract relations. Giovanni Michelucci's design for Florence railway station (1934–6) was evidence of the presence of modern architecture in the field of major public commissions, while between 1934 and 1937 the enlightened patronage of Adriano Olivetti

(director of the business machines company) allowed the creation of an entire centre at Ivrea (designed largely by Figini and Pollini) in which industrial buildings, products and housing were conceived as an integrated form.

In retrospect the outstanding architectural figure of the 1930s in Italy was Giuseppe Terragni. Born in 1904 near Como, he soon outstripped the academicism of his education and by the mid-1920s was aware of the modern movement then crystallizing in northern Europe. His earliest works were characterized by a struggle to reconcile a species of classical figuration with the construction techniques and abstraction that seemed to him synonymous with 'modernity'. His designs of the late 1920s for urban buildings were suave reinterpretations of international examples, while those for tombs (notably the Stecchini and Pirovano Tombs, both in Como) revealed Terragni's intense simplification of classical forms. From his student days, he had been in the habit of sketching and transforming buildings from the past (some of his finest drawings are of Michelangelo's more bizarre details, or of the stark volumes of classical ruins). It is scarcely surprising, then, that of all foreign modern architects, Terragni should have admired Le Corbusier the most. His understanding of the French-Swiss architect, who was a generation older than himself, went far deeper than that of most Italian modernists, who imbibed the technological imagery and the purity of form, but did not always grasp the deeper principles of organization and the links with tradition. Terragni was a traditionalist

448

in much the same way that Le Corbusier was: he believed that 'essential' architectural values could be rethought and successfully incorporated into a modern mode of expression. More than that, Terragni was at heart a classicist and was able to perceive in Le Corbusier's buildings and writings qualities of proportion, abstraction, and urbane reference that the cruder Italian modernists missed.

This combination of aptitudes and circumstances made Terragni uniquely endowed to forge a bond between the progressivist and traditionalist aspects of Fascist mythology, and to give to these patterns of thought and feeling a form. This is already evident in the Casa del Fascio (the local headquarters of the Fascist party) of 1932–6 in Como, which stands not far from the traditional urban institutions, facing on to a piazza. The façade is a taut, linear design, in which architectural effect is created by crisp contrasts of thin planes and voids. Frame and walls are juxtaposed in a manner which suggests that the architect has rigorously redefined the fundamental meanings of such perennial elements as 'support', 'opening' or 'enclosure'. However, the iconography of this frame façade, with its subtle net of layered space, has less to do with the technological 'objectivity' of much architecture in the 1920s than it has to do with a sort of abstracted, Latin mode. This is a classical façade in modern spatial terms, with a portico rethought to give a suitably open image to a modern institution in an urban setting. Terragni wrote of his own building:

Here is the Mussolinian concept that Fascism is a glasshouse into which everyone can peer giving rise to the architectural interpretation that is the complement of that metaphor; no encumbrance, no barrier, no obstacle, between the political hierarchy and the people.

The vital and creative tension between the modern and the classical extends from the overall arrangement of the plan to the image of the façade, to the choice of materials and to the character of proportions (square in plan, with the façade height equal to one half side). The inner atrium, a space for public assembly linked easily with the piazza outside, is disposed in a manner which recalls the *cortile* of a Renaissance *palazzo*, while the building is clothed in a finely cut marble which avoids mechanistic reference and suggests an honorific character, yet is detailed in such a way that the banal massiveness of so much Fascist neo-classicism is avoided. There is no mistaking that this is a building made from modern materials with slender structural members, but there is also the sense of a wall-like block from which openings have been subtracted and cut. Details such as the spandrels and ledges, or the joints in the stone, are handled sharply to pick up accents of light and lines of shade. While there is an emphasis on craft, this is not for its own sake, but to enhance the overall image and give a tactile presence to the guiding ideas.

The Casa del Fascio derives part of its visual tension from the contrast between its rectangular geometry and the upward curvature of the piazza (in practical terms a solution to drainage). The external articulation reinforces the idea of front, back and sides, and manages the transition through the façade plane to the active layers of structure inside. The main elevation is both symmetrical and asymmetrical, a fact which allows the Casa del Fascio to live on several scales with its setting, but which also prepares the visitor for an indirect line of approach, an entrance off-axis, through the transitional foyer where one grasps the lateral positions of the stairs and of the monument to the

449 Giuseppe Terragni, Casa del Fascio, Como, 1932–6, proportional system and plan

450 Casa del Fascio

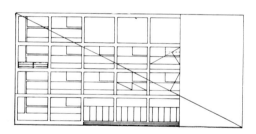

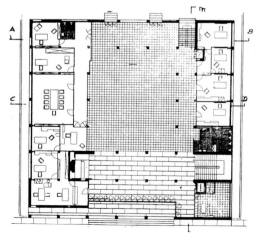

449

450

Fascist martyrs to one side. The roof of the atrium is split open symmetrically to admit light, and the structural piers are also grouped to reinforce the central axis of the building, but it is an axis which is directed *out* again through the retractable glass doors to the piazza. Thus the 'axis of the state' and the 'axis of the people' become one and the same – the Casa del Fascio belongs to all – and this feeling of reconnection with the urban space beyond the building is reinforced by the polished stone soffits over the lobby which read almost as mirrors, and which therefore help to dissolve the main façade away when one is looking out to the piazza.

Le Corbusier had used the phrase *'une maison / un palais'* – 'a house, a palace' – to refer to an ennobled institution, and Terragni's building developed a similar theme. The Casa del Fascio crystallized (and idealized) the social situation which gave rise to it, but also transcended these conditions in generic architectural terms. Presumably this is one of the reasons why the building has been able to excite the admiration of people who find the political system it represented repugnant. The Casa del Fascio, the contemporary High Point I flats in London by Lubetkin, and Aalto's near contemporary Sanatorium at Paimio were clear evidence of the way an authentic modern tradition was taking shape in the early 1930s, in which seminal ideas of the modern movement were being blended with new impulses and metaphors. The same period, of course, witnessed the rapid devaluation of white forms and flat roofs into banal formulae and mannered clichés.

By the mid-1930s, Terragni was able to work with a consistent architectural language on large and small scales, in which delicate rectangular frames were used as frontispieces, and internal structure was deployed as a series of parallel layers and transparencies. The villa projects of 1933 and 1936 were variations upon this theme, as were several apartment schemes, most notably the Casa Rustici in Milan of 1936, in which a frame of slender horizontal concrete terraces was used to link the two lateral blocks and to generate a modern version of an urban screen. In the Asilo Sant'Elia, a nursery school in Como of 1936–7, the transition from the urban edges of the site to the public lobby and continuous patio at the centre of the plan was handled by parallel 'veils' (real or implied), engendered by shifting the glazed partitions off the lines of the column grid. In this way, individual classrooms at the edges were each given a shaded terrace (enhanced by retractable awnings), while the main hall and corridors became, in effect, covered outdoor spaces. Extending horizontal slabs and 'sliding' planes were used to reinterpret the ideas of entrance, portico and patio with surrounding loggias. Thus Terragni took over traditional types and reinvigorated them by inverting the expected relationships of solid and void, load and support, mass and transparency, and by introducing shifts, asymmetries and rotations. Among the stimuli which enabled him to enact these dynamic transformations were the perceptual ambiguities of coloured rectangles found in the paintings of his close friend Mario Radice.

451 Giuseppe Terragni, Asilo Sant'Elia, Como, 1936–7

452 Giuseppe Terragni and others, competition project for the Palazzo Littorio, Rome, 1934

451

452

If the displaced rectangles and dense screens of the Casa del Fascio revealed ways for handling the rhetoric of the modern 'transparent monument', they also suggested subtle surrogates for the classical apparatus of the multi-layered façade. Terragni revealed further implications of all this in his several proposals for major state buildings in the mid-1930s. Chief among these was the entry (at the head of a team of architects) for the competition for the Palazzo Littorio in Rome of 1934. The building was to combine the functions of Fascist headquarters and memorial to Italian civilization, and the site was adjacent to the Basilica of Maxentius and Constantine, with lateral views to the Colosseum. Terragni envisaged a curved façade over 260 feet (80 metres) wide hovering above the ground and covered in polished black porphyry, with its upper part split open by a tribune where Mussolini would be seen silhouetted against the sky by the populace massed below. The façade surface would have been partly dematerialized by light and was incised with the isostatic lines of tension found in stress models: a haunting articulation, splicing together the iconography of modern structural science with a vaguely geological metaphor of the expanding empire. (Porphyry, which had been used in the columns of the Pantheon, came only from Egypt, and Egypt was among the Duce's territorial ambitions.) In his diagrams accompanying the proposal, Terragni used overlays of the ruins in the Roman Forum to explain the antique resonances of his scheme, and drawings of the curved 'entasis' of the Parthenon to demonstrate his interest in the visual tensions and distortions of ancient Greek architecture. In effect, Terragni seems to have seen the Fascist programme as an opportunity to return to the basics of Mediterranean civilization, and to reinvestigate some of the generating ideas from which later stages of classicism sprang. For him the poetic and the political were inseparable. His unbuilt project for the Palazzo dei Congressi of 1937 (designed with Pietro Lingeri and Cesare Cattaneo) resorted to the idea of skeletal transparencies, combining structural frames and piers in syncopated rhythms over a basically classical armature of base, *piano nobile*, cornice and visually reinforced corners. It should not be forgotten that, in the hands of Louis Sullivan, the steel structural frame had excited analogies with classical schemata, that

453

Le Corbusier's Dom-ino in reinforced concrete of 1914 was a structural genotype with the potential of being 'cross-bred' with ideas of load and support drawn from the past, and that Mies van der Rohe had already exhibited an interest in parallelisms between modern structural frames and classical forms. Thus Terragni's researches into architectural syntax, however locally motivated, had a more general aspect related to the entire problem of modernity and classicism.

In the late 1930s Terragni's creative endeavours were nourished increasingly by intellectual ruminations on history and on the beginnings of architecture in archetypical institutions. The ever more complex levels of his imagery found an outlet eventually in a curious scheme, never built, for a monument to Dante, to stand in the Roman Forum and to be an emblem of the continuity of Italianate culture, the unity of the new empire, and its parallels

with earlier ones. The 'Danteum' (as it was to be called) was to include a Dante study centre and was to stand on a site next to the Basilica of Maxentius. The scheme was commissioned in 1938 by Rino Valdameri, Director of the Brera in Milan, and an early version was approved by Mussolini, but both the patron and the architect were killed in the war.

In essence, Terragni's project was a sort of analogue to Dante's *Divine Comedy* and was arranged around an ascending processional route which linked rectangular compartments of different mood and articulation, representing the Inferno, Purgatory, and Paradise, the last being a space open to the sky with a grid of glass columns in it. The basic formal elements were walls and cylindrical columns disposed in proportional relationships based upon the Golden Section, the dimensions of the nearby Basilica of Maxentius, and an abstruse

453 Giuseppe Terragni
and Pietro Lingeri,
Danteum project, 1938,
perspective drawing,
Paradise

454 Danteum project,
plans of upper level (at 10
metres) and lower level (at
6 metres)

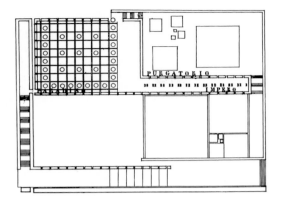

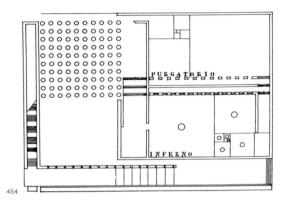

454

numerological symbolism of Terragni's own, which he believed to be consonant with Dante's thought. But the grids and hypostyles of columns were in turn allied to the architect's notions of the beginnings of architecture, and incorporated what he felt to be archetypical forms (e.g. cylinders, rectangles), archetypal relationships (e.g. rows, grids), basic types (e.g. free-standing columns, porticoes, hypostyles), and fundamental institutional types (e.g. temple, palace). Indeed, the building blended together, subtly and beautifully, sources derived from Egyptian temple design with the vocabulary of modern architecture, with the abstraction of modern painting, with the basic elements of the neighbouring Roman buildings. The Danteum was intended as a sort of microcosm of the Duce's empire, its pan-Mediterranean ambition, its triumph, its cultural achievement, and its divine sanction, which supposedly linked

the era of Fascism with other great eras in Italy's history. This was a case, clearly, where modern devices of abstraction were employed not to escape the past, but to enter it more fully on a number of levels simultaneously.

Despite the fact that it was never built, the Danteum project must rank as one of the most subtle and complex ideas to be conceived within the tradition of the modern movement; it demonstrated one possible way of blending the ancient and the modern without ending in a betrayal of both. After inspecting Terragni's *oeuvre* as a whole, and sensing the depth with which he investigated the roots of architecture and addressed the problem of fusing modern space and structure with classical schemes of representation, one is left guessing whether this architect, had he been a German, would have surmounted the strictures of ideological prejudice and created a similar rich mix of meanings under Nazi patronage. By contrast, Speer's architecture was banal and obvious; but was this due to its trumped-up content or to the artist's lesser talents? The prejudices of early modernist historiography used to require that one see modern architecture as an expression of liberal ideologies, but the case of Terragni flies in the face of this cosy theory by presenting an architecture of a high order, indisputably modern, profoundly linked to the past, in the service of Fascism.

The totalitarian critiques of modern architecture bit deep and revealed problems and rifts between avant-garde culture and some of the traditional, preservationist and institutional functions of monumental architecture. These dilemmas were not the exclusive property of the dictatorships, as the continuing use of classical models in the democracies in the 1930s suggests. The repression of the modern movement at such an early stage of its development in Germany forced some of its protagonists to emigrate and to take their forms with them to foreign soils; it also had the curious side-effect of pressurizing the lone figure of Mies van der Rohe into laying the basis of a new language of modern monumentality that would profit him and the Western democracies after the war. In Italy, modernism was embroiled in the contradictions of Fascism, but it too made parallels with classicism to which a post-war generation working in a different political system would return.

21

international, national, regional: the diversity of a new tradition

... a classical stage cannot long endure. It can only be extended, in the twofold sense of spreading over more and more territory and of being brought to bear on more and more problems, in an effort to think through to the end the new principles in all their various manifestations.
Paul Frankl, 1914

455 Oscar Niemeyer restaurant at Pampulha, Minas Gerais, Brazil, 1943

After periods of drastic innovation in the history of forms, it is not unusual for there to be a phase of reflection in which foundation myths are set in place, lines of descent are sanctified and claims of universality are made. Something of the kind happened for modern architecture in the 1930s, when several histories were formulated which contributed to the modern movement's understanding (and misunderstanding) of itself. Inevitably the early accounts reproduced some of the rhetoric that modern architects had themselves used to promote and defend their own work; inevitably too they reflected the biases, allegiances, even geographical situations of their authors. The construction of lineages for modern architecture could scarcely be a neutral operation; it was, in fact, a highly charged exercise in retrospective selection relying upon both personal preference and (mostly undeclared) theories about the nature of historical development.

While some writers reiterated 'functionalist' explanations of the new architecture, others preferred to concentrate on matters of form. In a book with the slightly misleading title *Gli elementi dell'architettura funzionale* (1932), Alberto Sartoris actually contributed to the discussion on style, while Emil Kaufmann (in *Von Ledoux bis Le Corbusier*, 1933) developed the notion of long-range classical continuities within modernism, even hinting at the possible existence of 'autonomous' architectural values transcending time. Hitchcock and Johnson (1932) focused on the general features of what they took to be an 'International Style', while Walter Curt Behrendt, in a book called, pointedly, *Modern Building, its Nature, Problems and Forms* (1937) emphasized the social relevance of the new architecture: what he called 'identity between the form and content of life'.

Ideas about the pedigree of modern architecture also varied. Pevsner's *Pioneers of the Modern Movement* (1936) stressed the rejection of revivalism, and a moral commitment to design quality extending from William Morris to Walter Gropius. Lewis Mumford's *The Brown Decades* (1931) offered a less Eurocentric view, tracing an American strand of authenticity through Olmsted and Richardson to Sullivan, Root and Wright; and Giedion (in his early writings at least) drew a direct line from the era of the *grands constructeurs* in iron and glass, to the reinforced concrete structures, transparencies and hovering volumes of the architecture of his own time.

In Giedion's writings of the 1930s, the nineteenth century emerged as a divided age; modernism as a resolution and synthesis of earlier contradictions and antitheses. Individual creators such as Le Corbusier or Mies van der Rohe took their place in an almost evolutionary historical process. The scheme was exclusive, and had little place for the 'Expressionism' of a Mendelsohn, or for the 'Romanticism' of Wright's California houses of the 1920s. Regionalist or classicizing influences upon the formation or ensuing development of the select cast of 'modern masters' were ignored. National traditions were played down, a figure like Aalto emerging as a sort of agent of biomorphic abstraction. Giedion was little interested in the Soviet Union of the 1920s, and the Italian modern architecture of the 1930s was virtually taboo. He tended to see the matter of modernism in a transnational or pan-cultural way. By the time he formulated *Space, Time and Architecture* (1941), Giedion realized that the ideals he stood for were under threat of extinction in Europe. Perhaps with one eye on the United States, he was prepared to present modern architecture in deterministic, not to say Hegelian terms, as the inevitable 'true' expression of the unfolding spirit of the modern age.

Enough has been said in previous chapters to suggest that a phenomenon as complex as modern architecture cannot be reduced to a single generating principle or to an exclusive stylistic description. Even in its phase of crystallization, in the 1920s, there was a basic tension between the shared and the individual, the universal and the unique. To understand the patterns of invention, extension, reaction, dissemination, and absorption in the 1930s it is necessary to go beyond obvious resemblances of style to the level of underlying types and informing ideas. It is not unreasonable to posit a 'universalizing' aspect to modernism in this period, so long as one strips away the Western bias and progressive assumptions which lurk behind this formulation, and so long as one also takes into account national and regional histories with their own logic and momentum. In the 1930s there was a species of 'cross-fertilization' in which modern architecture was drawn into a variety of local agendas, and in which regional preoccupations were also given an international stamp. Generic modern devices such as the steel frame, the concrete skeleton, the free façade, the hovering horizontal and the planar wall were moved around the world, encountering diverse climates, societies, technologies, traditions, architectural languages, even varying definitions of modernity. Sometimes the new simply collided with the old; sometimes there was mutual transformation. Modern forms made a break with what had gone immediately before, but they also allowed the substructures of national or regional cultures to be understood in new ways.

As has already been seen with cases as diverse as Italy, Finland and Britain, the reasons for introducing modern architecture varied considerably. Sometimes it was a matter of individual preference; sometimes it had to do with entire schemes of social and cultural 'renewal'. Sometimes it answered to ideological needs; modern architecture clearly had its uses in both Democratic and Fascist states. Remarkable individual artists like Aalto and Terragni were even able to make 'microcosms' of their respective societies in their works of art. The 'universalizing' aspect of modernism could also be interpreted in quite different ways, responding to a classical inheritance in one case, to a vernacular tradition in another. Paradoxically, this same aspiration towards 'universality' could be used to further the causes of particular national identities, as happened in Brazil.

Contrary to the myth of an even and uniform development, modern architecture in the 1930s sometimes responded to cultural nuances and territorial differences within individual countries. An interesting case of this is provided by Switzerland. If Geneva and the Suisse Romande were most open to French influence, Zurich and the industrial zones of the North had an orientation towards Germany and towards a somewhat clinical idea of functionalism, which could no longer flourish under the Nazi regime but which already had its Swiss adherents. The Doldertal Apartments of 1934–6 by Alfred and Emil Roth with Marcel Breuer gave a competent, if prosaic, rendering of International Style themes such as the box on stilts or the cantilevered terrace, while the Neubühl Siedlung of 1932 by Max Haefeli, Werner Moser,

Hans Schmidt and others took the restraint of the 'new objectivity' to a puritan extreme. The Hallenstadion (indoor stadium) in Zurich of 1938–9 by Karl Egender revealed what could be achieved when an architect approached the practical problems of a wide span and daylight in a direct and unpretentious way. With its naked concrete frame, its huge interior steel stanchions, its horizontal rim of industrial glazing, and its deep roof overhang, it raised straightforward constructive facts to the level of architecture. It was in these years that Sigfried Giedion, the historian who was also Secretary of CIAM, lived and taught in Zurich, and this helped to ensure a range of international contacts and connections for the architectural community there. But he was not alone in reflecting and writing upon the history and contemporary direction of modern architecture: in 1940 Alfred Roth published a book entitled *The New Architecture* which collected together an array of recent buildings without insisting upon an exclusive stylistic dogma.

Basle, one of the most naturally cosmopolitan of Swiss cities, by dint of its history and situation, was also most catholic in its architectural outlook, harbouring both the functionalist abnegations of Hannes Meyer and the mystical extravagances of Rudolf Steiner. A pronounced classical substratum extending both French and German influences could be felt in, for example, Karl Moser's Church of St Anthony of 1926 (a building also notable for its reinforced concrete) or in the later works of Hans Bernoulli, which resembled those of Auguste Perret. If the cultural and educational sectors were relatively conservative (e.g. the restrained classicism of Roland Rohn's Kollegiengebäude of 1939 in the University), the industrial sector was clearly open to aesthetic and technological experiment. This may be gauged by, for example, the works undertaken by Otto Salvisberg for the Hoffmann-La Roche Company, including a warehouse with bold concrete mushroom columns and continuous glazing in 1936–7.

Among the most daring of modernist experiments in Switzerland in the 1930s was the St. Johannes-Kirche in Basle of 1936 by Karl Egender and E. F. Burckhardt, for here the problem of a church was handled through an 'abstract' modern vocabulary combining steel frame, masonry and glass. Swiss architects were able to select their external models

456

with some distance and discrimination, and the house at Schnitterweg (1935) by Otto and Walter Senn seemed to combine poetic lessons from Le Corbusier with a delicate handling of trellis and frame suggesting Italian Rationalist influence. The connection with Italian Rationalism was pursued more deliberately by Alberto Sartoris, who was a practising architect as well as a historian. Most of his works were built in the Valais, a French-speaking canton of Switzerland bordering Italy. Sartoris was a friend of Terragni and was attracted by a certain 'Mediterraneanism'; he was also quick to sense the possibility of a friendly pact between the functional and geometrical disciplines of modernism, and the basic principles of rural vernacular architecture (an intuition which would be of use to a later generation of Swiss architects based in the Italian-speaking canton of the Ticino (see Chapter 33)). As a rule, Swiss modern architecture of the 1930s did not engage in a committed way with the problem of 'Alpine Regionalism'. Nor did it set out to achieve statements of high poetic intensity. Its hallmarks were technical rigour, functional clarity and formal restraint.

Switzerland might have gained a public modern architecture of a certain timeless character if Le Corbusier's League of Nations project of 1927 (Chapter 15), or his Mundaneum proposal of 1929, both to stand close to Geneva, had been built. These were projects conceived on the symphonic landscape scale of Lac Léman and the Alps – a landscape which evoked Mediterranean parallels for Le Corbusier; even the small house which he

designed for his parents on the lake at Vevey in 1924 celebrated the mythical view to the south towards the classical world in its small framed opening through the garden wall. The Mundaneum was intended to combine some modern vision of an Acropolis with a reinterpretation of the pastoral vision of Rousseau, its prisms and spaces resonating with the epic vistas of water, mountains, and sky. The dominant building in the ensemble was the 'World Museum' which resembled a stepped pyramid rising by means of ascending ramps over a square spiral geometry. This monument was to have been approached ritualistically between formally grouped glazed towers. But Le Corbusier's symbol of universal world culture was not to be. As it was, he had more success with the Clarté Apartments in Geneva constructed in the early 1930s, an elegant glazed slab with an underlying steel frame extending balconies, some double-height living rooms, stone clad entry-ways and stairs with glass-brick treads and landings. Conceived as a piece of a larger urban plan for that part of Geneva, the Clarté constituted a virtual manifesto on steel fabrication: a level of technological realization that it would have been hard to equal in any other country at the time.

Even in a culture which placed a high value on industrial craftsmanship and precision engineering, Robert Maillart was a case of his own. In the 1930s he designed a series of exquisite concrete bridges which appeared to float above the Alpine landscape. These were stripped to their structural bones and attenuated in their overall form. The Salginatobel

Bridge (1930) near Schiers was a hollow-box, three-hinged arch which sprang lightly across a ravine in a clear span of over 300 feet (90 metres). If one is to search for parallels with Maillart's structural forms, one is most likely to find them in abstract sculpture or else in nature. He continued to insist upon structural engineering as an art, as well as a science, against the dogmas of an academic establishment committed to the cult of calculations. Towards the end of the decade, Maillart experimented with concrete shell construction, which allowed a reduction to the thinnest of planar surfaces. The Cement Hall built for the National Exhibition in Zurich of 1939 was parabolic in section and stood on four slender piers. Like a curved blade in extreme tension, it was entirely smooth inside and out, without ribs of any kind.

By contrast, the series of aircraft hangars designed by the Italian engineer Pier Luigi Nervi between 1936 and 1939 for the Italian Air Force were formed from two-way ribs as a lattice supported on tapered diagonal piers. Nervi characterized his solution as 'a unified structural system … in vaulted form'. The roofs of the hangars, which gave uninterrupted spans 114 feet (35 metres) wide and more than 325 feet (100 metres) long, illustrated his general principle of bringing dead and live loads down to foundations with the minimum use of materials. The external cladding, using tiles,

was applied as a separate skin. Nervi, no less than Maillart, saw structure as an art. He emulated the visual tension of Gothic ribs and flying buttresses, as well as the principle of classical coffering in antique examples such as the dome over the Roman Pantheon constructed in the second century AD. Nervi was an engineer with a developed historical sense: he bridged the worlds of modern technology and antiquity, at the level of principles rather than just appearances.

Far from being totally 'objective', the engineer of a high order works in part with *a priori* images and reveals both personal style and national accent. The Spanish engineer Eduardo Torroja extended a Mediterranean artisanal tradition of laminated ceramic surfaces and saddle vaults. The slender, wave-like roofs of his Zarzuela Racecourse near Madrid of 1935, were only 4 inches (10 centimetres) thick and were constructed using segments of hyperboloids in the wafer-thin shells. The enormous spans were achieved by combining the principle of the cantilever with intersecting curvatures that generated the necessary stiffness without recourse to beams. Some of this echoed the Catalan vaulting systems used by Gaudí at the turn of the century. Torroja's ideas were absorbed in several Latin American countries, and contributed in the course of time to a culture of expressive engineering based upon limited technological means.

459

460 André Lurçat, Karl Marx School, Villejuif, near Paris, 1931–3

461 Jean Prouvé (with Eugène Beaudouin, Marcel Lods and Vladimir Bodiansky), Maison du Peuple, Clichy, Paris, 1937–9

462 Le Corbusier, project for an Agricultural Estate, Cherchell, North Africa, 1942

France in the 1930s offers a virtual case-study in the way that modernism might be accepted in some sectors of a nation but not in others. The field of monumental and civic commissions remained, for the most part, in the hands of a Beaux-Arts establishment which became increasingly fatigued in its classical devaluations, even if these were sometimes given the allure of Art Deco veneers (e.g. the Trocadéro, the Musée d'Art Moderne). Le Corbusier's steel and glass experiments (Chapter 18) were in a class of their own, as was Chareau and Bijvoet's Maison de Verre of 1928–31 (Figs. 327–9). Otherwise, modern architecture in France followed several different paths. The chic apartment blocks and department stores of Michel Roux Spitz developed a streamlined aspect of the International Style, while the housing at La Muette, Drancy, of 1932 by Eugène Beaudouin and Marcel Lods combined earnest social intentions with a somewhat ponderous approach to form. Modern architecture became a plaything of the rich in several seaside villa and garden designs, but also stimulated interesting commercial inventions such as Oscar Nitzschké's unbuilt project for a Maison de la Publicité of 1935, with a steel-frame façade carrying flashing advertisements and projected images.

One of the most probing and formally inventive buildings of the early 1930s in France was the Karl Marx School at Villejuif of 1931–3 by André Lurçat. This radicalized the educational programme, not only by introducing new standards of lighting,

heating, ventilation and use of space, but also by opening up the plan and breaking down old class barriers. The school was even to function as a forum for the surrounding community. The Maison du Peuple at Clichy of 1937–9 (designed by the engineer/architect Jean Prouvé (with the collaboration of Beaudouin, Lods and Bodiansky) also explored the notion of transparency as a sign of social emancipation, but in a language of steel girders, moving components and glass. Built for the socialist *Mairie* of a working-class area of Paris, the Maison du Peuple combined the functions of market hall, auditorium and *salle des fêtes*. Several structural systems were combined, and some parts were moveable to allow adjustable interior uses. Like Prouvé's slightly earlier Roland Garros Aero-Club at Buc, the Maison du Peuple worked with a direct aesthetic of bolts, joints and connections. The 'normative' modern solution of the steel skeleton was inflected to convey the notion of an egalitarian instrument. Prouvé's building welded together the French structural Rationalist tradition with a populist factory of culture. It may be that the 'brutal' expression of metallic fabrication was intended to express a 'social realism' of a kind. But the totality was nevertheless composed with a degree of formality that kept it within the bounds of institutional conventions. It was more radical in its content than in its form.

When the subject of 'Regionalism' was addressed in the France of the 1930s it was normally through an obvious imitation of local styles or a pastiche of the native forms of colonized countries. The sort of probing analysis of mechanization and regional values attempted by Le Corbusier in his French rural works, his North African proposals or his more generalized evocations of 'peasantism' was more the exception than the rule. In his reading of the vernacular, Le Corbusier looked to the type and the principle beyond the particular example, whether for the disposition of the plan, the handling of sun or rain, or the use of materials. The combined steel and masonry of the house at Le Pradet in Provence of 1929–32 (Fig. 388) touched upon the dilemma of combining the 'universal' types of centralized, urban, technocratic culture with the vernacular types that had emerged over the centuries in each region through the application of handicraft to local materials, and in direct response to climate, landscape and way of life.

Climate was one of the great modifiers of the language of international modern architecture in the 1930s. During these years there were several proposals for French colonies or French areas of interest, which attempted to deal with tropical or semi-tropical conditions in a rigorously modern form. Paul Nelson's unbuilt project for a hospital in Ismailya, Egypt (1936), relied upon a slender pier and slab construction to open up airy luminous interiors protected from the glare and direct rays of the sun by an adjustable double-skin of moveable grilles, slats and louvres. Michel Écochard in Syria and Louis Miquel in Algeria each evolved vocabularies attuned to the climates of their respective locations. They learned from local tradition but did not resort to a direct imitation of local forms.

Implicit in Le Corbusier's several plans for Mediterranean locations in the 1930s was a grandiose vision combining a syndicalist Utopia and a hedonistic fusion with nature. Realities of nationalism and colonialism were conveniently laid aside in favour of some vague idea of cultural destinies, based upon common geographical groupings and upon the mythology of a modernity rooted in a return to the land. Le Corbusier's vaulted projects of the 1930s evoked a 'female principle', and explored a middle ground between industrial usage and the abstraction of rural and antique sources, such as the aggregate forms of the Tunisian vaulted vernacular, or the structural repetitions of antique Roman markets. The unbuilt project for an Agricultural Estate at Cherchell, North Africa of 1942 (using low vaults, thick walls, courtyards and water channels) was conceived as 'an enclosure with high walls – and several independent gardens irrigated in the Arab way'. Le Corbusier explained that he was 'opposed to a passive, backward Regionalism' and that his project would have created a subtle interplay of solids, voids, light and shade that was modern but based upon 'the most fundamental forms of Mediterranean tradition'. He summed up his overall position and gave important hints about his post-war direction when he declared: 'Building in a modern way one has found harmony with the landscape, the climate and tradition.'

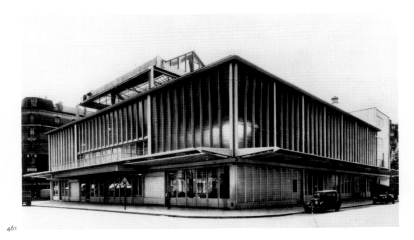

461

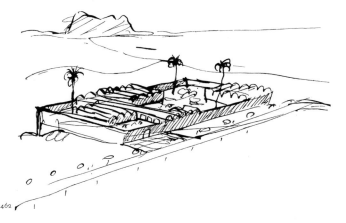

462

The theme of 'Mediterraneanism' was pervasive in the 1930s, and took on several quite different political complexions and architectural forms. Some of the Italian Rationalists and their more traditionalist counterparts addressed the question of 'Mediterranean constants' within the context of an imperialist design upon the Mediterranean itself. But one of the buildings to be most successful at distilling antique maritime memories was conceived quite outside such nationalist calculations. This was Casa Malaparte, perched on a rocky promontory above the Tyrrhenian sea near Capri, designed by Adalberto Libera together with his client Curzio Malaparte between 1938 and 1942. The house was oblong and tapered in shape and russet in colour; a wedge-shaped stair leading to the platform on top was integrated with the main volume. Casa Malaparte was reached by means of a meandering path of small stepping-stones cut into the sharp crests of the rock. The slight distortions of horizontals and verticals, as well as the white curved plane on the terrace (evoking a sail), launched the eye towards a hazy infinity, but also drew the horizon into the composition. Casa

Malaparte suggested how a building could be treated as a geometrical accent, focusing the lines of force in a wider landscape. Views from the interiors were controlled to give glimpses of rocks and waves in the middle distance, or close-ups of geological details. Malaparte was a writer and an aesthete who had become disaffected with, and imprisoned by, the Fascist regime, and he wanted nothing less than a spiritual retreat. His house was not without its metaphysical, even surrealist aspects, and it was these which pushed the inheritance of Italian Rationalism towards an unusual intensity. Casa Malaparte evoked, simultaneously, a ritual stair, a ceremonial platform, a boat and a shelf of rocks, but its sheer abstraction resisted any simplistic reading and reasserted its presence and mystery as a dynamic shape of ambiguous scale reacting to its surroundings. Although there were no direct allusions to classicism in the Casa Malaparte, the plan was like a condensed Pompeian house, while the red colours and the wall-less terrace open to the sky evoked an antique ruin poised above the sea.

A modern architecture with Mediterranean accents was also developed in and around Barcelona

463

464

in the 1930s, but here it was directed at the problems of the largest number and at the need to find an equilibrium between the forces of rapid urbanization and the requirements of a particular landscape, climate and culture. In its early phase, the Spanish modern movement was principally a socialist and Catalan effort with a strong reformist commitment. It was cut short when Franco won the Spanish Civil War in 1939 and insisted thereafter on a reactionary nationalist style based upon revered models such as the Escorial. From the beginning, Spanish Modern architecture addressed regional questions but without being overtly Regionalist. Among the key personalities were Josep Lluís Sert, Josep Torres Clavé and Joan Subirana, who together helped to found the Spanish wing of CIAM called GATEPAC (Grupo de Arquitectos para el Progreso de la Arquitectura Contemporanea). They maintained close links with Le Corbusier, and were committed to finding viable urbanistic solutions for Barcelona. Their Master Plan of 1933 for the city was intended to achieve high density but with a low-rise pattern of courtyard housing – essentially a transformation of Cerdà's nineteenth-century grid and patio typology. Their seven-storey 'Casa Bloc', constructed in 1933, was a variant of Le Corbusier's *à redent* housing, but adjusted to the warm climate and to the rich Mediterranean vegetation. The

Dispensario Central Antituberculoso of 1934–8 (by Sert, Subirana and Torres) developed a similar language; it was L-shaped in plan, and used a steel skeleton as the armature for a health-giving instrument in which the most was made of natural light and ventilation. This 'modern' technology was combined with traditional Catalan construction using vaults made from ceramic tile.

The Spanish Pavilion by Sert and Luis Lacasa at the 1937 Paris International Exhibition was also constructed on the basis of a steel frame, but had a patio covered by an awning of double thickness at its centre, and was cut through by a serpentine ramp. This was the structure which housed Picasso's *Guernica*, and which was intended to demonstrate to the world at large the liberal values of the struggling (but doomed) Spanish Second Republic. Overall, the building resembled a brightly coloured 'agitprop' stand. Both the interior and exterior frames were used to support photomontages, paintings, sculptures, maps, statistics, diagrams and objects proclaiming a progressive and populist ethos in which peasant, proletarian, soldier and artist were represented on an equal footing. The anti-authoritarian message was clear enough, and was given extra emphasis through an immediate contrast with the heavy-handed monumentality and state realism of the nearby Soviet and Third Reich

465

pavilions. While the architecture and the contents amounted to an 'Internationalist' statement of sorts, there were also Spanish touches – the crude peasant matting on the floors, the colours of the Republican flag, the patio with its awning, the shading slats and ventilating screens. Sert wrote of his ideal of a 'meridional architecture' in which 'new materials and systems of construction in universal use' would be adjusted to particular climatic and natural conditions, and in which local principles and traditional devices – terraces, loggias, screens, awnings, etc. – would be transformed in modern terms. There were echoes here of the aims of an earlier Catalan generation, but without the National Romantic imagery and without the vernacular folklore.

The forms of modern architecture were more likely to marry with some local traditions than with others. The latent 'Mediterraneanism' and 'Hellenism' in certain of Le Corbusier's works of the 1920s were not lost on those Greek architects who, towards the end of the decade, turned against revivalism and embraced the new international language. This they attempted to 'root' in the social habits, spatial patterns and landscape of their own country. Analogies between the cubic white volumes and flat roofs of modern architecture and the vernaculars of the Greek islands were not so hard to make. The Elementary School on Lycabettus Hill, Athens, designed by Dimitris Pikionis in 1933, used reinforced concrete, metal windows and whitewashed plaster to create simple planar shapes gashed by strong shadow, but also disposed the elements of the plan around a precinct of platforms

cascading down the hill, in a manner loosely recalling the topography of a Cycladic hill town. The same architect's Experimental School in the northern Greek city of Thessaloniki (1935) attempted to take the more rainy climate of this northern region into account by using tiled roofs and timber-framed balconies recalling the Macedonian vernacular, although here the marriage was less successful. Among the other Greek architects who wished to seek out some common ground between a modernist simplification and popular roots were Stami Papadaki and Aris Konstantinidis (e.g. the latter's Eleusis House of 1938).

Ironically, the whitewashed cube and the concrete frame were destined to come together, not as part of some cultural regeneration, but in a devalued form, as the standard kit of the building contractor and the real-estate developer in the post-war years. Already in the 1930s a species of seaside vernacular emerged around the Mediterranean from Tel Aviv and Alexandria at

466

465 Dimitris Pikionis,
Elementary School,
Lycabettus Hill, Athens,
1933

466 Hassan Fathy,
house in mud-brick for
an artist, Cairo, 1942

467 Sedad Hakki Eldem,
Taslik Coffee House,
Istanbul, 1947–8

one end, to the '*nouvelles villes*' (the 'new towns'
built by colonists outside traditional centres)
of Morocco and Algeria at the other. Among those to
be highly critical of the situation was the Egyptian
architect Hassan Fathy, who saw the 'International
Style' as just one more foreign intrusion in the
already fragmented and colonized culture of his
own country. Far from perceiving 'modernism' as
an instrument for universal liberation, critics liks
Fathy saw it as a destructive force that was reducing
the whole world to a hollow sameness. He also felt
that the wide windows, concrete construction and
free-standing boxes of modern architecture made
no sense in extreme heat, and in societies with
long-standing courtyard traditions embodying
well-tried devices for excluding the sun and
for dealing with privacy. Fathy's position was
articulated through a 'Pharaonic' ideal: a notion of
returning to the basis of Egyptian culture in the mud
vernacular of the southern part of the country.
His hope was to regenerate architecture from the

ground up, by encouraging the peasant to build for
himself, with forms and techniques that were cheap
and had stood the test of time.

The struggle to reconcile modernity and national
identity was central to the work and the thought
of the Turkish architect Sedad Hakki Eldem, who
rejected both a superficial Orientalism of applied
domes and arches, *and* a thoughtless importation
of the International Style. He wished instead to
give new life to basic Turkish traits but in a widely
applicable modern architectural grammar based
upon reinforced-concrete construction. He studied
indigenous timber buildings for their underlying
types, their characteristic forms and their living-
patterns. He also sought out relevant parallels in
modern architecture, especially in the works of
Frank Lloyd Wright and Auguste Perret. Eldem's
oscillations back and forth between national and
international models can be traced throughout
the 1930s and need to be understood against the
background of much broader cultural dilemmas
concerning the need of the Turkish Republic
to find a sound balance between the forces of
modernization and secularism on the one hand
and the weight of Ottoman and Islamic traditions
on the other. Eldem had written in 1939:

Although the same new architectural attitudes and elements are
adopted and applied by many different nations, when it comes to
ideas and ideals, they all look for ways of maintaining, developing
and expressing their own identities. And for this they look back to
tradition, they commit themselves to a new ideal or they try to
synthesize the two.

It was in the following decade (in buildings such as
the Istanbul Palace of Justice of 1948 or the Taslik
Coffee House of 1947–8) that he succeeded in just
such a synthesis of the concrete frame, a grammar
drawn from timber examples, and certain constants
of local tradition (visible in monument and
vernacular alike) to forge a language of his own that
could be used on a small or large scale. These works
of the 1940s were indisputably 'modern' buildings
but with a distinctive Turkish character and sobriety.

The architecture of Erich Mendelsohn erected
in British Mandate Palestine (or 'Eretz Israel', as
Jewish settlers preferred to call it) in the mid- to
late 1930s embodied a similar attempt at a mating of
the 'new ideal' with tradition – in fact with several
traditions, since Mendelsohn saw the emerging
order of the Middle East in terms of the blending

467

of modern Western rationalism and ancient Eastern mysticism, even in terms of the reuniting of Jew and Arab in a single Semitic cultural and political entity. At a less nebulous level there were the facts of climate, geography, landscape and materials, and it is striking how quickly Mendelsohn realized the need for inward-turning buildings, shaded precincts, thick walls, small apertures and protective exteriors. By 1935, he had established some of the terms of his Levantine synthesis in the Weitzman House at Rehovot (with terraces open to breezes and orchards, but a central patio linked to the garden) and in several projects for Jerusalem (the Schocken House, the Schocken Library, the Anglo-Palestine Bank) which used sober, cubic volumes clad on the outside in the local honey-coloured stone. The interiors, by contrast, were characterized by a limpid space and a cool, filtered light, as if the 'transparency' of the 1920s had been turned outside in.

Already by the early 1930s a feverish construction was taking place in coastal towns such as Tel Aviv and Haifa which followed the general directives of the International Style. Recently arrived European architects (many of them from Germany) brought with them the whitewashed planes, wide windows and concrete supports of the new architecture. Some Zionists saw in this evidence of a 'new society', or at least a fresh start ('an apartment free from past memories', as the historian Julius Posener put it); others were more caustic and referred to Tel Aviv as 'Bauhaus by the Sea'. While there were notable individual buildings (such as the Engel House of 1933 by Zeev Rechter which received inspiration from Corbusian and Italian sources), there was also a general pattern which established streets, squares and junctions using the vocabulary of simple, flat-topped buildings with concrete balconies and airy throughways. By the time Mendelsohn arrived in 1934, he was surprised to discover straight imitations of his own Berlin buildings.

Mendelsohn was as little interested in repeating the sanctioned tricks of the International Style as he was in following the Orientalist eclecticism of architects like Alexander Baewald who, several years earlier, had tried to mix together several Middle Eastern influences. It was Erich Mendelsohn's ambition to make a great East–West synthesis –

468

a fusion of new and old, regional and universal – and to reconcile the world of science with that of revelation. His chance to attempt this came with the commission to build the Hadassah Hospital and Medical School at Mount Scopus (1934–9) to the east of Jerusalem on an epic site with views across the great geological divide containing the River Jordan. Mendelsohn organized the building as a series of parallel bars running east to west, an arrangement that left several residual spaces between the wings, some of them with the character of courtyards, others more open, allowing a panorama of the desert landscape. Seen from a distance the hospital was like a long, low slab of rock, perforated here and there by small apertures. In fact it was a frame building clad in a stone veneer, and the main entrance was marked by a portico with slender piers and a slab roof with three flat saucer-domes protruding from it, perceived from beneath as concave, lens-like shapes. These set in motion a circular theme which would be rediscovered elsewhere in the building as one moved gradually (and somewhat indirectly) across the site through a series of 'layers' of varying light and intensity: in skylights, in pools, in the circular shaft rising the full height of the stairs, and in the curved balconies of the last structure in the

468 Erich Mendelsohn, Schocken Library, Jerusalem, 1934–6

469 Erich Mendelsohn, Hadassah Hospital and Medical School, Mount Scopus, Jerusalem, 1934–9

470 Hadassah Hospital and Medical School, ground-floor plan

471 Hadassah Hospital and Medical School, nurses' wing

469

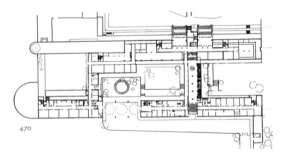

470

471

sequence, the Nurses' Wing. These were delicate, even feminine, touches in the otherwise rectilinear geometry.

Mendelsohn's Mount Scopus complex was a relative of some of his earlier European buildings that also used long, low slabs linked by necks of circulation. It reiterated his guiding preoccupations with space, light, movement and internal tranquillity, but avoided any excessive play with dynamism. Like his other buildings in Jerusalem, it was sober and restrained on the outside, and shaded but luminous within. A modern city of science for healing and research, it none the less abstracted features of the Old City not far away: the tawny cubes of stones and buildings, the city walls and their gates, the streets, squares, courts, the free-standing pavilions, the continuous façades, and the different sizes and depths of openings. There were even some (probably unintentional) similarities in plan with the Muristan quarter of Old Jerusalem, an ancient hospital which stood upon a Roman foundation. Mendelsohn was not blind to the richness and relevance of the architectural heritage surrounding him, transforming it to fit his own ideas; the façade of his Nurses' Wing, for example, recalled the proportions and secretiveness of a convent. The portico with the three abstract domes

472

was a symbolic form of some complexity, since it was at the same time a shelter, a tripartite entry-way and a modern gesture towards tradition. Beyond it, on axis with the central bay, was a single round pool with a still surface which reiterated the circular theme. Perhaps this was Mendelsohn's symbol of the unity of the three great civilizations flowing from a single source? He wrote of the Mount Scopus Hospital: 'No one will be disappointed who regards it in the light of the monumental austerity and serenity of the greatest spiritual creations of this part of the world – the Bible, the New Testament, the Koran.'

The modern movement in British-occupied Palestine had something of the character of a broad social transformation. By contrast, modern architecture in South Africa was the aesthetic property of a restricted élite. There was no firmly established tradition to extend or reject, although in the years leading up to the First World War Herbert Baker had made a viable synthesis of local sources, the Mediterranean vernacular, and the English Arts and Crafts. South Africa was remote from the innovatory centres, and culturally dependent on Britain (which lacked a modern movement of its own until the 1930s). It was in the mid-1920s that contacts began to be made with avant-garde developments in Europe. Rex Martienssen, probably the most interesting of the South African architects, travelled to Holland and France, even establishing a dialogue with Le Corbusier. In the

early 1930s, Martienssen was a co-founder of the Transvaal group, and set up a practice with John Fassler and Bernard Cooke. Together they designed a number of buildings of high quality, among them the Peterhouse Flats and Funeral Home in Johannesburg (1934–5), which reflected a variety of influences from Europe, most notably those of Gropius and Le Corbusier, but which also possessed a logic and power of its own arising from the ingenious combination of diverse functions on an urban site, and from the tight control of proportion and detail. The composition was crowned by a majestic curved solarium recalling the one in the Villa Savoye, and the strong South African sunlight provided dramatic gashes of shadow in the voids cut through the taut planes of the walls. Martienssen understood the classical and Mediterranean echoes in Le Corbusier's work, and in his own architecture celebrated the sensuous qualities of the South African climate, vegetation and landscape. His unusual intellectual gifts assured a firm basis of principle in his activities as a creator and an educator. His writings on ancient Greek sites (later published as *The Idea of Space in Greek Architecture,* 1956) revealed his interest in basic elements such as the platform and the wall, and in the spatial drama linking temples to their wider setting. He realized that modern architecture should embody artistic fundamentals as well as a revolution in technology, social attitudes and forms.

473

In Japan the establishment of a modern movement was inseparable from a broader process of technological and institutional modernization involving considerable ambivalence towards Western influence. Eclectic works such as Katayama Toyu's Hyokekan Museum in Tokyo of 1908 (which combined the French seventeenth century with English Palladianism) stood out in all their agonized and foreign self-consciousness against a setting in which religious and vernacular structures continued to be built in traditional styles and with a craftmanship that stretched back uninterruptedly for centuries. Even imported methods of construction (particularly those which substituted brick for the usual wood) were sometimes regarded with suspicion. In 1909, the architect Chinto Itoh, who had immersed himself in the old styles of East Asia, argued that Japan should purify itself, rid itself of harmful occidental images and revive its own traditions. He claimed that a new-found language would arise automatically once truly indigenous forms were cross-bred with imported building methods. A year later, Yashukura Ohtsuka put the opposite argument: that Japan should welcome Western visual models but modify them to local conditions, crafts and means of construction. Both men had essentially the same aim – the creation of a specifically Japanese modern style.

Western modern architecture owed more than a little to Japanese aesthetics in the first place. Frank Lloyd Wright had been drawn to the disciplines of Japanese design when forming his own architectural language, but his Imperial Hotel in Tokyo of 1912–23 ended up being highly ornate and mannered. Despite its obvious debts to Japanese prototypes, it exerted a limited local influence. Even after the hotel's completion, 'progressive' Japanese architects were eagerly taking up Art Nouveau – a full two decades after it had dropped out of favour with the European avant-garde. Mamoru Yamada's Central Telegraph Office in Tokyo of 1926 still had a vaguely Secessionist air. It was through publications like Gropius's *International Architektur* and Le Corbusier's *Oeuvre complète, 1910–29*, and detailed reports on tendencies such as De Stijl and Esprit Nouveau, that Western modern architecture gradually became known in Japan. Foreigners such as Bruno Taut pointed out affinities between the modular simplicity of indigenous forms and the reductivism of modern design. Analogies were also made between timber and steel frames.

By the mid-1930s the germ of a Japanese modern movement existed which was not just a copy of earlier Western developments. In his design for the Okada House and gardens of 1933, for example, Sutemi Horiguchi blended the thin planes of the new architecture with traditional qualities of lightness and airiness. The garden, with its slight level-changes and rectangular pools continuing the patterns and dimensions of the straw mats in the interior, had as much to do with historical examples like the moon-viewing platform of the Katsura Imperial Villa as it did with abstract modern art. The Japanese Pavilion at the Paris 1937 International Exhibition, designed by Junzo Sakakura, restated the slender steel frame (which Sert had identified as a 'universal' norm) in a way which recalled the modules, proportions and delicate carpentry of traditional Japanese construction. Sakakura and Kunio Mayekawa had both worked in Le Corbusier's atelier in the late 1920s and brought home an understanding of inner principles rather than just surface effects. They helped to establish the intellectual scaffolding for a distinctly Japanese modern architecture, but their efforts were severely undermined by a resurgence of extreme nationalism (which, ironically, turned to Western classical models) and then by the outbreak of war.

474

Among the foreign architects to be interested in an 'East–West' synthesis was Antonin Raymond, a Czech-American who helped to supervise the Imperial Hotel and who set up his office in Japan in 1920. His own house in Tokyo of 1924 recalled the geometry of Wright's Unity Temple, while the interior spaces and details blended machine imagery with Japanese finesse, especially in the screens and trellises. At the start of the 1930s Raymond turned to a direct expression of the concrete frame (in a manner recalling both Perret and indigenous timber-work) in his search for a valid modern East–West synthesis. Something of the kind was achieved in the Fukui Residence at Atami Bay in 1935. In 1936 Raymond began work on the 'Golconde Dormitory' at the Aurobindo Ashram in the French colony of Pondicherry in southern India. Here he adjusted a modern vocabulary to tropical conditions. The building had a reinforced concrete skeleton, and the 'free façade' was interpreted as a continuous screen of adjustable louvres, an image of vibrant but tranquil abstraction. The roof was constructed with a double shell in concrete for insulation against the heat, and the partitions on the inside were made from timber grille-work to permit the flow of air. Beyond the basic idea of an adjustable climatic membrane for tropical conditions, the Golconde Dormitory possessed an evocative stillness, enhanced by a soft interior light, a direct but subtle mix of materials, and a vital connection to the daily and seasonal rhythms of nature. Raymond stated modestly that an architect should 'deal directly with conditions growing out of the work itself and its location'.

The fuller cultural implications of a 'tropical modernism' were developed in countries such as Brazil, where an ideal of national progress was combined with a quest for 'national origins', not by copying the past, but by reinvigorating basic spatial patterns responsive to the hot climate and the sumptuous landscape. The idea that Brazil should be purged of the 'foreign' forms imported in the nineteenth century gained momentum in the 1920s, especially in the writings of Gilberto Freyre, who advocated an authentically 'Brazilian' artistic expression based on a thorough understanding of tangible and intangible aspects of a national way of life. Needless to say, much of this was mythical, but it is on myth that architectural meaning is partly based.

475

While the first tentative moves towards modern architecture were made in the 1920s, the consolidating event where the future of Brazilian modernism was concerned was the reversal of the jury's original decision to give the commission for the Ministry of Education in Rio de Janeiro to traditionalist architects. This initiative was taken by the Minister of Education himself (Gustavo Capenema) in 1936. Instead, he diverted this crucial task symbolizing the direction of the nation after the revolution of 1930 to a team of modern architects including Lúcio Costa, Oscar Niemeyer, Jorge Machado Moreira and Affonso Eduardo Reidy. They in turn invited Le Corbusier to be their consultant architect. The resulting building was one of the earliest attempts at providing a fully glazed prismatic skyscraper with a protective screen of *brises-soleil*. In effect, the Ministry was a demonstration of the way that a concrete skeleton could be turned into a naturally ventilated grille: windows were made operable by hand, and the free plan used partitions which did not reach to the ceilings. But it was also a public affirmation of local materials and of Brazilian modern art. Solid walls and floors were clad in native granite or Portuguese-style faïence tiles, while the complex curves embodied both a sensual rhythm and an echo of the exuberance of the eighteenth-century Brazilian Baroque. The *pilotis* lifting the superstructure into space rose a full ten metres, allowing air to pass beneath the building and

475 Antonin Raymond, 'Golconde Dormitory', Aurobindo Ashram, Pondicherry, 1936–48

476 Lucio Costa, Oscar Niemeyer and others (with Le Corbusier), Ministry of Education, Rio de Janeiro, 1936–45

476

477

framing views of the tropical landscaping designed
by Roberto Burle Marx in a style blending
biomorphic abstraction and indigenous varieties
of plants.

    The Brazilian modern architecture of the ensuing
two decades expanded this formal and metaphorical
repertoire. Oscar Niemeyer took over the principle
of the free plan and employed it with unparalleled
verve, even exploding the curves beyond the
building edge as dynamic ramps, cantilevered
canopies, convex and concave partitions. The
Brazilian Pavilion at the New York World's Fair of
1939 (designed by Niemeyer with Costa and Paul
Wiener) was a perforated box lifted up on *pilotis*,
with a curved approach ramp and fluid transitions
from one part to the next. Niemeyer's Casino at
Pampuhla of 1942–3 translated the idea of
sequential movement into a series of pirouettes
geared to the 'high life' function of the building.
While the exteriors were sedate and coated in
juparana stone and travertine, the interiors were
suave and luxurious, finished in tinted glass, satin,
and ceramic tile. The ramps and levels swirled
across the building towards the roulette wheels,
dance floor and bars. A slightly theatrical quality
was underlined by the manner in which curves were
used to differentiate the routes of gamblers from
those of staff. The Church at Pampuhla (1943), also

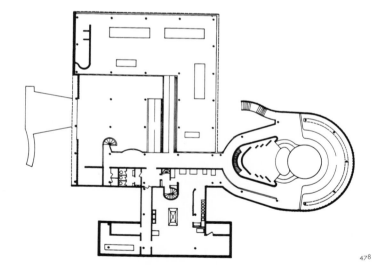

478

477 Oscar Niemeyer,
Pampulha Casino (now
Pampulha Museum of
Arts), Pampulha, Minas
Gerais, 1942–3

478 Pampulha Casino,
plan

479 Oscar Niemeyer,
Church of St Francis
of Assisi, Pampulha,
Minas Gerais, 1943,
axonometric drawing

480 Church of St Francis
of Assisi

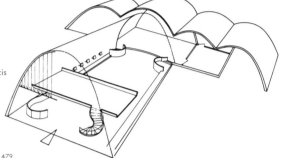

479

designed by Niemeyer, had thin, parabolic shell
vaults and brightly coloured mosaics. In a way
that echoed Le Corbusier's poetic reaction to the
Brazilian landscape and rivers seen from the air
('the law of the meander') Niemeyer declared his
passion for the serpentine and the organic:

Right angles created by man, hard and inflexible, do not attract me.
What draws my attention are free, sensual curves – curves which I
encounter in the mountains of my own country, in the sinuosity of
its rivers, in the clouds in the sky and the waves of the sea. The
whole universe is made of curves …

In Brazil, modern architecture was adopted by
the state to symbolize 'forward-looking' policies
of centralization and industrialization, and even
to reflect a long-standing preoccupation with
'universalizing' models of culture derived from the
European Enlightenment. Something analogous was
true of modern architecture in Mexico, although
its introduction needs to be understood against
the background of the revolution of 1910 and the
ensuing rejection of 'imposed' foreign cultural
models such as those of the French Belle Époque.
Mexico possessed an active avant-garde in the
other arts in the 1920s and 1930s, as epitomized by

480

the work of the 'muralist' painters. Diego Rivera in particular combined a Marxist vision of emancipation and harmony with nature with an evocation of supposed 'Golden Ages' before the arrival of colonialism. The gradual and almost unconscious absorption of deep-rooted continuities in the minds of ensuing generations of Mexican modern architects may be understood in the light of an 'inclusive' national mythology, binding together city and country, new and old, international and indigenous.

The father-figure of Mexican modern architecture was José Villagran Garcia, who was born in 1901, and whose outlook blended functionalism with an interest in modern abstract art and theories of perception. Villagran was a teacher as well as a practitioner and helped to form the outlook of the following generation, including figures like Mario Pani or Enrique del Moral who would come to prominence in the years after the Second World War (Chapter 27). Villagran's Institute of Hygiene at Popotla of 1925 was a straightforward utilitarian building, while his school designs of the 1930s made extensive use of standardized fabrication. Among his most brilliant pupils was Juan O'Gorman, whose studio for Diego Rivera of 1929–30 was modelled on Le Corbusier's Atelier Ozenfant of 1923 and on Russian Constructivist sources, yet possessed a crude vitality of its own with its almost exaggerated structural volumes, bold colours, industrial skylights and spiral concrete stairs.

While modern architecture was absorbed into the national programme of modernization in the 1930s, and so used as an instrument of social planning in the construction of clinics, housing and schools, it also had a role in the unlocking of new perceptions of vernacular and pre-Columbian traditions. Here one of the pivotal figures was Luis Barragán who was drawn more to the poetic and spiritual aspects of modernism than to the technical or functionalist ones. His earliest houses in his native Guadalahara, designed in the late 1920s, were based upon Andulucian and Moroccan sources, and were built around patios in a neo-colonial style. By degrees Barragán absorbed the lessons of modern architecture (especially from Le Corbusier and Mies van der Rohe), which enabled him to make a radical simplification of his vocabulary. His work in Mexico City, executed in the mid- to late 1930s, was frankly in the International Style, but he soon moved beyond this sparse, planar vocabulary towards an architecture of greater visual weight, texture and emotional presence, epitomized by his landscape designs at El Pedregal to the south of Mexico City, of the mid-1940s. Here Barragán created an architecture of abstract rectangular planes, volcanic-rock walls and sliding surfaces of water, which brought together a modern sense of space with a metamorphosis of such recurrent Mexican types as the outdoor room, the platform and the secret interior. Modern abstraction gave Barragán the means to distil personal memories and enter the past on several levels.

481 Juan O'Gorman, studio houses in San Angel, Mexico City, 1929–30: left, rear view of studio for Diego Rivera; right, studio for Frida Kahlo

482 Luis Barragán, El Pedregal landscape gardens, Mexico City, 1945–50

481

482

In contrast to the legend of a seamless, unified and inevitable 'International Style', the picture that emerges from the 1930s is one of dissemination in which newly invented paradigms possessing an aura of modernity and universality were simultaneously extended and criticized, and in which new uses and meanings were found for generating ideas and generic principles. While the new architecture encountered fierce opposition and rejection in some quarters, it was welcomed and adopted as an appropriate basis for cultural expression in others. The clichés of modernism were even absorbed here and there into the common usages of the urban vernacular. Although prototypical solutions to housing were given several regional interpretations in warm and cold climates, the grandiose Utopian plans for new cities remained on paper, and would have to wait for the emergence of post-colonial India or post-war Brazil to come to fruition. At the scale of the individual building or landscape, several works of high intensity were achieved which evoked half-veiled societal myths. One has only to think of the haunting forms and multilayered meanings of such buildings as Wright's Taliesin West, Le Corbusier's Pavillon Suisse, Aalto's Villa Mairea, Asplund's Woodland Crematorium or Mendelsohn's Mount Scopus Hospital to realize that the 1930s had its fair share of timeless works.

When the First World War broke out in 1914, the pioneering phase of modern architecture had belonged, principally, to several European and North American cities and industrial centres. In the tumult of the 1920s, modernism crystallized its basic forms, extended its functional and geographic range, and served a variety of social visions and ideological programmes for renewal on a wide political spectrum. Gradually the hold of earlier symbols and styles was loosened as the new forms took their place. In the 1930s, the expansion, extension and diversification continued, as connections were made with other traditions, recent and ancient, and as distant points were touched in Africa and Asia, Latin America and the Middle East. Despite the checks of political reaction and traditionalism, modern architecture established itself on wide-spaced foundations. In effect, this was a new tradition with several intellectual and territorial strands, which would continue to be developed and transformed in the post-war world.

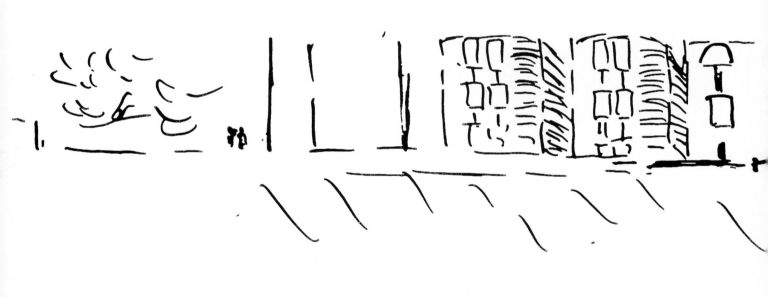

part 3

transformation
and
dissemination
after
1940

22

modern architecture in the u.s.a.: immigration and consolidation

In the 1920s one was forced to do away with nineteenth-century tendencies, when one had to begin again from scratch. Today the situation is completely different. We stand at the beginning of a new tradition. One need no longer destroy what the preceding generation accomplished, but one has to expand it...
Sigfried Giedion, 1955

483 Ludwig Mies van der Rohe, Lake Shore Drive Apartments, Chicago, 1948–51

Even now it is difficult to assess the full impact of the Second World War on architecture. Like the earlier world war, it destroyed a previous social and economic order, and to that extent eroded some of the impulses which had brought modern architecture into existence. It went some way to discredit technology with the avant-garde and so disrupted a key element in an earlier Utopia. It also brought with it a severe physical and cultural destruction, especially in Europe, the Soviet Union and Japan. Rebuilding was necessary, but optimism in architectural innovation had been severely undermined. Hasty construction for the largest number left little room for urban sensitivity. In some quarters existential probings led to a vein of primitivism or archaism requiring a new examination of the past. The intellectual climate varied considerably from country to country, but there was little to compare with the creative quest for a brave new world which had filled a certain vacuum after the First World War in Europe.

Despite radically altered circumstances, the 'new tradition' was not so easily defeated, though; all the masters of modern architecture were still alive, and so were many of their guiding ideas. There was no going back and pretending that the architectural revolution of the 1920s had not happened, no use pretending that another revolution of equal depth was likely to occur. The architect seeking forms in the late 1940s found himself in the position of an extender of tradition. Whatever new meanings might be sought, whatever functions might need handling, whatever regional traditions might need respecting, transformation could occur only on the basis of, or in reaction to, the earlier modern movement.

It has to be stressed that creative transformation was a necessity; simply to have repeated the solutions of the interwar period would have been to court the worst form of academicism. Unfortunately, this often happened, offering a classic case of 'symbolic devaluation' and of the misapplication of prototypes. One of the striking features of the years between the end of the war and about 1960 was a battle between factions intent on a tired international formula, and factions seeking a revitalization on the basis of a new post-war state of mind. Even the 'masters' themselves were faced with the problem of simultaneously extending their

earlier discoveries and seeking new solutions.

Another feature of the broad picture after the war was the international 'victory' of modern architecture. From Rio de Janeiro to Sydney, from Tokyo to Beirut, the inheritance of pre-war architecture began to pop up. In part the spread of images (many of them bastardized and stereotyped) was the result of the internationalization of trade, with the United States supplying many of the standard emblems of 'modernization'. But it also stemmed from the need of indigenous élites to break with earlier nineteenth-century colonial traditions, or else with earlier national or regional tendencies which they found too restrictive. In some countries – e.g. most of Western Europe, the USA, Japan among the 'industrialized' nations; Mexico and Brazil in the 'developing world' – post-war architecture could build on pre-war beginnings, though the contrast between countries which had industrialized gradually and those which had done so in a single generation was dramatic. In other parts of the world such as India or even Australia, modern

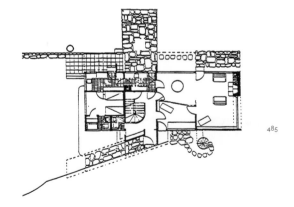

architecture had to begin virtually from scratch. When examining the international picture, it is crucial to understand at what stage of maturity, and with what depth of content, modern forms first entered a local scene; then to try and gauge how the foreign body was received, rejected, or made amenable to pre-existing cultural matter.

Some of the dramas of transmigration were already being played out in the 1930s, when architects as diverse as Aalto, Niemeyer, Sakakura, Barragán and Sert (to mention only a few) were concerned with finding forms attuned to local climates and ways of life. The work of the seminal figures in the 1930s (such as Wright and Le Corbusier) also reflected a new sensitivity to 'nature' and to locale. The emigration of some of the modern masters added another dimension to the process of change. Mies van der Rohe and Walter Gropius, for example, both arrived in the United States in 1937; Mendelsohn in 1941. They brought with them mature philosophies and vocabularies, and their arrival gave immense prestige to the International Modern movement in North America. However, they still entered a culture quite foreign to their original aims; they changed it, but it also changed them. Arguably, Mies van der Rohe survived the shock of the transatlantic crossing best.

Gropius left Germany in 1934, realizing that Nazism and modern architecture were irreconcilable, and spent three years in England before being invited by Joseph Hudnut, Dean of the Harvard Graduate School of Design, to direct the

Department of Architecture there. Soon after his arrival in Massachusetts in 1937, he built a house for himself and his wife in Lincoln, just beyond the Boston suburbs. The crisp white forms, wide openings and free plan marked this out as a foreign, Internationalist intrusion; however, there were some respectful regional touches, such as indigenous wooden framing and white-painted New England siding. It seems that Gropius may have sensed, in the stripped forms of the early Massachusetts vernacular, a concentration on essentials akin to his own. Marcel Breuer, Gropius's colleague from the Bauhaus, soon followed him to Boston, and he too built himself a house combining ideas derived from the collective housing experiments of the 1920s, with curious rustic intrusions such as a rubble wall of local stone. Compared with the taut, machine-age designs of a decade earlier, there was a considerable mellowness, which perhaps betokened a loss of polemical edge. The historian William Jordy has described this character well with the phrase 'the domestication of modern'. Both Breuer and Gropius had experienced the upheaval of the diaspora; some loss of intensity was probably inevitable; forms which had been created to deal with the social conditions of Weimar were bound to mean something different in the vicinity of Walden Pond.

As important as their individual buildings was their influence as teachers. At Harvard (a school with both national and international influence) an era of Beaux-Arts-inspired instruction came to an

486

end. The past, once the source of all wisdom, came to be regarded with suspicion. Suave manipulation of inherited elements of tradition was replaced by a nuts-and-bolts rationality, allied to more nebulous notions of a 'new architecture' supposedly in tune with the dictates of contemporary social and technological reality. An appealing progressivist sentiment was also implied (though the original ideological imperatives were never spelt out), and when the apologist and historian of modern architecture, Sigfried Giedion, presented the work of his European friends as the only true tradition of the modern epoch in his Charles Eliot Norton lectures at Harvard of 1938 (later published as the monumental *Space, Time and Architecture*), it seemed as if manifest destiny must have singled out Massachusetts.

Of course, there had been modern developments in the United States before this date, as we have seen. The buildings of Howe and Lescaze, Neutra and Schindler, the uncategorizable middle works of Wright, the experiments of Buckminster Fuller and Kocher and Frey, and Hitchcock and Johnson's book *The International Style* of 1932 had done something to change taste. But Gropius brought with him the full authority of one of the founding fathers, and into a region of the United States (the north-east) which had lacked major architectural innovations for over a generation. With the dousing of the modern movement in Europe in the 1930s, it seemed as if the liberal generosity of America was allowing a flame to keep burning which might otherwise have gone out. A new generation of young Americans, sickened by the weak eclecticism rife in America, flocked to Cambridge to hear the new gospel. Paul Rudolph, Edward L. Barnes, Ieoh Ming Pei, Philip Johnson, and Benjamin Thompson were among the first disciples.

In its American beginnings, the new architecture imported from Europe was primarily a suburban matter. But after the war came more general acceptance and larger commissions. In 1948, Gropius and his firm TAC (The Architects Collaborative) designed a new Graduate Center complex for Harvard University, comprising low dormitory blocks and a 'commons' building (with open-plan lounges and canteen) at an amplified scale. In the local context, the intrusion of the 'factory aesthetic', the flat roofs, strip windows and asymmetrical forms, was a symbolic event of some importance, since the same university had favoured neo-Georgian in its dormitory designs two decades earlier. In the same period Breuer designed Ferry House dormitory at Vassar College (1948–51), in a softer, less demanding modern mode, while Aalto's Baker House at Massachusetts Institute of Technology (1947–8, Fig. 564) already pointed the way beyond the rigidities of the International Style.

Gropius stressed teamwork and the necessity to seek a sort of anonymity arising, supposedly, from the logic of programme and structure and from a sense of 'objectivity' about modern conditions. In the wrong hands this quest for simplicity could very easily become mere banality; the rationality could all too easily degenerate into the wilderness of real-estate values and management science. To trace Gropius's American development from the hopeful beginnings (which even then lacked the force and conviction of his earlier works) to such designs of the mid-1960s as the Pan Am skyscraper in New York or the J. F. Kennedy building in Boston, is to see a loss of expressive power and to be made aware of a decline. Can this be accounted for in merely biographical terms, or is it perhaps symptomatic of a larger situation in the post-war period when the 'alternative' vision of modern architecture was gradually absorbed by the institutions of consumer capitalism? The 'victory' of modern forms certainly brought with it the onus of representing the establishment; and once the devalued International Style became a tired orthodoxy, another rejection and re-evaluation became necessary.

In America the process was already under way by the late 1950s, with divergent results. On the one hand there were those 'Expressionists' who, like Eero Saarinen, sought 'to extend the ABC' of modern architecture into curvaceous, occasionally powerful, sometimes delectable, but all too often mannered realms of expression. Then again, there were reversions to historicism; the Beaux-Arts was never far beneath the surface, and a bland neo-classicism was pursued by Philip Johnson, Edward Durell Stone, Wallace Harrison and Max Abramovitz, perhaps because the monumental tasks handed to these architects seemed to require a greater degree of rhetoric and reference than the spindly forms of Gropian modernism allowed. Or

487

again, there were forceful new integrations, like
those of Louis I. Kahn, who achieved a synthesis
of the modern and the ancient.

The historiography of American architecture
has tended to reflect a Yankee bias, as if the only
worthwhile cultural forms were those which moved
from the north-eastern seaboard towards the west.
Giedion unwittingly played into this tradition when
he overstressed the importance of Gropius's earliest
American works in and around Boston, even though
in reality these were evidence of decline. During the
1940s and 1950s in the United States there were, of
course, several vital strands of modern architecture
each with its own momentum. Aside from Wright's
extraordinarily far-ranging production and
influence in this period at home (on certain 'organic'
architects such as Bruce Gough) and abroad (on
figures as diverse as Jørn Utzon and Carlo Scarpa),
there were the later works of Schindler and
Neutra on the West Coast, and various pockets of

'Regionalism' such as the Bay Region School around
San Francisco (for example, the work of William
Wurster). Schindler tended towards an ever more
complex manner, delighting in the oddities of
hillside sites, eccentric clients and unusual building
materials such as corrugated plastic sheeting, which
he used in combination with exposed timber. In
contrast to this 'shed aesthetic', Neutra became even
more involved with an architecture of precise steel,
plate glass, transparency and illumination. His
vision of a 'health house' – a mechanism serving
mind and body, and linking the individual in a
sensual way to the rhythms of nature – was perhaps
most clearly expressed in the Desert House at
Palm Springs of 1946, which opened out across
a rectangular pool to the surrounding desert
landscape of cacti, crags and palms. Here the
minimalist, hovering planes of the International
Style were given a distinct expression in response to
climate and topography.

488

489

In the Midwest, the Finnish-born Eliel Saarinen and his son Eero were responsible for some of the most alluring work of this period. Eliel's American career was founded upon his Cranbrook School in Bloomfield Hills, Michigan, of 1924–30, and consolidated in buildings such as the Tabernacle Church in Columbus, Indiana, of 1939–42, which combined a lingering Scandinavian feeling for brick craftsmanship with a 'cool rationality'. Eero established his own reputation by winning the competition for the Jefferson National Expansion Memorial in St Louis, Missouri, in 1947 with a monumental sculptural statement: a parabolic arch 631 feet (192 metres) high straddling an east-west axis and rising above the western bank of the Mississippi. This was an idea conceived on a transcontinental scale which might very well have been a cliché. But the finished object possessed extraordinary visual force and tension, enhanced by the impeccable control of profiles and overall proportions, and by the polished stainless-steel surfaces reacting to light, shadow and weather. At times it was a dark silhouette, at times a mercurial arc, and even the steel surfaces buckled and shimmered slightly in changing temperatures. Aside from the distant reference to the idea of a triumphal arch, Saarinen's monument evoked the local aviation technology and suggested a metaphor for the bridge between East and West.

The 1950s in the United States was a period of unparalleled prosperity and relative optimism, in which scientific and technological ingenuity allowed an increasing sophistication in the construction, servicing and detailing of buildings. Among the seminal works in this respect was the General Motors' Technical Center in Warren, Michigan, begun in 1948 by Eliel Saarinen and carried on by his son Eero after the father's death in 1950. Here, the abstract, mechanical processes of American management and industry were translated into a vocabulary combining reductivist volumes and a neutral, yet poetic handling of standardized steel and glass components. The spirit was Miesian, but the aesthetic had long American roots in the frame vernacular, and the style was distinctly Eero Saarinen's own. Among the most memorable of the individual buildings was the Dynameter Building where engines were tested. Saarinen grouped cylindrical stacks in front of the planar curtain wall as a species of functional colonnade. In his later buildings such as the Kresge Auditorium and the Multidenominational Chapel at the Massachusetts Institute of Technology (from the mid-1950s) or the TWA Terminal at Idlewild (now J. F. Kennedy) Airport of 1956–62, Saarinen moved towards an increasingly personal, not to say wilful, expression, sometimes using shell vaults as the basis of fantastic curvatures.

The picture of dissemination in the America of the 1950s cannot be understood at all without reference to the late works of Mies van der Rohe and Frank Lloyd Wright. Mies van der Rohe appears to have had fewer problems of adjustment in the diaspora than did Gropius. Indeed, his arrival in Chicago, the home of the steel frame, seems to have been engineered by fate. Like Gropius, he owed one of his earliest commissions to university patronage; from 1939 to 1956 he redesigned the campus of the Armour Institute, renamed the Illinois Institute of Technology. The idea shows most clearly in the model. The main functions were grouped in rectangular steel-framed boxes on a podium, in a composition combining neo-classical axiality with the asymmetrical planning ideas of the 1920s. It was as if a sort of industrialized

abstraction had strayed from some foreign land into the grid of the surrounding south side of Chicago. The lower buildings in the hierarchy were like elegant factories, and may well have been partially inspired by Albert Kahn's steel-frame factory designs or, perhaps, by Berlin industrial structures of the 1920s such as Mendelsohn's Boiler House for the Rudolf Mosse Building of 1928. With their brick-panel infills, their tight steel detailing, their sober proportions, and their air of straightforward 'factuality', they were a unique blend of Mies van der Rohe's stern intellectual quest for impersonality and of high-quality American steel craftsmanship. The local fire codes required that steel be coated in a layer of fireproofing, so that in order to express the structure 'honestly', the architect had to adopt the artifice of an extra veneer of steel around the fireproof casing. At the corners of the buildings this led to a curious detail in which the recessed core of steel was hinted at in a cut-away involving a steel veneer over concrete fireproofing, itself overlying the actual structure within the wall. This was variously praised for its 'structural clarity' and its supposed Mondrianesque, metaphysical implications – as if such a corner implied 'lines running on to infinity'.

490

491

492

At the head of the campus was Crown Hall (1950–6), destined to become the architecture building. Once again the image of the factory was dominant – the idea for this vast, uninterrupted 'universal' space seems traceable directly to Albert Kahn's Bomber Assembly Plant of 1939, which also employed a dramatic truss system. The 'glass box' seemed to imply a generalized view of human function: a space good for everything, in which there was little response to individual incident or to a sense of place. However, the neo-classical qualities of Mies van der Rohe's design were also crucial; these were schematic and relied on an interpretation of such essentials as symmetry, proportion, the clear expression of load and support, and a certain honorific mood. Crown Hall was approached up a grand flight of steps and was detailed with all the

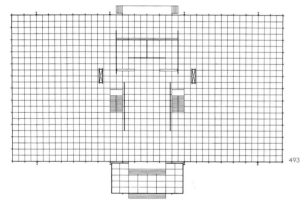

493

492 Ludwig Mies van
der Rohe, Crown Hall,
Illinois Institute of
Technology, Chicago,
1950–6

493 Crown Hall, plan

494 Ludwig Mies van
der Rohe, Farnsworth
House, Plano, Illinois,
1945–51

495 Philip Johnson,
Glass House, New
Canaan, Connecticut,
1949–50

care and clarity that Schinkel might have mustered in similar circumstances. The primary structure was a series of bridge-like trusses from which the roof plane was, in effect, suspended. The secondary articulation was provided by slender I-shaped girders attached to the outside of the horizontal steel bands of the main box. This detail, combined with the floating horizontals of the podium and steps, lent a weightless feeling to the whole. In reducing a building to its essence, Mies believed it possible to transform naked construction into the most basic underlying form. This is surely what was implied by his well-known statement, 'less is more'. Such a simplicity was the result of a prodigious abstraction, and indeed a highly idealistic view of architecture's spiritual mission. One is only too aware how easily less could become *less* rather than more, in the hands of Mies's followers. In much the same way Mondrian's followers managed to reduce his sublime abstractions to mere checkerboard or tablecloth patterns.

In the Farnsworth House of 1945–51, Mies van der Rohe indicated how a similar idea could be applied to the domestic pavilion in a natural setting. Here the crystalline steel box was again merged with a classical ideal. In overall form and detail what Wright had called architecture's 'lowest elements' were distilled into a mechanistic, hovering version of plinth, support and architrave. But the composition also made the house and its deck 'slide' past each

other in a way which recalled the abstract painting of the 1920s. This design, for all its idiosyncrasy and impracticalities, fathered a host of imitations around the world, the most notable being, probably, Philip Johnson's erudite Glass House at New Canaan of 1949–50. The 'machine in the garden' had been an image of some insistent meaning in American culture since the early nineteenth century, and here it was restated. Johnson claimed a multiplicity of 'sources' for his design, from Mies van der Rohe, to Schinkel, to Palladio, to the brick-stack/ wooden-frame constructions of the earliest settlers. However one assesses the references, the fact remains that a Miesian aesthetic was here being transformed into a chic and rather static evocation of high living different in tone from the originals. The historian Colin Rowe attempted to express such a shift in meaning in American modern architecture when he later wrote:

The revolutionary theme was never a very prominent component of American speculation about building. European modern architecture, even when it operated within the cracks and crannies of the capitalist system, existed within an ultimately Socialist ambiance; American modern architecture did not. And it was thus, and either by inadvertence or design, that when in the 1930s, European architecture came to infiltrate the United States, it was introduced simply as a new approach to building – and not much more. That is: it was introduced, largely purged of its ideological or societal content; and it became available not as an evident manifestation (or cause) of Socialism in some form or other, but rather as a 'décor de la vie' for Greenwich, Connecticut, or as a suitable veneer for the corporate activities of 'enlightened capitalism'.

494

495

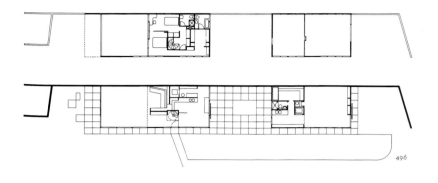

496

497

498

499

However, the steel and glass box could have
other domestic applications than Johnson's
quasi-classical one, especially when broken open,
irregularized, or cross-bred with more sprawling
domestic plan types. Charles Eames's own house
in California of 1945–9 was, in a sense, the obverse
of Mies van der Rohe's Platonism – the building
was assembled from standard parts and composed
with a sensitive irregularity which reflected an
interest in Japanese wooden-frame traditions.
The Eames 'shed' was subtly placed alongside a
row of eucalyptus trees which filtered the light into
an interior where judiciously selected objects were
as much part of the architecture as the building
itself. The aesthetic effect arose from the careful
juxtaposition of 'ready-made' structural elements
such as webbed trusses, from reflections and
transparencies, and from an understatement which
aspired towards ordinariness; while the Eames
design achieved a poetry of form, it did so by means
that were at variance with the absolutism of Mies.

In the same period in California, the Case Study
Program houses by Craig Ellwood, Raphael Soriano,
Pierre Koenig, Ralph Rapson and others showed
how standardization could be applied to the
problem of the individual family home. Initially
encouraged by John Entenza, editor of *Arts and
Architecture* magazine, the Case Study experiment
began in 1945 as an attempt at formulating low-cost,
steel-frame prototypes for houses responsive to

immediate post-war social conditions and to the
landscape of southern California. The minimal
skeleton was used to 'frame' and intensify
suburban existence, and (in combination with
trellis, screen and deck) to make delicate pavilions
poised in the trees, with fine views of city and
nature. Interiors were usually open, efficient and
transparent, catering to a casual way of life, and to
an independence allowed by the automobile. While
the designers of the Case Study houses pretended
to have no interest in style, their vocabulary of thin
wall, slender pier and interlocking beam was a
simplified, linear version of the interlocking volumes
of Neutra, Schindler and Wright. There were even
longer-distant memories of the extending verandas
and Orientalist timber-work of Greene and Greene.
Here perhaps was a case of certain underlying
spatial patterns of regional adaptation being
transformed generation by generation; with the
Case Study houses they were again reinterpreted,
but in a terminology reliant upon the planar
abstraction of the mid-twentieth century.

The steel frame with glass infill or with glazed
curtain wall seems to have had the status of a
leitmotif in the United States in the first decade after
the war. But it was capable of supporting a wide
range of functions, philosophies, architectural ideas
and individual forms. The Equitable Life Assurance
Building in Portland, Oregon of 1944–7 by Pietro
Belluschi took the rectangular order implicit in the
frame and explored its relevance to the American
office building. It was a slender, twelve-storey slab
of lustrous green glass, reflective aluminium and
smooth marble. The resulting surface was sensitive
to local light and weather conditions, maintaining
its sheen under overcast skies, and darkening
towards a deep, forest green in the bright sunlight
of the summer. The curtain wall was, in fact, double-
layered, and the entire building was air-conditioned,
glare being excluded by the glass itself, which was
similar to that used in windscreens of American
cars. The Equitable Building derived part of its
elegance and visual tension from slight variations
on a standardized module. The lower storey was
amplified to supply a base; the crowning horizontal
was increased in height to mark the termination;
the corners were emphasized to stress the edges.
Within the framework there were secondary
rhythms deriving from window mullions and the

illusion of recessions of coloured planes on a flat field. Belluschi's celebration of high technology may possibly be related to the presence of the aircraft industry in the region, while the idea of a 'weightless' volume made up of hovering, semi-transparent planes recalls Mies's unbuilt glazed projects from the late 1920s (e.g. the Adam Building of 1928). Equally, the Equitable Building fitted an American lineage stretching back to the PSFS Building of 1926–32 by Howe and Lescaze, to the remarkable double-glazed curtain wall of Willis Jefferson Polk's Hallidie Building in San Francisco of 1918, and ultimately to the geometrical simplifications of the Chicago School (e.g. Jenney's Second Leiter Building of 1889–90). To construct a pedigree in this way is in no sense to diminish the distinction and originality of Belluschi's solution. It is rather to acknowledge that the gradual elaboration of the possibilities inherent in a type may take several generations to work out, and that individual inventions may rest upon a transformation of earlier discoveries. In this case,

the inherited schemata were distilled and purified to a minimal grid of light traced in the Oregon air.

Mies van der Rohe's contributions to the art and craft of the tall building are sometimes discussed as if he had managed to invent the steel-framed skyscraper on his own. In fact, he collaborated with an American construction vernacular, out of which he was able to extract poetic statement. With the twin towers of apartments at 860 and 880 Lake Shore Drive, Chicago, of 1948–51, the theme of the rectangular prism on stilts was stated with unparalleled clarity. These stood on a triangular lot with views across Lake Michigan, rose to 26 storeys, and were the same in plan and size, but disposed on adjacent sites so that the oblong forms faced different ways and were perceived in constant tension; the towers were linked at the lower levels by hovering steel overhangs, and the transparent lobbies with fine views of the Lake were finished in polished steel and marble. Elevators rose through the centre of each block and gave access to luxury apartments situated around the edges.

The uniformity of interior plans was expressed in a repeated bay system on the façades. However, there were minute variations in the dimensions of the window bays at the end of each horizontal row of four, where the vertical structural posts passed up the façade. These resulted in an increase of vertical stress visually, and in an illusionistic sense of depth and movement. Further visual subtleties were introduced by the slender I-beams attached at regular intervals. These had little practical structural function, but what might be called a mainly 'visual-structural' role: they emphasized the verticality of the building and preserved a uniform rhythm and texture over what were in fact a variety of interior structural realities. The main structural posts were once again clad in concrete fireproofing which was then in turn wrapped in steel; and where the façades came together at the corner, adjacent I-beams conspired to produce a sharp visual emphasis on the theme of two attached planes linked to an underlying armature. The 'Rationalist puritan' might be upset by the extent of these 'artificialities', but they were employed precisely to heighten one's awareness of the inner nature of the frame.

But the I-beams attached to the trabeated rectangular skeleton seemed to have more meaning than that. These exquisitely rolled industrial

500

501

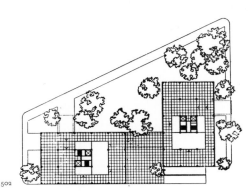

502

elements, smooth blue-black against the glint of glass and the silver chrome, were themselves celebrated as objects of machine production. At the same time they gave emphasis to visual lines of force, to the dominant geometrical order and driving idea. Writing in the 1950s, Colin Rowe suggested that the structural frame 'established relationships, defined a discipline, and generated form …' and that it had come to 'possess a value for contemporary architecture equivalent to that of the column for classical antiquity and the Renaissance'. For the I-beams of Mies it might be more precise to speak of pilasters or even of Gothic fluting. Whatever the historical analogies, they were what they were: commonplace steel beams. They called to mind Oud's suggestion made thirty years earlier that the new architecture should lead to the experience of 'higher things' through a ruthless objectivity. Mies himself tried to express a similar thought when he stated: 'I believe that architecture has little or nothing to do with the invention of interesting forms or with personal inclinations. True architecture is always objective and is the expression of the inner structure of our time from which it springs.'

There can be little doubt that Mies van der Rohe was stimulated in his search for simplicity by the more transparent frame buildings of the early Chicago School and by the romanticization of American garage and factory structures which had been so prevalent among the European avant-garde in the 1920s. It was a position in which the 'true' products of American culture were seen to be the anonymous vernacular creations, while the self-conscious, and usually eclectic, creations of 'artist architects' were rejected as an aberration. Such transatlantic myths played a central role in determining the appearance of some of the European entries to the *Chicago Tribune* competition (Chapter 13). Mies van der Rohe's arrival in Chicago in the late 1930s, his later commissions in the city and his enormous influence ensured that a version of the 1920s European avant-garde dream of the crystal tower became a reality in the America of the 1950s – admittedly with a change in meaning. His architecture caught a post-war American mood and even had loose affiliations with the spiritualized abstractions of American painters such as Ellsworth Kelly. But Mies's glass-slab prototypes also became parents of a worldwide

503

503 Ludwig Mies van
der Rohe, Seagram
Building, New York,
1954–8

504 Skidmore, Owings
and Merrill, designer
Gordon Bunshaft, Lever
House, New York, 1951–2

progeny. His imagery conjured up efficiency, cleanliness, organization and standardization, and so fitted the bill for big-business America. However, the crudely handled imitations were in the majority, and these reproduced many of the limitations and few of the qualities of the originals.

The Seagram Building on Park Avenue in New York, designed by Mies and Philip Johnson between 1954 and 1958, must be counted one of the seminal works of the post-war period in defining an image for the prestige office building. The skyscraper here achieved a grand and honorific character, sober and symmetrical, with elegant materials such as rust-coloured bronze, amber-grey glass, travertine and polished green marble. The attached I-beams gave the façades density and opacity, while also enhancing the vertical lines of the whole. It was another variation on the core and envelope theme, and this idea was pursued rigorously in the fabric and details: for example, in the way that the adjacent façade planes were brought together on the corner piers. Just as Sullivan, over half a century earlier, had adjusted appearance to express an *idea* of structure, so Mies 'lied in order to tell the truth' about the steel frame; in this case the rectangular aesthetic of the curtain wall disguised diagonal wind-bracing within. The Seagram Building stood opposite McKim, Mead and White's palatial Racquets Club of 1918, but an affinity could be sensed between old and new in terms of nobility and classical restraint. One approached along a main axis between symmetrical rectangular pools flanked by ledges of marble. The travertine plinth on which the building stood introduced a moment of calm in the busy street life of New York and recalled the platform of the Barcelona Pavilion. Even though Seagram was a commercial headquarters, the stance was monumental. A portico was implied by the overhanging slab, and this then guided the visitor to the main lobby, a somewhat tight space preceding the lifts. Details of the interior design were carefully considered in relation to the whole; and, as at Lake Shore Drive, attached vertical mullions had a variety of visual and symbolic attributes. The Seagram Building contributed some of the terms of American corporate style in the 1950s, but it also recalled ideas stemming from the Deutscher Werkbund of half a century before, especially the notion that standardized industrial technique should

be elevated to the level of ideal form. Mies van der Rohe seemed able to make of the repetitious and abstract qualities of modern urban existence a sort of sublime order, but the imitators reduced this to technical uniformity, ending up (to paraphrase Muthesius) with 'a merely brutish world'. The result was the slickness and alienation of the glass-box 'downtown', a phenomenon which was reproduced world-wide in the 1960s and 1970s.

Not that Mies van der Rohe's prototypes were entirely blameless. For all its sensitivity to its site, the Seagram Building offered a limited urban language and took the theme of repetition close to its limits: bigger buildings would require an intermediary formal hierarchy which they were rarely given. The Farnsworth House was impractical in the extremes of the Midwestern climate, and Lake Shore Drive derived part of its clarity from the architect's insistence that all tenants use the same outer curtain material. Arguably too, Mies's forms were more likely to be workable with wealthy clients. The stilts, slabs, uniform windows and rectilinear geometries could only too easily be reduced to a drab formula when money, proportion and controllable urban space were lacking. For all the arresting beauty of

504

his individual buildings, Mies would later be criticized for excluding too much of the mess of life and for putting constraints upon the possibilities of architectural representation (Chapter 30).

Between the sublimities of Mies van der Rohe and the emptiness of the mere glass box there were, of course, gradations of quality. In particular one thinks of the school of architects best represented by firms like Skidmore, Owings and Merrill (SOM), whose Lever House of 1951–2 (for which Gordon Bunshaft was chief designer) stands almost opposite the Seagram Building on Park Avenue in Manhattan. By contrast it was weightless, almost planar, in appearance. Perhaps following some of the hints of the PSFS Building twenty years earlier, the Lever Building employed a podium for its mezzanine offices, which created a courtyard at ground level, and a roof terrace on top. The main slab then rose clear as a hovering volume clad in a network of chrome lines and blue and green tinted glass. The machine rooms containing the air-conditioning plant at the top were expressed by a variation in pattern, while the presence of the individual floor slabs was hinted at through the horizontal banding. An effect of weightlessness and dematerialization was achieved by recessing the main vertical supports within the skin, by reducing mullions to the thinnest of lines, and through the use of polished, shimmering surfaces and semi-reflecting glass. Of course, such a sealed-box solution relied totally on air conditioning and mechanical ventilation for its environmental quality. Modifications of the slab, using sunshades, balconies and other natural climatic devices, would emerge later on the American skyline. For the moment, Lever, Seagram, and such buildings as Belluschi's Equitable Building and Eero Saarinen's 'horizontal skyscrapers' for the General Motors Technical Center set the pattern for forward-looking commercial architecture in North America. And, as happens when a stylistic norm is briefly dominant, efforts could concentrate upon variations and refinements. In their solution for the Inland Steel Building in Chicago of 1955 (for example) SOM shifted the core and the vertical structure outside the slab, expressing the latter as a row of glinting stainless-steel columns which effectively advertised the company product.

The glazed skyscraper could also be employed in

505

non-commercial contexts too. In the United Nations complex by Wallace Harrison and Max Abramovitz of 1947–50, the Secretariat was housed in a semi-transparent slab overlooking the East River and providing the dominant image of the scheme. The end walls were clad in stone, the side ones in lustrous green glass held in place by a textured network of mullions. The compositional effect of the ensemble arose from the way the main elements (glazed tower, curved Assembly, oblong Members' Lounge etc.) were disposed as sculptural objects on a platform, with walkways, a small park and other public facilities interwoven. Lewis Mumford doubted the appropriateness of a slab to the symbolic aspirations of the new post-war congress of nations, until he reflected that perhaps the bureaucracy would be the most notable feature of the organization. If the United Nations complex had been carried out as originally intended, however, a poetry and power appropriate to the idealism of the institution might have been achieved. For there can be little doubt that Harrison and Abramovitz adapted their building from an original idea by Le Corbusier (enshrined in a wooden model and some notebook sketches) known as 'Project 23A' (1947). It was not the first time that this architect had set his mind to the design of a world parliament, as we have seen in his League of Nations proposal of 1927 (Fig. 321), and it is notable that an analogous distinction was made between the honorific Assembly and the less intense, standardized offices of the Secretariat.

The idea of putting the Secretariat in a tower may have owed something to Hannes Meyer's proposal for the League of Nations of 1927 (Fig. 320), and probably reflected Le Corbusier's experience of

506

working with Niemeyer, Costa and others on the Ministry of Education in Rio de Janeiro of 1936. It also served to demonstrate to Americans the 'true' urban function of the skyscraper – the liberation of the city for light, space and greenery – by realizing a fragment of the Ville Radieuse on the edge of Manhattan. Evidently Le Corbusier intended to follow the lead of his Algiers tower of 1938–42 and to integrate *brises-soleil* with the UN façades. These constituted a major modification of the glass-box formula, adding new possibilities for monumental articulation and sculptural expression. Le Corbusier proposed to regulate the dimensions of the building with yet another recent invention, his proportional system – the 'Modulor', which drew together the Golden Section, a six-foot human figure, and harmonic proportions in an elaborate Corbusian theorem supposedly reconciling mechanization and 'natural order'. When one bears in mind that the architect also envisaged a Museum of World Culture in the form of a spiral ziggurat alongside the United Nations, one realizes the extent to which this project excited his universal aspirations. But this is to discuss a proposal which was never built or of which only a shadow was constructed; Le Corbusier's advice was accepted freely, but he did not receive the commission and returned to Europe empty-handed and embittered. The present building is a diluted concept in search of appropriate articulation and details; the lobbies with their curvaceous cantilevers, and their abstract-art adornments, speak more of the clichés of the 'international hotel style' of the 1950s than they do of dignified places of assembly. To grasp how Le Corbusier would handle civic monumentality, one has to turn to his Capitol in Chandigarh (Chapter 23).

The late works of Frank Lloyd Wright reveal both an endless capacity for invention and an uneven level of realization. When the Second World War came to an end, he was nearly eighty, but he still had a decade and a half of experimentation to go before his death in 1959. Despite Wright's haughty disdain for 'mobocracy' he could not remain entirely aloof from mass values. Suburban America took over the image of the Usonian house and turned it into a popular cliché of overhanging roofs, extending decks and eat-in kitchens. Wright's own production could descend to the science-fiction

Orientalist kitsch of the projects for Baghdad (1957) or could rise to the desert magic of some of his houses in Arizona from the 1950s. At his best he was capable of realizing gems like the V. C. Morris Gift Shop in San Francisco (1948–9). But whatever the occasion, Wright demonstrated that he was not spent, that he could come up with fresh spatial ideas, and that he could elaborate these with geometrical schemes of great formal and metaphorical richness.

One cannot do justice to Wright's wide range, but it is possible to suggest how lifelong themes were reactivated and recombined in individual buildings. The Price Tower in Bartlesville, Oklahoma, of 1952–6, for example, at last afforded him the chance to construct a habitable skyscraper, and drew upon ideas from the Johnson Wax Laboratory Tower of 1943–5 and the unbuilt St Mark's-in-the-Bouwerie Tower project of 1927–31. Wright's concept of a skyscraper involved the complete rejection of the box/frame/grid idea in favour of a core with extending cantilevered trays which allowed some double-height spaces with

507

507 Frank Lloyd Wright, Price Tower, Bartlesville, Oklahoma, 1952–6

508 Price Tower, section

mezzanines. The essential analogy was that of the tree; the central idea, an organism rather than a mechanism. The Price Tower combined apartments and offices and was on a radiating plan. The stratified section and complex geometry of the plan were expressed directly on the outside as diagonal, interlocking trays. The façades were covered in slender copper slats which kept out the direct rays of the sun and weathered to an iridescent green. The Price Tower acted as a beacon for miles around, and allowed views in all directions. Seen from a distance over the flat landscape, it recalled some of Wright's drawings of Broadacre City. While it offered an alternative to the glass box, its idiosyncrasies did not immediately recommend it as a general prototype, though some of its lessons were developed by others.

The design which occupied Wright most in the 1940s and 1950s was the Guggenheim Museum in New York. This was to stand on a site opposite Central Park in Manhattan and was to house an extensive collection of non-objective art. Wright's initial reaction was to suggest a 'center for the arts',

including attached studios, but by degrees he reverted to a more conventional programme, though by no means a conventional solution. The building as it stands is organized around an expanding spiral ramp which rises through a central volume in ever wider bands. Ancillary volumes containing offices and the director's apartment are fashioned in the same smooth, curved layers, and from the outside the building is a complete contrast with the grid of the city. One passes through a low zone of transition (which loosely recalls the Johnson Wax entry) and comes into a stunning space with light streaming in from the top. Wright himself declared something of his intention:

Here for the first time architecture appears plastic, one floor flowing into another (more like sculpture) instead of the usual superimposition of stratified layers cutting and butting into each other by way of post and beam construction.

The whole building, cast in concrete, is more like an eggshell – in form a great simplicity … The light concrete flesh is rendered strong enough everywhere to do its work by embedded filaments of steel either separate or in mesh. The structural calculations are thus those of the cantilever and continuity rather than the post and beam. The net result of such construction is a greater repose, the atmosphere of the quiet unbroken wave; no meeting of the eye with abrupt changes of form.

The Guggenheim Museum drew together several of Wright's preoccupations. The inward-looking atrium was a circular descendant of Johnson Wax and Larkin, while the cantilevered horizontal layers were variants of a pervasive stratification. Circular forms had also occurred earlier in Wright's work – initially in the mural for the Coonley House playroom of 1912 where they emerged as mysterious floating coloured discs, not unlike Kandinsky's nearly contemporary abstract paintings. As for the spiral, this was a visual metaphor for growth and change in nature and was the generating idea in several projects (e.g. the Sugar Loaf Mountain project of 1925, in which a spiral traffic-ramp was envisaged encircling a domical Planetarium, or the Morris Gift Shop in San Francisco, a petite showroom for jewellery where an interior spiralling ramp was used to exhibit precious objects on display). But a building is more than the sum of an architect's earlier motifs and bears the imprint of new intentions. With the Guggenheim Wright hoped to design a 'total work of art' in harmony with 'non-objective' painting and sculpture. He declared:

508

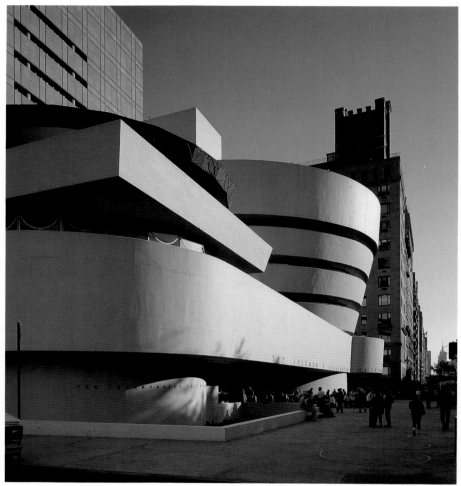

509

The building was intended by Solomon R. Guggenheim to make a
suitable place for the exhibition of an advanced form of painting
wherein line, color and form are a language in themselves …
independent of reproduction of objects animate or inanimate, thus
placing painting in a realm hitherto enjoyed by music alone.

This advanced painting has seldom been presented in other
than the incongruous rooms of old static architecture. Here in the
harmonious fluid quiet created by this building interior the
new painting will be seen for itself under favorable conditions.

Despite these lofty spatial ambitions, there was some
wishful thinking in this assessment, since the
outward-sloping walls, the 'lobster bisque' colours,
and the lighting system were found to be at odds
with what some considered to be the basic need of
neutral vertical surfaces for looking at paintings; the

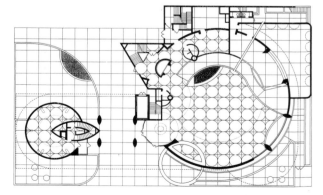

510

sloping floor was not ideal either. Wright evidently thought of architecture as the mother art, and of furniture, paintings, and sculptures almost as internal ornament. None the less, the Guggenheim constituted a full demonstration of his ideal of an 'organic' architecture, in which form, structure and space were fused. Space, of course, had been central to his vision from the beginning, as the defining feature of architecture itself, and as a means for touching the mind and ennobling human action. Years before, he had written of the Unity Temple in terms which could refer equally well to the Guggenheim Museum: 'You will find the sense of the great room coming through – space not walled in now but more or less free to appear … the new reality, that is *space* instead of matter.'

Thus the Guggenheim Museum was an apotheosis of Wright's organic philosophy, in which plan, section, and elevation ideas of his earlier experimentation were brought together in a cogent, three-dimensional weave of form, space and abstraction. It was the old theme of the vase as an image of spiritual containment which had so intrigued the architect in the 1920s, but restated at an institutional scale. In this connection, Wright liked to cite the ancient Chinese sage Lao Tze who 'first declared that the reality of the building consisted not in the four walls and the roof … but in the space within'. Perhaps only a spiral in concrete could have embodied his full range of intentions, for this form combined centrality and procession, equilibrium and movement, and an inherent sense of growth and aspiration. The

511

building was an 'organism' of a kind; an antidote perhaps to the brutality and gridded uniformity of the American industrial city. Even so, the Guggenheim lacked the force of many of Wright's earlier works. The painted concrete surfaces were curiously lifeless, as if an idea had failed to find its proper material expression and texture. The mannered fussiness of certain of the joints and ornaments anticipated the flimsy arches and weak profiles of the later Marin County Court House (1957–62), completed after the architect's death in 1959. Wright's immediate followers tended to reproduce this formalism and to copy the surface effects of his style, but without much grasp of the generating principles, and there was little immediate impact on American architecture as a whole. Seen in a longer perspective though, his contribution was obviously vast, and altered the ground rules of architecture itself. Wright influenced several generations worldwide during his own lifetime, and even now the full implications of his discoveries have hardly been be explored.

The decade and a half between the end of the Second World War and the outset of the 1960s was a propitious time for the development of modern architecture in the United States. Economic, cultural and institutional energies were channelled through patronage into several individual works of a high order, although the fate of the capitalist city, its internal contradictions and its lack of coherence were scarcely addressed. Some of the most effective buildings of the period were characterized by an equilibrium between individual intentions and technical norms, between fresh interpretations and inherited types, between imported images and native realities. The 'masters' attempted to bring to fruition ideas which had been with them since pre-war years. This is scarcely surprising, since the late works of any artist of calibre are liable to show a balance of both retrospection and innovation. Gropius's work revealed a gradual loss of impulse, and Wright's sometimes erred towards the idiosyncratic, while Mies van der Rohe's achieved moments of high intensity, but had the mixed blessing of acceptance in the general currency of the commercial world. The 'Modern Project' achieved something of a popular victory on American soil, but in the process lost something of its soul.

23

form
and
meaning
in the
late
works
of
le corbusier

The principle which
gives support to a work
of art is not necessarily
contemporary with it.
It is quite capable of
slipping back into the
past or forward into
the future ... The
artist inhabits a time
which is by no means
necessarily the history
of his own time.
Henri Focillon, 1939

512 Le Corbusier,
Chapel of Notre-Dame-
du-Haut, Ronchamp,
1950–4, detail of rain
spout and water splash

Between 1945 and his death in 1965, Le Corbusier
produced a series of elusive masterpieces, each of
them characterized by a complex interweaving of
old themes and new means of expression, by a sense
of primitivism, and by a deliberate cultivation of
ancient associations. There was none of the loss of
nerve manifest in the late works of Gropius, nor the
mannerist exaggeration which seemed to afflict
Wright, nor the technological perfectionism of
Mies van der Rohe. Like the ageing Michelangelo,
Le Corbusier entered an increasingly private and
mystical world of poetry in his last years. But any
tendency to expressionistic wilfulness was held
in check by a strong intellectual discipline and
a refinement of earlier type-forms and themes.
The introduction of new devices like *béton brut*
(bare concrete), the Modulor (p. 412) or complex
curved 'acoustic' forms, should not blind one to the
elaboration of earlier principles, such as the Five
Points of a New Architecture, the collective slab on
pilotis, or the *brise-soleil* (sun breaker). This was an
architect who, like Picasso, worked and reworked
basic ideas. Part of the richness of Le Corbusier's
late works lies, precisely, in the tension between
well-worn formulations and new patterns of form
and meaning.

There were already hints of Le Corbusier's later
direction in some of his designs of the 1930s, such as
the Petite Maison de Weekend. In these the brittle
and pristine world of Purism had been broken open
to reveal something more archaic, deliberately
crude, and rooted in the organic. The mechanical
slaughter of the Second World War may have gone
further to disrupt Le Corbusier's confidence in the
machine and its 'progressive' potential. The poet
of the machine age spent the early 1940s in rustic
seclusion in the Pyrenees, emerging from his retreat
in fitful and unsuccessful attempts at persuading
the Vichy authorities to build his Algiers plan. It
was during this period that he made his proposal
for an Agricultural Estate in North Africa in
'harmony with the landscape, the climate and
tradition' (p. 377), and also painted a series
of biomorphic monsters known simply as 'Ubus'
after Alfred Jarry's well-known and preposterous
character 'Ubu Roi'. These paintings seemed to sum
up the artist's mixed feelings of futility and irony,
and to correspond to a mental state of withdrawal.
In these years Surrealism also held out an appeal

513

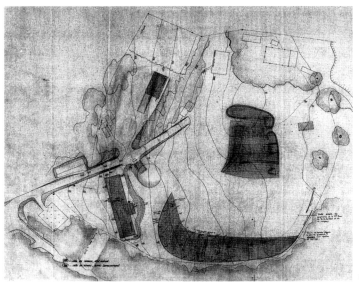

514

515

in the search for primal subject-matter and subconscious imagery; one notes a loose parallel between Le Corbusier's 'biological' forms and developments in avant-garde painting and sculpture in the United States (e.g. early Jackson Pollock or David Smith), in which totemic and primitivist features also came to the fore. By the end of the war, when he returned to Paris, Le Corbusier was in his late fifties; he had not built for over a decade. It is scarcely surprising, then, that each of his post-war commissions should have been treated as an opportunity to cram together many levels of ideas. He became increasingly obsessed with leaving behind him autobiographical mementoes and lexicons of principle.

The late 1940s in France was not the most propitious time for an architect of Le Corbusier's formal calibre. Of course, there were vast programmes of rehousing, but he failed in his ambition of becoming France's 'chief architect / urbanist of reconstruction'. Instead of seeing his grand models adopted, he had to be content, once again, with piecemeal demonstrations. Thus the Unité d'Habitation at Marseilles (and the handful of other Unités he was called upon to design during the 1950s) were fragmentary realizations compared with his expectations (see Chapter 24). Even so, these buildings did effectively serve as prototypes. The

Marseilles Unité had as powerful a hold over the post-war imagination as Mies van der Rohe's glass towers; these were among the seminal images of the 1950s. At the same time the 'theorems' embodied in the United Nations skyscraper and the Modulor proportional system failed to have the grand societal impact which their creator had craved.

It was almost as if the post-war world conspired to stop the Le Corbusier of 'standards' and industrialized prototypes from having an effect, leaving, presumably, the idiosyncratic poet of form to dig ever deeper into private worlds of metaphor. The society at which the artist had directed his pre-war Utopias had undoubtedly changed. He seemed now to seek inspiration less in the 'miracles of contemporary life' than in a fraternity with nature and with the great works of the past. A nostalgia for the giant ruins of antiquity began to creep in. Of course, the search for perennial and unchanging values had always been a primary motivation; now it went on less disturbed by a quest for 'modernity'.

Such preliminary remarks seem appropriate to the Chapel of Notre-Dame-du-Haut at Ronchamp of 1950–4. This stands brooding on a hilltop in the Vosges mountains with views across valleys of evergreens towards the far horizons. A dark roof with pointed angle and complex curvature rests uneasily on convex and concave battered-rubble

516

walls punctured by irregular openings and sprayed in whitewashed gunnite concrete. The fluidity of the resulting composition is held in check by three hooded towers facing in varying directions. These and the undulating surfaces echo the pressures of the surrounding landscape. The interior is hollowed out like a cave and has a sloping floor which focuses attention towards the altar. The smaller chapels are top-lit within the towers, while the perforated south wall pours light into an otherwise sober interior. The junction between roof and walls is handled deftly with a slight gap so that a crack of daylight gleams through; what seemed solid from outside becomes planar and thin from within. Such ambiguities of mass and space, support and supported, are basic to the formal character of the chapel, and the readings vary as one changes position. Ronchamp is a sculpture to be seen in the round; exterior and interior movements of the spectator become involved with the dynamics of the composition and are central to the concept of the work.

Typical of this sense of unfolding ambiguity is the space outside the east wall, where an open-air altar sits under the boat-shaped roof. This outdoor sanctuary is replete with pulpit and an image of the Madonna in a glazed box embedded in the wall (so that it can be seen from the inside too). The grass platform stretching to the edge of the hill now becomes the 'nave' of a church in open nature. There is the stunning backdrop of woods and hills, while, to one side, a ziggurat of old stones marks the spot where a previous church was destroyed in the final years of the war. The site had traditionally been a place of pilgrimage (even in pre-Christian times), and Le Corbusier managed to capture the spirit of the place. The gradual ascent up the hill has a ritualistic character, which the architect turned to good effect by organizing the building as a sequence of *évènements plastiques* ('sculptural events') incorporating the setting and the surrounding horizons. The culmination of the procession might vary: it might be a Mass in the open air or a private prayer in the interior with its numinous space and filtered light.

At the time of its completion in 1954, the Chapel at Ronchamp shocked the critics who flocked to see it. Pevsner complained of a retreat into 'irrationality' (thus betraying his prejudice that Le Corbusier's earlier works had been somehow 'rational'), while

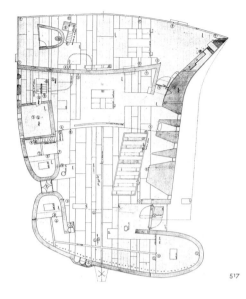

517 Le Corbusier, Chapel of Notre-Dame-du-Haut, Ronchamp, 1950–4, plan

518 Chapel of Notre-Dame-du-Haut, interior

517

the young British architect James Stirling was dismayed by 'conscious imperfectionism' and 'mannerism', and questioned whether the building 'should influence the course of modern architecture'. One thing seemed to be clear amidst these confused reactions: the master of European modern architecture had changed direction profoundly. The commentators seemed to forget that these changes had been in the making for some time; that the architect's ideas and forms had been in gradual transition for two decades, since his works of the 1920s, which they seemed to regard as 'normative'. The inventions of Ronchamp were not without precedent in Le Corbusier's paintings, in his rugged wooden sculptures of the late 1940s, in his sketches of shells and boats of the early 1930s (the roof structure was, in fact, directly inspired by a crab-shell), in the landscape sculptures of the buildings in his Algiers schemes, and in the curved rubble wall of the Pavillon Suisse. His recently completed Unité d'Habitation at Marseilles was entirely constructed from bare concrete, and was crowned by a roofscape of totemic service stacks and sculpted landscape forms which echoed the distant crags of rock.

Le Corbusier was not a member of any particular faith, yet his outlook was fundamentally idealistic. He later wrote that he was interested in 'the effect of architectural forms and the spirit of architecture in the construction of a vessel of intense concentration and meditation', and in what he called 'an acoustic component in the domain of form'. In other words, he sought to evoke religious emotions through the play of form, space and light, and without recourse to any obvious church typology. The patronage conditions were well suited to this kind of free interpretation, since Father Alain Couturier (with whom Le Corbusier liaised throughout the design) believed that a vital, existential expression of religious consciousness was best achieved, not by forcing an artist into a traditional ecclesiastical straitjacket, but by allowing the free play of imagination. Le Corbusier seemed to mirror this intention of the client when he wrote: 'I have not experienced the miracle of faith but I have often known the miracle of inexpressible space, the apotheosis of plastic emotion.'

In fact some of Le Corbusier's inspirations at Ronchamp were heathen in tone. The attitude to landscape and to natural forms provided the key to his sacral interpretation. As a young man he had soaked himself in nature worship, in the writings of Ruskin, in the symbolic allegories of Art Nouveau, and had even had the vision of a sort of temple to nature to stand on a Jura mountain-top. The chapel at Ronchamp speaks of a similar pantheism; this was an artist for whom natural forms were capable of a divine and magical character. Immediately before he received the commission, Le Corbusier had been giving thought to the design of a shrine at St-Baume in the mountains of Provence (never built), which he had envisaged as a sort of top-lit cave embedded among boulders. Ronchamp was pervaded by a sense of primitive animism.

Other connections can be found with a great variety of 'sources'. It seems that the top lighting of the 'Canopus' at Hadrian's Villa (sketched in 1911) may have inspired the lighting system of the towers; certain mud buildings from the Mzab, seen in Algeria in the mid-1930s, may have influenced the main perforated wall; a fascination with sluices may have registered in the water scoop of the Ronchamp roof. Dolmens and Cycladic vernacular structures have even been adduced as other clues, and it is possible that the procession to the Parthenon was

519

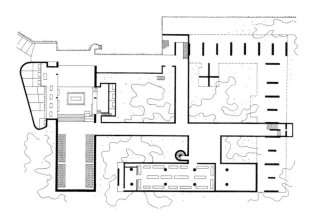

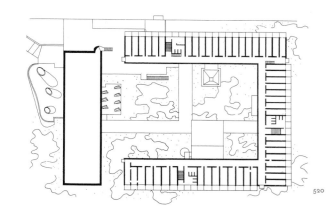

520

once again inspirational. But, whatever the sources and other memories, the important point is that they were here brought together in a coherent work of art; they became inseparable elements of a synthesis.

It was while Ronchamp was under construction that Le Corbusier was asked to design another religious structure, the Dominican monastery of La Tourette at Eveux-sur-l'Arbresle, not far from Lyons. Again Father Couturier was instrumental in Le Corbusier's receiving the commission. The editor of *L'Art sacré*, Couturier was one of several Dominicans to advocate a return to the timeless qualities of French rural Romanesque churches. He recommended to Le Corbusier that he go to see the twelfth-century Cistercian monastery of Le Thoronet in Provence, a building which he thought epitomized monastic rule, and which relied upon the most elemental means of light, proportion, stone, space and music to evoke a sense of the sacred. Monasteries had, of course, had a strong hold over Le Corbusier's imagination ever since his visit to the Charterhouse at Ema in Tuscany in 1907, when he had been deeply impressed by the ordered rule of the architecture, the balance between public and private, and the framed views of nature from the cells. During the '*voyage d'Orient*', he had also visited the monastic communities on Mount

Athos in Greece, which had interior courts and overhanging balconies extending towards the landscape. For La Tourette Le Corbusier was therefore able to draw on years of researches in his reinterpretation of an ancient type. It is striking that he employed vestiges of the traditional enclave in his plan and that his use of bare concrete and stark forms was intended as an equivalent to the stonework of old buildings. However, the site – a slope overlooking meadows – required considerable modification of the inherited device of the cloistered court. The resulting monastery did not ape the prototypes but transformed them, restating them in a new structural terminology in concrete.

The form of La Tourette addressed the theme of a well-regulated community living towards a common, ideal purpose. The individual cells were placed around the crowning overhang, wrapped around three of the outside edges, and expressed as deep-cut rectangular embrasures. Each monk had his individual balcony framing a private view over trees or far-distant hills to the west. The communal areas were set in the recessed lower levels, the most public (e.g. the small oratory under a pyramidical roof and the library) being placed close to the entrance. The refectory was situated at one level

521

down from the entrance floor, but since the site sloped so steeply, it seemed poised above the meadows. The main church was entered one level further down, but was entirely inward-looking and a full triple volume in height. It made a solid block along one side of the building, holding its own against the slope, and its interior (to paraphrase Le Corbusier) was '*d'une pauvreté totale*' ('of a total poverty'). In other words, it possessed a stern moral beauty arising from the interplay of stark concrete surfaces, colour and light.

What gave these variously articulated functions the power of architecture was the way they were linked by platforms and corridors, and orchestrated within a clear overall form. There was precision in the relationship of plane and volume, of the dense and the transparent, of the heavy and the light. No less than the Chapel at Ronchamp, or the roof terrace at Marseilles, the Monastery of La Tourette revealed Le Corbusier's interest in weaving together institutional ritual with an intensified experience of the surrounding landscape.

Seen from outside, the roof plane of the block-like church was inclined, so as to draw the distant hills into the action of the building's forms. The double-curved, battered wall of the side chapel (containing individual altars where the monks might say daily Mass) was surmounted by splayed cylindrical skylights ('light cannons') which also gestured towards the horizon. The stark exterior north wall of the church – a total blank – signalled a private precinct, and was described at the time as 'a great dam holding back a reservoir of spiritual energy'. The visitor was guided beyond this barrier and towards the entrance by carefully controlled visual cues, then led into the more and more private areas in a downward-spiralling movement through spaces of varying light and intensity. In a sense, this was a route of initiation, from the secular world outside to the daily rituals of the community within. The path continued to descend by means of inclined, transparent walkways to the grave interior of the church, then even further down (for those who were initiated) into the cave-like space of the curved chapel seen in the first view. The plan and section provided a series of transitions which corresponded to the stripping away of the persona, the submission to the Rule, and the direct confrontation with God.

522

Much of the necessary experimentation for the use of bare concrete had gone on at Marseilles – half a decade before – but La Tourette still succeeded in extending the vocabulary. One may recognize the old Le Corbusier theme of the box on stilts, but dismembered and rearranged in a sort of collage composition in which 'found objects' – a triangular skylight, a stack, a protruding balcony – introduced staccato incidents. Moreover, La Tourette was still based on the principles of the Five Points of a New Architecture, but the number and type of architectural elements had increased. Instead of just cylindrical *pilotis*, there were now directional piers as well; instead of the thin planes of stucco of the earlier works, there were robust walls; instead of the plate-glass or strip windows, there were now *brises-soleil*, *ondulatoires* (the rhythmically positioned concrete struts laid out according to the Modulor), and *aérateurs* – the last being vertical, wooden ventilating panels inserted into the fenestration membrane. Le Corbusier's *recherche patiente* ('patient search') proceeded in this way: each new project became a testing ground for new ideas, as well as an extension of old ones. La Tourette demonstrated how the increase in the number of elements allowed a greater variety of articulation both functionally and formally. Apart from the obvious features – like rough concrete, stepping overhangs, and slab-like piers – it was this conceptual richness which endeared La Tourette to followers seeking a way out of the limitations of the inherited 'International Style'.

Two little houses designed at approximately the same time as La Tourette – the Maisons Jaoul in Neuilly-sur-Seine (1951–4) – were also widely imitated. Here the contrast with Le Corbusier's early works was even more dramatic, for these deliberately crude brick dwellings, with their rough concrete frames, their curved 'Catalan' vaults and their turf roofs, stood less than two miles from the Maison Cook and the Villa Stein/de Monzie at Garches, and could not be explained away as rustic religious sprees. Peter Smithson, the English architect, characterized the combination of sophistication and primitivism nicely when he spoke of the Maisons Jaoul as being 'on the knife edge of peasantism'. Stirling once again registered nervousness in a well-known comparison of Jaoul with Garches, in which he suggested that the polemical drive of early modern architecture, the expression of a new way of life in built forms, was giving way to a more comfortable, less challenging view of social progress. Once again, though, the

themes of the houses had already been evident in the Petite Maison de Weekend nearly twenty years earlier, and Le Corbusier had already written rhapsodically in the early 1940s of the lessons to be learned from the peasant vernacular. The machine-age polemic had gone, but it had been replaced by new attitudes concerning the primal relationship between man and nature. Stirling himself seems to have sensed the cogency of the vision, for his Ham Common flats of 1955–8 (Fig. 673) adopted rough brick and concrete. Indeed, the Jaoul houses became one of the canonical works of the so-called 'New Brutalists' in Britain and elsewhere – a younger generation sensing the devaluation of the heroic vision of the earlier modern movement into something smooth and ersatz, and seeking a visual language to give body to their own rough awakening to the social realities of the post-war years.

The Maisons Jaoul were on the drawing board at the same time as two dwellings for India – the Sarabhai House and the Villa Shodhan in Ahmadabad – where effects of precision were out of the question, even had the architect wanted them, and where handmade sun-baked brick and rough concrete were right for the labour conditions, for the climate and for the ethos Le Corbusier was trying to express in a country recently liberated from colonial rule. It seems that India entered his mythology as a place destined to side-step the chaos of the 'first machine age' and to enter directly the phase of natural harmony of the *deuxième ère machiniste* ('the second machine age') in which the industrial superstructure and the rural base would achieve a happy equilibrium. These houses of Ahmadabad's well-to-do could, of course, be only partial vehicles for such ideas. The Sarabhai House (1951–5) was built for Manorama Sarabhai, sister-in-law of Guatam Sarabhai (who was director of the National Institute of Design in the town), and the site stood on a tree-filled estate. Mrs Sarabhai belonged to the Jain sect, which stressed the inviolability of all forms of life. Le Corbusier's design was a variant on his Monol type of 1919 (of which the Petite Maison de Weekend had also been a descendant), with low vaults and an earth-hugging character. It also incorporated his researches into hot climate vernaculars (such as the project for an Agricultural Estate in Cherchell, North Africa, of 1942). Le Corbusier oriented the house to catch the

523

prevailing winds and designed the façade with deep-cut piers which acted as *brises-soleil* and porticoes simultaneously. The Catalan vault system was again employed for the shaded interiors, while the roof had a thick mat of turf traversed by water channels (to cope with the monsoons) laid over it. There was even a dramatic scoop/slide sluicing the rainwater down into a pool. The Indian architect Charles Correa later characterized the humility and spatial fluidity of the Sarabhai House in these terms: 'a masterwork as complex, as amorphous, and as open-ended as a banyan tree, as an Indian joint family'.

The Villa Shodhan (1951–4) descended in the long run from the Maison Citrohan. Originally it was designed for Surrotam Hutheesing, the president of the Millowners' Association (for which Le Corbusier also designed a building), but it was then sold at the planning stage to Shyamubhai Shodhan and transferred to another site. The building's cubic form was carved out with dramatic concrete *brises-soleil* and overhangs to create a textured, dynamic composition, an ascending route and a habitation traversed by breezes. The whole was capped by a hovering slab on piers – recalling the image of the Dom-ino but incorporating as well the concept of a parasol against rain and sun. A similar device had been used in the Maison Baizeau near Carthage of 1928, but here it was restated in

a more rugged form. Le Corbusier had decided that this should be one of the central elements of any new Indian architecture; variations of parasol ideas could be found in several phases of the history of Indian architecture.

The Millowners' Association Building of 1951–4 was on a site on the west bank of the Sabramati River opposite the Old City of Ahmadabad, and here Le Corbusier chose to reinterpret the old theme of *'une maison/un palais'* at an institutional scale. The building was organized as a *promenade architecturale* rising up a ramp, then weaving back and forth between the main façades of deep-cut *brises-soleil*. At the top was a meeting hall enfolded in a complex curved partition and roofed by the bowing underside of a convex parasol descending through the top of the building. This space, with its indefinite, even ineffable character, revealed the extent to which Le Corbusier was still elaborating the idea of the free plan, and still working out of the spatial dynamism of Cubism, but with a more tactile sense of the movement of the human figure. But there were also echoes in the building as a whole of local Gujarati examples, such as the timber grilles of indigenous houses, or the stone trabeation of both Muslim and earlier Hindu architecture. Like a large loom combining the weft and warp of horizontal and vertical elements, the Millowners' Association Building was a demonstration of the idea of a

524 Le Corbusier, Villa Shodhan, Ahmadabad, 1951–4

525 Le Corbusier, Millowners' Association Building, Ahmadabad, 1951–4, east façade

526 Le Corbusier, Chandigarh, plan of city, 1951. Fondation Le Corbusier, Paris

527 Chandigarh, view from the south-east towards the Parliament and Secretariat

524

525

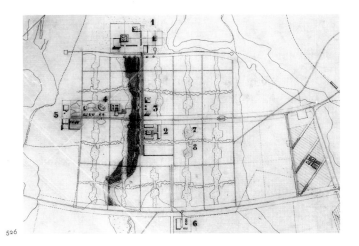

526

527

shaded, transparent frame encouraging the flow of breezes. The architect called it 'a little palace: genuine evidence of an architecture for modern times adjusted to the climate of India'.

These Ahmadabad commissions were relatively marginal to Le Corbusier's main Indian commitment: the design of the new city of Chandigarh, which occupied him from 1951 up to his death in 1965. In 1948 Western Punjab and the traditional state capital of Lahore were ceded to the newly created Pakistan, leaving the Indian Punjab and a large number of Hindu refugees in need of a capital. A scheme was drawn up by Albert Mayer and Matthew Nowicki, but in 1950 the latter was killed in a plane crash. The chief engineer, P. L. Varma, and the state administrator of public works, P. N. Thapar, toured Europe in search of an architect/planner, and on the recommendation of the British architects Jane Drew and Maxwell Fry (who both eventually played a major role in the design of the housing sectors) turned to Le Corbusier. In February 1951, in a little rest-house on the road to Simla, close to the small village of Chandigarh, the blueprint for the new capital was drawn up in a matter of days. Le Corbusier had been ruminating on the history and meaning of cities for over forty years, and came supplied with his own pre-existing vision of a modern urban ideal ready to be modified by particular conditions.

The main body of the city was planned on a grid of circulation (in fact, there were seven different 'hierarchies' of movement in the design) dividing up a variety of rectangular sectors containing neighbourhoods of relatively low-rise dwellings in a sort of Garden City arrangement. In the course of time, a variety of hot-climate housing types, using cheap, labour-intensive materials would be worked out for the different social levels and sectors. Several of these were designed by Le Corbusier's cousin and associate Pierre Jeanneret, others by Fry and Drew. At the 'heart' of the urban body was the commercial centre, located just off the main artery which ran up to the 'head' containing the main state buildings: the Governor's Palace, the Parliament (or Assembly) Building, the High Court (or Palace of Justice), and the Secretariat. The University, the Museum, the Stadium and other 'leisure and educational' activities were disposed on a cross-axis extending to the north, while out to the south-east, separate from the main body, was the railway station with its depots.

The rationale for this overall plan embodied Le Corbusier's major principles: his belief in the ordered distinction of urban functions, his notion of the essential joys of 'light, space, and greenery', his conception of social order and rationalization, his dream of a *polis* inhabited by forward-looking technicians and bureaucrats of high cultural aspiration. The form was a variant on the basic layout of the Ville Radieuse, but without *à redent* housing blocks, and with free-standing sculptural monuments instead of glass towers symbolizing government at the head. However, Chandigarh also incorporated ideas from Paris – the grand

boulevards and focal points; from ancient Peking –
in the overall geometrical form; and from Lutyens's
New Delhi, with its own extraordinary blend of
Garden City principles and Baroque vista planning.
Le Corbusier fully appreciated another aspect of
New Delhi, evident in the Viceroy's House and
other monumental buildings: the way they fused
the European and the Indian traditions in an
iconography of state magnificence (Chapter 17).

Much of Le Corbusier's attention over the
subsequent years would be devoted to the Capitol
complex, in which he allowed his ideas on
monumental expression free rein. Like Lutyens,
he learned his lessons from the Mogul tradition,
with its generous provision of deep loggias,
romantic roofscapes, and water. The crescent-
shaped 'parasol', upturned against water and sun,
incorporating a traditional image of authority but
also inverting it in an anti-authoritarian gesture,
became a sort of shared leitmotif at Chandigarh.
It recurred on top of the Governor's Palace and the
Secretariat, transformed into the colossal scoop of
the Parliament Building portico, and became the
very form of the Justice basilica itself. Indeed, the
genesis of Le Corbusier's monumental vocabulary
seems to have involved a prodigious feat of
abstraction in which devices from the classical
tradition – the grand order, the portico – were
fused with his own general system of forms in
concrete and in turn cross-bred with Indian
devices like the 'chattri' (a dome on slender
supports), the trabeated terraces, balconies and
loggias of Fahtepur Sikri. In turn, this architectural
language, rich in references and associations of a
public institutional kind, was suffused with the
artist's private cosmological themes – the fantasy
of water dousing and splashing over giant concrete
roofs and surfaces, the image of the sun's path at
the solstice and the equinox attached to the colossal
lighting-tower of the Parliament, and the curious
'Valley of Contemplation', emblazoned with signs
representing different aspects of the architect's
philosophy.

The Capitol itself was a diagram of institutional
hierarchies, with the Governor's Palace at its head,
the High Court and the Parliament facing one
another lower down, and the Secretariat off to one
side in a subordinate position. The buildings and
spaces between were conceived as integral parts of a

528

529

530

531

sort of cosmic landscape, in which mounds, valleys, bodies of water, platforms and the roofscapes of the main structures were juxtaposed with the foothills of the Himalayas in the distance, and attuned to reflect the passage of the sun, the changing angles of shadows, and the light of the moon. The relationship between objects near and far was enlivened by tensions and spatial ambiguities. To one side of the Governor's Palace, there was a modern version of a formal Mogul garden. (Le Corbusier had projected something similar for the roof of the Museum which he designed for the city of Ahmadabad.) The flat roofs of the monumental institutions were conceived as gathering-places, and on the top of the Governor's Palace (which was never built) there was an upturned crescent shape, which combined an open-air theatre, a shaded undercroft, and a political and cosmic symbol open to multiple readings – bulls' horns, the path of the sun, a parasol of authority.

The apotheosis of this new state imagery drenched in Corbusian references was perhaps the 'Open Hand', a monument designed to stand close to the Governor's Palace (and eventually on its own when the latter function was dropped because President Nehru found it 'undemocratic'). The Open Hand was a bizarre compound of a Picasso peace dove and a giant gesturing hand whose silhouette echoed the curved profiles of the buildings. Some of the meaning of the symbol was spelled out by the architect:

It was not a political emblem, a politician's creation … [but] an architect's creation … a symbol of peace and reconciliation…. Open to receive the wealth that the world has created, to distribute to the peoples of the world … It ought to be the symbol of our age. … The Open Hand will affirm that the second era of machinist civilization has begun; the era of harmony …

The High Court was another variation on the parasol theme, this time an open-sided box with a sculpted, protective roof in the form of a huge sluice, but also evoking the shape of an aeroplane wing. The Courtrooms themselves were slotted into a secondary system beneath this monumental portico, as a series of grille-like rectangles shaded by *brises-soleil*. The entrance to the main body of the building was towards one end of the low oblong, and took the form of three boldly coloured monumental piers that were curved in plan (like latter-day versions of the *pilotis* of the Pavillon Suisse), and followed by a lateral ramp zigzagging up to a terrace. While the High Court was consonant with the other primeval forms used at Chandigarh, it also seemed to distil some of Le Corbusier's early observations and sketches of Roman ruins (e.g. the Basilica of Constantine), and to involve a characteristic transformation of a relevant Indian type: the Mogul Diwan-I-Am, or public audience hall, with its open sides and overhanging roofs.

The Parliament Building itself was also loaded with symbolism and enriched with ancient references. Basically, it was designed as a large box with a grid of columns inside and the large 'objects' of the main Assembly and Senate chambers set down into it. These were made visible on the exterior through the sculptural roofscape forms, a tilted pyramid for the Senate and a dynamic funnel-like shape for the main Assembly. Rugged concrete, with all the signs and enrichment of rough handicraft, was used throughout; the searing climate soon added its own patina. If the result has the appearance of a colossal, grave and dignified ruin, this was probably intended; one has the sensation that these buildings must have stood on this plateau for centuries. The sides of the box were perforated by the repeated shadows of *brises-soleil*, while the main façade (on the cross-axis of the Capitol plateau facing the High Court in the distance) provided a gesture of considerable formality: a scoop-shaped portico on lateral piers, with a large enamelled door bearing solar diagrams designed by Le Corbusier. Inside one left behind the blazing heat and the jagged shadows for a cool, serene world of smooth cylinders rising to a black soffit. The light filtered in from the sides of this hovering element to reveal a space the ancient Egyptians might have revered. The mushroom columns looked as if they had been inspired by hypostyle halls. Concrete was here endowed with the density and *gravitas* of hewn and polished stone. With the awe-inspiring volume of the great funnel containing the Assembly descending into it, with the rising sequences of ramps and the vast floors, this was a sure demonstration that monumentality had not died in the modern age.

The Assembly room itself was a hyperbolic funnel exploding through the roof towards the sky. Top-lit, it was reached through the hypostyle by a latter-day version of the traditional circumambulation, and its axis was aligned with the path of the sun at the zenith rather than with the grid of the building or that of the city as a whole. Its inner surfaces were ornamented with curved plaques of soundproofing panel, conceived as abstractions of clouds. The sublime spatial drama of the Assembly chamber was somewhat at odds with its function as a place for democratic, political debate. Nevertheless, it is interesting to probe the genesis of the 'funnel' concept as this gives clues concerning the way Le Corbusier translated images and ideas into forms.

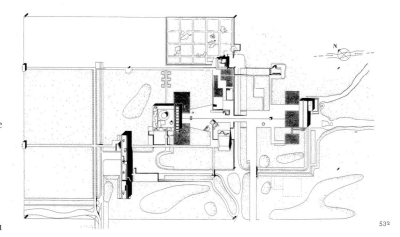

532

533

In the earliest stages, the Parliament Building was a close relative of the Supreme Court opposite: a large box under a massive parasol in concrete. By degrees the theme of the portico emerged naturally from the expression of the rectangular trabeation within. At this stage the main chambers were submerged in the box as two gland-shaped rooms enclosed by free-form curved partitions set into the grid of supports. A key breakthrough was made in mid-1953 when the architect began to envision the dramatic possibility of sun- and moonlight penetrating the roof; there were even vague hints of 'nocturnal festivals' and 'solar celebrations'. It was then that the idea of the light-tower – an object within the bigger object of the box – began to emerge, its form partly inspired by the hyperboloid shape of power-station cooling towers (ventilation concerns may have triggered the analogy). In the placement of a stack-like form in the centre of a box, one recognizes a basic Corbusian habit of mind extending back at least as far as the villas of the 1920s. The suggestion has been made that the architect may have been inspired by the plan of Schinkel's Altes Museum in Berlin (Fig. 3), where the theme of portico, grid and circular form had been stated with great clarity and force. The choice of these forms far transcended utilitarian concerns (in fact, the solution was never entirely practical); they arose rather from the architect's aim of creating a sort of modern equivalent to the dome – an emblem of state authority and rule. Among the early sketches, there were some showing the Chandigarh stack alongside a section of the dome of the imperial church of Hagia Sophia in Istanbul, and others showing the sun streaming down through the top in a manner inevitably recalling the Roman Pantheon. Whatever the precise 'sources', one is struck, once again, by the depth of the transformation into the stuff of the artist's own expression.

A funnel, a dome, a roofscape, a sculpture beckoning to the foothills of the Himalayas, the Chandigarh roof element partook of all of these things. From the earliest, too, Le Corbusier sought to incorporate some of his universalizing

534

535 Le Corbusier,
Parliament Building,
Chandigarh, 1951–63,
detail of roofscape
showing crescent forms on
funnel of Assembly
Chamber

536 Parliament Building,
section, drawn 1956.
Fondation Le Corbusier,
Paris

537 Parliament Building,
plan

538 Karl Friedrich
Schinkel, Altes Museum,
Berlin, 1824–8, plan

539 Parliament Building,
view up funnel

iconography. At one stage a spiral ramp was made
to run around it (useful for cleaning, but equally
a symbol of the Modulor); later a strange collage
of upturned curves was attached, referring to the
gesturing leitmotif of the whole scheme, as well
as to the path of the sun. It is probable that these
solar implications were prompted by a group
of sculptural abstractions that Le Corbusier
enormously admired: the astronomical devices of
the Jantar Mantar in Delhi, and at Jaipur (both
early eighteenth century). The architect spoke of his
invention as 'a true physics laboratory, equipped to
ensure the play of lights …' The solar symbolism
was linked in turn to the very notion of state
authority, and to the architect's own conception
of an all-embracing order of nature: the lighting
system was designed so that a beam would fall on
the speaker's chair on the day of the Opening of

539

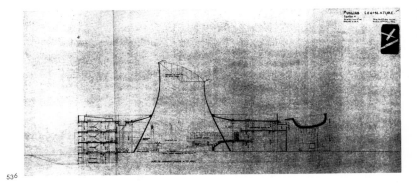

536

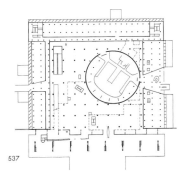

537

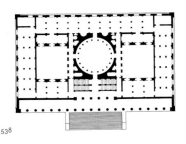

538

Parliament. On that occasion a procession would
proceed from the civic space outside, through the
great enamel door adorned with cosmic signs,
'reminding man once every year that he is a son of
the sun'. The Parliament Building exemplifies the
extraordinary depth and texture of Le Corbusier's
symbolic thinking in his late years.

At the inauguration of the Parliament in 1963,
President Nehru spoke of Chandigarh as 'a temple
of the new India': '… the first expression of our
creative genius, flowering on our newly earned
freedom … unfettered by traditions of the past –
reaching beyond the encumbrances of old towns
and old traditions …' There can be little doubt that
it was these 'progressive' qualities of the new city
and its buildings which were first to make their
mark. But Chandigarh, even though it was not
'fettered' by tradition, was still steeped in it; and
while in the Indian context it was an emblem of
the new, in Le Corbusier's mind it was equally a
symbol of values which transcended the Western
progressive mythology altogether.

By 1960 Le Corbusier was 73 and generally
acknowledged as the world leader in architecture.
His small atelier at 35 rue de Sèvres had become a
sort of breeding-ground for a new international
tradition. His own commissions involved him in
constant travel. The volumes of the *Oeuvre complète*
ensured a wide following. The late works soon

fostered a series of transformations in various countries. The 'New Brutalists' (to be discussed more fully later) learned from him the direct use of materials, to which they gave their own moral meaning. Architects as diverse as Kenzo Tange in Japan, Paul Rudolph in the United States and Balkrishna Doshi in India drew lessons from the monumental and rugged concrete expression and from the archaic echoes. And just as the seminal works of the 1920s were frequently devalued and turned into clichés, so the late works were often imitated for their surface effects without due attention to underlying principles: *brises-soleil* and rough concrete finishes could become a sort of façade cosmeticism just as easily as strip windows, thin *pilotis*, and glass and steel curtain walls.

Le Corbusier must have been aware of the dual pressure to consolidate principles and to continue experimenting. This seems to show in several of his later works and unrealized projects. The unconstructed project for Olivetti near Milan (1963) picked up on the sinuous circulation idea of Algiers (and perhaps on some of Niemeyer's buildings of the early 1940s), and restated it as an organism of routes and ramps penetrating the building. The steel and glass Heidi Weber Pavilion in Zurich (1961–5) gave material form to a structural idea which Le Corbusier had first crystallized over twenty years earlier. The (so far) unconstructed project for the Church of St-Pierre at Firminy developed further the idea of a top-lit funnel reacting in its form to distant hills. There were also proposals that demonstrated Le Corbusier's interest in particular urban settings. Among these was one for the Venice Hospital (1963–5), which remained only a project when the architect died. This was envisaged for a site half on the land, half in the water, not far from Venice railway station. Le Corbusier decided on a low project so as not to interfere with the historic skyline of the city. But the most striking aspect of his strategy is revealed by the plan or the model. For the hospital was a sort of modern analogue to the urban structure around it: an extension of the neighbouring order, yet an intensification of it in a new form. This was not just a matter of imitating local house types, but of penetrating intellectually to the typical pattern of Venetian urban spaces and reinterpreting them in the shape of the building. It was the opposite of what might be called 'object

540

planning' and indicated that Le Corbusier was sensitive when necessary to the historic tissue of a city. Perhaps, too, in setting the guidelines for the scheme he reflected awareness of the renewed debates of the Team X generation of architects, who identified a typical weakness of earlier CIAM planning as being its crass disregard for the sense of place, and for the unique qualities of context (see Chapter 24). Unfortunately the hospital was not built, but the project influenced several buildings of the early 1960s, in which platforms and routes became major generators of form.

The Carpenter Center for the Visual Arts in Cambridge, Massachusetts, of 1959–63 was built, however, and seems to have issued from a retrospective state of mind. The function was to house a new department of Visual Studies at Harvard University. The site was confined between neo-Georgian neighbours, close to the arcadian setting of 'Harvard Yard'. Le Corbusier's solution was a free-plan 'loft' building amply lit from the edges by a variety of fenestration devices, including *ondulatoires*, *aérateurs* and several types of *brise-soleil*. The heart of the idea was an S-shaped ramp linking the new function to the nearby streets, and implying a continuation of the diagonal paths of Harvard Yard opposite. The main studios were formed as freehand curves, extending from a cubic volume to the centre, the entire arrangement being twisted from the prevalent orthogonal geometry. The power of the scheme arose from the dramatic interpenetration of curved and rectangular volumes, of transparent and massive elements, whose dynamism was further varied by the fact of changing position. For the ramp supplied not only a showcase of the inner workings of the department (a response to a request in the programme), but an orchestrated sequence of architectural events. Using a limited number of elements, Le Corbusier created active spaces of great complexity.

The Carpenter Center was a rich amalgam of various earlier phases of Le Corbusier's evolution. It was as if the 'acoustic' forms of Ronchamp had been cross-bred with the elemental attitude to structure manifest in the early works (the extremely pure skeleton of smooth slabs and *pilotis* inevitably recalls the primary statement of the Dom-ino), or as if the free plan had been turned inside out so that extending curves could meet the surroundings in several dynamic ways. The evidence is abundant that the architect conceived the Carpenter Center as a demonstration of his vocabulary in concrete and as a sort of *summum* of structural principles. In line with this intention, the Quincy Street façade was

fitted with a barrage of different fenestration devices which far outstripped practical justification. Once again Le Corbusier was involving himself in demonstrations, in this case in a true 'teaching building'. The *Oeuvre complète* was right to claim that 'many of Le Corbusier's guiding ideas' found their place in the Carpenter Center.

But this was also Le Corbusier's only building in the United States and thereby achieved further significance. It was not industrially advanced America – spiritually poor in Le Corbusier's eyes – which gave him the opportunity to build a city, but the culturally rich, materially poor India. He had always hoped to persuade the American authorities to adopt his Ville Radieuse ideals, but without success. It seems possible that his didactic statement in the Carpenter Center did include urbanistic ideas, however; the S-shape of the ramp appears to refer to the ideogram for the rise and fall of the sun ('which regulates all our urban enterprises'), while the ramp itself may well be a metaphor for the American freeways Le Corbusier had so admired as potential tools for the realization of his urban ideal. It seems, in other words, that the Carpenter Center, despite its relatively humble size, was an emblem of Le Corbusier's philosophy – a building fusing his lifelong concerns as painter, sculptor, architect and urbanist.

In 1965, a little over two years after the completion of the Carpenter Center, Le Corbusier died in a swimming accident in his beloved Mediterranean, at Roquebrune, where he always spent his summers. Since then his ideas have continued to exert a great influence, but it is still difficult to assess them in a balanced way in the light of history. Some of the standard reactions against a great inventor who left a major imprint on his time have already occurred, and this only serves further to blur the picture. It seems likely, though, when the mists clear, that Le Corbusier will deserve to be considered as an artist of the highest calibre who identified key questions of his period and who invented prototypes to which others were virtually bound to react. Whether one agrees with this assessment or not, it must surely be clear that the architect reorganized the discipline of architecture in fundamental ways and realized his ambition of creating for the modern era an architecture which extended principles from the past.

541

24

the unité d'habitation at marseilles as a collective housing prototype

Every important work of art can be regarded both as a historical event and as a hard-won solution to some problem … other solutions to this same problem will most likely be invented to follow the one now in view. As the solutions accumulate the problem alters. The chain of solutions none the less discloses the problem.
George Kubler, 1962

A tradition is composed of features other than the sequence of personal styles within broadly shared themes. Some of its lines of continuity may also be defined in terms of the 'evolution' of building types. These may cut across a variety of individuals' vocabularies, yet still respond to certain kernel problems. It may even happen that a single building stands at the head of a sequence and takes on the role of a prototype. The Unité d'Habitation at Marseilles (1947–53) had something of this function in the field of collective housing. It was a difficult building to ignore for any later architect facing analogous tasks. To chart the lessons learned from it, and the various reactions to it, is to provide an extraordinarily clear summary of Western architectural attitudes over a period of nearly a quarter of a century.

The Unité stands off the boulevard Michelet on the outskirts of Marseilles. The first impression in early photographs is of a textured cliff towering above a dry landscape dotted with scrub, rocks and trees, though it now stands in a small park, hemmed in by later construction. In the summer, the deep crates of the *brises-soleil* are gashed with shadow and the concrete takes on the tawny colour of the Provençal mountains in the distance. The slab rises to twelve storeys excluding the undercroft and the roof terrace, and has an ingenious interlocking section. Each apartment possesses a double-height living room with a terrace, and a lower portion passing through to the smaller balconies on the opposite side. Access is from corridors running along the spine, and these give on to the lower part of some of the dwelling units, the upper part of others. There are 23 different apartment types catering for the entire range from the single individual to the family with four children. The elements of each are standardized, their combination varied. The factory-produced units are slotted into the overall lattice of the building's structural frame as wine bottles might be in a rack. But the aesthetic result is neither repetitious nor busy; banality is avoided, unity maintained, through judicious attention to proportion, rhythm, human scale and sculptural control of the mass.

The hierarchy of individual cells to overall form, of private spaces to public whole, has been handled deftly throughout. The colossal *pilotis* (tapered descendants of the ones at the Pavillon Suisse) define a communal undercroft to the slab, and create a zone of shadow on which the fully lit volumes appear to rest. Major verticals are created by the lift, service- and stair-towers and by the flange walls at the ends of the block. An interior street containing shops, a restaurant, even a hotel, is expressed halfway up the block as a glazed gap of increased transparency. The roof terrace on top is acknowledged by a series of sculptural objects – the gymnasium building, the crèche, and the bizarre form of the ventilator stack, a hollow version of the *pilotis* below, reminiscent in its surreal mood of a chimneyscape by Gaudí. This terrace, with its running track, its pool, and its odd concrete sculptures rhyming with the distant crags and rocky islands 'sliced off' by the parapet, is surely yet another celebration of Le Corbusier's Mediterranean myth. When the sun streams down on the bold concrete forms and flashes off the pool, when the trees rustle below and the bay is glimpsed in the distance, one is forcibly affected by the Corbusian dream of the good life – his antidote to the squalor of the industrial city. The memories of Greece are strong; this little acropolis of resounding silent objects in light seems set up to celebrate a healthy balance between the mental and the physical. The Unité as a whole is a synthesis of social and formal imagination, of geometrical order and intense plasticity. It is far more massive in its form and more robust in its materials than the pre-war works, yet the whole is regulated by the numerical abstraction of the Modulor.

If the Unité stands at the beginning of a typological tradition in the post-war years, it also represents the culmination of a long quest for a collective order in Le Corbusier's philosophy. The pedigree stretches back through the Algiers viaduct, to the *à redent* houses of the Ville Radieuse, to the Maison Clarté and Pavillon Suisse, and, even further, to the *immeubles villas* and the Maison

543 Le Corbusier, Unité d'Habitation, Marseilles, 1947–53

544 Unité d'Habitation, swimming pool and children's play area on roof terrace

545 Unité d'Habitation, axonometric drawing

543

544

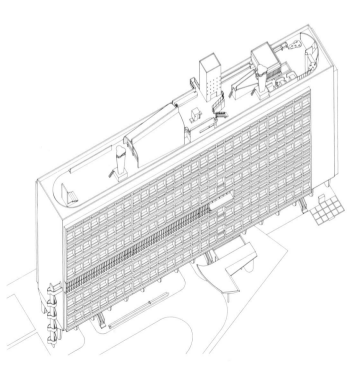

545

Citrohan. Each of these schemes considered different ways in which the modern building might anticipate the Utopian city. The Unité explored some of the main themes and may be interpreted as yet another demonstration of urbanistic principles, which also acted as a laboratory for experimentation. Central to the endeavour was the idea that mass production should be co-opted to deal with the housing shortage, and it was probably this that ensured the support of Eugène Claudius-Petit, Minister of Reconstruction. Le Corbusier's analysis began with the individual family. He sought to reconcile high-density urban living with the provision of the 'essential joys' of light, space and greenery. This was reflected in the 2:1 ratio of each apartment section. The living rooms were ample and spacious and had good views to the outside over balconies which (in Marseilles at least) could be used as living space. The kitchen, bathroom and bedrooms were half the height and tucked into the remaining part of each dwelling. It was the Citrohan section rethought; the Unité apartment even included a gallery, slung at the middle level of the double volume.

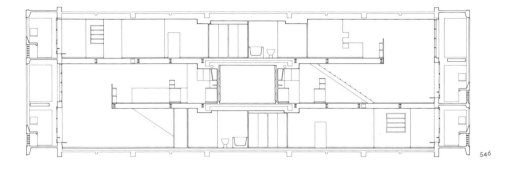

546   Le Corbusier, Unité
d'Habitation, Marseilles,
1947–53, section through
two interlocked apartment
units

547   Unité d'Habitation,
interior of typical
apartment

548   Unité d'Habitation,
plans of typical duplex
apartments

549   Unité d'Habitation,
'street' interior at middle
level of building

546

The communal aspects of the Unité were quite crucial to Le Corbusier's theorem. The individual apartments were ingeniously stacked so that the double-height part of one dwelling stood below or above the single-height part of another; the result was a jigsawed entity equal to three normal floor heights, with a corridor running through it. At the middle level of the building the corridor was amplified to become the *rue intérieure* or interior street, an element which recalled the walkways halfway up the Algiers viaduct of fifteen years earlier. The other major public domain was the roof terrace. It was hoped that this would be a safe place for people to sit and relax in the sun while their children played. As in Le Corbusier's Five Points of a New Architecture, the roof was thought of as a new level of ground in the air. The actual ground beneath the *pilotis* was reserved for circulation and had little of the intimacy of the analogous area in the Pavillon Suisse. The society of the Unité was lifted bodily into space.

The next scale of consideration was the relationship between the Unité and its physical setting. The theory behind the high-density vertical slab was the usual Corbusian one: modern techniques of construction and production were to be used to create high concentrations of population so as to liberate the ground for traffic and greenery; in the process, the old distinctions between country and city were to dissolve away. Le Corbusier had hoped to construct a number of Unités alongside one another in support of this idea. If he had done so, some of the drawbacks of his concept might well have been highlighted. For while each block expressed the notion of a unified

547

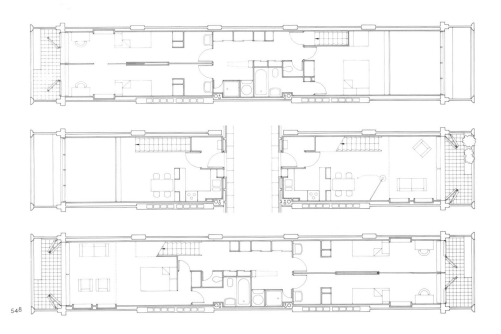

548

549

community, it is likely that a gulf would have existed between blocks. Mumford hinted at this problem when he criticized the interior street as an inadequate social equivalent to the traditional ground-level street in a dense urban setting. The particular Unité off boulevard Michelet may have been all right for Marseilles and the Midi; bu the *concept* of the Unité was liable to raise problems if applied indiscriminately in all situations. This was ironical; there can be no doubt that Le Corbusier thought his solution was normative and universal.

While the Unité stemmed from Le Corbusier's reflections on the sort of life possible for the majority in an industrial system, it drew on many earlier influences. It was no coincidence that 1,800 was the number posited by Le Corbusier as the ideal population for the mini-society of the Unité, since the same figure had been suggested by Charles Fourier for his '*phalanstère*' over a century before. There was another respect in which the Unité echoed its Utopian-socialist prototype: the idea of an interior street linking the building from one end to the other and expressing the notion of a united community. The double-height private dwellings looking out over nature recalled, once again, the monastery at Ema, while the disposition of decks, stacks, public and private areas was surely influenced by the image of the ocean liner. In his book *La Ville Radieuse* (1935), Le Corbusier had published a section of a Cunard transatlantic steamer and had called attention to its many admirable features as a model for collective living. The analogy between ship and Unité is, of course, an abstract one, but the image of a collective city 'floating' above the sea of verdure is none the less strongly felt at Marseilles.

In the 1920s Le Corbusier might have played up the mechanistic aspects of this metaphor, but at Marseilles the overtones were archaic and the concrete was rugged, as in the other late works. There is a rough similarity to the tawny forms of Roman ruins rising above the Provençal landscape, such as the Pont du Gard or the huge wall behind the antique theatre at Orange. In retrospect, it seems that the solution of highly textured concrete showing the imprints of the form-work planks was forced upon the architect by immediate post-war building conditions and by the fact that so many different contractors worked together on the project that it became impossible to hope for smooth transitions. Le Corbusier would probably have preferred to construct in steel. Even so, the architect turned these difficulties to good aesthetic use which accorded with changes in style and intention. At the opening of the building in 1953

he was happy to refer to concrete as a *natural* material and to compare it to stone. The *béton brut* of Marseilles was the finish appropriate to the ethos of the 'second machine age', the era of harmony in which a new contract would be formed between man and nature. The metaphor of mechanism was in retreat.

The opening of the Unité coincided with the 1953 meeting of the Congrès Internationaux de l'Architecture Moderne (CIAM IX) at Aix-en-Provence – the home of Cézanne, a founding father of the modern art faith. One wonders if the older members recalled the meeting twenty years previously on board the SS *Patris*, when they had sailed along the Mediterranean coastline and discussed the shape and politics of a new urban order. As they gathered together for the opening party on the roof terrace perhaps they realized that this robust concrete ship was the physical embodiment of the doctrines they had put together on that occasion as the Charter of Athens. But dry theories are one thing, life-enhancing forms another, and the younger generation at Aix were very clear about the difference. They saw a pallid version of the pre-war urban dream rising about them in the post-war reconstruction of Europe. They felt tricked, torn between disbelief in the tired doctrines of modern planning, and faith in the evocative power of the most poetic realizations of earlier modern architecture. This reaction, with its underlying dependence on the masters, led to the

550 Le Corbusier, sketch section of a typical cell of the Monastery at Ema, c.1907

551 Section through an ocean liner, illustration from Le Corbusier, *La Ville Radieuse*, 1935

552 Shadrach Woods, Vladimir Bodiansky and Georges Candilis, 'ATBAT' collective housing, Casablanca, Morocco, 1951–6

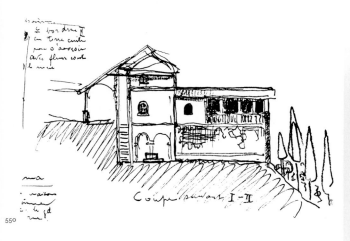

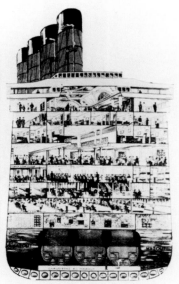

550

551

organization of the Dubrovnik meeting of CIAM in 1956 by 'Team X' (or Team Ten), an international affiliation of architects, mostly in their thirties, who wished to recapture the heroic moral drive of earlier modernism, yet channel it in ways relevant to an utterly transformed world. For them the Unité at Marseilles was charismatic; its philosophy was rooted in the Utopianism of the pre-war modern movement, but its forms embodied a new sensibility which suited their mood. Essentially their attitude was ambivalent. The same absolutism which gave the building its compelling power was also repellent to their pluralism. But as a prototype the Unité was unavoidable. The problem was to transform its fundamental lessons into a terminology more flexibly attuned to particular cities, societies and climates.

The Unité idea had been published long before the building was completed, so the theorem had already influenced numerous housing schemes of the late 1940s and early 1950s. The critical attitudes later embodied in Team X had also been fermenting for some time. One of the most cogent statements of a new attitude had been conceived even before the Aix meeting: the 'ATBAT' housing proposal for Morocco (1951–6) by Vladimir Bodiansky and Shadrach Woods. The idea had been to produce a collective habitat in tune with local climate, culture and context. The architects therefore attempted to abstract some of the spatial features of the traditional North African city and to cross-breed

the resulting order with such useful devices of the Unité idea as the street-in-the-air, the *brise-soleil*/balcony and the roof terrace. Evidently, the two sources could be blended; indeed, it is arguable that the tight aggregation of North African cities which Le Corbusier saw in the 1930s inspired some features of the Unité in the first place.

The Charter of Athens had separated urban functions into broad divisions of living, working, leisure and circulation. The new sensibility required something less simplistic and mechanical. A new formal pattern was needed to express a more complex image of the city and of social behaviour. In the mid-1950s words like 'association', 'neighbourhood' and 'cluster' began to replace the earlier abstract terminology, while organic analogies for growth and change began to supersede the rigid geometries of the Ville Radieuse. The younger generation was troubled by the grand-slam aspect of *tabula rasa* Utopian planning and sought a more complex and sympathetic relationship between old urban tissue and new functions. Even so, it has to be emphasized that the inherited schemata of earlier modern architecture were not completely rejected; quite the contrary, they were accepted as valuable and then modified.

The British situation in the decade after the war offered every opportunity for experiment, owing to the impact of the blitz and to the emergence of a socialist policy on public housing. Mostly bland blocks of flats soon rose up, although London boroughs like Richmond, Pimlico, Finsbury, and Paddington were fortunate in acquiring creditable reworkings of Unité ideas. The other major paradigm was the Garden City which was reinterpreted in the New Towns; again, little architecture of lasting value was achieved. Alison and Peter Smithson, two young architects who delighted in the role of *enfants terribles* and who were members of Team X, felt that none of these approaches captured the essence of British post-war life. With a little help from the critic Reyner Banham they indulged in the sensibility of the 'New Brutalism', a term which suggested their fascination with the toughness of British working-class existence and the 'art brut' of Dubuffet, as well as their rejection of the devalued version of modern architecture that they saw being built. It is a tribute to the power of the Unité image that it should have

553

intervened in what was a somewhat routine English
exercise in sentimental populism of the 'kitchen
sink' variety. But in their scheme for workers'
housing at Golden Lane in the East End of London
(1952) the hold of the prototype can be sensed in
the use of slabs with access streets in the air. Like
the ATBAT scheme for Morocco, Golden Lane
also implied a criticism of the free-standing block.
The slabs were linked together in a linear way and
disposed to respond to the surrounding street
patterns, while the interior street was brought to
the edge of the façade where it was repeated at
every third level. The 'street-deck' was intended
to encourage chance encounters, and was a
rather abstract attempt at restating traditional
working-class doorstep life in the air. In the same
period the Smithsons evolved designs with zigzags
of linear housing based on patterns of movement,
and designed a scheme for Sheffield University
(1953) in which the street-deck was the unifying
element. They pointed gleefully to the drip paintings
of Jackson Pollock and the grainy photographs of
Nigel Henderson as evidence of a new aesthetic,
blending change, coarseness and the primitive.
They insisted that they were seeking a new language
for urban design, and rejected the Garden City
and 'Rational' models as equally irrelevant. Of the
latter they wrote:

The social driving force of this movement was slum clearance, the
provision of sun, light, air and green space in the over-populated
cities.

This social content was perfectly matched by the form of
functionalist architecture, the architecture of the academic period
which followed the great period of Cubism and Dada and De
Stijl, of the Esprit Nouveau. This was the period of the minimum
kitchen and the four functions, the mechanical concept of
architecture.

Today in every city in Europe we can see Rational Architecture
being built. Multi-storey flats running north–south in parallel
blocks just that distance apart that permits winter sun to enter
bottom storeys, and just high enough to get fully economic density
occupation of the ground area – where the extent of development
is sufficient we can see the working out of the theoretical isolates,
dwelling, working, recreation (of body and spirit), circulation; and
we wonder how anyone can possibly believe that in this lay the secret
of town building.

Instead, the Smithsons claimed that they were
seeking an environment which would give 'form to
our generation's idea of order', and that Golden
Lane was a partial realization of this idea. Their
polemics were heavily laced with illustrations of
Greek islands, Bath, working-class backyards,
kasbahs, and other dwelling arrangements of the
past which seemed to be 'a direct expression of a
way of life', but it was obvious that the dominant
image was still the Unité d'Habitation; the vein of
'peasantism' that they detected in Le Corbusier
clearly allied his post-war works in their minds with
some of the traditional, pre-industrial qualities they

553 Alison and Peter
Smithson, 'street-deck'
scheme for Golden Lane,
London, 1952,
photomontage of
proposed decks on
actual site

554 Denys Lasdun,
'cluster block', Claredale
Street, Bethnal Green,
London, 1954

sought to reinterpret. However, they remained committed to the definition of images which would be 'counterforms' to a post-war, automobile world. At later Team X meetings in which they played a major role, the Smithsons were to discover that many of their enthusiasms and dilemmas were shared by the other members, despite their varied backgrounds.

Among the housing schemes actually built in this period in Britain, Denys Lasdun's 'cluster blocks' in Bethnal Green, London, embodied a new position most clearly. These were also an attempt at forming a new image of community, appropriate to the problems of post-war urban reconstruction, an undertaking in which it became increasingly clear that the new and the old must have a more complex symbiotic relationship than that proposed by 'diagrammatic' slab planning. Lasdun was older than the Smithsons, but younger than the generation of Lubetkin, and so straddled the pre- and post-war worlds. He remained aloof from the polemics of the 'Brutalists', and his own style was partly formed in the 1930s. A superficial inspection of the Usk and Claredale Street clusters (1952 and 1954 in design, respectively) reveals clear debts to Lubetkin's vocabulary, to the image of the modern tower, and to the ideal of well-lit, well-ventilated flats open to the view and the sun. However, such themes were overlaid with others which amounted to a rejection of the monolithic slab. The circulation and noisy service chutes were placed in a central core, while the 'maisonettes in the air' were located in four separate volumes linked to the core by bridges. Part of the rationale for this form was that it allowed maximum exposure of the living rooms to the sun; but it also involved the idea of turning the traditional Bethnal Green street on its end, re-creating some of the indigenous features (backyards for washing, etc.) in the air, and avoiding the bleakness of a tunnel-like corridor in the usual 'block' of flats. The actual dwellings were made two storeys high and were thus based on the typical local house-type, while the sills and proportions restated the scale and rhythms of the neighbouring nineteenth-century façades. Thus the sanitary and sculptural qualities of the Unité were employed, but in a way which incorporated the local social and physical context. The plan shape, with its splayed angles and its suggestions of stems

554

and arteries, relied on biological analogies at odds with the Cartesian geometries of the Ville Radieuse slab idea.

Among the eventual members of the loose Team X affiliation were two Dutch architects, Jacob Bakema and Aldo Van Eyck. Despite the tenor of his theoretical remarks, the former seemed to do relatively little in his actual works to modify pre-war housing tactics; but the latter was preoccupied with the contrast between the vapid post-war rebuilding of cities like Rotterdam and the close-knit traditional Dutch cities. Van Eyck realized that the way forward lay in the re-creation of basic psychological qualities of shelter, yet in a language attuned to modern realities. He spelled out the position clearly at the 1959 CIAM congress at Otterlo where Team X ideas began to dominate:

Each period requires a constituent language – an instrument with which to tackle the human problems posed by the period, as well as those which, from period to period, remain the same, i.e., those posed by man – by all of us as primordial beings. The time has come to gather the old into the new; to rediscover the archaic qualities of human nature. I mean the timeless ones …

Van Eyck's quest for these timeless qualities eventually took him far afield to Dogon mud communities in sub-Saharan Africa and into the field of linguistic anthropology. His approach to vernacular forms was mystical; he saw them as expressions of coherent spiritual mythologies which he felt were sorely missing from most industrial building. His analysis focused on the cosmic meaning of symbolic elements like gates and entrances and on the hierarchies of spaces. He was also fascinated by the way buildings and streets were woven together. The problem was to translate these qualities to deal with the realities of an increasingly affluent northern Europe. Van Eyck's Orphanage near Amsterdam (1957–62) revealed his attempt at forming equivalent architectural systems using modern means of construction (see Chapter 30). But the process by which an authentic vernacular was conceived and constructed was necessarily far away from the activities of even a sensitive mind seeking basic values in an industrial society which seemed increasingly committed to a trashy and insubstantial consumerism.

The preoccupation with primary qualities of shelter, enclosure and procession, grasped in part from the study of traditional urban structures, went hand-in-hand with an obsession with the notion of 'place' in numerous projects of the early 1960s. The Utopian ideas of the pre-war period had seemed to imply the imposition of a new, more 'rational' order on the texture of the metropolis, but the result had often been a dramatic rupture between new and old. The architects associated with Team X wished to deal with the demands of an automobile society and to construct with industrialized building materials, but in a way which maintained the sense of urban – or rural – identity. Forms had therefore to be found which allowed a gradual transition between the old tissue and the new object. Urban spaces and individual buildings needed to be merged in a more complex overlapping order than was usual in modern planning. It is no surprise to discover that the urban theories of Camillo Sitte were avidly restudied in this period. Moreover, the social meaning of the street (which Le Corbusier had overlooked in his destruction of the *rue corridor* or traditional 'corridor street') was given new emphasis. Even the 'street-deck' concepts of the

555 Shadrach Woods, with Georges Candilis, Alex Josic and Manfred Schiedhelm, Free University of Berlin, Berlin-Zehlendorf, 1964–79, plan

556 Atelier 5, Siedlung Halen, Berne, 1961

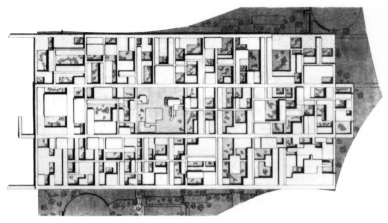

555

Smithsons seemed to lack a rich enough connection with pre-existing routes and with truly public urban space.

Something of this new urban consensus emerged in Alexis Josic, Georges Candilis and Shadrach Woods's unbuilt project for Frankfurt-Romerberg of 1963 that was based on a system of upper decks and streets linking the buildings together as a sort of pedestrian net above the services and automobiles beneath. One might perhaps see this order as an abstraction of the form of ancient Hellenistic cities like Priene (in Asia Minor), or as a relative (in procedure as well as form) of Le Corbusier's low-level Venice Hospital scheme. The buildings and the spaces between were locked together as a single system which attempted to restate the patterns of the neighbouring traditional city (but which never blended very well with the older fabric). The same architects worked with an analogous idea of a social network in their scheme for the Free University of Berlin of 1964–77. The theme of the upper walkway – a place preserving the social character of the street against modern vehicular functions – was pervasive in this period.

The 'mat' concept of architecture was the antithesis, obviously, of the free-standing slab; even so, it was still essentially part of the Unité tradition, as a fusion was still sought between concepts of city and individual building. Indeed, a number of models antithetical to the free-standing slab with a vacuum at its base were reactivated in this period: the perimeter courtyard block creating an interior precinct and reinforcing the shape of the street; the village, with its hierarchy of buildings and spaces; the hill town (or its conceptual relative the kasbah) with its apparent unity of topography, social hierarchy, built form and open space.

The prototype of a kasbah may have influenced the planning of the Siedlung Halen outside Berne (1961), by the Atelier 5 group, a 'squashed Unité' packed down to conform to the patterns of the landscape. (In fact, Le Corbusier had himself proposed a tight aggregation of dwellings and courts laid into a Mediterranean hillside in his proposal for 'Roq and Rob' holiday housing on the French Riviera in 1949.) The social relations of the Siedlung Halen were directly expressed in the gradual transition in scales, from the main piazza and street

557 Giancarlo de Carlo, Free University of Urbino, first phase, 1962–5

558 Josep Lluís Sert, Peabody Terraces married students' housing, Harvard University, Cambridge, Massachusetts, 1963–4

559 Minoru Yamasaki, Pruitt Igoe low-cost housing, St Louis, Missouri, 1950–4, demolished 1972

in the middle to the secondary routes, to the gardens, and then to the individual quarters. Giancarlo de Carlo's Free University of Urbino (1962–5) was another variant; indeed, universities were frequently employed as microcosms of urbanistic ideals, just as they had been in the interwar years. In this case the buildings were laid out on the crest of a low hill and splayed in a fan shape to maximize views and to harmonize with the contours. While the form probably reflected Aalto's 'organic' ideas, it was also a modern restatement of some of the typical elements and spaces of the medieval Italian city. A semi-enclosed space, rather than a free-standing object, became the main social focus, and everything possible was done to express the hierarchy of individual cells and social functions. A far less coherent version of this hill-town imagery was later pursued by Moshe Safdie in his 'Habitat' at Expo '67 in Montreal, while the most successful 'university city' of the period was probably Denys Lasdun's 'urban landscape' University of East Anglia of 1962–8 (see Chapter 29).

The combination of high-rise towers, perimeter blocks and courtyards was pursued in another variant of the 'Unité', also for university housing, but this time in the United States. This was Josep Lluís Sert's design for married-student housing at Harvard of 1962–4. Sert, it will be recalled (Chapter 21), had helped to found a Catalan branch of the Modern movement and had worked with Le Corbusier; from the beginning he had been concerned with the collaboration of architecture and urbanism. With the unfavourable outcome of the Spanish Civil War, Sert had emigrated to the United States. In 1942 he published the book *Can Our Cities Survive?* which spread CIAM pre-war urban doctrines in the English-speaking world; he was also, for a time, President of CIAM. The Harvard scheme, known as Peabody Terraces, was disposed as three main towers in a cluster around the traditional communal and collegiate device of a courtyard. The usual vacuum at the base of a tall building was avoided by gradations of scale between the main towers where lower perimeter dwellings stepped down to lawns, brick pathways and sheltered pedestrian routes. The structure combined poured and precast concrete and was detailed to give an idea of how the components were assembled; there was some analogy with timber construction. Delicate steel-framed balconies projected from the façades and were painted white. There were adjustable sunshading slats and small ventilating doors in primary colours. Together these supplied Peabody Terraces with human scale and a touch of life. Variation was achieved on the basis of a few standardized apartment types, ingeniously arranged in section, and linked by upper-gallery streets and bridges to the increasingly public spaces outside. One may see the scheme as an extension of the principles of the Unité, where such inherited ideas as the street-in-the-air, the *brise-soleil* and the roof terrace have been fused with the local courtyard tradition for student residences, and with the light wooden balconies of the nearby New England triple-decker houses. Thus a Utopian vision of an alternative city, in which an ideal harmony of man, nature and urban existence had been implied, was modulated, rendered less absolute, and wedded with a pre-existing context. The strategy was loosely similar to the one adopted a decade before in Lasdun's cluster conception, but it was expressed in a different personal style and with different regional responses in mind.

Sert's scheme was remarkable for the attention it gave to the quality of spaces between the buildings, to the disguise of parking, to townscape detail and ground materials, as well as to the expression of the actual forms of architecture. He was fortunate in having a client who intended the best, and was perhaps better able to achieve it than the usual public-housing agencies in the United States, and indeed most countries. The story of the inventive reinterpretation of the Unité ideal has, alas, the dreary and brutal backdrop of endless egg-crate high-rises built around the world in the 1950s and 1960s, in which minimum functional definitions were allowed to prevail over the rich elaboration of new communal images in touch with basic human needs. The problem must be traced to the over-simplification of a theorem: the Unité ideal needed all of its constituent parts to have a chance of succeeding. To reduce the matter to high density when no due attention was given to communal facilities was to court disaster; to create open space without greenery was to devalue the idea of the community living in contact with nature. The imitations of the Unité more often than not involved such drastic omissions. Does this mean that the prototype should be blamed for the later disastrous variations? Or is the blame to be laid on housing agencies and their architects for cutting corners in an over-simple response to the urban crises of the post-war era? However one answers these questions, the fact remains that the slang appellation 'vertical slum' fits many of the post-war experiments only too well. It is scarcely surprising that the now notorious arson (and eventual dynamiting by officials in 1972) of Minoru Yamasaki's low-cost housing scheme for St Louis, the Pruitt Igoe project of 1950–4, should have taken on the dimensions of a symbolic event; as the ultimate revenge of the populace for some supposed professional planning trick foisted upon them.

558

559

But it is hard to generalize about the 'high-rise' in the abstract. What may be good for Chicago's well-to-do may be bad, in its cheaper version, for the proletariat of Paris; what may be right for the outskirts of Copenhagen may be wrong for Willamaloo. Neither the proponents nor the opponents of high-rise ideas were very subtle in their arguments. Where the former, especially in the 1950s, had succeeded in constructing a vulgate of 'virtues' (cleanliness, density, greenery, order, replacement of slums, etc.), the latter, in the 1960s, assembled a standard set of complaints. It was argued that 'tall buildings' (all tall buildings, anywhere) caused 'social isolation', destroyed decent urban scale, were a strain for the very young and the very old, were lacking in domestic feeling, and represented the imposition of one social class on another. Whether or not these complaints were really traceable to architectural shortcomings, or to other forms of a *malaise*, it was evident that the charisma of the Unité, and of large-scale town planning, was beginning to fade.

The 1960s witnessed less sweeping critiques of the Unité that nevertheless reflected societal reactions against the free-standing slab. Neave Brown's Fleet Road Terrace Housing in London (1967) blended together new and old urban patterns and achieved high density on the basis of a low-rise solution. His project incorporated several features of the traditional London terrace but combined these with an entirely modern interlocking section based upon reinforced-concrete construction. Fleet Road relied upon certain long-standing London conventions for dealing with the front, side and entrances (plain façades with steps up and down over a light-well); the back (a mews with secondary accommodations over stables or garages); and the overall order (a neutral repetition of the basic module with parallel walls). At the same time it drew upon a modern inheritance (including Le Corbusier's Unité) which insisted upon tight functional planning, the provision of light deep within the dwelling through the use of a stepped section (permitting great flexibility) and the standardization of components. In Brown's solution, cars were tucked underneath the platforms, while private terraces with greenery were inserted adjacent to upper-level rooms. Customary layouts were sometimes inverted, so that in some units living rooms were placed alongside master bedrooms as a separate adult area up above. This was a realistic

560 Neave Brown, Fleet Road Terrace Housing, London, 1967

561 Fleet Road Terrace Housing, section

562 John Darbourne and Geoffrey Darke, Lillington Gardens housing, Pimlico, London, 1967–73

560

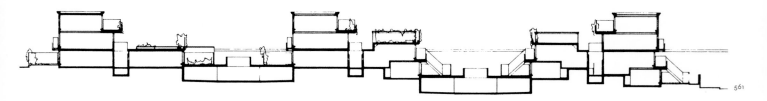

561

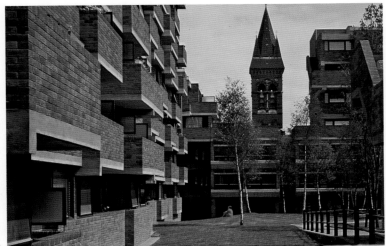

562

response to changing social habits of the 1960s involving greater independence for younger family members who could come and go freely. Fleet Road Terrace Housing was restrained, almost neutral in its architectural expression, but it contained many ingenious responses to the practical needs of daily existence, and rested upon a modern interpretation of the street as an *idea*: a type incorporating a social pattern and subtle gradations between public and private life. It constituted a demonstration, but one made quietly and without rhetoric.

The Lillington Gardens estate in Pimlico, London, by Darbourne and Darke, built between 1967 and 1973, was less disciplined and softer in its guiding thinking, and more picturesque in its form. Here the housing was wrapped around courtyards and precincts with sensitive level changes and vistas (recalling the townscape ideas of Gordon Cullen). The focus of the entire scheme was a pre-existing Gothic Revival church by G. E. Street. The new housing paid respect to its neighbour's coloured bricks and stone lintels with red-brick balconies and slender concrete beams. The street-deck principle was employed, but modified by planting and finely detailed brick surfaces. High density was achieved, but even the tallest parts of the estate had the feeling of connection with the surroundings and with the tree-filled courts. Traffic was excluded from the precinct by perimeter

blocks so that the idea of the traditional London square was restated in a new form which excluded the motor car. Courtyard type, hill town and Unité were thus cross-bred and blended with well-scaled responses to the Pimlico context. Standardization was still employed, but in support of the maximum visual variety, any sense of the free-standing monolith being avoided. The social make-up and ages of the residents were also varied, and such communal functions as a welfare centre, a pub, a clinic and an old people's home were included. A case could probably be made for the influence on Darbourne and Darke of Dutch housing schemes of the late 1910s such as the Eigen Haard by Michel de Klerk (Fig. 298), or of the red-brick vocabulary of Le Corbusier's Maisons Jaoul (Fig. 522). Equally one might see Lillington Street as a fully domesticated and thoroughly Anglicized version of the Unité: a fitting image for the well-meaning impulses and compromised Fabianism of the Welfare State. It may have lacked the visual unity and polemical challenge of its parent building, but it was a decent, socially responsible design none the less.

The history of the transformation of the Unité summarizes the process through which a major symbolic work, driven by an alternative Utopian dream, could gradually be softened and absorbed by the status quo. The Unité theorem was dragged from its initial heroic stance on the edge of a Mediterranean myth and forced to come to terms with the mess and complexity of faraway cities. In this process much fine housing was produced, and much that was disastrous, but in either case the contradictions of the avant-garde, visionary approach to planning were brought to the fore. Le Corbusier genuinely believed that his was the right universal formula for the regeneration of the community. But the very process of transmitting the formula left behind the aura of the original statement. Moreover, the societies in which the debased versions of his dream were built grew increasingly sceptical of both environmental determinism and social engineering, and became less and less able to project or define a sense of the possible social order in architecture. The single chapter of the Unité encapsulates the transition from the hopes of one era to the doubts, caution and cynicism of another.

25

alvar
aalto
and
scandinavian
developments

Nature, not the
machine, is the most
important model for
architecture.
Alvar Aalto, 1938

563 Alvar Aalto,
Vuoksenniska Church
(Church of the Three
Crosses), Imatra, 1956–9,
detail of east-side
windows

The process described in the last chapter whereby the ideas of a powerful prototype were transformed to meet various conditions was repeated many times throughout the 1950s and 1960s. Linked to this pattern of dissemination were self-conscious attempts at blending modern architecture with national and regional traditions. Uninventive modern building was dull and seemed to represent technological brashness and social anomy. It was a long way from the poetic power of the finest inter-war works to the dreary housing schemes, offices and schools that constituted the debased International manner prevalent in the 1950s. Some sort of regeneration was evidently necessary.

In the search for new inspirations and primal signposts, peasant vernaculars once again came into vogue. They evoked a reassuring, pre-industrial world in which men, things and natural forces seemed to work in unison. They also suggested keys for adapting to local environments, climates and traditions, and supplied possible correctives to the enfeebled versions of the International Style. Vague yearnings for archetypes were sensed in many of the arts in this period. Universalizing and transcultural psychological theories about 'Man' (derived from Carl Jung's ideas, for example) kept uneasy company with a quest for regional identity which steered carefully around overt nationalist positions. This was one of the ways in which a war-torn Europe sought internal equilibrium. The reverberations were felt by artists as diverse as Le Corbusier and Aalto; they emerged in the debates around the conference tables and in the musings of Team X.

Giedion baptized the mood the 'New Regionalism' and hastened to point out that it had nothing in common with inter-war 'blood-and-soil' ideologies such as those which had led to a neo-vernacular style under Nazism. The idea was to cross-breed principles of indigenous building with languages of modern design. A procured naïvety was evidently to be valued, and modern architecture was to show both greater respect for differences of climate and a more sensitive appreciation of 'place'. At its worst this could end up in tepid imitations of vernacular forms; at its best it led to Le Corbusier's Maisons Jaoul, or to Jørn Utzon's houses at Kingo, in Denmark, of 1956–60 (see below).

In Finland, in particular, the process of 'naturalization' of modern architecture had already begun in the 1930s, particularly in the work of Alvar Aalto. Indeed, the International Style had been a brief interlude and its lessons had soon been grafted to a substructure of national (or else National Romantic) building traditions. One is almost tempted to declare some Nordic genius for the sensitive handling of locale, landscape, light and natural materials. But then conditions were different from elsewhere in Europe: industrialization had less of a drastic impact; timber was plentiful; and the rural vernacular was a continuing point of reference.

Although Scandinavian modern design enjoyed a vogue in the 1950s and was associated with ovoid wooden salad bowls and organic banisters, this was not the whole story. There were also several strands of 'minimalism' which combined sparse abstraction and purity of form with a tactile sense of both natural and industrial materials. In Denmark, for example, Arne Jacobsen demonstrated how Miesian ideas could be refashioned in a steel and glass vocabulary combining elegance of detail with lightness of touch; he also designed furniture, glassware and other objects which were simplified, but sympathetic to the human hand. The manufacture of mass-produced models was aided by the strength of Scandinavian craft traditions, which perhaps took to industrialization with less fuss than had been the case in Germany and Britain.

There was never quite an Aalto School, but he hovered as a sort of father-figure over Scandinavian architecture none the less. His prototypes were well adapted to the scale of the landscape and to the stringencies of the Nordic climate; but he was also inimitable, and the architects who succeeded in translating his basic lessons and emerging with their own creative identities were few in number. Apart from their influence on others, Aalto's late works contained a drama of their own, and they need to be considered alongside the works of the other 'modern masters' in their maturity; as with them, new territories of expression were extended, while certain older themes continued to grow.

When the war came to an end, Aalto was 47 years old. He had managed to survive stagnant economic conditions in Finland by hazardous trips across the Atlantic to teach in Cambridge, Massachusetts, at the Massachusetts Institute of Technology (MIT),

only a mile away from Gropius at Harvard (but very far removed in spirit). Aalto's first notable post-war commission stemmed from this institutional connection: it was to design Baker House (1947–8), a student dormitory for MIT on a site to one side of the campus, with views over a busy road towards the broad basin of the River Charles. Aalto broke the programme down into its private and communal elements and disposed the former – the students' rooms – in a serpentine spine. This form was no mere whimsy, but had a variety of practical, aesthetic and symbolic justifications. It created considerable variety in the rooms and allowed diagonal views up and down the river; it made for an unmonolithic form of great sculptural vitality; and it marked out a small enclave to one side of the campus. The communal parts of the programme were enclosed in rectangular forms laid out on a diagonal axis at ground level; in fact the lounge and dining area was double-height and part buried below ground. This contrast in geometry was reinforced by contrasts in material between the

564 Alvar Aalto, Baker House student dormitory, Massachusetts Institute of Technology, Cambridge, 1947–8

565 Baker House student dormitory, pencil drawing showing trellising. Alvar Aalto Foundation, Helsinki

564

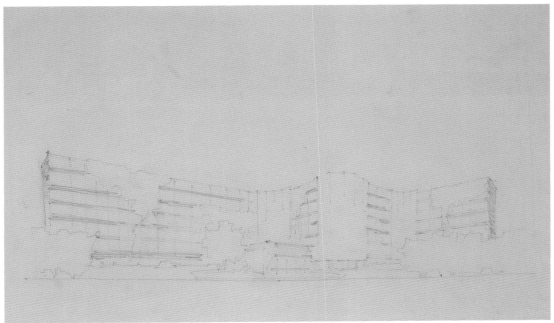

565

horizontal, hovering concrete and stone-clad roofs of the lounge/dining room area, and the rough red-brick textures of the serpentine wall punctured by the windows of the private rooms. Overall, the organization seemed to suggest that Aalto had taken the formula of the Pavillon Suisse – a hovering rectangular slab for the student rooms, curved rubble areas for the public functions – and turned it on its head. Indeed, the Baker House design started as an oblong block that was only gradually modified into a curved form.

Although Aalto was probably inspired by the local Boston tradition of red-brick houses with sinuous, curved sequences of bays, the thinking behind the building and its forms was rooted in his pre-war explorations. The curves were related to his continuous search for anthropomorphic forms and forms inspired by natural phenomena, in everything from furniture-design to the layout of large schemes on the Finnish landscape. Among the drawings for Baker House is one showing the building covered with trellises of thick greenery, like some geological formation. The rough, brick surfaces gave the impression that the building was already old, and the effects of weathering were anticipated and

invited. The contrast with the mechanical slickness then in vogue in America was extreme, and seemed to suggest a rejection of industrialism in favour of more lasting human themes. It is scarcely surprising that Baker House should have been perceived in America at the time as a challenge to the straitjacket of the International Style stemming from Gropius; it is equally notable that the building had little influence in the United States.

Aalto's idea of buildings as intermediaries between human life and the natural landscape was explored continuously in the post-war years. This was a period of rapid reconstruction and urbanization in Finland (whole villages and townships had been destroyed), and Aalto wished to find some way of blending modern architecture with topography in rural and semi-rural places. He reverted time and again to splayed volumes, to stratification, to layers of platforms and steps, and to irregular silhouettes arising from light-wells and sloping roofs. Behind these fragmentations of form was a larger idea of a democratic society gathering in an informal way within the loose framework supplied by public institutions such as town halls, churches and libraries. Aalto was acutely sensitive to

566 Alvar Aalto,
Town Hall, Säynätsalo,
1949–52

567 Town Hall,
Säynätsalo, plans of
ground-floor, courtyard
and council chamber
levels

568 Town Hall,
Säynätsalo, Council
Chamber

566

the contours of the land, to the angle and direction of winter sunlight, and to the need for convivial social settings linked directly to surrounding nature by meandering routes and framed views. He responded to the need for a new image of community and to a cultural condition between urbanity and rusticity.

Aalto felt that there were almost archetypal building configurations expressing the basic forms of human society. These he was able to intuit in both the vernacular and the most ancient monumental buildings; there was no opposition between 'high' and 'low' traditions where the search for fundamentals was concerned. One such archetype was the courtyard or, to be more precise, the 'harbour', formed by an inward-looking perimeter building on three sides, and linked to the surroundings by overflows of steps and levels. The Villa Mairea (1938–41) had been a variant on this scheme (Chapter 19) and Aalto's own 'experimental house' at Muuratsalo of 1953 was another. Variations on the idea recurred in many of his public (or quasi-public) schemes in the 1950s and 1960s when

a focus was needed which none the less had to be linked to a larger context. Aalto's sensitivity to vernacular precedent emerges in his description of the 'Karelian house' – a type of farmhouse aggregation with a scattering of dwellings, barns and pens around a loosely-defined enclosure – in the remote eastern province of Finland:

A dilapidated Karelian village is somehow similar in appearance to a Greek ruin, where, also, the materials' uniformity is a dominant feature, though marble replaces wood … Another significant special feature is the manner in which the Karelian house has come about, both its historical development and its building methods … The Karelian house is in a way a building that begins with a single modest cell or with an imperfect embryo building, shelter for man and animals, and which then figuratively speaking grows year by year. 'The expanded Karelian house' can in a way be compared to a biological cell formation …

This remarkable ability to grow and adapt is best reflected in the Karelian building's main architectural principle, the fact that the roof angle isn't constant.

It is interesting to carry this image in mind when one approaches Aalto's town centre at Säynätsalo of 1949–52. This was placed at the heart of an island community – the space at the centre becoming, in a sense, the focal point of the entire local society. The complex included a Council Chamber together with a public library. At ground level there were shops which could be transformed into government offices once the need arose. The Council Chamber was contained in an almost cubic volume with a slanted roof, and acted as the pivot of the scheme as one approached over the rising levels of land by means of a forest path, then up the stairs and across the court. Some variation of fenestration and texture was employed to articulate the different sides of the building: wooden-slatted windows and balconies were set off against predominant rough red-brick surfaces. With its steps overgrown with grass, its variation of silhouette, and its weathered materials, Säynätsalo had almost the air of an ancient complex of buildings which had grown gradually, bit by bit. The buildings blended with their forest setting and the varying levels of the site. Any lapse into the merely picturesque was held in check by an underlying formal discipline.

The Council Chamber at Säynätsalo had the character of a democratic meeting house and was reached by a circuitous route culminating in a narrow flight of stairs. It was entered off-axis and its naked brick walls, splayed timber roof-beams and broad wooden benches were arranged informally to encourage easy exchange and debate. The benches celebrated local craft (Saynätsalo was a timber town) but were also vivid symbols of egalitarian involvement. Their curved profiles recalled Alto's sketches of the mouldings in Greek theatres. A stark brick room, with light filtering in from above, the Council Chamber contained hidden presences and distilled both local and classical archetypes for political assembly: the Finnish sauna (where all were stripped to the same status and the sense of community was reinforced); and the type of rectangular state chamber for council meetings found in ancient Hellenistic cities such as Miletus or Priene. Säynätsalo was a casual building with

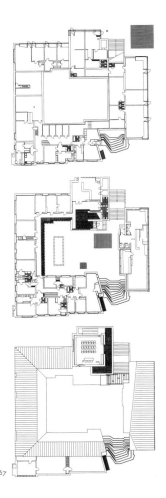

567

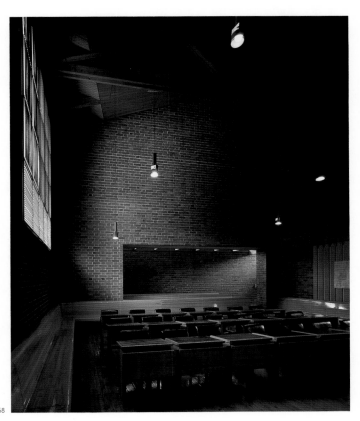

568

569   Alvar Aalto,
Vuoksenniska Church
(Church of the Three
Crosses), Imatra, 1956–9,
interior

570   Vuoksenniska
Church, sketch plan, 1956

571   Vuoksenniska
Church

572   Alvar Aalto,
Public Library, Rovaniemi,
1963–8, sketch plan

569

just a hint of ritual; it was civic without being
monumental, and lived between urban and rural
worlds. In Aalto's private terms it drew together the
Greek democratic city in its ruined shape with the
scraped glacial contours of the north.

Between 1950 and his death in 1973, Aalto
produced an extraordinary number of buildings
and projects, receiving commissions in places as far
apart as Oregon and Persia. Still, the majority of his
buildings were for Finland and other Scandinavian
countries. The range of tasks handled was also very
wide and included schools, libraries, churches,
housing schemes, university plans and entire urban
layouts. Each building was marked by a unique
response to the aspirations of the client, to the
anticipated character of human behaviour, and to
the configuration of the particular site whether in
countryside or city. Even so there were transcendent
themes and typical forms which added up to an
architectural language based upon a general corpus
of principles. This language represented a mythical

570

571

One of the recurrent Aalto configurations was a fan shape attached to a rectangle. This occurred in many of his designs for small public libraries (e.g. Rovaniemi, 1963–8) where the rectangle might contain offices, and the fan might radiate from a single central point, across a unified reading room with open book stacks, to finish in an irregular perimeter with small areas for individuals who wished to have privacy, a view and direct daylight. Variations on the fan could also be found in Aalto's many designs for auditoriums and concert halls (e.g. Finlandia Hall in Helsinki); even in the splayed plan forms of the unbuilt Museum of Modern Art for Shiraz in Persia. The fan could also be used to generate space between buildings, and in Aalto's own studio near Helsinki there was an outdoor, stepping precinct that was gently curved. Beyond practical considerations and programmatic distinctions, the combination of the hard-edged rectangle and the curved or fractured fan encapsulated Aalto's idea of the transition from town to landscape, from man-made to natural worlds. Here then was one of these basic patterns intrinsic to a true style. But each time the 'type-form' was employed it had to be rethought in the new context; it was not sufficient just to reuse it like a mechanical formula.

interpretation of society, and reflected the artist's ideas of both nature and history.

Like Wright, Le Corbusier, Mies van der Rohe or any other architect who achieved a genuine style, Aalto distilled many levels of meaning in his system of forms. A single sinuous line could blend the idea of a building as an illuminated vessel with the conception of a structure as a frozen wave of sound. For the Vuoksenniska Church near Imatra of 1957–9, these themes were brought together in a 'polyphonic' space resulting from the inter-penetration of uneven curves in plan and section. Slats and louvres over the windows reinforced the rhythm while fracturing the light over smooth white surfaces. In Aalto's late works, layers and levels were often combined in a complex stratification, while tactile details such as railings or handles reinforced the sense of the human body moving through space. The architect had less and less need for a 'rational' order; the vitality of the sketch seemed to be translated directly into the finished form.

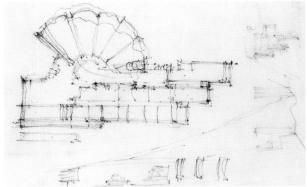

572

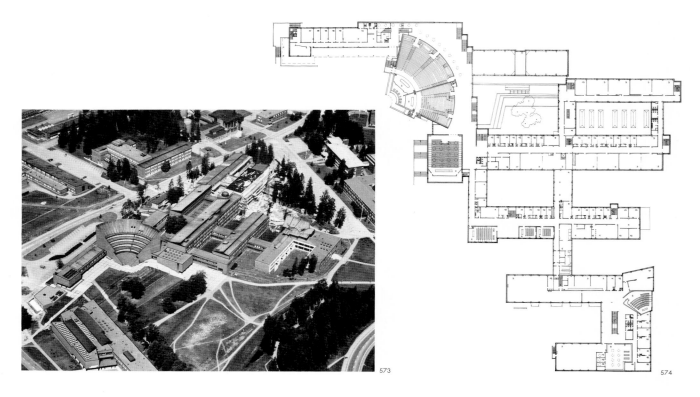

573

574

In the Helsinki University of Technology, Espoo, of 1949–66, the fan form appeared again in one of its most daring manifestations. The site was irregular, bordered on two sides by motorways, with a slight slope in the terrain. Aalto made the main auditorium the focus of the whole group of buildings and placed it in a prominent position, expressed as a wedge-shaped volume. This supplied a ceremonial centre to the project and acted as a pivot between the two directions of parallel, extendible strips containing classrooms, offices and laboratories. In effect, the wedge was also an outdoor theatre which gathered up the surrounding landscape in its stepping form. Light was brought in through the uprights of the steps, then reflected downwards into the lecture halls beneath by means of curved scoops which recalled Aalto's sketches of concave, sound-reflecting surfaces in antique theatres. In the far north, winter light was in short supply and this section was a way of maximizing its brief but life-enhancing presence. But the image of an outdoor theatre pierced by rays of light also corresponded to Aalto's vision of a liberal

academic institution dedicated to enlightenment. The University of Technology was like a small city in the landscape. Its plan implied both hierarchy and the separation of parts; a 'topographical' order which included stepping levels of ground and spaces between buildings. A similar approach to contours, fragments and interrelations informed many of Aalto's urban designs of the 1950s and 1960s (e.g. the city centre at Seinäjoki, or the plan for the area around Finlandia Hall in Helsinki). Beneath the surface of urban existence there was a basically geological metaphor. As early as 1926, Aalto had referred to the stratified rocks in Mantegna's paintings as a 'synthetic landscape', 'a small hint to our present-day urban planners on how they should approach their task'.

There was some affinity between Aalto's 'land-mass sculpture' approach to architecture, and the late works of Le Corbusier, particularly Ronchamp. Aalto was preoccupied with the idea of an architecture close to 'nature': more than just an insistence on natural materials and local topography, this meant that nature should be

573 Alvar Aalto, Helsinki University of Technology (formerly Finnish Technical Institute at Otaniemi), Espoo, 1949–66, aerial view

574 Helsinki University of Technology, plan

575 Helsinki University of Technology, main lecture theatre

576 Alvar Aalto, sketch of the amphitheatre at Delphi, Greece, 1953

575

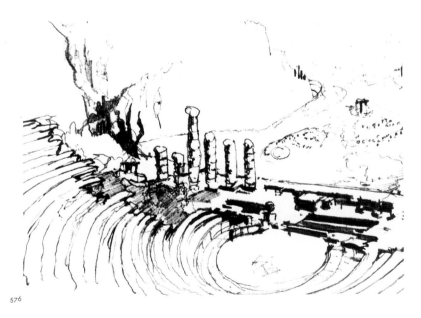

576

understood as a source of 'laws', as a 'model for architecture', in his own words. Like Le Corbusier, Aalto was drawn to the classical world, and to the forceful interaction of the intellectual with the sensual in the architecture of ancient Greece. But whereas for the Swiss the Parthenon was the prime exemplar (a 'pure creation of the mind'), for Aalto the chief inspiration lay in the way the Greeks arranged their urban sites with amphitheatres, stadia, and ceremonial platforms linked by paths and routes. It was an 'irregular' order of this kind – in which there was, none the less, a harmony of buildings, landscape and the spirit of place – that Aalto managed to evoke in his drawings of antique ruins, especially Delphi, and that he attempted to translate into his own architecture and urban designs. It may be that the final touchstone for the fan shape which so obsessed him was the Greek amphitheatre, fractured and eroded by time.

At this point it is worth attempting some generalizations about Aalto's sensibility in relation to other strands of the modern movement around 1960. In his late works, in those of Le Corbusier, in some projects by Team X, in the work of diverse individuals like Denys Lasdun, Louis Kahn or Jørn Utzon, even in the art of a painter such as Robert Rauschenberg, one senses a new complexity and ambiguity in the relationship between the art object and its surrounding spatial or cultural field. At some level this was a continuation of the fundamental changes made by Cubism at the turn of the century, but it seems also to have been related to an 'existential' frame of mind. Similarly there was a more overt acceptance of the past, but a past that was often seen in almost archaic terms. This was not a case of returning to nineteenth-century eclecticism, but of blending together, as it were, some of the primary devices of modern architecture with an ancient sensibility. Accompanying this development was a renewed interest in the unique qualities of materials and in the directness of things in themselves: slabs, gutters, rails, construction details. Finally, one notes a shift from mechanistic analogies to ones based upon geological or biological orders. Aalto (who was already working in some of these directions in the 1930s and 1940s) seems to have grasped and incorporated all these tendencies within one huge imaginative structure; but lesser talents paid increasing attention to similar questions at the same time.

Aalto's imitators, like those of Le Corbusier or Wright or Mies van der Rohe, tended to acquire some of the external mannerisms without grasping the underlying meaning or structure of thought. This was usual and to be expected. Nor was it always a bad thing: Aaltoesque pastiches did at least have a complexity and texture which would have been lacking without his influence. However, there were some artists capable of extending Aalto's principles, and using them to feed their own. Among these was the Finnish architect Reima Pietila, who evolved a metaphorical language of his own, nourished by primal images of the landscape. Aalto's influence spread well beyond national boundaries as well – to the rest of Scandinavia, and even to Spain and Portugal where certain 'Mediterranean' ingredients in his work stimulated architects such as Antonio Fernandez Alba and Alvaro Siza to make a fresh interpretation of their own situations (Chapter 26).

In the Nordic countries, what might be called an 'organic' tendency was accompanied by a precise minimalism which took several different forms, and which was inspired by the 'lucid quietude' of Mies van der Rohe, by the stern geometries of the vernacular, and by abstract painting. In Finland itself, Aulis Blomstedt was a key figure as a practitioner, theorist and teacher in encouring a mathematical discipline and a spirit of abnegation. Blomstedt spoke of architecture as 'the art of subordination' and evolved a methodology combining modular standardization and Pythagorean proportions. His terrace houses at Tapiola (1954) were self-effacing but harmonic in form. The Otaniemi Chapel at Espoo near Helsinki (1957), designed by Kaija and Heikki Siren, reduced structure to a sparse framework of walls, stilts, fences and roofs, adjusted to admit light and to frame the view of a free-standing cross in a forest glade beyond the altar. The building defined a geometrical precinct on the edge of the forest, and combined the abstraction of modernism with the tactile values of rural buildings in timber. The fence bounding the site was made of steel, but twig bindings were woven into it: the industrial and the rustic were sublimated by the order of the building. The chapel at Espoo extended an honourable lineage of Nordic courtyard types (including Aalto's unbuilt Funerary Church for Lyngby of 1952 and the smaller chapels in Asplund's Woodland Crematorium). Without rhetoric or forced symbolism, it also reinvestigated some of the earliest forms associated with congregation: the platform, the atrium and the assembly in a clearing.

577

578

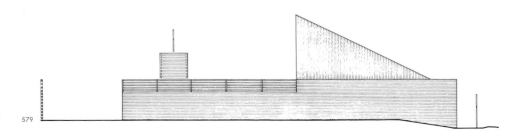

579

The Danish architect Arne Jacobsen laid the foundations of his architectural position in the 1930s, but soon moved beyond the obvious features of the International Style towards an architecture of formal restraint and material elegance, inspired by both the purity of the Danish vernacular and the disciplines of modern industrial design. The Town Hall at Rødovre of 1955 and the SAS Royal Hotel in Copenhagen of 1958–60 both made use of prismatic volumes and curtain walls in glass and steel, the latter being a fresh reinterpretation of North American models for the skyscraper. Even when constrained by standardization, Jacobsen was able to maintain a close attention to fabrication in steel, glass, stone, wood and brick. The suspended spiral staircases of several of his buildings, with their intricate expression of joints, connections, suspending-rods and slender treads, were virtually works of art in their own right. In parallel with these larger-scaled buildings using extensive glazing (and

580   Arne Jacobsen,
SAS Royal Hotel,
Copenhagen, 1958–60

581   Arne Jacobsen,
Carl Christensen Factory,
Aalborg, 1957

582   Jørgen Bo and
Vilhelm Wohlert,
Louisiana Museum of
Modern Art, Humlebaek,
1958

580

581

582

a vocabulary which owed something to both Mies and Eliel Saarinen), Jacobsen also developed the expressive potentials of the planar brick wall, starting with the funnel-like shapes of the Fish Smokehouse at Odden Harbour of 1942, and going on to the diagonal spatial dividers of the Søholm Terrace Houses at Klampenborg of 1950. In his best buildings, as in his furniture, glassware and cutlery designs, Jacobsen relied upon a clear, dominating idea, a reduced abstract form and a tense, linear silhouette. The Carl Christensen Factory at Aalborg, North Jutland of 1957 combined sharp-cut brick walls with a polished stainless-steel cylindrical stack, and worked along the line between industrialism and traditional craft.

The Louisiana Museum of Modern Art in Humlebaek designed by Jørgen Bo and Vilhelm Wohlert in 1958, drew upon several influences typical of this period in Danish architecture – Wright, Aalto, Mies van der Rohe, Japanese traditional architecture – but established its own ground rules in the exploration of spatial variety on the basis of a few standard pieces. The site was both demanding and rich in opportunity, in that a collection of modern paintings and sculptures needed displaying along a covered walkway between a fine eighteenth-century house and the sea, with the

Swedish coastline in the distance. Bo and Wohlert planned the building to take maximum advantage of this sequence without disrupting the landscape. Essentially the Louisiana Museum was a linear building defined by white planar walls and low wooden roofs; the result was a quiet but elegant structure from which the garden was grasped as a series of vignettes, and these, in turn, enhanced the works of art. One of the most stunning effects was achieved by placing the stick-like Giacometti sculptures in a double volume against a backdrop of marshland and reeds; this particular space was entered at an upper level. The Museum then gradually changed direction, to meander to the water's edge where a path continued (without the building over it) along a coastal way. The splay of the plan and the sensitivity to topography are reminiscent of Aalto. But the Louisiana design also had a certain regional sensitivity, since it seemed to fuse Miesian planar walls and spatial effects with the whitewashed enclosures and wooden structures of the Danish vernacular. The whole was permeated with a fine sense of proportion and a delicate scale which made it a comfortable neighbour for architecture of any age.

Another Danish architect to transform a variety of modern and ancient influences to good purpose

was Jørn Utzon, who was born in 1918 and studied at the Academy of Arts in Copenhagen under Steen Ejler Rasmussen and Kay Fisker. The period between the end of the war and 1957, when he won the Sydney Opera House competition, was one of constant travel, few commissions, and a vast absorption of impressions. He worked for a time with Aalto, absorbed much from the work of Asplund and visited Wright at Taliesin; he was also drawn to the sculpture of Henri Laurens, which provided basic lessons in abstraction and anthropomorphism. He travelled extensively in Mexico, the Far East, and North Africa, filling his sketchbooks with ideas and impressions. Among the strongest influences on him were the mud buildings he saw in Morocco and the cubic aggregate forms of Berber villages clustered around platforms and terraces in the High Atlas Mountains.

It is therefore insufficient to see Utzon as a mere follower of his Scandinavian mentors Asplund and Aalto, though he did draw on both in evolving qualities of subtle ordering and spatial complexity. In the Kingo Houses near Elsinore in Zeeland of 1956–60, he designed an L-shaped type, into the elbow of which a small garden was inserted. He disposed this standard in a variety of different ways over the topography to create a hierarchy between the individual home and the community, and to maximize a variety of site responses on a gently

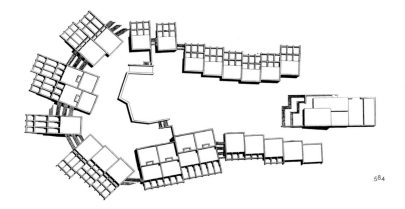

sloping terrain. The terrace houses at Fredensborg (1962–3) continued something of this theme, but created an even greater variety of rhythms through a more complex form including towers. The materials were humble brick and pantiles, and the effect was akin to the 'anonymous' vernacular buildings so much discussed at the time. The overall project layout of the Birkehoj at Elsinore (1963) introduced yet another pattern using standardized elements, grouping them around a loosely defined 'harbour' in which the sculpting of land-mass platforms helped to link the parts and give meaning to the spaces between. In this case it is possible to perceive the lingering debts to Aalto and to vernacular expressions of community, but the style was Utzon's own. Moreover, the arrangement also suggests loose parallels with some of the ideas being pursued by Van Eyck, De Carlo and others at about the same time.

Of course, the major building for which Utzon is internationally known is the extraordinary Sydney Opera House designed between 1957 and 1966, and then brought to completion in a modified form after his resignation. Here is not the place to untangle the only half-known personal and political complexities which led to this sad state of affairs. The results, so far as the architecture was concerned, were that the interior was quite different from Utzon's probable vision; that many of the details (of which he may have had an imprecise idea himself) were also gradually evolved by minds other than his own; and that the shells had a more vertical thrust than that envisaged in the earlier drawings.

But the image of these soaring white curves at the end of Bennelong Point, jutting out into the harbour and echoing the silhouette of the bridge and the sharp curves of the sails nearby, still has great power to move. They rise upwards from low platforms which themselves step up to their highest points at the water's edge. Into the platforms are laid the two main auditoriums on a slightly converging geometry, while a small space to the landward side contains a restaurant. The sails, butting into and slicing one another, rising and pitching against the sky, seem to transmit a visual force felt equally in their tense profiles and their smooth but slightly textured surfaces. The original idea for the interiors is best grasped from a section which shows a sort of counterwave motion of curved ceilings flowing beneath the vast roofs above. The fly-towers, finally, were buried under the highest of the shells, thus disturbing some hard-line puritans who were unable

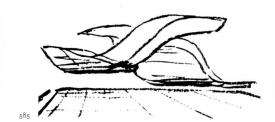

585

586

587 Jørn Utzon, Sydney
Opera House, 1957–73,
detail

588 Sydney Opera
House, section through
original scheme

589 Sydney Opera
House, plan

587

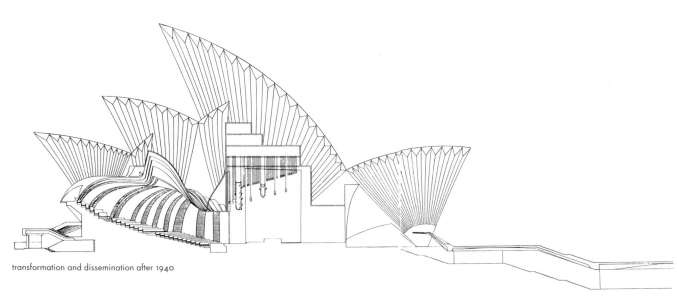

transformation and dissemination after 1940

588

to enjoy the contrasts and complexities between the interior and the exterior.

As is true of any original work of art, it serves only a limited purpose to list possible sources or analogies. The platform theme was on Utzon's mind anyway, as is clear from his housing designs, but in a monumental context it may have been specifically inspired by the artificial hills with ceremonial steps of Monte Alban, the ancient Mexican site which the architect had sketched during his travels. The shells were a staggering invention, perhaps partly influenced by Bruno Taut's curved crustacean abstractions of the 1920s, and perhaps partly prompted by the complex interlacing curvature which Utzon had seen in the work of Aalto; although here too were longer-range echoes, since Utzon's transformational sketches showed an Oriental temple roof hovering above a level plane, even clouds floating above a horizon. Whatever the historical or natural analogies, they were absorbed into a fresh synthesis, an idea which abstracted the waves and sails of the harbour even as it made visual reference to the flow of sound. It is curious that this *symbolic* expression of musical rhythms should in fact have posed considerable acoustic problems. Utzon's entire approach to design involved an oscillation back and forth between abstraction, metaphor and structural thinking. For example, the splayed window struts which were to reconcile the varying curvatures, and to stand up to structural and wind loads in the vast openings, were probably traceable to the architect's interest in the wing structures of birds.

But there were other levels to the symbolism of the building. It was in a sense a modern cathedral consecrated to a supremely important national art. One historian wrote of the concept that it '… concentrates the unconscious meanings of its urban context in the same way as Notre-Dame, situated on the Île de la Cité, does for Paris. It manifests the spirit of the city …' Utzon himself referred to the Opera House as a sort of church:

… if you think of a Gothic church you are closer to what I have been aiming at … looking at a Gothic church, you never get tired, you will never be finished with it … this interplay of light and movement … makes it a living thing.

Indeed, Utzon attempted to design a standardized system of parts which could eventually be assembled into his free-form design, in much the same way that Gothic architects had used repeated systems to achieve their sublime and complex spatial effects. At Sydney this eventually necessitated both a change in the geometry of the shells so that they conformed to a spheroid profile, and considerable experimentation with pre-cast concrete, in which the engineer Ove Arup played a major part. Many of the details remained to be realized at the time of Utzon's resignation, and the Opera House looked for a time as if it might be a white elephant. At last it opened in 1973, having already become an Australian national icon.

Long before this, the Sydney Opera House had become part of the folklore of modern architecture. Sigfried Giedion published the design in the later editions of *Space, Time and Architecture*, and conferred upon Utzon the mantle of the great tradition. The Opera House was presented alongside Le Corbusier's late works and Kenzo Tange's monumental buildings in Japan as evidence of a new elemental tendency in which the fusion of buildings with their context was held to be crucial to the emergent spatial conception. In a sense the choice was premature, as it was not clear what the Utzon design would really be like when finished; even so, this was judicious appreciation of a great architectural idea. Moreover, it was an idea which, in its combination of the abstract and the naturalistic, in its fusion of the complex and the simple, in its enrichment of the structural and spatial ideas of earlier modern architecture, and in its transformation of ancient monumentality, encapsulated some of the aims of a new generation.

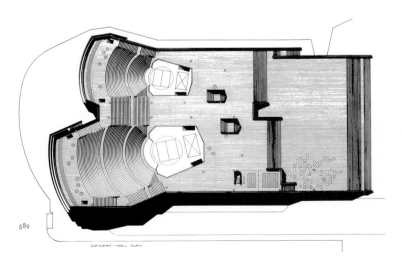

589

CONCERT · HALL · PLAN ·

26

disjunctions
and
continuities
in the
europe
of the
1950s

Considering history as
a process, one can
claim that it is subject
to continuity or crisis,
depending on whether
one wishes to emphasize
permanence or change
Ernesto Rogers, 1957

590 Hans Scharoun,
Berlin Philharmonie
Concert Hall, 1956–63,
auditorium

After 1945, in the war-damaged areas of Western and Eastern Europe, the first question had been survival, the second the guarantee of a roof over people's heads, so it was not altogether surprising that the emphasis should have been on prose rather than poetry, on norms rather than unique ideas. The remarkable individual inventions of figures such as Le Corbusier, Aalto, Utzon or Jacobsen stood out against a background of relatively neutral modern buildings which supplied solutions to the problems of shelter, hygiene and function but which often lacked humanity and urban sensitivity. The new economic order seemed destined, with or without architects, to create widely dispersed, free-standing objects which were inimical to the patterns of the traditional European city and which often lacked any sense of identity. The problem was not so much a shortage of talent, as the absence of an acceptable and pliable set of rules for putting together towns: some equivalent to the vernaculars of the past for handling buildings and urban spaces of medium to low intensity. The void was not filled by the diagrammatic versions of pre-war urban visions constructed in the 1950s, as these ignored variations of climate, culture and topography. It is little wonder that a critical position emerged whereby the modernist inheritance was to be revitalized through contact with the demands of particular situations and places.

Whether the architect was in Athens or Amsterdam, on the Atlantic coast of Portugal or close to the North Cape, he still needed an architectural language, and in the 1950s he was most likely to find it through a considered and critical re-examination of earlier modern architecture (which each would perceive in his own way), and through a distillation of those contemporary currents at home or abroad which seemed best to answer the practical and symbolic tasks at hand. Consensus was rare. The post-war years in Europe were characterized by a diversity of beliefs, forms and pedigrees, even by conflicting historical claims about what had really counted in earlier modernism. Schisms and oppositions were abundant between 'Rationalism' and 'organicism'; between those who advocated Mies van der Rohe, and those who advocated Le Corbusier (or Wright, or Aalto, or somebody else); between those who looked beyond national frontiers, and those who

looked within; between those who looked forward and those who looked back.

In most cases in Europe, post-war developments could build upon pre-war ones. Here a great deal depended upon the depth of the foundations and the relevance and resonance of the pre-war prototypes already in place. Finland was the unusual case of a country which, while it suffered severe war damage, none the less sustained a continuous development. Certainly this had to do with the sheer presence and inventiveness of Alvar Aalto, but beyond individuals there was an entire national endeavour of modernization in both private and public sectors which fostered a variegated modernism. Naturally, each country had its own passions and phobias arising from its particular history, culture, politics and pre-existing architectural traditions. In West Germany, for example, the main tasks were to house millions who had lost their homes in the war and to create an efficient new industrial system on a democratic base. Modern architecture held out the promise of a brave new world rising out of the ruins: a new Esperanto which might gloss over the nationalist evils of the 1930s. Cultural questions concerning the meaning of architecture in contemporary society, which plagued avant-gardes elsewhere in Europe, were mostly missing; so were Regionalist explorations, as these might have recalled Nazi obsessions. The dispersal of major talent in the 1930s left a void where there might have been a more continuous modern tradition (as was the case in Italy). For the general run of construction, American and international commercial influences supplied a safe middle way – a bland and rather uniform technocracy. One encountered a watered-down version of Mies van der Rohe from which the idealism and the classicism had been extracted. In Germany, at least, philosophical intensity was usually avoided, and the way to the past was temporarily barred.

If there was an internal debate within German practice, it concerned the status of the expressive image and its relation to the construction system employed. A puritan version of pre-war functionalism insisted on neutrality, but usually achieved it by spreading a thin technical veneer over all building types. One architect to transcend this limitation yet aspire towards a lucid poetry of silence was Egon Eiermann, who had studied with Poelzig before the war. The subtlety of his work lay in the way he disposed of a limited range of elements – frame, wall, opening, truss, stair – so that tension was maintained between part and whole, between idea and constructional means. Far from applying a formula, Eiermann reacted to the givens of each situation, and sought out a character appropriate to function and site. The building with which he set forth his position was the Handkerchief Mill at Blumberg of 1949–51, a work of stern abstraction enlivened by tectonic accents and bold incisions in the wall panels. However, the design which attracted most international attention, was the Neckermann Mail Order Company Building in

Frankfurt of 1958–61. Here the structural frame articulated the sculptural form, but without rhetorical excess. The neutral, industrial box was broken open to reveal layers of transparency, galleries, and the hierarchy of construction. The escape stairs and air-conditioning elements on the outside dramatized the sense of process and movement. Eiermann summed up his idea of architecture as 'making order visible, from the town plan to the smallest building'.

By contrast, Hans Scharoun tended to impose order rather than elicit it, and so represented another 'pole' of German architecture after the war. Scharoun's pedigree included the more extreme forms of Expressionism, and in the 1920s and 1930s he had rebelled against the strictures of the

International Style, evolving a personal manner of his own which relied upon angular or curved geometries, emphatic cantilevering and the concatenation of different structural systems in a single design. These features were brought to maturity in his project for the Berlin Philharmonie Concert Hall of 1956 (constructed in the early 1960s) in which the auditorium was conceived as a multifaceted vessel, with angular forms, tilted planes and stratified trays of seats floating at difference levels; overall it was an evocation of music in spatial terms. Eiermann on the one hand, Scharoun on the other: perhaps the difference between the two was emblematic of a broader dilemma in the European modern architecture of the 1950s, between those who tried to extract a minimalist aesthetic from the

592

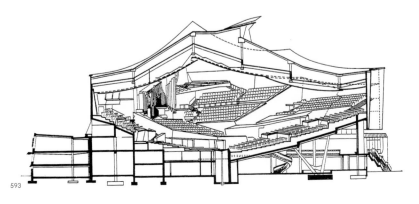

593

norms of technology, and those who pursued the path of personal expression. It was an old division, dating back at least to the days of debates in the Deutscher Werkbund before the First World War (Chapter 6).

In France the plan of modernization and reconstruction after the war was conceived on a broad territorial scale, although the relation between political intentions and architectural ones remained vague. Regionalist and neo-vernacular discourses were largely discredited owing to their proximity to Pétainist conservatism, and different towns were farmed out in the late 1940s to individual modern architects: Maubeuge to André Lurçat, the heart of St-Dié to Le Corbusier (eventually cancelled), Le Havre to Auguste Perret. Perret's buildings in Le Havre relied upon a simplified classical Rationalist vocabulary of frame and panel which did at least permit a degree of civic rhetoric in the handling of institutions and urban spaces, but the results were considered disappointing by many critics, who saw in them a drab repetition of an outmoded aesthetic. The first stages of urban reconstruction in France often worked with free-standing slabs in park-like settings. These constituted a strong counterform to pre-war slums but the vocabulary was sparse, diagrammatic, and limited: it was rare to encounter new urban ensembles with the topographical sensitivity of the best Scandinavian housing of the same period, and there was no equivalent to the bold 'social realism' of low-cost housing constructed around Rome and Madrid in the 1950s (see below). What seemed to be lacking was a theoretical reconsideration of the basic purposes of architecture.

594

Le Corbusier was curiously isolated from the general run of French practice. The Unité in Marseilles, indeed the late works as a whole, were more discussed, debated and reviled abroad than at home. The deeper resonances with tradition fell mostly on deaf ears. The most vivacious transformations of Le Corbusier's fusion of plastic and social imagination occurred close to the Mediterranean, or even on the other side of it. The Aérohabitat in Algiers of 1950–4 by Louis Miquel and Bourlier was an effective reinterpretation of the Unité theme, while Roland Simounet's remarkable stepped housing with vaulted units at Djenan el-Hassan (also in Algeria) of 1956–8 drew lessons from both the North African vernacular and Le Corbusier's Roq and Rob project of 1949. The latter was also the model for the holiday housing at Cap Camarat on the French Riviera (1958–65) designed by the Atelier de Montrouge (Jean Renaudie, Pierre Riboulet, Gérard Thurnauer and Jean-Louis Véret with Louis Arretche). This reiterated the kasbah theme and made a valid extension of Corbusian ideas, providing an ensemble of levels, terraces and courtyard buildings looking over the sea. Bodiansky and Woods's ATBAT housing for Morocco (1951–6; Fig. 552), was one of the rare cases of the 'universal type' of the Unité being adjusted to local climate and tradition.

While Regionalism was not on the 'official French agenda' (which tended to reflect the values of a centralized technocracy), there were several other architects who demonstrated an interest in the character and climate of particular geographical locations. Among these was the enigmatic figure of Fernand Pouillon, whose reconstruction of the area close to the Vieux Port of Marseilles in the 1950s was the antithesis of Le Corbusier's urbanism, in that it relied upon the traditional idea of the continuous urban façade, the block bounded by streets, and a simplified classical articulation in stone. But the result could not be written off as just a tired piece of traditionalism, as it possessed a durable quality in its handling of scale, proportion and material. Pouillon considered himself to be a follower of Perret, but his culture of architecture also extended to the North African world, and was suffused with a general Mediterranean sensibility. He realized several large projects in Algeria, most notably the huge housing scheme in Algiers known

594 Atelier de Montrouge with Louis Arretche, holiday housing at Cap Camarat, 1958–65

595 Bernard Zehrfuss, with Camelot and De Mailly, Centre National des Industries et des Techniques, La Défense, Paris, 1955

595

as Climat de France (1957) which was conceived
as a massive perimeter block surrounding a vast
interior courtyard. In this instance the domestic
programme was given an overtly monumental
treatment which echoed the walls and bastions of
old cities.

A recurrent preoccupation of French
architecture in the 1950s was the proper
relationship between 'art' and 'technique'. It was a
dilemma which was central to structural Rationalist
thinking and which in France, at least, was
emphasized by the institutional distinction between
the École Polytechnique and the École des Beaux-
Arts. The question of aesthetic expression in
engineering took on a new meaning in the post-war
years with the rapid creation of a new infrastructure
including airports, railway stations, power stations
and factories. On the other hand, a culture of
construction wedded to technological exploration
and to a mechanistic imagery also emerged in
French post-war architecture, notably in projects
such as the Maison de la Culture at Le Havre
(1952–61) by Lagneau and Weill, which sought a
balance between formal rhetoric and the desire to
treat a civic building as a flexible social instrument
in glass and steel. The Centre National des
Industries et des Techniques (CNIT) of 1958, at La
Défense, just to the west of Paris, designed by

Bernard Zehrfuss with Camelot and De Mailly, in
collaboration with Nicolas Esquillan and Jean
Prouvé employed a wide spanning system of
parabolic vaults and an attached curtain wall in
glass and steel. It combined architectural form
and engineering skill in a convincing synthesis.

Jean Prouvé drew upon, and contributed to, this
emerging French culture of construction, but he
was also a special case of his own. His best buildings
(such as his experimental houses at Meudon of
1951, or the exquisite Refreshment Room at
Evian of 1956) were endowed with an elegant
transparency and a limber sense of structure.
Prouvé had been brought up with metal in his
hands, and was an artist/craftsman as well as an
architect/engineer. Thus while his commitment to
evolving form both from systems of fabrication and
from the expression of the means of support placed
him in a structural-Rationalist lineage running back
to Viollet-le-Duc, there was also an artisanal side
to his work which made him a part-heir of Art
Nouveau. Prouvé revealed a commitment to the
ideal of transforming technology into socially
serviceable mechanisms in such pioneering
experiments of the 1930s as the Maison du Peuple at
Clichy (Fig. 461). While he designed numerous
prototypes for the mass production of everyday
objects and equipment in the 1950s (covering

everything from individual houses to bathroom cores, to furniture, to demountable Saharan shelters), he wished to avoid depersonalization. Prouvé's structures possessed a tensile, even anthropomorphic character, which reflected, in part, his overall intention of humanizing technology. His idea of structure went well beyond a neutral description of materials and forces to a virtually natural conception of limbs, knuckles, sinews, joints and connections. A thorough articulation of the regulating concept was accompanied by an exquisite control of detail. At a time when Le Corbusier's dense, sculptural buildings in reinforced concrete were dominating one side of French architecture, Prouvé reopened an alternative route of almost luxuriant metallic carpentry. The effect of this lingered on, manifesting itself in the steel and glass architecture of the 1980s in France.

The Dutch situation in the immediate post-war years was also dominated by the need for rapid reconstruction, especially in cities like Rotterdam which had been all but destroyed. But there was a divergence of positions between a group of traditionalists teaching in the Delft Technical College, chief among them G. M. Granpré Molière, who advocated a continuing craft tradition in brick; and remaining or new members of the Dutch modern persuasion (for example, J. J. P. Oud and Jacob Bakema). Granpré Molière's views were strongly influenced by Roman Catholicism and he saw 'functionalism' as a materialistic, degrading philosophy whereas the Dutch modern experiment between the wars had, in fact, tried to transcend the utilitarian with the spiritual. As it was, the new architecture won out, especially in Rotterdam where the activities of Bakema and J. H. van den Broek ensured an extension of pre-war principles rather than just an imitation of pre-war forms. Their several large-scale urban proposals for the poulders relied upon ordering grids over which bands of housing were placed, setting up a variety of spatial conditions between buildings. This system was not at odds with the largely artificial Dutch landscape, and was not without its memories of De Stijl. For the Lijnbaan shopping centre in Rotterdam (1954), the same architects worked out a wide pedestrian esplanade between low-rise buildings containing shops and offices, which formed a well-scaled foreground to high-rise buildings to the rear. These

Dutch architects were well aware of the doctrines of CIAM, but began to seek out a more complex urban image using 'layers' of public space. There was an anthropological flavour to their interpretation of the habitat, clearly expressed in the editorial policy of the journal *Forum*, to which both Bakema and Aldo van Eyck were contributors. Bakema's statement 'Architecture is the three-dimensional expression of human behaviour' was typical.

The Forum Group (some of whom became members of Team X) admired the work of Gerrit Rietveld, whose small pavilion of 1954 outside the Kröller-Müller Museum at Otterlo made exquisite use of rough concrete block and glass screens to create a tranquil environment against the background of sculptures and trees. Bakema's Montessori School in Rotterdam of 1955–60 also relied upon interpenetrating structure, floating elements and fluid spaces to evoke an open environment of visual and sensory enquiry. There were loose affinities with Japanese architecture, and with some of the Case Study Program houses in southern California; this could be another way of saying that the influence of Wright and of Mondrian continued silently in Dutch architecture. This legacy could be sensed too in the overlapping structural systems of Van Eyck, whose Orphanage of 1957–62 is discussed in Chapter 30. Behind these spatial conceptions there was an ideal of Social Democratic emancipation. In Van Eyck's case it was linked to a search for basic archetypes of shelter and community in vernacular forms. Evidently these 'patterns of association' were to be expressed in a

596 Jean Prouvé with Maurice Novarina, Refreshment Room, Source Cachat, Evian, 1956

597 Jacob Bakema, Montessori School, Rotterdam, 1955–60

596

597

rigorous abstraction and a polyphonic order which Van Eyck referred to as 'labyrinthine clarity'.

Post-war Italy had some of the same problems as Germany in disentangling itself from the totalitarian taint of the 1930s, but in many respects the situation was quite different. For one thing, Italy had not chased away its major talent and so possessed a stronger modern architectural culture to be continued, modified or even rejected. For another, the country had substrata of tradition which never entirely disappeared however radical the proposal. The overt use of classicism was, for the moment, a closed road (abstractions of classicism were another matter), but there were few foregone conclusions, and the decade after the war was characterized by vigorous debates and polemics concerning the direction that Italian architecture should take. Both theory and production were richer and more diverse than in Germany, and there were many political positions. Neorealists such as Mario Ridolfi and Ludovico Quaroni (influenced by the neorealism of Italian cinema) attempted to produce an imagery rooted in proletarian consciousness and 'everyday urban reality'. In their I. N. A. Casa planning for the Tiburtino district of Rome (1949–54), blocks of flats were laid out on an irregular plan and crowned with sloping 'Mediterranean' roofs. Here was an attempt at updating the vernacular on the basis of a populist

ideology and through a deliberate engagement with the problems of the rural poor who were streaming towards Italian cities. It was in these years that the historian and critic Bruno Zevi promoted the idea of an 'organic architecture' combining the spatial qualities of Wright with a vague reference to natural forms. What this meant in practice was uncertain, but it seemed that Zevi hoped to find an appropriate liberalizing catalyst for the newly democratic Italy, that would steer around the problematic recent past, avoiding both the aridity of mere technology and the temptations of revivalism.

In reality, several of the pre-war ideas and personalities continued to operate. Some of the best work extended the premises of the Italian 'Rationalism' of the 1930s (Chapter 20). The Termini Station in Rome (designed by Leo Calini, Eugenio Montuori and others between 1948 and 1952) was a clean-cut, modern structural idea integrated with a restrained rectangular exterior containing subliminal classical echoes. The long, sinuous trusses bridging the booking hall carried through towards the tracks, and the ensemble had an honorific character arising from its proportions, its slit-like openings, and its travertine facing. The main locus of Rationalist continuities from the pre-war days was Milan, where several names re-appeared and old positions re-emerged in a slightly altered guise. Among these architects was Ignazio Gardella, author of the Anti-Tuberculosis Sanatorium in Alessandria of 1937, who in 1952 designed a brick clad apartment building in the same city for employees of the Borsalino Company. This had deeply projecting sharp-cut eaves, angled walls with taut surfaces, and wooden-lattice shutters flush with the façades. It managed to convey domesticity without regressing into a facile neo-vernacularism, and without sacrificing conceptual and visual tension. Gardella's other major work of the early 1950s was the Museum of Modern Art in Milan, a neutral receptacle of light, in which a sparse steel and glass vocabulary was used with modesty but great effect. Luigi Figini and Gino Pollini (both of whom had been members of the original Gruppo 7 with Terragni in the 1920s) extended the Rationalist precept of poetic structure in their Church of the Madonna dei Poveri in Milan of 1952–6. Here, though, the expression was more tactile and robust. Rough concrete beams were deployed with textured walls, narrow light slits and compressions of space to create an aura of mystery and renunciation. This aesthetic of poverty resembled in some respects what Le Corbusier was intending for La Tourette at the same time.

Italian diversity was well represented by two skyscrapers which rose above Milan in the late 1950s: the Pirelli Building (1958–61) by Gio Ponti, and the Torre Velasca (1956–8) by Ernesto Rogers and Enrico Peressutti. The first was 33 storeys high and stood by the railway station. The plan was lozenge-shaped to accommodate lifts at the core and to convey the idea of the structure, which was not a steel cage but a double-vertebrate system (designed by the engineer Pier Luigi Nervi). These considerations led to a finely tapered form with an elegant, if stylized, metallic cladding. The result was a unique prestige office building which represented the high technical aspirations of the company; it showed that not all high-rise designs in Europe had to ape the American models. The Pirelli Building was witness to a new era of industrial design in Italy, also evident in the products and buildings of the Olivetti Company, which emerged as a major patron, as it had in the 1930s.

By contrast, the Torre Velasca stood close to Milan's Gothic cathedral, and contained both

599

offices and apartments. It rose to 26 storeys, but the top six (containing the domestic accommodation) were jettied outwards and expressed as a deep overhang supported on splayed buttresses. Variety was created in the façades through the straightforward revelation of interior needs. The verticality of the concrete structural frame was accentuated on the outside of the building to rhyme with the vertical shafts and pinnacles of the nearby cathedral, and a stone cladding with individual windows punched through it ensured that the tower did not depart too drastically from its lower neighbours. The overall image was vaguely reminiscent of a medieval *palazzo pubblico*. In short, Rogers and Peressutti had attempted to give a skyscraper 'urban identity' by making allusions to the historical context, and even by 'domesticating' it (there were massive chimneys protruding at the top). The Torre Velasca caused something of a furore in the international press because of its 'retreat from modernism' and its 'historicism'. Several Italian revivalist tendencies were submitted to a major broadside by the British critic Reyner Banham (who inaccurately labelled them 'Neo Liberty') and who much preferred contemporary works such as the Istituto Marchiondi of 1957 (also in Milan) by Vittoriano Vigano. With its bold expression of rough reinforced-concrete structure, and its distinct articulation of functional pieces, this was, in fact, a sculptural descendant of the Italian Rationalist lineage, but in Banham's eyes it was one of several works around the world (including, for example, Louis Kahn's Yale University Art Gallery

598

598 Leo Calini, Eugenio Montuori and others, Termini Station, Rome, 1948–52

599 Gio Ponti with Pier Luigi Nervi, Pirelli Building, Milan, 1958–61

600 Ernesto Rogers and Enrico Peressutti, Torre Velasca, Milan, 1956–8

600

of 1951–3) to embody the vaguely defined aspirations of his movement, the 'New Brutalism'.

The critical debates surrounding Italian work of the late 1950s revealed a typical worry of this period: the obsession with defining a 'true way' for modern architecture. The polemical atmosphere also risked over-simplifying the whole question of the effective use of the past, or rather, the avoidance of its abuse. As the founding members of the Rationalist Gruppo 7 had asserted in 1927, tradition was unavoidable for the Italian architect, who did not necessarily have to strain for references to the past to incorporate its lessons. A building like La Rinascente Store in Rome of 1957–62 by Franco Albini relied upon a frank expression of modern technical realities such as steel and glass, but also rhymed with the typical horizontal divisions of the Roman street façade (base, middle, cornice) in its overall organization. Even the engineer Pier Luigi

Nervi, who took pride in the purity of his intuitive and inductive methods of design, achieved buildings which seemed happy descendants of the grand constructions of antiquity. His numerous, stadiums, factories, exhibition halls, even *autostrada* bridges, demonstrated how engineering discipline and refined sculptural expression might achieve a high synthesis of an almost natural character. In the Agnelli Exhibition Hall in Turin of 1948, Nervi used open pre-cast concrete ribs with slender profiles resulting from the imprint of diamond-shaped pans, to realize a shell vault with an uninterrupted span of 262 feet (80 metres) over a room 328 feet (100 metres) long. A similar economy of means and richness of visual effect was achieved in the Gatti Wool Factory of 1951, in which the slender concrete columns had flared capitals and the concrete floor slabs were supported on a radiating network of two-way beams which gave visual expression to the

601 Pier Luigi Nervi, Gatti Wool Factory, Rome, 1951

602 Carlo Scarpa, Castelvecchio Museum, Verona, 1956–64, meeting of old and new with equestrian statue of Cangrande

601

602

pattern of underlying stresses. Nervi's engineering
aspired towards a clear statement of ideas, and in his
later Palazzo del Lavoro, for the Italia '61 exhibition
in Turin, he created an open space with a grid of
free-standing columns each supporting a square roof
unit on splayed beams. This solution allowed for an
entirely glazed perimeter and for strips of natural
light between the square roof elements, but it also
evoked an ancient hypostyle hall.

Carlo Scarpa was another designer to feel that
tradition and modernity could be interlaced.
Sometimes working on a tiny and intricate scale, he
drew upon a vast universe of forms from many eras
but developed a unique sensitivity to the Veneto,
and even described himself as 'a man of Byzantium
who came to Venice by way of Greece'. Scarpa
understood how Italian craftsmanship in stone,
plaster, wood, steel, glass and concrete might be
used to distil his vast reservoir of impressions
in materials. His architecture delighted in
stratification, layering and the dynamic interaction
of planes. Wright was a key influence on his
formation, but so were De Stijl painting and the
ancient architectures of Japan. There were even
hints in some of Scarpa's projects of the mid-1950s
of vegetal and geological analogies, which might
have fulfilled Zevi's yearnings for an 'organic'
architecture, except that Scarpa was scarcely an

artist to fit himself into a school. A central part
of his activity was the restoration and reuse of old
buildings, and here he developed a method of
juxtaposing new and old levels and fragments so
that the meaning of both was enhanced, and so that
the observer had the sensation of passing through
layers of time. Something of the kind was achieved
in his transformation of the Castelvecchio Museum
in Verona (1956–64), where interlocking floor and
slab patterns, paving and rough plastered walls
contributed to a sober setting for works of art
displayed on raw steel stands of Scarpa's own
design. The dramatic centrepiece of this historical
scenario was the junction between two of the
buildings, where Scarpa accentuated the fact of
the break by means of serrated masonry and
extending concrete platforms, one of them bearing
a medieval equestrian statue. With the Canova
Museum in the Veneto (1956–7), Scarpa created a
luminous modern space from the old structure by
the simple device of a cut-out skylight eating into
the top of the wall and the edge of the ceiling. He
managed to leave the fragments and deposits of
time in a sort of liquid suspension, where their
visual qualities could be isolated and scrutinized.

At a time when the whole matter of dealing
with a historical context – at the scale of an object,
a building or a piece of a city – ran the risk of

degenerating into a straight imitation of the old, Scarpa was able to demonstrate how it might be possible to create a 'counterform': a 'frame' for the past which harmonized in some ways, but separated in others. This corresponded to the way in which he looked at Venice: as a palimpsest combining networks of canals, positive and negative urban spaces, and strata of past civilizations. His architectural vocabulary delighted in the interweaving of water, light and solid matter, while the promenades that he threaded through old buildings were like miniaturized streets and squares. Scarpa's architectural language could be sensed at work in his drawing technique, with its overlays, coloured marks, and oscillations of figure and ground. While the graphic representation was a means for exploring the rationale of a building and the character of a site, it was also the map with which Scarpa traced his ideas. In the long run, this capacity to work with fragments and varying identities revealed a debt to Cubism, while the manner of conceiving space in architecture had much to do with Wright. But Scarpa had a myth and a language of his own. He was able to reveal the latent memories in a particular place and to hint at nuances and hermetic meanings which were, so to speak, embedded in the tactile nature of the materials of his buildings.

While the search for touchstones in the peasant vernaculars was a recurrent theme in the 1950s, it took several different directions. An architect like Van Eyck seemed to wish to find some 'universal' dimension of shelter and community, and it was this that took him eventually to the Dogon villages of North Africa. Utzon was also interested in these general qualities, but was 'eclectic' in the best sense, since in a project like the Kingo Houses (or the later Fredensborg houses) he was able to bridge similar courtyard types from different cultures (Mediterranean patio, Danish courtyard, Chinese farmhouse). But there were some cases, especially in southern Europe (and, one might add, in Turkey and Egypt), where more 'culturally specific' readings of peasant forms were intended, notably in Spain, Portugal and Greece.

In his pavilion next to his Church of St Dimitris Loumbardiaris (both of 1951–7) below the Acropolis in Athens, the Greek architect Dimitris Pikionis consolidated his earlier research into the

603

supposed origins of Greek Mediterranean culture by seeking out correspondences between the basis of classicism (visualized through a species of primitive hut) and the archetypes of the house. Beyond these matters of representation, Pikionis seemed to wish to explore an archaic and timeless sense of space which had nothing to do with the technological agendas of modernism at all, but which none the less relied on geometrical schemata with a partly modern pedigree. The park and promenade which he designed for the Philopappou Hill in Athens in 1950–7 incorporated bits of ruins, cyclopian slabs of rock and crude chippings in a pattern of varying textures, rhythms and intensities. Thus the ground was transformed into a series of highly charged 'places' – levels, ramps and routes – with something of the spiritual atmosphere of an ancient sacred way. Pikionis here worked with an aesthetic of fragments and traces which had loose affinities with the method, though not the actual form, of Scarpa's works at the same time. What these two artists had in common was an acute sensitivity to the *genius loci*.

Even as late as the 1950s, the less industrialized countries of southern Europe still possessed an active peasant culture and a living folklore which secreted the myths of past generations. For some artists and architects the tension between urban and rural worlds was vital and inspiring. The Portuguese architect Fernando Tavora (who worked in Oporto) attempted to cut through the prevailing eclecticism and provincialism of Portuguese architecture, and to return to local roots, while also attacking the social problems of his time. He sought an architecture that was modern but sensitive to a unique cultural landscape, and one of the keys for him was the Portuguese vernacular which he interpreted for its general principles and types. Another Portuguese architect, Alvaro Siza, adapted some features of this outlook, though in his case there was a greater attention to the lineaments of topography and to the spatial transition between buildings. Like Tavora, Siza had no intention of mimicking peasant architecture, but did wish to draw on its social pattern and sensitivity to both landscape and light. These qualities were subject to a rigorous transformation into an indisputably modern vocabulary, nourished in his case by a wide range of sources, including Aalto, Le Corbusier, Loos, Wright, Cubist painting and the Catalan architect José Antonio Coderch, who, during the 1950s, evolved a modern architecture with regional sensitivities. For Siza, modernism provided a route away from provincialism towards a certain

universality: he sought an equilibrium between the local and the general.

The first evidence of Siza's particular approach was provided by his designs for swimming pools and their attached buildings, at Quinta da Conceição, Matosinhos (1958-65), and at Leça da Palmeira (1961–6), both just north of Oporto, the latter on the actual coastline. At Leça da Palmeira, Siza reduced his intervention to minimal, linear incisions – concrete walls, platforms and soffits cut by grooves of shadow – drawing together buildings, landscape, rocks and sea. He seemed to wish to heighten the pre-existing forces in a place, and to find a delicate balance between new human uses and the pre-existing topography. The pool pavilion at Leça da Palmeira was reached down a ramp, and the visitor was steered along shaded passageways by bare concrete walls and hovering overhangs before being released along a diagonal towards the sky and the sea (both this device and the overall plan recalled Wright's Taliesin West). The structure then descended as a delicate web of terraces, steps and parapets – an informal theatre of a kind – on which groups of bathers gathered. Finally there were the pools themselves: taut sheets of water drawn between the rocks, standing before the sheen of the

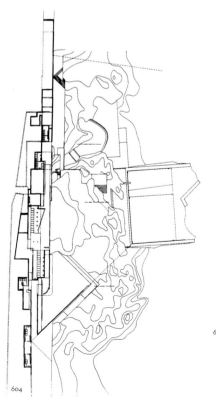

604

605

sea. Siza drew together the spatial ambiguities and tensions of Cubism with an architecture of abstract planes and contours to guide the human figure over the strata of a site and to intensify the experience of natural features in the setting.

Spain, like Portugal, remained isolated from most of the rest of Europe in the 1940s and 1950s. Its architectural culture was conditioned by the fleeting presence of a modernism with Mediterranean accents in the period before the Civil War, by the firmly traditionalist stance of the Franco regime (clear enough in retardative civic buildings of the late 1930s and 1940s), by a relatively backward technology, and by the country's dense layers of architectural history which lay for the most part dormant. If there were links to the outside world, they were tenuous ones with Italian modernism of several varieties, pre- and post-war. The former could be sensed in the Casa Syndicale in Madrid of 1949 by Francisco Cabrero, a work of forbidding presence with a brick-gridded 'Rationalist' façade on a stone-pier base, and an underlying scheme of classical organization.

The active reconsideration of the 'lost connection' with international modern architecture began in the late 1940s, principally in Barcelona (a little later in Madrid), and from the beginning was engaged with the question of local expression. Always more open to the outside world than any other Spanish city, Barcelona also gained from its recurring capacity both to integrate new ideas into its collective memory and to adjust the most general formulations to its specific landscape and culture. This resilience was no doubt reinforced by a certain political resistance against the centre, and by the consciousness of being a Catalan, a Mediterranean and a world city, as well as a Spanish one.

The architect who best grasped the nature and potential of these conditions was José Antonio Coderch. Over the course of the 1950s and 1960s he evolved a consistent modern architectural language of limited means but complex meanings. This was supple enough to address the typical conditions of apartment buildings in the heart of the city on the one hand, and those of individual residences resting in the verdant coastal landscape of the Costa Brava on the other. The Casa Ugalde at Caldes d'Estrac (1951) was perched above the sea on a spectacular site, with views across pines in several directions.

606

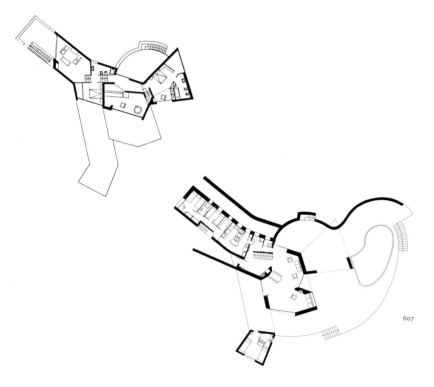

607

606 José Antonio
Coderch, Casa Ugalde,
Caldes d'Estrac, 1951

607 Casa Ugalde, first-
and ground-floor plans

608 José Antonio
Coderch, La Barceloneta
Apartment Building,
Barcelona, 1951

609 La Barceloneta
Apartment Building, plan

Coderch responded to the uneven terrain, the light, the sun and the sea with a fractured, organic plan blending together indoor and outdoor spaces on several levels. Like his Barcelona colleague Josep Sostres, Coderch had for several years studied the white-walled vernacular architecture of the Mediterranean coast and the Balearic Islands, and even in the late 1940s had designed projects with a direct echo of vernacular sources. With the Casa Ugalde he broke through to a new fluidity and abstraction which recalled both the hieroglyphic paintings of Miró and the long tradition of naturally inspired form running back to Jujol and Gaudí. At the same time, the Casa Ugalde spoke the language of International Modern architecture. Coderch's later houses pursued similar hedonistic and poetic themes, but in a vocabulary of increasing rectilinear precision which resembled in some ways the work of Schindler or Neutra in southern California.

What might be called Coderch's 'urban mode' was established in La Barceloneta Apartment Building in Barcelona of 1951. This was designed for retired seamen and had to fit together the maximum accommodation on a tight corner site. Coderch endeavoured to balance a series of

conflicting demands: exploiting the view over the port, yet maintaining privacy; letting light into the heart of the plan, but keeping out the direct rays of the sun; maintaining the urban edge, but signalling the presence of a separate modern building. These issues were resolved in a plan of splayed walls with slots of space along the perimeter behind wooden shutters, and an angled stair running up the centre of the building. Projected into space, this plan resulted in angled ceramic-clad walls, continuous grilles of shutters and a thin slab at the top, crowning the composition. Details were handled to minimize visual weight and to accentuate the sharp-edged planes, but far from being diagrammatic, La Barceloneta had vibrant, textured surfaces and a nautical character in tune with its purpose and setting. Coderch certainly drew upon the model of Gardella's Borsalino Apartment Building in Alessandria, but he transformed it to fit his own themes and grounded it in the almost unconscious continuities of Barcelona as a city. Thus in La Barceloneta there were echoes of Gaudí's idea of an undulating 'maritime' façade, and even of the long-standing Spanish tradition of miradors and screens. In the apartment building in Calle

608

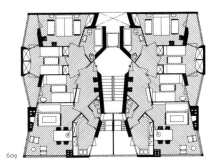

609

Compositor Bach of 1958, Coderch extended the white, louvred screen over the entire façade as a tense membrane, sharpening it with angled projections, and making it hover on slender concrete slabs. The result was both transparent and opaque: a thin, ambiguous line between the private life of the domestic interior and the public world outside, kept alive by flickering accents of light and shade.

In 1951, the young Catalan architect Oriol Bohigas published an essay entitled 'Possibilities for a Barcelona Architecture' in which he reflected on the pressing problems of rapid urbanization and on the need to go back in order to go forward – back to the spirit of the unfulfilled promise of the GATEPAC urbanistic reforms of the 1930s (Chapter 21), back even to some of the cultural agendas of National Romanticism at the turn of the century (Chapter 8). Bohigas was not advocating that past forms should be copied, but he was suggesting that it might be possible to reintegrate these agendas, and reinvigorate these traditions, in a way appropriate to the current situation. In architectural terms this meant reinterpreting regional means for handling the climate, reconsidering generic urban types, and extending Catalan craft and construction conventions based upon the use of ceramic and brick. As for the 'modern' side of the equation, this was to come from a dynamic spatial conception descending from Neo-Plasticism (an idea probably influenced by Bruno Zevi). In 1952, Bohigas and Sostres founded Grup R which concentrated on the need for buildings addressing public needs in a manner which recalled Italian neorealism. In effect, this was a plea for a modernist/Regionalist synthesis addressing both architecture and urbanism. Nowhere in all of this was there any reference to the 'International Style'.

These were the years of the great migrations from the poorer regions of the south of Spain into the industrializing cities of the north, and by the early 1950s there were shanty towns of hastily erected shacks on the fringes of Bilbao, Barcelona and Madrid. In effect this was a new proletariat with peasant roots, a situation that was understood by several architects responsible for elaborating housing types to relieve the social and political pressures of 'absorption'. In the case of Madrid, one of these models followed a similar route to that taken by the neorealists in Italy: that is, blending a domestic image of sloped roofs with brick boxes in a deliberate populist gesture. Disposed in the right way, even simple, rectangular, utilitarian forms using concrete frames, brick infills and simple timber details were capable of generating comfortable transitional spaces: for example, the Caño Roto housing of 1956 designed by Antonio Vázquez de Castro and José Luis Iñiguez. The Madrid housing projects were the result of political initiatives spurred in part by Catholic populist activism, in part by a desire within the government to avoid social disturbance. They provided a testing-ground for an emerging group of committed modern architects including José Luis Romany, Eduardo Mangada and Ramon Vázquez Molezún. Within a restrained language, and perhaps without intending to, the designers managed to distill the atmosphere of a period in neutral, almost 'objective' terms. Some of the schemes incorporated middle-rise solutions, but these were usually broken down in scale by means of platforms, perforated walls, steps and planting. Simple domestic touches like moving wooden lattices over windows were integrated with a geometrical order.

High densities were achieved in low-rise buildings by making intelligent use of planar brick walls, tight, logical plans, demountable metal elements, and small courtyards. In the Fuencarral A development of 1954, Francisco Saénz de Oíza employed a reductivist vocabulary of this kind to create an enclave of tight-knit alleys and patios. In the Fuencarral B development Alejandro de la Sota went further to evoke the rural vernacular, but in strict, reductivist terms: this was in effect an abstraction of an Andalusian village transposed to the industrializing edge of Madrid.

De la Sota was based in Madrid, but came from Galicia in the north-west of Spain, a remote region with a cold, clear light and a vernacular founded upon sharp granite masonry. When glass was used, it was as a sheet or screen flush with the stone, a planar surface, both tactile and abstract. De la Sota's mature works had just this quality of materiality and immateriality – as if there were a spiritual presence just beneath the surface of the simple facts of steel girders, plate glass or textured brick. Given this elusive sensibility and his other-worldly temperament, it is not surprising that de la Sota

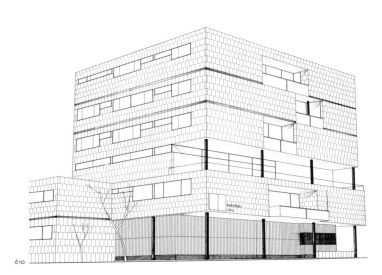

610

611

should eventually have been attracted to the architecture of Mies van der Rohe, which he knew only through books. His own private quest for 'essentials' within structure and technology happened to coincide with a growing dissatisfaction in Spanish society with the extreme traditionalism of the Franco regime. It was becoming clear that Spain should follow the Western industrial model of modernization, and the intelligentsia wished to escape a stifling isolation and provincialism. While not socially radical (he could be called a 'mystical conservative') de la Sota was radical in matters of art, and thirsted after the 'universality' of the major works of the modern movement which had been denied his generation in Spain. The sparse planarity and ideal forms of Mies van der Rohe thus took on the character of moral emblems to de la Sota: combining a progressive ethos with a spiritual core.

It was with the Government Centre (Gobierno Civil) in Tarragona of 1954–7, that de la Sota revealed his full powers of formal and intellectual control, as well as a certain wit in inverting customary expectations of civic monumentality. The Government Centre had the uncomfortable function of representing the central power of Madrid in Catalonia, and combined this honorific and symbolic role with those of a state office and a functionaries' residence. Essentially, de la Sota

combined an apartment slab with a schematized version of a public palace. But where such a building in the usual Francoist 'official' architecture would have had a solid base, a wall punctured by windows, a symmetrical façade and a crowning cornice, de la Sota's building had a transparent base, a planar wall of uncertain mass, and a counterpoint between symmetry and asymmetry, visual weight and transparency. It was a design which worked on the knife edge between presence and absence, which made a teasing interplay of light and shadow and which lived in perpetual tension between modern and classical schemata. De la Sota succeeded in distilling the latent memories of an ancient Mediterranean town in a work of precise and poetic Rationalism.

While the Government Centre in Tarragona probably had its debts to Terragni's Casa Del Fascio of 1932–6, the structural idea was quite different, since de la Sota did not express the frame as a lattice in the façade. In fact this was a concrete skeleton building pretending to be made of stone and steel. The steel columns in this instance were clearly of Miesian inspiration (from the Barcelona Pavilion) as probably was the use of polished travertine as a tactile but translucent surface. The main Governor's loggia was on axis and addressed the city, but the façade higher up was cracked open

612 Alejandro de
la Sota, Maravillas School
Gymnasium, Madrid,
1961–2

613 Maravillas School
Gymnasium, sketch
section by de la Sota
showing penetration of
light and passage of air

614 Maravillas School
Gymnasium, interior

in an interlocking fracture of shadow, not unlike the fissure in a Chillida sculpture. Details such as the planar glass ceiling on level one, or the governor's massive desk, reiterated the main compositional themes, while the back of the building took the form of a bold rectangle punched through the rear façade. Despite its original function, the Gobierno Civil in Tarragona was easily transformed into a democratic institution at the end of the Franco period, and even became a paragon of intellectual probity for a later generation of architects who detested everything it had stood for politically. Perhaps this is testimony to the building's intrinsic architectural quality; or perhaps it acknowledges de la Sota's success in impishly 'deconstructing' a previous iconography of power and rendering it more transparent and available.

In contrast to his Tarragona building, de la Sota's Maravillas School Gymnasium in Madrid of 1961–2 was without rhetoric, in fact it was so self-effacing as to be scarcely noticeable. The street façade was humble and utilitarian in character: a textured red-brick wall detailed as a skin; the hint of a steel frame; flat, industrial glazing; slightly protruding rectangular bays; and, on top, a wire-mesh fence on slender steel poles, suggesting the presence of a playground on the flat roof.

Behind this neutral and elusive mask, the interior was more dramatic, being a single volume of space bridged by inverted curved steel trusses. This single gesture achieved many results at once, as one may sense from de la Sota's spidery sketch of the section. It opened up a clear, uninterrupted span for the ball-court beneath, it funnelled air across the building, and it allowed light to be diffused off the convex ceiling without getting into the eyes of spectators. It made a kind of bridge into which classrooms could be inserted, their inclined seating fitting neatly into the curved section. The same steel beams in visual tension evoked the image of a trampoline or some other piece of equipment for physical education. If the profile of the curve recalled that of an aerofoil wing section, the manner in which it was detailed touched the memory of a canvas awning drawn across an ancient theatre. The Maravillas Gymnasium building was detailed rigorously to follow the theme of a skeletal frame-structure gradually detaching itself from a wall, so that grilles, climbing-bars, ceiling beams and railings all contributed to a single idea. Later in life, de la Sota wrote revealingly: 'Themes simplify and offer us possibilities. Architecture does not require that we have recourse to it; it will appear all by itself.'

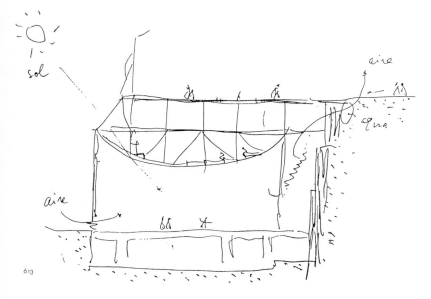

613

614

The spirit was 'functionalist' and 'objective', although the aim was to release a poetic tension in modern technology, allowing it to emerge as something virtually 'natural'. In the Maravillas Gymnasium, de la Sota was able to trace the main lines of his idea in the slender network of the structure itself: to reveal the anatomy of his intentions in the naked medium of steel. The quiet exterior, with its implied visual layers, and its projections and recessions, was a resolution of the many different internal requirements of lighting and ventilation but was also a silent abstraction made manifest in common, everyday materials. There was a sense of stark urban reality about the building, appropriate to its situation and to its purpose. Juan Navarro Baldeweg, a Spanish architect of a later generation who extended the principles (though not the forms) of de la Sota, wrote penetratingly of the ethos behind this attitude to architecture:

Each project exploits its own strategy of purification … One essential notion lies behind ever more free and complex embodiments. In the Maravillas Gymnasium the seemingly empirical appearance hides a radical formulation. The gymnasium is essentially a space stolen by scooping into the earth, rendered fit for sport by coaxing in light and air …

There is always the feeling of some underlying spark, something that is pervasive in the physical world, that has been perceived intensely and reborn in an object that retains the original emotion, now laden with associations and memory. This provides the support and renders natural those daring, even brutal, creative leaps we see in [de la Sota's] buildings, which coexist with the greatest refinement and delicacy … such ideas, in which each work has an underlying harmony and rhythm of its own, are close to the real spirit of the architecture of Alejandro de la Sota …

A tradition is made, not just from sequences of forms, but also from the linkage of underlying architectural ideas. De la Sota turned to Mies van der Rohe, not to mimic his style, but to transform his principles in the service of new intentions and another 'myth'. Similarly, de la Sota became a link in a chain for later generations of Spanish architects seeking their own balance of modernity and continuity. Taken together, the works of the more probing architects of the 1950s reveal an analogous process, whereby the driving ideas of the earlier modern movement were scrutinized, re-examined and reassessed in the light of new and particular situations. To the extent that these architects were able to touch on values transcending mere matters of style, they were also able to reinvigorate the longer tradition to which they all belonged.

the process of absorption: latin america, australia, japan

… the past reappears
because it is a hidden
present … The
history of every
people contains certain
invariable elements, or
certain elements whose
variations are so slow
as to be imperceptible.
Octavio Paz, 1968

615 Luis Barragán,
Plaza y Fuente del
Bebedero, Las Arboledas,
Mexico City, 1958–61

The modern movement, in its formative years, was scarcely a worldwide phenomenon; it was the intellectual property of certain countries in Western Europe, of the United States and of some parts of the Soviet Union. In retrospect this is scarcely surprising since the very conception of modern architecture was linked to the existence of 'avant-gardes' seeking authenticity within (so-called) 'advanced' industrial societies. But by the end of the 1950s, transformations, deviations and devaluations of modern architecture had found their way to many other areas of the world. The pattern of post-war economic development, including rapid industrialization and dissemination of 'progressive' Western ideas (whether capitalist or socialist in origin), certainly played an important role here. So did the reproducible media; architectural fashions were transmitted at a greater speed than before.

Many earlier inventions in architecture – the Gothic of the Île de France, the Renaissance of Florence – had gradually radiated their influences across frontiers. Although the speed of emigration was far more dramatic with modern architecture, some of the usual problems obtained. The first of these was not, strictly speaking, geographical by definition, since it had to do with the broader issue of prototypes being turned into clichéd imitations. A second problem concerned the relevance of forms in the new context: if an architecture had been right for Manhattan, could it be right for Malaya? If a form had emerged in Boulogne-sur-Seine, what would make it fit the conditions of Buenos Aires? In other words, what should be kept of the prototypes and what transformed to match new climates, cultures, beliefs, technologies and architectural traditions? A third problem was the complement of the second: if new ideas from abroad were accepted, which old or indigenous ones should be thrown out? Should one accept the avowed universality of modern design and bow down before it; or should one perhaps seek some fusion between the best of old and new, of native and of foreign?

One must beware of treating the 'modern invader' as some monolithic unchanging entity. The stage reached by ideas in the influencing countries conditioned, in some degree, the point of departure in influenced ones. Brazil, South

Africa, Mexico and Japan, for example, all received modern architecture when it was still young in the 1920s or 1930s, and produced their own variants in the inter-war period. To compare, say, Martienssen's house designs in Cape Town with Costa and Niemeyer's Ministry of Education in Rio de Janeiro (both of the mid-1930s) and to place the two alongside Sakakura's nearly contemporary design for the Japanese Pavilion in Paris is to be made aware of the extraordinary hold of the 'Internationalist vision', even with the subtle national accents mentioned earlier (Chapter 21); in this case, too, all three designs drew a great deal from Le Corbusier's works of the 1920s. By contrast, the two decades after the Second World War were characterized by a far greater diversity within the modern movement in its originating centres, and by a higher valuation of the indigenous, the variable, and the regional. The planarity of the International Style gave way to a more sculptural and robust form of expression in which bare brick and concrete, textured façades and the density of walls played a greater role. This broadening of the aesthetic spectrum permitted new alignments with the vernacular and the archaic and helped to stimulate fresh readings and interpretations of local identities.

It is as well, therefore, to avoid the caricature of modern architecture as the 'rootless cosmopolitan'. Like most earlier style phases with an international range and a 'universalizing' tendency, it possessed and provided for regional responses. The works of the modern masters themselves contained some clues for adjusting to foreign climates and cultures and even provided filters through which traditions in other parts of the world might be interpreted. Wright's pan-American investigations, Le Corbusier's essays on Mediterranean vernacular themes, even Mies van der Rohe's ideas for patio houses, touched chords in unexpected places where architects were grappling with the need to express modern aspirations, yet at the same time evoke some sense of regional or national continuity. But the route from prototype to later invention was rarely straightforward. Who could have imagined, for example, that Mies van der Rohe's extending planar walls and surfaces of water would have had such an impact on the Mexican architects of the 1940s, or that Le Corbusier's theme of the low

vaulted dwelling with a turf roof would have found 'indigenous' responses as far afield as India, Algeria and Uruguay? Territories of the imagination and national boundaries rarely coincided; an American or European work inspired by, say, Japanese traditions, might in turn prompt a Japanese modern architect to look at his own past afresh. Modernization brought with it a degree of rupture and deracination, but it also permitted the idea of a national culture to be framed and formulated in new ways. The very abstraction of modern architecture gave the penetrating architect the means to transcend provincialism and parochialism, while eliciting echoes from the basic forms and long-term myths of local traditions at a generalized level.

The majority of developing countries did not receive modern influences until the post-war years and therefore adapted not the formative models of the modern movement, but later modifications or inventions. India, for example, received the impact of the late works of Le Corbusier rather than the early ones, the more so as his own Indian buildings combined local and broader resonances. Louis Kahn's designs for Ahmadabad and Dacca would eventually fulfil an analogous parental role for Indian and Pakistani architects, while Wright's architecture tended to be more influential in

616 Enrique del Moral, Mario Pani, Carlos Lazo and others, Ciudad Universitaria (University City), Mexico City, 1946, site plan

617 Juan O'Gorman with Gustavo Saavedra and Juan Martinez de Velasco, University Library, University City, Mexico City, 1950–3

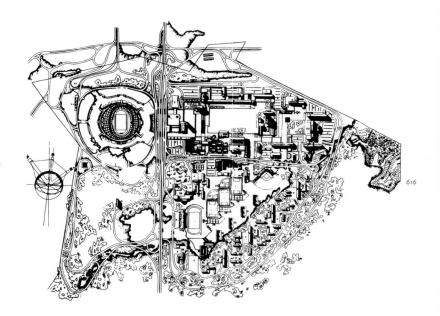

616

617

temperate zones such as south-east Australia. However, there was no obvious pattern of correspondences between prototypes and later absorptions and inventions – and one wonders if the whole picture of world architectural development might not have been different if, say, Wright rather than Le Corbusier had designed a major Indian city in his late years, or if Le Corbusier's vision of a *brise-soleil* skyscraper had been adopted by businesses and bureaucracies in the West, instead of Mies Van der Rohe's image of the steel and glass prism. When approaching the question of international exchange, it is as well to leave aside both simplistic notions of global hegemony and monolithic ideas of national identity; unexpected connections are found to work between one place and another.

The significance accorded to 'modernity' itself depended upon particular national histories and nationalist mythologies. In Mexico, for example, modern architecture had already played a role in post-Revolutionary reform in the 1920s and 1930s when aesthetic and social idealism had sometimes

been combined. Modernism had helped to dislodge the lingering Beaux-Arts influence and to emancipate visual culture from blatantly European models associated with foreign political control. It might itself have been perceived as just one more colonizing 'layer' from Europe, but was instead absorbed into the Mexican '*imaginaire*' as a vaguely universalizing force relevant to the causes of overcoming old social, racial and religious divisions and of achieving rapid technological 'progress'. It thus contributed to a style of national self-definition which required the integration of all past cultures within a single, unifying national ideal. In Latin America the construction of retrospective national 'histories' worked differently for countries with a visible ancient heritage (such as Mexico with its layers of Hispanic and pre-Columbian memories) than for countries lacking such tangible evidence of the distant past (Brazil for example). The ruins of Mexico's various past civilizations played a crucial role in transmitting some supposed 'constants' of national identity.

To follow Mexican architectural development from its modern beginnings in the 1920s up to the recent past is to sense how international types could be absorbed into these local patterns, and how Mexican traits could in turn be reinterpreted in modern ways. The Ciudad Universitaria (University City) to the south of Mexico City (1946 onwards) designed by several architects including Enrique del Moral, Mario Pani, Carlos Lazo, José Villagrán, Juan O'Gorman and the young Teodoro González de León, was a competent version of Le Corbusier's Ville Radieuse, adjusted to the institutions and technology of Mexico. The overall plan combined free-standing slabs, stadiums, open green spaces and transitional courts; bands of glazing, *pilotis*, curved entrance-ways, roof terraces, hovering horizontals and public murals completed the imagery of a 'progressive' educational ideal. There was something ample and broad about the handling of the ground plane which suggested subliminal echoes of the wide courts and landscape forms of pre-Columbian sites. The exterior walls of Juan O'Gorman's University Library (1950–3) were completely covered in richly coloured mosaics combining recognizable images, and abstract configurations based partly upon ancient motifs. These external surfaces expressed strong nationalist sentiments, but the anatomy of the architecture itself was little affected by traditional forms or by adjustments to the climate. As in other parts of Latin America, the University City was intended to symbolize the liberalizing and secularizing intervention of the state: 'integrating the thought, the hope and the labour of everyone through culture'. These 'micro-cities' of greenery, crystalline towers and official modern art, with their message of social emancipation, were like miniature Utopias – hypothetical urban models confronting the ever more daunting problems of the actual city undergoing the crisis of mass immigration from the countryside. They recalled a long-standing tradition in Latin American colonial development, whereby idealized urban visions based on bold geometry were used to further 'universalizing' schemes of modernization.

As Mexico had remained neutral in the Second World War, it was possible to continue the earlier modern development without interruption. The immediate problems stemmed from rapid urbanization and the influx of large numbers of people. Housing projects usually relied upon the pervasive international formula of high-rise slabs laid out in parallel, or else in indentations (for example, Mario Pani's Multifamiliar Aleman of 1949 in Mexico City, which also incorporated street decks), though there were some high-density, low-rise solutions (such as Teodoro González de León's low-cost housing using vaults and patios outside Guadalajara of 1957). In the commercial sector, an adequate version of the 'glass box' emerged in central Mexico City, enlivened here and there with murals or touches of coloured tiles. Typical were some of the skyscraper designs of Augusto Alvarez, which combined elegance of expression with technological standardization. The daring structural experiments of Felix Candela using concrete-shell technology opened up low-cost possibilities for market-halls and even churches, while the Mercado 'La Merced' of 1957 by Enrique del Moral showed how cheap ceramic and brick construction could combine utility and high formal quality. For institutional buildings the vague outline of a 'modern architecture with Mexican accents' began to emerge in the form of bold abstract masses, strident horizontals, platforms and steps. The Sports Pavilion of the University City, designed in 1953

618

by Espinosa Arai and Teruo Alberto, evoked the sloping walls and battered shapes of ancient Mexican pyramids.

The reconciliation of the 'general' and the 'local' was a recurrent theme in the late 1940s and the 1950s in Mexico. The main arena for such attempts at cultural interpretation was the suburban fringe of Mexico City where new wealth aspired to cosmopolitan values but still left the door open to tradition. There were several parallel directions in the field of Mexican domestic architecture in the 1940s and 1950s, which revealed the transformation of a variety of international influences. The house at Paseo de Reforma in Lomas, designed by Teodoro González de León in 1951 took over the Corbusian 'type' of the steel superstructure raised on a raft on *pilotis* (e.g. Pavillon Suisse), but reorganized the upper living areas in terms which accorded better with Mexican outdoor habits using sliding screens, transparent layers of structure and alternating roof gardens. The traditional Mexican type was the patio surrounded by blank walls, and this received several interpretations in modern forms. Enrique del Moral's own home of 1948–9 in Mexico City marked out an enclave using abstract planes and overlapping spaces to integrate the interiors with sheltered courts adjacent to private rooms and with a garden at the heart of the scheme. In this case, the design belonged, broadly speaking, in a Miesian lineage, but the inward-turning spaces, textured walls, earthy colours, bold planks, alabaster screens,

618 Enrique del Moral,
del Moral House,
Tacubaya, Mexico City,
1948–9

619 Luis Barragán,
Barragán House,
Tacubaya, Mexico City,
1947, roof terrace

volcanic rock ledges and exotic planting suggested a local interpretation of the international prototype. Here the sparseness and lightness of the International Style gave way to something more colourful, more massive, and more rustic.

The key figure in the discovery of a modern architecture full of Mexican echoes was Luis Barragán. Most of his works were for exclusive wealthy patrons on the suburban outskirts of Mexico City, and he discovered ways of endowing the well-to-do enclave with a certain urban solidity while also intensifying the experience of nature. As mentioned earlier (pp. 390–1), Barragán's mature style began to emerge in garden and landscape designs of the mid-1940s such as El Pedregal, in which austere platforms of lava and abstract wall planes channelled the flow of outdoor spaces and linked together cascades and pools. Among the major formative influences on him was the Alhambra in southern Spain (which he visited in 1924) with its dream-like vistas, water gardens, shifting axes and surreal atmosphere; he also

absorbed the stark walls of Mexican convents and peasant dwellings with their introspective patios and gardens. Barragán saw beyond the machine-age imagery of the International Style to something deeper. He developed a taste for the metaphysical strain of European Surrealism (e.g. De Chirico, Magritte) but also employed modernist devices of abstraction to distil hidden presences and to condense images from several eras of history. In his hands the inherited spatial patterns of modern architecture were used to serve a species of mystical conservatism – a poetry of retreat and private contemplation.

Barragán's own house of 1947 at Tacubaya laid down many of the themes of his mature architecture: cubic volumes, tranquil spaces, textured walls in uniform colours, ambiguous planes, variations on the platform, the patio, the terrace and the secret garden. His architecture worked with controlled views, transitions through layers of space, reflecting pools and hidden sources of light. The outside world was kept at bay behind

619

620

dense walls, with minimal openings allowing glimpses of interiors that withdrew from the mess and confusion of contemporary existence towards a still centre. Barragán called his own house a 'refuge', and claimed that: 'Any work of architecture which does not express serenity is a mistake.'

Taking a firm stance against functionalism, Barragán also spoke of the need for an 'emotional architecture'. For the Chapel of the Capuchin Convent at Tlalpan of 1952–5, he used grilles and screens to create veils between the various spaces in the plan, light taking on a mystical mood recalling, perhaps, the writings of St Teresa of Avila or those of St John of the Cross. The houses of the same period (e.g. the Galvez House at San Angel of 1955) linked together outdoor and indoor rooms in sequences of varying intensity and mood. The primary element of Barragán's architecture was the simple rectangular plane drenched in bright colour, and this could become a step, a floor, a wall, a ceiling, or a partition placed ambiguously between inside and outside. In effect, Barragán took the language of modern abstract painting and rendered it tactile and three-dimensional, transforming the real into the illusionistic, the illusionistic into the real. Slight distortions of edges were used to create subtle visual tensions and false perspectives, and space was compresssed and released through a careful control of thickness, mass and transparency. *Objets trouvés* from peasant culture – such as crude clay pots or log beams – made a vital contrast with this modern abstraction.

It is customary to think of Mexican modern art in terms of the realist muralist tradition stemming from Diego Rivera, but there was a parallel non-objective strand which concerned itself with 'spiritualized geometry' and 'private revelation', and it is this which is pertinent to Barragán. His houses were like silent, poetic puzzles in which time seemed to stop. Personal memory and cultural memory seemed to conspire. As well as articulating the rituals of the private interior, Barragán also addressed the problem of the larger landscape, and here too he attempted to intensify the experience of the observer but by working with the wider world of mountains and sky. In 1957, in collaboration with the sculptor Mathias Goeritz, he designed a cluster of shaft-like monumental towers that marked the exit of the northern highway from Mexico City and indicated the presence of the residential subdivision known as the Satellite City. The towers were solid monoliths in reinforced concrete, five in all, rising to 100, 120, 130, 150 and 165 feet respectively (31, 37, 40, 46 and 50 metres). They were triangular in plan, rough in texture, and originally painted in red, yellow, white and blue. Experienced from the passing car, they shifted into ever-changing alignments, one moment massive and solid, the next planar and immaterial. Ambiguous in size, the ensemble of coloured, abstract forms generated a field of energy on the scale of the wide central valley of Mexico, and were visible for miles around.

In Barragán's design for the riding stables at Las Arboledas (1958–61), the elegant rituals of equestrianism were organized as a sequence of shaded walks and outdoor rooms defined by geometrical planes in the landscape including a network of water tanks, pools, troughs and freestanding walls. Illusions of compression and depth, of size and perspective, were enhanced by contrasts of colour, ambiguously placed rectangles, controlled glimpses of distant landscapes seen

621

through horizontal openings, and the dappled play of light off water. Here the Islamic paradise garden and the discoveries of the Barcelona Pavilion or the illusionism of the roof terrace of the Unité at Marseilles came together in a labyrinth of curiously nostalgic character: a minimalist aesthetic was given an emotional charge. For Los Clubes (1963–4) and the Egerstrom Residence and Stables (1968), Barragán resorted to sliding spaces channelled by warm-coloured partition walls and wide horizontal proscenium openings with, on occasion, giant water troughs running above and discharging into extensive basins. Water was used to stir the memory and to release the imagination, as a smooth surface, a ruffled edge or a splashing cascade. In Barragán's work, abstraction was employed to concentrate meanings but also to hide them, leaving allusions just beneath the surface. The planar wall, a constituent element of earlier modernism, was embedded in a new set of metaphysical co-ordinates – a private myth that was personal in its references,

Mexican in its resonances, but universal in its underlying tone. To speak merely of the fusion of Regionalism and the International Style, or of the vernacular and Le Corbusier, is to trivialize Barragán: his style expressed a genuinely archetypical mood in touch with the tragic vein in Mexican cultural history.

In Brazil the foundations of a national modern movement were laid in the 1930s, when architects such as Lucio Costa and Oscar Niemeyer (taking Le Corbusier as one of their starting-points) focused the progressive ethos of the Brazilian state around the major project of the Ministry of Education in Rio de Janeiro (pp. 386). Modernism instituted a clean break with earlier eclecticism, but it also opened the way to an indigenous mythology based upon a metaphorical reaction to the landscape itself. Niemeyer's works of the early 1940s (such as those at Pampulha) were perhaps most successful in laying out the terms of a modern Brazilian language, relying, as they did, upon a practical and lyrical

622 Luis Barragán,
Egerstrom Residence and
Stables ('San Cristobal'),
Los Clubes, Mexico City,
1968

623 Oscar Niemeyer,
Niemeyer House, Gávea,
Rio de Janiero, 1953, plan

624 Niemeyer House,
interior

interpretation of tropical conditions in buildings of skeletal or transparent character activated by complex curvatures in plan and circulation. But Niemeyer was himself acutely aware of the limited social role played by his architecture in this early period, stating later that he would like to have made a 'more realistic achievement' reflecting 'not only refinements and comforts but also a positive collaboration between the architect and the whole society'. A dilemma of this kind would face several architects working in 'developing' countries: their architecture had frequently to become the chic plaything of a tiny and wealthy minority in order to be built at all.

In the late 1940s and early 1950s, the social basis of modern Brazilian architecture was broadened. The Pedregulho Housing Estate in Rio de Janeiro designed by Affonso Eduardo Reidy in 1947–52 was organized as a winding strip playing against the tumultuous topography in a manner recalling Le Corbusier's pre-war housing schemes for Algiers, or even for Rio itself (p. 325). In the Palace of Industry, Ibirapuéra Park, São Paulo (1951–4), designed by Niemeyer, the interiors were formed from dynamic interconnections

of curved ramps, making an almost operatic celebration of automobile circulation. The formal complexity of Brazilian modern architecture may be traced in part to the colonial Baroque, but it also drew upon the biomorphic abstraction of modern art (Hans Arp, Joan Miró, Alexander Calder). By using slender structural supports, louvres, transparencies and active curves, it was possible to reduce a building to a minimalist intervention through which people, air and vegetation could pass freely. Architecture and topography could also be fused together, planting and water taking on a special value. Roberto Burle Marx, the landscapist and painter, evolved a tropical style for gardens using indigenous varieties of plants, and serpentine pools, ledges and benches. Niemeyer's own house outside Rio de Janeiro (1953), with its impeccable control of free-form floating roofs, sinuous glass surfaces, and interconnections of indoor and outdoor spaces, summed up the hedonist possibilities of this phase of Brazilian modernism. The plan was like a hieroglyph of concave and convex incisions in the terrain: virtually an abstraction of landscape contours and tropical plant forms.

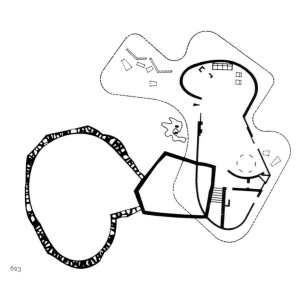
623

624

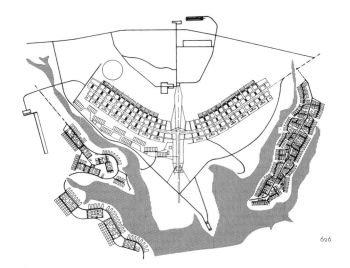

Where the architectural representation of the state was concerned in the Latin America of the 1950s, there was a dual pressure to symbolize progress and to celebrate national myths. The Mexican monumentality that emerged in this period had to do with the centralization of institutions and with the consolidation of an 'all-embracing' vision of national culture which drew upon the extensive pre-Columbian heritage. But Brazil possessed no equivalent to ancient ruins and when Lúcio Costa fixed the plan for the new city of Brasilia, and Oscar Niemeyer designed the main state institutions on the Capitol there, they worked out a generalized language of monumentality using largely modern means. The ideology latent in the programme implied a launch into an unknown future and something akin to a cosmic gesture for marking out a symbolic place on the vast virgin landscape of the Brazilian interior. Although the project for Brasilia was surrounded by mid-twentieth-century technocratic rhetoric, it also reiterated the old colonial dream of expanding towards the heart of the country. Costa's city plan resembled both an aeroplane with its wings spread out in a slight arc

625 Oscar Niemeyer,
Plaza of the Three Powers,
Brasilia, 1958

626 Lúcio Costa, master
plan for Brasilia, 1957.
The Plaza of the Three
Powers is on the main axis
towards the bottom of the
drawing

627 Oscar Niemeyer,
Cathedral of Our Lady
of Fatima, Brasilia,
1959–70

and a cross laid on the landscape. The focal point was the Plaza of the Three Powers, containing the Presidential Palace, the Supreme Court and the Congress with its Secretariat. The bifurcated slab of the Secretariat stood between the main State Chambers, which were expressed as saucer shapes, one face up, the other face down. The notch between the prisms carried the axis of the city on over the vast space of the continent towards infinity. Flanking the axis on each side were the Ministries, also oblong prisms with glazed façades, but this time lying on their sides. Completing this ensemble of abstract shapes was the Cathedral (1959–70), with its bundle of curved beams contributing to a hyperboloid shape but also evoking the image of a crown of thorns. Reflecting pools, level changes and ramps complemented the wide-open spaces, and launched the eye towards the sky.

Brasilia was the conception of a technocratic élite surrounding the figure of President Juscelino Kubitschek de Oliveira, and was intended to be a symbol of national commitment to industrial development. In its way it celebrated the romance

of the automobile and the freeway, at a time when Brazil was investing in the car industry and in a new infrastructure. The twin skyscrapers of the Secretariat with their lower accompanying volumes extended a typology which had already been announced in Hannes Meyer's League of Nations proposal of 1927, and which was to take yet another form in Le Corbusier's Project 23-A for the United Nations in New York of 1947 (Fig. 505, a project which Niemeyer may well have influenced). But the *superquadra* blocks of housing separated by wide spaces had the air of empty, theoretical speculations based upon earlier, unbuilt modernist Utopias remote from the Brazilian social realities of the day. The government élite commuted by plane from more urbane settings, while the poor flooded into the vacuum of a diagrammatic planning concept. The main ensemble of monuments was as ambitious as Le Corbusier's Capitol at Chandigarh, although Niemeyer was not able to maintain the same degree of formal intensity, perhaps because there was not the same depth of meaning. The Presidential Palace, for example, resorted to fussy, inverted arches in white marble, while the totality was curiously lacking in scale and articulation. The forms which had shown such vitality in the 1940s were beginning to show signs of fatigue.

Niemeyer's floating, curved roofs and dynamic interpenetrations marked one pole of post-war Latin American architecture; Barragán's dense walls and labyrinthine patios another. If the former established some of the terms of a modern tropical expression for hot/humid conditions, the latter did something analogous for hot/dry ones. The interpretation of climate was not just a geographical, practical exercise, but a cultural, poetic one as well, and some of the richest results were achieved when the entire spatial anatomy of a design was attuned to a way of life. The Casa Noval in Havana, Cuba (1952), by Mario Romañach and Silverio Bosch, drew its lessons from the tropical vernacular (overhangs, verandas, screens) without imitating the actual forms; instead, it worked with a modern syntax of hovering white planes, long horizontal openings, and layers of transparency perforated by eruptive vegetation. There were reminiscences of Neutra's idea for the 'Natural house', but these were transmuted to capture the mood of a Caribbean dwelling – something light, airy and overgrown.

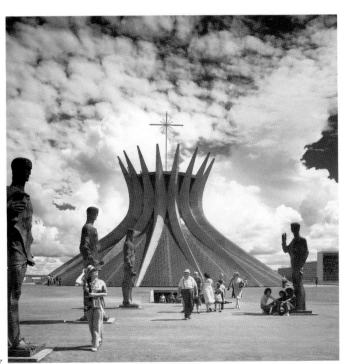
627

The Venezuelan architect Carlos Raúl Villanueva was intrigued by the spatial possibilities of reinforced concrete cantilevering and shell construction, and evolved an entire formal repertoire that was also attuned to a wet and sticky equatorial climate. But he saw climate in almost mythical terms and directed his formal inventiveness towards a progressive social vision for his country. Venezuela in the 1940s and 1950s was developing rapidly on the basis of an oil economy, and Villanueva was quick to grasp the need for an architecture that would be dynamically modern yet sensitive to tropical conditions. Although there were no long-standing architectural traditions to follow, he studied the relatively recent colonial buildings for their lessons in dealing with the local weather. He grasped the relevance of perforated boundaries, protective overhangs and a fluid transition of spaces. Villanueva studied at the École des Beaux-Arts in Paris in the 1930s, made friends with artists such as Fernand Léger and Alexander Calder, and, on his return to Caracas, attempted to give shape to the emergent social energies of Venezuela in a 'synthesis of the arts' – a fusion of modern architecture, painting, sculpture and urbanism.

While Villanueva drew from both Niemeyer and Le Corbusier, he succeeded in forming a distinctly personal style. His main works included the Ciudad Universitaria (University City), Caracas (1950–9), the Olympic Stadium (1950–1), his own house (1952), and several housing projects, all in Caracas. The University City encapsulated the idea of a landscaped enclave forming a liberal Utopia on the edge of the capitalist city, but here (in contrast to its Mexican equivalent) the vocabulary made extreme use of louvres, shades, grilles, coloured plaques and interlocking volumes. The walkways between the main institutions on the campus were formed from curved concrete overhangs that seemed suspended in mid-air. These floating forms guided movement, encouraged the free association of people, provided contact with the lush vegetation, and protected passing students from sun and rain. The *pièce de résistance* of the University City was the Aula Magna (1952–3), or main auditorium, with its suspended acoustic panels designed by Calder.

Equally impressive was the lobby preceding it, a space of indescribable complexity arising from the interpenetration of several levels, ramps and hovering, curved concrete roofs admitting cracks of daylight. Here the blending of inside and outside allowed the passage of breezes but also took on a social meaning to do with the democratization of the institutions of learning. The exposed concrete surfaces were enlivened by touches of bold colour supplied by works by Arp, Léger and others. Villanueva's architecture relied upon a poetic sense of structure, an intimate understanding of the interweaving of natural and climatic forces, a sense of the human figure moving through warm air, and a spatial concept which synthesized the discoveries of Cubism with cultural 'substructures' in his own land.

Part of the vitality of Latin American architecture in the 1950s derived from the inventive use of structural techniques such as parabolic vaulting, reinforced-concrete shells and extensive cantilevering – sometimes this inventiveness resulted in mere exhibitionism, sometimes in disciplined architectural ideas. The Berlingieri House at Punta Ballena, Uruguay (1947–8), designed by the Argentinian architect Antonio Bonet, was constructed from a rhythmic sequence of shell concrete roofs which helped to fit the building to the terrain. The idea evidently drew upon Le Corbusier's vaulted house typologies as well as upon vernacular examples. (Curiously enough,

Le Corbusier's Currutchet House at La Plata, Argentina of 1949 exerted slight local influence.) Another Argentinian architect, Amancio Williams, developed an entire morphology based upon structural ideas in reinforced concrete. His House on the Stream at Mar del Plata, Argentina (1943–5) was parabolic in section, a slender span which responded as an abstract form to the neighbouring topography. Williams's interest in attenuated bridge structures re-emerged in several unbuilt projects of the late 1940s, including one for an offshore airport for Buenos Aires raised on piles, and one for a skyscraper based not upon a conventional frame, but upon wide lateral trusses placed between pairs of piers: an idea which anticipated Norman Foster's Hong Kong and Shanghai Bank (Fig. 817) by thirty years. This strand of structural experimentation in Argentinian architecture was extended still further in such buildings of the early 1960s as the Bank of London and South America in Buenos Aires by Clorindo Testa, a work which pushed the elements of structure, servicing and circulation towards an almost Baroque plasticity.

The arrival of international ideas in a particular locale could generate considerable tension, as is revealed by the Australian situation in the years after the Second World War. The question of a specifically Australian 'tradition' was complicated by the relatively recent arrival of Europeans and by the fact that the Aboriginal population expressed

630

631

its ideas through other means than permanent buildings. As in the United States, the architecture of the settlers had emerged from the gradual adaptation of imported models to local conditions. There had been fragmentary modern influences between the wars, stemming especially from Walter Burley Griffin's introduction of Wrightian forms in the 1910s and 1920s, but a consolidated modern movement did not really get under way in Australia until the late 1940s. The problem of Australian cultural identity had been debated earlier in the century in connection with literature and the visual arts, and naturally raised the question of an 'authentic' response in content and form to the social, urban and geographical conditions of the country. These dilemmas did not disappear with the increasingly international cultural atmosphere of the 1940s and 1950s; if anything they intensified.

There were several positions in Australian modern architecture of the immediate post-war years, which ran from internationalism to a species of Regionalism. Harry Seidler's was the case of the cosmopolitan whose formation occurred under the impact of the waning International Style. He was born in Vienna and educated in Britain and Canada before entering the Graduate School of Design at Harvard, and appears to have thought of Gropius, Breuer and Josef Albers (the colour theorist) as fountainheads of modernist principle. His earliest houses in the Sydney suburbs (e.g. the Seidler House of 1948, or the Rose House of 1950) were clearly imitations of an architectural language which he had absorbed in the eastern United States and which (as we have seen) was already watered down by comparison with the seminal works of the 1920s. Seidler himself admitted that 'the pioneering days of modern architecture are over. We are now in a period of consolidation and development.' However, in a broader perspective it appeared that he was merely following the leaders in an all too obvious way. The American architect Paul Rudolph, who had also passed through the Graduate School of Design at Harvard, but who reacted more strongly against the puritanism of his mentors, singled out the Seidler house and described it as 'the Harvard house incarnate' transferred to Sydney 'without any modifications whatsoever', and made pleas for an enriching 'Regionalism' if modern architecture was to avoid an ersatz blandness.

In Australia it did not take long for a similar mood to surface, and for a certain 'foreignness' to be sensed about Seidler's taut white boxes poised on slender stilts among the boulders and eucalyptus trees. Instead a blend was sought between the principles of modern design and 'indigenous' features drawn from the informality of the vernacular. An example of this 'modern Regionalism' was the Muller House at Whale Beach of 1955 (designed by Peter Muller), which was formed from low wooden overhangs nestling among the trees. The rocks of the site were incorporated in the living room and an attempt was made to consult the special 'genius of the place'. Large areas of glass were used, but carefully hooded from the glare. The vocabulary clearly had a fundamentally Wrightian

632 Harry Seidler, Seidler House, near Sydney, 1948

633 Wilfred and Ruth Lucas, Lucas House, Castlecrag, New South Wales, 1957

634 Peter Johnson, Johnson House, Chatswood, New South Wales, 1964

632

633

634

character, and the strategy was not so very far from that being pursued in the more flexible of the Case Study Program houses on the West Coast of the United States. Indeed, there were several parallels between the temperate climate and hillside vegetation of coastal New South Wales and those of California. Muller also studied Japanese wooden architecture and was interested in Zen philosophy. His nature worship came through in a design which tried deliberately to respect the existing order of the hillside. The image of the International Style box was replaced by sprawling horizontal planes in local timber which evoked a casual, suburban way of life and intensified the views of trees and sea.

Before the arrival of the colonists, the Aboriginal population of Australia had made shelters from the most minimal materials, such as bark, branches and leaves. In this largely nomadic culture, the landscape itself (both visible and invisible) had supplied a monumental framework and an extended world of meanings. Little or nothing of this significance was understood by the settlers, who none the less evolved their own vernacular forms, adjusting timber frame, veranda and roof to rain, sun, heat, cold and vegetation in the different regions of the country. In the mid-twentieth century a certain mythology of the 'outback' was developed by the largely urban population, and settled around the image of a temporary shed, often with a timber veranda and a tin roof. Several Australian architects,

working in the late 1950s and 1960s, developed an analogous aesthetic of slender poles, open decks, trellises and suspension wires. One of the most remarkable examples was the Lucas House (1957) at Castlecrag near Sydney designed by Wilfred and Ruth Lucas, which was so understated that it virtually disappeared into its wooded setting. With its deliberately casual construction, it suggested some twentieth-century version of a tree house, although its 'simplicity' was, of course, born of extreme sophistication.

In the early 1960s, some Australian architects looked to Le Corbusier's late works for inspiration when seeking out their own image of a straightforward, semi-rural or suburban dwelling. In his own house at Chatswood of 1963, Peter Johnson reflected his interest in 'Brutalist ideology' and in the Maisons Jaoul, in the use of rough-and-ready clinker bricks and overhanging pitched roofs of a type found locally. The rooms became so many platforms, following the natural slope and open to a variety of views. Slender wooden balconies attached to the brick piers blended with the dense vegetation on all sides. Johnson sought to combine the image of some indigenous shack with cosmopolitan sources enriched by a vein of primitivism. Thus a variety of influences and ideas were brought together, all sited within a few miles of one another, in an attempt at producing, among other things, 'a new Australian architecture'.

At least these were cases in which the search for appropriate architectural forms had the benefit of minds intent on crystallizing a new cultural situation. But by the early 1960s the far more usual mode of influence was through straightforward exportation of forms to provincial centres. Moreover, it was usually a devalued style of industrial building, rather than an architecture of any formal value that was transmitted in this way. Thus the commercial offices of New York and London soon reproduced their imagery in cities as far apart as Hong Kong and Lagos. It was as if the steel or concrete rectangular frame, the air conditioner and the property developer conspired to reject national traditions overnight. This was not the true International Style – with its moral and aesthetic imperatives – so much as an 'international corporation style' – indeed, big business and tourism played a major part in the proliferation of the clichéd forms. It will be suggested later (Chapter 31) that this development was linked to rapid mechanization and to the confusion that was bound to ensue when countries proceeded in a single generation from peasant to industrial economies; the technocratic and Western style of education of new élites also played a part. The bland results around the world in the 1960s soon engendered a strong reaction in favour of Regionalism of various kinds in the 1970s. The sophisticated 'peasantism' of the European avant-garde would be only partially relevant to this backlash, which often sought a more direct evocation of the vernacular.

Japan, like Brazil and Mexico, laid the foundations of its modern movement between the Wars in a select number of buildings, and even established theoretical reference points that would continue to be relevant. The urban societies of Australia and Latin America had an almost automatic affinity with 'Western' concepts of modernity, since their history rested, to a degree, on the projections of earlier European colonialism; but in Japan the matter was more complicated, as modernization itself had involved a continual struggle between deeply ingrained Oriental traditions, and models that were perceived, even by the urban élite, as being alien. The scale of the construction crisis after military defeat and extensive war damage was almost beyond understanding. In 1945, at the time of the

635

surrender, 4.2 million new dwellings were needed. The architectural profession attempted to handle the problem by designing standardized, mass-producible, low-cost units based on the module of the tatami mat, buildable in less than a week. The late 1940s was characterized by a gradual democratization of Japanese life but long-standing dilemmas over Westernization and modernization were certainly not reduced by the American military presence or by the glaring contrast between imported forms and indigenous ones in the hasty reconstruction of cities. In architectural circles there were debates about the viability of reviving pre-war modernist tendencies and about the possibility of some form of 'Social Realism' in architecture.

635 Kunio Mayekawa,
Harumi Building, Tokyo,
1958

636 Kunio Mayekawa,
Kyoto Town Hall,
1958–60

In 1950, with the outbreak of the Korean War, an inflationary period came to an end with a boom, and at last paper projects could be set aside in favour of actual construction. Discussion returned to the question of a Japanese modern style. It was clear that this would have to address the realities of a rapidly industrializing society in which Western technocratic values were more and more in evidence, for Japanese life was being forcibly Americanized. Kunio Mayekawa's Nihon Sogo Bank or Antonin Raymond's more delicate Readers' Digest publishing house (both designed in Tokyo in 1950) reflected an attempt at continuing pre-war modernist experimentation. The Peace Treaty of San Francisco in the same year, which gave Japan her independence from the United States, strengthened the consciousness of national traditions which had, none the less, to be disentangled from earlier nationalism and imperialism. Once again the idea emerged that glib internationalism should be purged, but here the problem still lay in knowing quite how to *transform* earlier Japanese prototypes. The way forward seemed to lie in a sort of abstraction of indigenous spatial and structural concepts, and a mating of these principles with similar essential ideas of modern design of high quality – a notion which had already had some limited influence before the war. Noboru Kawazoe spelt out this position clearly, in a manner which bolstered national self-esteem, by suggesting that Japan had, in a sense, anticipated modern architecture:

Steel and concrete, in the form of columns and beams, provide framed structures and are, in this respect, akin to traditional timber constructions … A frame structure allows a room to be more open and flexible and obviates the need for solid walls as a structural element. In the continuity of interior and exterior, in the flexibility of a room design using movable partitions, traditional Japanese architecture has pioneered many solutions, such as the integration of the garden and the interior, the protection of the interior by oversailing roofs, the use of the veranda as a link between interior and garden, the connection of different parts of a building by corridors, the introduction of the sliding wall (fusama) by means of which a room can be enlarged or reduced in size, the use of screens (byobu) for visual protection, and the tatami mat serving as a module of floor area. Not only for the sake of industrialization, but also for the sake of flexibility, it is necessary to resort to standardization – something that the builders of the past have done. In traditional architecture 'kiwari' signified a modular order and a 'grammatical' determination of components for the layout and design of rooms …

While there might be analogies between traditional timber and modern frame construction, it was by no means obvious how old and new should be combined, especially for unprecedented building types on a large scale. Among these was the somewhat alien high-rise apartment building, of which Mayekawa's Harumi Building in Tokyo of 1958 was a notable example. This was modelled loosely on Le Corbusier's Unité d'Habitation, although the block was brought right down to the ground instead of having free passage between *pilotis*. Individual units were expressed as extending trays which were inserted into the larger frame of the whole, a robust articulation of the assembly of parts typical of advanced Japanese work. It was not unusual in the 1950s for Japanese dwellings to have Western-style rooms at the front and a traditional room to the back – evidence enough of a split state of mind in daily matters. The more inventive Japanese architects hoped to overcome this 'rift', and to establish a dialogue, if not a marriage, between traditional spatial concepts and modern ones.

Among the post-war Japanese architects to attempt this was Kenzo Tange, who had been a pupil of Mayekawa and Le Corbusier, and so was able to handle the inheritance of the West with less nervousness than his contemporaries. His Peace Memorial and Museum at Hiroshima of 1949–55 employed an updated version of the Five Points of a New Architecture, replete with delicate screens which were Japanese relatives of Le Corbusier's

636

brises-soleil. Similar devices were employed in the Kagawa Prefecture of 1955–8, where concrete columns and trellises revealed the hierarchy of structure in a way recalling the grammar of traditional timber buildings. Even the internal furnishings repeated the themes of the building but at a smaller scale. Tange combined a critical interpretation of an institutional building programme with a radical reassessment of Japanese monumental types. The ground floor of the Prefecture was entirely open to pedestrians, and there was easy access to the public functions in the low, lateral block. The offices were placed in a quadrangular tower, an object distinguished from commercial use by a certain rhetoric in the handling of exposed structural beams and railings.

In Japan in the late 1950s and early 1960s town halls and civic centres were planned as genuine attempts at expressing both the notion of citizens' forums in the recently created democracy, and a new feeling of national self-confidence. Delicate, screen-like effects gave way to a more monumental treatment and to a heavier articulation in rough concrete. Here again national precedents could be

identified – especially the giant logs and brackets of the Imperial treasure houses – though care had to be taken to avoid authoritarian overtones. There were also relevant prototypes in the international architectural culture of the period: Mayekawa and Tange were among the first in Japan to grasp the relevance of the rugged blend of Asian and European traditions at Chandigarh to a language of monumentality for their own country. One of the breakthrough buildings in the new genre was Mayekawa's Kyoto Town Hall of 1958–60, in which rough wooden patterns in the concrete and precast beams were used in a manner analogous to the 'kit-of-parts' approach of traditional Japanese timber construction. Joints were freely expressed to demonstrate and dramatize the process of building. In the Metropolitan Festival Hall in Tokyo of 1961, Mayekawa extended the same style further. Here the problem was to combine auditoriums and public areas in a suitably impressive visual framework, and there can be little doubt that the architect modelled his design on the Parliament Building at Chandigarh. The scooped overhangs, the deep porticoes, the bare concrete and the sculptural

637 Kenzo Tange,
Peace Memorial and
Museum, Hiroshima,
1949–55

638 Kenzo Tange,
Olympic Gymnasium,
Tokyo, 1961–4

roofscape elements expressing the auditoriums were all drawn from this source. Even so, there was a subtle difference: the silhouettes, shapes and proportions spoke a language evocative of Japanese monumental traditions.

Kenzo Tange took this tendency towards monumental expressionism still further in the Tokyo Olympic Gymnasium of 1961–4, in which he employed tensile steel roofs to create interwoven curves with an architectural effectiveness matched only by Utzon, Nervi, and Eero Saarinen at the time. By the mid-1960s it was clear to the rest of the world that a distinctive Japanese modern architecture had emerged which was based on a dramatic expression of structure and an almost aggressive use of modern technology. Japan's 'economic miracle' was proceeding so quickly that a glossy, uprooted urban culture was rapidly coming into being which seemed increasingly to threaten any sober assessment of the past and its meaning. In architecture this mood began to surface in schemes which celebrated industrial technique at the expense of all else.

Some of these were at an urban scale. The rapid post-war increase in population, combined with the finite habitable land of the country produced an apparently uncontrollable sprawl, and forced issues of town planning to the fore. Around 1960, Tange turned his mind to Tokyo's urban problems in a scheme which envisaged an extension of the urban network into the bay, with giant stanchions rising out of the water (containing services and lifts) and huge attached structural beams and bridges (supporting housing and other urban facilities). While the idea was loosely similar to some of the raised-deck proposals being made in Europe at the same time (e.g. by Team X), Tange's scheme had a far more forceful and megastructural character. Critics who were still keen to emphasize the 'Japaneseness' of this daunting technological wizardry pointed lamely to the similarities of the huge lattice of circulation to posts and brackets in wood. Tange's desperate attempt at simplifying and giving form to the chaos of a new industrial pluralism seemed to be emblematic of a larger question: how to find the deeper social meaning of an increasingly consumerist culture?

638

Grandiose Utopian schemes based on a fantastic deployment of technology became increasingly frequent in the early 1960s in Japan. A group of young architects calling themselves the 'Metabolists' announced their commitment to the very process of change in visionary urban projects which blended an obsession with mechanisms and a vaguely spaceship imagery. Kiyonori Kikutake, one of the key members of the 'Metabolist Group', declared:

Unlike the architecture of the past, contemporary architecture must be changeable, movable and … capable of meeting the changing requirements of the contemporary age. In order to reflect dynamic reality, what is needed is not a fixed, static function, but rather one which is capable of undergoing metabolic changes … We must stop thinking in terms of function and form, and think instead in terms of space and changeable function.

There was much in the Metabolist position that recalled the Futurists' suggestion that the modern city be made into a dynamic machine of moving and variable parts. Like their Archigram counterparts in Britain, the Japanese architects made much of the way pods and cells could be clipped on to lattice frames. The Metabolists also attempted to enforce the distinction between the fixed and changeable elements of a design, often resorting to towers of a monumental character to which less substantial-looking 'variable' standardized elements might be attached, as if 'plugged in' to a larger infrastructure. As early as 1958 Kikutake had anticipated some of Tange's ideas by suggesting marine cities in the form of vast discs on towers. While the rhetoric was mechanistic, there was also a hint of organic structures like cells and beehives. Although none of the extravagant visions of the Metabolists were realized, their ideas were sometimes carried out on a smaller scale and occasionally influenced other architects' schemes – for example, some of Arata Isozaki's buildings in the town of Oita, particularly the bank (1966–8) and the Girls' High School (1963–4), which made use of dramatic contrasts of structure and mechanical servicing.

In the above-mentioned designs there was the ever-present danger that architecture might simply degenerate into an arid technological fetishism. Tange seems to have sensed this danger, while still realizing that the new Japan was releasing energies that the architect must try to express. In the Yamanashi Press and Radio Centre at Kofu (1961–7), close to Mount Fuji, he managed to give images of a Metabolist character a dignified and monumental form. A variety of functions had to be accommodated – offices, shops, printing works, broadcasting studios and distribution points – so that the programme itself seemed to imply the notion of a building as a small city. The main elements of Tange's design were a grid of cylindrical service shafts containing air conditioning, stairs and lifts, and acting as a primary structural system; and large horizontal beams containing studios, offices, etc. set down in a secondary system of movable partitions. In plan the building gave the distinct impression of total flexibility within a fixed

639 Arata Isozaki, 'Metabolist' Group scheme for a modern city, 1963

640 Kenzo Tange, Yamanashi Press and Radio Centre, Kofu, 1961–7

639

640

framework, and the division between 'serving' towers and 'served' spaces inevitably recalled Louis Kahn's Richards Medical Laboratories in Philadelphia of 1957–65 (Fig. 650); indeed, the use of grand service towers and horizontal floors became a virtual leitmotif of the mid-1960s in many parts of the world. Something of the same idea of open-endedness was hinted at in the elevations of Tange's building as well, since some of the beams were 'left out', thus implying that they might be clipped on at some other time. The Yamanashi building flirted with the idea of total change, while still retaining the elemental dignity of a finite composition; it suggested the character of a modern technological mechanism, while still recalling traditional post and beam construction. It held the

forces of traditionalism and futurism, so basic to post-war Japan, in an anxious equilibrium.

The modern architectures which emerged in countries like Brasil, Mexico and Japan in the 1940s and the 1950s built upon pre-war foundations while also absorbing new stimuli from the outside. They did not reproduce international formulae slavishly, nor did they rest within the frontiers of exclusively national definitions of culture. They could not be explained by a merely Western version of development, or by the oversimplifications of regionalist rhetoric. They seemed to belong to a new kind of intellectual and artistic territory resulting from the processes of global modernization, in which the very notions of the local and the universal were themselves being redefined.

28

on monuments and monumentality: louis i. kahn

One should not be surprised to find, in fact one would expect to find an archaic quality in architecture today. This is because real architecture is just beginning to come to grips with a whole new order of artistic expression, growing in turn from the new set of tasks which society has set for the architect.
Louis I. Kahn, 1955

641 Louis I. Kahn, Kimbell Art Museum, Fort Worth, Texas, 1966–72, detail

Between the wars it was rare for modern architects to receive large commissions requiring monumental treatment. Certainly there were projects, such as Tatlin's Monument to the Third International (1919) or Le Corbusier's League of Nations (1927) and Mundaneum (1929), which suggested some ways in which the new architecture could be adapted to deal with the problems of size and symbolic expression posed by large institutions. But the hold of traditionalism over official taste remained strong between the wars in the United States, the Soviet Union and most of Western Europe, especially where civic ideals were involved. Perhaps this was understandable given that these were situations in which the need to *preserve* values and to suggest continuities with the past was pressing. This was particularly the case under the totalitarian regimes, where ancient models enjoyed a skin-deep revival in the search for imperial symbols. As shown earlier (Chapter 20), there were many similarities between Nazi Germany and Stalinist Russia in the choices of an 'official' monumental manner. Francoist Spain in the late 1930s and 1940s offers another case of a dictatorship insisting upon an all too obvious replication of hallowed national prototypes such as the Escorial. Only in Fascist Italy in the 1930s was there a concerted attempt at developing a modern architecture with echoes from tradition for the purposes of state representation.

In the circumstances it was understandable that monumentality should have been temporarily regarded with suspicion by the liberal-minded, as if it was, in and of itself, an inherently anti-democratic characteristic. By 1943, however, Sigfried Giedion and Josep Lluís Sert were already discussing a new monumentality to emerge in the post-war period. In a pronouncement entitled 'Nine Points on Monumentality' they referred to monuments as 'human landmarks … intended to outlive the period which originated them', and as 'the expression of man's highest cultural needs'. They also discussed the role of collective symbols and the need for an urbanism giving 'more than functional fulfilment'. A decade later Giedion pleaded for the creation of symbolic centres to cities. CIAM meetings shifted gear from the 'four functions' towards a more nebulous and 'emblematic' characterization of urban form. Perhaps this change of mood was linked to the more 'permissive' view of tradition and precedent expressed by Giedion in the same period.

Between 1945 and 1965, the dissemination of the modern movement around the world meant that it became, by degrees, the rule of the established order rather than a fringe product of the avant-garde. While it was sometimes co-opted to express 'progressive' ideals (e.g. the United Nations or Brasilia), it had also come to terms with some of the traditional rhetorical functions of architecture such as the embodiment of the state or the preservation of institutions. Monumentality is a quality in architecture which does not necessarily have to do with size, but with intensity of expression. In any event, the problem was to handle public buildings with the appropriate degree of presence and accessibility: to establish the terms of a democratic monumentality. Le Corbusier, Mies van der Rohe and Aalto gave indications in their works of the late 1940s and early 1950s of ways in which this might be done (e.g. Chandigarh, St-Dié, Crown Hall, Säynätsalo). External social conditions and the internal evolution of modern architecture were not out of step when it came to questions of civic representation and monumental expression.

There was still the problem bequeathed by the nineteenth century, that no clear language existed to distinguish one civic function from another, or from lesser functions in a hierarchy. The increase in the number of building types fostered by industrialization conspired with confusions over 'style' to create a babbling urban order which no longer legibly portrayed the relationships of society in the cityscape. Ideal cities of the early modern movement certainly brought their own version of clarity, but tended to concentrate on living and working, leaving monumental expression for skyscrapers and freeways; in the Ville Contemporaine, management and circulation had been the elements handled most forcefully. The designs for Brasilia revealed an attempt at using the skyscraper as a major symbolic element in a monumental state ensemble, but as part of a vast panorama of almost surreal objects set up on a virtually continental scale.

After the Second World War Le Corbusier's architecture began to possess a new visual weight and heroic force, which was not unconnected with his own need to solve problems of monumental expression. At both St-Dié (1946) and Chandigarh he seems to have been preoccupied with some new vision of an acropolis, at any rate with ceremonial urban spaces combining formality and symmetry with counterthemes of asymmetry and dynamism. Rough effects of *béton brut* and the strong articulation of shadow allowed him to create an allusive symbolic language in the service of an institutional pattern. In Chandigarh, particularly (as we have seen), he transformed various ancient types and formulations (e.g. the basilica and the *diwan* into the High Court, the dome/portico combination into the Parliament) in an attempt at providing images of a suitably honorific character. Pastiche of these prototypes was avoided by grasping their basic principles of organization and meaning, and by integrating these into a well-tried architectural vocabulary. The Five Points were amplified and given a new sense of scale and dignity; *brises-soleil* in vast repeating rows proved suitable to the *gravitas* of the artist's intentions; and his impeccable sculptural control and sense of visual order ensured that unity and diversity were held in balance.

This is not to suggest that a rugged sculptural treatment of the kind used at Chandigarh was an automatic recipe for good monumentality; the proposition is adequately disproved by the all too numerous examples around the world of concert halls, state monuments, parliaments, etc. in ungainly elephantine concrete forms surrounded by wildernesses of 'plazas', conceived between the

642 Pedro Ramírez Vázquez, National Museum of Anthropology, Chapultepec, Mexico City, 1963–4

643 Gerhard Kallmann, Michael McKinnell and Edward Knowles, Boston City Hall, 1962–8

642

643

water tumbling into a basin below: a combined image of tree of life, fountain of renewal, and national cultural unity. There were subtle allusions to pre-Columbian sources in the overall form, the dominant character and certain of the details of the building, such as the sun screens.

The Communist regimes in the Soviet Union and China both developed 'state' styles that combined a ponderous reuse of historical models with a light sprinkling of identifying features – hammers and sickles, stars, even traditional Chinese roofs in the latter case (e.g. the Nationalities Cultural Palace, Beijing, of 1958 by Zhang Bo). The Moscow State University by L. V. Rudnyev, S. J. Chernyshev, P. V. Abrosimov and S. J. Khryakov (1949) relied upon a skyscraper as its centrepiece but this was in a 'Stalinist Gothic' mode with a central spire rising to more than 820 feet (250 metres), the whole arranged upon a neo-classical plan. With the process of 'de-Stalinization' initiated by Khrushchev in 1956, Soviet architecture registered a slight change of direction. The Kremlin Palace of Congresses in Moscow of 1959–60 allowed for a version of the International Style in its lobbies,while the exterior colonnade was visibly a screen of slender, angled piers in front of a glass curtain wall. In other words, classical devices were here simplified in modern terms – a strategy which placed the Palace of Congresses in the same architectural world as many American official buildings of the same period.

In the North American city, the urban monument had to make its presence felt in the context of the downtown skyscraper. Devices were researched which might distinguish the public building from the private world of business. The Boston City Hall (1962–8) by Gerhard Kallmann, Michael McKinnell and Edward Knowles, relied upon a rugged sculptural language in rough reinforced concrete with red-brick ramps, floors and steps bringing the surrounding plaza in at the lower levels. The building tried to deal with the contradiction between authority and openness, combining visual weight with active interpenetrations of space. The main forms expressed the hierarchy of the enclosed institution clearly. The offices of the bureaucracy were on the top floors, legible in the repeated precast system of window elements, while the ceremonial functions (e.g. the mayor's office) were slung in amplified

late 1950s and the early 1970s. But Le Corbusier's forceful late style could prove useful as a starting point for some sensitive talents who took over not only the external effects, but also the intellectual strategies for the transformation of precedent. The Japanese examples cited in the last chapter suggest ways in which architects like Mayekawa and Tange were able to blend together Corbusian suggestions with a reinterpretation of Asian timber traditions, in creating a civic iconography for new democratic institutions such as town halls.

Modernism may have dislodged the classical apparatus for monumental representation, but it also allowed such fundamental devices as the grand portico, the processional axis and the ceremonial platform to be reinterpreted in fresh ways. Utzon's Sydney Opera House was evidence of the way in which a twentieth-century architect could take inspirations from one tradition (the ruins of ancient Mexico) and transform them to deal with a totally different setting and context. In the post-war years there was often a pressure towards 'national' expression using modern means. In Mexico itself, for example, a bold horizontality of great mass and gravity was developed to deal with the problem of public institutions. The National Museum of Anthropology in Mexico City of 1963–4 by Pedro Ramírez Vázquez embodied the ideal of 'national inclusiveness' in a monumental reinterpretation of the patio dominated by a colossal stone column/parasol on the main axis with a sheet of

644

volumes at the middle level; the most public facilities being at the ground level where they were most easily accessible. The programme seemed to suggest a rectangular plan around a court, but this basic diagram was then brought alive in the dynamic terms of what Kallmann called an 'action architecture' exploiting dramatic interior spaces, ascending movement and framed views of the surroundings. The whole was composed into an overall shape of considerable simplicity; at the top levels there was a marked horizontal emphasis which gave something of the character of a cornice, and supplied a strong contrast to the nearby skyscrapers. The concrete piers and variations in visual texture were clearly reliant on the model of Le Corbusier's monastery of La Tourette; while the lower brick mounds suggested the impact of Aalto. The architects were intrigued by those public palaces in Italy of the Middle Ages and Renaissance where piazzas penetrate a lower storey of arcades. The City Hall pulled together modern methods of component standardization with a restatement of classical rhetoric: the piers were a sort of 'grand order' in concrete, while the structural ceiling grid was reminiscent of coffering. These devices were firm reminders of the fact that the thin skins and slender *pilotis* of the International Style had proved themselves inadequate to handling a building of such scale. Boston City Hall grappled with a wide range of issues central to the problem of monumentality, and presented solutions which,

if not always totally resolved, were none the less propelled by serious thought.

Rough concrete was not the only material in which schematic devices derived from classicism could be restated. In his design for the New National Gallery in Berlin of 1962–8, Mies van der Rohe envisaged a glass and steel temple on a podium – a sort of shrine to modern art. The main effect arose from the way in which the steel supports were carefully proportioned and spaced in a way which suggested a latterday version of classical columns while the vast overhanging steel roof evoked the *idea* of an entablature. The rectangular ceiling grid recalled certain of Schinkel's designs for simplified coffering or trellises. In the interior the earlier Miesian notion of an abstract, 'universal' space was restated. In this case it was subdivided by columns and flexible planar partitions to bear pictures. Sculptures were left standing in the voids between. It was as if the trabeation, the overhangs and the thin planes of the Barcelona Pavilion had been cross-bred with the symmetry and spatial ideas of Crown Hall at the Illinois Institute of Technology (1950–6). Some features of the solution were even anticipated in Mies's unbuilt proposal of 1935 for the German Pavilion at Brussels (Chapter 20). The New National Gallery worked within the conventions of formality and *gravitas* which Mies had established for buildings of civic importance. Like Le Corbusier at Chandigarh, he was able to achieve monumentality by expanding a pre-existing architectural system based on rigorous intellectual and expressive rules. What stopped the historical allusions from being a game of mere quotation was the forceful expression of ideas in an abstract form brought alive by the tectonic emphases of structure. Certain essentials of classicism were rethought in a modern industrial material and in a new social context.

In the United States the expansive, optimistic, and, indeed, imperial undercurrents of the post-war years were manifest in many commissions for large-scale monuments. The influence of Beaux-Arts classicism certainly did not die with the introduction of modern architecture. At its deepest this tradition nourished an architect like Louis I. Kahn; but a more obvious, less expressive and often banal attempt at neo-classicism also emerged in the 1950s. This was no doubt part of a general mood of dissatisfaction with the restrictive minimalism of the American version of the International Style (a reaction expressed in other ways as well, e.g. in the 'modern Baroque' of Eero Saarinen's TWA terminal at Kennedy Airport, 1956–62). Thus architects like Edward Durell Stone (the American Embassy in New Delhi, 1954), Philip Johnson (the Sheldon Memorial Art Gallery in Lincoln, Nebraska, 1963), and Wallace Harrison and Max Abramovitz (with Johnson, the Lincoln Center in New York, 1961–5) indulged in grand axes, symmetry, expensive materials or tell-tale arches, to disguise an essentially bogus and skin-deep understanding of the nature of monumentality. These architects were well aware of the need to combine traditional schemata with modern technology, but were still unable to transcend a tendency towards 'camp'. Classical allusions were there in abundance; classical principles were almost entirely lacking.

Transformations of classicism were not the only viable ways for creating a new monumentality, as was well demonstrated by Utzon's Sydney Opera House, or by Hans Scharoun's Philharmonie in Berlin, which was in the 'Expressionist' free-form tradition. At Coventry Cathedral (1951–62), Basil Spence even attempted to design in an abstract Gothic manner, but his spindly supports and fussy details were expressive failures. What was lacking was not so much conviction, as an ability to translate that conviction into form. Nor were monumental tendencies in the late 1950s and early 1960s restricted to civic and religious programmes; especially in the United States there seems to have been a sort of inner will to grandeur affecting many architects and building tasks. The taut steel-frame skyscrapers gave way bit by bit to heavier-looking boxes clad in marble and adorned with massive slivers of stone not unlike pilasters. Even housing was overwhelmed by a wave of megastructural thinking. Thus the myth of 'total design' came together with elephantine forms in yet another attempt at giving a clear shape to the American city.

645

646

The master of monumentality in the United States in this period was, without a doubt, Louis I. Kahn. Monumentality was not, of course, his only preoccupation, but it was certainly a major one, and he evolved a philosophy and system of forms extraordinarily well suited to the expression of honorific themes and moods. Kahn was able to avoid some of the pitfalls mentioned in earlier examples; he was capable of handling problems of large size without degenerating into either an 'additive' approach or an overdone grandiosity; he knew how to fuse together modern constructional means with traditional methods; he was steeped in history but rarely produced pastiche; and his architecture was infused with a deep feeling for the meaning of human situations, which enabled him to avoid the mere shape-making of the formalists.

Kahn's formation took place before modern architecture had established a firm foothold in the eastern United States. He was trained in the Beaux-Arts system at Philadelphia under Paul Cret and was therefore fully acquainted with the classical grammar, with devices of axial organization, hierarchy and composition, and with an attitude to design which took it for granted that one should consult tradition for support. In Kahn's education great emphasis was placed upon the discovery of a central and appropriate generating *idea* for a building which was to be captured in a sketch rather like an ideogram (an '*esquisse*'). The attitude towards the past was not slavish and Cret was not blind to the need for a new architecture of some description, but one incorporating old lessons. The young Kahn certainly sensed the decadence of most American architecture of the 1920s and 1930s, and realized the need for a change which might better accommodate the needs and the means of the times. He absorbed almost unconsciously a structural-Rationalist emphasis on construction, and in later life several of his strongest ideas relied upon poetic interpretations of basic structural ideas. Kahn also studied Le Corbusier's *Vers une architecture* and learned much from Sullivan and Wright, and later from Mies van der Rohe. But he was a slow developer, and his house designs of the 1940s were mostly unexceptional extensions of the International Style. The crystallization seems to have occurred in the early 1950s, prompted in part by Kahn's stay at the American Academy in Rome, and by his travels

through Greece and Egypt. His sketchbooks of this period suggest he was trying to get back to basics – to probe the central meanings of architecture.

A key transitional work was the Yale University Art Gallery of 1951–3, in which Kahn responded to the many levels and textures of an eclectic urban environment with a subtle, inward-looking design. The interior spaces seemed to evoke an entirely different world from the brash mass-produced environment of standardized panels and suspended ceilings then prevalent in the United States, by subtle effects of light falling over the triangulated web of the concrete ceiling and by the direct use of materials, evident in the bare yet elegant concrete piers. The stair was contained in a cylindrical volume, and rose through a series of triangular changes of direction, thus hinting at the architect's later tendency to make strong formal distinctions between circulation and 'areas served'. The exterior took over the Miesian glass and steel façade, but gave it a new irregularity and softness; the side walls and qualities of interior space, meanwhile, were loosely evocative of Wright.

The Yale University Art Gallery was not a totally resolved work, and the sources were still not

647   Louis I. Kahn, Yale University Art Gallery, New Haven, Connecticut, 1951–3

648   Louis I. Kahn, sketch of San Gimignano, 1929. Watercolour and pencil, 12 × 9¼ in (30.5 × 23.5 cm). Williams College Museum of Art, Williamstown

649   Louis I. Kahn, Richards Medical Research Laboratories, University of Pennsylvania, Philadelphia, 1957–65, plan

650   Richards Medical Research Laboratories

647

648

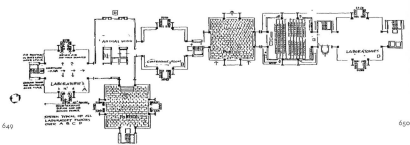

649

650

absorbed sufficiently for one to be able to speak of a coherent personal style. But the building still suggested a new archaic direction for American modern architecture. In the Richards Medical Research Laboratories at the University of Pennsylvania of 1957–65, Kahn pursued these qualities further. The laboratories required vast extract flues and flexible interiors, and the architect decided to express the distinction between the fixed and the variable, the serving and the served, by monumentalizing the service and stair-towers and treating the laboratories as attached cellular elements. The site was to one side of a main walkway through the campus, not far from a number of neo-Tudor buildings with varied tower silhouettes and windows with screens and panels, and it may be that Kahn was responding to this setting in making these moves. The plan was itself a subtle combination of the linear and the particulate, which also created harbours of space between the building and its surroundings, so that there was a gradual shift in scale from the context to the individual

details. The geometry of the plan and the use of towers containing services and stairs as monumental devices intermediate in scale between small and large parts of a design suggest that Kahn may have been influenced by Wright's Larkin Building.

But any influences there may have been were now absorbed into the internal logic of a personal style, and the formal and functional logic of a particular design. The structural system of the laboratory spaces was precast concrete, and Kahn attempted to show how the building was put together by accentuating joints and connections. This was no mere structural exhibitionism, for the intention was to give a suitable scale and character to the social organization of laboratory work. The approach was the opposite of the one which clothes everything in a single envelope; indeed, revulsion against the 'neutral box' was a widespread phenomenon of the period. Kahn was here supplying a variety of formal devices, just as Le Corbusier had done in the Unité and at La Tourette, for the articulation of complex social programmes. Moreover, the Richards

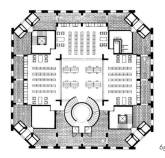

651

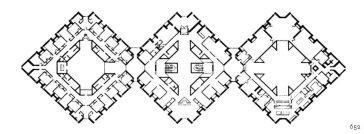

652

Laboratories used brick and concrete in a direct, uncompromising way which appealed to the sensibilities a new generation.

However powerful its forms and ideas, Kahn's building was not totally practical as a laboratory. The principal difficulties arose from lack of sun protection in the façades, and (despite all the effort of the design process) from a lack of functional flexibility. But a work which does not function properly may still be architecture of a high order. On the basis of a clear organizing idea and logical system of servicing and structure, Kahn had been able to create a building combining a bold 'objectivity' with generalized antique qualities he had admired in Roman ruins and in the towers and townscapes of medieval Italy. When the first stage was completed in the early 1960s, Kahn's building seemed to be a firm reminder of timeless architectural values in an era otherwise beset by extremes of meaningless formal gymnastics or arid functionalism. Kahn attempted to put his own sense of the basics of architecture into words:

> If I were to define architecture in a word, I would say that architecture is a thoughtful making of spaces. It is not filling prescriptions as clients want them filled. It is not fitting uses into dimensioned areas … It is a creating of spaces that evoke a feeling of use. Spaces which form themselves into a harmony good for the use to which the building is to be put …
>
> I believe that the architect's first act is to take the program that comes to him and change it. Not to satisfy it but to put it into the realm of architecture, which is to put it into the realm of spaces.

Kahn's architecture was based in part on a social vision: this was a challenge to the status quo not through some Utopian expectation of the future, but through a mystical conservatism. For Kahn believed there to be archetypal patterns of social relationship that it was the business of architecture to uncover and celebrate. A good plan would be one which found the central meaning, as it were, of the institution that it housed. Related to this notion of a higher meaning in social forms was the distinction between 'form' and 'design'. Basically, Kahn believed that any architectural problem had an 'essential' meaning which far transcended a mere functional diagram. This organization would be found through a probing and detailed analysis of requirements followed by an intuitive leap which would uncover the 'type' of the institution. Only when this was discovered and embodied in a suitable symbolic form could the architect proceed to the stage of design – of giving the central, intuitive concept a material shape. A good design would be one where the 'form', the underlying meaning, was coherently expressed through all the parts.

This idealistic position with regard to the spiritual roots of both the social and the aesthetic realms motivated Kahn's major designs of the early 1960s and led him to clarify a simple set of 'type-forms' based on primary geometries – the square, the circle, the triangle, etc. – which were capable of a vast variety of interrelationships over certain kernel patterns of form and meaning. When one examines the plans of such diverse schemes as the Erdman Hall Dormitories at Bryn Mawr near Philadelphia (1960–5), the Indian Institute of Management in Ahmadabad, India (1962–74), and the National Assembly building at Dacca, Bangladesh (1962–83), one is struck by the consistency of the approach. Time and again the architect reverts to a basic organization in which the primary meaning of an institution is expressed in a central space of a concentrated social character based on square, circle or diamond, and related hierarchically to the surroundings by axes. Secondary spaces tend to be set out as a fringe around the primary generator, marking out variations on the theme and containing smaller and more private functions. There is often a strong sense of the diagonal, with 90-degree and 45-degree directions combined. But these patterns of geometry – so like ornamental designs – are far from being arbitrary. They suggest crystals or mandalas or some other symbolic geometry. They remind one that Kahn, like Wright, had a pantheistic vision of nature which he attempted to express in universalizing abstractions. The strategy behind these plans may loosely recall Kahn's Beaux-Arts training, in which ceremonial routes of circulation tended to be laid out along the primary axis of the most important symbolic space of a scheme, but the finished buildings possess a spatial drama and other-worldly character which cannot be accounted for by pointing to particular influences. Kahn stated that he wished to evoke the 'immeasurable' in architecture, to translate his intentions of reality into a 'higher order' in which space, structure and light would be fused.

But to achieve the 'immeasurable' Kahn had to use the 'measurable' qualities of materials and construction. He never lost a feeling for the tangible presence of the wall as a major part of architecture, even when he employed reinforced concrete which might have allowed an open façade. But his walls took on the character of immaterial planes of light, while the shadows were modelled as if they were positive figures. Openings were reduced to simple voids cut deep through the outer skin, or to vertical slits where walls approached one another without actually touching. Sometimes the fundamental geometrical themes of a design – circles, squares, and so on, were reiterated in the secondary elements of cylindrical towers or in the shapes of apertures. Construction was supremely important to Kahn, and he detailed his buildings with great attention to joints, connections and the texture or colour of materials.

Kahn was just as interested in the spaces between buildings as he was in the buildings themselves. In fact his designs often involved sophisticated reversals of figure and ground, mass and void. At Ahmadabad, in the Indian Institute of Management (1962), the programme was translated into a dense citadel, a weave of 'streets', 'squares' and

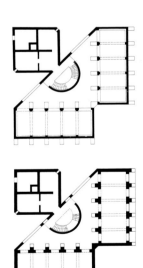

653

654

655

transitional spaces. The dormitories of the Institute were laid out in diagonal flotillas to catch the prevailing winds. The architect created a deep zone of transition between the outer edge and the interiors of individual buildings, to allow for shaded porticoes and walkways. The colossal cylinders of brick and concrete had something of the quality of the Roman ruins that Kahn had so admired. But it was a poetry of shapes which seemed to transcend the merely European tradition; Kahn, like Le Corbusier, was intrigued by the cosmological geometries of the Jaipur observatories, and these may have played a part in the distillation of his vocabulary.

In the project for the Jonas Salk Institute for Biological Sciences (1959–65), close to La Jolla, San Diego, California, Kahn had to design for a community of scientists involved in concentrated research. Another architect might have attempted to embody the forward-looking aspirations of such a programme. But Salk was no ordinary client and insisted that the human implications of science be explored. To Kahn the suitable references seemed to lie in such prototypes as monasteries or other forms of intellectual retreat. Three main clusters were planned standing apart from one another in the virgin landscape with views towards the Pacific: the community meeting and conference areas (the 'Meeting House'), the living quarters (the 'Village'), and the laboratories themselves (the only part built), contained in parallel blocks with a water garden between them. The laboratories were on an open plan and could be altered at will to fit the needs

of different experiments. They were spanned by perforated beams deep enough to accommodate an entire 'service floor' for adjustable ducts and tubes. The lowest storey was placed below ground level to bring down the height of the ensemble and was lit through sunken courts. The laboratories were linked by bridges to small studies which had views into the garden or out towards the sea; a distinction was made between the society of shared endeavour and the private world of thought. These studies were substantially furnished cells – or perhaps cabins – for contemplation. On the exterior they were expressed by teak-panel embrasures set into smooth concrete planes with refined joints and incisions which picked out shadows. The concrete was the same colour as the travertine used on the floor of the outdoor space, and the overall effect combined nobility with finesse. The diagonal fins in naked concrete clearly owed something to Le Corbusier, but the idea of the building had an internal life of its own.

Comparisons have sometimes been made between the Salk Institute and ancient Roman complexes such as Hadrian's Villa at Tivoli or Diocletian's Palace at Spalato, but this 'source hunting' does relatively little to explain the sublime order of the result. Kahn was steeped in history, but he also broke with it, aspiring towards a basic presence, a metaphysical state which he referred to obscurely as 'ground zero'. There can be no doubting the sense of antiquity or of the archaic in certain of Kahn's realizations (Salk included), but this was achieved by modern means, in which space, structure, materials and light were endowed with a resonant abstraction.

While the plan of the Salk Institute suggests an axial composition, the intentions and experience of the building are not so simple. As in several of Kahn's works, one approaches the site on an indirect path through the 'filter' of a grove of trees. The first impression is of a precinct separated from the outside world by a moat and by a central gate with steps. As one draws closer, the eye is launched towards the infinity of the Pacific horizon 'framed' as if by a proscenium. A thin, translucent line of water splits the platform down the middle, drawing sky and light down into the space. The route is then diverted off-axis by a stone bench blocking the way. The receding planes of concrete dissolve in light.

655 Louis I. Kahn, Jonas Salk Institute for Biological Sciences, La Jolla, California, 1959–65, model of 2nd scheme, 1961–2

656 Salk Institute, view towards sea

657 Salk Institute, ground-floor plan

656

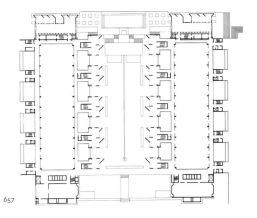

657

Shadows are almost tangible. It was Luis Barragán (that master of absence) who persuaded Kahn to plant no trees and to work with a void. With its low benches, its reflecting pools, its proportioned paving, and its air of ritual, the 'outdoor room' at the Salk Institute takes on the character of a philosopher's stage where ideas may be exchanged and the mysteries of nature studied. Steven Holl, an American architect of a younger generation, has caught the cosmic atmosphere of this space:

… there is a time of day when the sun, reflecting on the ocean, merges with light reflecting on the rivulet of water in the trough bisecting the central court. Ocean and courtyard are fused … Architecture and nature are joined in a metaphysics of place …

The abstract order of Kahn's buildings was usually achieved on the basis of simple structural ideas. The Kimbell Art Museum at Fort Worth in Texas (1966–72) was arranged as a series of parallel concrete vaults acting, in effect, as long beams liberating the space beneath. The curvature of the vaults was based upon a cycloid geometry (rather than the more obvious semicircle) and this added extra tension and vitality to the profiles. The plan was formal, virtually classical (suggesting the influence of such prototypes as Palladio's Palazzo Chierecati). But the interior space was anything but compartmentalized, flowing in a stately way from bay to bay, and allowing long diagonal views across the standardized structural system. Here and there, small light-courts were punctured through the

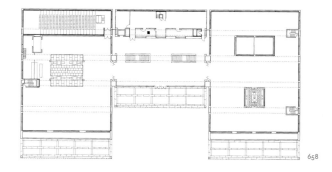

658

659

660

repeating vaults, while to the garden side the infill walls were absent from the last bay, so generating a species of vaulted portico. As at Salk, the architectural effect arose from the dignified pace of the primary geometrical themes, from the control of proportion and ratio, and from the evocative combination of a limited number of materials – in this case travertine, concrete, stainless steel, water and glass. But the essential magic of the Kimbell Art Museum resided in the fusion of structure and light. Each vault was bisected at the top by a narrow gap running the entire length. Daylight was spilled through the crack on to upturned stainless-steel reflectors, then dispersed as a silvery glow over the polished concrete undersides of the naked roof structure. Light, in Kahn's view, was an absence of shadow, a force capable of bringing matter to life. He referred to architecture itself as 'spent light'.

Kahn's capacity for effective monumental expression was revealed to the full in his design for the National Assembly Building at Dacca in what is now Bangladesh. For this architect, government was among the fundamental types of social order: the 'form' (in Kahn's sense of the word) would have to reflect the meaning of the institution. One is scarcely surprised to find that variations on a circular theme

were among the first to appear on paper, since the circle was the shape the architect used to express a coherent social grouping, a sense of unitary purpose, and a notion of 'centre'. In the plans of the overall layout of the Capitol, the Parliament was placed at the focal point, other buildings spreading away from it in descending echelons. The full panoply of Beaux-Arts rhetorical planning devices – primary and secondary axes, a sense of climax, variations in size and shape – was employed to reinforce this sense of the Parliament as the 'head' of the social order. There were echoes and schematizations of 'old friends' from several phases of the classical tradition: the Baths of Caracalla, Palladio's formal villas with their central blocks and symmetrical arms, even the plan of Garnier's Paris Opéra; but these were transformed into an entirely different spatial idea. Kahn absorbed what he needed from the monumental traditions of East and West to make a symbolic diagram of the state.

The Assembly at Dacca was placed on a vast brick platform surrounded by water, and was constructed in naked grey concrete with an overlay of thin white marble lines. These corresponded to the formwork divisions but they also had the effect of sharpening the image and picking out light. Kahn

himself described the building as a 'multifaceted jewel'. The Assembly Chamber was circled by a family of other functions – press galleries, members' rooms, etc. – smaller variations on the central formal themes. The main entrance was underneath the mosque; this had four cylindrical towers and was skewed slightly off the main axis to face Mecca, a deviation which served to reinforce the power of the prevalent geometrical order by contrast. The effect of these surrounding volumes when projected into space was of a jostling series of cylinders and oblongs grouped around the central mass.

Rather as Le Corbusier had also done at Chandigarh, Kahn amplified his earlier architectural system to achieve effects of massive grandeur. For the former this had meant working with the generating image of a protective parasol; for the latter it implied a centralized citadel with protective layers of vertical planes punctured by huge, shaded openings for ventilation. Where the exterior seemed solid, the interior dissolved away, the slots of structure being filled with light. With the deep cuts of shadow, the glaring force of the sun and the rudeness of the materials, the effect was entirely as if the buildings had been standing there for centuries.

The National Assembly Building in Dacca embodied Kahn's reaction to an Asian society's search for new institutions in a post-colonial stage of its history. Beyond the transient events of politics, it sought out a primary framework relating government to an idealized order. The plan

condensed several ideas relating to Kahn's interpretation of the state: a central space for debate and eventual consensus; a main axis running from the entrance, through the middle and out the other side again over the president's platform (from which an 'edict' might be transmitted to the outside world); a cross axis linking the orientation of the Parliament Chamber to prime minister and president; tertiary axes binding lesser functions; and the line to Mecca subordinating the institution to the co-ordinates of Islam. All these gestures were held in tense equilibrium in a form combining the qualities of a crystal with the resonances of a cosmic diagram or mandala. Kahn's plan distilled features of centralized organization from both Eastern and Western traditions: it was like a 'figure–ground' reversal of a centralized Mogul tomb (e.g. the Taj Mahal or the Tomb of Hummayum), as if the niches and corridors had been rendered as matter, and the solid masonry as space. The marble veins could be interpreted as a mimetic version of the reed and bamboo bindings of the typical Bengali hut, an association perhaps felt appropriate to a 'house of the state'. Whatever the sources and inspirations, they were absorbed into a modern work which aspired towards a timeless level of architectural order.

At Dacca, Kahn drew together new and old, regional and universal, in a building of haunting presence and magnificence. Without the underlying armature of his philosophy, his ruminations on the

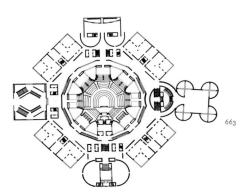

661 Louis I. Kahn,
National Assembly
Building, Dacca,
1962–75, aerial view

662 National Assembly
Building

663 National Assembly
Building, plan

664 National Assembly
Building, interior of
mosque

663

nature of man and architecture, and his ability to give these feelings a suitable and communicable symbolic form, the 'archaicizing' external textures would have been mere superficialities of patina, as skin-deep as the glossy intellectual packaging being employed by the devaluers of Mies van der Rohe at the same time. Kahn was able to make a convincing monumentality because his architectural system tended in that direction already and because his sensibility was open to the most ancient lessons of the great monuments of the past. Like Wright, Kahn believed in a 'Cause Conservative', invoking 'the elemental law and order inherent in all great architecture'; and (again like Wright) was able to achieve this spirit, not by copying the externals of past styles, but by probing into their underlying principles and attempting to universalize them in the service of modern aspirations. For Kahn, the aims of architecture did not change, only the means.

664

29

architecture and anti-architecture in britain

Whichever technique he chooses, the architect's function is to propose a way of life ...
Peter Smithson, 1963

665 James Stirling and James Gowan, Engineering Building, Leicester University, 1959–63, detail

When a long view is taken of the immediate post-war years, it is striking how each country had its own agendas where the introduction, use and formal elaboration of modern architecture were concerned. The case of Britain is revealing in this regard because the arrival of modernism in the 1930s, and its development in the following years, corresponded to an old pattern of absorbing then gradually modifying ideas imported from the Continent. At the start, the new architecture did not have the same broad support as in, say, Scandinavia, but in the years after 1945 this situation changed as it became less marginal to the culture at large, in fact quite central in the reconstruction of bombed cities and in the provision of social housing on a massive scale. In the circumstances, it is scarcely surprising that the relationship between architecture, urbanism and a new way of life should have become a dominant obsession in the search for forms. The British Welfare State provided more than a chance to build schools, hospitals and flats; it also suggested an ethos, a social ideal, to which architects were not blind. The well-meaning housing suggestions of the 1930s, with their vaguely socialist underpinnings, were at last able to come to fruition under a Labour government facing the post-war housing crisis. However, the limitations of those paradigms soon began to show and new ideas emerged that were supposedly better adjusted to British conditions and habits of mind.

Among the projects of the immediate post-war years were the 'New Towns'. Here the intellectual imperatives of Fabianism and the fading dreams of the Garden City movement were brought together in an adequate but uninspiring setting for the 'New Britain'. In the inner cities numerous repetitive blocks of flats rose from the rubble above the nineteenth-century slums. More often than not they were erected according to minimum standards. They seemed to embody a particularly modern and hygienic form of alienation. Certainly there were exceptions: one thinks of Lubetkin and Tecton's towers in Finsbury of 1946–50 which had elaborate curved roofscapes and almost decorative fenestration; of Philip Powell and John Hidalgo Moya's Churchill Gardens in Pimlico of 1946–62 which gave parallel slabs an elegant form and generated well-scaled spaces between them; or of the 'Mini-unités' of the Roehampton Estate close

666

to Richmond Park designed by the Architects' Department of the London County Council (1952–5), which made a creditable reinterpretation of Le Corbusier's seminal ideas; but the norm was lacking in richness and sat uncomfortably in the cityscape. It is scarcely surprising that those sectors of the avant-garde who sought to crystallize the inner meanings of working-class existence should have turned for inspiration to the dense street-life of the old slums which either bombs or bulldozers had done much to destroy.

In the Hertfordshire schools' programme of the early 1950s, standardization and clear planning came together in that 'quiet' and rational version of modern architecture which Pevsner so admired. Meanwhile at the Festival of Britain in 1951 the 'white forms of the thirties' went out with one last mannered fanfare. The Royal Festival Hall, designed by a team headed by Leslie Martin and Robert Matthew, was a fitting monument to the show as a whole, with its tidy elegance, its hooded roof so reminiscent of Lubetkin's High Point II, its attached coloured tiles and Scandinavian touches of detail. Here was public evidence of the way that the movement which had begun twenty years earlier under a polemical banner could become acceptable, sweetened, even a little academic.

A younger generation would have nothing of it. Among them were Alison and Peter Smithson, whose ideas of 'urban reidentification' have been referred to earlier. Before the Unité at Marseilles

captivated them, they relied on the example of Mies van der Rohe (whose buildings they knew only through photographs). In the Hunstanton School in Norfolk of 1949–54 they transformed the steel-frame vocabulary of Illinois Institute of Technology into an asymmetrical plan and made a point of leaving fixtures and materials deliberately crude. Without addressing the question of appropriateness to a junior school design, the critic Reyner Banham singled out 'the memorable quality of image' of Hunstanton, suggested that the building's materials were expressed 'as found', and implied that an ethical position (which he christened the 'New Brutalism') was on the point of emerging. Like the Smithsons, Banham was part of the '20th Century Group' in London, who admired the 'Art Brut' of Dubuffet, who were interested in the *béton brut* of Le Corbusier, and who were involved – along with the sculptor Eduardo Paolozzi and the photographer Nigel Henderson – in trying to convey the rough grain of modern urban life in a new art. The group were united in their distaste for the suavity of the English cultural élite and in their interest in Continental ideas stemming from, for example, Existentialist writers like Albert Camus and Jean-Paul Sartre.

Running through the Smithsons' thinking in the 1950s was also a strain of 'social realism' which led them to pin-point icons of contemporary life in such varied things as machine design, advertisements, and the bric-a-brac of street life (which they called the 'stuff of the urban scene'). In some ways this was a replay of what Le Corbusier had gone through

666 Leslie Martin, Robert Matthew and Peter Moro, Royal Festival Hall, London, 1951

667 London County Council Architects' Department, Alton West Estate, Roehampton, London, 1952–5

668 Alison and Peter Smithson, Hunstanton School, Norfolk, 1949–54, view over west playground to school (left) and gymnasium (right)

667

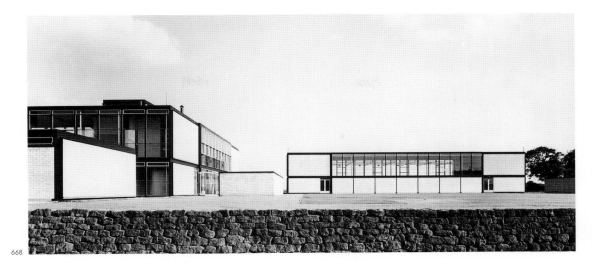

668

in his formative years, when he had battened on to ships and silos in his search for images expressing the nature of the times. But where Le Corbusier had attempted to invest the images of the machine age with a Platonic idealism, the Smithsons rejected any intimations of a closed aesthetic in favour of an aesthetic of change. This was manifest in their sprawling and incomplete plans for the Golden Lane housing project (see Chapter 24) and in their supposed disavowal of Renaissance symbolic proportions (many of their British contemporaries were influenced by Rudolf Wittkower's *Architectural Principles in the Age of Humanism*, 1949). Despite this rhetoric, the Smithsons had in fact revealed an interest in classical planning discipline in their Hunstanton design.

Apart from a scheme for a sort of science-fiction 'House of the Future' in 1956, the Smithsons had little chance to carry out their ideas until the late 1950s, when *The Economist* magazine asked them to design new offices on a site next to the eighteenth-century gentlemen's club Boodle's, off St James's Street in London. The context and the institution seemed to require a sedate solution somewhat at odds with the wilful brashness the architects had been cultivating. They broke the programme down into three separate towers of varying height, placing the largest one, containing *The Economist*'s offices, to the rear of the site where it would not challenge the scale of the main street front. In this way a small plaza, crossed by a

meandering route, was created. The middle-sized block was placed on the main street to the corner, and made to contain some elegant shops and a bank, which was inserted on a *piano nobile* of amplified scale and was reached up a moving staircase on the 45-degree angle. A third, much smaller block, containing apartments, was set back on the site to Boodle's side.

The main office block was organized around a core of circulation with intimate workspaces at the edges. The form was chamfered at the corners to give a distinctive image and to soften the relationship with neighbours. The architects claimed that the interior layout was influenced by monastic arrangements, and it may be that they were hoping to provide the place of work with a contemplative atmosphere. In any event, the Smithsons certainly wished to avoid the tackiness of the usual office building. Travertine slivers attached to the structural frame lent the *Economist* Building an honorific character; the honey-coloured stone also allowed it to blend with the numerous warm colours of the setting.

The ideas behind the plan as a whole reflected the Smithsons' earlier urban polemics: in their minds, the *Economist* group was a 'cluster', an image, a sign of the shape the future city might take. The asymmetry was a critique of the vapid, axial slab/plaza formula, and was felt to be one of the keys to a subtle relationship between old and new. The processional character of the walkway was

669

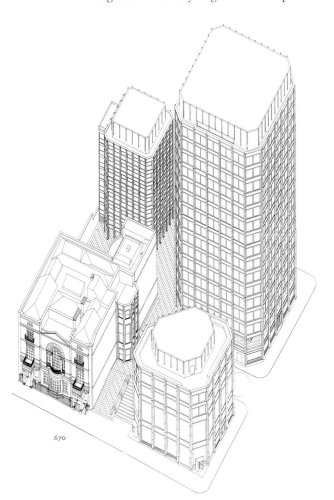

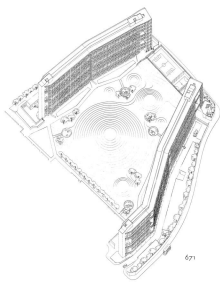

669 Alison and Peter
Smithson, *Economist*
Building, St James's
Street, London, 1959–64,
view of the plaza looking
west to St James's Street

670 *Economist* Building,
axonometric projection

671 Alison and Peter
Smithson, Robin Hood
Gardens, Robin Hood
Lane, London, 1966–72,
axonometric drawing

evidently inspired by a visit to Greece, while the
plaza had obvious Italian overtones. The bay widths
of each block were subtly differentiated to create
something like a tableau of the kind seen in the
background of some Renaissance pictures. The
placement of the bank on an upper level recalled
Howe and Lescaze's PSFS skyscraper (Fig. 291) in
Philadelphia of 1926–32, while the idea was also
related to the Smithsons' own Haupstadt scheme
for Berlin (1958), in which raised pedestrian streets
had been much in evidence. In turn, these ideas
recalled Team X urban theories. Seen in a longer
perspective, the *Economist* idea was an intelligent
solution to the problem of adapting a modern type
– the box skyscraper – to the peculiarities of a
particular place. This consultation of the *genius loci*,
and even the free asymmetrical massing with which
it was achieved, seemed to echo some features of the
eighteenth-century English Picturesque.

671

670

The Smithsons had to wait almost another
decade to test their housing theories in the
working-class context towards which they were
originally directed. In the meantime there was their
hall of residence for St Hilda's College, Oxford
(1970), but this was for a far softer and less
demanding visual and social environment. By
contrast Robin Hood Gardens (1966–72) was to
stand in Poplar, not far from the docklands of the
East End, a traditional Smithson stamping ground.
They arranged the housing in what amounted to yet
another reaction against the free-standing slab; two
serpentine spines marked off a green precinct
sheltered from the traffic and complete with an
artificial hillock. The individual dwellings were
made legible in the façades through attached
concrete fins, while the triple-level access system was
articulated by larger piers. In theory these devices
were supposed to be modern equivalents to the
standardized yet variable usages of classical orders
in such eighteenth-century prototypes as Bath; in
fact they appeared to be thin descendants of the
texturing devices employed in the Unité
d'Habitation. The street-decks themselves fell short
of their symbolic intention of expressing and
embodying the ideal community. Indeed, Robin
Hood Gardens as a whole seemed propelled by a
stark vision of working-class life more in tune
with the realities of the early 1950s than with the
consumerism of later years.

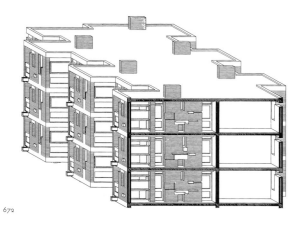

672

673

Another architect to feel dissatisfaction with the diluted modern architecture of the 1950s in Britain was James Stirling. Born in 1926, he was educated between 1945 and 1950 at Liverpool University, where he came into contact with the ideas of Colin Rowe, a historian acutely conscious of the Utopian and symbolic values in the architecture of the 1920s. From an early stage Stirling seems to have been conscious of his position in a modern tradition, and to have enjoyed employing references and quotations; even his student thesis was a clumsy but forceful reinterpretation of the Pavillon Suisse, replete with nautical analogies. Like Lasdun and the Smithsons, Stirling felt the need to recharge British modern architecture and, in a sense, to enrich it through contact with earlier national traditions. In his case the tough industrial vernacular of northern towns such as Liverpool was a particularly compelling inspiration. He also visited and wrote perceptive critical reviews of Le Corbusier's Chapel at Ronchamp and Maisons Jaoul. He was ambivalent towards the primitivism, and what he called the deliberate and 'mannered imperfectionism' of Le Corbusier's late works. Yet his own Ham Common Flats of 1955–8 (designed with James Gowan) were clearly influenced by them. Stirling was fully aware of Brutalist polemics, but kept a certain distance from the main group; even so, repeated attempts were later made to claim that his rough and ready machine poetics were 'Brutalist'.

Stirling's strong personal style emerged in the extraordinary Leicester University Engineering Building of 1959–63. This was formed from a slender tower on splayed legs, rising above the overhanging forms of the auditoriums and linked to a lower block of engineering workshops with saw-tooth factory glazing laid out on a 45-degree angle. As the programme called for a 100-foot (31-metre) hydraulic supply and the site was confined, a tower seemed reasonable. However, programmatic logic was only the starting point in a deliberate display of sculptural dynamics, in which individualized elements were played off against one another. Formal and functional considerations were in turn transcended by a preoccupation with mechanistic images and quotations from the 'heroic period' of modern architecture. Reminiscences of Hannes Meyer's 'factory' scheme for the League of Nations seemed to be blended with memories of Melnikov's Constructivism; battleship details were crammed together with Corbusian ramps and elements not unlike those employed by Wright in the Johnson Wax Laboratory Tower. There was about all this something almost too knowing, as if the architect were deliberately mannerizing the machine-age polemics of thirty years before. It was understandable that the term 'Futurist revival' was invoked.

Stirling attempted to apply some of the discoveries made at Leicester in the very different functional context of the History Faculty Building at Cambridge University of 1964–6. This commission came from a limited competition, and his design was the only one to attempt a complete integration of the library and the teaching spaces. This was done by placing the reading room in a quadrant under a glass tent roof leaning back against an L-shaped block containing seminar rooms, lounges and offices. Stirling put the largest and most public accommodation at the lowest levels, and this led naturally to a gradually stepping shape. The radial plan of the main reading room was also a response to a central demand of the programme: that there should be a single point of control from which the reading room and the book stacks of the library could be surveyed. It was perhaps a combination of logic and erudition which led Stirling to readapt the 'Panopticon' principle from the Utilitarian philosopher Jeremy Bentham, with its 'controlling eye' at the centre of a circle; this had frequently been employed in library designs throughout the nineteenth century. Several of Aalto's libraries in the 1950s had used a similar idea.

The polygonal stair-towers, industrial glazing, red quarry tiles, raised podiums, irregular silhouettes and engineering romanticism all recalled

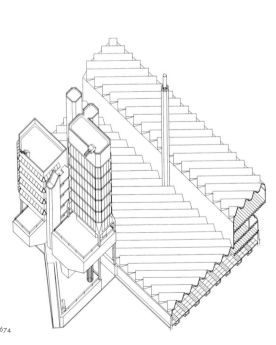

674

675

676

features used at Leicester. However, the glass tent over the reading room was a staggering invention reminiscent of a nineteenth-century greenhouse or of the rocket-assembly building at Cape Canaveral. The roof was formed as a double layer to incorporate an environmental cushion against extremes of heat and cold, and was supported on an elegant steel-truss system with adjustable louvres and other mechanical attachments. At the peak, above the point of command, an array of brightly coloured extractor fans was inserted above the smoked-glass inner layer of the roof. With its canted interior windows and its glazed galleries, the whole space was a bizarre evocation which seemed to oscillate between twentieth-century science fiction, the actualities of aircraft design, and nostalgia for the era of the *grands constructeurs* in steel and glass of the nineteenth century. As before, the imagery seemed suffused with Futurist poetry; but there was a once-removed quality about this heroic stance –

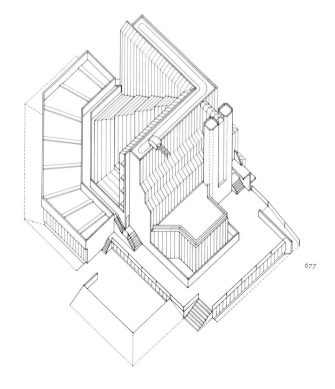

677

676 James Stirling,
History Faculty Building,
Cambridge University,
1964–6

677 History Faculty
Building, axonometric
drawing

678 History Faculty
Building, interior

as if Stirling wanted to employ the icons of the machine-age polemic without embracing the moral and Utopian commitments.

In presenting his own buildings Stirling tended to insist on their functional rationale rather than indulging in speculation about the meaning or sources of his forms. Factory patent glazing – so obviously evocative of the crystalline fantasies of the 1920s – was discussed in entirely pragmatic terms: 'Glass buildings are, I think, appropriate to the English climate. We are perhaps the only country where it is seldom too hot or too cold, and on a normal cloudy day, there is a high quality of diffused light in the sky. A glass covering keeps the rain out and lets the light through.' Even so, it was clear from the results that the architect was quite deliberate in his selection of precedents, and that associational and compositional criteria were sometimes uppermost; sloped glass was not ideal to keep rain out and extensive glazing could let in too much light, cold and heat and sound, as well as the prying eye. Both the advantages and the disadvantages were present in Stirling's Florey Building, a student residence designed for Queen's College, Oxford, (1966–71), a work which also underlined the architect's sophisticated stance towards seminal works of the early modern movement. The student

678

rooms were wrapped around a semi-open court looking towards fields and trees, were fully glazed from floor to ceiling, were ventilated by louvres and protected from the sun by roller blinds inside the glass. These same blinds were supposed to ensure privacy. Thus equipped, the Florey building had something of the character of a demonstration, as if a typical feature of the 'heroic period', the glass façade, was being given a new solution. The outer sides of the building, where the access corridors and circulation towers were positioned, were largely clad in Stirling's usual red tiles, while the building as a whole sat back on a splay-legged A-frame in concrete reminiscent of a grandstand. The main communal function – a breakfast room – was situated at the focal point, embedded in the court and surmounted by a swivelling extractor stack in the form of a wind vane, while the porter's lodge was contained in curved, free-plan shape tucked in under the box.

Inevitably, the image of the glass box lifted up on concrete supports and looking out over nature recalls the Pavillon Suisse; equally the stepping of the attached stair volumes and the placement of the breakfast room alongside a slab calls to mind Aalto's Baker House; finally, the 'cloister' under the A-frame at ground level and the vaguely courtyard-like plan are suggestive of the Oxbridge collegiate tradition. Thus the form of the Florey Building resulted not from a 'functionalist' position but from a deliberate cross-breeding of relevant types in tradition. Moreover, the solution adopted was beset with practical and acoustic problems and was seen by more traditional members of the local community as an imposition of machine-age obsessions on the gentility of Oxford life. Possibly this was Stirling's version of the challenging social character he had sensed in the architecture of the 1920s; however, the result smacked of a Mannerist manipulation of sanctioned sources of modernism. In his slightly earlier design for university halls of residence at St Andrews in Scotland (1964–8), he recalled and reworked another fetish of the 1920s, the collective image of the ship.

Stirling's mechanistic rhetoric seems to have come fully into its own in a number of prestige schemes for industrial concerns designed in the 1960s and early 1970s. For the steel company

Dorman Long at Middlesbrough (1965), he envisaged a linear building with a stepped form that was entirely sealed and which made a dramatic display of exposed steel girders; for Olivetti at Hazelmere (1969–72) he conjured up collages of architectural syntax and business-machine quotations; and for Siemens AEG (1969) he projected a computer centre outside Munich (never built) of a distinctly mechanomorphic character. The cylindrical shapes of the main office spaces were laid out as a grand axial composition with moving conveyors running along the spine, while rows of poplar trees gave the image a curiously eighteenth-century feeling. The whole thing seemed to be some cybernetic equivalent to Ledoux's Utopian Saltworks at Chaux, put together to celebrate the values of a new European technocratic class.

It is possible that Stirling's picturesque manipulation of machine-age images may have received stimulus from another branch of the British architectural avant-garde of the 1960s: the group known as 'Archigram'. This was founded around a nucleus consisting of Peter Cook, Warren Chalk, Ron Herron, Dennis Crompton, Michael Webb, and David Greene. The founding pamphlet, 'Archigram I', was put together in 1961 and spelled out many of the group's later fascinations with such things as 'clip-on' technology, the throwaway environment, space capsules and mass-consumer imagery. As early as 1959, Mike Webb had designed a project for a Furniture Manufacturers' Association Building in the form of pods and capsules plugged flexibly into a frame; and in 1961 his 'Sin Centre' for Leicester Square envisaged a cybernetic pleasure machine aping computer reels and comic-book spaceships. Robot fascination reached a peak in Ron Herron's 'Walking Cities' project of 1964, in which spider-shaped cities on legs were shown clambering over the water towards Manhattan. Then in 1964 Peter Cook drew together most of the group's themes in a sprawling but ever-changing megastructure: the 'Plug-in City'. This contained no buildings in the traditional sense, but 'frameworks' into which standardized components could be slotted. Functions were not fulfilled by forms any longer, but by mechanical and electronic 'services'.

There was a deliberately anti-heroic stance in Archigram which rejected the high-mindedness and

679

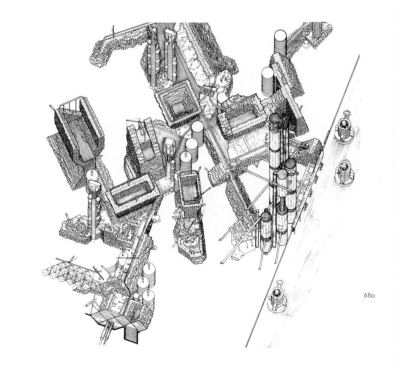

680

nature worship of the Team X generation. Archigram welcomed wholeheartedly, without moral stricture, the hedonistic possibilities of modern consumerism. There was certainly a rough parallel here to the Pop paintings of the early 1960s produced by Richard Hamilton, Andy Warhol, Robert Rosenquist, and Jasper Johns. The Archigram architects learned their lessons from the earlier '20th Century Group' (which had revelled in American advertisements) and from the engineer R. Buckminster Fuller, whose anti-monumentalism appealed to them. Broadly speaking, their aim was to portray and symbolize a new reality; as Warren Chalk stated:

We are in pursuit of an idea, a new vernacular, something to stand alongside the space capsules, computers and throwaway packages of an atomic electronic age …

We are not trying to make houses like cars, cities like oil refineries … this analogous imagery will eventually be digested into a creative system … it has become necessary to extend ourselves into such disciplines in order to discover our appropriate language to the present day situation.

Archigram pronouncements and images had a notably Futurist quality about them, and the group was certainly interested in Sant'Elia's descriptions of the city of the future as a dynamic machine. Their commentary on reality was mostly undertaken in the paper world of collages and drawings, which was probably just as well, for Archigram developed an anti-architectural philosophy towards the end of the 1960s. Thus the 'instant city' proposal of

1969 involved the sudden arrival of inflatable airships which would drop the minimal hardware necessary to create the 'true' urbanism – a software dream-world of electronic stimulation for the eye and the ear. The mythology of a non-oppressive environment rid of the tiresome weight of history, culture and architectural form was loosely entertained; it was an idea which blended well with the 'drop-out' consciousness of the decade.

The search for an anti-heroic imagery suitable to modern pluralism was given a considerable boost by the laconic ideas of Cedric Price in the same period. He maintained that society would, on the whole, be better off without the obsessions of form-makers. A typical Price project was the 'Potteries Thinkbelt' of 1964 – a design for a university in which he envisaged the reuse of an existing railway system in the Midlands as a new 'non-architectural' source of knowledge. Standardized modules containing books, recorded lectures, etc. were to be moved up and down the region to service different parts of it with 'information', but without buildings. Despite the anti-style pose, the position did crystallize a style of quiet ordinariness. A similar functionalist mood had been articulated by Reyner Banham at the end of his book *Theory and Design in the First Machine Age*, published in 1960: 'The architect who proposes to run with technology knows that he is in fast

681

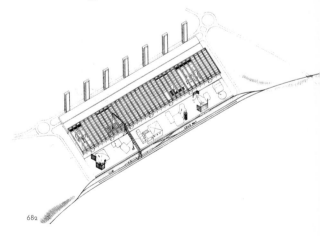

682

683

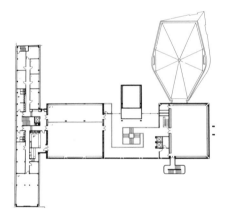

company and that in order to keep up, he may have
to emulate the Futurists and discard his whole
cultural load …' However, by the 1960s even the
Futurist position and imagery had become part of
a tradition. The paradox of the anti-architects was
that, in attempting to overthrow the bonds of the
past and the constraints of formal expression, they
drew on tradition and employed forms to get their
message across. Moreover, in the 1970s their
'anti-architectural' images became absorbed by
architects: Renzo Piano and Richard Rogers's
Pompidou Centre in Paris (1971–8) (Chapter 32),
for example, would have been inconceivable
without the legacy of Archigram.

One British architect whose work during the
1960s stood out in firm contrast to the obsessive
play with technological imagery was Denys Lasdun.
In his case, technology was regarded as a means
(rather than an end) towards the creation of what he
called an 'architecture of urban landscape'. Lasdun
was born in 1914 and experienced the seminal
buildings of the modern movement without the
historical and ironical distance of the generation
whose formation took place after the war. He
learned much from working with Lubetkin and
Coates, but most of all from his study of Le
Corbusier's buildings and ideas. Lasdun also knew

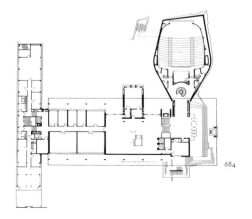

684

683 Denys Lasdun,
Royal College of
Physicians, Regent's Park,
London, 1959–61

684 Royal College
of Physicians, first-floor
and ground-floor plans

685 Royal College
of Physicians, interior of
main hall

Wright's architecture through drawings and photographs, and was deeply impressed by the English Baroque architect Nicholas Hawksmoor.

Lasdun's experimental cluster blocks at Bethnal Green of the mid-1950s have been mentioned earlier (p. 445) in connection with urbanistic reactions against the 'Unité'. In 1958 he designed some luxury flats in St James's in which he employed a 3:2 section to provide ample living room views and still make the most of expensive building land. The organization was expressed directly in the façades and handled adeptly through careful proportioning and fine detailing. The horizontal stratification also related to the adjacent building and to a neighbouring neo-Palladian town house. The sensitive relationship of new and old buildings had been a matter of relatively small importance to the majority of early modern movement masters, the more so as they were often keen to heighten the 'modernity' of their solutions through contrast; but in the 1950s and 1960s the matter of context became increasingly important.

Indeed the relationship of the individual building to its historical setting was a major motive force in Lasdun's next design, for the headquarters of the Royal College of Physicians (1959–61) – an august academic medical body – to stand close to Nash's neo-classical terraces in Regent's Park. The main, ceremonial part of the building was a white rectangular shell poised delicately on piers above its shadowy lower areas; this contained a grand hallway, the historic library and the focal 'Censor's room'. The transition in scale between these sharp, crisp forms and the setting was handled by a curved hump in purple brick containing the auditorium. Free in form, organic in association, this was intended to imply an ability to grow and to change. Behind the hump was a precinct, appropriate to an inward-looking community of scholars, while the main hallway contained a square spiral stair

685

which rose in ever-wider turns to join stepped levels, which then opened out on one side towards Nash's terraces. Thus the heart of the institution was defined by a well-scaled space that was sensed as being, at the same time, a piece of its surroundings.

Part of the subtlety of the Royal College of Physicians lay in the way the neo-classical setting was abstracted in its forms and finishes, without any recourse to a weak historical sentimentalism. Thus the main shell in white terrazzo was detailed in a manner recalling Nash's thin stucco surfaces, and the piers at the entrance were restatements of classical orders. The purple brick hump echoed the neighbouring slate roofs, and the sequence of spaces in the hall was analogous to the alleyways around the park. Lasdun expressed his intention clearly: it was to 'rhyme' with Nash and to make the new building a 'microcosm' of the surrounding city.

The classicism of the Royal College ran deeper than these witty references. At the Architectural Association in the 1930s Lasdun had been trained to deal with ceremonial sequences of space using Beaux-Arts devices like the axis, the vestibule and the grand stair. Moreover, he had studied the writings of Geoffrey Scott, who had stressed the anthropomorphic qualities of classical design and the vital sculptural character of good architecture. These were features which Lasdun had sensed in the architecture of Hawksmoor. The dynamic contrast of light and shade, and the dramatic use of space were probably inspired by this early eighteenth-century precedent.

Thus the Royal College of Physicians was a turning point for its creator which united the disparate strands in his background: his admiration for Le Corbusier and the English Baroque, his interest in biologically inspired patterns of growth, his fascination with the meaning of institutions, his concern with the sense of space. One of the main ideas to crystallize in the building was the concept of an 'urban landscape' of stepped levels linking spaces inside and outside an individual building so that it became part of its setting. This contextual obsession was carried through in Lasdun's next major design, for the University of East Anglia (1962–8) near Norwich.

The university was one of a number commissioned in the early 1960s in Britain to stand in rural settings near cathedral towns. The site was on open meadow stepping down slowly to the River Yare. The client required a nucleus capable of later extension, and eventually decided that traditional divisions between disciplines should be minimized. The architect therefore decided on a linear pattern based on circulation and adjusted to fit the contours. The main elements became the flexible, precast concrete 'teaching wall' (running along the back), the upper walkway (conceptual spine of the scheme), and the stepped residences (attuned to the landscape setting), which were grouped around a space at the centre called simply 'the harbour'. Clearly there were loose parallels between this organization and ideas being pursued by Utzon, Giancarlo de Carlo, and Shadrach Woods at the same time, but the East Anglia plan and its underlying strategies were equally an outgrowth of ideas which stretched back to Lasdun's cluster blocks, and even to the biologically inspired plan-form of Hallfield School at Paddington, London, of 1951.

The dominant architectural element of the University of East Anglia was the platform or raised level. The section was worked out ingeniously to minimize the use of lifts and to allow views from the upper walkways across the Norfolk landscape. Variation was achieved on the basis of a few standardized parts linked together by a strong overall idea and by a dominant geometry of 90-degree and 45-degree axes. The architect hinted at the underlying landscape romanticism and geological analogies when he referred to the platforms as 'strata'. Indeed, the University of East Anglia was nothing less than a demonstration of his 'urban landscape' philosophy:

Activities take place on 'platforms' – floors, paths, terraces, bridges, etc. (See Le Corbusier's pronouncement of 1915 – 'The actual ground of the town is a sort of (raised) floor, the streets and pavements as it were bridges. Beneath this floor and directly accessible are places for the main services.') A building can be looked at in the same way as a matter of platforms and connections and interlocking spaces. Sensitive gradations of levels and heights can be made to respond to site and function, creating an endless variety of rhythms and scales, satisfactory in themselves, and adaptable to any existing urban situation, including the architecture of the past.

The system of strata (with accompanying towers) was found to be relevant to Lasdun's next major commission, the National Theatre of 1963–76. In the earliest scheme (1965) a National Opera

686

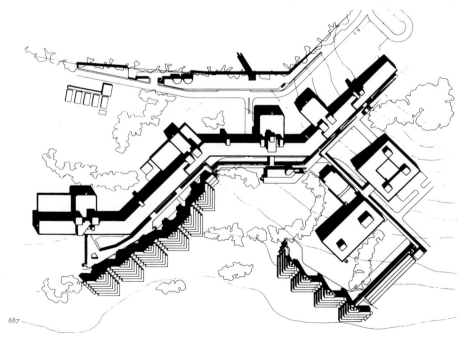

687

architecture and anti-architecture in britain

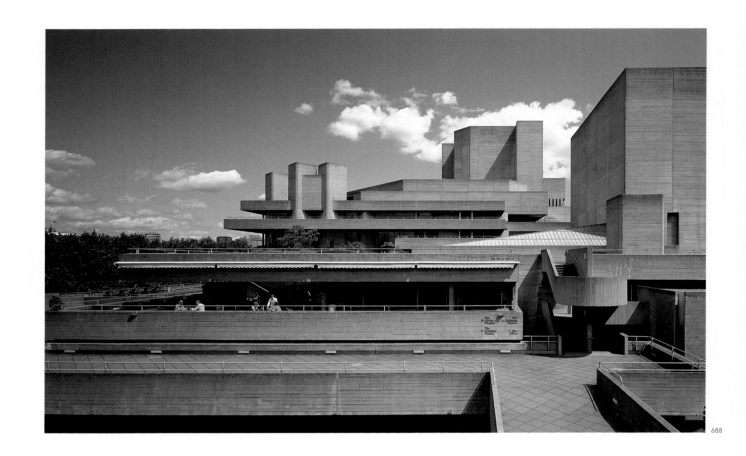

688

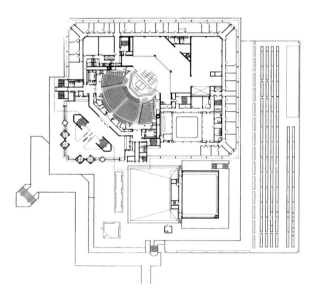

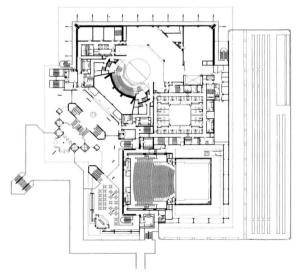

689

House was also to be included and the two were to stand together next to the River Thames in front of the monolithic shaft of the Shell tower. Platforms were this time used to create a series of interpenetrating spaces along the riverside with fine views towards the historic city, to blend the building with its setting, and to express the openness and public nature of the new institution. These themes were taken up in the final scheme (1967) for a theatre on its own to stand next to Waterloo Bridge; here the 'strata' supplied vantage points towards St Paul's and over the river, linked up with the bridge, and passed to the heart of the building where they supported the lobbies and auditoriums. They thus created a series of public 'stages' and social spaces with the cityscape itself as backdrop. Lasdun put the matter succinctly when he stated, 'the whole building could become theatre'. There were echoes of Baroque rhetoric and medieval silhouettes in the faceted towers (the architect was particularly intrigued by the polygonal shafts of Ely Cathedral), while the rhythms of horizontals hinted at his fascination with the ratios and divisions of classical mouldings. The strata underlined Lasdun's interest in the ceremonial meanings of platforms in ancient architecture, as well as his private myth concerning the roots of architecture in land-mass formations or strata of rock.

These themes were given added force through the powerfully expressive character of the National Theatre's form. The composition was dynamic, asymmetrical and ever variable in mood according to the spectator's changing position. Space and light were handled as positive features to lend drama to the sequences. The rugged silhouettes of the fly-towers gave the whole an effect of grandeur; at the same time the strata stopped the building from becoming an overbearing monolith and maintained the human scale. The theatre relied unapologetically on monumental rhetoric but also broke down the boundaries between a democratic institution and the public realm. Lasdun took the concrete cantilever from Le Corbusier's Dom-ino system and gave it a new meaning in the service of his own 'urban landscape' ideas.

The British situation in the quarter-century after the war was a pluralist one; none the less, there were shared preoccupations. One of these had to do with the expression of new social values; another with the cross-breeding of the international modern movement with national traditions; yet another with the relative human and architectural importance of technology. The National Theatre took a strong stand on all these issues; it is a good place to stop and consider how similar preoccupations were handled elsewhere.

690

30
extension
and
critique
in
the
1960s

I like complexity and
contradiction in
architecture ... based
on the richness and
ambiguity of modern
experience, including
that experience which
is inherent in art ...
Architects can no longer
afford to be intimidated
by the puritanically
moral language of
orthodox modern
architecture ...
Robert Venturi, 1966

691 Giancarlo de Carlo,
Faculty of Education,
Free University of Urbino,
1968–76

However diverse their approaches, however varied
their personal styles, the architects who came to
maturity in the early 1960s had certain broad
features in common. Their birth dates tended to fall
between 1915 and 1930, so their early years were
strongly impressed by the Second World War.
Their vocabularies were established against the
background of the declining International Style, and
they turned to the late works of the masters in their
own search for an architecture of greater robustness
and complexity. But while they respected some of
the guiding tenets of modern architecture, they did
not advocate a slavish orthodoxy. Their position was
characterized by tension between allegiance to the
founding fathers, the need to crystallize a changing
situation and the desire for self-expression. Faith
and scepticism were held in balance; dogma and
schism were equally to be avoided.

Looking back at the early 1960s from a distance
of three decades, one is struck by the genuine
optimism surrounding the production, criticism and
even the public reception of modern architecture.
The crises and introversions of the 1970s and
1980s were far away indeed. Singling out the work
of men like Utzon and Tange, and pointing to
the emergence of new civic monuments like the
Japanese town halls or the Sydney Opera House,
Sigfried Giedion even saw fit to announce the
presence of a 'third generation', as if his Grand
Tradition was now safely on its way. The idea was a
typical Giedionism in that it assumed the continuing
movement of an inner spirit of modern design with
the torch of inspiration being handed on from father
to son. But the post-war developments lacked linear
simplicity, and the individual architects within
it did not stagger their birth dates at convenient
twenty-year intervals. Sert, Lasdun, the young
Stirling, Tange, Utzon and Kahn may have shared
a certain consciousness, and even have exhibited
some stylistic similarities in their search for
sculptural enrichment, but they stopped far short
of constituting any unified movement. Even the
architects who rallied behind the banner of Team X
had widely different ways of interpreting the rough
consensus of ideas when it came to making forms.
Leitmotifs of the period, such as the elevated
platform, the directly expressed service tower, the
labyrinthine plan, the rough concrete surface, never
amounted to a coherent period style.

But in the fields of general construction (especially those of housing and of commerce), a banal international formula did triumph. The resultant dull reductivism was a mockery of the passionate simplicity of the seminal works of modern architecture. Functional discipline became confused with the instrumental purposes of real estate; planning bureaucracies took over *tabula rasa* images of the modern city and applied them with a confident, moralizing and stupid sense of certainty; what had started as an alternative urban dream was absorbed by an all too dreary status quo. The pioneer modern masters had had no difficulty in identifying their enemy: it had been the 'corrupt revivalism' of the nineteenth century. But by the 1960s good and evil had become harder to label and eclecticism was no longer a major issue. Now the enemy was cheapened modern architecture, and the critical exercise of distinguishing the genuine from the fake required greater subtlety; 'good' and 'bad' might even share the same features (simple geometrical forms, concrete frames, flat roofs). Thus the emerging young architect committed to quality was confronted with a series of dilemmas: should he believe that there was a core of modern architectural principles which he ought to uphold and extend? Should he maintain that the modern spirit required a constant quest for innovation in relationship to changing technologies and values? Or should he perhaps attempt to abandon the operation of modern architecture as too restrictive, and turn to other traditions in his formulation of a language?

The full force of these doubts would not be felt until the 1970s. For the two and a half decades after the War they were entertained by few. Modern architecture in its diverse manifestations continued to hold out the promise of social change, or at least to supply formal inspiration. As earlier chapters have shown, there was no single main line in the 1960s. Approaches and conditions varied considerably, and the period had its share of debate, dissension and criticism. But whatever the routes taken, they still extended some feature or another of an earlier modernism. In the 1960s, by degrees, this very continuity was questioned in some quarters, especially by those interested in a more overt use of the past, or in the lessons to be learned from the historical city.

692

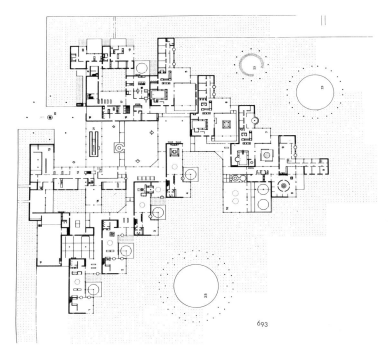

693

692 Aldo van Eyck,
Orphanage, Amsterdam,
1957–62

693 Orphanage,
Amsterdam, plan

694 Aldo van Eyck,
Sculpture Pavilion,
Arnhem, 1966, plan

695 Sculpture Pavilion,
interior

Some of the dilemmas of the 1960s stemmed from the materialism and off-handedness of rapid economic and technological development. The characteristic types of the new economic order were box-like offices and housing slabs, in any event isolated objects surrounded by a wilderness of roads and parking – a sprawl which not only lacked urbanity but also destroyed the countryside. Little wonder that so many of the critical discourses of the period addressed the need to create a viable public realm, to combine the new with the pre-existing patterns of streets and squares, to draw upon the layers of memory and social custom inherent in particular places. This was the period of raised

decks and streets for pedestrians; of plans as overlapping networks; of universities as small cities; of enclaves, clusters and precincts, and housing schemes as abstractions of hill towns. As suggested in the chapter on reactions to the Unité, the block was gradually eroded, flattened out, or in other ways enmeshed with its setting. It was the period, too, of Team X meetings on 'human association', and 'urban re-identification', of variety based upon standardization, of a 'less deterministic' version of modernism for a pluralistic and increasingly motorized society.

Team X was not the source of a rigid dogma. It was rather a loose affiliation of individuals from several nations who pooled ideas on broadly shared themes to do with architecture and urbanism. Each architect had his own language, pedigree and locus of activity, and each had his own place in a larger tradition. The Dutchman Aldo Van Eyck, for example, was acutely conscious of the high social and spiritual aims, and outstanding formal qualities, of the Dutch modern movement between the wars. He attempted to inject into his work a humanism which was a respectable (though less extreme) descendant of the Utopianism of the pre-war period. Preoccupied with the degradation brought about by technology ('mile upon mile of nowhere') he sought to counter this with an architecture founded on spiritual values and (what he took to be) archetypal meanings (see Chapter 24). Van Eyck's design for an orphanage near Amsterdam (1957–62), avoided the usual oppressive institutional image by making the building into a web of small pavilions looking into private courts, expressed as a repetitive but variable pattern. Using a phrase that summed up beautifully the aspirations of a period, he referred to this as 'labyrinthine clarity'. It was an order loosely reminiscent of an early Mondrian (rather than the later hardline images which had influenced De Stijl), or of the layout of a North African village: the intention was to create a field of spaces of different human pitch and intensity. Van Eyck detailed the Orphanage so that the elements flowed ambiguously into one another but the lattice of the structure could none the less be sensed. The ground plane was articulated by steps, levels and circular benches for multiple uses, while the vaults above were varied in size and strength of light. The regimentation of a systems building was avoided in a structure which

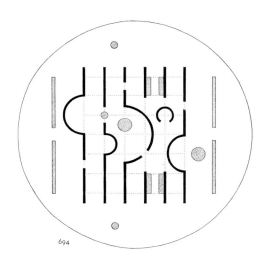

694

nevertheless employed standardization; richness was generated from repetition and layering. Van Eyck wrote:

Whatever space and time mean, place and occasion mean more. For space in the image of man is place, and time in the image of man is occasion … Provide that place, articulate the in between … make a welcome of each door and a countenance of each window … get closer to the shifting centre of human reality and build its counterform – for each man and all men …

Similar preoccupations inspired Van Eyck's Arnhem Sculpture Pavilion design of 1966 in which simple straight and semicircular partitions were set into an overall circular plan in such a way that the observer experienced a sequence of events and encounters that were held together by a firm geometrical discipline. The architect's mysticism emerged in the intense feeling for the psychological variation of space and in the imagery of the plan – a sort of talisman or emblem portraying a sequence of worlds within worlds. The building was like a small labyrinth and its shape recalled, once again, Van Eyck's interest in the cosmic symbolism of Dogon architecture (p. 446). He was trying to evoke underlying spatial 'constants', but using a modern architectural syntax, based upon the concrete frame, the textured wall and the glazed screen. Like most of his Team X contemporaries, Van Eyck gave relatively little attention to the urban façade, or to

696

the juncture between his buildings and the existing urban pattern. The 'micro-city' and the actual city remained curiously out of touch.

By the beginning of the 1960s, the days of even a semblance of the 'International Style' lay in the past. Even treated selectively, contemporary production did not lend itself to unitary descriptions. Reyner Banham (whose *Theory and Design in the First Machine Age*, 1960, did so much to reveal the theoretical complexity of the early modern movement) later tried to group together significant work of the late 1950s and early 1960s under the heading 'The New Brutalism', but was quick to qualify this somewhat vague 'ism' with the subtitle 'ethic or aesthetic?' If there was some broad period sensibility it perhaps manifested itself in the direct expression of materials, the separation of pieces and elements, the accentuation of service towers and circulation, the overlapping of geometries in plan, and the interlocking of spaces in section. In details there was insistence upon 'the thing itself', while the period cliché was the bare concrete surface procured with the aid of rough wooden formwork. Within these broad conventions many moods, meanings and levels of quality were achieved. Rough concrete might refer to the archaic in one case, to stark urban reality in another, to natural erosion in a third.

The themes of 'naked truth' and 'structural honesty' were interwoven in several remarkable buildings of the early 1960s, not all of them indulging in grandiose, monumental expression. The Nordic Pavilion at the Venice Biennale of 1962, designed by the Norwegian Sverre Fehn, combined a restrained minimalism and cool abstraction with the vibration of light on textured concrete planes. The Pavilion was to show Nordic works of art, and the roof was assembled from a lattice of apparently weightless concrete blades a metre deep but only six centimetres thick. One row of these blades rested laterally on another, so the effect was of a diapered pattern of floating shadows intended to create an equivalent to Scandinavian light, appropriate to the works of art on display. The concrete was made from white sand and crushed marble, and there were wafer-thin slices of translucent fibreglass for gutters. The plan relied upon a Miesian sense of absence ('almost nothing'), while the space conveyed a suitable 'Nordic silence'.

696 Sverre Fehn, Nordic Pavilion, Venice Biennale, 1962

697 Aarno Ruusuvuori, Tapiola Church, Espoo, Finland, 1965

698 Reima and Raili Pietilä, Dipoli Polytechnic Student Union Building, Helsinki University of Technology, Espoo, 1966

697

leaked in from unseen sources and enhanced a mood of grave intensity. This severity was alleviated by the lateral view out to the landscape (a device recalling Bryggman's funerary chapel of 1939 on the other side of the same cemetery) and by the stainless steel candlesticks catching the cross-light: six slender pins like wands marking the position where the coffin would stand during the Last Rites. What might be called the 'organic' strand of Finnish architectural culture was extended in the Dipoli Polytechnic Student Union Building at Espoo (1966) by Reima and Raili Pietilä, with its massive and fragmented forms in rough concrete opening towards the southern sunlight, but closing to the north. Evocative of shards of ice, of timber, and of rock, the Dipoli Building touched upon old National Romantic themes but via a set of formal conventions which – while deeply personal – owed much to Aalto. These Finnish institutional works were achieved against a general background in which modernism was the accepted norm for most areas of construction from housing and factories up to civic and religious types of building. Indeed, modern architecture was still considered an instrument of cultural transformation in the context of the Welfare State.

Spain in the 1960s reveals a pluralism of a different kind sometimes blending together diverse

In most European countries, in Japan and in the United States, it was normal for there to be several parallel, sometimes competing, strands of architectural development. Finland in the 1960s offers an interesting case of this diversity. The stern, minimalist tendency, initiated by Aulis Blomstedt and reinforced by geometrical abstract art, was carried forward by Aarno Ruusuvuori, for example, in the stark box and naked materials of the Tapiola Church at Espoo of 1965. The church combined a concrete frame with concrete block and sharp-cut steel details, but it was above all a building about light, space and sound. Another side of Finnish reductivism was well represented by the Funerary Chapel at Turku of 1966, by Pekka Pitkänen, a work which aligned itself with the late works of Le Corbusier. The naked concrete walls, ceilings and floors were smooth, almost polished, and were dematerialized in dense shadows. Daylight

698

features of the modern inheritance, sometimes responding to different climates and localities. In contrast to the silent and self-effacing works of De la Sota (Chapter 26), Madrid witnessed the eruptive, sculptural eclecticism of Francisco Javier Saénz de Oíza's Torres Blancas of 1966, an 'organic' tower with clustered shafts and curved balconies in *béton brut*, which owed much to Wright's late works if not to the clusters and pods of the Japanese Metabolists. In retrospect the building was seen as 'the greatest admirer of modernity and its greatest contester', since it drew together positions that were often opposed: 'a desire to be loyal to the principles of function and technology while simultaneously adhering to an organicist, expressionist and sculptural architectural language.' Some of the best Spanish architecture of the period managed to distil qualities of place or region but without adopting an overtly regionalist position, and without recourse to theoretical postures. The El Rollo Convent on the outskirts of Salamanca, designed by Antonio Fernandez Alba in 1963, restated the idea of the traditional monastic plan with court and cloister, in a bare vocabulary of simple rectangular windows cut through sandstone surfaces. The treatment was in harmony with the characteristic colour and texture of old Salamanca, but also owed something to Nordic architects such as Utzon or Asplund, while the plan contained certain Aaltoesque inflections. This transmission from north to south is itself worthy of comment, since these same Scandinavians had each in his own way drawn upon Mediterranean sources.

Although Josep Lluís Sert left Spain in the 1930s and eventually emigrated to the United States, he maintained his links with Catalonia and with the Balearic Islands (Ibiza in particular). The Mediterranean world continued to supply him with a basic source of inspiration in all of his works. The studio for the painter Joan Miró, outside Palma, Majorca (designed in 1955), was formed from interlocking Catalan vaults, textured rubble walls, a whitewashed concrete frame and deeply perforated grilles for protection against the fierce southern sunlight. A joyous and utterly straightforward building, the Miró studio succeeded in absorbing something of the playful spirit of the painter himself; it celebrated an analogous interest in the freshness of folk forms and the surrealism of peasant motifs. These preoccupations were filtered through a robust vocabulary indebted to both Le Corbusier and the curved shapes of Miró's or Léger's sculptures of the time.

Always a city with an internal momentum and memory of its own, Barcelona was the site in the 1960s of several mature realizations by José Antonio Coderch, notably the Banco Urquijo Apartment Complex of 1967, and the 'Las Cocheras' Apartments of 1968. In each of these Coderch employed a vocabulary of red-brick-clad walls and balconies over concrete frames. The serrated geometry allowed each unit to have a protective terrace (with wooden lattices in the first example, dense planting in the second), broke down the volumes to a human scale and enlivened the

699 Antonio Fernandez Alba, El Rollo Convent, Salamanca, 1963

700 El Rollo Convent, axonometric drawing

701 Josep Lluís Sert, Joan Miró Studio, Palma, Majorca, 1955–6

702 José Antonio Coderch, 'Las Cocheras' Apartments, Barcelona, 1968

699

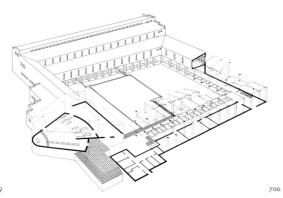

700

701

interstitial spaces. Thus the individual object was melted into a larger pedestrian enclave with a distinctly urbane quality. Coderch's late works reveal an enriching tension between cosmopolitan prototypes and local continuities: 'Las Cocheras' might well be considered as yet another counterform to Le Corbusier's 'Unité' slab, but in a Barcelona tradition.

In Germany in the 1960s several contrasting schools of thought also emerged, especially when it came to dealing with the city. The Interbau Exhibition of 1957 had had something of the function of a post-war Weissenhofsiedlung with contributions by well-known international architects like Aalto, Niemeyer and Le Corbusier alongside German offerings; Berlin acquired its own version of a Unité d'Habitation and a museum of modern architecture. But as the historian Wolfgang Pehnt suggested, there was 'a medley of remarkable individual buildings' without a relevant new town-planning principle. By the early 1960s German social and urban reconstruction had reached the point where civic monumentality (something of a taboo after the War) was once again broached. Scharoun's Berlin Philharmonie (Fig. 592) brought to fruition something of the Expressionist period of forty years before, while the New National Gallery by Mies van der Rohe

(Fig. 645) unapologetically asserted the German classical spirit. But poetic statements of this intensity were rare. The norm was a low-key architectural prose relying upon rectangular block, frame and curtain wall. In the 1960s, the urbanistic limitations of this language became increasingly clear, and reactions against it took several forms: romantic organicism reasserting handicraft and the past (e.g. the neo-medieval fortress forms of Gottfried Böhm's Town Hall at Bensberg of 1964); or the re-examination of traditional 'rules' for dealing with public urban space (e.g. in several unbuilt studies by Oswald Mathias Ungers carried out around 1963–5). Slowly but surely the problem of the past was reasserting itself in German architecture.

In Italy the past had never been totally banished, of course, but the post-war 'economic miracle' was achieved at a high cost to both city and country. The excessive technological rhetoric of devalued modernism continued to encounter resistance from several quarters: the vague 'organic architecture' championed by the historian and critic Bruno Zevi; an extravagant formalism (in the hands of architects like Paolo Portoghesi); a left-wing social critique in the historical writings of Leonardo Benevolo and the neo-Marxist texts of Manfredo Tafuri; and an almost unconscious continuation of some of the impulses of Italian Rationalism involving a fusion of abstract, classicizing discipline with modern construction means. As mentioned before, the problem of relating new buildings to their urban context had already been much discussed in the

702

703

1950s, and Ernesto Rogers continued to articulate his interest in tradition in his editorials in *Casabella*. These were the years too in which the art historian Giulio Carlo Argan published his ideas on 'typology' – ideas which would be of considerable interest to younger architects like Giorgio Grassi and Aldo Rossi, as may be sensed from the latter's *L'architettura della città*, published in 1966.

By contrast, the enigmatic figure of Carlo Scarpa avoided the Italian habit of theorizing. Yet his projects were among the most subtle when it came to inserting modern buildings into the old fabric. Scarpa's vocabulary of suspended fragments and stratified levels permitted him to 'excavate' a site for its underlying resonances and to explore the superimpositions of time. His conversion of an old Venetian palace, the Querini Stampalia, into a museum (1961–3) reiterated his technique of

working with 'layers', of separating the new from the old, and of guiding movement with interlocking planes in wall, floor and ceiling. The route through the museum ran from a small piazza in front of the building, over a canal by means of an exquisitely detailed bridge, through the interiors on a slightly raised floor, and out into the garden at the back where concrete screens were inset with small tesserae of mosaic. This path was a free-standing element in its own right, a modern intervention placed just above the level of the *acqua alta* – the winter high tide which periodically floods ground-floor rooms in the city. In the garden the theme of water encircling matter was reversed in the form of a slow-moving channel trickling along the top of a wall. A spring dribbled slowly into a white marble basin shaped as a labyrinth. The detail repeated the themes of the building in miniature but was also like an emblematic map of Venice, its canals, streets and squares. For Scarpa, ornament was a microcosm of larger worlds.

The reading of 'context' was central to the thinking of both Vittorio Gregotti (author of *Il territorio dell'architettura* of 1966) and Giancarlo de Carlo; but these were architects who also had to grapple with problems of large size and standardization in fabrication. De Carlo's response to topography and urban order involved a considerable abstraction (in contrast to the rather obvious mimicry of the historical setting evident in Ernesto Roger's Torre Velasca in Milan of 1958, Fig. 600), as was well revealed in the first stage of the Free University of Urbino (1962–5) clustered on a hillside outside the walls of the old city (Fig. 557). In later years De Carlo instituted a study of the entire building stock of the medieval and Renaissance core of Urbino with a view to sympathetic conversions and interventions. In effect he evolved a method for reading the forces latent in a place, a technique which was implicit in later additions such as the fan-shaped auditorium of the Faculty of Education (1968–76, Fig. 691) implanted in the old city among stone walls and tiled roofs with light dropping in several levels from above, its sloped glass roof and slightly fractured geometry reminiscent of Aalto. De Carlo was committed to the liberalization of institutions, and to social criticism, but he did not lose sight of architectural and urban values.

Although British developments in the 1960s were discussed in the last chapter, it is not idle to place them in the larger European context. Lasdun's 'urban landscape' ideas were never directly linked to Team X (to which he never belonged), but there were some analogous preoccupations, such as growth and change, the articulation of social relationships and the sense of place. The Smithsons, of course, were major figures in the group and with the other members eventually published the *Team 10 Primer* (1968) as a joint pronouncement of their philosophy. The technological romanticism of James Stirling had no direct parallels in Europe, but Archigram and the anti-architecture lobby were not a unique phenomenon. In Italy 'Archizoom' and 'Superstudio' articulated similar ideas, usually in glossy collages based on Pop imagery and surrealist aspects of advertising. The moral struggle for the 'deeper values' of the modern movement was put aside, and culture was reduced to a sort of consumer pluralism delighting in technology as a plaything. The Florentine group 'Superstudio' expressed a growing disaffection with the mores and values of mass capitalism by means of photomontages and surreal juxtapositions of glazed viaducts and wildernesses. One of their collages, entitled *A Journey from A to B*, showed groovy kids in bare feet walking through an ethereal perspective grid into a hazy desert landscape and bore the caption, 'There will be no further reason for roads or squares'. The forms and spaces of earlier architecture were to be rejected as so many pretensions towards an absolute order, which really masked oppressive social systems of power. Thus a curiously sensual attitude to technology was combined with the badinage of radical chic.

While the intention of the Team X generation was to 'humanize' technology, the actual architectural results were open to the criticism that they were too abstract – that to the man in the street, the manipulations of structure and plan were simply a more complex version of a basically alienating, modern way of building. The left-wing critique of modernism grew to a crescendo at the end of the 1960s with the claim that urban planning was simply a disguise for an ugly neo-capitalism, that it had become, in effect, a tool for pushing around the poor. Answers were supposed to lie in consulting the users; in adding neo-vernacular touches; in transforming the entire social system. Or else they were to lie in reconsidering the 'text' of the traditional city with all its latent meanings. The writings of urban theorists like Kevin Lynch (*The Image of the City*, 1960) were brought in to support a mapping of urban form in terms of 'landmarks' and 'edges'. More challenging to the progressive mythology of the technological city (and to the rupture and fragmentation which seemed to characterize the reality) were the writings of Aldo Rossi (e.g. *L'architettura della città*, 1966), which spoke unapologetically of 'memory' and 'monument', dealt with the social significance of traditional streets and squares, and advocated the transformation of long-standing historical types. At a time when science-fiction 'megastructures' such as those of the Japanese Metabolists or of the British Archigram group were in vogue, these reminders of urban continuity were disturbingly sane.

By the end of the 1960s, a total view of the city seemed less and less tenable, and the very idea of total planning was increasingly under siege. The 'megastructure' represented a last attempt at packaging the complexity of the city in a containable architectural form, and it brought the technological component of architecture to a huge exaggeration of structure, tubes and girders; grandiose gestures which became ever more excessive and vacuous. By degrees, the historical city was re-examined for its underlying structures and patterns, its continuities and conventions. The old city had had to adjust to the new, often with disastrous results; now the new would be asked to adjust to the old. In the minds of an emergent generation disturbed by the high price extracted by 'economic progress', the desirable paradigm became the city of spaces, rather than the city of objects. The island slab would be replaced in their attentions by the perimeter block with courtyard and urban façade. The modernist inheritance of idealized forms would be asked to obey traditional rules of urban conduct. Perhaps the mounting reaction against urban renewal revealed a broader dilemma arising from the collision between a faceless modern technology and the need for belonging and identity. In any event, by the end of the 1960s in the critical literature on the city, 'place' had become enthroned as the magic word.

In the United States between 1950 and the late 1960s, architecture pursued some parallel courses with Europe, though economic and patronage conditions required different reactions. In the business sector this was a boom period of construction, and firms such as Skidmore, Owings and Merrill evolved a standardized big-business heraldry incorporating a somewhat glib version of Miesian purity: the steel frame, tinted glass and refined finishes of chrome and marble. The engineer R. Buckminster Fuller succeeded in popularizing the geodesic dome and stimulated a school of technological wizardry which even came up with the fantastic notion of covering Manhattan with a giant environmental bubble. American confidence in high technology was also reflected in a megastructure compulsion which hit the architectural profession in the mid-1960s. This prompted Paul Rudolph to envisage a linear city of stepped section running for miles across the edge of New York. A scientific approach to the design process was argued

704 Bruce Goff, Bavinger House, Norman, Oklahoma, 1950

705 Kevin Roche and John Dinkeloo, College Life Insurance Building, Indiana, 1969

704

forcefully by Christopher Alexander (*Notes on the Synthesis of Form*, 1964), who restated some of the traditional functionalist arguments but with the help of mathematical models. And a certain admiration for social science was reflected in the foundation of numerous university departments with such titles as 'School of Environmental Studies'. The danger in all this was obvious: the role of intuition, imagination and tradition in the genesis of forms could become severely devalued. The later self-conscious and strenuous assertion of the primacy of aesthetic values which would bedevil the American avant-garde in the 1970s probably needs to be understood against the background of this largely spurious quasi-scientific methodology.

But the emulation of the processes and images of technology was only one strand of the complex American development. At another extreme was the wilderness romanticism of Bruce Goff, who delighted in *ad hoc* combinations of natural materials and *objets trouvés* from industrial waste. The Bavinger House of 1950, near Norman,

Oklahoma, was organized around a central mast with a swirling wooden roof and an idiosyncratic cable structure. It is not surprising that Goff should have been adopted as a sort of hero of the counterculture of the late 1960s, for his buildings implied a rejection of total design and of the corporate values that were associated with it in the American context.

Although there was no direct equivalent to Team X in America, the ideas of the group filtered in by a number of routes. Bakema, Woods and Jerzy Soltan taught in American architecture schools, while Sert (who was not a member, but whose ideas were not dissimilar) preached a new unity of architecture and town planning at Harvard Graduate School of Design (of which he was Dean) in the late 1950s. In his design for Peabody Terraces (Chapter 24) he gave form to his theories. Holyoke Center and the additions to Boston University (1960–7) dealt with similar ideas: the subtle linkage of townscaped spaces, tall towers, interior streets, intermediary buildings of transitional scale, the articulation of different uses through highly textured façades of louvres and balconies, the delicate composition of concrete frames and bright colours. As in Europe, these urban demonstrations remained the preserve of well-to-do universities, having little effect on the increasingly brutal development of the capitalist city. The 1960s witnessed the wholesale destruction of vast areas of historic fabric in the interests of 'economic development'. Earlier modern movement platitudes concerning the value of space and light (though rarely greenery) were co-opted to rationalize financial motives, to justify the construction of freeways, or else to support grotesque civic monuments with compulsory plazas. The American architect was constantly demoted to a sort of exterior decorator for business interests. Those housing agencies which existed encouraged simplistic, grand-slam solutions of an insensitive kind, and American architects had little tradition of radical criticism. The artist architect was thus forced into the gilded cage of upper-crust patronage: museums, prestigious university buildings, villas on Long Island. The aspirations towards an integrated society implicit in Team X thinking seemed foreign indeed.

If Mies van der Rohe dominated the early 1950s in America, late Le Corbusier dominated the early 1960s. Curiously enough his one American building, the Carpenter Center for the Visual Arts at Harvard (1959–63), was little understood, but replicas of La Tourette popped up all over the place as city halls or even department stores. Rough concrete piers, heavy crates of *brises-soleil*, and rugged overhangs were the order of the day. An elephantine tendency seems to have gripped America in the early 1960s in any case: veneers of *brises-soleil* or coatings of marble were laid over massive steel frames and trusses. Vincent Scully coined the phrase 'paramilitary dandyism' to describe it: and one

705

thinks of the grand monumentality of Kevin Roche and John Dinkeloo's Knights of Columbus Headquarters at New Haven (1965–9), or of the huge piers covered in expensive stone of their Ford Foundation in New York (1963–8), or again of the eerie surrealism of their sliced glass pyramids for College Life Insurance in Indiana (1967–71), where 'high tech' and the grandiose visions of Boullée seemed to come together. As always in American luxury commissions, the craftsmanship and detailing were of the highest level. Several tall buildings of this period used reflecting glass and a slender steel-mullion system of a precision unthinkable in Europe. Ieoh Ming Pei's Hancock Tower in Boston of 1969–73 (designed by Henry N. Cobb) took on the character of an angled mirror reflecting the sky. American corporations needed to express their power, their efficiency, their belief in advanced technology, their preoccupation with styling; the sharp-edged minimalist creations of the above-mentioned firms were able to supply them with just the right imagery.

The skyscraper remained a central preoccupation of American architecture, and the requirement of ever greater height stretched existing structural assumptions and formal conventions to the limit. As the office building grew taller, normal frame structures gave way to bundled tubes, mega-piers with intermediate beams, and diagonal lattices which gave frank expression to the need for lateral stability in strong winds. The usual compositional schemes no longer worked. Just adding up individual windows, spandrels and I-beams failed to give a sense of coherence to the tower, so the Miesian formula was gradually modified. The skyscraper which exhibited these new constraints and opportunities most clearly was the John Hancock Center in Chicago of 1968–70, designed by Bruce Graham of Skidmore, Owings and Merrill. The basic structural concept was decided by the engineer Fazlur Khan and was known as the 'diagonally braced tube', a system whose efficiency lay in the way the walls could be made to carry most of the vertical gravity loads while simultaneously dealing with the lateral forces of the wind. In effect, this led to a steel skyscraper of tapered form, combining a clear expression of corner piers and X-shaped bracing, and a secondary system of floors and window panels. Dramatic in silhouette, bold in

706

articulation, the John Hancock Tower took its place in a lineage of Chicago buildings in which structure supplied discipline and inspiration for form.

The rugged concrete tradition in monumental building was best represented by Kallmann, McKinnell and Knowles's Boston City Hall (Fig. 643) or by Paul Rudolph's works of the mid-1960s. These buildings were surely part of a robust reaction against the spindly International Style of the 1950s. Rudolph had been trained under Gropius at Harvard, and had soon rejected the reductivism of his mentor. The Jewett Arts Center at Wellesley College (1955) made references to its neo-Gothic setting, and was mannered in its use of ornamental sun-screens, but it still represented a quest for formal richness and contextual continuity. The late works of Le Corbusier, the spatial dramas of the Italian Baroque, and the complexities in section of Wright's works helped Rudolph to find his way.

706 Ieoh Ming Pei and
Associates (designer
Henry N. Cobb), Hancock
Tower, Boston, 1969–73

707 Skidmore, Owings
and Merrill (designer
Bruce Graham),
John Hancock Center,
Chicago, 1968–70

707

By the time he designed the Art and Architecture Building at Yale (1958–62), his personal style was assured: violent contrasts of scale and colossal piers in rough corduroy concrete gave the whole building a vaguely primitive air. Silhouettes and sequences were expressed in an exaggeratedly irregular external volume. The same vigorous style was taken still further in the buildings for Boston's Government Center (1962), a major 'urban renewal' project involving the destruction of acres of existing fabric and the creation of 'plazas'. In this case the complex was stepped in section with curved stairs and cascades of platforms linked to spiralling towers. But Rudolph's expressionism seemed overdone, giving the feeling that all these displays of virtuosity perhaps contained no social content. Once again, an American artist resorted to formalist gestures, albeit of considerable aesthetic interest.

Against this setting of the mechanistic at one end, and of dandyism at the other, the sober figure of Louis Kahn stood out like a sentinel of ancient sense and principle. As well as being the major talent of the post-war years in America (Chapter 28), he was also an inspiring teacher. In the 1950s he taught regularly at the University of Pennsylvania School of Architecture in Philadelphia, where he was a living link with the enlightened aspects of Beaux-Arts discipline. He encouraged a respect for the past and an understanding of the role of *ideas* in architectural expression. His pupils were presented with a very different diet from their Harvard contemporaries, who still laboured under the inheritance of Gropius. Among the younger architects to be taught by Kahn was Robert Venturi,

who won a scholarship to the American Academy in Rome, and then went into private practice in the late 1950s. He received few commissions and devoted much time to teaching and writing. His *Complexity and Contradiction in Architecture* (1966) pulled together the reflections of a decade, and functioned as both a personal 'Towards an Architecture' and a handbook of sensibility for a generation bored by the blandness of what they called 'orthodox modern architecture'.

'Orthodox modern architecture' turned out to mean not so much the entire architectural production of the previous half-century (Venturi singled out both Le Corbusier and Aalto for special praise) as the simplistic and skin-deep version of modern design that had become prevalent in America in the previous twenty years. Venturi took the well-known Miesian jingle 'Less is more' and parodied it with the retort 'Less is a bore'; however, he was quick to point out that the complexity he sought could not be found by simply sticking on more ornamental details. Rather he was in favour of a tension bred by perceptual ambiguity – a richness of both form and meaning – which should affect the overall character of a design:

The tradition 'either–or' has characterized orthodox modern architecture – a sun-screen is probably nothing else; a support is seldom an enclosure; a wall is not violated by window penetrations but is totally interrupted by glass; program functions are exaggeratedly articulated into wings or segregated pavilions … Such manifestations of articulation and clarity are foreign to an architecture of complexity and contradiction, which tends to include 'both–and' rather than exclude 'either–or'.
 If the source of the 'both-and' phenomenon is contradiction, its basis is hierarchy, which yields several levels of meanings among elements with varying values. It can include elements that are both good and awkward, big and little, closed and open, continuous and articulated, round and square, structural and spatial. An architecture which includes varying levels of meaning breeds ambiguity and tension.

Venturi supported his case with numerous illustrations of buildings and plans from past periods of architectural history: Lutyens, Hawksmoor, Le Corbusier or a humble stone building might all be used to illustrate a certain quality of complexity. The method was thus loosely similar to that pursued in *Vers une architecture*, but whereas the lesson of this earlier work had been the integration of certain underlying essentials of classicism with an imagery for the machine age, Venturi's approach seemed to imply a less profound synthesis and a more

708 Paul Rudolph,
Art and Architecture
Building, Yale University,
New Haven, Connecticut,
1958–62

709 Robert Venturi,
Vanna Venturi House,
Chestnut Hill,
Philadelphia, 1963

710 Vanna Venturi
House, first- and ground-
floor plans

708

709

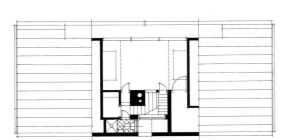

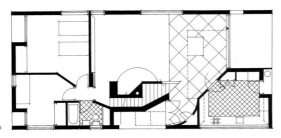

710

fragmented aesthetic. He claimed that his 'both-and' approach to architectural elements and meanings was more in tune with the complexity of modern experience than were the sterilities of the preceding generation, but gave little evidence of an underlying social vision or ideal. Clearly his sensibility had some loose links with contemporary painters such as Jasper Johns or Robert Rauschenberg, who deliberately confronted the spiritual heroics of the Abstract Expressionists with banalities drawn from everyday life; but there was no automatic step from such a sensibility to a set of architectural forms. Positive reviewers of Venturi claimed that he was all for enriching the language of modern design: detractors suggested that his forms were arbitrary and that he was simply opening the doors to eclecticism again. Whichever way you look at it, it was obvious that he was avoiding the arid sociological and technical definitions of architecture then prevalent, in favour of a discussion in which issues of form (and even meaning) did at least play a part.

Towards the end of the book Venturi applied some of his arguments to the American urban scene, claiming that 'Main Street is nearly all right' and that official planning (he might have called it 'orthodox modern urbanism') in the United States had done

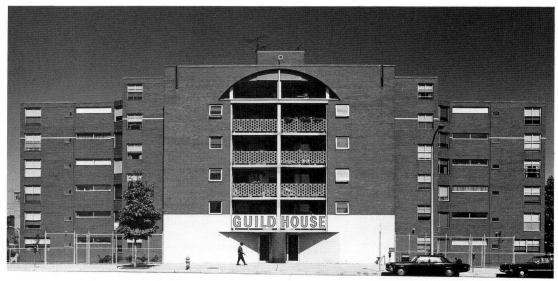

711

much to destroy street life and to subdue the vitality of flashing signs and advertisements. This mood of reaction against over-discrete and over-simple categories was in tune with the age: Jane Jacobs (in *The Death and Life of Great American Cities*, 1961) had praised the complex weave of meanings in the most 'ordinary' urban places, and the sociologist Richard Sennett would soon write in favour of 'disorder'. Venturi and his partners, Denise Scott Brown and Steven Izenour, continued to develop this point of view in *Learning from Las Vegas* (1972), in which they claimed that the coloured street-signs in front of the casinos were some native, indigenous form of expression of 'ordinary American people'. Thus populism and Pop Art sensibility came together in the curious illusion that products of Madison Avenue should be seen as a grass-roots, public, 'low art'.

There was a 'down home' flavour to Venturi's ideas which was related to his feeling that a truly American architecture should be created. The 'vernacular' to which he turned to find appropriately popular and reassuring images was artificial and mass-produced; it was provided by the commercial strip and the suburban cracker-box house, both areas traditionally despised by élitist planners with European pretensions. In his design for a house for his mother at Chestnut Hill,

Philadelphia (1963), Venturi had evaded the 1950s 'orthodox modern' cliché of the glass-box pavilion, in favour of an elusive image of the home replete with gable, sloped roof, attached mouldings, façade, back porch, etc. However, this was no mere replica of the standard suburban image, since the allusions to the humble American home were combined with witty and ambiguous quotations from Le Corbusier and Palladio. The façade had a deliberately deadpan character which disguised the welter of internal complexities and contradictions of the plan; Venturi praised the billboard character of American urban streets and coined the term 'decorated shed' to describe the type; this he contrasted to the concrete sculptural buildings of the early 1960s, which he referred to contemptuously as 'ducks'.

Despite Venturi's populist stance, his architectural jokes were obviously directed at the initiated. His buildings were even provided with his own elaborate explanatory texts. Of the small house just described he wrote:

This building recognizes complexities and contradictions: it is both complex and simple, open and closed, big and little: some of its elements are good on one level and bad on another; its order accommodates the generic elements of the house in general, and the circumstantial elements of a house in particular. It achieves the difficult unity of a medium number of diverse parts rather than the easy unity of few or many motival parts.

711 Robert Venturi, Guild
House, Philadelphia,
1962–6

712 Charles Moore,
Faculty Club, University
of California at Santa
Barbara, 1968, interior

In the Guild House, an old people's home in Philadelphia of 1962–6, Venturi adopted the same approach on a larger scale and for a function where his interest in 'commonly understood imagery' might be tested. The building had to include 91 apartments of varying types with a common recreation room; it was to house elderly folk from the neighbouring area. Venturi disposed the rooms in a symmetrical plan with a façade that came up to the street line. This elevation was also symmetrical, with the entrance doors placed tantalizingly on either side of the axis. A large arch was cut through the top of the façade, perhaps to try to give the building an image of openness and availability. Finally, on the very top was placed a gold-anodized television aerial, which could be interpreted (according to the artist) 'as a symbol of the aged, who spend so much time looking at TV'.

The Guild House was constructed from cheap bricks and simple standardized windows, and detailed so that a planar character was emphasized. The windows were chosen to rhyme with those in the area and were commonplace, standardized sashes of the kind found in the cheapest housing schemes. In the context of such a self-conscious architectural composition they recalled Venturi's observations on Pop artists who employed 'old clichés in new settings' and so gave 'uncommon meaning to common elements by changing their context or increasing their scale …' One scarcely needs to emphasize at this point the contrast between Venturi's approach and vocabulary, and those of Rudolph, Kallmann, Roche and Dinkeloo, and Pei at the same time. However, his ideas were usually more convincing in writing than when built. The agonized self-consciousness betrayed the lack of an instinctive feeling for form, space, or even proportion. Venturi set the tone for a literary conception of architecture in which more emphasis was put on imagery and quotation than on formal integration or material presence.

Another American architect to react against the blandness of clichéd modern architecture of the 1950s was Charles Moore, who was based in California, where the weight of imported European modernism of the Gropius variety was far less. Moore's and Donlyn Lyndon's houses at Sea Ranch on the Pacific coastline north of San Francisco of the 1960s were somewhat routine essays in redwood-cabin Regionalism. But by the end of the decade Moore had gone beyond this folksiness and absorbed some of the lessons of Pop Art. The interior of his Faculty Club for the University of California at Santa Barbara of 1968 was designed as a sort of stage set of thin planes and screens (planarity was once again in fashion), evoking simultaneously modern architectural icons (e.g. Van Doesburg's forms of the 1920s), the image of a baronial hall (replete with electric neon 'banners'), the standard effects of the American faculty club (portraits, stuffed animal heads), and Spanish colonial touches (a sort of tongue-in-cheek Regionalism). In this case it has to be said that too much complexity and contradiction ended up being simply a witty hotchpotch without underlying order or tension. But Moore's design was still symptomatic of an increasingly eclectic mood in

712

which all periods of the past (including the modern movement) were regarded as 'game' for quotations.

Venturi's and Moore's positions suggested that at least some of the guiding principles of modern architecture were losing hold, although, of course, their attitudes, styles and strategies would have been inconceivable without the numerous intellectual and formal inventions of the previous fifty years. None the less they could be portrayed as iconoclasts who were deliberately playing Mannerist games, and who were undermining some of the hard-won battles of the pioneers. In the circumstances, it was not surprising to find shrieks against their heresy, related to attempts at returning to 'the fundamentals of the faith'. This led to the curious situation of theorists arguing for a return to some mythical and crystalline principles of 'modernism', and of practitioners reviving some of the white forms of the 1920s.

Most of the architects involved in this exercise were linked to East Coast architecture schools such as Princeton and Cornell. Chief among them were five (briefly called the 'New York Five'): Peter Eisenman, Richard Meier, Charles Gwathmey, John Hejduk and Michael Graves. In the late 1960s most of these men were in their mid-thirties, and had therefore grown up with modern art and architecture as entirely established facts. They were loosely united by a strong feeling for the seminal works of the interwar years, like the Schröder House, the Villa Stein or the Casa del Fascio; by an obsession with formal issues at the expense of content and function (their formalist definitions of 'modernism' parroted those used by defenders of the American 'hard-edged' abstract painting of the late 1960s); and by their allegiance to the opinions of Colin Rowe, who taught in America from the late 1950s onwards, and who seems to have conveyed the 1920s to his acolytes as some lost Golden Age. But reviving the forms of the early International Style in the late 1960s, forty years afterwards, was by no means a simple exercise; it was every bit as dangerous as reviving any other set of forms of the past. The problem of pastiche hovered over the endeavour, and there was little evidence that the 'New York Five' were in any position to supply a cogent new content in their 'renaissance' of earlier forms.

Despite the insubstantiality of their philosophical positions, some of the New York Five architects achieved buildings of a dainty elegance. The Benacerraf House addition by Graves (1969) may stand as an example. This was a sort of pavilion attached to a residence in Princeton. Its architectural language was compounded from a variety of modern architectural sources, but elements were put in unexpected juxtapositions which challenged expectations concerning their usual role. Thus the knowledgeable observer might note that cylindrical *pilotis* turned up as horizontal handrails; or that coloured struts and exploding spatial effects derived from the Schröder House were being deliberately collided with free-plan curves recalling Le Corbusier's villas. Giulio Romano had relied, in the Palazzo del Tè (1530), on the knowledge of his audience, so that it might react with a frisson of shocked delight when it noticed his dropped keystones, and other breaks with the classical rules of the High Renaissance; in a similar way Graves relied on a historical perspective which made of the 1920s a classic age, and on an audience which, realizing this, would admire his virtuosity in breaking the rules. This was complexity and contradiction, but applied to revered prototypes of the modern movement, rather than to American domestic sources as with Venturi. It was an architect's architecture aimed at a profession thoroughly acquainted through coffee-table books and college art-history courses with the monuments of modernism. Philip Johnson characterized the Benacerraf rather aptly as 'a wonderfully sporty piece of lawn sculpture'. Indeed, it is arguable that the Graves style, with its interest in delicate coloured struts and a sort of backyard pastoralism, may have owed something to the abstract sculptures of Anthony Caro.

In the broad context of the 1960s in the United States it is possible to see the New York Five's self-conscious interest in formal issues as a reaction against the technological school on the one hand and the preoccupation with social scientific methodologies on the other. In turn, their stylistic emphasis on thinness, planarity and transparency may perhaps be seen as a formal reaction against the brutalist antics in heavy concrete of some of their predecessors. It is interesting, in retrospect, how little attention they devoted to late Le Corbusier, and how much they concentrated on the villas of the 1920s as sources. However, where the exemplars were often made of stuccoed concrete, and relied

on machine quotations, the replications were often
made of wood, were related to the American
timber-frame tradition, and were more spindly in
appearance. But it is not appropriate to treat the
group's work monolithically. Gwathmey, for
example, relied on bold contrasts of volume and
dumpy proportions for his effects. Meier was
preoccupied with the contrast and resolution of
vertical and horizontal layering in his house designs
(a concern which he claimed derived from the
inherent properties of Le Corbusier's Dom-ino
skeleton and Maison Citrohan respectively).
Hejduk built rarely and expressed his ideas through
crisp geometrical exercises based on a somewhat
academic view of Purism. Eisenman, a theorist as
well as a practitioner, modelled his style extensively
on that of Terragni, but disclaimed any cultural
significance in this choice of prototype or in the
resultant analogies between his work and Italian
Rationalism of the 1930s. Instead he argued
that such buildings as 'House II' (1969) were
explorations of basic formal syntax and the logical
structure of space. It seemed to matter little to
the New York Five architects that the forms they
imitated had been the outward expression of
Utopian philosophies and social visions. Discussions
of moral content were displaced by concentration
on issues of a purely formal kind. In their revulsion

against sociology they perhaps neglected the
different question of the idealization of a way of life
in symbolic form. In that respect they followed the
critical tradition of Clement Greenberg's writings
on abstract painting, or even the formalist version
of the International Style set by Hitchcock and
Johnson forty years before.

Indeed, the International Style revival was
cloaked in smoke screens of verbal rhetoric
implying that it was throwing aside false doctrines
of functionalism in favour, once again, of the 'art
of architecture'. Venturi and Moore tended to be
rejected for slumming it in Americana, and it
became customary by the early 1970s to contrast
the 'whites' (the New York Five) and the 'greys'
(Venturi *et al.*) in rather the same way that critics
had contrasted pure geometrical abstraction with
Pop Art, namely as a contest between modernism
and realism, or as a battle between exclusiveness
and inclusiveness. In fact the architectural
movements had a good deal in common:
both placed a high value on complex formal
manipulations of screens and planes; both were
involved with quotations and overt revival; both
were conceived (in part) as reactions against
debased modern design; and neither had much
to say about the general state of American society.
Both were precious-flower architectures, conceived
and concocted in the hothouses of the élite
American universities; and both were prone to a
bloodless and over-intellectualized academicism.

Broadly speaking, the path between 1955 and
1975 in Western Europe and the United States was
one from a loose consensus (which nevertheless
took many forms) to a position of greater scepticism,
in which various spectral versions of mythical
orthodoxy came under attack. The quest for deeper
meanings in the 1950s avant-garde gave way to a
brittle formalism proud to announce that it had
no social polemic, and dubiously supported by
intellectualizations derived from linguistics and
formalist criticism. The age of conviction gave way
to an era of broken faiths, where no strong, new
generating ideas seemed to emerge, leaving the
architect in a sort of suspension, free to stick
together fragments, but uncertain of the meaning of
their combination. It was symptomatic of the change
that, by the late 1970s, one could find the word
'revolutionary' applied to revivals of earlier styles.

713

3 1

modernity, tradition and identity in the developing world

Every people that has produced architecture has evolved its own favourite forms, as peculiar to that people as its language, its dress, or its folklore. Until the collapse of cultural frontiers in the last century, there were all over the world distinctive local shapes and details in architecture, and the buildings of any locality were the beautiful children of a happy marriage between the imagination of the people and the demands of the countryside.
Hassan Fathy, 1973

714 Balkrishna Doshi, low-cost housing, Ahmadabad, 1959–61

Modern architecture was created in Western industrialized countries where a progressivist world view flourished temporarily, and where avant-garde cliques attempted to produce an authentic modern style appropriate to rapidly changing social conditions. This curious pattern was rarely repeated elsewhere, but its results were copied all around the world, and were often misapplied. Moreover, as has been emphasized, it was not until the 1940s and 1950s that modern forms had any appreciable impact on the 'less developed' countries, and these forms were usually lacking in the poetry and depth of meaning of the masterworks of the modern movement. The dissemination of this degraded version of modern design occurred in a number of ways: through rapid economic development of a kind which fostered functions, technologies and urban circumstances where some sort of modern architecture seemed either relevant or unavoidable; through continuing colonization, in which case, images of modernity functioned as emblems of foreign economic or political control; and through the brainwashing of post-colonial élites (native-born but foreign-educated) with Western images and ideas that were upheld as 'progressive' counter-agents to an earlier era of 'backwardness and stagnation'.

Some sense of the problems following from rapid modernization has been given already in the examples of Japanese and Latin American architecture in the mid-twentieth century. In the decades immediately following the Second World War many other parts of the world, especially in Africa, and the Far and Middle East, were afflicted by similar difficulties of cultural identity. These were the years in which national liberation movements succeeded in overthrowing colonialism, only to be brought up short by the realization that they needed to rely upon their old masters for the tools of mechanization. Sometimes modernism was invited in as an instrument of social transformation (as was the case in India); sometimes it was simply part of the equipment of international investment, in which case its arrival was often linked to foreign businesses. While the multistorey, air-conditioned offices and the expensively clad airports may have served as instant status symbols for those intent on attracting international capital, the results were usually crude and lacking in sensitivity to local traditions, values and climates. Even had there been architects keen on reinterpreting national traditions, they would have had difficulty finding relevant local precedents for such functions. As it was, cultural introspection was not high on the list of priorities of the typical patron.

This collision of old and new was another version of the crisis of industrialization which Western European countries and the United States had themselves begun to experience in the nineteenth century. But there were at least two major differences: the 'advanced' nations had themselves invented the Industrial Revolution; and they had had over a century to adjust to the far-reaching social and cultural changes it brought with it. The rapidly developing Third World country of the 1960s or 1970s (e.g. Iran or Nigeria) could find itself passing from a rural and agricultural economy to an urban and industrial one in the course of a single generation. Moreover, the tools (including buildings) with which this rapid change was achieved were imported ones: little wonder that a form of cultural schizophrenia should have emerged at the same time.

Pleas on the part of 'sensitive' Western observers that national and rural traditions be preserved or used as the basis of a new Regionalism were liable to fall on deaf ears in these circumstances, since peasant vernaculars could easily be identified with backwardness and the exploitation of rural labour. The case in favour of preserving fine nineteenth-century colonial buildings (which might also possess subtle adjustments to local traditions and climates) was even harder to make. The new arriviste classes seemed to wish to dissociate themselves from the weight of their recent history and to experience nothing less than the consumer 'freedoms' of the West. They grew greedy for glossy images with technological and international overtones which could affirm their own position. Skin-deep modern building (rather than any substantial form of modern architecture) was waiting in the West, all too ready to overwhelm yet another area of the international market. The irony was that so many countries, at last liberated from overt colonial rule, should so quickly have been persuaded to adopt vulgar versions of Western architectural dress.

By the early 1960s city centres were springing up around the world which seemed closer in spirit to Manhattan or modern London than to local, national or colonial precedents. The new ersatz International modern design with its standard clichés – the glass-slab hotel with balconies and kidney-shaped pool, the air-conditioned lobby with tinted plate-glass windows, the whitewashed concrete frame, etc. – was not *just* the face of 'Western economic imperialism', for at the same time parallel developments occurred in countries under Soviet influence. Perhaps Le Corbusier had been right when he had suggested that the machine caused a revolution of its own transcending political ideologies. Some of the same distressing features which had crept up on the cities of the West during the nineteenth century, and to which modern architecture had been an attempted answer, now impinged on places where there was the added problem of a split between adapted Western models and native values. The safety valve of an avant-garde, or at least an élite intent on visual quality and symbolic depth, was usually missing or else a pale shadow of its Western relatives.

One way out of the impasse was to try to put together some combination of the indigenous and the imported. Here fake Regionalism – with a few gingerbread 'historical' attachments over an ill-conceived modern structural box – was a constant danger. A sounder approach lay in the sort of 'modern Regionalism' (or 'Regionalist modernism') that had already begun in some countries in the 1930s (see Chapter 21) and which continued in other forms in the 1940s and 1950s (see Chapter 27). Here an effort was made to unearth fundamental lessons in local tradition and to blend them with an already evolved modern language. The problem came in translating these basic features, expressing regional adaptation, into a form appropriate to changing social conditions; no set recipes existed which could guarantee success, and lesser talents ran the risk of producing buildings which were pastiches of both modern *and* traditional forms.

In the transactions between industrialized and industrializing nations there were also collisions in the ways buildings were designed and put up. Modern architecture presupposed a division of labour between architects, manufacturers, engineers and construction workers, but in many 'underdeveloped' countries there were fewer

715 Hassan Fathy, New Gourna Village, Luxor, 1946–53

715

conducted an experiment at New Gourna, close to Luxor in the Nile Valley, in which he had schooled the local peasantry in Nubian techniques of earth construction using mud-brick walls, vaults and simple domes. These elements had stood the test of time and were well attuned to the resources and climate of the region; by contrast, 'modern' solutions were often unfunctional and ill-fitted to the particular environment. Fathy expressed his scepticism of modern architecture succinctly:

Modernity does not necessarily mean liveliness, and change is not always for the better ... Tradition is not necessarily old-fashioned and is not synonymous with stagnation ... Tradition is the social analogy of personal habit, and in art has the same effect of releasing the artist from distracting and inessential decisions so that he can give his whole attention to the vital ones.

Fathy's critique of industrialization and its accompanying forms was thus basic. He simply refused to accept the myths of progress and claimed that in most Third World circumstances the peasant could build better for himself than any architect. He argued that each individual family should build to suit its own needs, employing the wisdom of tradition rather than the expensive whims of professionals. This sounded convincing enough until one encountered the problems of very large numbers of poor people living in cities. Not only did earth turn into a precious commodity to be kept for agricultural purposes, but population densities required new solutions using materials like concrete and industrial brick. There can be little doubt that Fathy's romanticization of the peasant was part of a larger ideological quest for national roots; his philosophy would have particular appeal wherever the rural past was idealized and treated as a source of cultural mythology.

Fathy's experiments were conducted in a country whose vernacular had, in fact, suffered severe disruption, first under Ottoman then under European rule, and his programme involved something of a self-conscious revival of indigenous craft. In many Third World rural areas no such revival was necessary, as local traditions endured on their own. But even in these cases mechanization of the techniques and means of production might eventually affect the remotest countryside by drawing peasants to the city in search of jobs, and by introducing labour-saving tools which interfered with the continuity of rural craft traditions. The

steps in the process between conception and construction. Thus a building conceived on a Parisian drawing-board might require imported and expensive mass-produced components which entirely ignored local patterns of construction and labour when built in the Persian Gulf. The resultant forms were immediately at odds with centuries-old traditions of craftsmanship in which specific methods had been evolved to handle local materials. The practical logic behind regional style was undermined, and the delicate details and intuitions of handicraft were replaced by tatty, industrial building components.

The problems attached to importing foreign technologies were compounded by others related to the imposition of alien social theories, especially in the field of housing. What were conceived in Europe as low-cost models might be inappropriate when built elsewhere. In Egypt, for example, the philosopher/architect Hassan Fathy discovered that concrete-frame housing schemes built by the government in the 1950s were liable to be far more expensive in terms of money, transport costs and salaries than local, traditional, self-build models, and that they were at odds with non-Western ways of life. In his *Architecture for the Poor, an Experiment in Rural Egypt* (1973), he summed up his critical position of the previous three decades by suggesting that labour-intensive construction methods using local materials were the obvious answer. Starting in the mid-1940s, Fathy had intricate fabric of myths behind genuine vernacular forms would be disrupted by a new spirit of rationality. The uprooted urban proletariat would be cut off from its countryside origins, but at the same time hard put to adjust to the chaos of industrial urban life.

A crisis of this kind was felt acutely in places as far apart as India and Brazil by the early 1960s. Architects were powerless in the face of it. Neither bland, low-cost housing slabs, nor agrarian romanticism of the type espoused by Fathy were of much use in dealing with this urban poverty and overcrowding. Vast new self-built slums made of tin cans, cardboard and industrial wastes grew around the urban fringes. In these circumstances, 'Architecture' – whether glass-boxed or regionally sensitive – was a luxury. It is scarcely surprising that urban theories should have reflected a feeling of hopelessness in the face of such chaos. Indeed, the argument was put forth that the squatter communities and shanty towns did at least provide shelter for the poor, which the official housing agencies were unable to do. Around Cairo (to take but one example) the illegal settlements even hinted at the shape of a new, half-industrialized vernacular, employing a rough-shod concrete frame with a flat roof, a courtyard and infill walls of pot-tile and brick.

By the late 1960s in any case, concepts of total planning were under attack. This anti-absolutist attitude was well reflected in an experiment conducted in Peru for 'Barriada' housing in 1968, when a variety of well-intentioned international architects supplied a rational plan based on the patterns of life which had emerged in the slums themselves, and left each family free to alter the individual house at will. In Papua New Guinea,

in towns like Port Moresby, native inhabitants who had recently arrived from the country were encouraged to transform rural vernacular patterns which coped well with a tropical climate, rather than follow the earlier way of dreary, ill-adapted, imported house-types. One theorist, Z. Plocki, even went so far as to propose a 'New Guinea' architectural style, advocating a sort of 'modern Regionalist' approach and arguing in favour of a new vernacular applicable to the broad range of building tasks, large and small:

Most architectural styles were the products of their own societies. Its religious values, climate, technology, social and political structures dictated the need and style of buildings. Shapes, proportions and decorations were symbolic and had meaning, often ending up with strict architectural orders. This 'internal stimulus' created cultures and architectural expressions that differed greatly from each other … Many of the better examples are being preserved, but rarely copied, and when they are it's apparent they have no meaning … Today, with jet travel, intercontinental news media, cinema, political structures and cultural exchanges, the world is smaller and the bulk of the influences which dictate a style are international, based on technology and economics … But, even accepting the International Style, technology and the stimulus from the outside, and not copying the traditional, rules can be formulated within which architects can create architecture and a character that can become the Niuginian style.

Here it was admitted that new urban patterns required a new architecture aping neither traditional tribal nor imported forms. The pretensions of the modern movement towards 'universality' showed up with embarrassing clarity, as did the limitations of a superficial and nostalgic Regionalism. Moreover, Plocki extended his arguments to simple and self-built structures, not just the creations of the well-to-do. The few touches of local colour required by the tourist industry were scarcely adequate to the problem of defining a new post-colonial style. This would have to come partly

716

717

716 'Industrialized
vernacular': outskirts of
Cairo, 1970s

717 Urban village,
Hahuabada, Port
Moresby, Papua New
Guinea, mid-1970s

718 Charles Correa,
Gandhi Ashram Memorial
Museum, Ahmadabad,
1958–63

718

from 'within' and be a direct expression of new
life-patterns.

Where basic shelter was the concern, Regionalist
sensitivities may have seemed a remote luxury,
but it was still possible to treat middle-class or
institutional commissions as a laboratory for the
exploration of ideas that could have a wider
application in the future. As always, architectural
value would reside in the convincing synthesis of
the practical, the aesthetic and the symbolic, and in
the creation of a unity in harmony with the setting.
Vernacular structures could provide some clues for
achieving these ends by revealing age-old patterns
of adaptation. But the intention was rarely to make
a merely 'local' architecture. It was rather to
draw upon vital currents in contemporary world
development and to adjust them to particular
circumstances. The principles behind peasant forms
and behind past monuments believed to exemplify
national or regional traits were to be translated into
quite different materials and vocabularies. In a post-
colonial circumstance, the search for 'roots' was
often accompanied by a strong need to belong to a
wider world. Architects in developing countries in
the 1960s and 1970s sometimes sought out parallels
between indigenous principles and modern ideas
with an archaic or primitivist character. The work of

Indian architects such as Charles Correa, Balkrishna
Doshi, Achyut Kanvinde, or Raj Rewal reveals a
cross-breeding of this kind. In India, modernism
seemed to provide a suitable expression for a
post-colonial, secular order beyond differences of
caste and creed (something which a short-lived
'Hindu Revival' in the 1950s was not able to do).
The rugged late works of Kahn and Le Corbusier
supplied a major stimulus, especially as these already
embodied a reaction to local culture, technology and
climate. However, the generation which came to
maturity in the 1960s did not copy these examples
slavishly. They rather took them as a general
reference point, while seeking, by degrees, a
different spatial pattern, more truly related to the
flux and ambiguity of Indian life and, of course, to
the extremes of the weather.

Charles Correa's Gandhi Ashram Memorial
Museum in Ahmadabad of 1958–63 revealed
something of the tension between imported and
native sources of inspiration. The building was laid
out as a labyrinth of courts, shaded walkways and
low pavilions traversed by an ambling route. This
weave of positive and negative spaces was held
together by a staggered grid of plain brick piers
bearing concrete lintels, waterspouts and pyramidal
tiled roofs. The scale and detailing were deliberately

719

Mechanization was relatively slight, steel was scarce, air conditioning a luxury; in any case there was an ethical imperative to work with natural climatic devices, hand labour and cheap local materials. One can gauge the contribution to a specifically Indian strand of modern architecture in such buildings of the 1960s as the YMCA Engineering Hostel in Faridabad (1966) by Ranjit Sabikhi and the Design Group (with its rough brick volumes and its shaded streets); the Peons' Housing in the compound of the French Embassy in New Delhi (1967) by Raj Rewal (with its ingenious reinterpretation of the section for hot/dry climates found in desert dwellings); the Lecture Halls in the University of Jodhpur (1969) by Uttam Jain (with their staggered volumes in rugged masonry evoking but transforming the local vernacular); or the International Centre in New Delhi (1960–2) by the American immigrant architect Joseph Allen Stein (with its stone walls, trellises and comfortable relationship to the natural environment).

Doshi's development epitomizes the search for a modern architecture adjusted to Indian conditions. He had worked with Le Corbusier, and had absorbed the notion that a harmony must be found between industrialism and nature, but he did not copy his mentor's forms, and by degrees established a philosophy and a vocabulary of his own. Doshi's Institute of Indology in Ahmadabad (1961) made a successful translation of Gujarat's stone or timber

719 Balkrishna Doshi, Institute of Indology, Ahmadabad, 1961

720 Balkrishna Doshi, with Joseph Allen Stein and Jai Bhalla, Indian Institute of Management, Bangalore, 1977–85, shaded interior street

721 Balkrishna Doshi, mixed-income housing for the Electronics Corporation of India, Hyderabad, 1968–71

humble and restrained, and the interlocking of voids was inspired, in part, by the 'outdoor rooms' of the typical village. It was part of Correa's intention to evoke Gandhi's search for truth and dedication to simplicity; in fact the new building stood alongside the modest vernacular structure which had housed the Ashram, a place of symbolic importance in the Indian movement towards Independence. The 'noble poverty' of the Gandhi Ashram Memorial Museum had obvious debts to Le Corbusier's Sarabhai House (only a short distance away) and to Kahn's Trenton Bath House (half way around the world), but it also probed towards a characteristically Indian conception: a network of pillars and terraces encouraging the flow of air and an ease of social communication. It was in the early 1960s that young Indian architects made their pilgrimages to places like the desert city of Jaisalmer or to the sixteenth-century palace at Fatehpur Sikri where they found ensembles with courts and interpenetrating levels, deep overhangs for shade and ledges and screens between inside and outside. These historical examples, in combination with the sort of labyrinthine space pursued by architects like Van Eyck, helped them to find their way beyond the social limitations and climatic inadequacies of buildings as free-standing objects.

The Indian architects were faced with the needs of a society undergoing the drastic transition from rural to urban life, and they wished to find a modern equivalent to traditional architectural languages. The polarity between Nehru's progressive vision of industrialization and Gandhi's mythologized version of rural integrity was inherent in this formulation.

720

721

balconies into a modern expression in concrete. His several townships and housing projects of the 1960s and early 1970s (some of them for industrial combines, others public) revealed his continuing research into the problems of dwelling and community. He established simple standardized systems of construction and patterns of plan-arrangement adapted to climate and use, and laid these out in variations which enlivened the spaces between. His housing in Hyderabad of 1968–71 employed terraces and overhangs derived from the rough stone vernacular of the region, careful thought being given to orientation, shading, water channels and natural cross-ventilation, as well as to gradations between public and private space. Doshi tried to avoid the gaping voids between buildings, such as had been made at Chandigarh, and to create something closer to the tight-knit and dense street-patterns of traditional Indian towns. He was acutely aware of the irrelevance of indulging in a merely romantic peasantism, especially in a country where the peasant's lot was anything but romantic. His buildings were sometimes constructed for an emergent bourgeoisie and were rigorously designed to meet the demands and habits of a new India combining local values and Western ways. Forms were needed which crystallized this situation, and Doshi also drew what he needed from contemporary international theory and practice. After all, much of the finest architecture in Indian history had emerged from the cross-breeding of foreign and local influences. Even the hardest-boiled nationalist might have to admit that not all the best things were entirely home-grown.

It was in the 1970s that modern architecture in India began to achieve a distinct character of its own. One sign of this was an ever more complex order, integrating inside and outside through ambiguous layers of structure; another was polychromy, using a variety of local materials or washed-grit finishes instead of the tired period uniform of brick and concrete; another was the evolution of devices for dealing with light, sun and air – shading lattices, screens, etc.; and yet another was a deeper integration with landscape and tradition. The Indian Institute of Management in Bangalore of 1977–85 (by Doshi, in association with Joseph Allen Stein and Jai Bhalla) summarized these developments, with its shaded precincts linked by galleries, courts and shifting axes, its transitional ledges for informal meetings, its interwoven gardens, pergolas and walls, and its variations of light, shade and texture. It was as if the network-planning ideas of Team X had been fused with the multilayered spatial polyphony of traditional Indian complexes such as Fatehpur Sikri or the labyrinthine temple cities of southern India. In this quest for Indian identity the emphasis was placed on continuous principles rather than the differences between periods or cultures (Buddhist, Hindu, Muslim, Jain etc.). The hope was to reinvigorate 'substructures' from the past in the present: to infuse modern buildings with a certain Indian spirit.

The Third World architect did not have access to 'high' technology but he could take advantage of relatively cheap materials and manual labour. This combination allowed solutions that were

722

unthinkable in the more industrialized countries.
The main trade exhibition halls in New Delhi, the
'Hall of Nations' and the 'Hall of Industries', both
designed by Raj Rewal in 1971 (with Mahendra
Raj as consultant engineer) demonstrated how a
normally 'high-tech' structural system using steel
rods and junctions – a 'space frame' inspired by the
geodesic lattices of Buckminster Fuller – could be
built out of 'low-tech' reinforced concrete struts
using a labour-intensive construction process. The
price of steel was far too high in India to consider
realizing such a system in the usual way; but the
cost of labour would have been prohibitive had one
tried to construct the idea out of concrete in Europe
or America. Rewal's hybrid solution combined
both worlds in a judicious way and generated vast,
naturally lit interior spaces and sloping, pyramidal
exteriors. As well as a rigid structure, the hexagonal
network of beams also provided a sun-shading grille
which reiterated the principle, and something of the
geometrical pattern, of the traditional Indian *jali*
or sun-shading screen, but on a large scale. The
plans of the exhibition halls demonstrated Rewal's
interest in finding some common ground between

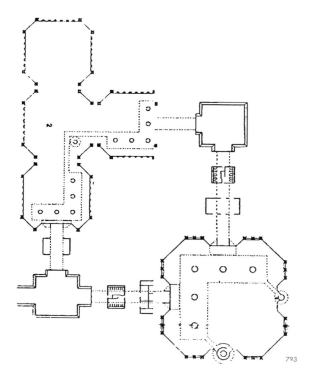

723

a latterday version of structural Rationalism, and the squares, circles and polygons which lay at the basis of so many Mogul and pre-Mogul buildings.

The Uruguayan architect/engineer Eladio Dieste thought of local technology as a basic feature of identity and was committed to the idea that Third World solutions 'must leave underdevelopment behind but without copying the processes and techniques of other countries'. His work relied upon structural systems in ceramic tile which were laminated together and combined as thin shell vaults, as wide-curved roof spans or as sinuous walls. These solutions mitigated the need for ribs and beams, and were much cheaper to construct than reinforced concrete. They were also adapted to the materials, labour and climate of Uruguay. Relying upon these basic principles, Dieste created, from the 1950s onwards, market halls, silos, towers, bus stations, houses, even churches, which were distinguished by their clear conceptual formulation, their powerful volumes, and their wafer-thin curved surfaces in tile with

rough mortar joints. In the long term, Dieste perhaps belonged to a tradition stretching back through Torroja to Gaudí, but even in his most utilitarian solutions he had the stamp of a genuine style: something rooted in his readings of contemporary 'agro-industrial' realities, and in a deep understanding of natural forces and pressures. The lateral thrusts of his market structures, for example, were held by bulging and undulating wall surfaces of impressive plasticity, while the continuous curved 'blades' of his self-supporting shells and tensile vaults were like 'sheets in space'. Dieste speculated upon the ethical and aesthetic implications of structural economy:

There are deep moral/practical reasons for our search which give form to our work: with the form we create we can adjust to the laws of matter with all reverence, forming a dialogue with reality and its mysteries in essential communion … For architecture to be truly constructed, the materials must be used with profound respect for their essence and possibilities; only thus can 'cosmic economy' be achieved … in agreement with the profound order of the world; only then can we have that authority that so astounds us in the great works of the past.

724

In Latin America the reinterpretation of tradition within modernity took diverse forms. Some of the most probing Mexican architects of the 1960s and 1970s sought out common ground between the vernacular and the monumental, while in no sense denying the inheritance of modern architecture. In this they relied upon the groundwork already done by the generation of Luis Barragán and Enrique del Moral, and upon visual filters provided by Mexican painters such as Rufino Tamayo. Together these revealed a plasticity charged with the primitive and the folkloric, and a 'palette' enriched by earthy or iridescent colours. Ricardo Legorreta extended these discoveries in an architecture of bold polychrome forms that provided a realistic response to large commissions while also evoking the magic of the Mexican vernacular. Legorreta's own studio in Lomas, Mexico City (1967), was inserted into a steep slope as a series of terraces and vaulted chambers, a maze of interior and exterior rooms. His Hotel Camino Real in Mexico City of 1968 was an inward-looking building of great spatial

725 Ricardo Legorreta, Hotel Camino Real, Mexico City, 1968, plan

726 Hotel Camino Real

727 Teodoro González de León with Abraham Zabludovsky, Colegio de Mexico, Mexico City, 1974–6, plan

728 Colegio de Mexico, interior

725

726

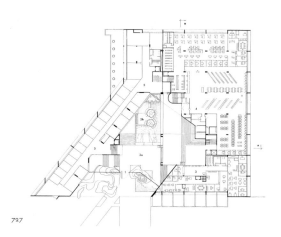

727

728

sophistication which combined bright-coloured, textured surfaces, filtered light, sequences of patios and sloping walls. With its wide entrance-ways for limousines sweeping around a turbulent pool between serrated coloured screens, and its broad glazing and ample stairs in the lobbies, it crystallized a certain image of the international high-life, but it also possessed a sense of calm and repose, and was undeniably Mexican in its mixture of sobriety and strong geometry. The gradual transition from active public areas to sequestered courts gave an atmosphere of retreat, even recalling the layout of old convents with their cloisters and courts. No less than India, Mexico possessed different strata of architectural history stretching back through colonial to pre-colonial eras. For Legorreta, the key to this heritage lay in a recurrent element which was shared by monument and peasant house alike: the wall:

Walls reflect our Mexican history. The pre-Hispanic wall – strong, ancient, stark and sometimes colourless – conveys the dignity of its makers and the magnificence of that civilization.

The Colonial wall has a different spirituality, not Spanish or Indian, but Mestizo, the blend of two races and religions …

Yet there is always a constant, humble, discreet wall that does not die … the glorious vernacular wall, a source of unlimited inspiration, strong, full of colour … decidedly Mexican.

In the same period, the Mexican architect Teodoro González de León (sometimes working with Abraham Zabludovsky) evolved a vocabulary for major institutional commissions using large portals, screens and pergolas in rough, bush-hammered concrete. There were certainly echoes of Le Corbusier's rugged late works (González de León had worked in the atelier in Rue de Sèvres in 1946), but there were also distinct and consistent spatial ideas such as the transition from the public to the private realm through covered walkways, or the organization of the plan around a central distributing-space containing layers of platforms, terraces and gardens. It was in buildings like the Mexican Embassy in Brasilia (1970), the Delegacion Cuauhtemoc (1972) or the Colegio de Mexico (1974–6) (the last two in Mexico City), that González de León brought his architecture to maturity. These worked with monumental themes such as the great portal made from hovering beams, the wide platform and the processional stair. There were subliminal echoes of the horizontal grandeur of pre-Columbian ruins, and of the angled shapes of ancient brackets, while the reinterpretation of the patio idea invoked a 'constant' type running through Mexican architecture from the beginning. González de León summed up his position as 'a continuing concern with "translating" the language of the International modern movement to a local reality'. In his mind, this was a latter-day version of a process of regionalization which other style-phases, such as the Romanesque or the Gothic, had undergone in their respective epochs.

729

This degree of confidence in the 'universalizing' aspect of modernism was not always present. Sometimes a more overt reference to local tradition was felt necessary. Sedad Hakki Eldem (see also p. 381) devoted his life's work to the formation of an authentic Turkish style blending national and international elements. His Social Security Complex at Zeyrek, Istanbul, designed in 1962–70, combined a modern expression of reinforced-concrete standardization (using stanchions, slabs and struts) with a subtle transformation of local timber frames and deep-cut overhangs, and even certain generic features of Ottoman stone monuments. The site for the building was a noisy street at the bottom of a hill of traditional wooden houses, and Eldem managed to respond to the dense scales and textures of the context while maintaining a coherent form. In plan, there was an interior street recalling something of a bazaar, while in volume and elevation the building managed to rhyme with Turkish prototypes in its proportions and articulation. The matter of 'identity' was not handled through a play with superficial imagery, but through a much deeper level of absorption of the past, manifesting itself in the character, rhythm, grammar and intonation of the finished building. Arguably, Eldem's achievement had relevance to a much broader dilemma of the 'developing world' succinctly formulated in the early 1960s by the French author Paul Ricoeur: 'This is the paradox: how to become modern and return to sources; how to revive an old, dormant civilization and take part in universal civilization.'

The Iraqi architect Rifat Chadirji, who constructed most of his buildings in and around Baghdad from 1960 to 1975, was committed to the notion of an architecture that was both modern and regionally sensitive. For him, it was a matter of bridging the gap between the liberating aspects of International modernism, and the elemental values which he sensed in the traditions of brick architecture in his own country running back through the severity of the earliest mosques to the ancient ziggurats of Ur and Nineveh. In projects

729 Sedad Hakki Eldem, Social Security Complex, Zeyrek, Istanbul, 1962–70

730 Rifat Chadirji, competition project for Tobacco Monopoly Offices and Stores, Baghdad, 1967. Ink on tracing paper. Chadirji Research Centre, Kingston upon Thames

such as the Tobacco Monopoly Offices and Stores for Baghdad (1967), he resorted to a vocabulary of stark brick rectangles and cylinders, punctured by arched openings and enlivened by a staccato rhythm of shaded accents. Beyond the evident features of composition there was a search for a certain national character emerging from the handling of massing, profile, silhouette and texture. Chadirji avoided the direct replication of traditional motifs, and also excluded conventional or rural technologies, because neither was compatible with what he called 'the mechanical-aesthetic mode'. In other words he wished to make an architecture that was right for rapidly changing social and urban conditions, that was authentically modern, that was unprovincial, and that might draw upon a powerful local tradition without just imitating it.

I hoped that my experiments would provide the raw materials for new architectural concepts, and thus leave a milestone on the road towards a regionalized international architecture.

While architectural positions were, in part, a matter of individual sensibility, they also reflected societal aspirations, myths and ideologies. The Indian, Mexican, Turkish and Iraqi examples just discussed were created in countries struggling in their respective ways with the question of modern national identities. These identities were formulated on the basis of 'unifying' secular ideals for the nation state, which sought to reconcile and integrate diverse religious and ethnic groups, regional and geographical differences, and strident contrasts between urban and rural worlds. The very notion of a 'national tradition' tended to mean an edited version of the 'local past' in which recent colonialism was seen as an alien intervention, but the remains of more ancient empires (some of them resulting from foreign occupation) were idealized as central to the national evolution. 'Modernization' usually implied mechanization of technology and a greater involvement with the global economy. Whatever the benefits, dependency and deracination were virtually part of the process. But there were places in the world that were more remote from the so-called 'norms' of industrial civilization, that were more inward-looking, and whose social and economic life relied more upon the rural base; in which case the continuity with local vernaculars was likely to be stronger. This was precisely the sort of 'integrity' which Fathy admired, and which he had attempted (without much success) to pit against the forces of rapid modernization in Egypt. From this perspective the question was less the modification of the modern movement to local inheritances than the slight adjustment of the continuing vernacular to modern ways and means.

The Medical Centre in Mopti, Mali, designed by André Ravereau in 1970, resulted from a transformation of sub-Saharan forms. The Centre had to be inserted between the fine old mud mosque and the River Niger. The solution was to distribute the functions in low, well-protected volumes, linked to one another by shaded walkways and disposed to maximize cross-ventilation. The style was simple

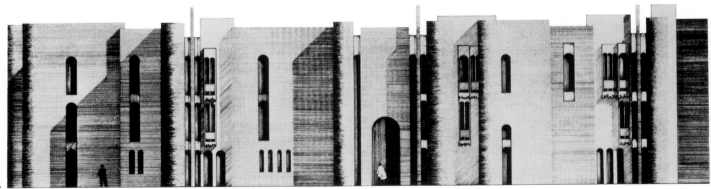

730

and unadorned, and in tune with local desert tradition. The typical rectangular geometries and flat roofs of the region, gashed by deep shadows and enlivened by repetitions and variations, might have been designed with a Cubist sensibility in mind. In the Medical Centre, the usual mud walls were strengthened (and given a longer life than normal) by the addition of cement. This technique was itself a happy mixture of the regional and the imported, since the mud and concrete could be cast together in wooden moulds. The contextual sensitivity of the scheme extended from its colour, materials, and shape (which merged with the neighbouring mosque), to the overall arrangement, which restated urban alleyways inside the building itself. Arguably these were strategies of a kind which had originated in the West (e.g. with Team X), but in Ravereau's design, the ideas were carried through to create a subtle blend of the old and the new, of the African and the European. Part of the richness of the building came from the use of local handicraft methods, which gave the forms a sensitive touch lacking in most industrialized buildings. To have achieved similar effects in the West would have been extremely expensive, as such craftsmanship was altogether rare. Ravereau attempted to incorporate the best qualities of both worlds.

The work of Geoffrey Bawa in Sri Lanka was attuned to the tropical landscape of the island and to its layers of architectural tradition, but also relied upon a cosmopolitan sensibility that was as open to the architecture of Wright as it was to ancient examples East and West. The local climate was hot and wet, so the relevant archetype was the hut on poles, with wide eaves protecting against sun and rain, and open edges permitting the flow of air. Over the ages, Sri Lanka had absorbed influences from elsewhere in Asia and from Europe, so that a characteristic vernacular of whitewashed walls and tiled roofs with openings for cross-ventilation had gradually emerged. Bawa's own studio in Colombo (designed in 1963 as a residence) reinvigorated this common usage in a unique poetic statement organized around a promenade through a sequence of alternating courts and enclosures protected by overhanging roofs. The moment one entered the forecourt one was drawn on to the axis by an alluring rectangle of greenery in the middle distance, and by the glimpse of a reflecting pool at the heart of the building. But the actual route was more circuitous, and linked laterally to gardens and open colonnades. Immediately above the pool was a gap through which air could circulate and monsoons pour –

731 André Ravereau, Medical Centre, Mopti, Mali, 1970

732 Geoffrey Bawa, Bawa Studio, Colombo, 1963

733 Bawa Studio, plan

731

732

733

a device found in the eighteenth-century southern
Indian palace of Padmanabhapuram, but which
also recalled a Roman 'impluvium'; a device which
Roman traders had brought to southern India nearly
two millennia ago. Meanwhile, the open range of
columns at the heart of the plan reinterpreted the
type of pillared hall (called '*dana salarwa*') found
in ancient Buddhist monasteries in Sri Lanka.
The Bawa Studio was thus a microcosm of an
island's architectural culture which fused together
influences from East and West while touching
upon the idea of architectural origins. It relied
upon local craftsmanship in stone and wood
(and so probably benefited from technological
insularity) and it contained ideas that would be
expanded by Bawa in buildings of greater size:
seaside hotels, a university, even the Sri Lankan
Parliament Building of 1981 (Fig. 800). The
traditional timber architectures of South East

Asia worked along the entire scale from hut, to house, to palace, to temple; in his way, Bawa investigated an analogous gradation but for buildings of modern function.

The view of tradition taken in Asian societies depended to some degree upon the historical, even political associations attached to past forms. After its Revolution in 1949, China embarked upon a tricky path of cultural self-definition that had to steer its way between Soviet influence, its own style of modernization and its ambivalence to its own great heritage. Grand state buildings such as the Great Hall of the People and the Museum of Chinese History and the Revolution built in the 1950s in Beijing reflected a classicizing line from Moscow, with mild touches here and there of bland ornament abstracted from the imperial tradition. The Building Ministry, erected in the 1950s, had more overtly nationalist overtones, but its Oriental touches were still skin-deep. Most matters of visual culture in China were highly controlled by the Ministry of Culture and by the propaganda arm of the Chinese Communist Party. A dogmatic framework of this sort did little to encourage visual excellence. Indeed, it was an ideological bias of the system that social function should usually be considered before formal quality. Evidently the idea that life-enhancing formal arrangements might have an elevating role to play in the formulation of a new society did not penetrate the official platitudes which stressed realism and obvious propaganda devices. Nor did Chinese tradition fare much better in Taiwan, the island to which most Chinese nationalists retreated after they lost the war to Mao Tse-tung. The main state monuments (e.g. the Monument to Chiang Kai-Chek in Taipei) revealed a similar awkward struggle to reconcile past images with new realities, and new images with past realities.

The dilemmas attached to the problem of public representation were not unique in any one society, creed or ideology: they were a basic feature of most societies facing rapid change. During the 1970s in the wealthier developing countries, there were several international competitions for 'cultural centres', museums, state palaces, and the like. One of these was organized in 1977 for the Royal National Pahlavi Library to stand in Tehran and embody (presumably) the magnificence of the

734

Shah's imperial court. Architects from all parts of the world made entries and indulged in confused efforts at 'cultural expression'. Alison and Peter Smithson, for example, departed from the safe path of their usual vocabulary (perhaps sensing that it lacked sufficient rhetoric to deal with the symbolic requirements of a state building which should be identifiable by the populace) and embarked upon a perilous road involving an imagery based upon the 'peacock feather' (a motif from the Shah's heraldry) and the dome (a traditional Persian symbol of authority). The result was a fussy Orientalism which failed entirely to capture the spirit of traditional monumentality. The mannered attempt at aping Islamic ornamental patterns recalled the Baghdad University scheme of over a decade before by Gropius and TAC, in which a bogus historicism took on the character of a Hollywood production of the Arabian Nights. Minoru Yamasaki's Dharan Airport in Saudi Arabia (1961) also came close to kitsch in its precast supports emulating palm trees, and its tracery screens supposedly modelled on traditional fenestration. However, the Western architect intent on even a genuine Regionalism might find himself faced by a client or an advisory body keen to have the latest from New York or London. For this scenario the theorist armed with his arguments about 'locale', 'identity' and 'genius of place' might be rejected as an agent of the West intent on holding the developing world back from 'progress'.

734 Beijing Institute of
Architectural Design,
Great Hall of the People,
Beijing, China, 1959

735 Minoru Yamasaki,
Dharan Airport, Saudi
Arabia, 1961

There were some situations in which the Western architect might be called in to design for religious or state institutions with highly defined traditional types of building such as mosques. In these cases, the conflict between new and old, imported and indigenous, was liable to be extreme. If the designer simply followed the formula of the traditional type he ran the risk of producing a sham, for his vocabulary and structural systems were not, in fact, traditional, and his forms lacked symbolic conviction. If he stuck to his own, modern vocabulary, he might fail to adhere sufficiently to the traditional elements and conventional meanings, and end up with a design that failed to communicate its purpose. The problem was not so very different in kind from that facing the architect in the West when presented with a cathedral: what was needed was an imaginative transformation of prototypes. However, it was rare that the Western architect working abroad grasped the spirit of the culture for which he was designing, and the employment of a native architect was no sure guarantee of authenticity either. At one extreme one might have a mosque that was indistinguishable from an office building; at the other, a bogus version of dome and minaret clumsily coated in industrial tiles and related uneasily to an entirely foreign constructional system in concrete.

Thus a major element of the architectural crisis of developing nations arose from a failure to establish an architectural language suitable to both modern and traditional tasks. It was no good pretending that modernization was not occurring, and hoping that the clock would stand still or even go backwards to some (entirely illusory) 'pure period', when foreign influences and chaotic changes were held not to have occurred. Even so, these fundamentalist sentiments were sometimes rehearsed in the confused search for 'cultural identity', whether this was defined in nationalist or pan-cultural terms. The architectural tradition in question might involve Islamic monuments or Melanesian wooden huts, but the traditionalist still shared all the predicaments of his revivalist counterpart in nineteenth-century Europe; even once a 'cultural essence' had been divined and linked to some 'Golden Age' or other in the past, there was still the problem of representing this core identity architecturally. One could not simply imitate the earlier forms; precedents needed transforming into meaningful images in the present.

1973 was a crucial year for the economies of the West because it was then that the 'oil crisis' came to a head. The revenue which subsequently flowed into the oil-producing countries was exchanged for Western expertise, including the talents of the architectural profession. A lull in Western production (often filled with paper projects and theoretical researches) corresponded with a boom in construction in previously undeveloped parts of the world which had usually been ignored by the West. It was not a happy contract of forces: get-rich-quick clients had little time to spend on niceties of architectural culture, and Western architects intent on financial gain were abysmally

735

736

ignorant of local customs and traditions. An epidemic of technological brashness hit the shores of the Persian Gulf and the fringes of the desert. The matter was further complicated by the relative lack of monumental and urban examples in once nomadic regions. What was needed was a thorough assessment, from first principles, of the formal suggestions inherent in climate, materials and social patterns. Unfortunately, such rigour was not usually applied, and the new buildings of Saudi Arabia or Kuwait looked as if they could have stood anywhere.

The boom in construction in the oil-rich states usually relied upon imported professional skills, imported ideas, imported manual labour, imported technologies, even imported materials. When 'local' expressions were attempted, they often took the form of veneers of horseshoe arches (which came, in any case, from Morocco) or attachments of fake screens placed in front of fully air-conditioned, sealed façades. But there were more intelligent responses to climate and to cultures in change. In his Intercontinental Hotel in Mecca of 1974 the German engineer Frei Otto incorporated the basic principles of a Bedouin tent but at a much larger scale, using steel cables and wooden slats instead of rope and cloth. The Hajj Terminal outside Jeddah in Saudi Arabia, designed by Skidmore, Owings and Merrill in 1980, also made use of the 'high-tech' tent, but this time on a grand scale and in a repeating module. The tent used a 'teflon' fabric

that combined great strength and durability with shade and insulation against solar radiation; it was held up on huge steel masts grouped in a formal way. The terminal was to shelter pilgrims who arrived by plane from all points of the world on their way to visit the Holy City of Mecca. Beyond the practical requirements of shade, circulation and standardized construction, the architects managed to deal effectively with the symbolic aspect of the task, evoking a space that was both egalitarian and dignified, and a structure that was traditional in its associations but on the cutting edge of technology.

The international resurgence in the cultural power and confidence of Islam was another major force to influence relationships between industrialized and less industrialized nations in the mid-1970s. It coincided with a period of soul-searching in the West, well reflected in a sort of architectural introversion and mannerism which sometimes replaced any serious attempt at expressing human values. 'Islamic revival' took many forms and was driven by many forces, among them a revulsion against the materialism which (it was held) could be traced to 'Western modernizing influences'. Architecture could not remain immune for long; the images of the debased International Style could easily be condemned as emblems of demonic secularism.

The backlash against 'modern values' implied nothing distinct beyond a greater reverence for traditional moral and aesthetic forms. Once again,

736 Louis Skidmore,
Nathaniel Owings and
John Merrill, Hajj
Terminal, Jeddah, 1980

737 Jørn Utzon,
National Assembly
Building, Kuwait, 1972

738 National Assembly
Building, sketch plan

the issue of identity was at stake, but Pan-Islamic sentiments could even be manipulated to imply a community of culture between Morocco and Manila; with the wave of a wand schisms, national boundaries and centuries of change could all be overlooked. It was a mood which was hard to translate into an architectural philosophy, let alone architectural forms. The traditionalist designer who pretended that 'modern' and 'Western' models could be expunged courted a number of teasing difficulties. He had to decide on the common denominators of 'Islamic architectural identity' (a tall order when one included the whole Muslim world, and when one admitted that many factors other than religion influenced forms). He felt compelled to believe that 'the nature of Islam' was some fixed and unchanging entity, which it clearly had not been. And, like any other revivalist, he had to decide which period of the arts was closest to the 'essential Islam', then to restate these forms without debasing them. There were other tricky issues arising from real changes in functions, technologies and needs. There was the further theoretical difficulty of deciding whether or not architectural quality might transcend religious dogmatism.

The pressure to look backwards did not have to lead to architectural regression, especially when tradition was probed for its underlying ideas. The National Assembly building in Kuwait, designed by Jørn Utzon in 1972, was one of the rare examples of an effective monumental statement in the Middle East, and gained much of its force from its success at combining local references, generic traditional types and a modern sense of space. The architect had the difficult task of giving shape to a unique governmental system combining regal, tribal, oligarchic and bureaucratic elements. At a practical level, it was a question of making all departments visible and available from the entrance, and it was this that led to the idea of a central street with the main assembly to one side and a vast hall open to the sea at the head. Individual departments were restricted to two storeys in height and were arranged round their own courtyards. These 'cellular' units could be added bit by bit, so that in plan the Assembly Building was like an abstraction of a Middle Eastern city with a main bazaar as a spine, but with amorphous edges extending towards the rectangular boundary. The entire complex was

737

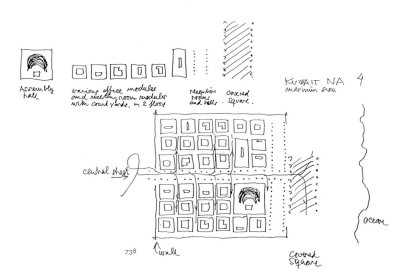

738

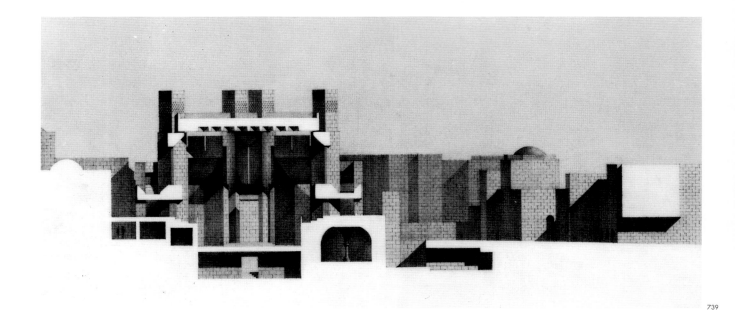

covered by a spreading roof, and in the case of
the main chamber and hall there was an uncanny
resemblance to the billowing forms of a tent, though
seen from a distance the bowing parasol over the
entrance also triggered associations with a dhow,
the national symbol of Kuwait. The structure was
conceived as a precast system in concrete, with
tapered columns of a unique curved plan visibly
and demonstrably holding the roof up. Utzon
referred to 'the purity of Islamic structure', but his
handling of concrete, light and space also echoed
the probity and *gravitas* of Le Corbusier's
Parliament at Chandigarh. The conception of the
sheltering roof as an image of the state invoked
tribal memories to do with the princely tent of the
elders. The following passage reveals the depth of
Utzon's penetration of a local archetype:

The dangerously strong sunshine in Kuwait makes it necessary to
protect yourself in the shade – the shade is vital for your existence –
and this hall which provides shade for the public meetings could
perhaps be considered symbolic of the protection a ruler extends
to his people. There is an Arab saying: 'When a ruler dies, his
shadow is lost.'

Denys Lasdun's unbuilt proposal for the
Hurva Synagogue of 1979 also relied upon the
interpretation of old ideas in modern forms and
upon the symbolic response to climate in order to
evoke an appropriate sense of ritual and assembly
for an institution. But in this case the context was
an ancient city combining many historical layers.
The site stood in the Old City of Jerusalem in the
Jewish Quarter over the ruin of a nineteenth-
century synagogue shelled in the 1948 war. It had
been occupied by the Jordanians until 1967 when
it had once again come under Israeli control, and
the decision had been taken to rebuild. Several
proposals were made by Louis Kahn in the early
1970s, with massive, sloped walls and a plan
probably intended to recall the First Temple.
Lasdun's solution was less forbidding but no
less monumental. The basic idea was a hovering
concrete parasol roof supported by polygonal
towers demarcating a shaded room and emerging
from enclosing stone walls cut by openings. The
lower part of the ruin was preserved at the base
and the new structure was made to grow from the
old. It absorbed the geological facets and fortress
forms of several eras of the city's history and took
on the character of a miniature citadel. Light was
filtered in under the overhanging roof, and the
faceted towers also functioned as ventilation shafts.
Lasdun thought of the main chamber as a 'piece
of the city', and of the building as a whole as an
intensified form of the surrounding urban patterns

of streets, squares and cubic buildings. There were
three main zones in the plan: the entrance, the
central chamber (with its upper, women's gallery)
and a final compartment glimpsed through a
vertical fissure in the structure. An 'abode of
vacancy', this was meant to be bathed in a golden,
otherworldly light. For the Hurva, no attempt was
made at employing domes or other elements of local
usage, because they were not specific to synagogues
as a type, and because they were not part of the
Lasdunian conviction and language. None the less,
the lighting system under the parasol gave a hooded
character to the interior, while the roof provided
an almost primeval feeling of shelter: in the most
elemental terms it restated the meaning of a sacred
umbrella marking a holy place. The silhouette of the
ensemble evoked associations with tabernacles and
ancient altars, but without relying upon devalued
signs. Lasdun 'rethought' the significance of a
synagogue in terms of an authentic architectural
language (strata and towers) already attuned to
the idea of 'congregation', and gave shape to an
institution in an idealized form. He sidestepped
caricatures of 'identity' by relying upon a resonant
abstraction which distilled memories of the place
and evoked a spiritual presence through the
articulation of space, geometry, structure and light.

The obsession with cultural representation
which came into focus in the 1970s was ever in
danger of ignoring issues of architectural quality
and authenticity. A building that fitted some
passing prescription, that illustrated values noisily
proclaimed as 'Islamic', 'Indian', 'Nationalist',
'Communist' (or whatever), was not necessarily
architecture of lasting quality. Indeed, too facile
an acceptance of conventional iconography could
lead quickly to kitsch. The post-Second World
War era began with the emancipation of various
architectural cultures from a debased international
formula; this was desirable and inevitable. But
Regionalism could easily become the facile tool of
religious and nationalist dogmatism of a sort which
left no room for the universal aspects of both the
human condition and the language of art. What was
needed was a blend of the local and the universal
which avoided the limitations of each and led to
forms of lasting symbolic resonance. Skin-deep
modernism and glib traditionalism were evils to
be avoided in every part of the world.

32
pluralism
in
the
1970s

740 Aldo Rossi,
Gallaratese Apartment
Block, Milan, 1969–76

One cannot pin a particular date to the emergence of a general state of mind, but sometime around 1970 there seems to have been a subtle shift in the ground of architectural thinking. By degrees a new status was accorded to the architectural image and to the role of the symbol in the making of forms. While the preoccupation with meaning often degenerated into a surface manipulation of signs and references, it also prompted reflections upon the basis of architectural language, and upon the role of precedent in design. The phenomenon called, loosely, 'Post-modernism' relied upon an obvious reuse of the past; but it did not have an exclusive tenure of tradition, and the re-examination of history took several paths, some of them extending discoveries already made in earlier modern architecture.

It is never safe to rely upon a period's own version of itself, since propaganda and polemic play such a large part in the formation of the 'official' picture. In the 1970s, the usual problems of separating reality from rhetoric were compounded by an increasing emphasis on the printed word and photograph. Movements and 'isms' were debated on the basis of a few drawings in magazines without so much as a brick being laid or a concrete slab poured. Factions of the avant-garde grappled for control over the media and over university departments to assert that their own ideas (rather than someone else's) were the 'right' ones for the times. Architects even developed the habit of writing their own histories (sources and all), thus leaving the impression that the most significant features of the period must be the ones most published and discussed.

By the end of the decade it was common enough to hear the refrain, 'modern architecture is dead.' This slogan encouraged the opinion that one period was in its decadence and that another one was about to dawn. Supporters of this view played down continuities with earlier modern architecture and did all they could to inflate the originality of architects selected to fit a 'postmodern' label. Opponents hung on to the habits of their upbringing, claiming that these stemmed from some core identity of 'modernism'. Neither was subtle about invention and its usual debts to the past, and each assumed a simplistic and monolithic version of modern architecture. In fact, both sides in the dispute were far too worried about superficial aspects of style, and both overlooked the level at which truly inspiring continuities were likely to exist: that of underlying principles and generating ideas. The 'newest' (and rarest) thing that one could hope for was a building that was simply very good, whatever its relationship to traditions near and far, however it fitted the prescriptions of the fashion-mongers or the yearnings of the old guard.

The backlash against what was called (simplistically) 'modernism' took several forms, but the most obvious target was the highly destructive 'urban renewal' which had been undertaken in the 1960s. The fact that this was often a travesty of modern planning ideas did nothing to alleviate the oppressive effect of the alienating results. The well-meaning frameworks supplied by Europe's welfare states or by wealthy patronage in the United States had exposed too many of their own contradictions for their adopted architecture to go unscathed. Modern architecture was blamed for disregarding human needs, for not blending in, for lacking signs of identity and association, for being an instrument of class oppression. The counterculture of the late 1960s had little time for modernist pretensions towards universality, and ideas derived from the theory of signs were drawn in to reveal the supposed 'arbitrariness' and 'conventionality' of architectural meanings. Relativism mounted its attacks on the sociological determinism which mattered to the functionalist wing of the modern movement, and revisionist art history undermined the legend of an inevitable modern development. Within the fold, the death of the modern masters may have had a further demoralizing effect by removing charismatic leaders. With progressive fervour doused and a profession increasingly uncertain of its aims, it is scarcely surprising that the word 'crisis' should have been everywhere in book titles and articles. For some it was a 'crisis' of consumer society, for others a 'crisis' of professional identity, for others again a 'crisis' of modernism. Increasingly, one encountered the suggestion that the way forward lay in going back; whether it was to the golden days of radiant modern architectural faith or to some earlier phase of supposed certainties.

But while there was all this vocal scepticism about the tenets of 'modern architecture' – or what were thought to have been the tenets – wholesale rejections of one aspect were often accompanied by unconscious continuations of another. In some cases (e.g. the designs of the New York Five or those of the Italian neo-Rationalist Aldo Rossi) there was actually a looping back, a re-examination of anterior forms. Even those happy to be called 'postmodernists' drew upon devices of fragmentation, collage and planarity with an obvious modern pedigree. One should be on the lookout, then, for a certain divergence between rhetoric and actual production, between words and forms. The tendency of avant-gardes to claim that they represent the essence of a period needs to be exposed for what it is: historical determinism in disguise. The historian who identifies with the interests of a single school or clique sacrifices the possibility of a balanced view. As time elapses, claims to revolutionary innovation usually seem excessive, and historical debts begin to show. Events, ideas, personalities blend into longer perspectives. Movements once claiming complete opposition to one another are found to have shared some common ground; even styles of criticism and rejection are seen to have a certain pedigree.

No single stylistic or ideological label can do justice to the range of ideas and buildings produced in the 1970s. A historical section sliced through the middle of the decade reveals the coexistence of several persuasions with varying lineages, all the way from 'high tech' to the cultivation of the archaic. As in most periods, the myths, obsessions and preoccupations of a number of generations and individuals lived side by side. Architects like Utzon, Kahn, Lasdun and Scarpa produced mature works of a high order which evaded changing fashion; this did not mean that they should be regarded as 'out-of-date'. Philip Johnson changed like a chameleon to keep his architecture adjusted to the latest trends; this did nothing to give his work the depth that it needed. James Stirling's style altered drastically as he tried to defer to context and precedent, and a younger generation intent on the self-conscious manipulation of formal language (e.g. Michael Graves, Arata Isozaki) began to receive major commissions. It was in these years, too, that Frank Gehry's buildings in southern California gave new life to the idea of Cubist assemblage, while Tadao Ando's minimalist houses in Japan opened the way to another link between modern reductivism and certain essentials of Japanese tradition. As the last chapter suggested, basically modern concepts were 'rethought' in diverse cultures and lands. Whatever else one may say about the 1970s, it entirely lacked uniformity. It would be futile to suggest a main line, unwise to attempt an equation between style and quality; parochial to fix one movement as the key one. In what follows, 'isms' are avoided as much as possible, broader tendencies being examined through individual works. Buildings of analogous function have been grouped together, as this provides some basis for comparison.

One can start with housing. An earlier chapter traced reactions to the Unité idea, and criticisms of it, unfolding around the need to give dwellings a greater sense of identity. Since it was felt that a major problem of pre-war housing had been a failure of communication between architects and users, several kinds of 'advocacy planning' were attempted in the 1960s. The Byker Wall Housing scheme for Newcastle (1969–75) by Ralph Erskine (yet another member of Team X) was designed on the basis of this sort of dialogue which included future inhabitants in the actual design process. The resulting Byker 'Wall' nevertheless bore the imprint of the Erskinian architectural style. The site was close to the path of an intended motorway and sloped down gently to rows of nineteenth-century houses. The solution was a serpentine wall: a long strip of varying height modulated to the uneven terrain, turning its back to the north against the noise of the traffic, and opening out to the south where smaller terraced houses with gardens were situated in a sheltered precinct. Byker combined solid pragmaticism with a certain Nordic Romanticism – a mood which was reinforced by brooding silhouettes and sombre brickwork – and from a distance it had something of the character of a rampart. The idea of a protective wall of housing had occurred already in Erskine's college design for Clare Hall, Cambridge (1969–70), but stretched back further to his schemes of the 1960s for settlements north of the Arctic Circle, where barriers against cold winds and a rugged, hostile landscape had been essential; it was even reminiscent of Aalto's perimeter walls and curved slabs (e.g. Baker House). At Byker, the collective

741

wall was mated with other typical Erskinian images: the shed roof (to suggest domesticity and to protect against rain), sprawling stick balconies in bright colours (to add human touch and variety), interwoven bricks of different colours (to break down the mass), and delicate entrance structures (to ensure a gradual transition from public to private worlds). Erskine's interest in defining territory and responding to local patterns of life recalled certain preoccupations of Team X. Of the various 'anti-heroic' housing schemes of the 1970s, Byker was one of the most successful socially and architecturally.

Despite the attempts of champions of Byker to argue that the good folk of Newcastle had virtually generated the architecture on their own, it was obvious that the imagery had resulted from a formal and symbolic interpretation. The populist camp rejected the strategy for precisely this reason, claiming that housing should be left to individuals, and not 'monumentalized' by architects with 'imposing concepts'. Radical criticism even went so far as to discount the role of formal planning altogether, as if good moral intentions on their own were sufficient to create a decent home. One brand of this anti-élitist opinion suggested that it would be better to imitate the types of existing 'vernaculars' than to allow any further housing schemes on the Unité model, but remained unclear about *which* vernaculars should be used as examples. It became politically respectable in the mid-1970s (especially in housing agencies in Western Europe) to ape hip-roofs and mouldings in the belief that this was an automatic guarantee of a 'humane image' of the dwelling.

The linear apartment block for the Gallarate district of Milan (1969–76) by Aldo Rossi was in strong contrast both to the Byker Wall and to the vernacular revival. The contrived complexities of Byker were replaced by a gaunt and repetitive simplicity; its serpentine form and picturesque accents were superseded by an obsessive linearity; its nooks and crannies were replaced by a monotonous street gallery running from one end to the other. The strip of housing marked off one edge of an enclave close to an autostrada intersection, and a bold gesture was needed in such a vacuous setting. It seems that Rossi's design strategy was situated between what he called 'inventory and memory' and involved the deliberate fusion of earlier types. In the Modena Cemetery (1972) the ancient mausoleum

742 Aldo Rossi, project for Modena Cemetery, 1972, planometric drawing

743 Aldo Rossi, Gallaratese Apartment Block, Milan, 1969–76

744 Josef Paul Kleihues, perimeter block housing project for Vinetaplatz, Berlin-Wedding, 1971–7

742

743

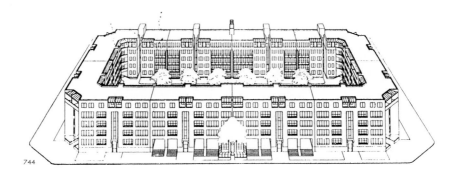

744

had been cross-bred with the abstract visions of Boullée or Ledoux from the late eighteenth century; in the Gallaratese, Rossi seemed to pull together the organization of the Unité, the street-deck, melancholy reminiscences of northern Italian arcades (with some help from Giorgio de Chirico's metaphysical cityscapes) and the idea of a viaduct:

… there is an analogical relationship with certain engineering works that mix freely with both the corridor typology and a related feeling I have always experienced in the architecture of the traditional Milanese tenement where the corridors signify a life style bathed in everyday occurrences, domestic intimacy and varied personal relationships.

Rossi's book of 1966, *L'Architettura della città*, had tried to establish the case for a set of urban archetypes, founded on 'basic' patterns, which were held to have existed before the chaos of industrialization. His idea was that one should transcend functionalism by an analogical mode of design, blending the earlier types with present-day needs in a language of simple geometries. Rossi's theory of urban types recalled Terragni's earlier reflections on the ancient beginnings of architecture, and there can be little doubt that Rossi's style, with its dead-pan rows of windows punched through simple white surfaces, owed a good deal to the prototypes of the Italian Rationalism of the 1930s. It was not entirely misleading then that the term 'neo-Rationalist' should have been coined to describe the work of Rossi and his movement named 'Tendenza'. The stripped forms of the 1930s were purged of their Fascist associations and given an almost nostalgic character. Neo-Rationalist sensibility delighted in axial composition and in reduction to the most primary geometries. Rossi's evocative sketches of beach cabins, lighthouses,

barns and vernacular structures in the Po Valley suggested a wistful involvement with northern Italy's past, and even a latent classicism. He wrote: 'The relationship between geometry and history, that is, the historical application of forms, is a constant characteristic of architecture.' Rossi's influence was considerable, especially in Spain and in the Ticino in southern Switzerland (e.g. Mario Botta), where a mood of revulsion against the technological aridity of so much modern design set in during the early 1970s. His ideas were also popularized in the United States where their classical undertones were rather wilfully linked to Italophile obsessions with Terragni and Palladio.

Rossi's insistence on 'locus, monument and type' was timely: it arrived when several others were reconsidering traditional ways of organizing urban space. German architects like Oswald Mathias Ungers and Josef Kleihues were confirmed in their belief that urban planning must reject the free-standing, island slab and rely instead upon the continuity of old typologies such as the street, the façade and the perimeter block with a courtyard (e.g. the IBA Housing in Berlin). The neo-Rationalist preoccupation with the transformation of monumental urban types such as the wall, the aqueduct, the bridge and the gate, found echoes far and wide. In France, for example, Paul Chemetov and Henri Ciriani evolved several projects which were like elongated bars raised on piers. Ciriani's Noisy-le-Grand Housing at Marne-la-Vallée (1978–83) was yet another descendant of the Unité (which had itself, after all, been partly inspired by ancient Roman aqueducts) that resorted to the theme of an extensive oblong, articulated in this case by rectangular screens and layers. The large

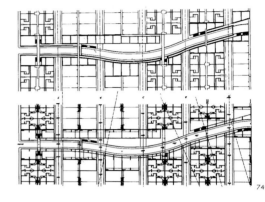

745

746

urban piece was here conceived as a device for anchoring the flux of the urban periphery in an increasingly sprawling suburban (or 'ex-urban') situation.

Alvaro Siza's restructuring of the entire quarter of Quinta da Malagueira on the outskirts of the Portuguese town of Evora (started in 1977) represented an attempt at giving a definite urban form to a peripheral area between the old city and the countryside. The whitewashed cubic forms, terraces and voids filled with deep shadow embodied a response to a particular landscape and place. Siza established a low-rise, high-density pattern which transformed the traditional patio and street from the Portuguese vernacular to deal with changing social realities. The new district was given a clear hierarchy and vertebrate order by means of elevated bridges carrying pipes and services (an allusion to local aqueducts running from the city walls out to the landscape). Siza's intentions were normative: he wished to establish elements and a system for handling the typical situations of the individual dwelling, its place in the community and the transitions from public to private. Quinta da Malagueira relied upon a personal reading of a climate and culture, upon

a common construction system using concrete and pot-tile, and upon a fresh interpretation of modern prototypes such as Oud's unbuilt Strandboulevard housing project of 1917 in Holland (Fig. 175). At the same time, the rows of rectangular units and parallel streets running through an archaic and virtually Mediterranean landscape of olive groves evoked more ancient memories, such as the grid layouts of Roman *insula* housing. Siza revealed something of his attitude to the past when he stated: 'Architecture is increasingly a problem of use and reference to models. Architects invent nothing. They work continuously with models which they transform in response to the problems they encounter.'

These three housing schemes – Byker, Gallaratese and Quinta da Malagueira – suggest different ways in which the inheritance of modern architecture could be extended into new expressive territories. A similarly broad range of ideological commitments and vocabularies emerges if one analyses architectural solutions to the workplace in the 1970s, particularly office buildings. By the late 1960s, of course, the standard modern types were the glass-box skyscraper and its suburban relative, the glass-box on its side. It is scarcely surprising that attempts should have been made to enrich these bald formulae by such means as atriums, gardens or balconies; the luxurious Ford Foundation by Roche and Dinkeloo in New York of 1963–8 incorporated all these devices and also tried to open the building to the street visually. Another approach was represented by the Willis Faber Dumas Building in Ipswich, England (1975), by Norman Foster. In this case no critique of modern technology was implied; quite the contrary, the imagery of the building rejoiced in the appearance of a precision mechanism. However, the partitioning and rigid grid of the usual type were broken open on the interior to create an entirely continuous work space, with moving staircases passing through it (the free plan taken to its logical, and not completely practical, conclusion). The finishes of chrome and stainless steel were matched by the glazed cladding, which embodied a similar ethos. The reflecting glass was clipped on without any intervening struts or mullions, and the resultant taut curtain-wall skin mirrored the setting. The building was curved in plan to fit the shape of the site, and this maximized the play of reflections. Foster's building combined executive 'chic' with a reinterpretation of Mies van der Rohe's 'universal space'; it drew on both the minimalist skyscrapers of the American 1960s and the original crystalline fantasies of the 1920s. The Willis Faber Dumas Building, and Foster's other designs of the period (e.g. the Sainsbury Centre for the Visual Arts at the University of East Anglia, 1978) thus represented an extension of the technological wing of the modern movement. However, with their elegant and crisp styling, they had an entirely different character from their 'first machine age' ancestors like the Van Nelle factory: the Utopian driving force was not recoverable; there was a (probably inevitable) loss of intensity in the later versions of mechanistic imagery.

747

748

The Centraal Beheer Office Building at Apeldoorn in Holland (1968–72) by Herman Hertzberger represented quite a different human position, which embodied scepticism about the values of a technocracy. Where the Willis Faber Building celebrated the continuous, open work space, the Centraal Beheer concentrated on the private domain of the individual worker; where the former worked inwards from a uniform envelope, the latter was assembled inside to out on the basis of small standardized units related to activity and human scale. The Hertzberger design was like a kasbah of alleyways, tortuous streets and level changes, but it was still based on a module. Where the high-tech position implied a total control of image and finish by designers and management, the rough concrete blocks, precast beams and

irregular trays of the 'workers' village' embodied an ideal of participation and implied that the structure would be incomplete until dressed in each individual's knick-knacks, plants and place-making symbols. The Centraal Beheer was a worthy descendant of Van Eyck's Orphanage of over a decade before and, like its prototype, sought to create a variety of ambiguous spaces on the basis of a small-scale standardized kit of parts. The idea of interior galleries and trays was perhaps traceable in the long run to Wright's Larkin Building; however, the Centraal Beheer lacked the coherence of this great example, especially on the exterior, where the forms were somewhat mute and confused.

By contrast, Denys Lasdun's European Investment Bank outside Luxembourg (1973–80) presented a clear and dominant overall form without destroying a sense of human scale. The building had to be a ceremonial headquarters as well as an office space, and the site, close to the ravines of the Val des Bons Malades, virtually demanded a scheme attuned to landscape. Lasdun modified his usual strata and towers to create a pinwheel plan with four low wings of horizontal emphasis cascading to meet the land masses at various levels. Where the four wings came together, the ceremonial zones were situated, traversed by a diagonal axis running from the *porte-cochère* at the entrance to the document-signing room at the far end; this was set under a low soffit supported on piers standing in a pool. The entrance-way was clearly signalled by directional piers and towers which set up a strong 45-degree axis; the sequence as a whole recalled the College of Physicians or the National Theatre, if not Lasdun's fascination with compressed and expanding spaces in Baroque architecture. The office wings were designed on the same system of horizontal floors and soffits but their treatment was sculpturally less intense. The slabs were designed to provide natural cooling and heating, and each office was given an opening window protected from glare with a view over nearby trees. The result was a building which countered the dullness of the usual glass box with humanity and dignity, but without loss of efficiency. The European Investment Bank was a palace among office buildings, but its forms were closely related to human purposes and to the geology and topography of a particular natural

setting. Devices derived in the long run from
Le Corbusier's Dom-ino skeleton or from the
stratification of Wright were given an entirely new
meaning.

Skyscraper design in the 1970s also reveals a
search for varied solutions on the basis of the
discoveries of the previous decades. Here was
a type in a true sense: a problem to which strings
of solutions had been worked out over nearly
a century. By the end of the 1960s, the curtain
wall/box formula for tall office building was
revealing its limits. Minoru Yamasaki's two
enormous slabs for the World Trade Center
at the base of Manhattan (1969) were an extreme
statement of the minimalist notion of the free-
standing object standing in a plaza. But they were
the end of a line, and in the 1970s new researches
were opened up. Two areas of skyscraper design
seem to have come in for particular scrutiny: the top
(either for practical reasons to do with servicing or
solar energy, or else for symbolic purposes), and
the bottom (frequently opened out as an atrium
connected to the street). The Citicorp Headquarters
in Manhattan (1978) by Hugh Stubbins was one
variant of this scheme, taking advantage of a zoning
law permitting extra floors in exchange for public
space at the base. Stylistically it was a sort of 'high-
tech' revival of the International Style, replete with
strip windows and taut volumes clad in a reflecting
metallic skin.

Another approach to the dull glass-box formula
was, of course, to adorn it but without severely
challenging its interior limitations. This dubious
form of 'enrichment' was pursued in the context of
the Manhattan skyscraper by Philip Johnson, in his
design for the American Telephone and Telegraph
building on Madison Avenue, 1979. Johnson
revived the tripartite division of the tall building so
often used in the American 1920s and traceable in
the long run to Sullivan's skyscrapers of the 1890s.
He emphasized the entrance-way with an arch
(intended to be reminiscent of Brunelleschi's early
fifteenth-century Pazzi Chapel in Florence), the
lobby with grand columns (supposedly based on
a hypostyle), and the top with a broken pediment
(which journalists compared to Chippendale
furniture). When the design was published it was
proclaimed as a wholesale rejection of modernism
and linked to so-called 'postmodernist' tendencies.
In fact Johnson had done little more than stick some
historical quotations on to a standard office space;
most of what was called 'postmodern' tended to be
cosmetic. The reduction of the skyscraper to a
cartoon-like sign in the cityscape was no doubt
symptomatic of a pressure to treat architecture as
a marketing device.

In the 1970s there were several skyscrapers which
relied upon an ingenious fusion of concepts drawn
from different prototypes within the modern
movement. The Banco de Bilbao in Madrid

749

750   Minoru Yamasaki,
World Trade Center,
New York, 1969

751   Hugh Stubbins,
Citicorp Headquarters,
New York, 1978

752   Philip Johnson,
American Telephone and
Telegraph Building, New
York, 1979

750

751

(1972–80), designed by Javier Saénz de Oíza, was broadly speaking in an 'organic/technological' tradition. Its structure was based upon the idea of cantilevered concrete rafts every six floors into which four-storey steel-framed armatures were inserted. This concept was expressed in an articulated, round-cornered tower in which the glazing was sliced by steel mesh balconies and rails for cleaning and shading the windows. There were echoes of the dense, bronze colours and sharp details of Mies's Seagram Building, although the guiding prototype was clearly Wright's Johnson Wax Laboratory Tower of 1943–5. The National Lottery Building (1971) in Mexico City by David Muñoz Suárez, Ramón Torres and Sergio Santacruz also worked with a staggered section (allowing some

triple-height public areas), and this was inserted into a triangular plan fitted to a site that was sliced off diagonally by roads. The main volume was lifted up into space on slender steel stanchions grouped towards the middle of each façade plane. These were laid into the glazing and rose the whole height of the building. The result was a tense pattern of visual forces in which aspiring verticals were combined with hovering horizontal planes. The sharp profiles and subtle transparencies inevitably recalled Miesian prototypes such as the crystalline Friedrichstrasse skyscraper proposal of 1921.

A comparison of museums in the 1970s reveals an analogous variety of architectural approaches and lineages, although the museum was scarcely a highly defined type like the skyscraper. Beyond

752

matters of lighting, display, sequence and organization, there was the tricky question of institutional representation, and here there were few fixed conventions. The Pompidou Centre in the Place Beaubourg, Paris, by Renzo Piano and Richard Rogers (1971–7) took the image of the flexible *machine à cultiver* to the extreme. The programme was for a mixed-use 'cultural centre' combining the old Musée de l'Art Moderne, a public library, an audio-visual centre and a large amount of exhibition space. The site was to one side of the Marais, facing a square not far from the mid-nineteenth-century market sheds (demolished just previously) of Les Halles. Evidently the aim was to make a 'popular' institution rather than a 'palace of culture', and it was this aspect of the brief which clearly appealed to Piano and Rogers (who were chosen by competition). They designed the building as a vast, serviceable hangar supported by a megastructural steel-tubed frame. The floor slabs were made to span adjustable interior spaces, and the elevations were entirely glazed. An appropriate

ornament was provided by festoons of mechanical tubes, including a long glass canister enclosing a moving staircase up the main façade. The imagery owed something to Archigram fantasies of a decade earlier, and was supposed to imply 'openness' and 'social pluralism'. The stylized play with technological effects and the exaggerated expression of tubes and ducts placed the Pompidou Centre in yet another tradition: the 'Futurist revival' of the 1960s in Britain with Reyner Banham, apostle of the architecture of mechanical services, at its head. At the same time it touched a live nerve in French engineering culture running back through Jean Prouvé's Maison du Peuple (Fig. 461) to the girders and machines of the nineteenth-century *grands constructeurs*.

The contrast with the Roman severity, *gravitas* and restraint of Louis Kahn's contemporary Kimbell Museum at Fort Worth, Texas (Fig. 659) could scarcely have been more complete. While Kahn was inimitable, he did emphasize certain timeless qualities to which others might aspire. Roland

753 Richard Rogers and
Renzo Piano, Centre
Georges Pompidou, Paris,
1971–7

754 Arata Isozaki,
Gunma Prefectural
Museum of Modern Art,
Takasaki City, 1971–4

Simounet's Musée de la Préhistoire at Nemours, France, of 1976–80 combined spatial and tectonic subtlety with a clear overall idea. Simounet worked with light and structure, articulating joints and connections and using technology as a means rather than an end. He tried to evoke a geometrical order transcending the materials used. His architecture was indelibly marked by his early days in North Africa, and he referred in many designs to a theme of overall unity based upon repetition and variation of simple cubic or rectangular units. However, as the Musée de Préhistoire suggests, the intention was to develop a fluid space beyond any merely additive system. In contrast to the array of neo-modernist mechanolatry characteristic of much French architecture in the 1980s, Simounet would continue to hold out for an architecture of relative silence.

In his Gunma Prefectural Museum of Modern Art, 1971–4, the Japanese architect Arata Isozaki addressed certain traditional conventions for dealing with the issues of façade, entrance and civic representation, but in a language relying upon a simple geometrical order, a clear structural system and a high level of industrial craftsmanship in detail. The building was organized as an oblong from which one wing was cranked at 22½ degrees, a device which served to define an urban space in front of the building. The end of the wing was raised on piers and resembled a pavilion; it gave a cue to passing traffic about the presence of a cultural institution while also signalling the entrance route. The entire design was based upon a cubic module, and the rectangular system was made visible through the network of rectangular joints between the metallic panels. Isozaki detailed the Gunma Prefectural Museum in a way that introduced teasing ambiguities between surface and volume, lightness and visual weight. He worked back and forth between abstraction and representation, and in other designs of the same period (e.g. the Fujima Country Club of 1977) Isozaki even transformed the basic theme of a long barrel vault floating above a transparent perimeter into an arched entrance-way which made witty inversions of Western classical devices. This degree of openness to Western tradition, and this mannerist stance would have been unthinkable in the Japan of the 1950s, when one of the main cultural tasks for architects had been the integration of Japanese tradition in modernism.

754

It was towards the end of the 1970s that modern architecture came increasingly under attack for its supposed lack of 'recognizable imagery'. The argument was put forth that the architect must make it a prime responsibility to communicate to his public through popularly established codes. This resembled the usual 'realist' complaint against abstraction, but in this instance the position was bolstered by a smattering of ideas from semiology and by a Pop sensibility perhaps derived from Venturi. Architects and critics were invited to climb down from the abstruse plane of formal concerns and to occupy themselves instead with easily legible images. It was in the late 1970s too that the term 'postmodern' began to be used in connection with architecture. Once again earlier modernism was reduced to a simplified demonology. The target of the postmodernist animus emerged as a composite caricature combining 'functionalism', simple forms, truth to structure, mute imagery and a belief in the *Zeitgeist*. Even at the theoretical level it was hard to be sure just what postmodernism proposed instead. One gathered that multivalence of meaning had some part to play and that buildings ought to be regarded as communications devices employing well-known and easily understood languages. Historical quotations were to be encouraged on the grounds that these would enrich architectural vocabulary. Eclecticism was no longer to be sneered at, indeed built commentaries on earlier architecture were to be considered valuable as a source of meaning. Under the new dispensation there was a shift towards the notion of architecture as a system of 'signs'.

Like its predecessor 'the New Brutalism', postmodernism was more a vague cluster of aspirations (or, at any rate, rejections) than a blueprint for a clearcut style. In a book on the subject of postmodern architecture, the critic Charles Jencks pulled together an odd assortment of buildings to illustrate the new tendencies. Kitsch neo-classical hotel lobbies appeared close to the buildings of architects such as Charles Moore and Kisho Kurokawa; Gaudí was brought in as historical support because of the 'multivalence' of his imagery, and Mies van der Rohe was castigated for designing buildings which did not 'signify' their uses clearly; garish images were gleaned from the commercial strip, and the illustrations were mostly in colour to reinforce the contrasts employed in the buildings. Most of the visual terminologies illustrated were simply extensions of movements which had started in the 1960s, many of them of quite divergent appearance and ideology, and some of the ideas had been rehearsed by Venturi some years before. However, one thing was entirely clear: neither the author nor his examples showed much concern for questions of expressive authenticity – the buildings illustrated shared a tendency towards superficiality which took earlier architectural precedents as a sounding board for references and quotations, but for little more.

The postmodern mood (perhaps it is best to call it that) was one of a number of revisionist tendencies which came to the fore from the mid-1970s onwards; ostensibly, these too were in favour of aesthetic and symbolic enrichment. The increase in historical self-consciousness was undoubtedly related to an erosion of faith in the validity and relevance of an abstract and unadorned aesthetic, but the clichés of the critique made no distinction between bland simplicity and the intense formal purification of the best modern architecture; this wholesale rejection fitted a public mood of dissatisfaction with bad modern buildings of all kinds, and it served the polemic *not* to attempt fine distinctions. In a similar manner, an immense literature flowed forth in the late 1970s of which the avowed aim was the undermining of 'modern movement assumptions'. Many of these 'assumptions' turned out to be illusory. One found anti-functionalist arguments rehearsed *ad nauseum* when modern architecture had been anything but functionalist. One found history being proudly reinstated when the best modern architects had remained rooted in tradition. One found the idea of a single monolithic style for the twentieth century being rejected when the notion had long before been abandoned. Utopianism also came under attack, despite the fact that it too had been gradually undermined in the previous three decades. Very little of this intellectual noise penetrated anywhere near the sources of inventive power which had led to Le Corbusier, Wright, Aalto, Kahn and the rest; and most of it was shooting at intellectual bodies which were already dead.

Theories and the productions of artists are interwoven in complex ways. Sometimes a theory

755 Charles Moore,
Piazza d'Italia,
New Orleans, 1975–9

755

emerges which is then taken up and translated into
a personal terminology of form; sometimes it is
the other way round, and a theory is invoked
as a post-rationalization. The free-wheeling
eclecticism of Charles Moore may have encouraged
the intellectual formulation of postmodernism;
equally, the critical writing may have prompted
further architectural licence. In the Piazza d'Italia,
New Orleans, 1975–9, Moore erected a fountain
from a series of brightly coloured curved screens of
classical columns, entablatures and arches, including
capitals made from reflecting materials and insets
bearing the self-portrait of the architect. The result
was scarcely a serious transformation of classical
order, having more the atmosphere of a piece of
fairground equipment or a stage-set assembled out

of literal quotations. Moore's building was greeted
by the criticism that it was a shallow joke, and a
self-indulgent one at that. The riposte was that
it was a suitable piece of festivalia to celebrate
the 'Italianness' of one of the city's ethnic
neighbourhoods. This was not very convincing
either, since it seemed, in this instance, that little
of sustaining power was left once the shock or
amusement had worn off.

The fashion for pictorial classicism spread
quickly in America. Another museum design, the
unbuilt project for the Fargo-Moorhead Cultural
Center between North Dakota and Minnesota of
1977 by Michael Graves may serve to illustrate the
changing intellectual atmosphere of the period.
Graves had originally been a member of the New

York Five, and in the 1970s the other architects associated with the group had continued to extend their pure geometrical vocabularies without drastic breaks. But Graves's development in the same period revealed an increasing preoccupation with naturalistic metaphors and with quotations from history. The Fargo-Moorhead project had to stand on each side of a river which was also the State line, and the bridge between was obviously pregnant with symbolic possibilities. Graves took his cue from Claude-Nicolas Ledoux's *architecture parlante* of the late eighteenth century, particularly from the project for a sluice house over the River Loue (Fig. 6): a shape which blended a semicircular abstraction, an arch, and the image of a sluice. This motif was adapted for the Fargo-Moorhead bridge, and Graves then assembled the rest of the building in geometrical overlays and fragments on each bank. In other schemes he organized entire plans around the 'reference' of the classical keystone. It must remain for history to decide whether this was simply a facile game of quotation and private daydreaming, or some more significant replay of classical values. One thing was certain: Graves's designs placed a personal lyricism high in the scale of values, and cocked a snook at 'functional appropriateness'.

To be sure, the new traditionalist mood was not much troubled by a search for rigour, and for that reason often degenerated into eclectic candyfloss. Imagery was high in its priorities; functional resolution was low. Formal sophistication was praised; social concern was denigrated. Conceptual exploration was prized; structural necessity was sneered at. In the circumstances, it was not surprising that some critics attempted to link the more facile aspects of postmodernism to the values of consumerism. Although the new trends were not restricted to the United States, they were strongest there and seemed to mirror a preoccupation with colourful packaging and bright commercial imagery. Another connection could be made with American nineteenth-century eclecticism of the type which had treated historical elements as a kit-of-parts to be stuck together in a new 'instant tradition'.

Despite the populist arguments that were used

756 Michael Graves, project for Fargo-Moorhead Cultural Center, North Dakota and Minnesota, 1977–8. Coloured pencil and ink on yellow trace

757 Robert Stern, 'House for an Academical Couple', Connecticut, 1974–6

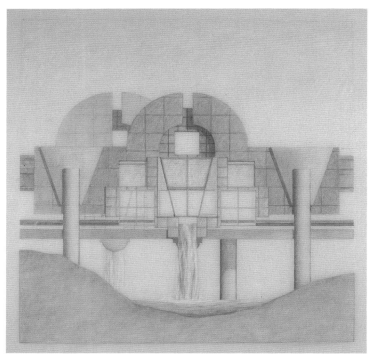

756

757

to launch 'radical eclecticism' (to use Jencks's term) against the haughtiness of earlier modern architecture, the evidence was slight that buildings employing historical references were any less obscure to the public than their 'modern' predecessors. It could even be argued that the manipulation of quotations required an in-crowd of *savants* for its full communicative effect. It was in architecture schools that the devices of commentary and allusion were most entertained, since these were places where the ground rules for communication could be learned or even enforced. There were also problems of craft and construction: the new images were really more at home in drawings than in building materials. Columns and entablatures of plywood scarcely possessed the presence of the originals, and traditional links between historical vocabularies and the building industries were long since dissolved. Robert Stern, a New York architect interested in historical quotation as a means of expression, had to resort to thin appliqués of mouldings and paint in his domestic designs of the mid-1970s. However photogenic they may have been, the results had a certain thinness. Perret,

Le Corbusier, Mies van der Rohe and Kahn (for example) had attempted to translate core principles of the classical tradition into modern terminologies rigorously disciplined by constructional and structural capabilities. But the 'radical eclectics' ran the risk of producing work of symbolic and material insubstantiality. Not even the craft of their nineteenth-century forebears was available to them in their attempts at a new ornamentation.

Postmodernism was by no means a uniquely American property, as was well demonstrated by two events in the Western architectural world of 1980. The first was an exhibition held at the Venice Biennale in the summer of that year and entitled 'The Presence of the Past'. The centrepiece of the show was an interior street (the Strada Novissima) lined with variations on classical façades in the form of large painted wooden models, designed by a selection of architects from various European centres as well as the United States (among those who contributed were Graves, Léon Krier, Hans Hollein and Paolo Portoghesi). The other public gesture of the new eclecticism was a rerun of the 1922 Chicago Tribune Competition conducted more or less as a stunt. The entrants (who came from far and wide) had a field day of revivalism, alongside which the original event seemed relatively restrained. The well-organized publishing industry saw to it that the new vogues and buzz phrases were transported quickly. The commercial world was alerted to the presence of a new design fashion, but beyond the superficial play something else was afoot: the emergence of a 'passéist avant-garde' signalling a loss of confidence in the modern project – social as well as architectural.

Postmodernism was much promoted and discussed in the late 1970s and early 1980s, but it was but one of several concurrent tendencies, and there were certain aesthetic devices such as fragmentation which crossed party lines. Frank Gehry, for example, used something like a technique of 'assemblage' in several of his designs of the late 1970s in and around Los Angeles. In his own house in Santa Monica of 1977, diagonal planes of plywood, chainlink fencing and metal siding were 'crashed' together in a way that disturbed normal expectations. In the Spiller House in Venice, California (Fig. 831), Gehry reacted to the mess of the urban surroundings, but without recourse to historical references. For him fragmentation was a means of exploring ambiguity. The Japanese architect Toyo Ito spoke of 'a syntax of space by collage which is peculiar to Japanese culture'; the layers of translucent planes and ambiguous walls in his architecture alluded simultaneously to the screens and membranes of traditional architecture, and to the shifting and evanescent realities of the modern oriental metropolis. The Viennese architect Hans Hollein used collage in a quite different way to play with levels of illusion and artificiality. In designs such as the Travel Agency in Vienna of 1976–8, he developed elaborate scenarios sticking together layers of reference and metaphor. The Travel Agency combined gold palm trees, eroded columns, high-tech details, and stone surfaces with varying degrees of roughness or polish. Fragmentation and layering were of course techniques with a long modern pedigree in painting, sculpture, photography and film, as well as in architecture, and they could serve many expressive purposes. Both Aalto and Scarpa had found ways of breaking down buildings and splaying their geometries to respond to contours and accidents of topography. Hollein used an analogous method in his Mönchengladbach Museum in Germany of 1972–82 where the individual pieces of the programme, instead of being unified in an overall volume, were separated and inflected across the site

as part of a continuous landscape running from the town and down a cascade of artificial terraces into a park. This fracturing of the building permitted the architect to respond to multiple scales in the setting.

The Neue Staatsgalerie in Stuttgart (1977–84) by James Stirling (with Michael Wilford) also relied upon fragmentation to pick up the scale and grain of the surroundings, and to direct movement, but here the pieces were spliced into a virtually neo-classical armature which responded to the symmetrical wings of the old museum next door, and which had a cylindrical open-air drum at its centre. Starting in the early 1970s, Stirling had employed increasingly overt historical allusions and metaphors. The unbuilt proposal for Derby Civic Centre (1970) already demonstrated a fascination with 'figure/ground' relationships between urban spaces and solids and with the idea of treating pre-existing monuments as *objets trouvés*. The juxtaposition of outdoor rooms and free-standing objects was continued in the scheme for Cologne Museum (1975), and in this case the ground plan of the neighbouring cathedral was restated as a sunken piazza along a sequence of vaguely surreal incidents. Evidently Stirling was also seeking inspiration from such things as ancient Roman plans with their sequences of curved rooms flowing into one another (the assumed collage character of Hadrian's 'fragmented' villa plan was much discussed at the

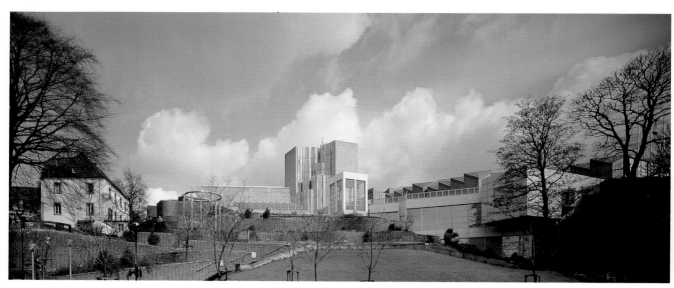

758

759

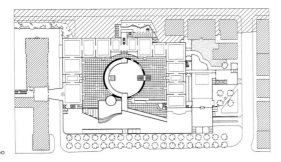

760

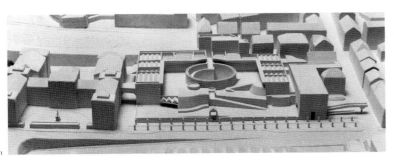

761

time), and in his design for the Staatsgalerie in Stuttgart all these features seem to have converged.

The Neue Staatsgalerie was an inclusive work which Stirling referred to in these terms: 'representational *and* abstract, monumental *and* informal, traditional *and* high tech'. It had its fair share of complexities and contradictions, combining as it did traditional rooms and a free plan; a masonry casket and 'high-tech' glazing; Cubist syntax and a centralized figure. It flirted with the taboo German subject of classical monumentality yet insisted on a democratic, even populist, interpretation of the institution by placing an urban space at its centre, and by threading a meandering public route through the drum from one side to the other. The plan was evidently modelled on the type of the Altes Museum by Schinkel but it was as if the dome and portico of this revered prototype had been 'sliced off' leaving a modern version of a ruin punctuated here and there by high-tech pieces and witty historical quotations and allusions. Stirling seems to have located the idea of a modern art museum somewhere between a people's palace and a supermarket for the 'consumption' of culture.

The bright, toy-like steel canopies and fat coloured railings set off against the curiously immaterial brown stone-striped veneers were intended as a 'user-friendly' ornament. The inflections of the main façade, with serpentine curves indicating the presence of the entrance, and ramps pointing the way along the ensuing sequence, recalled both earlier Stirling devices for handling analogous conditions and the Corbusian theme of the *promenade architecturale*. The large cylindrical void was as much a relative of the piston shapes of the Siemens scheme as it was a derivative from classical planning. Thus 'modern' and ancient were deliberately confronted but without being fused, in a technique of 'bricolage'. Curiously enough, Stirling still insisted on speaking of his designs in terms of their programmatic logic.

The Staatsgalerie addressed many issues that were in the air at the time (it was completed in 1984) – context, classicism, collage, typology, ornament, polychromy – and also made its 'winks' towards postmodernism. In the final analysis, though, it relied upon a modern planning discipline. Stirling's attitude to his modernist predecessors was Mannerist in a full sense. He took over devices from canonical buildings and placed them in 'quotation marks', inverting or reversing expectations about their usual role. The steel-tubed canopies, for example, were 'stolen' from Le Corbusier's Cité de Refuge but turned upside down; the sinuous gallery glazing with green mullions by the entrance seemed to be a transparent reinterpretation of the curved chapel at La Tourette or of Aalto's serpentine shapes; the rear wing was a piece of the nearby Weissenhofsiedlung redone. What resulted was a sophisticated and knowledgeable manipulation of stylistic elements rather than a profound transformation in the service of a new vision. To some critics Stirling's building had an appealing collagist aspect, but to others the forms seemed loosely resolved and lacking in expressive conviction. It was precisely the absence of ethical tension in this witty display of erudition which caused one writer to refer to Staatsgalerie as 'virtuosity around a void'.

What might be called a 'postmodern' idea of the city implied almost automatic respect for the existing context (sometimes verging on mimicry) and a preoccupation with pre-industrial models of urban form. These were seen as possible antidotes to the disruptive effects of economic development. By the 1970s the destruction of city centres around the world by motorways, skyscrapers and financial greed had reached the dimensions of a major crisis. While the causes were complex, it became common to blame the whole thing on 'modern architecture' and to point the finger at such Utopian schemes of the 1920s as the Ville Contemporaine because they happened to contain widely spaced skyscrapers and because they implied clean-sweep methods.

One result of the reaction against modernization was preservationism, and there were some quarters where anything old was valued over anything new. Another result was an obsession with streetscapes at the expense of individual buildings. This emerged in, for example, the writings and proposals of Léon and Robert Krier, whose *Stadtraum in Theorie und Praxis* (*Urban Space in Theory and Practice*) of 1975 assembled a morphological taxonomy of street and square types (e.g. boulevards, circuses, piazzas) as an antidote to the CIAM version of the city as a park filled with objects. Where Le Corbusier had posited the health of the city on the death of the old, choking 'corridor street', the opposite now happened. The Kriers returned to the street with a nostalgic revenge (any street type would do) and

762 Robert Krier, sketches from *Stadtraum in Theorie und Praxis*, 1975, showing historical variants of round open spaces

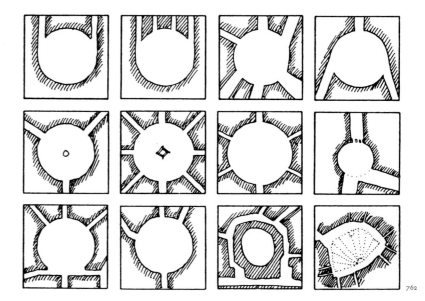

762

treated it as a virtual fetish, as if the refined design of open spaces and outdoor rooms would on its own guarantee life to the badly mauled urban body. They inveighed against zoning and praised the mixed living and working arrangements of traditional European cities. Their images had a vaguely eighteenth-century air, while their utterances suggested a somewhat impractical nostalgia for an era of handicraft.

Collage City (1978) by Colin Rowe and Fred Koetter was more sophisticated in its arguments. The authors attacked the determinism basic to Utopianism (with some help from *The Open Society and its Enemies* by Karl Popper), by exposing the totalitarianism implicit in holistic urban schemes. Against such large-scale social engineering they proposed a piecemeal and democratic metaphor which relied on 'collage' and 'bricolage' for its implementation and visual style. As a sort of allegory of this position they used such examples as Hadrian's Villa at Tivoli with its informality, its sprawling picturesque character, and its quotations from numerous places and times. They too emphasized the importance of 'spaces between' and criticized the object fixation of early modern urbanism – indeed a figure/ground conception of the city, which treated urban spaces with the same weight as buildings, was proposed as a more textured and complex antidote. The modern building was to blend with the patterns of the historic city. If any single building encapsulated all this, it was surely Stirling's Staatsgalerie.

In retrospect it is possible to see that *Collage City* relied for its full impact on the acceptance of a caricature of modernism as something holistic, teleological and essentially forward-looking. It did not do justice to the ideological and formal complexities of earlier twentieth-century Utopianism in urban design, let alone to the variegated role of tradition in the formation of Utopian images of the city; even the Ville Contemporaine, after all, had been a 'collage' of sorts, drawing together bits of Paris, New York, monasteries, ships and boulevards. None the less *Collage City* was symptomatic of a state of scepticism in which irony was a basic requirement, and any too positive or gushing a proposal was treated with dismay. As to its possible intentions in formulating an urbanistic or architectural language,

the book was circumspect. The plates and drawings encouraged admiration for complex urban tissues and reverence for certain key Renaissance squares; the fragmentation and ambiguity of Cubism were somehow linked to Camillo Sitte's love of outdoor rooms; 'object buildings' (i.e. those within the modern tradition) were severely castigated. However, even those who agreed with the rhetoric still had the problem of translating the book's insights into three dimensions, and it was noticeable that some of Rowe's acolytes took the allegory all too literally by spicing their plans with Uffizi corridors, Piazza Navonas and antique theatres. At his most facile the urban collagist could be just as vapid as the simple-minded adherent of radical eclecticism in architecture. But sticking little bits of history here and there into the modern urban fabric was scarcely a guarantee of environmental quality or even of spatial enrichment. Rowe's intentions were obviously more serious than those of his facile imitators, but even his own text positively encouraged flippancy.

… a collage technique, by accommodating a whole range of *axes mundi* (all of them vest pocket utopias – Swiss canton, New England village, Dome of the Rock, Place Vendôme, Campidoglio, etc.) might be a means of permitting us the enjoyment of utopian poetics without our being obliged to suffer the embarrassment of utopian politics … collage is a method deriving its virtue from its irony … it seems to be a technique for using things and simultaneously disbelieving in them …

The tone was knowledgeable, acutely self-conscious, and aware of both the dissolution of a past system of beliefs and the lack of any alternative ringing true; the result seemed to be an elegant parlour despair making the most of erudition by manipulating the outer shells of past kernels of meaning; the assumption was that greater conviction was not, for the moment, possible.

A similar mood of chic cynicism, and a suggestion (unwarranted but assumed) that that was the only possible viable one for the moment, is to be found in an essay by Jorge Silvetti written in 1977 in which he reflected upon the state of architecture in his own time:

… we find ourselves looking back on the Modern Movement itself from a real historical perspective. Its 'classicism' has now been experienced, its effects sensed, and its postulates questioned; yet with all this nothing seems to have appeared to replace it. Like the Mannerist architect, we can only manipulate the known. Such is, in my view, all that can be said in general terms about the state of architecture today.

Silvetti was right to suggest that the modern movement was still the most relevant source of paradigms, but wrong to insist that mannerism was the only possible stance. It can be seen from this cross-section of the 1970s that a variety of beliefs was in fact operative, and that several strands of modern architectural tradition continued to be extended in a vigorous way. That is why it may be relevant to draw to a close with two works conceived outside the realms of fashionable doubt, that were indisputably 'modern' yet steeped in the past; that were concerned with matters of form without sacrificing human meaning; that articulated complex feelings and ideas without forgetting the tectonic presence of construction. As it happens, both were also for religious purposes: the Brion Tomb at San Vito d'Altivole in the Veneto designed by Carlo Scarpa between 1969 and 1978; and the Bagsvaerd Church outside Copenhagen designed by Jørn Utzon between 1969 and 1976. Where the former was a private place of burial for a Catholic family, the latter was a parish church and meeting centre for a Protestant suburban community.

With the Brion Tomb, Scarpa created one of his most haunting and enigmatic works, evoking a field of the dead and the passage to the world beyond. It contained several individual family monuments and was wrapped around the back of the village graveyard in the form of an 'L'. The flat land was sculpted into a sequence of trenches, paths, platforms and pools, and was populated by sarcophagi in curious abstract shapes like large amulets. Concrete walls were faceted, weathered and submerged, lending the impression of an archaeological site scattered with remains and swamped by water. Pivotal structures such as the funerary chapel and the Brion couple's tomb were rotated on to a 45-degree geometry, while the rest of the cemetery relied upon Scarpa's usual devices of layering, striation and fragmentation. There was a poignant mood of time past, although slots of sky glimpsed through fractured openings hinted at infinity.

Rather than just a building, the Brion Tomb was a mythical landscape exploring the erosion of age and the soul-stirring effects of water. Squares, diamonds, circles and other emblematic shapes rested in a state of suspension, their historical identity ambiguous, their resonances with the past dimly felt. The funerary chapel stood in a sombre pond of lilypads flanked by cypresses and was like a latterday island of the dead. Marble and brass, smooth white plaster, glass and steel were set off against the patina of rough weathered concrete. Scalloped edges and striations followed obscure grammatical rules of their own but also touched

763 Carlo Scarpa, Brion Tomb, San Vito d'Altivole, Treviso, 1969–78, plan. Graphite and coloured pencil on blue print

764 Brion Tomb

763

764

connections with classical mouldings and fluting. The main tomb, containing the remains of the Brion couple, was inserted deeper in the precinct over a disc stepping down into the ground. Two tilted slabs leaned towards each other under a low, bridge-like form. The underside was covered in blue mosaic, suggesting a celestial soffit. Abstraction, instead of severing memory, allowed the recollection of several places and times. The Brion enclosure was like an aqueous ruin distilling Scarpa's beloved Veneto landscape of canals, islands and lagoons, but it was also haunted by more distant ghosts such as Buddhist perforated fences and ancient burial grounds.

The visitor to the Brion Tomb was drawn into a ritual movement through a maze of half-sunken paths allowing glimpses of funerary caskets. The route entered a dimly lit passageway, its walls cut by two intersecting rings – an allusion perhaps to the duration of the Brion marriage after death. The final enclosure was entered through a glass door sliding into the ground on pulleys. A cruciform plaque appeared to float on the still surface of the water. A tomb-like box on stilts recalling a medieval funerary monument stood on an island of its own, reached by a precarious pathway. But references were never obvious, and forms communicated before they were understood. Scarpa's work was a palimpsest of hermetic meanings, touching upon archetypal themes of transition and inner discovery, duality within unity, and the dark underwater world as an image of death. Fragmentation, far from being a device for establishing ironical distance, seemed to be the means for exploring the problems of faith and immortality.

Utzon's Bagsvaerd Church was formed from three main spaces, an atrium at the entrance, a main meeting hall with an altar, and an ancillary garden

765

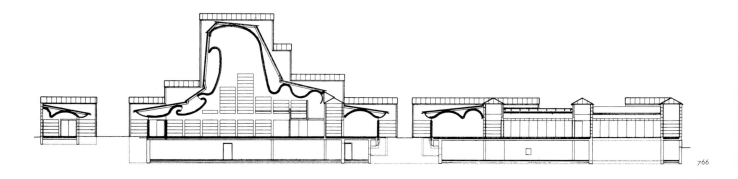

766

surrounded by small offices. These were contained by parallel cloisters running the entire length of the building and expressed as slender walls surmounted by triangular skylights. On the exterior the dominant church space was clearly visible towards the centre, and all parts of the building stepped up gradually towards it. However, unity was assured by a uniform structural treatment: a concrete frame with precast infill slabs of silver-grey colour. Within the building, the ceiling made a strong contrast with this stratified system, since it was formed from a white curved concrete surface which protruded over the entrance, then flowed gradually upwards in a wave motion that reached its peak over the main room and descended out of sight to the rear. This extraordinary organic shape modulated the light and contained the community within.

The aesthetic effects of the church were based on the simplest of means: fine proportions, contrast between similar elements, finesse in joints and craftsmanship, the play of light over plain materials. There was an elusive and quiet imagery which was at one with the idea of a religious 'meeting house'. This

767

was suggested by the small glass gables atop the parallel walls and by the stepping silhouette of the whole, which echoed the typical Zeeland country church with its characteristic stepped gables. The flowing ceiling, and even the plan as a whole, recalled Utzon's interest in Oriental religious buildings, while the section was like an abstraction of clouds hovering over a place of assembly. The corrugated aluminium attached to the tower introduced a bizarre but enriching note, along with associations that perhaps evoked the simplicity and sharpness of the modern agricultural vernacular. It was a house, a hall, a church, a barn, all in one, and its shapes recalled one aspect more than the other in different parts.

However, imagery was not overplayed and was supported by form. Form in turn arose directly from a simple structural means attuned to serve ideas. The driving concepts of the design were rooted in Utzon's own earlier solutions and in a style rich in metaphors and abstract images. The theme of the curved interior ceiling recalled the wave motion of the intended ceiling for the Sydney Opera House (which in turn relied on Aaltoesque precedent); the preoccupation with precast, modular discipline also returned to experiments like the Kingo Houses (Fig. 583). As before, the opposition and coalescence of the stratified and the curved implied two primary kinds of order and other layers of polarity – the rational and the organic, the supporting and the supported, the stable and the dynamic. The frame seemed to be a descendant both of the concrete, trabeated tradition stretching back to Perret, and of the wooden-frame tradition of the Scandinavian vernacular. However, all such allusions were tightly held in check in a design characterized by intellectual crispness and clarity.

Whatever the sources of Utzon's building, they were transmuted into a new terminology, a genuine style, based on private, intuitive rules. A guiding image informed all the parts and brought them into a tense unity. Without pretension or show, the lessons of the modern tradition, of the vernacular, and of old ecclesiastical types were fused. Surely this was what Van Eyck had in mind when he rejected 'the sentimental technocracy of the future' and 'the sentimental antiquarianism of the past' and suggested that 'past, present, and future must be active in the mind's interior as a continuum.'

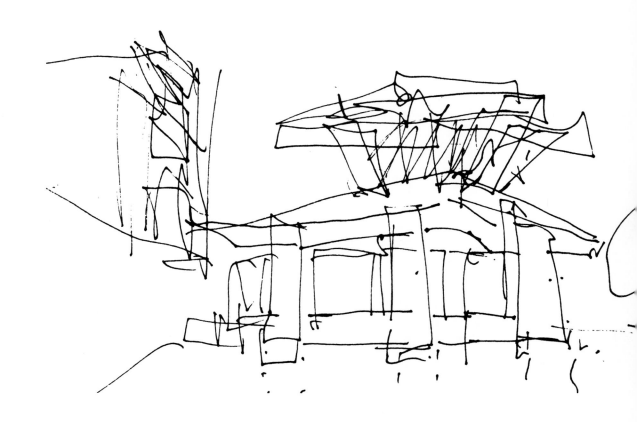

part 4

continuity and change in the late twentieth century

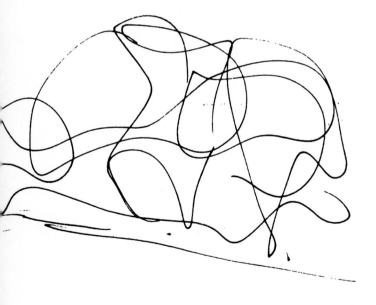

33

modern architecture and memory: new perceptions of the past

If you want to create
something new, search
for that which is ancient.
Aulis Blomstedt, 1957

It is a commonplace of art history that one should never try to write the history of the recent past. The reason given is that one is liable to be biased. Why this should not be true of the more distant past too is not explained; it is taken for granted that the true shape of history will somehow emerge on its own. Caution is obviously required when dealing with developments that are almost contemporary, but it is naïve to imagine that an acceptable consensus will come about naturally. If the historian steps back, the propagandist with an axe to grind steps in, usually with a polemical version of what is 'salient'.

Fifteen years have elapsed since the first edition of this book was written, and so much has happened in the interim that the time has now come to outline a preliminary historical map of the late twentieth century. This can only be approximate, but it can at least concentrate on the main lines of thought and on buildings which achieve a high architectural level while distilling broad concerns of the time. It is best not to rely too much upon 'isms' as these make no distinction between durable creations and weaker relatives that simply wear the fashionable dress. A balance must be found between innovation and inherited forms, between architectural values and the social role of buildings. The range must be wide, for some of the most vital architectural ideas of this period have emerged in places remote from the published discourse; the 'map' has to be able to chart works of substance in the Third World as well as the First.

There are no doubt many ways in which one could structure an investigation of recent architecture: through individual architects, through overall tendencies, through national cultures, through building types, through changing paradigms. The previous chapter suggested how one could reveal the pluralism of a decade (in that case the 1970s) by taking a cross-section through diverse strands of development. But architecture also evolves in response to generally sensed problems to which several answers are possible. This last part of the book is organized around broad themes such as the transformation of the past, the reading of context, the interpretation of cultural identity, the meaning of fragmentation, the expression of technology, the abstraction of topography, or the projection of different ideals of modernity. These subjects are not mutually exclusive, and they are not exhaustive, but they do supply a scheme of reference and research which can link internal concerns of the architectural discipline to wider realities of the recent past.

The time has long since elapsed when one could speak of a handful of cosmopolitan centres (mostly in the West) supplying the leading ideas behind which the rest of the world would run. The geographical disposition of key inventions has been redrawn, and cross-fertilizations now occur independently of the old intellectual trade routes which used to extend from the 'advanced industrial nations' to other regions of the globe. In truth this diversification of modern architecture has been in process for over half a century; it is the historiography and critical literature which have been guilty of clinging to a parochial vision. Vital regional and national strands of modern architecture were already being established in the 1930s and 1940s as far apart as Finland, Japan and Brazil, and some of them achieved their own momentum, their own resistance and their own capacity to absorb or reject external influences. In recent years outstanding buildings, even new paradigms with worldwide repercussions, have emerged in places sometimes relegated to the 'periphery' such as Spain and Portugal, or Mexico and India. These are places with distinctive modern architectural cultures and with experience at balancing internal inheritances with new ideas from the outside. Beneath the surface of the present lie layers of local memory and dormant agendas that may subtly insinuate themselves into projects of modernity.

Meanwhile the very definition of cultural 'territories' is undergoing constant change. With recent architecture it is sometimes more relevant to speak of an urban centre or a region than a nation. Outstanding buildings have emerged from the interstices of sprawl cities such as Los Angeles, Barcelona or Ahmadabad, or the urbanized valleys of the Ticino in southern Switzerland. These agglomerations have more and more in common with each other and reveal the homogenizing influence of worldwide networks of technology. The individual building has sometimes been conceived as a precinct of local memory or as a reminder of 'nature', in contrast to the surrounding transience. The pieces and parameters of a new global culture are beginning to take shape. These struggle to balance urbanization and topography, internationalization and identity. The collision and overlapping of new and old, artificial and natural, is intrinsic to the new pattern which goes even further to blur the distinction between urban and rural worlds.

The obvious needs restating: the architecture of the past fifteen years cannot be consigned to a single style of ideology. Nor can it be satisfactorily portrayed and analysed through current terms such as 'high-tech', 'Regionalism', 'neo-Rationalism', 'classicism', 'contextualism', 'minimalism'. These evoke rough allegiances but do little to penetrate to architectural ideas, still less to suggest the presence of actual buildings in all their uniqueness and complexity. As usual the key works refuse to fit the dictates or theoretical prescriptions of any movement. No easy formula will do when dealing with buildings as varied in form and intention as, say, Rafael Moneo's National Museum of Roman Art in Mérida, Spain (1980–6), Raj Rewal's National Institute of Immunology in New Delhi, India (1983–90), Fumihiko Maki's Fujisawa Gymnasium in Tokyo (1984–90), or Pierre Louis Faloci's Centre Archéologique Européen du Mont Beuvray in France (1991–5). These are works with their own ideas, order and lineages, that draw upon and contribute to the architectural culture of their time, even as they crystallize something of their respective places and societies. They embody different world-views in three-dimensional terms and have complex, even contradictory pedigrees in the earlier history of architecture.

The debate between 'modernism' and 'post-modernism' did little to clarify the true complexity of the 1980s. As predicted nearly fifteen years ago, postmodernism proved to be a short-lived and relatively localized phenomenon. The caricature of modern architecture as something rootless, functionalist and without meaning distorted the historical perspective. The primary works of the modern masters sometimes touched deep levels in tradition even as they innovated; their lessons continued to be developed in numerous, not necessarily obvious ways. The brief fashion for revivalism did little more than change the stylistic clothes, while the primary statements of modernism earlier in the century 'altered the very spatial anatomy of design' and reorganized 'the deep structures of the medium itself'. Despite the protestations of both traditionalists and neo-avant-gardists that they were bringing about major changes, the reality of architectural production in the 1980s and 1990s had more to do with evolution and reassessment than with revolution and radical breaks. This is said, not to denigrate inventiveness, or to insist upon a simplistic line of continuity, but to suggest a diverse and dynamic idea of a modern tradition.

To speak of inheriting and extending such a tradition does not mean copying what has gone before, or enforcing stylistic norms. It rather implies the absorption of principles behind earlier solutions and their transformation to meet different conditions and fit new intentions. In the period under review there were certainly crises and disjunctions, but diverse strands of modern architecture also continued to be extended, critiqued, mannerized, regionalized, even cross-bred with other traditions. The situation could be compared to a delta with the main currents flowing down dividing channels; some silted up, some were renewed by deep sources, others advanced with renewed strength; overall the river continued to move.

Whatever his architectural persuasion, the designer of the 1980s found himself confronted by a disturbing set of realities stemming from a new industrial revolution, one related to the electronic handling of information. The very status of the architectural object was bound to change when it was forced to compete in a field of rapidly transmitted optical patterns and flickering images. The dispersed megalopolis with no fixed centre, but multiple nodes linked by networks of communication, became the dominant urban model in the 'developing' countries as well as in the 'developed' ones. Global industrialization continued to undermine local traditions and to contribute to a new layer of transient gadgetry and to a mass kitsch. Little wonder that so many of the critical postures of the period had to do with reasserting the sense of place, or with creating enclaves of tranquillity and authentic experience. Proclamations could be found in favour of regional identity, structural integrity, indigenous craft, moral purpose, poetic presence – all things that were accorded a low priority in the new information city with its impermanence, its

arbitrary layers of references and 'signs', its lack of concern for direct human communication, its ebb and flow reacting to the forces of investment and marketing.

In the realm of ideas, old certainties and beliefs dissolved away. The determinisms which had helped to propel early modern architecture at the turn of the century had long since disappeared. Utopianism lay discredited. It was fashionable in the 1980s to proclaim that all 'grand historical narratives' of social progress and emancipation were exhausted. Even the most idealistic had to admit to uncertainties about the ultimate mission and content of architecture. These doubts reflected a wider scepticism about the capacity of languages to deal with 'realities' at all. It was a frame of mind which could lead quickly to a species of internalized architectural commentary. Rare indeed were distinctions between a merely superficial play with signs and references, and symbolic expressions emerging from a deeper mythic level. Quite aside from the erosion of earlier planning faiths, the architect was often reduced to a marginal position in deciding the overall shape and direction of the built environment. The obsession with collage, with fragments rather than urban totalities reflected a worthy intention of coming to terms with unique places, but it also betrayed a loss of nerve about projecting alternative images of the future at all.

While the declamatory rhetoric of post-modernism did little to touch or indicate the deeper creative forces of the period, it none the less bore witness to a wider preoccupation with the past, with the urban context, and with matters of convention and communication. Nor was the recycling of images and stylistic effects confined to postmodern classicism and traditionalism, since it also emerged in several 'neo-modernist' guises as well. Missing, usually, was some scheme of myths and beliefs that might help to take architecture to the higher levels. The formalist manipulations and witty gyrations implied a rejection of the progressive ethos and social planning associated with the 'modern project', but they also revealed a wider anxiety about the rootlessness of rapid technological change. Moreover, the obsession with the past took several other forms. The neo-Rationalist commitment to 'monument, locus and type' reflected a need to establish a more solid basis in history. The looping

769

attached uncomfortably to the façade of a curved apartment building supposedly modelled on an amphitheatre or the Roman Colosseum, but in fact smacking of a smart marketing trick to attract tenants. Michael Graves' Portland Building in Portland, Oregon, of the same period had colour renderings of a keystone and rustication stencilled onto what was otherwise a dumpy box with a shallow curtain wall. While promoters spoke of the reassertion of civic values, detractors referred to the building in disparaging terms (e.g. as 'a billboard dolled up with cultural graffiti'). Although architects like Graves and Bofill insisted upon the manipulation of architectural language, they actually had little meaning to convey and failed to touch the deeper values of classical architecture.

In the first half of the 1980s there was a boom in office building construction in the United States, and the tripartite formula with decorative headgear was the dominant fashion. Many were the American cities that were hit by pile-ups of arches, columns and stepped tops, clamouring for attention on the skyline. But the routine productions of the period were every bit as banal as the standardized glass and steel prisms they pretended to enrich. The American commercialization of postmodern classicism (dubbed up by one critic as 'hierarchies for hire') corresponded to the get-rich-quick mentalities of Reaganomics: the historical appliqués supplied a classy styling with suitably conservative undertones,

back to pre-colonial sources in several Third World societies was related to the need to establish post-colonial symbols of identity. In the West at least, the 'past' often meant the classical past, or some particular version or reading of it. Here there was a spectrum of positions from the abstract and geometrical to the representational and referential. While some were almost literal in their reuse of classical elements, others tried to transform underlying schemes of order; others again were whimsical, mannerist and somewhat arbitrary.

The postmodern classicists whose formation was discussed in the last chapter were mostly of the last kind. They played games of dislocation with the classical language but rarely approached the problem of an underlying order or discipline. In the early 1980s they had a chance to build, sometimes on a large scale, and the superficiality of their approach soon began to show. Typical were buildings such as Ricardo Bofill's housing at Marne-la-Vallée outside Paris (1978–83) in which giant columns in precast concrete and glass were

770

769 Ricardo Bofill, Le Palais d'Abraxas housing, Marne-la-Vallée, France, 1978–83

770 Michael Graves, Portland Building, Portland, Oregon, 1980–3

771 Quinlan Terry, Richmond Riverside development, Richmond, London, 1985–7

but this camouflage masked baser realities, and could scarcely disguise an underlying vacuity and inflation. The novelist Charles Newman caught the mood of an entire period in American culture when he wrote in *The Post Modern Aura* (1985):

What we invariably end up with is a gesture of historical pathos without content; the restoration of historical images with no co-ordinates – a romanesque arch which holds up nothing, a Greek pilaster in mid air, a trapezoid window in a neo-classical façade… testimony not to a new eclecticism but merely to the artists' erudition. What we have recently – in painting, music and architecture, no less than in literature, in opposition to an uncritical rejection of the past … is an uncritical reception, an all-embracing nostalgia, in which *all* historical styles are dredged up simultaneously, history as gesture to a 'pastness', which disguises the real pain of history and struggle for knowledge. The ideology of making it new becomes the ideology of making it (sort of) old. As Modernism has become the respectable culture, 'tradition' becomes the Avant-garde.

Attempts made in the 1980s at referring more directly to the classical language intersected with several cultural and political agendas, some of them reactionary in tone. In Britain, for example, a species of classical revival corresponded to a wave of neo-conservative values, and to a search by the New Right for a vehicle to replace earlier 'modernism' (identified over-simplistically with the Welfare State). Thus a figure like Quinlan Terry, who had been modestly pursuing a dull and rather literal version of classicism for two decades, suddenly found himself pushed into the limelight by a brand of cultivated opinion which perceived all modern

architecture as a nasty internationalist intrusion into the calm of English country life, and which imagined that 'taste' and 'traditional values' might somehow restore national glory. Terry's own buildings (e.g. the Richmond Riverside development, 1985–7) were polite and scholarly compositions using classical grammar and ornament, but they lacked the underlying order and measure that could be found in great classical works of the past. Nevertheless, he was one of several revivalists to touch a chord in the public imagination, and even to attract the attention of royalty; he helped to reinforce a general British insularity and suspicion about most aspects of modern architecture. Quinlan Terry did not consider himself to be a postmodernist, but a classical architect; in fact he distanced himself from postmodernism, saying that it was 'Satan's work' and 'even worse than modernism because done with irony'. The revivalist position which Terry represented substituted learning for inventiveness, nostalgia for a vital reinterpretation of tradition. 'Academic art', suggested Geoffrey Scott in *The Architecture of Humanism* (1914), 'sometimes implies a refusal to rethink the problems at issue… it attempts to make the imagination of the past do service for imagination in the present.'

The struggle to reconcile modernity and tradition has been a recurrent feature of twentieth-century architecture. Classicism runs like a subterranean

771

stream, sometimes coming to the surface on its own terms, sometimes mingling with the currents of modernism. In Italy and Germany in the post-war years, and in Spain in the immediately post-Franco period the direct reference to classical forms was virtually unthinkable because it might recall earlier dictatorial regimes. Even so, these were countries with a pronounced substratum of classical memories which could be integrated into the superstructures of modernism. The Italian neo-Rationalists (notably Aldo Rossi and Giorgio Grassi) supplied evidence of this process. For them the key to the past lay in the transformation of basic types and in the distillation of meaning in primary forms. Their approach relied upon a vein of classical values running through earlier modern architecture, and upon consonances with schemes of classical order; Le Corbusier and Ledoux, Terragni and Palladio, Kahn and Schinkel, all figured in their pantheon. There was a theoretical interest in possible 'natural' and vernacular origins of classicism and in metaphysical values supposedly cutting across time. Rossi's buildings of the late 1970s and early 1980s (eg. the Gallaratese Apartment Block, Fig. 743) were stripped down to the most elementary geometries of cube, cone and cylinder, were usually disposed over symmetrical plans, and were shorn of all ornament, although triangular skylights made subtle allusions to pediments, and formally grouped structural elements recalled rows of columns. Grassi's Project for Student Housing at Chieti (1979) relied upon the example of neo-classical arcaded streets, but restated this in a language of stern rectangularity, supplying the repeated concrete piers and horizontal overhangs with the accentuation of a portico.

Neo-rationalism wished to avoid both the emptiness of functionalism and the superficial 'remedy' of instant traditionalism by putting modern architecture back in touch with historical memory through a type of evocative abstraction. When the designer had sufficient intensity and control the results could be strong, but the simplicity could also end up being diagrammatic and drained of significance. In Germany, Oswald Mathias Ungers designed the Architecture Museum in Frankfurt (1983) under the overall dispensation of neo-Rationalism, working with the theme of buildings inside buildings, rectangular modules at several scales, and allusions to 'basic' elements such as the temple, the aedicule and the hut. However, the IBA housing in Berlin (to which Rossi, Ungers, the Kriers and Kleihues all made contributions) did not always fulfil the promise of a new urbanism based upon traditional typologies such as the street, the façade, the stressed entrance, the wall and the window. The ruptured city was stitched together but many of the individual buildings were banal and formulaic. What might be called a re-evaluation of the historical city exerted a wide influence in the 1980s, for example in the Villa Olimpica in Barcelona (co-ordinated by Oriol Bohigas towards

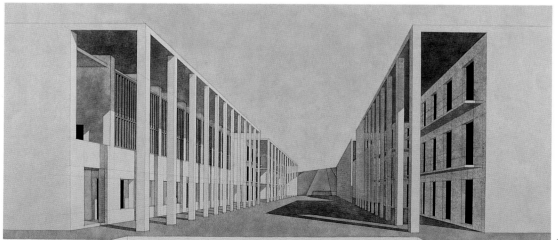

772

the end of the decade) which respected the historical grid and courtyard pattern and tried to institute a set of urbanistic rules. Only too often, neo-Rationalism was reduced to a set of clichés that were supposed to deliver up an instant urbanity: an easily reproduced style that soon turned up in a devalued form in many countries. Typical features of this new international manner were identified by Alan Colquhoun in an article of 1983:

… there has clearly been some (perhaps short-lived) compromise between the modernist tradition and new ideas based on a reassessment of the larger architectural tradition of classicism. This compromise usually avoids the literal quotation of those stylistic tropes handed down from the eclectic tradition, which were outlawed by the modern movement. For example, it still accepts the modernist rejection of ornament, or at least has reduced ornament to such devices as alternating materials and colours, which remain tectonic, geometrical and non-figurative. But at the same time, it clearly makes a connection with the architectural tradition through such generalized themes as 'column', 'room', 'corridor', 'window', 'roof', and is concerned with notions of surface, limit, symmetry and difference.

775

773

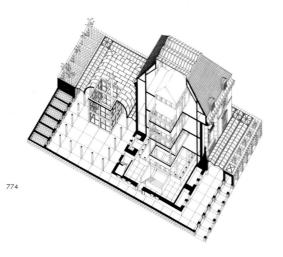

774

The significance of the new orientation to the past lay deeper than these sanctioned arrangements of perimeter blocks and symmetrical entrances. It lay in the penetration to the 'substructures' of regional and universal traditions; in the unearthing of historical memory in particular places; in the anchoring of territory against the onslaught of urban expansion; in the concentration upon geometry and type; and in the exploration of ideas of construction. Several of the most haunting buildings conceived in the first half of the 1980s emerged from preoccupations of this kind – Mario Botta's Casa Rotonda in the Ticino (1980–1), Rafael Moneo's National Museum of Roman Art in Mérida (1980–6), Juan Navarro Baldeweg's Congress Hall in Salamanca (1985–92) and Johan Otto von Spreckelsen's Grande Arche de la Défense in Paris (1981–7) could all be cited. These were buildings which drew something from neo-rationalist ideas and images even as they sought out resonances within their respective cultures. They crystallized a variety of contemporary social aspirations, but also harked back to ancient formulations and basic types in the history of architecture such as the hypostyle hall and the aqueduct (Mérida), the hovering dome with an oculus traversed by light (Salamanca) or the monumental gateway as a species of shelter or triumphal arch (La Défense).

One reason why Italian neo-Rationalism was influential was that it gave shape to aspirations which others already felt. Among those to be reinforced in this way was a small group of Swiss architects in the Italian speaking canton of Ticino, which had been developing an independent strand of modern architecture in the 1960s, inspired in part by Le Corbusier, Kahn, Scarpa and Terragni, in part by the local vernacular and alpine landscape. The early works of Luigi Snozzi, Aurelio Galfetti, Livio Vacchini and Mario Botta combined structural and geometrical discipline with a poetic evocation of the sense of place. In the late 1970s Botta gradually evolved a distinct personal style in a series of individual houses perched on the hillsides above Lugano or set down on the outskirts of increasingly industrialized villages. This style was characterized by bold rectangles and cylinders, symmetrical plans with slots for circulation, robust walls in concrete brick, and delicate superstructures in glass and steel. The attitude to the landscape was affirmative (Botta spoke of 'constructing the site'); attention was given to materials and joints; and there was a search for constants and continuities. The archaic mood and stark geometries punched by openings echoed the monumental rusticity of barns in the Ticino region, while the insistence on proportion and a dominant

idea incorporated something of Rossi's abstract vision of the classical past. Botta's architecture was sensitized to the light and landscape conditions of a particular locale but it was not overtly 'regionalist'. His forms seemed to emerge from a critical dialogue between a generalized typology for the modern dwelling, and the pre-existing order and topography:

The architecture I make is … very closely related to nature. It would please me if my architecture is perceived to be rooted in and tied to, the culture of my native land … I am trying to transform this reality, which is always unique. Every single house is a 'unicum' which communicates with a particular landscape, which in turn has its own history, its own culture, and which possesses its own stratification to be consolidated and transformed.

The Casa Rotonda at Stabio (1980–1) turned a two-car family home constructed from concrete blocks into a solid monument which defied the surrounding suburban sprawl, and which reaffirmed a more ancient set of co-ordinates linking old castellos and barns. The main cylinder of the building was cut in two by a slot admitting light deep into the structure. The skylight was triangular in shape, as if recalling a pediment or a roof. The circular plan was aligned to the compass points and suggested a solar calendar designed to catch the sun's rays at particular times of the day or the year. Views were controlled to cut out the immediate

776 Mario Botta, Casa Rotonda, Stabio, Switzerland, 1980–1, cut-away drawings

777 Casa Rotonda

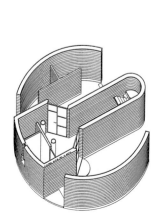
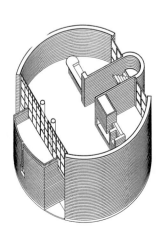
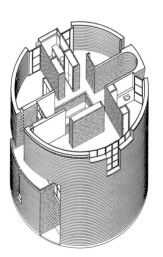
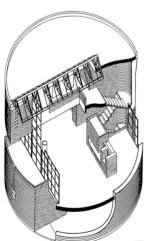

776

777

setting and to focus attention on the unblemished parts of the landscape. Casa Rotonda evoked an observatory or perhaps a tower for spiritual retreat. On the street side the walls stepped down and away to create room for cars each side but also to reveal the curved end of the stairs. Kahn's massive circulation towers or Le Corbusier's silo-shaped stairs come to mind, though the element was here embedded in a new expression with its own internal rules. The jointing to the larger cylinder of the house was handled adroitly by corbelling the bricks so that the form inevitably evoked a column, but one generated from within, functionally and in terms of ideas, not just an attached 'sign' or quotation. This curved form was resonant with the Romanesque as much as the Roman: it touched on the idea of the column in general, but also possessed the direct objectivity of modernity. Botta insisted that he wanted to make an architecture 'in harmony with our life and our time' and rejected post-modernism for its cynicism and superficiality. He stated that he

wished to discover: 'a new equilibrium between man and his surroundings … a series of elements which place man in relation with the earth itself, with the trajectory of the sun … with the awareness of the passing seasons' and that he hoped 'to recapture the initial values from which the dwelling was made'. He went on to say:

History is not a column, not a capital, and not the reuse of a form borrowed from the past. History in its profound meaning is an entity to which we are all indebted, but from which we must all attempt to free ourselves, in order to be able to respond to the needs of the times.

While Botta and several of his Ticinese contemporaries were sometimes grouped together as a movement, they in fact had different points of view and distinct personal styles within the area of their broadly shared concerns. Mario Campi owed much to the Italian Rationalists of the 1930s, often working with variations of rectangular frame, aperture and pier, around reinterpretations of ancient ideas such as the atrium house. Bruno

Reichlin's and Fabio Reinhardt's joint creations were almost overt in their reliance upon the plan types and proportional systems of Palladio's Villas. Although the Ticino was part of Switzerland, it also looked to Italy, in cultural and artistic matters; mythological links with the Mediterranean world were not so hard to imagine. After all, Le Corbusier had made analogous links between the Suisse Romande and the land to the south, and Alberto Sartoris, the historian/architect, had developed parallel themes in his writings (Chapter 21). This is not to say that every Ticinese architect of interest was obliged to work with classical analogies. Luigi Snozzi, for example, was more interested in making minimalist incisions into the hillside slopes and in organizing his buildings as topographical routes. He used sparse concrete planes to define limits or release space and to handle the transition from upper level entrances to the vast panoramas over lakes and mountains.

In the 1970s and 1980s, the Ticino developed rapidly, abandoning the last vestiges of rural existence and gradually turning into a vast megalopolitan network including motorways and new suburbs, pre-existing towns and villages, old farms and vineyards – all set against the majestic background of lakes, mountains and valleys. Aurelio Galfetti was sensitive to this larger topographical scale and endeavoured to create fixed points, monuments of a kind, to stem the flux of economic development, but also to echo prominent geological features and landmarks in the vicinity such as rocky outcrops or castles. His remodelling and transformation of the Castelgrande in Bellinzona (1981–8) was a sensitive exercise in combining new and old, concrete and stone, while his several apartment buildings of the 1980s (e.g. the 'Black' and 'White' blocks in Bellinzona of 1986) worked with bold cubic forms, polychrome banding and interlocking sections allowing individual terraces. Galfetti wished to make clear-cut objects which would mark out territory and resonate with ancient structures of analogous form and size in the landscape, even as they defined stabilizing elements in an emergent ex-urban sprawl. The Tennis Club in Bellinzona (1983) relied upon the theme of a long wall carrying a walkway, and was cut through by a rectangular portico at its mid-point. In reality, the 'wall' was not solid at all, but a slot defined by two parallel concrete planes that were deeply ribbed, and covered by hooped glass skylights. Galfetti described the Tennis Club in these terms: ' A strong, rough wall which resists the effects of the traffic and the wind. A wall to cross and pass along, like the footbridge of the swimming pool or the walls of the castle'.

778 Aurelio Galfetti, Tennis Club, Bellinzona, Switzerland, 1983

779 Livio Vacchini, Montagnola School, near Lugano, Switzerland, 1978–82

778

779

Like Botta and Galfetti, Livio Vacchini (who was based in Locarno) wished to 'urbanize' the suburban by lending it a certain civic substance. He also drew upon classical types and principles of organization, but, unlike most of his colleagues, developed the fact and idea of the modern structural frame in steel or concrete. The Maccioni Building in the centre of Lugano (1974–5) abstracted the rectilinear order, divisions and measure of a classical palace façade in a bold articulation of steel frame, plate glass and construction joints; it therefore continued a line of research into the tectonic expression of modern technology that had been initiated by the Chicago School and carried on by Mies van de Rohe. At the same time, the Maccioni Building addressed the grain and scale of its urban context. One should never forget that Como (and Terragni's Casa del Fascio, Fig. 450) were only a short distance from the Ticino, and ever present in the Ticinese architects' minds. It was perhaps their very frontier condition which encouraged them to explore the tension between local and more universal aspects of architecture.

Vacchini's School at Montagnola near Lugano (1978–82) revealed his approach to the problem of an educational institution, which he seems to have conceived in terms of a miniature city with walls, a gate, a platform, covered walkways, and a three-sided piazza opening out on the fourth side to a vista of distant mountains. Vacchini was intrigued by the ancient Roman presence in the Ticino, and

his School was like an unearthed forum with its attached civic spaces and functions. The layout also embodied his intention of expressing 'the three things that a building may be by nature: a limit created in the middle of the landscape; a door which leads to a different world; and a place to be at ease in'. These topographical and psychological nuances were explored in an active composition of rectangular volumes traversed by a route rising from the curved approach road, up a flight of steps and into the court where the view exploded unexpectedly and dramatically to the alpine setting.

The Montagnola School, like most of Vacchini's buildings, relied upon clarity of image and a precise control of solid, void, profile and material. Basic types were transformed into a language which held schemes of modern and classical order in a tense coexistence. The main façade worked with the compositional idea of a travée of pilasters and openings, but in terms distilled from Terragni, Mies and Kahn. There was all the traditional concern for part and whole, ratio and rhythm, the stress of elements and edges. What helped to bring the armature of the design alive was the choice and combination of materials: black polished marble, coarse granite, Roman and Sienese travertine, strips of reflective steel in the bevelled cornices. It was this unity of idea, form and craft, as well as the force of the underlying convictions, which set the best Ticinese work so far apart from the trashy confectionery of postmodern classicism.

Several of the modern masters had established links to classical antiquity by ruminating upon the scattered remains of ancient sites. In the 1980s there was a renewed interest in the naked structure of ruins, and in such themes as the roofless room, the theatre of memories and the revelation of historical strata and deposits. The Italian architect Francesco Venezia stated that he was 'interested in … everything that we have inherited from the past: techniques, precision, measurements, proportions, materials' and suggested that a ruin could be 'real or metaphorical':

The only possibility for classicism today is that it is bound to a melancholic view of reality, to a strong sense of change, of something being broken. Melancholy is the contemplation of an order which is returning to its previous nature. … ruins are so fascinating because they show us how a building grows up, how architecture forms. In Hadrian's Villa in Tivoli you can read, like an anatomic diagram, all the Roman ideas of structure …

Most of Venezia's projects were in the far south of Italy, in Sicily, in a landscape that was haunted by the archaic presence of early Greek temples and by the remnants of later civilizations broken by earthquakes. His Museum in Gibellina (1981–7) relied upon abstract geometry, a stark frame structure, and Antique fragments to reactivate the spirit of the place. The half-enclosed entrance structure with its stone bench and its small fountain dripping water was like a compression chamber focusing the mind. It relied for its effect upon the play of light and shade on elementary forms, and upon a surreal, serpentine sculpture squeezed into a vertical gap between the interior space and the wider view. Several of Venezia's buildings and projects resorted to the idea of geometrical incisions cutting back through the layers of time. The Small Open Air Theatre at Salemi (1983–6), also in Sicily, was inserted between an old town and a stern but beautiful landscape. The building was arranged as an outdoor room and delimited by walls: it was as if a theatre had been let down into a rectangular well open to the sky. The visitor was guided across the site by variations of walls and levels, by ramps, platforms and steps, the eye being launched from the upper walkway to the distant horizon. The Small Open Air Theatre was integrated with its rocky setting through the careful selection of materials: sandstone, travertine and rough concrete paving with a tufa aggregate. Pieces of broken column emerged from the platform as if from solidified lava, and the old town (setting of a collective tragedy as it had been damaged by an earthquake) emerged above the rim of the theatre like a backdrop. Venezia's geometrical abstraction and concentration of latent memories in a place recalled the technique of Terragni's unbuilt Danteum project of 1938 (Figs. 453–4), while the use of steps and platforms to resonate with the landscape owed something to Libera's Casa Malaparte of 1939–42 (Fig. 463). Thus a work which embodied several of the dominant preoccupations of the early 1980s looped back nearly half a century in order to achieve its own resonances with antiquity.

The National Museum of Roman Art in Mérida, Spain (1980–6), designed by Rafael Moneo spliced together real ruins with metaphorical ones, working its way back to the structural anatomy of ancient architecture and touching upon certain continuities in Spanish tradition. Mérida stood at the junction of

780

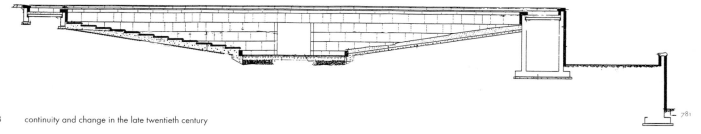

781

780 Francesco Venezia, Small Open Air Theatre, Salemi, Sicily, 1983–6

781 Open Air Theatre, Salemi, section

782 Rafael Moneo, National Museum of Roman Art, Mérida, Spain, 1980–6, sketch plan showing scheme in relation to urban context and ancient theatres

783 National Museum of Roman Art, basement with excavated ruins of Roman streets

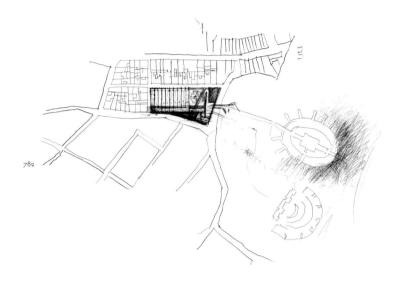

782

two major Roman roads. Under the early Empire it had been endowed with theatres, aqueducts and a long bridge. The Museum was across the road from a theatre and an amphitheatre and stood on top of excavated remnants of the old city which were visible in the basement. The design relied upon the insistent repetition of parallel concrete walls clad in Roman brick that were penetrated by different sized arches and surmounted by industrial skylights and tiled roofs. The result was a noble and airy hall, a cross between a turn of the century factory and something more ancient. The perspective between the main arches past rows of receding piers focused attention on white marble statues, Antique fragments and the *objet trouvé* of a classical column. Distances were hard to gauge and the effect of spatial illusion was dramatized by a beam of light falling across the end wall from an unseen source. To one side, concrete slab floors sliced through the main structure providing upper levels on a smaller scale for the display of jewellery, pottery and mosaics. Windows, doors and railings were in crude steel. The walls emerged on the exterior as a row of receding buttresses. The entrance was signalled by an arch in the lateral wing.

To the structural purist, the camouflaged concrete arches of the Mérida Museum were disturbing, but it was Moneo's intention to evoke associations with ancient structures rather than express the constructional realities of his own day. The building relied upon a series of analogies and displacements around the basic themes of Roman engineering and repeating arches; it alluded to aqueducts, baths, bridges or the flanges beneath Antique theatres. A museum was here conceived as an echo chamber of local history which also resonated with more distant sources and archaeological remains in the region. Moneo avoided the obvious references of academic classicism as well as the superficial graphic imagery of postmodernism, by establishing a strong formal and tectonic order, and by oscillating back and forth between abstract and figurative readings of tradition. The geometry of the Museum was shifted a few degrees off the excavated Roman street pattern underneath, and this accentuated the contrast between new and old. In those subterranean regions, the arches were denser, more numerous and less regular than above; they were

783

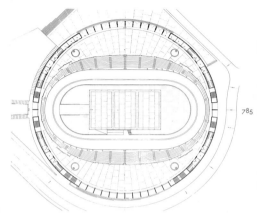

784

785

bathed in a dim, other-worldly light. The result was
something like an Antique cistern, though Kahn and
Piranesi also come to mind. Moneo's approach was
eclectic in a full sense; it drew images and ideas from
several periods, fusing or collaging them together.

The National Museum of Roman Art did not fit
comfortably with its immediate surroundings but
addressed a context in a much wider sense. The
reading of a place and its layers of memory involved
an imaginative excavation of past stages of a
civilization. There were even reminiscences of the
eighth-century Mosque at Cordoba (the 'Mezquita')
a columnated hall which itself blended the
inheritance of Roman aqueducts with the
metaphysical space of Islam. Moneo's building
touched upon deep continuities in Spanish
architecture ('*invariantes*', as an earlier generation
had called them) of a kind that had interested
architects in Spain around the turn of the century.
The hall of arches on a repetitive, modular plan was
a recurrent type in Spanish architecture, evident in
both the Gothic shipyards in Barcelona and in the
industrial vernacular of the late nineteenth century
(Chapter 8). Moneo took over the type and
reinterpreted it in a language that drew upon earlier
Spanish modernism and also engaged with the
questions raised by neo-Rationalism: he eroded and
adjusted the type to fit the purposes, context and
expressive intentions of a late twentieth-century

building. He wrote revealingly in 1979: 'The design
process is a way of bringing the elements of a
typology – the idea of a formal structure – into the
precise state that characterizes the single work.'

The past had never been totally banished from
earlier modernism in Spain, and there were some
buildings which extended the structural minimalism
of figures like de la Sota or Coderch (Chapter 26)
while also making a connection with more distant
traditions. The Velodrome in Barcelona (1982–4)
by Esteban Bonell and Francesc Rius managed to
combine new and old in an apparently effortless
way. It was placed on the outskirts of the city
on a prominent slope and worked at several
topographical scales, yet still maintained a clear
sense of unity. The Velodrome had something of the
tautness and straightforwardness of a bicycle wheel;
form and construction worked closely together,
and materials were handled in a direct and
unpretentious way. The building made a frank
display of its basic pieces and their interrelationship: the circular perimeter with access ways,
the oval disc and tilted surface of the bicycle track,
the leaning masts of floodlights, the restrained
structure using concrete, bricks and piers. Beyond
these functional facts, the form was brought to life
by subtle proportional and geometrical adjustments,
and by an underlying image combining associations
with amphitheatres or bullrings. The architects

hinted at the tension between modernity and tradition in their work:

If we had to define the velodrome in just a few words, we would say that it possesses a certain classicism, and at the same time an elaborated modernism. Classicism because of the way in which it sets itself on the landscape and because of the rotundity of its conception. Modernism because of its pragmatic and realistic appearance, because of its simplicity and the way in which construction is coherent with the materials used.

The best Spanish work of the 1980s succeeded in combining the exploration of ideas with a commitment to the material, spatial and sensuous aspects of architecture; in engaging with the past without regressing into pastiche; in responding to topography and context while without denying the need to express new social aspirations. Representative in all these respects was the Congress and Exhibition Hall in Salamanca (1985–92) by Juan Navarro Baldeweg, a work which also

addressed the dilemmas of modern monumentality in the increasingly democratic atmosphere of the post-Franco years. A simple composition of two boxes clad in warm-coloured sandstone, it was placed on a platform against the historic background of towers and spires. The typical urban pattern of Salamanca with its streets, squares and outdoor rooms continued inside in an abstracted state. The section expressed the intention of bringing the life of the city into the heart of a public institution. Over the main space hovered a flat saucer dome in ribbed concrete with an oculus at its centre. This massive roof was made from a single piece cast on the ground and lifted into place, but it was detailed so as to appear entirely weightless, floating in light and space without any apparent means of support; the beams holding it up were recessed and could not be seen. Where a traditional cupola rooted to the ground might have given an

787

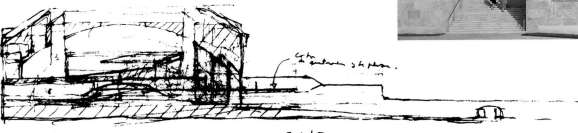

786

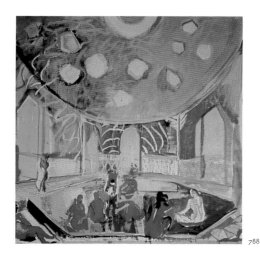

788

image of centralized, imperial authority, this was flattened and opened out, more like a parasol: it conveyed the notion of a hovering soffit over an open and democratic assembly, as if a piece of the city had been captured for social purposes.

The suspended saucer dome of the Salamanca Congress Hall echoed other top-lit roofs in the city's history, but also stemmed from Navarro Baldeweg's limited repertoire of forms, and from his previous experiments as an architect, painter and conceptual artist. In his paintings he explored such themes as the energy of light and water, or the conviviality of subterranean Arab baths with rays of light penetrating domes. In his conceptual pieces (which had a surreal, even Dadaist character) he dealt with more abstract ideas such as luminosity, gravity and weightlessness. Beyond the sphere of Navarro 's private concerns, the Congress Hall in Salamanca had much broader social and political implications. The central idea of the building engaged with the traditional iconography of authority only to subvert it: it provided an antidote to the ponderous weight of official Francoist classical culture, and gave monumentality a fresh interpretation. Likewise its orientation and debts to architectural tradition were complex and critical. It returned to a version of origins, to the basic type of a roof symbolizing the sky, but restated this in terms of a modern liberating space. It engaged with a long tradition of domical construction (including Islamic and Byzantine examples as well as Roman ones), but reversed normal expectations of load and support. It relied upon later 'filters' in the history of architecture such as John Soane's illusionistic domes of the early nineteenth century, but it used these as a basis for inspiration rather than imitation. The hovering soffit in Salamanca was tantalisingly simple, but in fact contained many echoes and ideas. It substantiated Juan Navarro's claim that works of art be thought of as 'physical, fabricated myths'.

If one were to investigate a specifically twentieth-century pedigree for the Congress Hall in Salamanca, one would find it more at the level of ideas and principles than at the level of forms. There were absorptions from the classicism of Asplund the archaicism of Kahn, even the formal intensity of Brancusi's sculptures. Without mimicking his Spanish mentor de la Sota, Navarro explored analogous questions of structural and visual ambiguity and subtle inversions of historical convention. He drew together two contrasting strands in Spanish modernism, the one concerned with historical types, the other with the intensified perception of natural forces in structure and in light. Essentially modern in its space, its structural idea and its social stance, the Congress Hall in Salamanca was none the less infused with what T. S. Eliot called 'the historical sense'.

The selection of works presented here by no means exhausts the range of architecture produced in the 1980s concerned with transforming the past. But it does serve to present several different approaches to the problem involving varying degrees of abstraction. Rather than a fixed pattern of frozen identities, a tradition reveals a constellation of pre-existing ideas and forms capable of unexpected new readings and alignments in the minds of later interpreters. Some of the richest creations of the 1980s and early 1990s were eclectic in the best sense: they drew upon and synthesized principles and types from several periods, even using the modernist inheritance as a lens through which to examine long-term themes and basic ideas in the history of architecture. 'Nothing old is ever reborn', stated Aalto. 'But it never completely disappears either. And everything that has ever been emerges in a new form.'

788 Juan Navarro Baldeweg, *El Baño*, 1985. Oil on canvas

789 Juan Navarro Baldeweg, Congress and Exhibition Hall, interior

789

34

the universal and the local: landscape, climate and culture

Every society possesses what is called an 'image of the world'. This image has its roots in the unconscious structure of society and requires a specific conception of time to foster it.
Octavio Paz, 1972

790 Tadao Ando, Koshino House, Hyogo, 1979–81

This book has gone to some lengths to demonstrate that modern architecture is not the rootless phenomenon which it is sometimes made out to be and that it has interacted with the inheritance of several cultures virtually from the beginning. The very notion of 'modernity' has inspired ideals reaching beyond nation, cast and creed, while the generation and dissemination of forms have involved a constant tension with local traditions. Sometimes these interactions of the international and the regional, the new and the old, have been implicated in schemes of national identity; sometimes they have contributed to the symbolic richness of individual works without specifically territorial aims; sometimes they have helped to crystallize myths about the origins of architecture, the human condition or the natural world.

The historiography of modern architecture has reflected a Western bias and continues to do so. This is not to dispute that the primary inventions of modernism occurred mostly in Europe and the United States. But it is to suggest that insufficient attention and credit have normally been given to the contribution of places remote from the points of origin. Already by the outbreak of the Second World War, strands of modern architecture existed in Mexico, Japan, Brazil, Palestine and South Africa (to mention only some), and several of these involved a judicious adjustment of generic features of modernism to the climates, cultures, memories and aspirations of their respective societies. Neither the concept of an International Style nor the myth of indigenous purity can do justice to this complex intermingling of elements, combining new visions of the future and new versions of the past.

The critical re-examination of modern architecture proceeded apace in the post-war years, sometimes in an attempt to find the right balance between progressive ideals of modernization and industrialization, national myths and the natural forces of particular regions. This was the period, after all, of the fine individual achievements of such architects as the Mexican Luis Barragán, the Japanese Kenzo Tange, the Brazilian Oscar Niemeyer, or the Turkish Sedad Hakki Eldem, each of whom worked in the tension between international influence and the interpretation of his particular society. The term 'Regionalism' has sometimes been used to describe these developments, but it does not do them justice, as it can imply something provincial or peripheral. Both the aims and the achievements of such architects transcended their local situations. If anything they wished to blend different 'universalisms' – those which they sensed in the seminal works of modern architects, and those they sensed in the substructures of their respective cultures, some of which (e.g. Mexico, Turkey, Japan) rested upon the foundations of ancient civilizations and grand traditions. In turn these architects contributed vital new ideas to the wider world of architecture.

By the 1970s, both the political map and the architectural universe had altered, with greater status and validity being accorded to non-Western traditions, and with a far more permissive attitude towards the use of the past. Earlier chapters attempted to outline the range of options and positions in various parts of what Nehru called the 'Third World' – the world other than the two main power blocks. In ways that echoed, to some degree, the earlier discourses of National Romanticism in the West, new models were proposed for cross-breeding modernism with distinctive images of national pasts. Sometimes it was the internal impetus which gained, in which case buildings might move more towards a direct engagement with some phase or another of local tradition; sometimes it was the external impetus which gained, in which case the local was transformed more in the direction of international models. The examples of individuals such as Geoffrey Bawa, Balkrishna Doshi, Eladio Dieste or Teodoro González de León have served to demonstrate a range of ways of grappling with these dilemmas.

It needs to be said straightaway that the struggle to reconcile modern and ancient, regional and universal, was by no means restricted to questions of identity in developing societies, but played (and continues to play) a central role in the work of several major architects with more generalized aims. One cannot imagine dealing with figures like Wright, Le Corbusier, Aalto, Kahn (or Utzon, Van Eyck and Coderch in a later generation) without coming to terms with their prodigious capacity to absorb and transform diverse sources and civilizations into their own work. A great architectural creation is like a symbolic world with its own empires of the imagination, its own mental

regions and its own inner landscapes; it has diverse historical and human currents flowing through it, even as it responds to its particular place and time. One of the reasons why buildings such as Wright's Prairie Houses, Aalto's urban complexes, or Le Corbusier's and Kahn's late works on the Indian subcontinent continue to radiate a powerful influence, is that they managed to distil the myths of their respective societies, while also blending fundamentals from several traditions; they combined a response to the local with a certain universality.

In recent years, the question of what constitutes a region or a nation has, if anything, become even more confused. For this has been a period characterized by a worldwide standardization of products, images, fashions and ideas on the one hand, and by an ever greater pluralism of identities, factions, confederations and territorial allegiances on the other. Some of these regroupings have occurred independently of the previous structure of nation states, and others have sought to balance the cosmopolitanism of the new kind of megalopolis with echoes of old cultural units (for example, Catalonia and the Ticino). At the same time urbanization has proceeded at a great pace and the rural base (once supposed to have secreted the 'essence' of local identity according to thinkers like Hassan Fathy) has been gradually eroded, depopulated, exploited by international agri-business, or submitted to the ravages of extra-urban development. In the process, the inner life of vernacular languages – whether spoken or built – has been further destroyed.

If the preoccupation with classicisms in the early 1980s perhaps reflected a need to reground the disciplines of architecture in the past, the interest in 'regionalisms' revealed anxiety about the pervasive erosion and deracination of particular cultures and places by the homogenizing forces of modern commercial and technological development. Most (though not all) of these regionalisms were quick to distance themselves from the instant history of post-modernism, (which they identified as part of the disease rather than the cure) and from the blood and soil regionalisms of the 1930s. What Alexander Tzonis and Lliane Lefaivre called a 'critical regionalism' seemed to imply an anxious recognition that most folk and vernacular traditions were

791 Judith Chafee, Ramada House, Tucson, Arizona, 1980

791

irretrievably lost, but that some modern manoeuvre must be set (or reset) in motion to retrieve old knowledge at a distance. Kenneth Frampton used the same term 'critical regionalism' to reject 'consumerist iconography masquerading as culture' and to criticize the postmodernist reduction of architecture to the mere 'communicative or instrumental sign'. Frampton instead advocated both the deconstruction of 'universal modernism in terms of values or images that are locally cultivated', and an adulteration of 'autochthonous elements with paradigms drawn from alien sources'. In fact, several of the modern masters, and several regional strands of modern architecture, had been doing something of the kind for more than half a century. The regionalist discourse of the early 1980s even

served up some of the old wine of National Romanticism in new bottles, but with the bitter taste of nationalism removed. When it came to illustrating what was meant by a critical regionalism, there was usually a selection of creditable modern architects whose work embodied a vital synthesis of the local and the general – figures like Coderch and Barragán in the middle distant past, or like Botta, Siza or Ando in the then recent world of architecture.

Theoretical post- (and pre-) rationalizations are one thing; works giving shape to ideas, insights, and intuitions, another. In the 1980s several buildings were created which responded intelligently to climate, place, memory and landscape, without ignoring social and technological change. Some of these emerged from the dramatic contrast between urban and rural worlds in developing countries where matters of cultural identity were a conscious part of the intention; others emerged in remote corners of the industrialized world where native architectures were still visible, even if native cultures had been seriously undermined. The best of these buildings seemed able to draw upon indigenous wisdom, but without simply imitating vernacular forms: to penetrate beyond the obvious features of regional style to some deeper mythical structures rooted in past adjustments to landscape and climate.

The Ramada House in Tucson, Arizona (1980), by Judith Chafee, combined the space, structure and abstraction of modernism with a recall of ancient methods for dealing with the hot/dry desert climate and the fierce sunlight of the American Southwest. The building was formed from a protective parasol made from slender wooden poles, and shading slats placed above an adobe substructure of planar whitewashed walls half-buried in the ground. The Ramada House lived in tension with its desert setting, the mood and light changing from minute to minute. The skeletal structure framed views near and far, and the roof was a stable horizontal incident in a turbulent landscape of cacti, sand and crags. In drawings, the Ramada House was an uncompromisingly modern design which blended Corbusian ideas such as the free plan, the grid of pilotis and the shading slab, with concepts derived from Wright (Taliesin West) or Schindler (El Pueblo Ribera Courts), but it engaged with these precedents at the level of

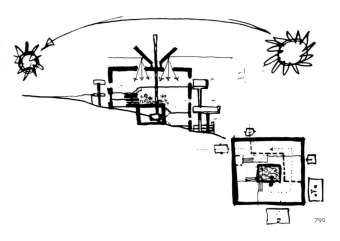

principles rather than just appearances. In the same spirit it dug up desert archetypes from the Native American tradition: the simple cactus, log and twig shelters of the nomads (reinterpreted in Spanish Colonial ranches as a raft of saguarro fronds on poles called a '*ramada*'), and the half-buried earth or masonry dwellings of the more sedentary communities. Chafee rejected the term 'Regionalist' as too limiting; the Ramada House captured the spirit of a place using means drawn from near and far, interpreted natural conditions through the inheritance of myth, and engaged with the very idea of architectural origins.

While mechanized devices for the control of climate became ever more sophisticated, some architects considered it a moral duty to respond to the extremes of heat and cold in the form and organization of their buildings. Ralph Erskine's projects for the North of Scandinavia and for the Polar wastes took on the character of a virtual 'sub-Arctic Regionalism', so consistently did they address the problems of new communities in frigid zones. Erskine had evolved a set of devices to exclude the North winds and blizzards, to admit the most of low winter sunlight, to stop snow from obstructing openings, and to allow social life to continue in entirely closed, but naturally lit spaces during the midnight months. The precincts, irregular geometries and uneven silhouettes of his buildings reacted to the topography and micro-climate of each landscape, while the extending slats, balconies and shelters provided gradual transitions from public to private space. Like many designers working out

of a Scandinavian modern tradition, Erskine was indebted to the humanism and 'poetic functionalism' of Alvar Aalto, who had found ways of adjusting modernism to his own geography and culture. The Finnish architect and critic Marja-Riitta Norri has evoked the physical and mental impact of the climate and landscape in northern latitudes:

The Nordic countries are united above all, by natural conditions, the changing seasons, and light. Nowhere does light act more strongly on people's states of mind than in the North: the lengthening of the days seems equally dramatic and real every Spring, after the winter darkness. The clarity and fragility of the light when the days are at their longest, and its meagreness at the dark time of the year, are of central importance as a starting point in building. In the North, earth, air and water meet on a large scale. The interplay of these basic landscape elements differs in each country according to topography … With the cycle of the seasons, the elements of the Nordic landscape change their forms. The gentle waters of summer freeze in winter to hard, sharp ice, the soft breezes become icy winds, the sun's stride through the sky – weeks on end in the far North – shrinks to a couple of hours, or disappears entirely below the horizon.

The Norwegian architect Sverre Fehn developed a sparse, minimalist architecture from concrete, glass, wood and steel, that was often embedded in the terrain in order to handle these exacting conditions. His project for an Art Gallery at Verdens Ende (World's End) of 1988 envisaged a building inserted into the crevices of a rocky shoreline facing the vastness of ocean and sky. The flat roofs were tilted, or sliced, to let light down into the stepped, subterranean section. Fehn's architecture worked with wall planes and platforms. His sharp, linear abstractions seemed to

792 Ralph Erskine, Villa Ström, Stocksund, 1961, sketch section showing reflectors on roof for low winter sun, and plan showing separated balconies for summer use

793 Sverre Fehn, Norsk Bremuseum, Fjaerland, Norway, 1991

794 Rick Leplastrier, Palm House, Sydney, 1974

contain subliminal echoes of ships or geological formations. His reading of the Nordic landscape included a mythical interpretation of its creation under the impact of sea, snow, ice, wind and rain. The Norsk Bremuseum (Norwegian Glacier Museum) at Fjaerland (1991) was organized as a low bar with interior and exterior walkways, and a diagonal stair carrying the visitor to the upper level which allowed long views across the Fjords towards the mountains. The site was on the last projection of the Josstedal Glacier – a delta running out of the Sogne complex of inlets. The splintered angles and shards of the building suggested something between a wreck and a shattered piece of ice, although the architect spoke of a long, low slab of rock deposited by a glacier. Fehn considered glaciers to be almost living creatures sliding across the land. Like museums, they contained layers of memory: 'Lying in the content of this mass are secrets of the past in the transparent invisibility.'

When 'Regionalism' was broached in the European context in the 1980s it often had to do with a populist or kitsch imitation of the vernacular. But there were developments of a more demanding intellectual nature which addressed the particular character of topographies and loosely defined 'regions'. The work of Mario Botta and his colleagues in the Ticino (discussed in the last chapter) has some relevance here since it attempted to translate the elemental character of the local vernacular into an architecture of pure forms arranged to make the most of the southern Alpine aspect; but its aspirations were obviously more general, engaged with both classical echoes, and the universal inheritance of modernism. A sensitivity to climate, context and geographical location was woven into Spanish modern architecture as well, and when certain Catalan architects in the 1980s revealed a modernism with Mediterranean accents (e.g. José Antonio Martinez Lapeña, Elías Torres, Josep Llinas, Carlos Ferrater) they in fact extended a string of earlier solutions to analogous problems stretching back through Coderch and Gaudí. At the same time they were alert to a wide range of stimuli in contemporary thinking and to worldwide developments in modern architecture (see Chapter 35).

By the last quarter of the twentieth century most truly regional traditions – most authentic

794

vernaculars – were dead, and the rest were under threat of extinction. In any case, the architect in the modern condition could not reuse these languages directly without devaluing them and producing a fake version. But he could invent new worlds full of resonances with a particular cultural or natural landscape. Australian domestic architecture of the 1970s and 1980s reveals several poetic interventions of this kind: The Palm House to the north of Sydney, designed by Rick Leplastrier (1974) was pivotal in this development. This was inserted into a dense patch of tropical rain forest between land and sea, and was formed from a copper hooded roof riding on timber struts above a substructure of russet coloured adobe walls. Canvas awnings and steel tackle suggested nautical inspirations, while the image of a primeval shelter assembled from both industrial and pre-industrial materials touched upon several resonances in the Australasian past. Le Plastrier was of a generation which inherited the local expressions of the 1960s, but which also sought nourishment far and wide in the modern movement, and in several world vernacular traditions.

The Australian architect Glenn Murcutt responded to the different climatic zones in which he worked in delicate buildings combining slender metal frames, corrugated iron roofs and shading devices. Without straining for a particular image of 'an Australian way of life', Murcutt succeeded in creating buildings which could have stood hardly anywhere else. His architecture extended and rejected features of earlier Australian modernism, and looked inwards to corrugated tin shacks, wool shearing sheds, Aboriginal bark shelters, and the inspiration of the Australian landscape itself; at the same time it maintained a cosmopolitan tension by looking outwards to a Miesian lineage stressing abstraction and precision in steel. Light – its admission, exclusion, and transmission through filters and blinds – took on a poetic dimension, related in turn to the architect's understanding of foliage and natural forces. The wafer-like metallic roofs and tensile structures of Murcutt's buildings suggested subtle connections with bark or leaves, but he rejected 'natural references' as sentimental, insisting instead upon a more penetrating reading of what he called the 'legible landscape':

I want my buildings to use natural light and ventilation to the greatest extent possible, and so I adjust their orientation to maximize the potential cross ventilation from prevailing breezes, and I shift roof-lines and pitches to gain maximum winter sun and minimize summer sun ...The natural stresses on an environment, and the responses of the land, are the keys to the incredible emotional power of a place ... In Australia the light is so intense, so clear and sharp that it separates and isolates elements in the landscape in harsh contour. The physical as well as the visual effect of that light on the land is extraordinary. In parts of the Australian desert, the leaves of the trees, unlike leaves in European and North American temperate zones which curl and turn their faces towards the sun, instead face away from it, hanging down to reduce the evaporation of surface moisture. And the edge of the leaf picks up the track of the sun and follows it through the day ... If we understand ... why a thing looks the way it does, or why it works the way it does, then we understand the principle, and that principle, not the form it produces, is transferable.

The architect's reading and interpretation of basic concepts and patterns in his own part of the world could in fact, be focused by his version of what was universal in modernism; equally his transformation of relevant features in the modern tradition could be influenced by his intuition of what was archetypal in his own national or regional past. The Japanese architect Tadao Ando is revealing in this respect. Using modern means, he attempted to restate 'the unity between house and nature that Japanese houses have lost in the process of modernization'. His buildings supplied a minimalist alternative to the visual cacophony and sprawling mess of the modern megalopolis. They also distilled a sense of identity in subtle ways. Ando's houses of the late 1970s and early 1980s (e.g. the Koshino House in Hyogo of 1979–81) turned their back on the

795

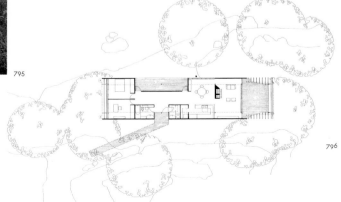

796

797

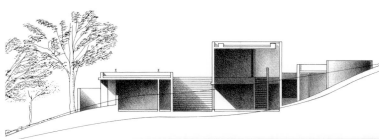
798

outside world and (rather like Barragán's dwellings a quarter of a century before) worked within the secrecy of blank but emotionally charged walls. They opened up tranquil precincts in which the individual might re-establish contact with the inner life and with the rhythms of the seasons. Ando's vocabulary was stripped down to essentials – planar, smooth concrete walls, frames, vaults, glazing, glass bricks – but these were merely the material means for revealing an underlying sense of order, a spiritualized abstraction, intensified by light, shade and space. The sequences of passageways, rooms and courts were bathed in gentle light admitted through restricted openings that focused attention on small incidents. As in the traditional Japanese teahouse, a sophisticated simplicity was used to heighten the sense of the natural world. While Ando's architecture drew on long-established concepts in his own culture, it also owed much to Le Corbusier, Kahn and abstract sculptors like Richard Serra. It also recalled Mies van der Rohe's suggestion that modern architecture should bring man and nature together in a 'higher unity'. Of his own work, Ando wrote: 'Architecture of this sort is likely to alter with the region in which it sends down roots … still it is open in the direction of universality.'

799

800 Geoffrey Bawa,
Parliament Building,
Colombo, Sri Lanka,
1980–3

801 Henning Larsen,
Ministry of Foreign
Affairs, Riyadh, Saudi
Arabia, 1979–84, interior

802 Ministry of
Foreign Affairs, plan

803 Ministry of
Foreign Affairs,

The re-examination of local traditions took on a special meaning in developing countries recovering from colonial occupation which wished to establish distinct natural identities in their architecture. In the 1980s a mood gathered momentum in the Third World which rejected the glib reproduction of international formulae and sought out symbolic forms rooted in the past that might also express contemporary aspirations. At its worst this tendency resulted in skin-deep instant history (aided and abetted by Western postmodernism) in which national stereotypes were combined with pastiches of the vernacular. At its best it succeeded in penetrating to the substructures of local traditions (some of them with grand imperial pasts) and in transforming these in ways which were right for the social order of the present. It was a matter of sensing beneath the surface the memories, myths and ideals giving a society its coherence and energy, and then of providing these with an architectural arrangement. The hope was to produce buildings of a certain timeless character fusing old and new, local and universal. The excavation of history in traditional societies involved a penetration of different layers, and a selection of points of reference by modernizing élites. The Indian historian Romila Thapar described this process well when she suggested that 'each generation chooses the past on which it wishes to draw.'

The formulation of modern ideals of national identity involved a balancing act between the need to communicate through a locally understood language, and the need to belong to the broader tendencies of the contemporary world. The greater permissiveness towards the past which was felt in

the late 1970s allowed architects to blend several associations, some legible, some less so, into a single design. When designing the Sri Lankan Parliament Building outside Colombo in 1980, Geoffrey Bawa was confronted with the problem of providing a national democratic symbol for a country of many castes and creeds in a post-colonial state, a nation whose institutions were eclectic mixtures of ancient rituals and modern Western ways. The Parliament Building was set on an island approached formally over a causeway, and it evoked the feeling of an Oriental shrine, yet the main chamber was modelled on that of the Houses of Commons in London. The wide roofs and deep overhangs suggested the indigenous image of a collective meeting house from a village. The monumentalization of the vernacular fitted with Bawa's own sensitivity to the tropical environment of the island and to the traditional architectures of southern Asia, and was an amplified version combining industrial materials and handicrafts of the vocabulary he had discovered in smaller buildings such as his own studio (Fig. 732), but it also responded to the expectations of a largely traditional society for an appropriate image of itself.

When grappling with the task of a legible political representation, Bawa was able to rely upon the existing conventions of a local style of building which still had some vital vernacular basis. But with rapid urbanization and the loss of rural traditions this was not always available and the architect had to invent by synthesizing relevant prototypes. The Ministry of Foreign Affairs in Riyadh, Saudi Arabia (1974–84) designed by the Danish architect Henning Larsen combined modernist simplicity,

801

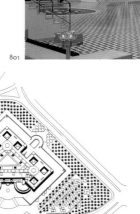

802

regional innuendoes and Pan-Islamic references in its interpretation of the enclosed institution. The Saudis wanted a building that would combine offices and ceremonial spaces, that would act as 'gateway to the nation' for visiting dignitaries or diplomats, and that would reflect the stern moral values of the heartlands as well as the central position of Saudi Arabia in the Islamic world. Larsen made an inward-looking building with a large triangular hall at its centre, and a perimeter of offices which looked down into courtyard gardens or into tall, top-lit corridors with galleries. The exteriors were of brown stone imported from Italy and were fully insulated. Small windows were punched in them and light was admitted through a baffle to cut down glare. The actual structure was a frame, not a traditional wall, and the Ministry was packed with up-to-the-minute technology for ventilation, fire control and security. The low towers at the corners and the bastions flanking the main entrance hinted at the mud fortresses of the Nejd, thus alluding to the home region and foundation myths of the Saud royal family. The interiors were chaste, white and luminous, filled with the sound of fountains. Allusions to the Alhambra or the Magreb mingled with abstract surfaces and transparencies with a Corbusian pedigree. The hovering ceiling over the central space, with light creeping around its edges, even recalled Ronchamp.

Larsen's Ministry of Foreign Affairs was an eclectic work fusing together many sources, some of them recognisable, some of them hermetic. He tried to understand tradition at the level of types, not just images, and even to seek out analogies between different periods and styles. In that respect, his

803

approach (and even his forms) owed something to Aldo Rossi and to neo-Rationalism. At the core of his interpretation was the archetype of the Arab house with its blank exteriors excluding the heat and the prying eye, and its rich interior life around a courtyard reached through several transitions. Around this theme he worked with others such as the fabric of streets and squares in desert towns, or geometrical water gardens. The plan was an ingenious combination of spaces in masses, and masses in spaces, that owed something to the geometry of Mogul tombs in India, and even to the neo-classical Police Headquarters in Copenhagen of 1919–24 (Fig. 160). Beneath the more obvious manipulations of references and sources (sometimes too theatrical) there was an inventive reinterpretation of the spatial layering and visual ambiguity of Islamic architecture. Larsen's Ministry of Foreign Affairs emerged from a basic tension which existed in several of the wealthy Arab nations between Westernization and modernization on the one side, and the pull of traditional values on the other. It steered its way carefully between international influences and a traditionalism which could only too easily regress into a surface manipulation of Orientalist imagery.

It could be argued that some building types were more international than others by definition. Skyscrapers, for example, could be thought of as rootless pieces of standardized equipment like Boeing 747s. Even so, there were attempts at 'regionalizing' the tall building which went deeper than just attaching a few horseshoe arches or traditional screens to the façade. The National Commercial Bank in Jeddah, Saudi Arabia (1979–83), designed by Gordon Bunshaft of Skidmore, Owings and Merrill, crossbred the international type with principles for dealing with a hot climate that was sometimes dry, sometimes humid, and prone to sandstorms. The building was placed between a lagoon , the business district, and what remained of the old 'Medinah'. The plan was triangular with an attached lift shaft on one side, and it had originally been intended that the sharp edge should face out to sea like a prow. The curiously scaleless monolith was punctured by huge rectangles of shadow behind which internal trays of offices were retracted, so being protected from heat, glare and sand-laden gusts of wind. The terraces behind

the openings were planted like oases in the air. At the core was a shaft which siphoned warm air upwards and drew cool air in below, reducing the internal temperature and the need for air conditioning. Thus the section drew upon local climatic devices – found in courtyard houses, wind-towers etc. – but without imitating their form. Bunshaft's design took its place in a line of researches adjusting tall buildings to the sun (e.g. Le Corbusier's unbuilt Algiers skyscraper of the early 1940s), but it also explored a new anatomy for the skyscraper, and expressed it in a bold external form that evoked seaside landmarks or ancient forts. The National Commercial Bank rose out of the flat landscape declaring wealth and self-assurance but without exterior show. It managed to make serious architecture out of the unlikely combination of green microprocessor screens and palm trees, international finance and national prestige, the tools and mores of a new technocratic class, and desert traditions of building.

In most countries of the Middle East modern architecture was a recent foreign import, and there was no local modern tradition to build upon. In countries like India or Mexico, it was possible to extend themes which had emerged in previous decades. There was never quite a modern Mexican style, but there were recognizable devices and accents nevertheless: a certain breadth and grandeur

804 Gordon Bunshaft, National Commercial Bank, Jeddah, Saudi Arabia, 1979–83, section

805 Ricardo Legorreta, Renault Factory, Monterrey, Mexico, 1984

806 Ricardo Legorreta, Museum of Contemporary Art, Monterrey, 1989–92

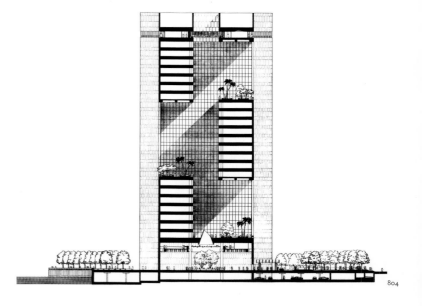

804

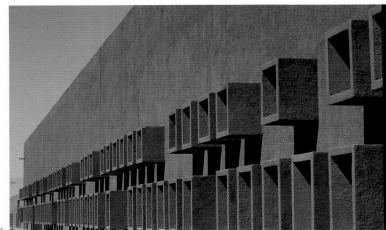
805

monumental, not so say rhetorical treatment. As
mentioned earlier (Chapter 31), he drew much from
the archaic late works of Le Corbusier, but also
crystallized a language of his own rooted in Mexican
realities and myths. The Tabasco Government
Centre in the tropical city of Villahermosa (1986–8),
was organized as a wide portal in reinforced
concrete preceding an interior street covered by a
pergola of hovering structural beams which allowed
air to circulate while casting deep shadows over
the public precinct below. The building reiterated
several of the architect's themes – the gate, the
patio, the shading roof – but also contained
Mayan echoes in its proportions and accentuation.
References to this local past were more overt in
González de León's other major realization in
Villahermosa, a tropical landscape garden called
the Parque Tomás Garrido Canabal (1984–7). The
landscape design combined formal and informal
modes, Pre-Colombian and classical memories,
modern materials and spatial effects. At the centre,
on the main axis was a two-sided arch referring to

to the best work which combined a monumental
abstraction with almost unconscious echoes
of primary elements from the past such as the
platform, the patio, the wide horizontal plane
and the stark wall. In the 1980s Ricardo Legorreta
continued to extend his basic language of bold
volumes, coloured walls and precincts. Many
of his buildings were for the industrial sector,
and here he resorted to daring statements of
abstract geometry which were carried through in
processional sequences, structural piers, hovering
planes and controlled effects of natural light and
transparency. The Renault Factory at Monterrey
(1984) was placed behind a long rust-coloured wall
set down in the stark landscape, punctured by
minimal openings, and preceded by mounds of
rough boulders and flints. Legorreta's architecture
continued to draw inspiration from Barragán, but
he had his own touchstones in the polychromy of
the Mexican vernacular and the vibrancy of
modern colour-field painting. The Museum of
Contemporary Art in Monterrey (1989–92), which
was modelled on a convent-type with stern exterior
walls and welcoming patios, rejoiced in the play
of light on textured surfaces, in the movement of
water, and in the telescoping of interior perspectives
with framed views of the landscape. Indisputably
modern, it also engaged with the emotive values
of traditional Mexican forms.

González de León's main commissions
were in the Mexican public sector and required

806

the unity of European and Meso-American culture. The central promenade continued over a bridge through a monumental version of a Mayan hut roof, then ended at a slender mirador tower with a spiral stair. Rusticated concrete pergolas, steps, mounds and water cascades were overrun with tropical vegetation, and an alleyway of palms was drawn into a play of perspectival illusions. The Parque Tomás Garrido Canabal combined legible and abstract elements in a single idea and unearthed ancient Mexican themes to do with the origins of architecture in platforms, hills and valleys. A modern version of a Meso-American ruin, it fused together regional and cosmopolitan sources, but also worked with fundamentals of the landscape art. González de León's works in Villahermosa reflected a new spirit of decentralization – a Regionalism in the true sense – which even stirred old rumours of an ancient Mayan nation.

With the Supreme Court in Mexico City (1987–92), González de León achieved one of his strongest statements of civic monumentality, reverting to the idea of a public building as a wide opening on a grand but accommodating scale leading to a species of interior street covered by a pergola. The courtrooms themselves were laid out along a central spine of circulation, and the plan suggested an anthropomorphic figure with a head, a body and feet. The structure was again made from

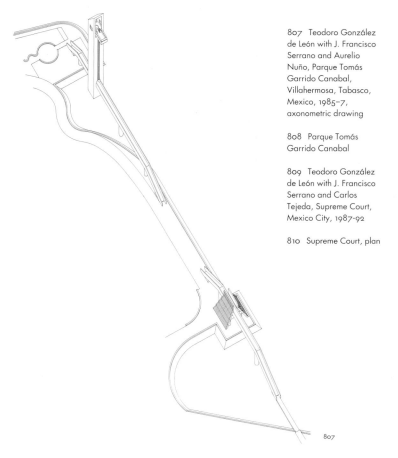

807

807 Teodoro González de León with J. Francisco Serrano and Aurelio Nuño, Parque Tomás Garrido Canabal, Villahermosa, Tabasco, Mexico, 1985–7, axonometric drawing

808 Parque Tomás Garrido Canabal

809 Teodoro González de León with J. Francisco Serrano and Carlos Tejeda, Supreme Court, Mexico City, 1987-92

810 Supreme Court, plan

808

809

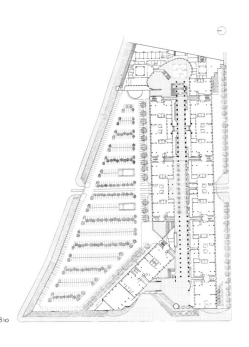

810

rough, bush-hammered concrete with large chips of stone in several colours, a finish that was sensitive to light and weathering, labour intensive (and therefore relatively cheap in Mexico), and resistant to the corrosive effects of pollution. The striations around the main entrance recalled Carlo Scarpa, but were also inspired by details on the niches of the pyramid at Tajin. The building as a whole contained Corbusian echoes, in fact was a worthy descendant of the High Court in Chandigarh (Chapter 23), while its repetitive geometry and bold surfaces revealed González de León's study and absorption of ideas from Aldo Rossi. The Supreme Court was a building with a presence and standing of its own which relied upon ancient types to do with the idealization of social order: the portico, the platform and the hypostyle hall. For González de León these were generalized ideas cutting across particular cultures or periods, and he transformed them with the mind and eye of a modern painter interested in both Cubism and the development of mathematical and geometrical themes. The Mexican painter Rufino Tamayo put the matter succinctly: 'Art is universal, the accent is local.'

Another architect to start with Le Corbusier and
then move on to his own cultural space was the
Colombian Rogelio Salmona. In the 1960s and
1970s, Salmona evolved an architecture based upon
indigenous brick construction. His Torres del
Parque in Bogota of 1964–70 created an entire
enclave of considerable urban substance out of
angles, shafts and towers in this material. By the
1980s, Salmona was aware of a general shift in
architectural thinking towards a more overt cultural
representation in architectural form, but was equally
conscious of the danger of reducing tradition to
a superficial transfer. His Casa de Huespedes de
Colombia at Cartagena (1983–7) on the coastline
of the Caribbean was organized as a series of
interlocking courts and levels and was woven into
the pre-existing fabric of fortifications and tropical
planting. Sober stone walls were punched with
simple rectangular openings and on the interior
there was a counter-theme of brick vaults. The
courts were cut across by water channels and the
sequence through the building was orchestrated by
an alternating rhythm of light and shade. There was
the intimation of an Arab space as if a memory of
the Alhambra had been transported across the
waters to Latin America; and in fact just this did
occur in the early colonial architecture of Colombia
which came from southern Spain. But the
distillation of patio ideas included another
archetype, a reference point in the quest for

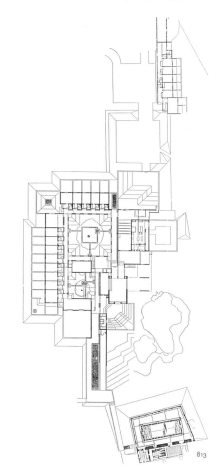

universality in Meso-American architecture, namely the 'Nuns' Quadrangle' at Uxmal, the ninth-century Mayan site in the Yucatan. Commentators on the Casa de Huespedes referred to a 'distillation of place', but it in fact distilled many other places than just its own, and achieved a poetic presence through the compression of these memories in a sensuous and tactile form. In effect the building was a constructed myth resonant with echoes and far transcending any merely 'Regionalist' agenda, although it was fashionable in the 1980s to refer to Latin American architecture with Regionalist labels of various kinds. With reference to Salmona's work, Tejeda suggested in 1989 that:

Latin American ideological regionalism or localism is recent in the field of architecture. It began by a descent from the universalist doctrine ... to seek a presumed but uncertain 'regional identity' ... Salmona's architecture is more vital, important and valuable because of its universal dimension, its permanence and its roots in the past, than for its presumed regional character ... His creations in the formidable presence of the natural space of his adaptive country, show an emotional and spiritual consciousness ... [they] require all the senses for a true understanding of the hidden intentions and the implicit meanings of his particular poetic code ... his architecture will occasionally grant the observer a sensuous pleasure which can only come from a formidable mastery of constructed forms.

The best Indian work of the 1980s and early 1990s also managed to maintain a certain tension between international and regional, modern and ancient, and to blend local responses with more universal dimensions. One reason that it was able to do this was that it continued to evolve in a creative symbiosis with the powerful prototypes generated by Le Corbusier and Louis Kahn in the 1950s and

1960s; another was that it probed towards generic features of the Indian architecture of the past without resorting to trivial stylistic quotations. The pressure to investigate tradition came not just from the architects' own desire to enrich their work by re-rooting it in principles appropriate to climate and culture, but also from an ideological transition in Indian society which insisted more and more upon some vaguely defined 'Indianness' in artistic and even political matters. The retrospective understanding of national pasts was influenced not only by the weight of artistic heritage (which was enormous in the case of countries like Mexico and India), but also by contemporary belief which might accord very different meaning and value to 'modernity' and 'tradition'. A nation like Pakistan, that was committed to a notion of Islamic identity, had a different perspective on the grand inheritance of south Asian architecture from that of a nation like India which exerted itself to maintain a secular ideal.

India had received and absorbed many foreign influences in the past, and it is arguable that the adjustment of modernism to fit Indian ways and mentalities corresponded to an old pattern. Something of this can be sensed in the transition of a number of Indian architects' work between the late 1970s and the late 1980s. Charles Correa's basic commitment was to 'open to sky space', and this was already revealed in his Gandhi Ashram Memorial Museum completed at the beginning of the 1960s (Fig. 718). Gradually Correa began to emancipate himself from the hold of Le Corbusier and Kahn, exploring overlaps between new and old, monumental and folk. His kit of parts for Indian conditions included platforms and terraces, sunken courts and outdoor rooms, sections for natural ventilation, and balconies, overhangs or screens for shade; like most modern Indian architects he used a simple construction system of concrete frame and rough brick, sometimes with coloured grit or paint. In effect he evolved a basic grammar using piers, slabs, columns, walls, soffits, slats and skylights. This could be adjusted to programme, place or regional climate, with one inflection for a low-cost housing scheme in a hot/dry area, another for a middle-class hotel in a damp tropical zone. The Bharat Bhavan in Bhopal (1976–82) combined an arts centre and museum in a low series of terraces

814

and sunken courts flowing gently down to a lake.
The hooded skylights were descendants in the long
run of Le Corbusier's funnel in the Chandigarh
Parliament, but adjusted to the distant skyline of
white domes.

In the 1980s, Correa made more overt use of
historical precedents. The Madhya Pradesh State
Assembly (1981–7) and the Nehru Museum in
Jaipur (1988), both relied upon Mandala-like plans.
Some of the details of the former mimicked those
on the nearby Buddhist stupas at Sanchi, while the
central court of the latter was modelled on a temple
tank with steps. Correa wrote of the need to make
'transformations' of the 'deep structures' of the past
rather than just 'transfers' of images; in these two
projects he ran the risk of doing the latter. Correa
was well aware of international tendencies in design,
and his works of the late 1980s and early 1990s
revealed a struggle to reconcile a modernist
abstraction with a layer of communicable references.
As important as his forms, were his ruminations
upon 'the forces that generate architecture and their
crucial relationship with each other'.

The first of these forces is Culture. In our model it is like a giant
reservoir, calm and continuous, changing only gradually over
the years.

The second is Aspirations. This force can be quite different
from Culture – though they of course interact continuously.
Aspirations are dynamic and volatile, often quite ephemeral.

The third force acting on architecture is Climate. It
is fundamentally an unchanging force … a very thorough
understanding of climate … must go far beyond the merely
pragmatic. For at the deep-structure level, Climate conditions
Culture and its expression, its rites and rituals. In itself, Climate
is the source of myth. the metaphysical qualities attributed to
open-to-sky space in the cultures of India and Mexico are
concomitants of the warm climate in which they exist …

The fourth force acting on architecture is Technology …
In architecture, … the prevailing technology changes every few
decades. And each time this happens, architecture must re-invent the
expression of the mythic images and values upon which it is based.

In India modern architecture played a major
role in the public sector and in planning for large
numbers. The problem of designing housing prototypes to deal with mass urbanisation was never
far from the thoughts of the committed Indian
architect. The Asian Games Housing in New Delhi
(1980–2) by Raj Rewal was a hypothesis of this kind
which rejected the free-standing block of flats
surrounded by open space in favour of aggregations
of courts, precincts and terraces with separating

gates. Standardized units of several types were
combined in ways which created variety of form
and aspect, and layers of transition from public to
private space. This reflected Rewal's interest in
the spatial and social structure of desert cities like
Jaisalmer in which houses, terraces, streets and
courts were locked together in a single system based
upon variations of a limited number of structural
elements. Even the individual units were inspired,
in part, by *havelis* – courtyard dwellings with tall
rooms, small openings and interpenetrating levels.
But Rewal did not revert to a merely picturesque
townscape: vistas were controlled by axes, and
irregularities of external form were a direct
expression of inner logic. Combinations of types
followed almost systematic rules. The structure of
the Asian Games Housing was a concrete frame
with an infill of brick covered by a washed terrazzo
finish of rough grit that was durable and sensitive to
light. The textured surfaces were amber in colour
and incised with grooves which indicated the actual
structure, marked the human scale, and suggested
analogies with the honey-coloured sandstone panels
of traditional architecture.

Most of Rewal's buildings were in and around
Delhi and several of them were for large institutions
or bureaucracies. In these he resorted to variations
on courtyards with interlocking galleries or terraces,
and transitional layers of structure to supply shade.

815 Charles Correa,
Madhya Pradesh State
Assembly Building,
Bhopal, 1981–7, model

816 Raj Rewal, Asian
Games Housing, New
Delhi, 1980–2

817 Raj Rewal, National
Institute of Immunology,
New Delhi, 1983–90,
view across scholars'
court

815

The National Institute of Immunology (1983–90) to the south of Delhi, was one variant upon this pattern. Here Rewal provided a community of scientists with a series of courtyard clusters linked to each other by shaded walkways, planting, levels and steps. In effect this was a micro-city blending up-to-the-minute laboratory technology with traditional devices for dealing with climate and social space. The National Institute of Immunology was marked by a clear theme of horizontal stratification which echoed the rise and fall of the land. The plan was embedded in a geometrical discipline which worked with variations on square and polygon. The pale brown and pink bands of washed terrazzo helped to clarify the tectonic order of the buildings while also recalling the polychrome marble stripes of so many past eras of Delhi architecture. Rewal explored certain parallels between modern, concrete trabeation and the pier and lintel masonry of the Mogul urban/palace complexes such as Fatehpur Sikri, or Rajput forts like Datia. The scholars' court of the Institute had galleries on several levels looking down onto an open-air theatre, while the Laboratory block continued the same idea in reverse with stepping terraces on the wings. The view towards nature – the scientist's province – was dramatically framed along a diagonal axis. Rewal's work resonated with the past without imitating it. He used a Rationalist discipline and geometrical

817

order, but went beyond the merely utilitarian to a continuous Indian spirit of construction – a presence or mood referred to by the term '*rasa*'. Beyond the particular example, Rewal sought out types and organizational principles that he might transform. He wrote:

Our generation has been trying to discover the common thread in which the fabric of Indian architecture has been woven in the past and its significance for our times.

It has been a basic theme of this book that individual architects gradually form their own vocabularies by distilling lessons from pre-existing seminal works. Anant Raje's Indian Institute of Forest Management in Bhopal (1986–91) returned to a theme of Kahn's Indian Institute of Management at Ahmadabad two decades earlier: the idea of a modern educational institution as a species of monumental citadel. In the prototype, several geometrical and spatial systems were overlaid, and outdoor and indoor spaces formed part of a continuous pattern of figure and ground. Raje's

816

818 Anant Raje, Indian
Institute of Forest
Management, Bhopal,
1986–91

819 Balkrishna Doshi,
sketch plan for Vidyadhar
Nagar, Jaipur, 1984,
studying orientation,
circulation and irrigation

820 Balkrishna Doshi,
Sangath, Ahmadabad,
1979–81, sketch section

818

building was broken down into separate pieces such
as curved auditoria and rectangular teaching blocks,
that were then reunited on the sloping contours so
that axes were inflected to respond to wind, views
and topography. Parallel slots of structure were used
to create complex interpenetrations in plan and in
section, and these interstitial ambiguous spaces
extended across the complex as galleries,
courtyards, passageways and pavilions. Raje's
vocabulary was connected directly to the means of
construction – concrete piers, arches and beams,
with walls in stone and brick – but there were
echoes none the less of past complexes, Islamic and
Roman: the ruins at Mandu (fifteenth century), a
dream world of roofless halls and ruined water tanks
overrun by jungle, or the fragments and courts of
Hadrian's Villa at Tivoli (second century). Raje thus
bridged East and West, and worked with generic
themes binding the two.

The flight of the poor from country to city was a
basic fact of life in all parts of the developing world.
In India this crisis of urbanization resulted from
large-scale 'crisis immigration': the gradual
abandonment of villages by the poor, and the
growth of vast squatter settlements in and around
the main cities. Although decentralized models
involving a better balance between industry and the
rural base were sometimes proposed, these rarely
took root. In fact, these were problems so vast that
no single architectural proposal or urban plan could
begin to encompass them. Both Charles Correa (*The
New Landscape*, 1985) and Balkrishna Doshi (in his
project for Indore of 1984, for example) suggested
that the squatter settlements themselves supplied a
new sort of vernacular, a resource which might be
combined with professional expertise in a more
satisfactory meeting of services, public spaces and
self-built dwellings. Doshi's proposal for Vidyadhar
Nagar (1986), a satellite city of 350,000 people, to
stand close to the old city of Jaipur (early eighteenth
century) combined these insights with a more formal
geometrical plan. The old city had been laid out on
the basis of a nine-square mandala and relied upon a
revival of ancient Hindu texts on urbanism. Doshi
absorbed something of this cosmological lore into
his own ideal city which otherwise put emphasis
upon energy conservation (windpower, solar
orientation, planting and water), transitions from
the public to the private realm, and the elaboration
of several courtyard typologies within a legible
overall hierarchy. In effect, Doshi's Vidyadhar
Nagar combined features of Le Corbusier's utopian
urbanism with a more ancient philosophical
tradition.

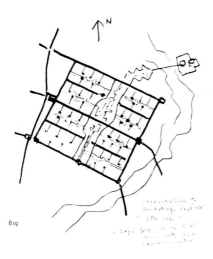

819

Doshi's own studio known as 'Sangath' (1979–81), on the outskirts of Ahmadabad, was an emblem of his world-view and drew together several of his guiding themes. 'Sangath' means 'moving together through participation' and the building was conceived as a meeting place for reflection, research and the exchange of ideas as well as an architectural studio. It marked out a grassy precinct where country and city meet, and was formed from low parallel vaults rising from earth mounds and platforms traversed by channels of water. The interiors were half buried in the ground where they were better protected from the heat, the dust and the monsoons: a transverse section gives almost the feeling of a primeval shelter. In plan, Sangath worked with several overlapping structural systems and parallel axes. The building was approached along a circuitous route which continued through the interiors where double, even triple volumes were combined. On the outside, the longitudinal geometry of 'Sangath' was eroded by a shallow outdoor theatre for informal meetings, its low steps evoking a communal space in a village. The vaults were constructed from ceramic tubes covered in concrete and broken white tiles, a roof insulation which helped to reduce the temperature in the hottest months. A natural cooling system was used inside, and glare was reduced by filtering light indirectly under hooded overhangs or through skylights. In the rainy season water would swirl off the shiny white china surfaces of the curved roof through spouts and gutters into channels and pools. Giant peasant pots in the garden rhymed with

the curved silhouettes and rounded rims, hinting at analogies between concrete construction and traditional buildings in mud. Sangath was on the knife edge between industrialism and primitivism, between modern architecture and vernacular form. It was a microcosm of a kind, celebrating Doshi's ideal of harmony between the individual, community and nature.

More than that, Sangath was a virtual manifesto of a 'new Indian architecture' in its spatial order, its guiding concepts and its several levels of meaning. It relied upon the discoveries of modernism to excavate tradition, and upon a deep reading of local culture and climate to achieve a modern architectural idea of a certain generality. Doshi wrote of the need for an architecture 'reflecting social lifestyles and spiritual convictions', and referred to 'constant elements of Indian architecture: the village square, the bazaar, the courtyard'. He also alluded to 'pauses, transitional spaces and threshholds', to 'multi-functional elements', and to 'duality and ambiguity'. His sketches and models for Sangath reveal his interest in the sculpting of landscape forms for human uses and interactions, and his employment of structural elements such as vaults, walls and piers to create sequences of shaded spaces and multiple, overlapping rhythms. Doshi evidently drew inspiration from the labyrinthine plans of southern Indian temple cities, the circuitous themes of traditional music, the earthbound forms of the rural vernacular, even the vaulted *chaitya* halls of Buddhist architecture. But this penetration of the Indian past was none the less achieved using

820

821

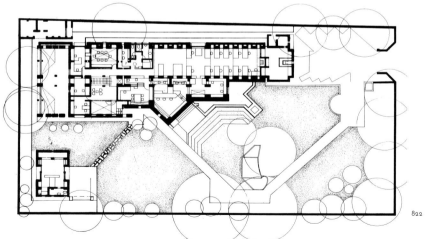

822

821 Balkrishna Doshi,
Sangath, Ahmadabad,
1979–81

822 Sangath, plan

823 Sangath, water
spout

modern means. Sangath extended a string of earlier Corbusian solutions for vaulted and irrigated precincts including the nearby Sarabhai House in Ahmadabad (Fig. 523), and the unrealized Agricultural Estate for Cherchell, North Africa, Fig. 462 ('building in a modern way one has found harmony with the landscape, the climate and tradition'). One may also sense the influence of Kahn's Kimbell Museum (with its rows of parallel vaults), Wright's Taliesin West (with its landscape echoes, low roofs and diagonal platform), Gaudí's Park Güell (with its rounded surfaces in broken china), even the Arts Centre in Giza, Egypt, by Wissa Wassef (a crafts complex made from mud vaults and domes). But whatever the foreign or indigenous influences, they were here welded together in the terminology of a new myth: an architectural idea which gave shape to the flux and ambiguity of contemporary Indian existence, even as it proposed a return to roots.

The preoccupation with the specific character of particular places and regions which played such an important part in the architecture of the 1980s responded to a crisis of deracination, a sense that the whole world was becoming more and more the same. But while the emotions and conditions were new, the strategies adopted had a long pedigree within the history of modern architecture. The struggle to reconcile the local and the universal had taken many forms earlier in the century, even if the very definition of these terms continued to change. But the world of the 1980s and 1990s was becoming ever more fluid in its exchanges, and was being irremediably transformed by international technology, and by the shifting of mental and political frontiers. Even the most fervent supporters of the notion of separate identities tended to draw upon an international discourse of ideas. It was one of the paradoxes of global modernization that the architect committed to the interpretation of his local cultural landscape should have relied upon foreign sources to fulfil his task. The Finnish architect Juhani Pallasmaa caught the complexity of the situation when he wrote in 1989:

The present concern with Regionalism has the evident danger of turning into sentimental provincialism, whereas vital products of art in our specialized culture are always drawn from an open confrontation between the universal and the unique, the individual and the collective, the traditional and the revolutionary.

823

35

technology, abstraction and ideas of nature

824 Renzo Piano, Menil Collection, Houston, Texas, 1981–6, detail of louvres

Architecture in the late twentieth century has evidently followed many channels, and has been characterized by both geographical diversity and intellectual pluralism. But this does not mean that the attempt at discerning broader patterns and longer lines of development should be abandoned. Little is gained by inventing fictive movements, especially when these are described or analysed using the rhetorical terminology of the participants themselves. Nevertheless, there may be communities of concern, overlaps of intention or shared territories of expression. 'The artist no less than the scientist or the philosopher … works in a structured area of problems.' Some of these 'problems' are internal to the architectural discipline and are reflected in formulations and fashions of the moment; others are inherited from earlier seminal buildings, leaving a string of questions and answers in their wake; others again stem from the outside world, changes in society or shifts in technology. Each artist has a particular stance and makes a singular contribution, but the dilemmas facing him are generic. The power of a new paradigm resides, precisely, in its ability to crystallize the underlying concerns of a period.

To come to terms with recent architecture one needs to read through such seminal statements to the sensibilities and societal myths which they exemplify; to take into account both a building's unique intentions and its position in the overall field of architectural investigation. This means working at several focal lengths from close-ups to wide-angle views. Chapter 33 did this for dominant issues of the early 1980s such as the transformation of the past; Chapter 34 considered interpretations of climates, cultures and traditions; this chapter explores parallel themes to do with new myths of modernity, poetic expressions of technology, the re-emergence of abstraction, and analogies between architecture and other realms: minimalist sculpture, landscape art and 'nature'.

Architecture oscillates between the unique and the typical. Even a concept of great originality may rely upon features that are common to its time, and upon lines of thought that run back from the recent to the more distant past. In the inner recesses of the mind time is telescoped; old and new unite in unexpected ways. Examples like Navarro Baldeweg's Congress Hall in Salamanca or Doshi's

'Sangath' in Ahmadabad serve to underline the complexity of ideas, fantasies, memories and aspirations that may operate in a single creation, and the range of influences on which an artist may draw to fit his own configuration. If these interconnections work on the surface the result will be stylish and superficial; if they work in depth, a new synthesis of form and content becomes possible. The entire pattern of an inheritance is then reorganized, and a new set of principles and generating ideas is opened to others. It is unique creations embodying personal and collective myths in forms of a certain timeless character which keep a tradition alive.

This is as true of forward-looking, futurist buildings, as it is of buildings with an evident orientation to the past. The very distinction is problematic, since even those architects who assert the romanticism of engineering or the rhetoric of a new avant-garde have pedigrees and belong to traditions. In the 1980s 'neo-modernists' were sometimes as 'retrospective' in their actual forms as their supposed enemies in the postmodern camp, except that instead of looking back to classicism and using pink keystones on the surface of their buildings, they looked back to once revolutionary modern works and used acceptable modernist 'tropes' (white floating planes, sinuous curves, mechanistic images) in a superficial and uncommitted way. When casting an eye over the wide range of buildings relying upon features of earlier modernism, it is important to carry a general distinction in mind between mere 'signs' referring to past modernities, and the substantial transformations resulting in resonant 'symbols' – inventions that are vital extensions of earlier lines of thought. It is, once again, the distinction between principle and pastiche, between the integration of meaning and the shallow manipulation of form, but applied to works employing 'modernist conventions', such as transparency, skeletal structure or dynamic space. In reality there was no clear 'canon' of modern architecture, the distinguishing quality of a building lying beyond its adherence to any one 'school' at the level of its underlying order and driving ideas.

An earlier chapter referred to the multiple traditions of the modern as a 'delta' comprising the several channels of a river. In the 1980s one of the

most vigorous of these streams was so-called 'high-tech', a label used sweepingly to refer to figures like Norman Foster, Richard Rogers and Renzo Piano (the latter two designers of the Centre Pompidou in Paris in the 1970s). While these architects shared a commitment to the poetics of structure, transparency and technology, and a pedigree which included Jean Prouvé, nineteenth-century engineering and revered icons such as the Crystal Palace (1851), they diverged in important ways. The Lloyds Building (1978–86) in London by Richard Rogers, for example, tended towards techno-romanticism in its almost picturesque handling of shiny silver ducts, tubes and mechanical services. By contrast, Rogers's ex-partner, Renzo Piano, aspired towards the natural inevitability of forms arising from considerations of structure, function, daylighting and assembly, and was less pre-determined on the matter of style. Norman Foster was somewhere between the two: his ideas were often rooted in structural facts or metaphors, but he was also concerned with light, space and the elaboration of detail. Mechanical and natural analogies were woven into Foster's work, and technology was frankly idealized: 'not an exploitation of nature, but a fusion of nature and the human spirit into a new kind of creation which transcends both'.

Foster's Hong Kong and Shanghai Bank (1979–85) was a virtual manifesto of his position, and emerged in strong contrast to the post-

825 Richard Rogers, Lloyds Building, London, 1978–86

826 Norman Foster, Hong Kong and Shanghai Bank, Hong Kong, 1979–85

827 Hong Kong and Shanghai Bank, preliminary sketches

825

826

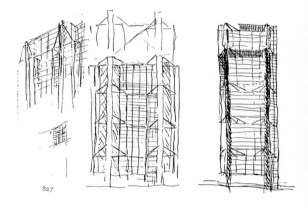

827

modernist packaging of skyscrapers then in vogue. The anatomy of the tall building was here re-examined in terms of an open plan, and the articulation of structure and mechanical services. The usual notion of a stack of floors around a central core was exploded open to accommodate a vertical atrium at the centre and to provide a new vision of the workspace in an age of electronic communications. The main structural piers were pushed out to the corners to maximize stability in typhoons. Rather than a frame, this was a ladder of megatrusses from which intermediate floors were suspended – an idea which suggested knowledge of Jean Prouvé's unbuilt project for the National Ministry of Education in Paris of 1970, although the piers of the Golden Gate Bridge in San Francisco

also come to mind. Within Hong Kong itself, the Bank building functioned as a virtual gateway, and its main body was lifted up on structural legs so that the public could pass through at street level. Moving staircases (their angle determined by Chinese geomancers) rose from this space, penetrating a slung glass membrane before emerging in the atrium which expanded dramatically upwards past layers of floors. A giant reflecting scoop on the outside captured the zenithal light and transmitted it through the layers of transparency to the heart of the structure. While Foster made appeals to a 'structural rationalist' philosophy, it was obvious that his architecture existed somewhere between commercial fact and technocratic fantasy. The Bank had a complex pedigree which included the Futurist

828

notion of a building as a dynamic mechanism,
Constructivist paper projects from the 1920s, the
rocket launching platforms at Cape Canaveral,
Wright's conception of a textured tower as an
abstraction of a tree, and Le Corbusier's idea of a
louvred skyscraper with upper-level social floors
(e.g. Algiers, 1938–42). There were even subtle
Oriental undertones in the modular order and the
delicate, screen-like façades. The Hong Kong and
Shanghai Bank looked back over the water towards
Kowloon and the Chinese mainland proclaiming
high technology and capitalist ingenuity – a building
for 'the Pacific century'.

Renzo Piano's museum for the Menil Collection
in Houston, Texas (1981–6), might just as easily be
described as 'high-craft' as 'high-tech'; in fact it was
characterized by a restraint which had little to
do with technocratic exhibitionism. The basic
gestures of the building were a slender steel frame
supporting an aluminium superstructure holding a
series of ferro-cement 'leaves' filtering solar heat and
glare, and letting a cool light into the exhibition
halls beneath; and a wooden box for more closed
areas of the museum at the lower level. The Menil
Museum was a non-monumental institutional
building which harmonized with the domestic scale
of its Texan suburban neighbourhood and which
picked up on the slender white-painted balconies

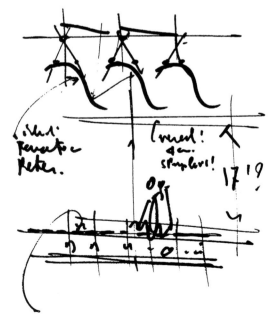
829

and verandas in the immediate setting. It had a certain tropical delicacy about it, while the solution for filtering and distributing the strong local light obviously recalled Louis Kahn's Kimbell Museum, also in Texas. No less than his predecessor, Piano set out to achieve the distillation of the modern and the old in forms that were poetically attuned to climate and light. The stilted steel, refined proportions, and hovering 'cornice' of blades drew together a Miesian instinct for classical order in structure, with an American frame tradition (e.g. Case Study Houses or the work of Eames), a faint reminiscence of timber Greek Revival porches, and a vernacular quietness. The light blades, meanwhile, contributed to a vertebrate, 'natural' repetition recalling nineteenth-century analogies between animal skeletons and metallic elements of construction, but also extending an Aaltoesque theme: the light scoop as a rethought antique moulding. They exemplified Piano's tendency to generate a building by repeating a highly articulate and multifunctional part. The architect wrote:

> Building is about putting together material elements. I feel that one needs to invent something new but at the same time quite old within our craft; to return to the close association between thinking and doing …

The expression of technology was a long-standing modern architectural theme which sometimes achieved a Utopian character, and sometimes merely illustrated the mechanics of engineering. 'High-tech' continued to reflect this ambiguity, as it often worked with the basic commercial building type of the mechanically serviced shed, which it either 'decorated' with excessive displays of tubes and coloured struts, or else elevated to the level of structural art through spatial imagination and the discovery of geometrical order. Both Foster and Piano designed airport terminals which dealt with these dilemmas by combining technical standardization and the control of an overall formal idea. Foster's Stansted Terminal to the north of London (1981–91) was somewhere between an elegant piece of equipment and a poetic expression, with its floating superstructure of silvery parasol roofs, its cool light, and its structural / servicing columns starting as compact 'trunks' in the ground and then gradually opening out into splayed 'branches' whose struts recalled the tubular elements of aircraft. Piano's Kansai Terminal on an island in Osaka Bay (1988–94) was a linear, transparent building whose elongated form and sinuous section arose from the repetition of a standardized, structural piece – a tensile beam and glazed membrane of uneven curvature. This aviomorphic profile permitted uninterrupted interiors, conveyed a sense of dynamism, and responded to external forces such as wind, gravity and light. It suggested Piano's interest in the principles behind man-made inventions like the aerofoil section, and those behind natural forms.

The same economic forces which led to the commercialization of postmodernism, pushed 'high-tech' towards seductive visual effects emulating those of product design. Consumerism shifted attention from function and structure towards external styling and associative imagery. The American architect Hellmuth Jahn endowed the mechanical entrails and kaleidoscopic glazing of his designs with an air of science fiction (e.g. the Illinois State Center in Chicago of 1985, with its vast atrium, red lattice structure and curved, curtain wall in glass of several colours and opacities). Even the discipline of engineering was affected by the desire for sensationalist effects. The biomorphic bridges, stations and airports designed by the Spanish engineer Santiago Calatrava in the late 1980s and early 1990s aimed well beyond technical neutrality, and even beyond the calm balance of means and ends achieved by Maillart earlier in the century, towards a species of structural expressionism relying

830

upon the dynamic accentuation of elements of construction, streamlining and obvious metaphors (e.g. his design for the TGV station at Lyons-Satolas Airport (1989–92) which was crowned by an engineered version of a bird spreading its wings).

Mechanical analogies might be blended with organic ones, or else become part of a system of polarities between the 'technological' and the 'natural'. The Lucille Halsell Conservatory in San Antonio, Texas (1988) by Emilio Ambasz was formed from a scattering of glazed pyramids and cones poking out of grassy mounds which evoked simultaneously fragments of palm houses and a surreal landscape of transparent prisms. His work reflected an interest in the metaphysical abstraction of Luis Barragán, and in the environmental sculptures of artists like Robert Smithson, Mary Miss or Robert Long, which evoked a cosmic link between land and sky. For Ambasz, technology was 'an instrument for evoking architectural presences', not an end in itself; an ally of natural processes, rather than an enemy. The Japanese architect Tadao Ando suggested that Ambasz revealed a new kind of

environmental architecture … drawing nature into abstraction … and using nature on a massive scale … His work promises an ample domain where the found and the made, the natural and the artificial, coexist …

In effect the periphery of the sprawl city was expanding to absorb remnants of the countryside, a development which required a broad redefinition of the boundaries of architecture. By the second half of the 1980s the obsessions with typology, with traditional urban space and with various kinds of classical figuration were on the wane. The paradigms of neo-Rationalism gradually lost their hold. A new abstraction that had been waiting in the wings while postmodernism carried out its brief performance gradually insinuated itself as the prevalent mode, sometimes in minimalist forms, sometimes in works which made new claims on the interpenetrating section, the dynamic diagonal or the plan made up from fragments set in a field of space. It is never wise to tie down changes in perception or visual convention to a single body of ideas, or even to a single artist, and these new directions in fact overlapped with contrasting beliefs, all the way from those who were looking for an expression of late twentieth-century rootlessness and dissolution (connected in some vague way to the

philosophical ideas of 'deconstruction'), to those who were seeking a new topographical model for embedding buildings on the edges of cities into the contours of landscapes.

One of the seminal figures in the discovery of a new fragmentation was Frank Gehry, who had already been working in that direction in the 1970s (Chapter 32). Gehry lived in Los Angeles, and part of his inspiration came from his encounter with southern California and its culture of sensual immediacy ('the bright present of the Pacific beaches'), part from his exchange with painters, sculptors and conceptual artists, part from his direct engagement with 'ordinary' techniques of construction in which he found extraordinary possibilities of expression. But the attempt to restrict Gehry's architecture to a locality should be resisted, since it expressed a much more general shift in sensibility beyond dogmatic frameworks of modernity and in favour of the individual's direct perceptions of an ever more confused world. Confronted by the mess of the megalopolis, Gehry did not retreat towards quietism, or revert to idealized types, but responded openly in a technique of bricolage abstracting bits and pieces of the confused urban environment. His buildings resembled non-representational film sets that were soothing and hedonistic, yet disquieting and destabilizing. They did not rely upon 'composition' but were rather assemblages of different fragments

831 Frank Gehry, Spiller House, Venice, California, 1979

832 Frank Gehry, Schnabel House, Brentwood, California, 1990, plan

833 Schnabel House

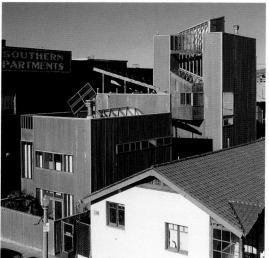

831

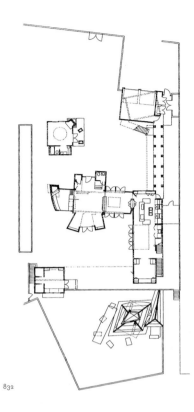

832

833

held together by lines of force. This was not the postmodernist indulgence in 'signs' but something more akin to Kurt Schwitter's or Robert Rauschenberg's earlier attempts at blending the rubbish and detritus of industrialism into a sublimated collage.

Gehry's distinctive vocabulary began to emerge in works like the Ron Davis Studio of 1972 or the Spiller House in Venice, California, of 1979, in which angled planes and tilting volumes introduced visual tensions and ambiguities, while 'materials as found' (stud frames, corrugated metal sheets, chain link fencing, drywall wooden panels) were handled in a deliberately casual way which exposed the process of assembly. There were echoes of Schindler's shed-like late buildings with their crude carpentry and plastic sheeting, even of the steel net fences of the environmental artist Robert Irwin.

Gehry's later buildings gained part of their ambiguity from their break with normal conventions, from their fractured geometry, from their acceptance of banal features in the surroundings, and from their resemblance to abstract sculptures. With the Ignatius Loyola Law School in Los Angeles (1986), some forced efforts were made at historical and civic references, but the real interest of the project still lay in its collision of disparate pieces and scales. The Winston Guest House in Wayzata, Minnesota (1983), took the separation of curved and rectangular parts even further and resembled a constructed Cubist still life, while the Schnabel House in Brentwood, California (1990), had the mood of a psychic projection of disturbing dream fragments. Gehry's larger-scale projects (such as the Disney Concert Hall in Los Angeles (1989), the Furniture Display Centre for Vitra at Weil-am-Rhein, Germany (1987), or the project for the Guggenheim Museum in Bilbao, Spain, 1991) relied upon the dynamic interpenetration of walls, floors, ceilings and skylights, as well as the explosion of convex and concave planes. These floating facets, which were sometimes clad in stainless steel, were capable of evoking multiple associations, musical and nautical, but they also extended the spatial researches initiated by Le Corbusier and Aalto in some of their late works. Gehry's architecture was personal and inimitable, and was without a social or ideological programme, yet it still caught the mood of a widespread uncertainty in which public frameworks and supports were falling away, leaving the individual in a state of suspension.

Another route towards fragmentation and abstraction lay through the work of 'neo-modernist' architects like Richard Meier or Peter Eisenman (both of whom had been associated with the New York Five, p. 564), but their intentions diverged considerably. In the 1980s, Meier established a signature style that was characterized by layers of wall planes and transparencies, fractured structural grids, interpenetrating ramps, and spaces of varying luminosity. These devices were all on display in the Museum für Kunsthandwerk in Frankfurt (1981–5), a building of painterly delicacy which picked up on the scale and proportions of its historical neighbours while also achieving a complex internal order based upon the intersection of geometries derived from the setting. In later works such as Canal Plus Television Headquarters in Paris (1988–91), Meier seemed to reduce his architecture to an easy formula of Corbusian trills and formalist gestures which lacked both visual and ethical tension. The result was a species of official modernism, clean-cut and devoid of challenging content. Peter Eisenman was involved in a self-conscious struggle at realizing some late twentieth-century equivalent to an avant-garde, but in the unlikely context of an American East Coast establishment which had long since abandoned the idea that modernism might have a role to play in social transformation. In the late 1970s he gradually abandoned his earlier fascination with hermetic formal studies based upon transparency and planarity, instead developing a method for 'mapping' sites. This had little to do with the usual pieties of contextualism since it used a variety of grids and overlaid geometries that had no particular topographical or functional justification. Eisenman wished to liberate architecture from simplistic considerations of use and context, and to investigate its internal mechanisms as a language. His Cannaregio proposal for Venice (1978) relied upon the laconic repetition of a grid traced selectively from the previous 'text' of Le Corbusier's unbuilt Venice Hospital (Fig. 540). Both the form and the attitude owed something to minimalist sculptors like Donald Judd, while the exercise in 'intertextuality' fitted with the then fashionable notion that languages have no necessary connection to sense or to the outside world.

Eisenman's trajectory in the 1980s was influenced by the fact that he received large commissions and so had to find ways of translating his theories into forms that could work on several scales. His Wexner Center for the Visual Arts in Columbus, Ohio (1983–9), was formed from a long transparent trellis which sliced through the old fabric on a diagonal, and set up new co-ordinates with such

834 Richard Meier, Museum für Kunsthandwerk, Frankfurt, 1981–5

835 Peter Eisenman, Wexner Center for the Visual Arts, Ohio State University, Columbus, Ohio, 1983–9

836 Bernard Tschumi, Parc de la Villette, Paris, 1984–9

834

835

random things as an airstrip several miles away. Complementing this Dadaist interest in arbitrary 'rules' of composition was a fictional 'historical' façade of broken castellated forms, an invented fragment of 'context' which mocked the earnest civic intentions of other architects of the time. The Wexner Centre was calculated and contrived in its overlays and fragmentations, but once the intellectualizations were stripped away it was obvious that the vocabulary continued to extend Terragni's idea of a public building as a transparent perforated frame, while distorting it in a deliberately anti-classical way. Eisenman's later projects (e.g. the Hotel for Banyoles in Spain, 1988) usually dispensed with grids, taking on an increasingly stratified appearance with sinuous curves and broken pieces. In Eisenman's view, architecture had entered a 'post-humanist' era in which 'place' and 'tradition' had less and less meaning, and in which the fracturing of the city and the landscape could be seen as part of an inevitable 'atopia' – a modern placelessness – into which fragments of architectural discourse could be inserted virtually as mannerist games. While this position was proposed as an avant-garde critique, it in fact corresponded to the devaluation of history and topography that extra-urban capitalist development was achieving on its own.

The Parc de la Villette in Paris (1984–9) by Bernard Tschumi revealed another aspect of the neo-modernist stance, the parody of past Utopian forms, since it borrowed the imagery of revolutionary machinism from the 1920s, and rendered it as an amusing exercise in radical chic. The Parc was one of President Mitterand's 'grands projets' and was conceived as a new kind of landscape for the 'twenty-first century', which

rejected past, romantic notions of nature. Tschumi's basic strategy of co-ordinates, sinuous lines and boundaries suggested a latter-day version of Kandinsky's elements of abstract painting (points, lines and planes), or perhaps the score for an avant-garde film in which the same shot-pieces were repeated in different montages. Marking the main intersections of the grid were red, cubic 'follies' resembling Soviet 'agitprop' stands of the 1920s but also recalling Eisenman's Cannaregio project. These cubes were varied according to arbitrary 'rules', so that one would have a ramp, another a stair, another an attached wheel. The coloured steel lattices, hovering walkways and sinuous roofs bordering the site recalled past mechanistic fantasies such as Tchernikov's sketches of around 1929. The 'follies' were like giant red toys scattered across the grass. The language of an earlier revolutionary polemic was thus anaesthetized, while leaving just enough edge for the 'official' modernism of the French left-wing cultural establishment. Like Eisenman, Tschumi was interested in destabilizing simplistic

836

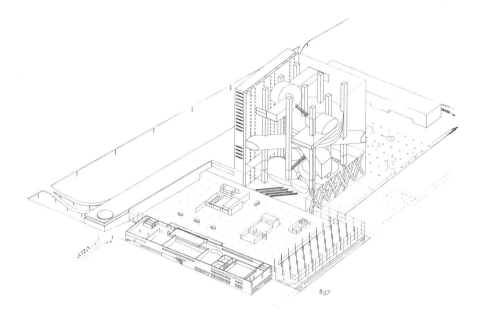

assumptions about the relationship between form, function and meaning, and his results distanced themselves from the idea of a deeper significance, even taking on the aspect of caricatures. A voguish terminology drawn from the philosophy of deconstruction (e.g. the writings of Jacques Derrida) was used to sanction a series of displaced ironies upon the supposed inability of architecture to carry a cogent cultural content: a discourse about the impossibility of discourse that caused a shimmer of delight in the intellectual salons of Paris and New York. Neo-avant-gardism was adept at recycling images but rarely struggled to crystallize an ideal of its own. Tschumi's manipulation of the known, with its implicit mannerism, recalls Colin Rowe's observation on the ironical distance of collage: 'a technique for using things and simultaneously disbelieving in them'.

The Parc de la Villette was one of several schemes to emerge in the mid-1980s which projected spatial concepts supposedly attuned to the 'age of information' or the 'post-industrial society'. In these years, the Dutch architect Rem Koolhaas moved gradually away from his earlier cartoon-like projects for multi-use skyscrapers towards a more complex idea of the urban building as a transparent framework made up of pieces suspended illusionistically in mid air. The National Dance Theatre in The Hague (1981), combined a graphic scenario of modernist clichés with intersecting oval

839

trays and diagonals of a certain dynamism.
Koolhaas delighted in the artificiality of the big
city and its numerous overlays and screens of
reality and illusion. His proposals for the Grande
Bibliothèque in Paris and the Centre for Art and
Technological Communication in Karlsruhe (both
1989) re-investigated the syntax of the Corbusian
free plan but in terms which made much of floating
volumes of complex curvature, layers of opaque
or transparent glazing and dramatic ramps for
movement. Koolhaas's interest in the cinema
as a key to modern experience was translated
metaphorically into frames, screens and 'clips',
and the façades of his buildings were sometimes
designed to receive projections of changing
electronic information. But the attitude was far
from being openly technocratic. In fact, Koolhaas's
architecture seemed to mirror a state of doubt about
the direction of advanced industrialism, even to
replace the social conviction of the previous Dutch
avant-garde with a modernism of quick sensations
and ironical asides. His Kunsthal in Rotterdam
(1987–92), for example, relied upon staged
quotations from revered prototypes in the history of
modern architecture, such as Mies van der Rohe's
Berlin National Gallery, or Rietveld's Schröder
House, and was lacking in tectonic or symbolic
substance. On the other hand, his giant Congress
and Exhibition Hall ('Congrexpo') on the outskirts
of Lille (1991–5), with its curious oval plan and its

sinuous façades in cheap materials like corrugated
metal and plastic, caught the atmosphere of
'Euromarketing' capitalism in a convincing way.

While it was fashionable in the late 1980s to
group together architects who used fragmented
forms as 'deconstructivist', it was obvious that the
implied connection between Soviet Constructivism
and the late twentieth-century philosophy of
deconstruction was little more than an intellectual
sleight of hand, and that there were several
contrasting directions and theoretical agendas.
Gehry, for example, was an intuitive artist with little
time for the kind of arcane theorizing that interested
Eisenman, and had anyway been pursuing his own
version of assemblage for years. Zaha Hadid's
paintings and architectural projects (e.g. the Hong
Kong Peak proposal of 1983) used floating shards
and dynamic planes in a way which suggested
extraterrestial lines of force, but her rather
decorative re-use of Lissitzky's or Malevich's
spatial discoveries was devoid of any radical social
content. The Viennese architects Wolf Prix and
Helmut Swiczinsky (known as 'Coop Himmelblau')
employed slicing diagonals, glazed angles and
tensile structures to cut through the conventions of
traditional forms, and had a virtually Expressionist
idea of design which contrasted with the studied
variations of Tschumi. Daniel Libeskind, who had
developed a private calligraphy of interwoven lines
in the 1970s, gradually evolved an architectural
language which made use of tilting volumes and
converging planes. His Jewish Museum in Berlin
(1989–96) was a zigzag incision in which nothing
was quite stable. Like a bolt of lightning, it cut
through societal complacency to repressed but
disturbing memories beneath the surface. Its
vast planar walls in concrete were sliced by small
openings admitting gashes of light to the interiors.
Several routes were overlaid in the complex
geometry of both plan and section, each of them
referring to different departures and transitions in
Jewish history; one of them inspired by *The One
Way Street*, a text of Walter Benjamin, a writer who
did not live to see the full horror of the Holocaust
but understood only too well the racist implications
of Fascism. In effect, Libeskind evolved a complex
political metaphor in space, light, matter and
dematerialization to evoke the universality of Jewish
civilization, and the void left in Western culture by

the destruction of the Jews in the Second World War. Far from being an exercise in neo-modernist formalism, this was a work of chilling authenticity, drawing together in its lines of thought both grave, apocalyptic themes, and radical reassessments of the meaning of human destiny.

In the late 1980s, fragmentation and layering were sometimes discussed as if they were contemporary inventions, whereas in fact they stemmed in the long run from Cubism, and had anyway been employed in several senses in the 1970s. While they seemed to be abstract devices without 'territory', they did in fact help architects to 'read' their respective situations in fresh ways. The Japanese architect Toyo Ito, for example, thought that they were particularly relevant to the complexity of the Far Eastern city, and conceived of buildings as delicate super-impositions of semi-transparent screens in industrial materials like glass, brick or perforated stainless steel (e.g. his Silver Hut in Tokyo of 1984). Already in 1978, he had suggested that the skin of a building might be thought of 'as a screen upon which various lights and shadows are projected.' The screen even became a kind of mental map for reading the layers of traditional Japanese space and the fleeting realities of modern urban life:

These elements, carrying fragmentary meaning, are treated lightly as if they were made from paper. No matter how deliberately we trace over a screen as thin as paper, we only slide on the surface and never see the depth of the substance. This turns out to be the structure of our cities, where we just skim across the surface. Whether in buildings or in cities, we walk through a realm where symbols are drifting about and with these we weave the space of our own significance.

Another Japanese architect, Kazuo Shinohara, tried to draw a dissonant order from the 'disorder' and energy of the information city. His Zen acceptance of the accidental was revealed in buildings which brought together disparate geometries, materials and '*objets trouvés*' in complex compositions and which were held together by the individual artist's sense of visual tension rather than by any external system of rules or typologies. His Tokyo Institute of Technology Centennial Hall (1987) slammed together several forms in a dynamic interplay of transparent boxes and hovering curves suspended in mid-air. It was as if the diverse scales of a confused environment had imploded on the inner space of a building, or as if the object had exploded to respond to invisible lines of force in the 'third nature' of electronic industrialization. The large scoop shape (vaguely recalling the roof of Le Corbusier's Ronchamp but in high-tech terms) penetrated the Centennial Hall and generated

840

841

interiors with a feeling of instability. Shinohara's attitude to technology was far from being celebratory; it was as if he wished to reveal a repressed violence, an underlying societal disturbance. Nevertheless, he was committed to the idea of a kind of visual coherence: an 'aesthetic of chaos' that was both 'dynamic and unified'.

The Japanese modern architecture of the 1980s and early 1990s revealed several ways of reacting to a rapid technological transformation of the environment. Fumihiko Maki responded to the new Japanese industrial landscape by combining bold structural concepts with the high level of craftsmanship in steel, glass, plastic and concrete typically available in his own country. Maki realized that the outer appearance of the Japanese sprawl city masked subtle filters of cultural space and memory, and tried to establish points of intensity in the mess of freeways, buildings, signs and wastelands. The Spiral Building in Minato, Tokyo (1985), combined a free-flowing movement on the inside with a fragmented collage of different-sized openings on the outside which responded to several overlays of scale in the setting. For larger buildings such as stadia, Maki worked with the theme of curved steel roofs coated in silvery membranes

which seemed to float like luminous bands above the surroundings. The Fujisawa Gymnasium of 1984–6 had a steel skeleton of interlacing girders which permitted an uninterrupted span of 263 feet (80 metres). The outer skin of reflective stainless steel was less than half a millimetre thick. The interior was experienced as slender planes dematerialized in light, while the exterior established a clear image of a place of social gathering. The lunging silhouettes suggested temple roofs, Japanese armour, even space technology (to mention some of the architect's own associations) but the imagery was held in check by a coherent sculptural form and a clear structural idea. The Fujisawa was a majestic work, a worthy descendant of Tange's Olympic Gymnasium of two decades earlier, which reflected the complex mentalities of a society suspended between a commitment to technological invention and a continuing reverence for tradition. It reaffirmed Maki's belief in an expanded modernism combining 'a search for a more subtle relationship between structure and expression, a search for the power that details within abstract figures seem to possess, a study of the dynamic equilibrium between part and whole, the expression of the present that comes about from the simultaneous awareness of past and future'.

Tadao Ando's response to the artificiality of capitalist, consumerist sprawl was to reassert the connection with nature, either in closed enclaves within the city or else in subtle landscape interventions in the countryside. In his Church-on-the-Water at Tomamu (1985–8) and his Children's Museum at Himeji (1987–9) he used polished concrete planes, platforms and levels of water to intensify the experience of the surroundings and to draw the vistas of hillsides, islands or sea into the field of energy activated by his buildings. The minimalist incisions recalled both modern abstract sculpture and traditional ideas concerning the spirit of place ('*ma*'), the linkage of foreground and background ('*shakkei*') and the fusion of the artificial and the natural ('*oku*'). In Ando's work the inheritance of modernism was distilled to reinforce metaphysical values within a particular culture, but at a level which far transcended mere visual references. His desire to help man 'discover a new relationship with nature' revealed a critical reaction to the transience of late industrialism that was none

the less typical of its time in its preoccupation with soothing inner states of mind and a generalized 'spirituality'. However, some of Ando's projects also revealed the intention of defining new kinds of public institution, sometimes alongside historic sites in the countryside. His Chikatsu-Asuka Historical Museum at Minami-Kawachi near Osaka (1990–4) was formed from ascending platforms and wide banks of steps which gave the ensemble the air of a dignified place of ritual. In fact this structure, which was a form of artificial landscape, was intended as an open-air theatre for drama festivals with the surrounding hills as a backdrop. It also controlled the entry to the neighbouring ancient tombs and tumuli of the Kofan culture, offering vantage points across the site, and intensifying the geometry of the remains. Ando wished to help the visitor encounter history as well as nature:

Architecture delivers a place's memory to the present, and transmits it to the future … Architecture differentiates nature, and also integrates nature. Through architecture, nature is reduced to its elements and then drawn into unity. Thus nature is architecturalized, and man's confrontation with nature is refined.

842

842 Tadao Ando,
Church-on-the-Water,
Tomamu, 1985–8

843 Tadao Ando,
Chikatsu-Asuka Historical
Museum, Minami-
Kawachi, 1990–4

844 Chikatsu-Asuka
Historical Museum, plans

843

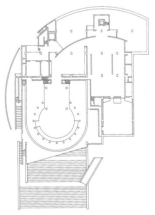
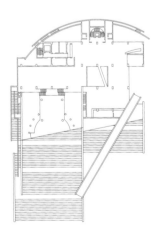

844

technology, abstraction and ideas of nature   671

Like the modern architectural culture of Japan, that of France in the 1980s combined several contrasting strands and positions. Overall it was influenced by a renewed interest in the meaning of the city, by a re-examination of the seminal works of modernism on the part of a younger generation, and by the extensive institutional and housing patronage offered by a socialist government in the public sector. Even though postmodernism had a relatively slight though sensationalist impact on France (e.g. Ricardo Bofill's works around Paris and Montpellier), there were plenty of other schisms and divisions over the direction that modern architecture should take. While Henri Ciriani advocated the reinterpretation of a basically Corbusian canon (e.g. his own Musée de la Grande Guerre at Péronne, 1987–92), younger architects like Dominique Perrault or Jean Nouvel were drawn to the mechanical analogies and transparency of 'high-tech' and to the tradition of steel and glass construction running back from the Centre Pompidou, to Jean Prouvé, the Maison de Verre and the nineteenth-century *grands constructeurs*. Roland Simounet continued to pursue an architecture characterized by restrained plasticity, and the control of space and light, while emerging architects such as Yves Lion or Christian Devillers avoided the fashion for slick, technocratic imagery in an unrhetorical modernism that was responsive to both context and the logic of construction.

In contrast to the 'privatized' cultural sectors of Britain and the United States, modernism in France received the support of the state. This was most obvious from the Parisian *grands projets* which were conceived as public institutions endowing the

capital with a modernized cultural infrastructure and with monuments to celebrate the Bicentennial of the French Revolution of 1789. While there was never an official 'Mitterand Style', many of the projects were characterized by bold geometry, transparent layers, mechanistic details in glass and polished steel, and forms which derived in the long run from the early modern movement and from Russian Constructivism. Responses varied from free-standing prisms like I. M. Pei's glass pyramid at the Louvre (1983–7), J. O. von Spreckelsen's perforated cube for the Grande Arche de la Défense (1984–9) or the four Cartesian skyscrapers marking out the precinct of Dominique Perrault's Grande Bibliothèque (1989–95), to inflected urban pieces combining readings of the structure of the city with a variety of modern expressions. The Cité de la Musique at La Villette (1985–92) by Christian de Portzamparc, for example, relied upon complex fragmentation to create a species of eroded gateway to the Parc de la Villette, and combined lessons from Le Corbusier's sculptural late works with mannerized curves and obvious musical analogies. The Institut du Monde Arabe (1981–7) by Jean Nouvel and the Architecture Studio responded to a bend in the Seine and to the orthogonal geometry of the pre-existing buildings, by uniting a transparent oblong volume with a curved one around an inner court. With its multiple layers of glazing, shiny metallic surfaces, exposed machinery, and electronically controlled sun-shading diaphragms like mechanistic versions of traditional Arab

845 Dominique Perrault, Grande Bibliothèque, Paris, 1989–95

846 Jean Nouvel, Institut du Monde Arabe, Paris, 1981–7

847 Johan Otto von Spreckelsen, Grande Arche de la Défense, Paris, 1983–9

847

visual tension and made it seem to address the distant Eiffel Tower (the main monument of the Centennial of the Revolution a century before) across space and time. What the latter had been for the age of steam and steel, the former was for the age of electronic information, and in Spreckelsen's early studies the inner faces of the sides of the building were detailed to resemble an abstraction of a micro-chip, while the low transparent 'clouds' (realized eventually as a suspended tent) were like waves of energy passing through the air. The programme stressed that this should be a '*carrefour*' or 'crossroads' of communications and a symbol of the Universal Rights of Man, and Spreckelsen took the ideal form of a cube to reflect these intentions, opening it out as a 'window to the future' and as a species of 'shelter' for all peoples of the world. While the Arche suggested a minimalist sculpture of vast scale and pure proportions, its geometrical form was capable of carrying many meanings and allusions simultaneously. There were echoes of Le Corbusier's giant porticoes from Chandigarh, of a classical triumphal arch with coffering, of a rocket launching platform, even of Boullée's sublime and grandiose geometrical visions from the period of 'Revolutionary Classicism' in the late eighteenth century. The Arche de la Défense touched upon several subliminal themes in the French collective *imaginaire* from the glorification of military might, and the celebration of reason and Republican virtues, to the centralization of state power.

Despite this concentration of patronage in Paris, some of the most interesting French buildings of the 1980s and 1990s were realized in the provinces, and several of them were museums. Ciriani's Musée de l'Arles Antique (1984–95) was triangular in plan and established a firm identity for a new institution to one side of an historic centre already containing the bold imprints of the Roman past (e.g. an amphitheatre and an aqueduct). A skin of blue glazing over a concrete armature defined the walls of the new building as semi-reflective planes responsive to the light and sky of the Midi. The interior elaborated the Corbusian theme of a *promenade architecturale* through a grid of *pilotis* by means of ramps, and at the centre of the scheme was a species of atrium with reflecting surfaces of water at its base. Despite its almost too obvious allegiances to Le Corbusier, Ciriani's building gave convincing shape

mashrabiya screens, Nouvel's design supplied evidence of a new panache in French architecture, a somewhat theatrical version of high-tech.

The Grande Arche de la Défense, designed by the Danish architect Johan Otto von Spreckelsen, (realized in a slightly modified form by Paul Andreu and Peter Rice) stood at the west end of the historic axis running from the Louvre through the Place de la Concorde and the Arc de Triomphe, and fused together the image of a monumental urban gateway with a celebration of the prowess of French technology. It gave a clear focus to the business district of La Défense, and was shifted a few degrees off the urban axis, a practical move to accommodate subterranean railway lines which also introduced

848 Pierre-Louis Faloci, Musée du Centre Archéologique Européen du Mont Beuvray, Glux-en-Glenne, Autun, 1991–5

849 Mikko Heikkinen and Markku Komonen, Chancery, Finnish Embassy, Washington DC, 1990–4

848

to his notion of '*une abstraction cultivée*' – literally 'a cultivated abstraction': a geometrical order reiterating basic architectural ideas such as the façade and the procession, but without the use of direct historical references. The Musée du Centre Archéologique Européen du Mont Beuvray (1991–5) by Pierre-Louis Faloci also relied upon a species of abstraction, but one more attuned to topography and geology. This building used planar walls, platforms, terraces and soffits to capture the space of the rural setting and to resonate with the surrounding landscape. The programme was broken into separate pieces, the largest being a museum, and these were handled as delicate incisions into hillside sites which responded to each other across the valley. Faloci's Museum abstracted the geometry of the nearby archeological excavations in its plan, while working its way up from a rusticated base through several textures of masonry to smooth stone walls and a hovering steel superstructure. The section thus expressed the notion of different layers of time, while the experience of moving through the spaces of varying intensity brought together long views with close-up vignettes of the ancient site with its pre-Roman, Gallic and Celtic remains. The parentage of Faloci's building included Mies van der

Rohe's Barcelona Pavilion of 1929, and Terragni's works of the 1930s, buildings of modern form and structure with a certain classical resonance. But Faloci avoided neo-modernist formalism, giving precise expression to new ideas in geometry, light and material. He took over basic themes from the modern tradition such as sliding planes and layers of transparency, and gave them a fresh significance with respect to the historical and geological strata of a particular place.

Modernisms might fit different schemes of modernization yet still evoke half-buried memories and myths. The Finnish modern architecture of the 1980s continued to address the diverse functions of an industrialized Welfare State from schools and housing to churches and institutional buildings, while still reacting to the ever-present forest landscape, to the Nordic light and climate, and to deeply embedded social patterns and ways of using space. Grand classical monumentality had no place in this society, and the basic model for institutions continued to be the inflected artificial landscape as discovered by Aalto, although this 'woodland order' could be expressed in many different ways. From the start, modernism in Finland had been associated with national identity and its internal energies were still sufficient in the 1980s to ensure that postmodernism only made a slight impact, but this does not mean that mental frontiers were closed. The best work continued to reflect a healthy tension between the local and the international, extending principles and discoveries from within a Finnish modern tradition, but remaining open to fresh ideas.

Earlier Finnish modernism was far from being a monolithic entity, and there were contrasting lines of thought within it, from Aalto's unique trajectory to the sparse minimalism represented by Blomstedt and later Ruusuvuori. In the 1980s there was, in fact, a reaction against the rather dull standardization which had been evident in the general run of building in the previous decade, and this was accompanied by a reinvestigation of some of the primary statements of modern architecture. Here too perspectives varied. Reima and Raili Pietilä continued their own path towards an idiosyncratic architecture of great geometrical complexity drawing upon natural analogies. Kristian

849

Gullichsen believed in 'the reinterpretation of concepts that have proved good' and practised a species of modern eclecticism; his Church complex at Kauniainen near Helsinki (1979–83) was an amalgam of images from sources as diverse as Le Corbusier's Maison Ternisien (1924), Bryggman's Resurrection Chapel at Turku (1938) and Ruusuvuori's Tapiola Church at Espoo (1964–5). Timo Vormala's buildings were more linear and abstract, deriving part of their structural elegance from a native functionalism in industrial architecture, part from a reconsultation of Rietveld and Russian Constructivism. In a younger generation, Mikko Heikkinen and Markku Komonen combined some features of the 'new abstraction' from abroad with topographical erosions which descended in the long run from Aalto. Their buildings made use of interlacing fields of structure, sharp-cut steel and glass details, overlapping geometries and rays of light: the Finnish Science Centre, 'Heureka' at Vantaa (1986–8) had a rainbow glass wall that changed colour as one moved, while the Rovaniemi Airport on the Arctic Circle (1988–92) traced the annual path of the midday sun on the floor in a figure 8. The acknowledgement of natural forces did not have to mean 'naturalistic' uses of materials, and their Chancery for the Finnish Embassy in Washington DC (1990–4) relied upon a cool abstraction of suspended planes, green glass, oxidized bronze and granite to intensify the experience of the woodland site. The grid of the building was continued across the downhill slope as a series of light-topped poles; at night the floor plane of the reception hall extended into the trees as a field of luminous points.

The work of Juha Leiviskä revealed other lines of continuity within Finnish modernism while engaging with a more universal idea of tradition, but his buildings did not rely upon technological imagery and were usually constructed from slender brick walls, white-painted wooden ceilings, double glazing with mullions and simple trellises. The extending lines and multiple rhythms of his plans recalled the fields of energy in Mondrian's early paintings, if not the spatial devices of Mies van der Rohe and Wright, but they were also distillations of childhood, countryside memories, and of basic patterns of the Finnish vernacular, for farmsteads were often organized in an analogous way, with gradual transitions from house and yard to barns, poles, fences and trees. Leiviskä's church designs (notably the Myyrmäki Church near Helsinki of 1984–7 and the Männistö Church at Kuopio of 1988–93) combined a vibrant abstraction of overlapping planes and multiple rhythms, with a deep feeling for the spiritual power of light, and for the contours of the landscape. In the Myyrmäki Church, the route towards the main space of assembly was threaded back and forth between walls and ceilings of varying size and intensity, and the gradual loosening of the geometry towards the entrance expressed the intention of opening the institution to the public while blending the building with the birch trees next to the site. The main brick wall separating the church from a railway line also functioned as a dam holding back the pressure of light and hinting at the 'world beyond'. Leiviskä drew upon a Nordic tradition and combined the luminosity and layering of Aalto with the minimalism of Siren, Blomstedt or Ruusuvuori, but he still had a distinctive vocabulary of his own. He reconsidered the significance of modern space while also deriving inspiration from several 'light vessels' in the history of architecture, and from the polyphony of music. His churches aspired to a sublime order, dissolving the boundaries of the senses and elevating the mind. For Leiviskä, the fundamentals of architecture did not change:

I believe in the permanency of the basic factors of architecture, the so-called eternal values. I do not therefore believe that there has been anything in recent years which could revolutionize the basic tenets of architecture or its central task.

850

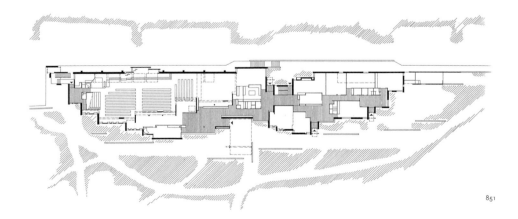
851

The Finnish Pavilion at the Seville World's
Exhibition of 1992 was designed by a group of
architects in their late twenties known collectively as
MONARK (Juha Jääskeläinen, Juha Kaakko, Petri
Rouhiainen, Matti Sanaksenaho and Jari Tirkkonen)
and consisted of a polished steel slab with a curved
wooden element alongside it, and a converging slot
of space between. The design was characterized by
an extreme discipline of means, but this apparently
simple configuration compressed together many
ideas. The steel oblong was known as the 'Machine',
the timber curve as the 'Keel', and both were
hollowed out to allow a route through a series of
exhibition spaces inside; the cleavage between the
two had the character of a deep ravine, a veritable
'Shaft of Hell' with restorative powers in Finnish
mythology. The basic contrast between industrial
and natural materials touched upon an old dialogue
within Finnish culture between mechanization and
the landscape, but it also recalled the themes of
earlier Finnish pavilions, including Aalto's from the
1930s; in fact it took over a fundamental type from
the history of modern architecture – the slab with
curved attachment – and gave it a new charge of
meaning.

In the 1980s 'abstraction' was often equated with
an empty formalism, with a retreat into internal

853

puzzles of architectural language, but some of the
most probing architects of an emerging generation
used it to intensify the significance of their forms, to
heighten experience, even to resonate with natural
forces or with the invisible spirit of place. The
American architect Steven Holl held out against
the successive fashions of postmodernism and
deconstructivism, pursuing lines of thought and
feeling that drew together personal interpretations
of modern 'mentors' with a close concentration
upon mythical, poetic and tactile aspects of
architecture. His unbuilt proposal for the American
Library in Berlin, Germany (1988), enmeshed the
banal existing slab in a counterpoint of interlocking
and hovering pieces which responded to several
scales in the setting and to past traces in the city,
and opened up an internal promenade of changing
volumes and intensities of light, a sort of route of
exploration. The childrens' library was suspended in
a prominent position in an elliptical membrane of
opaque and transparent materials, and had sloping
floors so that the children could read while lying
down. The curtain walls of the building were
envisaged in several tints and tones of sand-blasted
glass, and there were tiny framed views of the
outside world. Holl's buildings were sensitized to
natural rhythms and the hidden qualities of sites:
they fused together ideas, intuition and material
presence.

The essence of a work of architecture is an organic link between
concept and form. Pieces cannot be subtracted or added without
upsetting fundamental properties ... the organizing idea is a hidden
thread connecting disparate parts with exact intention ... From this
position experiential phenomena are the material for a kind of
reasoning that joins concept and sensation ... Outer perception (of
the intellect) and inner perception (of the senses) are synthesized in
an ordering of space, light and material.

852

The Swiss architects Jacques Herzog and Pierre de Meuron also tried to discover a poetic link between a building's form, structure and idea which might reinforce the sense of a site without making gratuitous references to context. Most of their work was in and around Basle, and so gained from the fact that this city had been a crossroads of modern architectural culture since the 1920s, but with certain lines of continuity of its own. Herzog and De Meuron's architecture drew upon Rossi's ideas but not his forms, upon conceptual art but without neo-modernist trickery, and upon the disciplines of structure and construction without retreating from the materialization of ideas. It combined the Protestant sparseness of northern Swiss modernism with something more tactile and evocative containing hidden echoes of classicism (transmitted via earlier Basle classical rationalists like Bernoulli), resonances with both the timber and the industrial vernacular, even subliminal geological echoes. The building which really announced Herzog and De Meuron's direction was the mysterious Ricola Storage Building at Laufen (1986–7), a refrigerated warehouse for stocking chocolates and caramels, standing on the outskirts of the village between an industrial building and the face of a disused limestone quarry. This hermetically sealed box was clad in horizontal striations of wood-cement angled slightly to function as drip mouldings, and supported on wooden struts locked into the underlying steel frame. The timber appeared again at the top of the building as a splayed superstructure which had the effect of an overhanging cornice, while a raft of concrete beams supplied a base. The façade between was defined by the repeating horizontal lines of splayed panels which diminished in size towards the bottom of the building and expanded towards the top in three sets of dimensions. These subtle variations and ratios (which had the character of a simplified rustication) introduced a strong visual tension and added to the haunting ambiguity of an overall form apparently assembled from humble, 'off the peg' materials and standardized elements. The Ricola Storage Building was on the knife edge between a mute 'objectivity' and an abstraction enlivened by hermetic images; it was somewhere between the rural, the industrial and even the natural, for the adjacent quarry in limestone underlined a parallelism with horizontal strata of rock. In 1989 Herzog wrote:

854

If you are looking for pantheism or naturalism in our work … you will find it, but only on the structural level which interests us, never on an analogical or figurative level.

Every natural object, all organic and inorganic matter, such as plants and stones, possesses a highly complex structure of visible and invisible images.

It was at one time possible for traditional architecture to bring together the various different facets of the construction, the images, the materials and so on, but as this now no longer exists it is necessary to fill the emptiness left between these different aspects with another kind of energy: the energy of thought, of the reflections of the architect, the artist and the scientist; and, equally, with the perceptual energy of the observer.

Another Swiss architect, Peter Zumthor, also concentrated upon the direct materiality of architecture, on 'the thing in itself', and in this was stimulated by the German conceptual artist Josef Beuys, as well as by his intuition of the presence of

buildings as objects in the landscape. His Chapel of
Sogn Benedetg near Sumvitg, in the eastern part of
Switzerland (1988–9), was a haunting elongated
oval in timber and shingles which evoked spiritual
qualities of the local vernacular without imitating the
external image, and which worked with the primary
means of material, light, space and abstract form.

There was all the evidence in these Swiss
buildings of a wider reaction against both
consumerist kitsch and fake neo-modernism: a
search, in fact, for more solid touchstones in the
material and conceptual order of buildings.
Analogous experiments emerged in several parts
of the world in the late 1980s and early 1990s, and
constituted a sort of 'tactile minimalism' in which
simplification was used to increase visual tension
and to intensify significance, and in which buildings
were sometimes conceived as topographical accents
reacting to features well beyond their immediate
site. One could mention here works as varied in
their situation and background as the Cultural
Centre in Oporto, Portugal, by Eduardo Souta de
Moura (1989–92), the Queen's Music Building at
Emmanuel College, Cambridge, by Michael
Hopkins (1991–4), the Public Library in Phoenix,
Arizona by Will Bruder (1992–5) or the Musée du
Centre Archéologique Européen du Mont Beuvray,
by Pierre-Louis Faloci (1991–5, Fig. 848) – all of
which relied upon heightened perceptions induced
by a resonant geometrical order and by direct
(though metaphorical) uses of materials. Overall
this was a sensibility attuned to a new meeting
of the mechanical and the natural, which drew
parallels between contemporary abstraction
and 'metaphysical' geometries in early modern
architecture, and which, if it made historical
allusions at all, distilled them to the essence.

Spanish architecture in the late twentieth
century reveals yet another pattern combining
the absorption of new ideals from the outside
with subliminal continuities of indigenous themes.
The pitfalls of instant traditionalism and skin-deep
neo-modernism were mostly avoided in a complex
and rooted modern architectural culture that was
open to conceptual exploration, but which also
addressed the public realm and the city. The best
work reflected the energetic social and institutional
transformations of the post-Franco years, but still
continued to develop lines of thought laid down by

earlier figures such as Sert, de la Sota, Coderch
and Saénz de Oíza. The spectrum of architectural
interests was wide, all the way from classicizing
tendencies in the Basque country, through the sort
of transformations of types and contexts mentioned
in Chapter 33 (Moneo, Navarro Baldeweg etc.)
to a range of works which combined a certain
abstraction with a close attention to construction,
and topography. High-tech was a rarity in Spain
until the Olympic Games in Barcelona and the
World's Exhibition in Seville, both of 1992, and the
normative techniques relied upon concrete, steel,
brick, ceramic and timber. This fact alone provided
Spanish work with a certain tactile directness at
odds with the flux of consumerism, and in strong
contrast to the polished machinism of French
technocratic modernism.

A concern for urban space was never far from
Spanish architects' minds and the major
transformations of Barcelona in the 1980s and 1990s
were indicative in this respect. To begin with, these
were piecemeal interventions, plazas, streets, parks,
negotiated out of the conflict between public and
private interest by the political skill of architect /
urbanists like Oriol Bohigas. They represented a
civic reaction against the destructiveness of past
laissez-faire development and allowed a degree of
avant-garde experimentation, evident for example in
the Plaza de la Estación de Sants (1981–3) by Helio
Piñón and Albert Viaplana (with Enric Miralles).
This relied upon a delicate minimalism, a tracing of

855

856

steel lines in light and air, which defined a slender pergola and an extending field of geometrical incisions and markings. While there were debts to contemporary environmental sculpture, the aesthetic also had a Spanish pedigree in the sharp Miesian aesthetic of de la Sota, notably in the fences and netting of the Maravillas School Gymnasium of 1965 (Figs. 612–14). But Barcelona also underwent larger-scale transformations towards the end of the 1980s, particularly in preparation for the Olympic Games of 1992. Among the most successful of the housing schemes in the 'Villa Olimpica' were the three courtyard blocks designed by Carlos Ferrater, which responded to the pre-existing Cerdá grid and to Mediterranean courtyard typologies, while also introducing counter-themes in the form of ground-planes extending under *pilotis*, lavish planting, and ingenious manipulations of the stepped section in the interiors. In effect, Ferrater's solution recalled some of the agendas of GATEPAC in the 1930s, and his Garbi Apartment Building at Estartit on the Costa Brava (1988–9) recalled aspects of Coderch's architecture in its taut maritime façade, its angled planes, and its sharp details in white brick, wood and stainless steel.

But there was no single direction to Catalan architecture; rather there were identifiable areas of investigation. Ignacio Paricio and Lluis Clotet remained committed to an architecture of historical resonances, bold construction and traditional brick craftsmanship (e.g. their Bank of Spain in Gerona of

1981–9). Esteban Bonell and Francesc Rius (p.630) continued to develop an architecture combining functional restraint and a certain modernist abstraction. Pedro Llinas was closer to Ferrater in his development of an incisive Rationalism employing structural ideas, hovering planes and precise, linear details. Miralles and Pinós (who were born in the mid-1950s) were more open to avant-garde experimentation abroad, but still reacted to the internal momentum of Spanish modernism (see below). Catalan architects built mainly in Mediterranean conditions, dealing with urban, suburban and rural sites in the Barcelona region or in the Balearic Islands. They drew almost unconsciously upon the resources of a Barcelona tradition, at the same time opening themselves to vital ideas in the international field. Elias Torres Tur and José Antonio Martinez Lapeña, for example, developed a controlled but poetic Rationalism that was responsive to the maritime environment, to the lush vegetation and to straightforward techniques of

857

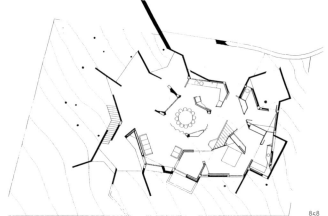

858

construction in brick and concrete. Their larger projects such as the Mora d'Ebre Hospital near Tarragona (1982–8) relied upon a humanized standardization, while their smaller interventions such as the Gili House on Ibiza (1988) developed an aesthetic of angled planes and transitional spaces which absorbed something from the 'new abstraction' abroad, even as it reinforced resonances with Coderch, Gaudí, and the Mediterranean vernacular. Their plaza below the Cathedral in Palma de Majorca (1983–92) was a delicate intervention, a network of triangular lines and allusive fragments, which seemed to give shape to invisible lines of force in the context, making evocative use of a polychrome tent-structure, palm trees and surreal incidents to intensify the experience of a historical place; here again, hermetic images of organic inspiration were combined with a species of topographical abstraction.

Spanish architecture responded to differences of region without being overtly 'Regionalist'. While much of the energy was concentrated in Madrid and Barcelona, vital centres also emerged in places as diverse as Galicia on the northwest Atlantic coast, Andalucia in the far south, and Navarre in the area around Pamplona. Galician architects like Manuel Gallego or César Portela evolved distinct responses to the severe granite landscape and rainy atmosphere of their remote corner of Spain, the former extending the primary lessons of de la Sota in works that were carefully inflected to their sites, the latter transforming the ideas and images of Aldo Rossi and blending them with the stern archetypes of the local stone vernacular. Andalucian architects such as Guillermo Vazquez Consuegra, or the partners Antonio Cruz and Antonio Ortiz, had to deal with entirely different cultural and climatic conditions, in particular the fierce light and heat of the south. While they were little involved in the layers of Arab architectural history, they none the less developed a species of 'contextual rationalism' combining straightforward construction, sensitive urbanistic

859

860

responses, and a variety of ledges, terraces, courts or screens for shade (e.g. Cruz and Ortiz's Baluarte de la Candelaria Maritime Museum (1986–9) inserted in the walls of the seaside fortress at Cadiz). Navarre, on the other hand, emerged as a testing ground for a restrained modernism which returned to the disciplines of function, structure and simplified form (e.g. the works of Roberto Ercilla). Whatever the varied local reactions of Spanish modern architecture, there did seem to be certain common denominators: these lay in its constructive discipline, its tectonic order, its inventive reinterpretation of generic modern themes, and its capacity to distil context and memory in abstract forms.

The Spanish interest in the sense of place, and in the meeting of artificial and natural orders, received much stimulus from the work of the Portuguese architect Alvaro Siza, whose mature buildings were like vectors of light and space holding together the fragments of the city or landscape. His Centro Galego de Arte Contemporaneo in Santiago de Compostela, Spain (1988–94), reinvoked the topographical sensitivity of his earliest buildings while responding to the civic ambitions of a regional culture. The site was to one side of the historical city, and Siza used fragmentation to respond to multiple scales and textures in the setting. The exterior was in the sober granite typical of the place, but this was attached to a structural frame which lifted the main superstructure free of the ground allowing routes and levels to penetrate the interiors at a number of angles. The cool Atlantic light was brought in through a variety of cracks, openings and skylights, and bathed the pure white interiors, picking out edges, shadows and hovering planes. Spatial tensions, vistas and shifting perspectives developed an argument in visual and tactile terms. Devices drawn in the long run from Cubist painting and from Aalto were used to enhance the experience of works of art and the feeling for the *genius loci*. Far from being a device for ironical commentary, fragmentation was here a means for holding ambiguities in equilibrium, for enriching the experience of an historic site, and for placing the human figure back at the centre of architecture.

The Igualada Cemetery (1985–92) outside

860 Alvaro Siza,
Centro Galego de
Arte Contemporaneo,
Santiago de Compostela,
1988–94, roof terrace

861 Enric Miralles and
Carme Pinós, Igualada
Cemetery, Barcelona,
1985–92, plan

862 Igualada Cemetery

Barcelona by Enric Miralles and Carme Pinós also relied upon dynamic diagonals, erosions and fractures to concentrate a topographical gesture and to heighten a sense of ritual. The cemetery was defined as a procession into the earth, an angular cut or descending route that was channelled between sculpted embankments in concrete containing the rows of burial caskets. The textured paving had scattered wooden railway ties embedded in it, like logs moving in a stream, and conveyed the notion of a river of souls. Although the Igualada Cemetery had no obvious resemblance to Scarpa's Brion Tomb, it relied upon analogous themes to do with the scraping away of layers and the confrontation with the reality of death. At the bottom of the main ramp was a curved enclosure with rubble walls, like an ancient burial ground. The re-ascent towards an abstraction of a cross invoked the themes of Calvary and of Resurrection, recalling the ideas, though not the forms, of Asplund's Woodland Crematorium at

Enskede. Miralles and Pinós's 'building' was in fact somewhere between architecture, landscape and environmental sculpture. It fused together the archaicism and curved profiles of Le Corbusier's late works, the slicing planes of Richard Serra, and the pantheistic landscape art of Gaudí, while grappling with a spatial expression appropriate to a late twentieth-century culture combining secular structures with religious roots. Here, avant-garde experimentation and institutional norms achieved a vital interchange: a mental map containing numerous ideas was translated into a social landscape.

The multiple modernisms of the late twentieth century were rarely embedded in some large-scale social project and could do little to suggest alternative forms for the city at a time when the city was, in fact, in a state of dissolution and when the surrounding landscape was itself undergoing drastic redefinition. Modern architecture in its many manifestations seemed to flourish best in the tension

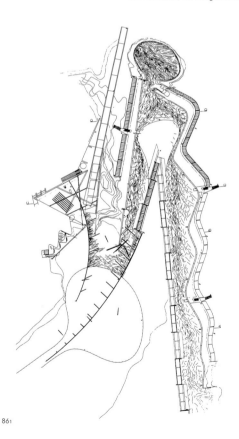

861

862

between public and private interests, especially in social democracies struggling to reconcile the forces of technological modernization with the demands of liberal institutions. The economic infrastructure rested at the level of mere mechanisms and networks of information while critical architectures aspired to the level of poetic forms and enduring symbols. Cataclysmic changes – the collapse of Soviet Communism, the emergence of new political and religious identities, the ever-deepening ecological crisis with its crying need for new conceptual models of 'nature' – were slow to register at the level of visual and metaphorical interpretation. Even so, the growing perception of a shared planet offered hints of new conceptions of universality, while the appreciation of local differences prompted new formulations of 'modernity' and revised schemes of history. Perceptions were less idealistic and less Utopian than in the early 'heroic period', but were also more realistic about the possible scope of architecture. The most probing works in the 1980s and early 1990s took on the character of eloquent fragments, condensed worlds, standing out against a rabid technological development, and evoking idealized relationships between people, things and ideas: microcosms of a kind.

Despite vast changes in intention, ideology, function and technology, the invention of forms continued to rely upon the major revolutions that occurred earlier in the century. These exerted obvious and less obvious influence, since they affected the underlying structures of conception and perception, as well as actual forms. The lines of continuity turned out to be more complex, diverse and enduring than some had thought. As time moved on and as historical consciousness of earlier phases developed, the entire configuration reorganized itself into unexpected patterns and alignments, and new links were made to diverse cultures and past forms. But the most challenging architecture still emerged in the tension between individual intentions and collective myths, between unique ideas and universal aims. One may leave the uncompleted and open sequences of late twentieth-century architecture with a thought from Viollet-le-Duc which continues to be a challenge, although formulated over a century ago when modern architecture was just an idea for the future: 'Style is the manifestation of an ideal based on principle.'

conclusion: modernity, tradition, authenticity

Every artist finds certain
visual possibilities
before him, to which
he is bound. Not
everything is possible
at all times.
Heinrich Wölfflin, 1915.

The early propagandists of modern architecture were convinced that a century-old problem had been solved in their own times, that a genuine modern style rather than a revival of past forms had at last been achieved. They may have been wrong in treating this 'style' as monolithically as they did, and they certainly oversimplified its relationship to previous traditions, but they were probably right in stressing its epic significance. The revolution in sensibility which affected all of the arts around the turn of the century constituted a profound reorientation in ways of seeing and thinking, as well as in the universe of forms. In the late twentieth century the implications are still not exhausted, in fact core ideas continue to be revised and reinterpreted. The overall historical significance accorded to modernism also varies greatly, all the way from postmodernists, who dismiss the whole thing as a temporary aberration, to legitimists who claim to see in the modernist revolution some latterday equivalent to the invention of Gothic or the onset of the Renaissance.

Whatever value one places on modern architecture, it clearly has the character of a major transformation. With hindsight modernism emerges as a radical intervention in the world historical process. Its universalizing ambition is traceable to the Enlightenment. Like de Tocqueville's version of the French Revolution, it used 'the debris of the old order for building up the new' and 'aspired to be world-wide', creating 'an intellectual fatherland whose citizenship was open to men of every nationality'. Modernism purged defunct authority, reordered the fundamentals of the discipline, and instated new liberties for the future. It struggled to reconcile idealism with material progress, science with history, the city with nature. In many of its Utopian endeavours it failed, becoming ensnared in the ideological contradictions of mass industrialization and urbanization in capitalist and socialist societies, and in the Third World. Its 'universalism' was co-opted by nationalisms and imperialisms, although it also served as a refracting prism through which local traditions (some of them with a universality of their own) could be re-examined in the post-colonial world. Inevitably modernism partook of the crises and conflicts of the process of modernization itself.

If one refers to modernism as a historical abstraction in this way, it is because it now plays several roles: an activating ideal almost outside time; a renewable charter of intentions; an incomplete cultural project; an evolving tradition of ideas, forms and actual buildings. The epic adventure of modernism is clearly not over, especially in a world grappling with the implications of a global economy, the universalization of technology, the redefinition of identities and territories, and the question of how the future should be planned. To judge by the work presented in the last part of this book, it is even entering a new phase where several of its generative principles are being re-examined and reactivated. As the process is still going on, and as the historian is part of it, it is hard to write a conclusion. But one can at least outline the shape of an unfolding modern tradition as it appears from the shifting perspective of an evolving present.

This book has been at some pains to explain that there is nothing simple or predestined about the development of modern architecture. One may be tempted to impose a sequential structure upon it – a formative phase, a crystallization, a 'classic moment', an extension of principles, a mannerism, a decadence – but there are too many exceptions that refuse to fit the scheme. Or one may care to speak of new paradigms and their ensuing transformation, but this always risks underrating the unpredictable invention, the unique spark of individual artistic personality. There may be a case for shared elements of style and recurrent types, but disjunctions are sometimes as important as continuities, and there can be a sudden revival of a lost agenda; buildings of real interest transcend the norms of their period. An evolutionary scheme may be suggested, but works of art scarcely behave biologically; they also fit into different lengths of duration. There are clearly geographical components to the modern architectural development, but these have to be treated with caution, as they can be distorted by the political imperatives of internationalization on the one side, of regionalisms on the other. The book has done its best to negotiate these difficulties, and to portray the diverse strands of modernism in all their subtlety and complexity, in space and in time.

Any new ideal has its period of self-definition, in which inherited elements and partial experiments are resumed in forms that seem to posses an air of general relevance. The crucial decade for modern architecture in this respect was the 1920s. To say this is not to ignore outstanding works before and since; it is rather to suggest that there is a time when basic themes come to a point of clarity, and new ground rules are set in place. Periods of this creative intensity are altogether rare in the history of architecture. They rely on uncommon coincidences of talent, patronage and luck, and on phases of cultural transition in which new world-views strive for expression. The generation which came to maturity after the First World War happened to contain individuals of the calibre of Le Corbusier, Walter Gropius and Mies van der Rohe, each of them obsessed with the problem of defining an architectural language appropriate to industrialized society. They inherited this problem, and some of the means of solving it, from an earlier generation containing artists of the order of Frank Lloyd Wright, Charles Rennie Mackintosh, Peter Behrens and Auguste Perret. But the protagonists of the modern movement of the 1920s had other ideas in common. They shared a commitment to social improvement through design and a feeling for the progressive potential of modern technology. They were fascinated by the spatial possibilities inherent in Cubism and in steel and concrete construction. They were united in their belief in a universal and international language of form, and in their hope that lessons might be abstracted from the past without facile imitation. Despite a degree of alienation intrinsic to their avant-garde position, they thought of themselves as the prophets of a new society and as preservers of higher values; their Utopias combined apocalyptic expectation with a vein of nostalgia. The bringing of art to life, of form to industrialism seemed a worthwhile and meaningful cultural programme in the service of human betterment. And while each artist chose to express these euphoric sentiments in his own way, the results had certain broad features in common.

This happy coincidence of historical circumstance and aesthetic intentions was brief, but it still changed many of the formal, spatial, structural and symbolic bases of architecture. Since the early days of this century conditions and intentions have continued to change, and the conventions of modern architecture have been stretched and agitated into new combinations, but they have not been fundamentally revised. The architects who first inherited the modern tradition in the 1930s, Aalto, Terragni, Martienssen, Niemeyer, Barragan, Lubetkin and the rest, absorbed the principles of the seminal buildings and extended their lessons. Even the reformulations necessitated by the cataclysmic event of the Second World War did not dislodge the majority of the premises laid out in the 'heroic' period. The modern masters themselves extended their vocabularies on some levels, while maintaining core qualities from their earlier works. Lesser figures built the skyscrapers and housing schemes envisaged on paper in the 1920s in a much debased form three decades later. Probing inheritors of the tradition took over some concepts and rejected others; the ideas of Team X or artists as individual as Kahn, Van Eyck, Tange, Lasdun and Utzon were characterized by a tense recognition of the continuing relevance of modern architectural schemata, combined with a feeling that new expressive territories should be discovered. This is not to denigrate such figures for a lack of originality; it is rather to emphasize that an inventor's task may vary according to the point at which he enters a tradition, and to stress that creative individuals and traditions need one another if they are to stay alive.

Despite the noisy proclamations of 'postmodernists' in the early 1980s about the end of an era, their actual vocabularies involved little more than the sticking-together of pre-existing pieces of modern architecture, with appliqués here and there of skin-deep historicism. This scarcely amounted to a basic critique; it was rather a change of clothes. By contrast, the inventions of the masters, of Le Corbusier and Wright in particular, altered the very spatial anatomy of design and constituted a fundamental reorganization of the deep structures (so to say) of the medium itself. As Picasso, Braque, Matisse and Kandinsky had done for painting, they made available new expressive languages of vast range and applicability on which others, whether faint-hearted or intensely intelligent, could build. The world-wide production of the past half-century tends to confirm this. There are airport buildings in remote parts of Africa which would not have their present appearance without the prototypes of Mies van der Rohe, and recent buildings of high poetic intensity which rely upon spatial concepts inherent in the Dom-ino skeleton of eighty years ago. For better or for worse, the modern movement has become the dominant tradition of our time.

But this tradition is neither monolithic nor static. It is composed from the creations of individual artists of varying belief and from buildings which each have a unique life; it encompasses considerable regional variety and a very broad spectrum of quality; it interacts with several cultures and pasts. The architect of the present inherits this tradition whether he likes it or not, but the way in which he sees it will depend on the obsessions dominant in his time and even on the filters created by historians. What he chooses to do with his inheritance will in turn vary according to his temperament, the possibilities made available by patronage, and the relevance of prototypes to new situations. The average talent will take over a little piece and trot out an imitation of it: that is what average artists have always done throughout history whether they built with pointed arches, columns or steel frames. But the original mind is bound to grapple with his version of his tradition, rejecting some of it, welcoming part of it, and taking a good deal of it for granted. Gradually he will move from imitation of his forefathers to the crystallization of a personal style, blending his own preoccupations with solutions appropriate to the new problems which face him. The quality of his results will depend in some degree on his ability to avoid repeating the mere surface effects of his predecessors, and on his capacity to inject new meaning into the basic formulations of his tradition.

If the available style is beginning to show signs of fatigue, to become irrelevant, or to stand in the way of a valid or vital interpretation of reality, then it may have to be cast away. Surely this is the combination of reasons which led to the formulation of modern architecture in the first place: the existing forms were inadequate to the task of containing the new functions, materials, aspirations and ideologies fostered by the Industrial Revolution. There are those who claim that modern architecture is also in a period of profound malaise. The introverted mannerism and symbolic devaluation portrayed in the latter part of this book, whether postmodernist or neo-modernist in appearance, are scarcely signs of health. But alongside these jaded version of modern design (really no worse than the decadent versions of earlier styles) are buildings of high quality; as ever they are in a minority and their excellence transcends mere period concerns.

From the vantage point of the late twentieth century it is the dynamism and diversity of the modern tradition that are most striking. Formative principles have now been disseminated world-wide, and continue to pass through metamorphoses in places remote from the points of origin. Influences cross and recross frontiers, encountering varying resistance, blending regional, national and international elements, extending existing lines of research and opening up new ideas for the future. In the process, the modern tradition rethinks itself, both through historical and critical texts, and through actual buildings and projects. This implies both an internal inheritance of underlying types, and an active 'rereading' of seminal buildings and core ideas. Each generation poses different questions, has different problems to solve, and sees the same buildings differently. There is a sort of accumulation of historical layers as prototypes are reinterpreted through later filters, and as potentials latent within them are revealed. The resilience of a tradition is gauged by the capacity of its schemata to go on transforming in time, achieving new connections of myth and meaning, new syntheses of ideas and forms. It provides 'mental maps' throught which actuality, history and nature may be read and interpreted in symbolic terms.

The underlying conceptual structures of modern architecture are more insistent than is usually admitted. The architect who is convinced otherwise still has the problem of formulating an architectural language. Perhaps he will attempt (as some have attempted) to turn back to earlier phases in history for support. If so he will have the problem of reviving an earlier style without pastiche. He must rethink the past in terms of present-day tasks, techniques and meanings. Along the way he may discover that superficial mimicry of past forms is really no better than skin-deep modernity and that past forms had their own reasons for being, most of which no longer apply. If the resolution of this problem is sought in an intuition of past principles, then the artist will still need a language in the present through which he can abstract precedent.

He will then be face to face with the problem of modern architecture again and, perhaps, with the realization that its formal and spatial conceptions are closer to present functions and meanings than he had hoped. There is a solid core of wisdom to Malraux's observation that 'no man builds on a void, and a civilization that breaks with the style at its disposal soon finds itself empty-handed'.

The problems that the inventors of modern architecture set out to solve are still very much with us. As the whole world gradually industrializes it confronts difficulties similar to the ones which first faced the West a century ago, some of which remain. New building problems emerge to which pre-existing traditions have no adequate solution; changing techniques undermine the reason for traditional forms and the craft systems in which they were made; new patterns of life lead to new needs and values which cry out for an adequate architectural home. Neither regressive sentimentalism nor slick technocracy hold out adequate answers ideologically or achitecturally. Evidently forms have to be found which are equal to the new problems but which embody lasting values as well. Muthesius's observation made just after the turn of the century continues to ring true:

Far higher than the material is the spiritual; far higher than function, material and technique stands Form. These three material aspects might be impeccably handled but – if Form were not – we would still be living in a merely brutish world.

Since the loss of authority of classical norms in the eighteenth century, architects have lacked a vocabulary which appeared to have a universal sanction. This remains the position today. But where the architect at the turn of the century had to battle to formulate a new style, the architect of the present has the intervening chain of discoveries of the modern tradition to rely on. It seems sensible to build on the wisdom embodied in works of quality in this tradition and to avoid the mistakes of the lesser creations. This does not imply the imitation or mannerization of earlier architectural forms, but the rigorous redefinition of the principles behind them in the context of new problems. Modern architecture is intrinsically neither better nor worse than past architectures; all depends on how it is used in any one case. There is no short cut in the creation of quality; no recipes will do; and a preoccupation with passing fads will only result in work of transient value. Indeed, 'modernity' can become a distraction since what really counts is authenticity.

Authenticity suggests genuineness and probity – the opposite of the fake. It implies forms based on principle, forms which avoid arbitrariness, and which are appropriate on a number of levels. Whether it uses pilotis or piers, rectangles or curves, the authentic building transcends the convention in which it was conceived. It possesses a sublime unity subsuming part and whole, revealing different aspects of a dominating image, and suggesting a character of almost natural inevitability. Through a marvellous abstraction, its materials, details, spaces and forms reveal the hierarchy of intentions. It is never merely a rational structural solution, nor merely an elegant play with shapes, but an embodiment of a social vision, an intuitive interpretation of a human institution, an idealization of a kind. Its forms may conform to the regulations of a period, a style, or a building type, but the authentic work will cut through the customary to reveal new levels of significance.

Such authenticity is inconceivable without the basis of a genuine personal style. In the vocabularies of Wright, Le Corbusier, Mies van der Rohe, Aalto, Kahn (and a few others) one recognizes some of the necessary features: a limited family of forms capable of rich variation on the foundation of consistent patterns of thought; a system of type-forms blending the practical, the aesthetic and the symbolic; shapes pregnant with meaning embodying a mythical interpretation of the world. The genuine style is the opposite of a cliché: it is a vital formula and a source of discipline, and it functions as a filter through which the artist draws experience and translates it into form; it places limits on any new problem and provides the shape of hypotheses while reflecting the artist's most obsessive themes.

When a style possesses this prodigious power of abstraction, it becomes a tool for transforming precedent. Its external physiognomy may relate to contemporary relatives, but its inner life will rely on nourishment from tradition. A single abstract shape may derive simultaneously from a dome, a funnel, a cooling-tower, an Indian observatory, a syntax for concrete, a favourite form in painting and a particular institutional interpretation, as happened with the curved volume at the heart of Le Corbusier's Parliament at Chandigarh. A modern solution to the roof may blend the wisdom of the classical cornice with an intuition about a basic order in nature, and even with the shape of a Froebel block, as happened in the architectural system of Wright. And as each new task is faced, the range of a style is extended a little, but without a loss of consistency; the chemistry of a genuine poetic language continues to fuse new unities out of well-tried parts.

The Robie House, the Villa Savoye, the Barcelona Pavilion, the town centre at Säynätsalo, the Kimbell Art Museum, the church at Bagsvaerd, the Congress Hall in Salamanca – these are among the buildings in the modern tradition which possess such extraordinary depth. To slot them into the modern movement is to miss much of their value for they are also relatives of past works of excellence. It was this timeless character to which Le Corbusier referred in 1923 when he wrote: 'Architecture has nothing to do with the various styles.'

bibliographical note

Like architecture, scholarship has its traditions: the historian both extends and rejects the work of predecessors while incorporating new evidence and insights. Theories suggest general questions and areas of investigation; particular observations in turn test and modify theories. The footnotes to individual chapters list relevant monographs and articles, while the present 'Bibliographical Note' is reserved for more general works on modern architecture which have helped me to form a picture of overall development even when I have disagreed with the point of view or have felt that crucial material was missing. Not to say that this book takes its place in any obvious historiographical lineage, or that its underlying aims and ideas can be accounted for in terms of prior publications. However attentive the writer may be to new researches and discoveries, the essence of historical thinking eludes any simple additive process of facts and interpretations. If a work of history has any claim to lasting value it is surely at the level of its basic understanding of its subject and in its literary structure and form.

The following bibliography makes no claim at being complete: it rather concentrates upon books which are referred to frequently in the notes. It would be quite impossible to include even a fair representation of the vast and ever-growing bibliography on architecture this century without writing another, separate volume. The reader who seeks a more detailed coverage is referred to Dennis Sharp, ed., *Sources of Modern Architecture* (Architectural Association, London, Paper no. 2), London and New York, 1967; to Muriel Emanuel, ed., *Contemporary Architects*, New York, 1980, new edn, 1995; to A.K. Placzek, ed., *Macmillan Encyclopedia of Architects* (New York, 1982); to Vittorio Magnago Lampugnani, ed., *The Thames and Hudson Encyclopedia of Twentieth Century Architecture*, London, 1986; and to Jean-Paul Midant, ed., *Dictionnaire de l'architecture du vingtième siècle*, Paris, 1996.

The picture is necessarily less complete the earlier one goes. One might begin with the modern movement's initial attempts at understanding itself, such as Walter Gropius's *Internationale Architektur*, Munich, 1925; Walter C. Behrendt's *Der Sieg des neuen*

Baustils, Stuttgart, 1927; Ludwig Hilberseimer's *Internationale neue Baukunst*, Stuttgart, 1927; Gustav Platz's *Baukunst der neusten Zeit*, Berlin, 1927; Sigfried Giedion's *Bauen in Frankreich*, Leipzig, 1928; or Bruno Taut's *Die neue Baukunst in Europa und Amerika*, Stuttgart, 1929. It is possible that some of these influenced the selection of buildings in, even the title of, Henry-Russell Hitchcock and Philip Johnson's slightly later *The International Style, Architecture Since 1922*, New York, 1932, although the thinking behind each book was different. Where Hilberseimer, for example, stressed attitudes to design rather than prescribing a set of forms, Hitchcock and Johnson attempted to characterize the predominant visual modes in a selection of modern architectural works, and to relate these to structural effects of concrete and steel. As the title suggests, the emphasis was stylistic; ideological aspects of the new architecture were ignored, as were buildings which did not conform visually.

Lewis Mumford's *The Brown Decades* (New York, 1931) was an important milestone in understanding a specifically American contribution to the emergence of modern architecture in the late nineteenth century, giving due emphasis to the work of individuals such as Henry Hobson Richardson, Louis Sullivan, John Wellborn Root and Frank Lloyd Wright. Walter Curt Behrendt's *Modern Building, its Nature, Problems and Forms*, New York, 1937, also stressed the ethical and social implications of modern architecture, while writers such as Emil Kaufmann, in *Von Ledoux bis Le Corbusier, Ursprung und Entwicklung der autonomen Architektur*, Vienna, 1933–4, suggested long-term connections with the late eighteenth century and with a heritage of basically classical values. Despite the title of his book, *Gli Elementi dell'architettura funzionale*, Milan, 1932, Alberto Sartoris dealt with issues well beyond function, contributing in the course of time to the perception of 'Mediterranean' echoes in modernism.

In 1932 P. Morton Shand published a series of articles in the *Architectural Review* (London) dealing with the evolution of modern architecture in the late nineteenth and early twentieth centuries. These may have influenced the picture given by Nikolaus Pevsner in his better-known *Pioneers of the Modern Movement*, London, 1936. Pevsner traced the impact of Morris's moral ideas and of nineteenth-century engineering on formulations around the turn of the century. He examined Art Nouveau, the work of Perret, Behrens, Hoffmann and Wright, and brought his story to a close in 1914, with buildings like Gropius's Werkbund Pavilion at Cologne of that year. The implication seemed to be that these individual buildings were part of a saga, resulting in what Pevsner felt was the true, rational style of the twentieth century.

Sigfried Giedion's *Space, Time and Architecture*, Cambridge, Mass., 1941, had something of this character too. Perhaps influenced by historicists like Heinrich Wölfflin, he believed it was the historian's task to characterize the 'constituent' facts of a period, those which supposedly represented the 'spirit of the age', and to ignore the rest. As he wrote, his new Grand Tradition of modern architecture was under threat of extinction in Europe: his tone was lofty and apostolic. His view of the origins of modern architecture did

much to emphasize the role of new materials like iron, glass, steel and concrete in the nineteenth century, and of a new 'space conception' stemming from Cubism and culminating in the rich spatial ambiguities of modern architecture. His treatment went further than Pevsner's in that it covered urbanism and architecture in the 1920s and 1930s. Expressionist tendencies were played down; rationalist ones emphasized; extensions of nineteenth-century revivalism ignored. Even the later editions of the book, which included buildings of the 1940s and 1950s, were selective tracts in favour of a cause with which Giedion was directly involved.

The perspective altered drastically after the war as a new younger generation of historians looked back at the 'heroic' years as a separate period of history, and became more conscious of the symbolic and ideological flavour of modern architecture. The most notable products were the fragmentary essays of Colin Rowe written in the late 1940s (e.g., 'The Mathematics of the Ideal Villa: Palladio and Le Corbusier Compared', *Architectural Review*, 1947) and the remarkable *Theory and Design in the First Machine Age*, London, 1960, by Reyner Banham. This was on a sounder documentary foundation than its predecessors, as it was based on theoretical texts of the first three decades of this century. It is probably pointless to blame Banham's work for its cursory treatment of Wright, its Eurocentrism and its near-avoidance of politics, as these were not close to its central aims. However, the book did draw to a close around 1930, and analysed texts more than it did forms.

Banham's book was conceived in parallel with Henry-Russell Hitchcock's magisterial *Architecture, Nineteenth and Twentieth Centuries*, which appeared in the Pelican History of Art series in 1958. This was sound scholarship of an undaring kind belonging to that tradition of art history which concentrates on the description of stylistic movements. Only the last third of the book was devoted to the twentieth century and it closed in the early 1950s. There was little sense of the social role of architecture and even individual artistic personalities were blended into 'phases' and 'developments'. However, the treatment of Art Nouveau was extensive, and the book retains its function as a weighty reference work with a good bibliography and useful notes.

Bruno Zevi's *Storia dell'architettura moderna*, Turin, 1950, issued from an entirely different historiographical tradition, and was pervaded by the author's strong commitment to dynamic spatial values as a measure of a supposedly 'organic' cultural synthesis. In Zevi's scheme, Frank Lloyd Wright took on a central role that had been denied him by several historians of an earlier generation. Aside from the datable aspects of Zevi's polemics, his reading of modern architecture indicated underlying spatial concepts beyond the outer features of style.

Leonardo Benevolo's *History of Modern Architecture*, 2 vols., Cambridge, Mass., 1971; original Italian edition 1960, amplified both Giedion's and Zevi's treatment of the nineteenth century. It stressed the reformist roots of modern architecture and urbanism, and the crises following from industrialization. Volume 2, dealing with the twentieth century, took a broad view and included political debates surrounding the modern movement, and the impact of Nazi and Fascist critiques. As he was writing in the late 1950s, his treatment of the years after the Second World War was cursory, although it did include Brazil and Japan; he also abstained from a close analysis of individual works.

Peter Collins's *Changing Ideals in Modern Architecture*, London, 1965, must be counted among the seminal works of modern architectural scholarship. In this case the emphasis was on the intellectual history of the nineteenth century and on the emergence of the idea, rather than the forms, of modern architecture. This was seen against the background of the various philosophical debates underlying nineteenth-century styles. Collins provided the most succinct treatment of Rationalism, an attitude to design which would be rethought in the modern movement of the twentieth century. A similar interest in the role of ideas emerged in the fragmentary writings of Alan Colquhoun in the 1960s – 1980s, later collected together as the anthology of essays entitled *Essays in Architectural Criticism, Modern Architecture and Historical Change*, New York and Cambridge, Mass., 1981.

For coverage of the period up to the end of the 1960s, one has to resort to lesser works than those mentioned so far. Charles Jencks's *Modern Movements in Architecture*, New York, 1973, was written by a critic who has made no bones about the propaganda value of 'history' writing. The book reflects the agonies and hesitations of the convinced pluralist. Jencks was determined to avoid the 'single strand' method of Giedion and Pevsner, and implied instead (with the aid of charts and diagrams) a series of 'discontinuous movements'; six in all. These had names like 'The Idealist', 'The Intuitive' and 'The Activist'. Architecture covering half century or more was thus parcelled rather uncomfortably into arbitrary categories. The result of all the straining after relativism was a confused picture which clearly acknowledged the difficulty of *selection* and the need to avoid presenting modern architecture as a monolithic entity.

In the mid-1970s the publications on 'Modern Architecture and Design' of the BBC Open University course A305, run by Tim and Charlotte Benton, began to appear. The eighteen 'units' on architecture from 1890 to 1939 presented some previously unpublished facts, sources, images and opinions. Most useful too were the two anthologies of source material: *Architecture and Design, 1890-1939, an International Anthology of Original Articles*, New York, 1975 (eds. Tim Benton and Charlotte Benton, with Dennis Sharp) and *Documents, a Collection of Source Material on the Modern Movement*, Milton Keynes, 1975 (ed. Charlotte Benton). A curious habit seems to have developed in the architectural history confraternity, of not acknowledging the 'units' as publications; I have avoided this in my own references.

Also in the 1970s, Manfredo Tafuri and Francesco Dal Co published *Modern Architecture*, New York, 1979 – translated from the Italian *Architettura Contemporanea*, Milan, 1976. The emphasis of this lavish book was on the evolution of the modern industrial city more than on individual buildings or artists. The authors were proud to announce their Marxist affiliations and to mar any pretence at objectivity in a social polemic. Even so their treatment of American and Soviet city planning was most useful.

However, the years after 1950 were given little coverage and next to nothing was said about architecture outside Europe and the United States. Another book which emphasized ideology at the expense of other matters and which did not address the problems of 'developing countries', was Kenneth Frampton's *Modern Architecture, a Critical History*, New York, 1980, nearly half of which was devoted to architecture before 1914. I have recorded my reactions to the strengths and weaknesses of these two books in a review in the *Journal of the Society of Architectural Historians*, 40, no. 2, May 1981), pp. 168-70.

So far little has been done to clarify the overall shape of the years since around 1970, although some attempt is made in Josep Maria Montaner's *Después del movimiento moderno, arquitectura de la segunda mitad del siglo XX*, Barcelona, 1993. This book is most valuable for its analysis of the 1950s in Southern Europe (especially Italy) but the closer it gets to the present the more it relies upon questionable critical categories, and the less it analyses actual buildings or specifically architectural ideas. While it includes a wide range of recent production in the 'advanced industrial nations', it has little on the cultures of the third world.

the third edition of modern architecture since 1900

The first edition of *Modern Architecture since 1900* was written at the end of the 1970s and the beginning of the 1980s, being published in 1982. The governing ideas were first formulated in earlier monographs and articles, then in broader outlines and essays. It seemed necessary to avoid the various determinisms (historical or social) of some previous authors, and to elaborate a more complex picture of both the internal order of a modern tradition, and of longer-range debts to the past. An 'integrated' approach seemed desirable, something that might address the multiple aspects of the architectural totality (social, technical, symbolic, material, mental etc.) but without losing sight of the unique order and presence of the individual work. It was also clear that the historiography suffered from a Western bias, and that whole areas of the 'developing world' remained to be charted.

For the second edition (1987) the book remained unchanged except for a single new chapter at the end entitled 'Search for Substance: Recent World Architecture'. This was worked out against the drift of critical opinion then current, avoiding the usual, but misleading postures concerning 'modernism' and 'postmodernism'. This addendum relied upon primary research and the evidence of the buildings themselves. Aside from a short section of notes for this chapter, the end-matter of the book remained as in the first edition.

The main intention in writing a revised third edition has been (to cite the Preface): 'to integrate new knowledge and experience in an existing structure and to accentuate themes that were left undeveloped'. In the past fifteen years there has been an explosion of literature on modern architecture, all the way from detailed studies on individual buildings and architects, to theoretical speculations on the cultural landscape, the industrial city and the political aspects of

architecture. The materials of archives have made themselves felt through publications and microfiches of documents and drawings, and through a gradual sifting in the writings of scholars. There have been retrospective exhibitions on most of the major figures of modern architecture (e.g. Le Corbusier, Frank Lloyd Wright, Louis Kahn, Mies van der Rohe), sometimes coinciding with centenaries, and these have in turn fostered catalogues full of essays and new information. Given all this there might be a temptation to retreat into obsessive detail, abandoning any attempt at larger-scale interpretation. In fact, the scholarship has sometimes been accompanied by literature of a more speculative kind, much of it specious. Lacking, as a rule, has been a satisfactory synthesis of the general and the particular.

In the same period, the author's own explorations have taken him into many new geographical and intellectual territories. As well as monographs on Le Corbusier, Denys Lasdun and Balkrishna Doshi, he has written numerous catalogue essays, critical articles, introductions and book reviews on aspects of recent world architecture, on historiography and on principles of design (some of these in the Bibliography and Notes). Intensive travels have opened up dialogues with diverse architectural cultures in India, Mexico, Spain, Finland among others and these researches have in turn led to publications. Some have been concerned with the transformation of cultural 'substructures' in non-Western traditions into modern terms. The combination of these personal investigations and of new discoveries by others has inevitably led to reformulations about the overall shape of twentieth-century architectural history.

The current third edition (started in late 1993) is one of the results of this process of intensive re-examination, a process which has also gained from both formal and informal criticisms by others. More emphasis has now been given to: architecture and the city; to interactions between personal and period style; to the transformation of the past in Western and non-Western contexts; to the interplay between individual inventions and technological or vernacular norms; to the tension between 'local' and 'universal' within modernism; to the concept of a modern tradition; and to the underlying structure of problems and solutions (emerging and inherited) within world architectures of the recent past; to the effects of modernization in the Third World.

The preface to the first edition has been reproduced in its entirety. The Introduction and the Conclusion have been altered slightly to accommodate a longer historical perspective. Together these hint at the underlying intentions of the book which are intrinsic to its structure and which remain basically unchanged. A new Preface has been added for the third edition and this gives an outline of additions, deletions and revisions; a more complete rationale follows in this Bibliographical Note. The rest of the book, including bibliography and footnotes, has been revised, more in some parts than in others. The most obvious modification is the addition of seven new chapters (2, 8, 21, 26, 33, 34, 35), but there are some other changes of order and of emphasis.

Certain of these changes have been made to accommodate recent discoveries on subjects already treated, others to include buildings, individuals or ideas that were previously unknown to the author; more has also been done to discuss the cultural role of architecture and to deal with interactions between the individual building and the wider environment. For example, a new Chapter (2) has been inserted near the beginning of Part 1 which deals with the late nineteenth-century industrial city and with the architectural and philosophical dilemmas posed by an emergent building type, the skyscraper. While this is largely an American story (even a Chicago story), it also serves to outline some of the basic structures and generic contradictions of the capitalist city. A further chapter (8) has been added to Part 1, dealing with national myths and classical transformations soon after the turn of the century. These are subjects with their own interest, but they also explain some of the formative influences on the 'modern masters', and hint at the later continuation of regional and classical influences within modern architecture itself. More attention has been given, as well, to the inheritance of theories from the nineteenth century (e.g. the writings of Gottfried Semper), and to diverse conceptions of nature.

In the same spirit, Part 2 has been reordered and reorganized to emphasize the range and diversity of modern architectural developments between the wars, to underline the various cultural, political and aesthetic agendas of seminal figures like Wright, Le Corbusier, Mies van der Rohe and Aalto, and to re-evaluate individual architects who never fit period pigeonholes, such as Schindler, Terragni and Mendelsohn. It was always an intention of the book to deal with the question of style in a deep sense, rather than abandoning the problem of style altogether as others have done. The first edition already expressed scepticism about the relative superficiality of the categories used in the formulation of a so-called 'International Style'. The third edition has gone further to clarify the underlying spatial concepts, mental structures and modes of organization at work in the architectures of the 1920s. It delves into similarities and differences, generic types and particular variations, elements of personal and period style. A new chapter has been added to the end of Part 2 which deals with the foundation of branches of the modern movement in countries such as Spain, Denmark, Sweden, Japan, Brazil, South Africa, Palestine and Mexico in the 1920s and 1930s. This addresses the themes of extension, 'naturalization' and cultural adaptation in short, the entire process of global dissemination.

When the book was first written the literature on the years after the Second World War was sparse and somewhat distorted by an apparent obsession with (mostly illusory) 'movements'. Over the past decade there have been several valuable studies of individual architects, buildings, national cultures and building types which have filled out the picture with greater accuracy. A new chapter (26) on the European situation in the years of reconstruction (which hopefully compensates for the thin treatment of Italy, Germany, Spain and Scandinavia in the earlier editions) has been added to Part 3, and more has also been done to portray the significant contribution of countries in Latin America and Asia. Some reviewers of the first edition suggested that *Modern Architecture*

since 1900 was one the few general studies to broach the problems of modernization, urbanization and identity in the 'developing world'; the third edition expands upon these themes, notably for India, North Africa and the Middle East.

There is now just enough distance from the 1970s to portray the crises of the period without falling prey to the polemics, but for developments since then this is more difficult. The Preface to the second edition (1987) suggested that 'in many parts of the world, primary lessons learned earlier in this century are being extended and transformed better to deal with the claims of context, region and tradition'. A new Part 4, 'Continuity and Change in the Late Twentieth Century', explores this assertion in three entirely new chapters, examining a broad range of recent work in such places as Spain, Finland, Japan, France, India, the United States and Mexico. Rather than relying on the self-inflationary rhetoric of 'isms', this part develops its themes around individual buildings and architectural ideas that seem seminal in the creation of a contemporary architectural culture. It examines the underlying structure of recent history by seeking out shared problems and by suggesting how diverse talents have attempted to solve them.

On the whole, the first edition of *Modern Architecture since 1900* was given a warm reception by reviewers in its various language editions. But there were several useful criticisms. I did listen when told that not enough was said about Mies van der Rohe, about the city, about the inheritance of nineteenth-century ideas and about the architecture of the Spanish-speaking world. But in the end the historian must be his own critic and one of the most direct and enjoyable ways of having one's prejudices upset is through the experience of buildings. A few months living in the remnants of Schindler's Pueblo Ribera Courts in Southern California helped me to realize how important ideas of 'origins' were to several architects of the 1920s. A visit to Mendelsohn's Mount Scopus Hospital outside Jerusalem reinforced an existing interest in regional inflections beyond the International Style. A cold morning in Madrid looking at the Maravillas Gymnasium by Alejandro de la Sota set in motion a revised vision of an entire decade and led to a major engagement with Spanish Modern architecture since. Time living in Doshi's 'Sangath' in Ahmadabad, India, focused attention on a larger range of Asian continuities, and on creative tensions between countryside and city in the Third World. A historian may construct his own abstractions but these must rely (ultimately) on the solid existence of actual buildings.

The writing of history does not reduce itself to any simplistic formula. Nor can the relationship between architectural objects, texts, and the interpretation of both, be pinned down with precision. To form a mental picture of the past, or of the intentions behind a building, involves a degree of intuition, an act of historical imagination. It requires that one penetrate through the individual creation to the original context and process of thought. At least for a moment, the accretions of later interpretation, and the knowledge of hindsight, need to be stripped away. The historian C.V. Wedgwood has suggested that 'History is lived forwards but it is written in retrospect. We know the end before we consider the beginning and we can never

wholly recapture what it is to know the beginning only.'

As time moves on, the entire kaleidoscope of developments earlier in this century takes on new patterns and reveals unexpected connections with the more distant past. There can be little doubt that modern architecture has constituted a major revolution in the history of forms, but it has also allowed basic types and ideas to be reinterpreted in new ways. Works of a high order give shape to contemporary aspirations, but they may also draw upon and transform diverse pasts. Thus the task of reformulating the concept a 'modern tradition' in the late twentieth century requires more than ever that one avoid determinism, that one sidestep the excessive claims of both avant-gardes and reactionary cliques, that one admit the likelihood that this is neither the end of an era nor the beginning of a new one. For works of great intensity it may even be necessary to work at several temporal scales, some recent, some old, cutting through the strata of time to recurrent sources of meaning beneath.

books referred to in shortened form in notes

Aalto, Alvar   *Complete Works* in 3 vols., ed. Hans Girsberger, Zurich, 1963-78.

Banham, Reyner   *The New Brutalism – Ethic or Aesthetic?*, New York, 1966;   *Theory and Design in the First Machine Age*, London, 1960.

Behrendt, Walter Curt   *Modern Building, its Nature, Problems and Forms*, New York, 1937.

Benevolo, Leonardo   *A History of Modern Architecture*, 2 vols., Cambridge, Mass., 1971, translated from *Storia dell'architettura moderna*, 1960.

Benton, Charlotte   ed., *Documents, a Collection of Source Material on the Modern Movement*, Milton Keynes, 1975.

Benton, Tim and Charlotte, eds., with Dennis Sharp *Architecture and Design, 1890–1939: an International Anthology of Original Articles*, New York, 1975: also published as *Form and Function: a Source Book on the History of Architecture and Design 1890-1939*, Milton Keynes, 1975. I have followed the Bentons' translations unless otherwise stated.

Bolon, Carol, Nelson, Robert, and Seidel, Linda, eds. *The Nature of Frank Lloyd Wright*, Chicago, 1988.

Brooks, H. Allen, ed.   *The Le Corbusier Archive*, New York and Paris, 1982 (32 volumes, some with introductory essays).

Brownlee, David, and De Long, David G.   *Louis I. Kahn – in the Realm of Architecture*, New York, 1991.

Burchard, J. and Bush-Brown A.   *The Architecture of America, a Social and Cultural History*, Boston, 1961.

Collins, Peter   *Changing Ideals in Modern Architecture*, London, 1965.

Colquhoun, Alan   *Essays in Architectural Criticism: Modern Architecture and Historical Change*, Cambridge, Mass., 1981.

Curtis, William J.R.   *Le Corbusier/English Architecture 1930s*, Milton Keynes, 1975; *Le Corbusier: Ideas and Forms*, Oxford and New York, 1986;   *Balkrishna Doshi, an Architecture for India*, Ahmadabad and New York, 1989;   *Denys Lasdun: Architecture, City, Landscape*, London, 1994.

Curtis, William J.R., and Sekler, Eduard, ed. *Le Corbusier at Work, the Genesis of the Carpenter Center for the Visual Arts*, Cambridge, Mass., 1978.

Drew, Phillip   *The Third Generation: Changing Meaning in Architecture*, London, 1972.

Egbert, Donald Drew   *Social Radicalism and the Arts*, New York, 1970.

Frampton, Kenneth   *Modern Architecture, a Critical History*, London, 1980; 3rd edn., 1992.

Giedion, Sigfried   *Space, Time and Architecture*, Cambridge, Mass., 1941: 5th edn., 1967.

Hatje, Gerd, ed.   *Encyclopedia of modern architecture*, New York, 1964.

Hays, Michael and Burns, Carol, eds.   *Thinking the Present, Recent American Architecture*, New York, 1990.

Hitchcock, Henry-Russell   *Architecture, Nineteenth and Twentieth Centuries*, Harmondsworth, 1958.

Hitchcock, H.R., and Johnson, Philip   *The International Style: Architecture since 1922*, New York, Museum of Modern Art, 1932.

Jencks, Charles   *Modern Movements in Architecture*, New York, 1973.

Jordy, William H.   *American Buildings and their Architects*, vol. 3, *Progressive and Academic Ideals at the Turn of the Twentieth Century*, New York, 1972; *American Buildings and Their Architects*, vol. 4, *The Impact of European Modernism in the Mid Twentieth Century*, New York, 1972.

Lasdun, Denys, ed.   *Architecture in an Age of Scepticism*, London, 1984.

Le Corbusier (Jeanneret, Charles Edouard)   *Vers une architecture*, Paris, 1923. Translated by Frederick Etchells as *Towards a New Architecture*, London, 1927, and frequently republished thereafter.

Le Corbusier and Pierre Jeanneret   *Oeuvre complète* in 8 volumes: *1910–1929; 1929–1934; 1934–1938; 1938–1946; 1946–-1952; 1952–1957; 1957–1965*; editors W. Boesiger, M. Bill, O. Stonorov, Zurich, 1929–70. These have been translated as the *Complete Works*, and into numerous languages other than English.

Lucan, Jacques, ed.   *Le Corbusier: une encyclopédie*, Paris, 1987.

Mallgrave, Harry Francis, ed., trans.and Introduction *Otto Wagner, Modern Architecture*, California, 1988.

Monnier, Gérard   *L'Architecture en France, une histoire critique, 1918-1950, architecture, culture, modernité*, Paris, 1990.

Montaner, Josep Maria   *Después del moviemento moderno, arquitectura de la segunda mitad del siglo XX*, Barcelona, 1993.

Mumford, Lewis   *The Brown Decades, a Study of the Arts in America 1865-1895*, New York, 1931.

Pevsner, Nikolaus   *Pioneers of the Modern Movement*, London, 1936; republished as *Pioneers of Modern Design from William Morris to Walter Gropius*, New York, 1949.

Rossi, Aldo   *L'architettura della città*, Padua, 1966; English ed. Cambridge, Mass., 1982.

Rowe, Colin   *The Mathematics of the Ideal Villa and Other Essays*, Cambridge, Mass., 1976.

Schulze, Franz, ed.   *Mies van der Rohe, Critical Essays*, New York, 1989.

Sherwood, Roger   *Modern Housing Prototypes*, Cambridge, Mass., 1978.

Smith, Norris Kelly   *Frank Lloyd Wright, a Study in Architectural Content*, Englewood Cliffs, N.J., 1966.

Smithson, Alison, ed.   *Team 10 Primer*, Cambridge, Mass., 1968.

Tafuri, Manfredo and Dal Co, Francesco   *Modern Architecture*, New York, 1979: translated from *Architettura contemporanea*, Milan, 1976.

Venturi, Robert   *Complexity and Contradiction in Architecture*, New York, 1966.

Viollet-le-Duc, Eugène   *Entretiens sur l'architecture*, Paris, 1863-72. Translated as *Discourses on Architecture*, Boston, 1876;   *Dictionnaire raisonné de l'architecture*, Paris, 1854-68.

Von Moos, Stanislaus   *Le Corbusier: Elemente einer Synthese*, Frauenfeld and Stuttgart, 1968: translated as *Le Corbusier, l'architecte et son mythe* (1974) and as *Le Corbusier, Elements of a Synthesis*, Cambridge, Mass., 1979.

Walden, Russell, ed.   *The Open Hand, Essays on Le Corbusier*, Cambridge, Mass., 1977.

Wright, Frank Lloyd   *In the Cause of Architecture, Wright's Historic Essays for Architectural Record 1908-1952*, ed. Frederick Gutheim, New York, 1975; *Wasmuth Volumes: Ausgeführte Bauten und Entwürfe von Frank Lloyd Wright*, Berlin, Ernst Wasmuth, 1910, with introduction by Wright; *Frank Lloyd Wright, Ausgeführte Bauten*, Berlin, Ernst Wasmuth, 1911, introduction by W.R. Ashbee.

Zevi, Bruno   *Storia dell'architettura moderna*, Turin, 1950.

notes

introduction

11 Motto: Ernst Kris, *Psychoanalytic Explorations in Art*, New York and London, 1952, p. 21.

Modern Age: the conception of history as a sequence of ages, each with a dominating spirit owes a good deal to the theories of Hegel. For impact of historicist thought on modern architecture, see Norris Kelly Smith, *On Art and Architecture in the Modern World*, Victoria, BC, 1971. Also Georg Henrik von Wright, 'The Myth of Progress. A Contribution to the Debate on Modernity', *Architecture and Cultural Values, The 4th International Alvar Aalto Symposium*, ed. Maija Kärkkäinen, Jyväskylä, Finland, 1988, pp. 64ff. See also Chapter 1 below.

12 Propagandists: for a refutation of determinist thinking in such historians as Henry-Russell Hitchcock, Sigfried Giedion and Nikolaus Pevsner, see David Watkin, *Morality and Architecture*, Oxford 1977; for distortions in modernist historiography and in writings of revisionists such as Watkin, see William J.R. Curtis, review of David Watkin, *Morality and Architecture*, *Journal of Society of Architectural Historians*, October 1979.

Pioneers: Pevsner's title of 1936, *Pioneers of the Modern Movement*; that of the 1949 edition: *Pioneers of Modern Design from William Morris to Walter Gropius*.

13 Architecture, complex art: the theoretical framework informing this book was worked out in a series of courses taught at Harvard University from 1976 to 1982, entitled 'Towards an Integrated Theory of Design', 'Towards an Integrated Theory of Form', and 'From Idea to Form'.

14 Starting points in earlier histories: see Bibliographical Note.

15 Origins: a distinction is deliberately drawn between theoretical formulations of modern architecture, and eventual architectural forms, the relation between theory and later invention and practice being far from direct. Since the 1970s attempts have been made to locate conceptual roots of modernism in the eighteenth century, e.g. Joseph Rykwert, *The First Moderns*, Cambridge, Mass., 1980; these usually develop the subtle parallelisms made by Emil Kaufmann, *Von Ledoux bis Le Corbusier*, Vienna,

1933. Like any complex phenomenon, modern architecture drew upon several intellectual and formal heritages in defining itself and combined different historical wavelengths and temporal levels.

16 Tradition: the avant-garde myth tends to imply a constant rejection of the past, but modern architecture, like any other gradual development in time, has relied on exemplars and transformations, as well as on the restrictive bonds of slowly changing stylistic conventions. The view of tradition presented in this book owes something to T.S. Eliot, 'Tradition and the Individual Talent', *Collected Essays 1917–1932*, London, 1932; to Henri Focillon, *The Life of Forms in Art*, New Haven, 1949; to Karl Popper, *The Logic of Scientific Discovery*, London and New York, 1959; to E.H. Gombrich, *Art and Illusion*, London; 1960, to George Kubler, *The Shape of Time*, New Haven, 1962. The author also admits a long-standing fascination with Giorgio Vasari's attempt at presenting a coherent development of the Renaissance to which he still belonged in his *Le Vite de' più eccelenti pittori, scultori ed architettori* written in the mid-sixteenth century.

Introduction: see first edition *Modern Architecture Since 1900*, p. 11; in the third edition later parts of the introduction have been changed.

chapter 1   the idea of a modern architecture in the nineteenth century

21 Motto: Viollet-Le-Duc, *Dictionnaire raisonné*, vol. 1, p. ix.

Modern: Collins, *Changing Ideals*, see particularly chapter 13, 'The Demand for a New Architecture', pp. 128ff. This chapter is heavily indebted to Collins's approach. For a subtle treatment of 'modernity' in a particular cultural milieu, see Karl E. Schorske, *Fin de Siècle Vienna, Politics and Culture*, New York, 1981.

Spiritual Core: for a discussion of determinist theories in historiography, see Karl Popper, *The Open Society and Its Enemies*, London, 1945, also R.G. Collingwood, *The Idea of History*, Oxford, 1946, and M. Bury, *The Idea of Progress*, London, 1920. For the concept of the *Zeitgeist* ('spirit of the times') in art historiography, see E.H. Gombrich, 'Art History and the Social Sciences', in *Ideals and Idols*, Oxford, 1979. For the relationship of determinism to modern architecture, see N.K. Smith, *On Art and Architecture in the Modern World*, Victoria, BC, 1971, D. Watkin, *Morality and Architecture*, Oxford, 1977 and Colquhoun, *Essays in Architectural Criticism*, pp. 152ff. It needs to be stressed that a belief in determinism does not determine things.

Absolute Authority: see John Summerson, 'The Case for a Theory of Modern Architecture', *RIBA Journal*, 64 (June 1957), pp. 307–13. See also Rudolf Wittkower, *Architectural Principles in the Age of Humanism*, London, 1949 for an attempt at explaining the idealist world-view supposedly underlying Renaissance forms; and Alberto Pérez-Gomez, *Architecture and the Crisis of Modern Science*, Cambridge, Mass., 1983 for an attempt at explaining the gradual collapse of this framework of ideas.

22 New Methods: Collins, *Changing Ideals*, Ch. 20,

'New Planning Problems'; also Giedion, *Space, Time and Architecture*, and Benevolo, *History of Modern Architecture*, Vol. I, for the impact of industrialism on architecture and engineering in the nineteenth century. Also, Francis D. Klingender, *Art and the Industrial Revolution*, London, 1947.

Nineteenth-century Moralists: see Paul Thompson, *The Work of William Morris*, London, 1960 and Edward P. Thompson, *William Morris: Romantic to Revolutionary*, London, 1955. Also: John Ruskin, *The Stones of Venice*, London, 1851–3. For Morris's role in the evolution of modern architectural ideas: Pevsner, *Pioneers*, and Watkin, *Morality and Architecture*.

23 Alternative Social and Urban Structures: see Egbert, *Social Radicalism*, especially pp. 117ff. for Saint-Simon, pp. 133ff. for Fourier, and pp. 87ff. for Karl Marx.

24 Concept of modern architecture: for fuller discussion see Collins, *Changing Ideals*, pp. 128ff; Colquhoun, *Essays in Architectural Criticism*; Harry Francis Mallgrave, 'Introduction', *Modern Architecture, Otto Wagner*, California, Getty Center, 1988, especially pp. 10ff. for Heinrich Hübsch, and Hübsch's book *In welchen stil sollen wir bauen?* Karlsruhe, 1828; see also Werner Oechslin, *Stilhülse und Kern, Otto Wagner, Adolf Loos und der evolutionäre Weg zur modernen Architektur*, Zürich, 1994.

Schinkel; new element: see Karl Friedrich Schinkel, *Aus Schinkels Nachlass*, ed. Alfred Freiherr von Wolzogen, 4 vols., Berlin, 1862, vol. 2, pp. 211–12; for Schinkel's ideas on modernity and tradition see Alex Potts, 'Schinkel's Architectural Theory', *Karl Friedrich Schinkel: a Universal Man*, ed. Michael Snodin, New Haven and London, 1991, pp. 47ff.

Semper: see Mallgrave, 'Introduction', p. 15. Also Gottfried Semper, *Der Stil in den technischen und tektonischen Künsten oder praktische Aesthetik*, 2 vols., Frankfurt, 1860–3, vol. 1, p. xx, and Mallgrave and Wolfgang Herrmann, *Gottfried Semper: The Four Elements of Architecture and Other Writings*, Cambridge, 1988.

Greek, Gothic, Egyptian: for a detailed account of the various style phases of nineteenth-century European architecture see Hitchcock, *Architecture*, Stefan Muthesius and Roger Dixon, *Victorian Architecture*, New York, 1979, and J. Mordaunt Crook, *Style*, London, 1988. For more probing analysis of the basis of stylistic choice in nineteenth century see e.g. David Brownlee, *The Law Courts, The Architecture of George Edmund Street*, New York and Cambridge, Mass., 1984; Colin Rowe: 'Character and Composition; or Some Vicissitudes of Architectural Vocabulary in the Nineteenth Century', *The Mathematics*, pp. 59ff.; for particular retrospective interpretation of Gothic see, for example, the polemics employed by A.W. Pugin in *An Apology for the Revival of Christian Architecture in England*, London, 1843; for later phase Gothic Revival, see George L. Hersey, *High Victorian Gothic*, Baltimore, 1972.

25 Eclecticism: see Collins, *Changing Ideals*; Nikolaus Pevsner, *Some Architectural Writers of the Nineteenth Century*, Oxford, 1972; 'tireless mind', quote is from A.E. Richardson, 'The Style Néo Grec', *Architectural Review*, xxx, July-Dec. 1911, p. 28.

26 Labrouste: see Neil Levine, 'The Book and the

Building: Hugo's Theory of Architecture and the Bibliothèque Sainte Geneviève', *The Beaux Arts*, ed. Robin Middleton, London, 1982, pp. 138ff.; also David van Zanten, *Designing Paris, The Architecture of Duban, Labrouste, Duc and Vaudoyer*, Cambridge, Mass., 1987, for perceptive analysis of transformation of historical principles, and motives behind use of forms.

Schinkel, spiritual principle: Goerd Peschken, *Das architektonische Lehrbuch*, Berlin, 1979, p. 58; also Potts, op. cit.

Primitive Hut: M.A. Laugier, *Essai sur l'architecture*, Paris, 1753: W. Herrmann, *Laugier and Eighteenth-Century French Theory*, London, 1962; J. Rykwert, *On Adam's House in Paradise; the Idea of the Primitive Hut in Architectural History*, New York, 1972; Anthony Vidler, *The Writing of the Walls, Architectural Theory in the Late Enlightenment*, New York, 1987; also Vidler, *L'Espace des lumières, architecture et philosophie de Ledoux à Fourier*, Paris, 1995.

Rationalism: see Chapter 19 of that title, in Collins, *Changing Ideals*. See also Colquhoun, 'Rationalism, a Philosophical Concept in Architecture', *Modernity and the Classical Tradition Architectural Essays, 1980–1987*, Cambridge, Mass., 1989, pp. 57ff. For Durand, J.N.L. Durand, *Précis des leçons d'architecture données à l'Ecole Royale Polytechnique*, Paris, 1819.

27 Truth to programme and methods of construction: for a succinct discussion of Viollet-le-Duc's rationalism see John Summerson, *Heavenly Mansions*, London, 1949, pp. 135ff. For Viollet's own arguments see particularly, *Entretiens sur l'architecture*, Chapter 10; for a critique of functional determinism, Alan Colquhoun 'Typology and Design Method', *Perspecta*, 12 (1969), pp. 71–4.

Viollet-le-Duc: *Discourses*, p. 448; see also M.F. Hearn, ed., *The Architectural Theory of Viollet-le-Duc, Readings and Commentrary* (Cambridge, Mass., 1990); see also Barry Bergdoll, *E.E. Viollet-le-Duc, The Foundation of Architecture. Selections from the Dictionnaire raisonné*, New York, 1990.

28 Beaux-Arts: for a somewhat fragmented treatment see Arthur Drexler, ed., *The Architecture of the École des Beaux-Arts*, New York, 1977. Modern architects like Le Corbusier and Walter Gropius lumped the École together unfairly and monolithically. Their principal objections were against a formulaic use of precedent, axial plans of a decorative sort, the extensive use of ornament, and an ignorance of modern technologies. In short they took the Beaux-Arts to exemplify traditionalism in the worst sense of the word. However, as Banham (*Theory and Design*, Chapter 1) has shown, ideas of Academic extraction influenced the pioneers of modern architecture much more than they would have admitted.

Abstraction of Tradition: it is instructive that the original French title of Le Corbusier's *Towards a New Architecture* of 1923 was *Vers une architecture* (without the 'New'). His aims were radical: they were revolutionary but also involved returning to roots. Walter Gropius concluded *The New Architecture and the Bauhaus*, 1926 with the following thoughts : '… my conception of the role of the New Architecture is nowhere and in no sense in opposition to Tradition properly so called … It means and always has meant,

the preservation of essentials.' For another view of the pertinence of the past to modern experimentation, see Frank Lloyd Wright, 'In the Cause of Architecture', *Architectural Record*, 23 March 1908.

Ledoux, Boullée: see Claude-Nicholas Ledoux, *L'Architecture considérée sous le rapport de lart, des moeurs et de la législation* (Paris, 1804), and Étienne-Louis Boullée, *Architecture* (Paris, 1868).

29 Universal Formal Values: see Adolf von Hildebrand, *Das Problem der Form in der bildenden Kunst*, Strasbourg, 1893 and Heinrich Wölfflin, *Die klassische Kunst*, Munich, 1899.

Type: see Chrysostome Quatremère de Quincy's essay on type, *Encyclopédie méthodique*, III, 2, 1825; also Anthony Vidler, 'The Idea of Type: the Transformation of the Academic Ideal 1750–1830', *Oppositions 8*, IAUS, New York (Spring 1977); for subtle treatment of analogous themes, Sylvia Lavin, *Quatremère de Quincy and the Invention of a Modern Language of Architecture*, Cambridge, Mass., 1992.

Schinkel, Le Corbusier, typological pattern: see Martin Goalen, 'Schinkel and Durand: The Case of the Altes Museum', in Snodin, ed., *Karl Friedrich Schinkel*, pp. 37ff.; for Le Corbusier's rethinking of the same basic type, see Rowe, *The Mathematics of the Ideal Villa*, p. 16 (addendum 1973); also William J.R. Curtis, *Le Corbusier: Ideas and Forms*, pp. 188ff.

Gottfried Semper: *Der Stil*, cited Banham, *Theory and Design in the First Machine Age*, p. 143, in the context of H.P. Berlage, *Grundlagen und Entwicklung der Architektur*, Berlin, 1908. For Semper's basic elements see Mallgrave and Herrmann, *Gottfried Semper: The Four Elements of Architecture*, and Edgar Kaufmann, jr., 'Frank Lloyd Wright and Gottfried Semper', *Nine Commentaries on Frank Lloyd Wright*, New York and Cambridge, Mass., 1989, pp. 129ff.

Ideas of nature: in the nineteenth century see, for example, John Ruskin, *The Stones of Venice*, London, 1853, pp. 102ff. on abstract lines, crystals, waves, shells etc. as sources of inspiration for architect; and Owen Jones, *The Grammar of Ornament*, London, 1856, Plates IV, V, VI for influence of Nile Valley plants such as Lotus on ancient Egyptian ornament and column forms. In the twentieth century, ideas and abstractions of 'nature' take many forms; see, for example, Bolon, ed., *The Nature of Frank Lloyd Wright*; William J.R. Curtis, 'Le Corbusier: Nature and Tradition', *Le Corbusier, Architect of the Century*, London, 1987, 'Introduction', pp. 13ff.; the Aalto quotation is from Alvar Aalto, 'The Influence of Structures and Materials on Modern Architecture', *Alvar Aalto 1896–1976*, Helsinki, Architectural Museum of Finland, 1981.

30 Analogies: Collins, *Changing Ideals*. See also analyses of individual architectural languages of Wright, Le Corbusier, Aalto (and others) below.

chapter 2 industrialization and the city: the skyscraper as type and symbol

33 Motto: Louis Sullivan, 'The Tall Office Building Artistically Considered', *Lippincotts Magazine*, March 1896, cited Benton and Benton, *Architecture and Design*, p. 11.

34 Industrial City: see Lewis Mumford, *The City in History, its Origins, its Transformations and its Prospects*, New York, 1961; John Reps, *The Making of Urban America*, Princeton University Press, 1968; Asa Briggs, *Victorian Cities*, London, 1965; Manfredo Tafuri, Francesco dal Co, Giorgio Ciucci, Mario Manieri-Elia, *The American City from the Civil War to the New Deal*, Cambridge, Mass. 1983.

Haussmann: speech of 1864, cited Françoise Choay, *Espacements*, Paris, 1969, p. 82; see also Howard Saalman, *Haussmann: Paris Transformed*, New York, 1971.

Middle landscape: the term was suggested to me by Daniel Bluestone in a remarkable unpublished student essay of 1973 on H.H. Richardson and F.L. Olmsted at North Easton.

Railway Station: see Carol Meeks, *The Railroad Station*, New Haven, 1984; see also Nikolaus Pevsner, *A History of Building Types*, Princeton, 1976.

35 Schinkel and city: in effect Schinkel seems to have developed a latter-day version of decorum to deal with the whole range of building types from city to country, a formulation with classical roots which may have influenced H.H. Richardson, Sullivan and Wright in their respective notions of American centre city and suburb.

Pugin: A.W.N. Pugin, *Contrasts, or a Parallel between the Architecture of the 15th and the 19th Centuries*, London, 1836; in fact the illustrations were varied in later editions.

Row upon row: from George Gissing, *The Nether World* (1889), cited by Raymond Williams, *The County and the City*, London 1985, p. 223.

36 Urban reform; see L. Benevelo, *The Origins of Modern Town Planning*, Cambridge, 1967; Anthony Sutcliffe, *Towards the Planned City*, Oxford, 1981; for Marx, Engels, Utopian Socialism etc., Egbert, *Social Radicalism and the Arts*.

37 Crystal Palace: quotations are : first two, Lothar Bucher, cited Giedion, *Space, Time and Architecture*, p. 252–3; Semper, *Wissenschaft, Industrie und Kunst*, Braunschweig, 1852; Building Committee, W. Bridges, 'Adams', *Westminster and Foreign Quarterly Review*, April 1850, cited John Hix, *The Glass House*, Cambridge, Mass., 1974, p. 133. For retrospective historical importance of Crystal Palace, see Henry-Russell Hitchcock, 'The British Nineteenth Century and Modern Architecture', *Modern Architecture in England*, New York, 1937, p. 10, 'often hailed with pardonable exaggeration as the first modern building'. For a fresh interpretation, Andrea Kahn, 'The Invisible Mask', in Andrea Kahn, ed., *Drawing, Building, Text, Essays in Architectural Theory*, New York, 1991, pp. 85ff.

38 Benjamin: Walter Benjamin, 'Paris Capital of the Nineteenth Century', in Peter Demetz, ed., *Reflections : Essays, Aphorisms, Autobiographical Writings*, New York, 1978, p. 161. See also Kurt W. Forster, 'Walter Benjamin: Residues of a Dream World', *On the Methodology of Architectural History, AD Profile*, New York, 1981, pp. 68–71.

39 Frames, iron steel: for Giedion's early orientation, *Bauen in Frankreich, Eisen, Eisenbeton*, Leipzig, 1928; for Labrouste, see reference Chapter 1; for Deane and Woodward, Trevor Garnham, *Oxford Museum, Oxford 1855–60* (Architecture in Detail),

London, 1992; Colin Rowe, 'Chicago Frame', *Architectural Review*, 1956, reprinted in *The Mathematics of the Ideal Villa*, pp. 90ff.

Emergence of skyscraper: best general treatments still found in Mumford, *The Brown Decades*; Frank Alfred Randall, *History of the Development of Building Construction in Chicago*, Urbana, 1949. Carl W. Condit, *The Chicago School of Architecture*, Chicago, 1964; and Jordy, *American Buildings and Their Architects*, vol. 3; for competent overview of nineteenth-century America, Burchard and Bush-Brown, *American Architecture*; for mechanization and nature, Tafuri, Dal Co, Ciucci, Manieri-Elia, *The American City*; and Leo Marx, *The Machine in the Garden*, New York, 1964.

41 H.H. Richardson: this reading is very much the author's own; and extends suggestions on Richardson's architectural language made in William J.R. Curtis's review of James O'Gorman, *The Architecture of Henry Hobson Richardson and his Office*, Cambridge, Mass., 1974, in *Journal of Society of Architectural Historians*, Dec. 1975; valuable still is Mariana G. van Rensselaer, *Henry Hobson Richardson and his Works*, Boston, 1888; also James O'Gorman, *Three American Architects, Richardson, Sullivan and Wright, 1865–1915*, Chicago, 1991; and O'Gorman, *H.H. Richardson, Architectural Forms for an American Society*, Chicago, 1987.

42 Four square: quotation on Marshall Field, Louis H. Sullivan, *Kindergarten Chats*, New York, 1947, pp. 28–30; 'Vitality of the rising city', Giedion, *Space, Time and Architecture*, p. 294.

44 Sullivan: for his philosophy, see Jordy, *American Buildings and their Architects*, vol. 3, especially Chapter 2, 'Functionalism as Fact and Symbol: Louis Sullivan's Commercial Buildings, Tombs and Banks'; also Sullivan, *Kindergarten Chats; The Autobiography of an Idea*, New York, 1924; and *A System of Architectural Ornament According with a Philosophy of Man's Powers*, New York, 1924.

45–6 Monadnock: quotation, Montgomery Schuyler, *American Architecture*, New York, 1892, cited in Mumford, *Brown Decades*, p. 62; Egyptian, cited Harriet Monroe, *John Wellborn Root*, Boston, 1896, p. 141; ideals business life, cited in Mumford, *Brown Decades*, p. 63; Root, quotation 'free of artistic traditions', cited in Mumford, *Brown Decades*, pp. 60–1. For Root's debts to Semper see e.g. John W. Root, 'Style', *Inland Architect*, Jan. 1887, p. 100; Owen Jones, see note in Chapter 1. Fine appreciations of Monadnock are found in Mumford, *Brown Decades*; in Walter C. Behrendt, *Modern Building*, New York, 1937, p.120; and in Donald Hoffmann, *The Architecture of John Wellborn Root*, Chicago, 1973.

46 Reliance: see Giedion, *Space, Time and Architecture*; Rowe, 'Chicago Frame'; and William J.R. Curtis, 'Der Wolkenkratzer Realität und Utopie', in *Die Zwanziger Jahre: Kontraste eines Jahrzehnts*, Zürich, 1973, pp. 44–7.

47–9 Sullivan skyscraper ideas; quotation, 'The Tall Office Building Artistically Considered'; see also Jordy, *American Architects*, vol. 3; and Hugh Morrison, *Louis Sullivan: Prophet of Modern Architecture*, New York, 1935. Viollet-le-Duc, Semper's and Greenough's ideas (viz. *Form and Function*, New York, 1846) were all known in the Chicago milieu; and Sullivan's

'functionalist' explanations fit into an intellectual tradition (see E.R. De Zurko, *Origins of Functionalist Theory*, New York, 1957); however, Sullivan's actual forms emerged from several intentions and inspirations, including abstractions of classicism and of nature; see Collins, *Changing Ideals*, on mechanical and biological analogies, also William J.R. Curtis, 'Modern Transformations of Classicism', *Architectural Review*, August 1984. Schinkel's work was probably known in Chicago through the drawings published in *Sammlung architektonische Entwürfe* and may have influenced both Sullivan and Wright at architectural and urban scales; see also note on Schinkel in Chapter 7 on Frank Lloyd Wright.

50 Bourget: quotation, Paul Bourget, *Outre Mer*, as translated by Montgomery Schuyler, 'Architecture in Chicago: Adler and Sullivan' ('Great American Architects Series', no. 2, part 1), *Architectural Record*, December 1895, p. 8.

Columbian Exhibition: see e.g. Giedion, *Space, Time and Architecture* for notion that Beaux Arts Fair was major set-back to development of modern architecture; also Dimitri Tselos, 'The Chicago Fair and the Myth of the Lost Cause', *Journal of the Society of Architectural Historians*, no. 4, Dec. 1967, p. 259.

51 Skyscraper, Suburb: in the American city there is a strong interconnection between the two, a theme developed in several seminars by the author on the skyscraper as a type, in late 1970s and early 1980s.

chapter 3 the search for new forms and the problem of ornament

53 Motto: Otto Wagner, *Moderne Architektur*, Vienna, 1895, from the preface. The expanded version of this book, entitled *Die Baukunst unserer Zeit. Dem Baukunstjünger ein Führer auf diesem Kunstgebiet*, 4th edn., Vienna, 1914, contains the quotation, on p. 76.

Friedrich Nietzsche: *The Use and Abuse of History*, trans. Adrian Collins, Indianapolis, 1957.

54 Hitchcock: *Architecture*, p. 416.

Pevsner: *Pioneers*, p. 90.

55 Ornament: Owen Jones, *The Grammar of Ornament*, London, 1856.

56 Maison du Peuple: Victor Horta, 'Reminiscences of the Maison du Peuple' (undated), Benton and Benton, *Architecture and Design*, p. 65.

57 Horta: 'Reminiscences of the Maison du Peuple'.

Van de Velde: for a concise assessment see P. Morton-Shand, 'Van de Velde to Wagner', *Architectural Review*, October 1934, pp. 143–5.

58 Van de Velde: 'A Chapter on the Design and Construction of Modern Furniture', 1897: Benton and Benton, *Architecture and Design*, pp. 17–18.

Turin Art Nouveau: Silvius Paoletti, 'For the Workers', *L'Arte decorativa moderna*, 1, no. 2, February 1902.

59 Hector Guimard: 'An architect's Opinion of l'Art Nouveau', *Architectural Record*, June 1902, pp. 130ff.

Gaudí: for neo-Gothic antecedents see T.G. Beddall, 'Gaudi and the Catalan Gothic', *Journal of Society of Architectural Historians*, 34, no. 1, March 1975, p. 48. Also George Collins, *Antoni Gaudí*, New York and London, 1960 for an interpretation of the architect's

guiding principles.

Gaudí, cultural context: see David Mackay, *Arquitectura moderna a Barcelona 1854–1939*, Barcelona, 1989; Ignasi de Solà-Morales, *Gaudí*, Barcelona, 1983, and *Eclecticismo y vanguardia. El caso de la arquitectura moderna en Catalunya*, Barcelona, 1980; for regional aspects see M.A. Leblond, 'Gaudí et l'architecture méditerranéenne', *L'Art et les artistes*, 1910, and Sert and James Johnson Sweeney, *Antonio Gaudí*, Buenos Aires, 1961.

62 Baldachino, Palma: the particular interpretation is hypothetical; the general suggestion is that Gaudí's vocabulary relies upon a complex abstraction, like a system of hieroglyphics.

63 Dragons: see Charles Jencks, *The Language of Post-modern Architecture*, New York, 1977, p. 99–100 for an idiosyncratic interpretation of the roof shape.

64 Mackintosh: see T. Howarth, *Charles Rennie Mackintosh and the Modern Movement*, London 1952; also W. Buchanan, ed., *Mackintosh's Masterwork: The Glasgow School of Art*, Glasgow, 1989; and James Macaulay, *Glasgow School of Art, Glasgow 1897–1909 Charles Rennie Mackintosh* (Architecture in Detail), London, 1992.

65 Spatial Effects of Library: Pevsner, *Pioneers*, p. 167; quotation, Denys Lasdun, 'Charles Rennie Mackintosh: a Personal View', *Mackintosh and His Contemporaries*, ed. Patrick Nuttgens, London, 1988.

66 Mackintosh, Vienna: see Eduard F. Sekler, 'Mackintosh and Vienna', in *The Anti-Rationalists*, eds. Nikolaus Pevsner and J.M. Richards, New York, 1973, pp. 136–42.

August Endell: 'Formenschönheit und dekorative Kunst', *Dekorative Kunst*, 2, 1898, p. 119; translated as 'The Beauty of Form and Decorative Art' in Benton and Benton, *Architecture and Design*, p. 2.

Wagner: for translation of *Moderne Architektur*, see Mallgrave, *Modern Architecture,* 1988; for Viennese context, Karl E. Schorske, *Fin de Siècle Vienna,* New York, 1981; for bolts on Post Office Savings Bank, Peter Haiko, 'Otto Wagner: Die Postsparkasse und die Kirche Am Steinhof', *Traum und Wirklichkeit, Wien 1870–1930*, catalogue, Museen der Stadt Wien, 1985, pp. 88–105; see also Iain Boyd White, introduction, *Otto Wagner: Vienna 1841–1918, Designs for Architecture*, exhibition catalogue, Oxford Museum of Modern Art, 1985.

68 Stoclet: Eduard F. Sekler, 'The Stoclet House by Josef Hoffmann', *Essays in the History of Architecture Presented to Rudolf Wittkower*, London, 1967; see also Sekler, *Josef Hoffmann, The Architectural Work, Monograph and Catalogue of Works*, Princeton, 1985.

70 Adolf Loos: 'beauty only in form', 'The Luxury Vehicle', *Neue Freie Presse*, 3 July 1898, in Adolf Loos, *Spoken Into the Void, Collected Essays 1897–1900*, translated from *Ins Leere gesprochen* (1932), by Jane O. Newman, John H. Smith, Cambridge, Mass., 1982, p. 40; see also Yehuda Safran, Kenneth Frampton, D. Steiner, *The Architecture of Adolf Loos*, London, 1985; see also Juan Miguel Hernandez Leon, *La casa de un solo muro*, Madrid, 1990; and Max Risselada, ed., *Raumplan versus Plan Libre*, Delft, 1987.

71 Ornament: Adolf Loos, 'Ornament und Verbrechen', may be found in the original in A. Loos, *Trotzdem*, Innsbruck, 1930. I have followed Banham's translation in *Theory and Design*, p. 93.

Loos, architectural language: see Leslie van Duzer and Kent Kleinman, *Villa Müller: A Work of Adolf Loos*, New York, 1994. This building dates from 1930 but distils many of the architect's previous themes. Mention should also be made of Loos's unbuilt project for the Lido in Venice of 1923 which, in its overall disposition and dynamic sequence of spaces, may have influenced Le Corbusier's Villa Stein/de Monzie at Garches; see Chapter 10 below.

chapter 4   rationalism, the
engineering tradition, and reinforced
concrete

73 Motto: from the preface of the first issue of the periodical *L'Architecture vivante*, Paris, 1923.
74 Viollet-le-Duc: *Entretiens*, vol. 1, p. 186.
Auguste Choisy: See Banham, *Theory and Design*, pp. 23ff., for a concise discussion of Choisy's ideas. The role of nineteenth-century engineering in the formation of modern architecture is discussed most obsessively by Giedion, *Space, Time and Architecture*, but he has insufficient to say about the *symbolic transformation* of these sources into architecture in the modern movement. See also P. Morton-Shand, 'Architecture and Engineering', *Architectural Review*, November 1932.
Rationalism: see notes to Chapter 1; for eighteenth-century traditions of engineering, Antoine Picon, *Architectes et ingénieurs au siècle des lumières*, Marseilles, 1988.
Durand, Hübsch, Schinkel: see notes to Chapter 1.
75 Bridges: David P. Billington, *The Tower and the Bridge, the New Art of Structural Engineering*, Princeton, 1983, pp. 60ff. for Eiffel, pp. 72ff. for Roebling. See also Alan Trachtenberg, *Brooklyn Bridge: Fact and Symbol*, New York, 1965, and Montgomery Schuyler, 'The Bridge as a Monument', *Harper's Weekly*, 27, May 1883, p. 326, cited in Schuyler, *American Architecture and Other Writings*, eds. William H. Jordy and Ralph Coe, New York, 1964, p. 164.
Sullivan: see notes to Chapter 2.
76 Concrete: see Peter Collins, *Concrete, the Vision of a New Architecture, a Study of Auguste Perret and his Precursors*, London, 1959.
Hennebique: Gwenaël Delhumeau, 'Hennebique, les architectes et la concurrence', *Culture constructive, les cahiers de la recherche architecturale 29*, Marseilles, 1992, pp. 33ff.
Reinforced cement: Collins, *Concrete, the Vision of a New Architecture*, pp. 113ff.
Gothic skeleton: Kenneth Frampton, 'Graeco-Gothic and Neo-Gothic: The Anglo-French Origins of Tectonic Form', *Arkkitehti, Finnish Architectural Review*, 4, 1989, pp. 25ff.
77 Julien Guadet: *Eléments et théories de l'architecture*, Paris, 1902.
Structure and form: see Geoffrey Scott, *The Architecture of Humanism*, London, 1914, especially Chapter entitled 'The Mechanical Fallacy'; see also Eduard F. Sekler, 'Structure, Construction, Tectonics', in Gyorgy Kepes, ed., *Structure in Art and Science*, London, 1965, pp. 84ff.

80 Auguste Perret on ornament: Collins, *Concrete, the Vision of a New Architecture*, p. 199.
Kahn: see Grant Hildebrand, *Designing for Industry; the Architecture of Albert Kahn*, Cambridge, Mass., 1974.
81 Maillart: Billington, *The Tower and the Bridge*, pp. 147ff.; also Billington, *Robert Maillart's Bridges, The Art of Engineering*, Princeton, 1979.
82 Tony Garnier: *Une Cité Industrielle: Étude pour la construction des villes*, Paris, 1917; see also Dora Wiebenson, *Tony Garnier: The Cité Industrielle*, New York, 1969.
84 Dom-ino: see Paul Turner, 'Romanticism, Rationalism and the Domino System', in Walden, ed., *The Open Hand*; also Eleanor Gregh, 'The Dom-ino Idea', *Oppositions*, 15–16, Cambridge, Mass., 1979, pp. 61ff.
85 Le Corbusier's copy of Viollet-le-Duc: *Dictionnaire raisonné*, vol. 1, p. 66, is covered with notes. The page illustrates the principle of the flying buttress in Gothic architecture, a skeleton of sorts. See Curtis, *Le Corbusier: Ideas and Forms*, p.28.

chapter 5   arts and crafts ideals in
britain and the u.s.a.

87 Motto: Hermann Muthesius, 'The Meaning of the Arts and Crafts', 1907, from his speech given at the Berlin commercial academy in spring of that year.
Pevsner: *Pioneers*; see also 'William Morris and Architecture', *RIBA Journal*, 64, 1957, by same author.
Arts and Crafts values: see Gillian Naylor, *The Arts and Crafts Movement*, London, 1990; Andrew Saint, *Richard Norman Shaw*, London, 1978; Peter Davey, *Arts and Crafts Architecture*, London, 1995; Mark Girouard, *Sweetness and Light: the Queen Anne Movement 1860–1900*, London, 1977. Mention should also be made of W.R. Lethaby's remarkable book, *Architecture, Mysticism and Myth*, London, 1892.
88 Voysey: Nikolaus Pevsner, 'C.F.A. Voysey 1858–1941', *Architectural Review*, 1941; A. Johnson, 'C.F.A. Voysey', *Architectural Association Quarterly*, 4, 1977, pp. 26–35; see also Wendy Hitchmough, *C.F.A. Voysey*, London, 1995.
89 Pevsner: *Pioneers*, p. 150. See also David Gebhard, 'The Vernacular Transformed', *RIBA Journal*, 78, March 1971, pp. 98ff.
90 Mackintosh, frosty air: see Denys Lasdun, 'Charles Rennie Mackintosh: a Personal View', in Patrick Nuttgens, ed., *Mackintosh and His Contemporaries*, London, 1988.
Lutyens: The best treatments of Lutyens are to be found in A.S.G. Butler and Christopher Hussey, *The Architecture of Sir Edwin Lutyens*, London, 1950, and L. Weaver, *Houses and Gardens by E. Lutyens*, London 1913; see also Colin Amery, ed., *Lutyens*, London, 1981 (exhibition catalogue).
92 Hermann Muthesius: *Das englische Haus*, Berlin, 1902–5: quotation from the conclusion of vol. 2, 'The Development of the English House'.
W.R. Lethaby: 'Modern German Architecture and what we may Learn from it', a talk given at the Architectural Association, London, 1915; cited by Benton and Benton, *Architecture and Design*, p. 55.

93 Vincent Scully: *The Shingle Style and the Stick Style*, New Haven, 1971.
American Architecture: valuable still is Mumford's *The Brown Decades*; see also Burchard and Bush-Brown, *The Architecture of America*; David Handlin, *The American Home, Architecture and Society 1851–1915*, Boston, 1979; and Gwendolyn Wright, *Moralism and the Modern Home: 1870–1913*, New York, 1980.
94 Frank Lloyd Wright: 'The Art and Craft of the Machine', a talk given to the Chicago Arts and Crafts Society, at Hull House, on 6 March 1901; cited by Edgar Kaufmann, *Frank Lloyd Wright: Writings and Buildings*, New York, 1960, p. 55.
The Craftsman: ran from 1901 to 1916 and bore the sub-title 'an illustrated monthly magazine for the simplification of life'.
Greene Brothers: see Jordy, *American Buildings and their Architects*, vol. 3, Chapter 4, pp. 217ff., for detailed analysis of the Gamble House; also Edward Bosley, *Gamble House Pasadena 1907–8: Greene and Greene* (Architecture in Detail), London, 1992.
96 Maybeck: Jordy, *American Buildings and their Architects*, vol. 3, Chapter 5.
97 Irving Gill: *The Craftsman*, vol. 30, May 1916, pp. 142ff., for both quotations. For further treatment of Gill's ideas see Esther McCoy, *Five California Architects*, New York, 1960; Jordy, *American Buildings and their Architects*, vol. 3, pp. 246ff.

chapter 6   responses to
mechanization: the deutsche
werkbund and futurism

99 Motto: Antonio Sant'Elia, 'Messagio', 1914; see Banham, *Theory and Design*, p. 128.
100 Hermann Muthesius: 'Wo stehen wir?', a speech given at the Werkbund congress, 1911; cited and translated by Banham, *Theory and Design*, p. 73. For further discussion of Werkbund ideology see J. Campbell, *The German Werkbund: the Politics of Reform in the Applied Arts*, Princeton, 1978; Tilmann Buddensieg, *Industriekultur: Peter Behrens und die AEG. 1907–1914*, Berlin, 1979; Stanford Anderson, 'Modern Architecture and Industry: Peter Behrens and the Cultural Policy of Historical Determinism', *Oppositions 2*, Winter 1977.
101 A.E.G.: see Standford Anderson, 'Modern Architecture and Industry: Peter Behrens and the AEG Factories', *Oppositions 23*, 1981, pp. 53–83; see also 'The Turbine Hall of the AEG, 1910', Benton, *Documents*, pp. 56–57.
103 Walter Gropius: 'Die Entwicklung moderner Industriebaukunst', *Deutscher Werkbund Jahrbuch*, Jena, 1913, pp. 19–20, translated by Benton and Benton, *Architecture and Design*, p. 53, as 'The Development of Modern Industrial Architecture'.
Werkbund Debate 1914: excerpts are published in English translation in Benton, *Documents*, pp. 5ff.; see also Francesco Dal Co, *Some Figures of Architecture and Thought: German Architectural Culture 1880–1920*, 1990.
104 Fagus Factory: for a detailed discussion of the design process see Tim Benton, Stefan Muthesius and

Bridget Wilkins, *Europe 1900–1914*, Open University, Milton Keynes, Units 5–6, 1975.

106 Paul Scheerbart, *Glasarchitektur*, Berlin, 1914. See also Dennis Sharp, ed., *Glass Architecture by Paul Scheerbart and Alpine Architecture by Bruno Taut*, London, 1972.

107–11 Futurism: see Banham, *Theory and Design*, pp. 99ff. for acknowledgement of contribution of Futurism; I have followed Banham's translations of the various manifestoes. The Manifesto of Futurist architecture is reproduced in full in Ulrich Conrad's *Programmes and Manifestoes on 20th-Century Architecture*, London, 1970. See also M. Martin, *Futurist Art and Theory 1909–1915*, Oxford, 1968 and U. Apollonio, *Futurist Manifestoes*, London, 1973 for further analysis of texts.

chapter 7   the architectural system of frank lloyd wright

113 Motto: Frank Lloyd Wright, 'In the Cause of Architecture', *Architectural Record*, 23 March 1908, p. 158, republished in Frederick Gutheim, ed., Hugh Donlan and Martin Filler, co-eds., *In the Cause of Architecture, Frank Lloyd Wright, Wright's Historic Essays for Architectural Record 1908–1952*, New York, 1975, p. 53.

Historical Views of Wright: Mumford, *The Brown Decades*, laid the basis for numerous later attempts at placing Wright in the context of late nineteenth-century American culture; Pevsner, *Pioneers of the Modern Movement*, was content to treat Wright as a pioneer of modern design. Hitchcock (*In the Nature of Materials: The Buildings of Frank Lloyd Wright 1887–1941*, New York, 1942) simply described the externals of Wright's style; in *Architecture Nineteenth and Twentieth Centuries*, he slotted early Wright into a chapter entitled 'The Detached house in England and America', and abstained from generalizing about his historical significance. Bruno Zevi, *Frank Lloyd Wright*, Milan, 1947 concentrated upon spatial concepts in Wright, extending ideas from his earlier book, *Towards an Organic Architecture*, 1945. Vincent Scully, *Frank Lloyd Wright*, New York, 1960, developed themes to do with the American landscape and several traditions in history. Norris Kelly Smith's *Frank Lloyd Wright* forcibly removed Wright from any simplistic evolutionary scheme by concentrating on the institutional metaphors of his buildings and their suburban cultural context. Banham, in *Theory and Design*, treated Wright only in so far as he was relevant to the European modern movement. David Handlin, *The American Home,* Boston, 1979, placed Wright's domestic architecture in a long American tradition of home-building and emphasized some of the classical influences on his architectural grammar. Mention should also be made of Grant Manson, *Frank Lloyd Wright to 1910: the First Golden Age*, New York, 1958, for its precise and evocative analyses of Wright's houses; of Jordy, *American Buildings and Their Architects*, vol. 3, for its detailed account of the Robie House; and of Frederick Gutheim, *Frank Lloyd Wright on Architecture, Selected Writings*, New York, 1941. Since the early 1980s there has been a boom in Wright

publications including general anthologies of essays such as Bolon, ed., *The Nature of Frank Lloyd Wright*; Robert McCarter, ed., *Frank Lloyd Wright: a Primer of Architectural Principles*, New York, 1991; Terence Riley, ed., *Frank Lloyd Wright, Architect*, Catalogue of MOMA exhibition on Wright, New York, 1994; drawings and documents, such as Y. Futagawa, ed., *Frank Lloyd Wright: Drawings from the Taliesin Fellowship Archive,* Tokyo, 1987, or Bruce Brooks Pfeiffer's several publications of primary material, e.g. *Frank Lloyd Wright, Letters to Clients*, London, 1987; detailed monographs on individual buildings such as Jack Quinan, *Frank Lloyd Wright's Larkin Building, Myth and Fact*, New York and Cambridge Mass., 1987, or Joseph Connor's *The Robie House of Frank Lloyd Wright*, Chicago, 1986; or general themes, for example, Herbert Muschamp, *Man About Town: Frank Lloyd Wright in New York City*, London and Cambridge, Mass., 1983; and Anthony Alofsin, *Frank Lloyd Wright: The Lost Years, 1910–1922*, Chicago, 1993. For a reflection on the Wright literature of the 1980s, see William J.R. Curtis 'Naturally Mechanical', *Times Literary Supplement*, March 24–30, 1989. This by no means exhausts the Wright bibliography, but it serves to demonstrate the range of views about him.

Wright's Biography: see R. Twombly, *Frank Lloyd Wright, an Interpretative Biography*, New York, 1973; the inaccurate but gripping *Autobiography*, New York, 1932 by Wright himself; more recently, Brendan Gill, *Many Masks: a Life of Frank Lloyd Wright*, London, 1987.

116 William Channing Gannett, *The House Beautiful*, River Forest, Ill., 1897.

Institutional Metaphor: Smith, *Frank Lloyd Wright*.

Winslow House: quotation from R. Spencer, 'The Work of Frank Lloyd Wright', *Architectural Review*, 7, June 1900, p. 65.

Tripartite Division: Handlin, *The American Home*, discusses the relationship to classical base, shaft and cornice, pp. 305ff.

Clients: Leonard K. Eaton, *Two Chicago Architects and their Clients*, Cambridge, Mass., 1969, p. 62; see also Gwendolyn Wright, 'Architectural Practice and Social Vision in Wright's Early Designs', in Bolon, ed., *The Nature of Frank Lloyd Wright*, pp. 98ff.

117–18 Japan: see Manson, *Frank Lloyd Wright to 1910*, p. 39; also catalogue of exhibition *Frank Lloyd Wright and Japan*, Phoenix, Arizona, 1995; and Julia Meech-Pekarik, 'Frank Lloyd Wright's Other Passion', in Bolon, ed., op. cit. pp. 125ff.; and Trevor Nute, *Frank Lloyd Wright and Japan, The Role of Traditional Japanese Art and Architecture in the work of Frank Lloyd Wright*, London, 1993.

118 Abstraction: see Frank Lloyd Wright, *The Japanese Print: an Interpretation*, Chicago, 1912.

Home in Prairie Town: *Ladies' Home Journal*, February 1901.

120 Frank Lloyd Wright: 'The Cardboard House', 1931, cited by Benton and Benton, *Architecture and Design*, p. 60; see also H. Allen, Brooks, 'Wright and the Destruction of the Box', *Journal of the Society of Architectural Historians*, 38, March 1979, pp. 7–14.

122 Villa: it is instructive to compare the Dana, Martin and Coonley Houses to a plate of Schinkel's Court Gardener's House, Charlottenhof, in Schinkel, *Sammlung architektonische Entwürfe*, part 24, 1835, pl.

145: see note on Schinkel in Chapter 2. See also James Ackerman, *The Villa, Form and Ideology of Country Houses*, London, 1990, especially Chapter 11.

123 Style and system: several attempts have been made at revealing geometrical systems in Wright, e.g. Richard D. MacCormac, 'The Anatomy of Wright's Aesthetic', *Architectural Review*, 143, February 1968, pp. 143–6; or else typological continuities and variations, e.g. Paul Laseau, James Tice, *Frank Lloyd Wright, between Principle and Form*, New York, 1992; these touch upon the language, but little of the meaning and magic of Wright's buildings.

123–6 Robie: for reminiscences by the client of his intentions see Eaton, *Two Chicago Architects and their Clients*; for the climatic functions of the roof see R. Banham, 'Frank Lloyd Wright as Environmentalist', *Architectural Design*, April 1967; for detailed analysis of house, Jordy, *American Buildings and Their Architects*, vol. 3, p. 180; also Connor's *The Robie House*, and Donald Hoffmann, *Frank Lloyd Wright's Robie House, the Illustrated Story of an Architectural Masterpiece*, New York, 1984.

126 Strata: see, for example, Thomas H. Beeby, 'Wright and Landscape: a Mythical Interpretation', in Bolon, ed., *The Nature of Frank Lloyd Wright*, pp. 154ff.; also James O'Gorman, *Three American Architects* Chicago, 1991, p. 154, which speaks of Wrights debts to Richardson and of his 'conventionalized geological analogy'. See Chapter 18, below, especially on Wright's Fallingwater.

Semper: Kaufmann, 'Frank Lloyd Wright and Gottfried Semper', cited above, note to p. 29.

126–7 Larkin: see Quinan, *Frank Lloyd Wright's Larkin Building*, Appendix L. 'Reply to Mr. Sturgis's Criticism', on pp. 164ff. for Wright quotation.

127 Unity Temple: Wright, *Autobiography*, pp. 138ff.; Kakuzo Okakura, *The Book of Tea*, Rutland, Vermont and Tokyo, 1906.

128 Lowest elements: Letter of Charles White Jr. to Walter Willcox, 13 May 1904, in *Writings on Wright*, ed. H. Allen Brooks, Cambridge, Mass., 1981, p. 86; the letter is illustrated with sketches. See also Edward Ford, *The Details of Modern Architecture*, Cambridge, Mass., 1991.

Schinkel: see Handlin, *The American Home*, pp. 317ff.; it is instructive to compare Wright's formal, symmetrical buildings with Schinkel's urban monuments (e.g. the Schauspielhaus in Berlin, or The Neue Wache); his asymmetrical, dynamic suburban or even rural houses with Schinkel's park pavilions, belvederes and villas; it is also instructive to compare Wright's use of line drawings, in publications of his work, with Schinkel's.

129 Wasmuth Volumes: *Ausgeführte Bauten und Entwürfe von Frank Lloyd Wright*, Berlin, Ernst Wasmuth, 1910, with introduction by Frank Lloyd Wright; *Frank Lloyd Wright Ausgeführte Bauten*, Berlin, Ernst Wasmuth, 1911, introduction by W.R. Ashbee.

Taliesin: for an interpretation see Neil Levine, 'Frank Lloyd Wright's Own Houses and His Changing Concept of Representation', in Bolon, ed., *The Nature of Frank Lloyd Wright*, pp. 20ff.

Prairie School: see H. Allen Brooks, *The Prairie School*, Toronto, 1972.

131 Motto: John Ruskin, *The Stones of Venice*,
London, 1853.
Ruskin, Viollet-le-Duc, nation, nature: see, for
example, Ruskin's essay (written under the pseudonym
'Kata Phusin'), 'The Poetry of Architecture: the
Architecture of the Nations of Europe Considered in
its Association with Natural Scenery and National
Character', *Loudon's Architecture Magazine*, London,
1853, considering English cottages, Swiss Chalets etc.
as distillations of national character; for further
discussion of 'national' formulations in opposition to
'international' tendencies of the academies, in second
half of the nineteenth century, see Rykwert, *On Adam's
House in Paradise*, New York, 1972, pp. 33ff. For
Viollet-le-Duc's ideas concerning national and even
regional ingredients in French medieval architecture,
see his critique of 1853 of Vaudoyer's project for
Marseilles Cathedral, analysed with finesse in Van
Zanten, *Designing Paris*, Cambridge, Mass., 1987,
pp. 137ff. For abstraction of nature as basis for
architectural ornament see Ruskin, *Stones of Venice*,
p. 104; Jones, *Grammar of Ornament*; Sullivan,
A System of Architectural Ornament; for landscape as
source of form and meaning, notes on Prairie and on
Le Corbusier: Jura Regionalism below; and on strata in
Chapter 7.
132 National Romanticism: The term has more
currency in literary or painting studies than in histories
of architecture. It is used by Hitchcock (*Architecture
Nineteenth and Twentieth Centuries*, pp. 534ff) mainly
to refer to certain Nordic tendencies of the last decades
of the nineteenth century and the early stages of the
twentieth. The majority of writers on modern
architecture have avoided questions of national
identity or of national *imaginaires*, tending to present
modernism in terms of trans-national even pan-cultural
ideals. In doing so they have ignored tensions between
national traditions (or mythical versions of them), and
more 'universal' aspirations attached to notions of
modernity in the formative phases of modern
architecture. Classicisms play various roles, often in
opposition to regionalizing tendencies, although not
always, (see below, Le Corbusier: Jura Regionalism).
Nation and region do not mean the same thing, and
nationalism sometimes insists upon hegemony and
centralization at the expense of regional differences;
equally regions may assert their identity against the
nation state.
Catalonia: see for example David Mackay,
L'arquitectura moderna a Barcelona, 1854–1939,
Barcelona 1989; Ignasi de Solà-Morales, *Architecture
fin de siècle à Barcelone*, Barcelona, 1992. For early
formulation of local identity see Lluis Domenech, 'A la
recerca d'una arquitectura nacional', *La Renaixenca*,
Barcelona, 1878.
133 Substructures, Spanish tradition: for notion of
constants ('invariantes') denoting 'Spanishness' and
cutting across the various periods, see, for example,
Fernando Chueca, *Invariantes Castizos
del'Arquitectura Espagnola*, Madrid, 1943.
Catalan vaulting: for interesting reflection on Gaudí's
techniques and on cultural aspects of a local
engineering tradition, see David Billington, *The Tower

and the Bridge,* Princeton, 1983, p. 183.
133–4 Jujol: see issues 179, 178 of *Quaderns
d'arquitectura*, Barcelona, Oct–Dec. 1988, Feb–March
1989, devoted to this architect; also Ignasi de Solà-
Morales, *Jujol*, Barcelona, 1990.
134 Copenhagen: for historical perspectives on
Nyrop's Town Hall, Tobias Faber, *Danish
Architecture*, Copenhagen, 1975; also Knud Millech
and Kay Fisker, *Danske arkitekturstrømninger
1850–1950*, Copenhagen, 1951, still the best overall
treatment.
Stockholm Town Hall: see E. Cornell, *Ragnar
Ostberg, Svensk Arkitekt*, Stockholm, 1965.
135 Sonck: see monograph *Lars Sonck, Arkkitehti,
1870–1956*, Museum of Finnish Architecture, 1981,
especially essay by Paula Kivinen, 'Early Period –
National Romanticism 1894–1907', which deals with
design process of St Johns Tampere; see also Marc
Treib, 'Lars Sonck', *Journal of the Society of
Architectural Historians*, 3, September 1975, pp. 3–13.
136 Richardson: influence in Nordic countries, see
Leonard K. Eaton, *American Architecture Comes of
Age: European Reaction to H.H. Richardson and Louis
Sullivan*, London, 1972.
137 Saarinen: criticisms of his Helsinki Railway
Station by Strengell and Frosterus, see Riitta Nikula,
Architecture and Landscape, The Building of Finland,
Helsinki, 1993, p. 104; Albert Christ-Janer, *Eliel
Saarinen*, Chicago, 1979; see also William J.R. Curtis,
'Romantic and Geological', *Arquitectura y vivienda*, 95,
Madrid, 1995, p. 34.
Grundtvig: for Jensen-Klint's vision of a revived craft
system, see, for example, his *Bygmesterskolen*,
Copenhagen, 1911.
138 Prairie: see Larzer Ziff, 'The Prairie in Literary
Culture and the Prarie Style of Frank Lloyd Wright', in
Bolon, ed., *The Nature of Frank Lloyd Wright*, p. 173;
also Donald Hoffmann, *Frank Lloyd Wright:
Architecture and Nature*, New York, 1986, for
responses to Midwestern landscape; see also H. Allen
Brooks, *The Prairie School*, Toronto, 1972.
Irving K. Pond: *The Meaning of Architecture*, Boston,
1918, p. 174.
Owatonna: see Lauren S. Weingarden, *Louis H.
Sullivan: The Banks*, Cambridge, Mass., 1987.
139 Louis Sullivan: 'Suggestions in Artistic
Brickwork', 1910; cited in Weingarden, op. cit., p. 11.
140 Classical values: While 'classicism' is sometimes
proposed as a universal ideal, the classical tradition is
not monolithic, and individual inventions rely upon
particular readings and transformations of the diverse
models, types, and linguistic elements of classical
architecture. For a flavour of Blomfield's traditionalist
position, see his *Memoirs of an Architect*, London,
1932; for Lutyens's transformations of the English
Baroque, see Colin Amery, ed., *Lutyens*; for
Scandinavian perspectives on classicism, see note
below on Nordic classicism. The subject of
substructures from the classical tradition within
modernism now has an extensive literature; see, for
example, Rowe, *The Mathematics of the Ideal Villa*,
Collins on classical rationalism in *Changing Ideals*,
Banham on 'Academic' survivals in *Theory and Design*,
Curtis on Le Corbusier's transformation of several
'levels' in antiquity and later phases of classicism in *Le
Corbusier: Ideas and Forms*, Colquhoun on aspects of

classical rationalism in *Modernity and the Classical
Tradition*, Cambridge, Mass., 1989. See also John
Summerson, *The Classical Language of Architecture*,
London, 1964, and Alexander Tzonis and Liane
Lefaivre, *Classical Architecture, the Poetics of Order*,
Cambridge, Mass., 1986, for certain underlying
schemata of classicism.
141 Amédée Ozenfant: *The Foundations of
Modern Art*, Trans. John Rodker, New York, 1931.
Hoffmann: see Sekler, *Josef Hoffmann*, pp. 121ff,
for discussion of renewed interest in classicism.
142 Mies: for formative ideas and classical
influences see Fritz Neumeyer, *Mies van der Rohe: das
kunstlose Wort, Gedanken zur Baukunst*, Berlin, 1986,
translated by Mark Jarzombek, *The Artless Word. Mies
van der Rohe on the Building Art*, Cambridge, Mass.,
1991; see also Fritz Neumeyer, 'Space for Reflection:
Block Versus Pavilion', in *Mies van der Rohe, Critical
Essays*, ed. Franz Schulze, New York, 1989, pp. 148ff.;
for Mies's ideas on 'civilization' see Francesco dal Co,
'Excellence: The Culture of Mies as seen in his Notes
and Books', *Mies Reconsidered: his Career, Legacy and
Disciples*, Chicago, 1986 (Art Institute exhibition
catalogue), pp. 72ff.; also Rowe, 'Neo-"Classicism"
and Modern Architecture', 1 and 2, *The Mathematics
of the Ideal Villa*, pp. 120ff.
143 Le Corbusier; Jura Regionalism: see Mary
Patricia May Sekler, 'Le Corbusier, Ruskin, the Tree
and the Open Hand', in Walden, ed., *The Open Hand*,
pp. 42ff.; for Le Corbusier's formative years and
absorptions from the past, as well as classicizing
elements in his early work, see Curtis, *Le Corbusier:
Ideas and Forms*, especially first three chapters; for
Cingría-Vaneyre's theories, Paul Turner, *The
Education of Le Corbusier*, New York, 1977.
Le Corbusier, The past as master: *Le Corbusier,
Précisions sur un état présent de l'architecture et de
l'urbanisme*, Paris, 1930, p. 34.
145 Danish neo-classicism: Jørgen Sestoft and
Jørgen Hegner Chrisiansen, *Guide to Danish
Architecture 1, 1000–1960*, Copenhagen, 1991, p. 33.
See also Anne-Louise Sommer, 'Vitale forbindelser –
et dansk svensk mellemspil', *Proces*, Kunstakademiets
Arkitektskole, no. 3, Copenhagen, June 1994.
Woodland Cemetery: see Janne Ahlin, *Sigurd
Lewerentz, Architect, 1885–1975*, Cambridge, Mass.,
1987, pp. 38ff.; Stuart Wrede, 'Landscape and
Architecture: the Work of Erik Gunnar Asplund',
*Perspecta, 20,*1983, pp. 195ff., and Stuart Wrede,
The Architecture of Erik Gunnar Asplund, Cambridge,
Mass., 1980; Caroline Constant, *The Woodland
Cemetery: Towards a Spiritual Landscape*, Stockholm,
1994.
146 Nordic classicism: see Colin St John Wilson and
others, *Erik Gunnar Asplund 1885–1940: the Dilemma
of Classicism*, London, 1988; also St John Wilson, A.P.
Smithson and others, *Sigurd Lewerentz 1885–1976:
the Dilemma of Classicism*, London, 1989; Dimitri
Porphyrios, *Sources of Modern Eclecticism: Studies
on Alvar Aalto*, London, 1982; see also William J.R.
Curtis, 'Erik Gunnar Asplund: a Distilled Classicism',
'Sigurd Lewerentz, The Meaning of Order', 'Erik
Bryggman, Between Two Traditions', and 'Alvar Aalto,
The Nordic Myth', in *Arquitectura y vivienda*, 95, 1995,
pp. 38ff.
Core to surface: Aulis Blomstedt, 'Prospects in

Architecture', note from 1950s (precise date
uncertain), published in Scott Poole, *The New Finnish
Architecture*, New York, 1992, p. 46.

chapter 9 cubism and new conceptions of space

149 Motto: T. van Doesburg, G. Rietveld, C. van
Eesteren, 'Vers une construction collective', *de Stijl*,
1924, columns 91, 92.

150 Avant-Garde: see Renato Poggioli, *The Theory
of the Avant-Garde*, Cambridge, Mass., 1968.
W. Kandinsky: *Über das Geistige in der Kunst*,
Munich, 1912.
Spirit of Times: see notes on 'modern age' and
'propagandists' in Introduction and on 'spiritual core'
in Chapter I. It is evident that Le Corbusier, for
example, saw himself as a revealer of the true nature
of his own epoch. See Chapter 10.
Henri Matisse: 'Notes of a Painter' (1908), in Alfred
H. Barr Jr., *Matisse, his Art and his Public*, New York,
1951, pp. 119ff.
150–1 Geoffrey Scott: *The Architecture of
Humanism*, London, 1914, p. 210. This book was
supposedly a defence of 'humanist' values in classicism,
but it can equally be read as a critique of ethical,
literary, functionalist and other 'fallacies', and an
assertion of the primacy of spatial relationships and
'empathy' in the experience of architectural order.
151–2 Cubism, Abstract Art, Architecture: Banham,
Theory and Design, pp. 106–213. See also Giedion,
Space, Time and Architecture for a different emphasis
which makes much of the so-called space–time
conception intrinsic to Cubism and modern
architecture.
152 Wright, space: see, for example, *Storia
dell'architettura moderna*; 'A Language After Wright',
in Gutheim, ed., *Frank Lloyd Wright: In the Cause of
Architecture*, pp. 34ff.; and (for influences on Holland),
Poetica dell architettura neoplastica, Milan, 1953.
153 Berlage: *Grundlagen und Entwicklung der
Architektur*, Berlin, 1908; I have followed Banham's
translation, *Theory and Design*, p. 141; for Berlage on
Wright, lecture given in Zurich, March 1912, cited H.
de Fries, *Frank Lloyd Wright*, Berlin, 1926, and
Banham, op. cit, pp. 145–6. See also note on 'Wasmuth
volumes' at end of Chapter 7
Dutch Expressionists: see Ulrich Conrads and H.G.
Sperlich, *Phantastische Architektur*, Stuttgart, 1960;
Suzanne S. Frank, *Michel de Klerk, 1884–1923*, UMI
Research Papers, Ann Arbor, Michigan, 1984; also the
Dutch periodical *Wendingen* between 1919 and 1925.
154 J.J.P. Oud: 'Architectural Observations
Concerning Wright and the Robie House', *De Stijl*, 4,
1918, pp. 39–41, translated Elsa Scharbach.
Van Doesburg: see Jean Badovici, 'Entretiens sur
l'architecture vivante: la couleur dans la nouvelle
architecture', *L'architecture vivante*, spring/summer
1924, pp. 17–18; for abstraction in painting,
architecture, design, see Nancy Troy, *The De Stijl
Environment*, Cambridge, Mass., 1983.
155 De Stijl: see the ever useful Hans Ludwig C.
Jaffé, *De Stijl 1917–1931, the Dutch Contribution to
Modern Art*, Amsterdam, 1956. This formulation, 'The

Style', resonates with a range of contrasting earlier
writings on the problem of style in architecture,
including, possibly, Berlage's *Gedanken uber Stil*,
Leipzig, 1905; Alois Riegl's *Stilfragen*, Berlin, 1893; and
both Viollet-le-Duc's and Semper's writings on style
earlier in the nineteenth-century (of which Riegl's were
in part a critique). 'De Stijl' rejected both the
limitations of rationalism and those of 'naturalism',
insisting upon an Idealist notion of abstraction and
space-relations as projections of an evolving *Zeitgeist*.
This stress on the primacy of formal and spatial
relationships finds some loose parallels in art-historical
writings soon after the turn of the century, notably
those of Heinrich Wölfflin and Paul Frankl.
156 The Machine: see Banham, *Theory and Design*,
pp. 151ff.
156–7 Number and Measure: J.J.P. Oud, 'Der
Einfluss von Frank Lloyd Wright auf die Architektur
Europas', in *Holländische Architektur* (Bauhausbuch
10), Munich, 1926.
157–9 Schröder House: T. Brown, *The Work of
Gerrit Rietveld, Architect*, Utrecht and Cambridge,
Mass., 1958.
159 Barren Rationalism: J.J.P. Oud, 'Über die
zukünftige Baukunst und ihre architektonischen
Möglichkeiten', 1912, eventually published in Oud,
Holländische Architektur, 1926.

chapter 10 le corbusier's quest for ideal form.

163 Motto: Le Corbusier, *Towards a New
Architecture*, p. 31. I have altered Etchell's translation
of the French volumes, from 'masses' to 'volumes', as
this seems more precise.
International Style: see below, Chapter 15 for a more
intricate discussion of 'this shared language of
expression'.
Le Corbusier Formative Years: for general
treatments and further bibliography see: Stanislaus
Von Moos, *Le Corbusier, Elements of a Synthesis*,
Cambridge, Mass., 1979 (originally *Le Corbusier:
Elemente einer Synthese*, Frauenfeld and Stuttgart,
1968); Maurice Besset, *Who was Le Corbusier?*,
Geneva, 1968; and Curtis, *Le Corbusier: Ideas and
Forms*. For useful anthologies: Peter Serenyi, *Le
Corbusier in Perspective*, Englewood Cliffs, N.J., 1975;
Russell Walden, ed., *The Open Hand, Essays on Le
Corbusier*, Cambridge, Mass., 1977; Kenneth
Frampton, ed., *Oppositions 15/16* and *19/20*, double
issue on Le Corbusier, 1978 and 1980. H. Allen
Brooks, ed., *The Le Corbusier Archive*, New York and
Paris, 1982, (32 volumes, some with introductory
essays); *Le Corbusier, Architect of the Century*,
exhibition catalogue, Arts Council, London, 1987;
Jacques Lucan, ed., *Le Corbusier: une encyclopédie*,
Paris, 1987. For early years see also M. Gauthier, *Le
Corbusier – ou l'architecte au service de l'homme*, Paris,
1934; Mary Patricia May Sekler, *The Education of Le
Corbusier, a Study of the Development of Le Corbusier's
Thought 1900–1920*, New York, 1977; Paul Turner,
'The Beginnings of Le Corbusier's Education, 1902–7',
Art Bulletin, 53, June 1971, pp. 214–24. For the
gradual emergence of Le Corbusier's architectural

system see William J.R. Curtis, 'Le Corbusier: the
Evolution of his Architectural Language and its
Crystallization in the Villa Savoye at Poissy', *Le
Corbusier/English Architecture 1930s*, Milton Keynes,
1975. Throughout this chapter it is useful to consult the
Oeuvre complete 1910–29.
165 Travel: Charles Edouard Jeanneret, *Le Voyage
d'Orient*, Paris, 1966; also Giuliano Gresleri, *Le
Corbusier, Viaggio in Oriente*, Venice, 1984.
166 Own Antiquity: The historian in question is
James Ackerman.
Italy, graveyard: C.E. Jeanneret letter to William
Ritter 1 Nov. 1991; see Eleanor Gregh, 'The Domino
Idea', *Oppositions 15/16*, pp. 61ff.
Amédée Ozenfant, *The Foundations of Modern Art*,
Trans. John Rodker, New York, 1931.
167 Ozenfant and Charles E. Jeanneret: *Après le
Cubisme*, Paris, 1919. See also Christopher Green and
John Golding, *Léger and Purist Paris*, London, 1970.
168 Platonism: best treatment is still Banham,
Theory and Design, p. 211.
L'Esprit Nouveau, Paris, 1919–25. The quotation is
from no. 1, October 1920, reproduced in *Towards a
New Architecture*, p. 83; see also Stanislaus Von Moos,
ed., *L'Esprit Nouveau, Le Corbusier et l'Industrie
1920–1925*, exhibition catalogue, Zurich and
Strasbourg, 1987.
168–9 Le Corbusier: *Towards a New Architecture*,
pp.16, 31.
170 Le Corbusier: *Towards a New Architecture*,
pp. 124–5.
171 Henry IV: Le Corbusier, 'Conséquences de
Crise', *L'Esprit Nouveau*, 22, 1924, also in Le
Corbusier, *L'Art décoratif d'aujourdhui*, Paris, 1925,
p. 43; for ideas on types etc. see also Le Corbusier,
Almanach d'architecture moderne, Paris, 1924.
Pessac: Brian Brace Taylor, *Le Corbusier at Pessac*,
Cambridge, Mass., 1972.
Wyndham Lewis: *Time and Western Man*, New York,
1929, for 'upper middle class bohemia'.
172 Le Corbusier: *Towards a New Architecture*,
p. 92.
172–3 La Roche-Jeanneret House: see R. Walden's
article in Walden, ed., *The Open Hand*; Tim Benton,
Les Villas de Le Corbusier 1920–1930, Paris, 1984,
pp. 43ff.
172 Type: see A. Ozenfant and C.E. Jeanneret,
La Peinture moderne, Paris, 1926, passage cited and
translated, Banham, *Theory and Design*, p. 211
173 Good plan: Le Corbusier, *Towards a New
Architecture*, p. 166.
174 Events from history: see Benton, *Les Villas de
Le Corbusier*, p. 43; also Kurt Forster, 'Antiquity and
Modernity in the La Roche Jeanneret Houses of 1923',
Oppositions 15–16, pp. 131ff.
175–7 Cook: Le Corbusier, *Oeuvre complète
1910–1929*, p. 130; for Cook as demonstration, Curtis,
Le Corbusier/English Architecture 1930s, p. 32.
177 Guiette, Baizeau: see Guy Schraenen, *Les
Peupliers, Maison Guiette, Le Corbusier*, 1926,
Brussels, 1987; and Tim Benton, 'La Villa Baizeau et
le Brise-soleil', in *Le Corbusier et la Mediterranée*,
exhibition catalogue, Marseilles, 1987, pp. 125ff.
178 Les Terrasses, design process: Max Risselada,
ed., *Le Corbusier and Pierre Jeanneret, Ontwerpen voor
di woning*, Delft, 1980; also Benton, *Les Villas*; and

James Ward 'Le Corbusier's Villa "Les Terrasses" and the International Style', PhD Thesis, New York, 1984.

179   Perceptual Layers: see Colin Rowe (with Robert Slutzky), 'Transparency: Literal and Phenomenal', *Perspecta*, 1963; republished Rowe, *The Mathematics of the Ideal Villa*, pp. 160ff.

180   Le Corbusier: *Oeuvre complète 1910–1929*, p. 140; *Towards a New Architecture*, p. 89.

181   Classical villa: see Rowe, *The Mathematics*, pp. 2ff.; see also James Ackerman, *The Villa, Form and Ideology of Country Houses*, London, 1990, Chapter 11; and Curtis *Le Corbusier: Ideas and Forms*, Chapter 6.

chapter 11   walter gropius, german expressionism, and the bauhaus

183   Motto: Gropius, 'The Development of Modern Industrial Architecture', 1913: the same sentiments were expressed in almost exactly the same words by Gropius in *Idee und Aufbau des Staatlichen Bauhausses Weimar*, Weimar, 1923.

Walter Gropius: essay in *Ja Stimmen des Arbeitsrates für Kunst in Berlin*, Berlin, 1919, p. 32.

Bruno Taut: *Alpine Architektur*, 1919; for translation see D. Sharp, ed., *Glass Architecture by Paul Scheerbart and Alpine Architecture by Bruno Taut*, London, 1972; *Die Stadtkrone*, Jena, 1919.

184   Bauhaus Proclamation: Walter Gropius, 'Idee und Aufbau … ' ('Programme of the Staatliche Bauhaus in Weimar'), April 1919; cited by Banham, *Theory and Design*.

185   For ideas and events leading to the Bauhaus, Marcel Franciscono, *Walter Gropius and the Creation of the Bauhaus in Weimar: the Ideals and Artistic Theories of its Founding Years*, Urbana, 1971.

Adolf Behne: review of Scheerbart's *Glas-architektur*, 1918–19; see Benton and Benton, *Architecture and Design*, p. 77; also Rosemarie Bletter, 'The Interpretation of the Glass Dream Expressionist Architecture and the History of the Crystal Metaphor', *Journal of Society of Architectural Historians*, 40, 1981, pp. 20–43.

186   Strygowski: see Joseph Rykwert *On Adam's House in Paradise*, pp. 23ff.

Expressionism: for a simple introduction, Dennis Sharp, *Modern Architecture and Expressionism*, London, 1966; see also W. Pehnt, *Expressionist Architecture*, London, 1973; J.M. Richards and N. Pevsner, eds., *The Anti-Rationalists*, London, 1973.

186–8   Mendelsohn: see Arnold Whittick, *Eric Mendelsohn*, Leonard Hill, 1964; O. Beyer, ed., *Erich Mendelsohn: Letters of An Architect*, New York, 1967; E. Mendelsohn, *Das Gesamtschaffen des Architekten – Skizzen, Entwürfe, Bauten*, Berlin, 1930; published in English as *Erich Mendelsohn, The Complete Works*, New York, 1992; also Hans Rudolf Morgenthaler, *The Early Sketches of German Architect Erich Mendelsohn, 1887–1953*, New York, 1992

187   Einstein Tower: Erich Mendelsohn, lecture given to Architectura et Amicitia, 1923, cited by Banham, *Theory and Design*, p. 182, and reproduced in original in Mendelsohn, *The Complete Works*, as 'The International Consensus on the New Architectural Concept, or Dynamics and Function', p. 24.

188   Mendelsohn, light: op. cit. p.31; Mendelsohn, function plus dynamics: letter to his wife, 1919, cited Banham, *Theory and Design*, p. 181.

Mendelsohn, stress-free horizontal: *Complete Works*, p. 24.

189   Mies: Philip Johnson, *Mies van der Rohe*, New York, 1947; P. Westheim, 'Mies van der Rohe: Entwicklung eines Architekten', *Das Kunstblatt*, 2, February 1927, pp. 52ff.; Ludwig Hilberseimer, *Mies van der Rohe*, Chicago, 1956; Peter Carter, 'Mies van der Rohe', *Architectural Design*, 31, March 1961, pp. 65–121; Werner Blaser, *Mies van der Rohe, The Art of Structure*, London, 1965. In the 1980s there was a reassessment of Mies, making use of archives and relying upon a longer historical perspective. Among the results were: Franz Schulze, *Mies van der Rohe, a Critical Biography*, Chicago, 1985; Schulze, ed., *Mies van der Rohe, Critical essays*; John Zukowsky, ed., *Mies Reconsidered: his Career, Legacy and Disciples*, Chicago, Art Institute, 1986; Neumeyer, *Mies van der Rohe*; and Wolf Tegethoff, *Mies van der Rohe, the Villas and Country Houses*, New York and Cambridge, Mass., 1985; the latter translated from the German edition of 1981; see also note to p. 142.

190   Utopian Content in Glass Skyscrapers: William J. R. Curtis, 'Der Wolkenkratzer – Realität und Utopie', in *Die zwanziger Jahre Kontraste eines Jahrzehnts*, Zurich, 1973, pp. 44–7.

Mies Skyscrapers: see Mies van der Rohe, 'Hochhaus-projekt für Bahnhof Friedrichstrasse in Berlin', in *Frühlicht*, ed. B. Taut, 1922; translated in Johnson, *Mies van der Rohe*, p. 182, as 'Two Glass Skyscrapers of 1922'.

Le Corbusier: *Towards a New Architecture*, p. 28.

Mies van der Rohe: 'Working Theses 1923', G, vol. 1, 1923; translated in Uhlrich Conrads, *Programs and Manifestos of 20th Century Architecture*, London, 1970, p. 74.

193–4   Walter Gropius: *Idee und Aufbau des Staatlichen Bauhausses Weimar*, 1923; I have followed Banham's translation, *Theory and Design*, pp. 279ff.; for detailed treatment of Bauhaus, Hans Maria Wingler, *The Bauhaus: Weimar, Dessau*, Berlin, Chicago, Cambridge, Mass., 1969; for analysis of ideas, Gillian Naylor, *The Bauhaus Reassessed: Sources and Design Theory*, London, 1985; see also Reginald Isaacs, *Gropius, an Illustrated Biography*, Boston, 1991.

195   Bauhaus Criticisms: K. Nonn, 'The State Garbage Supplies (The Staatliche Bauhaus in Weimar)', 1924; cited by Benton and Benton, *Architecture and Design*, p. 129. For further discussion of the Bauhaus see Hans Wingler, *Das Bauhaus, 1919–1933*, Cologne, 1962; for political debates see Barbara Miller-Lane, *Architecture and Politics in Germany, 1918–1945*, Cambridge, Mass., 1968.

195–6   Bauhaus buildings: see Dennis Sharp, *Bauhaus, Dessau, 1925–6, Walter Gropius* (Architecture in Detail), London, 1993.

196   Golden Age: see particularly L. Moholy-Nagy, *Von Material zu Architektur*, Munich, 1928; O. Schlemmer, L. Moholy-Nagy and F. Molnar, *The Theatre of the Bauhaus*, Middletown, Conn., 1964; G. Adams, 'Memories of a Bauhaus Student', *Architectural Review*, September 1968, pp. 192ff.; W. Kandinsky, *Punkt und Linie zu Fläche*, Munich, 1925; P. Klee, *Pädagogisches Skizzenbuch*, Munich,

1926; W. Gropius, I. Gropius and H. Bayer, *Bauhaus 1919–1928*, New York, 1938; W. Gropius, *Internationale Architektur*, Munich, 1925; W. Gropius, *The New Architecture and the Bauhaus*, London, 1935.

198   Mies van der Rohe, Objectivity: see Banham, *Theory and Design*, p. 271; see also F. Schmalenbach, 'The Term Neue Sachlichkeit', *Art Bulletin*, 22, September 1940.

Weissenhofsiedlung: see Karin Kirsch, *Die Weissenhofsiedlung, Werkbund-Ausstellung Die Wohnuug – Stuttgart 1927*, Stuttgart, 1987; also Richard Pommer and Christopher Otto, *Weissenhof 1927 and the Modern Movement in Architecture*, Chicago, 1991. For Weissenhof as Kasbah, see Benton and Benton, *Architecture and Design*, ill. 23; also Chapter 20 below.

199   Hannes Meyer: C. Schnaidt, *Hannes Meyer, Buildings, Projects and Writings*, London, 1965; see also O. Birkner, J. Herzog and P. de Meuron, 'Die Petersschule in Basel, 1926–29', *Werk/Architbèse*, 13/14, Jan.–Feb. 1978, pp. 6–8; Michael Hays, *Modernism and the Post-humanist Subject: the Architecture of Hannes Meyer and Ludwig Hilberseimer*, London, 1992.

chapter 12   architecture and revolution in russia

201   Motto: A. and V. Vesnin, from *Sovremennaya Arkhitectura* (*Contemporary Architecture*), 1926. This chapter is particularly indebted to Anatole Kopp, *Town and Revolution, Soviet Architecture and City Planning 1917–1935*, New York, 1970, originally published as *Ville et Revolution*, Paris, 1967; and to the articles and recollections of El Lissitzky, Hans Schmidt and Berthold Lubetkin (see below); for points of detail, Selim Khan-Magomedov, *Pioneers of Soviet Architecture. The Search for New Solutionsin the 1920s and 1930s*, Trans. A. Lieven, London, 1987.

202   Proletcult: see El Lissitzky, *Russia: an Architecture for World Revolution*, London, 1970 (originally published as *Russland: Die Reconstruktion der Arckitektur in der Sowjetunion*, Vienna, 1930), pp. 14ff., 'Translator's Introduction', by Eric Dluhosch; see also Camilla Gray, *The Great Experiment: Russian Art, 1863–1922*, London, 1962.

Visual language: When examining avant-garde production in the 1920s in the Soviet Union it is crucial to avoid making over-simplistic equations between theoretical positions and declarations, and the actual architectural forms. Visual thinking has some internal rules of its own which work by another logic than that of ideology; the problem is to unravel the levels of meaning, and to find the links between the 'iconological', the iconographic (to use Erwin Panofsky's terms) and the expressive; a distinction needs to be made between the social *content* of a work and the social reality within which it emerges.

203   El Lissitzky: see J. Lissitzky-Küppers, ed., *El Lissitzky, Maler, Architekt, Typograf, Fotograf*, Dresden, 1967.

205   Tatlin's Monument: N. Punin, 'Tatlin's Monument', 1922; cited by Benton and Benton, *Architecture and Design*, p. 86; for further discussion of the symbolic implications of spirals see Berthold Lubetkin, 'Architectural Thought since the Revolution', *Architectural Review*, May 1932, pp. 210–14; see also Paul Zygas, 'Tatlin's Tower Reconsidered', *Architectural Association Quarterly*, 2, 1976, pp. 15–27; and L. A. Zhadova, *Tatlin*, 1988; see also Serge Eisenstein, *Film Form*.

207 Melnikov: see Frederick Starr, *Konstantin Melnikov. Solo Architect in a Mass society*, Princeton, 1978; also William J. R. Curtis, section on Melnikov's 1925 Paris Exhibition Pavilion in *Search for Total Construction: Art, Architecture and Townplanning. USSR 1917–1932 – Fragments of a Development*, exhibition catalogue, Carpenter Center, Harvard University, Cambridge, Mass., 1971, pp. 11ff.

208 F. Yalovkin: 'OSA [Union of Contemporary Architects] Vopra and OSA', 1929, cited by Benton, *Documents*, p. 30; for Ginzburg's search for a language, see Moisei Ginzburg, *Stil i Epokha*, 1924; trans. and intro. A. Senkevitch, *Style and Epoch*, Cambridge, Mass., 1982. For an incisive discussion of different ideological positions in the 1920s in the Soviet Union, see Lubetkin, 'Architectural Thought since the Revolution'; for documentation, see Catherine Cooke, *Russian Avant-garde Theories of Art, Architecture and the City*, London, 1995.

Constructivist: for slightly contrasting uses of this term, see George Rickey, *Constructivism – Origins and Evolution*, London, 1967; Kopp, *Town and Revolution*, pp. 94ff.; J.-L. Cohen, 'Constructivisme', in Lucan, ed., *Le Corbusier, une encyclopédie*, pp. 101ff.; and Berthold Lubetkin, 'The Origins of Constructivism', cited John Allan, *Berthold Lubetkin, Architecture and the Tradition of Progress*, London, 1992, pp. 24ff. and Cooke, op. cit., pp. 121ff. In reality, a range of definitions was already operative in the 1920s; for example, A. Gan, *Konstruktivizm*, Tver' 1922; and Moisei Ginzburg, 'Constructivism in architecture', *Sovremennaya Arkhitektura*, 5, 1928, pp. 143–5.

209 Narkomfin: see Kopp, *Town and Revolution*, pp. 143ff.; and V. Quilici, *L'architettura del costruttivismo*, Bari, 1969, p. 164; Sherwood, *Modern Housing Prototypes*, p. 118ff.; Karel Teige, *Nejmenski Byt*, Prague, 1932, p. 323; and Curtis, 'Housing Between 1926 and 1930', *Search for Total Construction*, pp. 17–18. For architects' design approach, 'The Constructivist Architects' Functional Method', *Sovremennaya Arkhitektura*, 6, 1927, p. 160, cited in Cooke, op. cit., p. 121; see also 'Narkomfin, Method of Analysis', Cooke, p. 120. For essays on theme of 'Das Kollektivwohnhaus – la maison collective, 1900–1930', see *Archithèse 12*, Niederteufen, Dec. 1974; notably Martin Steinmann, 'Das Laubenganghaus', pp. 3–12; and Stanislaus Von Moos, 'Wohnkollektiv, Hospiz und Dampfer', pp. 30–42.

210 Le Corbusier, Centrosoyus: see Curtis, *Le Corbusier: Ideas and Forms*, Chapter 7; also Tim Benton, 'The Era of the Great Projects', in *Le Corbusier Architect of the Century*, Arts Council Exhibition Catalogue, London, 1987, pp. 164ff.; Jean-Louis Cohen, *Le Corbusier et la mystique de l'URSS: théories et projets pour Moscou 1928–1936*, Paris, 1987; and Alan Colquhoun, 'The Strategies of the Grands Travaux', *Modernity and the Classical Tradition*, Cambridge, Mass., pp. 121ff.

211 Leonidov: Lenin Institute: see Andrei Gozak, *Andrei Leonidov, Ivan Leonidov*, London, 1988, ed. Catherine Cooke, p. 44, where Leonidov describes glass sphere as a 'Planetarium: a scientific optical theatre', and as 'a speaking platform for mass gatherings when one half opens up and the walls and seats withdraw into the remaining half'. For an appreciation of Leonidov's individual qualities as an architect see Le Corbusier, 'Défense de l'architecture', 1929, published in *Architecture d'aujourdhui*, 10, 1933, pp. 58–60; see also S. Khan-Magomedov, *Ivan Leonidov*, New York, 1981 (IAUS Catalogue, no. 8).

Soviet planning: see Kopp, *Town and Revolution*; also Curtis, 'Townplanning and the Five Year Plan', *Search for Total Construction*, pp. 19–20; and Kenneth Frampton, 'Notes on Soviet Urbanism 1917–32', *Architects' Year Book*, 12, 1968, pp. 238–52; see also Chapter 14, below.

212–15 Palace of Soviets competition: see *Architectural Review*, 71, May 1932, pp. 199ff.; also Giorgio Ciucci, 'Concours pour le palais des soviets', *VH IOI*, nos. 7–8, 1972; for discussion of change of Soviet official policy see Hans Schmidt, 'The Soviet Union and Modern Architecture', in English edition of Lissitzky, *Russia: an Architecture for a World Revolution*, p. 218. One reason that Le Corbusier's project was rejected was its 'machinism', see Curtis, *Le Corbusier: Ideas and Forms*, p. 92; for monumentality and representation of state in Stalinist period, see *Art and Power: Europe under the Dictators 1930–45*, exhibition catalogue, Hayward Gallery, London, 1995; for imagery of Iofan's building project, see William J.R. Curtis, 'Modern Architecture, Monumentality and the Meaning of Institutions', *Harvard Architectural Review*, no. 4, 1984.

chapter 13 skyscraper and suburb: america between the wars

217 Motto: Calvert Vaux, 'A New Scale of Values', *Villas and Cottages*, New York, 1857, pp 13–32; also Lewis Mumford, ed., *Roots of Contemporary American Architecture*, New York, 1952, pp. 57ff.

'291': this was the name of the gallery opened by Alfred Stieglitz in 1908, in which he showed the avant-garde work of the 'Photo Secessionist' movement.

218 Marsden Hartley: 'Art and the Personal Life', *Creative Art*, 2, June 1928.

Lewis Mumford: *The Brown Decades: A Study of the Arts in America, 1865–1895*, New York, 1931.

Le Corbusier: *Towards a New Architecture*, p. 42.

219 Skyscrapers: see Carl Condit, *The Chicago School of Architecture*, Chicago, 1964, specially for the early stages of the type; Vincent Scully, *American Architecture and Urbanism*, London, 1969, is a useful overview, as is J. Burchard and Bush Brown, *American Architecture: a Social and Cultural History*, Boston, 1961; see also W. Weisman, 'A New View of Skyscraper history', in Edgard Kaufmann, Jr., ed., *The Rise of an American Architecture*, New York, 1970.

Tribune: *Chicago Tribune Competition*, Chicago, 1922, contains illustrations of the entries and the programme sent to competitors.

222 Glass Skyscrapers: for the contrast in ideology between Europe and USA, see Curtis, 'Der Wolkenkratzer – Realität und Utopie', in *Die zwanziger Jahre Kontraste eines Jahrzehnts*, Zurich, 1973, and Manfredo Tafuri, 'La Dialectique de l'absurde Europe-USA: les avatars de l'idéologie du gratte-ciel 1918–1974', *Architecture d'aujourdhui*, 178, March/April 1975, pp. 1–16.

223 Reliance Building: see Giedion, *Space, Time and Architecture*, p. 386.

223–4 New York Skyscrapers: see Rosemary Bletter and Cervin Robinson, *Skyscraper Style – Art Deco New York*, New York, 1975; also Jordy, *American Buildings and Their Architects*, vol. 4, and W.A. Starrett, *Skyscrapers and the Men who Built Them*, New York, 1928. See also Jean-Louis Cohen, *Scenes of the World to Come, European Architecture and the American Challenge 1893–1960*, Montreal, 1995.

225 Louis Sullivan: *Kindergarten Chats and other Writings*, New York, 1947, p. 77; written in 1918.

Skyscraper as Tool: Le Corbusier, *Quand les cathédrales étaient blanches: voyage aux pays des timides*, Paris, 1937, p. 62, author's translation.

Hugh Ferris: *The Metropolis of Tomorrow*, New York, 1929.

226 Erich Mendelsohn: 'Synthesis – World Architecture' (with Bernard Hoetyer), Berlin, 1928, cited Ulrich Conrads, *Programs and Manifestoes on 20th Century Architecture*, Frankfurt, 1966, pp. 106–7.

227 Rockefeller Center: see Jordy, *American Buildings and Their Architects*, vol. 4, and C. Krinsky, *Rockefeller Center*, London and New York, 1978. For urbanistic problems of skyscraper, Werner Oechslin, 'Zwischen Amerika und Deutschland: Hegemanns städtebauliche Vorstellungen jenseits der Frage nach der "Moderne"', in Wolfgang Böhm, ed., *Das Bauwerk und die Stadt (The Building and the Town), Aufsätze für Eduard F. Sekler*, Vienna, 1994; also Tafuri et al., *The American City from the Civil War to the New Deal*, Cambridge, Mass., 1983.

229 Hollyhock: for diverse interpretations see Neil Levine, 'Hollyhock House and the Romance of Southern California', *Art in America*, 71, no. 8, September 1983; Kathryn Smith, *Frank Lloyd Wright, Hollyhock House and Olive Hill 1915–1919*, New York, 1992; also James Steele, *Barnsdall (Hollyhock) House Los Angeles 1921* (Architecture in Detail), London, 1992.

230 Frank Lloyd Wright: *A Testament*, New York, 1972, p. 111; for Wright's possible debts to Meso-America, Dimitri Tselos, 'Exotic Influences in the Architecture of Frank Lloyd Wright', *Magazine of Art*, 46, April 1953, pp. 166ff. and William J. R. Curtis, 'Paisajes miticos: la arquitectura moderna y el pasado mexicano', in Alicia Azuela, ed., *Hechizo de Oaxaca*, exhibition catalogue, Museo de Arte Contemporaneo de Monterrey, 1991, pp. 329ff.

231 Concrete blocks and geometry: Kenneth Frampton, 'The Text-tile Tectonic', in Robert McCarter, ed., *Frank Lloyd Wright, A Primer on Architectural Principles*, New York, 1991; also Otto Graf, *Die Kunst des Quadrats, Zum Werk von Frank Lloyd Wright*, Vienna, 1983.

234 Rudolf Schindler: 'Modern Architecture: a Programme', Vienna, 1912, in August Sarnitz, *R. M. Schindler Architect 1887–1953, a Pupil of Otto Wagner between International Style and Space Architecture*, New York, 1988, p. 42; see also Esther McCoy, *Five*

California Architects, New York, 1960; David Gebhard, *Schindler*, London, 1971; Reyner Banham, *Los Angeles, the Architecture of the Four Ecologies*, Harmondsworth, 1971; Lionel March, Judith Sheine, eds., *R. M. Schindler: Composition and Construction*, London, 1993; and Kathryn Smith (with foreward by Robert L. Sweeney), *R.M. Schindler House 1921–22*, Los Angeles, Friends of Schindler House West Hollywood, California, 1987 (brochure).
235 Technik: Schindler notebook 1928, in McCoy, op.cit., p. 167.
El Pueblo Ribera: The author lived with his family in the remnants of Schindler's complex during the winter of 1992–3, and this analysis is partly based upon this experience; the interpretation of Schindler has also been influenced by an extensive correspondence between the author and Pauline Schindler (Schindler's widow) during the early 1970s.
Lovell Beach House: Stefanos Polyzoides, 'Schindler, Lovell and the Newport Beach House, Los Angeles, 1921–1926', *Oppositions 18*, Fall 1979, pp. 60–73.
237 Richard Neutra: *Wie Baut Amerika?* Stuttgart, 1927, see also Thomas Hines, *Richard Neutra and the Search for Modern Architecture*, New York, 1982.
238 PSFS: George Howe, cited by Jordy in *American Buildings and Their Architects*, vol. 4, pp. 47–83.
239 Hitchcock and Johnson: *The International Style*, p. 20.

chapter 14 the ideal community: alternatives to the industrial city

241 Motto: Karel Teige, 'Contemporary International Architecture', 1928, in Benton and Benton, *Architecture and Design*, p. 200.
Industrial City: see L. Benevolo, *Le origini dell'urbanistica moderna*, Bari, 1963, translated into English as *The Origins of Modern Town-Planning*, Cambridge, Mass., 1967; Françoise Choay, *The Modern City, Planning in the 19th Century*, New York, 1969; also Lewis Mumford, *The City in History, its Origins, its Transformations and its Prospects*, New York, 1961, especially chapters 14–18 (still a magisterial work).
Friedrich Engels: *The Condition of the Working Classes in England in 1844* (tr. Wischnewetzky), London, 1952, p. 49.
242 Critiques of Industrial City: see Benevolo, *History of Modern Architecture*, pp. 127ff., and Egbert, *Social Radicalism*, pp. 133–43 for Fourier, pp. 67–77 for Marx, p. 104 for Engels, also pp. 117–19. For Fourier's phalanstère see Benevolo, *The Origins of Modern Town-Planning*, p. 56, and Charles Fourier, *Traité de l'association domestique-agricole* in *Oeuvre complète*, Paris, 1841, vol. 4, pp. 500–2; also Anthony Sutcliffe, *Towards the Planned City; Germany, Britain, the United States and France 1780–1914*, London, 1981; see also R. H. Guerrand, *Les Origines du logement social en France*, Paris, 1967; and in Italian edition of same (Rome, 1981), essay by Georges Teyssot, 'La casa per tutti: per una genealogia del tipi'; also Peter Rowe, *Modernity and Housing*, London, 1993.

243 Camillo Sitte: *Der Städtebau nach seinem künstlerischen Grundsätzen*, Vienna, 1889, translated as *City Planning according to Artistic Principles*, London, 1965. See G. and C. Collins, *Camillo Sitte and the Birth of Modern City Planning*, London, 1965.
Soria y Mata: see George Collins, 'Linear Planning Throughout the World', *Journal of Society of Architectural Historians*, 18, October 1959, pp. 74–93.
Ebenezer Howard: *Tomorrow: a Peaceful Path to Real Reform*, London, 1898, reissued with slight changes as *Garden Cities of Tomorrow* in 1902.
John Ruskin: *Sesame and Lilies*, London, 1865.
244 Garnier: *Une Cité Industrielle*, Paris, 1917; see also D. Wiebenson, *Tony Garnier: the Cité Industrielle*, New York, 1969.
245 Tafuri and Dal Co: *Modern Architecture*, p. 110.
246 Catherine Bauer: *Modern Housing*, Boston, 1934, p. 110.
Patrick Geddes: for sense of his planning ideas, *Cities in Evolution*, London, 1915.
246–8 Le Corbusier City Planning: see Le Corbusier, *Urbanisme*, Paris, 1925, translated as *The City of Tomorrow*, Cambridge, Mass., 1971; Norma Evanson, *The Machine and the Grand Design*, New York, 1969; Robert Fishman, *Urban Utopias in the Twentieth Century*, New York, 1977; P. Boudon, *Lived-in Architecture*, Cambridge, Mass., 1972; B. Taylor, *Le Corbusier at Pessac*, Cambridge, Mass., 1972; Anthony Vidler, 'The Idea of Unity and Le Corbusier's Urban Form', *Architects' Year Book 15*, 1968; Anthony Sutcliffe, 'A Vision of Utopia: Optimistic Foundations of Le Corbusier's doctrine d'urbanisme', in Walden, ed., *The Open Hand*, p. 216; Manfredo Tafuri, 'Machine et Mémoire: City in the Work of Le Corbusier', in H. Allen-Brooks, ed., *The Le Corbusier Archive*, New York and Paris, 1982, vol. 10; Curtis, *Le Corbusier: Ideas and Forms*, especially Chapters 5, 10.
248 Monastery: see Peter Serenyi, 'Le Corbusier, Fourier, and the Monastery of Ema', *Art Bulletin*, 49, 1967, pp. 277–86.
249 Frankfurt: see B. Miller-Lane, *Architecture and Politics in Germany, 1919–1945*, Cambridge, Mass., 1968, Tafuri and Dal Co, *Modern Architecture*, and G. Uhlig, 'Town Planning in the Weimar Republic', *Architectural Association Quarterly*, 11, no. 1, 1979, pp. 24ff.; V. Fischer et al., *Ernst May und das neue Frankfurt, 1925–1930*, 1986; H. Hirolina, ed., *Neues Bauen, neue Gesellschaft: das neue Frankfurt die neue Stadt. Eine Zeitschrift zwischen 1926–1933*, 1984.
251–2 Oud, housing: Hitchcock, *J.J.P. Oud*, Paris, 1931.
252 Soviet Urbanism: see Berthold Lubetkin, 'Recent Developments of Town-Planning in the USSR', *Architectural Review*, May 1932, pp. 215ff.; K. Frampton, 'Notes on Soviet Urbanism 1917–32', *Architects' Year Book*, 12, 1968, pp. 238–52. Manfredo Tafuri, M. de Michelis, J.L. Cohen, *URSS 1917–1978: la ville, l'architecture*, 1978; see also notes to Chapter 12.
El Lissitzky: *Russia: an Architecture for World Revolution*, London, 1970, p. 59.
253 N. A. Milyutin: *Socgorod, Problema Stroitel 'stva Socialisticskih Gorodov*, Moscow, 1930, translated as *Sotsgorod: the Problem of Building Socialist Cities*, Cambridge, Mass., 1974.

254 Karl Marx-Hof: Tafuri and Dal Co, *Modern Architecture*, p. 193.
C.I.A.M.: 'Declaration of Aims', La Sarraz, Switzerland, 1928; see Benton and Benton, *Architecture and Design*, for excerpts; also Benevelo, *History of Modern Architecture*, vol. 2, p. 497; and Martin Steinmann, *CIAM Dokumente 1928–1939*, Basle and Stuttgart, 1979.
255 Charter of Athens: see Benevelo, *History of Modern Architecture*, vol. 2, p. 539; for Gropius on high-rise dwellings see 'Flach, Mittel-oder Hochbau?', *Rationelle Behauungsweisen*, Stuttgart, 1931, p. 26. The doctrines of the Athens Charter later appeared as José Luis Sert, *Can Our Cities Survive?*, Cambridge, Mass., 1942.

chapter 15 the international style, the individual talent, and the myth of functionalism

257 Motto: Gombrich, *Art and Illusion*, London, 1960. For a penetrating essay on the notion of style, Meyer Schapiro, 'Style', *Anthropology Today*, ed. A. L. Kroeber, Chicago, 1953, p. 302.
Hitchcock and Johnson: *The International Style*, p. 19.
259 Weissenhofsiedlung: Karin Kirsch, *Die Weissenhofsiedlung, Werkbund-Austellung 'Die Wohnung' – Stuttgart 1927*, Stuttgart, 1987; also Pommer and Otto, *Weissenhof 1927*.
260–1 El Lissitzky: *Russia: an Architecture for a World Revolution*, London, 1970, p. 32.
261 Van Nelle: for Le Corbusier's panegyric see *Plans*, 12, February 1932, p. 40.
263 Kenneth Frampton: 'The Humanist versus the Utilitarian Ideal', *Architectural Design*, 38, 1968, pp. 134–6.
Hannes Meyer and Wittwer: Report on League of Nations Entry, cited by Frampton, 'The Humanist versus the Utilitarian Ideal'.
264 Le Corbusier: for his competition entry and its design process, see Werner Oechslin, ed., with a Foreword by Alfred Roth, *Le Corbusier und Pierre Jeanneret, Das Weltbewerbsprojekt für die Völkerbundspalast in Genf 1927*, Zurich, 1988.
Czechoslovakia: Gustav Peichl and Vladimir Slapeta, *Czech Functionalism 1918–1938*, 1987.
265 Eileen Gray: Peter Adam, *Eileen Gray: Architect Designer*, London, 1987; Brigitte Loye, *Eileen Gray 1879–1976*, Paris, 1984; for house E1027 see Colin St John Wilson, *The Other Tradition of Modern Architecture, the Uncompleted Project*, London, 1995, pp. 109ff.; also Jean Badovici, and Eileen Gray, 'Maison au bord de la Mer', special issue *Architecture Vivante*, 1929; for quote, see Joseph Rykwert, *The Necessity of Artifice*, London, 1982.
266 R. Buckminster Fuller: passage cited by Banham, *Theory and Design*, p. 325. See also R.W. Marks, *The Dymaxion World of Buckminster Fuller*, New York, 1960.
267 William Jordy: on 'objectivity' in *American Buildings and their Architects*, vol. 4, p. 182; by the same author, see 'The Symbolic Essence of Modern European Architecture of the Twenties and its

Continuing Influence', *Journal of the Society of Architectural Historians*, 22, October 1963, pp. 177–87. See also Le Corbusier, *Towards a New Architecture*, p. 187: 'By the use of inert materials and *starting from* conditions more or less utilitarian, you have established certain relationships which have aroused my emotions. This is Architecture.'
Rudolf Schindler: letter to Philip Johnson, 9 March 1932, cited in Sarnitz, *R.M. Schindler*, p. 209.
268 Maison de Verre: for a somewhat technocratic reading of the building, see Reyner Banham, *The Architecture of the Well-Tempered Environment*, London, 1969; see also Paul Nelson, 'Maison de Verre', *L'Architecture d'aujourdhui*, 9, 1933, pp. 11ff.; and Kenneth Frampton, 'Maison de Verre', *Perspecta 12*, 1969; Marc Vellay and Kenneth Frampton, *Pierre Chareau*, Paris, 1984; and Gérard Monnier, *L'Architecture en France, une histoire critique 1918–1950*, Paris, 1990, pp. 113ff.
270 Henri Focillon: *The Life of Forms in Art*, trans. G. Kubler, New York, 1958, p. 74.
271 Mies van der Rohe: the passage was written in 1928 but is clearly relevant to the Barcelona Pavilion, see 'Zum Thema Austellungen', *Die Form*, 121, 1928. For Schnitzler quote, see Wolf Tegethoff, *Mies van der Rohe, the Villas and Country Houses*, New York and Cambridge, Mass., p. 73, note 15; Tegethoff's researches have revealed much about the original social and physical context of the Barcelona Pavilion. See also J. Bier, 'Mies van der Rohe's Reichs pavilion in Barcelona', *Die Form*, August 1929, pp. 23–30. For analysis of critical and historical interpretations of the Barcelona Pavilion, see Juan Pablo Bonta, *Anatomia de la interpretacion in arquitectura: resegne semiotica de la critica de la Pabellon de Barcelona de Mies van der Rohe*, Barcelona, 1975. For four contrasting 'readings' of the building see: Banham, *Theory and Design*, pp. 321ff.; Steven K. Peterson, 'Idealized Space: Mies – Conception or Realized Truth?' *Inland Architect*, 21, no. 5, May 1977, pp. 4–11; José Quetglas, *Imagenes de Pabellon de Alemania, Mies van der Rohe*, Montreal, 1991; and Caroline Constant, 'The Barcelona Pavilion as Landscape Garden, Modernity and the Picturesque', *Architectural Association Files*, 20, 1990, pp. 47–54.
273 Mies van der Rohe, 'Baukunst und Zeitwille', *Der Querschnitt*, 4, 1924, pp. 31–2, translated as 'Architecture and the Times', Johnson, *Mies van der Rohe*, p. 191; for classical echoes in Mies see Chapter 8 and notes to Chapter 8; also William J. R. Curtis, 'Modern Transformations of Classicism', *Architectural Review*, August 1984.

chapter 16 the image and idea of le corbusier's villa savoye at poissy

275 Motto: Le Corbusier, *Towards a New Architecture*, p. 165. The basis of the interpretation given in this chapter was laid in Curtis, 'Le Corbusier: the Evolution of his Architectural Language and its Crystallization in the Villa Savoye at Poissy', in *Le Corbusier/English Architecture 1930s*, 1975.
279 Fresh Air: for one of Le Corbusier's own descriptions of the Villa Savoye, see *Précisions sur un état présent de l'architecture et de l'urbanisme*, Paris,

1930, pp. 136ff. 'Air circulates freely, light abounds and penetrates everywhere.'
280 Construction spirituelle: see Giedion, *Space, Time and Architecture*, 5th edn., 1967, p. 525.
281 Le Corbusier: Villa Savoye, *Oeuvre complète 1929–34*, p. 24.
Standards: Le Corbusier, *Towards a New Architecture*, p. 189.
282 Their idea: *Oeuvre complète 1929–34*, p. 24.
Design Process: see Tim Benton, 'Radiovision, Villa Savoye: Preliminary Drawings', Open University, 1975, and Max Risselada, 'Le Corbusier and Pierre Jeanneret, *Ontwerpen voor de woning 1919–1929*', exhibition catalogue, School of Architecture, Delft, 1980; see also Benton, *Les Villas de Le Corbusier 1920–1930*, Paris, 1984, pp. 191ff., for an attempt at reconstructing steps of the design.
284 Purist still life: see Banham, *Theory and Design*, p. 325. Referring to both the Barcelona Pavilion and the Villa Savoye, Banham suggested: 'Their status as masterpieces rests, as it does with most other masterpieces of architecture, upon the authority and felicity with which they give expression to a view of men in relation to their environment.'
285 Le Corbusier: *Towards a New Architecture*, p. 189.
Idealism, Rationalism: see Rowe, *The Mathematics of the Ideal Villa*; also P. Turner, 'The Beginnings of Le Corbusier's Education', *Art Bulletin*, June 1971; Curtis, *Le Corbusier: Ideas and Forms*, Chapter 5; and Curtis, *Le Corbusier/English Architecture 1930s*, pp. 38–40.

chapter 17 the continuity of older traditions

287 Motto: Reginald Blomfield, 'Is Modern Architecture on the Right Track?', *The Listener*, 10, 1933, p. 124.
Continuations of earlier traditions: it is to Hitchcock's credit that he included a chapter entitled 'Architecture Called Traditional in the Twentieth Century' in *Architecture 19th and 20th Centuries*. Instead of terms like 'traditionalism', 'revivalism', 'eclecticism', Hitchcock preferred the term 'historicism'. This he used in a special sense to mean 'the re–use of forms borrowed from the architectural styles of the past, usually in more or less new combinations', op. cit., p. 624, note 1.
Frank Lloyd Wright: 'In the Cause of Architecture', 1908, see note to motto to Chapter 7. For valuable essay on Wright's transformations of the past, see Vincent Scully, Introduction to Bolon, ed., *The Nature of Frank Lloyd Wright*, 1988, pp. xiiiff.
Le Corbusier: *Précisions*, p. 34 (see notes to Chapter 8). For essay on Le Corbusier's transformations, William J.R. Curtis, 'Le Corbusier: Nature and Tradition', *Le Corbusier Architect of the Century*, exhibition catalogue, Arts Council, London, 1987, pp. 13ff.; also Curtis, *Le Corbusier: Ideas and Forms*, 'Conclusion'.
Mies van der Rohe: see, for example, Colin Rowe, 'Neo-"Classicism" and Modern Architecture', in *The Mathematics of the Ideal Villa*, pp. 120ff.; see also notes

to Chapter 8.
288 'Traditional' architecture in Germany: see, for example, V. Magnago Lumpugnani and R. Schneider, *Moderne Architektur in Deutschland 1900 bis 1959. Reform und Tradition*, exhibition catalogue, Frankfurt, 1992.
289 Goetheanum: see, for example, Colin Wilson, *Rudolph Steiner, the Man and his Vision*, Wellingborough, 1985, especially pp. 125ff.; see also Rudolf Steiner, *Wege Zu einem neuen Baustil*, Dornach, 1926, and *Der Baugedanke des Goetheanum*, Dornach, 1932; for sketches of building see Hagen Biesante, Arne Klingberg, *Das Goetheanum,Der Bau-Impuls Rudolph Steiners*, Dornach, 1978.
290 Art Deco: see G. Veronesi, *Style and Design 1909–29*, New York, 1968; D. Gebhard, *The Richfield Building 1926–1928*, Los Angeles, 1970; Bevis Hillier, *Art Deco in the 1920s and 1930s*, London, 1968. For Guevrekian and The Garden of the Villa Noailles, see Dorothée Imbert, *The Modernist Garden in France*, New Haven and London, 1993, pp. 125ff.
292 Ralph Adams Cram: *My Life in Architecture*, Boston, 1936, pp. 126ff.; the ensemble of Rice Institute was designed by the New York and Boston firm of Cram, Goodhue and Ferguson, but while Goodhue may have been more responsible for the overall layout of the campus, Cram was responsible for the actual architectural expression; see Stephen Fox, *The General Plan of the William M. Rice Institute and its Architectural Development*, Architecture at Rice, Monograph 29, Houston, 1980; see also W. Kidney, *The Architecture of Choice, Eclecticism in America 1880–1930*, New York, 1974.
293 Lincoln Memorial: for details of the commission see US Office of Public Buildings and Public Parks of the National Capital, *The Lincoln Memorial, Washington, DC*, Washington, 1927; for a conservative view of late nineteenth-century and early twentieth-century American architecture, see Fiske Kimball, *American Architecture*, Indianapolis, 1928.
294 Goodhue, Lincoln State Capitol: aptly characterized by Hitchcock as 'an eclectic sort of semi-modernism … vaguely Byzantinesque', *Architecture, Nineteenth and Twentieth Centuries*; see also Richard Oliver, *Bertram Grosvenor Goodhue*, New York, 1983, p. 195. A perspective of the project was reproduced in W. Hegemann, *Neue Amerikanische Baukunst*, Berlin and Hamburg, 1926; for a non-avant-gardist perception of American architecture, see also Hegemann, *Amerikanische Architektur und Stadtbaukunst*, Berlin, 1925, and Hegemann and E. Peets, *The American Vitruvius: an Architects' Handbook of Civic Art*, New York, 1922. These 'traditionalist' 'versions' of the American city can be contrasted with those of modernists such as Richard Neutra, *Wie Baut Amerika?*, 1927, or Erich Mendelsohn, *Amerika Bilderbuch eines Architekten*, Berlin, 1926.
294–5 Plecnik: François Burkhardt, Claude Eveno, Boris Podrecca, eds., *Jozé Plecnik, Architect: 1872–1957*, Cambridge, Mass., 1989, especially essays by Prelovsek, 'The Life and Work of Jozé Plecnik', pp. 26ff.; and Vladimir Slapeta, 'Jozé Plecnik and Prague', pp. 82ff.
296 New Delhi: see Robert Grant Irving, *Indian Summer: Lutyens, Baker and Imperial India*, New

Haven and London, 1981; also Giles Tillotson, *The Tradition of Indian Architecture*, New Haven and London, 1989, and Robert Byron, 'New Delhi', *Architectural Review*, 49, Jan. 1931, pp. 1–30.

298 Garrison Church: one of the author's 'discoveries' in the course of extended visits and researches in India, 1980–8.

Ecclesiastical architecture: for German examples, see Walter Müller-Wulckow, *Architektur der zwanziger Jahre in Deutschland*, Leipzig, 1929, pp. 91ff.

299 Griffin: there is some risk in placing Griffin (and his partner and wife, Marion Mahony) in a Chapter entitled 'The Continuity of Earlier Traditions', but Newman College is one of the most effective transformations of Gothic in the early twentieth century. The Canberra project makes less overt use of the past, and relies upon a greater degree of abstraction, reminding one of the Chicago lineage stretching back through Wright to Sullivan. See James Birrell, *Walter Burley Griffin*, Brisbane, 1964, and David van Zanten, *Walter Burley Griffin, Selected Designs*, Palos Park, 1970.

300 Asplund, imagery: see S. Wrede, *The Architecture of Erik Gunnar Asplund*, Cambridge, Mass., 1979.

302 Blomfield: 'Is Modern Architecture on the Right Track?'. The fact that Blomfield identified modern architecture with 'functionalism' is not entirely his own fault. In Britain in the 1930s the functional and moral aspects of modern architecture were stressed by its supporters at the expense of formal and symbolic qualities. See, for example, the critical writings of N. Pevsner and J.M. Richards in this period, or F.R.S. Yorke, *The Modern House*, London, 1934.

chapter 18   nature and the machine, mies van der rohe, wright and le corbusier in the 1930s

305 Motto: Charles L'Eplattenier, 1906, cited by Le Corbusier, *L'Art décoratif d'aujourdhui*, Paris, 1925, p. 198; rather than 'nature' this chapter is, of course, concerned with artistic and philosophical conceptions of nature; see R.G. Collingwood, *The Idea of Nature*.

307 Lapidary clarity: the phrase is borrowed from Philip Johnson referring to Mies's prose, 'Epilogue: Thirty Years After', in Johnson, *Mies van der Rohe*, 1947, p. 209.

307–9 Tugendhat: useful information in W. Tegethoff, *Mies van der Rohe, the Villas and Country Houses*, pp. 90ff.; quotations from Fritz Tugendhat, Tegethoff, *Mies van der Rohe*, p. 98; Frampton, 'Modernism and Tradition in the Work of Mies van der Rohe, 1920–1968', *Mies Reconsidered*, pp. 35ff.

311 Nature, unity: Mies from: 'Talks with Mies van der Rohe', *L'architecture d'aujourd'hui*, 29, no. 79, September 1958, p. 100. For Mies's spiritual attitudes (and the possible influence upon him of theologian, philosopher Romano Guardini), see Fritz Neumeyer, *Mies van der Rohe: Das kunstlose Wort Gedanken zur Baukunst*, Berlin, 1986, p. 265.

Mies 1930s: for politics, see Richard Pommer, 'Mies van der Rohe and the Political Ideology of the Modern Movement in Architecture', in Schulze, ed., *Mies van*

der Rohe, Critical Essays, pp. 96ff.; Mies's reaction to Taliesin, a verbal recollection was made by William Wesley Peters over forty years later.

312 Edgar Kaufmann Jr.: 'Introduction' to D. Hoffmann, *Frank Lloyd Wright's Fallingwater, the House and its History*, New York, 1978; see also Bruno Zevi, 'Alois Riegl's Prophecy and Frank Lloyd Wright's Fallingwater', *l'Architettura*, August 1962, pp. 220–1; and William J.R. Curtis, 'Naturally Mechanical', *Times Literary Supplement*, 24 March 1989.

Frank Lloyd Wright, 'The Cardboard House', 1931; cited in Benton and Benton, *Architecture and Design*, p. 61.

313 Frank Lloyd Wright: cited by Olgivanna Lloyd Wright, *Frank Lloyd Wright: his Life, his Work, his Words*, New York, 1966, p. 159.

Frank Lloyd Wright, on rock ledges, 'The Meaning of Materials – Stone', *Architectural Record*, 63, April 1928, pp. 350, 356; see also note on 'Strata', Chapter 7 above.

Ralph Waldo Emerson: 'The Poet' (1844) in *Essays: Second Series, Complete Works*, Boston and New York, 1903, p.13.

314 Johnson Wax: for interpretation as 'institutional metaphor' see Norris Kelly Smith, *Frank Lloyd Wright: a Study in Architectural Content*, Englewood Cliffs, New Jersey, 1966; for detailed monograph, Jonathan Lipman, *Frank Lloyd Wright and the Johnson Wax Buildings*, New York, 1986.

316 Wright, prophet: Frank Lloyd Wright, 'Broadacre City, a New Community Plan', *Architectural Record*, 77, no. 4, April 1935, pp. 243–4; for flavour of Wright's urban thinking, see Wright, *The Disappearing City*, New York, 1932; also R. Fishman, *Urban Utopias in the Twentieth Century*, New York, 1977; for criticism of Broadacre, see Meyer Schapiro, 'Architects' Utopia', *Partisan Review*, 4, March 1938, pp. 42–7; see also S. Stillman, 'Comparing Wright and Le Corbusier', *American Institute of Architects Journal*, 9, April–May 1948, pp. 171–8, 226–33.

Eye, hand: Frank Lloyd Wright, *When Democracy Builds*, Chicago, 1945, p. 67; 'great city', cited Lionel March, 'An Architect in Search of Democracy', BBC talk, Jan. 1970, in H. Allen Brooks, ed., *Writings on Wright*, Cambridge, Mass., 1981, p. 202.

317 Usonian Houses: see J. Sergeant, *Frank Lloyd Wright's Usonian Houses: the Case for Organic Architecture*, New York, 1976.

317–18 Taliesin West: for two evocative and related interpretations, Vincent Scully, *Frank Lloyd Wright*, New York, 1960, p. 28; Neil Levine, 'Frank Lloyd Wright's Own Houses and his Changing Concepts of Representation' in Bolon, ed., *The Nature of Frank Lloyd Wright*, 1988, especially pp. 47ff.

319 Le Corbusier, 1930s: for two general treatments of changes, Peter Serenyi, 'Le Corbusier's Changing Attitude towards Form', *Journal of Society of Architectural Historians*, 24, March 1965, pp. 15–23; and Curtis, *Le Corbusier: Ideas and Forms*, Chapter 9.

320 Cité de Refuge: see Brian Taylor, *Le Corbusier, Cité de Refuge*, Paris, 1980; for climate problems, Reyner Banham, *the Architecture of the Well Tempered Environment*, London, 1969.

Natural order: Le Corbusier, *La Ville Radieuse*, Paris, 1935, p. 6.

321 Universal technology, local craftsmanship: see

below, notes to Chapter 21. pp. 377, 379.

Petite Maison: for male, female, Le Corbusier, *The Modulor*, Cambridge, Mass., 1954, p. 224; 'ironic grotto', Vincent Scully, 'Le Corbusier 1922–1965', *The Le Corbusier Archive*, vol. 2, p. xiii; see also Tim Benton, 'Six Houses', *Le Corbusier Architect of the Century*, exhibition catalogue, Arts Council, London, pp. 65–6.

322 Geometry, nature: see Stanislaus von Moos, 'Natur und Geometrie im Werk von Le Corbusier', *Kunstnachrichten*, 2, no. 6, March 1966.

Pavillon Suisse: for extensive discussion of design process and meaning see William J.R. Curtis, 'Ideas of Structure and the Structure of Ideas: Le Corbusier's Pavillon Suisse, 1930–1931', *Journal of Society of Architectural Historians*, 40, December 1981.

323 Urbanistic meaning of pilotis: see *Oeuvre complète 1929–34*, p. 84 for illustration; for individual buildings as urbanistic laboratories, p. 19. For 'à redent' housing, see Le Corbusier, *La Ville Radieuse*, Paris, 1935, p. 158.

Syndicalism and the Ville Radieuse: see Kenneth Frampton, 'The City of Dialectic', *Architectural Design*, 39, October 1969, pp. 515–46; also R. Fishman, *Urban Utopias in the Twentieth Century*, New York, 1977.

325 Reyner Banham: for CIAM doctrines and reactions against them see *The New Brutalism, Ethic or Aesthetic?*, New York, 1966, especially pp. 70ff.

Algiers: Stanislaus Von Moos, 'Von den Femmes d'Alger zum Plan Obus', *Archithèse*, 1, 1971, pp. 25–37; see also unpublished essay by Catherine J. Dean on the various Algiers schemes, their political context , and Le Corbusier's sensitivity to the pre-existing site and culture, MIT, School of Architecture, 1978; for a syndicalist reading of Algiers, see M. Macleod, 'Le Corbusier's Plans for Algiers 1930–1936', *Oppositions 16/17*, 1980.

326 Invention of brise-soleil, Le Corbusier, *Oeuvre complète 1938–46*, p. 103; see also Harris J. Sobin, 'Le Corbusier in North Africa: the Birth of the Brise-Soleil', *Desert Housing*, eds. K. Clark, P. Paglore, Phoenix, Arizona, pp. 155ff.; see also note on Baizeau, Chapter 12, above.

Manhattan: see William J.R. Curtis, 'Le Corbusier, Manhattan et le rêve de la ville radieuse', *Archithèse*, 17, 1976, pp. 23–8; also Le Corbusier, *When the Cathedrals Were White*, New York, 1947, the English translation of *Quand les cathédrales étaient blanches: voyage aux pays des timides*, Paris, 1937.

chapter 19   the spread of modern architecture to britain and scandinavia

329 Motto: Hitchcock, *The International Style*, Preface to 1966 edition, p. xiii.

330–1 Britain in the Thirties: H.R. Hitchcock and L.K. Bauer, *Modern Architecture in England*, exhibition catalogue, Museum of Modern Art, New York, 1937, New York; J.M. Richards, *An Introduction to Modern Architecture*, Harmondsworth, 1940; Anthony Jackson, *The Politics of Architecture, a History of Modern Architecture in Britain*, London, 1970; William J.R. Curtis, 'The Modern Movement in

England 1930–9; Thoughts on the Political Content and Associations of the International Style', in *Le Corbusier/English Architecture 1930s*, Milton Keynes, 1975. Tim and Charlotte Benton, 'Architecture, Contrasts of a Decade', *Thirties*, exhibition catalogue, London, 1979.

331 Royal Corinthian Yacht Club: see Rosemary Ind, *Emberton*, London and Berkeley, 1983, pp. 20–1.
Lubetkin: R. Furneaux Jordan, 'Lubetkin', *Architectural Review*, July 1955, pp. 36–44; William J.R. Curtis, 'Berthold Lubetkin or "Socialist" Architecture in the Diaspora', *Archithèse*, 12, 1974, pp. 42–8; Peter Coe and Malcolm Reading, *Lubetkin and Tecton: Architecture and Social Commitment*, exhibition catalogue, Bristol and London, 1981; John Allan, *Berthold Lubetkin, Architecture and the Tradition of Progress*, London, 1992.

333 Le Corbusier: 'The Vertical Garden City', *Architectural Review*, 79, January 1936, pp. 9–10.
Lawn Road: see Sherban Cantacuzino, *Wells Coates, a Monograph*, London 1978; and Laura Cohn, ed., *Wells Coates, Architect and Designer*, 1895–1958, Oxford, 1979.

334 Connell, Ward, Lucas: see *Architectural Association Journal*, November 1956, special issue.

336 J.M. Richards: 'The Condition of Modern Architecture and the Principle of Anonymity', in N. Gabo, J. L. Martin, B. Nicholson, eds., *Circle*, London, 1937.

337 High Point II: *Architectural Review*, 83, October 1938, pp. 161–4; also, Anthony Cox, 'High Point Two, North Hill, Highgate', *Focus*, 2, 1938, pp. 76–9.

338 Denmark: Knud Millech and Kay Fisker, *Danske arkitekturstømninger 1850–1950*, Copenhagen, 1951; for Jacobsen, Bellavista, Anne-Louise Sommer, *Arkitektur og Design*, Copenhagen, 1995, p. 109ff.

339 Asplund: see Caroline Constant, *The Woodland Cemetery: Toward a Spiritual Landscape*, Stockholm, 1994; also Stuart Wrede, *The Architecture of Erik Gunnar Asplund*, Cambridge, Mass., 1980 (who suggests a womb analogy for the main chapel, in the context of death as 'rebirth').

341 Bryggman: see Riitta Nikula, ed., *Erik Bryggman 1891–1951, Architect*, Helsinki, 1991, especially Nikula, 'Erik Bryggman and his Architecture', pp. 70ff.; and Janey Bennett, 'Sup Specie Aeternitatis, Erik Bryggman's Resurrection Chapel', ibid., pp. 243ff.

341–9 Aalto: for general treatments, see, for example, Giedion, *Space, Time and Architecture*, 4th edn; also Benevelo, *A History of Modern Architecture*, vol. 2, pp. 607ff.; Tafuri and Dal Co, in their *History of Modern Architecture*, are curiously dismissive of Aalto. For biography: Göran Schildt, *Alvar Aalto: The Early Years*, New York, 1984; *Alvar Aalto, The Decisive Years*, New York, 1986; *Alvar Aalto, The Mature Years*, New York, 1991; for general study, see Alvar Aalto, *The Complete Works*; also Aarne Ruusuvuori, Juhani Pallasmaa, eds., *Alvar Aalto 1898–1976*, exhibition catalogue, Museum of Finnish Architecture, Helsinki, 1981; and Göran Schildt, ed., *Alvar Aalto, Sketches*, Cambridge, Mass., 1978; Malcolm Quantrill, *Alvar Aalto, a Critical Study*, Helsinki, 1983; and Richard Weston, *Alvar Aalto*, London, 1995.

343 Viipuri: P. Morton Shand, 'Viipuri Library, Finland', *Architectural Review*, 1936, pp. 107–14; see also Richard Weston, *Alvar Aalto*, London, 1995; see also essays on Viipuri by Kristina Nivari, Simo Paavilainen, Sergei Kravchenzo, in Marjja-Riita Norri, ed., *Acanthus*, Helsinki, 1990, Museum of Finnish Architecture.

345 Paimio: see P. Morton Shand, 'Tuberculosis Sanatorium, Paimio, Finland', *Architectural Review*, September 1933, pp. 85–90; for influence of Duiker, P.D. Pearson, *Alvar Aalto and the International Style*, New York, 1978, p. 87.

346 Alvar Aalto: see essay entitled 'National Planning and Cultural Goals', 1949, for his reflections on nature, excerpt in Schildt, ed., *Alvar Aalto, Sketches*.

346–9 Villa Mairea: see Alvar Aalto, *Complete Works*, vol. 1, pp. 108–123, where architect states that 'the new building, according to the express desire of the clients, had to be a symbol of our times.' See also Juhani Pallasmaa, 'Image und Form – The Villa Mairea as a Cubist Collage', *Studio International*, 200, no. 1018, 1987, who has suggested another 'layer' of meaning to do with Japanese ideas of landscape.

chapter 20 totalitarian critiques of the modern movement

351 Motto: Adolf Hitler, 'Speech on Art', 11 September 1935, cited by R. Taylor, *The World in Stone, the Role of Architecture in National Socialist Ideology*, Berkeley, 1974, p. 31. For the totalitarian manipulation of the visual arts, see for example, *Art and Power: Europe under the Dictators 1930–45*, exhibition catalogue, Hayward Gallery, London, 1995.

352 Bauhaus Criticisms: see B. Miller-Lane, *Architecture and Politics in Germany 1919–1945*, Cambridge, Mass., 1968, p. 69ff.
Anti-Semitism: see, for example, P. Schultze-Naumburg, *Kunst und Rasse*, Munich, 1929: for Bolshevist innuendoes see Alexander von Senger, *Krisis der Architektur*, Zurich, 1928.

353 Adolf Hitler: speech delivered 1 September 1933, published in Hitler, *Die deutsche Kunst als stolzeste Verteidigung des deutschen Volkes*, Munich, 1934. For a particular view of architectural tendencies in Germany in this period, see Philip Johnson, 'Architecture in the Third Reich', *Hound and Horn 7*, October–December, 1933, pp. 137–9.
Mies: for the Reichsbank competition, see Winfried Nerdinger, 'Versuchung und Dilemma des Avantgarde im Spiegel der Architekturwettbewerbe 1933–1935', in Hartmut Frank, ed., *Faschistische Architekturen, Planen und Bauen in Europa 1930 bis 1945*, Hamburg, 1985, pp. 65–73. See also, Richard Pommer, 'Mies van der Rohe and the Political Ideology of the Modern Movement in Architecture', in Schulze, ed., *Mies van der Rohe, Critical Essays*, pp. 118ff. For the ideological range of modernism in Germany, see Jeffrey Herf, *Reactionary Modernism: Technology, Culture and Politics in Weimar and the Third Reich*, Cambridge, 1984; for the ideological range of traditionalism in Germany, Vittorio Magnago Lampugnani and R. Schneider, *Moderne Architektur in Deutschland 1900 bis 1959. Reform und Tradition*, Frankfurt, 1992.

354 Linz: Hitler's interest in architecture is already evident in *Mein Kampf* (1925); an early sketch project of his for a triumphal arch at the entry of Linz was transposed into his and Speer's grand plan for Berlin at the end of the 1930s (see fig. 437).
Half-baked art history: see Taylor, *The Word in Stone*, pp. 83ff.; also *Art and Power*. In 1937 two exhibitions were staged in Troost's newly completed House of German Art in Munich: one on 'Degenerate Art' (including modern painters like Paul Klee); one on 'Great German Art'.

355 Speer: for his own version of events see Albert Speer, *Inside the Third Reich*, New York, 1970.

357 Regionalism: the intention was to follow local styles and patterns of building. Roofs of different angles and depths of eaves reinforced the message of the 'homeland' in contrast to the 'internationalist' flat roof which was portrayed as a foreign, rootless import.

358 Soviet Union in 1930s: see Anatole Kopp, *L'architecture de la périod stalinienne*, Grenoble, 1978. For the reaction against the avant-garde and the reuse of classicism see the retrospective analysis of the Palace of the Soviets Competition by M.P. Tsapenko, *O Realisticheskykh Osnovakh Sovietskoi Arkhitektury*, Moscow, 1952, pp. 73ff. The Committee in charge announced on 28 February 1932 that 'both new techniques and the best methods of "Classical" architecture should be employed henceforth'.

359 Official criticism of avant-garde: registered by Vzik, the Central Executive Committee of the Communist Party, 1930, cited by Lubetkin, 'Recent Developments of Town-planning in the USSR', *Architectural Review*, May 1932; see also *Art and Power*.

360 Mussolini and Town-Planning: see Spiro Kostoff, *The Third Rome*, Berkeley, 1977. For general discussions of Italian architecture in the Fascist period, see Benevelo, *History of Modern Architecture*, pp. 561ff.; Tafuri and Dal Co, *Modern Architecture*; Richard Etlin, *Modernism in Italian Architecture 1890–1940*, Cambridge, Mass., 1991; and Dennis Doordan, *Building Modern Italy: Italian Architecture 1914–1936*, New York, 1988; and the crucial Cesare de Seta, *La cultura architettonica in Italia tra le due guerre*, Bari, 1972.
Mediterranean: Sarfatti was a close confidante of Mussolini; at the second Novecento exhibition of 1929 she wrote of 'the attempt to arrive at a formula to mediate between the traditional and the modern'.

361 Classicisms: Giorgio Ciucci, 'Italian Architecture During the Fascist Period: Classicism between Neoclassicism and Rationalism: the Many Souls of the Classical', *The Harvard Architectural Review*, 6, 1988, pp. 77ff.; see also Ciucci, 'The Classicism of the E42: Between Modernity and Tradition', *Assemblage*, 8, 1989, pp. 79–87.

362 Gruppo 7: see 'Architettura' in *Rassegna italiana*, December 1926. One of the Group's pronouncements was: 'That the new architecture could be compared with that of the distant past'. See also A. Sartoris, *Gli elementi dell'architettura funzionale*, Milan, 1932, and Silvia Danesi and Luciano Patetta, *Rationalisme et architecture en Italie 1919–1943*, Venice, 1976.
Libera: V. Quilici, 'Adalberto Libera', *Lotus*, 16, 1977, pp. 55–8; see also Francesco Garofalo and Luca Veresani, *Adalberto Libera*, New York, 1992.

363–9 Terragni: only a selection can be mentioned :

Alberto Sartoris and Mario Radice et al., *Ritratto di Giuseppe Terragni*, Como, 1949 (first retrospective catalogue); Panos Koulermos, 'The Work of Lingeri, Terragni, and Italian Rationalism', *Architectural Design*, March 1963; Enrico Mantero, *Giuseppe Terragni e la città del razionalismo italiano*, Bari, 1969; Bruno Zevi, *Giuseppe Terragni*, Bologna, 1980; Daniel Vitale, 'An Analytic Excavation: Ancient and Modern, Abstraction and Formalism in the Work of Giuseppe Terragni', *9H7*, 1985, pp. 5–24; Thomas L. Schumacher, *Surface and Symbol, Giuseppe Terragni and the Architecture of Italian Rationalism*, New York, 1990.

364 Casa del Fascio: for Terragni quotation see Thomas Schumacher, 'From Gruppo 7 to the Danteum: a Critical Introduction to Terragni's Relazione sul Danteum', *Oppositions*, 9, 1977, p. 92.; for political iconography, see Diane Ghirardo, 'Politics of a Masterpiece: The "Vicenda" of the Decoration of the Façade of the Casa del Fascio, Como, 1936–39', *Art Bulletin*, 62, no. 3, 1980, pp. 466–78; for an abstract reading of Terragni, Peter Eisenman, 'From Object to Relationship', *Casabella*, 344, Jan. 1970, pp. 38–41, also *Perspecta 13/14*, 1971.

366 Le Corbusier: 'une maison – un palais', *Précisions*, p. 159.

368–9 Danteum: for analysis of Terragni's intentions in his 'Relazione sul Danteum', see Schumacher, 'From Gruppo 7', pp. 92–105; and Schumacher, *Surface and Symbol*, pp. 192ff.

chapter 21   international, national, regional: the diversity of a new tradition

371 Motto: Paul Frankl, *Principles of Architectural History*, trans. James O'Gorman, Cambridge, Mass., 1968, p. 190; translated from Frankl's work on the Renaissance and Post-Renaissance, *Die Entwicklungsphasen der neuren Baukunst*, Stuttgart, 1914.

Early historians: see Bibliographical Note p. 690; also Ludwig Hilberseimer, *Internationale neue Baukunst*, Dessau, 1927; Gustav Platz, *Baukunst der neusten Zeit*, Berlin, 1927; Walter C. Behrendt, *Der Sieg des neuen Baustils*, Stuttgart, 1927; Bruno Taut, *Die neue Baukunst in Europa und Amerika*, Stuttgart, 1929; Sigfried Giedion, *Bauen in Frankreich*, Leipzig, 1928. For a reflection on early historical formulations, see Werner Oechslin, 'A Cultural History of Modern Architecture 2, Modern Architecture and the Pitfalls of Codification: the Aesthetic View', *A + U*, Tokyo, June 1990, pp. 29–38.

372 Giedion, determinism: for two overstated critiques, Norris Kelly Smith, *On Art and Architecture in the Modern World*, Victoria, B.C., 1971; and David Watkin, *Morality and Architecture*, Oxford, 1977; for reflection on Giedion's assumptions, Werner Oechslin, 'Fragen um Sigfried Giedion's kunsthistorichen Prämissen', in catalogue, *Sigfried Giedion 1888–1968. Der Entwurf einer modernen Tradition*, Zurich, 1989, pp. 191ff.; for problem of determinism in historiography, see E.H. Gombrich, 'In Search of Cultural History', in *Ideals and Idols*, Oxford, 1979.

Modern forms, regional cultures: on the problem of the emergence of a new formal system crossing frontiers see, for example, Oleg Grabar, *The Formation of Islamic Art*, New Haven and London, 1973, p. 2: 'It would be like a special overlay, a deforming or refracting prism which transformed, at times temporarily and imperfectly, at other times permanently some local energies or traditions.'

372–4 Switzerland: see, for example, Max Bill, *Moderne Schweizer Architektur 1925–1949*, Basle, 1949; G.E. Kidder Smith, *Switzerland Builds*, London and New York, 1950; and Jacques Gubler, *Nationalisme et internationalisme dans l'architecture moderne de la Suisse*, Lausanne, 1975.

373 Alfred Roth: *Die neue Architektur. La Nouvelle Architecture. The New Architecture*, Zurich, 1940.

374 Mundaneum, Lac Léman, see Le Corbusier, *Précisions*, p. 50; also Dorothée Imbert, *The Modernist Garden in France*, New Haven and London, pp. 174ff.

374–5 Engineering: see David P. Billington, *Robert Maillart's Bridges, the Art of Engineering*, Princeton, 1979; Nervi quotation, Pier Luigi Nervi, *Aesthetics and Technology in Building*, trans. Robert Einaudi, Cambridge, Mass., 1965, p. 25; Torroja, *The Structures of Eduardo Torroja: an Autobiography of Engineering Accomplishment*, New York, 1958. For the notion of different national cultures of engineering, see Billington, *The Tower and the Bridge*, Chapter 10, 'Roof Vaults and National Styles'.

376 France 1930s, for analysis of the varying social roles of architecture, Gérard Monnier, *L'Architecture en France, une Histoire Critique, 1918–1950, architecture, culture, modernité*, Paris, 1990; see also Pierre et Robert Joly, *L'Architecte André Lurçat*, Paris, 1995; and Jean-Louis Cohen, *André Lurçat, autocritique d'une moderne*, Mardaga, 1995.

377 Le Corbusier, 'universal' technology and vernacular: see for example Bruno Reichlin, '"Cette Belle Pierre de Provence". La Villa de Mandrot', *Le Corbusier et La Méditerranée*, exhibition catalogue, Marseilles, 1987, p. 131.

Nelson: Pavillon de Chirurgerie, Hôpital à Ismailia, Compagnie du Canal de Suez, 1936; for isometric drawing of this remarkable unbuilt project (a tropical cousin of the Maison de Verre), see Monnier, op. cit., p. 163; see also, Terence Riley and Joseph Abram, eds., *The Filter of Reason, Work of Paul Nelson*, exhibition catalogue, Columbia University, New York, 1990.

Le Corbusier: *Oeuvre complète 1938–46*, p. 116.

378 Casa Malaparte, for an interpretation which credits the client Curzio Malaparte with a major role in the genesis of the design, see Marida Talamona, *Casa Malaparte*, Milan, 1990; for a review of arguments concerning the attribution of the house, Jean-Paul Robert, 'Cap Malaparte', *L'Architecture d'aujourdhui*, 289, October, 1993, pp. 117ff.

379 Spain, see Oriol Bohigas and Carlos Flores, *Arquitectura espanola de la Segunda Republica*, Barcelona, 1970; also Edgardo Mannino and Ignacio Paricio, *J.L. Sert: construccion y arquitectura*, Barcelona, 1983, especially for combination of local and more general construction techniques.

379 1937 Pavilion, Spanish Republic: see Catherine B. Freedberg, *The Spanish Pavilion at the Paris World's Fair of 1937*, New York, 1986; also *Pabellon Espanol, Exposicion International de Paris, 1937*, exhibition

catalogue, Ministry of Culture and Centro de Arte Reina Sofia, Madrid, 1987, especially pp. 40ff., for Sert's intentions and his notion of a meridional architecture.

380 Pikionis, see *Dimitris Pikionis, Architect 1887–1968, a Sentimental Topography*, exhibition catalogue, Architectural Association, London, 1989.

381 Fathy, see Hassan Fathy, *Architecture for the Poor, an Experiment in Rural Egypt*, Chicago, 1973, for essence of his building philosophy; and J.M. Richards, I. Serageldin, D. Rastorfer, *Hassan Fathy*, Singapore and London, 1985, for a reading in terms of Islamic identity which does not do enough to explain the role of Egyptian nationalism in Fathy's thinking.

Sedad Hakki Eldem: 'Milli Mimari Meselesi', *Arkitekt*, 1939, p. 220; for Eldem's formulation of a 'national architecture', see Sibel Bozdogan, 'Modernity in Tradition, Works of Sedad Hakki Eldem', in Suha Ozkan, ed., *Sedad Eldem, Architect in Turkey*, Singapore and New York, 1987, pp. 61ff.

381–4 Palestine, see Julius Posener, 'Traditionelles und modernes Bauen in Palastina', *Das Werk*, 1938, p. 257; Michael Levin, *White City, International Style Architecture in Israel*, Tel Aviv, 1984; Winfried Nerdinger, ed., *Tel Aviv neues Bauen 1930–1939*, Tubingen, 1993.

384 Mendelsohn, Middle East, see Ita Heinze-Greenberg, 'Erich Mendelsohn in Palestine, the Search of Architectural Roots', and Gilbert Herbert, 'The Divided Heart: Erich Mendelsohn and the Zionist Dream', in *Erich Mendelsohn in Palestine*, Technion exhibition catalogue, Haifa, 1987; for Mendelsohn quotation, see Heinze-Greenberg, p. 7; my reading of Hadassah has also been reinforced by Mendelsohn's remarkable essay on his vision of the future for the Eastern Mediterranean, *Palestine and the World of Tomorrow*, Jerusalem, 1940.

Rex Martienssen: *The Idea of Space in Greek Architecture*, Johannesburg, 1956; see also Gilbert Herbert, *Martienssen and the International Style: the Modern Movement in South African Architecture*, Cape Town, 1975; and Gilbert Herbert, 'Le Corbusier and the South African Modern Movement', *Architectural Association Quarterly*, Winter 1972, pp. 16ff.

385 Japan: see Bruno Taut, *Grundlinien japanischer Architektur*, Tokyo, 1935, translated the same year as *Fundamentals of Japanese Architecture*; see also Arthur Drexler, *The Architecture of Japan*, New York, 1955; and D.B. Stewart, *The Making of a Modern Japanese Architecture 1868 to the Present*, Tokyo, 1987.

386 Antonin Raymond: 'An Architect Comes Home from Japan', *Architectural Forum*, February 1939, p. 129; for Golconde also Malay Chatterjee, 'The Evolution of Contemporary Indian Architecture', in Jean-Louis Véret, ed., *Architecture in India*, Festival of India exhibition catalogue, Paris, 1985, pp. 124ff.

386–9 Brazil: for cultural background, see Henrique E. Mindlin, *Modern Architecture in Brazil*, Amsterdam, 1956; for review of work then recent, Philip Goodwin, *Brazil Builds*, New York, 1943.

389 Niemeyer, see Stamo Papadaki, *The Work of Oscar Niemeyer*, New York, 1950; the statement on curves is cited Peter Buchanan, 'Formas flotantes, espacios fluidos, La poética de Oscar Niemeyer', *Arquitectura y vivienda*, 13, 1988, pp. 28ff.

389–91 Mexico, see I.E. Meyer, *Mexico's Modern*

Architecture, New York, 1952; Emilio Ambasz, *The Architecture of Luis Barragán*, New York, 1976; Louise Noelle Mereles, 'Precursores de La Arquitectura Contemporánea Mexicana', *Discurso de Ingreso a la Academia de Artes*, Mexico, 1993.

chapter 22   modern architecture
in the usa: immigration and
consolidation

395 Motto: for Giedion on tradition see *Architecture You and Me*, Cambridge, Mass., 1958. For overview of the decade and a half after the Second World War: Giedion's and Benevelo's fragmentary accounts are filled out somewhat by J. Jacobus, *Twentieth Century Architecture: the Middle Years 1940–65*, New York, 1966, and J. Joedicke, *Architecture since 1945*, London and Stuttgart, 1969. Drew's *Third Generation* is useful for some aspects of the 1960s. Otherwise the series, *New Directions in Architecture*, published by Braziller, New York, in the late 1960s (e.g., *New Directions in Swiss Architecture … in British Architecture … in Italian Architecture*, etc.), is most useful. See also G.E. Kidder Smith, *The New Architecture of Europe*, New York, 1961. For competent résumés close in time to their subjects, see Hatje, *Encyclopedia of Modern Architecture*.
397 Gropius and Breuer in America: see particularly Giedion, *Space, Time and Architecture*, vol. 4; also William J.R. Curtis, *Boston: Forty Years of Modern Architecture*, exhibition catalogue, Institute of Contemporary Arts, Boston, 1980; for discussion of diaspora see William Jordy, 'Aftermath of the Bauhaus: Mies, Gropius and Breuer', in Bernard Bailyn and Donald Fleming, eds., *The Atlantic Migration*, Cambridge, Mass., 1964; and Jordy, *American Buildings and their Architects*, vol. 4 for Breuer's problems of transplanting modern architectural ideas from Europe to America.
397–8 Harvard: among those to study under Gropius in his early years as a teacher were Barnes, Rudolph, Johnson, and Pei. The version of modern architecture they absorbed was somewhat puritanical; for a polemical assessment, Klaus Herdeg, *The Decorated Diagram, Harvard Architecture and the Failure of the Bauhaus Legacy*, Cambridge, Mass., 1983.
399 1950s USA: see Ian McCallum, *Architecture USA*, New York and London, 1959.
400 Saarinen, Eliel, Churches: see Hitchcock, *Architecture: Nineteenth and Twentieth Centuries*, p. 486; also Eliel Saarinen, *Search for Form*, New York, 1949; and Albert Christ-Janer, *Eliel Saarinen*, Chicago, 1949.
400–1 Saarinen, Eero: see A. Temko, *Eero Saarinen*, New York, 1962.
401 Mies van der Rohe: see notes to Chapters 8, 11, 18; for general treatment, Peter Blake, *The Master Builders: Le Corbusier, Mies van der Rohe, Frank Lloyd Wright*, New York, 1960; and Peter Carter, *Mies van der Rohe at Work*, New York, 1974; for his teaching activities and influence at IIT, Alfred Swenson and Pao-Chi Chang, *Architectural Education at IIT 1938–1978*, Chicago, 1980; see Franz Schulze, *Mies van der Rohe, a Critical Biography*, Chicago, 1985,

especially Chapter 8, 'America: The Triumph of Steel and Glass, 1949–58', pp. 239ff.
402–3 Mies and classicism, see Colin Rowe, 'Neo-"Classicism" and Modern Architecture', *Oppositions 1, 2*, republished *The Mathematics of the Ideal Villa*, pp. 120–56; see also notes to Chapter 8 above.
403 Machine, garden: see Leo Marx, *The Machine in the Garden, Technology and the Pastoral Ideal in America*, New York, 1964.
Colin Rowe: 'Introduction', *Five Architects*, New York, 1975.
405 Eames and Case-Study Houses: see Esther McCoy, *Case-Study Houses 1945–1962*, Los Angeles, 1977, 2nd edn., pp. 54ff., see also James Steele, *Eames House, Charles and Ray Eames* (Architecture in Detail), London, 1994; and David Dunster, ed., *Key Buildings in the Twentieth Century*, vol. 2, *Houses: 1945–1989*, London, 1990.
406 Belluschi, see *Architectural Forum*, September 1948, pp. 97–106; also Walter Creese, 'The Equitable Revisited', *Architectural Forum*, June 1968, pp. 40–5; Belluschi himself traced the idea for the Equitable to one of his earlier projects of 1943, see Belluschi '194X', *Architectural Forum*, May 1943, pp. 108–12.
Lake Shore: see Jordy, 'The Laconic Splendor of the Metal Frame: Ludwig Mies van der Rohe's 860 Lake Shore Apartments and his Seagram Building', *American Buildings and their Architects*, vol. 4, pp. 221ff.; for quotation, Colin Rowe, 'Chicago Frame', *Architectural Review*, 1956, republished *The Mathematics of the Ideal Villa*, pp. 90ff.; for 'I' beams, Peter Carter, 'Mies van der Rohe: an Appreciation on the Occasion, this Month, of his 75th Birthday', *Architectural Design*, March 1961, p. 108; also Thomas H. Beeby, 'Vitruvius Americanus, Mies's Ornament', *Inland Architect*, 21, May 1977, pp. 12–15; see also Kenneth Frampton, *Case Studies in Tectonic Culture: the Poetics of Construction in the Nineteenth and Twentieth Centuries*, Cambridge, Mass., 1995.
407 Mies van der Rohe: 'Prologue' to Werner Blaser, *Mies van der Rohe, the Art of Structure*, New York, 1965.
409 Seagram: see Lewis Mumford, 'Skyline: the Lesson of the Master', *The New Yorker*, 34, 13 September 1958, p. 141; also William J.R. Curtis, 'Der Wolkenkratzer – Realität and Utopie', *Die zwanziger Jahre Kontraste eines Jahrzehnts*, Zurich, 1973, pp. 44–7; for Muthesius quote, see note to page 100.
Imitations of Mies: For American construction, James Marston Fitch, *American Building: the Forces that Shape it*, Boston, 1948. For polemical treatment of the problem of devaluation of Mies, Stanley Tigerman, 'Mies van der Rohe and his Disciples, or the American Architectural Text and its Reading', in *Mies Reconsidered: his Career, Legacy, and Disciples*, pp. 99ff.; see also James Ingo Freed interviewed by Franz Schulze, 'Mies in America', in Schulze, ed., *Mies van der Rohe, Critical Essays*, New York, 1989, pp. 172ff.; and Denys Lasdun and John H.V. Davies, 'Thoughts in Progress: Detail', published anonymously, *Architectural Design*, September 1957; for theoretical aspects of replication, see Françoise Choay, *La règle et le modèle*, Paris, 1980.
410 Lever House, air conditioning: see Banham, *The Architecture of the Well-Tempered Environment*, London, 1969, pp. 226ff.

UN: see Le Corbusier, *UN Headquarters*, New York, 1947; also Victoria Newhouse, *Wallace K. Harrison*, New York, 1989; see also George Dudley, 'Le Corbusier's Notebook Gives Clues to the United Nations Design', *Architecture*, September 1985, p. 40.
412 Modulor: Le Corbusier, *Modulor*, Paris, 1948; translated as *The Modulor*, Cambridge, Mass., 1954; *Modulor 2*, Paris, 1955. See also Peter Collins, 'Modulor', *Architectural Review*, 116, July 1954, pp. 5–8; Rudolf Wittkower, 'Le Corbusier's Modulor', *Four Great Makers of Modern Architecture*, New York, 1970, pp. 196–204.
Wright, Price Tower: see N.K. Smith, *Frank Lloyd Wright*, for metaphorical interpretation; see also *Frank Lloyd Wright, The Story of the Tower*, New York, 1956.
413 Guggenheim: for Wright's own statement of intention, *Solomon R. Guggenheim Museum* (brochure pull-out); for detailed analysis see Jordy, 'The Encompassing Environment of Free-Form Architecture: Frank Lloyd Wright's Guggenheim Museum', *American Buildings and their Architects*, vol. 4, pp. 279ff.; for Wright's unbuilt spiral ramp scheme of 1925, see Mark Reinberger, 'The Sugarloaf Mountain Project and Frank Lloyd Wright's Vision of a New World', *Journal of Society of Architectural Historians*, March 1984, pp. 38ff.; for the theme of continuity, Edgar Kaufmann, Jr., 'Frank Lloyd Wright: Plasticity, Continuity, and Ornament', *9 Commentaries on Frank Lloyd Wright*, New York, 1989, pp. 119ff.
414 Frank Lloyd Wright: in *Solomon R. Guggenheim Museum*.
415 Wright, space: quotation refers to Unity Temple, *Autobiography*, New York, 1932, pp. 138ff. For Lao Tze, see Wright, *An Organic Architecture: the Architecture of Democracy*, London, 1939, p. 30; for metaphorical reading in terms of 'immurement in the ideal hollow, and … the conquest of time itself through the use of the continuous spiral', see Scully, *Frank Lloyd Wright*, p. 30; for discussion of vase analogy, Jordy, op. cit., and Neil Levine, 'Frank Lloyd Wright's Own Houses and his Changing Concepts of Representation', in Bolon, ed., *The Nature of Frank Lloyd Wright*, pp. 20ff. There can be little doubt that Wright was also aware of Le Corbusier's concepts for spiralling museums, and of ancient prototypes such as the 'Caracol' at Chichen-Itza.

chapter 23   form and meaning in
the late works of le corbusier

417 Motto: Henri Focillon, *The Life of Forms in Art*, trans., G. Kubler, C. Hogan, New York, 1958, p. 74.
Surrealism: arguably the totemic fascinations of the Surrealists influenced the primitivism already visible in Le Corbusier's paintings and buildings of the 1930s. One suspects that his interests in multiple meanings and hermetic erotic references may be related too. For the invention of the bizarre 'Ubu' sculptures, see Le Corbusier, *New World of Space*, New York, 1948, p. 23.
417–19 Le Corbusier, late works: see William J.R. Curtis, '"Maturité", Le moderne et l'archaïque, ou les dernières oeuvres', in Jacques Lucan, ed., *Le Corbusier, une Encyclopédie*, Paris, 1987, pp. 246ff.; valuable primary material in *Le Corbusier Sketchbooks*,

Cambridge, Mass., and New York, 1981 (4 vols.); for a useful recollection, Jerzy Soltan, 'Working with Le Corbusier', in Brooks, ed., *The Le Corbusier Archive*, vol. 17, pp. ixff.

420 Pevsner, irrationality: see, for example, 'Nikolaus Pevsner on the Anti-Pioneers', *The Listener*, 29 December 1966.
James Stirling: 'Ronchamp: Le Corbusier's Chapel and the Crisis of Rationalism', *Architectural Review*, 119, March 1956, pp. 155–61. For patronage see Martin Purdy, 'Le Corbusier and the Theological Program', in Walden, ed., *The Open Hand*, p. 286.
421 Le Corbusier: *Oeuvre complète 1946–52*, p. 88.
Le Corbusier: *The Modulor*, Cambridge, Mass., 1954, p. 32. For influences on Ronchamp, see Von Moos, *Le Corbusier, Elemente einer Synthese*, p. 323; Danièle Pauly, *Ronchamp: lecture d'une architecture*, Paris, 1980; Peter Buchanan, 'La Caverne, L'horizon', in *La Méditerranée de Le Corbusier*, Marseilles, 1991.
423 La Tourette: see Serenyi, 'Le Corbusier, Fourier, and the Monastery of Ema', *Art Bulletin*, 1967. Purdy, 'Le Corbusier and the Theological Program'; Colin Rowe, 'Dominican Monastery of La Tourette, Eveux-sur-Arbresle, Lyons', *Architectural Review*, 129, 1961, pp. 400–1; Tim Benton, 'The Sacred and the Search for Myths', in *Le Corbusier Architect of the Century*, pp. 238ff.; and Peter Buchanan, 'La Tourette and Le Thoronet', *Architectural Review*, January 1987.
424 Ondulatoires: Le Corbusier, *Modulor 2*, pp. 321ff. for explanation of 'musical glazed panels'; see also Yannis Xenakis, 'The Monastery of La Tourette', in Brooks, ed., *The Le Corbusier Archive*, vol. 28, pp. ixff. for genesis of these elements and use of Modulor.
425 A. and P. Smithson: *Ordinariness and Light*, London, 1970, p. 169.
James Stirling: 'Garches to Jaoul: Le Corbusier as Domestic Architect in 1927 and 1953', *Architectural Review*, 118, 1955, pp. 145–51. For vault typologies, especially Roq and Rob, see Jean-Lucien Bonillo, 'L'Architecture est le site', *Le Corbusier et La Méditerranée de Le Corbusier*, Marseilles, 1987, pp. 143ff.
Second machine Age: for the epochal style of Le Corbusier's historical and social thinking and philosophy underlying his late works see William J.R. Curtis in Curtis and Sekler, ed., *Le Corbusier at Work*.
Sarabhai: for Ahmadabad patronage, Peter Serenyi, 'Timeless but of its Time: Le Corbusier's Architecture in India', *Perspecta*, 20, 1983; and Curtis, *Le Corbusier: Ideas and Forms*, Chapter 14.
426 Charles Correa, 'Chandigarh: the View from Benares', Brooks, ed., *The Le Corbusier Archive*, vol. 22, New York, 1983.
427 Millowners as little palace: letter, Le Corbusier to Mr Kaul (Secretary to President Nehru), 17 March 1953, Fondation Le Corbusier, Paris.
Chandigarh: for the broad principles of the urban layout see Norma Evenson, *Chandigarh*, Berkeley, 1966; for a sceptical analysis, Sten Nilsson, *The New Capitals of India, Pakistan and Bangladesh*, Lund, 1973; for housing and daily life, M. Sarin, 'Chandigarh as a Place to Live in', in Walden, ed., *The Open Hand*; for general context, Sunand Prasad, 'Le Corbusier in India', in *Le Corbusier Architect of the Century*, pp. 278ff.
428 Capitol and monuments: see William J.R. Curtis, 'Authenticity, Abstraction, and the Ancient

Sense: Le Corbusier and Louis Kahn's Ideas of Parliament', *Perspecta*, 20, 1983; Serenyi, 'Timeless but of its Time'; Curtis, 'The Ancient in the Modern' in Jean-Louis Véret, ed., *Architecture in India*, Festival of India exhibition catalogue, Paris, 1985, pp. 81ff.; and Pierre Riboulet, 'Concerning the Composition of the Capitol at Chandigarh', op. cit., pp. 91ff.; also Alexander Gorlin, 'An Analysis of the Governor's Palace at Chandigarh', *Oppositions 19/20*, New York, 1980.
429 Open Hand: see Patricia Sekler, 'Le Corbusier, Ruskin, the Tree and the Open Hand' and S. Von Moos, 'The Politics of the Open Hand: Notes on Le Corbusier and Nehru at Chandigarh', in Walden ed., *The Open Hand*, pp. 42ff. and 412ff. The Le Corbusier quotation is from a letter cited by Von Moos, note 65.
429–31 Parliament, Sources and Meaning: see Von Moos, 'The Politics of the Open Hand'; Curtis, 'The Ancient in the Modern'; also Curtis, 'Fragments of Invention', *The Sketchbooks of Le Corbusier*, Cambridge, Mass., 1981; also Curtis, *Le Corbusier: Ideas and Forms*, Chapter 13; see also notes to Chapter 1 above, 'Schinkel, Le Corbusier, typological pattern'.
433 Observatory, sun etc.: see Le Corbusier, *Oeuvre complète 1952–57*, p. 94; for Jantar Mantar, Le Corbusier Sketchbook E18, *Le Corbusier Sketchbooks*, vol. 2, p. 330.
Nehru: from the inauguration speech, 1963, see Von Moos, The 'Politics of the Open Hand'.
434 Venice: see Alan Colquhoun, 'Formal and Functional Interactions: a Study of Two Late Projects by Le Corbusier', *Architectural Design*, 36, May 1966, pp. 221–2.
434–5 Carpenter Center: see Curtis and Sekler, ed., *Le Corbusier at Work*, particularly Curtis, 'Descriptions of the Building', pp. 9–36, and 'History of the Design', pp. 37–226; and Sekler, 'The Carpenter Center in Le Corbusier's Oeuvre: an Assessment', pp. 229–60.
435 Le Corbusier: *Oeuvre complète 1957–65*, p. 54.

chapter 24   the unité d'habitation
at marseilles as a collective
housing prototype

437 Motto: George Kubler, *The Shape of Time*, New Haven and London, 1962, p. 33.
Unité: see Le Corbusier, *l'Unité d'Habitation de Marseille*, Souillac, 1950.
441 Lewis Mumford: The Sky Line: 'The Marseille "Folly"', *New Yorker*, 5 October 1957, pp. 76ff.
441–2 Influences and analogies: for ships see Von Moos, 'Wohnkollektiv, Hospiz und Dampfer', *Archithèse*, 12, 1971, pp. 30–41; for monasteries, see Serenyi, 'Le Corbusier, Fourier and the Monastery of Ema', *Art Bulletin*, 1967; for analogical thinking, Alan Colquhoun, 'Displacement of Concepts in Le Corbusier', *Architectural Design*, 43, April 1972, pp. 220–43; for prototypes, Reyner Banham, 'La Maison des hommes and la misère des villes: Le Corbusier and the Architecture of Mass Housing', and André Wogenscky, 'The Unité d'Habitation at Marseilles', both in H. Allen Brooks, ed., *Le Corbusier: the Garland Archive*; for overviews see Jacques Sbriglio, *L'Unité d'habitation de Marseille (Le Corbusier)*, Marseille,

1992, and David Jenkins, *Unité d'Habitation Marseilles, Le Corbusier*, (Architecture in Detail), London, 1993; see also Curtis, *Le Corbusier: Ideas and Forms*, Chapter 11, 'The Modulor, Marseilles and the Mediterranean Myth', pp. 162ff.
442 Béton Brut: see Curtis, in Curtis and Sekler, ed., *Le Corbusier at Work*, pp. 157ff., especially letter, cited p. 166, from Le Corbusier to J.L. Sert 26 June 1962 on Marseilles.
CIAM IX, Aix: for the importance of this meeting to the new, younger generation see Banham, *The New Brutalism*, p. 70.
443 Team X or Team Ten: see Alison Smithson, *Team 10 Primer*, London, 1968 for a collection of maxims and theories.
ATBAT: 'Atelier de Bâtisseurs'. The Moroccan housing envisaged courtyards in the air. The architects were aware that many of the future users would come from the south of the Atlas and therefore studied vernaculars from that region when preparing their design; for other housing sensitive to climate and culture in North Africa, see for example, Roland Simounet's Nouvelle agglomération, Timgad, Algeria, 1958–62. Simounet, 'Itineraire', *Werk, Bauen und Wohnen*, 6, Zurich, June 1981, pp. 30ff.
New Brutalism: evidently the term was invented before there were buildings to constitute a movement: see A. and P. Smithson, 'The New Brutalism', *Architectural Review*, April 1954, pp. 274–5; also Banham, *The New Brutalism*; for a sceptical analysis of the very notion of 'Brutalism' see Denys Lasdun and John H.V. Davies, 'Thoughts in Progress: the New Brutalism', published anonymously in *Architectural Design*, April 1957.
444 Alison and Peter Smithson: 'The Built World, Urban Re-Identification', first published *Architectural Design*, June 1955, then in *Ordinariness and Light*, London, 1976, pp. 105–6.
445 Clusters: see William J.R. Curtis, 'A Language and a Theme', in Denys Lasdun, ed., *A Language and a Theme, the Architecture of Denys Lasdun and Partners*, London, 1976, pp. 9ff.; also William J.R. Curtis, *Denys Lasdun: Architecture, City, Landscape*, London, 1994, pp. 47ff.; the Smithsons published an article entitled 'Cluster City – a New Shape for the community', in *Architectural Design*, 1957, some three years after Lasdun's first clusters.
446 Van Eyck: see J. Joedicke, ed., *CIAM '59 in Otterlo*, London, 1961; for a full flavour of his ideas, Smithson, *Team 10 Primer*.
Team X, place identity: see Kenneth Frampton, 'Des Vicissitudes de l'idéologie', *L'Architecture d'aujourd'hui*, 177, January–February 1975, pp. 62ff.; see also Jencks, *Modern Movements*, pp. 310ff.
447 Atelier 5: The architects were Erwin Fritz, Samuel Gerber, Rolf Hesterberg, Hans Hostettler, Niklaus Morgenthaler, Alfredo Pini; see also, J. Blumer, 'Modern Swiss Architecture since 1945', *Architects' Year Book 10*, London, 1962, pp. 143–5.
448 Urbino: see Lamberto Rossi, *Giancarlo de Carlo, Architettura*, Milan, 1988, pp. 65ff.; 'Urbino, Collegio delle Colle', in *Giancarlo De Carlo, Immagini e frammenti*, Catalogue of Milan Triennale, Milan, 1995, pp. 42ff.; also Giancarlo de Carlo, *Planificazione e disegno dell'università*, Venice, 1968.
Expo: Safdie's inspirations included not only

vernacular hill towns, but also the prototype of Le Corbusier's *immeubles villas* of 1922 (conversation with author, May 1992); see also, Safdie, *Beyond Habitat*, Cambridge, Mass., 1973.

Sert, Peabody Terraces: see Catherine J. Dean, 'The Design Process and Meaning of J.L. Sert's Peabody Terraces at Harvard', unpublished senior thesis, Harvard, 1976; also Knud Bastlund, *José Luis Sert*, New York, 1967, pp. 220–31; and Roger Sherwood, *Modern Housing Prototypes*, Cambridge, Mass., 1978, pp. 159ff.

450 Fleet Road: see *Architectural Design*, September 1967, pp. 423ff.; also Sherwood, *Modern Housing Prototypes*, pp. 66ff.

451 Lillington Street: see William J.R. Curtis, '"A Century Spanned": Lillington Street Housing, Pimlico by Darbourne and Darke', *Connoisseur*, May 1970, p. 45; for Gordon Cullen's ideas, see *Townscape*, London, 1966.

chapter 25   alvar aalto and scandinavian developments

453 Motto: Aldo Van Eyck, in Smithson, ed., *Team 10 Primer*, p. 9.

New Regionalism: see, for example, Sigfried Giedion, 'The New Regionalism', 1954, an essay published in *Architecture You and Me, Diary of a Development*, Cambridge, Mass., 1958, p. 138.

454 Aalto, Baker House: see Giedion, *Space, Time and Architecture*; also Curtis, *Boston Forty Years of Modern Architecture*, Boston, 1980; for sketches and hints at design process, see Marja-Riitta Norri, ed., *Viiva, Linjen, the Line, Original Drawings from the Alvar Aalto Archive*, Helsinki, 1993, pp. 56ff.

456 Karelian House: see Alvar Aalto, 'Karjalan rakennustaide', *Uusi Suomi*, 1941, translated in Goran Schildt, ed., tr. Stuart Wrede, *Alvar Aalto, Sketches*, Cambridge, Mass., 1978, p. 82. See also R. Glanville, 'Finnish Vernacular Farmhouses', *Architectural Association Quarterly*, 9, no. 1, 1977, pp. 36–52 for analysis of precinct forms in the Nordic vernacular; and George Baird's useful introduction to *Alvar Aalto*, London, 1970.

457 Säynätsalo: see William J.R. Curtis, 'The Idea of a Modern Tradition', in Maija Kärkäinen, ed., *Functionalism: Utopia or the Way Forward? The 5th International Alvar Aalto Symposium*, Jyväskylä, 1992; also Richard Weston, *Town Hall Säynätsalo, 1951, Alvar Aalto* (Architecture in Detail), London, 1992.

458 Levels of meaning: Hints at Aalto's intuitive approach to design are found in, for example, his own essay 'The Trout and the Mountain Stream' (1947), in Schildt, ed., *Alvar Aalto, Sketches*; See also Andres Duany, 'Principles in the Architecture of Alvar Aalto', *Harvard Architectural Review 3. Precedent and Invention*, New York, 1986, pp. 104–19.

460 Synthetic landscape: see fragment of text written by Alvar Aalto c. 1926 concerning Mantegna frescoes in Church of Eremitani, Padua, cited Goran Schildt, ed., *Alvar Aalto, The Decisive Years*, New York, 1986, pp. 11–13.

461 Delphi: see Schildt, ed., *Alvar Aalto, Sketches*, particularly ills. 9 and 11, drawn in 1953. Aalto seems

to have been preoccupied with earth-forms, platforms, steps and public places in Delphi. Analogous elements were used in many of his own civic schemes. Once again one finds a 'modern' architect returning to some of the most archaic roots of architecture.

462 Precise minimalism: see Scott Poole, 'The Construction of Silence', in *The New Finnish Architecture*, New York, 1992, pp. 28ff.; also Juhani Pallasmaa, '"Man, Measure and Proportion", Aulis Blomstedt and the Tradition of Pythagorean Harmonics', in *Focus*, Helsinki, 1992, pp. 5ff.

464 Jacobsen: J. Pedersen, *Arkitekten Arne Jacobsen*, Copenhagen, 1954; see also Tobias Faber, 'Jacobsen', in Hatje, ed., *Encyclopedia of Modern Architecture*, pp. 159ff.; and William J.R. Curtis, 'Arne Jacobsen, Minimalist Elegance', *Arquitectura y vivienda*, 55, 1995.

465 Louisiana: see P.E. Skriver, 'Contemporary Danish Architecture', *Architects' Year Book 10*, London, 1962; also Tobias Faber, *New Danish Architecture*, New York, 1968.

466 Utzon, Kingo, Fredensborg: see K. Helmer-Petersen, 'A Visit to Denmark: a New Personality, Jørn Utzon', *Zodiac*, 5, October 1957, pp. 80–5; also Sherwood, *Modern Housing Prototypes*, pp. 45ff.; and Tobias Faber, *Jørn Utzon, Houses in Fredensborg*, Berlin, 1991, which considers the influence of both Danish and Chinese farm courtyard prototypes.

Utzon, general: see for example, Giedion, 'Jørn Utzon, and the Third Generation', in 1967 edition of *Space, Time and Architecture*; also Jørn Utzon 'The Importance of Architects', in Denys Lasdun, ed., *Architecture in an Age of Scepticism*, London, 1984, pp. 214ff.; Utzon is an architect who evades categories, and who still awaits an appropriate historical assessment.

469 Platforms: see 'Platforms and Plateaux: Ideas of a Danish Architect', *Zodiac*, 10, Milan, 1962.

One Historian: Philip Drew, *The Third Generation: Changing Meaning in Architecture*, London, 1972.

Utzon: 'The Sydney Opera House', *Zodiac*, 14, Milan, 1965, p. 49.

chapter 26   disjunctions and continuities in the europe of the 1950s

471 Motto: Ernesto Nathan Rogers, 'Continuitá o crisi?', *Casabella-Continuità*, 215, April–May 1957.

472–3 Germany, 1950s: see G. Hatje, H. Hoffman, K. Kaspar, *New German Architecture*, London, 1956; Ulrich Conrads and W. Marshall, *Modern Architecture in Germany*, London, 1962; and Wolfgang Pehnt, 'Germany', in Hatje, ed., *Encyclopedia of Modern Architecture*, pp. 122ff.; see also Pehnt, 'Eiermann', in Hatje, ed., op.cit., pp. 89–90. For Scharoun, Peter Blundell Jones, *Hans Scharoun*, London, 1995 .

474–5 France, 1950s: for reconstruction, see Monnier, *Histoire critique de l'architecture en France*, pp. 353ff.; also Anatol Kopp, F. Boucher, Danièle Pauly, *L'Architecture de la reconstruction en France, 1945–53*, Paris, 1982; for historical perspective on earlier modernism, see Michel Ragon, *Le Livre de l'architecture moderne*, Paris, 1958; for Atelier de Montrouge, Christian Devillers, 'Les Dernières Puritains', *Architecture, mouvement et continuité*, 11,

April 1986; for Pouillon, see Fernand Pouillon, *Mémoires d'un architecte*, Paris, 1968; also Bernard Dubor, Jacques Lucan and Bernard Huet, *Fernand Pouillon*, Paris, 1986; for Prouvé, François Burkhardt, ed., *Jean Prouvé, constructeur*, CCI Pompidou exhibition catalogue, Paris, 1990; for Simounet, Devillers, 'Entrétien avec Roland Simounet', *Architecture, mouvement et continuité*, 8, May 1983, pp. 52–73; also Roland Simounet, 'Itinéraire', *Werk, Bauen und Wohnen*, 6, Zurich, June 1981, pp. 30ff.

476 Netherlands; see J.J. Vriend, *Nieuvere Architectuur*, Amsterdam, 1957, and *Algemeen Overzicht Architectuur van deze Eeuw*, Amsterdam, 1959; for traditionalist perspective, see G.M. Granpré Molière, *Woorden en Werken*, 1949; for views of Bakema and Van Eyck, see especially *Forum* magazine at end of 1950s and in 1960s.

477 Aldo Van Eyck, 'Labyrinthine Clarity', in John Donat, ed., *World Architecture 3*, London, 1966, pp. 121–2. For an overview of Dutch modern architecture, R. Blijstra, *Netherlands Architecture since 1900*, Amsterdam, 1960. For conception of a Dutch modern tradition, see Peter Buchanan, 'The Current Situation of a Man-made Land', *Arquitectura y vivienda*, 19, 1989; see also Hans Ibelings, *20th Century Architecture in the Netherlands*, Rotterdam, 1995.

Italy, post-war: see, for example, G.E. Kidder Smith, *Italy Builds*, London, 1955, and A. Pica, *Architettura italiana recente*, Milan, 1959. For discussion of different ideological positions (eg. neo-'Realism') see Manfredo Tafuri, *Storia dell'architettura italiana 1945–1985*, Turin, 1982. For Zevi's views, see *L'Architettura*, of which he was and is editor; also *Verso un'architettura organica*, Turin, 1945 (English translation, *Towards an Organic Architecture*, London, 1950); *Poetica dell'architettura neoplastica*, 1953; *Architecture as Space*, 1957; for Zevi's *Storia dell'architettura moderna*, 1950, see Bibliographical Note.

478 Ernesto Rogers: for his re-evaluation of the past while editor of *Casabella-Continuità* in the 1950s, see Montaner, *Después del movimiento moderno*, pp. 99ff.; for Reyner Banham attack, see 'Neoliberty: the Italian Retreat from Modern Architecture', *Architectural Review*, 125, April 1959, pp. 230–5.

480 Nervi: see Pier Luigi Nervi, *Scienze o arte del costruire?* Rome, 1945, also his later *Aesthetics and Technology in Building*, trans. R. Einaudi, Cambridge, Mass., 1965, for his views on intuition, rationality, tradition and invention.

481 Scarpa, Byzantium: cited by Giuseppe Zambonini, 'Process and Theme in the Work of Carlo Scarpa', *Perspecta*, 20, 1983, p. 22; for a useful monograph containing a catalogue of works and an anthology of critical reactions, see Francesco Dal Co and Giuseppe Mazzariol, eds., *Carlo Scarpa, The Complete Works*, Milan, 1984.

482 Pikionis: see *Dimitris Pikionis Architect 1887–1968, a Sentimental Topography*, London, 1989.

483 Portugal, Tavora: see Nuno Portas, 'Arquitecturas marginadas en Portugal', *Cuadernos summa – nueva vision*, 43, April 1970; interview with Fernando Tavora, *Arquitectura*, 261, 1986; also Kenneth Frampton, 'In Search of a Laconic Line: a Note on the School of Porto', in Kärkäinen, ed., *Architecture and Cultural Values, the Fourth*

International Alvar Aalto Symposium, Jyväskylä, 1988, pp. 100ff., see also Fernando Tavora, ed., *Arquitectura popular en Portugal*, 1961, a study of vernacular types.
Siza: see, for example, Peter Testa, *The Architecture of Alvaro Siza, Thresholds Working Paper 4*, Cambridge, Mass., MIT Dept. of Architecture, 1986; L. Beaudouin and C. Bousselot, 'Entretien avec Alvaro Siza', *Architecture, mouvement et continuité*, 44, 1978; for topographical abstraction and spatial concepts at basis of Siza's architectural language, see William J.R. Curtis, 'Alvaro Siza, una arquitectura de bordes. Alvaro Siza, an Architecture of Edges', *Alvaro Siza 1958–1994, El Croquis, 68/69*, Madrid, 1994; also Curtis, 'Alvaro Siza – paisajes urbanos', in *Alvaro Siza, obras y proyectos*, exhibition catalogue, CGAC, Madrid and Compostela, 1995.
484–9 Spain, 1940s and 1950s: see for example, Carlos Flores, *Arquitectura Espanola Contemporanea*, Madrid, 1960; Josep Maria Montaner, 'Espana', article in Spanish edition, Leonardo Benevelo, *Historia de la arquitectura moderna*, Barcelona, 1982, pp. 842ff.; 'Arquitectura para después de una guerra 1939–1949', exhibition catalogue, published *Cuadernos de arquitectura*, 121, January 1977; and Antón Capitel, *Articulos y ensayos breves 1976–1991*, Madrid, 1993.
484–6 Catalonia, Bohigas, Coderch: see A. Cirici Pellicer, *Arquitectura catalana*, Barcelona, 1974; Oriol Bohigas, *Polemica d'arquitectura catalana*, Barcelona, 1970; Carlos Fochs, ed., *Coderch 1913–1984*, Barcelona, 1989; V. Elio Pinon, 'Tres décadas en al obra de José Antonio Coderch', *Arquitecturas bis*, 11, January 1976; also Capitel, 'José Antonio Coderch, del mar a la ciudad', op. cit., pp. 133ff.; see also Alberto Sartoris, *Encyclopédie de l'architecture nouvelle: ordre et climat méditerranéens*, Milan, 1957.
486 Madrid housing: see Luis Fernandez-Galiano, Justo Isasi, Antonio Lopera, *La quimera moderna, los poblados dirigidos de Madrid en la arquitectura de los 50*, Madrid, 1989.
De la Sota: see Miguel Angel Baldellou, *Alejandro de la Sota*, Madrid, 1975; also, *Alejandro de la Sota*, Madrid, 1989; and Pedro de Llano, *Alejandro de la Sota, o nacemento dunha arquitectura*, Pontevedra, 1994.
487 Gobierno Civil, Tarragona: see William J.R. Curtis, '"Harmonic, hierarchical and noble": de la Sota's Civil Government Building in Tarragona', in Wolfgang Böhm, ed., *Das Bauwerk und die Stadt. The Building and the Town, Essays for Eduard F. Sekler*, Vienna, 1994, pp. 73–86.
488 Maravillas: see William J.R. Curtis, 'Anatomia de intenciones, el Gimnasio Maravillas', *Arquitectura viva*, November 1988, pp. 33ff; also Curtis, 'Dúas obras', *Grial*, 109, 1991, pp. 7–27.
Alejandro de la Sota, 'Introduction', Rafael Moneo, ed., *Alejandro de la Sota*, exhibition catalogue, Harvard Graduate School of Design, Cambridge, Mass., 1987.
489 Juan Navarro Baldeweg, 'Alejandro de la Sota', in Peter Buchanan, ed., 'Madrid: Masters and Disciples', *Architectural Review*, 179, May 1986, special issue on Spain.

chapter 27   the process of absorption: latin america, australia, japan

491 Motto: Octavio Paz, 'Critique of the Pyramid', 1968, initially published in *The Other Mexico*, Grove Press, 1972; republished, *The Labyrinth of Solitude*, enlarged edition, London, 1985.
492 National histories, nationalist mythologies: relevant formulations in Clifford Geertz, *The Interpretation of Cultures*, New York, 1973, above all Chapter 9, 'After the Revolution: The Fate of Nationalism in the New States'; also in Paul Ricoeur, 'Universal Civilisation and National Cultures', in *History and Truth*, Evanston, 1961, pp. 276ff. Ricoeur's use of the term 'Universal' seems to have less to do with any notion of the 'universality' of humankind, than with the homogenizing effects of internationalization.
493 Ciudad Universitaria: see Mario Pani and Enrique del Moral, *La construccion de la ciudad Universitaria de Pedregal*, Mexico City, 1979; for quotation, see Piedra sobre Piedra, *Pensiemento y destino de la CU 1952*, Mexico City, 1983, p. 5; for Ville radieuse as prototype, discussions in late 1980s between author and Téodoro González de León (who was also involved with design of CU, and who worked with Le Corbusier in 1946–7); see also Le Corbusier's unbuilt proposal for 'la Cité Universitaire du Brésil', Rio de Janeiro, 1936, in *Oeuvre complète 1934–38*, pp. 42–45.
494 Housing: see Manuel Larrosa, *Mario Pani, arquitecto de su epocha*, Mexico City, 1985 for housing projects in Mexico City; and Teodoro González de León, *Barrio de Navidad, estudio de un área*, Jalisco, 1958, for a wide-ranging study in regional, ecological and urban planning, including detailed proposals for low-cost house types adjusted to local climate, economy and materials.
Del Moral House: William J.R. Curtis, 'The "General and the Local": Enrique de Moral's Own House, Calle Francisco Ramirez 5, Tacubaya, Mexico, D.F., 1948' (1994), forthcoming in Ed Burian, ed., book on modern Mexican architecture, to be published by University of Texas, Austin, 1997; see also del Moral, 'Lo general y lo local', *Espacios*, 2, October 1948, and Louise Noelle Mereles, ed., and 'Introduction', *Enrique del Moral, imagen y obra escogida*, Mexico City, 1984; and Salvador Pinoncelli, *La obra de Enrique de Moral*, Mexico City, 1983.
495–8 Luis Barragán, cited Emilio Ambasz, *The Architecture of Luis Barragán*, New York, 1976, p. 8; Antonio Toca Fernandez, ed., *Barragán, obra completa*, Seville, 1995, for useful bibliography; see also William J.R. Curtis, 'Laberintos intemporales: Luis Barragán', *Arquitectura y vivienda*, July 1988, reprinted *Vuelta*, Octavio Paz, ed., January 1989 as an obituary to Barragán; see also William J.R. Curtis, 'Mythical Landscapes: Modern Architecture and the Mexican Past', in Alicia Azuela, ed., *Hechizo de Oaxaca*, Monterrey, 1991.
498 Oscar Niemeyer: statement made in introduction to S. Papadaki, *The Work of Oscar Niemeyer*, New York, 1950; see also P.L. Goodwin, *Brazil Builds*, New York, 1943: Oscar Niemeyer, *Work in Progress*, New York, 1956; H.R. Hitchcock, *Latin American Architecture since 1945*, New York, 1955.

Also, for a general overview, Benevelo, *History of Modern Architecture*, vol. 2, Ch. 20, 'The New International Field', pp. 748ff. For a rather puritanical reaction see Max Bill, lecture in Sao Paulo, mid-1950s: 'Architecture in your country stands in danger of falling into a parlous state of anti-social academicism. I intend to speak of architecture as a social art...', 'Report on Brazil', *Architectural Review*, 116, 1957, p. 234.
499 Abstraction of landscape: for Niemeyer, see Peter Buchanan, 'Formas flottantes, espacios fluidos, la poética de Oscar Niemeyer', *Arquitectura y vivienda*, 13, 1988, pp. 28ff.; David Underwood, *Oscar Niemeyer and the Architecture of Brazil*, New York, 1994; see also Roberto Burle Marx, *Arte y paisagem conferencias escolhidas*, São Paulo, 1987, and S. Eliovson, *The Gardens of Roberto Burle Marx*, 1991; for Burle-Marx and biomorphic abstraction, as well as influence on such North American landscapists as Garrett Eckbo or Thomas Church, see Marc Treib, 'Axioms for a Modern Landscape Architecture', in Treib, ed., *Modern Landscape Architecture, a Critical Review*, Cambridge, Mass., 1993;
500 Brasilia: see Oscar Niemeyer, *Minha experiência em Brasilia*, Rio de Janeiro, 1961; also James Holston, *The Modernist City, an Anthropological Critique of Brasilia*, Chicago, 1989, especially Chapter 3, 'The Plan's Hidden Agenda'.
501 Havana, Casa Noval: see Roberto Segre, *America latina, fin de milenio, raizes e perspectivas de sua arquitetura*, São Paulo, 1991, p. 189, who discusses impact of Neutra's and Le Corbusier's ideas; in the Cuba of the post-revolutionary years, on the other hand, the Marxist-materialist functionalism of Hannes Meyer influenced large-scale modernization.
502 Villanueva: Hitchcock, *Latin-American Architecture since 1945*, New York, 1955; and Sibyl Moholy-Nagy, *Carlos Raul Villanueva*, Caracas, 1964.
503 Argentina: see Segre, op. cit.; also Jorge Glusberg, *Clorindo Testa, pintor y arquitecto*, Buenos Aires, 1983. For possible connection between Amancio Williams's suspended building for offices, 1948, and Foster's later Hong Kong and Shanghai Bank, see Alan Colquhoun, 'Regionalism and Technology', *Casabella*, 491, May 1983.
504 Harry Seidler, *Houses, Interiors and Projects*, Sydney, 1954, p. ix. For Paul Rudolph's criticisms of Seidler, see 'Regionalism in Architecture', *Perspecta*, 4, 1957, p. 13. For general treatment of arrival of modern architecture in Australia, see Donald L. Johnson, *Australian Architecture 1901–51, Sources of Modernism*, Sydney, 1980, the numerous writings of Robin Boyd on the Australian environment; and J. M. Freeland, *Architecture in Australia*, Ringwood, 1968.
505 Regionalism and international influences: for ideas behind houses in the Sydney area reflecting a concern with 'place' and 'identity', see Jennifer Taylor, *An Australian Identity, Houses of Sydney 1953–63*, Sydney, 1972; see also, Winsome Callister, 'Dealing with the "Sydney School": Perspectives on Australian Architecture in the 1950s and 1960s', *Transition*, September 1987, pp. 6–12; for absorption of international 'models' (Wright, Mies and Neutra in the case of Neville Gruzman, Le Corbusier in the case of Johnson, Case-study houses in the case of the Lucases, Japanese dwellings in the case of Muller), discussions between author and both Neville Gruzman and Peter

Johnson, Sydney 1980–1.

506 Japan: see Shinji Koike, *Contemporary Architecture of Japan*, Tokyo, 1953; Arthur Drexler, *The Architecture of Japan*, New York, 1955; Manfredo Tafuri, *L'Architettura moderna in Giappone*, Bologna, 1965; Robin Boyd, *New Directions in Japanese Architecture*, New York, 1968; and D.B. Stewart, *The Making of a Modern Japanese Architecture, 1868 to the Present*, Tokyo, 1987.

507 Noboru Kawazoe, 'Modern Architecture Confronts Functionalism, New Buildings of Japan', *Zodiac*, 3, Milan, 1958, pp. 117ff. In the same article Kawazoe hinted at the difficulties of creating an authentic architecture under a regime of neo-colonialist American influence: 'It is a fact that in capitalist society, concrete products are treated as abstract values. This is the reason why modern architecture is inhuman and de-nationalized …'; for problem of modernity and Japanese traditions in 1950s, see also Benevelo, *A History of Modern Architecture*, vol. 2; for problem of homogenization of modern technology, Kunio Mayekawa, 'Thoughts on Civilization in Architecture', *Architectural Design*, May 1965, pp. 229–30.

510 Metabolism: Kikutake's statement is quoted in J. Donat, ed., *World Architecture 2*, London, 1965, p. 13. See also, K.N. Kurokawa, and K. Kikutake, *Metabolism, Proposals for a New Urbanism*, Tokyo, 1960, and Kurokawa, 'Metabolism: the Pursuit of Open Form', in Donat, ed., *World Architecture 1*, London, 1964; for continuing reflection on analogies between modern architecture and past Japanese concepts, see Kawazoe, 'Metabolism 1', *The Japan Architect*, 44, December 1969, pp. 191–8; 'Metabolism 2: the Progress of Modern Architecture: Architectural Values and Pragmatic Values', ibid., January 1970, pp. 97–101.

Tange: see Robin Boyd, *Kenzo Tange*, New York, 1962; also Shinji Koike, 'Tange', in Hatje, ed., *Encyclopedia of Modern Architecture*, pp. 288–9; also Udo Kultermann, ed., *Kenzo Tange 1946–69*, London, 1970.

chapter 28   on monuments and
monumentality: louis i. kahn

513 Motto: Louis I. Kahn, 1955, cited by Jordy, *American Buildings and Their Architects*, vol. 4, p. 361.
Monumentality: see Giedion, *Architecture You and Me*, Cambridge, Mass., 1958, p. 25, for 'The Need for a New Monumentality', formulated in 1943–4. 'The Core of the City' was taken as the theme for CIAM 8 at Hoddesdon, England, July 1951. Giedion recorded his reactions to the proceedings in an essay, 'The Humanization of Urban Life', 1951, in *Architecture You and Me*, p. 125. For other views on civic monumentality in this period see Henry Hope Reed, 'The Need for Monumentality', *Perspecta*, 1, 1950. See also William J.R. Curtis, 'Modern Architecture, Monumentality and the Meaning of Institutions', *Harvard Architectural Review*, 4, 1984.

515 National Museum of Anthropology, Mexico City: designed by Pedro Ramirez Vazquez, Jorge Campuzano and Rafael Mijares. See Louise Noelle

Mereles, *Arquitectos contemporàneos de México*, Mexico City, 1989, pp. 131ff.; see also Pedro Ramirez Vazquez, *The National Museum of Anthropology*, Geneva, 1968.

China: for a useful survey, see The Academy of Building Research, *New China Builds*, Beijing, 1976; also Musgrove, ed., *Sir Banister Fletcher's A History of Architecture*, 19th edn., pp. 1450ff.

516 Action Architecture: see G. Kallmann, 'The "Action Architecture" of a New Generation', *Architectural Forum*, 3, October 1959, pp. 132–7. For discussion of Boston City Hall and a sketch of the scheme, see William J.R. Curtis, *Boston, Forty Years of Modern Architecture*, Boston, 1980, p. 10.
Mies: for New National Gallery commission, see Schulze, *Mies van der Rohe, a Critical Biography*, pp. 305ff.; for technical aspects, Carter, *Mies van der Rohe*, pp. 95–9.

518–27 Kahn: for a general introduction, Vincent Scully, *Louis I. Kahn*, New York, 1962; also Heinz Ronner and Sharad Jhaveri, *Louis I. Kahn: Complete Work 1935–1974*, 2nd edn., Basle and Boston, 1987, especially for sketches and drawings; and Brownlee and De Long, *Louis I. Kahn in the Realm of Architecture*, particularly valuable for resumés of research on individual projects, and for bibliography.

519 Richards: see Jordy, 'What the Building "Wants To Be": Louis I. Kahn's Richards Medical Research Building at the University of Pennsylvania', *American Buildings and Their Architects*, vol. 4, pp. 361ff.

520 Kahn: for quotation and other statements of intention, see Jan C. Rowan, 'Wanting to Be', *Progressive Architecture*, April 1961, pp. 130–49; for Kahn's writings, see for example, Alexandra Tyng, *Beginnings: Louis I. Kahn's Philosophy of Architecture*, New York, 1984; Alessandra Latour, *Louis I. Kahn: Writings, Lectures, Interviews*, New York, 1991; and Richard S. Wurman, ed., *What Will Be Has Always Been: the Words of Louis I. Kahn*, New York, 1986; for a reflection on monumentality by Louis Kahn, 'Monumentality', in Paul Zucker, ed., *New Architecture and City Planning, a Symposium*, New York, 1944; for concepts 'form' and 'design', see Kahn, 'Form and Design', 1961, reprinted Scully, op. cit.

521 Immeasurable: see, for example, Kahn, 'Order Is', *Perspecta*, 3, 1955, pp. 59ff.; for a suggestive interpretation of Idealist and mystical strands in the architect's outlook, see Joseph Burton, 'Notes from Volume Zero: Louis Kahn and the Language of God', *Perspecta*, 20, 1983, pp. 69ff.
IIM: see Christian Devillers, 'Indian Institute of Management, Ahmedabad', *Casabella*, 571, September 1990, pp. 36–58.

522 Ruins: see Scully, op. cit. for ancient Rome; and Kahn, 'Louis Kahn: the Baths of Caracalla, Rome' in 'What is Your Favourite Building?' *New York Times Magazine*, 21 May 1961, p. 34; for oversimplification of Kahn's attitude to the past, see Heinrich Klotz, *The History of Post-Modern Architecture*, trans. Radka Donnell, Cambridge, Mass., and London, 1988, p. 111. Klotz seems to have wished to turn Kahn into a father of post-modernism. For a critique of this tendency, see Christian Deviller's review of Brownlee and De Long, *Louis I. Kahn in The Realm of Architecture*, 'Louis Kahn il grande contemporaneo', *Casabella*, 684, November 1991, pp. 40–5.

523 Salk: Steven Holl, *Anchoring*, New York, 1989, pp. 9–10; see also James Steele, *Salk Institute, La Jolla 1959–1965, Louis I. Kahn* (Architecture in Detail), London, 1992.

524 Kimbell: Nell Johnson, ed., *Light is the Theme: Louis I. Kahn and the Kimbell Art Museum*, Fort Worth, 1975; also David Brownlee, 'Light the Giver of All Presences', in Brownlee and De Long, op., cit. pp. 126–41; for Kahn's distillation of classical principles, see William J.R. Curtis, 'Omm att Transformera Palladio' ('On Transforming Palladio'), *Palladio Idag*, Stockholm, 1985; for 'spent light', see Kahn, 1972, in Latour, op. cit., p. 273.

526 Dacca, Parliament or National Assembly: basic outline of commission, stages of project, and something of Kahn's intentions, see Peter S. Reed, 'Sher-e-Bangla Nagar: Capital of Bangladesh', in Brownlee and De Long, op. cit., pp. 374–83 and pp. 78–92; for symbolic interpretation, see William J.R. Curtis, 'Authenticity, Abstraction and the Ancient Sense', *Perspecta*, 20; Curtis, 'Modern Architecture, Monumentality and the Meaning of Institutions', op. cit.; Curtis, 'Regionalism in Architecture, Session III', in Suha Ozkan, ed., *Exploring Architecture in Islamic Societies, Regionalism in Architecture*, Proceedings of Seminar Held in Dacca, Bangladesh, 17–22 December 1985, Singapore, 1985, pp. 73ff.; and Curtis, 'Cosmos y estado: la Asemblea Nacional de Dhaka, Cosmos and State. The National Assembly in Dhaka', *Arquitectura y vivienda*, special issue on Kahn, 44, 1993, pp. 16–21; for Wright quotation, see Motto, Chapter 7.

chapter 29   architecture and
anti-architecture in britain

529 Motto: Peter Smithson, in Smithson, ed., *Team 10 Primer*, p. 42.
530 British Architecture in 1950s: contrasting and partial accounts of this period are supplied by Jackson, *The Politics of Architecture*; Banham, *The New Brutalism*; Jencks, *Modern Movements*; Frampton, *Modern Architecture, a Critical History*. The pages of the *Architectural Review* supply a fairly precise synopsis of the debates and concerns of the decade.
Reyner Banham published an article entitled 'The New Brutalism' in *Architectural Review*, December 1955, pp. 355–62. It was an era in Britain which delighted in 'isms' (e.g., the 'New Empiricism'). For further analysis of Hunstanton, see Philip Johnson, 'Comment on School at Hunstanton, Norfolk', *Architectural Review*, September 1954, pp. 148–62; also A. and P. Smithson, 'The New Brutalism', *Architectural Review*, April 1954, pp. 274–5; see 'New Brutalism' in notes to Chapter 24.
Smithsons: for their reflections on 'Urban Re-identification' throughout the 1950s, see series of articles in *Architectural Design*, republished in *Ordinariness and Light*.
531 Rudolf Wittkower, the architectural historian, was teaching at the Warburg Institute in the 1940s and seems to have influenced the theory, practice and historiography of modern architecture, e.g. Colin Rowe's 'The Mathematics of the Ideal Villa'. For analogies between Le Corbusier's Modulor and Renaissance harmonic proportions, see H. Millon,

'Rudolf Wittkower, *Architectural Principles in the Age of Humanism*: its Influence on the Development and Interpretation of Modern Architecture', *Journal of the Society of Architectural Historians*, 31, no. 2, May 1972, pp. 83–91.

Economist: for the role of the Smithsons' earlier urban theories in this design, see Kenneth Frampton, 'The Economist and the Hauptstadt', *Architectural Design*, 1965, pp. 61–2; also Reyner Banham, 'Revenge of the Picturesque: English Architectural Polemics 1945–65', in John Summerson, ed., *Concerning Architecture*, Baltimore, 1968, p. 265.

533 Robin Hood: Alison and Peter Smithson, 'Thirty Years of Thoughts on the House and Housing', in Lasdun, ed., *Architecture in an Age of Scepticism*, pp. 172–92.

534 Futurist Revival: This tag was in gossip circulation in the London of the late 1960s but the source is not certain. However, it suggests the impact of Banham's 'rediscovery' of Futurism in *Theory and Design in the First machine Age*, and his own 'Neo-Futurist' arguments concerning the 'progressive' role of technology. For further discussion of Stirling's sources see J. Jacobus, *James Stirling, Buildings and Projects, 1950–1974*, New York, 1975; see also, Kenneth Frampton, 'Leicester University Engineering Laboratory', *Architectural Design*, 2, 1966, pp. 61ff.

537 James Stirling, 'Architect's Approach to Architecture', *Zodiac*, 16, Milan, 1966, p. 161.

Typology: for the influence of Pavillon Suisse on later university dormitories see William J.R. Curtis, 'L'Université, la ville et l'habitat collectif, reflections sur un thème de l'architecture moderne', *Archithèse*, 14, 1975, p. 29. See also Mark Girouard, 'Florey Building, Oxford', *Architectural Review*, 1972, p. 260.

538 Warren Chalk: 'Architecture as Consumer Product', *The Japan Architect*, 165, 1970, p. 37. For further taste of Archigram polemics, see *Archigram I–IX* (published from 1961 to 1970, London) and Peter Cook, *Experimental Architecture*, London, 1970.

539 Thinkbelt: see C. Price, 'Potteries Thinkbelt', *Architectural Design*, November 1967, pp. 507ff.; the quotation is from Banham, *Theory and Design*, pp. 329–30.

540 British 1960s: for two overviews steered by theoretical positions, Royston Landau, *New Directions in English Architecture*, London, 1968; and Robert Maxwell, *New British Architecture*, London, 1973.

541 Lasdun: for study of his work starting with 1930s, see William J.R. Curtis, *Denys Lasdun: Architecture, City, Landscape*, London, 1994; also Curtis, *A Language and a Theme, the Architecture of Denys Lasdun and Partners*, RIBA catalogue, London, 1976. Denys Lasdun and Partners was founded in 1960 with Alexander Redhouse and Peter Softley as partners, Graham Lane, Harry Pugh, Peter McKinley, Stefan Kuszell and Donald Mill becoming associates. For Lasdun's intellectual outlook in the 1950s, see series of anonymous articles co-authored with John H.V. Davies, entitled 'Thoughts in Progress', from *Architectural Design*, December 1956 to December 1957 (appendix to Curtis, *Denys Lasdun*); see also 'An Architect's Approach to Architecture', *RIBA Journal*, April 1965; and Denys Lasdun, 'The Architecture of Urban Landscape', in Lasdun, ed., *Architecture in an Age of Scepticism*, pp. 134ff. For the theme of 'rhetoric'

in Lasdun's architecture see Maxwell, op. cit.

542 Denys Lasdun, 'The Evolution of a Style', *Architectural Review*, May 1969.

545 National Theatre: For Lasdun's intentions see 'Building Vistas/1', a conversation between Lasdun and Peter Hall, in *The Complete Guide to Britain's National Theatre*, ed. J. Goodwin, London, 1976, p. 25; also William J.R. Curtis, 'Description', 'Past Perspective', 'Criticism', in *Architectural Review*, January 1977, National Theatre Special Issue.

chapter 30   extension and critique in the 1960s

547 Motto: Robert Venturi, *Complexity and Contradiction in Architecture*, New York, 1966, p. 16.

Third Generation: Throughout the 1950s Giedion attempted to define the essence of a new post-war sensibility as exemplified in the inheritors of the modern movement. Since he thought of architects like Perret and Behrens as pioneers, and architects like Le Corbusier and Gropius as the next stage, those who came to maturity around 1950–60 were regarded as a 'third generation'. In an essay entitled 'Spatial Imagination', 1957, Giedion referred to the concrete vaulting techniques of Catalano and Utzon as evidence of a new dimension to the 'space-time' conception at the heart of modern architecture; this he compared to the vaulting and grand interior spaces of Roman antiquity. He expanded his reflections on recent world architecture in the introduction to the 1962 edition of *Space, Time and Architecture*, where he included Tange, and spoke of a new consciousness binding the traditions of East and West. He also pointed to an emergent civic monumentality and a synthesis of the rational and the organic. Jørn Utzon became the hero of the third phase in an article written in 1962–3, entitled 'Jørn Utzon and the Third Generation', eventually published in the 1967 edition of *Space, Time and Architecture*. A similar theme was picked up by Philip Drew, *The Third Generation: Changing Meaning in Architecture*, London, 1972.

550 Aldo Van Eyck: in Smithson, ed., *Team 10 Primer*, p. 43. For further clues concerning this architect's insights see: 'Labyrinthine Clarity', in J. Donat, ed., *World Architecture 3*, London, 1966, pp. 121–2; and 'Interior Time/a Miracle in Moderation', in George Baird and Charles Jencks, eds., *Meaning in Architecture*, London, 1969, pp. 171ff.

Fehn, see Per Olaf Fjeld, *The Thought of Construction*, New York, 1983; for Nordic sensibility, see Marja-Riitta Norri, Maija Kärkkäinen, eds., *5 Masters of the North*, Helsinki, 1992, set of five catalogues of Museum of Finnish Architecture, particularly *Sverre Fehn, the Poetry of the Straight Line*.

551 Finland: for Ruusuvuori, see Norri and Kärkkäinen, *5 Masters*, catalogue entitled *Aarno Ruusuvuori, Structure is the Key to Beauty*; for minimalist tendencies, Scott Poole, 'The Construction of Silence', in Poole, *The New Finnish Architecture*, New York, 1992; for Pietilä, for example Malcolm Quantrill, *Reima Pietilä, Architecture, Context, Modernism*, 1985; also Quantrill, *Finnish Architecture and the Modernist Tradition*, London, 1995.

552 Oíza, Torres Blancas: see Antón Capitel, 'The Modern Adventure of Spanish Architecture', in Capitel and Ignacio Solà-Morales, *Contemporary Spanish Architecture: an Eclectic Panorama*, New York, 1986, p. 16.; for Fernandez Alba, Antón Capitel, 'La arquitectura de Antonio Fernandez Alba en el interior de la aventura Espanola Moderna', in Capitel, *Articulos y Ensayos Breves, 1976–1991*, Madrid, 1993.

Sert, see Edgardo Mannino, Ignacio Paricio, *J.L. Sert: contrucción y arquitectura*, Barcelona, 1983, especially pp. 24ff. for Coderch, for intentions behind Las Cocheras, see Enric Soria Badia, ed., *Conversaciones con José Antonio Coderch de Sentmenat*, Barcelona, 1979, p. 144; also Fochs, ed., *Coderch 1913–1984*, pp. 126–35.

553 Wolfgang Pehnt, 'Germany', in Hatje, ed., *Encyclopedia of Modern Architecture*, p. 126; for gradual reorientation to past, see, for example, Unger's project for Student Residences, Enschede, Netherlands, 1963, reproduced, Klotz, *The History of Post modern Architecture*, pp. 277–8; also important, the restoration and enhancement of the Alte Pinakothek, Munich by Hans Döllgast in the 1950s, see Winfried Nerdinger, 'Hans Döllgast: an Outsider of Modern Architecture', in Rosamund Diamond and Wilfried Wang, eds., *9H No. 9. On Continuity*, Cambridge, Mass., and Oxford, 1995.

553–4 Italy, critical positions: see, for example, Zevi, editorials in review *L'Architettura* (Rome); Manfredo Tafuri, *Teorie e storia dell'architettura*, Bari, 1968; Ernesto Rogers, *Editoriali di architettura*, Turin, 1968 (editorials from review *Casabella-Continuità*); Giulio Carlo Argan, *Progetto e destino*, Milan, 1965 (see particularly his article on the concept of 'typology'); Aldo Rossi, *L'architettura della città*, Padua, 1966.

554 Scarpa: see Dal Co and Mazzariol, eds., *Carlo Scarpa, the Complete Works*; also Richard Murphy, *Querini Stampalia Foundation, Venice 1961–3, Carlo Scarpa* (Architecture in Detail), London, 1991.

555 De Carlo: see Giancarlo De Carlo, 'The University Centre, Urbino', in Lasdun, ed., *Architecture in an Age of Scepticism*, pp. 50ff; also Vittorio Gregotti, *New Directions in Italian Architecture*, New York, 1969.

Superstudio: see A. Natalini, 'Description of the Micro-event', in Emilio Ambasz, ed., *Italy: the New Domestic Landscape*, New York, 1972, p. 242.

City: see Kevin Lynch, *The Image of the City*, Cambridge, Mass., 1960; Reyner Banham, *Megastructure, Urban Futures of the Recent Past*, London, 1976; see also Joseph Rykwert, 'Preface to the Paper Edition', *The Idea of a Town*, Cambridge, Mass., 1988.

556 USA, post-war: see Burchard and Bush Brown, *The Architecture of America, a Social and Cultural History*; Alan Gowans, *Images of American Living*, Philadelphia, 1964; Vincent Scully, *American Architecture and Urbanism*, New York, 1969; Mario Manieri Elia, *L'architettura del dopoguerra in USA*, Bologna, 1976; and for a polemical view of the 1960s, Robert M. Stern, *New Directions in American Architecture*, New York, 1969.

557 Paramilitary dandyism, Scully, op. cit., p. 200.

558 Khan: see Fazlur R. Khan, '100-Storey John Hancock Center in Chicago – a Case Study of the

Design Process', *IABSE Journal*, J–16/82, August 1982, see particularly p. 28, 'a significant architectural statement may have a transcendental value and quality far beyond arbitrary forms and expressions that reflect the fashion of a time.'

558–60 Kallmann, Rudolph, Boston: see William J.R. Curtis, *Boston, Forty Years of Modern Architecture*, Boston, 1980; Rudolph's early career in the 1950s, and periods of crystallization in the 1960s, have been distorted and obscured by retrospective polemics, and deserve historical re-evaluation.

560 Robert Venturi: *Complexity and Contradiction in Architecture*, New York, 1966, pp. 23, 104. It is likely that Venturi was influenced by T.S. Eliot's ideas on tradition, and those of William Empson on ambiguity.

562–3 Venturi, op. cit., p. 118; p. 116; pp. 43–4.

564 New York 5: see Peter Eisenman, ed., *Five Architects*, New York, 1972.

Twenties as Classic Age: once again one senses the influence of a historian on practising architects; Graves's 'mannerist' exercises on the elements of an earlier tradition illustrate, in some degree, the insights of Colin Rowe in 'Mannerism and Modern Architecture', *Architectural Review*, 107, May 1950, pp. 289ff.

chapter 31   modernity, tradition and identity in the developing world

567 Motto: Hassan Fathy, *Architecture for the Poor, an Experiment in Rural Egypt*, Chicago, 1973, p. 19. The existing historiography of 19th- and 20th-century architecture and building continues to reflect a Western bias. The term 'developing world' has been used in this chapter heading with some hesitation as it too seems to carry a cultural bias in favour of the values and historical trajectories of the so called 'developed' countries.

568 Modern Regionalism, Regionalist Modernism: these are evolving concepts which apparently reflect ever-changing notions of 'centre' and 'periphery' (see, for example, Chapters 8, 21, 27 above). For design strategies suggested for the 'developing countries' in the 1950s, see Josep Luis Sert, housing proposals for Bogata in the 1950s; or, Maxwell Fry and Jane Drew, *Tropical Architecture*, New York, 1956, and their *Village Housing in the Tropics*, London, 1953.

569 Hassan Fathy, *Architecture for the Poor*, p. 24.

Romanticization of Peasants: for further discussion of peasantism and nationalism, see William J.R. Curtis, 'Type and Variation: Berber Dwellings of the Northwestern Sahara', in Oleg Grabar, ed., *Muqarnas 1*, New Haven, 1983; also Curtis, 'Towards an Authentic Regionalism', *Mimar*, 19, January 1986.

570 Self-build housing: see J.F. Turner, *Housing by People, towards Autonomy in Building Environments*, London, 1976.

Barriadas: In 1967 the Peruvian government approached the United Nations Development Programme for support of 'PREVI' (Proyecta Experimental de Vivienda). See *Architectural Design*, April 1970, pp. 187ff.; also W. Mangin, 'Urbanisation Case History in Peru', *Architectural Design*, August 1963, pp. 366–70; for Van Eyck in particular, see 'Aldo van Eyck Wasted Gain', in Lasdun, ed., *Architecture in an Age of Scepticism*, pp. 234ff. Possibly the 'PREVI' programme was influenced by Turner's theories; he worked in Peru in the late 1950s and early 1960s; see also the writings of Peter Land (e.g., 'Houses for the Horizontal city', *Process Architecture*, 14). For a housing theory based on the idea of a fixed infrastructure and variable components (in this instance for Industrialized nations), see N.J. Habraken, *Supports: an Alternative to Mass housing*, New York, 1972.

Z. Plocki: *Towards a Melanesian Style of Architecture*, Institute of Papua-New Guinea Studies, Boroko, 1975, p. 22.

571 Early modernism in India: for contrasting views, see Malay Chaterjee, 'The Evolution of Contemporary Indian Architecture', in J.L. Veret, ed., *Architecture in India*, Paris, 1985, pp. 124ff.; G.N.R. Tillotson, *The Tradition of Indian Architecture*, New Haven and London, 1989, pp. 127ff.; Norma Evenson, *The Indian Metropolis, a View Toward the West*, New Haven and London, 1989; Peter Serenyi, 'A.P. Kanvinde. Ethics and Aesthetics: an Architect and His Values', *Architecture and Design* (Delhi), May–June 1985, pp. 14ff.; William J.R. Curtis, 'Modernism and the Search for Indian Identity', *Architectural Review*, August 1987; and Peter Scriver and Vikram Bhatt, *After the Masters*, Ahmedabad, 1991.

572 Correa: see Sherban Cantacuzino, *Charles Correa*, Singapore, 1984; also Correa, 'The Roots of Architecture', *Conspectus*, Delhi, 1965, and 'Architecture in Hot Dry Climates', 1973.

573 Doshi: see William J.R. Curtis, *Balkrishna Doshi: an Architecture for India*, Ahmadabad and New York, 1988; see also Balkrishna Doshi, 'The Proliferating City and Communal Life: India', *Ekistics*, 1968.

574 Rewal: see William J.R. Curtis, 'Architecture Moderne, racines indiennes', in D. Treiber, ed., *Raj Rewal, architecture climatique*, Paris, 1986; English version in *Architecture and Design* (Delhi), March–April 1989, pp. 42ff.

575 Eladio Dieste, 'Tecnica y Desarollo' and 'Arquitectura y Construccion', in D. Ivakhoff, ed., *Eladio Dieste: La Estructura Ceramica*, Bogota, 1987, pp. 160ff.

577 Ricardo Legorreta, 'Walls', in Wayne Attoe, ed., *The Architecture of Ricardo Legorreta*, Austin, 1991, p. 62.

Teodoro González de León, 'Conferencia, 1987', cited in William J.R. Curtis, 'Modern Architecture, Mexican Conditions', in Louise Noelle Mereles, ed., *Teodoro González de León, la voluntad del creador*, Bogota, 1994, p. 32; see also Paul Heyer, *Mexican Architecture, the Work of Abraham Zabludovsky and Teodoro González de León*, New York, 1978. For notion of 'constants' in Mexican tradition, González de León, 'On Two Constants in our Architectural Work', unpublished essay, Mexico City, 1985.

578 Sedad Eldem: see Suha Ozkan, ed., *Sedad Eldem, Architect in Turkey*, Singapore and New York, 1987, pp. 88ff.; also Dogan Kuban, 'A Survey of Modern Turkish Architecture', in S. Cantacuzino, ed., *Architecture in Continuity*, New York, 1985; for problems of 'regionalism and universalism', Bülent Ozer, *Rejyonalizm, Üniversalizm ve Cagdas Mimarimiz Uzerine Bir Deneme*, Istanbul, 1964.

Paul Ricoeur, 'Universal Civilization and National Cultures', in *History and Truth*, Evanston, 1961, pp. 276ff.; for nation state, rural base etc., see Curtis, 'Towards an Authentic Regionalism', op. cit.

579 Rifat Chadirji, *Concepts and Influences. Towards a Regionalized International Architecture*, London, 1986, p. 51, p. 49.

580 Ravereau, Mopti: for Ravereau's absorption of lessons from the vernacular, see André Ravereau, *Le M'zab, une leçon d'architecture*, 1981; Ravereau, 'Apprendre de la tradition', *Techniques et Architecture*, 365, 1983; Ravereau, 'Mesures de l'homme, et représentation: l'abri ou le temple', *Poiesis*, 1, Toulouse, 1994, pp. 59ff. For a general survey of African tendencies, see Udo Kultermann, *New Directions in African Architecture*, New York, 1969, p. 40.

580–1 Geoffrey Bawa: see Curtis, 'Towards an Authentic Regionalism', op. cit.; see also Brian Taylor, ed., *Geoffrey Bawa*, Singapore and New York, 1986.

582 Great Hall of People, Beijing: designed 1959 by Beijing Institute of Architectural Design; for People's Republic of China, see Academy of Building Research, *New China Builds*, Beijing, 1976; see also, 'Beijing', Architectural Information Bulletin, in *Mimar*, 19, January 1986.

Smithsons: see 'Pahlavi National Library', *Architectural Review*, 166, August 1978, pp. 79–85.

584 Hajj Terminal: see catalogue of Aga Khan Award for Architecture, 1983, section 8; Ravereau's Mopti Medical Centre received an Aga Khan Award in 1980.

585 Pan-Islamic Sentiments: see, for example, S.H. Nasr, 'The Contemporary Muslim and the Architectural Transformation of the Urban Environment of the Islamic World', *Proceedings of the Aga Khan Award for Architecture*, 1, Philadelphia, 1978. The subtitle of the proceedings was: 'Toward An Architecture in the Spirit of Islam'. Some of the intellectual and historical difficulties lurking in this formulation were raised by other participants. For incisive studies of problems of cultural identity in the Middle East, see Abdullah Laroui, *The Crisis of the Arab Intellectuals: Tradionalism or Historicism?*, trans. Cammell, Berkeley, 1976, and Fouad Ajami, *The Arab Predicament*, Cambridge, 1981. For valuable etymological distinctions between 'Islamic' and 'Muslim', see Kamil Khan Mumtaz, 'The Islamic Debate, Architecture in Pakistan', in *Mimar*, 19, January 1986; see also Mohammed Arkoun, 'Muslim Character: the Essential and the Changeable', in Ismail Seageldin, ed., *Space for Freedom, the Search for Excellence in Muslim Societies*, London, 1989.

586 Jørn Utzon, 'A House for Work and Decisions, Kuwait National Assembly Complex', in Lasdun, ed., *Architecture in an Age of Scepticism*, pp. 222ff. The dhow, incidentally, is the national symbol of Kuwait.

586–7 Hurva Synagogue: for architect's intentions see Denys Lasdun, 'The Architecture of Urban Landscape', in Lasdun, op. cit., pp. 134ff; also William J.R. Curtis, *Denys Lasdun: Architecture, City, Landscape*, London, 1994.

589 Motto: Aldo Van Eyck: 'The Interior of Time', Jencks and Baird, eds., *Meaning in Architecture*, New York, 1969, p. 171; this chapter grows out of a less extensive version in the first edition: Chapter 28, 'The Traditions of Modern Architecture in the Recent Past'.
590 Rejection of absolutism: One thinks of the popularization of the ideas of Ivan Illich (e.g., *De-schooling Society*) and Karl Popper (e.g. *The Open Society and its Enemies*); of the increasing scepticism about the dominant values of Western industrial nations; of the increased respect for architectural vernaculars (Bernard Rudofsky's *Architecture Without Architects*, 1964, must be counted a cult book); of a pervasive distrust of cultural élites in the 'counter-culture' of the late 1960s; and so on.
Crisis: for example, M. MacEwen, *Crisis in Architecture*, London, 1974. For a more probing critique, this time of the avant-garde and from a somewhat confused Marxist standpoint, see Manfredo Tafuri, *Architecture and Utopia: Design and Capitalist Development*, Cambridge, Mass., 1976. For the erosion of closed frameworks of aesthetic reference see, for example, Leo Steinberg, *Other Criteria*, New York, 1972.
591 Byker: see *Architectural Design*, November-December, 1974, special issue on Erskine; see also Ralph Erskine, 'Democratic Architecture: the Universal and Useful Art', in Lasdun, ed., *Architecture in an Age of Scepticism*, pp. 72ff.
Radical critiques of planning: see, for example, the ideas of John Turner cited in the notes to the last Chapter; also Martin Pawley, *Architecture Versus Housing*, New York, 1971, and Jacobs, *The Death and Life of Great American Cities*, New York, 1961.
592 Vernacular revival: for a sample of pop sociology combined with the myth of a grass-roots architectural expression, see Conrad Jameson, 'Modern Architecture as an Ideology', *Architectural Association Quarterly*, October–December 1975.
593 Aldo Rossi, 'An Analogical Architecture', *A+U*, May 1976, p. 74. For his urban theories, *L'architettura della città*, Padua, 1960; see also *Architettura razionale*, exhibition catalogue, Madrid, 1973, and *Scientific Autobiography*, trans. Lawrence Venuti, Cambridge, Mass., 1981. For a far from dispassionate treatment of Rossi, see Rafael Moneo, 'Aldo Rossi: the Idea of Architecture and the Modena Cemetery', *Oppositions* 5, Summer 1976, pp. 1–30. For influence and affinities and for a quote on 'geometry and history', see Klotz, *The History of Post Modern Architecture*, pp. 263ff.; for Kleihues, pp. 290ff.; for Ungers, pp. 213ff.; also Oswald Mathias Ungers and Reinhard Gieselman, 'Zu einer neuen Architektur', *Der Monat*, 174, 1963, p. 96, for absorption of past. For Ciriani and Chemetov urban ideas, see Jacques Lucan, *France, architecture 1965–1988*, Paris, 1989, pp. 91ff.
Types and typology: in Italian architectural culture, see writings of Rossi, Argan, in 1960s (notes to Chapter 30); in Anglo-Saxon world, see, for example, Alan Colquhoun, 'Typology and Design Method', *Arena*, 83, June 1967, republished, *Essays in Architectural Criticism*, pp. 43ff. It seems likely that Colquhoun (like Gombrich in his notion of 'schemata' in *Art and Illusion*), was influenced by the ideas of Karl Popper on

the role of pre-existing theories and of deduction in invention (viz. Popper's *The Logic of Scientific Discovery*), in this instance as a critique of the 'functionalist' proposition that form may follow from function.
Berlin IBA: see *Internationale Bauaustellung Berlin, 1984, die Neubaugebiete, Dokumente Projekte*, Berlin, 1981; also 'Berlin IBA', *Architectural Review*, April 1987, and 'Berlin IBA '87', in *Arquitectura y vivenda*, 1 and 2, 1985.
594 Alvaro Siza, 'Interview', *Plan Construction*, PAN, 11 May 1980; see also Peter Testa, *The Architecture of Alvaro Siza, Thresholds Working Paper 4*, MIT, Dept. of Architecture, 1984, Chapter 4; and William J.R. Curtis, 'Alvaro Siza: an Architecture of Edges', *El Croquis*, 68, 69, 1994; and Wilfried Wang, *Alvaro Siza, Figures and Configurations – Buildings and Projects*, New York, 1988.
595 Norman Foster: see T. Nakamura, 'Foster and Associates', *A+U*, September 1975, particularly essay by Reyner Banham.
596 Centraal Beheer: see Alan Colquhoun, 'Centraal Beheer', *Architecture Plus*, September–October 1974, pp. 49–54. For a sample of Hertzberger's ideas, see 'Place, Choice and Identity', *World Architecture 4*, London, 1967, pp. 74ff.
European Investment Bank: see William J.R. Curtis, *Denys Lasdun: Architecture, City, Landscape*, London, 1994; also Curtis 'Modernism, Nature, Tradition', in *Denys Lasdun Architect*, exhibition catalogue, EIB, Luxembourg, 1995; see also Peter Buchanan, 'Lasdun Landmark', *Architectural Review*, November 1981.
597–9 Skyscraper, type and variation: see William J.R. Curtis, 'The Skyscraper and the City', in Margaret Sevçénko, ed., *Design for High Intensity Development*, Cambridge, Mass., 1986, pp. 15ff.; for design of structure of Citicorp, see engineer's own account, William Le Messurier, 'Designing High-Rise Buildings', ibid., pp. 45ff.; for AT and T, William J.R. Curtis, 'On Appearing to be Classical', in Curtis, 'Principle versus Pastiche: Perspectives on Some Recent Classicisms', *Architectural Review*, August 1984; for Banco de Bilbao, see Antón Capitel, 'Las ideas organicas como instrumentos de proyecto. Torres Blancas y Otros obras de Saenz de Oiza', *Articulos y ensayos breves, 1976–1991*, Madrid, 1993, pp. 197ff.; National Lottery, Mexico, see 'Edificio de Oficinas', in *Modern Mexican Architecture*, special issue of *Process: Architecture*, 39, 1983, pp. 45–6. For unified and contextually sensitive use of tripartite order in skyscrapers, see Bill Pedersen's (adjunct Alexander Ward), 333 Wacker Drive, Chicago, 1979–83, in Sonia Chao, ed., *Kohn Pedersen and Fox, Buildings and Projects 1976–86*, New York, 1987; for emphasis on appearances, see Paul Goldberger, *The Skyscraper*, New York, 1981; and Ada Louise Huxtable, *The Tall Building Artistically Reconsidered: the Search for a Skyscraper Style*, New York, 1984.
600 Beaubourg: for a generous criticism of a problematic work, see Reyner Banham, 'The Pompidolium – Criticism', *Architectural Review*, May 1977, pp. 277ff.; for museums, see for example, *Josep M. Montaner, nuevas museos – espacios para el arte y la cultura*, Barcelona, 1990.
601 Simounet: see *Roland Simounet, pour une invention de l'espace*, Paris, 1986; Jacques Lucan,

France Architecture 1965–1988, Paris, 1989, pp. 159ff., 'L'architecture comme recherche patiente'; also Claude Schnaidt, 'Roland Schweitzer, Roland Simounet', *Werk, Bauen und Wohnen*, 6, June 1981, pp. 11ff.; Schweitzer, e.g. Centre de vacances, Le Four (Limousin), 1972, is another French architect born in the mid-1920s to have side-stepped fashion, and to have developed a sensitivity for place and topography.
602 Postmodern: see, for example, Charles Jencks, 'The Rise of a Post-Modern Architecture', *Architectural Association Quarterly*, October–December 1975 – a trial run of ideas later published as his book, *The Language of Post-Modern Architecture*, New York, 1977; see also Klotz, op. cit., pp. 128ff.
Postmodernism and Linguistic Analogies: The interest in 'conventions' and 'signs' undoubtedly reflects linguistic theories in vogue at the time (e.g. those of Ferdinand de Saussure); the importance of 'conventions' may also be found in the influential writings of E.H. Gombrich (e.g. 'The Vogue of Abstract Art', *Meditations on a Hobby Horse*, London, 1963, p. 143) who in turn stressed the limitations of 'expressionist' theories, and of abstraction as a means of communication. See Alan Colquhoun, 'Form and Figure', *Oppositions 12*, Spring 1978; and Stanislaus von Moos, ed., *Archithèse*, 19, 1976, special issue 'Realismus in der Architektur'.
Revisionist tendencies: ideological criticism was not the exclusive property of left-wing critics. For a conservative view, see David Watkin, *Morality and Architecture*, Oxford, 1977, p. 115; 'Our conclusion is that an art-historical belief in the all-embracing *Zeitgeist*, combined with a historicist emphasis on progress and the necessary superiority of novelty, has come dangerously close to undermining, on the one hand, our appreciation of the imaginative genius of the individual and, on the other, the importance of artistic tradition.' For the severe limitations of Watkin's rather caricatured version of 'modern architecture', see my review of Watkin's book in *Journal of Society of Architectural Historians*, 38, October 1979, pp. 304ff. For a flip opinion see Tom Wolfe, *From Bauhaus to Our House*, New York, 1981.
603 Piazza d'Italia, for praise, see Charles Jencks, ed., 'Post-Modern-Classicism', *Architectural Design*, 5 and 6, 1980; for criticism, see Curtis, 'Principle versus Pastiche', *Architectural Review*, August 1984.
604 Graves: see *Architectural Design*, Architectural Monographs, 5, 1979. For a stab at the increasing introversion of the American architectural world of the 1970s, see Manfredo Tafuri, 'Architecture dans le boudoir: the Language of Criticism and the Crisis of Language', *Oppositions 3*, May 1974, pp. 37–62.
605 Presence of the Past: see 'La presenza del passato. I Mostra Internazionale di architettura della Biennale di Venezia', special issue of *Contraspazio*, nos. 1–6, 1980.
Consumerism: see Stanley Tigerman, ed., *Chicago Tribune Tower Competition [and Late Entries]*, New York, 1981.
606 Hans Hollein, see Klotz, op. cit., pp. 130ff., and pp. 337–54; also Peter Cook, *Experimental Architecture*, London, 1970; also *Hans Hollein: métaphores et métamorphosis*, exhibition catalogue, CCI Pompidou, Paris, 1987; and F. Achleitner, 'Viennese Positions', *Lotus*, 29, 1989, pp. 5–27.

Figure/Ground: this method of urban analysis seems traceable to Colin Rowe, Stirling's one-time mentor. See below, 'Collage City'. The concept of 'bricolage' (derived from Lévi-Strauss on the 'savage mind') is also traceable to Rowe, and reflects an interest in composition from pre-existing stylistic, typological and urban 'fragments'.

606–8 Neue Staatsgalerie, James Stirling: 'The Monumentality Informal', in *Neue Staatsgalerie und Kammertheater Stuttgart*, Stuttgart, 1984, p. 17, the phrases originally used at a lecture Rice University, 1979; see also special off-print of *Architectural Review*, December 1984, 'Monument in the City', with critical essays by Alan Colquhoun, 'Democratic Monument'; Reyner Banham, 'Celebration of the City'; Emilio Ambasz, 'Popular Pantheon'; Oriol Bohigas, 'Turning Point'; and William J.R. Curtis, 'Virtuosity Around a Void'.

608 Kriers: see Rob Krier, *Stadtraum in Theorie und Praxis*, Stuttgart, 1975, and Leon Krier, *Reconstruction of the European City*, Brussels, 1978; for revisionist view of city, see Alan Colquhoun, 'Twentieth Century Concepts of Urban Space', in Joan Ockman, ed., *Architecture, Criticism, Ideology*, Princeton, 1985.

609 Collage City: Rowe's critique of Utopianism seems to have been influenced by Karl Popper's critique of the notion of 'ideal states'; see particularly Popper, *The Open Society and its Enemies*.

Jorge Silvetti: 'The Beauty of Shadows', *Oppositions* 9, Summer 1977, pp. 44ff.

610 Brion: for a sensitive appreciation, see George Ranalli, 'Introduction', *Carlo Scarpa, Drawings for the Brion Family Cemetery*, exhibition catalogue, Yale School of Architecture, New Haven, 1984; see also untitled essay by Francesco dal Co in same catalogue; and Dal Co and Mazzariol, *Carlo Scarpa, Complete Works*.

611–13 Utzon, Bagsvaerd: see Jørn Utzon, 'The Importance of Architects', in Lasdun, ed., *Architecture in an Age of Scepticism*, pp. 230–3; for 'meeting house', see Denys Lasdun, speech on occasion of Utzon's RIBA Gold Medal, 20 June 1978.

613 Aldo Van Eyck: 'The Interior of Time', see note to motto of this chapter.

chapter 33 modern architecture and memory: new perceptions of the past

617 Motto: Aulis Blomstedt, 'Studies in Harmony', *c.* 1957, cited Scott Poole, *The New Finnish Architecture*, New York, 1992, p. 46.

618–19 Spatial anatomy: see 'Conclusion' to first edition of this book, 'Modernity, Tradition and Authenticity', written in 1981, and included in third edition with slight changes.

619 Delta: see William J.R. Curtis, 'Contemporary Transformations of Modern Architecture', *Architectural Record*, June 1989; also, Curtis, 'The Idea of a Modern Tradition', in Marja Kärkäinen, ed., *Functionalism – Utopia of the Way Forward? The Fifth International Alvar Aalto Symposium*, Jyvaskyla, 1992, pp. 120ff.

Grand historical narratives exhausted: see for example the writings of Jean-François Lyotard, Jacques Derrida, Jean Baudrillard, Gilles Deleuze, Michel Foucault; for ruminations on 'modern project', see particularly writings of Jürgen Habermas, e.g. 'Die Moderne ein unvollendetes Projekt', in *Kleine politische Schriften*, 1981.

620 Post-modern classicism: see Charles Jencks, ed., 'Post-Modern Classicism', *Architectural Design*, 5–6, 1980; and Jencks, *Free Style Classicism*, London 1982.

Billboard, cultural graffiti: William J.R. Curtis, 'Principle versus Pastiche, Perspectives on Some Recent Classicisms', *Architectural Review*, August 1984; for an antidote to the stylistic manipulations of the early 1980s, see Alexander Tzonis and Liane Lefaivre, *Classical Architecture, the Poetics of Order*, Cambridge, Mass., 1986.

Critical disillusionment: see, for example, the review by Paul Gapp, 'Post-Modern Promise Turns into a Hulking High-Rise Dud', *Chicago Tribune*, 31 October 1982, which rejected Portland as a 'dud'.

Hierarchies for hire: see Martin Filler, 'Hierarchies for Hire. The Impact of Big Firms since 1976', in Hays and Burns, eds., *Thinking the Present, Recent American Architecture*, New York, 1990, pp. 23ff.

621 Charles Newman: *The Post-Modern Aura, the Act of Fiction in an Age of Inflation*, Evanston, 1985, p. 182.

Neo-conservative: see William J.R. Curtis, '"Clipper Class Classicism", Venturi's National Gallery Extension', *Architects' Journal*, 17 June 1987; also Mary McLeod, 'Architecture and Politics in the Reagan Era: from Post-Modernism to Deconstructivism', *Assemblage*, 8, 1989.

Royalty: HRH The Prince of Wales, *A Vision of Britain: a Personal View of Architecture*, London and New York, 1989.

Quinlan Terry: 'Twentieth Century Renaissance' (interview), *Architects' Journal*, 14 December 1983, p. 40; see also Clive Aslet, *Quinlan Terry. The Revival of Architecture*, Harmondsworth and New York, 1986.

Geoffrey Scott: *The Architecture of Humanism*, London, 1914, p. 199.

622 Neo-rationalists: see notes to chapters 30, 32, also Peter Arnell and Ted Bickford, *Aldo Rossi, Works and Projects*, New York, 1985; Giorgio Grassi, *La costruzione logica dell'architettura*, Padova, 1967, and Carlos Aris and Agostino Rema, *Giorgio Grassi, Projekte und Entwurfe 1960–1980*, Berlin, 1980; Vittorio Magnago Lampugnani, 'Ungers' Boxes; Museum, Frankfurt, West Germany', *Architectural Review*, August 1984.

Berlin, Barcelona, traditional typologies: for IBA, Berlin, see notes to Chapter 32; for Barcelona, Oriol Bohigas, Mackay, Martorell, Puigdomènech, *La Villa Olimpica, transformacion de una frente maritimo*, Barcelona, 1988.

623 Alan Colquhoun: 'A Way of Looking at the Present Situation', *Casabella*, 490, April 1983; reproduced in Colquhoun, *Modernity and the Classical Tradition*, pp. 193ff. The interrelationships between theory and practice, historical research and artistic invention, are never straightforward, but it may be relevant to mention a certain concentration upon theoretical problems of the late eighteenth century and early nineteenth, in the writings of, e.g., Joseph Rykwert, Anthony Vidler, Neil Levine, David van Zanten and Robin Middleton, in the late 1970s and early 1980s. For example, Anthony Vidler, 'The Idea of Type. The Transformation of the Academic Ideal 1750–1830', *Oppositions 8*, 1977, or Rykwert, *On Adam's House in Paradise*.

624–5 Mario Botta: quotations from, 'Architecture and Morality: an Interview with Mario Botta', by Livio Dimitriu, in *Perspecta*, 20, 1983, pp. 119–38; the literature on Botta is extensive: see, for example, Pierluigi Nicolin and François Chaslin, *Mario Botta 1978–1982*, Milan, 1983, and Tita Carloni, 'The Architect of the Wall and not of the Trilith Building and Mario Botta', *Lotus International*, 37, January 1983, pp. 34–46. Relevant too is Aldo Rossi, Eraldo Consolascio, Max Bosshard, *La Costruzione del territorio – uno studio sul Canton Ticino*, Milan, 1985 (first version, 1979), for a way of conceiving a 'local tradition' through its rural and urban vernacular types. For Casa Rotonda, see also R. Trevisiol, ed., *La casa rotonda*, Milan, 1982, and William J.R. Curtis, 'Orders without Order and Order without Orders', in 'Principle versus Pastiche', op. cit.

625–6 Ticino: for emergence of new tendencies in 1970s, *Tendenzen: neuer Architektur in Tessin*, exhibition catalogue, ETH, Zurich, 1975; see also Vittorio Gregotti, *Luigi Snozzi*, Milan, 1984; Werner Seligmann and Jorge Silvetti, *Mario Campi and Franco Pessina*, New York, 1987.

626 Galfetti: see Mario Botta and Mirko Zardini, 'Introductions', *Aurelio Galfetti*, Barcelona, 1989, quotation is from p. 50.

627 Vacchini: see Ch. Norberg-Schulz, and Jean Claude Vigato, 'Introductions' *Livio Vacchini*, Barcelona, 1987, Vacchini quotation from p. 44.

627–8 Francesco Venezia: 'Contemplations on Architecture. A Series of Monologues', in Marja-Riitta Norri, ed., *Acanthus*, 1990, pp. 57ff.; see also Alvaro Siza, 'Introduction', *Francesco Venezia*, Barcelona, 1988.

629–30 Moneo: see William J.R. Curtis, 'Pieces of City, Memories of Ruins', *El Croquis 64, Rafael Moneo 1990–1994*, Madrid, 1994; also Francesco Dal Co, 'Roman Brickwork, The Museum of Roman Art of Merida, by Rafael Moneo', *Lotus International, 46, Interpretazione del passato*, 1985, pp. 23ff.; Peter Buchanan, 'Rafael's Spanish Romans', *Architectural Review*, November 1985, p. 43; for Moneo quotation, see Rafael Moneo, 'On Typology', *Oppositions 13*, 1978. For 'invariantes', see note to p. 133.

630 Esteban Bonell and Francesc Rius: 'Velodromo de Horta', in Richard C. Levene, Fernando Márquez Cecilia, Antonio Ruiz Barbarin, eds., *Arquitectura espanola contemporanea 1979/1990*, Madrid, 1989, p. 447. For other points of view on Spanish 1980s, see William J.R. Curtis, 'Una perspectiva historica, Espana durante los ochenta', *Arquitectura y vivienda*, 24, 1990, pp. 4ff.; Thomas Reese, 'Figuras canonicas, la imagen de la Espana rectente'; and Peter Buchanan, 'Tras la década dorada', ibid., pp. 10ff. (with English translations); see also Joseph Rykwert, 'Introduction', *Arquitectura espanola contemporanea, la decada de los 80*, Barcelona, 1990 (which actually says more about the 1950s and 1960s); and essays by Antón Capitel, Ignasi de Solà-Morales, Victor Pérez Escolano, Kenneth Frampton, in Martha Thorne and Pauline Saliga, eds., *Building in a New Spain, Contemporary Spanish Architecture*, Madrid, 1992 (Art Institute of

Chicago, exhibition catalogue).

631–2 Salamanca: see William J.R. Curtis, 'A Patient Search: the Art and Architecture of Juan Navarro Baldeweg', *El Croquis*, 54, *Juan Navarro Baldeweg, 1982/1992*, Madrid, 1992, pp. 6ff.; for paintings, ideas and architecture, see also Mirko Zardini, ed., *Juan Navarro Baldeweg, Opere e progetti*, Milan, 1990; and Juan Navarro Baldeweg, 'The Convention and Exhibition Center of Salamanca', especially 'An Object is a Section', in *Perspecta*, 27, 1992.

632 T.S. Eliot; 'Tradition and the Individual Talent', *Collected Essays 1917–1932*, London, 1932.

Alvar Aalto, 'Painters and Masons', *Jousimies*, 1921, cited in 'Tradition', Ruusuvuori and Pallasmaa, eds., *Alvar Aalto 1898 1976*, exhibition catalogue, Museum of Finnish Architecture, Helsinki, 1981, p. 69.

chapter 34   the universal and the
local: landscape, climate and culture.

635 Motto: Octavio Paz, 'The New Analogy', lecture, New York, Cooper Union, 1972.

635–6 Regionalisms, universalisms etc.: for discussion of related problems, see William J.R. Curtis, 'Towards an Authentic Regionalism', *Mimar*, 19, January 1986, in effect, developing themes spelt out in Chapters 25, 27 of the first edition of this book.

636–7 Critical regionalism: for contrasting uses of this never very precise term, see Alexander Tzonis and Lliane Lefaivre, 'The Grid and the Pathway: an Introduction to the Work of Dimitris and Susana Antonakakis, with Prolegomena to a History of the Culture of Modern Greek Architecture', *Architecture in Greece*, 15, 1981, pp. 164ff.; and Kenneth Frampton, 'Prospects for a Critical Regionalism', *Perspecta*, 20, pp. 147ff. For one of several critiques of critical regionalism, see Testa, *The Architecture of Alvaro Siza*, Cambridge, Mass., 1986; see also note on Pallasmaa below.

637 Judith Chafee: 'The Region of the Mindful Heart', *Arts Quarterly*, Spring 1982, pp. 27ff., for rejection of restrictive definitions of 'regionalism'.

638 Erskine, Arctic: see Ralph Erskine, 'The Impact of Climate', in Lasdun, ed., *Architecture in an Age of Scepticism*, pp. 82ff.

Marja-Riitta Norri: 'Preface', *Five Masters of the North*, exhibition catalogue, Museum of Finnish Architecture, Helsinki, 1992.

638–9 Sverre Fehn: in Norri, ed., *Five Masters of the North, Sverre Fehn, The Poetry of the Straight Line*, p. 24.

639 Modernism, Mediterranean accents: see William J.R. Curtis, 'Lines of Thought, Fragments of Meaning, the Architecture of José Antonio Martinez Lapena and Eliás Torres Tur', *El Croquis*, 61, *Elias Torres and Martinez Lapena 1988–1993*, Madrid, 1993, pp. 7ff. 'When one takes an overview of recent Spanish architecture, it is striking how much of the best work is concerned with matters of place and identity but without involving itself in overt regionalism or in the caricature that contextualism has now usually become.'

Australia: observations on Leplastrier based on visits and discussions with architect, early 1980s; see also, Françoise Fromonot, 'Contexte, influences', in *Glenn*

Murcutt, oeuvres et projets, Paris, 1995, for useful observations on the Sydney milieu of 1970s; see also Fromonot, guest ed., 'Australie', special issue of *L'Architecture d'aujourd'hui*, 285, February 1993; and Leon Paroissien and Michael Griggs, *Old Continent, New Building, Contemporary Australian Architecture*, Sydney, 1983.

640 Legible landscape: see Glenn Murcutt, 'The Museum of Broken Hill', *Perspecta*, 27, 1993 pp. 168ff.; see also Fromonot, *Oeuvres et Projets*, for cultural implications of Murcutt's ideas about 'nature'; also Elizabeth M. Farrelly, *Glenn Murcutt – Three Houses* (Architecture in Detail), London, 1993, and Philip Drew, *Leaves of Iron, Pioneer of an Australian Architectural Form*, Sydney, 1985.

640–1 Tadao Ando: 'From Self–Enclosed Modern Architecture Toward Universality', *The Japan Architect*, 301, May 1982, pp. 8–12; see also Ando, 'Mon architecture moderne, du moi à l'universel', and François Chaslin, 'Matière à réflexions', in *Tadao Ando, Minimalisme*, Paris, 1982, pp. 10ff. and p. 9; and Kiyoshi Takeyama, 'Tadao Ando: Heir to a Tradition', *Perspecta*, 20, pp. 163ff.

642 Post-colonial identities: see, for example, Curtis, 'Towards an Authentic Regionalism'; also Clifford Geertz, *The Interpretation of Cultures*, New York, 1973, pp. 243ff., particularly with reference to what he calls 'Essentialism and Epochalism': 'Nationalist ideologies built out of symbolic forms drawn from local traditions – which are, that is, essentialist – tend like vernaculars, to be psychologically immediate but socially isolating; built out of forms implicated in the general movement of contemporary history – that is epochalist – they tend, like lingua francas, to be socially de-provincializing but psychologically forced' and p. 242: 'What, from the ordinary speaker's view, is the natural vehicle of thought and feeling (and particularly in cases like Arabic, Hindi, Amharic, Khmer, or Javanese – the repository of an advanced religious, literary, and artistic tradition to boot) is, from the view of the main current of twentieth-century civilization, virtually a patois. And what from that current are the established vehicles of its expression, are for that ordinary speaker at best but half-famililar languages of even less familiar peoples.'

Romila Thapar: 'Tradition and Change', in Brian Taylor, ed., *Raj Rewal*, London, 1992, p. 20: 'Societies have many pasts and each society chooses the past on which it wishes to draw.'

Bawa: see Curtis, 'Towards an Authentic Regionalism'; and Taylor, ed., *Geoffrey Bawa*, pp. 164ff. for 'New Parliamentary Complex, Sri Jayawardenepura, Kotte'; also Peter Scriver, 'Decoding the Discourse – Late Modern Luddism and the Notion of Third World Architecture', in *Architecture 1990, Montréal UIA XXVIII, Culture and Technologies*, Montréal, 1990, pp. 415ff.

643–4 Ministry, Riaydh: for detailed analysis and assessment, William J.R. Curtis, 'Technical Review Report, Ministry of Foreign Affairs, Riaydh', 1986, on file at Aga Khan Awards, Geneva; see also 'Third World Myths and First World Fashions', review of Aga Khan Awards, 1986, *Architectural Record*, January 1987; also, Anders Nyborg, *Ud Af Det Bla, Henning Larsen*, Rungsted, 1986, especially for sketches and

thought process of architect.

644 Jeddah: for NCB see Arthur Drexler, *Three New Skyscrapers*, New York, 1983; also William J.R. Curtis, 'Technical Review Report, National Commercial Bank, Jeddah', 1986, on file at Aga Khan Awards, Geneva.

645 Mexico, primary elements: see William J.R. Curtis, 'Paisajes miticos: la arquitectura moderna y el pasado mexicano', in Alicia Azuela, ed., *Hechizo de Oaxaca*, Monterrey, 1991, pp. 329ff.

Legorreta: for his absorption of tradition, see Louise Noelle Mereles, *Ricardo Legoretta, Tradition y Modernidad*, Mexico City, 1989; for a visual primer of basic elements and themes of language, Wayne Attoe, ed., *The Architecture of Ricardo Legorreta*, Austin, 1990; see also, Antonio Toca, 'Presencia prehispanica en la arquitectura moderna Mexicana', *Basa*, 10, Las Palmas, July 1989; and Pedro C. Sondreguer, *Memoria y utopia en la arquitectura mexicana*, Mexico City, 1990.

645–7 González de León: see Louise Noelle Mereles, 'Teodoro González de León', and William J.R. Curtis, 'Arquitectura moderna: condiciones mexicanas, Modern Architecture, Mexican Conditions', in Mereles, ed., *Teodoro González de León, la voluntad del creador*, Bogota, 1994; see also Teodoro González de León, 'On Two Constants in our Architectural Work', unpublished essay, Mexico City, 1985, especially interesting for his idea of the patio.

647 Tamayo: cited Paul Heyer, *Mexican Architecture, the Work of Abraham Zabludovsky and Teodoro González de León*, New York, 1978, p. 67.

649 Salmona: quotation, from essay by Tejeda, 'Rogelio Salmona: arquiteto latino americano o arquiteto en latina america?', in Carlos Morales, G. Carbonell, eds., *Rogelio Salmona, arquitectura y poetica del lugar*, Bogota, 1991, pp. 342ff.

India, Le Corbusier, Kahn: see, for example, William J.R. Curtis, 'Le Corbusier et l'architecture moderne en Inde. Le Corbusier and Modern Architecture in India', in Catherine Coustols, ed., *Passeurs d'Orient, Encounters between India and France*, Paris, Ministère des Affaires étrangères, 1991, pp. 96–106; see also note on 'Early Modernism in India', Chapter 31; also Vikram Bhatt and Peter Scriver, *After The Masters*, Ahmadabad, 1991.

Indianness, see William J.R. Curtis, 'The Construction of the East, Myths of Indian Architecture', *Times Literary Supplement*, 30 August 1991; also Curtis, 'Modernism and the Substructures of Indian Tradition', *Architecture 1990 Montréal UIA XVII, Culture and Technologies*, Montreal, 1990, and Curtis, 'Modernism and the Search for Indian Identity', *Architectural Review*, August 1987; for Pakistan and Muslim Conceptions of identity, see Kamil Mumtaz, *Architecture in Pakistan*, Singapore, 1985.

650 Charles Correa: 'On Regionalism', *Thresholds*, 4, MIT School of Architecture Newsletter, Cambridge, Mass., 3 December 1992; for notions of 'deep structure', see Correa 'Vistas', in James Steele, ed., *Architecture for Islamic Societies Today*, London, 1994, pp. 12ff. For 'transformations' and 'transfers', see, for example, special issue of *Architectural Review* on India, August 1987.

651 Raj Rewal, 'The Relevance of Tradition in Indian Architecture', in Jean-Louis Véret, ed., *Architecture in India*, Paris 1985, p. 12; for Rewal, see also William J.R. Curtis, 'Architecture moderne, racines indiennes: Raj Rewal' (English version, 'Raj Rewal Modern Architecture, Indian Roots', *Architecture & Design* (Delhi), March–April 1989; also Daniel Treiber, 'Un régionalisme du plus grand nombre', in *Raj Rewal, architecture climatique*, Paris, 1986; also Rewal, 'Evolution and Metamorphosis', in Taylor, ed., *Raj Rewal*, London, 1992, pp. 25ff., for concept of 'rasa' and for architect's reading and transformation of basic Indian types.

Anant Raje: the assessment here is based on study of his projects as well as discussions with the architects, mid-1980s in India. See 'Building on Tradition, Anant Raje', *Architecture & Design*, November–December 1987.

652 Indian city: see Charles Correa, *The New Landscape, Urbanisation in the Third World*, Bombay, 1985; also Balkrishna Doshi, *How the Other Half Builds*, Ahmadabad and Montreal, 1984; see also Doshi, 'Low-Cost Housing Township at Indore', 1984; and *New Town Studies, Vidyadhar Nagar, Jaipur*, 1986, both Ahmadabad, Vastu Shilpa Foundation.

653 Doshi, Sangath: see William J.R. Curtis, *Balkrishna Doshi: an Architecture for India*, Ahmadabad and New York, 1988, especially pp. 118–35 for Doshi quotation; see Le Corbusier, *Oeuvre complète 1938–46*, p. 116, for Cherchell, North Africa, project.

655 Juhani Pallasmaa: 'Tradition and Modernity', *Architectural Review*, May 1988.

chapter 35   technology, abstraction
and ideas of nature

657 Motto: Berthold Lubetkin, 'Notes of a Talk Given to AA, London, 1967', Peter Coe and Malcolm Reading, *Lubetkin and Tecton: Architecture and Social Commitment, A Critical Study*, London, 1981, pp. 76–9.
Structured area of problems: see Ernst Kris, motto, note to p. 11, Introduction above.

658 Signs, Symbols: see Carl Jung, 'Definitions, 51: Symbol', in Violet S. de Laszlo, ed., *The Basic Writings of C.G. Jung*, Princeton, 1990, p. 28.ff.
Foster, technology, nature: the quotation is from Robert Pirsig, *Zen and the Art of Motor Cycle Maintenance, an Enquiry into Values*, and is cited approvingly by Foster in text of speech at opening of Jean Prouvé exhibition, IFA, Paris, 1983, see *Foster*, exhibition catalogue, Barcelona, 1989, p. 128; for design process of Hong Kong and Shanghai Bank, see 'Norman Foster, 1 QRC Extracts from a Project Diary', in Lasdun, ed., *Architecture in an Age of Scepticism*, pp. 112ff; for a particular interpretation, Chris Abel, 'A Building for the Pacific Century', *Architectural Review*, April 1986; for possible connection with 1949 project by Amancio Williams, see note to p. 503, Chapter 27, above.

661 Renzo Piano: in an interview with Vittorio Gregotti, 4 June 1986, cited in Renzo Piano, *The Process of Architecture*, exhibition catalogue, 9H Gallery, London, 1987, p. 3. For more extensive discussion of Piano's design philosophy, see Peter Buchanan, *Renzo Piano Building Workshop*, London, 1994 (vol. 1), 1996 (vol. 2).

662 Ambasz: quote on technology, Ettore Sottsass,

in *Emilio Ambasz: the Poetics of the Pragmatic*, New York, 1988; for Tadao Ando quotation see *Emilio Ambasz, Architecture and Design, 1973–1993*, Tokyo, 1993, pp. xxxvi–vii; see also Terence Riley, 'Emilio Ambasz: Landscape of the Marvellous', ibid., pp. ix–xvi.

Gehry, bright present of Pacific beaches: see David Cohn, 'Singing the Light Electric', *El Croquis*, 45, *Frank Gehry*, p. 120; see also Carol Burns, 'The Gehry Phenomenon', in Hays and Burns, eds., *Thinking the Present, Recent American Architecture*, pp. 72ff., and James Steele, *Los Angeles Architecture, the Contemporary Condition*, London, 1993, especially pp. 73ff.; my perceptions of Gehry's earlier works owe something to discussions with Joseph Giovannini, Venice, California, early 1980s.

664 Meier: see Michael Brawne, *Museum für Kunsthandwerk, Frankfurt am Main 1984* (Architecture in Detail), London, 1993; also Joseph Rykwert, *Richard Meier, Architect*, vol. 1, 1986, vol. 2, 1991; and Philip Jodidio, *Richard Meier*, Berlin, 1995; on the question of the 'neo-modern' see also Jorge Glusberg, ed., *Vision of the Modern*, London, 1988.

665 Eisenman, changes of emphasis: see Eisenman, *La fine del classico*, Venice, 1977 (essays on 'end of classicism', 'post-functionalism' etc); also K. Michael Hays, 'From Structure to Site to Text: Eisenman's Trajectory', in Hays and Burns, op. cit., pp. 61ff.; see also Rafael Moneo, 'Inesperados coincidencias, Unexpected Coincidences', *El Croquis*, 41, *Peter Eisenman*, 1989, pp. 52ff., and David Cohn, 'Erase una vez en el oeste, Once Upon a Time in the West', ibid., pp. 120ff.; see also Cohn interview with Eisenman, ibid., pp. 7ff. On the 'algebraic', virtually laconic aspects of minimalism and for a particular conception of 'modernity', see Rosalind Krauss, 'LeWitt in Progress', 1977, in Krauss, *The Originality of the Avant-Garde and other Modernist Myths*, Cambridge, Mass., 1985, pp. 244ff., for example: 'To get inside the systems of this work, whether LeWitt's or Judd's or Morris's, is precisely to enter a world without center, a world of substitutions and transpositions nowhere legitimated by the revelations of a transcendental subject. This is the strength of this work, its seriousness, and its claim to modernity.'

665–6 Tschumi: see Philip Johnson and Mark Wigley, *Deconstructivist Architecture*, exhibition catalogue, MOMA, New York, 1988; also review of this exhibition by Roger Kimball, *Architectural Record*, August 1988. For La Villette, see Tschumi, *The Manhattan Transcripts*, London, AA, 1985; and 'La Villette', *Pratt Journal of Architecture, 'Form Being, Absence'*, New York, 1988; see also, Anthony Vidler, 'Trick/Track', *The Architecture of the Uncanny*, Cambridge, Mass, 1992. For intellectual smoke-screens, Christopher Norris and Andrew Benjamin, *What is Deconstruction?*, London, 1988; for intellectual clarity, Jessie Marshall, 'A Critique of the Architectural Idea', unpublished dissertation, Diploma in Architecture, Emmanuel College, Cambridge University, 1993. For ambiguities of political meaning and problems of 'neo avant-gardist' stance, see William J.R. Curtis, 'Les Grands Projets parisiens: monumentalité et machines d'état', *Techniques et Architecture*, Paris, Sept. 1989, pp. 116ff.; for Rowe quote on ironical distance, see notes Chapter 32.

667 Koolhaas: see interview with Alejandro Zaera Polo, in *El Croquis*, 53, *OMA/Rem Koolhaas, 1987/1992*, pp. 6ff.; OMA is short for 'Office for Metropolitan Architecture'. For Lille, setting, see Jean-Paul Robert, 'Fiction de Ville', and Françoise Fromonot, 'Gros plans', in *L'Architecture d'aujourdhui*, 298, April, 1995; see also Koolhaas, *Delirious New York*, New York, 1978 for early position; Koolhaas and Bruce Mau, *S, M, L, XL*, Rotterdam, 1995, for more recent.

Daniel Libeskind, for his Jewish Museum, see 'Libeskind, el centro es una ausencia …', in José Maria Lozano, ed., *Arquitectura de la razon, actas Congresso Internacional, 1992*, Jaen, 1992, pp. 65ff.

668 Fragmentation: layering, for an undiscriminating round-up of projects and buildings of the 1980s, see Aaron Betsky, *Violated Perfection, Architecture and the Fragmentation of the Modern*, New York, 1990; among other architects to explore fragmentation, the German Günther Behnisch; the American partnership 'Morphosis' (Michael Rotondi, Thom Mayne); the American firm Scogin, Elam and Bray; the American Rob Quigley; the German-based partnership, Peter Wilson and Bolles; and the British, William Alsop and John Lyall.

Toyo Ito, 'Collage and Superficiality in Architecture', in Frampton, ed., *A New Wave of Japanese Architecture*, New York, 1978.

Kazuo Shinohara: see Shinohara, 'Chaos and Machine', *Japan Architect*, 373, May 1988, pp. 25–32, and Shinohara, 'Tokyo Institute of Technology Centennial Hall', op. cit. pp. 6–24; also B. Bognar, 'An Art and Architecture of Fragmentation: the New Urban Architecture of Japan', in Bognar, ed., *The New Japanese Architecture*, New York, 1990.

669–70 Fumihiko Maki: expanded modernism, 'New Directions in Modernism', *Space Design*, 256, January 1986, pp. 6ff.; for reading of layers in urban environment, see Maki, 'The City and Inner Space', in Bohm, ed., *Das Bauwerk und die Stadt. The Building and the Town*, Vienna, 1994, pp. 173ff.

670 Tadao Ando: 'Suspension and Precipitation', and 'Differentiation and Integration', in *El Croquis*, 558, *Tadao Ando, 1989–1992*, 1993, p. 155 (place & memory) and p. 17 (nature); see also Francesco Dal Co, *Tadao Ando, Complete Works*, London, 1995 (Italian edition, 1994).

672 France, 1980s: see Jacques Lucan, *France Architecture 1965–1988*, Paris and Milan, 1989; and Sébastien Marot, ed., *Le Visiteur*, 1, Paris, 1995, pp. 3ff. editorial, and pp. 88ff, critical reflections by Bernard Huet, Jean-Louis Cohen, Jacques Lucan, François Chaslin.

672–3 Grands Projets: see François Chaslin, *Le Paris de François Mitterand, histoire des grands projets architecturaux*, Paris, 1985; also *Grands Travaux*, with preface by François Mitterand, special issue of Philip Jodidio, ed., *Connaissance des arts*, 1992; Curtis, 'Les Grands Projets parisiens, monumentalité et machines d'état'; François Chaslin and Virginie Picon-Lefebvre, *La Grande Arche de la Défense*, Paris, 1989; Jacques Lucan, 'Bibliothèque Nationale de France', *Moniteur Architecture AMC*; Frederic Edelmann, 'La Bibliothèque nationale de France que le public pourra découvrir en 1997', *Le Monde*, 28 March 1995, pp. 18–19.

673 Henri Ciriani: see *L'Architecture d'aujourdhui*, September 1992, Special issue; also William J.R. Curtis, *Architecture*, August 1995, note on Arles museum; for perspectives on different 'modernisms' in France, see Luis Fernandez-Galiano, ed., *Arquitectura viva*, 37, July–August, 1994, 'Francia en Formas'.

674 Pierre-Louis Faloci, Mont Beuvray: see William J.R. Curtis, 'Abstraction du lieu, mémoire d'architecture', *L'Architecture d'aujourdhui*, 301, October, 1995, pp.88–9.

675 Finland: see William J.R. Curtis, 'Concepts and Continuities, Finnish architecture of the 1980s', Introduction to Maija Kärkkäinen, ed., *Suomi rakentaa 8, Finland byyger 8, Finland Builds 8*, Helsinki, 1992, pp. 10ff.; see also Scott Poole, *The New Finnish Architecture*, New York, 1992, and Vilhelm Helander and Simo Rista, *Suomalainen Rakennustaide, Modern Architecture in Finland*, Helsinki, 1990; see also journal *Arkkitehti*, including Addenda on architectural competitions; and the French journal *Le Carré bleu* for continuous interest in Finland.

Pietila: see Malcolm Quantrill, *Reimi Pietila, Architecture, Context, Modernism*, 1985; also Roger Connah, *Writing Architecture: Fantômas, Fragments, Fictions. An Architectural Journey through the Twentieth Century*, Cambridge, Mass., 1989.

Kristian Gullichsen: see *Gullichsen/Kairamo. Vormala*, Barcelona, 1991.

Heikkinen, see *Heikkinen and Komonen*, Barcelona, 1994.

676 Juha Leiviska: see Curtis 'Concepts and Continuities', p. 12; also Armelle Lavalou, 'Juha Leiviska, Portrait', and William J.R. Curtis, 'Variations sur un thème', *L'Architecture d'aujourdhui*, 30, October 1995, pp. 53ff. and pp. 64ff.

677 Finnish Pavilion: see 'Suomi Sevillan Maailmannäyttelyssä 1992', *Architectural Competitions in Finland 1.90*; also Peter Mackeith and Kerstin Smeds, *The Finland Pavilions: Finland at the Universal Expositions 1900–1992*, Kustannus Oy City, 1993.

Steven Holl: 'Anchoring', in *Anchoring, Steven Holl Selected Projects 1975–1988*, New York, 1989, pp. 10–11. Holl's emphasis on perception and experience no doubt reflects his interest in phenomonology.

678 Jacques Herzog: 'Ideas of Design', 'Conversation with José Luis Mateo' in *Herzog and de Meuron*, Barcelona, 1989, p. 12; see also Wilfried Wang, ed., *Herzog and de Meuron: Projects and Buildings 1892–1990*, Cambridge, Mass., 1989.

679 Abstraction, material and conceptual order: see, for example, Martin Steinmann, 'La presencia de las cosas', and Peter Zumthor, 'El prado y la caverna, residencia de ancianos en Chur y termas en Vals', in *Arquitectura viva*, 41, March–April 1995, 'Grado Cero, Suizos del norte, una nueva simplicidad'; also Wilfried Wang, Alvaro Siza, 'Introductions', *Souto de Moura*, Barcelona, 1990, and William J.R. Curtis, 'Desert Illumination, Phoenix Central Library, Bruder D.W.L. Architects', *Architecture*, October 1995, pp. 56ff.; see also Josep Maria Montaner, 'Minimalismos, Minimalisms', *El Croquis*, 62/63, for a somewhat forced and reductivist attempt at linking together disparate artists and architects under the heading of an 'ism'.

679–83 Spain 1980s, 1990s: see notes to Chapter 33 for several overviews and perspectives. Useful coverage found in journals such as *Arquitectura y vivienda*, and *Arquitectura viva* (both Madrid, both edited Luis Fernandez-Galiano); *Quaderns* (Barcelona), *El Croquis* (Madrid), *Peripheria* (Grenada). Also relevant are numerous catalogues published by local Colegios or Associations of Architects, for example, series of monographs, 'documentos de arquitectura', produced by Colegio de Arquitectos de Almeria. For more conservative orientation, the independent *Composicion arquitectonica* (Bilbao). For early 1990s see for example, Luis Fernandez-Galiano, ed., *Anuario. Yearbook 1993, arquitectura espanola, Spanish Architecture*, Madrid, 1993; *Quaderns d'arquitectura i urbanisme*, 187, 1993 (special issue on Barcelona, especially periphery); see also *1993/1994, III Bienal de arquitectura espanola*, Madrid, 1995, including William J.R. Curtis, 'La crisis de la normalidad, The Crisis of Normality', pp. 19ff.; as well as essays by Juan Antonio Cortés, Luis Fernandez-Galiano, Ignasi de Solà-Morales, Antón Capitel, Juan José Lahuerta.

680 Barcelona: see Helio Pinon, *Arquitectura de las neovanguardias*, Barcelona, 1984; also *Arquitectura y vivienda*, 37, 1992, 'Barcelona Olimpica', notably articles by Oriol Bohigas, 'A New Barcelona. Reflections on the Last Ten Years', and Ignasi de Solà-Morales, 'Use and Abuse of the Historical City. Barcelona's Olympic Village'; see also William J.R. Curtis, 'Modern Architecture in a Barcelona Tradition' in *Carlos Ferrater*, Barcelona, 1989; and Carlos Ferrater, *Tres mansanes vora la vila olimpica: l'eixample maritim de Barcelona*, Barcelona, 1990, booklet.

681 Torres/Lapena: see Peter Buchanan, José Quetglas, *M. Lapena/Torres*, Barcelona, 1990; and William J.R. Curtis, 'Lines of Thought, Fragments of Meaning', *El Croquis*, 61, *Elias Torres and Martinez Lapena 1988–1993*, Madrid, 1993.

Spain, Regions: see thematic treatments in *Arquitectura y vivienda*, also Gili Catalogos de Arquitectura Contemporanea on *Cruz/Ortiz*, Barcelona, 1988; *J.I. Linazasoro*, 1989; *Vazquez Consuegra*, 1992; *J. Manuel Gallego*, 1992; etc.

682 Siza, Compostela: see William J.R. Curtis, 'Paisajes urbanos. Urban Landscapes', *Alvaro Siza Obras y proyectos*, exhibition catalogue CGAC, Madrid and Compostela, 1995; and Curtis, 'Alvaro Siza: an Architecture of Edges', *El Croquis*, 68/69, *Alvaro Siza 1958–1994*, Madrid 1994.

683 Miralles/Pinos: William J.R. Curtis, 'Mapas mentales y paisajes sociales: la arquitectura de Miralles y Pinos. Mental Maps and Social Landscapes. The Architecture of Miralles and Pinos', *El Croquis*, 49/50, *Enric Miralles/Carme Pinos 1988/1991 en construction. Under Construction*, Madrid, 1991, pp. 6ff.; for possible relevance of Serras larger landscape pieces to achitecture or landscape architecture, see e.g. Richard Serra, 'Shift', 1973, in *Richard Serra, Writings, Interviews*, Chicago, 1994, pp. 11ff.; see also Curtis, 'Contours of the "Secret Cause". The Cultivation of Meaning in Landscape Design', *Times Literary Supplement*, 30 December 1994.

684 Eugène Viollet-Le-Duc: *Dictionnaire*, Chapter 8; cited Bergdoll, *E.E. Viollet-Le-Duc: the Foundations of Architecture*, p. 233, italics are Viollet-Le-Duc's.

conclusion   modernity, tradition, authenticity (1995)

685 Motto: Heinrich Wölfflin, *Kunstgeschichtliche Grundbegriffe*, Munich, 1915, trans. M. Hottinger, *Principles of Art History*, New York and London, 1932, p. 11.

Alexis de Tocqueville, *L'Ancien Régime et la revolution*, Paris, 1856, trans. Stuart Gilbert, The *Old Régime and the French Revolution*, Garden City, NY, 1955, 'Foreword', p. vii, and p. 10.

686–8 Development of modern architecture: see note on 'Tradition' in Introduction above; also William J.R. Curtis, The Idea of a Modern Tradition, in Marja Kärkäinen, ed., *Functionalism – Utopia or the Way Forward? the Fifth International Alvar Aalto Symposium*, Jyväskylä, 1992, pp. 120ff.; and Hans Van Dijk, 'Dutch Modernism and its Legitimacy', in *Architectuur in Nederland Jaarbock, 1991–1992*, Amsterdam, 1992, pp. 6ff. for reflection on author's method: 'Curtis has history unfold in a number of gradually developing traditions. Individual works play a crucial role in these evolutionary processes. They transform and integrate latent tendencies into sensorial experiences. Great masterpieces have an exemplary effect. They can end traditions, bend them and summon new ones into being. For Curtis the assimilation, imitation and amendment of these works can explain more of architectural history than the verbal constructions with which they are presented or criticised. He does not have modern architecture arising out of the polemics of the historic avant-gardes. And it is therefore not surprising that he is equally unimpressed by the diatribes which nowadays announce its demise. According to him, on the whole, we are not at the end of an era or the beginning of a new one. We are in the middle of the multiform tradition of the modern.'

688 André Malraux: *The Voices of Silence*, trans. S. Gilbert, New York, 1953, p. 281.

Hermann Muthesius: 'Wo stehen Wir?', 1911.

689 Authenticity: the word was used in the initial version of the Conclusion (1981). For several approaches towards and definitions of authenticity, see *Perspecta*, 20, 1983, especially Karsten Harries, 'Thoughts on a Non-Arbitrary Architecture', pp. 9ff.; and William J.R. Curtis, 'Authenticity, Abstraction and the Ancient Sense: Le Corbusier's and Louis Kahn's Ideas of Parliament', pp. 181ff.

Idealization: see William J.R. Curtis, 'L'Enigme de l'objet', interview with Jean-Paul Robert and Armelle Lavalou, *L'Architecture d'aujourdhui*, 229, June 1995, pp. 4ff., for a statement of critical principles.

Le Corbusier, *Towards a New Architecture*, pp. 27ff.

index

Numbers in **bold** refer to the illustrations

picture credits

Illustrations numbers are in **bold**

Museum of the City of New York/The Wurts Collection: **266, 271**

Museum of Finnish Architecture: **148, 418, 419, 420, 429, 573** (Rauno Karhu), **698** (Martti I. Jaatinen)

The Museum of Modern Art, New York, gift of Nelson A. Rockefeller, 1979: **110**

The Museum of Modern Art, New York, Van Gogh Purchase Fund. Photograph © 1995: **187**

Photograph courtesy of the Museum of Modern Art, New York: **125, 131, 217** (Mies van der Rohe Archive), **368, 369, 431**

Nebraska State Historical Society: **355**

Coll. Ned. Doc. Centrum, Amsterdam: **171, 173, 175, 305, 306, 307, 308**

Netherlands Architecture Institute: **174, 317**

New-York Historical Society, New York City: **267**

Louise Noelle: **618**

Norwegian Glacier Museum/photo Ole Martin Korsen: **793**

Jean Nouvel: **846**

Novosti: **238, 243, 246, 251, 256, 318, 442**

Paul Ockrassa: **559**

Öffentliche Kunstsammlung Basel, gift of Dr H.C. Raoul La Roche, 1952/ photo Martin Bühler: **167**

Lennart Olson/Tiofoto, Stockholm: **524**

Open University: **325**

Pancro-2000 S.L./Andreu Català, Barcelona: **608, 701**

Richard Pare: **790**

Pei Cobb Freed & Partners: **706**

Dominique Perrault/photo Georges Fessy: **845**

Renzo Piano Building Workshop: **828** (Paul Hester), **829, 830** (Skyfront)

Radisson SAS Royal Hotel, Copenhagen: **580**

Anant Raje: **818**

Raj Rewal Associates: **722**

Rice University Archives, Houston: **353**

Simo Rista, Helsinki: **421, 427, 563, 566, 568, 569, 571, 575, 578**

Kevin Roche, John Dinkeloo & Associates: **705**

José Rodrigues, Évora: **745**

Roger-Viollet: **15, 17**

Aldo Rossi: **742**

A. & E. Roth: **456**

Anna J. Ruusuvuori: **697**

Armando Salas Portugal: **482, 615**

Rogelio Salmona: **811, 812, 813**

Jordi Sarrà Arau, Barcelona: **145**

Scala, Florence: **598, 600**

Archivio Carlo Scarpa: **602, 763, 764**

Harry Seidler & Associates: **632**

Sert, Jackson & Gourley Associates/© Pholkion Karas, Mass: **558**

Josep Luis Sert Collection, Frances Loeb Library, Harvard University, Graduate School of Design: **464**

Shinkenchiku-sha Co, Tokyo: **840** (Masao Arai), **841** (Taisuke Ogawa)

Julius Shulman: **96, 257, 281, 288, 487, 497, 499, 504, 627, 631**

Siedlung Italien: **556**

Eric Sierins: **586**

Skidmore, Owings & Merrill: **804**

Alison & Peter Smithson: **553, 668, 669, 670, 671**

Society for Cooperation in Russian & Soviet Studies: **441**

Stapleton Collection: **14**

Stato Maggiore Aeronautica: **443**

Stedelijk Van Abbemuseum, Eindhoven: **236**

Stedelijk Museum, Amsterdam: **176, 181**

Robert Stern/photo Edmund Stoecklein: **757**

© Ezra Stoller/Esto: **90, 272, 489, 503, 564**

Tim Street-Porter: **93, 274, 277, 278, 279, 284, 287, 290, 498, 622, 831, 833**

Strüwing Reklamefoto: **582**

Hisao Suzuki: **605, 854, 855, 859, 862**

Swedish Museum of Architecture: **162, 366, 412**

Kenzo Tange Associates: **637, 638, 640**

Toledo Museum of Art, Ohio, purchased with funds from the Florence Scott Libbey Bequest in Memory of her Father, Maurice A. Scott: **2**

Elias Torres Tur and José Antonio Martinez Lapena: **857**

Rauno Träskelin, Helsinki: **425, 428**

Archives of the Triennale, Milan: **448**

Rupert Truman: **47**

Professor Turnbull, University of Melbourne: **362**

Ullstein Bilderdienst, Berlin: **233, 304, 434, 437**

O.M. Ungers: **774**

Unità locale socio sanitaria 11 Venezia: **540**

United Nations: **506**

University Art Museum (Architectural Drawing Collection), University of California, Santa Barbara: **285**

University of Witwaterstrand, Johannesburg: **472**

V&K Publishing: **241**

Livio Vacchini: **779**

Aldo van Eyck: **692, 695**

Francesco Venezia: **780, 781**

Venturi, Scott Brown & Associates: **709, 710, 711**

Jean-Louis Véret: **594**

Michael Wilford & Partners Ltd: **761**

Williams College Museum of Art, Museum purchase 94.14/photo Michael Agee: **648**

Bertram D. Wolfe Collection/Hoover Institution Archives: **381**

Charlotte Wood: **83**

F.R. Yerbury: **72, 196, 198, 203, 207.**